Dear West Customer:

West Academic Publishing has changed the look of its American Casebook Series®.

In keeping with our efforts to promote sustainability, we have replaced our former covers with book covers that are more environmentally friendly. Our casebooks will now be covered in a 100% renewable natural fiber. In addition, we have migrated to an ink supplier that favors vegetable-based materials, such as soy.

Using soy inks and natural fibers to print our textbooks reduces VOC emissions. Moreover, our primary paper supplier is certified by the Forest Stewardship Council, which is testament to our commitment to conservation and responsible business management.

The new cover design has migrated from the long-standing brown cover to a contemporary charcoal fabric cover with silver-stamped lettering and black accents. Please know that inside the cover, our books continue to provide the same trusted content that you've come to expect from West.

We've retained the ample margins that you have told us you appreciate in our texts while moving to a new, larger font, improving readability. We hope that you will find these books a pleasing addition to your bookshelf.

Another visible change is that you will no longer see the brand name Thomson West on our print products. With the recent merger of Thomson and Reuters, I am pleased to announce that books published under the West Academic Publishing imprint will once again display the West brand.

It will likely be several years before all of our casebooks are published with the new cover and interior design. We ask for your patience as the new covers are rolled out on new and revised books knowing that behind both the new and old covers, you will find the finest in legal education materials for teaching and learning.

Thank you for your continued patronage of the West brand, which is both rooted in history and forward looking towards future innovations in legal education. We invite you to be a part of our next evolution.

Best regards,

Louis H. Higgins
Editor in Chief, West Academic Publishing

CONTEMPORARY FAMILY LAW

Second Edition

■ ■ ■

By

Douglas E. Abrams
Associate Professor of Law
University of Missouri
School of Law

Naomi R. Cahn
John Theodore Fey Research Professor of Law
The George Washington University Law School

Catherine J. Ross
Professor of Law
The George Washington University Law School

David D. Meyer
Professor of Law
University of Illinois
College of Law

AMERICAN CASEBOOK SERIES®

WEST®
A Thomson Reuters business

Mat #40762950

American Casebook Series is a trademark registered in the U.S. Patent and Trademark Office.

© West, a Thomson business, 2006
© 2009 Thomson Reuters
 610 Opperman Drive
 St. Paul, MN 55123
 1–800–313–9378
Printed in the United States of America

ISBN: 978-0-314-19565-4

 TEXT IS PRINTED ON 10% POST CONSUMER RECYCLED PAPER

To my parents, Barbara and Saul D. Abrams,
who led our family.

D.E.A.

To Louisa, Abigail, and Tony, for always teaching me about family.

N.R.C.

To the three men in my life:
In loving memory of my father, Alexander I. Ross, a pioneer in paternal
custody, and
To my husband Jon and son Daniel, who cheerfully lived with the
demands of this project, with love and thanks.

C.J.R.

To Amy, Michael, and Matthew, with love of family.

D.D.M.

*

PREFACE

Contemporary family law is experiencing a revolution. The profound changes that have transformed the field over the past four decades are arguably unmatched in any other area of the law. Nor does the pace of change seem to be slowing. As we observed in the Preface to the first edition of this book, questions that appeared merely academic to many just a few decades ago—for example, the permissibility of same-sex marriage, the desirability of government support for marriage generally, the definition of parenthood, and indeed the meaning of "family" itself—now press urgently on courts and legislatures and feature prominently in the public discourse. These issues are even more the focus of legislative, political and judicial attention today than they were when this book first appeared in 2006. Indeed, as we go to press, the outcome of a number of specific controversies at the state level over issues such as same-sex marriage remains unclear. We have done our best to capture the status of these emerging issues as of the time the book went to press, but readers will need to remain alert to later developments. It is undeniably an exciting time to study and practice family law.

This is the first family law casebook entirely conceived and written in the twenty-first century. The book captures the rapid evolution of doctrine, introduces students to emerging policy debates, and explores issues that arise in family law practice.

Solid grounding in legal analysis and reasoning is indispensable to family law study because court decisions, statutes and administrative regulations are the lawyer's basic legal tools. Study of doctrine carries legal education only so far, however, because much of today's doctrine will be tomorrow's history. Family law doctrine continues to develop, particularly because of fast-paced social and cultural change concerning family life and intimate relationships. By conveying a solid sense of the recent trajectory of doctrinal change, this book provides students a foundation for anticipating, understanding and participating in future developments.

Policy study is particularly central in disciplines such as family law, where broad discretionary standards enunciated by the legislature compel practitioners and judges to grapple with policy considerations when they apply doctrine to the immediate circumstances of individuals who seek the law's protection. It is impossible to determine the "best interests" of a child or an "equitable" division of a couple's marital assets, for example, without considering public policy. Policy considerations will also help shape future doctrinal evolution in contentious areas largely unmentioned in family law courses only a few years ago—areas such as same-sex marriage, assisted reproductive technology, joint custody of children, cohabitants' rights and obligations, and indeed the very definition of the "family" itself. Because many family law policy issues now sharpen political debate (the so-called "culture wars"), the book encourages students and their teachers to analyze not only what the law is, but also what the law should be. To help inform this analysis, notes in several chapters introduce some comparative material.

Over the past decade, legal education has increasingly recognized that lessons in practice are central to the challenges most students will face in client representation. Practical legal education is a lifelong process honed by experience, but the process begins in law school. To help students apply doctrine to practical problems, the casebook includes questions and exercises inviting classroom resolution.

We have attempted to reconceptualize family law to reflect ongoing developments by integrating four themes that help shape contemporary discussions of family law, and by organizing the chapters differently than most other family law casebooks.

The first theme, appearing in virtually every chapter, is that families take a variety of forms, including marital and nonmarital heterosexual and same-sex relationships. The second theme is that constitutional law has become increasingly integrated into familial rights and responsibilities through such issues as the right to marry, the right of parents to control their children's upbringing, and other rights of individual and family privacy. Third, we pay particular attention to the ways a variety of biases—such as gender, culture, race, and class—have affected family law's development and application.

The fourth theme belongs at the forefront of the contemporary family law curriculum. More than ever before, family law practice depends on lawyers' collaboration with professionals trained in disciplines that complement and enrich our own. The roles of marriage counselors, mental health professionals, child psychologists, experts in abuse and neglect and juvenile delinquency, and professionals in other specialties loom large amid the emotions that frequently attend family distress or dissolution. Some of these specialties are staples of the children and the law course, which remains a useful adjunct to the family law course. This casebook's interdisciplinary materials explore non-legal issues that arise in domestic relations practice, not to provide expertise, but to accustom readers to the general concepts, and to prepare lawyers to collaborate with other professionals.

This book recognizes significant developments in the theory and practice of family law with several chapters that do not appear in many other family law casebooks. For example, we devote separate chapters to lawyering, private ordering, and alternative dispute resolution. And, although family law case-books usually treat alimony and property distribution together, we consider them in separate chapters to emphasize the distinctive theoretical and practical aspects of each topic. Finally, we devote two chapters to child custody arrangements, which lead to some of the most acrimonious legal disputes in family law. The first custody chapter treats the initial custody decision, and the second explores post-custody disputes, including legal battles that arise over visitation.

Casebook readers might be interested to know something more about the collaboration that led to the book that will occupy them for an entire semester. Co-authorship provides an opportunity to collaborate from beginning to end with colleagues who share professional interests, and the four of us have made the most of this enriching opportunity. We hope the book reflects not only our own enthusiasm for family law, but also the enjoyment we have derived from designing and producing the final product together. Each of us began with primary responsibility for particular chapters:

> Professors Ross and Cahn co-authored chapters 1 and 4; Professor Ross authored chapters 9, 12, and 13; Professor Meyer authored chapters 3, 7, 8, and, with Judith Helfman, 14; Professor Cahn wrote chapters 5, 6, 10, and 16; and Professor Abrams wrote chapters 2, 11, 15, and 17.

Each author assumes responsibility for the contents of his or her chapters, but each draft chapter was read and commented on by several of the other authors.

Like law itself, books about law thrive on continuous reexamination and refinement. To help students and faculty remain current in family law, we anticipate periodic supplements and new editions. We invite comments and suggestions from readers because you are truly collaborators in our joint project. Your input will benefit the next generation of family law practitioners and the families whose lives they touch.

* * *

Writing a book, like teaching in the classroom, is a team effort that depends on valuable contributions from others. Our "team" is comprised of all-stars who deserve to share the limelight.

We have accumulated a number of debts in preparing the second edition of this book. Our deans–Frederick Lawrence at George Washington University, R. Lawrence Dessem at Missouri, and Bruce Smith at Illinois–as always encouraged and supported our work. Law students at George Washington University–Lauren Birzon, Paul William Kraczek, Lindsey Nelson, Christiana Samuels, Elizabeth Szabo, Laura Valden, Christine Williams, and Christy Zlatkus–provided excellent research assistance, as did Gregory Cassens, Amanda Haahr, Matthew Morris and Ryan Neal at the University of Missouri. Kasia Solon, reference librarian at George Washington University, answered countless inquiries with expertise and good humor. Angela Martin at the University of Illinois provided expert administrative and technical assistance in assembling and preparing the manuscript and page proofs throughout the production of the book. The students who have studied family law with the four of us since this book first appeared have helped us to refine our ideas and (we hope) to share them more clearly where greater clarity was needed.

Working with the Thomson Reuters editors and their staffs in preparing both editions has been a pleasure. We particularly thank Pamela Siege Chandler, Roxy Birkel, Staci Herr, Louis Higgins, and Bonnie Karlen.

This second edition would not have come to fruition without the support we received from so many people in the harder work of crafting the first edition.

We owe a special debt of gratitude to Editorial Consultant Judith Helfman, whose expert editorial assistance on the manuscript for the first edition went well above and beyond all reasonable expectations. She drew from her own family law practice experience to suggest and integrate additional materials and ideas that greatly enriched the book, and she also zealously ensured the consistency of citation form, style and formatting throughout the book.

We continue to acknowledge the support of the others who made the first edition possible. Our deans—R. Lawrence Dessem at Missouri, Heidi M. Hurd at Illinois, and Frederick M. Lawrence and Michael Young at George Washington University—encouraged and supported our efforts from beginning to end. Professor Andrew I. Schepard graciously reviewed the entire manuscript and shared his knowledge and experiences. Professors James R. Devine, Suzanne Jackson, John Lande, and Sarah H. Ramsey reviewed individual chapters, while Professors Cheryl Block, Karen Brown, Joan Meier and Miriam Galston generously lent their expertise. Research assistance at Missouri and Illinois was ably provided by Kathleen M. Birkhofer, Ellen Jean Brooke, Kathleen E. Goddard, Amy Tomaszewski, and Tamara Ann Wallace. At GW, Veronica Wayner led a superb team of research assistants including Reetuparna Dutta, Karen Goff, Cecilia Isaacs–Blundin, Blake Johnson, Elizabeth Ann Kopley, Cynthia Landesberg, Josh Levy, Melissa Liebman, Scott Minneman, Katherine Mullane, Erin Murphy, Naomi Porter, Marissa Shuback, Bonnie Vanzler, and Rachel Marie Wilhelm. Professional staff members at each of our institutions—particularly Stacey Ballmes, Elsie–Denise Lejano, Cheryl Poelling, and Germaine Leahy—provided tireless and crucial assistance throughout, while Jo Ann Roberts, Ulla Sochman, and Kasia Solon helped us cross the finish line. Students in Professor Ross' fall 2005 Family Law class at George Washington University were a thoughtful "focus group" that tested the manuscript and provided valuable comments. Professor Cahn's spring 2006 Family Law class at GW and Professor Meyer's spring 2006 Family Law class at Illinois also added their insights to the manuscript.

We thank our own families for enriching our appreciation of the meaning of family law and for supporting our work on this book.

We also thank the family law students all of us have taught throughout our careers. Classroom give-and-take with these thoughtful men and women has helped refine our own thoughts about the important issues this book treats. Many of our students enroll in the course because they plan to devote their professional energies to family law after graduation. Others expect to practice family law as part of a broader general practice. Others will choose government service in the executive, legislative or judicial branch. Still others will serve on bar association committees, law revision commissions and similar bodies committed to improving family law in the public interest. To whatever stops and destinations their career paths lead, our students will continue to make us proud that we were their teachers.

DOUGLAS E. ABRAMS
NAOMI R. CAHN
CATHERINE J. ROSS
DAVID D. MEYER

May 2009

Authors' Note: Footnotes and textual citations of courts and commentators have been omitted without so specifying. Numbered footnotes are from the original materials and retain the original numbering. Notes designated by ''a'' indicate that the text was written by the authors.

*

ACKNOWLEDGMENTS

ABA Section of Family Law Working Group on Same–Sex Marriages and Non–Marital Unions, *A White Paper: An Analysis of the Law of Same–Sex Marriage, Civil Unions, and Domestic Partnerships*, 38 FAM. L.Q. 339, 349–50 (2004). Copyright by American Bar Association. Reprinted with permission.

American Law Institute, *Principles of the Law of Family Dissolution: Analysis and Recommendations*, §§ 2.03(1)(b), 2.03(c), 2.03 (Comment b. (iii), Illustration 13), 2.08, 2.17 (4), 6.03 (Comments and Illustrations). © 2002 by the American Law Institute, Philadelphia, Pennsylvania. Reprinted with permission. All rights reserved.

American Psychological Association, Presidential Task Force On Violence and the Family, *Issues and Dilemmas in Family Violence, Issue 5: When Parents Separate After an Abusive Relationship,* http://www.apa.org/pi/pii/familyvio/issue5.html. © 1998 American Psychological Association, Washington, DC. Reprinted by permission.

ANTOKOLSKAIA, MASHA, CONVERGENCE OF DIVORCE LAWS IN EUROPE 3–4 (2004). Copyright by M.V. Antokolskaia. Reprinted by permission of M.V. Antokolskaia.

Appleton, Susan Frelich, *Missing in Action? Gender Talk in the Same–Sex Marriage Debate*, 16 STAN. L. & POL'Y REV. 97, 106–09 (2005). Copyright by Stanford Law & Policy Review. Reprinted by permission of *Stanford Law & Policy Review*.

Atwood, Barbara Ann, *The Uniform Representation of Children in Abuse, Neglect and Custody Proceedings Act: Bridging the Divide Between Pragmatism and Idealism*, 42 FAM. L. Q. 63 (2008). Reprinted by permission of the author and the American Bar Associcaiton.

Bahr, Stephen J., *Social Science Research on Family Dissolution*, 4 J. L. & FAM. STUD. 5, 7–8 (2002). Copyright by Journal of Law & Family Studies. Reprinted by permission of *Journal of Law & Family Studies*.

BARTHOLET, ELIZABETH, FAMILY BONDS: ADOPTION, INFERTILITY, AND THE NEW WORLD OF CHILD PRODUCTION 73–74 (1999). Copyright by Beacon Press. Reprinted by permission.

Basch, Norma, *Invisible Women: The Legal Fiction of Marital Unity in Nineteenth Century America,* 5 FEMINIST STUD. 350 (1979). © 1979 Feminist Studies, College Park, Maryland. Reprinted by permission.

Brinig, Margaret F., *Domestic Partnership: Missing the Target?*, 4 J. OF L. & FAM. STUD. 28 (2002). © 2002 Journal of Law and Family Studies, Salt Lake City, Utah. Reprinted by permission.

———, *In Search of Prince Charming*, 4 J. GENDER, RACE & JUST. 321, 331–32 (2001). Copyright by Margaret Brinig. Reprinted by permission of Margaret Brining.

———, *Does Mediation Systematically Disadvantage Women?*, 2 WM. & MARY J. WOMEN & L. 1 (1994). Copyright by The College of William and Mary. Reprinted by permission.

Buel, Sarah, *Effective Assistance of Counsel for Battered Women Defendants: A Normative Construct*, 26 HARV. WOMEN'S L.J. 238 (2003). © 2003 by the President and Fellows of Harvard College and The Harvard Women's Law Journal, Cambridge, Massachusetts. Reprinted with permission.

Cahn, Naomi, *Perfect Substitutes or the Real Thing?*, 52 DUKE L.J. 1077, 1139–40 (2003). Copyright by Duke Law Journal. Reprinted by permission of Duke Law Review.

Cahn, Naomi & Jana Singer, *Adoption, Identity and the Constitution: The Case For Opening Closed Records*, 2 U. PA. J. CONST. L. 150 (1999). Copyright by The University of Pennsylvania Journal of Constitutional Law. Reprinted by permission.

Carbone, June, *The Futility of Coherence: The ALI's Principles of the Law*, 4 J. OF L. & FAM. STUD. 78–79 (2005). © 2005 Journal of Law and Family Studies, Salt Lake City, Utah. Reprinted by permission.

Carbone, June & Naomi Cahn, *Which Ties Bind? Redefining the Parent–Child Relationship in an Age of Genetic Certainty*, 11 WM. & MARY BILL RTS. J. 1011, 1042 (2003). Reprinted by permission.

Case, Mary Anne, *How High the Apple Pie? A Few Troubling Questions About Where, Why, and How the Burden of Care for Children Should Be Shifted*, 76 CHI.-KENT L. REV. 1754–55, 1765–66 (2001). © 2001 Chicago–Kent Law Review, Chicago, Illinois. Reprinted by permission.

Cere, Dan, *The Future of Family Law: Law and the Marriage Crisis in North America, A Report from the Council on Family Law,* pp. 5–8, 39–40 (2005). © 2005 Institute for American Values, Institute for Marriage and Public Policy, and Institute for the Study of Marriage, Law and Culture, New York, New York. Reprinted by permission.

Chambers, David L., *Polygamy and Same–Sex Marriage*, 26 HOFSTRA L. REV. 53, 79–81 (1997). Copyright by David Chambers. Reprinted by permission of the Hofstra Law Review Association.

CLARK, HOMER H., JR., THE LAW OF DOMESTIC RELATIONS IN THE UNITED STATES 406 (1988). Copyright by Thomson West. Reprinted with permission of Thomson West.

COONTZ, STEPHANIE, MARRIAGE: A HISTORY (2005). (c) 2005 by the S.J. Coontz Company. Used by permission of Viking Penguin, a division of Penguin Group (USA) Inc. Reprinted by permission.

Corbett, William R., *A Somewhat Modest Proposal To Prevent Adultery and Save Families: Two Old Torts Looking for a New Career*, 33 ARIZ. ST. L.J.

985, 988–89 (2001). Copyright by William R. Corbett. Reprinted by permission of the Arizona State Law Journal and Professor William R. Corbett.

COTT, NANCY F., PUBLIC VOWS: A HISTORY OF MARRIAGE AND THE NATION 3, 30–31, 208–09 (2000). Copyright by Harvard University Press. Reprinted by permission of the Harvard University Press.

Crenshaw, Kimberle, *Mapping the Margins: Intersectionality, Identity Politics, and Violence Against Women of Color*, 43 STAN. L. REV. 1257 (1991). © 1991 The Stanford Law Review, Stanford, California. Reprinted by permission.

Dubler, Ariela R., *Wifely Behavior: A Legal History of Acting Married*, 100 COLUM. L. REV. 957, 968–69 (2000). Copyright by Columbia Law Review. Reprinted with permission of *Columbia Law Review*.

Eisenberg, Melvin A., *Disclosure in a Contract Law*, 91 CAL. L. REV. 1645, 1682 (2003). Copyright by California Law Review. Reprinted by permission of the *California Law Review*.

———, *Why There is No Law of Relational Contracts*, 94 NW. U. L. REV. 805, 808 (2000). Copyright by Northwestern University Law Review. Reprinted by special permission of Northwestern University School of Law, *Northwestern University Law Review*.

———, *The Limits of Cognition and the Limits of Contract*, 47 STAN. L. REV. 211 (1995). Copyright by Stanford Law Review. Reprinted by permission.

Ellman, Ira Mark & Stephen D. Sugarman, *Spousal Emotional Abuse as a Tort?*, 55 MD. L. REV. 1268, 1302, 1328–29, 1343 (1996). Copyright by Ira Mark Ellman. Reprinted by permission of Ira Mark Ellman and the *Maryland Law Review*.

Ellman, Ira Mark and Sharon Lohr, *Marriage as Contract, Opportunistic Violence, and Other Bad Arguments for Fault Divorce*, 1997 UNIV. OF ILL. L. REV. 743. © 1997 The Board of Trustees of the University of Illinois, Champaign, Illinois. Reprinted by permission.

ESPENSHADE, THOMAS J., INVESTING IN CHILDREN: NEW ESTIMATES OF PARENTAL EXPENDITURES 1–4 (1984). Copyright by the Urban Institute. Reprinted by permission.

Martha L. Fineman and Anne Opie, *The Uses of Social Science Data in Legal Policymaking: Custody Determinations at Divorce*, 1987 Wis. L. Rev. 112–113. © 1987 Wisconsin Law Review, Madison, Wisconsin.

Finn, Margot, *Women, Consumption and Coverture in England, c. 1760–1860, The Historical Journal,* 39,3 (1996), pp.703–722. Copyright ©1996 Cambridge University Press. Reprinted with the permission of Cambridge University Press.

Freud, Anna, "Painter v. Bannister: *Postscript by a Psychoanalyst,*" in PROBLEMS OF PSYCHOANALYTIC TRAINING, DIAGNOSIS, AND THE TECHNIQUE OF THERAPY 1966–1970 (1971). Reprinted from Writings of Anna Freud, Vol. 7, pages 247–255, International Universities Press, Inc. Copyright 1971 by Anna Freud.

Galston, William, *What About the Children?*, BLUEPRINT MAGAZINE, May 21, 2002. Copyright by Blueprint Magazine. Reprinted by permission Blueprint Magazine.

Garrison, Marsha, *Is Consent Necessary? An Evaluation of the Emerging Law of Cohabitant Obligation*, 52 UCLA L. Rev. 815, 817–819 (2005). © 2005 UCLA Law Review, Los Angeles, California. Reprinted by permission.

Gische, Hon. Judith J., *Domestic Violence as a Factor in Child Custody Determinations in New York*, 27 Ford. Urb. L.J. 937, 939–943 (2000). © 2000 Fordham Urban Law Journal, New York, New York. Reprinted by permission.

Glennon, Theresa, Still Partners? Examining the Consequences of Post–Dissolution Parenting, 41 Fam. L. Q. 105 (2007). Reprinted by permission of the author and the American Bar Association.

Goelman, Deborah M., *Shelter from the Storm: Using Jurisdictional Statutes to Protect Victims of Domestic Violence after the Violence Against Women Act of 2000*, 13 Colum. J. of Gender and L. 105 (2004). © 2004 Columbia Journal of Gender and Law, New York, New York. Reprinted by permission.

Goldberg, Steven, *MRIs and the Perception of Risk*, 33 Am. J. L. & Med. 229 (2007). Copyright by the American Society of Law, Medicine & Ethics and the Boston University School of Law. Reprinted by permission.

GOLDSTEIN, JOSEPH, ANNA FREUD & ALBERT J. SOLNIT, BEYOND THE BEST INTERESTS OF THE CHILD. Copyright © 1973, 1979 by the Free Press. Reprinted with the permission of The Free Press, a Division of Simon & Schuster Adult Publishing Group. All rights reserved.

GOLDSTEIN, JOSEPH, ANNA FREUD, ALBERT J. SOLNIT & SONJA GOLDSTEIN, THE BEST INTERESTS OF THE CHILD. Copyright © 1986 by the Free Press. Reprinted with the permission of The Free Press, a Division of Simon & Schuster Adult Publishing Group. All rights reserved.

Grillo, Tina, *The Mediation Alternative: Process Dangers For Women*, 100 YALE L.J. 1545, 1545–1610 (1991). Reprinted by permission of *The Yale Law Journal Company* and William S. Hein Company.

GUGGENHEIM, MARTIN, WHAT'S WRONG WITH CHILDREN'S RIGHTS 162–63 (2005). Copyright © 2005 by the President and Fellows of Harvard College. Reprinted by permission of Harvard University Press.

Harris, Leslie Joan, *The ALI Child Support Principles: Incremental Changes to Improve the Lot of Children and Residential Parents*, 8 DUKE J. L. & POL'Y 245 (2001). Copyright by Leslie Joan Harris. Reprinted by permission.

HARTOG, HENDRICK, MAN AND WIFE IN AMERICA: A HISTORY 24 (2000). Copyright by Harvard University Press. Reprinted by permission of Harvard University Press.

Herman, Stephen P., *Child Custody Evaluations and the Need for Standards of Care and Peer Review*, 1 J. of the Center for Child. & the Courts 141 (1999). © 1999 Stephen P. Herman. Judicial Council of California, San Francisco, California. Reprinted by permission.

HILL, CATHERINE & ELENA SILVA, PUBLIC PERCEPTIONS OF THE PAY GAP 4–9 (2005). © 2005 American Association of University Women, AAUW Educational Foundation, Washington, DC. Reprinted by permission.

HOCHSCHILD, ARLIE & ANN MACHUNG, THE SECOND SHIFT. Copyright (c) 1989, 2003 by Arlie Hochschild. Used by permission of Viking Penguin, a division of Penguin Group (USA) Inc.

Joyce, Holly, *Mediation and Domestic Violence: Legislative Responses*, 14 J. of Amer. Acad. of Matrimonial Law. 451–452 (1997). © 1997 American Academy of Matrimonial Lawyers, Chicago, IL. Reprinted by permission.

Kapalla, Lara Lenzotti, *Some Assembly Required: Why States Should Not Adopt the ALI's System of Presumptive Alimony in Its Current Form*, 2004 MICH. ST. L. REV. 207, 234–235. © 2005 Michigan State Law Review, East Lansing, MI. Reprinted by permission.

Kay, Herma Hill, *From the Second Sex to the Joint Venture: An Overview of Women's Rights and Family Law in the United States During the Twentieth Century*, 88 CAL. L. REV. 2048–2049, 2062–2064, 2088, 2090, 2093 (2000). © 2000 by the California Law Review, Berkeley, California. Reprinted by permission of the University of California, Berkeley.

Kisthardt, Mary Kay, *Rethinking Alimony: The AAML's Considerations for Calculating Alimony, Spousal Support or Maintenance*, 21 J. AM. ACAD. MATRIMONIAL L. 61 (2008). Copyright American Academy of Matrimonial Lawyers. Reprinted by permission.

Klarman, Michael J., Brown *and* Lawrence *(and* Goodridge*)*, 104 MICH. L. REV. 431 (2005). Copyright by Michigan Law Review and Michael J. Klarman. Reprinted with permission.

Lande, John & Gregg Herman, *Fitting the Forum to the Family Fuss: Choosing Mediation, Collaborative Law, or Cooperative Law for Negotiating Divorce Cases*, 42 FAM. CT. REV. 280 (2004). Copyright Blackwell Publishing, Inc. Reprinted by permission.

Lehrman, Frederica, *Factoring Domestic Violence into Custody Cases*, 32 TRIAL Mag. 34–35 (1996). © 1996 Association of Trial Lawyers of America, Washington, DC. Reprinted by permission.

Larson, Jane E., *"Women Understand So Little, They Call My Good Nature 'Deceit' "*: *A Feminist Rethinking of Seduction*, 93 COLUM. L. REV. 374, 379–80 (1993). Copyright by Columbia Law Review. Reprinted with permission of *Columbia Law Review*.

McCluskey, Martha, *Caring for Workers,* 55 Me. L. Rev. 321 (2003). © 2003 Maine Law Review, Portland, Maine. Reprinted by permission.

McDonnell, Brett, *Is Incest Next?*, 10 CARDOZO WOMEN'S L.J. 337, 354–55 (2004). Copyright by Cardozo Women's Law Journal. Reprinted by permission of *Cardozo Women's Law Journal*.

Mnookin, Robert H., *Divorce Bargaining: The Limits on Private Ordering*, 18 U. MICH. J. L. REF. 1015, 1015–16 (1985). Reprinted with the permission of LexisNexis.

Mnookin, Robert H. & Lewis Kornhauser, *Bargaining in the Shadow of the Law*, 88 YALE L.J. 950 (1979). Copyright by Robert H. Mnookin. Reprinted by permission.

National Marriage Project, The State of Our Unions (2007). Reprinted by permissioin.

Neely, Richard, *The Primary Caretaker Parent Rule: Child Custody and the Dynamics of Greed*, 3 YALE L. & POL'Y REV. 177 (1984). © 1984 Yale Law and Policy Review, New Haven, Connecticut. Reprinted by permission.

Note, *The Unnecessary Doctrine of Necessaries*, 82 MICH. L. REV. 1773–75 (1984). © 1984 Michigan Law Review, Ann Arbor, Michigan. Reprinted by permission.

Papke, David Ray, State v. Oakley, *Deadbeat Dads, and American Poverty*, 26 W. NEW ENG. L. REV. 9 (2004). Copyright by The Western New England Law Review and David Ray Papke. Reprinted by permission.

Perry, Twila L., *Alimony: Race, Privilege, and Dependency in the Search for Theory*, 82 GEO. L.J. 2489–2490, 2519 (1994). © 1994 Georgetown Law Journal, Washington, DC. Reprinted with permission of the publisher, Georgetown Law Journal © 1994.

Pratt, Robert A., *Crossing the Color Line: A Historical Assessment and Personal Narrative of* Loving v. Virginia, 41 HOW. L.J. 229, 236 (1998). Copyright by Howard Law Journal. Reprinted with permission of *Howard Law Journal*.

Ravdin, Linda J., *Prenups to Protect Children*, 24 FAM. ADVOC. 32, 33–36 (Winter 2002). Copyright by American Bar Association. Reprinted by permission.

Roberts, Dorothy E., *Spiritual and Menial Housework*, 9 YALE J. OF L. & FEMINISM 55, 59, 61, 63, 70, 73, 79 (1997). © 1997 Yale Journal of Law and Feminism, New Haven, Connecticut. Reprinted by permission.

Ross, Catherine J., *From Vulnerability to Voice: Appointing Counsel for Children in Civil Litigation*, 64 FORD. L. REV. 1615–1616 (1996).© 1996 Fordham Law Review, New York, New York. Reprinted by permission.

———, *United Family Courts: Good Sense, Good Justice*, 35 TRIAL Mag. 30–31 (1999). © 1999 Association of Trial Lawyers of America, Washington, DC. Reprinted by permission.

SCHEPARD, ANDREW I., CHILDREN, COURTS, AND CUSTODY: INTERDISCIPLINARY MODELS FOR DIVORCING FAMILIES 45–46, 167–169 (2004). © 2004 Cambridge University Press, New York, New York. Reprinted by permission.

Schontzler, Gail, *E-wedding in Montana Unites Couple Thousands of Miles Away*, BOZEMAN DAILY CHRONICLE, Dec. 23, 2005. Copyright by Bozeman Daily Chronicle. Reprinted by permission of the *Bozeman Daily Chronicle*.

Silbaugh, Katharine B., *Marriage Contracts and the Family Economy*, 93 NW. U. L. REV. 65, 78 (1998). Copyright by Northwestern University Law

Review. Reprinted by special permission of Northwestern University School of Law, *Northwestern University Law Review.*

Singer, Jana B., *The Privatization of Family Law*, 1992 Wis. L. Rev. 1443. Copyright by the Wisconsin Law Review. Reprinted by permission.

Singer, Jana B. & William Reynolds, *A Dissent on Joint Custody*, 47 Md. L. Rev. 503–504 (1988). © 1988 Maryland Law Review, Baltimore, Maryland. Reprinted by permission.

Smith, Peggie R., *Elder Care, Gender, and Work: The Work–Family Issue of the 21st Century*, 25 Berkeley J. of Employ. & Lab. L. 352–353, 360, 370, 379, 382 & 386 (2004). © 2004 by The Regents of the University of California, Berkeley, California. Reprinted by permission of The Regents of the University of California.

Spaht, Katherine Shaw & Symeon C. Symeonides, *Covenant Marriage and the Law of Conflict of Laws*, 32 Creighton L. Rev. 1120 (1999). Copyright © 1999 by Creighton University. Reprinted by permission.

Spector, Robert G., *Marital Torts: The Current Legal Landscape*, 38 Fam. L.Q. 745, 760–61 (1999). Copyright by American Bar Association. Reprinted with permission.

Starnes, Cynthia Lee, *Swords in the Hands of Babes: Rethinking Custody Interviews After Troxel*, 2003 Wis. L. Rev. 117. © 2003 Wisconsin Law Review, Madison, Wisconsin. Reprinted by permission.

————, *Mothers as Suckers*, 90 Iowa L. Rev. 1513 (2005). Reprinted by permission.

Stewart, Monte Neil, *Judicial Redefinition of Marriage*, 21 Can. J. Fam. L. 11, 81 (2004). Copyright by the Canadian Journal of Family Law. Reprinted with permission of Canadian Journal of Family Law.

Stutzman, Rene, *Wife Says Divorce Is News To Her*, Orlando Sun-Sentinel, Jan. 3, 2006. Copyright by Orlando Sentinel. Reprinted with the permission of *Orlando Sentinel.*

Strub, Rochelle, *Marital Property Division in Divorce Proceedings: Full Faith & Credit Clause and Jurisdiction*, 11 J. of Contemp. Legal Issues 222–223 (2000). © 2000 Journal of Contemporary Legal Issues, San Diego, California. Reprinted with the permission of the Journal of Contemporary Legal Issues.

Teitelbaum, Lee, *Rays of Light: Other Disciplines and Family Law*, 1 J. of L. & Fam. Stud. 2 & 10 (1999). © 1999 Journal of Law and Family Studies, Salt Lake City, Utah. Reprinted by permission.

Turley, Jonathan, *Polygamy Laws Expose Our Own Hypocrisy*, USA Today, Oct. 4, 2004, at 13A. Copyright by Jonathan Turley. Reprinted with the permission of Jonathan Turley.

Waggoner, Lawrence, *The Uniform Probate Code's Elective Share: Time for a Reassessment*, 37 Univ. of Mich. J. L. Ref. 1 (2003). © 2003 University of Michigan Journal of Law Reform, Ann Arbor, Michigan. Reprinted by permission.

Warren, Elizabeth, *The New Economics of the American Family*, 12 Amer. Bankr. Inst. L. Rev. 14–16, 19–20 (2004). © 2004 American Bankruptcy Institute Law Review, Alexandria, Virginia. Reprinted with permission of the American Bankruptcy Institute (www.abiworld.org).

Wasserman, Rhonda, *Divorce and Domicile: Time to Sever the Knot*, 39 WM. & MARY L. REV. 32–33 (1997). © 1997 College of William and Mary, William and Mary Law Review, Williamsburg, Virginia. Reprinted by permission.

————, *Parents, Partners, and Personal Jurisdiction*. 1995 UNIV. OF ILL. L. REV. 813–815. © 1995 The Board of Trustees of the University of Illinois, Champaign, Illinois.

WILLIAMS, JOAN, UNBENDING GENDER: WHY FAMILY AND WORK CONFLICT AND WHAT TO DO ABOUT IT (1999). Copyright © 1999 by Oxford University Press, Inc. Used by permission of Oxford University Press, Inc.

Williams, Joan & Nancy Segal, *Beyond the Maternal Wall: Relief for Family Caregivers Who Are Discriminated Against on the Job*, 26 HARV. WOMEN'S L.J. 90–98, 100–101 (2003). © 2003 Harvard Women's Law Journal, Cambridge, Massachusetts. Reprinted by permission.

Zainaldin, Jamil S., *The Emergence of a Modern American Family Law: Child Custody, Adoption, and the Courts, 1796–1851*, 73 Nw U. L. Rev. 1035 (1979). Reprinted by special permission of Northwestern University School of Law, *Northwestern University Law Review*

SUMMARY OF CONTENTS

———

*

TABLE OF CONTENTS

———

TABLE OF CASES

The principal cases are in bold type. Cases cited or discussed in the text are in roman type. References are to pages. Cases cited in principal cases and within other quoted materials are not included.

CONTEMPORARY FAMILY LAW

Second Edition

*

CHAPTER 1

MARRIAGE, FAMILY AND PRIVACY IN CONTEMPORARY AMERICA

■ ■ ■

The family is central to many political and legal debates. Family policy dominates the front pages of our newspapers and debates about judicial appointments, political elections and congressional actions. Family policy, of course, also vitally affects the day-to-day lives of adults and children. In prominent front-page coverage, social commentators have warned that the nuclear family is receding and being fast eclipsed by a variety of more unconventional family forms.

"Nuclear" families comprised of married couples living with their children—the family form long venerated as the social norm—now constitute less than a quarter of all American households. In their place, the U.S. Census Bureau has found dramatic growth in alternative family arrangements, particularly in the number of households headed by single mothers. Even more to the point, the Census Bureau finds a shift toward what it calls "nonfamily" households. These households—consisting of single adults living alone or with others not related by marriage, birth or adoption—already comprise nearly a third of all households, and their numbers are growing at twice the rate of "family" households. This increase in the number of nonfamily households, moreover, does not fully capture the growing frequency of unconventional living arrangements. Some households classified by the Census Bureau as "family households" (because they contain two or more people related by birth, adoption or marriage) nevertheless contain broader intimate groupings that the Bureau does not recognize as "families"—for instance, unmarried partners living with a child who is related by birth or adoption to only one partner. Thus, even the ranks of "family households" include a growing number of what might be called "nonfamily families."

For many years now, changes in the patterns and forms of family life have attracted intense, very public and sometimes acrimonious discussion. In different quarters, the discussion has occasioned both hand-wringing and celebration that individuals are choosing to marry later, or to forgo marriage altogether for a widening array of nontraditional alternatives. For some decades, legislation and administrative policy concerning the family have shown a sustained trend toward permitting individuals great-

1

er freedom to define the content and terms of their own relationships. The law of no-fault divorce, for instance, has comprehensively shifted decisional power from legislators and judges—who for years intensively regulated precisely which human foibles or failures would permit dissolution of a marriage—to the marriage partners themselves.

This course explores issues concerning what the family is, and the legal rights and obligations of belonging to a family. Family law (and traffic violations) are the most common points of contact between most individuals and the justice system. This course is rich in human emotions, and its lessons are useful even if you do not ultimately specialize in family law practice. Because everyone is somehow involved with one or more families, your friends, family members and clients will likely ask you, either formally or informally, about subjects covered in this course. Because family law overlaps with so many other areas of substantive law, ranging from tax to real property to closely held corporations to poverty law, you are likely to use your learning from this course regardless of what area of legal practice you eventually enter.

This Chapter sets the stage for ongoing discussions about the contemporary American family. It includes an overview of changes in the family in the last half-century and then examines how the law structures and affects families. As you will see, the law is integrally involved in the family.

To show how the law structures families, this Chapter's decisions focus on the contours of family privacy. There are three reasons for this focus. First, the right to privacy is closely entwined with the rights and obligations of family members. Second, this Chapter introduces the central characters and debates that recur throughout family law. The materials raise the interests of the family unit itself, the individual, the married couple, the unmarried, wives, husbands, parents, children, fetuses, and the state and federal governments. The materials also present conflicts among these persons and interests. Third, this Chapter emphasizes the lack of consensus that pervades family law. As you read the concurring and dissenting opinions in the Supreme Court's family privacy decisions, you will see the intense disagreements that family law issues evoke. These disagreements hold both societal interest in public policy formulation and practical significance for client representation.

SECTION 1: THE AMERICAN FAMILY TODAY

The structure of the family has changed dramatically over the past century as individuals live longer, marry at a later age, and have fewer children. In the United States, the median age of first marriage is 25.5 for women and 27.5 for men. U.S. Census Bureau, Table MS–2: Estimated Median Age at First Marriage, by Sex: 1890–Present (2007), avail. at http://www.census.gov/population/socdemo/hh-fam/ms2.xls. These demographics have changed dramatically since 1960, when the median age at first marriage was 20.3 for women, and 22.8 for men. On the other hand, in 1890, the median age at first marriage for men was 26.1, and 22.0 for women. *Id.* The number of couples who live together without marrying increased by more than 1,000% from 1960 to 2006. The National Marriage Project, The State of Our Unions, 2007, at 19–20 (2007). This Section offers contrasting views on the changing American family.

A. PROPONENTS OF CHANGE

STEPHANIE COONTZ

Marriage, a History: From Obedience to Intimacy or How Love Conquered Marriage.
243, 250, 263–64, 275–76 (2005).

As late as 1963 nothing seemed more obvious to most family experts and to the general public than the preeminence of marriage in people's lives and the permanence of the male breadwinner family. * * *

It is impossible to sort out neatly in order of importance all the factors that rearranged social and political life between the 1960s and the 1990s and in the process transformed marriage as well. Sometimes it is even hard to say which changes caused the transformation and which were consequences. But the changes were not effected by a single generation or a particular political ideology. * * *

In 1977, sociologist Amitai Etzioni warned that if present trends in divorce continued, "not one American family" would be left intact by the 1990s. By 1980 the divorce rate stood at 50 percent. Half of all people who married could be expected to divorce.

The divorce revolution, as some people have called it, transformed the lives of millions of people. But the surge in divorce was only an early precursor of the bigger storm that swept across marriage and family life between the late 1970s and the end of the century.

As long as rates of marriage and remarriage remained high, the increase in divorce did not threaten the universality of marriage, however disruptive and painful those divorces and remarriages were to the particular families involved. But at the end of the 1970s the impact of high divorce rates was accelerated by a plunge in the number of remarriages and a whole flood of new alternatives to marriage.

After 1981, divorce rates leveled off and began a slow decline, despite the fact that by then no-fault divorce was ubiquitous. But fewer people remarried after divorce. A generation earlier, in the 1950s, two-thirds of divorced women in the United States married again within five years. By the end of the century only half of divorced women were married or even living with partners five years later.

* * *

Equally dramatic was the number of people who waited past their mid-twenties to marry for the first time. In 1960 only one in ten American women aged twenty-five to twenty-nine was single. In 1998, nearly 40 percent of women in that age group were unmarried.

An even more momentous change was the number of couples who lived together without marrying. Between 1970 and 1999 the number of unmarried couples living together in the United States increased seven-fold. When this trend began, most couples married if the woman got pregnant. But by the 1990s, marriage was no longer regarded as the obvious response to pregnancy or childbirth.

The repercussions were staggering. In 1960, one American child in twenty was born to an unmarried woman. By the end of the century it was one child in three. In 2003, the U.S. census reported that almost 40 percent of cohabiting couples had children under eighteen living with them, a figure nearly as high as the 45 percent of married couples with children under eighteen.

In the late 1990s the pace of change began to slow, leading some observers to hope that the storm had passed and marriage would soon return to "normal." By 1998 the divorce rate was 26 percent lower than in 1979. Birthrates for unmarried white women stabilized in the 1990s, and those of black and Hispanic women actually declined. Also, more out-of-wedlock babies were now born to cohabiting couples than to women living alone, the earlier pattern. In popular culture, marriage and family life seemed to be regaining some of their luster. * * *

One-third of female same-sex households and more than one-fifth of male same-sex households include biological children under eighteen. Eight U.S. states and the District of Columbia currently allow a child to have two legal mothers or two legal fathers. And 40 percent of the nation's adoption agencies report that they have placed children with gay or lesbian parents. This is a reality that won't go away. In 2002 the American Academy of Pediatrics called for legalizing partner adoptions in families where the biological parent of a child lives with a same-sex partner. In 2004 the American Psychological Association endorsed same-sex marriage.

* * *

The reproductive revolution has shaken up all the relationships once taken for granted between sex, marriage, conception, childbirth, and parenting. People who could not become parents before can now do so in such bewildering combinations that a child can potentially have five different parents: a sperm donor, an egg donor, a birth mother, and the social father and mother who raise the child. On the other hand, some married couples use new reproductive technologies to avoid having chil-dren altogether. Seen in this light, a childless marriage is just as much a challenge to the tradition that children are the central purpose and glue of a wedded relationship as is a gay union.

The many young people who delay marrying until their late twenties or early thirties also contribute to the diminishing role of marriage in organizing social and personal life. Today, in contrast with medieval Europe and colonial America, most young people go through an extended period when they do not live with and are not under the control of their parents or any other married people. However, as singles they can exercise most of the political and economic privileges of adulthood when they turn eighteen and twenty-one.

This large pool of single youth, along with the extension of the life span, has contributed to a stunning explosion of solitary living in Western societies. More than one-quarter of all U.S. households now contain only one person. At various times and in various places in history, rates of nonmarital sex, divorce, cohabitation, or out-of-wedlock childbearing have been higher than they are today. But never before have so many people lived alone. And never before have unmarried people, living alone or in couples, had the same rights as married adults. The spread of solitary living and cohabitation reduces the social weight of marriage in the economy and polity; creating tastes, habits, expectations, and voting blocs that are not tied to the role of wife or husband.

In the 1950s married couples represented 80 percent all households in the United States. By the beginning of the twenty-first century they were less than 51 percent, and married couples with children were just 25 percent of all households. For the first time ever, there were more single-person households than those with a married couple and children. Married persons were still a majority of the workforce and of the home buyers in 2001, but unmarried individuals were gaining fast, accounting for 42 percent of the workforce and 40 percent of home buyers.

* * *

B.   RESERVATIONS ABOUT CHANGE

In response to the developments chronicled by Coontz and the perception that many legal scholars and institutions have embraced or even promoted a revolution in social practices concerning marriage and parenthood, 21 legal scholars from the United States and Canada offered a critique of current family law trends. The following excerpt summarizes their argument that the lack of "conceptual clarity about marriage and its meanings" in both professional and popular debate has resulted in diminished understanding of the stakes at issue in the transformation of the family.

COUNCIL ON FAMILY LAW
DANIEL CERE, PRINCIPAL INVESTIGATOR

The Future of Family Law: Law and the Marriage Crisis in North America.
5–8, 39–40 (2005).

* * * [F]amily law is headed in one or more of at least four troubling directions. Some of these changes have already been implemented in some jurisdictions in the United States and Canada.

1. Equivalence Between Cohabitation and Marriage

Many now argue that marriage and cohabitation should be treated equally under the law. This approach denies that some couples might intentionally choose not to marry. Most dramatically, it would have the law treat the two institutions similarly when social science data show that, when it comes to the well-being of children, cohabitation is on average much less stable and safe.

2. Redefining Marriage as a Couple–Centered Bond

In order to accommodate same-sex couples, this approach redefines marriage as a gender-neutral union of two persons. By doing so it neutralizes the law's ability to say that children need their mothers and fathers, and reifies a new conception of marriage that is centered on the couple rather than the children.

3. Disestablishment, or the Separation of Marriage and State

Given serious and seemingly irresolvable cultural and political clashes between competing visions of marriage, increasing numbers of advocates on the left and the right are calling for disestablishment of marriage, or getting the state "out of the marriage business." This approach denies the state's legitimate and serious interest in marriage as our most important child-protecting social institution and as an institution that helps protect and sustain liberal democracy.

4. Why Just Two?

The gendered definition of marriage has already met serious challenges (and been defeated) in some U.S. and Canadian courts. Challenges to the two-person definition of marriage are only a matter of time. * * *

Clashing Models of Marriage

What are the competing models of marriage that are at odds in today's family law debates?

1. The Conjugal View

The model of marriage broadly reflected in law and culture until quite recently can be called the "conjugal model." Marriage in this view is a sexual union of husband and wife who promise each other sexual fidelity, mutual caretaking, and the joint parenting of any children they may have. Conjugal marriage is fundamentally child-centered. Theorists of liberal democracy from John Locke to John Rawls have underlined the important, generative work that conjugal marriage does for society. This normative model of marriage is under attack.

2. The Close Relationship Model

This competing vision of marriage has emerged in recent decades. In it, marriage is a private relationship between two people created primarily to satisfy the needs of adults. If children arise from the union, so be it, but marriage and children are not seen as intrinsically connected. * * *

This view of marriage radically sidelines the main feature that makes marriage unique and important as a social institution–that is, the attempt to bridge sex difference and struggle with the generative power of opposite-sex unions, including the reality that children often arise (intentionally or not) from heterosexual unions.

* * *

Delinking parenthood from marriage, embracing the variety of relationships that adults construct as the new "standard," and conceptualizing the parent-child relationship as just another "close relationship," may free adults to live in the diverse family types they choose, but it seriously undermines the law's historic role to seek to protect the best interests of children. Children need and desire, whenever possible, to be raised by their own parents. Though fallible, marriage is society's best known way to try to fulfill that need. * * *

* * * Institutions like marriage and parenthood are not simply mechanisms to fulfill individual needs and aspirations. They are also thick, multi-layered realities that speak to the needs for meaning and identity within human community. Marriage is the complex cultural site for opposite-sex bonding. A rich heritage of symbols, myths, theologies, traditions, poetry, and art has clustered around the marital bond. To change the core features of marriage is to impact real people, adults and children, whose lives will be significantly shaped by the renewal or decline of this institution. * * *

* * *

NOTES AND QUESTIONS

1. *The role of marriage.* The authors of these commentaries express very different views of the changing American family and the function of marriage. *See* Vivian Hamilton, *Mistaking Marriage For Social Policy*, 11 Va. J. Soc. Pol'y & L. 307, 314–23 (2004) (describing conflicting perspectives). Which view of the contemporary family is closer to your own? What is the purpose of marriage? What should it be? In answering these questions, consider how your own family experiences influence your answer. Also consider whether there are any distinctions between the scope of your personal views and the scope of the appropriate level of legal intervention in personal choices.

This course deals with legal definitions of marriage. Common usage may take a different view. In 2009 Merriam–Webster's Collegiate Dictionary joined other dictionaries in adding a secondary definition of marriage: "the state of being united to a person of the same sex in a relationship like that of a traditional marriage." Martha Neil, *Webster Makes It Official: Definition of Marriage Has Changed.* Mar. 23, 2009 ABA Journal, Law News Now. http://www.abajournal.com/weekly.

2. *The contemporary family.* As you will see later in this Chapter, the family exists as a legal entity. Yet the individuals within the family also have rights. Balancing these legal rights, of families and of individual family members, creates a significant tension throughout family law. How do the two commentaries respond to this tension?

3. *What constitutes a family?* Some commentators have argued that the law should respect a broader range of close personal relationships outside of marriage—including friendships without sexual relationships—and accord these relationships legal protections resembling those accorded to marital families. *See, e.g.,* Maxine Eichner, *Marriage and the Elephant: The Liberal Democratic State's Regulation of Intimate Relationships Between Adults,* 30 Harv. J.L. & Gender 25 (2007).

C. TWO AMERICAS: THE IMPORTANCE OF SOCIAL AND DEMOGRAPHIC DIFFERENCES

Regardless of which view of marriage dominates, the propensity to marry, to have children only within marriage, and to remain married is not evenly distributed across social and economic groups. Recent social science research suggests a growing divide in which "class differences in marital dissolution rates [ ] exacerbate some effects of socioeconomic inequality * * *." Steven P. Martin, *Trends in Marital Dissolution by Women's Education in the United States,* 15 Demographic Research 537, 538 (2006). Professor Martin finds that educational attainment—closely tied to income and earning potential—increasingly predicts marital stability. Marital stability is also correlated with marrying for the first time at a later age and waiting to have children. The decline in the divorce rate that began in the 1970s, he reports, is limited to individuals with a four-year college degree. *Id.* at 537. In contrast, the divorce rate for less educated women is rising; "their marriages are becoming more unstable even as marriages become more stable for highly educated women." *Id.* at 553. The rate of cohabitation is higher among persons with "lower educational and income levels" than for college graduates, as is the rate of childbirth before or outside of marriage. The National Marriage Project, 2007, *infra* at 20, 16. The following excerpt summarizes this increasing social divide.

THE NATIONAL MARRIAGE PROJECT
The State Of Our Unions.
16 (2007).

The Marriage Gap

There is good news and bad news on the marriage front. For the college-educated segment of our population, the institution of marriage appears to have gained strength in recent years. For everyone else, however, marriage continues to weaken. Thus there is a growing "marriage gap" in America, between those who are well educated and those who are not.

Recent data indicates that, for the college-educated, the institution of marriage may actually have strengthened. * * * College-educated women are now marrying at a *higher* rate than their [less educated] peers. Not only that, but the divorce rate among these women is relatively low and has been dropping. This may be due partly to the fact that college-educated women, once the leaders of the divorce revolution, now hold a more restrictive view of divorce than less well educated women. The out-of-wedlock childbearing of college-educated women has always been well below that of other segments of the population. Now, among those who delay marriage past age 30, this is the only group becoming more likely to have children *after* marriage rather than before.

There is more good news. The marriages of the college-educated have become more egalitarian than ever, both in the sense that husbands and wives are matched more equally in their educational and economic backgrounds, and that they hold more egalitarian attitudes about marital gender roles. As icing on the cake, all of this may add up to greater marital happiness. The percentage of spouses among this group who rate their marriage as "very happy" has held fairly steady over recent decades, whereas for other parts of the population the percentage has dropped significantly.

In large numbers, * * * the college-educated part of America is living the American dream—with happy, stable, two-parent families. * * *

* * *

For the non college-educated population, unfortunately, the marriage situation remains gloomy. Marriage rates are continuing to decline, and the percentage of out-of-wedlock births is rising. In the year 2000, fully forty percent of high-school drop-out mothers were living without husbands, compared with just twelve percent of college-grad mothers. Because of the many statistically well-documented benefits of marriage in such areas as income, health, and longevity, this gap is generating a society of greater inequality. America is becoming a nation divided not only by educational and income levels, but by unequal family structures.

NOTES AND QUESTIONS

1. *The risks of divorce are not randomly distributed.* "[Y]our chances of divorce may be lower than you think" because the "background characteristics of people entering a marriage have major implications for their risk of divorce." *Id.* at 20. The "percentage point decreases in the risk of divorce * * * during the first ten years of marriage" is based on various factors. For example, an annual income over $50,000 diminishes the risk of divorce by 30% when compared to a person with an annual income below $25,000. *Id.* Delaying child bearing until marriage (including becoming pregnant in the two months prior to marriage) decreases the likelihood of divorce by 24%, as does waiting until age 25 to marry. *Id.*

2. *The fertility gap.* College-educated women have significantly fewer children than women with less education. "In 2004, for example, twenty-four percent of women 40 to 44 years old with a bachelor's degree were childless, compared to only fifteen percent of those without a high school degree." The National Marriage Project, 2007, *supra*, at 16. Since children's educational attainment and social class often replicate that of their parents, "[s]ome expect the marriage gap to grow larger in the future * * *. Children of the

educated and financially comfortable are better socialized to marry successfully and to contain childbearing within marriage, whereas children of the lower classes often do not have this advantage." *Id.* at 7.

3. *Unequal family structures.* If, as some have argued, one primary function of marriage is to provide a stable setting for raising children, how concerned are you about the documentation of unequal family structures? To the extent that education is what social scientists call a "proxy" for socioeconomic status, what government policies might help stem the marriage gap? Should government play a role in encouraging marriage, at least for couples who have, or plan to have, children? If so, on what basis?

As you read the next Section of this Chapter consider how the law treats families that do not resemble the idealized nuclear family.

SECTION 2: THE RELATIONSHIP BETWEEN FAMILIES AND THE LAW

A. PUBLIC LAW

The law affects the family in many different ways, ranging from tax and bankruptcy to education to regulation of the actual formation and dissolution of the family as a legal unit. By deciding what groups constitute a family, the law has a significant impact on the benefits of different familial structures.

MOORE v. CITY OF EAST CLEVELAND

Supreme Court of the United States, 1977.
431 U.S. 494.

MR. JUSTICE POWELL announced the judgment of the Court, and delivered an opinion in which MR. JUSTICE BRENNAN, MR. JUSTICE MARSHALL and MR. JUSTICE BLACKMUN joined.

East Cleveland's housing ordinance, like many throughout the country, limits occupancy of a dwelling unit to members of a single family. § 1351.02.[1] But the ordinance contains an unusual and complicated definitional section that recognizes as a "family" only a few categories of related individuals. § 1341.08.[2] Because her family, living together in her home,

---

1. All citations by section number refer to the Housing Code of the city of East Cleveland, Ohio.

2. Section 1341.08 (1966) provides:

" 'Family' means a number of individuals related to the nominal head of the household or to the spouse of the nominal head of the household living as a single housekeeping unit in a single dwelling unit, but limited to the following:

"(a) Husband or wife of the nominal head of the household.

"(b) Unmarried children of the nominal head of the household or of the spouse of the nominal head of the household, provided, however, that such unmarried children have no children residing with them.

"(c) Father or mother of the nominal head of the household or of the spouse of the nominal head of the household.

"(d) Notwithstanding the provisions of subsection (b) hereof, a family may include not more than one dependent married or unmarried child of the nominal head of the household or of the

fits none of those categories, appellant stands convicted of a criminal offense. The question in this case is whether the ordinance violates the Due Process Clause of the Fourteenth Amendment.

I

Appellant, Mrs. Inez Moore, lives in her East Cleveland home together with her son, Dale Moore, Sr., and her two grandsons, Dale, Jr., and John Moore, Jr. The two boys are first cousins rather than brothers; we are told that John came to live with his grandmother and with the elder and younger Dale Moores after his mother's death.

In early 1973, Mrs. Moore received a notice of violation from the city, stating that John was an "illegal occupant" and directing her to comply with the ordinance. When she failed to remove him from her home, the city filed a criminal charge. Mrs. Moore moved to dismiss, claiming that the ordinance was constitutionally invalid on its face. Her motion was overruled, and upon conviction she was sentenced to five days in jail and a $25 fine. * * *

II

The city argues that our decision in *Village of Belle Terre v. Boraas*, 416 U.S. 1 (1974), requires us to sustain the ordinance attacked here. Belle Terre, like East Cleveland, imposed limits on the types of groups that could occupy a single dwelling unit. Applying the constitutional standard announced in this Court's leading land-use case, *Euclid v. Ambler Realty Co.*, 272 U.S. 365 (1926),[6] we sustained the Belle Terre ordinance on the ground that it bore a rational relationship to permissible state objectives.

But one overriding factor sets this case apart from *Belle Terre*. The ordinance there affected only unrelated individuals. It expressly allowed all who were related by "blood, adoption, or marriage" to live together, and in sustaining the ordinance we were careful to note that it promoted "family needs" and "family values." 416 U.S. at 9. East Cleveland, in contrast, has chosen to regulate the occupancy of its housing by slicing deeply into the family itself. This is no mere incidental result of the ordinance. On its face it selects certain categories of relatives who may live together and declares that others may not. In particular, it makes a crime of a grandmother's choice to live with her grandson in circumstances like those presented here.

---

spouse of the nominal head of the household and the spouse and dependent children of such dependent child. For the purpose of this subsection, a dependent person is one who has more than fifty percent of his total support furnished for him by the nominal head of the household and the spouse of the nominal head of the household.

"(e) A family may consist of one individual."

6. *Euclid* held that land-use regulations violate the Due Process Clause if they are "clearly arbitrary and unreasonable, having no substantial relation to the public health, safety, morals, or general welfare." 272 U.S. at 395. Later cases have emphasized that the general welfare is not to be narrowly understood; it embraces a broad range of governmental purposes. But our cases have not departed from the requirement that the government's chosen means must rationally further some legitimate state purpose.

When a city undertakes such intrusive regulation of the family, neither *Belle Terre* nor *Euclid* governs; the usual judicial deference to the legislature is inappropriate. "This Court has long recognized that freedom of personal choice in matters of marriage and family life is one of the liberties protected by the Due Process Clause of the Fourteenth Amendment." *Cleveland Bd. of Educ. v. LaFleur,* 414 U.S. 632, 639–40 (1974). A host of cases, tracing their lineage to *Meyer v. Nebraska,* 262 U.S. 390, 399–401 (1923), and *Pierce v. Soc'y of Sisters* 268 U.S. 510, 534–35 (1925), have consistently acknowledged a "private realm of family life which the state cannot enter." *Prince v. Massachusetts,* 321 U.S. 158, 166 (1944). *See, e.g., Roe v. Wade,* 410 U.S. 113, 152–53 (1973); *Stanley v. Illinois,* 405 U.S. 645, 651 (1972); *Griswold v. Connecticut,* 381 U.S. 479 (1965); *Poe v. Ullman,* 367 U.S. 497, 542–44, 549–53 (1961) (HARLAN, J. dissenting); *cf. Loving v. Virginia,* 388 U.S. 1, 12 (1967). Of course, the family is not beyond regulation. But when the government intrudes on choices concerning family living arrangements, this Court must examine carefully the importance of the governmental interests advanced and the extent to which they are served by the challenged regulation.

When thus examined, this ordinance cannot survive. The city seeks to justify it as a means of preventing overcrowding, minimizing traffic and parking congestion, and avoiding an undue financial burden on East Cleveland's school system. Although these are legitimate goals, the ordinance before us serves them marginally, at best. For example, the ordinance permits any family consisting only of husband, wife, and unmarried children to live together, even if the family contains a half dozen licensed drivers, each with his or her own car. At the same time it forbids an adult brother and sister to share a household, even if both faithfully use public transportation. The ordinance would permit a grandmother to live with a single dependent son and children, even if his school-age children number a dozen, yet it forces Mrs. Moore to find another dwelling for her grandson John, simply because of the presence of his uncle and cousin in the same household. We need not labor the point. Section 1341.08 has but a tenuous relation to alleviation of the conditions mentioned by the city.

III

The city would distinguish the cases based on *Meyer* and *Pierce.* It points out that none of them "gives grandmothers any fundamental rights with respect to grandsons," and suggests that any constitutional right to live together as a family extends only to the nuclear family—essentially a couple and their dependent children.

To be sure, these cases did not expressly consider the family relationship presented here. They were immediately concerned with freedom of choice with respect to childbearing, e.g., *LaFleur, Roe v. Wade, Griswold,* or with the rights of parents to the custody and companionship of their own children, *Stanley v. Illinois,* or with traditional parental authority in matters of child rearing and education. But unless we close our eyes to the basic reasons why certain rights associated with the family have been accorded shelter under the Fourteenth Amendment's Due Process Clause, we cannot avoid applying the force and rationale of these precedents to the family choice involved in this case.

Understanding those reasons requires careful attention to this Court's function under the Due Process Clause. Mr. Justice HARLAN described it eloquently:

> Due process has not been reduced to any formula; its content cannot be determined by reference to any code. The best that can be said is that through the course of this Court's decisions it has represented the balance which our Nation, built upon postulates of respect for the liberty of the individual, has struck between that liberty and the demands of organized society. If the supplying of content to this Constitutional concept has of necessity been a rational process, it certainly has not been one where judges have felt free to roam where unguided speculation might take them. The balance of which I speak is the balance struck by this country, having regard to what history teaches are the traditions from which it developed as well as the traditions from which it broke. That tradition is a living thing. A decision of this Court which radically departs from it could not long survive, while a decision which builds on what has survived is likely to be sound. No formula could serve as a substitute, in this area, for judgment and restraint.

> ... [T]he full scope of the liberty guaranteed by the Due Process Clause cannot be found in or limited by the precise terms of the specific guarantees elsewhere provided in the Constitution. This 'liberty' is not a series of isolated points pricked out in terms of the taking of property; the freedom of speech, press, and religion; the right to keep and bear arms; the freedom from unreasonable searches and seizures; and so on. It is a rational continuum which, broadly speaking, includes a freedom from all substantial arbitrary impositions and purposeless restraints, ... and which also recognizes, what a reasonable and sensitive judgment must, that certain interests require particularly careful scrutiny of the state needs asserted to justify their abridgment.

Poe v. Ullman, [367 U.S.] at 542–43 [(HARLAN, J., dissenting)].

Substantive due process has at times been a treacherous field for this Court. There are risks when the judicial branch gives enhanced protection to certain substantive liberties without the guidance of the more specific provisions of the Bill of Rights. * * * [T]here is reason for concern lest the only limits to such judicial intervention become the predilections of those who happen at the time to be Members of this Court. That history counsels caution and restraint. But it does not counsel abandonment, nor does it require what the city urges here: cutting off any protection of family rights at the first convenient, if arbitrary boundary—the boundary of the nuclear family.

Appropriate limits on substantive due process come not from drawing arbitrary lines but rather from careful "respect for the teachings of history [and] solid recognition of the basic values that underlie our society." *Griswold,* 381 U.S. at 501 (HARLAN, J. concurring). Our decisions establish that the Constitution protects the sanctity of the family precisely because the institution of the family is deeply rooted in this Nation's history and tradition. It is through the family that we inculcate and pass down many of our most cherished values, moral and cultural.

Ours is by no means a tradition limited to respect for the bonds uniting the members of the nuclear family. The tradition of uncles, aunts, cousins, and especially grandparents sharing a household along with parents and children has roots equally venerable and equally deserving of constitutional recognition. Over the years millions of our citizens have grown up in just such an environment, and most, surely, have profited from it. Even if conditions of modern society have brought about a decline in extended family households, they have not erased the accumulated wisdom of civilization, gained over the centuries and honored throughout our history, that supports a larger conception of the family. Out of choice, necessity, or a sense of family responsibility, it has been common for close relatives to draw together and participate in the duties and the satisfactions of a common home. Decisions concerning child rearing, which *Yoder, Meyer, Pierce* and other cases have recognized as entitled to constitutional protection, long have been shared with grandparents or other relatives who occupy the same household indeed who may take on major responsibility for the rearing of the children. Especially in times of adversity, such as the death of a spouse or economic need, the broader family has tended to come together for mutual sustenance and to maintain or rebuild a secure home life. This is apparently what happened here.[16]

Whether or not such a household is established because of personal tragedy, the choice of relatives in this degree of kinship to live together may not lightly be denied by the State. *Pierce* struck down an Oregon law requiring all children to attend the State's public schools, holding that the Constitution "excludes any general power of the State to standardize its children by forcing them to accept instruction from public teachers only." 268 U.S. at 535. By the same token the Constitution prevents East Cleveland from standardizing its children—and its adults—by forcing all to live in certain narrowly defined family patterns.

Reversed.

MR. JUSTICE BRENNAN, with whom MR. JUSTICE MARSHALL joins, concurring.

I join the plurality's opinion. I agree that the Constitution is not powerless to prevent East Cleveland from prosecuting as a criminal and

---

16. We are told that the mother of John Moore, Jr., died when he was less than one year old. He, like uncounted others who have suffered a similar tragedy, then came to live with the grandmother to provide the infant with a substitute for his mother's care and to establish a more normal home environment.

jailing a 63–year–old grandmother for refusing to expel from her home her now 10–year–old grandson who has lived with her and been brought up by her since his mother's death when he was less than a year old. I do not question that a municipality may constitutionally zone to alleviate noise and traffic congestion and to prevent overcrowded and unsafe living conditions, in short to enact reasonable land-use restrictions in furtherance of the legitimate objectives East Cleveland claims for its ordinance. But the zoning power is not a license for local communities to enact senseless and arbitrary restrictions which cut deeply into private areas of protected family life. East Cleveland may not constitutionally define "family" as essentially confined to parents and the parents' own children. The plurality's opinion conclusively demonstrates that classifying family patterns in this eccentric way is not a rational means of achieving the ends East Cleveland claims for its ordinance, and further that the ordinance unconstitutionally abridges the "freedom of personal choice in matters of . . . family life [that] is one of the liberties protected by the Due Process Clause of the Fourteenth Amendment." *LaFleur*, 414 U.S. at 639–40. I write only to underscore the cultural myopia of the arbitrary boundary drawn by the East Cleveland ordinance in the light of the tradition of the American home that has been a feature of our society since our beginning as a Nation—the "tradition" in the plurality's words, "of uncles, aunts, cousins, and especially grandparents sharing a household along with parents and children." The line drawn by this ordinance displays a depressing insensitivity toward the economic and emotional needs of a very large part of our society.

In today's America, the "nuclear family" is the pattern so often found in much of white suburbia. The Constitution cannot be interpreted, however, to tolerate the imposition by government upon the rest of us of white suburbia's preference in patterns of family living. The "extended family" that provided generations of early Americans with social services and economic and emotional support in times of hardship, and was the beachhead for successive waves of immigrants who populated our cities, remains not merely still a pervasive living pattern, but under the goad of brutal economic necessity, a prominent pattern—virtually a means of survival—for large numbers of the poor and deprived minorities of our society. For them compelled pooling of scant resources requires compelled sharing of a household.

The "extended" form is especially familiar among black families. We may suppose that this reflects the truism that black citizens, like generations of white immigrants before them, have been victims of economic and other disadvantages that would worsen if they were compelled to abandon extended, for nuclear, living patterns. Even in husband and wife households, 13% of black families compared with 3% of white families include relatives under 18 years old, in addition to the couple's own children.[8] In black households whose head is an elderly woman, as in this case, the contrast is even more striking: 48% of such black households, compared

---

8. R. Hill, The Strengths of Black Families 5 (1972).

with 10% of counterpart white households, include related minor children not offspring of the head of the household.

I do not wish to be understood as implying that East Cleveland's enforcement of its ordinance is motivated by a racially discriminatory purpose: The record of this case would not support that implication. But the prominence of other than nuclear families among ethnic and racial minority groups, including our black citizens, surely demonstrates that the "extended family" pattern remains a vital tenet of our society. It suffices that in prohibiting this pattern of family living as a means of achieving its objectives, appellee city has chosen a device that deeply intrudes into family associational rights that historically have been central, and today remain central, to a large proportion of our population.

Moreover, to sanction the drawing of the family line at the arbitrary boundary chosen by East Cleveland would surely conflict with prior decisions that protected "extended" family relationships. For the "private realm of family life which the state cannot enter," recognized as protected in *Prince*, 321 U.S. at 166, was the relationship of aunt and niece. * * *

[The concurring opinion of STEVENS, J., and the dissenting opinions of BURGER, C.J., STEWART, J. (joined by REHNQUIST, J.), and WHITE, J., are omitted.]

NOTES AND QUESTIONS

1. *Family relationship.* What family relationship is not considered a family for purposes of the housing ordinance? Should the law's definition of family change depending on the context?

2. *Rationale for the housing restriction.* The city offered various justifications for the ordinance, none of which the Court found persuasive. What standard of review did the Court use? Why?

3. *The meaning of "family."* *Moore* contains expansive language concerning historical respect for the extended family. But consider the views of Professor Robert Burt, writing two years after the decision was issued:

At first glance, the East Cleveland ordinance might appear anti-black and constitutionally suspect on that ground. * * * Mr. Justice Stewart, in a footnote to his dissenting opinion, explains why: "In point of fact, East Cleveland is a predominantly Negro community, with a Negro City Manager and City Commission." * * * The plurality did not consider that the purpose of the ordinance was quite straightforward: to exclude from a middle-class, predominantly black community, that saw itself as socially and economically upwardly mobile, other black families most characteristic of lower-class ghetto life. * * * The Court in *Moore* myopically saw the case as a dispute between "a family" and "the state" rather than as a dispute among citizens about the meaning of "family."

Robert A. Burt, *The Constitution of the Family*, 1979 Sup. Ct. Rev. 329, 388–89, 391; *see also* C. Quince Hopkins, *The Supreme Court's Family Law Doctrine Revisited: Insights From Social Science on Family Structures and*

Kinship Change in the United States, 13 Cornell J.L. & Pub. Pol'y 431, 434–35 (2004) (criticizing the Court's historical inquiry for "fail[ing] to account for the true richness of Americans' historical and present-day family-related kinship practices and beliefs").

PROBLEM 1–1

Imagine that you are the head of a city's housing department, and that the city council has recently enacted an ordinance that limits occupancy of a dwelling unit to a single "family." You are responsible for drafting a definition of "family" for purposes of this ordinance. (Someone else is defining the definition of "dwelling unit.") What would you write? How do you define "family"? Does a family include grandparents? Heterosexual or homosexual cohabitants? Cohabitants who have lived together for a certain period of time? Cohabitants with children? Foster families? Three roommates attending your law school? Is a family limited by biology or contract?

B. THE EVOLUTION OF THE RIGHT TO PRIVACY

Moore's plurality opinion discusses the "basic reasons why certain rights associated with the family have been accorded shelter under the Fourteenth Amendment's Due Process Clause." The decisions in this Section explore the scope and origins of the right to privacy that attaches to families and to individuals within them. Some arguments supporting a right to family and personal privacy rely on the Fourteenth Amendment, but the Justices have also found this right elsewhere in the Constitution. As you read this Section, try to sort out the sources of the rights being discussed.

The origins of the right to privacy within the family are often traced to *Meyer v. Nebraska*, 262 U.S. 390 (1923), and *Pierce v. Society of the Sisters*, 268 U.S. 510 (1925). These decisions, which concerned parents' rights to make decisions about their children's education, contained frequently cited dicta concerning a parent's Fourteenth Amendment substantive due process liberty interest in the "care, custody and control" of children.

Meyer struck down a state statute that barred teaching in the German language to children who had not yet reached the eighth grade. The case was brought by a teacher convicted of teaching in the German language, but the Court stressed the Fourteenth Amendment liberty interests of parents who wanted their children to study German:

> While this Court has not attempted to define with exactness the liberty thus guaranteed, the term has received much consideration and some of the included things have been definitely stated. Without doubt, it denotes not merely freedom from bodily restraint but also the right of the individual to contract, to engage in any of the common occupations of life, to acquire useful knowledge, to marry, establish a home and bring up children, to worship God according to

the dictates of his own conscience, and generally to enjoy those privileges long recognized at common law as essential to the orderly pursuit of happiness by free men.

Meyer, 262 U.S. at 399.

Decided just two years after *Meyer, Pierce* overturned an Oregon statute that provided that parents could satisfy the state's compulsory education law only by enrolling their children in public schools. A coalition of sectarian and non-sectarian independent schools challenged the statute as a threat to their businesses. As in *Meyer*, no parent or child was a party to the action. The Court nonetheless applied the earlier decision, which, it held, made it "entirely plain" that the statute "unreasonably interferes with the liberty of parents and guardians to direct the upbringing and education of children under their control. * * * The child is not the mere creature of the state; those who nurture him and direct his destiny have the right, coupled with the high duty, to recognize and prepare him for additional obligations." *Pierce*, 268 U.S. at 534–35.

A third decision, *Prince v. Massachusetts*, 321 U.S. 158 (1944), is frequently cited along with *Meyer* and *Pierce* as recognizing family privacy. "It is cardinal with us," Justice Rutledge wrote in *Prince*, "that the custody, care and nurture of the child reside first in the parents, whose primary function and freedom include preparation for obligations the state can neither supply nor hinder. And it is in recognition of this that [our] decisions have respected the private realm of family life which the state cannot enter." *Id*. at 166.

These decisions provide the early framework for the Supreme Court's return to family privacy in the 1960s.

GRISWOLD v. CONNECTICUT

Supreme Court of the United States, 1965.
381 U.S. 479.

MR. JUSTICE DOUGLAS delivered the opinion of the Court.

Appellant Griswold is Executive Director of the Planned Parenthood League of Connecticut. Appellant Buxton is a licensed physician and a professor at the Yale Medical School who served as Medical Director for the League at its Center in New Haven—a center open and operating from November 1 to November 10, 1961, when appellants were arrested.

They gave information, instruction, and medical advice to *married persons* as to the means of preventing conception. They examined the wife and prescribed the best contraceptive device or material for her use. * * *

The statutes whose constitutionality is involved in this appeal are §§ 53–32 and 54–196 of the General Statutes of Connecticut (1958 rev.). The former provides:

Any person who uses any drug, medicinal article or instrument for the purpose of preventing conception shall be fined not less than fifty dollars or imprisoned not less than sixty days nor more than one year or be both fined and imprisoned.

Section 54–196 provides:

Any person who assists, abets, counsels, causes, hires or commands another to commit any offense may be prosecuted and punished as if he were the principal offender.

The appellants were found guilty as accessories and fined $100 each, against the claim that the accessory statute as so applied violated the Fourteenth Amendment. * * *

We think that appellants have standing to raise the constitutional rights of the married people with whom they had a professional relationship * * * [b]y reason of a criminal conviction for serving married couples in violation of an aiding-and-abetting statute. * * *

* * *

Coming to the merits, we are met with a wide range of questions that implicate the Due Process Clause of the Fourteenth Amendment. Overtones of some arguments suggest that *Lochner v. New York*, 198 U.S. 45 [(1905)], should be our guide. But we decline that invitation. * * * We do not sit as a super-legislature to determine the wisdom, need, and propriety of laws that touch economic problems, business affairs, or social conditions. This law, however, operates directly on an intimate relation of husband and wife and their physician's role in one aspect of that relation.

The association of people is not mentioned in the Constitution nor in the Bill of Rights. The right to educate a child in a school of the parents' choice—whether public or private or parochial—is also not mentioned. Nor is the right to study any particular subject or any foreign language. Yet the First Amendment has been construed to include certain of those rights.

By *Pierce v. Society of Sisters* [268 U.S. 510 (1925)], the right to educate one's children as one chooses is made applicable to the States by the force of the First and Fourteenth Amendments. By *Meyer v. Nebraska*, [262 U.S. 390 (1923)], the same dignity is given the right to study the German language in a private school. In other words, the State may not, consistently with the spirit of the First Amendment, contract the spectrum of available knowledge. The right of freedom of speech and press includes not only the right to utter or to print, but the right to distribute, the right to receive, the right to read and freedom of inquiry, freedom of thought, and freedom to teach—indeed the freedom of the entire university community. Without those peripheral rights the specific rights would be less secure. And so we reaffirm the principle of the *Pierce* and the *Meyer* cases.

In *NAACP v. Alabama*, 357 U.S. 449, 462 [(1958)], we protected the "freedom to associate and privacy in one's associations," noting that freedom of association was a peripheral First Amendment right. * * * In other words, the First Amendment has a penumbra where privacy is protected from governmental intrusion. In like context, we have protected forms of "association" that are not political in the customary sense but pertain to the social, legal, and economic benefit of the members. * * *

* * *

The foregoing cases suggest that specific guarantees in the Bill of Rights have penumbras, formed by emanations from those guarantees that help give them life and substance. *See Poe v. Ullman*, 367 U.S. 497, 516–22 [(1961) (DOUGLAS, J., dissenting)]. Various guarantees create zones of privacy. The right of association contained in the penumbra of the First Amendment is one, as we have seen. The Third Amendment in its prohibition against the quartering of soldiers "in any house" in time of peace without the consent of the owner is another facet of that privacy. The Fourth Amendment explicitly affirms the "right of the people to be secure in their persons, houses, papers, and effects, against unreasonable searches and seizures." The Fifth Amendment in its Self–Incrimination Clause enables the citizen to create a zone of privacy which government may not force him to surrender to his detriment. The Ninth Amendment provides: "The enumeration in the Constitution, of certain rights, shall not be construed to deny or disparage others retained by the people."

The Fourth and Fifth Amendments were described in *Boyd v. United States*, 116 U.S. 616, 630 [(1886)], as protection against all governmental invasions "of the sanctity of a man's home and the privacies of life." We recently referred in *Mapp v. Ohio*, 367 U.S. 643, 656 [(1961)], to the Fourth Amendment as creating a "right to privacy, no less important than any other right carefully and particularly reserved to the people."

We have had many controversies over these penumbral rights of "privacy and repose." These cases bear witness that the right of privacy which presses for recognition here is a legitimate one.

The present case, then, concerns a relationship lying within the zone of privacy created by several fundamental constitutional guarantees. And it concerns a law which, in forbidding the *use* of contraceptives rather than regulating their manufacture or sale, seeks to achieve its goals by means having a maximum destructive impact upon that relationship. Such a law cannot stand in light of the familiar principle, so often applied by this Court, that a "governmental purpose to control or prevent activities constitutionally subject to state regulation may not be achieved by means which sweep unnecessarily broadly and thereby invade the area of protected freedoms." *NAACP v. Alabama*, 377 U.S. [288], 307 [(1964)]. Would we allow the police to search the sacred precincts of marital bedrooms for telltale signs of the use of contraceptives? The very idea is repulsive to the notions of privacy surrounding the marriage relationship.

We deal with a right of privacy older than the Bill of Rights—older than our political parties, older than our school system. Marriage is a coming together for better or for worse, hopefully enduring, and intimate to the degree of being sacred. It is an association that promotes a way of life, not causes; a harmony in living, not political faiths; a bilateral loyalty, not commercial or social projects. Yet it is an association for as noble a purpose as any involved in our prior decisions.

Reversed.

MR. JUSTICE GOLDBERG, whom THE CHIEF JUSTICE and MR. JUSTICE BRENNAN join, concurring.

I agree with the Court that Connecticut's birth-control law unconstitutionally intrudes upon the right of marital privacy, and I join in its opinion and judgment. Although I have not accepted the view that "due process" as used in the Fourteenth Amendment includes all of the first eight Amendments, I do agree that the concept of liberty protects those personal rights that are fundamental, and is not confined to the specific terms of the Bill of Rights. My conclusion that the concept of liberty is not so restricted and that it embraces the right of marital privacy though that right is not mentioned explicitly in the Constitution is supported both by numerous decisions of this Court, referred to in the Court's opinion, and by the language and history of the Ninth Amendment. In reaching the conclusion that the right of marital privacy is protected, as being within the protected penumbra of specific guarantees of the Bill of Rights, the Court refers to the Ninth Amendment. I add these words to emphasize the relevance of that Amendment to the Court's holding.

* * *

This Court, in a series of decisions, has held that the Fourteenth Amendment absorbs and applies to the States those specifics of the first eight amendments which express fundamental personal rights. The language and history of the Ninth Amendment reveal that the Framers of the Constitution believed that there are additional fundamental rights, protected from governmental infringement, which exist alongside those fundamental rights specifically mentioned in the first eight constitutional amendments. The Ninth Amendment reads, "The enumeration in the Constitution, of certain rights, shall not be construed to deny or disparage others retained by the people." * * *

* * *

While this Court has had little occasion to interpret the Ninth Amendment,[6] "[i]t cannot be presumed that any clause in the constitution is intended to be without effect." *Marbury v. Madison*, 1 Cranch 137, 174 [(1803)]. * * * The Ninth Amendment to the Constitution may be regarded by some as a recent discovery and may be forgotten by others, but since 1791 it has been a basic part of the Constitution which we are sworn to uphold. To hold that a right so basic and fundamental and so deeprooted in our society as the right of privacy in marriage may be infringed because

---

6. This Amendment has been referred to as "The Forgotten Ninth Amendment," in a book with that title by Bennett B. Patterson (1955).... * * * As far as I am aware, until today this Court has referred to the Ninth Amendment only in [three cases]. * * *

that right is not guaranteed in so many words by the first eight amendments to the Constitution is to ignore the Ninth Amendment and to give it no effect whatsoever. Moreover, a judicial construction that this fundamental right is not protected by the Constitution because it is not mentioned in explicit terms by one of the first eight amendments or elsewhere in the Constitution would violate the Ninth Amendment, which specifically states that "[t]he enumeration in the Constitution, of certain rights shall not be *construed* to deny or disparage others retained by the people." (Emphasis added.)

* * * [T]he Ninth Amendment shows a belief of the Constitution's authors that fundamental rights exist that are not expressly enumerated in the first eight amendments and an intent that the list of rights included there not be deemed exhaustive. As any student of this Court's opinions knows, this Court has held, often unanimously, that the Fifth and Fourteenth Amendments protect certain fundamental personal liberties from abridgment by the Federal Government or the States. The Ninth Amendment simply shows the intent of the Constitution's authors that other fundamental personal rights should not be denied such protection or disparaged in any other way simply because they are not specifically listed in the first eight constitutional amendments. * * *

* * *

In determining which rights are fundamental, judges are not left at large to decide cases in light of their personal and private notions. Rather, they must look to the "traditions and [collective] conscience of our people" to determine whether a principle is "so rooted [there] * * * as to be ranked as fundamental." *Snyder v. Massachusetts*, 291 U.S. 97, 105 [(1934)]. The inquiry is whether a right involved "is of such a character that it cannot be denied without violating those 'fundamental principles of liberty and justice which lie at the base of all our civil and political institutions' ...." *Powell v. Alabama*, 287 U.S. 45, 67 [(1932)]. "Liberty" also "gains content from the emanations of ... specific [constitutional] guarantees" and "from experience with the requirements of a free society." *Poe v. Ullman*, 367 U.S. 497, 517 [(1961) (Douglas, J., dissenting].

I agree fully with the Court that, applying these tests, the right of privacy is a fundamental personal right, emanating "from the totality of the constitutional scheme under which we live." *Id.* at 521. Mr. Justice Brandeis, dissenting in *Olmstead v. United States*, 277 U.S. 438, [478 (1928)], comprehensively summarized the principles underlying the Constitution's guarantees of privacy:

> * * * The makers of our Constitution undertook to secure conditions favorable to the pursuit of happiness. They recognized the significance of man's spiritual nature, of his feelings and of his intellect. They knew that only a part of the pain, pleasure and satisfactions of life are to be found in material things. They sought to protect Americans in their beliefs, their thoughts, their emotions and their sensations. They conferred, as against the government, the right to be let alone—

the most comprehensive of rights and the right most valued by civilized men.

The Connecticut statutes here involved deal with a particularly important and sensitive area of privacy—that of the marital relation and the marital home. * * *

I agree with MR. JUSTICE HARLAN's statement in his dissenting opinion in *Poe*, 367 U.S. at 551–52:

> Certainly the safeguarding of the home does not follow merely from the sanctity of property rights. The home derives its pre-eminence as the seat of family life. And the integrity of that life is something so fundamental that it has been found to draw to its protection the principles of more than one explicitly granted Constitutional right. . . . Of this whole 'private realm of family life' it is difficult to imagine what is more private or more intimate than a husband and wife's marital relations.

The entire fabric of the Constitution and the purposes that clearly underlie its specific guarantees demonstrate that the rights to marital privacy and to marry and raise a family are of similar order and magnitude as the fundamental rights specifically protected.

Although the Constitution does not speak in so many words of the right of privacy in marriage, I cannot believe that it offers these fundamental rights no protection. * * *

* * *

Although the Connecticut birth control law obviously encroaches upon a fundamental personal liberty, the State does not show that the law serves any "subordinating [state] interest which is compelling" or that it is "necessary . . . to the accomplishment of a permissible state policy." The State, at most, argues that there is some rational relation between this statute and what is admittedly a legitimate subject of state concern—the discouraging of extra-marital relations. It says that preventing the use of birth-control devices by married persons helps prevent the indulgence by some in such extra-marital relations. The rationality of this justification is dubious, particularly in light of the admitted widespread availability to all persons in the State of Connecticut, unmarried as well as married, of birth-control devices for the prevention of disease, as distinguished from the prevention of conception. But, in any event, it is clear that the state interest in safeguarding marital fidelity can be served by a more discriminately tailored statute, which does not, like the present one, sweep unnecessarily broadly, reaching far beyond the evil sought to be dealt with and intruding upon the privacy of all married couples. * * * The State of Connecticut does have statutes, the constitutionality of which is beyond doubt, which prohibit adultery and fornication. These statutes demonstrate that means for achieving the same basic purpose of protecting marital fidelity are available to Connecticut without the need to "invade the area of protected freedoms." *NAACP* [*v. Alabama*], 377 U.S. [288,] 307 [(1964)].

* * *

In sum, I believe that the right of privacy in the marital relation is fundamental and basic—a personal right "retained by the people" within the meaning of the Ninth Amendment. Connecticut cannot constitutionally abridge this fundamental right, which is protected by the Fourteenth Amendment from infringement by the States. I agree with the Court that petitioners' convictions must therefore be reversed.

MR. JUSTICE HARLAN, concurring in the judgment.

I fully agree with the judgment of reversal, but find myself unable to join the Court's opinion. * * *

* * *

In my view, the proper constitutional inquiry in this case is whether this Connecticut statute infringes the Due Process Clause of the Fourteenth Amendment because the enactment violates basic values "implicit in the concept of ordered liberty," *Palko v. Connecticut*, 302 U.S. 319, 325 [(1937)]. * * * I believe that it does. While the relevant inquiry may be aided by resort to one or more of the provisions of the Bill of Rights, it is not dependent on them or any of their radiations. The Due Process Clause of the Fourteenth Amendment stands, in my opinion, on its own bottom.

* * *

MR. JUSTICE WHITE, concurring in the judgment.

In my view this Connecticut law as applied to married couples deprives them of "liberty" without due process of law, as that concept is used in the Fourteenth Amendment. I therefore concur in the judgment of the Court reversing these convictions under Connecticut's aiding and abetting statute.

* * * Surely the right invoked in this case, to be free of regulation of the intimacies of the marriage relationship, "come[s] to this Court with a momentum for respect lacking when appeal is made to liberties which derive merely from shifting economic arrangements." *Kovacs v. Cooper*, 336 U.S. 77, 95 [(1949) (FRANKFURTER, J., concurring)].

The Connecticut anti-contraceptive statute deals rather substantially with this relationship. * * *

An examination of the justification offered, however, cannot be avoided by saying that the Connecticut anti-use statute invades a protected area of privacy and association or that it demands the marriage relationship. The nature of the right invaded is pertinent, to be sure, for statutes regulating sensitive areas of liberty do, under the cases of this Court, require "strict scrutiny" * * *. But such statutes, if reasonably necessary for the effectuation of a legitimate and substantial state interest, and not arbitrary or capricious in application, are not invalid under the Due Process Clause.

* * * [T]he State claims but one justification for its anti-use statute. * * * [T]he statute is said to serve the State's policy against all forms of promiscuous or illicit sexual relationships, be they premarital or extramarital, concededly a permissible and legitimate legislative goal.

Without taking issue with the premise that the fear of conception operates as a deterrent to such relationships in addition to the criminal proscriptions Connecticut has against such conduct, I wholly fail to see how the ban on the use of contraceptives by married couples in any way reinforces the State's ban on illicit sexual relationships. * * *

* * *

Mr. Justice Black, with whom Mr. Justice Stewart joins, dissenting.

I agree with my Brother Stewart's dissenting opinion. And like him I do not to any extent whatever base my view that this Connecticut law is constitutional on a belief that the law is wise or that its policy is a good one. In order that there may be no room at all to doubt why I vote as I do, I feel constrained to add that the law is every bit as offensive to me as it is my Brethren of the majority and my Brothers Harlan, White and Goldberg who, reciting reasons why it is offensive to them, hold it unconstitutional. There is no single one of the graphic and eloquent strictures and criticisms fired at the policy of this Connecticut law either by the Court's opinion or by those of my concurring Brethren to which I cannot subscribe—except their conclusion that the evil qualities they see in the law make it unconstitutional.

Had the doctor defendant here, or even the nondoctor defendant, been convicted for doing nothing more than expressing opinions to persons coming to the clinic that certain contraceptive devices, medicines or practices would do them good and would be desirable, or for telling people how devices could be used, I can think of no reasons at this time why their expressions of views would not be protected by the First and Fourteenth Amendments, which guarantee freedom of speech. * * * The Court talks about a constitutional "right of privacy" as though there is some constitutional provision or provisions forbidding any law ever to be passed which might abridge the 'privacy' of individuals. But there is not. * * *

* * * I like my privacy as well as the next one, but I am nevertheless compelled to admit that government has a right to invade it unless prohibited by some specific constitutional provision. For these reasons I cannot agree with the Court's judgment and the reasons it gives for holding this Connecticut law unconstitutional.

* * *

* * * My disagreement with the Court's opinion holding that there is such a violation here is a narrow one, relating to the application of the First Amendment to the facts and circumstances of this particular case.

But my disagreement with Brothers HARLAN, WHITE and GOLDBERG is more basic. I think that if properly construed neither the Due Process Clause nor the Ninth Amendment, nor both together, could under any circumstances be a proper basis for invalidating the Connecticut law. * * *

The due process argument which my Brothers HARLAN and WHITE adopt here is based, as their opinions indicate, on the premise that this Court is vested with power to invalidate all state laws that it consider to be arbitrary, capricious, unreasonable, or oppressive, or this Court's belief that a particular state law under scrutiny has no "rational or justifying" purpose, or is offensive to a "sense of fairness and justice." If these formulas based on "natural justice," or others which mean the same thing, are to prevail, they require judges to determine what is or is not constitutional on the basis of their own appraisal of what laws are unwise or unnecessary. The power to make such decisions is of course that of a legislative body. * * * But perhaps it is not too much to say that no legislative body ever does pass laws without believing that they will accomplish a sane, rational, wise and justifiable purpose. * * *

* * *

I realize that many good and able men have eloquently spoken and written, sometimes in rhapsodical strains, about the duty of this Court to keep the Constitution in tune with the times. The idea is that the Constitution must be changed from time to time and that this Court is charged with a duty to make those changes. For myself, I must with all deference reject that philosophy. The Constitution makers knew the need for change and provided for it. Amendments suggested by the people's elected representatives can be submitted to the people or their selected agents for ratification. That method of change was good for our Fathers, and being somewhat old fashioned I must add it is good enough for me. * * *

* * *

MR. JUSTICE STEWART, whom MR. JUSTICE BLACK joins, dissenting.

Since 1879 Connecticut has had on its books a law which forbids the use of contraceptives by anyone. I think this is an uncommonly silly law. As a practical matter, the law is obviously unenforceable, except in the oblique context of the present case. As a philosophical matter, I believe the use of contraceptives in the relationship of marriage should be left to personal and private choice, based upon each individual's moral, ethical, and religious beliefs. As a matter of social policy, I think professional counsel about methods of birth control should be available to all, so that each individual's choice can be meaningfully made. But we are not asked in this case to say whether we think this law is unwise, or even asinine. We are asked to hold that it violates the United States Constitution. And that I cannot do.

In the course of its opinion the Court refers to no less than six Amendments to the Constitution: the First, the Third, the Fourth, the

Fifth, the Ninth, and the Fourteenth. But the Court does not say which of these Amendments, if any, it thinks is infringed by this Connecticut law.

* * *

What provision of the Constitution, then, does make this state law invalid? The Court says it is the right of privacy 'created by several fundamental constitutional guarantees'. With all deference, I can find no such general right of privacy in the Bill of Rights, in any other part of the Constitution, or in any case ever before decided by this Court.

At the oral argument in this case we were told that the Connecticut law does not "conform to current community standards." But it is not the function of this Court to decide cases on the basis of community standards. * * * If, as I should surely hope, the law before us does not reflect the standards of the people of Connecticut, the people of Connecticut can freely exercise their true Ninth and Tenth Amendment rights to persuade their elected representatives to repeal it. That is the constitutional way to take this law off the books.

NOTES AND QUESTIONS

1. *Classic impact litigation. Griswold* offers a classic example of well-crafted impact litigation and a stark reminder of the rapidity of social change. By the 1950s, Connecticut was the only state which still imposed an absolute ban on contraceptive devices. Some doctors in private practice apparently ignored the law and offered advice to their married patients, who could obtain birth control in neighboring states. Other doctors followed the law. Single persons and people too poor to afford private medical care had no options. Estelle Griswold, who had just become the executive director of the Planned Parenthood League of Connecticut, enlisted the help of two Yale professors, C. Lee Buxton of the Medical School and Fowler Harper who taught family law at the Law School. They enlisted well-chosen patients for the initial suit, entitled *Poe v. Ullman*, 367 U.S. 497 (1961). Jane Poe, a 25–year–old house-wife, was a patient of Dr. Buxton's. Admitted to the emergency room for complications of pregnancy, she had had a stroke which left her partially paralyzed, with a damaged kidney and speech impairment. Her pregnancy led to a stillbirth. Dr. Buxton believed she could not survive another pregnancy. Two other married couples were also named plaintiffs. One couple had already lost three children in infancy, all of whom had been born with genetic problems. The other had been advised that blood tests indicated that they would not be able to have a healthy child.

In the initial round of litigation in the Connecticut courts, the plaintiffs sought a declaratory judgment that would allow birth control clinics for married patients, but did not raise the privacy argument.

They lost in the Connecticut courts, and the Supreme Court declined to reach the merits on the ground that no realistic threat of criminal prosecution existed. *See Poe v. Ullman*, 367 U.S. 497 (1961). However, two *Poe* dissenters, Justices Douglas and Harlan, emphasized the patient's right to privacy. Regrouping, the plaintiffs decided to open one clinic in New Haven, which led within ten days to Dr. Buxton's arrest and closure of the clinic. In this new procedural posture, the defense relied heavily on the thinking of the *Poe* dissenters, leading to the result in *Griswold*. *See* Catherine G. Roraback, *Griswold v. Connecticut: A Brief Case History*, 16 Ohio N.U. L. Rev. 395 (1989).

2. *Constitutional grounding for the right to privacy.* You have read all six opinions issued in *Griswold*, four supporting the right to privacy in the marital relationship, and two opposed. Which Amendments did the supporters rely on to find a constitutional right to privacy? What constitutional standards and level of scrutiny did they apply? Did they apply the correct level of scrutiny? What are the essential differences between Justice Douglas' opinion for the Court and the two concurrences? Do the dissenters disagree with the majority about the text of the Constitution, the role of the Court, or both?

3. *Contours and strength of the right to privacy.* How far does the right to privacy expounded in *Griswold* extend? What questions does *Griswold* leave unanswered? How solid is the jurisprudential basis for the right to privacy set forth in the majority and concurring opinions? How strong is the right to privacy within the family? Outside the context of a "family"?

4. *The right to privacy for families on public welfare.* In 1971, the Supreme Court decided *Wyman v. James*, 400 U.S. 309 (1971). Barbara James, a public welfare recipient, refused to allow her caseworker to visit her home, explaining that she would provide any information relevant to her continued receipt of welfare, but without a home visit. At the time, New York state law required home visits to public welfare recipients once every three months to verify information concerning eligibility for welfare, provide professional counseling, and prevent welfare fraud. Moreover, New York law specified that a child would be eligible for aid only "if his home situation is one in which his physical, mental and moral well-being will be safeguarded and his religious faith preserved and protected." The *James* majority distinguished between a true Fourth Amendment search and the "visitation" at issue, which it found neither forced nor compelled, nor sanctionable with criminal penalties. Even if the home visit was a search in some sense, the majority held it not unreasonable under the Fourth Amendment. The majority upheld termination of Ms. James's welfare benefits because of her refusal to comply with the home visit requirement.

In dissent, Justices Marshall and Brennan disparaged the argument that the home visit was justified "to protect dependent children from 'abuse' and 'exploitation.'" *Id.* at 341 (Marshall, J., dissenting). "These are heinous crimes, but they are not confined to indigent households. Would the majority sanction, in the absence of probable cause, compulsory visits to all American homes for the purpose of discovering child abuse? Or is this Court prepared to hold as a matter of constitutional law that a mother, merely because she is poor, is substantially more likely to injure or exploit her children?"

As these questions show, family privacy means different protections for various kinds of families. Jacobus tenBroek identified this problem more than 40 years ago. *See* Jacobus tenBroek, *California's Dual System of Family Law: Its Origin, Development and Present Status* (pts. 1 & 3), 16 Stan. L. Rev. 257 (1964), 17 Stan. L. Rev. 614 (1965). Professor Jill Elaine Hasday argues that "welfare law and family law" have been placed "in entirely distinct legal categories [which] has helped legal authorities avoid explaining why different rules should govern familial rights and responsibilities in poor families." Jill Elaine Hasday, *The Canon of Family Law*, 57 Stan. L. Rev. 825, 898 (2004). Do the decisions you have read so far in this Chapter support this statement? The Supreme Court revisited some of the questions left unanswered in *Griswold* in the following decision, that arose out of a lecture at Boston University in 1967.

EISENSTADT v. BAIRD

Supreme Court of the United States, 1972.
405 U.S. 438.

MR. JUSTICE BRENNAN delivered the opinion of the Court.

Appellee William Baird was convicted at a bench trial in the Massachusetts Superior Court, under Massachusetts General Laws Ann., c. 272, § 21, first, for exhibiting contraceptive articles in the course of delivering a lecture on contraception to a group of students at Boston University and, second, for giving a young woman a package of Emko vaginal foam at the close of his address. The Massachusetts Supreme Judicial Court unanimously set aside the conviction for exhibiting contraceptives on the ground that it violated Baird's First Amendment rights, but by a four-to-three vote sustained the conviction for giving away the foam. * * * [T]he Court of Appeals for the First Circuit vacated the dismissal and remanded the action with directions to grant the writ discharging Baird. We affirm.

Massachusetts General Laws Ann., c. 272, § 21, under which Baird was convicted, provides a maximum five-year term of imprisonment for "whoever ... gives away ... any drug, medicine, instrument or article whatever for the prevention of conception," except as authorized in § 21A. Under § 21A, "[a] registered physician may administer to or prescribe for any married person drugs or articles intended for the prevention of pregnancy or conception. [And a] registered pharmacist actually engaged in the business of pharmacy may furnish such drugs or articles to any married person presenting a prescription from a registered physician." As interpreted by the State Supreme Judicial Court, these provisions make it a felony for anyone, other than a registered physician or pharmacist acting in accordance with the terms of § 21A, to dispense any article with the intention that it be used for the prevention of conception. The statutory scheme distinguishes among three distinct classes of distributees—first, married persons may obtain contraceptives to prevent pregnancy, but only from doctors or druggists on prescription; second, single persons may not obtain contraceptives from anyone to prevent pregnancy; and, third, married or single persons may obtain contraceptives from anyone to prevent, not pregnancy, but the spread of disease. This construction of state law is, of course, binding on us.

The legislative purposes that the statute is meant to serve are not altogether clear. In *Commonwealth v. Baird*, the Supreme Judicial Court noted only the State's interest in protecting the health of its citizens: "[T]he prohibition in § 21," the court declared, "is directly related to" the State's goal of "preventing the distribution of articles designed to prevent conception which may have undesirable, if not dangerous, physical consequences." In a subsequent decision, the court, however, found "a second and more compelling ground for upholding the statute"—namely, to protect morals through "regulating the private sexual lives of single persons." The Court of Appeals, for reasons that will appear, did not consider the promotion of health or the protection of morals through the deterrence of fornication to be the legislative aim. Instead, the court concluded that the statutory goal was to limit contraception in and of itself—a purpose that the court held conflicted "with fundamental human rights" under *Griswold v. Connecticut*, where this Court struck down Connecticut's prohibition against the use of contraceptives as an unconstitutional infringement of the right of marital privacy.

We agree that the goals of deterring premarital sex and regulating the distribution of potentially harmful articles cannot reasonably be regarded as legislative aims of §§ 21 and 21A. And we hold that the statute, viewed as a prohibition on contraception per se, violates the rights of single persons under the Equal Protection Clause of the Fourteenth Amendment.

* * *

The basic principles governing application of the Equal Protection Clause of the Fourteenth Amendment are familiar. * * *

The question for our determination in this case is whether there is some ground of difference that rationally explains the different treatment accorded married and unmarried persons under [the Massachusetts statute].[7] For the reasons that follow, we conclude that no such ground exists.

First. Section 21 stems from Mass. Stat. 1879, c. 159, § 1, which prohibited without exception, distribution of articles intended to be used as contraceptives. In *Commonwealth v. Allison*, 227 Mass. 57, 62 (1917), the Massachusetts Supreme Judicial Court explained that the law's "plain purpose is to protect purity, to preserve chastity, to encourage continence and self restraint, to defend the sanctity of the home, and thus to engender in the State and nation a virile and virtuous race of men and women." Although the State clearly abandoned that purpose with the enactment of § 21A, at least insofar as the illicit sexual activities of married persons are concerned, the court reiterated in *Sturgis v. Attorney General*, that the object of the legislation is to discourage premarital sexual intercourse. Conceding that the State could, consistently with the Equal Protection Clause, regard the problems of extramarital and premar-

---

7. Of course, if we were to conclude that the Massachusetts statute impinges upon fundamental freedoms under *Griswold*, the statutory classification would have to be not merely *rationally related* to a valid public purpose but *necessary* to the achievement of a *compelling* state interest. But ... we do not have to address the statute's validity under that test because the law fails to satisfy even the more lenient equal protection standard.

ital sexual relations as "[e]vils ... of different dimensions and proportions, requiring different remedies," *Williamson v. Lee Optical Co.*, 348 U.S. 483, 489 (1955), we cannot agree that the deterrence of premarital sex may reasonably be regarded as the purpose of the Massachusetts law.

It would be plainly unreasonable to assume that Massachusetts has prescribed pregnancy and the birth of an unwanted child as punishment for fornication, which is a misdemeanor under Massachusetts General Laws Ann., c. 272, § 18. Aside from the scheme of values that assumption would attribute to the State, it is abundantly clear that the effect of the ban on distribution of contraceptives to unmarried persons has at best a marginal relation to the proffered objective. What Mr. Justice Goldberg said in *Griswold*, 381 U.S. at 498, (concurring opinion), concerning the effect of Connecticut's prohibition on the use of contraceptives in discouraging extramarital sexual relations, is equally applicable here. "The rationality of this justification is dubious, particularly in light of the admitted widespread availability to all persons in the State of Connecticut, unmarried as well as married, of birth-control devices for the prevention of disease, as distinguished from the prevention of conception." * * * Nor, in making contraceptives available to married persons without regard to their intended use, does Massachusetts attempt to deter married persons from engaging in illicit sexual relations with unmarried persons. Even on the assumption that the fear of pregnancy operates as a deterrent to fornication, the Massachusetts statute is thus so riddled with exceptions that deterrence of premarital sex cannot reasonably be regarded as its aim.

Moreover, §§ 21 and 21A on their face have a dubious relation to the State's criminal prohibition on fornication. As the Court of Appeals explained, "Fornication is a misdemeanor [in Massachusetts], entailing a thirty dollar fine, or three months in jail. Violation of the present statute is a felony, punishable by five years in prison. We find it hard to believe that the legislature adopted a statute carrying a five-year penalty for its possible, obviously by no means fully effective, deterrence of the commission of a ninety-day misdemeanor." Even conceding the legislature a full measure of discretion in fashioning means to prevent fornication, and recognizing that the State may seek to deter prohibited conduct by punishing more severely those who facilitate than those who actually engage in its commission, we, like the Court of Appeals, cannot believe that in this instance Massachusetts has chosen to expose the aider and abetter who simply gives away a contraceptive to 20 times the 90–day sentence of the offender himself. * * *

Second. Section 21A was added to the Massachusetts General Laws by Stat. 1966, c. 265, § 1. The Supreme Judicial Court in *Commonwealth v. Baird* held that the purpose of the amendment was to serve the health needs of the community by regulating the distribution of potentially harmful articles. It is plain that Massachusetts had no such purpose in mind before the enactment of § 21A. As the Court of Appeals remarked, "Consistent with the fact that the statute was contained in a chapter dealing with 'Crimes Against Chastity, Morality, Decency and Good Order,' it was cast only in terms of morals. * * * Nor did the Court of Appeals "believe that the legislature [in enacting § 21A] suddenly reversed its field and developed an interest in health. Rather, it merely made what it thought to be the precise accommodation necessary to escape the *Griswold* ruling."

Again, we must agree with the Court of Appeals. If health were the rationale of § 21A, the statute would be both discriminatory and overbroad. Dissenting in *Commonwealth v. Baird*, Justices Whittemore and Cutter stated that they saw "in § 21 and § 21A, read together, no public health purpose. If there is need to have a physician prescribe (and a pharmacist dispense) contraceptives, that need is as great for unmarried persons as for married persons." * * *

* * *

But if further proof that the Massachusetts statute is not a health measure is necessary, the argument of Justice Spiegel [dissenting below] is conclusive * * *. [The statute is not necessary in light of the] federal and state laws *already* regulating the distribution of harmful drugs. * * *

Third. If the Massachusetts statute cannot be upheld as a deterrent to fornication or as a health measure, may it, nevertheless, be sustained simply as a prohibition on contraception? * * * The Court of Appeals went on to hold:

> To say that contraceptives are immoral as such, and are to be forbidden to unmarried persons who will nevertheless persist in having intercourse, means that such persons must risk for themselves an unwanted pregnancy, for the child, illegitimacy, and for society, a possible obligation of support. Such a view of morality is not only the very mirror image of sensible legislation; we consider that it conflicts with fundamental human rights. In the absence of demonstrated harm, we hold it is beyond the competency of the state.

We need not and do not, however, decide that important question in this case because, whatever the rights of the individual to access to contraceptives may be, the rights must be the same for the unmarried and the married alike.

If under *Griswold* the distribution of contraceptives to married persons cannot be prohibited, a ban on distribution to unmarried persons would be equally impermissible. It is true that in *Griswold* the right of privacy in question inhered in the marital relationship. Yet the marital couple is not an independent entity with a mind and heart of its own, but an association of two individuals each with a separate intellectual and emotional makeup. If the right of privacy means anything, it is the right of the individual, married or single, to be free from unwarranted governmental intrusion into matters so fundamentally affecting a person as the decision whether to bear or beget a child.

On the other hand, if *Griswold* is no bar to a prohibition on the distribution of contraceptives, the State could not, consistently with the Equal Protection Clause, outlaw distribution to unmarried but not to married persons. In each case the evil, as perceived by the State, would be identical, and the underinclusion would be invidious. * * *

* * * We hold that by providing dissimilar treatment for married and unmarried persons who are similarly situated, Massachusetts General Laws Ann., c. 272, §§ 21 and 21A, violate the Equal Protection Clause. * * *

MR. JUSTICE POWELL and MR. JUSTICE REHNQUIST took no part in the consideration or decision of this case.

MR. JUSTICE DOUGLAS, concurring.

While I join the opinion of the Court, there is for me a narrower ground for affirming the Court of Appeals. This to me is a simple First Amendment case, that amendment being applicable to the States by reason of the Fourteenth.

Under no stretch of the law as presently stated could Massachusetts require a license for those who desire to lecture on planned parenthood, contraceptives, the rights of women, birth control, or any allied subject, or place a tax on that privilege. * * *

* * *

Baird addressed an audience of students and faculty at Boston University on the subject of birth control and overpopulation. His address was approximately one hour in length and consisted of a discussion of various contraceptive devices displayed by means of diagrams on two demonstration boards, as well as a display of contraceptive devices in their original packages. In addition, Baird spoke of the respective merits of various contraceptive devices; overpopulation in the world; crises throughout the world due to overpopulation; the large number of abortions performed on unwed mothers; and quack abortionists and the potential harm to women resulting from abortions performed by quack abortionists. Baird also urged members of the audience to petition the Massachusetts Legislature and to make known their feelings with regard to birth control laws in order to bring about a change in the laws. At the close of the address Baird invited members of the audience to come to the stage and help themselves to the contraceptive articles. We do not know how many accepted Baird's invitation. We only know that Baird personally handed one woman a package of Emko Vaginal Foam. He was then arrested and indicted (1) for exhibiting contraceptive devices and (2) for giving one such device away. The conviction for the first offense was reversed, the Supreme Judicial Court of Massachusetts holding that the display of the articles was essential to a graphic representation of the lecture. But the conviction for the giving away of one article was sustained. * * *

Had Baird not "given away" a sample of one of the devices whose use he advocated, there could be no question about the protection afforded him by the First Amendment. A State may not "contract the spectrum of available knowledge." However noxious Baird's ideas might have been to the authorities, the freedom to learn about them, fully to comprehend their scope and portent, and to weigh them against the tenets of the "conventional wisdom," may not be abridged. Our system of government requires that we have faith in the ability of the individual to decide wisely, if only he is fully apprised of the merits of a controversy.

* * *

It is irrelevant to the application of these principles that Baird went beyond the giving of information about birth control and advocated the use of contraceptive articles. The First Amendment protects the opportunity to persuade to action whether that action be unwise or immoral, or whether the speech incites to action.

In this case there was not even incitement to action. There is no evidence or finding that Baird intended that the young lady take the foam home with her when he handed it to her or that she would not have examined the article and then returned it to Baird, had he not been placed under arrest immediately upon handing the article over.

First Amendment rights are not limited to verbal expression. The right to petition often involves the right to walk. The right of assembly may mean pushing or jostling. Picketing involves physical activity as well as a display of a sign. A sit-in can be a quiet, dignified protest that has First Amendment protection even though no speech is involved. * * * Putting contraceptives on display is certainly an aid to speech and discussion. Handing an article under discussion to a member of the audience is a technique known to all teachers and is commonly used. * * * But passing one article to an audience is merely a projection of the visual aid and should be a permissible adjunct of free speech. * * *

I do not see how we can have a Society of the Dialogue, which the First Amendment envisages, if time-honored teaching techniques are barred to those who give educational lectures.

MR. JUSTICE WHITE, with whom MR. JUSTICE BLACKMUN joins, concurring in the result.

In *Griswold*, we reversed criminal convictions for advising married persons with respect to the use of contraceptives. As there applied, the Connecticut law, which forbade using contraceptives or giving advice on the subject, unduly invaded a zone of marital privacy protected by the Bill of Rights. The Connecticut law did not regulate the manufacture or sale of such products and we expressly left open any question concerning the permissible scope of such legislation.

Chapter 272, § 21, of the Massachusetts General Laws makes it a criminal offense to distribute, sell, or give away any drug, medicine, or article for the prevention of conception. Section 21A excepts from this prohibition registered physicians who prescribe for and administer such articles to married persons and registered pharmacists who dispense on medical prescription.

Appellee Baird was indicted for giving away Emko Vaginal Foam, a "medicine and article for the prevention of conception...." The State did not purport to charge or convict Baird for distributing to an unmarried person. No proof was offered as to the marital status of the recipient. The gravamen of the offense charged was that Baird had no license and therefore no authority to distribute to anyone. As the Supreme Judicial Court of Massachusetts noted, the constitutional validity of Baird's conviction rested upon his lack of status as a "distributor and not ... the marital status of the recipient." * * *

* * * Had Baird distributed a supply of the so-called "pill," I would sustain his conviction under this statute. Requiring a prescription to obtain potentially dangerous contraceptive material may place a substantial burden upon the right recognized in *Griswold*, but that burden is justified by a strong state interest. * * *

* * *

Baird, however, was found guilty of giving away vaginal foam. * * * Due regard for protecting constitutional rights requires that the record contain evidence that a restriction on distribution of vaginal foam is essential to achieve the statutory purpose, or the relevant facts concerning the product must be such as to fall within the range of judicial notice.

Neither requirement is met here. * * *

That Baird could not be convicted for distributing Emko to a married person disposes of this case. * * *

MR. CHIEF JUSTICE BURGER, dissenting.

The judgment of the Supreme Judicial Court of Massachusetts in sustaining appellee's conviction for dispensing medicinal material without a license seems eminently correct to me and I would not disturb it. It is undisputed that appellee is not a physician or pharmacist and was prohibited under Massachusetts law from dispensing contraceptives to anyone, regardless of marital status. To my mind the validity of this restriction on dispensing medicinal substances is the only issue before the Court, and appellee has no standing to challenge that part of the statute restricting the persons to whom contraceptives are available. There is no need to labor this point, however, for everyone seems to agree that if Massachusetts has validly required, as a health measure, that all contraceptives be dispensed by a physician or pursuant to a physician's prescription, then the statutory distinction based on marital status has no bearing on this case.

* * *

NOTES AND QUESTIONS

1. *Extending the privacy doctrine. Eisenstadt* confronted two questions that *Griswold* left unanswered. First, was the right to privacy restricted to the confines of marriage? Second, did the right to sexual privacy attach only to a couple, or also to the individuals who might comprise a couple? To answer this question, the Court turned to yet another constitutional provision it had not considered in *Griswold*, the Equal Protection Clause. Does the application of the Equal Protection Clause affect the level of scrutiny the Court must apply, or the terms of the analysis? If *Griswold* had not opted for substantive due process analysis, would equal protection also have been a sound basis for that decision? What classification would have provided a basis for an equal protection decision?

2. *Narrower grounds.* Justice Douglas suggested that *Eisenstadt* could have been resolved as a speech case. Chief Justice Burger, dissenting, argued that the case could have been construed more narrowly as involving the practice of medicine without a license. If the Court had used Justice Douglas' approach, what questions would have been answered, or left unanswered? If the Court had followed Chief Justice Burger's lead, would it have had sufficient factual findings or would a remand have proved necessary? If the Court had all the necessary findings, which questions would it have been able to resolve, and which would have remained for another day?

3. *Recent developments.* The Supreme Court revisited the scope of family and personal privacy in two recent decisions. In *Lawrence v. Texas*, 539 U.S. 558 (2003), discussed in Chapter 3, the Court held that the right to personal privacy extends to consensual intimate relations between adults of the same sex. In *Troxel v. Granville*, 530 U.S. 57 (2000), Justice O'Connor's plurality opinion reaffirmed *Meyer*, *Pierce*, and the stature of parents' liberty interest in making decisions regarding their children, although some of the Justices did not agree with her summary of the doctrine. You will read *Troxel* in Chapter 13 in connection with a discussion of rights to visit children.

PROBLEM 1–2

Pick the Justice whose *Griswold* opinion you find most interesting. If you were a clerk for that Justice, and you also received the briefs in *Eisenstadt* as a hypothetical, would you advise your Justice to revise his opinion? How and why? You might be interested to know that Justice Stephen Breyer was a law clerk to Justice Goldberg during the 1964 Term and wrote the first draft of Goldberg's concurring opinion.

Chapter 2

Practicing Contemporary Family Law

■ ■ ■

SECTION 1: THE STATUS AND CONDITIONS OF FAMILY LAW PRACTICE

At the dawn of the twenty-first century, "the practice of family law is as intellectually demanding as mergers and acquisitions or intellectual property." Monroe L. Inker, *Changes in Family Law: A Practitioner's Perspective*, 33 Fam. L.Q. 515, 516 (1999). "There is no longer a 'one-size-fits-all' approach to family law." Nancy Van Steegh, *Innovations in Family Law Education: Using Externships to Introduce Family Law Students to New Professional Roles*, 43 Fam. Ct. Rev. 137, 137 (2005).

The outlook was not always so bright because much of the bench and bar traditionally perceived family law practice as a low-status field, largely because family law was seen primarily as "divorce law." Much of this perception stemmed from broader societal forces beyond the control of individual domestic relations lawyers. Divorce itself carried a profound stigma, which sometimes reflected adversely on the lawyers who practiced in the area. Major law firms rarely handled divorce cases, creating a vacuum that left the field to lawyers sometimes excluded from prestigious firms because of religion, ethnicity, race or gender. Sanford N. Katz, *Prologue*, 33 Fam. L.Q. 435, 435 (1999).

The traditional low status of family law practice, however, also derived from the sordid procedural and substantive law. By the 1930s and 1940s, divorce procedure was "rotten to the core." Lawrence M. Friedman, *A Dead Language: Divorce Law and Practice Before No–Fault*, 86 Va. L. Rev. 1497, 1536 (2000). The literal strictness of fault-based divorce statutes was belied by the overt reality that "[c]ollusive divorces [were] the rule rather than the exception," marked by sham proceedings besmirched with perjury and other "highly dubious" evidence that would not have been routinely admitted in any other category of civil action. Fowler V. Harper, *The Myth of the Void Divorce*, 2 Law & Contemp. Probs. 335, 347 (1935).

In the middle of the twentieth century, "distaste for handling divorce cases appear[ed] to be universal among judges." Maxine Boord Virtue, Family Cases in Court 84 (1956). Before no-fault divorce, "the average divorce case was garbage. It was who committed adultery and how many times and what kinds of pictures could you produce." Georgia Dullea, *Wide Changes in Family Life Are Altering the Family Law*, N.Y. Times, Feb. 7, 1983, at A1. According to one respected commentator, "[i]n the whole administration of justice there is nothing that even remotely can compare in terms of rottenness with divorce proceedings." Reginald Heber Smith, *Dishonest Divorce*, Atl. Monthly 42, 43 (Dec. 1947).

The image of family law practice brightened in the mid–1970s with the advent of no-fault divorce and equitable property distribution. "Constitutional principles now impinge on all aspects of traditional family law," former Chief Justice Edward F. Hennessey of the Massachusetts Supreme Judicial Court explained, "from questions about state jurisdiction in case of divorce, alimony, child custody and support, to state regulations of the right to marry, the right to procreate, rights associated with divorce and child custody, the rights of parents to control the upbringing of their children and the rights of children." Dullea, *supra*, at A1.

Much of this Chapter focuses on divorce, but the family lawyer's repertoire also includes a wide variety of other recurrent issues covered in this casebook, including cohabitation agreements, domestic violence, international abductions, and adoption. Estate planning and other tax issues may also loom large. "[F]amily lawyers must be knowledgeable in such fields as tax, contracts, ERISA, real estate, and health insurance continuation (COBRA), as well as family systems theory, child psychology, and family violence." Mary E. O'Connell & J. Herbie DiFonzo, *The Family Law Education Reform Project Final Report*, 44 Fam. Ct. Rev. 524, 525 (2006). Family lawyers also play a special role in public debate about such questions as work/family balance, abortion and other procreative issues, children's rights and obligations, and access to rapidly-evolving assisted reproductive technologies.

In contemporary America, domestic relations practitioners play a variety of new roles, including these:

(1) Mediator—A third-party neutral who meets with the parties, with or without counsel, seeking to facilitate voluntary settlement.

(2) Arbitrator—A third-party decisionmaker appointed by the parties to reach binding resolution.

(3) Collaborative Lawyer—An attorney who negotiates on behalf of one party, with the understanding that if negotiation fails and the case proceeds to court, the attorney will withdraw and be replaced by litigation counsel.

(4) Guardian *Ad Litem* (GAL)—An advisor appointed by the court to speak on behalf of the child's best interests.

(5) Parent Educator—An attorney instructing divorcing parents in a classroom setting about post-divorce matters involving child custody and visitation.

(6) Parent Coordinator—An attorney providing intensive case management for high-conflict families with children.

Today, as Justice Sandra Day O'Connor has observed, "family law is—and must be—a collaborative enterprise" because the practice "poses special challenges and requires judges and attorneys, as well as other professionals like psychologists and social workers, to study and work together." Sandra Day O'Connor, *Remarks: The Supreme Court and the Family*, 3 U. Pa. J. Const. L. 573, 573, 576 (2001). "[T]he family court of the early twenty-first century is often an interdisciplinary enterprise, where psychologists, social workers, non-lawyer mediators, and others may wield extraordinary power. At times, these professionals may work as partners with the attorney, providing both help and insight in the resolution of a family dispute. In other cases, the attorney's role is to help the client navigate the often bewildering world of mandatory mediation, mandatory divorce education, court-appointed custody evaluation, parenting coordination, and more." O'Connell & DiFonzo, *supra,* at 525.

One "special challenge" still facing family lawyers is the raw emotion that characterizes many domestic relations proceedings. Parties contemplating dissolution approach law offices at fragile moments in their lives. The marriage may have been marked by significant power imbalance between the spouses, ongoing personal strife, and even physical confrontation or assault. Neither spouse may ever have consulted a lawyer before, except to make a will or close on a home purchase. Most spouses have never entered a courtroom except to serve jury duty or argue a traffic violation, but they generally sense that they will never again be involved in a legal matter with such high stakes for themselves and the persons closest to them.

Whether marital dissolution will ultimately be by settlement or court determination, the lawyers whom people select to represent them may have tremendous impact on the rest of their lives and on the futures of other family members. Unlike business and commercial parties that typically litigate about money, divorcing spouses are at odds over "failed relationships, bittersweet memories, disputed finances, and arguments over valued personal possessions. In many cases, child custody becomes an issue * * *." Sherrie Bourg Carter, *When the Enemy Lies Within: Risk for Professional Burnout Among Family Lawyers*, 20 Am. J. Fam. L. 160, 162 (Fall 2006).

The client's emotional fragility may infect the lawyer-client relationship. For example, a demoralized client, bent on establishing his or her innocence and the other spouse's guilt for the family's breakup, may misinterpret the lawyer's more dispassionate focus on tangible factors in a no-fault regime usually dominated by the property and child-related issues. The client may resist the lawyer's explanations for why emotion-laden representation will likely backfire.

Uncomfortable intimacy may also impose a barrier between lawyer and client. "Dealing with a divorce lawyer means having to expose the most intimate details of one's personal and financial life to a stranger. It means having to trust the lawyer's commitment and loyalty at a time when a far stronger set of commitments and loyalties have proven untrustworthy. It is not surprising then that clients are often wary or suspicious of their own lawyers." Austin Sarat & William L.F. Felstiner, Divorce Lawyers and Their Clients: Power and Meaning in the Legal Process 4 (1995).

Domestic relations cases comprise about one quarter of the total civil caseload in the state trial courts. *See* Nat'l Center for State Courts, *Examining the Work of State Courts, 2003*, at 29 (2008). Many trial judges reportedly still disdain these cases for the emotions they often arouse, and for the broad discretion they vest in the court to intrude into family members' lives. California's Advisory Committee on Gender Bias in the Courts, for example, has likened service on the family court bench to an "assignment to Siberia." Judicial Council of California, Achieving Equal Justice for Women and Men in the California Courts, Final Report 160–62 (Gay Danforth & Bobbie L. Welling eds. July 1996), http://www.courtinfo. ca.gov/programs/access/documents/f-report.pdf. The Committee's survey of the state's sitting judges found that by a wide margin, family law was the respondents' least favorite assignment. Lawyers participating in a state bar focus group suggested that "judges feel they become too personally involved in the proceeding; they find it unpleasant, too personal, too fraught with bickering; and they may incorporate a general societal bias that accords more importance to issues of property and money than to issues affecting people." *Id.*

This article summarizes the emotions that distinguish family law practice from practice in other fields.

HOWARD S. ERLANGER, ET AL.

Participation and Flexibility in Informal Processes: Cautions From the Divorce Context.
21 Law & Soc'y Rev. 585, 594–96 (1987).

* * *

Although disputes in other informal settings are subject to financial, procedural, and emotional pressures, the informal divorce process is arguably unique in its vulnerability to the idiosyncrasies of interpersonal conflict. Nearly every lawyer we interviewed distinguished divorce from other types of cases, observing that divorce was by far the most emotionally draining area of their practice. As one lawyer quipped, "Divorce is 99 percent psychotherapy, 1 percent law." The very intimacy that supposedly makes divorce well-suited to informal resolution may instead hamper rational negotiation of terms. As one practitioner observes:

> Your client in a personal injury action, they generally don't know the person who ran them over. Their only contact with them was for that brief fleeting moment when they were hit by the car. And they probably haven't seen them since, and maybe will never see them

again. They therefore don't have much of an opportunity to generate strong emotional feelings toward them. They may be very dissatisfied with what happened, the fact that they ended up being injured, and went through pain and suffering and all of this and it was that person's fault. But generally speaking, a large dose of money is going to cure a lot of [that]. I have never had a personal injury case where the client has said at any time during the proceedings, you know "that person is a real son-of-a-gun and I don't care about the money, I don't care about anything. I just want you to get him. I want to go to trial and stand up and tell the whole world what a rotten driver he or she may be." ... If you switch over to a divorce action, obviously the parties know each other.... In the vast majority of cases, they have strong feelings.

Even in other legal actions involving long-term relationships, such as contract disputes in business, the negotiation context may be qualitatively different than it is in divorce. One lawyer points out that

in business and such, the major tool is your ability to walk out, but in divorce, you are going to have to have a resolution someday.... And in divorce the concept of fairness arises whereas in business it doesn't make any difference, because it just doesn't apply. I mean if you want to buy some real estate you don't have to give them a fair price, you can just offer them half of what you think it is worth.... If he agrees, fine; and if he doesn't, fine.

The emotional intensity of divorce is particularly evident when the decision to end the marriage is not mutual. Like financial and procedural pressures, emotional pressures can affect parties differently; one party may be eager to settle while the other is reluctant to proceed. * * * Clearly, if one party wants out of the marriage, [the irretrievable-breakdown] requirement is met; thus, there is no guarantee that divorce is a mutual decision. In a number of our cases, while one party was extremely impatient to finalize the divorce, the other party wanted nothing less than a "day in court"—a chance to vilify the initiating spouse. These emotional conflicts can color the whole settlement process. * * *

Similar observations have led [to the statement] that "lawyers and clients are in effect largely occupied with two different divorces: lawyers with a legal divorce, clients with a social and emotional divorce."[1]

* * *

NOTES AND QUESTIONS

1. *Clients' perceptions of their domestic relations lawyer.* Each year clients file more ethics complaints against family lawyers than against lawyers in other fields of practice. *See* Nancy Ver Steegh, *Yes, No, and Maybe: Informed Decision Making About Divorce Mediation In the Presence of Domes-*

---

1. John Griffiths, *What Do Dutch Lawyers Actually Do in Divorce Cases?*, 20 Law & Soc'y Rev. 135, 155 (1986).

tic Violence, 9 Wm. & Mary J. Women & L. 145, 163 (2003). Family lawyers are also named in about 10% of malpractice claims filed each year, a percentage exceeded only by personal injury lawyers and real estate lawyers. *See* Am. Bar Ass'n, *Profile of Legal Malpractice Claims, 2000–2003*, at 4, tbl. 1 (2005).

The relatively high rates of ethics complaints and malpractice claims likely indicate significant client dissatisfaction with the quality of family law representation. In one study of divorcing parents with young children, 20% of the respondents believed the divorce process would work better without lawyers. These parents felt that attorneys heightened antagonism and contributed to lasting feelings of hardship and frustration. *See* Marsha Kline Pruett & Tamara D. Jackson, *The Lawyer's Role During the Divorce Process: Perceptions of Parents, Their Young Children, and Their Attorneys*, 33 Fam. L.Q. 283, 303, 306 (1999).

Pruett and Jackson suggest, however, that much client frustration with counsel may stem from frustration with divorce litigation itself, and from the parties' own unrealistic expectations about the outcome. Many spouses emerge embittered from the divorce process because they entered with unrealistic expectations that property, alimony and child-related issues would be resolved to everyone's satisfaction. "It is inescapable that divorces are among the most stressing and debasing experiences faced by a broad section of American families. It is difficult to conceive how most parents, with all the anger and hurt attendant to divorce, could reach agreement without attributing much of their pain to the legal process and to legal personnel themselves. * * * [I]t is so much easier to kill the messenger than to change * * * the conditions within the family that led to the divorce itself." *Id.* at 307.

2. *High job satisfaction among domestic relations attorneys.* Despite the emotional intensity frequently experienced by family law practitioners in their client representation, a clinical study examining job satisfaction among lawyers in twelve primary areas of law found that family lawyers had one of the highest job satisfaction scores, while corporate and real estate practitioners had the lowest scores. Lawrence R. Richard, *Psychological Type and Job Satisfaction Among Practicing Lawyers in the United States*, 29 Cap. U. L. Rev. 979, 1014, 1057 (2002). This result is due largely to the nature of contemporary family law practice. Family law is a people-oriented practice that enables its practitioners to help one family at a time. Family law is typically practiced in smaller firms, or in smaller departments within larger firms. Unlike lawyers in larger corporate firms, domestic relations lawyers typically do not have high billing demands. Family lawyers are encouraged to become active in the local family law associations and to participate in *pro bono* activities.

3. *Self-representation in divorce cases.* Many divorcing spouses, particularly ones with modest incomes, proceed without counsel. In 2001, for example, Florida's Family Court Steering Committee found that at least one party appeared *pro se* in 60% of divorce cases filed in the state, and in 80% of post-judgment matters. *See In re Report of the Family Court Steering Committee*, 794 So.2d 518 (Fla. 2001). The findings were consistent with the results of

earlier studies, which found *pro se* divorce rates between 68% and 80%. *See* Ver Steegh, *supra*, at 165.

A 1990 American Bar Association study of Maricopa County, Arizona divorce cases found that at least one party was unrepresented in 88% of the cases. In a 1994 ABA study, nearly half the divorcing parties studied chose self-representation because they thought the case was simple, and others chose self-representation because they could not afford a lawyer. Parties were more likely to appear *pro se* if they had no children, were not homeowners, had limited personal property, had household incomes less than $50,000, or were married less than ten years. *See* ABA Standing Comm. on the Delivery of Legal Servs., Responding to the Needs of the Self–Represented Divorce Litigant 2–3 (1994).

Some divorcing spouses, particularly those with few marital assets in uncontested proceedings, have recently sought to avoid lawyers and higher costs by working with on-line companies that provide forms, which the spouse or the company itself fills out and files in court. *See, e.g.,* Grant Schulte, *More Iowans Handle Legalities Solo*, Des Moines Register, Mar. 24, 2008, at 1A. Because these "dot.com" divorce companies typically do not customize the papers to satisfy the specific procedural requirements of a particular state's family courts, however, couples may incur higher costs than if they retained lawyers for an uncontested divorce.

Many courts have responded to the needs of *pro se* filers by providing model complaints, answers, and other basic filings with easy-to-follow instructions, available on-line and at the courts. *See, e.g.,* Maryland Judiciary Domestic Relations Forms, http://www.courts.state.md.us/family/forms/domred.html. Some courts also provide case managers to help guide unrepresented parties through the divorce process. In 2006, a New York commission identified the high rate of *pro se* representation as "a substantial barrier to the efficient, effective and timely movement of contested matrimonial cases" in that state. *See* Report of the Matrimonial Commission to the Chief Judge of the State of New York 57 (2006).

The 1994 ABA study found that compared to represented litigants, *pro se* litigants were as satisfied with the terms of their divorce decrees, more satisfied with the legal process, and more satisfied with judges. On the other hand, *pro se* litigants often had trouble filling out forms and working their way through the legal system. *Pro se* litigants were also less likely than represented litigants to receive marital counseling or dispute resolution services, to receive advice about the tax consequences of their divorce, to receive advice about pension or insurance matters, to request spousal maintenance, and to pursue temporary orders or post-decree modification. ABA Standing Comm., *supra,* at 10–12.

Should states enact legislation or procedural rules authorizing courts to appoint counsel for divorcing parties who cannot afford to retain counsel? Should any such authority be plenary, or should it be limited to uncontested divorces? To contested divorces?

SECTION 2: ETHICS IN FAMILY LAW PRACTICE

A. ETHICAL FOUNDATIONS

Like lawyers practicing in other fields, domestic relations lawyers regularly face vexing ethical questions in their relationships with clients, courts, opponents and third parties. Questions can arise under the full range of ethical rules. This Section complements the required professional responsibility course by treating major ethical questions that frequently surface in domestic relations practice.

Family law practitioners serve their clients in four primary roles. The lawyer is an *advisor* who "provides a client with an informed understanding of the client's legal rights and obligations and explains their practical implications." The lawyer is an *advocate* who "zealously asserts the client's position under the rules of the adversary system." The lawyer is a *negotiator* who "seeks a result advantageous to the client but consistent with requirements of honest dealings with others." Finally, the lawyer is an *evaluator* who "acts by examining a client's legal affairs and reporting about them to the client or to others." Model Rules of Prof'l Conduct, Preamble (2008).

Domestic relations lawyers face multiple layers of professional and legal influences. Most prominent is each state's mandatory code of ethics, which regulates all lawyers. Most states have enacted the ABA's Model Rules of Professional Conduct (sometimes with amendments), though some states retain codes patterned largely on the earlier Model Code of Professional Responsibility. Unless otherwise specified, this Chapter cites and applies the 2008 version of the ABA Model Rules, as amended.

Unofficial sources may also influence domestic relations lawyers. For example, the American Academy of Matrimonial Lawyers (AAML) has promulgated the aspirational *Bounds of Advocacy, Goals For Family Lawyers*, which is directed at AAML members. These guidelines may urge higher standards than those imposed by the Model Rules, and may influence other lawyers through endorsement by state bar associations, http://www.aaml.org/files/public/Bounds_of_Advocacy.htm. The American Law Institute has promulgated the Restatement (Third) of the Law Governing Lawyers, which, like other restatements, assembles principles gleaned from official sources such as statutes, decisions and codes. Lawyers serving as mediators or arbitrators also feel the influence of unofficial ethical codes, discussed in Chapter 15, that relate to such service.

Family lawyers have several basic ethical obligations to clients, including these:

(1) *Competence.*

"A lawyer shall provide competent representation to a client. Competent representation requires the legal knowledge, skill, thoroughness and preparation reasonably necessary for the representation." Model Rule 1.1.

Model Rule 1.1 may impose particular obligations on domestic relations lawyers now that no-fault divorce has steered dissolution proceedings away from proof of wrongdoing and more toward often-complex property and child-related issues, and now that family law practice frequently includes nonmarital families. Some cases may raise legal issues beyond the lawyer's immediate competence, or issues requiring expertise from other fields. Family lawyers "need to understand family dynamics and the impact of divorce on all of the parties, in addition to all of the complexities of pensions, corporate valuation, taxation and child support. Lawyers who want to help families should have additional training in child development, child abuse and neglect, domestic violence and alternative conflict resolution. In addition, family lawyers should be knowledgeable in cross-disciplinary issues affecting their high-conflict custody cases, such as competencies of other professionals and availability of community resources." Linda D. Elrod, *A Minnesota Comparative Family Law Symposium: Reforming the System to Protect Children in High Conflict Custody Cases*, 28 Wm. Mitchell L. Rev. 495, 536–37 (2001).

In light of the complexities that mark contemporary family law practice, law students seeking a career compass should resist the assumption that "any lawyer can handle a divorce." In *Attorney Grievance Comm'n v. Kreamer*, 946 A.2d 500, 516 (Md. 2008), for example, the lawyer was disbarred for, among other violations, "abject failure to understand and comprehend how to calculate child support." The lawyer claimed that most of her practice was in family law, but she based calculations on a form she had created, rather than on the intricate child support guidelines worksheet required by law and well-known to practitioners in the field. (The child support guidelines are treated in Chapter 11.)

(2) *Diligence.*

"A lawyer shall act with reasonable diligence and promptness in representing a client." Model Rule 1.3. A family lawyer's failure to heed this injunction can be particularly serious because "[c]lients in contested divorce proceedings, especially involving child custody disputes, need expeditious resolution of the issues in order that they may get on with their lives." *In re Daugherty*, 83 P.3d 789, 793 (Kan. 2004). In *Kentucky Bar Ass'n v. Bock*, 245 S.W.3d 206 (Ky. 2008), a lawyer was suspended for thirty days for failing to file the client's divorce petition, failing to communicate with the client concerning the matter, and failing to return the client's fee for work not done.

(3) *Informing the client.*

"A lawyer shall explain a matter to the extent reasonably necessary to permit the client to make informed decisions regarding the representation." Model Rule 1.4(b).

Because so many domestic relations clients are laypersons who lack experience with lawyers and the legal system, counsel may need to take particular steps to assure that the client understands the process and its likely ramifications. The AAML also recommends that lawyers "should advise the client of the emotional and economic impact of divorce and explore the feasibility of reconciliation," including marriage counseling or therapy. AAML, *Bounds of Advocacy* § 1.2. "Although few attorneys are qualified to do psychological counseling, a discussion of the emotional and monetary repercussions of divorce is appropriate." *Id.* cmt.

(4) *Communicating with the client.*

"Reasonable communication between the lawyer and the client is necessary for the client effectively to participate in the representation." Model Rule 1.4 cmt.1. "The lawyer must keep the client reasonably informed about the matter," and must "promptly comply with a client's reasonable requests for information." ALI Restatement (Third) of the Law Governing Lawyers § 20 (2000). Maintaining communication may pose particular challenges because "[m]any clients come to family law attorneys defeated and depleted, and expect and request the attorney to make decisions for them (no matter how informed the client may be). One of the most challenging parts of communicating with the family law client then, is empowering those clients who do not want to participate in decision-making, and doing so in a manner that allows dispute resolution to move forward in a timely manner." Barbara Glesner Fines & Cathy Madsen, *Caring Too Little, Caring Too Much: Competence and the Family Law Attorney*, 75 UMKC L. Rev. 965, 980–81 (2007).

Regardless of stress or emotion, regular contact with the client remains an ethical imperative. "Lawyer failure to maintain effective contact with clients may be one of the most serious complaints that clients have about lawyers." Charles W. Wolfram, Modern Legal Ethics 164 (West 1986). Domestic relations lawyers sometimes suffer discipline for failing to respond to clients' phone calls and requests for information. *See, e.g., Office of Lawyer Regulation v. Christnot*, 685 N.W.2d 788, 789 (Wis. 2004) (lawyer suspended for six months for failing to respond for two years to divorce client who telephoned the lawyer twenty times, tried to visit the lawyer at her office approximately four times, and sent correspondence to her office asking about the status of the matter).

(5) *Fraud.*

Model Rule 8.4(c) provides that a lawyer may not "engage in conduct involving dishonesty, fraud, deceit or misrepresentation." The Model Rules define "fraud" as "conduct that is fraudulent under the substantive or procedural law of the applicable jurisdiction and has a purpose to deceive." Model Rule 1.0(d).

Other more specific ethical rules concerning fraud may also apply. Model Rule 1.2(d), for example, provides that "[a] lawyer shall not counsel a client to engage, or assist a client, in conduct that the lawyer knows is criminal or fraudulent, but a lawyer may discuss the legal consequences of any proposed course of conduct with a client and may counsel or assist a client to make a good faith effort to determine the validity, scope, meaning or application of the law." Model Rule 4.1 provides: "In the course of representing a client a lawyer shall not knowingly: (a) make a false statement of material fact or law to a third person; or (b) fail to disclose a material fact when disclosure is necessary to avoid assisting a criminal or fraudulent act by a client," unless the Rules otherwise prohibit disclosure relating to representation of the client.

In *In re Belding*, 589 S.E.2d 197 (S.C. 2003), the court suspended the husband's lawyer for one year for drafting a fictitious, but apparently authentic, set of divorce documents designed to "shock" the wife into mending the parties' marriage. The documents included a summons and complaint with a fictitious docket number and a fictitious filing stamp from the clerk's office, a fictitious consent order to change venue with the signatures of the family court judge and lawyers forged by the suspended lawyer, and fictitious discovery requests with counsel's signature also forged. Forging a judge's signature usually results in disbarment or indefinite suspension, but *Belding* opted for a lesser sanction because the wife found the fictitious documents in the husband's car and the lawyer never presented the documents as authentic. *Id.* at 200–01.

NOTES AND QUESTIONS

1. *Contingent fees.* In the typical contingent-fee arrangement, lawyer and client agree that the lawyer will receive a fixed percentage of the client's recovery in a settlement or judgment (usually about one-third), but nothing if there is no recovery. Lawyer and client sometimes agree instead that the lawyer will be paid by the hour, but with a bonus for a specified favorable result.

Contingent-fee agreements are most commonly used in personal injury actions by plaintiffs, including plaintiffs who might not otherwise be able to afford a lawyer. Model Rule 1.5 generally permits arrangements for reasonable contingent fees, but the Rule specifically prohibits contingent fees "in a domestic relations matter, the payment or amount of which is contingent upon the securing of a divorce or upon the amount of alimony or support, or property settlement in lieu thereof." Model Rule 1.5(d)(1). Because the Model Rule and its predecessors specify divorce, the prohibition has generally not been interpreted to preclude contingent-fee arrangements in actions between unmarried cohabitants or in paternity proceedings. *See, e.g.*, Mont. Ethics Op. 990119 (undated).

The rule prohibiting contingent fees in most domestic relations cases is grounded in policy concerns. A contingent-fee arrangement, for example, might induce the lawyer to "ignore the possibility of reconciliation and to press, for personal gain, the dissolution of a marriage which patience and effort might salvage." Louis Parley, The Ethical Family Lawyer 47 (1995). Contingent fees, sometimes negotiated with clients otherwise unable to pay, are assertedly unnecessary in divorce cases because common law and statutes authorize courts to assess fees and costs against the other spouse. A contingent-fee arrangement might permit lawyers to overreach emotionally vulnerable clients by taking unfairly high percentages of the recovery. In property distribution, a contingent-fee arrangement might create a conflict of interest between the lawyer who may want to maximize the value of property obtained, and the client who may want lower values placed on the property. Contingent fees might divert too much money from post-divorce support for ex-spouses and children. *Id.* at 47–48.

Model Rule 1.5 does not preclude contingent-fee agreements "in connection with the recovery of post-judgment balances due under support, alimony or other financial orders because such contracts do not implicate the same policy concerns." Model Rule 1.5 cmt.6. These post-judgment actions are seen as collection proceedings, with the parties' respective rights and obligations already determined by the divorce decree. The contingent fee diverts funds from the intended recipients, but a successful post-judgment action provides the recipients funds they otherwise might not receive.

The AAML *Bounds of Advocacy* are less inclusive than the Model Rules. Goal 4.5 provides that a lawyer should not charge a fee that is contingent on (a) obtaining a divorce; (b) particular custody or visitation provisions; or (c) the amount of alimony or child support awarded. An attorney may charge a contingent fee for all other matters (such as property distribution issues), provided that the client is informed of the right to have the fee based on an hourly rate, and that the client has an opportunity to seek independent legal advice concerning the desirability of the contingent fee arrangement. Which approach to contingent fees, the Model Rules' or the AAML's, do you prefer?

2. *Competence as stated in Model Rule 1.1.* Do you agree with Professor Linda D. Elrod's recommendation that "[f]amily law is a specialty area and lawyers who practice family law should be required to meet additional requirements, i.e. board certification or some type of state or bar-approved specialization"? Elrod, *supra,* 28 Wm. Mitchell L. Rev. at 536.

B. CLIENT CONFIDENCES

Model Rule 1.6(a) states the general rule that "[a] lawyer shall not reveal information relating to the representation of a client unless the client gives informed consent [or] the disclosure is impliedly authorized in order to carry out the representation." Confidentiality, which aims to encourage persons to seek legal advice by assuring that lawyer and client can communicate freely and frankly with one another, is central to the consultation, negotiations and drafting that characterize the typical domestic relations proceeding. The Model Rule reaches both the lawyer's communications with the client and other information concerning the representation. *See, e.g., In re Disciplinary Proceedings Against O'Neil,* 661 N.W.2d 813 (Wis. 2003) (lawyer publicly reprimanded for revealing to police, during their probe into the wife's apparent murder, the lawyer's conversations with the client husband and his file on the pending divorce proceedings); *State ex rel. Counsel for Discipline v. Wilson,* 634 N.W.2d 467 (Neb. 2001) (lawyer suspended for eighteen months for threatening to disclose confidential information from a former client's divorce case unless the client paid the lawyer fees allegedly due for a variety of matters).

Where the lawyer suspects that the client is abusing the children, the lawyer may struggle with impulses to report the abuse to child protective or law enforcement authorities. State child abuse reporting statutes create classes of "mandatory reporters," persons such as educators, medical personnel and law enforcement agents, who must report suspected child abuse or face possible criminal punishment for non-reporting. The reporting statutes also permit reports of suspected abuse from any other person. Reporting statutes normally do not list lawyers in the enumeration of mandatory reporters.

Model Rule 1.6(b)(1), however, provides a limited exception to the lawyer's obligation to maintain client confidences: "A lawyer may reveal information relating to the representation of a client to the extent the lawyer reasonably believes necessary * * * to prevent reasonably certain death or substantial bodily harm." The literature amply demonstrates the substantial physical and emotional harm that child abuse can cause victims in the short-term and the long-term. Does the Model Rule, which is grounded in "the overriding value of life and physical integrity," require or permit domestic relations lawyers to report physical or sexual abuse that they reasonably suspect their clients are perpetrating? *Id.* cmt.6. To the extent that the Model Rules would prevent lawyers from reporting, do the Rules serve the best interests of children?

In family law representation, allegations that the other spouse is committing child abuse may also present a lawyer with an ethical dilemma. A client locked in contentious litigation may seek the upper hand by making vindictive, and unsupported, child abuse claims. Rates of reported child sexual abuse seem to be about six times higher in families involved in custody disputes than in the general population, either because rates of abuse are higher in divorced families, or because custody disputes produce higher rates of emotional distress and anxiety. Andrew I. Schepard, Children, Courts and Custody 97 (2004). The lawyer's participation in making abuse claims may implicate Model Rule 3.1: "A lawyer shall not bring or defend a proceeding, or assert or controvert an issue therein, unless there is basis in law and fact for doing so that is not frivolous, which includes a good faith argument for an extension, modification or reversal of existing law." Where the client insists on making claims that the lawyer believes are baseless, the lawyer may consider withdrawing from the representation because "the client insists upon taking action that the lawyer considers repugnant or with which the lawyer has a fundamental disagreement." Model Rule 1.16(b)(4).

PROBLEM 2–1

You are representing Paula Perkins, the mayor of your city, in her divorce proceedings. Because of her official position and the pointed statements she and her estranged husband have made, the impending divorce has attracted considerable media attention. A reporter phones and asks you to comment on reports that the marriage has been marked by the husband's intermittent domestic violence, and that the children have missed several days of school in the last two months. What will you say to the reporter? Would your answer be any different if the husband's lawyer called and wanted to know whether Paula was seeing another man?

C. CONFLICTS OF INTEREST

"In representing a client, a lawyer shall exercise independent professional judgment and render candid advice." Model Rule 2.1. Model Rule 1.7(a) prohibits a lawyer from representing a client if the representation involves a "concurrent conflict of interest"—that is, if "the representation of one client will be directly adverse to another client," or if "there is a significant risk that the representation of one or more clients will be materially limited by the lawyer's responsibilities to another client, a former client or a third person or by a personal interest of the lawyer."

Where a concurrent conflict of interest exists, however, Model Rule 1.7(b) permits a lawyer to represent a client if:

(1) the lawyer reasonably believes that the lawyer will be able to provide competent and diligent representation to each affected client;

(2) the representation is not prohibited by law;

(3) the representation does not involve the assertion of a claim by one client against another client represented by the lawyer in the same litigation or other proceeding before a tribunal; and

(4) each affected client gives informed consent, confirmed in writing.

NOTES AND QUESTIONS

1. *Common representation.* May a lawyer represent both the husband and the wife in their dissolution proceeding? Despite genuine potential for conflicts of interest as the parties grapple with property and child-related issues, common representation "occurs more often than one might want to imagine." Louis Parley, The Ethical Family Lawyer 16 (1995).

Some lawyers represent parties who appear to be cooperating in seeking a no-fault divorce, particularly when the parties seek to save money and reduce adversary tensions by retaining a shared lawyer and each party provides informed written consent to common representation. Despite the temptation that might follow insistent requests from seemingly reasonable spouses, common representation comes with potential pitfalls. For one thing, common representation may provide a ground for rescinding the separation agreement for overreaching, thereby upsetting the reasonable expectations of at least one of the parties. *See, e.g., Levine v. Levine*, 436 N.E.2d 476 (N.Y. 1982).

For another, if the common representation fails before entry of the divorce decree because the spouses' potentially adverse interests cannot be reconciled, the lawyer must ordinarily withdraw from representing either spouse. The result can be additional cost, embarrassment and recrimination. *See* Model Rule 1.7 cmt.29. In *Lawyer Disciplinary Bd. v. Frame*, 479 S.E.2d 676 (W. Va. 1996), for example, the court imposed a public reprimand on the husband's lawyer, who prepared the divorce complaint and (at the request of the husband, who said the divorce was amicable) also prepared the wife's answer. The answer recited that the wife was appearing *pro se*. When the wife informed the lawyer several weeks later that the husband was abusing her, the lawyer withdrew as the husband's counsel and refunded his fee. The couple then employed separate lawyers and obtained the divorce.

In states that determine the propriety of common representation of divorcing spouses on a case-by-case basis, lawyers undertaking such representation "advanc[e] at their own peril" because dissolution proceedings apparently amicable today may be marked by disagreements before the court enters the final decree. "Where there is a potential conflict in interest between the parties, as is true in every domestic dispute, it is inappropriate to attempt to represent them both. This is true even where the parties appear to be in full accord at the time." *Blum v. Blum*, 477 A.2d 289, 296 (Md. 1984).

In some states, common representation of divorcing spouses establishes a *per se* ethical violation. In *Walden v. Hoke*, 429 S.E.2d 504 (W. Va. 1993), for example, the court held that a lawyer may not represent both spouses at any stage of the separation and divorce proceeding, even with informed written consent from both. "The likelihood of prejudice is so great with dual representation so as to make adequate representation of both spouses impossible, even where the separation is 'friendly' and the divorce uncontested." *Id*. at 509. The *Hoke* majority included Chief Justice Richard Neely, who had warned nine years earlier that common representation "works if there are no children, little property, and no alimony—and if both parties have almost no disagreements. Couples with that degree of mutual concern and understanding usually don't get divorced." "There is no getting around the fact," he wrote, "that divorce is adversarial. In any given family, the hours that children spend with their parents, the future earning capacities of the husband and wife, and all the accumulated property constitute a pie of a given size. Divorce splits up that pie, and a larger slice for one person necessarily means a smaller slice for the other. It is impossible for one lawyer simultaneously to advise each party to a divorce to demand a bigger slice of the pie." Richard Neely, The Divorce Decision: The Legal and Human Consequences of Ending a Marriage 140–41 (1984).

Even in an evidently amicable divorce, does Model Rule 1.7 permit common representation of divorcing spouses? Is the parties' relationship "directly adverse" within the meaning of Rule 1.7(a)(1)? Is there a "significant risk" that representation of one spouse will be "materially limited by the lawyer's responsibilities" to the other? Is common representation "consentable" under Model Rule 1.7(b)?

2. *Duties to current clients.* Domestic relations lawyers sometimes face potential conflicts of interest because one or both spouses, facing the severe personal crisis inherent in divorce, have grown comfortable with the lawyer through prior personal or professional dealings. The spouses may even have come to regard the lawyer as the "family attorney." One spouse, for example, may seek to retain a lawyer whose earlier representation of the other spouse or both spouses, in a business venture or other matter unrelated to the divorce proceeding, has not concluded. The other divorcing spouse is a current client of the lawyer. With narrow exceptions, "[a] lawyer shall not use

information relating to representation of a client to the disadvantage of the client unless the client gives informed consent." Model Rule 1.8(b). Such use would violate the duty of loyalty the lawyer owes to the client.

In one case, the lawyer was representing a husband and wife as co-executors of an estate in which they were beneficiaries of a substantial minority interest in a valuable piece of real estate. The lawyer had obtained no confidential information from the husband individually, and had never represented the husband or wife on any other matter. The state bar association's ethics committee concluded that the lawyer could not represent the wife in divorce proceedings unless the lawyer held the requisite reasonable belief and the husband gave the requisite written consent. "If the divorce proceedings are going to be 'amicable' so that those proceedings will not produce any rancor that might spill over into the estate matter, then perhaps the [reasonable belief] test can be met. The possibility of contention in the divorce proceedings would, by contrast, point in the opposite direction." The ethics committee also concluded that the lawyer could not cure a conflict by withdrawing from representing the husband as co-executor. *See* Mass. Formal & Informal Ops. 2002–1.

3. *Duties to former clients.* Model Rule 1.9(a) provides that "[a] lawyer who has formerly represented a client in a matter shall not thereafter represent another person in the same or a substantially related matter in which that person's interests are materially adverse to the interests of the former client unless the former client gives informed consent, confirmed in writing." Even with this consent, "[a] lawyer who has formerly represented a client in a matter or whose present or former firm has formerly represented a client in a matter shall not thereafter * * * use information relating to the representation to the disadvantage of the former client except * * * when the information has become generally known * * *." Model Rule 1.9(c)(1).

Two matters are "substantially related" where the lawyer "reasonably could have learned confidential information in the first representation that would be of significance in the second." Information the lawyer could reasonably have learned is presumed to have been learned. The presumption is generally not rebuttable because "if the lawyer was permitted to contest the point, the former client would have to reveal the very information that he sought to protect." Geoffrey C. Hazard, Jr. & W. William Hodes, The Law of Lawyering § 13.5, at 13–13 (3d ed. 2001). The lawyer may be disciplined for using confidential information even if the lawyer does not otherwise publicly disclose the information. *See, e.g.,* Md. Ethics Op. 2002–10 (prior representation of the husband and wife in preparing and filing a bankruptcy petition during the marriage created conflict of interest because the bankruptcy filing required each party to reveal all assets, income potential, and debts to the lawyer).

A divorcing spouse might seek to retain a lawyer who previously represented the other spouse, or both spouses, in a matter concerning, for example, a family-owned business or other family affairs. Even where the former representation has concluded, representing either spouse in the divorce proceeding may present a conflict of interest because the other spouse is a former client who may have provided significant confidential information. *See, e.g.,*

Florida Bar v. Dunagan, 731 So.2d 1237 (Fla. 1999) (suspending for three months a lawyer who represented the husband in a divorce after having represented the husband and wife jointly in their acquisition and maintenance of a restaurant business during the marriage).

Mere consultation may create a "former client" conflict of interest. In *In re Conduct of Knappenberger*, 108 P.3d 1161 (Or. 2005), for example, the court suspended for ninety days a lawyer who represented the wife in a divorce proceeding less than two months after the husband had interviewed the lawyer for two hours about representing him in that proceeding. During the interview, the husband gave the lawyer a copy of the property settlement agreement the spouses had signed, told the lawyer about the restraining orders the spouses had obtained against one another, described the main issues in the divorce, and told the lawyer about the husband's goals in the divorce proceeding. The court held that an attorney-client relationship existed during the two-hour interview because the lawyer provided the husband substantive advice on aspects of the divorce proceeding, the husband reasonably believed the interview was confidential, the lawyer also believed the interview was confidential, and the lawyer billed the client for the interview.

In *Camuto v. Camuto*, 1999 WL 956688 (Conn. Super. Ct. Oct. 7, 1999), however, the court refused to disqualify the wife's lawyer based on the husband's interview with a member of the lawyer's firm three and a half years earlier concerning the condition of the marriage. The court found that the interview was one of several the husband conducted with lawyers to help select the right attorney to represent him in the divorce proceedings, without intending to establish an attorney-client relationship. During the interview, the husband did not provide confidential financial information or the names of his wife or the children. The court concluded that any information the husband provided during the interview could not significantly harm him in the divorce proceedings.

A domestic relations lawyer may face a "former client" conflict of interest where other lawyers in the firm previously represented or consulted with the other spouse about any matter, even if the lawyer himself did not conduct the former representation or consultation. *See* Model Rule 1.10. The "former client" rule applies regardless of the size of the firm, and it is one reason why most large firms do very little divorce work.

In *Hosack v. Hosack*, 2002 WL 31687232 (Conn. Super. Ct. Nov. 12, 2002), for example, the wife consulted about a possible divorce with a partner of the lawyer the husband retained in divorce proceedings a year later. The wife and partner discussed financial issues and her difficulty in getting her husband to attend counseling sessions. The partner did not bill the wife for the consultation, which lasted between twenty-four minutes and an hour. The court disqualified the husband's lawyer because the wife was a "former client" of the partner. The wife disclosed confidential matters to the partner concerning the spouses' domestic problems while seeking professional aid, even though she did not employ him.

4. *Duties to prospective clients.* Where a spouse consults with a lawyer concerning the possibility of creating a client-lawyer relationship, the spouse may be a "prospective client" entitled to protection from conflicts of interest,

even if no such relationship is created. Model Rule 1.18 provides that with limited exceptions, the lawyer "shall not use or reveal information learned in the consultation," or "represent a client with interests materially adverse to those of a prospective client in the same or a substantially related matter if the lawyer received information from the prospective client that could be significantly harmful to that person in the matter."

5. *Sexual relations between domestic relations lawyer and client.* In 2003, the ABA added Model Rule 1.8(j), which provides that "[a] lawyer shall not have sexual relations with a client unless a consensual sexual relationship existed between them when the client-lawyer relationship commenced." In the next few years, this new prohibition will likely be a matter of spirited debate as states decide whether to adopt it.

Sexual relations with clients are not confined to domestic relations lawyers, but the problem has been called a "systemic, unchanging and consistent trend" in the domestic relations field. 1990 Report of the Illinois Task Force on Gender Bias in the Courts 54 (1990). Sex with clients draws particular attention in domestic relations cases because of the intimate nature of the issues, and because of the asserted dependence and emotional vulnerability of some clients.

Because neither the ABA Model Rules of Professional Conduct nor the ABA Model Code of Professional Responsibility explicitly addressed sexual relations with clients before 2003, discipline has generally depended on application of general ethical rules. In 1992, an American Bar Association ethics opinion concluded that lawyers "would be well advised to refrain from" sexual relations with clients. The ABA stated that sexual relations with a client "may involve unfair exploitation of the lawyer's fiduciary position, and/or significantly impair lawyer's ability to represent the client competently * * *." "The roles of lover and lawyer are potentially conflicting ones as the emotional involvement that is fostered by a sexual relationship has the potential to undercut the objective detachment that is often demanded for adequate representation." ABA Comm. on Ethics and Prof'l Responsibility, Formal Op. 92–364 (1992). The American Academy of Matrimonial Lawyers similarly advises that a lawyer "should not have a sexual relationship with a client * * * in the case during the time of the representation." *See* AAML, *Bounds of Advocacy* § 3.4.

In New York, "[a] lawyer shall not * * * in domestic relations matters, enter into sexual relations with a client during the course of the lawyer's representation of the client." N.Y. Comp. Codes R. & Regs. tit. 22 § 1200.29–a(b)(3) (2008). In states without ethical rules expressly addressing the sexual relations question, lawyers face discipline under generally applicable rules for "put[ting] the lawyer's own personal feelings ahead of the objectivity that must be the hallmark of any successful attorney-client relationship." *Butler County Bar Ass'n v. Williamson*, 884 N.E.2d 55, 56 (Ohio 2008) (lawyer indefinitely suspended for sexual relations with divorce client).

Sexual relations with a domestic relations client in a fragile emotional or physical condition, for example, may establish a violation of Model Rule 1.14 (a) ("When a client's capacity to make adequately considered decisions in connection with a representation is diminished, whether because of minority, mental impairment or for some other reason, the lawyer shall, as far as reasonably possible, maintain a normal client-lawyer relationship with the client.") *See, e.g., In re Hoffmeyer*, 656 S.E.2d 376, 378 (S.C. 2008) (lawyer suspended for nine months for sexual relations with divorce client). Sanctions may be imposed on a lawyer who suggests to a prospective client that he will represent her in return for sexual favors. *See, e.g., In re Stewart*, 563 S.E.2d 859 (Ga. 2002) (lawyer suspended for eighteen months). Sanctions may also be imposed on a lawyer who maintains "a substantial social relationship" with the client's spouse during dissolution proceedings. *In re Disciplinary Proceedings Against Inglimo*, 740 N.W.2d 125, 132 (Wis. 2007) (lawyer suspended for three years). Where aggravating circumstances appear, the sanction for sexual relations during representation may be disbarment. *See, e.g., In re Frick*, 694 S.W.2d 473 (Mo. 1985) (lawyer disbarred because he had an affair with a divorce client and later pursued a campaign of embarrassment, intimidation, vandalism, harassment and violence against her).

In *In re Disciplinary Proceeding Against Halverson*, 998 P.2d 833 (Wash. 2000), the court suspended a veteran domestic relations lawyer for one year for having sexual relations with a client while the married lawyer was president of the Washington State Bar Association. The court held that the sexual relationship violated ethical canons concerning the lawyer's duty to avoid conflicts of interest, duty to communicate with the client, and duty to exercise independent professional judgment on the client's behalf. Do you agree with dissenting Justice Richard B. Sanders, who accused the majority of "demonstrating its paternalistic perception of female dissolution clients"?:

> Viewing female dissolution clients as "victims" who need the support, assistance and guidance of their powerful male attorneys is degrading because it undermines women's right of independent self-determination. Moreover it does not accurately portray the dynamics of an attorney-client relationship. Rather it is the *client* who has the power to choose her attorney from the multitude of attorneys competing to gain her business. It is the *client* who has the power to determine the objectives of the representation and whether to accept or reject an offer of settlement. It is the client who has the power to terminate the services of her lawyer for any reason or no reason at all. It is the client who has the power to sue an attorney if he fails to adequately represent her wishes * * * .

> While rules governing attorney-client sex appear to control male sexuality—by disciplining attorneys who engage in the sexual relationships, the vast majority of whom are male—they indirectly control female sexuality by denying self-determination to female clients who desire a dual relationship with an attorney. Thus, characterizing [the female] client as a defenseless victim subject to the overwhelming power of her attorney is * * * inconsistent with the legal entitlements of all concerned.

Id. at 851–52 (Sanders, J., concurring in part, dissenting in part). Where a lawyer has sexual relations with a domestic relations client during the client's divorce proceedings, should consent be available as a defense to the lawyer in a disciplinary proceeding? Should the answer depend on whether the state has adopted Model Rule 1.8(j), or otherwise prohibits lawyers from having sexual relations with clients during representation?

Should states adopt Model Rule 1.8(j)? Consider the American Psychological Association's Ethical Principles of Psychologists and Code of Conduct, which provide: "Psychologists do not engage in sexual intimacies with current therapy clients/patients," § 10.05; "Psychologists do not engage in sexual intimacies with individuals they know to be close relatives, guardians, or significant others of current clients/patients," § 10.06; "Psychologists do not accept as therapy clients/patients persons with whom they have engaged in sexual intimacies," § 10.07; and "Psychologists do not engage in sexual intimacies with former clients/patients for at least two years after cessation or termination of therapy. * * * Psychologists do not engage in sexual intimacies with former clients/patients even after a two-year interval except in the most unusual circumstances," § 10.08. Do these APA principles have any bearing on the unique characteristics of domestic relations proceedings?

PROBLEM 2–2

Bob and Roberta Ricketts, acquaintances of yours from the country club, visit your law office together one afternoon to say that they wish to dissolve their marriage after fourteen years. They would like you to represent both of them in the divorce proceedings and begin drawing up the papers as soon as possible. They assure you that the divorce is "amicable," and that they have talked through the issues and have reached agreement about the property and child-related issues. What questions would you ask Bob and Roberta, and how would you respond to their request?

D. OBLIGATIONS TO COURTS, THIRD PARTIES, AND OPPONENTS

NOTES

1. *Candor toward the court.* Model Rule 3.3(a) provides that a lawyer may not knowingly "make a false statement of fact or law to a tribunal or fail to correct a false statement of material fact or law previously made to the tribunal by the lawyer." The Rule further provides that the lawyer may not knowingly "offer evidence that the lawyer knows to be false." In matrimonial cases, the first provision may be particularly relevant when the lawyer drafts the separation agreement, which the parties generally submit to the court as the basis for the decree. The second provision relates to any document or testimonial evidence entered during the proceeding. *See, e.g., Iowa Sup. Ct. Bd. of Prof'l Ethics & Conduct v. Alexander*, 574 N.W.2d 322 (Iowa 1998) (domestic relations lawyer suspended indefinitely for submitting an order for modification to the trial court and saying that it was agreed to by the adversary, who had no knowledge of the order).

2. *The family lawyer's relations with third parties: improper purpose.* Model Rule 4.4(a) provides: "In representing a client, a lawyer shall not use means that have no substantial purpose other than to embarrass, delay, or burden a third person, or use methods of obtaining evidence that violate the legal rights of such a person." *See, e.g., In re Dvorak*, 611 N.W.2d 147 (N.D. 2000) (lawyer who represented a client in a divorce action and bitter custody

dispute suspended for one year for telling a witness' employer that the witness admitted providing false information to the guardian *ad litem*).

3. *The family lawyer's ethical obligations to represented and unrepresented opponents.* In the heat of emotional domestic relations proceedings, the client may ask the lawyer to "try to reason with" the other spouse, who may or may not be represented by counsel.

Where the other spouse is represented by counsel, any such communications between the lawyer and the other spouse would invite professional discipline. Model Rule 4.2 provides that "[i]n representing a client, a lawyer shall not communicate about the subject of the representation with a person the lawyer knows to be represented by another lawyer in the matter, unless the lawyer has the consent of the other lawyer or is authorized to do so by law or a court order."

The lawyer's communications with an unrepresented person might also violate Model Rule 4.3 ("Dealing With Unrepresented Person"). The Model Rule provides that the lawyer may not state or imply that the lawyer is disinterested; must make reasonable efforts to correct any misunderstanding where the lawyer knows or reasonably should know that the unrepresented person misunderstands the lawyer's role in the matter; and may not give the unrepresented person legal advice, other than the advice to secure counsel, if the lawyer knows or reasonably should know that the person's interests are, or have a reasonable possibility of being, in conflict with the client's interests. Model Rule 4.3 is central to domestic relations practice because *pro se* appearances in divorce cases are common in many places, and lay divorce litigants are typically inexperienced in legal matters.

"So long as the lawyer has explained that the lawyer represents an adverse party and is not representing the person, the lawyer may inform the person of the terms on which the lawyer's client will enter into an agreement or settle a matter, prepare documents that require the person's signature and explain the lawyer's own view of the meaning of the document or the lawyer's view of the underlying legal obligations." Model Rule 4.3 cmt.2.

BARRETT v. VIRGINIA STATE BAR

Supreme Court of Virginia, 2005.
611 S.E.2d 375.

AGEE, JUSTICE.

This case presents an appeal of right from a ruling of the Virginia State Bar Disciplinary Board ("the Board"). Timothy M. Barrett challenges the Board's order of August 5, 2004, suspending his license to practice law in the Commonwealth for a period of three years * * *.

* * *

I. RULE 4.3(b)

Timothy M. Barrett and Valerie Jill Rhudy were married in 1990. Barrett was admitted to practice law in the Commonwealth of Virginia in

1996 and operates as a sole practitioner in the City of Virginia Beach. Rhudy served as his secretary during their marriage.

In the summer of 2001, Barrett and Rhudy separated. She took the couple's six children and moved from the marital home in Virginia Beach to her parents' home in Grayson County.

Rule 4.3(b) provides as follows:

A lawyer shall not give advice to a person who is not represented by a lawyer, other than the advice to secure counsel, if the interests of such person are or have a reasonable possibility of being in conflict with the interest of the client.

The Board found that Barrett violated this rule because it concluded certain statements in two electronic mail ("e-mail") communications he wrote to Rhudy after the separation, but before she retained counsel, constituted legal advice. On July 25, 2001, Barrett sent an e-mail to Rhudy containing the following:

Venue will not be had in Grayson County. Virginia law is clear that venue is in Virginia Beach.

. . . .

Under the doctrine of imputed income, the Court will have to look at your skills and experience and determine their value in the market-place. . . . You can easily get a job . . . [making] $2,165.00 per month. . . .

In light of the fact that you are living with your parents and have no expenses . . . this income will be more than sufficient to meet your needs. I . . . just make enough to pay my own bills . . . Thus, it is unlikely that you will . . . obtain spousal support from me.

I . . . will file for . . . spousal support to have you help me pay you [sic] fair share of our $200,000+ indebtedness. Since I am barely making it on my income and you have income to spare, you might end up paying me spousal support.

. . .

In light of the fact that . . . I . . . am staying in the marital [sic] home . . . I believe that I will obtain the children. . . . [Y]ou will have to get a job to pay me my spousal support. . . . The Court will prefer the children staying with a [parent], . . . there is no question that I can set up a home away from home and even continue to home school our kids. Therefore, it is likely that you will lose this fight. And of course, if I have the kids you will be paying me child support. . . .

I am prepared for the fight.

("July e-mail").

Barrett sent Rhudy another e-mail on September 12, 2001, in which he included the following:

I will avail myself of every substantive law and procedural and evidentiary rule in the books for which a good faith claim exists. This means that you, the kids and your attorney will be in Court in Virginia Beach weekly . . . You are looking at attorney's expenses that will greatly exceed $10,000. . . . I will also appeal . . . every negative ruling . . . causing your costs to likely exceed $30,000.00. . . .

You have no case against me for adultery. . . . [The facts] show[ ] that you deserted me. . . . Your e-mails . . . show . . . that you were cruel to me. This means that I will obtain a divorce from you on fault grounds, which means you can say goodbye to spousal support. . . .

I remain in the marrital [sic] home . . . I have all the kids [sic] toys and property, that your parents' home is grossly insufficient for the children, that I can home school the older kids while watching the younger whereas you will have to put the younger in day care to fulfill your duty to financially support the kids, I believe that I will get the kids no problem. . . .

[T]he family debt . . . is subject to equitable distribution, which means you could be socked with half my lawschool [sic] debt, half the credit care [sic] debt, have [sic] my firm debt, etc.

("September e-mail").

The foregoing e-mail passages were interwoven with many requests from Barrett to Rhudy to return home, professing his love for her and the children and exhorting Rhudy for reasons of faith to reunite the family because it was God's will. * * *

In finding that Barrett gave unauthorized legal advice to an unrepresented person in violation of Rule 4.3(b), the Board opined that "Barrett cannot send those two e-mails stating what he did." Barrett contends that Rule 4.3(b) was not meant to bar communications between a husband and wife, and that construing it as such interferes with the sanctity of marriage. He further contends the e-mails only stated his opinions and were not advice to Rhudy.

* * *

* * * Comment [1] to Rule 4.3 of the Virginia Rules of Professional Conduct cautions that "[a]n unrepresented person, particularly one not experienced in dealing with legal matters, might assume that a lawyer is disinterested in loyalties or is a disinterested authority on the law."

* * *

* * * In the case at bar, * * * Barrett expressed only his opinion that he held a superior legal position on certain issues in controversy between himself and Rhudy. His statements may have been intimidating, but he did not purport to give legal advice. Rhudy knew that Barrett was a lawyer and that he had interests opposed to hers. We find that the concern articulated by the Comment to Rule 4.3 is not borne out in this case.

While the Bar argues that there is no "marital" exception to Rule 4.3(b), neither does it ask us to set out a per se rule that all communication by a lawyer, to his or her unrepresented spouse in a divorce proceeding discussing legal issues pertinent to the divorce, is prohibited under Rule 4.3(b). We do not find there is such a per se rule, but it is otherwise unnecessary for us to address that point because upon our independent review of the entire record, we find that there was not sufficient evidence to support the Board's finding that Barrett's e-mail statements to Rhudy were legal advice rather than statements of his opinion of their legal situation. Therefore, we will set aside the Board's finding that Barrett violated Rule 4.3(b).

* * *

JUSTICE KEENAN, with whom CHIEF JUSTICE HASSELL and SENIOR JUSTICE COMPTON join, concurring in part and dissenting in part.

* * *

I would hold that [Barrett's] explanations constituted legal advice intended to influence the conduct of a party who had conflicting legal interests and who was not represented by counsel. Without question, Barrett's conduct would have been a violation of Rule 4.3(b) had he communicated this advice to a pro se litigant whose spouse Barrett was representing. Thus, the majority's conclusion necessarily implies that there is a "spousal exception" to Rule 4.3(b), under which an attorney may attempt to influence his or her spouse's conduct by imparting legal advice in a harassing manner regarding the parties' conflicting legal interests.

Such a conclusion, however, is contrary to the plain language of Rule 4.3(b), which provides no "spousal exception." Moreover, Barrett's use of legal advice as a "sword" in his marital conflict is clearly a type of conduct that Rule 4.3(b) is designed to discourage. It is hard to imagine a situation in which an attorney would be in a stronger position to improperly influence another's conduct by giving legal advice.

* * *

NOTES AND QUESTIONS

1. *Model Rule 4.3*. Virginia has not adopted Rule 4.3 of the ABA Model Rules, which provides:

In dealing on behalf of a client with a person who is not represented by counsel, a lawyer shall not state or imply that the lawyer is disinterested. When the lawyer knows or reasonably should know that the unrepresented person misunderstands the lawyer's role in the matter, the lawyer shall make reasonable efforts to correct the misunderstanding. The lawyer shall not give legal advice to an unrepresented person, other than the advice to secure counsel, if the lawyer knows or reasonably should know that the interests of such a person are or have a reasonable possibility of being in conflict with the interests of the client.

2. *Constitutional and policy questions.* (a) When states apply disciplinary rules against *pro se* lawyers for communicating with their unrepresented spouses about their impending dissolution, do the disciplinary rules interfere unduly (or perhaps even unconstitutionally) with the marital relationship? (b) Does such application of the rules diminish prospects for reconciliation or inhibit the spouses' ability to manage their affairs and raise their children? Or does application help level the playing field between the lawyer spouse and the lay spouse? (c) If Barrett had been a layperson rather than a lawyer, would he likely have had the legal knowledge to make some of the statements he made in his e-mails? Would a recipient in his wife's position reasonably have given the e-mail statements more credence because they were made by a lawyer rather than a layperson? (d) If Rhudy had been represented by counsel at the time of Barrett's e-mails to her, would Barrett's e-mails have violated Model Rule 4.2, which is quoted in note 3 above? Should they?

3. *May a lawyer represent a domestic relations client against an opponent represented by the lawyer's spouse?* In Formal Opinion 340 (1975), the ABA declined to mandate disqualification in all cases: "Where both husband and wife are lawyers but they are not practicing in association with one another, they are not necessarily prohibited from representing different interests or from being associated with firms representing differing interests. * * * In any situation where a client or potential client might question the loyalty of the lawyer representing him, the situation should be fully explained to the client and the question of acceptance or continuance of representation left to the client for decision." Formal Opinion 340 advised lawyers to weigh whether the marital relationship would impair their ability to heed ethical rules relating to conflict of interest, breach of client confidences, and ability to exercise independent professional judgment on the client's behalf.

The Model Rules continue the Formal Opinion's case-by-case approach, but emphasize the informed consent of both clients: "[E]ach client is entitled to know of the existence and implications of the relationship between the lawyers before the lawyer agrees to undertake the representation. Thus, a lawyer related to another lawyer, e.g., as parent, child, sibling or spouse, ordinarily may not represent a client where that lawyer is representing another party, unless each client gives informed consent." Model Rule 1.7 cmt. 11.

PROBLEM 2–3

You are representing Frank Friedman in his divorce proceedings against his wife, Dolores, who you know is proceeding *pro se.* You have scheduled a negotiating session for the parties, which you plan to attend. What should you say to Dolores about your relationship with Frank and her, and when and how should you say it?

E. OBLIGATIONS TO THE PARTIES' CHILDREN

1. OBLIGATIONS WHEN REPRESENTING A PARENT

A significant percentage of dissolutions involve parents with minor dependent children. The children are not parties to the dissolution, but the outcome will inevitably affect their emotional and perhaps financial well-being.

May a lawyer representing a parent seek an outcome that serves the best interests of the children, even where the outcome would be inconsistent with the client's wishes? Model Rule 1.2(a) states the essence of the attorney-client relationship: generally "a lawyer shall abide by a client's decisions concerning the objectives of representation." "[L]awyers in a divorce proceeding owe a duty to their clients—the parents—not to the children of their clients." *Person v. Behnke*, 611 N.E.2d 1350, 1355 (Ill. App. Ct. 1993). Decisions such as *Person* "generally reject the notion that a lawyer for a parent has any duty to a child. Their rationale is that the lawyer would not be able to represent his or her client effectively if required to advocate for another party—the child—with adverse interests. A child's representative can represent the child so that his or her best interests are protected." Andrew Schepard, Kramer v. Kramer *Revisited: A Comment on* The Miller Commission Report *and the Obligation of Divorce Lawyers for Parents to Discuss Alternative Dispute Resolution with Their Clients*, 27 Pace L. Rev. 677, 693 (2007).

The lawyer's ethical obligation to abide by the client's decisions concerning the objectives of representation, imposed by Model Rule 1.2, may cause discomfort to a lawyer who senses that the client is inattentive to or unconcerned about the children's best interests as the lawyer perceives them. The American Academy of Matrimonial Lawyers urges that "[a]n attorney representing a parent should consider the welfare of, and seek to minimize the adverse impact of the divorce on, the minor children." *See* AAML, *Bounds of Advocacy* § 6.1. This aspirational goal may clash with mandatory ethical standards, but the AAML suggests that it is consistent with parents' "continuing fiduciary duty * * * toward their children, to serve their children's best interests."

What if the lawyer believes that the client does not wish to have custody of the children, but wishes to seek custody as a bargaining chip to induce the other spouse to accept a lower property settlement or forego maintenance? The Model Rules of Professional Conduct do not yield a definitive answer, but Model Rule 2.1 permits a lawyer rendering advice to "refer not only to law but to other considerations such as moral * * * [and] social * * * factors, that may be relevant to the client's situation." The AAML *Bounds of Advocacy* provides directly that "[a]n attorney should not permit a client to contest child custody, contact or access for either financial leverage or vindictiveness." Goal 6.2. "Proper consideration for the welfare of the children requires that they not be used as pawns in the divorce process. * * * If despite the attorney's advice the client persists, the attorney should seek to withdraw." *Id.* cmt.

Professor Lewis Becker argues that using children as bargaining chips should be viewed as a "burden" under Model Rule 4.4(a) ("In representing a client, a lawyer shall not use means that have no substantial purpose other than to embarrass, delay, or burden a third person * * * "). Model Rule 3.1 provides further that a lawyer may not assert or controvert an issue in a legal proceeding unless there is a non-frivolous basis for the position, but the Rule applies only in a legal proceeding. Professor Becker suggests that the lawyer advise the client about the hurt children may suffer from bad-faith custody claims, and about the "immorality of a terroristic threat directed to an area of especial vulnerability." If the client refuses to abandon the bad-faith claim, the lawyer might withdraw from representation under Model Rule 1.16(b)(4) because the client insists on taking action that the lawyer considers repugnant, or with which the lawyer has a fundamental disagreement. "Moreover, even a lawyer who decides to continue to represent the client should advise the client, unless there is clear state law to the contrary, that some judicial decisions have upheld an attack on the validity of an agreement where the consent of the party attacking the agreement was secured by a threat to contest custody." *See* Lewis Becker, *Ethical Concerns in Negotiating Family Law Agreements*, 30 Fam. L.Q. 587, 628–29 (1996).

2. OBLIGATIONS WHEN REPRESENTING A CHILD

Section 310 of the Uniform Marriage and Divorce Act authorizes the court to "appoint an attorney to represent the interests of a minor or dependent child with respect to his support, custody, and visitation." The court may make the appointment on either parent's motion or on its own motion. *Id.* cmt. By statute in most states today, courts hold this authority in proceedings for divorce, legal separation, or in other proceedings that raise any of the three children's issues. The court's authority is generally discretionary, though some states mandate appointment of a representative for the child when custody or visitation is in issue and a party charges abuse or neglect. Some courts exercise inherent appointment authority even without a statute. The appointed attorney may be called a Guardian *Ad Litem* (GAL), though trained volunteer non-attorneys may also serve as GALs. A GAL is charged with representing the child's best interests, even where these interests conflict with the child's stated preferences. Where the court holds discretionary authority to appoint counsel for the child, what factors should the court consider in deciding whether to make an appointment in a particular case?

Lawyers for children report great satisfaction in their work because they feel they "make a difference." In a 1999 study, however, many lawyers called the process for appointing counsel for children in divorce cases "inadequate." A few said that appointed counsel often do not meet with the child and instead form their opinions based on which parent they prefer. Children's cases are often assigned to young lawyers, who are inadequate advocates for the child's best interests because they are inexperienced in practice and children's issues. *See* Marsha Kline Pruett & Tamara D. Jackson, *The Lawyer's Role During the Divorce Process: Perceptions of Parents, Their Young Children, and Their Attorneys*, 33 Fam. L.Q. 283, 302 (1999).

Confusion continues to surround not only the attorney-appointee's obligations to the child-client, but also the question whether the child is really a client at all. If the child is a client, does the lawyer represent the child's wishes, or does the lawyer represent what the lawyer believes is in the child's best interests?

The ABA Model Rules of Professional Conduct leave the confusion unresolved because they do not grant lawyers authority to make their own best-interests determination for their young "clients." Model Rule 1.2 states that generally "a lawyer shall abide by a client's decisions concerning the objectives of representation." Model Rule 1.14(a) provides that "[w]hen a client's capacity to make adequately considered decisions in connection with a representation is diminished * * * because of minority, * * * the lawyer shall, as far as reasonably possible, maintain a normal client-lawyer relationship with the client." The latter rule recognizes that "[w]hen the client is a minor, * * * maintaining the ordinary client-lawyer relationship may not be possible in all respects," but also that "a client with diminished capacity often has the ability to understand, deliberate upon, and reach conclusions about matters affecting the client's own well-being." *Id*. cmt.1. "For example children as young as five or six years of age, and certainly those of ten or twelve, are regarded as having opinions that are entitled to weight in legal proceedings concerning their custody." *Id*.

Determining the child's capacity remains central, but uncertain in many cases. "The Child's Attorney should abide by the client's decisions about the objectives of the representation with respect to each issue on which the child is competent to direct the lawyer, and does so. The Child's Attorney should pursue the child's expressed objectives, unless the child requests otherwise, and follow the child's direction, throughout the case." ABA Section of Family Law, *Standards of Practice for Lawyers Representing Children in Custody Cases*, 37 Fam. L.Q. 131, 143 (2003) (approved by ABA House of Delegates, Aug. 2003).

F. DOMESTIC MISCONDUCT BY LAWYERS

1. EMOTION AND LAWYERS' SELF–REPRESENTATION IN DOMESTIC RELATIONS PROCEEDINGS

The rules of professional conduct, which regulate lawyers when they represent clients, also generally apply to lawyers who represent themselves. *Pro se* lawyers caught up in their own divorce proceedings (as in *Barrett*) sometimes suffer discipline because, like other spouses facing divorce, they may let their emotions get the better of them. One writer calls lawyers' self-representation in divorce cases an "ethical minefield." Louis Parley, *Lawyers, Their Divorces, and Legal Ethics*, 30 Fam. L.Q. 661, 676 (1996).

In *In re O'Meara's Case*, 834 A.2d 235 (N.H. 2003), for example, the court publicly censured the *pro se* lawyer for two pleadings he filed in divorce and custody proceedings against his wife. The first pleading misrepresented the date on which he sent a subpoena, and the second pleading (a motion to modify custody of the couple's two children) contained allegations about his wife that the disciplinary committee found to be gross embellishments on the truth and lacking sound factual predicates. The lawyer conceded that he had no independent information or evidence indicating a basis for the allegations, which he based primarily on conversations with his children.

O'Meara weighed the lawyer's violations and mitigating factors before imposing censure. "The responsibility to the court is certainly not diminished when a lawyer appears *pro se*," but the court stressed that O'Meara made his false statements "in the context of a personal, highly charged and emotional proceeding in which he served as his own counsel, a circumstance that is not likely to repeat itself and one which pressures a lawyer's good judgment in a way that would not occur when involved only as an advocate." *Id.* at 237.

Lawyers representing themselves in their own divorce proceedings may also run afoul of ethical obligations having little directly to do with emotion. Where the lawyer convinces the spouse not to retain counsel, for example, the lawyer may be found to have assumed a lawyer-client relationship with the spouse. The lawyer may then be found not to have rendered competent representation to the spouse, or to have created an impermissible conflict of interest with the spouse. *See, e.g., Williams v. Waldman*, 836 P.2d 614 (Nev. 1992).

2. DOMESTIC MISCONDUCT BY FAMILY LAWYERS UNRELATED TO REPRESENTATION

"A lawyer, as a member of the legal profession, is * * * an officer of the legal system and a public citizen having special responsibility for the quality of justice." Model Rules, Preamble [1]. Ethical lapses in the lawyer's "personal life" may lead to charges because "[a]n attorney is subject to [discipline] even for actions committed outside the professional capacity." *In re Warren*, 704 A.2d 789 (Vt. 1997). Discipline may result where the lawyer "commit[s] a criminal act that reflects adversely on the lawyer's honesty, trustworthiness or fitness as a lawyer in other respects"; "engage[s] in conduct involving dishonest, fraud, deceit or misrepresentation"; or "engage[s] in conduct that is prejudicial to the administration of justice." Model Rule 8.4.

Lawyers may face professional discipline for committing domestic violence. Sometimes the violence is unaccompanied by family law proceedings. *See, e.g., In re Jacoby*, 945 A.2d 1193 (D.C. Ct. App. 2008) (lawyer suspended for sixty days after pleading guilty to assault on his wife). Lawyers caught up in the emotions of their own divorces also frequently suffer discipline for domestic violence, even when other lawyers represent them in the divorce proceedings. *See, e.g., In re Grella*, 777 N.E.2d 167, 169 (Mass. 2002) (lawyer was suspended for two months after pleading guilty to a misdemeanor for savagely beating his estranged wife while the children were at home).

A lawyer's failure to pay court-ordered child support or alimony, or a lawyer's other domestic misconduct, may also lead to professional discipline for violating Model Rule 8.4. *See, e.g., Disciplinary Counsel v. Redfield*, 878 N.E.2d 10, 12–13 (Ohio 2007) (lawyer suspended for two years for failure to pay child support); *In re Disciplinary Action Against Giberson*, 581 N.W.2d 351 (Minn. 1998) (lawyer suspended indefinitely for willful failure to pay court ordered child support and alimony).

Sanctions may also arise from a lawyer's misconduct directed at non-family members. In *Warren*, for example, the lawyer suffered a public reprimand for writing to the wife of the man who was living with the lawyer's wife during their divorce proceedings. Lawyer Warren wrote that he wanted to make the man's life "a living hell," and that he could help the man's wife get a divorce "at no cost to you but at great expense to him." One letter urged the man's wife to help Warren "hit [the man] so hard that he will join me in wishing he was never born." 704 A.2d at 790.

SECTION 3: THE RELATIONSHIP BETWEEN ETHICS AND MALPRACTICE

A client's legal malpractice claim alleges that the lawyer failed "to use such skill, prudence and diligence as lawyers of ordinary skill and capacity commonly possess and exercise in the performance of the tasks which they undertake." *Koeller v. Reynolds*, 344 N.W.2d 556, 560 (Iowa Ct. App. 1983). The claim generally alleges that the lawyer negligently rendered professional services, negligently handled the lawyer-client relationship, or committed a breach of fiduciary duty.

The ABA Model Rules of Professional Conduct take the position that "[v]iolation of a Rule should not itself give rise to a cause of action against a lawyer nor should it create any presumption in such a case that a legal duty has been breached." Model Rules, Preamble [20]. The rules' effect in malpractice suits, however, differs from state to state. In some states, ethical rules are inadmissible to establish the duty of care in legal malpractice actions because they affect only discipline; the client seeking to establish a right of recovery is left to ordinary negligence or fiduciary principles. In other states, the trier of fact may consider ethical rules in establishing the duty of care in malpractice claims. In many states, the lawyer's violation of the rules of professional conduct may directly establish the rule of decision in a malpractice action.

Regardless of the ethical rules' effect on establishing malpractice, malpractice claims against domestic relations lawyers may be grounded in ethical lapses, such as ones arising from representing both spouses, representing one spouse after having represented the other in previous matters, engaging in sexual relations with a client, or disclosing the client's confidences without authorization. *See* Ronald E. Mallen & Jeffrey M. Smith, Legal Malpractice ch. 27 (West 5th ed. 2000). Malpractice claims may also arise from the lawyer's alleged failure to understand and apply the substantive law, such as failure to grasp a property settlement's tax or pension consequences. Most malpractice claims against domestic relations lawyers arise from property settlements, but clients also frequently allege negligence in drafting or negotiating premarital agreements, or in resolving custody and spousal or child support matters. *Id.* § 27.2.

A malpractice action grounded in negligence may lie even where the family lawyer has acted perfectly ethically. For example, a lawyer may honestly but negligently fail to consider all of the opposing spouse's assets in making a claim for a property settlement. *Ziegelheim v. Apollo*, 607 A.2d 1298 (N.J. 1992), a principal case in Chapter 15, provides an apt illustration.

* * *

Issues in lawyering and ethics are central guideposts on an attorney's career path. Consider the issues raised in this Chapter as the course now proceeds to substantive family law.

CHAPTER 3

ENTERING MARRIAGE

■ ■ ■

Marriage today is a battleground of ideas. From one perspective, marriage is increasingly seen as an exclusively private concern of the marital partners. One poll of young adults, for instance, found that "[e]ight out of ten agree that marriage is nobody's business but the two people involved." Nat'l Marriage Project, The State of Our Unions 2001: The Social Health of Marriage in America 13 (2001), http://marriage. rutgers.edu/Publications/SOOU/NMPAR2001.pdf. Nearly half believed that the government should have no role in licensing marriages. *Id.* Marriage, after all, has long been described as a *contract*, a relation based upon the consent of the parties. *See Travers v. Reinhardt*, 205 U.S. 423 (1907). Thus, the Supreme Court was surely correct when it observed that special expectations of "privacy" have long attended the marriage relationship. *Griswold v. Connecticut*, 381 U.S. 479, 486 (1965) (discussed in Chapter 1).

Yet, extensive public regulation of the relationship has long co-existed—in some obvious tension—with social and legal norms that describe marriage as occupying a "private realm of family life which the state cannot enter." *Prince v. Massachusetts*, 321 U.S. 158, 166 (1944). What legal historian Hendrik Hartog writes, in describing the reality of marriage in the nineteenth century, remains true of marriage today:

> A marriage was both legally constructed and private. Law was not everything in a marriage. Love, lust, hatred, duty, friendship, affection, abandonment, commitment, greed, and self-sacrifice, all the feelings and practices that made up a nineteenth-century marriage, were not primarily legal. But law was there as well. Law was there when a marriage began; it was there when it ended. And in between: law was there when a husband and wife struggled or negotiated over the terms of power between them; law was there when a married couple constructed or reconstructed a relationship with a world of others—including children, parents, and third party creditors; law was there when husbands or wives thought about themselves as husbands or wives; law was also there when those same husbands or wives denied or repressed their identities as husbands or wives.

Hendrik Hartog, Man and Wife in America: A History 24 (2000).

By regulating the institution of marriage—determining who may marry, how they shall marry, which obligations and entitlements are required, and whether conditions permit a marriage to end—lawmakers have sought to define and reinforce foundational social values relating to citizenship, morality, child-rearing, gender and race. For this reason, the Supreme Court has long accepted that "the public is deeply interested" in maintaining the "purity" of marriage. *Maynard v. Hill,* 125 U.S. 190, 211 (1888). "Marriage, as creating the most important relation in life, as having more to do with the morals and civilization of a people than any other institution, has always been subject to the control of the legislature." *Id.* at 205.

For much of our nation's history, broad consensus concerning basic social values allowed legal regulation of marriage formation to be kept to a relatively compact list of "rules." To marry, a person had to consent, be at least a certain minimum age, not already be married to someone else, and not have a close familial relation with the intended marriage partner. The procedural requirements were also straightforward: a formal marriage required obtaining a marriage license and participating in a religious or civil ceremony exchanging vows of commitment, but informal marriage (also called common-law marriage) was also widely practiced and permitted. Through common-law marriage, parties could legally marry simply by expressing their mutual intentions to be married and establishing a community reputation as a married couple. Beyond these few requirements, much regulation—such as the prohibition against same-sex marriage—was simply left unstated, out of the conviction that it was needless to commit universal assumptions to paper.

In recent decades, however, as consensus undergirding long-established social values has eroded, traditional marriage regulations have faced repeated challenges, and we have entered a period in which age-old assumptions about marriage are being scrutinized and reconsidered. *See* Linda C. McClain, *Love, Marriage, and the Baby Carriage: Revisiting the Channelling Function of Family Law,* 28 Cardozo L. Rev. 2133 (2007). Legislatures have scaled back restrictions on entry into marriage and liberalized exit through divorce, and courts have cast aside still other marriage regulations on constitutional grounds.

Two developments have contributed significantly to the trend toward "deregulation" of marriage. The first has been a fundamental transformation of the understanding about the central purposes of marriage. For much of American history, marriage was primarily valued as an institution that provided important social and communal benefits. Marriage permitted the establishment of kinship alliances, it provided a measure of economic security for women in a society with limited opportunities for self-support, and it provided a stable environment for the expression of sexual desire and, consequently, for the rearing of children. *See* Harry D. Krause, *Marriage for the New Millennium: Heterosexual, Same–Sex—or Not at All?*, 34 Fam. L.Q. 271 (2000). In modern times, however, these outward-looking justifications for marriage have arguably yielded to an inward-looking notion that values marriage for its ability to facilitate the bonding of intimate adult partners. *See* Nat'l Marriage Project, *supra* at 6 (reporting that in a Gallup poll of young adults, "[a]n overwhelming majority (94%) of never-married singles agree that 'when you marry you want your spouse to be your soul mate, first and foremost'"). This shift in focus for a significant number of Americans has raised personal expectations about marriage to new highs and posed new questions about the propriety of legal standards obstructing personal choice in marriage. *See* Stephanie Coontz, Marriage, A History: From Obedience to Intimacy, or How Love Conquered Marriage (2005).

A second major contributor to the retreat of marriage regulation has been the recognition in the past half-century of significant constitutional limitations on government power over family life (a development briefly surveyed in Chapter 1). *See* David D. Meyer, *The Constitutionalization of Family Law,* 42 Fam. L.Q. 529 (2008). The emergence in the 1960s of a robust constitutional doctrine protecting "privacy" rights in family relationships opened new lines of attack on traditional marriage regulation, just as the 1970s ushered in a new understanding of the Equal Protection Clause that directly challenged the government's ability to enforce gender roles through family law. These twin developments in constitutional law have required states to place marriage law on a more gender-neutral footing and to articulate strong public reasons for marriage laws that had once seemed natural and self-evident. This process of reconstructing the law of marriage is very much ongoing, and the present debate over same-sex marriage is only the most visible illustration.

The materials that follow survey, first, the substantive rules that define who is eligible to marry (e.g., limitations of age), and second, the procedural rules that prescribe the means by which eligible parties may enter into marriage (e.g., requirements of a license and a ceremony). As you read these materials, consider whether the law appropriately navigates the tension between the understandings of marriage as a public institution and as a private sphere of intimate freedom. Are traditional restrictions on individual choice concerning entry into marriage justified in view of the public purposes marriage is now understood to serve? What role should remain for government in policing the institution of marriage?

SECTION 1: SUBSTANTIVE REQUIREMENTS FOR ENTRY INTO MARRIAGE

A. THE EBB AND FLOW OF MARRIAGE REGULATION

For the most part, state law restrictions on eligibility to marry have been few. All states have barred bigamous and incestuous marriages and have set certain minimum ages for persons capable of giving consent. Until quite recently, all states likewise have taken for granted that marriage required a union of one man and one woman. Beyond these universal limitations, the extent of public regulation of entry into marriage varied both from place to place and over time. The tide ran against expansive marriage regulation for the first 100 years of American history. Indeed, "the first half of the nineteenth century witnessed a pervasive relaxation of formal legal restrictions on marriage." Lee E. Teitelbaum, *Family History and Family Law*, 1985 Wis. L. Rev. 1135, 1158. During this period, in recognition of the practical difficulties with rigid enforcement of marriage restrictions in a frontier society, state law took a largely permissive attitude toward marriage formation. Michael Grossberg, Governing the Hearth: Law and Family in Nineteenth–Century America 69–70 (1985). Couples were widely permitted to form marriages on their own, informally, and often "[t]he boundary between the legally constituted and the non- and illegally constituted was porous and fuzzy." Hendrik Hartog, Man and Wife in America: A History 23 (2000). "Even for those not married by any of the standard rules, even for those who could not marry because of some civil disability like slavery or infancy, the technical illegality still might not matter," because courts were sometimes generous in blurring or overlooking legal barriers. *Id.*

The closing decades of the nineteenth century and opening decades of the twentieth century, however, were marked by a surging interest in public control of marriage. A handful of states had prohibited interracial marriage since colonial times, but anti-miscegenation laws sprouted up in additional jurisdictions during and after the Civil War. Later, the Progressive Era inspired efforts in many states to regulate marriage for reasons of eugenics or public health. For most of the 1800s, states showed little or no interest in the health of persons embarking on marriage; by the 1930s, however, more than a third of the states had enacted laws denying marriage to persons with epilepsy, venereal disease, active tuberculosis, or certain other diseases. *See* Matthew J. Lindsay, *Reproducing a Fit Citizenry: Dependency, Eugenics, and the Law of Marriage in the United States, 1860–1920*, 23 Law & Soc. Inquiry 541 (1998). During the same period, states moved to raise the minimum legal age for marriage to ensure that the partners possessed sufficient maturity to fulfill their marital obligations.

Since World War II, the tide of public regulation of marriage has again turned. Many state legislatures have rolled back age restrictions, abandoned mandatory health screening, and repealed certain other gatekeeping regulations aimed at maintaining the moral purity of marriage, such as a Louisiana law that barred subsequent marriage between an adulterer and his or her "accomplice in adultery." La. Civ. Code Ann. art. 161 (repealed 1991); *see* Katherine Shaw Spaht, *The Last One Hundred Years: The Incredible Retreat of Law from the Regulation of Marriage*, 63 La. L. Rev. 243, 255–57 (2003). Much of this "deregulation" has been propelled by shifts in public opinion through the political process and legislative repeal. Since 1965, with the Supreme Court's recognition in *Griswold* of a constitutional right of privacy within marriage, courts have accelerated the trend on constitutional grounds. This Chapter examines the origins of the constitutional "right to marry" and its impact on the traditional legal restrictions on access to marriage.

B. THE RIGHT TO MARRY

LOVING v. VIRGINIA

Supreme Court of the United States, 1967.
388 U.S. 1.

MR. CHIEF JUSTICE WARREN delivered the opinion of the Court.

* * *

In June 1958, two residents of Virginia, Mildred Jeter, a Negro woman, and Richard Loving, a white man, were married in the District of Columbia pursuant to its laws. Shortly after their marriage, the Lovings returned to Virginia and established their marital abode in Caroline County. At the October Term, 1958, of the Circuit Court of Caroline County, a grand jury issued an indictment charging the Lovings with violating Virginia's ban on interracial marriages. On January 6, 1959, the Lovings pleaded guilty to the charge and were sentenced to one year in jail; however, the trial judge suspended the sentence for a period of 25 years on the condition that the Lovings leave the State and not return to Virginia together for 25 years. He stated in an opinion that:

> "Almighty God created the races white, black, yellow, malay and red, and he placed them on separate continents. And but for the interference with his arrangement there would be no cause for such marriages. The fact that he separated the races shows that he did not intend for the races to mix."

After their convictions, the Lovings took up residence in the District of Columbia [and thereafter filed suit challenging the validity of their convictions on the ground that Virginia's law banning interracial marriage violated the Equal Protection and Due Process Clauses of the U.S. Constitution]. * * *

* * *

Virginia is now one of 16 States which prohibit and punish marriages on the basis of racial classifications. Penalties for miscegenation arose as an incident to slavery and have been common in Virginia since the colonial period. The present statutory scheme dates from the adoption of the Racial Integrity Act of 1924, passed during the period of extreme nativism which followed the end of the First World War. The central features of this Act, and current Virginia law, are the absolute prohibition of a "white person" marrying other than another "white person," a prohibition against issuing marriage licenses until the issuing official is satisfied that the applicants' statements as to their race are correct, certificates of "racial composition" to be kept by both local and state registrars, and the carrying forward of earlier prohibitions against racial intermarriage.

I.

In upholding the constitutionality of these provisions in the decision below, the Supreme Court of Appeals of Virginia referred to its 1955 decision in *Naim v. Naim*, [87 S.E.2d 749 (1955),] as stating the reasons supporting the validity of these laws. In *Naim*, the state court concluded that the State's legitimate purposes were "to preserve the racial integrity of its citizens," and to prevent "the corruption of blood," "a mongrel breed of citizens," and "the obliteration of racial pride," obviously an endorsement of the doctrine of White Supremacy. The court also reasoned that marriage has traditionally been subject to state regulation without federal intervention, and, consequently, the regulation of marriage should be left to exclusive state control by the Tenth Amendment.

While the state court is no doubt correct in asserting that marriage is a social relation subject to the State's police power, the State does not contend in its argument before this Court that its powers to regulate marriage are unlimited notwithstanding the commands of the Fourteenth Amendment. * * * Instead, the State argues that the meaning of the Equal Protection Clause, as illuminated by the statements of the Framers, is only that state penal laws containing an interracial element as part of the definition of the offense must apply equally to whites and Negroes in the sense that members of each race are punished to the same degree. Thus, the State contends that, because its miscegenation statutes punish equally both the white and the Negro participants in an interracial marriage, these statutes, despite their reliance on racial classifications do not constitute an invidious discrimination based upon race. * * *

Because we reject the notion that the mere "equal application" of a statute containing racial classifications is enough to remove the classifications from the Fourteenth Amendment's proscription of all invidious racial discriminations, we do not accept the State's contention that these statutes should be upheld if there is any possible basis for concluding that they serve a rational purpose. * * * [In cases] involving distinctions not drawn according to race, the Court has merely asked whether there is any rational foundation for the discriminations, and has deferred to the wisdom of the state legislatures. In the case at bar, however, we deal with statutes containing racial classifications, and the fact of equal application does not immunize the statute from the very heavy burden of justification which the Fourteenth Amendment has traditionally required of state statutes drawn according to race.

* * *

There can be no question but that Virginia's miscegenation statutes rest solely upon distinctions drawn according to race. The statutes proscribe generally accepted conduct if engaged in by members of different races. Over the years, this Court has consistently repudiated "[d]istinctions between citizens solely because of their ancestry" as being "odious to a free people whose institutions are founded upon the doctrine of equality." *Hirabayashi v. United States*, 320 U.S. 81, 100 (1943). At the very least, the Equal Protection Clause demands that racial classifications, especially suspect in criminal statutes, be subjected to the "most rigid scrutiny," *Korematsu v. United States*, 323 U.S. 214, 216 (1944), and, if they are ever to be upheld, they must be shown to be necessary to the accomplishment of some permissible state objective, independent of the racial discrimination which it was the object of the Fourteenth Amendment to eliminate. * * *

There is patently no legitimate overriding purpose independent of invidious racial discrimination which justifies this classification. * * * There can be no doubt that restricting the freedom to marry solely because of racial classifications violates the central meaning of the Equal Protection Clause.

II.

These statutes also deprive the Lovings of liberty without due process of law in violation of the Due Process Clause of the Fourteenth Amendment. The freedom to marry has long been recognized as one of the vital personal rights essential to the orderly pursuit of happiness by free men.

Marriage is one of the "basic civil rights of man," fundamental to our very existence and survival. *Skinner v. State of Oklahoma*, 316 U.S. 535, 541 (1942). To deny this fundamental freedom on so unsupportable a basis as the racial classifications embodied in these statutes * * * is surely to deprive all the State's citizens of liberty without due process of law. The Fourteenth Amendment requires that the freedom of choice to marry not be restricted by invidious racial discriminations. Under our Constitution, the freedom to marry, or not marry, a person of another race resides with the individual and cannot be infringed by the State.

These convictions must be reversed. It is so ordered.

[The concurring opinion of STEWART, J., is omitted.]

NOTES AND QUESTIONS

1. *The* Loving *case.* Richard Loving and Mildred Jeter grew up together in rural Central Point, Virginia. They fell in love as teenagers with no intention of becoming civil rights pioneers. Professor Robert Pratt, who grew up nearby and knew their families, recounts the origins of their landmark case:

> Mildred did not know that interracial marriage was illegal in Virginia, but Richard did. This explains why, on June 2, 1958, he drove them across the Virginia state line to Washington, D.C., to be married. With their union legally validated by the District of Columbia, Mr. and Mrs. Loving returned to Central Point to live with Mildred's parents; however, their marital bliss was short-lived. Five weeks later, on July 11, their quiet life

was shattered when they were awakened early in the morning as three law officers "acting on an anonymous tip" opened the unlocked door of their home, walked into their bedroom, and shined a flashlight in their faces. Caroline County Sheriff R. Garnett Brooks demanded to know what the two of them were doing in bed together. Mildred answered, "I'm his wife," while Richard pointed to the District of Columbia marriage certificate that hung on their bedroom wall. "That's no good here," Sheriff Brooks replied. He charged the couple with unlawful cohabitation, and then he and his two deputies hauled the Lovings off to a nearby jail in Bowling Green.

Robert A. Pratt, *Crossing the Color Line: A Historical Assessment and Personal Narrative of* Loving v. Virginia, 41 How. L.J. 229, 236 (1998). After their conviction and banishment from their home state, they spent five years of exile living in Washington, D.C. Two young lawyers, acting *pro bono*, filed suit on the Lovings' behalf; Philip Hirschkop was not yet three years out of law school when he argued the case before the Supreme Court.

After the Supreme Court unanimously ruled in their favor, the Lovings returned to Central Point with their three children. Tragically, Richard was killed by a drunk driver shortly after the couple's seventeenth wedding anniversary in 1975. For the next 33 years, until her death in 2008, Mildred continued to live "in the same house that Richard built for her," generally seeking to avoid the limelight their case generated. "All we ever wanted was to get married, because we loved each other," she told Professor Pratt in 1994. "I married the only man I had ever loved, and I'm happy for the time we had together." *Id.* at 243–44. For additional background on the case, see Phyl Newbeck, Virginia Hasn't Always Been for Lovers: Interracial Marriage Bans and the Case of Richard and Mildred Loving (2004).

2. *Public attitudes toward interracial marriage.* Interracial marriage laws were already in retreat when *Loving* was decided (in the 15 years preceding the decision, 13 states had repealed their anti-miscegenation laws), but public support for the laws remained substantial. A 1965 Gallup poll showed that 72 percent of Southern whites and 42 percent of Northern whites favored laws banning interracial marriage. Public attitudes about the propriety of interracial marriage surely should not affect the courts' judgment about whether anti-miscegenation laws unconstitutionally discriminate based on race. Are public attitudes relevant, however, to whether the laws violate the fundamental right to marry under due process? Why or why not?

3. *Constitutional scrutiny of family law: basic doctrine.* Loving recognized two constitutional defects in Virginia's anti-miscegenation law: that it discriminated based on race in violation of the Equal Protection Clause and that it impermissibly burdened the "fundamental freedom" to marry in violation of the Due Process Clause. The decision thus illustrates each of the two primary avenues of constitutional attack on family law regulations.

The Equal Protection Clause of the Fourteenth Amendment provides that no state may "deny to any person * * * the equal protection of the laws."[1]

---

1. The Fourteenth Amendment reaches only actions of state governments, but the Supreme Court has interpreted the Fifth Amendment's Due Process Clause to encompass a parallel equal

The Equal Protection Clause therefore provides a basis for challenging discriminatory laws, including marriage laws. As *Loving* indicates, however, not all forms of discrimination are equally objectionable as a matter of law. As a general rule, the Constitution permits government to differentiate among people in a multitude of ways—based on their age, for example, or their place of residence, or their income or occupation—so long as there is a rational reason for the distinction. Under the "rational basis test," such classifications are presumed to be constitutional and will be struck down only if a litigant challenging the law can show that the differential treatment bears no rational relationship to a legitimate public interest.

As *Loving* also states, however, the Supreme Court has recognized that some government classifications, such as discrimination based on race or gender, should be subject to more skeptical judicial review. "Suspect" classifications, relating to race, national origin or alienage, are subjected to "strict scrutiny," under which the challenged law is presumed to be invalid unless the state can carry the extraordinary burden of proving that the discrimination is necessary, or "narrowly tailored," to achievement of a public interest that is not merely legitimate, but "compelling." Classifications based upon gender or the "illegitimate" status of a nonmarital child are considered "quasi-suspect" and are subjected to a middle tier of scrutiny. Under this intermediate scrutiny, government may overcome the presumption of unconstitutionality by carrying the somewhat lesser burden (as compared with strict scrutiny) of establishing that the classification is "substantially related" to the achievement of an "important" state interest. Through these forms of "suspect class" scrutiny, courts have struck down a wide range of traditional family laws drawn on gender or racial lines.

Loving also held, however, that Virginia's anti-miscegenation law violates the guarantee of due process. The Fourteenth Amendment, applicable to state governments, and the Fifth Amendment, applicable to the federal government, each contains a Due Process Clause prohibiting government from depriving any person of "life, liberty, or property, without due process of law." The Supreme Court has long understood these clauses not only to entitle individuals to fair procedures when facing a loss of liberty, but also to impose some substantive limitations on government power no matter how much process is provided. Since 1938, and the demise of the *Lochner* era (named for a 1905 decision, *Lochner v. New York*, 198 U.S. 45, which invalidated a state regulation of labor conditions), the Supreme Court has pointedly kept "substantive due process" review of most government action to minimal proportions. Like the rule for equal protection review of "nonsuspect" classifications, the general rule for substantive due process review is now the deferential "rational basis" test. Consequently, the government is broadly permitted to limit the liberty of individuals—insisting, for example, that pedestrians cross streets only at a cross-walk, or that drivers wear seat belts—so long as the imposition can be rationally supposed to advance a legitimate state interest.

---

protection component applicable to the federal government. *See Bolling v. Sharpe*, 347 U.S. 497, 499 (1954).

Over the past 50 years, however, the Supreme Court has resurrected a more aggressive form of substantive due process review where the government acts to deprive a person of an aspect of liberty deemed "fundamental." *Griswold v. Connecticut*, 381 U.S. 479 (1965), effectively recognized one such "fundamental" liberty in a married couple's freedom to decide whether to use contraception (discussed in Chapter 1). *Loving* recognizes another, the "fundamental freedom" to marry. As detailed in other chapters of this casebook, the Court has recognized fundamental rights in other family contexts as well, including a parent's liberty to rear her children as she sees fit, *see Troxel v. Granville*, 530 U.S. 57 (2000) (discussed in Chapter 13), and an extended family's decision to live together in a common home, *see Moore v. City of East Cleveland*, 431 U.S. 494 (1977) (discussed in Chapter 1). It is often said that, under modern substantive due process review, significant government burdens on such "fundamental rights" are subject to "strict scrutiny," requiring government to justify its action by showing that the burden on individual liberty is "narrowly tailored" to the achievement of a "compelling" state interest. As the next decision, *Zablocki v. Redhail*, illustrates, however, the precise standard of constitutional review is sometimes ambiguous. What is also often unclear is the precise scope of the "fundamental rights" recognized in these cases.

Zablocki began in September 1974, when the Milwaukee County Clerk refused to issue a marriage license to Roger Redhail because he had failed to support a daughter he had fathered three years earlier, while he was still in high school. Indigent and unemployed, he had paid none of his $109 monthly child support obligation since admitting paternity two years before. As you read *Zablocki*, consider carefully the different ways in which the various Justices understand the "right to marry."

ZABLOCKI v. REDHAIL

Supreme Court of the United States, 1978.
434 U.S. 374.

MR. JUSTICE MARSHALL delivered the opinion of the Court.

At issue in this case is the constitutionality of a Wisconsin statute, Wis. Stat. § 245.10(1), (4), (5) (1973), which provides that members of a certain class of Wisconsin residents may not marry, within the State or elsewhere, without first obtaining a court order granting permission to marry. The class is defined by the statute to include any "Wisconsin resident having minor issue not in his custody and which he is under obligation to support by any court order or judgment." The statute specifies that court permission cannot be granted unless the marriage applicant submits proof of compliance with the support obligation and, in addition, demonstrates that the children covered by the support order "are not then and are not likely thereafter to become public charges."
* * *

[Roger Redhail was ineligible to marry under the statute because he was more than $3,700 in arrears on his child support obligations and, even if he had made all mandated payments, his daughter would still have qualified as a public charge. After the state denied Redhail a marriage license, he sued and a three-judge federal district court held the statute unconstitutional.]

* * *

II.

In evaluating § 245.10(1), (4), (5) under the Equal Protection Clause, "we must first determine what burden of justification the classification created thereby must meet, by looking to the nature of the classification and the individual interests affected." *Mem'l Hosp. v. Maricopa County*, 415 U.S. 250, 253 (1974). Since our past decisions make clear that the right to marry is of fundamental importance, and since the classification at issue here significantly interferes with the exercise of that right, we believe that "critical examination" of the state interests advanced in support of the classification is required.

The leading decision of this Court on the right to marry is *Loving v. Virginia*, 388 U.S. 1 (1967). In that case, an interracial couple who had been convicted of violating Virginia's miscegenation laws challenged the statutory scheme on both equal protection and due process grounds. The Court's opinion could have rested solely on the ground that the statutes discriminated on the basis of race in violation of the Equal Protection Clause. But the Court went on to hold that the laws arbitrarily deprived the couple of a fundamental liberty protected by the Due Process Clause, the freedom to marry. * * *

Although *Loving* arose in the context of racial discrimination, prior and subsequent decisions of this Court confirm that the right to marry is of fundamental importance for all individuals. Long ago, in *Maynard v. Hill*, 125 U.S. 190 (1888), the Court characterized marriage as "the most important relation in life," and as "the foundation of the family and of society, without which there would be neither civilization nor progress." In *Meyer v. Nebraska*, 262 U.S. 390 (1923), the Court recognized that the right "to marry, establish a home and bring up children" is a central part of the liberty protected by the Due Process Clause, and in *Skinner v. Oklahoma ex rel. Williamson*, [316 U.S. 535, 541 (1942),] marriage was described as "fundamental to the very existence and survival of the race."

More recent decisions have established that the right to marry is part of the fundamental "right of privacy" implicit in the Fourteenth Amendment's Due Process Clause. In *Griswold v. Connecticut*, 381 U.S. 479 (1965), the Court observed:

"We deal with a right of privacy older than the Bill of Rights—older than our political parties, older than our school system. Marriage is a coming together for better or for worse, hopefully enduring, and intimate to the degree of being sacred. It is an association that promotes a way of life, not causes; a harmony in living, not political faiths; a bilateral loyalty, not commercial or social projects. Yet it is an association for as noble a purpose as any involved in our prior decisions."

Id. at 486.

* * *

It is not surprising that the decision to marry has been placed on the same level of importance as decisions relating to procreation, childbirth, child rearing, and family relationships. As the facts of this case illustrate, it would make little sense to recognize a right of privacy with respect to other matters of family life and not with respect to the decision to enter the relationship that is the foundation of the family in our society. The woman whom appellee desired to marry had a fundamental right to seek an abortion of their expected child or to bring the child into life to suffer the myriad social, if not economic, disabilities that the status of illegitimacy brings. Surely, a decision to marry and raise the child in a traditional family setting must receive equivalent protection. * * *

By reaffirming the fundamental character of the right to marry, we do not mean to suggest that every state regulation which relates in any way to the incidents of or prerequisites for marriage must be subjected to rigorous scrutiny. To the contrary, reasonable regulations that do not significantly interfere with decisions to enter into the marital relationship may legitimately be imposed. *See Califano v. Jobst*, [434 U.S. 47, 55 n.12 (1977)]. The statutory classification at issue here, however, clearly does interfere directly and substantially with the right to marry.

Under the challenged statute, no Wisconsin resident in the affected class may marry * * * without a court order * * *. Some of those in the affected class, like appellee, will never be able to obtain the necessary court order, because they either lack the financial means to meet their support obligations or cannot prove that their children will not become public charges. These persons are absolutely prevented from getting married. Many others, able in theory to satisfy the statute's requirements, will be sufficiently burdened by having to do so that they will in effect be coerced into forgoing their right to marry. And even those who can be persuaded to meet the statute's requirements suffer a serious intrusion into their freedom of choice in an area in which we have held such freedom to be fundamental.[12]

---

12. The directness and substantiality of the interference with the freedom to marry distinguish the instant case from *Califano v. Jobst*. [*Ed.'s note*: The U.S. Supreme Court heard oral arguments for *Jobst* and *Zablocki* on the same day, October 4, 1977.] In *Jobst*, [434 U.S. 47 (1977),] we upheld sections of the Social Security Act providing, *inter alia*, for termination of a dependent child's benefits upon marriage to an individual not entitled to benefits under the Act. As the opinion for the Court expressly noted, the rule terminating benefits upon marriage was not "an attempt to interfere with the individual's freedom to make a decision as important as marriage." The Social Security provisions placed no direct legal obstacle in the path of persons desiring to get married, and—notwithstanding our Brother REHNQUIST's imaginative recasting of the case [in dissent]—there was no evidence that the laws significantly discouraged, let alone made "practically impossible," any marriages. Indeed, the provisions had not deterred the individual who challenged the statute from getting married * * *.

III.

When a statutory classification significantly interferes with the exercise of a fundamental right, it cannot be upheld unless it is supported by sufficiently important state interests and is closely tailored to effectuate only those interests. Appellant asserts that two interests are served by the challenged statute: the permission-to-marry proceeding furnishes an opportunity to counsel the applicant as to the necessity of fulfilling his prior support obligations; and the welfare of the out-of-custody children is protected. We may accept for present purposes that these are legitimate and substantial interests, but, since the means selected by the State for achieving these interests unnecessarily impinge on the right to marry, the statute cannot be sustained.

* * * Even assuming that counseling does take place—a fact as to which there is no evidence in the record—this interest obviously cannot support the withholding of court permission to marry once counseling is completed.

With regard to safeguarding the welfare of the out-of-custody children, appellant's brief does not make clear the connection between the State's interest and the statute's requirements. At argument, appellant's counsel suggested that, since permission to marry cannot be granted unless the applicant shows that he has satisfied his court-determined support obligations to the prior children and that those children will not become public charges, the statute provides incentive for the applicant to make support payments to his children. This "collection device" rationale cannot justify the statute's broad infringement on the right to marry.

First, with respect to individuals who are unable to meet the statutory requirements, the statute merely prevents the applicant from getting married, without delivering any money at all into the hands of the applicant's prior children. More importantly, regardless of the applicant's ability or willingness to meet the statutory requirements, the State already has numerous other means for exacting compliance with support obligations, means that are at least as effective as the instant statute's and yet do not impinge upon the right to marry. Under Wisconsin law, whether the children are from a prior marriage or were born out of wedlock, court-determined support obligations may be enforced directly via wage assignments, civil contempt proceedings, and criminal penalties. And, if the State believes that parents of children out of their custody should be responsible for ensuring that those children do not become public charges, this interest can be achieved by adjusting the criteria used for determining the amounts to be paid under their support orders.

There is also some suggestion that § 245.10 protects the ability of marriage applicants to meet support obligations to prior children by preventing the applicants from incurring new support obligations. But the challenged provisions of § 245.10 are grossly underinclusive with respect to this purpose, since they do not limit in any way new financial commitments by the applicant other than those arising out of the contemplated marriage. The statutory classification is substantially overinclusive as well: Given the possibility that the new spouse will actually better the applicant's financial situation, by contributing income from a job or otherwise, the statute in many cases may prevent affected individuals from improving their ability to satisfy their prior support obligations. And, though it is true that the applicant will incur support obligations to any children born during the contemplated marriage, preventing the marriage may only result in the children being born out of wedlock, as in fact occurred in appellee's case. Since the support obligation is the same whether the child is born in or out of wedlock, the net result of preventing the marriage is simply more illegitimate children.

The statutory classification * * * thus cannot be justified by the interests advanced in support of it. The judgment of the District Court is, accordingly,

Affirmed.

* * *

MR. JUSTICE STEWART, concurring in the judgment.

* * *

I do not agree with the Court that there is a "right to marry" in the constitutional sense. That right, or more accurately that privilege, is under our federal system peculiarly one to be defined and limited by state law. A State may not only "significantly interfere with decisions to enter into [the] marital relationship," but may in many circumstances absolutely prohibit it. Surely, for example, a State may legitimately say that no one can marry his or her sibling, that no one can marry who is not at least 14 years old, that no one can marry without first passing an examination for venereal disease, or that no one can marry who has a living husband or wife. But, just as surely, in regulating the intimate human relationship of marriage, there is a limit beyond which a State may not constitutionally go.

The Constitution does not specifically mention freedom to marry, but it is settled that the "liberty" protected by the Due Process Clause of the Fourteenth Amendment embraces more than those freedoms expressly enumerated in the Bill of Rights. And the decisions of this Court have made clear that freedom of personal choice in matters of marriage and family life is one of the liberties so protected.

It is evident that the Wisconsin law now before us directly abridges that freedom. The question is whether the state interests that support the abridgment can overcome the substantive protections of the Constitution.

* * *

* * * The Wisconsin law makes no allowance for the truly indigent. The State flatly denies a marriage license to anyone who cannot afford to fulfill his support obligations and keep his children from becoming wards of the State. We may assume that the State has legitimate interests in

collecting delinquent support payments and in reducing its welfare load. We may also assume that, as applied to those who can afford to meet the statute's financial requirements but choose not to do so, the law advances the State's objectives in ways superior to other means available to the State. The fact remains that some people simply cannot afford to meet the statute's financial requirements. To deny these people permission to marry penalizes them for failing to do that which they cannot do. Insofar as it applies to indigents, the state law is an irrational means of achieving these objectives of the State.

As directed against either the indigent or the delinquent parent, the law is substantially more rational if viewed as a means of assuring the financial viability of future marriages. * * * But the State's legitimate concern with the financial soundness of prospective marriages must stop short of telling people they may not marry because they are too poor or because they might persist in their financial irresponsibility. * * * A legislative judgment so alien to our traditions and so offensive to our shared notions of fairness offends the Due Process Clause of the Fourteenth Amendment.

* * *

MR. JUSTICE POWELL, concurring in the judgment.

* * * I write separately because the majority's rationale sweeps too broadly in an area which traditionally has been subject to pervasive state regulation. The Court apparently would subject all state regulation which "directly and substantially" interferes with the decision to marry in a traditional family setting to "critical examination" or "compelling state interest" analysis. Presumably, "reasonable regulations that do not significantly interfere with decisions to enter into the marital relationship may legitimately be imposed." The Court does not present, however, any principled means for distinguishing between the two types of regulations. * * *

I.

On several occasions, the Court has acknowledged the importance of the marriage relationship to the maintenance of values essential to organized society. "This Court has long recognized that freedom of personal choice in matters of marriage and family life is one of the liberties protected by the Due Process Clause of the Fourteenth Amendment." *Cleveland Bd. of Educ. v. LaFleur*, 414 U.S. 632, 639–40 (1974). * * *

Thus, it is fair to say that there is a right of marital and familial privacy which places some substantive limits on the regulatory power of government. But the Court has yet to hold that all regulation touching upon marriage implicates a "fundamental right" triggering the most exacting judicial scrutiny.

The principal authority cited by the majority is *Loving v. Virginia*. Although *Loving* speaks of the "freedom to marry" as "one of the vital personal rights essential to the orderly pursuit of happiness by free men," the Court focused on the miscegenation statute before it. * * * Thus, *Loving* involved a denial of a "fundamental freedom" on a wholly unsupportable basis—the use of classifications "directly subversive of the principle of equality at the heart of the Fourteenth Amendment...." It does not speak to the level of judicial scrutiny of, or governmental justification for, "supportable" restrictions on the "fundamental freedom" of individuals to marry or divorce.

In my view, analysis must start from the recognition of domestic relations as "an area that has long been regarded as a virtually exclusive province of the States." *Sosna v. Iowa*, 419 U.S. 393, 404 (1975). The marriage relation traditionally has been subject to regulation, initially by the ecclesiastical authorities, and later by the secular state. As early as *Pennoyer v. Neff*, 95 U.S. 714, 734–35 (1878), this Court noted that a State "has absolute right to prescribe the conditions upon which the marriage relation between its own citizens shall be created, and the causes for which it may be dissolved." The State, representing the collective expression of moral aspirations, has an undeniable interest in ensuring that its rules of domestic relations reflect the widely held values of its people.

> "Marriage, as creating the most important relation in life, as having more to do with the morals and civilization of a people than any other institution, has always been subject to the control of the legislature. That body prescribes the age at which parties may contract to marry, the procedure or form essential to constitute marriage, the duties and obligations it creates, its effects upon the property rights of both, present and prospective, and the acts which may constitute grounds for its dissolution."

Maynard v. Hill, 125 U.S. 190, 205 (1888).

State regulation has included bans on incest, bigamy, and homosexuality, as well as various preconditions to marriage, such as blood tests. Likewise, a showing of fault on the part of one of the partners traditionally has been a prerequisite to the dissolution of an unsuccessful union. A "compelling state purpose" inquiry would cast doubt on the network of restrictions that the States have fashioned to govern marriage and divorce.

II.

State power over domestic relations is not without constitutional limits. The Due Process Clause requires a showing of justification "when the government intrudes on choices concerning family living arrangements" in a manner which is contrary to deeply rooted traditions. Due process constraints also limit the extent to which the State may monopolize the process of ordering certain human relationships while excluding the truly indigent from that process. * * *

The Wisconsin measure in this case does not pass muster under either due process or equal protection standards. * * * The opinion of the Court amply demonstrates that the asserted counseling objective bears no relation to this statute. * * *

The so-called "collection device" rationale presents a somewhat more difficult question. * * * To the extent this restriction applies to persons who are able to make the required support payments but simply wish to shirk their moral and legal obligation, the Constitution interposes no bar to this additional collection mechanism. The vice inheres, not in the collection concept, but in the failure to make provision for those without the means to comply with child-support obligations. * * *

* * *

* * * [The statute] tells the truly indigent, whether they have met their support obligations or not, that they may not marry so long as their children are public charges or there is a danger that their children might go on public assistance in the future. Apparently, no other jurisdiction has embraced this approach as a method of reducing the number of children on public assistance. Because the State has not established a justification for this unprecedented foreclosure of marriage to many of its citizens solely because of their indigency, I concur in the judgment of the Court.

* * *

MR. JUSTICE REHNQUIST, dissenting.

I substantially agree with my Brother POWELL's reasons for rejecting the Court's conclusion that marriage is the sort of "fundamental right" which must invariably trigger the strictest judicial scrutiny. I disagree with his imposition of an "intermediate" standard of review, which leads him to conclude that the statute, though generally valid as an "additional collection mechanism" offends the Constitution by its "failure to make provision for those without the means to comply with child-support obligations." * * * I would view this legislative judgment in the light of the traditional presumption of validity. * * * [Under the "rational basis test," the statute] is a permissible exercise of the State's power to regulate family life and to assure the support of minor children, despite its possible imprecision in the extreme cases envisioned in the concurring opinions.

* * *

[The concurring opinions of BURGER, C.J., and STEVENS, J., are omitted.]

NOTES AND QUESTIONS

1. *Basis for the constitutional right to marry.* Since marriage and family are not specifically mentioned in the text of the Constitution, on what basis does the Court in *Loving* and *Zablocki* conclude that personal choices concerning marriage are an aspect of individual "liberty" warranting especially sensitive constitutional protection? Is it because the ability to marry a partner of one's choice is essential to personal "happiness," as *Loving* might be read

to suggest? Or is it solely because our country has a deeply rooted social tradition of honoring freedom of choice in marriage, as Justice Powell suggests in his concurring opinion in *Zablocki*? What is the significance of the choice between these rationales?

2. *Scope of the fundamental right to marry. Zablocki* distinguishes between statutes that "interfere directly and substantially" with the choice to marry—which are subject to heightened constitutional scrutiny—and "reasonable regulations that do not significantly interfere" with free choice, which are not. Which category do you think most substantive marriage prohibitions fall into? Justice Powell criticizes the majority's differentiation among marriage regulations as unprincipled, but agrees that not all marriage restrictions should be subject to heightened scrutiny. Does he offer a principled basis for exempting "bans on incest, bigamy, and homosexuality, as well as various preconditions to marriage, such as blood tests"?

3. *What level of scrutiny for restrictions burdening the fundamental right to marry? Zablocki* subjects Wisconsin's restriction on marriage to what it calls "rigorous scrutiny," under which it must be "closely tailored" to advance "sufficiently important state interests." Is this the same as "strict scrutiny," under which courts require proof that a challenged law is "narrowly tailored" to achieve a "compelling state interest"? Lower courts routinely cite *Zablocki* for the principle that strict scrutiny applies to state laws restricting entry into marriage. *E.g.*, Andersen v. King County, 138 P.3d 963, 976 (Wash. 2006). Some commentators, on the other hand, have seen potential significance in the Court's use of ambiguous synonyms in *Zablocki* and other "family privacy" cases, concluding that the Court means to adopt a standard of review somewhat more flexible than strict scrutiny. *See* Naomi R. Cahn, *Models of Family Privacy*, 67 Geo. Wash. L. Rev. 1225, 1231 (1999); David D. Meyer, *The Paradox of Family Privacy*, 53 Vand. L. Rev. 527, 539–41 (2000). Does society have "compelling" interests in regulating marriage? What are they?

4. *Prison marriages.* In *Turner v. Safley*, 482 U.S. 78 (1987), Missouri prison inmates challenged the constitutionality of a state policy that permitted an inmate to marry only with permission of the prison superintendent and only for "compelling reasons," such as pregnancy or the birth of a child. The Court applied *Zablocki* to hold that "the marriage rule is constitutionally infirm," *id.* at 99–100:

> It is settled that a prison inmate "retains those [constitutional] rights that are not inconsistent with his status as a prisoner or with the legitimate penological objectives of the corrections system." The right to marry, like many other rights, is subject to substantial restrictions as a result of incarceration. Many important attributes of marriage remain, however, after taking into account the limitations imposed by prison life. First, inmate marriages, like others, are expressions of emotional support and public commitment. These elements are an important and significant aspect of the marital relationship. In addition, many religions recognize marriage as having spiritual significance; for some inmates and their spouses, therefore, the commitment of marriage may be an exercise of religious faith as well as an expression of personal dedication. Third, most

inmates eventually will be released by parole or commutation, and therefore most inmate marriages are formed in the expectation that they ultimately will be fully consummated. Finally, marital status often is a precondition to the receipt of government benefits (*e.g.*, Social Security benefits), property rights (*e.g.*, tenancy by the entirety, inheritance rights), and other, less tangible benefits (*e.g.*, legitimation of children born out of wedlock). These incidents of marriage, like the religious and personal aspects of the marriage commitment, are unaffected by the fact of confinement or the pursuit of legitimate corrections goals.

Id. at 95–96.

Because the state's legitimate interests in prison security and inmate rehabilitation could be as effectively served by alternative means having less restrictive effect on inmates' freedom to marry, the Court concluded that the regulation failed constitutional scrutiny even under the more deferential "reasonable relationship" test typically used to review correctional policies.

Is the Court's willingness to find a "constitutionally protected marital relationship in the prison context" consistent with Justice Powell's suggestion in *Zablocki* that the right of marriage extends only where societal traditions have honored free choice? What about *Loving*'s recognition of substantive due process protection for interracial marriage? Do these decisions signal the Court's acceptance of a right to marry that extends beyond deeply rooted historical consensus? Or does *Loving* rest solely on the specific repugnance of racial classifications under the Constitution?

5. Zablocki *redux?* David Oakley was convicted of willfully failing to support his nine children. As a condition of his probation, the trial judge ordered him to have no more children unless he could show that he was in fact supporting all his children. The Wisconsin Supreme Court upheld the probation condition under *Zablocki*. The constitutional rights of convicted criminals, the court reasoned, may be restricted more easily than those of other individuals, and the condition on Oakley's probation was not "overbroad":

> [B]ecause Oakley can satisfy this condition by not intentionally refusing to support his current nine children and any future children as required by the law, we find that the condition is narrowly tailored to serve the State's compelling interest of having parents support their children. It is also narrowly tailored to serve the State's compelling interest in rehabilitating Oakley through probation rather than prison. The alternative to probation with conditions—incarceration for eight years—would have further victimized his children. And it is undoubtedly much broader than this conditional impingement on his procreative freedom for it would deprive him of his fundamental right to be free from physical restraint.

State v. Oakley, 629 N.W.2d 200, 212 (Wis. 2001). The *Oakley* case is treated more fully in Chapter 11, concerning child support.

SECTION 2: SAME–SEX MARRIAGE?

Until 2004, no state permitted couples of the same sex to marry. For decades, courts had consistently upheld the denial of marriage to same-sex couples against sporadic constitutional attacks. Early decisions reasoned that the constitutional right to marry simply had no application to same-sex couples because the very idea of marriage necessarily assumed a union of one man and one woman. A Kentucky court, for instance, briskly concluded that a same-sex couple's demand for marriage raised "no constitutional issue" because "[i]n substance, the relationship proposed by the appellants ... is not a marriage." *Jones v. Hallahan*, 501 S.W.2d 588, 590 (Ky. Ct. App. 1973); *see also Baker v. Nelson*, 191 N.W.2d 185 (Minn. 1971).

The U.S. Supreme Court has never directly addressed the constitutionality of laws banning same-sex *marriage*, but has considered whether the right of privacy recognized in *Griswold v. Connecticut*, 381 U.S. 479 (1965) (discussed in Chapter 1), protects *sexual intimacy* between same-sex partners more generally. In *Bowers v. Hardwick*, 478 U.S. 186 (1986), the Court upheld a Georgia law that criminalized sodomy between consenting adults. *Bowers* held significant implications for the question of same-sex marriage. First, as a general matter, the Court embraced a narrow test for recognizing "fundamental rights" under the Constitution: to qualify for heightened judicial protection, a claimed liberty must be " 'deeply rooted in this Nation's history and tradition' " or " 'implicit in the concept of ordered liberty,' such that 'neither liberty nor justice would exist if [it] were sacrificed.' " *Id.* at 191–92. *Bowers* then dismissed the suggestion that "homosexual conduct" could qualify for constitutional protection under this test as "at best, facetious." *Id.* at 194. The five-Justice majority distinguished earlier precedents protecting family privacy on the ground that "[n]o connection between family, marriage, or procreation on the one hand and homosexual activity on the other has been demonstrated." *Id.* at 191.

The *Bowers* holding that the Constitution permitted states to criminalize sexual intimacy between same-sex couples posed obvious difficulty for those asserting a constitutional privacy right for other aspects of same-sex conduct, including a right to marriage. Accordingly, after *Bowers*, several courts rejected privacy-based challenges by same-sex couples under the federal or state constitutions on the ground that same-sex marriage could not be said to be a right " 'deeply rooted in this Nation's history and tradition.' " *E.g., Dean v. District of Columbia*, 653 A.2d 307, 333 (D.C. 1995); *Baehr v. Lewin*, 852 P.2d 44, 57 (Haw. 1993).

In 2003, however, the Supreme Court overruled *Bowers* in *Lawrence v. Texas*, which struck down as a violation of substantive due process a Texas law criminalizing same-sex sodomy. As you read the Court's opinion, consider whether it bolsters claims for constitutional protection for same-sex marriage as well.

LAWRENCE v. TEXAS

Supreme Court of the United States, 2003.
539 U.S. 558.

JUSTICE KENNEDY delivered the opinion of the Court.

* * *

The question before the Court is the validity of a Texas statute making it a crime for two persons of the same sex to engage in certain intimate sexual conduct.

In Houston, Texas, officers of the Harris County Police Department were dispatched to a private residence in response to a reported weapons disturbance. They entered an apartment where one of the petitioners, John Geddes Lawrence, resided. The right of the police to enter does not seem to have been questioned. The officers observed Lawrence and another man, Tyron Garner, engaging in a sexual act. The two petitioners were arrested, held in custody over night, and charged and convicted before a Justice of the Peace [of violating a Texas statute making it a crime to engage in oral or anal sex with a person of the same sex. On appeal, they argued that the Texas statute violated the Due Process and Equal Protection Clauses of the Fourteenth Amendment.]

* * *

II

* * *

There are broad statements of the substantive reach of liberty under the Due Process Clause in earlier cases, * * * but the most pertinent beginning point is our decision in *Griswold v. Connecticut,* 381 U.S. 479 (1965).

In *Griswold* the Court invalidated a state law prohibiting the use of drugs or devices of contraception and counseling or aiding and abetting the use of contraceptives. The Court described the protected interest as a right to privacy and placed emphasis on the marriage relation and the protected space of the marital bedroom.

After *Griswold* it was established that the right to make certain decisions regarding sexual conduct extends beyond the marital relationship. In *Eisenstadt v. Baird,* 405 U.S. 438 (1972), the Court invalidated a law prohibiting the distribution of contraceptives to unmarried persons. * * * It [stated] * * * :

> "It is true that in *Griswold* the right of privacy in question inhered in the marital relationship.... If the right of privacy means anything, it is the right of the *individual,* married or single, to be free from unwarranted governmental intrusion into matters so fundamentally affecting a person as the decision whether to bear or beget a child."

Id. at 453.

* * *

In *Carey v. Population Services Int'l*, 431 U.S. 678 (1977), the Court [invalidated] a New York law forbidding sale or distribution of contraceptive devices to persons under 16 years of age. * * * Both *Eisenstadt* and *Carey,* as well as the holding and rationale in *Roe* [*v. Wade,* 410 U.S. 113 (1973) (striking down a Texas law banning abortion)], confirmed that the reasoning of *Griswold* could not be confined to the protection of rights of married adults. This was the state of the law with respect to some of the most relevant cases when the Court considered *Bowers v. Hardwick* [478 U.S. 186 (1986) (upholding a Georgia anti-sodomy law against a nearly identical constitutional challenge)].

* * *

The Court began its substantive discussion in *Bowers* as follows: "The issue presented is whether the Federal Constitution confers a fundamental right upon homosexuals to engage in sodomy and hence invalidates the laws of the many States that still make such conduct illegal and have done so for a very long time." *Id.* at 190. That statement, we now conclude, discloses the Court's own failure to appreciate the extent of the liberty at stake. To say that the issue in *Bowers* was simply the right to engage in certain sexual conduct demeans the claim the individual put forward, just as it would demean a married couple were it to be said marriage is simply about the right to have sexual intercourse. The laws involved in *Bowers* and here are, to be sure, statutes that purport to do no more than prohibit a particular sexual act. Their penalties and purposes, though, have more far-reaching consequences, touching upon the most private human conduct, sexual behavior, and in the most private of places, the home. The statutes do seek to control a personal relationship that, whether or not entitled to formal recognition in the law, is within the liberty of persons to choose without being punished as criminals.

This, as a general rule, should counsel against attempts by the State, or a court, to define the meaning of the relationship or to set its boundaries absent injury to a person or abuse of an institution the law protects. It suffices for us to acknowledge that adults may choose to enter upon this relationship in the confines of their homes and their own private lives and still retain their dignity as free persons. When sexuality finds overt expression in intimate conduct with another person, the conduct can be but one element in a personal bond that is more enduring. The liberty protected by the Constitution allows homosexual persons the right to make this choice.

Having misapprehended the claim of liberty there presented to it, and thus stating the claim to be whether there is a fundamental right to engage in consensual sodomy, the *Bowers* Court said: "Proscriptions against that conduct have ancient roots." In academic writings, and in many of the scholarly *amicus* briefs filed to assist the Court in this case, there are fundamental criticisms of the historical premises relied upon by the majority and concurring opinions in *Bowers*. We need not enter this debate in the attempt to reach a definitive historical judgment, but the following considerations counsel against adopting the definitive conclusions upon which *Bowers* placed such reliance.

At the outset it should be noted that there is no longstanding history in this country of laws directed at homosexual conduct as a distinct matter. * * * [E]arly American sodomy laws were not directed at homosexuals as such but instead sought to prohibit nonprocreative sexual activity more generally. This does not suggest approval of homosexual conduct. It does tend to show that this particular form of conduct was not thought of as a separate category from like conduct between heterosexual persons.

* * *

* * * [Thus, t]he longstanding criminal prohibition of homosexual sodomy upon which the *Bowers* decision placed such reliance is as consistent with a general condemnation of nonprocreative sex as it is with an established tradition of prosecuting acts because of their homosexual character.

The policy of punishing consenting adults for private acts was not much discussed in the early legal literature. We can infer that one reason for this was the very private nature of the conduct. Despite the absence of prosecutions, there may have been periods in which there was public criticism of homosexuals as such and an insistence that the criminal laws be enforced to discourage their practices. But far from possessing "ancient roots," *Bowers*, 478 U.S. at 192, American laws targeting same-sex couples did not develop until the last third of the 20th century. * * *

* * *

It must be acknowledged, of course, that the Court in *Bowers* was making the broader point that for centuries there have been powerful voices to condemn homosexual conduct as immoral. The condemnation has been shaped by religious beliefs, conceptions of right and acceptable behavior, and respect for the traditional family. For many persons these are not trivial concerns but profound and deep convictions accepted as ethical and moral principles to which they aspire and which thus determine the course of their lives. These considerations do not answer the question before us, however. The issue is whether the majority may use the power of the State to enforce these views on the whole society through operation of the criminal law. "Our obligation is to define the liberty of all, not to mandate our own moral code." *Planned Parenthood of Southeastern Pa. v. Casey,* 505 U.S. 833, 850 (1992).

* * * In all events we think that our laws and traditions in the past half century are of most relevance here. These references show an emerging awareness that liberty gives substantial protection to adult persons in deciding how to conduct their private lives in matters pertaining to sex.

"[H]istory and tradition are the starting point but not in all cases the ending point of the substantive due process inquiry." *County of Sacramento v. Lewis,* 523 U.S. 833, 857 (1998) (KENNEDY, J., concurring).

This emerging recognition should have been apparent when *Bowers* was decided. In 1955 the American Law Institute promulgated the Model Penal Code and made clear that it did not recommend or provide for "criminal penalties for consensual sexual relations conducted in private." ALI, Model Penal Code § 2.13.2, cmt. 2, p. 372 (1980). * * *

In *Bowers* the Court referred to the fact that before 1961 all 50 States had outlawed sodomy, and that at the time of the Court's decision 24 States and the District of Columbia had sodomy laws. Justice Powell pointed out that these prohibitions often were being ignored, however. Georgia, for instance, had not sought to enforce its law for decades. [*Bowers,* 478 U.S.] at 197–98, n.2 ("The history of nonenforcement suggests the moribund character today of laws criminalizing this type of private, consensual conduct").

* * *

* * * [T]he deficiencies in *Bowers* became even more apparent in the years following its announcement. The 25 States with laws prohibiting the relevant conduct referenced in the *Bowers* decision are reduced now to 13, of which 4 enforce their laws only against homosexual conduct. * * *

Two principal cases decided after *Bowers* cast its holding into even more doubt. * * * The *Casey* decision again confirmed that our laws and tradition afford constitutional protection to personal decisions relating to marriage, procreation, contraception, family relationships, child rearing, and education. [*Planned Parenthood of Southeastern Pa. v. Casey,* 505 U.S. 833, 851 (1992).] In explaining the respect the Constitution demands for the autonomy of the person in making these choices, we stated as follows:

> "These matters, involving the most intimate and personal choices a person may make in a lifetime, choices central to personal dignity and autonomy, are central to the liberty protected by the Fourteenth Amendment. At the heart of liberty is the right to define one's own concept of existence, of meaning, of the universe, and of the mystery of human life. Beliefs about these matters could not define the attributes of personhood were they formed under compulsion of the State."

[*Id.*] Persons in a homosexual relationship may seek autonomy for these purposes, just as heterosexual persons do. The decision in *Bowers* would deny them this right.

The second post-*Bowers* case of principal relevance is *Romer v. Evans,* 517 U.S. 620 (1996). There the Court struck down class-based legislation directed at homosexuals as a violation of the Equal Protection Clause. *Romer* invalidated an amendment to Colorado's constitution which named as a solitary class persons who were homosexuals, lesbians, or bisexual either by "orientation, conduct, practices or relationships," and deprived them of protection under state antidiscrimination laws. We concluded that the provision was "born of animosity toward the class of persons affected" and further that it had no rational relation to a legitimate governmental purpose. *Id.* at 634.

* * *

The foundations of *Bowers* have sustained serious erosion from our recent decisions in *Casey* and *Romer.* * * *

* * *

The rationale of *Bowers* does not withstand careful analysis. In his dissenting opinion in *Bowers*, Justice STEVENS came to these conclusions:

> "Our prior cases make two propositions abundantly clear. First, the fact that the governing majority in a State has traditionally viewed a particular practice as immoral is not a sufficient reason for upholding a law prohibiting the practice; neither history nor tradition could save a law prohibiting miscegenation from constitutional attack. Second, individual decisions by married persons, concerning the intimacies of their physical relationship, even when not intended to produce offspring, are a form of 'liberty' protected by the Due Process Clause of the Fourteenth Amendment. Moreover, this protection extends to intimate choices by unmarried as well as married persons."

478 U.S. at 216. Justice STEVENS' analysis, in our view, should have been controlling in *Bowers* and should control here.

Bowers was not correct when it was decided, and it is not correct today. It ought not to remain binding precedent. *Bowers v. Hardwick* should be and now is overruled.

The present case does not involve minors. It does not involve persons who might be injured or coerced or who are situated in relationships where consent might not easily be refused. It does not involve public conduct or prostitution. It does not involve whether the government must give formal recognition to any relationship that homosexual persons seek to enter. The case does involve two adults who, with full and mutual consent from each other, engaged in sexual practices common to a homosexual lifestyle. The petitioners are entitled to respect for their private lives. The State cannot demean their existence or control their destiny by making their private sexual conduct a crime. Their right to liberty under the Due Process Clause gives them the full right to engage in their conduct without intervention of the government. "It is a promise of the Constitution that there is a realm of personal liberty which the government may not enter." *Casey*, [505 U.S.] at 847. The Texas statute furthers no legitimate state interest which can justify its intrusion into the personal and private life of the individual.

Had those who drew and ratified the Due Process Clauses of the Fifth Amendment or the Fourteenth Amendment known the components of liberty in its manifold possibilities, they might have been more specific. They did not presume to have this insight. They knew times can blind us to certain truths and later generations can see that laws once thought necessary and proper in fact serve only to oppress. As the Constitution endures, persons in every generation can invoke its principles in their own search for greater freedom.

The judgment of the Court of Appeals for the Texas Fourteenth District is reversed, and the case is remanded for further proceedings not inconsistent with this opinion.

It is so ordered.

JUSTICE O'CONNOR, concurring in the judgment.

The Court today overrules *Bowers v. Hardwick,* 478 U.S. 186 (1986). I joined *Bowers,* and do not join the Court in overruling it. Nevertheless, I agree with the Court that Texas' statute banning same-sex sodomy is unconstitutional. Rather than relying on the substantive component of the Fourteenth Amendment's Due Process Clause, as the Court does, I base my conclusion on the Fourteenth Amendment's Equal Protection Clause.

The Equal Protection Clause of the Fourteenth Amendment "is essentially a direction that all persons similarly situated should be treated alike." *Cleburne v. Cleburne Living Ctr., Inc.,* 473 U.S. 432, 439 (1985). Under our rational basis standard of review, "legislation is presumed to be valid and will be sustained if the classification drawn by the statute is rationally related to a legitimate state interest." [*Id.*] at 440.

* * * We have consistently held, however, that some objectives, such as "a bare ... desire to harm a politically unpopular group," are not legitimate state interests. *Dep't of Agric. v. Moreno,* 413 U.S. 528 (1973)[; *see also Cleburne,* 473 U.S.] at 446–47; *Romer v. Evans,* [517 U.S. 620 (1996)]. When a law exhibits such a desire to harm a politically unpopular group, we have applied a more searching form of rational basis review to strike down such laws under the Equal Protection Clause.

We have been most likely to apply rational basis review to hold a law unconstitutional under the Equal Protection Clause where, as here, the challenged legislation inhibits personal relationships. * * *

* * *

The Texas statute makes homosexuals unequal in the eyes of the law by making particular conduct—and only that conduct—subject to criminal sanction. * * *

* * *

Moral disapproval of a group cannot be a legitimate governmental interest under the Equal Protection Clause because legal classifications must not be "drawn for the purpose of disadvantaging the group burdened by the law." [*Romer,* 517 U.S.] at 633. Texas' invocation of moral disapproval as a legitimate state interest proves nothing more than Texas' desire to criminalize homosexual sodomy. * * *

* * *

That this law as applied to private, consensual conduct is unconstitutional under the Equal Protection Clause does not mean that other laws distinguishing between heterosexuals and homosexuals would similarly fail under rational basis review. Texas cannot assert any legitimate state interest here, such as national security or preserving the traditional institution of marriage. Unlike the moral disapproval of same-sex relations—the asserted state interest in this case—other reasons exist to promote the institution of marriage beyond mere moral disapproval of an excluded group.

A law branding one class of persons as criminal based solely on the State's moral disapproval of that class and the conduct associated with that class runs contrary to the values of the Constitution and the Equal Protection Clause, under any standard of review. * * *

JUSTICE SCALIA, with whom THE CHIEF JUSTICE and JUSTICE THOMAS join, dissenting.

* * *

Most of the rest of today's opinion has no relevance to its actual holding—that the Texas statute "furthers no legitimate state interest which can justify" its application to petitioners under rational-basis review. Though there is discussion of "fundamental proposition[s]," and "fundamental decisions," nowhere does the Court's opinion declare that homosexual sodomy is a "fundamental right" under the Due Process Clause; nor does it subject the Texas law to the standard of review that would be appropriate (strict scrutiny) if homosexual sodomy *were* a "fundamental right." Thus, while overruling the *outcome* of *Bowers,* the Court leaves strangely untouched its central legal conclusion: "[R]espondent would have us announce ... a fundamental right to engage in homosexual sodomy. This we are quite unwilling to do." 478 U.S. at 191. Instead the Court simply describes petitioners' conduct as "an exercise of their liberty"—which it undoubtedly is—and proceeds to apply an unheard-of form of rational-basis review that will have far-reaching implications beyond this case.

* * *

Our opinions applying the doctrine known as "substantive due process" hold that the Due Process Clause prohibits States from infringing *fundamental* liberty interests, unless the infringement is narrowly tailored to serve a compelling state interest. We have held repeatedly, in cases the Court today does not overrule, that *only* fundamental rights qualify for this so-called "heightened scrutiny" protection—that is, rights which are " 'deeply rooted in this Nation's history and tradition.' " All other liberty interests may be abridged or abrogated pursuant to a validly enacted state law if that law is rationally related to a legitimate state interest.

* * *

* * * Not once does [the majority] describe homosexual sodomy as a "fundamental right" or a "fundamental liberty interest," nor does it subject the Texas statute to strict scrutiny. Instead, having failed to establish that the right to homosexual sodomy is " 'deeply rooted in this Nation's history and tradition,' " the Court concludes that the application of Texas's statute to petitioners' conduct fails the rational-basis test, and overrules *Bowers'* holding to the contrary. * * *

* * *

* * * [The Court's examination of the history of sodomy laws] in no way casts into doubt the "definitive [historical] conclusion" on which *Bowers* relied: that our Nation has a longstanding history of laws prohibiting *sodomy in general*— regardless of whether it was performed by same-sex or opposite-sex couples * * *.

* * *

* * * [A]n "emerging awareness" is by definition not "deeply rooted in this Nation's history and tradition[s]," as we have said "fundamental right" status requires. Constitutional entitlements do not spring into existence because some States choose to lessen or eliminate criminal sanctions on certain behavior. Much less do they spring into existence, as the Court seems to believe, because *foreign nations* decriminalize conduct. * * *

IV

I turn now to the ground on which the Court squarely rests its holding: the contention that there is no rational basis for the law here under attack. This proposition is so out of accord with our jurisprudence—indeed, with the jurisprudence of *any* society we know—that it requires little discussion.

The Texas statute undeniably seeks to further the belief of its citizens that certain forms of sexual behavior are "immoral and unacceptable," *Bowers*, [478 U.S.] at 196—the same interest furthered by criminal laws against fornication, bigamy, adultery, adult incest, bestiality, and obscenity. *Bowers* held that this *was* a legitimate state interest. The Court today reaches the opposite conclusion. * * * This effectively decrees the end of all morals legislation. If, as the Court asserts, the promotion of majoritarian sexual morality is not even a *legitimate* state interest, none of the above-mentioned laws can survive rational-basis review.

V

Finally, I turn to petitioners' equal-protection challenge, which no Member of the Court save Justice O'CONNOR embraces: On its face

§ 21.06(a) applies equally to all persons. Men and women, heterosexuals and homosexuals, are all subject to its prohibition of deviate sexual intercourse with someone of the same sex. To be sure, § 21.06 does distinguish between the sexes insofar as concerns the partner with whom the sexual acts are performed: men can violate the law only with other men, and women only with other women. But this cannot itself be a denial of equal protection, since it is precisely the same distinction regarding partner that is drawn in state laws prohibiting marriage with someone of the same sex while permitting marriage with someone of the opposite sex.

The objection is made, however, that the antimiscegenation laws invalidated in *Loving v. Virginia,* 388 U.S. 1, 8 (1967), similarly were applicable to whites and blacks alike, and only distinguished between the races insofar as the *partner* was concerned. In *Loving,* however, we correctly applied heightened scrutiny, rather than the usual rational-basis review, because the Virginia statute was "designed to maintain White Supremacy." *Id.* at 6, 11. * * *

* * *

Justice O'CONNOR simply decrees application of "a more searching form of rational basis review" to the Texas statute. The cases she cites do not recognize such a standard, and reach their conclusions only after finding, as required by conventional rational-basis analysis, that no conceivable legitimate state interest supports the classification at issue. * * *

This reasoning leaves on pretty shaky grounds state laws limiting marriage to opposite-sex couples. Justice O'CONNOR seeks to preserve them by the conclusory statement that "preserving the traditional institution of marriage" is a legitimate state interest. But "preserving the traditional institution of marriage" is just a kinder way of describing the State's *moral disapproval* of same-sex couples. Texas's interest in § 21.06 could be recast in similarly euphemistic terms: "preserving the traditional sexual mores of our society." In the jurisprudence Justice O'CONNOR has seemingly created, judges can validate laws by characterizing them as "preserving the traditions of society" (good); or invalidate them by characterizing them as "expressing moral disapproval" (bad).

* * *

Let me be clear that I have nothing against homosexuals, or any other group, promoting their agenda through normal democratic means. Social perceptions of sexual and other morality change over time, and every group has the right to persuade its fellow citizens that its view of such matters is the best. * * *

One of the benefits of leaving regulation of this matter to the people rather than to the courts is that the people, unlike judges, need not carry things to their logical conclusion. The people may feel that their disapprobation of homosexual conduct is strong enough to disallow homosexual marriage, but not strong enough to criminalize private homosexual acts— and may legislate accordingly. The Court today pretends that it possesses a similar freedom of action, so that that we need not fear judicial imposition of homosexual marriage, as has recently occurred in Canada (in a decision that the Canadian Government has chosen not to appeal). *See Halpern v. Toronto*, [[2003] 65 O.R. (3d) 161] (Ontario Ct. App.). At the end of its opinion—after having laid waste the foundations of our rational-basis jurisprudence—the Court says that the present case "does not involve whether the government must give formal recognition to any relationship that homosexual persons seek to enter." Do not believe it. More illuminating than this bald, unreasoned disclaimer is the progression of thought displayed by an earlier passage in the Court's opinion, which notes the constitutional protections afforded to "personal decisions relating to *marriage,* procreation, contraception, family relationships, child rearing, and education," and then declares that "[p]ersons in a homosexual relationship may seek autonomy for these purposes, just as heterosexual persons do." Today's opinion dismantles the structure of constitutional law that has permitted a distinction to be made between heterosexual and homosexual unions, insofar as formal recognition in marriage is concerned. If moral disapprobation of homosexual conduct is "no legitimate state interest" for purposes of proscribing that conduct; and if, as the Court coos (casting aside all pretense of neutrality), "[w]hen sexuality finds overt expression in intimate conduct with another person, the conduct can be but one element in a personal bond that is more enduring," what justification could there possibly be for denying the benefits of marriage to homosexual couples exercising "[t]he liberty protected by the Constitution"? Surely not the encouragement of procreation, since the sterile and the elderly are allowed to marry. This case "does not involve" the issue of homosexual marriage only if one entertains the belief that principle and logic have nothing to do with the decisions of this Court. Many will hope that, as the Court comfortingly assures us, this is so.

* * *

NOTES AND QUESTIONS

1. *What is the holding of* Lawrence? The Court's opinion in *Lawrence* is surprisingly opaque. Some have adopted Justice Scalia's view that *Lawrence* found no fundamental right and invalidated the Texas law solely on the ground that it failed rational-basis review. *See, e.g., Standhardt v. Superior Court*, 77 P.3d 451, 457 (Ariz. Ct. App. 2003). Others have read the majority opinion as striking down the Texas sodomy law on the ground that it violated a fundamental privacy right relating to family or intimate association. *See, e.g.,* Mark Strasser, *The* Lawrence *Reader:* Standhardt *and* Lewis *on Women in Love*, 24 St. Louis U. Pub. L. Rev. 59 (2005); Laurence H. Tribe, Lawrence v. Texas: *The "Fundamental Right" That Dare Not Speak Its Name*, 117 Harv. L. Rev. 1893 (2004).

Professor Cass Sunstein has suggested that *Lawrence* is best understood as an exceptional response to the fact that sodomy laws, like the contraception laws struck down in *Griswold*, had fallen into desuetude and were "hopelessly out of touch with existing [popular] convictions." *See* Cass R. Sunstein, *What Did* Lawrence *Hold? Of Autonomy, Desuetude, Sexuality, and Marriage*, 55 Sup. Ct. Rev. 27 (2003). Is Justice Scalia correct that *Lawrence* calls into question other laws, such as those regulating same-sex marriage, incest, and polygamy? If not, then what is the distinction?

2. *Individual or familial privacy? Griswold* appeared to ground the right of privacy in the intimate associational bond between married partners, while *Eisenstadt* (also discussed in Chapter 1) emphasized the rights of single persons as individuals. What about *Lawrence*? Professor David Meyer contends that the expansion of the right of privacy in *Lawrence* is based on "a broadening conception of family," rather than on a broader conception of protection for sexual liberty; "the Court ultimately appeared to link constitutional protection to contemporary society's acceptance of the legitimacy of the family bonds constructed by gays and lesbians." David D. Meyer, *Domesticating* Lawrence, 2004 U. Chi. L. Forum 453, 454–55. What type of privacy is protected post-*Lawrence*? For thoughtful exploration of the foundations and boundaries of autonomy within the family, see David J. Herring, The Public Family: Exploring Its Role in Democratic Society (2003); Linda C. McClain, The Place of Families: Fostering Capacity, Equality, and Responsibility (2006).

3. Lawrence *and Marriage. Lawrence* does not expressly call into doubt the constitutionality of laws prohibiting same-sex marriage. Indeed, Justice O'Connor, concurring in the judgment, made a point of insisting that "other reasons exist to promote the institution of marriage [as limited to opposite-sex couples] beyond mere moral disapproval of an excluded group." Nevertheless, as Justice Scalia's dissent predicted, *Lawrence*'s willingness to protect private intimacy between same-sex partners has led some courts to rethink the permissibility of laws banning same-sex marriage.

In the following decision, *Goodridge v. Department of Public Health*, the Massachusetts Supreme Judicial Court found support in *Lawrence* for the conclusion that, under the state constitution, denial of marriage to same-sex couples is unrelated to any legitimate public purpose. As you read the case, consider the types of arguments that each party makes to support its claims.

GOODRIDGE v. DEPARTMENT OF PUBLIC HEALTH

Supreme Judicial Court of Massachusetts, 2003.
798 N.E.2d 941.

MARSHALL, C.J.

Marriage is a vital social institution. The exclusive commitment of two individuals to each other nurtures love and mutual support; it brings stability to our society. For those who choose to marry, and for their children, marriage provides an abundance of legal, financial, and social benefits. In return it imposes weighty legal, financial, and social obligations. The question before us is whether, consistent with the Massachusetts Constitution, the Commonwealth may deny the protections, benefits, and obligations conferred by civil marriage to two individuals of the same sex who wish to marry. We conclude that it may not. * * *

* * *

I

The plaintiffs are fourteen individuals from five Massachusetts counties [who were each denied marriage licenses because they wished to marry a partner of the same sex]. * * *

* * *

[The plaintiffs filed a lawsuit challenging the denial and the trial judge granted summary judgment for the Commonwealth, concluding that] * * * the marriage exclusion does not offend the liberty, freedom, equality, or due process provisions of the Massachusetts Constitution, and that the Massachusetts Declaration of Rights does not guarantee "the fundamental right to marry a person of the same sex." He concluded that prohibiting same-sex marriage rationally furthers the Legislature's legitimate interest in safeguarding the "primary purpose" of marriage, "procreation." [The Supreme Judicial Court granted direct review.] * * *

* * *

III

A

* * * We have recognized the long-standing statutory understanding, derived from the common law, that "marriage" means the lawful union of a woman and a man. But that history cannot and does not foreclose the constitutional question.

* * * In matters implicating marriage, family life, and the upbringing of children, the two constitutional concepts [of equality and liberty] frequently overlap, as they do here. Much of what we say concerning one standard applies to the other.

We begin by considering the nature of civil marriage itself. Simply put, the government creates civil marriage. In Massachusetts, civil marriage is, and since pre-Colonial days has been, precisely what its name implies: a wholly secular institution. No religious ceremony has ever been required to validate a Massachusetts marriage.

In a real sense, there are three partners to every civil marriage: two willing spouses and an approving State. While only the parties can mutually assent to marriage, the terms of the marriage—who may marry and what obligations, benefits, and liabilities attach to civil marriage—are set by the Commonwealth. Conversely, while only the parties can agree to end the marriage (absent the death of one of them or a marriage void *ab initio*), the Commonwealth defines the exit terms.

* * *

Without question, civil marriage enhances the "welfare of the community." It is a "social institution of the highest importance." Civil marriage anchors an ordered society by encouraging stable relationships over transient ones. It is central to the way the Commonwealth identifies individuals, provides for the orderly distribution of property, ensures that children and adults are cared for and supported whenever possible from private rather than public funds, and tracks important epidemiological and demographic data.

Marriage also bestows enormous private and social advantages on those who choose to marry. Civil marriage is at once a deeply personal commitment to another human being and a highly public celebration of the ideals of mutuality, companionship, intimacy, fidelity, and family. * * * Because it fulfils yearnings for security, safe haven, and connection that express our common humanity, civil marriage is an esteemed institution, and the decision whether and whom to marry is among life's momentous acts of self-definition.

* * *

The benefits accessible only by way of a marriage license are enormous, touching nearly every aspect of life and death. The department states that "hundreds of statutes" are related to marriage and to marital benefits [including laws governing property rights, tax status, insurance and leave coverage, and other topics]. * * *

* * *

It is undoubtedly for these concrete reasons, as well as for its intimately personal significance, that civil marriage has long been termed a "civil right." *See, e.g., Loving v. Virginia,* 388 U.S. 1, 12 (1967). The United States Supreme Court has described the right to marry as "of fundamental importance for all individuals" and as "part of the fundamental 'right of privacy' implicit in the Fourteenth Amendment's Due Process Clause." *Zablocki v. Redhail,* 434 U.S. 374, 384 (1978).

Without the right to marry—or more properly, the right to choose to marry—one is excluded from the full range of human experience and denied full protection of the laws for one's "avowed commitment to an intimate and lasting human relationship." *Baker v. State*, [744 A.2d 864, 889 (Vt. 1999)]. Because civil marriage is central to the lives of individuals and the welfare of the community, our laws assiduously protect the individual's right to marry against undue government incursion. Laws may not "interfere directly and substantially with the right to marry." *Zablocki*, [434 U.S. at 387].

* * *

B

* * *

The Massachusetts Constitution protects matters of personal liberty against government incursion as zealously, and often more so, than does the Federal Constitution, even where both Constitutions employ essentially the same language. * * *

* * * Whether and whom to marry, how to express sexual intimacy, and whether and how to establish a family—these are among the most basic of every individual's liberty and due process rights. And central to personal freedom and security is the assurance that the laws will apply equally to persons in similar situations. * * * The liberty interest in choosing whether and whom to marry would be hollow if the Commonwealth could, without sufficient justification, foreclose an individual from freely choosing the person with whom to share an exclusive commitment in the unique institution of civil marriage.

The Massachusetts Constitution requires, at a minimum, that the exercise of the State's regulatory authority not be "arbitrary or capricious." Under both the equality and liberty guarantees, regulatory authority must, at very least, serve "a legitimate purpose in a rational way"; a statute must "bear a reasonable relation to a permissible legislative objective." Any law failing to satisfy the basic standards of rationality is void.

* * *

The department argues that no fundamental right or "suspect" class is at issue here, and rational basis is the appropriate standard of review. For the reasons we explain below, we conclude that the marriage ban does not meet the rational basis test for either due process or equal protection. Because the statute does not survive rational basis review, we do not consider the plaintiffs' arguments that this case merits strict judicial scrutiny.

The department posits three legislative rationales for prohibiting same-sex couples from marrying: (1) providing a "favorable setting for procreation"; (2) ensuring the optimal setting for child rearing, which the department defines as "a two-parent family with one parent of each sex"; and (3) preserving scarce State and private financial resources. We consider each in turn.

The judge in the Superior Court endorsed the first rationale, holding that "the state's interest in regulating marriage is based on the traditional concept that marriage's primary purpose is procreation." This is incorrect. Our laws of civil marriage do not privilege procreative heterosexual intercourse between married people above every other form of adult intimacy and every other means of creating a family. General Laws c. 207 contains no requirement that the applicants for a marriage license attest to their ability or intention to conceive children by coitus. * * * While it is certainly true that many, perhaps most, married couples have children together (assisted or unassisted), it is the exclusive and permanent commitment of the marriage partners to one another, not the begetting of children, that is the sine qua non of civil marriage.[23]

---

23. It is hardly surprising that civil marriage developed historically as a means to regulate heterosexual conduct and to promote child rearing, because until very recently unassisted heterosexual relations were the only means short of adoption by which children could come into the world, and the absence of widely available and effective contraceptives made the link between

Moreover, the Commonwealth affirmatively facilitates bringing children into a family regardless of whether the intended parent is married or unmarried, whether the child is adopted or born into a family, whether assistive technology was used to conceive the child, and whether the parent or her partner is heterosexual, homosexual, or bisexual. If procreation were a necessary component of civil marriage, our statutes would draw a tighter circle around the permissible bounds of nonmarital child bearing and the creation of families by noncoital means. * * *

* * *

The department's first stated rationale, equating marriage with unassisted heterosexual procreation, shades imperceptibly into its second: that confining marriage to opposite-sex couples ensures that children are raised in the "optimal" setting. Protecting the welfare of children is a paramount State policy. Restricting marriage to opposite-sex couples, however, cannot plausibly further this policy. * * *

The department has offered no evidence that forbidding marriage to people of the same sex will increase the number of couples choosing to enter into opposite-sex marriages in order to have and raise children. There is thus no rational relationship between the marriage statute and the Commonwealth's proffered goal of protecting the "optimal" child rearing unit. Moreover, the department readily concedes that people in same-sex couples may be "excellent" parents. These couples (including four of the plaintiff couples) have children for the reasons others do—to love them, to care for them, to nurture them. But the task of child rearing for same-sex couples is made infinitely harder by their status as outliers to the marriage laws. * * * Excluding same-sex couples from civil marriage will not make children of opposite-sex marriages more secure, but it does prevent children of same-sex couples from enjoying the immeasurable advantages that flow from the assurance of "a stable family structure in which children will be reared, educated, and socialized." [Cordy, J., dissenting, *infra*.]

* * *

The third rationale advanced by the department is that limiting marriage to opposite-sex couples furthers the Legislature's interest in conserving scarce State and private financial resources. The marriage restriction is rational, it argues, because the General Court logically could assume that same-sex couples are more financially independent than married couples and thus less needy of public marital benefits, such as tax advantages, or private marital benefits, such as employer-financed health plans that include spouses in their coverage.

---

heterosexual sex and procreation very strong indeed. Punitive notions of illegitimacy and of homosexual identity further cemented the common and legal understanding of marriage as an unquestionably heterosexual institution. But it is circular reasoning, not analysis, to maintain that marriage must remain a heterosexual institution because that is what it historically has been. * * *

An absolute statutory ban on same-sex marriage bears no rational relationship to the goal of economy. First, the department's conclusory generalization—that same-sex couples are less financially dependent on each other than opposite-sex couples—ignores that many same-sex couples, such as many of the plaintiffs in this case, have children and other dependents (here, aged parents) in their care. * * * Second, Massachusetts marriage laws do not condition receipt of public and private financial benefits to married individuals on a demonstration of financial dependence on each other; the benefits are available to married couples regardless of whether they mingle their finances or actually depend on each other for support.

The department suggests additional rationales for prohibiting same-sex couples from marrying, which are developed by some amici. It argues that broadening civil marriage to include same-sex couples will trivialize or destroy the institution of marriage as it has historically been fashioned. Certainly our decision today marks a significant change in the definition of marriage as it has been inherited from the common law, and understood by many societies for centuries. But it does not disturb the fundamental value of marriage in our society.

* * *

* * * As a public institution and a right of fundamental importance, civil marriage is an evolving paradigm. * * * Alarms about the imminent erosion of the "natural" order of marriage were sounded over the demise of antimiscegenation laws, the expansion of the rights of married women, and the introduction of "no-fault" divorce. Marriage has survived all of these transformations, and we have no doubt that marriage will continue to be a vibrant and revered institution.

* * *

IV

We consider next the plaintiffs' request for relief. We preserve as much of the statute as may be preserved in the face of the successful constitutional challenge.

Here, no one argues that striking down the marriage laws is an appropriate form of relief. Eliminating civil marriage would be wholly inconsistent with the Legislature's deep commitment to fostering stable families and would dismantle a vital organizing principle of our society.[34] We face a problem similar to one that recently confronted the Court of Appeal for Ontario, the highest court of that Canadian province, when it considered the constitutionality of the same-sex marriage ban under the Canadian Charter of Rights and Freedoms (Charter), part of Canada's Federal Constitution. *See Halpern v. Toronto*[, [2003] 65 O.R. (3d) 161].

---

34. Similarly, no one argues that the restrictions on incestuous or polygamous marriages are so dependent on the marriage restriction that they too should fall if the marriage restriction falls. Nothing in our opinion today should be construed as relaxing or abrogating the consanguinity or polygamy prohibitions of our marriage laws. * * *

* * * In holding that the limitation of civil marriage to opposite-sex couples violated the Charter, the Court of Appeal refined the common-law meaning of marriage. We concur with this remedy, which is entirely consonant with established principles of jurisprudence empowering a court to refine a common-law principle in light of evolving constitutional standards.

We construe civil marriage to mean the voluntary union of two persons as spouses, to the exclusion of all others. This reformulation redresses the plaintiffs' constitutional injury and furthers the aim of marriage to promote stable, exclusive relationships. It advances the two legitimate State interests the department has identified: providing a stable setting for child rearing and conserving State resources. It leaves intact the Legislature's broad discretion to regulate marriage.

* * * Entry of judgment shall be stayed for 180 days to permit the Legislature to take such action as it may deem appropriate in light of this opinion.

So ordered.

GREANEY, J. (concurring).

I agree with the result reached by the court, the remedy ordered, and much of the reasoning in the court's opinion. In my view, however, the case is more directly resolved using traditional equal protection analysis.

* * *

Analysis begins with the indisputable premise that the deprivation suffered by the plaintiffs is no mere legal inconvenience. The right to marry is not a privilege conferred by the State, but a fundamental right that is protected against unwarranted State interference. * * *

Because our marriage statutes intend, and state, the ordinary understanding that marriage under our law consists only of a union between a man and a woman, they create a statutory classification based on the sex of the two people who wish to marry. *See Baehr v. Lewin,* [852 P.2d 44, 60] (1993) (plurality opinion) (Hawaii marriage statutes created sex-based classification). * * * Stated in particular terms, Hillary Goodridge cannot marry Julie Goodridge because she (Hillary) is a woman. * * *

* * *

The equal protection infirmity at work here is strikingly similar to (although, perhaps, more subtle than) the invidious discrimination perpetuated by Virginia's antimiscegenation laws and unveiled in the decision of *Loving v. Virginia.* In its landmark decision striking down Virginia's ban on marriages between Caucasians and members of any other race on both equal protection and substantive due process grounds, the United States Supreme Court soundly rejected the proposition that the equal application of the ban (*i.e.,* that it applied equally to whites and blacks) made unnecessary the strict scrutiny analysis traditionally required of statutes drawing classifications according to race and concluded that "restricting the freedom to marry solely because of racial classifications violates the central meaning of the Equal Protection Clause." That our marriage laws, unlike antimiscegenation laws, were not enacted purposely to discriminate in no way neutralizes their present discriminatory character.

With these two propositions established (the infringement on a fundamental right and a sex-based classification), the enforcement of the marriage statutes as they are currently understood is forbidden by our Constitution unless the State can present a compelling purpose furthered by the statutes that can be accomplished in no other reasonable manner. This the State has not done. The justifications put forth by the State to sustain the statute's exclusion of the plaintiffs are insufficient for the reasons explained by the court * * *.

* * *

Sosman, J. (dissenting, with whom Spina and Cordy, JJ., join).

In applying the rational basis test to any challenged statutory scheme, the issue is not whether the Legislature's rationale behind that scheme is persuasive to us, but only whether it satisfies a minimal threshold of rationality. * * *

* * *

* * * Conspicuously absent from the court's opinion today is any acknowledgment that the attempts at scientific study of the ramifications of raising children in same-sex couple households are themselves in their infancy and have so far produced inconclusive and conflicting results. * * * The Legislature can rationally view the state of the scientific evidence as unsettled on the critical question it now faces: are families headed by same-sex parents equally successful in rearing children from infancy to adulthood as families headed by parents of opposite sexes? Our belief that children raised by same-sex couples *should* fare the same as children raised in traditional families is just that: a passionately held but utterly untested belief. The Legislature is not required to share that belief but may, as the creator of the institution of civil marriage, wish to see the proof before making a fundamental alteration to that institution.

* * *

* * * Absent consensus on the issue (which obviously does not exist), or unanimity amongst scientists studying the issue (which also does not exist), or a more prolonged period of observation of this new family structure (which has not yet been possible), it is rational for the Legislature to postpone any redefinition of marriage that would include same-sex couples until such time as it is certain that that redefinition will not have unintended and undesirable social consequences. Through the political process, the people may decide when the benefits of extending civil marriage to same-sex couples have been shown to outweigh whatever risks—be they palpable or ephemeral—are involved. However minimal the risks of that redefinition of marriage may seem to us from our vantage

point, it is not up to us to decide what risks society must run, and it is inappropriate for us to arrogate that power to ourselves merely because we are confident that "it is the right thing to do."

* * *

CORDY, J. (dissenting, with whom SPINA and SOSMAN, JJ., join).

* * *

The Massachusetts marriage statute does not impair the exercise of a recognized fundamental right, or discriminate on the basis of sex in violation of the equal rights amendment to the Massachusetts Constitution. * * *

* * *

The marriage statute, which regulates only the act of obtaining a marriage license, does not implicate privacy in the sense that it has found constitutional protection under Massachusetts and Federal law. It does not intrude on any right that the plaintiffs have to privacy in their choices regarding procreation, an intimate partner or sexual relations. The plaintiffs' right to privacy in such matters does not require that the State officially endorse their choices in order for the right to be constitutionally vindicated.

Although some of the privacy cases also speak in terms of personal autonomy, no court has ever recognized such an open-ended right. "That many of the rights and liberties protected by the Due Process Clause sound in personal autonomy does not warrant the sweeping conclusion that any and all important, intimate, and personal decisions are so protected...." *Washington v. Glucksberg,* 521 U.S. 702, 727 (1997). Such decisions are protected not because they are important, intimate, and personal, but because the right or liberty at stake is "so deeply rooted in our history and traditions, or so fundamental to our concept of constitutionally ordered liberty" that it is protected by due process. *Id.* * * *

While the institution of marriage is deeply rooted in the history and traditions of our country and our State, the right to marry someone of the same sex is not. No matter how personal or intimate a decision to marry someone of the same sex might be, the right to make it is not guaranteed by the right of personal autonomy.

* * *

* * * Indeed, it is not readily apparent to what extent contemporary values have embraced the concept of same-sex marriage. * * * No State Legislature has enacted laws permitting same-sex marriages; and a large majority of States, as well as the United States Congress, have affirmatively prohibited the recognition of such marriages for any purpose.

Given this history and the current state of public opinion, as reflected in the actions of the people's elected representatives, it cannot be said that "a right to same-sex marriage is so rooted in the traditions and collective conscience of our people that failure to recognize it would violate the fundamental principles of liberty and justice that lie at the base of all our civil and political institutions. Neither . . . [is] a right to same-sex marriage . . . implicit in the concept of ordered liberty, such that neither liberty nor justice would exist if it were sacrificed." *Baehr v. Lewin,* [852 P.2d 44, 57] (Haw. 1993). * * *

* * * In his concurrence, Justice Greaney contends that the marriage statute constitutes discrimination on the basis of sex * * *. Such a conclusion is analytically unsound and inconsistent with the legislative history of the ERA.

The central purpose of the ERA was to eradicate discrimination against women and in favor of men or vice versa. Consistent with this purpose, we have construed the ERA to prohibit laws that advantage one sex at the expense of the other, but not laws that treat men and women equally. The Massachusetts marriage statute does not subject men to different treatment from women; each is equally prohibited from precisely the same conduct.

Of course, a statute that on its face treats protected groups equally may still harm, stigmatize, or advantage one over the other. Such was the circumstance in *Loving v. Virginia,* 388 U.S. 1 (1967), where the Supreme Court struck down a State statute that made interracial marriage a crime, as constituting invidious discrimination on the basis of race. While the statute purported to apply equally to whites and nonwhites, the Court found that it was intended and structured to favor one race (white) and disfavor all others (nonwhites). * * *

By contrast, here there is no evidence that limiting marriage to opposite-sex couples was motivated by sexism in general or a desire to disadvantage men or women in particular. Moreover, no one has identified any harm, burden, disadvantage, or advantage accruing to either gender as a consequence of the Massachusetts marriage statute. In the absence of such effect, the statute limiting marriage to couples of the opposite sex does not violate the ERA's prohibition of sex discrimination.

* * *

[Because the ban on same-sex marriage does not involve a fundamental right or discrimination against a suspect class, it is constitutional so long as it is rationally related to a legitimate state purpose. The marriage statute satisfies that test.]

Paramount among its many important functions, the institution of marriage has systematically provided for the regulation of heterosexual behavior, brought order to the resulting procreation, and ensured a stable family structure in which children will be reared, educated, and socialized. Admittedly, heterosexual intercourse, procreation, and child care are not necessarily conjoined (particularly in the modern age of widespread effective contraception and supportive social welfare programs), but an orderly society requires some mechanism for coping with the fact that sexual intercourse commonly results in pregnancy and childbirth. The institution of marriage is that mechanism.

The institution of marriage provides the important legal and normative link between heterosexual intercourse and procreation on the one hand and family responsibilities on the other. The partners in a marriage are expected to engage in exclusive sexual relations, with children the probable result and paternity presumed. * * *

* * *

Taking all * * * available information into account, the Legislature could [also] rationally conclude that a family environment with married opposite-sex parents remains the optimal social structure in which to bear children, and that the raising of children by same-sex couples, who by definition cannot be the two sole biological parents of a child and cannot provide children with a parental authority figure of each gender, presents an alternative structure for child rearing that has not yet proved itself beyond reasonable scientific dispute to be as optimal as the biologically based marriage norm. Working from the assumption that a recognition of same-sex marriages will increase the number of children experiencing this alternative, the Legislature could conceivably conclude that declining to recognize same-sex marriages remains prudent until empirical questions about its impact on the upbringing of children are resolved.

* * *

That the State does not preclude different types of families from raising children does not mean that it must view them all as equally optimal and equally deserving of State endorsement and support. * * * The Legislature may rationally permit adoption by same-sex couples yet harbor reservations as to whether parenthood by same-sex couples should be affirmatively encouraged to the same extent as parenthood by the heterosexual couple whose union produced the child.

In addition, the Legislature could conclude that redefining the institution of marriage to permit same-sex couples to marry would impair the State's interest in promoting and supporting heterosexual marriage as the social institution that it has determined best normalizes, stabilizes, and links the acts of procreation and child rearing. While the plaintiffs argue that they only want to take part in the same stabilizing institution, the Legislature conceivably could conclude that permitting their participation would have the unintended effect of undermining to some degree marriage's ability to serve its social purpose.

* * *

There is no reason to believe that legislative processes are inadequate to effectuate legal changes in response to evolving evidence, social values, and views of fairness on the subject of same-sex relationships. * * * It is not enough that we as Justices might be personally of the view that we have learned enough to decide what is best. So long as the question is at all debatable, it must be the Legislature that decides. * * *

* * *

[Dissenting opinion of SPINA, J., is omitted.]

NOTES AND QUESTIONS

1. *Backlash to* Goodridge. The political reaction to *Goodridge*, coming less than five months after the Supreme Court's decision in *Lawrence v. Texas*, was swift and strong:

> In the end, the political backlash ignited by *Lawrence*—and, even more so, by *Goodridge*—had several direct consequences. First, thirteen states added to their constitutions language defining marriage as a union between a man and a woman; before 2004, only four states had such provisions in their constitutions. * * *

> Second, opposition to same-sex marriage mobilized conservative Christians to turn out at the polls in 2004 in unprecedented numbers, leading one social conservative to joke the day after the election that "President Bush should send a bouquet of flowers" to the members of the Massachusetts Supreme Court. * * * Thus, the backlash ignited by *Goodridge* possibly ensured the reelection of a president whose judicial appointments will almost certainly delay the legal recognition of same-sex marriage.

Michael J. Klarman, Brown *and* Lawrence *(and* Goodridge*)*, 104 Mich. L. Rev. 431, 466–68 (2005); *but cf.* Carlos A. Ball, *The Backlash Thesis and Same–Sex Marriage: Lessons from* Brown v. Board of Education *and Its Aftermath*, 14 Wm. & Mary Bill Rgts. J. 1493, 1494 (2006) (concluding that "despite the harmful backlash experienced by the gay rights movement following marriage cases such as *Goodridge*, lesbians and gay men are nonetheless better off as a result of those cases").

2. *Reaction in other state courts: a developing split.* In 2006, the New York Court of Appeals delivered what the *New York Times* described as "a legal rebuke" to *Goodridge*. *See* Patrick Healy, *For Gay Rights Movement, a Key Setback*, N.Y. Times, July 7, 2006, at A1. In *Hernandez v. Robles*, 855 N.E.2d 1 (N.Y. 2006), the court upheld New York's prohibition against same-sex marriage in an opinion that disagreed broadly with *Goodridge*. The court held that (1) there is no fundamental right to same-sex marriage under the due process clause of the state's constitution; (2) bans on same-sex marriage do not discriminate based on gender; (3) gays and lesbians do not comprise a "suspect class" so that discrimination against them would trigger heightened scrutiny under the equal protection clause; and (4) prohibitions against same-sex marriage are adequately supported by legitimate state interests under rational-basis review. The highest courts of Maryland and Washington followed suit in interpreting their own state constitutions. *See Conaway v. Deane*, 932 A.2d 571 (Md. 2007); *Andersen v. King County*, 138 P.3d 963 (Wash. 2006).

Commentators suggested that *Hernandez* and *Andersen* had blunted the momentum of *Goodridge*, perhaps setting back the quest for same-sex marriage rights nationally by a decade or more. *See* Healy, *supra*. Yet, within the next three years, the supreme courts of California, Connecticut and Iowa each ruled that their state constitutions required that gays and lesbians be allowed to marry. *See In re Marriage Cases*, 183 P.3d 384 (Cal. 2008); *Kerrigan v. Commissioner of Public Health*, 957 A.2d 407 (Conn. 2008); *Varnum v. Brien*, ___ N.W.2d ___, 2009 WL 874044 (Iowa Apr. 3, 2009). All three courts concluded that laws withholding marriage from same-sex couples discriminate on the basis of sexual orientation in violation of equal protection guarantees. Additionally, the California Supreme Court held that the ban on same-sex marriage violated the fundamental right to marry. In expressly recognizing heightened constitutional protection for same-sex couples, the California, Connecticut and Iowa courts took a significant step beyond the Massachusetts court's holding in *Goodridge*, which applied only rational-basis review.

For a few weeks in October 2008, same-sex couples were able to marry in three states: California, Connecticut and Massachusetts. But the California Supreme Court's decision resulted in a popular backlash of its own. In November 2008, less than six months after the court's ruling, voters approved a ballot measure known as Proposition 8, thereby amending the state's constitution to reinstate the ban on same-sex marriage. The amendment resulted in an immediate halt to same-sex marriages in California. Two weeks after the election, the California Supreme Court agreed to hear a legal challenge to the validity of Proposition 8. *See Strauss v. Horton*, Nos. S168047/S168066/S168078 (Cal. review granted Nov. 19, 2008).The challenge contends that the ballot measure so radically altered the constitution's equality guarantee as to constitute a "revision" rather than an "amend-ment," requiring additional legislative approval. (An Oregon court in 2008 rejected a similar challenge to a voter-sponsored constitutional amendment against same-sex marriage there. *See Martinez v. Kulongoski*, 185 P.3d 498 (Or. App. 2008).) The California litigation will also address the continuing validity of approximately 18,000 same-sex marriages solemnized in the state between the court's decision and the voter referendum.

Notwithstanding the reversal in California, a national public opinion poll conducted after the election found "growing public support for gay marriage and civil unions." Arian Campo–Flores, *A Gay Marriage Surge*, Newsweek, Dec. 5, 2008, http://www.newsweek.com/id/172399. The poll also found that support for same-sex marriage increased markedly among younger respon-dents, suggesting that approval will gain strength in the years ahead.

Indeed, in April 2009, just a few days after the Iowa Supreme Court made same-sex marriage available in that state on constitutional grounds, the Vermont legislature overrode the governor's veto to permit same-sex couples to marry. Significantly, the action in Vermont marked the first time that a legislature elected to allow same-sex marriage on its own initiative without prompting by a court decision, bringing to four the number of states where same-sex marriage is permitted (Connecticut, Iowa, Massachusetts and Ver-mont).

3. *Fundamental right to marry.* Courts have differed on whether gays and lesbians have a fundamental right to marry. Reflecting the majority approach, New York's intermediate appellate court rejected the claim in *Hernandez*, reasoning:

Fundamental rights are defined as those "which are, objectively, deeply rooted in this Nation's history and tradition ... and implicit in the concept of ordered liberty, such that neither liberty nor justice would exist if they were sacrificed." Courts are admonished to "exercise the utmost care" in conferring fundamental-right status on a newly asserted interest lest we transform the liberty protected by due process into judicial policy preferences rather than principles born of public debate and legislative action.

Hernandez v. Robles, 805 N.Y.S.2d 354, 262 (App. Div. 2005) (quoting *Washington v. Glucksberg*, 521 U.S. 702, 720–21 (1997)), *aff'd*, 855 N.E.2d 1 (N.Y. 2006). Affirming, the New York Court of Appeals added: "[W]hether the right in question is 'fundamental' depends on how it is defined. The right to marry is unquestionably a fundamental right. The right to marry someone of the same sex, however, is not 'deeply rooted'; it has not even been asserted until relatively recent times." *Hernandez*, 855 N.E.2d at 9.

The California Supreme Court, however, disagreed:

In light of the fundamental nature of the substantive rights embodied in the right to marry—and their central importance to an individual's opportunity to live a happy, meaningful, and satisfying life as a full member of society—the California Constitution properly must be interpreted to guarantee this basic civil right to *all* individuals and couples, without regard to their sexual orientation.

Marriage Cases, 183 P.3d at 427.

In rejecting the claim of a fundamental right to marry for gays and lesbians, *Hernandez* and Justice Cordy's dissent in *Goodridge* relied on the U.S. Supreme Court's 1997 decision in *Washington v. Glucksberg* for the proposition that fundamental rights should be narrowly construed and anchored in "deeply rooted * * * history and traditions." Is *Glucksberg*'s formulation still the governing test for identifying fundamental rights after *Lawrence*? The New York Court of Appeals answered yes, at least for the question of same-sex marriage:

The difference between *Lawrence* and *Glucksberg* is that in *Glucksberg* the relatively narrow definition of the right at issue was based on rational line-drawing. In *Lawrence*, by contrast, the court found the distinction between homosexual sodomy and intimate relations generally to be essentially arbitrary. Here, there are * * * rational grounds for limiting the definition of marriage to opposite-sex couples. This case is therefore, in the relevant way, like *Glucksberg* and not at all like *Lawrence*.

Hernandez, 855 N.E.2d at 10; *see also* Brian Hawkins, Note, *The* Glucksberg *Renaissance: Substantive Due Process Since* Lawrence v. Texas, 105 Mich. L. Rev. 409, 424 (2006) (surveying case law since *Lawrence* and finding "numerous courts applying the *Glucksberg* Doctrine to substantive due process claims as if *Lawrence* never happened"). Do you agree?

4. *What "other reasons" are there for banning same-sex marriage?* Concurring in *Lawrence*, Justice O'Connor suggested that "other reasons," besides moral disapproval of homosexuality, might legitimately support laws banning same-sex marriage. In *Hernandez,* the New York Court of Appeals found "at least two grounds that rationally support the limitation on marriage":

First, the Legislature could rationally decide that, for the welfare of children, it is more important to promote stability, and to avoid instability, in opposite-sex than in same-sex relationships. * * * Despite the advances of science, it remains true that the vast majority of children are born as a result of a sexual relationship between a man and a woman * * * . The Legislature could also find that such relationships are all too often casual or temporary. It could find that an important function of marriage is to create more stability and permanence in the relationships that cause children to be born. It thus could choose to offer an inducement—in the form of marriage and its attendant benefits—to opposite-sex couples who make a solemn, long-term commitment to each other.

The Legislature could find that this rationale for marriage does not apply with comparable force to same-sex couples. These couples can become parents by adoption, or by artificial insemination or other technological marvels, but they do not become parents as a result of accident or impulse. * * *

There is a second reason: The Legislature could rationally believe that it is better, other things being equal, for children to grow up with both a mother and a father. Intuition and experience suggest that a child benefits from having before his or her eyes, every day, living models of what both a man and a woman are like.

Hernandez, 855 N.E. at 7. Do these observations convincingly answer the court's analysis in *Goodridge*?

5. *Whose burden of proof?* Should states be required to prove the factual suppositions they offer in support of traditional marriage? *Goodridge* rejected the state's child-welfare rationale partly because the state offered "no evidence" to support its suppositions. *Hernandez*, on the other hand, held that the burden of proof rested on those challenging the law:

Plaintiffs seem to assume that they have demonstrated the irrationality of the view that opposite-sex marriages offer advantages to children by showing there is no scientific evidence to support it. Even assuming no such evidence exists, this reasoning is flawed. In the absence of conclusive scientific evidence, the Legislature could rationally proceed on the common-sense premise that children will do best with a mother and father in the home.

Id. at 8. Which view is correct? At least under federal constitutional doctrine, the answer depends on the applicable level of scrutiny: under heightened scrutiny, the state is required to prove its claims of necessity; under rational-basis review, by contrast, "[s]tates are not required to convince the courts of the correctness of their legislative judgments. Rather, 'those challenging the legislative judgment must convince the court that the legislative facts on which the classification is apparently based could not reasonably be conceived to be true by the governmental decisionmaker.'" *Minnesota v. Clover Leaf Creamery Co.*, 449 U.S. 456, 464 (1981) (quoting *Vance v. Bradley*, 440 U.S. 93, 111 (1979)).

Summing up the available evidence about the welfare of children raised by same-sex couples, *Hernandez* wrote that "the studies on their face do not establish beyond doubt that children fare equally well in same-sex and opposite-sex households. What they show, at most, is that rather limited observation has detected no marked differences." *Hernandez*, 855 N.E.2d at 8;

see also Charlotte J. Patterson, *Lesbian and Gay Parents and Their Children: Summary of Research Findings*, in Lesbian & Gay Parenting 5, 15 (Amer. Psych. Ass'n 2005) (concluding that "[n]ot a single study has found children of lesbian or gay parents to be disadvantaged in any significant respect relative to children of heterosexual parents").

6. *Sex discrimination.* Justice Greaney's concurrence in *Goodridge* contends that the state's ban on same-sex marriage is best understood as unconstitutional gender discrimination. The Hawaii Supreme Court had earlier come to the same conclusion in *Baehr v. Lewin*, 852 P.2d 44 (Haw. 1993). Like the New York Court of Appeals in *Hernandez*, *Baehr* ruled that the state's ban passed due process review because the fundamental right to marry is limited to traditional marriage and does not extend to same-sex couples; like Justice Greaney in *Goodridge*, however, *Baehr* also concluded that the law should be subject to heightened equal protection scrutiny as gender discrimination under the state constitution. (The case was ultimately mooted when voters later amended the Hawaii constitution to ratify and preserve the traditional bar against same-sex marriage.)

Is it accurate to describe the traditional ban on same-sex marriage as gender discrimination? From one perspective, the ban plainly involves a formal gender classification, in that marriages are allowed or prohibited based directly on the gender of the partners. At the same time, however, the prohibition against same-sex marriage arguably does not express a preference for one gender over another. Indeed, to the contrary, it might be said that the "dual-gender" requirement expresses the view that *both* genders are equally essential to the formation of a valid marriage.

Should such "even-handedness" toward the genders immunize the prohibition from scrutiny on grounds of sex discrimination? *Loving v. Virginia* rejected a somewhat similar argument in striking down an anti-miscegenation law that equally punished persons of all races for crossing the color line in marriage. Does *Loving* suggest that any use of a gender line in marriage, like any use of a race line, is presumptively unconstitutional? Or might *Loving* be distinguished on the ground that Virginia's law was only nominally "neutral" toward different races and was, in fact, indisputably meant to express and enforce constitutionally repugnant notions of racial hierarchy? In *Hernandez*, the New York Court of Appeals reasoned: "This is not the kind of sham equality that the Supreme Court confronted in *Loving*; the statute there, prohibiting black and white people from marrying each other, was in substance anti-black legislation. Plaintiffs do not argue here that the legislation they challenge is designed to subordinate either men to women or women to men as a class." *Hernandez*, 855 N.E.2d at 11. The California Supreme Court agreed, holding that the sex-discrimination argument "improperly conflates two concepts—discrimination on the basis of sex, and discrimination on the basis of sexual orientation." *Marriage Cases*, 183 P.3d at 439. For differing views on these questions, compare Andrew Koppelman, *Why Discrimination Against Lesbians and Gay Men is Sex Discrimination*, 69 N.Y.U. L. Rev. 197 (1994), with Edward Stein, *Evaluating the Sex Discrimination Argument for Lesbian and Gay Rights*, 49 UCLA L. Rev. 471 (2001).

Is it possible that bans on same-sex marriage do in fact reinforce stereotypical notions of gender hierarchy, in much the same way that Virginia's enforcement of a color line in marriage reinforced prevailing notions of white supremacy? Professor Susan Frelich Appleton writes:

> [A]ny temptation to assert that same-sex marriage bans do not discriminate because they apply equally to men and women alike must give way in view of males' traditional position of superiority in law, society, and family life. Moreover, like the racial caste system in *Loving*, the gender hierarchy requires clearly defined categories, male and female. The work of establishing these categories and policing their boundaries is accomplished by gender roles and gender norms, which provide the scripts for performing as a man or a woman. Laws prohibiting same-sex intimacy and marriages impose just such a "gender script" because they specify that each sexual and marital relationship must have one woman and one man—requirements that two men or two women would appear unable to satisfy.

Susan Frelich Appleton, *Missing in Action? Searching for Gender Talk in the Same–Sex Marriage Debate*, 16 Stan. L. & Pol'y Rev. 97, 107–08 (2005); *see also* R.A. Lenhardt, *Beyond Analogy:* Perez v. Sharp, *Antimiscegenation Law, and the Fight for Same–Sex Marriage*, 96 Cal. L. Rev. 839 (2008). Deborah Widiss, Elizabeth Rosenblatt and Douglas NeJaime contend that courts often uncritically rely on such gender scripts in upholding traditional marriage laws. "Courts, for example, have upheld different-sex marriage requirements on the grounds that men and women, simply by virtue of their gender, provide distinct role models for children; that men and women play 'opposite' or 'complementary' roles within marriage; and that marriage is essential to protect vulnerable women from irresponsible men who, absent the bonds of marriage, would abandon their children." Deborah A. Widiss, Elizabeth L. Rosenblatt & Douglas NeJaime, *Exposing Sex Stereotypes in Recent Same–Sex Marriage Jurisprudence*, 30 Harv. J. L. & Gender 461, 463 (2007). Does the state's insistence on dual-sex marriage necessarily rely on sex stereotypes? Does the fact that gender classifications are considered only "quasi-suspect" under federal equal protection doctrine suggest a greater constitutional tolerance of "gender scripts" than is permitted for (fully "suspect") racial classifications?

7. *Sexual-orientation discrimination.* Whether or not bans on same-sex marriage are properly understood to involve sex discrimination under the Equal Protection Clause, is it not clear that they at least involve discrimination based on sexual orientation? In 2008 and 2009, the California, Connecticut and Iowa Supreme Courts ruled in favor of same-sex marriage on this basis. *See Marriage Cases*, 183 P.3d at 440–44; *Kerrigan*, 957 A.2d at 472–73; *Varnum*, 2009 WL 874044. For supporters of same-sex marriage, the difficulty with this line of constitutional attack is that sexual orientation, unlike gender and race, has not been established as a "suspect" basis of classification under equal protection analysis. Many lower courts have rejected the idea that gays and lesbians constitute a suspect class, *see, e.g., Lofton v. Secretary of Dep't of Children & Fam. Servs.*, 358 F.3d 804, 818 (11th Cir. 2004), and the U.S. Supreme Court has repeatedly declined to decide the question. The California,

Connecticut and Iowa courts, however, concluded that gays and lesbians meet the criteria for heightened protection under equal protection principles:

> Gay persons have been subjected to and stigmatized by a long history of purposeful and invidious discrimination that continues to manifest itself in society. The characteristic that defines the members of this group—attraction to persons of the same sex—bears no logical relationship to their ability to perform in society, either in familial relations or otherwise as productive citizens. Because sexual orientation is such an essential component of personhood, even if there is some possibility that a person's sexual preference can be altered, it would be wholly unacceptable for the state to require anyone to do so. * * * [A]s a minority group that continues to suffer the enduring effects of centuries of legally sanctioned discrimination, laws singling them out for disparate treatment are subject to heightened judicial scrutiny to ensure that those laws are not the product of such historical prejudice and stereotyping.

Kerrigan, 957 A.2d at 432.

Although they agreed that gays and lesbians qualify for heightened protection, the California and Connecticut courts disagreed about the strength of the scrutiny to be applied. The Connecticut Supreme Court held that gays and lesbians constitute a "quasi-suspect" class triggering intermediate constitutional scrutiny (under which discrimination is permissible only if "substantially related" to achievement of an "important" state interest)—the same test used for sex discrimination under the federal Constitution; the California Supreme Court held that gays and lesbians constitute a fully "suspect" class warranting strict scrutiny (under which any discrimination must be "narrowly tailored" to a "compelling" state interest)—the same test used for sex discrimination under the California Constitution. (The Iowa Supreme Court stopped short of resolving the matter, holding that the bar on same-sex marriage failed even intermediate scrutiny.) Should sexual-orientation discrimination receive the same level of scrutiny as sex discrimination? Even if the Court was not explicit, does *Lawrence* signal tacit acceptance of gays and lesbians as a "quasi-suspect" class?

8.   *International developments.* The majority opinions in *Lawrence* and *Goodridge* both draw support from recent legal developments in other countries. By court decision or legislative action, same-sex marriage is now legal in Canada, Belgium, the Netherlands, Norway, South Africa, Spain and Sweden. *See* Katharina Boele–Woelki, *The Legal Recognition of Same–Sex Relationships Within the European Union*, 82 Tul. L. Rev. 1949 (2008). A still larger number of counties permit same-sex couples to register as domestic partners with rights and obligations substantially identical to those attending marriage. The trend began in Denmark in 1989 and since has spread throughout Scandinavia. More recently, other European nations—including France, Germany, and the United Kingdom—and some countries outside Europe—including Brazil, Costa Rica, Israel, and New Zealand—have permitted same-sex couples to claim some of the benefits of marriage through domestic partnerships. What relevance, if any, might these developments have in deciding

whether U.S. jurisdictions are constitutionally required to permit same-sex marriage or civil unions?

9. *Civil unions.* In 1999, the Vermont Supreme Court ruled that the state's restriction of marriage to opposite-sex couples violated the state constitution. *See Baker v. State*, 744 A.2d 864 (Vt. 1999). Although the court found insufficient the state's reasons for denying same-sex couples the benefits of marriage, it did not order the state to issue marriage licenses to same-sex applicants. Instead, the court declared that the legislature should be given a reasonable opportunity to craft a solution that would give same-sex couples an opportunity to obtain comparable benefits without necessarily allowing same-sex couples to obtain a marriage license. In response, the Vermont legislature enacted a statute permitting same-sex couples to enter into state-recognized "civil unions." Partners to a "civil union" under the law are treated in virtually all legal respects as if they were married. Thus, partners are entitled to "receive the benefits and protections and be subject to the responsibilities of spouses," Vt. Stat. Ann. tit. 15, § 1201(2) (2005); once formed, a civil union can be dissolved only in a legal proceeding resembling divorce, *see id.* § 1206. Yet, "civil unions" under the law are explicitly *not* "marriages." The same statute that confers substantively identical legal status for same-sex "civil unions" specifies that "marriage" shall remain "the legally recognized union of one man and one woman." *Id.* § 1201(4).

Three other states have since followed Vermont's lead. In 2005, Connecticut became the second state to offer "civil unions" to same-sex couples. New Jersey followed suit in 2007, after the state supreme court ruled that "the unequal dispensation of rights and benefits to committed same-sex partners can no longer be tolerated under our State Constitution." *Lewis v. Harris*, 908 A.2d 196, 200 (N.J. 2006). New Hampshire began offering civil unions in 2008. Notably, legislators in both Connecticut and New Hampshire acted to authorize civil unions without prodding from a court decision. (Connecticut and Vermont subsequently changed their laws, in 2008 and 2009 respectively, to permit same-sex couples to *marry* as well.)

Still other states, including California, Hawaii, Maine, Oregon, Washington and New Jersey (before it offered civil unions), have enacted laws permitting same-sex couples to register as "domestic partners" or "reciprocal beneficiaries." The domestic partnership registries vary in the extent to which they extend marriage-like status to domestic partners. In California, domestic partners—like participants in civil unions—are treated for virtually all state-law purposes as if they were married. The California Supreme Court found that the new law reflects the clear intent of the legislature "to equalize the status of registered domestic partners and married couples." *Koebke v. Bernardo Heights Country Club*, 115 P.3d 1212, 1219 (Cal. 2005). Other domestic partnership laws do not go quite as far, but still afford partners a wide range of marriage benefits. The laws also vary in whether they allow opposite-sex couples to qualify. Vermont, for example, limits civil unions to same-sex couples, for whom marriage is not legally an option; Hawaii, by contrast, permits any couple to register as domestic partners, while California and New Jersey make domestic partnerships available to same-sex partners of any age and opposite-sex partners who are at least 62 years old.

10. *Marriage or civil unions—what's in a name?* Public opinion polls have shown substantial support for the sort of compromise reflected in

domestic partnership and reciprocal beneficiary laws: permitting committed same-sex couples to claim most or even all legal benefits of marriage, while reserving "marriage" itself to opposite-sex couples. *See* Arian Campos–Flores, *A Gay Marriage Surge*, Newsweek, Dec. 5, 2008, http://www.newsweek.com/id/ 172399 (reporting that "[f]ifty-five percent of respondents favored legally sanctioned unions or partnerships, while only 39 percent supported marriage rights"). Does the availability of civil unions satisfy constitutional objections to denial of marriage to same-sex couples? Several state supreme courts recently have answered "no," emphasizing the unique cultural significance of *marriage*. The California Supreme Court reasoned:

> [B]ecause of the long and celebrated history of the term "marriage" and the widespread understanding that this term describes a union unre- servedly approved and favored by the community, there clearly is a considerable and undeniable symbolic importance to this designation. Thus, it is apparent that affording access to this designation exclusively to opposite-sex couples, while providing same-sex couples access to only a novel alternative designation, realistically must be viewed as constituting significantly unequal treatment to same-sex couples.

Marriage Cases, 183 P.3d at 445; *accord Kerrigan*, 957 A.2d at 474; *Opinion of the Justices to the Senate*, 802 N.E.2d 565, 572 (Mass. 2004). What public purpose is served by withholding the status of "marriage" from same-sex couples while extending to them all substantive legal incidents of marriage? Is that purpose compatible with *Lawrence*'s holding that enforcement of popular moral objections to homosexuality could not justify laws criminalizing sod- omy? Given that marriage is such a loaded term, would it be better if states simply "abandon[ed] the marriage label in favor of another civil status" for all couples? Melissa Murray, *Equal Rites and Equal Rights*, 96 Cal. L. Rev. 1395, 1399 (2008).

A NOTE ON INTERSTATE RECOGNITION OF SAME–SEX UNIONS

An important and unresolved question is whether other states will give legal effect to same-sex marriages or civil unions validly contracted elsewhere. In California alone, an estimated 18,000 same-sex couples wed between June and November 2008, many of whom reside elsewhere. In Massachusetts, a state law that effectively limited same-sex marriage to Massachusetts resi- dents was repealed in 2008, permitting same-sex couples from all other states to marry there. The question of interstate recognition is therefore of immedi- ate and growing significance.

With respect to marriages contracted in another jurisdiction, most states follow the general rule found in section 283(2) of the Second Restatement of Conflict of Laws: "A marriage which satisfies the requirements of the state where the marriage was contracted will everywhere be recognized as valid unless it violates the strong public policy of another state which had the most significant relationship to the spouses and the marriage at the time of the marriage." Restatement (Second) of Conflict of Laws § 283(2) (1971). This means that states ordinarily bend their own marriage policies to uphold the validity of foreign marriages unless doing so would offend an exceptionally strong policy of the forum state.

In the context of same-sex marriage, 41 states in recent years have enacted statutes or constitutional amendments to specify that they do indeed have such policies and so will refuse to recognize same-sex marriages no matter where contracted. *See* Andrew Koppelman, *Interstate Recognition of Same–Sex Marriages and Civil Unions: A Handbook for Judges*, 153 U. Pa. L. Rev. 2143, 2165 (2005). This would seem to provide a clear answer to the question of recognition at least in these jurisdictions. *See Wilson v. Ake*, 354 F. Supp. 2d 1298 (M.D. Fla. 2005) (refusing to recognize same-sex marriage contracted in Massachusetts); *Burns v. Burns*, 560 S.E.2d 47 (Ga. Ct. App. 2002) (refusing to recognize Vermont civil union). In states that have failed to enact such laws, the answer is less clear. A New Jersey court ruled that a same-sex couple married in Canada in 2003 would be recognized as married in New Jersey prior to the legislature's creation of civil unions in 2007, but would thereafter be recognized as having a civil union. *See Quarto v. Adams*, 929 A.2d 1111 (N.J. Super. Ct. 2007). In New York, Governor David Paterson in May 2008 issued an order (excerpted in Chapter 16) directing all state officers to recognize the validity of same-sex marriages contracted in other states and countries. *See Martinez v. County of Monroe*, 850 N.Y.S.2d 740 (App. Div. 2008) (holding that a Canadian same-sex marriage is entitled to recognition in New York); Linda Silberman, *Same–Sex Marriage: Refining the Conflict of Laws Analysis*, 153 U. Pa. L. Rev. 2195 (2005).

Questions remain, however, about whether it is constitutional for states to refuse recognition of out-of-state marriages in this context. The first such question concerns the application of the Full Faith and Credit Clause of the federal Constitution. The Clause provides: "Full Faith and Credit shall be given in each State to the public Acts, Records, and Judicial Proceedings of every other State. And the Congress may by general Laws prescribe the Manner in which such Acts, Records, and Proceedings shall be proved, and the Effect thereof." U.S. Const. art. IV, § 1. This provision might be read to require states to give full faith and credit to marriages validly created in other states, notwithstanding their own policy preferences. There is some doubt concerning the Clause's application to marriage licenses. *See* Joanna L. Grossman, *Resurrecting Comity: Revisiting the Problem of Non–Uniform Marriage Laws*, 84 Or. L. Rev. 433, 452 (2005) (observing that "[h]istorically speaking, . . . full faith and credit principles have never been understood to compel one state to recognize another's marriages"). Some commentators have contended that the Clause requires full faith and credit only for final judgments entered by the courts of other states, and so is not triggered simply by the issuance of a marriage license in another state. *See, e.g.*, Koppelman, *Interstate Recognition, supra* at 2146–47. Even if the Clause does command some respect for foreign marriage licenses, moreover, it has long been assumed that the Clause grants states at least some leeway to refuse enforcement on policy grounds. *See, e.g.*, R. Lea Brilmayer, Testimony before the U.S. Senate Committee on the Judiciary Subcommittee on the Constitution, Civil Rights, and Property Rights, Full Faith and Credit, Family Law, and the Constitutional Amendment Process (Mar. 3, 2004), http://www.law.yale.edu/ outside/html/Public_Affairs/452/senatetestimony.pdf.

Notwithstanding these uncertainties about the applicability of the Full Faith and Credit Clause, however, Congress acted to quell all doubt in 1996 by enacting the Defense of Marriage Act (DOMA). The federal DOMA has two key provisions. The first provides that a same-sex couple married under state law will not be recognized as married for any purposes of federal law, such as determining eligibility for federal welfare benefits or tax obligations. 1 U.S.C. § 7 (2007). The second states:

> No State, territory, or possession of the United States, or Indian tribe, shall be required to give effect to any public act, record, or judicial proceeding of any other State, territory, possession, or tribe respecting a relationship between persons of the same sex that is treated as a marriage under the laws of such other State, territory, possession, or tribe, or a right or claim arising from such relationship.

28 U.S.C. § 1738C (2007). Through DOMA, therefore, Congress meant to exercise the authority granted it by the Full Faith and Credit Clause to prescribe the "manner" and "effect" of full-faith enforcement by directing that *no* effect need be given. Some scholars have contended that this exceeds Congress' power by effectively nullifying the Full Faith and Credit obligation, *see, e.g.*, Mark Strasser, Baker *and Some Recipes for Disaster: On DOMA, Covenant Marriages, and Full Faith and Credit Jurisprudence*, 64 Brooklyn L. Rev. 307 (1998), but courts so far have disagreed. *See Wilson v. Ake*, 354 F. Supp. 2d 1298, 1303 (M.D. Fla. 2005); *Hennefeld v. Township of Montclair*, 22 N.J.Tax 166, 186 (N.J. Tax Ct. 2005).

And, quite apart from the Full Faith and Credit Clause, non-recognition of out-of-state marriages or civil unions raises other constitutional issues. Most obviously, of course, non-recognition might be challenged on the same constitutional grounds used to challenge bans on same-sex marriage in the first instance. *See Morrison v. Sadler*, 821 N.E.2d 15 (Ind. Ct. App. 2005) (rejecting challenge under the Indiana constitution to state courts' refusal to recognize validity of Vermont civil union). Additionally, a forum state's refusal to recognize a temporary visitor's marital status might be challenged as a violation of the fundamental right to interstate travel guaranteed by the federal Constitution. *See* Koppelman, *Interstate Recognition, supra* at 2159–62.

A related question now arising is whether same-sex couples who enter into marriages, civil unions or domestic partnerships under the laws of one state may dissolve them in another state. Not surprisingly, states that refuse to recognize same-sex unions have so far also refused to permit same-sex divorce. *See O'Darling v. O'Darling*, 188 P.3d 137 (Okla. 2008). Yet, even states without clear policies against recognition have refused to provide a forum for the dissolution of same-sex unions. *See Chambers v. Ormiston*, 935 A.2d 956 (R.I. 2007) (holding that state courts had no jurisdiction to dissolve Massachusetts same-sex marriage); *Rosengarten v. Downes*, 802 A.2d 170 (Conn. Ct. App. 2002) (declining, prior to Connecticut's allowance for same-sex marriage and civil unions, to recognize Vermont civil union for purposes of conferring dissolution jurisdiction). *But see C.M. v. C.C.*, 867 N.Y.S.2d 884 (Sup. Ct. 2008) (concluding that same-sex couple married in Canada could divorce in New York). As a result, same-sex couples may be considered married under the laws of one state, but effectively unable to divorce. Limitations on divorce jurisdiction affecting same-sex couples are addressed in Chapter 16.

SECTION 3: POLYGAMY

Many Americans tend to view polygamy as an oddity of marginal significance, but it is a practice with deep historical roots and broad contemporary reach in many non-Western cultures:

> Originally, polygamy * * * was common in ancient civilizations in the Middle East. In the Bible, for example, marriage was traditionally polygamous. Abraham was married to both Sarah and Hagar and had children with both. Jacob married Leah and Rachel, and then married two of their maidservants. He had children with all of them. Solomon was said to have had more than one thousand wives. The Bible also recites that a deceased husband's brother was to marry his widow, even if he was already married. The Code of Hammurabi, written in approximately 1780 B.C., also makes reference to a man being able to take a second wife. When referring to marriage, the code refers to "man and wife" or "woman and husband."

> Polygamy was, and still is, common in Islamic cultures. The Quran permits a man to have up to four wives. Indeed the Prophet Mohamed was said to have taken four wives. Even today, polygamy is found throughout the Middle East.

> * * *

> Polyandry (having more than one husband) was practiced in Central Asia, particularly in Tibet, Sri Lanka, and Southern India, and a few areas in Africa. This practice is believed to have arisen from a demographic imbalance: men far outnumbered women or were absent for long periods * * *.

ABA Section of Family Law, *A White Paper: An Analysis of the Law Regarding Same–Sex Marriage, Civil Unions, and Domestic Partnerships*, 38 Fam. L.Q. 339, 349–50 (2004).

In the American experience, of course, the practice of polygamy is most closely associated with the history of the Church of Jesus Christ of Latter–Day Saints, also known as the Mormon Church, which encouraged polygyny (the marriage of one man to more than one woman) as a part of its faith before finally rejecting the practice in 1890. In the late nineteenth century, the Church's practice was aggressively targeted by a series of congressional enactments that criminalized polygamy in the U.S. Territories, compelled Utah to prohibit the practice as a condition of statehood, and even confiscated Church property. The Supreme Court repeatedly upheld these measures against constitutional attack. *E.g.*, *Davis v. Beason*, 133 U.S. 333 (1890); *see* Sarah Barringer Gordon, The Mormon Question:

Polygamy and Constitutional Conflict in Nineteenth–Century America (2002).

In *Reynolds v. United States*, 98 U.S. 145 (1878), the Court upheld the criminalization of polygamy against a claim that it punished religious conduct in violation of the First Amendment. The Court reasoned that the Free Exercise Clause entitled polygamists to *believe* in polygamy as a tenet of their faith but not to *act* on that belief if the conduct would otherwise be "in violation of social duties or subversive of good order." *Id.* at 164. And polygamy, the Court concluded, was plainly offensive to good order:

> Polygamy has always been odious among the northern and western nations of Europe, and, until the establishment of the Mormon Church, was almost exclusively a feature of the life of Asiatic and of African people. At common law, the second marriage was always void, and from the earliest history of England polygamy has been treated as an offence against society. * * *

> By the statute of 1 James I. (c. 11), the offence, if committed in England or Wales, was made punishable in the civil courts, and the penalty was death. * * * From that day to this we think it may safely be said there never has been a time in any State of the Union when polygamy has not been an offence against society, cognizable by the civil courts and punishable with more or less severity. In the face of all this evidence, it is impossible to believe that the constitutional guaranty of religious freedom was intended to prohibit legislation in respect to this most important feature of social life. Marriage, while from its very nature a sacred obligation, is nevertheless, in most civilized nations, a civil contract, and usually regulated by law. Upon it society may be said to be built, and out of its fruits spring social relations and social obligations and duties, with which government is necessarily required to deal. In fact, according as monogamous or polygamous marriages are allowed, do we find the principles on which the government of the people, to a greater or less extent, rests. Professor Lieber says, polygamy leads to the patriarchal principle, and which, when applied to large communities, fetters the people in stationary despotism, while that principle cannot long exist in connection with monogamy.

Id. at 164–66; *see also Late Corp. of the Church of Jesus Christ of Latter-Day Saints v. United States*, 136 U.S. 1, 49 (1890) ("The organization of a community for the spread and practice of polygamy is, in a measure, a return to barbarism.").

The Mormon Church has formally rejected polygamy for more than 100 years, but breakaway sects continue to adhere to the practice. It is estimated that between 10,000 and 100,000 Americans are currently living in polygamous unions, scattered mostly in rural settlements in Western states. *See* Brook Adams, *LDS Splinter Groups Growing*, Salt Lake Trib., Aug. 9, 2005, at B1. Far from these Western enclaves, the practice of polygamy may also be growing among African–American and immigrant

Muslim families in East Coast cities. *See* Barbara Bradley Hagerty, *Philly's Black Muslims Increasingly Turn to Polygamy*, National Public Radio, May 27, 2008, http://www.npr.org/templates/story/story.php?storyId= 90886407; Nina Bernstein, *In Secret, Polygamy Follows Africans to N.Y.*, N.Y. Times, Mar. 23, 2007.

Apart from a politically disastrous raid on a polygamist community in Short Creek, Arizona, in 1953, prosecutors and police mostly ignored polygamists through the second half of the twentieth century. Recently, however, invigorated enforcement efforts and significant national attention have been drawn to the issue of polygamy by various developments. In 2000, after Thomas Green made a series of national television appearances boasting of his plural marriages—including at least one to a 13–year–old girl—Utah launched its first criminal prosecution of polygamy in 50 years. *See State v. Green*, 99 P.3d 820 (Utah 2004) (upholding Green's conviction for criminal nonsupport of his 25 children and four counts of bigamy). In 2006, Warren Jeffs, then-president of the Fundamentalist Church of Jesus Christ of Latter Day Saints (FLDS), became the subject of intense media coverage after the FBI placed Jeffs on its Ten Most Wanted List while he was on the run from charges of arranging polygamous marriages involving underage girls. (He was later convicted of being an accessory to child rape and sentenced to between 10 years and life in prison.) In 2008, an FLDS compound outside Eldorado, Texas, known as the Yearning for Zion Ranch, became the target of a highly publicized raid that led to the temporary removal of all 468 children living there into state custody. The next month, the Texas Supreme Court ruled that the blanket removal of children was not warranted, although three dissenting justices would have sustained the removal of all post-pubescent girls from the compound. *See In re Texas Dep't of Fam. & Protective Servs.*, 255 S.W.3d 613 (Tex. 2008). The dissenting justices found that pubescent girls in the compound were endangered by a widespread practice of arranged "spiritual" marriages. *See id.* at 616–17 (O'Neill, J., dissenting).

Recent enforcement activities and even popular television programs, such as the HBO series *Big Love* chronicling a fictional polygamous family in suburban Utah, have focused new scrutiny on both the practice of polygamy and traditional state policies prohibiting it. As you read the following decision upholding a conviction arising from one recent prosecution, consider whether a blanket prohibition against all polygamous marriages remains defensible given modern trends toward acceptance of broader family diversity.

STATE v. HOLM
Supreme Court of Utah, 2006.
137 P.3d 726.

DURRANT, JUSTICE:

In this case, we are asked to determine whether Rodney Hans Holm was appropriately convicted for bigamy and unlawful sexual conduct with a minor. * * *

BACKGROUND

Holm was legally married to Suzie Stubbs in 1986. Subsequent to this marriage, Holm, a member of the Fundamentalist Church of Jesus Christ of Latter-day Saints (the "FLDS Church"), participated in a religious marriage ceremony with Wendy Holm. Then, when Rodney Holm was thirty-two, he participated in another religious marriage ceremony with then-sixteen-year-old Ruth Stubbs, Suzie Stubbs's sister. After the ceremony, Ruth moved into Holm's house, where her sister Suzie Stubbs, Wendy Holm, and their children also resided. By the time Ruth turned eighteen, she had conceived two children with Holm, the second of which was born approximately three months after her eighteenth birthday.

* * *

At trial, Ruth Stubbs testified that although she knew that the marriage was not a legal civil marriage under the law, she believed that she was married. Stubbs's testimony included a description of the ceremony she had participated in with Holm. Stubbs testified that, at the ceremony, she had answered "I do" to the following question:

> Do you, Sister [Stubbs], take Brother [Holm] by the right hand, and give yourself to him to be his lawful and wedded wife for time and all eternity, with a covenant and promise on your part, that you will fulfill all the laws, rites and ordinances pertaining to this holy bond of matrimony in the new and everlasting covenant, doing this in the presence of God, angels, and these witnesses, of your own free will and choice?

Stubbs testified that she had worn a white dress, which she considered a wedding dress; that she and Holm exchanged vows; that Warren Jeffs, a religious leader in the FLDS religion, conducted the ceremony; that other church members and members of Holm's family attended the ceremony; and that photographs were taken of Holm, Stubbs, and their guests who attended the ceremony.

Stubbs also testified about her relationship with Holm after the ceremony. She testified that she had moved in with Holm; that Holm had provided, at least in part, for Stubbs and their children; and that she and Holm had "regularly" engaged in sexual intercourse at the house in Hildale, Utah. Evidence was also introduced at trial that Holm and Stubbs "regarded each other as husband and wife."

* * *

[Holm was convicted of one count of bigamy and three counts of unlawful sexual contact with a 16– or 17–year–old based on his relationship with Ruth Stubbs.] * * * The trial court sentenced Holm to up to five years in state prison on each conviction, to be served concurrently, and imposed a $3,000 fine. Both the prison time and the fine were suspended in exchange for three years on probation, one year in the county jail with work release, and two hundred hours of community service.

Holm appealed his conviction on all charges. * * *

* * *

ANALYSIS

* * *

I. WE AFFIRM HOLM'S CONVICTION FOR BIGAMY

Holm was convicted pursuant to Utah's bigamy statute, which provides that "[a] person is guilty of bigamy when, knowing he has a husband or wife or knowing the other person has a husband or wife, the person purports to marry another person or cohabits with another person." Utah Code Ann. § 76–7–101 (2003). The jury weighing the case against Holm indicated on a special verdict form its conclusion that Holm had both "purported to marry another person" and "cohabited with another person" knowing that he already had a wife.

* * * First, Holm argues that his conviction under the "purports to marry" prong of the bigamy statute was improper as a matter of statutory interpretation. Specifically, Holm argues that he did not "purport to marry" Ruth Stubbs, as that phrase is used in the bigamy statute, because the word "marry" in subsection 76–7–101(1) refers only to legal marriage and neither Holm nor Stubbs contemplated that the religious ceremony solemnizing their relationship would entitle them to any of the legal benefits attendant to state-sanctioned matrimony. * * *

* * *

* * * We hold that the term "marry," as used in the bigamy statute, includes both legally recognized marriages and those that are not state-sanctioned because such a definition is supported by the plain meaning of the term, the language of the bigamy statute and the Utah Code, and the legislative history and purpose of the bigamy statute.

First, the common usage of "marriage" supports a broader definition of that term than that asserted by Holm. The dictionary defines "marry" as "to join in marriage according to law or custom," or "to unite in close and [usually] permanent relation." * * *

* * *

Second, when we look, as we must, at the term "marry" in the context of the bigamy statute, as well as statutes in the same chapter and related chapters of the Utah Code, it is clear that the Legislature intended "marry" to be construed to include marriages that are not state-sanctioned. * * * Specifically, the bigamy statute does not require a party to enter into a second marriage (however defined) to run afoul of the statute; cohabitation alone would constitute bigamy pursuant to the statute's terms.

* * *

Third, although we need not look at other interpretive tools when the meaning of the statute is plain, our construction of "marry" is supported by the legislative history and purpose of the bigamy statute. * * * [T]he well-documented legislative history of this State's attempts to prevent the formation of polygamous unions supports our conclusion that the bigamy statute was intended to criminalize both attempts to gain legal recognition of duplicative marital relationships and attempts to form duplicative marital relationships that are not legally recognized. This court has previously recognized that the legislative purpose of the bigamy statute was to prevent "all the indicia of marriage repeated more than once." *State v. Green*, 99 P.3d 820 (Utah 2004). In *Green*, we allowed an unsolemnized marriage to serve as a predicate marriage for purposes of a bigamy prosecution. If an unlicensed, unsolemnized union can serve as the predicate marriage for a bigamy prosecution, we are constrained to conclude that an unlicensed, solemnized marriage can serve as a subsequent marriage that violates the bigamy statute.

* * *

Applying the definition of "marry" outlined above to the facts presented in this case, there can be no doubt that Holm purported to marry Stubbs. * * *

* * *

* * * The crux of marriage in our society, perhaps especially a religious marriage, is not so much the license as the solemnization, viewed in its broadest terms as the steps, whether ritualistic or not, by which two individuals commit themselves to undertake a marital relationship. Certainly Holm, as a result of his ceremony with Stubbs, would not be entitled to any legal benefits attendant to a state-sanctioned marriage, but there is no language in the bigamy statute that implies that the presence of or desire for such benefits should be determinative of whether bigamy has been committed. Holm, by responding in the affirmative to the question placed to him by his religious leader, committed himself to undertake all the obligations of a marital relationship. The fact that the State of Utah was not invited to register or record that commitment does not change the reality that Holm and Stubbs formed a marital bond and commenced a marital relationship. The presence or absence of a state license does not alter that bond or the gravity of the commitments made by Holm and Stubbs.

Accordingly, we hold that Holm's behavior is within the ambit of our bigamy statute's "purports to marry" prong.[7] Having so concluded, we

---

7. Because we conclude that Holm's behavior violates the "purports to marry" prong of the bigamy statute, we need not reach Holm's arguments relating to the validity of the cohabitation prong. As indicated above, the jury convicted Holm under both prongs of the bigamy statute, and if, as we conclude, Holm was properly convicted pursuant to the "purports to marry" prong of the bigamy statute, it is of no consequence whether the cohabitation prong was properly applied to him.

now turn to Holm's arguments attacking the constitutional legitimacy of his bigamy conviction. * * *

B. The Utah Constitution Does Not Shield Holm's Polygamous Behavior from State Prosecution

It is ironic indeed that Holm comes before this court arguing that the Utah Constitution, despite its express prohibition of polygamous marriage, actually provides greater protection to polygamous behavior than the federal constitution, which contains no such express prohibition. * * *

* * *

* * * [T]he Utah Constitution offers no protection to polygamous behavior and, in fact, shows antipathy towards it by expressly prohibiting such behavior. Specifically, article III, section 1, entitled "Religious toleration-Polygamy forbidden," states as follows: "First:—Perfect toleration of religious sentiment is guaranteed. No inhabitant of this State shall ever be molested in person or property on account of his or her mode of religious worship; but polygamous or plural marriages are forever prohibited." This language, known commonly as the "irrevocable ordinance," unambiguously removes polygamy from the realm of protected free exercise of religion. * * *

* * *

C. Holm's Conviction Does Not Offend the Federal Constitution

* * *

Although the United States Supreme Court, in *Reynolds v. United States*, 98 U.S. 145 (1879), upheld the criminal prosecution of a religiously motivated polygamist as nonviolative of the Free Exercise Clause, Holm contends on appeal that his federal free exercise right is unduly infringed upon by his conviction in this case. Holm argues that *Reynolds* is "nothing more than a hollow relic of bygone days of fear, prejudice, and Victorian morality," and that modern free exercise jurisprudence dictates that no criminal penalty can be imposed for engaging in religiously motivated polygamy. * * *

As we pointed out in *Green, Reynolds*, despite its age, has never been overruled by the United States Supreme Court and, in fact, has been cited by the Court with approval in several modern free exercise cases, signaling its continuing vitality. * * * As we noted in *Green*, the United States Supreme Court held in *Employment Division, Department of Human Resources v. Smith*, 494 U.S. 872 (1990), that a state may, even without furthering a compelling state interest, burden an individual's right to free exercise so long as the burden is imposed by a neutral law of general applicability. * * * In *Green*, we concluded that Utah's bigamy statute is a neutral law of general applicability and that any infringement upon the free exercise of religion occasioned by that law's application is constitutionally permissible.

* * *

Holm [further] argues that the State of Utah is foreclosed from criminalizing polygamous behavior because the freedom to engage in such behavior is a fundamental liberty interest * * * .

In arguing that his behavior is constitutionally protected as a fundamental liberty interest, Holm relies primarily on the United States Supreme Court's decision in *Lawrence v. Texas*, 539 U.S. 558 (2003). In that case, the United States Supreme Court struck down a Texas statute criminalizing homosexual sodomy, concluding that private, consensual sexual behavior is protected by the Due Process Clause of the Fourteenth Amendment. Holm argues that the liberty interest discussed in *Lawrence* is sufficiently broad to shield the type of behavior that he engages in from the intruding hand of the state. Holm misconstrues the breadth of the *Lawrence* opinion.

Despite its use of seemingly sweeping language, the holding in *Lawrence* is actually quite narrow. Specifically, the Court takes pains to limit the opinion's reach to decriminalizing private and intimate acts engaged in by consenting adult gays and lesbians. In fact, the Court went out of its way to exclude from protection conduct that causes "injury to a person or abuse of an institution the law protects." * * *

In marked contrast to the situation presented to the Court in *Lawrence*, this case implicates the public institution of marriage, an institution the law protects, and also involves a minor. In other words, this case presents the exact conduct identified by the Supreme Court in *Lawrence* as outside the scope of its holding.

* * * [T]he behavior at issue in this case is not confined to personal decisions made about sexual activity, but rather raises important questions about the State's ability to regulate marital relationships and prevent the formation and propagation of marital forms that the citizens of the State deem harmful.

* * *

The dissent states quite categorically that the State of Utah has no interest in the commencement of an intimate personal relationship so long as the participants do not present their relationship as being state-sanctioned. On the contrary, the formation of relationships that are marital in nature is of great interest to this State, no matter what the participants in or the observers of that relationship venture to name the union. * * *

* * *

* * * [M]arital relationships serve as the building blocks of our society. The State must be able to assert some level of control over those relationships to ensure the smooth operation of laws and further the proliferation of social unions our society deems beneficial while discouraging those deemed harmful. The people of this State have declared monogamy a beneficial marital form and have also declared polygamous relationships harmful. As the Tenth Circuit stated in [*Potter v. Murray City*, 760 F.2d 1065, 1070 (10th Cir. 1985)], Utah "is justified, by a compelling interest, in upholding and enforcing its ban on plural marriage to protect the monogamous marriage relationship."

Further, this case features another critical distinction from *Lawrence*; namely, the involvement of a minor. Stubbs was sixteen years old at the time of her betrothal, and evidence adduced at trial indicated that she and Holm regularly engaged in sexual activity. Further, it is not unreasonable to conclude that this case involves behavior that warrants inquiry into the possible existence of injury and the validity of consent. *See, e.g., Green*, 99 P.3d 820 ("The practice of polygamy ... often coincides with crimes targeting women and children. Crimes not unusually attendant to the practice of polygamy include incest, sexual assault, statutory rape, and failure to pay child support.").

Given the above, we conclude that *Lawrence* does not prevent our Legislature from prohibiting polygamous behavior. * * *

* * *

* * * Accordingly, we affirm the judgment of the trial court.

DURHAM, CHIEF JUSTICE, concurring in part and dissenting in part:

I join the majority in upholding Holm's conviction for unlawful sexual conduct with a minor. As to the remainder of its analysis, I respectfully dissent. * * *

The majority upholds Holm's criminal bigamy conviction based solely on his participation in a private religious ceremony because the form of that ceremony—though not its intent—resembled what we think of as a wedding, a ritual that serves to solemnize lawful marriages and in which the parties formally undertake the legal rights, obligations, and duties that belong to that state-approved institution. In resting its conclusion on that basis, the majority, in my view, ignores the legislature's intent that the concept of marriage in Utah law be confined to a legally recognized union. I also believe that the majority's reasoning fails to distinguish between conduct that has public import of a sort that the state may legitimately regulate and conduct of the most private nature.

* * *

I. INTERPRETATION OF "PURPORTS TO MARRY" IN SECTION 76–7–101

The majority concludes that Holm may be found guilty of "purport[ing] to marry another person" while already having a wife because he entered a religious union with Ruth Stubbs that the two of them referred to as a "marriage," even though neither believed, represented, or intended

that the union would have the legal status of a state-sanctioned marriage.
* * *

* * *

I do not believe it is appropriate to interpret the term "marry" when it appears in a state statute as providing what is essentially an anthropological description of human relationships. To do so is to ignore the fact that the law of our state and our nation has traditionally viewed marriage as denoting a legal status as well as a private bond.

* * *

As for the "cohabits" prong of section 76–7–101, the majority fails to explain why the breadth of that provision should conclusively determine our interpretation of the parallel "purports to marry" prong. I perceive no justification for judicial speculation that the legislature intended a uniquely "expansive definition" of "marry" in section 76–7–101, especially given the legislature's express statement to the contrary in another Utah Code provision, section 30–1–4.1. That provision explains that Utah "recognize[s] as marriage only the legal union of a man and a woman as provided in this chapter." As a matter of simple grammatical extrapolation, if only a "legal union of a man and a woman" is "marriage," then "purporting to marry," must be purporting to enter into such a legal union.

* * *

The majority claims that "[t]he crux of marriage in our society, perhaps especially a religious marriage, is not so much the license as the solemnization" * * * . It is apparent that the majority wishes to emphasize the importance of the private commitment between two partners who pledge to each other lifelong love, companionship, and support. The majority also alludes to the sanctification such a commitment receives when the partners participate in a religious ceremony in accord with their faith. Undoubtedly, a couple may feel it is their commitment before God that gives their relationship its legitimacy or permanence. However, it is beyond dispute that such private commitments alone, even when made before God, do not constitute "marriage" in our state or in our legal system. * * *

* * *

I next address the majority's treatment of Holm's state and federal constitutional claims and explain why I consider Holm's conviction for engaging in private religiously motivated conduct unconstitutional.

II. STATE CONSTITUTIONAL CLAIMS

* * *

B. Religious Freedom Claim

Holm essentially argues that the State may not subject him to a criminal penalty under a generally applicable criminal law for his religiously motivated practice of polygamy because imposing that penalty is inconsistent with our constitution's protection of religious freedom. The State does not dispute the sincerity of Holm's religious motivation * * * . * * *

* * *

* * * I believe that governmental burdens on religiously motivated conduct should be subject to heightened scrutiny * * * .

* * *

Applying heightened scrutiny, I conclude that imposing criminal penalties on Holm's religiously motivated entry into a religious union with Ruth Stubbs is an unconstitutional burden under our constitution's religious freedom protections. * * * I do not believe that any of the strong state interests normally served by the Utah bigamy law require that the law apply to the religiously motivated conduct at issue here—entering a religious union with more than one woman.

* * *

* * * [T]he State has emphasized its interest in "protecting" monogamous marriage as a social institution. I agree that the state has an important interest in regulating marriage, but only insofar as marriage is understood as a legal status. In my view, the criminal bigamy statute protects marriage, as a legal union, by criminalizing the act of purporting to enter a second legal union. Such an act defrauds the state and perhaps an innocent spouse or purported partner. It also completely disregards the network of laws that regulate entry into, and the dissolution of, the legal status of marriage, and that limit to one the number of partners with which an individual may enjoy this status. The same harm is targeted by criminalizing the act of cohabiting with a partner after purportedly entering a second legal marriage with that partner.

However, I do not believe the state's interest extends to those who enter a religious union with a second person but who do not claim to be legally married. For one thing, the cohabitation of unmarried couples, who live together "as if" they are married in the sense that they share a household and a sexually intimate relationship, is commonplace in contemporary society. Even outside the community of those who practice polygamy for religious reasons, such cohabitation may occur where one person is legally married to someone other than the person with whom he or she is cohabiting. Yet parties to such relationships are not prosecuted under the criminal bigamy statute, the criminal fornication statute, or, as far as I am aware, the criminal adultery statute, even where their conduct violates these laws.

* * *

The second state interest served by the bigamy law, as recognized in *Green*, is in preventing "marriage fraud," whereby an already-married individual fraudulently purports to enter a legal marriage with someone else, "or attempts to procure government benefits associated with marital status." * * * This interest is simply not implicated here, where no claim to the legal status of marriage has been made.

In *Green*, the court cited "protecting vulnerable individuals from exploitation and abuse" as the third state interest served by the bigamy statute. The court concluded that this was a legitimate state interest to which the criminal bigamy statute was rationally related * * * . The court rested this conclusion on the idea that perpetrators of other crimes "not unusually attendant to the practice of polygamy"—such as "incest, sexual assault, statutory rape, and failure to pay child support"—could be prosecuted for bigamy in the absence of sufficient evidence to support a conviction on these other charges. * * * [R]eviewing this assessment in light of the heightened scrutiny I believe is called for here, I cannot conclude that the restriction that the bigamy law places on the religious freedom of all those who, for religious reasons, live with more than one woman is necessary to further the state's interest in this regard. * * * The State has provided no evidence of a causal relationship or even a strong correlation between the practice of polygamy, whether religiously motivated or not, and the offenses of "incest, sexual assault, statutory rape, and failure to pay child support," cited in *Green*. Moreover, even assuming such a correlation did exist, neither the record nor the recent history of prosecutions of alleged polygamists warrants the conclusion that section 76–7–101 is a necessary tool for the state's attacks on such harms. * * *

* * *

* * * The State of Utah has criminal laws punishing incest, rape, unlawful sexual conduct with a minor, and domestic and child abuse. Any restrictions these laws place on the practice of religious polygamy are almost certainly justified. However, the broad criminalization of the religious practice itself as a means of attacking other criminal behavior is not.

* * *

III. FOURTEENTH AMENDMENT DUE PROCESS CLAIM

* * * [T]he Court in *Lawrence* stated the principle that "absent injury to a person or abuse of an institution the law protects," adults are free to choose the nature of their relationships "in the confines of their homes and their own private lives." The majority concludes that the private consensual behavior of two individuals who did not claim legal recognition of their relationship somehow constitutes an abuse of the institution of marriage, thus rendering *Lawrence* inapplicable. On that

basis, the majority summarily rejects Holm's due process claim as beyond the scope of *Lawrence*'s holding. I disagree with this analysis.

* * *

The majority also offers the view that "[t]he state must be able to . . . further the proliferation of social unions our society deems beneficial while discouraging those deemed harmful." The Supreme Court in *Lawrence*, however, rejected the very notion that a state can criminalize behavior merely because the majority of its citizens prefers a different form of personal relationship. * * *

* * *

The majority does not adequately explain how the institution of marriage is abused or state support for monogamy threatened simply by an individual's choice to participate in a religious ritual with more than one person outside the confines of legal marriage. Rather than offering such an explanation, the majority merely proclaims that "the public nature of polygamists' attempts to extralegally redefine the acceptable parameters of a fundamental social institution like marriage is plain." It is far from plain to me.

I am concerned that the majority's reasoning may give the impression that the state is free to criminalize any and all forms of personal relationships that occur outside the legal union of marriage. While under *Lawrence* laws criminalizing isolated acts of sodomy are void, the majority seems to suggest that the relationships within which these acts occur may still receive criminal sanction. Following such logic, nonmarital cohabitation might also be considered to fall outside the scope of federal constitutional protection. Indeed, the act of living alone and unmarried could as easily be viewed as threatening social norms.

In my view, any such conclusions are foreclosed under *Lawrence*. Essentially, the Court's decision in *Lawrence* simply reformulates the longstanding principle that, in order to "secure individual liberty, . . . certain kinds of highly personal relationships" must be given "a substantial measure of sanctuary from unjustified interference by the State." *Roberts v. U.S. Jaycees*, 468 U.S. 609, 618 (1984). Whether referred to as a right of "intimate" or "intrinsic" association, as in *Roberts*, a right to "privacy," as in *Griswold v. Connecticut*, 381 U.S. 479, 485 (1965), a right to make "choices concerning family living arrangements," as in *Moore v. City of East Cleveland*, 431 U.S. 494, 499 (1977) (plurality), or a right to choose the nature of one's personal relationships, as in *Lawrence*, this individual liberty guarantee essentially draws a line around an individual's home and family and prevents governmental interference with what happens inside, as long as it does not involve injury or coercion or some other form of harm to individuals or to society. * * *

* * *

* * * I agree with the majority that because Holm's conduct in this case involved a minor, he is unable to prevail on his individual liberty claim under the Due Process Clause. However, I disagree with the majority's implication that the same result would apply where an individual enters a private relationship with another adult.

* * *

[Concurring opinion of NEHRING, J., omitted.]

NOTES AND QUESTIONS

1. *The Free Exercise claim. Reynolds* grounded its rejection of the Free Exercise claim in part on a distinction between religious belief (which the Court conceded was protected by the Constitution) and religiously motivated conduct (which the Court held was outside the scope of Free Exercise protection). Subsequent Supreme Court decisions abandoned the belief-action distinction. In *Wisconsin v. Yoder*, 406 U.S. 205 (1972), for example, the Court found that the Free Exercise Clause protected the religiously motivated decision of Amish parents to educate their children at home notwithstanding a state law requiring education in a state-approved school. *Yoder*'s implications for *Reynolds* were blunted, however, by the Court's later decision in *Employment Division v. Smith*, 494 U.S. 872 (1990), which upheld the state's power to punish drug use without regard for the sincere religious motivations of the user. Citing *Reynolds, Smith* held that "neutral, generally applicable laws may be applied to religious practices even when not supported by a compelling governmental interest," so long as the laws are not meant to target religion specifically. *City of Boerne v. Flores*, 521 U.S. 507, 514 (1997). Given the close historical association of anti-polygamy laws in Utah with overt hostility to the Mormon Church, is *Holm* correct to regard the state's bigamy laws as religiously "neutral" and therefore subject only to rational-basis review under the Free Exercise Clause? Moreover, *Smith* suggested that even neutral laws might be subject to more searching scrutiny if they burdened both religious exercise and another fundamental constitutional right, presenting a so-called "hybrid" constitutional claim. Should religiously motivated polygamy trigger heightened scrutiny on the ground that it involves a hybrid of Free Exercise rights and the fundamental right to marry? *See* Mark Strasser, *Marriage, Free Exercise, and the Constitution*, 26 L. & Inequality 59, 87 (2008) (concluding on this basis that "even under *Smith*, many polygamy bans would be appropriately subjected to strict scrutiny").

2. *The privacy claim.* Concurring separately in *Zablocki v. Redhail, supra,* Justices Stewart and Powell each stated that laws banning polygamy should be considered constitutional without triggering heightened scrutiny. The "principled means" by which Justice Powell would place polygamy outside the scope of the fundamental right to marry is the notion of "deeply rooted" social consensus: because society has not long and widely regarded polygamy as a fundamental liberty, it warrants no special protection under substantive due process. Is this limiting principle still viable after *Lawrence v. Texas*? On what basis, besides tradition and popular morality, might polygamy be distinguished from monogamous marriage?

3. *Criminal and civil prohibitions against polygamy.* States typically have both criminal and civil prohibitions against polygamy. *Holm* involved a felony prosecution for bigamy, while civil law classifies bigamous marriages as void. Chief Justice Durham's dissent suggests that consenting adults might have a fundamental constitutional right to cohabit in a self-described polygamous "marriage" as long as the participants made no claim to legal recognition of their union. But she appears to accept that states may withhold legal recognition from such relationships (and even prosecute those who do seek recognition). In *Bronson v. Swensen*, 500 F.3d 1099 (10th Cir. 2007), a married couple and another female partner—all consenting adults—challenged a county clerk's refusal to issue a marriage license for their intended plural marriage. The Tenth Circuit avoided a decision on the merits, ruling that the plaintiffs had "forfeited any argument that Utah's refusal to give civil recognition to polygamous marriages is unconstitutional" by failing to brief it adequately. *Id.* at 1105. What result in a properly presented case? What state interests justify the civil bar against such marriages?

4. *The analogy to same-sex marriage.* Was *Holm* correct that *Lawrence* provides no support for a fundamental privacy right to polygamous marriage? If the Constitution is ultimately construed to recognize a fundamental right to same-sex marriage, is there a principled basis for distinguishing polygamous marriage? In recognizing a right to same-sex marriage under the Massachusetts constitution, *Goodridge* made clear that it would find no similar protection for polygamous marriage, but why not?

After reviewing the history of public campaigns against polygamy and evidence about life within contemporary polygamous families, Professor David Chambers considered several possible bases for distinguishing polygamy from same-sex marriage:

> * * * Andrew Sullivan offers as the principal distinction between polygamy and same-sex marriage: "Almost everyone seems to accept, even if they find homosexuality morally troublesome, that it occupies a deeper level of human consciousness than a polygamous impulse." * * *

> Sullivan's reasoning is unsatisfying as a basis for distinguishing polygamous marriages. * * * [S]upporters of gay marriage are simply wrong to claim that gay peoples' need for a union with another person of the same sex is more compelling than the needs of others who already have a spouse and who want to add a second or a third. History suggests that, for many Mormons, the desire to take an additional spouse grows out of deeply held beliefs central to their conceptions of themselves and their purposes in life. * * *

> William Eskridge, another advocate of same-sex marriage, relies on other grounds for claiming that the case for same-sex marriage is superior to the case for polygamy. Drawing on the writings of Richard Posner, he argues that polygamy can lead to harms that society has a legitimate interest in preventing. If people could take more than one spouse, "the central goals of marriage, namely, its companionate and social insurance features, would be compromised." He speculates that "the intensity of [the] emotional bond" between the husband and any of his plural wives would be diminished, and that serious rivalries and tensions would likely

result. Moreover, he claims that polygamy may promote an authoritarian, male-dominated hierarchy within the marital relationship, thereby undermining "the companionate goal of marriage [and] contribut[ing] to gender inequality."

* * *

Like Sullivan, Eskridge makes his point without examining the actual reported experiences of polygamous families in this country. * * * To my reading, the actual experiences of American men and women in plural marriages seems more complex and less sinister than * * * Eskridge imagines them. Many people in plural marriages find temporal and religious satisfactions that greatly outweigh their disadvantages.

David L. Chambers, *Polygamy and Same–Sex Marriage*, 26 Hofstra L. Rev. 53, 79–81 (1997).

Professor Susan Frelich Appleton points out that refocusing the constitutional argument for same-sex marriage toward a claim of sex discrimination, rather than one grounded in the right to marry under substantive due process, might spare "same-sex marriage proponents [the need to] * * * distinguish opponents' red herring, an asserted right to polygamous or incestuous unions * * *." Susan Frelich Appleton, *Missing in Action? Searching for Gender Talk in the Same–Sex Marriage Debate*, 16 Stan. L. & Pol'y Rev. 97, 103 (2005). Does this approach solve the "red herring" problem?

5. *How strong are the state interests in monogamy?* Are the public concerns recounted by Professor Chambers, or cited in *Holm*, strong enough to justify withholding marriage from polygamous families? Should any of these concerns qualify as "compelling" under strict scrutiny? The attempted marriage in *Bronson* appeared to involve consenting adults; at least one of the marriages in *Green*, the Utah case cited in *Holm*, involved a 13–year–old girl. What difference, if any, is there if the plural wives are underage when the marriage commences? If some of the wives are related to one another? Mother and daughter?

Even if states have a compelling interest in preventing exploitation of women and children, is a blanket ban on polygamous marriage narrowly tailored to that goal? Professor Elizabeth Emens observes that, whatever one thinks of the polygamy practiced by Rodney Holm, some adults form enduring, consensual relationships with more than one partner in circumstances that are free from coercion or exploitation. "Contrary to the common view of multiparty relationships as either oppressive or sexual free-for-alls," she writes, "at least some set of individuals—polyamorists, or 'polys' for short—seems to be practicing nonmonogamy as part of an ethical practice that shares some of its aspirations with more mainstream models of intimate relationships." Elizabeth F. Emens, *Monogamy's Law: Compulsory Monogamy and Polyamorous Existence*, 29 N.Y.U. Rev. L. & Soc. Change 277, 283 (2004). What state interest justifies withholding marriage from such persons? Child abuse laws, of course, might address directly any concerns with predation on children. And, as Professor Chambers points out, society's concern for exploitation of women is arguably qualified given that society makes no effort to withhold marriage from "large numbers of conservative Christians, Muslims, and Jews in monogamous marriages in the United States today [who] accept a view of wives as subordinate to their husbands." Chambers, *supra*, at 82.

Finally, is it defensible to prosecute polygamists while tolerating multiple-partner intimacy outside of marriage and the increasingly common practice of "serial monogamy," in which persons marry multiple partners in succession? Professor Jonathan Turley writes:

> [S]omeone such as singer Britney Spears can have multiple husbands so long as they are consecutive, not concurrent. Thus, Spears can marry and divorce men in quick succession and become the maven of tabloid covers. Yet if she marries two of the men for life, she will become the matron of a state prison.

Jonathan Turley, *Polygamy Laws Expose Our Own Hypocrisy*, USA Today, Oct. 4, 2004, at 13A. Is Professor Turley right that "[t]he difference between a polygamist and the follower of an 'alternative lifestyle' is often [nothing more than] religion"?

PROBLEM 3–1

John and Mary Jones "married" two years ago even though (unbeknownst to Mary) John has never been divorced from his first wife, who is still alive. Last month, John was indicted for a felony. The spousal testimonial privilege provides that one spouse may not testify for or against the other spouse without the other spouse's consent. John refuses to give his consent. May John prevent Mary from testifying?

SECTION 4: INCESTUOUS MARRIAGE

Incest has been prohibited in every U.S. jurisdiction since colonial times. Sexual relations between two persons sharing a sufficiently close family relationship is punishable as a crime, although three states (Ohio, New Jersey and Rhode Island) have no criminal prohibition for consensual contact between adults. *See* Jennifer M. Collins, Ethan J. Leib & Dan Markel, *Punishing Family Status*, 88 B.U. L. Rev. 1327, 1343 & n.83 (2008). The civil law also sanctions incest by denying marriage to such persons. There is no universal agreement among the states about which family relationships qualify as sufficiently close to trigger the incest bar, and the definition of incest sometimes varies within a single jurisdiction depending upon whether the statute provides for criminal or civil sanctions. *See id.* at 1343–44; Leigh B. Bienen, *Defining Incest*, 92 Nw. U. L. Rev. 1501 (1998).

At the core, the crime of incest in all states includes marriage between certain close family members—including parent and child, grandparent and grandchild, and between siblings. Moving outward from that core, however, more variation appears. Many, but not all, states treat relations by affinity (*i.e.*, by marriage) the same as relations by consanguinity (*i.e.*, by blood)—so that marriage would be denied, for instance, to a step-father and step-daughter. Likewise, most states treat relations created by adoption in the same manner as those created by blood—so that marriage would be denied, for instance, to adoptive siblings. For example, the Missouri criminal incest statute provides that "[a] person commits the crime of incest if he marries or purports to marry or engages in sexual intercourse or deviate sexual intercourse with a person he knows to be, without regard to legitimacy: (1) His ancestor or descendant by blood or adoption; or (2) His stepchild, while the marriage creating that relationship exists; or (3) His brother or sister of the whole or half-blood; or (4) His uncle, aunt, nephew or niece of the whole blood." Mo. Ann. Stat. § 568.020(1) (2004).

When it comes to marriage of first cousins, the states are split nearly evenly. Not quite half prohibit such marriages in all circumstances; a handful prohibit them but make exceptions for marriages between cousins incapable of procreation; and a substantial minority allow first-cousin marriages without restriction. Missouri legislates, in a civil domestic relations statute, that all attempted marriage between "parents and children, including grandparents and grandchildren of every degree, between brothers and sisters of the half as well as the whole blood, between uncles and nieces, aunts and nephews, first cousins" are "presumptively void," thereby going beyond the reach of the criminal prohibition to prohibit marriages between first cousins as well. *Id.* § 451.020.

The following decision, *Smith v. State*, considers the public interests justifying incest laws. It does so in the context of a criminal prosecution of an uncle-niece relationship close to the core of the incest prohibition. As you read it, consider whether the interests it relies upon are sufficient to support incest regulations—both criminal and civil—closer to the periphery of the taboo, such as a marriage of first cousins. Also, note that *Smith* was decided before *Lawrence v. Texas*, 539 U.S. 558 (2003), held unconstitutional a criminal ban on same-sex sodomy. Does *Lawrence* now require a stronger justification of traditional incest laws?

SMITH v. STATE

Court of Criminal Appeals of Tennessee, 1999.
6 S.W.3d 512.

Hayes, Judge.

* * *

On March 13, 1997, the appellant entered a guilty plea to one count of incest[1] and was sentenced to three years supervised probation. [She was

---

1. The indictment charged and it is not disputed that the appellant was involved in an incestuous relationship with her paternal uncle. The appellant does not deny this relationship. We are able to glean from the sparse record before us that the incestuous relationship began while the appellant was still a minor and continued into her majority. Her uncle was in his mid-thirties when the relationship began. No children were born as a result of this relationship. The appellant's brief indicates that she suffers from various psychological disorders and was eighteen years old when charged with this offense.

subsequently sentenced to prison when she violated the conditions of her probation]. * * *

* * *

* * * [A]ppellant's sole assignment of error is whether [Tennessee's criminal incest statute] is unconstitutional under the protections provided by the Constitution of the State of Tennessee. Specifically, the appellant relies upon the Court of Appeals decision in *Campbell v. Sundquist,* 926 S.W.2d 250, 262 (Tenn. App.), *perm. to appeal denied,* (Tenn. 1996) (finding the Homosexual Practices Act unconstitutional), for the proposition that "an adult's right to engage in consensual and noncommercial sexual activities in the privacy of that adult's home is a matter of intimate personal concern which is at the heart of Tennessee's protection of the right to privacy."

The right to privacy is addressed within the context of due process guaranties. Protection against infringement of fundamental rights is guaranteed by both the United States and Tennessee Constitutions. When a challenge is made alleging infringement of a fundamental right, "strict scrutiny" of the legislative classification is only required when the classification interferes with the exercise of a "fundamental right" or operates to the peculiar disadvantage of a suspect class. However, if no fundamental right or suspect class is affected, the court must determine whether there is some rational basis to justify a classification set out in a statute. There is no dispute that the challenged statutory provision does not involve a suspect class, thus, our initial determination remains whether the appellant's right to privacy encompasses a guaranteed protected "fundamental right" to engage in incestuous sexual activity.

* * *

* * * It is clear from the precedent established by the Supreme Court that the constitutional right of privacy places limits on a state's right to interfere with a person's most basic decisions regarding family and parenthood.

Notwithstanding the individual rights heretofore recognized as embraced within the right to privacy, there is no general endorsement of an "all-encompassing 'right of privacy.' " * * * Rather, if the right cannot be logically deduced from the text of the Constitution, "the court must look to the traditions and collective conscience of our people to determine whether a principle is so rooted as to be ranked as fundamental." [*Griswold v. Connecticut,* 381 U.S. 479, 493 (1965) (Goldberg, J., concurring in the judgment).] * * *

* * *

Incest is the sexual intercourse or marriage between persons related to each other in any of the degrees of consanguinity or affinity that is prohibited by law.[9] The taboo against incest has been a consistent and

---

9. Tenn. Code Ann. § 39–15–302 provides:

almost universal tradition with recorded proscriptions against incest existing as early as 1750 B.C.[10] The incest taboo has been characterized as one of the most important human cultural developments and is found in some form in all societies. Being primarily cultural in origin, the taboo is neither instinctual nor biological and has little to do with actual blood ties. Anthropologists and sociologists claim the significance of the incest taboo is twofold: (1) the restriction forces family members to go outside their families to find sexual partners, requiring people to pursue relationships outside family boundaries that help form important economic and political alliances, and (2) to maintain the stability of the family hierarchy by protecting young family members from exploitation by older family members in positions of authority and by reducing competition and jealous friction among family members.

Although the ban on incest was widely followed in all societies, incest was not a common law crime in England; rather, punishment was left solely to the ecclesiastical courts. The ecclesiastical courts followed the interdiction of Levitical law which prohibited marriages between persons more closely related than fourth cousins unless a dispensation was procured from the Church of Rome; no distinction was made between persons related by affinity or consanguinity. In 1540, after England's separation from the Church of Rome, legislation was enacted to correct "an unjust law of the bishop of Rome" relating to the degrees in which marriages were permitted. The revised statutes limited prohibitions against marriage to relatives closer than first cousins. The ecclesiastical courts proclaimed the statute to be a return to "God's law."

The English tradition prohibiting incest within certain degrees was adopted by the American colonists. American jurisprudence, however, deviated from the ecclesiastical law in two respects: the majority of American jurisdictions extended the proscriptions beyond that of first cousins while others only imposed criminal penalties where the relationship was consanguineous. Specific to our concern, Tennessee has traditionally recognized the proscription against incest as a punishable offense. *See, e.g.*, Ch. 23, Section 18, Code of Tennessee (1829). The proscription continues as evidenced by today's challenged statutory provision. Regardless of the manner of the proscription, the crime of incest is governed by specific statutes in every American jurisdiction. There is nothing to suggest a movement away from the historical treatment of incest; Tennessee, as other states, continues to condemn it as a grave public wrong.

"(a) A person commits incest who engages in sexual penetration as defined in § 39–13–501, with a person, knowing such person to be, without regard to legitimacy:

(1) The person's natural parent, child, grandparent, grandchild, uncle, aunt, nephew, niece, stepparent, stepchild, adoptive parent, adoptive child; or

(2) The person's brother or sister of the whole or half-blood or by adoption."

10. Discovered in 1901, the Code of Hammurabi, a Babylonian king, punished the incestuous relationship between mother and son by burning of both parties at the stake. See Sara Robbins, Law: A Treasury of Art and Literature 20–22 (1990).

To conclude that there exists a "fundamental right" to engage in an incestuous relationship, this court would be called upon to contradict centuries of legal doctrine and practice[,] which this court declines to do. The evidence is plain; the incest taboo is deeply rooted in Anglo–American history and traditions. Although one does have a general right to privacy, this right does not, by itself, warrant the sweeping conclusion that all intimate and personal decisions are so protected. Accordingly, we are led to conclude that the asserted "right" to participate in adult consensual incest is not a fundamental liberty interest protected by the Tennessee Constitution.

In the absence of a fundamental right, a rational basis test is used to examine the statute's constitutional validity. A legislative enactment will be deemed valid if it bears a real and substantial relationship to the public's health, safety, morals or general welfare and it is neither unreasonable nor arbitrary.

There is little doubt that the prohibition against incest is directly reflective of the moral concerns of our society. Some argument has been made that this is an inadequate rationale to support the ban. The law, however, is constantly based on notions of morality, and if all laws representing essentially moral choices are to be invalidated, the courts would be very busy. *Bowers v. Hardwick,* 478 U.S. at 196. * * * [C]riminal statutes prohibiting incestuous relationships reflect the belief that incest is a wrong against the public largely because of its potential to destabilize the family, traditionally regarded as society's most important unit.

* * *

The prohibition against incest is aimed at the protection of children and of the family unit. Society is concerned with the integrity of the family because society cannot function in an orderly manner when age distinctions, generations, sentiments, and roles in families are in conflict. The state has a legitimate and rationally based objective in prohibiting sexual relations between those related within the proscribed degrees of kinship to promote domestic peace and purity. We conclude that the state, in the exercise of its legislative function, may legitimately proscribe against acts which threaten public order and decency, including prohibitions against interfamilia[l] sexual relations. Our pronouncements of these principles are consistent with and not contrary to deeply rooted traditions. We, therefore, hold that Tenn. Code Ann. § 39–15–302 does not violate the Constitution of the State of Tennessee.

* * *

NOTES AND QUESTIONS

1. *The impact of* Lawrence v. Texas. *Smith* relies directly on *Bowers v. Hardwick* for two propositions: first, that traditional social consensus defines the scope of fundamental privacy rights, so that traditional penalties for

incest are subject only to rational-basis review; and, second, in applying rationality review, that the state's interest in enforcing popular notions of morality provides a sufficient basis for incest prohibitions. Do these premises require reconsideration after *Lawrence v. Texas*? If Texas may not criminalize private, consensual sexual conduct between two persons of the same sex, on what basis may Tennessee punish appellant Smith? *See* Courtney Megan Cahill, *Same–Sex Marriage, Slippery Slope Rhetoric, and the Politics of Disgust: A Critical Perspective on Contemporary Family Discourse and the Incest Taboo*, 99 Nw. U. L. Rev. 1543, 1549 (2005) (contending that "the emotion of disgust is the only way to comprehend the depth and breadth of the incest taboo"). So far, courts in Tennessee and elsewhere have rejected the suggestion that *Lawrence* protects incestuous relations. *See, e.g., Beard v. State*, 2005 WL 1334378, at *2 (Tenn. Ct. Crim. App. June 7, 2005) (concluding that "the *Lawrence* decision in no way alters our holding in *Smith*"); *State v. Freeman*, 801 N.E.2d 906, 909 (Ohio Ct. App. 2003) ("In the case of incest, as opposed to a consensual homosexual relationship, there is injury to persons. * * * Additionally, the state has a legitimate interest in preventing incest: protecting the family unit. The same cannot be said for homosexual relationships.").

In *Muth v. Frank*, 412 F.3d 808 (7th Cir. 2005), the Seventh Circuit held that *Lawrence* provided no basis for overturning the incest conviction of a man who had married his adult sister. The two had apparently obtained a marriage license without revealing their familial relationship, which later came to light during neglect proceedings involving one of their children. The state then terminated their parental rights based on their incestuous relationship and later prosecuted them for incest. The brother was sentenced to eight years in prison and his sister (and wife) received five years in prison. *Lawrence*, the court wrote, "did not announce * * * a fundamental right, protected by the Constitution, for adults to engage in all manner of consensual sexual conduct, specifically in this case, incest." *Id.* at 817.

Smith and *Freeman* involved incestuous relationships that began when one of the parties was a minor; the brother and sister in *Muth* met when the sister, who had spent her childhood in foster care, was 18 years old. Can concerns over intrafamilial sexual exploitation justify statutes punishing the *minor*, who is the object of the law's concern and who, as a matter of law, is incapable of consenting to sexual activity or being a party to a contract? (Note that in *Smith* and *Muth*, the state convicted and incarcerated even the younger participants who would have been the victims of any exploitation.)

Would punishment be justified in the case of a relationship that, at all times, involved genuine consent by the adult participants? In 2005, Michigan prosecutors brought charges against a 46–year–old man and his 24–year–old daughter for engaging in what police, prosecutors and the parties involved described as a consensual relationship. In fact, the woman had not known her father until they met when she was an adult; they later moved in together and had a child. Christy Arboscello, *Father, Daughter Face Incest Charge*, Detroit Free Press, Dec. 9, 2005, at 6. Sustaining the conviction of a father for incest involving his 18–year–old daughter, a California appeals court distinguished *Lawrence* based on doubts about the validity of consent in cases involving even adult daughters and fathers. *See People v. Scott*, 68 Cal.Rptr.3d

592, 595 (Ct. App. 2007) (noting that *Lawrence*, by its own terms, did not apply to cases involving " 'persons who might be injured or coerced or who are situated in relationships where consent might not easily be refused,' " and that "[t]his aptly describes adult daughters, who are typically in positions of vulnerability vis-à-vis their older, and thus more authoritative fathers, 'in matters pertaining to sex' ").

Professor Brett McDonnell, examining the various incest prohibitions after *Lawrence*, concludes:

> The core of incest statutes—parent/child, sibling, and probably aunts et. al.—would most likely appear safe from *Lawrence*, both because the behavior may not fall within the liberty interest, and because adequate state interests justify such rules (although if strict scrutiny applies, the states might be in a difficult situation even here). Prohibitions on step-parent and step-child sex are harder to justify, but I would guess would still pass muster, for now. Step-siblings and other sorts of step-relations or adoptive relations, though, are harder to justify, and the few remaining prohibitions on cousin incest could also be vulnerable, though only if the courts push *Lawrence* pretty aggressively. Most actual prosecutions for incest involve a father's contact with an under-age daughter, which can clearly still be criminalized under *Lawrence*.

Brett H. McDonnell, *Is Incest Next?*, 10 Cardozo Women's L.J. 337, 354–55 (2004).

2. *Interstate recognition of incestuous marriages.* In most states, an attempted marriage between persons falling within the prohibited class of incest statutes is both a crime and void for all civil purposes. Nevertheless, as discussed in the material on same-sex marriage, the general rule is that a state will recognize as valid a marriage legally contracted in another state, unless recognition would offend very strong public policies of the recognizing state. Consequently, states will sometimes—though not always—recognize the validity of an incestuous marriage legally undertaken elsewhere. *See, e.g., Ghassemi v. Ghassemi*, 998 So.2d 731, 747 (2008) (concluding that "Louisiana does not have a strong public policy against recognizing a marriage between first cousins performed in a state or country where such marriages are valid").

In *Cook v. Cook*, 104 P.3d 857 (Ariz. Ct. App. 2005), two first cousins had legally married in Virginia before moving in 1989 to Arizona, where first-cousin marriage is prohibited. Legislation enacted in Arizona in 1996 directs courts to withhold recognition of incestuous marriages, even if they were legally formed under the law of another state. The court declined to apply that rule to invalidate the Cooks' marriage, reasoning that they had established a "vested right" in their marital status before enactment of the law, but held that the law would apply to married couples who moved to Arizona *after* enactment of the law in 1996. What "strong public policy exceptions" might impel Arizona to treat first-cousin couples arriving after 1996 as unmarried? Indeed, Arizona's policy goes beyond denying marriage recognition; Arizona is one of eight states that criminalizes intercourse or attempted intermarriage between first cousins. *See* Ariz. Rev. Stat. Ann. § 13–3608 (West 2007); McDonnell, *supra*, at 349 & n.80. Does concern for sexual or emotional exploitation within the family warrant laws preventing marriage among cousins? Is it permissible for the state to aggressively extend the incest prohibition to first cousins to inculcate a stronger incest taboo generally, with the ultimate aim of erecting stronger internal curbs against incest closer to the family core, as between siblings for example?

3. *Health risks of incestuous procreation.* It is often said that special risks of genetic defects relating to intrafamily childbearing support laws banning incest. *Smith* downplayed this concern, but it is evidently a significant basis for Arizona's law prohibiting incestuous marriages, which makes an exception for first cousins who are incapable of procreation. Procreation between close relatives indisputably elevates the risk of passing on some medical conditions associated with recessive genes, but the most recent scientific evidence suggests the risks are quite small in pairings of first cousins. *See* Robin Bennet et al., *Genetic Counseling and Screening of Consanguineous Couples and Their Offspring: Recommendations of the National Society of Genetic Counselors*, J. Genetic Counseling 11, 97–118 (2002). Indeed, Professor Sanford Levinson writes, "[t]he standard 'genetic' argument that is often trotted out with regard to adult incest * * * is riddled with holes," and might even be dismissed as "bogus." Sanford Levinson, *Thinking About Polygamy*, 42 San Diego L. Rev. 1049, 1052 (2005). Does the latest evidence suggesting only modest genetic risks warrant rethinking incest laws such as Arizona's?

4. *Application to adoptive and stepfamily relationships.* The Tennessee statute at issue in *Smith*, like the laws in many states, includes parent-child and sibling relationships founded on adoption within the scope of prohibited incestuous relations. The laws are more varied with respect to stepfamily relationships. Stepfamily relations were once broadly included within the scope of incest laws, but many states have since eliminated coverage of step-relations, leaving "a striking lack of consensus" in state law. *See* Margaret M. Mahoney, *A Legal Definition of the Stepfamily: The Example of Incest Regulation*, 8 BYU J. Pub. L. 21, 26 (1993). Where these prohibitions exist, they are clearly not founded on genetic concerns in childbearing. Given the prevalence of stepfamilies in modern society, the effect of incest statutes on step relationships is of more than academic interest.

In *Israel v. Allen*, 577 P.2d 762 (Colo. 1978), the Colorado Supreme Court held that a law prohibiting marriage between adoptive siblings was unconstitutional because it was not rationally related to a legitimate state interest. With genetic concerns absent, the court dismissed the state's asserted concern for avoiding intrafamily rivalries and tensions with the assertion that "it is just as likely that prohibiting marriage between brother and sister related by adoption will result in family discord." *Id.* at 764. Was the Colorado court right to find no rational basis supporting the incest prohibition? What about the state interest in normalizing fully the family relationships created by adoption? As Professor Naomi Cahn writes:

> If incest is a crime between a parent and a child, and if adoption creates one parent-child relationship and disrupts another, then in which relationship are otherwise incestuous acts a crime? Depending on the policy supporting the incest prohibition, states could proscribe two kinds of

relationships: (1) those between adopted parents and children; or (2) those between biological parents and their subsequently adopted children.

Naomi Cahn, *Perfect Substitutes or the Real Thing?*, 52 Duke L.J. 1077, 1139–40 (2003).

When it comes to marriage regulation, are some step or adoptive relationships different from others? Where the marriage act's incest provision prohibits marriage between a man and a woman without specifying whether the prohibition extends to persons related only because of a step or adoptive relationship, should courts construe the prohibition as inapplicable where neither marriage partner created the step or adoptive relationship? For example, should the prohibition be construed as inapplicable to step-siblings after the marriage of one's father and the other's mother? Or to a man and woman who assume the relationship of uncle and aunt after the uncle's brother married the niece's mother? Would state prohibition of these marriages be constitutional? Might these situations differ from, for example, a stepfather's effort to marry his stepdaughter?

5. *"Accidental" incest.* In January 2008, newspapers reported the story of twin siblings who had been adopted into different families at birth but who met years later as adults and, unaware of their genetic ties, fell in love and married one another. According to David Alton, the British legislator who disclosed the tale, "It's a tragedy for the couple who are involved, a terrible tragedy. Everyone's hearts will go out to people caught up quite unwittingly in a case of incest of this kind." Alton, who said he learned of the case from a judge who presided over the annulment of the marriage after the twins discovered their common origin, had used the case to illustrate the need for legislation mandating that children conceived through assisted reproduction be informed of their genetic parents. *See Separated Twins Marry, Then Are Forced to Break Up*, Boston Globe, Jan. 12, 2008. The scenario of the married twins seems wildly improbable, but Professor Naomi Cahn observes that "with more than 40,000 children born from donor eggs and sperm [in 2007], concerns about what is now called 'inadvertent consanguinity' are quite real." Naomi Cahn, *Accidental Incest: Drawing the Line—or the Curtain?—for Reproductive Technology*, 32 Harv. J. Gender & L. 109 (2009). Criminal incest statutes usually provide a defense for persons who were reasonably unaware of the incestuous relationship, but should pairings of adults sharing an unknown genetic connection be considered "incest" that would absolutely create a void marriage under a marriage statute? Would states be justified in limiting the number of children conceived from a single donor in order to reduce incest risks?

PROBLEM 3–2

In 2000, Huck married Wilma in Springfield, Missouri. At the time of their marriage, Huck had sole custody of a 15–year–old son, Sam, and Wilma had sole custody of a 12–year–old daughter, Darla. Six years later, when Darla was 18 years old, Wilma died. If Huck and Darla were now to marry one another in Missouri, what would be the legal implications? If they cohabited without formally marrying, would that change the legal implications? Could

Darla and Sam marry in Missouri? In answering, refer to the Missouri incest statutes discussed on p. 137. Would it affect your answers if Huck had adopted Darla in 2001?

SECTION 5: MINIMUM AGE AT MARRIAGE

To marry, each spouse must be of sufficient age. Most states have statutes prescribing the minimum age for marriage, although the question remains a matter of common law in a few. Most jurisdictions follow a graduated approach to defining the minimum age for marriage, setting the minimum age at 18 years, while allowing minors to marry with parental or judicial consent. *See Roper v. Simmons*, 543 U.S. 551, 585 app. D (2005) (listing minimum age statutes for all 50 states and the District of Columbia). Most states permit a minor who is 16 or 17 years old to marry with approval either from a parent or from a court. Minors under 16 may marry in exceptional cases (generally construed to mean when the girl is pregnant) with approval *both* from a parent *and* from a court. *See, e.g.*, N.J. Stat. Ann. § 37:1–6 (West 2006); Nev. Rev. Stat. § 122.025 (2007).

The obvious premise of the dual-consent requirement for minors under 16 is that as the minor's age diminishes, the state becomes less trusting of the parents' good judgment in the matter. Indeed, at some point, the question melds into one of child abuse, although states disagree on the tipping point. In North Carolina, for instance, more than 200 13–year–olds reportedly were permitted to marry in 1998. *See* Ann Laquer Estin, *Toward a Multicultural Family Law*, 38 Fam. L.Q. 501, 507 n.31 (2004). In New Jersey, on the other hand, parents who applied for court approval to allow their 13–year–old daughter to marry her 19–year–old boyfriend were charged and convicted of child abuse for acquiescing in her sexual relationship. *See New Jersey Div. of Youth & Fam. Servs. v. RW*, 641 A.2d 1124 (N.J. Super. Ct. 1994).

Conflicting rules on age requirements for marriage, moreover, make statutory rape of a spouse a recurring real-world scenario. In one recent case, a pregnant 14–year–old Nebraska girl traveled to Kansas to marry her 22–year–old boyfriend because Kansas law then allowed marriage without parental consent for persons as young as 12 years old. *See* Gretchen Ruethling, *Husband Pleads Guilty to Sex Assault of Child*, N.Y. Times, Dec. 14, 2005, at A24; *see also In re Pace*, 989 P.2d 297, 298 (Kan. Ct. App. 1999) (upholding marriage between 16–year–old girl and 20–year–old man and suggesting that Kansas law, following the common-law rule, fixes the age of consent for marriage as 14 for males and 12 for females). Their marriage did not, however, affect the husband's liability for statutory rape under Nebraska law, and he ultimately pled guilty to first-degree sexual assault. After the case attracted national publicity, Kansas amended its law in 2006, setting the minimum age at 15 years and requiring a judge's agreement that marriage is in the minor's best interests.

In another well-publicized case, a pregnant 37–year–old Georgia woman was arrested for child molestation one day after marrying her 15–year–old husband. *See* Wendy Koch, *More Women Charged in Sex Cases*, USA Today, Nov. 30, 2005, at 3A. A similar case in Georgia, involving a 21–year–old woman and a 13–year–old boy, occurred in 2000. *See Georgia Woman Arrested for Having a Baby by Teen Husband*, CNN.com, Aug. 23, 2000, http://archives.cnn.com/2000/US/08/23/teen.father.ap. Georgia law allowed minors of any age to marry without parental consent if the bride-to-be was pregnant. *See* Ga. Code Ann. §§ 19–3–2(2), 19–3–37(b) (2004). In 2006, Georgia lawmakers raised the state's minimum age for marriage to 16 years with judicial approval in all cases.

It was formerly common for states to distinguish between men and women in setting marriage age, setting a lower age for females than for males. These distinctions have been invalidated on equal protection grounds, *see Phelps v. Bing*, 316 N.E.2d 775 (Ill. 1974); *cf. Stanton v. Stanton*, 421 U.S. 7 (1975) (striking down law that set different ages of majority for purposes of terminating child support obligation), but linger on the books of a handful of states, *see, e.g.*, Miss. Code Ann. § 93–1–5(d) (2008) (fixing minimum age for marriage at 17 for boys and 15 for girls). Constitutional attacks on other aspects of marriage-age regulation have mostly proved unavailing. The Equal Protection Clause permits states to discriminate on the basis of age so long as the state has rational reasons for the lines it draws. And, in 1982, the Second Circuit held that "the right of minors to marry has not been viewed as a fundamental right deserving strict scrutiny." *Moe v. Dinkins*, 669 F.2d 67, 68 (2d Cir. 1982). Applying the rational basis test, the court held that the state's age restrictions on marriage plainly served "New York's important interest in promoting the welfare of children by preventing unstable marriages among those lacking the capacity to act in their own best interests." *Id.*

More recently, the Nevada Supreme Court rejected the argument that a state law authorizing a minor to marry by obtaining the consent of only one parent violates an objecting parent's fundamental right to participate in basic childrearing decisions. *See Kirkpatrick v. Eighth Jud. Dist. Ct.*, 64 P.3d 1056 (Nev. 2003).

In 2006, a Colorado appeals court held that the state's minimum-age statute—requiring judicial approval for any marriage of a minor under the age of 16—applied only to ceremonial marriages. *See In re Marriage of J.M.H.*, 143 P.3d 1116 (Colo. Ct. App. June 15, 2006). For common-law marriages, the court concluded, "in the absence of a statutory provision to the contrary, it appears that Colorado has adopted the common law age of consent for marriage as fourteen for a male and twelve for a female, which existed under English common law." *Id.* at 1120. Accordingly, the court held that a lower court was wrong to have invalidated the marriage of a man to a 15–year–old girl on the ground that they failed to obtain judicial approval. In response, Colorado legislators swiftly amended state law to set a minimum age of 18 for common-law marriages. In 2008, the couple whose case stirred the controversy were back in court, this time suing state officials for damages for interfering with their marriage. They complained that officials wrongly prosecuted and incarcerated the husband, sought to annul their marriage, and imposed a continuing obligation on the husband to register as a sex offender. *See Rouse v. Ritter*, 2008 WL 1746978 (D. Colo. Apr. 10, 2008).

SECTION 6: CONSENT TO MARRIAGE

In the United States, a valid marriage has always required mutual consent of the spouses. Each party must have the mental capacity to consent, and any expression of consent must be voluntary and free from duress or fraud.

IN RE ESTATE OF SANTOLINO

Superior Court of New Jersey, Chancery Division, 2005.
895 A.2d 506.

LYONS, J.

The issue before the court is may a court annul a marriage after the death of one party to the marriage. * * *

The decedent and the petitioner first met in January 2000, when the petitioner moved into the decedent's home as a tenant. On or about March 11, 2004, the decedent was admitted to Trinitas Hospital. During his hospitalization, he was diagnosed with lung cancer. He was released from the hospital on April 1, 2004, at which time he returned to his Elizabeth residence. The petitioner and the decedent were married on April 27, 2004, in the Elizabeth Municipal Court. At the time of the marriage, the decedent was 81½ years old, and the petitioner was 46 years old. He was readmitted to Trinitas Hospital on May 11, 2004, where he expired on May 20, 2004. No will of the decedent has ever been found.

His heirs are his sister, Mercedes Tabor, the respondent. The respondent filed a caveat against letters granting administration. The respondent claims that the marriage to the petitioner is a nullity pursuant to N.J.S.A. 2A:34–1. * * * Counsel for the petitioner has filed the instant motion to dismiss under R. 4:6–2(e) claiming * * * that * * * the death of the decedent terminated the marriage, and the validity of the marriage, therefore, can no longer be questioned.

* * *

A survey of the law in other states shows that the prevailing rule continues to provide that a void marriage may be annulled after the death of one of the parties in the absence of a statute to the contrary. * * *

* * *

N.J.S.A. 2A:34–1 provides:

Judgments of nullity of marriage may be rendered in all cases, when:

* * *

c. The parties, or either of them, were at the time of marriage physically and incurably impotent, provided the party making the application shall have been ignorant of such impotency or incapability at the time of the marriage, and has not subsequently ratified the marriage.

d. The parties, or either of them, lacked capacity to marry due to want of understanding because of mental condition, or the influence of intoxicants, drugs, or similar agents; or where there was a lack of mutual assent to the marital relationship; duress; or fraud as to the essentials of marriage; and has not subsequently ratified the marriage.

* * *

The respondent attacks the marriage on four different grounds: (1) the deceased was impotent; (2) he was unable to consent to the marriage; (3) the marriage was based on fraud as to the essentials of the marriage; and (4) there exist equitable reasons to declare the marriage void.

Each claim will be addressed in turn.

IMPOTENCY CLAIM:

This court interprets N.J.S.A. 2A:34–1(c) as providing that impotency, when the condition meets the statutory criteria, makes a marriage voidable at the election of the party to the marriage who did not know of the other's condition at the time of the marriage. * * *

* * *

* * * [O]nly a party to the marriage can be an applicant for annulment on the ground of impotency.

* * * Unlike parties marrying within degrees prohibited by law or when one of the parties has another wife or husband at the time of the marriage—both situations in which the State's interest in protecting the health and welfare of the public, including potential children of such marriage or another spouse or family, is strong—here, it is logical that the parties to the marriage, alone, would determine whether their marriage shall be annulled due to impotency unknown to one, though existing at the time of the marriage.

The unique proofs required for this ground lend credence to the notion that this is a private right of the parties to the marriage. * * *

* * *

LACK OF CONSENT:

N.J.S.A. 2A:34–1(d) provides that an annulment may be granted

"where the parties, or either of them, lacked capacity to marry due to want of understanding because of mental condition, or the influence of intoxicants, drugs, or similar agents; or where there was a lack of mutual assent to the marital relationship; duress; or fraud as to the essentials of marriage; and has not subsequently ratified the marriage.''

The clause can be broken down into (1) inability to give consent; (2) lack of mutual assent; (3) duress; and (4) fraud as to the essentials of the marriage. Respondent argues that her brother did not have the mental capacity to give his consent and that the marriage constituted a fraud as to its essentials.

* * * The plain language of subsection d does not preclude a posthumous cause of action for lack of consent and further does not require that the action be brought only by one of the parties to the marriage. * * *

* * *

* * * With regard to capacity to consent, the courts of this state have held that where there is a lack of capacity to consent, the incapacitated party is not capable of contracting the marriage and the marriage is void ab initio.

In this case, Mr. Santolino was 81 1/2 years old; he was hospitalized on March 4, 2004 and diagnosed with lung cancer; he was released on April 1, only to be readmitted on May 11, where he expired on May 20. Respondent argues that during this time, Mr. Santolino was heavily medicated, was undergoing chemotherapy, required the daily assistance of an in-home nurse and was hooked up to an oxygen tank during his wedding to the petitioner. Under this factual setting, an argument certainly can be made that Mr. Santolino lacked the capacity to consent to the marriage.

* * *

FRAUD AS TO THE ESSENTIALS OF THE MARRIAGE:

Respondent's third argument for annulling the marriage is that it was the product of a fraud as to the essentials of the marriage. The courts have defined "fraud in the essentials" to include a number of different factual scenarios in which one spouse omits to mention or misrepresents an issue so material that it goes to the very essence of the marriage relationship constituting grounds for annulment.[2] * * * However, a deter-

---

    2. For example, evidence that after plaintiff entered into contract for marriage by proxy with defendant, a resident of Cuba, defendant repeatedly refused to join plaintiff in the United States, evidence that marriage was not consummated and that defendant did from inception of marriage form fixed determination not to consummate marriage established that defendant committed such fraud as to constitute ground for annulment. *Lopez v. Lopez*, 102 N.J.Super. 253 (Ch. Div.1968). Where plaintiff had been a deeply religious Orthodox Jew throughout her life and, in light of the far-reaching requirements of that religion, could not properly have performed the duties of wife and mother following the rules and teachings of her faith without the support of a husband holding the same beliefs, and where defendant knowingly misrepresented to plaintiff that he was also a practicing Orthodox Jew, and thereby induced plaintiff to marry him, plaintiff was entitled to annulment on ground of "gross and far-reaching" fraud, though the marriage had been consummated. *Bilowit v. Dolitsky*, 124 N.J.Super. 101 (Ch. Div.1973). Husband's concealment prior to marriage of intent to have children contrary to expressed antenuptial agreement

mination of whether a spouse's fraud goes to the essentials of a marriage warranting an annulment must be decided on a case-by-case basis since what is essential to the relationship of the parties in one marriage may be of considerably less significance in another.

While respondent raises this claim, her papers do not articulate any particulars to support same. * * *

* * * Accordingly, respondent's claim of fraud as to the essentials of the marriage is dismissed without prejudice. Respondent will be afforded the opportunity to amend her pleading should discovery reveal any specifics that will support such a claim.

* * * [The court further held that respondent could seek to avoid the petitioner's marriage on other grounds under the court's general equity jurisdiction by demonstrating that the marriage was "somehow illicit."]

CONCLUSION:

Based upon the foregoing analysis, petitioner's motion to dismiss is granted with prejudice as to the claim of impotency; granted without prejudice as to the claim of fraud in the essentials of the marriage; and denied without prejudice as to the claims of inability to consent and as to those permitted under the court's general equity jurisdiction. * * *

NOTES AND QUESTIONS

1. *"Void" versus "voidable" marriages.* The New Jersey statute in *Santolino* lists both impotence and mental incapacity as grounds establishing the "nullity" of a marriage. But the court holds that impotence will nullify a marriage only if the other spouse requests annulment, while mental incapacity renders a marriage void *ab initio*, regardless of the parties' wishes. The court's different treatment of the two marriage defects illustrates the distinction between marriages that are "void" and those that are merely "voidable."

"Void" marriages are those that offend very strong public policies; because of the state's overriding policy objection, such marriages are considered to be absolutely void even without a request for annulment. Because the union is of no legal effect, no formal dissolution is required, although parties often find it advisable to obtain a judicial declaration of invalidity to avoid any uncertainty. "Voidable" marriages, by contrast, offend less strident public policies relating to marriage formation. A "voidable" marriage is considered legally valid *unless* and *until* one party goes to court to have it annulled. *See, e.g., In re Marriage of Glatfelter,* 2005 WL 950472 (Cal. Ct. App. Apr. 26, 2005); *Dodrill v. Dodrill,* 2004 WL 938476 (Ohio Ct. App. Apr. 28, 2004).

The categories of "void" and "voidable" marriages vary somewhat from state to state. Most states regard attempted same-sex, bigamous and incestuous marriages as void. On the other hand, most treat a marriage in which one party is underage, lacks physical capacity or was induced by fraud or duress to be merely voidable. *See, e.g.,* Del. Code Ann. tit. 13, § 101 (1999); Wyo. Stat.

---

not to have children was a fraud which went to essentials of marriage and warranted annulment. *V.J.S. v. M.J.B.,* 249 N.J. Super. 318 (Ch. Div.1991).

Ann. § 20–2–101 (2008); *Estate of DePasse*, 118 Cal.Rptr.2d 143, 154 (Ct. App. 2002).

2. *Mental capacity.* Courts have held that to give valid consent to marriage, a party must be capable of "understand[ing] the rights, duties, and responsibilities of marriage at the time of the marriage contract." *Nave v. Nave*, 173 S.W.3d 766, 774–75 (Tenn. Ct. App. 2005). Several decisions have found this capacity wanting and have nullified attempted marriages where a party suffers from dementia or Alzheimer's disease, typically at the behest of the party's adult child or legal guardian. *See, e.g., id.; Brown v. Watson*, 2005 WL 1566541 (Tenn. Ct. App. July 5, 2005). Statutes and case law also recognize the possibility that a party might lose mental capacity temporarily "because of the influence of alcohol, drugs or other incapacitating substances." Del. Code Ann. tit. 13, § 1506(a)(1) (1999). In 1998, former basketball star Dennis Rodman unsuccessfully sought to annul his marriage to actress Carmen Electra one day after their wedding for having an "unsound mind" attributable, his agent said, to being drunk. The couple remained married, however, for five more months until divorcing. A few months after their divorce, they were arrested for battering each other after a late-night fight in a Miami Beach hotel. *See Rodman, Wife Electra Arrested*, CBSNews. com, http://www.cbsnews.com/stories/1998/12/08/archive/main24601.shtml. A party who enters marriage without capacity to consent but later regains mental competence can then validate the marriage by ratifying the decision to marry. *See, e.g., Hunt v. Hunt*, 412 S.W.2d 7 (Tenn. Ct. App. 1965).

3. *Mutual assent.* To effect a valid marriage, competent parties must demonstrate their mutual assent to be married. With mixed success, parties sometimes seek to avoid an attempted marriage by claiming that it was undertaken in jest or without serious thought. A notable example involved pop singer Britney Spears, just eight months prior to her marriage to Kevin Federline in September 2004. In the wee hours of a Saturday morning on January 3, 2004, after a night of carousing on the Las Vegas strip, Spears married a childhood friend, Jason Alexander, at an all-night wedding chapel. According to Alexander, "[W]e were just looking at each other and said, 'Let's do something wild, crazy. Let's go get married, just for the hell of it.' " It was, agreed a publicist for Spears, "a joke [taken] too far." Glenn Puit, *Britney Spears' 55–hour Marriage Annulled*, Las Vegas reviewjournal.com, Jan. 6, 2004, http://www.reviewjournal.com/lvrj_home/2004/Jan–06–Tue–2004/news/ 22935262.html. Later that day Spears signed papers seeking to annul the marriage on the ground that she "lacked understanding of her actions to the extent that she was incapable of agreeing to the marriage because the Plaintiff and Defendant did not know each other[']s likes and dislikes, each other[']s desires to have or not to have children, and each other[']s desires as to State of residency." She further alleged that "[u]pon learning of each other[']s desires, they are so incompatible that there was a want of understanding of each other[']s actions in entering into this marriage." Compl. for Annulment, ¶ 8, *Spears v. Alexander*, No. D311371 (Clark Co., Nev. Dist. Ct. Jan. 5, 2004). A Las Vegas district court agreed and, finding "no meeting of the minds in entering into this marriage contract," granted an annulment within hours. Decree of Annulment, ¶ 9, *Spears v. Alexander*, No. D311371 (Clark Co., Nev. Dist. Ct. Jan. 5, 2004).

Should Spears have been so easily released from the obligations of marriage? (Note that, in contrast to Dennis Rodman, she did not claim that her judgment was impaired when she obtained a marriage license and exchanged vows.) A handful of other decisions have allowed parties to annul a marriage undertaken on a dare or "in jest," *see, e.g., Davis v. Davis*, 175 A. 574 (Conn. 1934), but not all courts are so indulgent. In one early case, for example, the Georgia Supreme Court declined to annul the marriage of a 15–year–old girl who, "in a spirit of hilarity, and without serious intent," agreed with her date and another young couple at the conclusion of a dinner-dance to drive to a neighboring state, rouse a local probate judge from bed and marry. *Hand v. Berry*, 154 S.E. 239, 239 (Ga. 1930). "[A]lthough the marriage was agreed upon and took place in a spirit of levity and joke," the court explained, "nevertheless there was no fraud on the part of either party as against the other." *Id.* at 240.

As a general matter, how compliant should courts be when an adult seeks to annul a marriage for lack of mutual assent? Should the answer be influenced by the length of the marriage, or by whether the marriage has produced minor dependent children? Does the New Jersey statute, quoted in *Santolino*, answer this question to your satisfaction?

4. *Fraudulent inducement.* A party's consent to marriage is legally ineffective if induced by fraud. In most jurisdictions, however, the fraud must relate to "the essence of the marriage." *See, e.g.*, 13 Del. Code § 1506(a)(4) (1999). *Santolino* allows that "the essentials of the marriage" vary from case to case, depending upon the values and priorities of the individuals involved. This understanding is similar to the way that courts define "material" fraud under the common law of torts and some federal criminal and securities laws. *See, e.g., Coldwell Banker Whiteside Assocs. v. Ryan Equity Partners*, 181 S.W.3d 879, 888 (Tex. Ct. App. 2006) (to recover for real-estate fraud, "[a] fact is material if it would likely affect the conduct of a reasonable person concerning the transaction in question"); *Basic Inc. v. Levinson*, 485 U.S. 224, 231 (1988) (in federal securities fraud, "[a]n omitted fact is material if there is a substantial likelihood that a reasonable shareholder would consider it important in deciding how to vote").

Other jurisdictions, however, have defined "the essentials of the marriage" in narrower terms. Where a man falsely led his fiancée to believe that he was "a well-educated millionaire with expertise in real estate and finance," for example, a California appellate court held that "the fraud * * *, as a matter of law, was not of the type that constitutes an adequate basis for granting an annulment." *In re Marriage of Meagher*, 31 Cal.Rptr.3d 663, 664, 669 (Ct. App. 2005). The court wrote:

> * * * Meagher does not contend that there is any evidence that Maleki [her husband] lied to her about his marital history, or that he concealed an intention not to have sexual relations with her, not to live with her after the marriage, or not to discontinue an intimate relationship with a third party. On the contrary, the parties began living together even before their marriage and continued to do so for well over two years thereafter, and Meagher cites to no evidence in the record that she ever expressed any dissatisfaction with the intimate aspects of their relation-

ship. Instead, she argues that the financial fraud at issue in this case is "at least as contrary to the essence of marriage" as the types of fraud that have been held sufficient to justify annulment. She cites no authority, however, either in California or elsewhere, for the proposition that annulment can be granted based on fraud or misrepresentation of a purely financial nature. * * * [T]he cases are entirely to the contrary. *Id.* at 668–69; *accord Stepp v. Stepp*, 2004 WL 626116, at *1 (Ohio Ct. App. Mar. 31, 2004) (following the " 'general rule that false representation as to character, health, wealth and external conditions do not constitute such fraud as will annul a marriage contract' ").

The Michigan Supreme Court, while seeming to agree that " '[f]raudulent representations of wealth, or connections, or health, or temper and disposition' " do not justify annulment, held further that a wife's "fraudulent conduct in failing to inform [her husband] that she remained romantically involved with another man" was likewise insufficient. *Chudnow v. Chudnow*, 2001 WL 672571, at *1 (Mich. Apr. 27, 2001). The court reasoned that a misrepresentation qualifies as " 'subversive of the true essence of the marriage relationship' " only if it demonstrates that the "party has no intention of ever fulfilling his or her marriage 'vows' or that such are impossible." *Id.* at **1–2. Thus, as long as the wife intended ultimately to abandon her adulterous relationship, her fraud did not concern the essentials of the marriage.

More remarkable still, a California court denied an annulment where a woman alleged that her husband had "created an entirely false portrait of his character, nature, previous conduct, behavior, and past," by saying, among things, that he was a former partner in a major accounting firm and a war hero who had won the Congressional Medal of Honor. *Summers v. Renz*, 2004 WL 2384845 (Cal. Ct. App. Oct. 26, 2004). She further alleged that after 10 years of marriage, she learned that he had attempted to murder his first wife by shooting her as she slept and was suspected of arson and other violent crimes. The court found that "the fraud did not go to the essence of the marriage relationship," reasoning that " 'Husband'[s] criminal record played no part at all in the marriage until Wife became aware of it in September of 1996, i.e. six months following their tenth wedding anniversary,' " and that " '[d]uring the first ten years of their marriage, by Wife's own admission, Husband lived up to Wife's expectations.' " *Id.* at *9 n.3 (quoting trial court's opinion).

As these decisions suggest, many courts agree that " '[f]alse representations as to fortune, character, and social standing are not essential elements of the marriage, and it is contrary to public policy to annul a marriage for fraud or misrepresentations as to personal qualities.' " *Elliott v. James*, 977 P.2d 727, 731 n.14 (Alaska 1999) (quoting *Wolfe v. Wolfe*, 389 N.E.2d 1143, 1144 (Ill. 1979)). What public policies are served by this rule? Would you favor permitting annulment any time a misrepresentation *actually* induced the other party to agree to marry? Why or why not?

5. *"Who Wants To Marry a Millionaire?"* On February 15, 2000, as 22 million viewers watched, Darva Conger and Rick Rockwell were married on the Fox television show, *Who Wants To Marry a Millionaire?*. *See Rebroadcast of Marriage Show Is Cancelled,* N.Y. Times, Feb. 21, 2000, at A8. In the show,

Rockwell was presented as a multi-millionaire real estate developer in search of a wife. Conger, then a 34–year–old emergency room nurse, beat out 49 other contestants to win the prize of Rockwell's hand in marriage, and the two were married at the conclusion of the program. Because Rockwell, 42, was hidden behind a screen for most of the program, Conger had laid eyes on him for only about a minute before the ceremony. After the on-air wedding, the couple was dispatched on a Caribbean cruise honeymoon arranged by the network. While Conger and Rockwell were on the cruise, *The Smoking Gun* website disclosed that a Los Angeles court had entered a temporary restraining order against Rockwell in 1991, after a former fiancée had alleged that he threatened to kill her. *Id.* About the same time, news outlets began reporting that—whatever the truth of Rockwell's claimed exploits in the world of real estate development—his "resume was deep in show business moments, including stand-up appearances in Las Vegas and a stint on a television sketch-show as a love-starved beach nerd." *Id.*

After learning of these developments, Conger refused to have any further contact with Rockwell and sought an annulment for fraud. "He was not honest and did not represent those restraining orders," Conger testified in a court hearing on her petition. *Judge Grants Annulment to TV Bride*, Las Vegas reviewjournal.com, Apr. 6, 2000, http://www.reviewjournal.com/lvrj_home/2000/Apr–06–Thu–2000/news/13317568.html. Rockwell did not appear to answer the petition, but he did tell reporters: "[I]f she takes the time to get to know me, she'll find me to be a kind and considerate person. . . . You just have to know in your heart whether you're doing the right thing or not. Remember the title of the show was not 'Who Wants to Marry a Millionaire with an Unblemished Background?' " *Game Show Bride Loses Job, Seeks Annulment,* Gaming Magazine, Mar. 9, 2000, http://gamingmagazine.com/ManageArticle.asp?C=540 & A=311.

In April 2000, the court granted Conger's request for an annulment, although the judge called the televised ceremony "a very legal wedding." Was the court correct to annul the marriage based on fraud? If it had turned out that Rockwell was not a millionaire, would that have been a sufficient misrepresentation to annul the marriage?

SECTION 7: MARRIAGE FORMALITIES

States generally prescribe two formal requirements to establish a valid ceremonial marriage: a marriage license and solemnization. These requirements serve important purposes, but they are meant to reflect what most marrying parties would normally expect to do. States do not expect parties to consult a lawyer to determine how to be married.

Statutes set out the basic requirements for obtaining a marriage license. Ordinarily, parties must submit an application providing information about their identities, marital histories, age and other information needed to determine their eligibility to marry. A Minnesota statute, for example, provides:

Application for a marriage license shall be made upon a form provided for the purpose and shall contain the following information:

(1) the full names of the parties and the sex of each party;

(2) their post office addresses and county and state of residence;

(3) their full ages;

(4) if either party has previously been married, the party's married name, and the date, place and court in which the marriage was dissolved or annulled or the date and place of death of the former spouse;

(5) if either party is a minor, the name and address of the minor's parents or guardian;

(6) whether the parties are related to each other, and, if so, their relationship;

(7) the name and date of birth of any child of which both parties are parents, born before the making of the application, unless their parental rights and the parent and child relationship with respect to the child have been terminated;

(8) address of the bride and groom after the marriage to which the court administrator shall send a certified copy of the marriage certificate;

(9) the full names the parties will have after marriage and the parties' social security numbers. * * *

* * *

Minn. Stat. Ann. § 517.08(1a) (Supp. 2008).

As the following excerpt from the Uniform Marriage and Divorce Act (UMDA) illustrates, the legal requirements for solemnization are typically flexible and forgiving.

UNIFORM MARRIAGE AND DIVORCE ACT
9A U.L.A. 182 (1998).

§ 206. Marriage

(a) A marriage may be solemnized by a judge of a court of record, by a public official whose powers include solemnization of marriages, or in accordance with any mode of solemnization recognized by any religious denomination, Indian Nation or Tribe, or Native Group. Either the person solemnizing the marriage, or, if no individual acting alone solemnized the marriage, a party to the marriage, shall complete the marriage certificate form and forward it to the [appropriate county or municipal] clerk.

(b) If a party to a marriage is unable to be present at the solemnization, he may authorize in writing a third person to act as his proxy. If the person solemnizing the marriage is satisfied that the absent party is unable to be present and has consented to the marriage, he may solemnize the marriage by proxy. If he is not satisfied, the parties may petition the [appropriate] court for an order permitting the marriage to be solemnized by proxy.

(c) Upon receipt of the marriage certificate, the [designated] clerk shall register the marriage.

(d) The solemnization of the marriage is not invalidated by the fact that the person solemnizing the marriage was not legally qualified to solemnize it, if either party to the marriage believed him to be so qualified.

NOTE AND QUESTION

Rationale for requiring a ceremony. Given the very loose requirements for a valid ceremony, what is the purpose of requiring solemnization at all? As you read the following decision, consider how forgiving courts should be regarding defects in proper solemnization.

PERSAD v. BALRAM

Supreme Court of New York, Queens County, 2001.
724 N.Y.S.2d 560.

DARRELL L. GAVRIN, J.

The plaintiff commenced this action seeking a declaration that the parties were never married or in the alternative for a divorce. * * *

* * *

FACTS

On May 22, 1994, the plaintiff and defendant participated in a Hindu marriage or "prayer" ceremony at the home of the defendant's family in Brooklyn, New York. The Hindu prayer ceremony was presided over by Moscan Persad and was attended by 100 to 150 guests. At the time, the plaintiff and defendant were approximately 32 and 28 years old, respectively. During the ceremony, the parties were adorned in traditional Hindu wedding garments, prayers were articulated, the defendant's parents symbolically gave her to the plaintiff, vows were made and rings and a flower garland were exchanged. The ceremony lasted approximately two hours. At the conclusion of the marriage ceremony, Mr. Persad said a benediction.

Mr. Persad testified that he is an ordained Hindu priest or "pandit" sanctioned since February 21, 1993 to perform wedding ceremonies. Two certificates, issued by USA Pandits' Parishad, Inc., were introduced into evidence certifying Mr. Persad as a "Hindu Priest" and "competent in Kamkand (rituals) and Purohitkarm (priesthood)." Both certificates predate the marriage ceremony in this action.

Immediately following the nuptials, a reception was held for 275 friends and family at Terrace on the Park in Corona, Queens. A photo album was introduced into evidence wherein the plaintiff and defendant are depicted in photographs wearing Hindu marriage garments. In other photos, the plaintiff is wearing a white-on-white tuxedo and the defendant is wearing what appears to be a traditional white wedding gown. At the reception, the parties had a wedding cake and received wedding gifts. After the ceremony and reception the defendant sent the guests "thank you" notes.

It was not disputed that the parties lacked a valid marriage license on May 22, 1994. On three separate occasions, once immediately prior to the ceremony and twice subsequently (January & April 1995), the parties began proceedings to obtain a marriage license, but each time it was not properly secured. Each party blamed the other for the failure to obtain the marriage license. It was also not contested that Moscan Persad was not licensed by the City or State of New York to perform marriage ceremonies.

* * *

CONCLUSIONS OF LAW

There is an old cliche that goes "if it walks like a duck and quacks like a duck, and looks like a duck, it's a duck." This familiar maxim appears perfectly suited to the case at the bar, as it conforms with the intent underlying the statutory structure enacted by the Legislature. Essentially, the Domestic Relation[s] Law establishes that where parties participate in a solemn marriage ceremony officiated by a clergyman or magistrate wherein they exchange vows, they are married in the eyes of the law. It is the opinion of the court that this is precisely what occurred in the instant case.

The parties' failure to obtain a marriage license does not render their marriage void. Section 25 of the Domestic Relations Law provides that "[n]othing in [Article 3 of the DRL] shall be construed to render void by reason of a failure to procure a marriage license any marriage solemnized between persons of full age ..." Likewise, Moscan Persad's failure to register with the City of New York pursuant to Domestic Relations Law § 11–b prior to performing the marriage ceremony did not render the parties' marriage void. In New York, a marriage may be solemnized by a "[a] clergyman or minister of any religion ..." (DRL § 11[1]). * * *

* * *

Accordingly, as the plaintiff has failed to overcome the strong presumption favoring the validity of marriages, the marriage is adjudged lawful and the court directs that a declaration be entered to that effect.

NOTES AND QUESTIONS

1. *Qualified officiant. Persad* is representative of the highly deferential approach taken by many courts (and section 206(a) of the UMDA) in determining the qualifications of persons to officiate at marriage ceremonies. *See, e.g., Hassan v. Hassan*, 2001 WL 1329840 (Conn. Super. Ct. Oct. 9, 2001).

The deference, however, is neither absolute nor universal. Some states consider a marriage performed by an unauthorized officiant to be voidable and a few even hold them to be void. *See Dodrill v. Dodrill*, 2004 WL 938476

(Ohio Ct. App. Apr. 28, 2004). One recurring issue that has divided the courts is the validity of marriages officiated by members of the Universal Life Church (ULC). *Compare, e.g., In re Blackwell,* 531 So.2d 1193 (Miss. 1988) (holding that ULC ministers are empowered to officiate at weddings), *with Ranieri v. Ranieri,* 539 N.Y.S.2d 382 (App. Div. 1989) (holding ULC marriages void); *State v. Lynch,* 272 S.E.2d 349 (N.C. 1980) (same); *Cramer v. Commonwealth,* 202 S.E.2d 911 (Va. 1974) (same); *cf.* N.C. Gen. Stat. § 51–1.1 (2008) (validating only ULC marriages contracted before July 3, 1981). Jurisdictions refusing to credit such marriages point out that the ULC allows any person to become an ordained minister upon payment of a nominal fee, and reason that a "church which consists of all ministers, and in which all new converts can become instant ministers, in fact has no 'minister' within the contemplation of [the marriage laws]." *Ranieri,* 539 N.Y.S.2d at 388 (quoting *Cramer,* 202 S.E.2d at 914–15).

2. *Marriage by proxy.* Consistent with section 206(b) of the UMDA, several states permit marriage by proxy when one party is unable to be present at the ceremony. One state, Montana, goes further and permits "double proxy" solemnization at which *both* spouses are absent:

> Francie Mercado, 25, wearing a white lace wedding gown at the University of Florida, and Jason Druding, 26, wearing Marine desert camouflage fatigues at a base in Djibouti, Africa, got married Thursday in a ceremony held thousands of miles away at Montana State University.

> Although they were eight times zones and two continents apart, the jovial groom and smiling, tearful bride were able to see and hear each other's vows, thanks to a video-conference signal carried over the Internet.

Gail Schontzler, *E-wedding in Montana Unites Couple Thousands of Miles Away,* Bozeman Daily Chron., Dec. 23, 2005, http://www.bozemandaily chronicle.com/articles/2005/12/23/news/01internetwedding.txt. A justice of the peace officiated at the ceremony in Montana.

A California statute provides that "[n]o particular form for the ceremony of marriage is required for solemnization of the marriage, but the parties shall declare, in the presence of the person solemnizing the marriage and necessary witnesses, that they take each other as husband and wife." Cal. Fam. Code § 420(a) (Supp. 2006). In 2003, an appellate court considered it uncertain whether this law countenanced a marriage ceremony at which a San Quentin prison inmate was "present 'via the telephone.' " *See People v. Tami,* 2003 WL 22235337 (Cal. Ct. App. Sept. 30, 2003) (reserving judgment on validity of marriage). Thereafter, in September 2004, California enacted emergency legislation to permit "a member of the Armed Forces of the United States who is stationed overseas and serving in a conflict or a war" to participate in a valid marriage ceremony by proxy. *See* Cal. Fam. Code § 420(b) (Supp. 2006). What sorts of circumstances should qualify as "inability to be present" at the ceremony, thus validating a proxy marriage?

3. *Licensing defects.* Contrary to *Persad,* some jurisdictions require strict compliance with licensing requirements. Emphasizing the need to avoid "uncertainty [as to] who is lawfully married," these jurisdictions have held that ceremonial marriages undertaken without a valid marriage license are legally ineffective. *See Stovall v. City of Memphis,* 2004 WL 1872896 (Tenn.

Ct. App. Aug. 20, 2004); *In re Khalil*, 2003 WL 1873739 (D. V.I. Apr. 4, 2003) (construing Virgin Islands law, but acknowledging that majority rule is to the contrary); *Parks v. Martinson*, 694 So.2d 1386 (Ala. Ct. Civ. App. 1997).

As in *Persad*, however, most jurisdictions take a more permissive view toward the failure to comply with marriage licensing requirements, emphasizing instead the public interest in upholding marriage and the expectations of family members and others in the apparent marriage. *See, e.g., Mayfield v. Mayfield*, 2005 WL 497263 (Ky. Ct. App. Mar. 4, 2005); *Accounts Mgt., Inc. v. Litchfield*, 576 N.W.2d 233 (S.D. 1998). A Connecticut court explained:

> Marriage is strongly favored by the law, and existing marriages are presumed to be valid and that presumption has been described by the courts as very strong. It is a presumption that grows stronger with the passage of time, is especially strong when the legitimacy of children is involved, and can only be negated by disproving every reasonable possibility that it is valid.

Hassan v. Hassan, 2001 WL 1329840, at *8 (Conn. Ct. App. Oct. 9, 2001). Thus, the Connecticut Supreme Court declined to hold a marriage void for lack of a license where "the parties exchanged marital vows before a priest according to the rite of the Roman Catholic Church," and "[t]hereafter * * * had four children, and essentially conducted themselves as a married couple" for the next two decades. *Id.* at * 5 (discussing *Carabetta v. Carabetta*, 438 A.2d 109 (Conn. 1980)). Where reliance interests are less substantial, however, courts are sometimes less tolerant of non-compliance. In *Harlow v. Reliance National*, 91 S.W.3d 243 (Tenn. 2002), for example, the Tennessee Supreme Court declined to find a valid marriage where a couple had reconciled a year after divorcing and "participated in a 'remarriage' ceremony at a church in which marriage vows were exchanged under the direction of a minister." *Id.* at 244. In reaching its conclusion that the putative wife was not entitled to claim survivors benefits after her (former) husband's death, the court noted that the husband's conscious refusal to obtain a new license raised doubts about whether they truly intended to be married. *See id.* at 246. If parties fail to satisfy *both* formal requirements for marriage—*i.e.,* if they lack both a license and solemnization—may the court excuse the failure and uphold the marriage as valid?

4. *Premarital waiting periods and counseling.* Most states require a short waiting period (typically, 72 hours) between the issuance of a marriage license and the marriage ceremony. In recent years, more than a half dozen states have enacted legislation to encourage couples to obtain premarital counseling, waiving waiting periods or lowering license fees for couples who complete an approved educational program. *See* Matthew J. Astle, *An Ounce of Prevention: Marital Counseling Laws as an Anti–Divorce Measure*, 38 Fam. L.Q. 733 (2004).

5. *Health screening.* At one time, states scrutinized the health of persons to determine their suitability for marriage. Many states refused to permit persons with certain conditions—venereal disease or epilepsy, for example—to marry. *See* Matthew J. Lindsay, *Reproducing a Fit Citizenry: Dependency, Eugenics, and the Law of Marriage in the United States, 1860–1920*, 23 L. & Soc. Inquiry 541 (1998). In recent decades, however, such laws have been in

rapid retreat. To the extent that states continue to mandate blood tests and screening for disease, it is now typically only to inform the marital partners about their health status, not to police access to marriage. Michigan's statute is representative of the modern trend:

(1) An individual applying for a marriage license shall be advised through the distribution of written educational materials by the county clerk regarding prenatal care and the transmission and prevention of venereal disease and HIV infection. The written educational materials shall describe the availability to the applicant of tests for both venereal disease and HIV infection. * * *

(2) A county clerk shall not issue a marriage license to an applicant who fails to sign and file with the county clerk an application for a marriage license that includes a statement with a check-off box indicating that the applicant has received the educational materials * * *.

(3) If either applicant for a marriage license undergoes a test for HIV or an antibody to HIV, and if the test results indicate that an applicant is HIV infected, the physician or a designee of the physician * * * immediately shall inform both applicants of the test results, and shall counsel both applicants regarding the modes of HIV transmission, the potential for HIV transmission to a fetus, and protective measures.

* * *

Mich. Comp. L. Ann. § 333.5119 (West 2007).

PROBLEM 3–3

Anthony and Roberta obtained a marriage license and participated in a marriage ceremony. The minister signed the marriage license at the ceremony, but the parties never filed it with the county clerk's office, as required by state law. Anthony claims that the couple lived together for two months following the ceremony before separating.

Roberta insists that the parties never intended to file the marriage license or to become legally married. She alleges that Anthony told her that his mother and daughter knew that the couple had a sexual relationship and believed he would go to hell if he did not marry her. Thus, she claims Anthony proposed a "fake" ceremony to be performed by his cousin and represented to her that the marriage would not be valid. Roberta states that, following the ceremony, she took possession of the marriage license and burned it. She alleges that the license was destroyed with Anthony's full knowledge and consent. She further claims that the parties never lived together as husband and wife. In the alternative, Roberta asserts that, if the court does find the parties were legally married, the marriage should be annulled and declared void. She claims that, at the time of the ceremony, she was emotionally vulnerable due to the recent death of her husband and that she relied on Anthony's misrepresentations that the marriage would not be valid.

If you were the trial judge, would you find a valid marriage? Which factual disputes, if any, would you need to resolve in order to decide?

SECTION 8: COMMON–LAW MARRIAGE

The preceding section considered the consequences for an attempted marriage of non-compliance with the formal requirements of solemnization and a license. At one time, defects in a formal marriage were of less concern because "common-law marriage" stood as a backstop in most states to validate such marriages. Even without solemnization or a license, parties could contract a valid common-law marriage simply by (1) living together and (2) holding themselves out as married with (3) the mutual intention to be married. Once formed, a common-law marriage was fully valid for all legal purposes, and could be dissolved only through formal divorce.

For much of American history, common-law marriage was widely practiced and permitted as a necessary response to frontier conditions. Professor Nancy Cott writes:

> Informal marriage, in which couples lived together as husband and wife without the requisite official license and ceremony—"self-marriage" or "common-law" marriage as it came to be called—was the most frequent [marriage] irregularity. Despite stipulation of appropriate marriage ceremonies, informal marriage was common and validated among white settlers from the colonial period on. The dispersed patterns of settlement and the insufficiency of officials who could solemnize vows meant that couples with community approval simply married themselves. Acceptance of this practice testified to the widespread belief that the parties' consent to marry each other, not the words said by a minister or magistrate, mattered most. Neighbors' awareness of the couple's cohabitation and reciprocal economic contributions figured a great deal in establishing that a marriage existed between a man and a woman, but consent was the first essential.

Nancy F. Cott, Public Vows: A History of Marriage and the Nation 30–31 (2000).

Beyond these concerns with the impracticality of strict compliance with marriage formalities in a frontier society, Professor Ariela Dubler suggests that the widespread embrace of common-law marriage in the eighteenth and nineteenth centuries was propelled by additional public policies:

> The doctrine of common law marriage provided judges with a way to privatize the financial dependency of economically unstable women plaintiffs. By declaring a woman to be a man's wife or widow at common law, courts shielded the public fisc from the potential claims of needy women, effectively deflecting those claims inward to a particular private, family unit. In addition, holding a couple married at common law avoided branding their children with the legal status of illegitimacy.

Moreover, common law marriage served another purpose: The doctrine allowed judges to efface the potentially threatening nature of nonmarital domestic relationships by labeling them marriages. Common law marriage thus transformed potentially subversive relationships—subversive in their disregard for the social and legal institution of marriage—into completely traditional relationships. In recognizing common law marriages, therefore, courts reinforced the supremacy of the institution of marriage by demonstrating that it could subsume under its aegis almost all long-term domestic forms of ordering.

Ariela R. Dubler, *Wifely Behavior: A Legal History of Acting Married*, 100 Colum. L. Rev. 957, 969 (2000).

Beginning in the late 1800s, the tide began to turn against common-law marriage and most states have now enacted legislation abolishing the institution. Today, common-law marriage is permitted in less than a dozen jurisdictions: Alabama, Colorado, District of Columbia, Iowa, Kansas, Montana, Oklahoma, Rhode Island, South Carolina, and Texas. *See Staudenmayer v. Staudenmayer*, 714 A.2d 1016, 1020 n.3 (Pa. 1998) (collecting authorities). New Hampshire and Utah recognize common-law marriages under limited circumstances. The latest blow came in 2003, when a Pennsylvania lower court claimed to abolish the doctrine of common-law marriage in the state prospectively:

Many sound reasons exist to abandon a system that allows the determination of important rights to rest on evidence fraught with inconsistencies, ambiguities and vagaries. The circumstances creating a need for the doctrine are not present in today's society. A woman without dependent children is no longer thought to pose a danger of burdening the state with her support and maintenance simply because she is single, and the right of a single parent to obtain child support is no longer dependent upon his or her marital status. Similarly, the marital status of parents no longer determines the inheritance rights of their children. Access to both civil and religious authorities for a ceremonial marriage is readily available in even the most rural areas of the Commonwealth. The cost is minimal, and the process simple and relatively expedient. Under Pennsylvania's statutory scheme, the fee for the issuance of a license is $3.00.

PNC Bank Corp. v. Workers' Comp. App. Bd., 831 A.2d 1269, 1279 (Pa. Cmwlth. Ct. 2003). In 2004, the Pennsylvania legislature resolved initial doubts about the statewide effect of the lower court's decision by formally abolishing common-law marriages beginning in 2005. *See* 23 Pa. Consol. Stat. Ann. § 1103 (Supp. 2008).

Do you agree with *PNC Bank* that common-law marriage has outlived its utility? The court suggests that women no longer need the paternalistic protection of common-law marriage. Professor Cynthia Grant Bowman, however, points out that "common law marriage * * * benefitted women—protected their welfare when they were vulnerable (widowed, abandoned), protected their reliance upon and investment in long-term relationships of trust, and recognized their contributions of labor and commitment that were not embodied in money, property, or title." She further argues that common-law marriage "in fact was more effective at protecting the interests of women, especially poor women and women of color, than any of the theories suggested to handle the problems created by its abolition." Cynthia Grant Bowman, *A Feminist Proposal To Bring Back Common Law Marriage*, 75 Or. L. Rev. 709, 711–12 (1996). What are the social costs of abolishing common-law marriage?

Despite widespread abolition of common-law marriage, conflicts-of-laws rules provide for upholding a common-law marriage as valid throughout the United States provided it was successfully created in a state that recognized the institution when the marriage was formed. *See, e.g., In re Estate of Gernold*, 800 N.Y.S.2d 329, 329 (Sur. Ct. 2005); *Knight v. Super. Ct.*, 26 Cal.Rptr.3d 687, 690–91 (Ct. App. 2005). In addition, common-law marriages created before statutory abolition (e.g., 2005 in Pennsylvania, 1997 in Georgia, 1991 in Ohio) remain valid. *See, e.g., In re Estate of Love*, 618 S.E.2d 97 (Ga. Ct. App. 2005); *Perrotti v. Meredith*, 868 A.2d 1240 (Pa. Super. Ct. 2005). Accordingly, the institution of common-law marriage continues to have broad significance, even in states that do not permit creation of such marriages within their borders.

IN RE ESTATE OF HUNSAKER

Supreme Court of Montana, 1998.
968 P.2d 281.

NELSON, J.

Anne Barnett (Anne) appeals from the July 17, 1997 Findings of Fact, Conclusions of Law and Order of the District Court for the First Judicial District, Broadwater County, determining that she was not the common-law wife of decedent Maurice L. Hunsaker (Maurice) and was therefore not an heir to his estate. * * *

Factual and Procedural Background

Sometime in 1985, Maurice and Anne met at a restaurant where Anne worked as a waitress. At that time, Anne was married to Raymond Price; Maurice had never married. Maurice and Anne became close friends initially, but they did not share an intimate relationship until sometime later. Anne separated from her husband in December 1986 and was divorced on February 30, 1987.

After Anne separated from her husband, she moved into a mobile home that Maurice bought for her. Maurice and Anne moved her personal effects into the mobile home the week prior to Christmas 1986. Anne testified that Maurice gave her a gift on every day of that week and that, on Christmas Day, Maurice gave her an engagement ring along with a matching wedding band and asked her to marry him. Anne wore the engagement ring at times, but she did not wear the wedding band. Anne stated that she never wore the wedding band because she did not believe that she had the right to wear it since she and Maurice did not have a formal wedding ceremony.

Maurice stayed nights with Anne at the mobile home until October 1987, when they moved into Maurice's house near Toston. The title and mortgage on the house were in Maurice's name alone. Maurice and Anne lived together in the house until Maurice's death on September 27, 1996.

* * *

Leonard Lambott (Lambott), a Toston area farmer and grain-elevator operator who knew Maurice and Anne for many years, testified at the bench trial on this matter that a sign in front of the house read, "Hunsakers, Home of the Classics" (referring to Maurice's and Anne's classic car collection). Lambott further testified that the message on the telephone answering machine, recorded by Anne, stated, "this is the Hunsaker residence."

Anne testified that she and Maurice purchased a large grandfather clock together and displayed the clock in the living room of the house. Maurice had the pendulum of the clock engraved with an "H" for Hunsaker in the center of the pendulum and an "M" for Maurice intertwined with the left side of the "H" and an "A" for Anne intertwined with the right side of the "H." Anne stated that she and Maurice were proud of the clock and showed it to people who came to the house.

* * *

Even though they lived together and did many activities together, Anne and Maurice kept separate bank accounts. Because Maurice had poor credit, Anne purchased many personal items for Maurice and he bought many items with Anne's credit. Anne testified that Maurice generally reimbursed her for these purchases.

Maurice and Anne owned shares of stock in two companies as joint tenants. They also owned a time-share condominium at Island Park, Idaho as joint tenants. Maurice listed Anne as the secondary beneficiary to his sister on his Department of Veterans Affairs life insurance policy. Anne was listed as Maurice's spouse on the Designation of Beneficiary forms for that policy. Although most of one form was filled in by Maurice, Anne testified that she filled in the word "spouse" on that form. Maurice had another life insurance policy that listed Shorland as the sole beneficiary.

Maurice and Anne filed separate income tax returns each year listing themselves as single instead of married. Anne testified that they filed as single persons because Maurice told her that he was in trouble with the IRS and that he did not want to get her involved with his financial problems. Anne testified that she did not know that she could have filed as married filing jointly. Gary Spitzer (Spitzer), the accountant who prepared Maurice's income tax returns until 1993, testified that Maurice did not indicate to him that Maurice was married.

Steven Shapiro (Shapiro), a Montana City attorney who represented Maurice in several matters starting in the fall of 1993, testified that he once introduced Anne to a mediator as "Annie Hunsaker, Morrie's wife." Shapiro stated that neither Maurice nor Anne corrected his introduction. Shapiro sent Christmas cards to Maurice and Anne and addressed the cards to "Maurice and Anne Hunsaker." * * *

* * *

Anne testified that she felt that she was married to Maurice during their relationship. She also testified that she thought that Maurice felt married to her.

* * *

Lee Stokes, a Bozeman attorney, represented a client that was purchasing land from Maurice and two of his brothers and their spouses. He testified that, in trying to make sure that the title to the land was clear, he asked Maurice if he had any premarital agreements with Anne and that Maurice responded that Anne was not his wife and that he did not involve her in business.

Shorland testified that Maurice called Anne his "sweetheart," but not his wife. Shorland also testified that he was close enough to Maurice that if Maurice had been married, he would have told Shorland. * * *

Maurice was listed as Anne's "significant other" on two hospital consent forms that Anne signed. One of the consent forms initially listed Maurice as Anne's "husband." However, the word "husband" was crossed out and replaced with "significant other." Betsie Rasmussen, the nurse who filled out the consent forms, testified that she filled them out with information that Anne gave her.

* * *

On September 25, 1997,[a] Maurice contacted Stonecipher about preparing a will. Stonecipher testified that Maurice told him that Anne was his "common-law wife" and that he wanted to leave everything to her. Stonecipher further testified that Maurice said that he did not have a will and that his family would "eat [Anne] alive" if he died without a will leaving his estate to her. Because Stonecipher usually does not prepare wills, he and Maurice decided to speak again the following week to make arrangements for the preparation of a will. However, two days after their initial conversation and before a will could be drafted, Maurice died. He was 63 years old. At the time of his death, Maurice had five surviving brothers and one surviving sister. One brother, Harper Hunsaker, died shortly after Maurice.

* * *

---

a. [Ed. Note: The court's opinion is inconsistent about whether Maurice died in September 1996 or September 1997. In addition, the court states that Anne separated from her first husband on February 30, 1987, a non-existent date. Nevertheless, the errors appear to be immaterial to the court's decision.]

* * * [T]he District Court * * * concluded that Anne was not Maurice's common-law wife. The court therefore ruled that Anne was not an heir to Maurice's estate and it denied Anne's petition to be named personal representative of that estate. * * *

Standard of Review

* * *

We have reviewed the record and conclude that, although substantial evidence exists to support the District Court's findings of fact, the District Court misapprehended the effect of the evidence.

Discussion

* * *

We have long held that the party asserting that a common-law marriage exists has the burden of proving: (1) that the parties were competent to enter into a marriage; (2) that the parties assumed a marital relationship by mutual consent and agreement; and (3) that the parties confirmed their marriage by cohabitation and public repute. *Matter of Estate of Alcorn* (1994), 868 P.2d 629, 630. The party asserting the existence of a common-law marriage must prove all three elements. Public policy generally favors the finding of a valid marriage.

In the case at bar, we first consider whether Maurice and Anne were competent to enter into a marriage. * * * [A] party may not enter into a marriage prior to the dissolution of an earlier marriage. Thus, Anne was not competent to enter into a marriage with Maurice, as a matter of law, until her dissolution of marriage from Price was finalized on February 30, 1987. After Anne's divorce was finalized, the record shows that both she and Maurice were competent to enter into marriage. Thus, Anne has carried her burden as to this element.

Second, we consider whether Maurice and Anne assumed a marital relationship by mutual consent and agreement. The mutual consent of the parties does not need to be expressed in any particular form. Mutual consent can be implied from the conduct of the parties. This Court has stated that the mutual consent "must always be given with such an intent on the part of each of the parties that marriage cannot be said to steal upon them unawares."

In *Alcorn*, Kathee, who asserted that she was common-law married to Fred, proved that she and Fred mutually consented and agreed to marriage. Fred gave Kathee a wedding ring that he designed. The ring contained two interlocking horseshoes made with Yogo sapphires, which reflected the couple's shared interest in horses. Kathee testified that Fred designed the ring and gave her a matching bracelet. The couple also used the interlocking horseshoe design at their home by cementing horseshoes into the walkway leading to their house and etching their names below the horseshoes. Kathee also testified that she and Fred agreed that they were husband and wife. The combination of these factors led to our holding in that case that they mutually consented and agreed to a marriage.

Similar evidence found in the record in the case at bar shows that Maurice and Anne agreed to a marital relationship. Anne wore an engagement ring that Maurice gave her. While we recognize that Anne did not wear the accompanying wedding band, she explained that she did not wear the wedding band only because they did not have a "formal" wedding ceremony.

Likewise, the grandfather clock engraved with Maurice's and Anne's initials that they prominently displayed in their home has the same effect as the horseshoe design in the walkway in *Alcorn*. Both of these displays are evidence that the parties living together in the home mutually consented and agreed to a marital relationship. Finally, Anne testified that she felt married to Maurice. Anne also testified that she believed that Maurice felt married to her. The engraving on the pendulum of the grandfather clock is evidence of this in that Maurice considered Anne a Hunsaker. Thus, the effect of the evidence in the record is that Anne carried her burden of proving that she and Maurice mutually consented and agreed to a marital relationship.

Finally, we consider whether Anne proved that she and Maurice confirmed their marriage by cohabitation and public repute. There is no dispute that Maurice and Anne lived together for almost nine years. As to public repute, we consider how the public views the couple. Relevant to this inquiry is whether the couple held themselves out to the community as husband and wife. A common-law marriage does not exist if the parties have kept their marital relationship secret.

In *Alcorn*, the record was clear that Fred and Kathee lived together for nine years. That, in turn, led us to focus in that case on whether Fred and Kathee established a common-law marriage by public repute. We noted that Kathee never changed her last name to Fred's last name; that she did not list Fred as a beneficiary on her life insurance, health insurance, or retirement forms; that she filed her tax returns as a single person during the term of her relationship with Fred; that Fred stated in his will, which left Kathee one-half of the net value of his ranch and all of his household furniture and goods, that he was single; that two of Fred's friends testified that Fred told them that he was not married to Kathee, and that Fred indicated to an attorney who drafted three wills for him, that he was single.

Nevertheless, we held in *Alcorn* that Fred and Kathee held themselves out to be husband and wife. In support of this holding, we set out that they spent all of their free time together, that Kathee wore the wedding ring that Fred gave her, that they regularly hosted people at the house, that Kathee spent time with Fred and cared for him during an extensive illness, that Kathee's family referred to Fred as "Uncle Fritz," that several witnesses testified that they considered Fred and Kathee to be married, and that Fred and Kathee held themselves out as a married couple to those witnesses.

In the case at bar, the record shows that Anne and Maurice held themselves out as a married couple and, therefore, had a reputation as such. The sign in the front of their home and the pendulum of the grandfather clock are evidence that Maurice and Anne held themselves out as husband and wife to those who visited their home. The answering machine message is evidence that Maurice and Anne held themselves out as husband and wife to those who called their home. Maurice's brother Richard stated in a petition filed with the District Court that Anne was Maurice's "surviving spouse." One witness testified that Maurice called Anne "my wife." An attorney who represented Maurice thought that Maurice and Anne were married. * * * The cumulative effect of this evidence is that Maurice and Anne held themselves out to the community as husband and wife and, consequently, had a reputation as a married couple.

* * *

* * * The party asserting the existence of a common-law marriage must * * * prove that the three elements of common-law marriage all existed at one time. The record in the instant case reflects that although Anne could not prove an exact date when all three elements were satisfied, there was a period of time, prior to Maurice's death, when all three elements of common-law marriage existed.

In sum, although there was substantial evidence to support the District Court's findings of fact, our review of the record leads us to the conclusion that the court misapprehended the effect of the evidence.

Accordingly, we hold that the District Court erred in ruling that the evidence presented did not establish that Anne was the common-law wife of Maurice.

Reversed and remanded for further proceedings consistent with this opinion.

GRAY, J., dissenting.

* * * It is my view that the Court has merely substituted its judgment for that of the District Court in weighing conflicting evidence and determining the credibility of the witnesses. * * *

* * *

* * * Anne's testimony that she "felt" married to Maurice, and that she "believed" he "felt" married to her, reflects how she and Maurice felt; it does not rise to mutual consent and agreement to a marital relationship. I daresay that many people who live together in an emotionally and physically monogamous relationship "feel" married. That is a far cry, however, from parties actually mutually consenting and agreeing to enter into a marital relationship. * * *

* * *

NOTES AND QUESTIONS

1. *Origin of the* Hunsaker *marriage.* When do you think the Hunsakers' marriage began (if at all)? On Christmas day in 1986 when Anne accepted Maurice's proposal and began wearing his ring? Later, when the parties moved into Maurice's house? In September 1997, when Maurice resolved to execute a will in Anne's favor? To determine Anne's status as an heir, pinning down a specific date of marriage formation may have been unnecessary. In many cases, however, the timing of marriage creation will dramatically affect the parties' entitlements. In *Staudenmayer v. Staudenmayer*, 714 A.2d 1016 (Pa. 1998), for instance, establishing an earlier common-law marriage would have reclassified a substantial tort settlement won by the husband as marital property in the parties' later divorce. In *In re Estate of Antonopoulos*, 993 P.2d 637 (Kan. 1999), establishing an earlier common-law marriage increased the wife's elective share of her husband's estate from 15% to 30% based on the length of the marriage.

2. *Present agreement to marry.* The issue did not arise in *Hunsaker,* but some decisions specify that the agreement to marry must be a "present agreement," that is, that the parties must agree to marry today, not a week or a month from now. Could Anne have had a present intention to be married even though she mistakenly believed that nothing short of a formal marriage could legally bind the parties? *Hunsaker* appears to say yes. *Compare Callen v. Callen*, 620 S.E.2d 59, 63 (S.C. 2005) ("A party need not understand every nuance of marriage or divorce law, but he must at least know that his actions will render him married as that word is commonly understood. If a party does not comprehend that his 'intentions and actions' will bind him in a 'legally binding marital relationship,' then he lacks intent to be married."). Would it be better to require proof of a written agreement to marry?

The Montana Supreme Court is one of the most liberal courts in its willingness to find the elements of common-law marriage. *See, e.g., In re Estate of Ober*, 62 P.3d 1114, 1116 (Mont. 2003) (finding common-law marriage despite evidence that "(1) Selma did not assume John's last name; (2) John and Selma maintained separate property and bank accounts; (3) John and Selma filed their taxes as 'single' taxpayers; (4) John and Selma filed documents with the Farm Service agency as 'single' persons; (5) John did not designate Selma as the beneficiary on his life insurance policy; (6) John did not report Selma as his spouse to his employer; (7) John granted his brother Benno Ober power of attorney in three separate documents; (8) John continued to pay rent on an apartment in Conrad, Montana, after he moved into Selma's home near Power, Montana; and (9) Selma continued to receive her widow's survivor benefit from the Social Security Administration under the name of her deceased husband, Frank Klein").

Other jurisdictions demand stronger proof of the parties' mutual intentions. Out of concern for the danger of fraudulent or unsubstantiated claims, most demand that the elements of common-law marriage be proved by "clear and convincing evidence." *E.g.*, *Sulfridge v. Kindle*, 2005 WL 1806482 (Ohio Ct. App. July 28, 2005); *Perrotti*, 868 A.2d at 1244; *Davis v. State*, 103 P.3d 70 (Okla. Ct. Crim. App. 2004); *DeMelo v. Zompa*, 844 A.2d 174 (R.I. 2004). And, while most states agree with *Hunsaker* that the parties' agreement to marry may be demonstrated by circumstantial evidence relating to their conduct, Pennsylvania generally requires (for claimed common-law marriages predating the legislature's prospective abolishment in 2005) an "exchange of words in the present tense, spoken with the specific purpose that the legal relationship of husband and wife is created by that [exchange]." *Staudenmayer,* 714 A.2d at 1021; *see also Hutton v. Brink*, 798 N.Y.S.2d 378, 379 (App. Div. 2005) (finding insufficient evidence of agreement under the Pennsylvania rule where "during a dinner they were having with two friends, [the couple] 'toasted to one another as "Husband" and "Wife" and publicly avowed our mutual commitment to one another as a loving married couple' ").

3. *Holding out as married.* In addition to capacity to marry and present agreement, the states also require evidence that the parties "held themselves out," or established a community "reputation," as a married couple. The evidence consulted in *Hunsaker*—*e.g.*, the understandings of neighbors, business associates, and family members; filing status on tax returns, real estate deeds or leases, loan applications, and other official documents; use of common names; the intermingling of financial affairs—is typical of the cases. In contemporary America, it is not difficult for parties to an asserted common-law marriage to hold themselves out as married if they truly wish to do so.

The absence of "holding out" is often persuasive evidence that the parties never actually regarded one another as spouses. *See, e.g., Mesa v. United States*, 875 A.2d 79, 84 (D.C. 2005). But suppose that a case presented powerful evidence of the cohabiting parties' mutual intention to be married— a written contract, for instance—but the parties had kept their understanding private? *Hunsaker* and other decisions suggest no common-law marriage could be found for want of public "holding out." What is the purpose of insisting on evidence of "holding out," at least where the other elements of common-law marriage are clearly met?

4. *Common-law marriage preceding or following a formal marriage.* Occasionally, a party to a formal marriage seeks to establish that the couple established a common-law marriage before the wedding ceremony. That the parties saw fit to establish a formal marriage might belie the existence of a preexisting understanding that they were already married. This circumstance may impose an extra burden on the party seeking to prove present agreement, but it is not necessarily preclusive. *Compare, e.g., Staudenmayer,* 714 A.2d at 1022 (finding no antecedent common-law marriage and observing that wife "offered no explanation as to why she thought this civil ceremony [was] necessary" given her claim of a preexisting common-law marriage), *with Antonopoulos*, 993 P.2d at 648 (finding sufficient evidence of common-law marriage where, five years before their ceremonial marriage, parties moved in together and "Nick gave Barbara rings in a private ceremony witnessed by Barbara's two young daughters").

Parties have also claimed to establish common-law marriages with a former spouse following a divorce and reconciliation. Courts, however, have demanded proof of a new agreement to marry, cohabitation, and holding out after the dissolution of the formal marriage. In an Iowa case, for example, a woman claimed that she and her husband had divorced solely "as a means for her to qualify for various forms of public assistance, including financial aid, to enable her to attend college." *In re Marriage of Martin*, 681 N.W.2d 612, 615 (Iowa 2004). The parties resumed living together for the next 10 years, however, frequently holding themselves out as married; when they ultimately separated, even their teenaged daughter was "surprised" to learn that they had previously divorced. Nevertheless, the Iowa Supreme Court agreed that the facts—especially the couple's inconsistency in the way they described their relationship to others and the fact that the man had specifically refused the woman's request to remarry formally—showed no mutual intent to be married following their divorce. *See id.* at 618.

5. *Capacity to marry.* A common-law marriage is a marriage. As with any marriage, parties to a common-law marriage must have the legal capacity to marry. Thus, no common-law marriage can be created where the relationship would be bigamous, incestuous, or violative of some other substantive prohibition. Similarly, no common-law marriage can occur where one party is mentally incapable of giving consent, or suffers from some other incapacity. *See, e.g., Parks v. Martinson*, 694 So.2d 1386 (Ala. Ct. Civ. App. 1997) (terminal cancer patient who was in "intense pain" and under the influence of medication that impaired her cognitive abilities lacked the mental capacity to enter into a valid common-law marriage). Where the incapacity or impediment to marriage is later removed, most courts insist upon renewed acts following attainment of capacity establishing the requisite elements of common-law marriage. *See, e.g., Callen v. Callen*, 620 S.E.2d 59 (S.C. 2005) (holding that previous conduct of parties in other jurisdictions not recognizing common-law marriage could not be used to create a common-law marriage upon the parties' move to South Carolina, a jurisdiction allowing common-law marriage; parties must engage in new conduct in South Carolina establishing the necessary elements).

PROBLEM 3–4

John Smith and Judy Jones, domiciliaries of Missouri residing in St. Louis, decided to attend a weekend dog show in Pueblo, Colorado. John and Judy had both been divorced from their respective spouses a few years earlier. Colorado recognizes common-law marriages created in that state, but Missouri abolished common-law marriage nearly a century ago.

While they were in Colorado for the dog show, John and Judy agreed to become husband and wife and they told several of their Colorado friends about the agreement. John gave Judy a wedding ring, and she put it on her finger. They registered at a Pueblo hotel as "Mr. and Mrs. John Smith." At the end of the weekend, they returned home to St. Louis, where they have lived for the past two months and have told other friends about their agreement.

Must Missouri recognize the Smiths as married?

SECTION 9:   THE PUTATIVE
SPOUSE DOCTRINE

So far, we have explored the limits of the law's willingness to validate attempted formal and common-law marriages. What happens if a court finds a defect in marriage formation to be simply too big to forgive (such as where one party is at all times married to another)? The putative spouse doctrine provides an equitable remedy where an innocent spouse has relied in good faith on a mistaken belief in the validity of the marriage. The putative spouse doctrine does *not* validate the defective marriage. The attempted marriage remains void, but the doctrine provides for relief that may closely resemble the relief the party would have received if the attempted marriage had ended in divorce. Where the doctrine does not apply (either on the facts of the case or because the relevant jurisdiction does not recognize the doctrine), the parties are left to whatever relief the jurisdiction affords cohabiting, nonmarital partners (discussed in Chapter 5).

In *Williams v. Williams,* the Nevada Supreme Court considered for the first time whether to adopt the putative spouse doctrine. As you read the decision, consider what functions the doctrine serves and whether it might undermine other policies distinguishing between valid and invalid marriages.

WILLIAMS v. WILLIAMS
Supreme Court of Nevada, 2004.
97 P.3d 1124.

Per curiam.

This is a case of first impression involving the application of the putative spouse doctrine in an annulment proceeding. Under the doctrine, an individual whose marriage is void due to a prior legal impediment is treated as a spouse so long as the party seeking equitable relief participated in the marriage ceremony with the good-faith belief that the ceremony was legally valid. A majority of states recognize the doctrine when dividing property acquired during the marriage, applying equitable principles, based on community property law, to the division. However, absent fraud, the doctrine does not apply to awards of spousal support. While some states have extended the doctrine to permit spousal support awards, they have done so under the authority of state statutes.

We agree with the majority view. Consequently, we adopt the putative spouse doctrine in annulment proceedings for purposes of property division and affirm the district court's division of the property. However, we reject the doctrine as a basis of awarding equitable spousal support. Because Nevada's annulment statutes do not provide for an award of support upon annulment, we reverse the district court's award of spousal support.

FACTS

On August 26, 1973, appellant Richard E. Williams underwent a marriage ceremony with respondent Marcie C. Williams. At that time, Marcie believed that she was divorced from John Allmaras. However, neither Marcie nor Allmaras had obtained a divorce. Richard and Marcie believed they were legally married and lived together, as husband and wife, for 27 years. In March 2000, Richard discovered that Marcie was not divorced from Allmaras at the time of their marriage ceremony.

In August 2000, Richard and Marcie permanently separated. In February 2001, Richard filed a complaint for an annulment. Marcie answered and counterclaimed for one-half of the property and spousal support as a putative spouse. In April 2002, the parties engaged in a one-day bench trial to resolve the matter.

At trial, Richard testified that had he known Marcie was still married, he would not have married her. He claimed that Marcie knew she was not divorced when she married him or had knowledge that would put a reasonable person on notice to check if the prior marriage had been dissolved. Specifically, Richard stated that Marcie should not have relied on statements from Allmaras that he had obtained a divorce because Marcie never received any legal notice of divorce proceedings. In addition, Richard claimed that in March 2000, when Marcie received a social security check in the name of Marcie Allmaras, Marcie told him that she had never been divorced from Allmaras. Marcie denied making the statement.

Marcie testified that she believed she was not married to her former husband, John Allmaras, and was able to marry again because Allmaras told her they were divorced. Marcie further testified that in 1971, she ran into Allmaras at a Reno bus station, where he specifically told her that they were divorced and he was living with another woman. According to Marcie, she discovered she was still married to Allmaras during the course of the annulment proceedings with Richard. * * *

During the 27 years that the parties believed themselves to be married, Marcie was a homemaker and a mother. From 1981 to 1999, Marcie was a licensed child-care provider for six children. During that time, she earned $460 a week. At trial, Marcie had a certificate of General Educational Development (G.E.D.) and earned $8.50 an hour at a retirement home. She was 63 years old and lived with her daughter because she could not afford to live on her own.

* * *

The district court found that Marcie had limited ability to support herself. The district court also concluded that both parties believed they were legally married, acted as husband and wife, and conceived and raised two children. Marcie stayed home to care for and raise their children. Based upon these facts, the district court granted the annulment and awarded Marcie one-half of all the jointly-held property and spousal support. * * * Richard timely appealed the district court's judgment.

DISCUSSION

Annulment

A marriage is void if either of the parties to the marriage has a former husband or wife then living. Richard and Marcie's marriage was void because Marcie was still married to another man when she married Richard. * * * An annulment proceeding is the proper manner to dissolve a void marriage and resolve other issues arising from the dissolution of the relationship.

* * *

Putative spouse doctrine

Under the putative spouse doctrine, when a marriage is legally void, the civil effects of a legal marriage flow to the parties who contracted to marry in good faith. That is, a putative spouse is entitled to many of the rights of an actual spouse. A majority of states have recognized some form of the doctrine through case law or statute. States differ, however, on what exactly constitutes a "civil effect." The doctrine was developed to avoid depriving innocent parties who believe in good faith that they are married from being denied the economic and status-related benefits of marriage, such as property division, pension, and health benefits.

The doctrine has two elements: (1) a proper marriage ceremony was performed, and (2) one or both of the parties had a good-faith belief that there was no impediment to the marriage and the marriage was valid and proper. "Good faith" has been defined as an "honest and reasonable belief that the marriage was valid at the time of the ceremony." Good faith is presumed. * * * However, when a person receives reliable information that an impediment exists, the individual cannot ignore the information, but instead has a duty to investigate further. Persons cannot act " 'blindly or without reasonable precaution.' " Finally, once a spouse learns of the impediment, the putative marriage ends.

We have not previously considered the putative spouse doctrine, but we are persuaded by the rationale of our sister states that public policy supports adopting the doctrine in Nevada. Fairness and equity favor recognizing putative spouses when parties enter into a marriage ceremony in good faith and without knowledge that there is a factual or legal impediment to their marriage. Nor does the doctrine conflict with Nevada's policy in refusing to recognize common-law marriages or palimony suits. In the putative spouse doctrine, the parties have actually attempted to enter into a formal relationship with the solemnization of a marriage ceremony, a missing element in common-law marriages and palimony suits. As a majority of our sister states have recognized, the sanctity of marriage is not undermined, but rather enhanced, by the recognition of the putative spouse doctrine. We therefore adopt the doctrine in Nevada.

We now apply the doctrine to the instant case. The district court found that the parties obtained a license and participated in a marriage ceremony on August 26, 1973, in Verdi, Nevada. The district court also found that Marcie erroneously believed that her prior husband, Allmaras, had terminated their marriage by divorce and that she was legally able to marry Richard. * * *

* * * The district court was free to disregard Richard's testimony, and substantial evidence supports the district court's finding that Marcie did not act unreasonably in relying upon Allmaras' representations. The record reflects no reason for Marcie to have disbelieved him and, thus, no reason to have investigated the truth of his representations. * * * We conclude that the district court did not err in finding that Marcie entered into the marriage in good faith. She therefore qualifies as a putative spouse. We now turn to the effect of the doctrine on the issues of property division and alimony.

Property division

* * *

* * * In this case, the district court treated the parties' property as quasi-community property and equally divided the joint property between the parties. Substantial evidence supports the district court's division, and we affirm the district court's distribution of the property.

Spousal support

States are divided on whether spousal support is a benefit or civil effect that may be awarded under the putative spouse doctrine. Although some states permit the award of alimony, they do so because their annulment statutes permit an award of rehabilitative or permanent alimony. * * *

* * *

Nevada statutes do not provide for an award of alimony after an annulment. Thus, the cases in which alimony was awarded pursuant to statute are of little help in resolving this issue. * * *

* * *

The putative spouse doctrine did not traditionally provide for an award of spousal support. Extensions of the doctrine have come through statute or findings of fraud and bad faith. As neither is present in this case, we decline to extend the doctrine to permit an award of spousal support when both parties act in good faith. * * *

CONCLUSION

* * * We adopt the putative spouse doctrine and conclude that common-law community property principles apply by analogy to the division of property acquired during a putative marriage. However, the putative spouse doctrine does not permit an award of spousal support in the absence of bad faith, fraud or statutory authority. Therefore, we affirm that portion of the district court's order equally dividing the parties' property and reverse that portion of the order awarding spousal support.

NOTES AND QUESTIONS

1. *Good faith and termination of putative spouse status.* As *Williams* states, a finding of "good faith" for these purposes is a fact-intensive inquiry. A party cannot recover if he or she is willfully blind to red flags warning of serious defects in the marriage. And, if the party undertook the putative marriage in good-faith ignorance of its invalidity, subsequent discovery of the impediment terminates the party's status as a putative spouse. Accordingly, any property or support rights cease to accrue after the truth comes to light. *See* Uniform Marriage and Divorce Act (UMDA) § 209, 9A U.L.A. 192 (1998) ("Any person who has cohabited with another to whom he is not legally married in the good faith belief that he was married to that person is a putative spouse *until knowledge of the fact that he is not legally married terminates his status and prevents acquisition of further rights.*") (emphasis added).

2. *Property and support rights.* Contrary to *Williams*, many other states do allow putative spouses to recover alimony or spousal support as well as an equitable distribution of community or marital property. *See* UMDA § 209 ("A putative spouse acquires the rights conferred upon a legal spouse, including the right to maintenance following termination of his status, whether or not the marriage is prohibited * * * or declared invalid * * *."). What principle—equitable or otherwise—might support withholding future support from putative spouses while according them a spouse-like property distribution? *Williams* pointed to decisions, many of them older, reasoning that with no valid marriage, there could be no basis for imposing an ongoing obligation of support. *See Williams,* 97 P.3d at 1130–31. But, by the same token, then, what basis is there for forcing a marriage-like division of property between putative spouses?

3. *Putative common-law marriage. Williams* limits the scope of Nevada's putative spouse doctrine to cases in which one party relies in good faith on a defective *ceremonial* marriage. *Accord* 750 Ill. Comp. Stat. Ann. § 5/305 (West 2007) (modifying UMDA provision by limiting relief to "[a]ny person, *having gone through a marriage ceremony,* who has cohabited with another * * *") (emphasis added). This limit would exclude the possibility of a putative common-law marriage, as for example where one party genuinely but mistakenly believed the couple had succeeded in establishing a valid common-law

marriage. Why limit relief to putative ceremonial marriages? Some states—particularly those few that continue to recognize common-law marriage—extend the putative spouse doctrine to defective common-law marriages. *See, e.g., In re Estate of Marson*, 120 P.3d 382 (Mont. 2005).

CHAPTER 4

SOCIAL AND ECONOMIC RIGHTS AND OBLIGATIONS

■ ■ ■

This Chapter chronicles the profound changes that have taken place over time in the relationship of gender to American family life. As you study this ongoing evolution, consider whether social change prompted legal change, whether legal change prompted social change, or whether each helped prompt the other.

SECTION 1: CHANGING VIEWS ON THE SOCIAL AND ECONOMIC STATUS OF WOMEN

A. THE COMMON LAW

Until the mid-nineteenth century, American and British women's legal rights—or lack of rights—depended heavily on the commentaries of Sir William Blackstone, which defined a married woman and man as one person under the law. Blackstone continued to hold considerable influence in the United States throughout most of the nineteenth century, when most lawyers entered the profession by "reading law"—that is, by reading Blackstone (and American commentaries written by James Kent and Joseph Story). Here is what Blackstone wrote in 1765:

WILLIAM BLACKSTONE

Commentaries on the Laws of England.
Vol. 1, 442–45 (1765).

By marriage, the husband and wife are one person in law: that is, the very being or legal existence of the woman is suspended during the marriage, or at least is incorporated and consolidated into that of the husband; under whose wing, protection, and *cover*, she performs every thing; and is therefore called in our law-French a *feme-covert, foemina viro co-operta*; is said to be *covert-baron*, or under the protection and influence of her husband, her *baron*, or lord; and her condition during her marriage is called her *coverture*. Upon this principle, of a union of person in

178

husband and wife, depend almost all the legal rights, duties, and disabilities, that either of them acquire by the marriage. I speak not at present of the rights of property, but of such as are merely *personal*. For this reason, a man cannot grant any thing to his wife, or enter into covenant with her: for the grant would be to suppose her separate existence; and to covenant with her, would be only to covenant with himself: and therefore it is also generally true, that all compacts made between husband and wife, when single, are voided by the intermarriage. * * * And a husband may also bequeath any thing to his wife by will; for that cannot take effect till the coverture is determined by his death. The husband is bound to provide his wife with necessaries by law, as much as himself: and, if she contracts debts for them, he is obliged to pay them; but, for any thing besides necessaries, he is not chargeable. Also if a wife elopes, and lives with another man, the husband is not chargeable even for necessaries; at least if the person who furnishes them, is sufficiently apprized of her elopement. If the wife be indebted before marriage, the husband is bound afterwards to pay the debt; for he has adopted her and her circumstances together. If the wife be injured in her person or her property, she can bring no action for redress without her husband's concurrence, and in his name, as well as her own: neither can she be sued without making the husband a defendant. There is indeed one case where the wife shall sue and be sued as a feme sole, *viz.* where the husband has abjured the realm, or is banished: for then he is dead in law; and the husband being thus disabled to sue for or defend the wife, it would be most unreasonable if she had no remedy, or could make no defence at all. In criminal prosecutions, it is true, the wife may be indicted and punished separately; for the union is only a civil union. But, in trials of any sort, they are not allowed to be evidence for, or against, each other: partly because it is impossible their testimony should be indifferent; but principally because of the union of person. * * *

But, though our law in general considers man and wife as one person, yet there are some instances in which she is separately considered; as inferior to him, and acting by his compulsion. And therefore any deeds executed, and acts done, by her, during her coverture, are void; except it be a fine, or the like manner of record, in which case she must be solely and secretly examined, to learn if her act be voluntary. She cannot by will devise lands to her husband, unless under special circumstances; for at the time of making it she is supposed to be under his coercion. And in some felonies, and other inferior crimes, committed by her, through constraint of her husband, the law excuses her: but this extends not to treason or murder.

The husband also, by the old law, might give his wife moderate correction. For, as he is to answer for her misbehaviour, the law thought it reasonable to intrust him with this power of restraining her, by domestic chastisement, in the same moderation that a man is allowed to correct his apprentices or children; for whom the master or parent is also liable in some cases to answer. But this power of correction was confined within reasonable bounds, and the husband was prohibited from using any violence to his wife. * * * But, with us, in the politer reign of Charles the second, this power of correction began to be doubted: and a wife may now have security of the peace against her husband; or, in return, a husband against his wife. Yet the lower rank of people, who were always fond of the old common law, still claim and exert their ancient privilege: and the courts of law will still permit a husband to restrain a wife of her liberty, in the case of any gross misbehaviour.

These are the chief legal effects of marriage during the coverture; upon which we may observe, that even the disabilities, which the wife lies under, are for the most part intended for her protection and benefit. So great a favourite is the female sex of the laws of England.

NOTES AND QUESTIONS

1. *Rationale.* Blackstone's approach to marriage and the status of women was based primarily on an economic rationale. "Marriage was an arrangement of property for the propertied and their children, who were the conduits for family wealth. In Blackstone's rendition of marital unity, women and men approached marriage as theoretical equals to a contract. After marriage, nothing remained of that equality because of the very nature of the contract." Norma Basch, *Invisible Women: The Legal Fiction of Marital Unity in Nineteenth Century America*, 5 Fem. Studies 346, 350 (1979). Was Blackstone's approach relevant to the life circumstances of the vast majority of British and American spouses, who were not members of a landed gentry?

2. *Disabilities or protection?* Blackstone asserted that married women's disabilities were intended for their "protection and benefit." Did this rationale have any support? What support did Blackstone provide?

3. *Coverture in America.* Professor Linda McClain points out that, in early America, the "colonists' rejection of hierarchy and insistence upon equality in politics did not extend to rejection of these rules of family governance. All free women, married or unmarried, lacked the right to participate formally in democratic self-government." Moreover, she notes that "African Americans held in slavery" did not even have "legal access to marriage" nor to other forms "of protection of family life." Linda McClain, The Place of Families: Fostering Capacity, Equality and Responsibility 57 (2006).

B. THE CHANGING VIEWS OF MARRIED WOMEN'S STATUS

The next two selections describe changing perspectives on the social and economic status of married women.

HERMA HILL KAY

From the Second Sex to the Joint Venture: An Overview of Women's Rights
and Family Law in the United States During the Twentieth Century.
88 Calif. L. Rev. 2017, 2048–49, 2062–64, 2088, 2090, 2093 (2000).

* * *

The movement of twentieth century family law in the United States
has been away from a patriarchical model and toward a more egalitarian
one. Formerly, the husband was the legal head of the household, responsible for its support and its links to the external society, while the wife was
the mistress of the home, responsible for the day-to-day management of
its internal affairs and the care and education of children. More recently,
these roles have tended to converge and the family is sometimes characterized as a partnership or a family firm. This trend did not, of course,
begin in the twentieth century. * * *

F. THE REEMERGENCE OF THE WOMEN'S MOVEMENT IN THE 1960s:
FOCUS ON CIVIL RIGHTS, THE BIRTH CONTROL PILL, AND N.O.W.

The period of the 1960s was one of extraordinary social and political
ferment in the United States. In 1960, the Federal Drug Administration
approved the first birth control pill for contraceptive use, thus for the first
time providing women with a reliable method of controlling their fertility.
African–American students began their lunch counter sit-ins in Greens-
boro, North Carolina in February 1960, adding a new element to the civil
rights movement. * * *

Responding to the efforts of liberals and African Americans under the
leadership of the Reverend Martin Luther King, Jr., and pressured by the
Birmingham riots in April and May of 1963, President Kennedy sent a
civil rights bill to Congress on June 19, 1963. It was enacted in 1964 after
his assassination made Lyndon Johnson President. The Civil Rights Act of
1964, meant to redress the situation of African Americans, contained an
unexpected bonus for women. Title VII of the Act, as originally drafted,
forbade discrimination in employment based on "race, color, religion, or
national origin." As enacted, however, it also applied to discrimination
based on "sex." These favorable federal laws and comparable state laws
may have facilitated the entry of women into the labor force in dramatically increased numbers: between 1960 and 1980, the number of women
workers almost doubled, from 23 million in 1960 to 45.5 million in 1980.
* * *

* * *

I. CONSTITUTIONAL CAMPAIGNS FOR WOMEN'S
EQUALITY AND SELF-DETERMINATION

1. Ruth Bader Ginsburg and the Equal Protection Clause

During the 1970s, while the state legislatures were occupied with
divorce reform, abortion reform, and ratification of the [proposed Equal

Rights Amendment to the Constitution ("ERA"), which ultimately failed to become federal law, falling three states short when the ratification period expired on June 30, 1982], a quiet campaign was underway in the federal courts to create a secure place for women in the United States Constitution. This campaign was conceived, implemented, and carried out by the Women's Rights Project of the American Civil Liberties Union, under the leadership of [then] law professor Ruth Bader Ginsburg. When the campaign began, the United States Supreme Court's interpretation of the Equal Protection Clause consisted of a two-tier review process: claims were tested either under the deferential or "rational relationship" standard, or under the "strict scrutiny" standard. The first standard was said to be "offended only if the classification rests on grounds wholly irrelevant to the achievement of the State's objective.... A statutory discrimination will not be set aside if any state of facts reasonably may be conceived to justify it." [*McGowan v. Maryland*, 366 U.S. 420, 425 (1961)]. The higher standard was reserved for "suspect classifications" such as race or national origin, as well as where "fundamental interests," such as voting, were involved. In such cases, the government was required to show a much closer fit between ends and means: that it was pursuing a "compelling" state interest and that the classification was necessary to promote that interest. * * *

Equal protection claims brought by women had been relegated to the lower tier of this approach and were decided under the "rational relationship" standard. Not surprisingly, most of these claims were unsuccessful. * * * [T]he feminist strategists of the ACLU undertook the ambitious task of changing the Court's interpretation of the Equal Protection Clause to make sex, like race, a "suspect classification." Their argument received its first hearing in the Supreme Court in *Reed v. Reed*, 404 U.S. 71 (1971), and resulted in the creation of a new tier of review, one that came to be known as an "intermediate" standard. Two years later, in *Frontiero v. Richardson*, 411 U.S. 677 (1973), the Court came within one vote of classifying sex as a "suspect classification." Ginsburg later described her strategy in choosing cases to bring before the Court as "basic education," explaining that the 1970s cases ... all rested on the same fundamental premise: that the law's differential treatment of men and women, typically rationalized as reflecting "natural" differences between the sexes, historically had tended to contribute to women's subordination—their confined "place" in man's world—even when conceived as protective of the fairer, but weaker and dependent-prone sex. Ginsburg's strategy succeeded brilliantly. When she left the academy to accept appointment to the federal bench in 1980, the intermediate scrutiny standard was well established and, with it, women's enhanced ability to assert constitutional claims for equality.

* * *

III.   CHALLENGES FOR THE TWENTY-FIRST CENTURY

Carl Degler characterized the differing attitudes of nineteenth-and early twentieth-century men and women toward their work:

Although women have been a part of the industrial system in the United States virtually from its inception, their relation to that system has always been different in certain fundamental ways from that of men. From the outset woman's employment was shaped around the family, while man's work, in a real sense, shaped the family. The family moved, lived, and functioned as man's work decreed; woman's employment, on the other hand, ceased when the family began, and from then on, as we have seen, it adjusted to the needs of the family, for the family was a woman's first responsibility.[466]

As the twenty-first century opens, this observation has lost much of its force for a relatively small, but growing, number of career women working in the professions, politics, and business. These women come from all racial and ethnic backgrounds and all socioeconomic classes. Unlike many of their mothers and grandmothers, they do not expect to forego family life to take on full-time careers, nor do they derive their identities from their husbands or companions. They are no longer the "second" sex. Their influence as trend-setters has not yet spread to all women, but their example as role models is powerful.

* * *

* * * The trend towards independence and self-sufficiency for women described above has made clear, however, that traditional marriage is not well-adapted to dual-career couples. Laws governing married names, domicile, and marital property all assume a primary breadwinner/dependent homemaker model of marriage, while the current marriage tax and anti-nepotism policies could serve as deterrents to marriage. If the couple has children, the assumption that a mother has primary responsibility for their care, combined with the difficulties associated with performing that function while juggling a demanding job in the absence of available and affordable child care, creates enormous pressure. * * *

The other side of this story—its impact on men—has as yet been only imperfectly explored. * * * As women sought to break down barriers to their own participation in the public sphere, some men sought expression for their nurturing capacities in the private sphere. This pattern is reflected in the early Supreme Court sex discrimination litigation, which exhibited a two-way exchange of power, with women gaining access to job opportunities formerly limited to men, while men acquired a larger role in the family, formerly the exclusive province of women.

This vision of equality between men and women in the home as well as the market-place, however, has not yet been realized. Fathers who have primary child care responsibility are unusual in our culture. The work force, especially at the most prestigious and highly rewarded levels, continues to be organized along a male model and to feature a "glass ceiling" hindering the advancement of women. Dual-career couples typi-

---

466. Carl N. Degler, *At Odds* 395 (1980).

cally do not share the home front duties. Instead, women work a "second shift" at home, or, if they can afford to do so, hire mother-substitutes.

* * *

The challenges of the twenty-first century cannot be met by a return to nineteenth-century family law, which required women to function as the "second sex." The fundamental changes in women's opportunities highlighted in this paper were hard-won and will not be abandoned by tomorrow's women. Young girls growing up today have very different expectations about their lives than their mothers did. Their daughters are likely to be even less constrained, either by the law, the marketplace, or social arrangements. Still, it is a safe prediction that family life will continue to be attractive. If it is to continue to offer the best opportunity for happiness and fulfillment for adults and children, it must receive more than society's blessing. Defining and facilitating family life in egalitarian terms must become a high priority on the national agenda as we approach the new millennium.

CATHERINE HILL & ELENA SILVA

Public Perceptions of the Pay Gap. American Association
of University Women Educational Foundation.
2, 4–9 (2005).

Women have made gains toward closing the gender pay gap during the past two decades. Much of the progress occurred during the 1980s, with smaller gains in the 1990s. Women's achievements in higher education are partly responsible for narrowing the pay gap in the 1980s and 1990s. As more women earned college and professional degrees, women's overall earnings increased, even while individuals continued to face a pay gap at every educational level.

* * *

Economists agree that there is a gender pay gap among full-time workers, but disagree on the size of the gap and the factors driving the disparities. Among full-time, year-round workers ages 18 and older, the median earnings for men in 2003 was $40,683 and the median earnings for women was $30,733 for an earnings ratio of 75.5 percent.

* * *

Many economists agree that women's decision to put their family first, manifested as taking time out of the labor force or reducing hours at various times to care for children or other family members, accounts for part of the gender pay gap. A recent study by the U.S. General Accounting Office found the following:

> Of the many factors that account for the differences in earnings between men and women, our model indicates that work patterns are key. Specifically, women have fewer years of work experience, work

fewer hours per year, are less likely to work a full-time schedule, and leave the labor force for longer periods of time than [do] men.

* * *

While parenthood appears to affect men's and women's careers differently, a majority of mothers do continue working, even while they have young children. [Research shows that] three-fourths (76 percent) of mothers work for pay and more than one-third (39 percent) work 40 hours per week, year-round[,] women who received pay during their maternity leave are more likely to return to the workplace than are those who have to finance the leave themselves [and] that workplace flexibility, including scheduling flexibility and maternity leave, has either a positive or no effect on mothers' wages.

Occupational segregation is often cited as a reason for pay disparities between men and women. * * * Despite women's progress in many nontraditional jobs, occupational segregation remains widespread. An analysis * * * found that more than half of women (or men) would have to change jobs to completely eradicate occupational segregation. * * *

With the remarkable educational gains by women during the past 40 years, there should be no dispute that women have the credentials for higher paying jobs. Today, women make up a majority of college students. Overall, men are only slightly more likely to have a college degree, and among young adults, these differences disappear altogether.

Women have made considerable advancements in the fields traditionally considered male. The most dramatic changes occurred in professional programs such as medicine, law, and business, where the proportion of women shot up from 9 percent in 1970 to 47 percent in 2000. * * *

During the past three decades, women have made significant gains in nontraditional fields including biology, physical sciences, business, and mathematics. * * *

[However, a] comparison of recent college graduates who work full time offers one indication that differences in skills and education are not a key factor in the gender pay gap. It is notable that the gap is greatest in engineering, math, and science and lowest among traditionally female occupations.

* * *

Economists agree that individual differences in negotiating skills can lead to pay variation among workers with similar skill sets, although they differ on the relative importance of this factor. * * *

Most economists agree that some part of the pay gap is unaccounted for and thus could result from employer discrimination, although there is disagreement on the extent to which pay differences are not explained by other factors. [The U.S. General Accounting Office] found that about 20 percent of the pay gap is unexplained and hence could be attributed to discrimination (or other factors not included in their analysis):

When we account for differences between male and female work patterns as well as other key factors, women earned, on average, 80 percent of what men earned in 2000. * * *

* * *

Women's progress throughout the past 30 years attests to the possibility of change. * * *

Before Title IX of the Education Amendments of 1972 and Title VII of the Civil Rights Act of 1964, employers could, and did, refuse to hire women for occupations deemed unsuitable, fire women when they became pregnant, or limit their work schedule because they were female. Schools could, and did, set quotas for the number of women admitted or refuse women admission altogether. In the decades since these civil rights laws were enacted, women have made remarkable progress in fields such as law, medicine, and business as well as in nontraditional blue-collar jobs like airplane pilots, fire fighters, and auto mechanics.

C. CONSTITUTIONAL LAW

As Professor Kay's commentary indicates, American constitutional law was slow to shed Blackstone's view of women's social and economic status. The Fourteenth Amendment, which became part of the Constitution in 1868, prohibited states from denying "any person" equal protection of the laws. Do you think the framers of the Fourteenth Amendment intended the Equal Protection Clause to protect women?

For decades, the Supreme Court did not think so. When the Amendment was barely five years old, the Court expressed "doubt * * * whether any action of a State not directed by way of discrimination against the negroes as a class, or on account of their race, will ever be held to come within the purview of" the Clause. *Slaughter–House Cases*, 83 U.S. 36, 81 (1872). A year later, the Court denied the claims (under the Fourteenth Amendment's Privileges and Immunities Clause) of a married woman who sought admission to the Illinois Bar. *Bradwell v. Illinois*, 83 U.S. 130 (1873). Justice Joseph B. Bradley, concurring in *Bradwell*, explained that "[t]he paramount destiny and mission of woman are to fulfil the noble and benign offices of wife and mother. This is the law of the Creator." *Id.* at 141 (Bradley, J., concurring). Justice Bradley's discussion left no room for gender equality as we conceive it today:

> Man is, or should be, woman's protector and defender. The natural and proper timidity and delicacy which belongs to the female sex evidently unfits it for many of the occupations of civil life. The constitution of the family organization, which is founded in the divine ordinance, as well as in the nature of things, indicates the domestic sphere as that which properly belongs to the domain and functions of womanhood. The harmony, not to say identity, of interests and views which belong, or should belong, to the family institution is repugnant

to the idea of a woman adopting a distinct and independent career from that of her husband.

Id.

The Court remained inhospitable to gender equity well into the 1960s. In *Hoyt v. Florida*, the Court, applying rational basis scrutiny to an equal protection claim, upheld a state statute that granted women (but not men) an absolute exemption from jury service. 368 U.S. 57 (1961). "Despite the enlightened emancipation of women from the restrictions and protections of bygone years, and their entry into many parts of community life formerly considered to be reserved to men," wrote Justice John M. Harlan, "woman is still regarded as the center of home and family life." *Id.* at 61–62. *Hoyt* was subsequently overruled. *Taylor v. Louisiana*, 419 U.S. 522 (1975).

The next decision recounts the constitutional change that began in the early 1970s and articulates the Court's current approach to equal protection claims alleging gender discrimination.

UNITED STATES v. VIRGINIA

Supreme Court of the United States, 1996.
518 U.S. 515.

Justice Ginsburg delivered the opinion of the Court.

Virginia's public institutions of higher learning include an incomparable military college, Virginia Military Institute (VMI). The United States maintains that the Constitution's equal protection guarantee precludes Virginia from reserving exclusively to men the unique educational opportunities VMI affords. We agree.

I.

Founded in 1839, VMI is today the sole single-sex school among Virginia's 15 public institutions of higher learning. VMI's distinctive mission is to produce "citizen-soldiers," men prepared for leadership in civilian life and in military service. VMI pursues this mission through pervasive training of a kind not available anywhere else in Virginia. Assigning prime place to character development, VMI uses an "adversative method" modeled on English public schools and once characteristic of military instruction. * * *

VMI has notably succeeded in its mission to produce leaders; among its alumni are military generals, Members of Congress, and business executives.

* * *

VMI produces its "citizen-soldiers" through "an adversative, or doubting, model of education" which features "physical rigor, mental stress, absolute equality of treatment, absence of privacy, minute regulation of behavior, and indoctrination in desirable values." * * *

VMI cadets live in spartan barracks where surveillance is constant and privacy nonexistent; they wear uniforms, eat together in the mess hall, and regularly participate in drills. Entering students are incessantly exposed to the rat line, "an extreme form of the adversative model," comparable in intensity to Marine Corps boot camp. * * *

* * *

In 1990, prompted by a complaint filed with the Attorney General by a female high-school student seeking admission to VMI, the United States sued the Commonwealth of Virginia and VMI, alleging that VMI's exclusively male admission policy violated the Equal Protection Clause of the Fourteenth Amendment. Trial of the action consumed six days * * *.

In the two years preceding the lawsuit, the District Court noted, VMI had received inquiries from 347 women, but had responded to none of them. "Some women, at least," the court said, "would want to attend the school if they had the opportunity." The court further recognized that, with recruitment, VMI could "achieve at least 10% female enrollment"—"a sufficient 'critical mass' to provide the female cadets with a positive educational experience." And it was also established that "some women are capable of all of the individual activities required of VMI cadets." In addition, experts agreed that if VMI admitted women, "the VMI ROTC experience would become a better training program from the perspective of the armed forces, because it would provide training in dealing with a mixed-gender army."

The District Court ruled in favor of VMI, however, and rejected the equal protection challenge pressed by the United States.

* * *

* * * [The Fourth Circuit vacated the lower court's judgment and] suggested these options for the Commonwealth: Admit women to VMI; establish parallel institutions or programs; or abandon state support, leaving VMI free to pursue its policies as a private institution. * * *

C

In response to the Fourth Circuit's ruling, Virginia proposed a parallel program for women: Virginia Women's Institute for Leadership (VWIL). The 4–year, state-sponsored undergraduate program would be located at Mary Baldwin College, a private liberal arts school for women, and would be open, initially, to about 25 to 30 students. Although VWIL would share VMI's mission—to produce "citizen-soldiers"—the VWIL program would differ, as does Mary Baldwin College, from VMI in academic offerings, methods of education, and financial resources.

* * *

* * *. In lieu of VMI's adversative method, the VWIL Task Force favored "a cooperative method which reinforces self-esteem." In addition to the standard bachelor of arts program offered at Mary Baldwin, VWIL

students would take courses in leadership, complete an off-campus leadership externship, participate in community service projects, and assist in arranging a speaker series.

Virginia represented that it will provide equal financial support for in-state VWIL students and VMI cadets, and the VMI Foundation agreed to supply a $5.4625 million endowment for the VWIL program. * * *

D

Virginia returned to the District Court seeking approval of its proposed remedial plan, and the court decided the plan met the requirements of the Equal Protection Clause. The District Court again acknowledged evidentiary support for these determinations: "The VMI methodology could be used to educate women and, in fact, some women ... may prefer the VMI methodology to the VWIL methodology." But the "controlling legal principles," the District Court decided, "do not require the Commonwealth to provide a mirror image VMI for women." The court anticipated that the two schools would "achieve substantially similar outcomes." * * *

A divided Court of Appeals affirmed the District Court's judgment. * * *

* * *

In 1971, for the first time in our Nation's history, this Court ruled in favor of a woman who complained that her State had denied her the equal protection of its laws. *Reed v. Reed*, 404 U.S. 71, 73 [1971] (holding unconstitutional Idaho Code prescription that, among " 'several persons claiming and equally entitled to administer [a decedent's estate], males must be preferred to females' "). Since *Reed*, the Court has repeatedly recognized that neither federal nor state government acts compatibly with the equal protection principle when a law or official policy denies to women, simply because they are women, full citizenship stature—equal opportunity to aspire, achieve, participate in and contribute to society based on their individual talents and capacities.

Without equating gender classifications, for all purposes, to classifications based on race or national origin, the Court, in post-*Reed* decisions, has carefully inspected official action that closes a door or denies opportunity to women (or to men). To summarize the Court's current directions for cases of official classification based on gender: Focusing on the differential treatment or denial of opportunity for which relief is sought, the reviewing court must determine whether the proffered justification is "exceedingly persuasive." The burden of justification is demanding and it rests entirely on the State. The State must show "at least that the [challenged] classification serves 'important governmental objectives and that the discriminatory means employed' are 'substantially related to the achievement of those objectives.' " *Mississippi Univ. for Women*, 458 U.S. at 724. The justification must be genuine, not hypothesized or invented *post hoc* in response to litigation. And it must not rely on overbroad generalizations about the different talents, capacities, or preferences of males and females.

* * *

Measuring the record in this case against the review standard just described, we conclude that Virginia has shown no "exceedingly persuasive justification" for excluding all women from the citizen-soldier training afforded by VMI. We therefore affirm the Fourth Circuit's initial judgment, which held that Virginia had violated the Fourteenth Amendment's Equal Protection Clause. Because the remedy proffered by Virginia—the Mary Baldwin VWIL program—does not cure the constitutional violation, *i.e.*, it does not provide equal opportunity, we reverse the Fourth Circuit's final judgment in this case.

* * *

Single-sex education affords pedagogical benefits to at least some students, Virginia emphasizes, and that reality is uncontested in this litigation. Similarly, it is not disputed that diversity among public educational institutions can serve the public good. But Virginia has not shown that VMI was established, or has been maintained, with a view to diversifying, by its categorical exclusion of women, educational opportunities within the Commonwealth. In cases of this genre, our precedent instructs that "benign" justifications proffered in defense of categorical exclusions will not be accepted automatically * * *.

Mississippi Univ. for Women is immediately in point. There the State asserted, in justification of its exclusion of men from a nursing school, that it was engaging in "educational affirmative action" by "compensating for discrimination against women." 458 U.S. at 727. Undertaking a "searching analysis," *id.* at 728, the Court found no close resemblance between "the alleged objective" and "the actual purpose underlying the discriminatory classification," *id.* at 730. Pursuing a similar inquiry here, we reach the same conclusion.

Neither recent nor distant history bears out Virginia's alleged pursuit of diversity through single-sex educational options. In 1839, when the Commonwealth established VMI, a range of educational opportunities for men and women was scarcely contemplated. Higher education at the time was considered dangerous for women * * *. * * *

* * *

* * * A purpose genuinely to advance an array of educational options, as the Court of Appeals recognized, is not served by VMI's historic and constant plan—a plan to "afford a unique educational benefit only to males." However "liberally" this plan serves the Commonwealth's sons, it makes no provision whatever for her daughters. That is not *equal* protection.

B

Virginia next argues that VMI's adversative method of training provides educational benefits that cannot be made available, unmodified, to women. Alterations to accommodate women would necessarily be "radical," so "drastic," Virginia asserts, as to transform, indeed "destroy," VMI's program. * * *

The District Court forecast from expert witness testimony, and the Court of Appeals accepted, that coeducation would materially affect "at least these three aspects of VMI's program—physical training, the absence of privacy, and the adversative approach." And it is uncontested that women's admission would require accommodations, primarily in arranging housing assignments and physical training programs for female cadets. * * *

* * *

The United States does not challenge any expert witness estimation on average capacities or preferences of men and women. Instead, the United States emphasizes that time and again since this Court's turning point decision in *Reed v. Reed*, 404 U.S. 71 (1971), we have cautioned reviewing courts to take a "hard look" at generalizations or "tendencies" of the kind pressed by Virginia, and relied upon by the District Court. State actors controlling gates to opportunity, we have instructed, may not exclude qualified individuals based on "fixed notions concerning the roles and abilities of males and females." *Mississippi Univ. for Women*, 458 U.S. at 725.

It may be assumed, for purposes of this decision, that most women would not choose VMI's adversative method. * * * The issue, however, is not whether "women—or men—should be forced to attend VMI" [as Fourth Circuit Judge Motz observed in her dissent from denial of rehearing en banc]; rather, the question is whether the Commonwealth can constitutionally deny to women who have the will and capacity, the training and attendant opportunities that VMI uniquely affords.

The notion that admission of women would downgrade VMI's stature, destroy the adversative system and, with it, even the school, is a judgment hardly proved, a prediction hardly different from other "self-fulfilling prophec[ies]," see *Mississippi Univ. for Women*, 458 U.S. at 730, once routinely used to deny rights or opportunities. When women first sought admission to the bar and access to legal education, concerns of the same order were expressed. * * *

* * *

* * * Virginia, in sum, "has fallen far short of establishing the 'exceedingly persuasive justification,'" *Mississippi Univ. for Women*, 458 U.S. at 731, that must be the solid base for any gender-defined classification. * * *

VI

In the second phase of the litigation, Virginia presented its remedial plan—maintain VMI as a male-only college and create VWIL as a separate program for women. * * *

A

A remedial decree, this Court has said, must closely fit the constitutional violation; it must be shaped to place persons unconstitutionally denied an opportunity or advantage in "the position they would have occupied in the absence of [discrimination]." See *Milliken v. Bradley,* 433 U.S. 267, 280 (1977) (internal quotation marks omitted). * * *

* * *

In contrast to the generalizations about women on which Virginia rests, we note again these dispositive realities: VMI's "implementing methodology" is not "inherently unsuitable to women," "some women . . . do well under [the] adversative model" * * *. It is on behalf of these women that the United States has instituted this suit, and it is for them that a remedy must be crafted, a remedy that will end their exclusion from a state-supplied educational opportunity for which they are fit, a decree that will "bar like discrimination in the future." *Louisiana v. United States*, 380 U.S. [145, 154 (1965)].

* * *

Virginia * * * has failed to provide any "comparable single-gender women's institution." Instead, the Commonwealth has created a VWIL program fairly appraised as a "pale shadow" of VMI in terms of the range of curricular choices and faculty stature, funding, prestige, alumni support and influence. * * *

* * *

The Fourth Circuit plainly erred in exposing Virginia's VWIL plan to a deferential analysis, for "all gender-based classifications today" warrant "heightened scrutiny". Valuable as VWIL may prove for students who seek the program offered, Virginia's remedy affords no cure at all for the opportunities and advantages withheld from women who want a VMI education and can make the grade. In sum, Virginia's remedy does not match the constitutional violation; the Commonwealth has shown no "exceedingly persuasive justification" for withholding from women qualified for the experience premier training of the kind VMI affords.

* * *

JUSTICE THOMAS took no part in the consideration or decision of these cases.

CHIEF JUSTICE REHNQUIST, concurring in the judgment.

The Court holds first that Virginia violates the Equal Protection Clause by maintaining the Virginia Military Institute's (VMI's) all-male admissions policy, and second that establishing the Virginia Women's Institute for Leadership (VWIL) program does not remedy that violation. While I agree with these conclusions, I disagree with the Court's analysis and so I write separately.

* * *

Our cases dealing with gender discrimination also require that the proffered purpose for the challenged law be the actual purpose. It is on this ground that the Court rejects the first of two justifications Virginia offers for VMI's single-sex admissions policy, namely, the goal of diversity among its public educational institutions. While I ultimately agree that the Commonwealth has not carried the day with this justification, I disagree with the Court's method of analyzing the issue. * * *

* * *

* * * [I]n 1971, we decided *Reed v. Reed,* which the Court correctly refers to as a seminal case. But its facts have nothing to do with admissions to any sort of educational institution. An Idaho statute governing the administration of estates and probate preferred men to women if the other statutory qualifications were equal. The statute's purpose, according to the Idaho Supreme Court, was to avoid hearings to determine who was better qualified as between a man and a woman both applying for letters of administration. This Court held that such a rule violated the Fourteenth Amendment because "a mandatory preference to members of either sex over members of the other, merely to accomplish the elimination of hearings," was an "arbitrary legislative choice forbidden by the Equal Protection Clause." * * *

* * *

Before this Court, Virginia has sought to justify VMI's single-sex admissions policy primarily on the basis that diversity in education is desirable, and that * * * there should also be room for single-sex institutions. I agree with the Court that there is scant evidence in the record that this was the real reason that Virginia decided to maintain VMI as men only. * * *

Even if diversity in educational opportunity were the Commonwealth's actual objective, the Commonwealth's position would still be problematic. The difficulty with its position is that the diversity benefited only one sex; there was single-sex public education available for men at VMI, but no corresponding single-sex public education available for women. * * *

I do not think, however, that the Commonwealth's options were as limited as the majority may imply. * * * Had Virginia made a genuine effort to devote comparable public resources to a facility for women, and followed through on such a plan, it might well have avoided an equal protection violation. I do not believe the Commonwealth was faced with the stark choice of either admitting women to VMI, on the one hand, or abandoning VMI and starting from scratch for both men and women, on the other.

* * *

* * * An adequate remedy in my opinion might be * * * two institutions [that] offered the same quality of education and were of the same overall caliber.

* * *

* * * [T]he women's institution Virginia proposes, VWIL, fails as a remedy, because it is distinctly inferior to the existing men's institution and will continue to be for the foreseeable future. * * *

JUSTICE SCALIA, dissenting.

Today the Court shuts down an institution that has served the people of the Commonwealth of Virginia with pride and distinction for over a century and a half. To achieve that desired result, it rejects (contrary to our established practice) the factual findings of two courts below, sweeps aside the precedents of this Court, and ignores the history of our people. * * *

* * *

* * * For almost all of VMI's more than a century and a half of existence, its single-sex status reflected the uniform practice for government-supported military colleges. Another famous Southern institution, The Citadel, has existed as a state-funded school of South Carolina since 1842. And all the federal military colleges—West Point, the Naval Academy at Annapolis, and even the Air Force Academy, which was not established until 1954—admitted only males for most of their history. Their admission of women in 1976 (upon which the Court today relies), came not by court decree, but because the people, through their elected representatives, decreed a change. * * * [T]he assertion that either tradition has been unconstitutional through the centuries is not law, but politics-smuggled-into-law.

And the same applies, more broadly, to single-sex education in general, which, as I shall discuss, is threatened by today's decision with the cutoff of all state and federal support. Government-run *non*military educational institutions for the two sexes have until very recently also been part of our national tradition. * * * These traditions may of course be changed by the democratic decisions of the people, as they largely have been. * * *

* * *

NOTES AND QUESTIONS

1. *Questions about* United States v. Virginia. (a) As Professor Kay notes, four Justices in *Frontiero v. Richardson*, 411 U.S. 677 (1973), would have

identified gender as a suspect classification, triggering strict scrutiny of due process and equal protections claims. Should the Court continue to decide gender discrimination claims by applying intermediate scrutiny, or should the Court apply strict scrutiny? (b) What is wrong with "separate but equal" in gender discrimination cases? Is "sufficiently comparable" (the Fourth Circuit's test in the lower court's decision) sufficient to assure women equal social and economic status? (c) Should VMI's history of all-male enrollment policies (which began in 1839, while Virginia also maintained slavery) have counted in the school's favor here? Would a history of racial discrimination have counted in VMI's favor if it discriminated between white and black cadets today? (d) What effect, if any, does gender discrimination in higher education have on the social and economic status of women in American society generally? Do you think any such effect applies to military education? (e) Given VMI's rich history, could the state of Virginia ever provide truly separate, equal programs for male and female cadets? (f) Now that the major service academies all admit women, what "exceedingly persuasive reason" could the Commonwealth of Virginia proffer for excluding women or maintaining separate programs at VMI? (g) Was the dual-track military education program created by the state of Virginia grounded in gender-based stereotypes? Regardless of its grounding, would the dual-track program have perpetuated such stereotypes? (h) Should regulation of gender discrimination depend on the Court's application of equal protection, or should regulation (as dissenting Justice Scalia suggests) depend on action by "the people, through their elected representatives"?

2. *Standard for single-sex education.* In *Mississippi Univ. for Women v. Hogan*, 458 U.S. 718 (1982), the Court developed the guidelines for determining the constitutionality of single-sex education. That decision concerned the exclusion of men from Mississippi University's all-female nursing school. Joe Hogan, who was denied admission, brought suit, claiming that while Mississippi did offer alternative nursing schools that admitted men, none was located within a reasonable distance from his home. Writing for the Court, Justice O'Connor acknowledged that gender-favored classifications may be acceptable, but only if there is an "exceedingly persuasive justification for the classification," which can be met by showing that the classification "serves 'important governmental objectives and that the discriminatory means employed are substantially related to the achievement of those objectives.'" *Id.* at 724. However, such classifications may not act simply to advance gender-based stereotypes, such as that nursing is a woman's job.

3. *Other challenges.* In 1993, there was a similar challenge to admission policies at The Citadel, an all-male military college in Charleston, South Carolina. Shannon Faulkner was initially admitted based on a gender-neutral application. However, when The Citadel learned that Faulkner was in fact female, it promptly revoked her acceptance. The trial court rejected the state's argument that it could not provide any public military education to women due to the minimal demand for female training. As in *VMI*, the Fourth Circuit held that public single-sex education violates the Equal Protection Clause of the Fourteenth Amendment. *Faulkner v. Jones*, 10 F.3d 226 (4th Cir. 1993). After the Supreme Court's *VMI* decision, The Citadel abandoned its single-sex admission policy, and Shannon Faulkner was ultimately admitted, only to

resign within one week of enrolling. *United States v. Jones*, 136 F.3d 342 (4th Cir. 1998).

The lawyer who represented Shannon Faulkner later reflected on her experiences, observing that she had initially argued that admitting women would not materially change The Citadel; however, "on the frontline of this gender war," she realized "that The Citadel was right—the admission of women would require fundamental changes in this masculine institution. * * * I saw that its exclusion of women was * * * its essential and defining feature. Its mission was to create the 'whole man' through a military-style system structured around a hyper masculinity." Valorie K. Vojdik, *Gender Outlaws: Challenging Masculinity in Traditionally Male Institutions*, 17 Berkeley Women's L.J. 68, 69–71 (2002). Do you agree that the admission of women would require "material changes" in the operation of these military academies?

4.   *Female cadet training.* VMI began to admit women in 1996, but VWIL continues as an alternative for military education in Virginia. In 2004–2005 [update], VWIL included 135 cadets compared to 65 female cadets at VMI. VWIL continues to receive public funding despite the fact that women now receive equal access to VMI. Does this funding violate the Equal Protection Clause by providing additional opportunities only to women?

5.   *Debate about single-sex education.* Single-sex education remains a divisive topic. Feminists do not speak with one voice on the advantages and disadvantages of single-sex schools that are designed to promote gender equality and empowerment. Some argue that the Equal Protection Clause and Title IX permit single-sex education intended to remedy past wrongs, provided certain criteria are satisfied to ensure that the programs will withstand legal challenge. *See* Dawinder S. Sidhu, *Are Blue and Pink the New Brown? The Permissibility of Sex–Segregated Education as Affirmative Action*, 17 Cornell J.L. & Pub. Pol'y 579 (2009).

D.   FAMILY NAMES

Family surnames can tell much about the social and economic status of husbands and wives. Based on the modern Anglo–American tradition, most women adopt their husband's last name, but this has not always been the case. In thirteenth and fourteenth century England, for example, it was "not unusual for a married heiress to maintain her father's family name." Roslyn Goodman Daum, *The Right of Married Women to Assert Their Own Surnames*, 8 U. Mich. J.L. Reform 63, 67 (1974). Based on common law, men and women could generally change their names in any manner although, under the law of coverture, it was customary for a married woman to use her husband's last name. This custom did not become law until the middle of the nineteenth century, primarily as a result of judicial decisionmaking; apparently only one state—Hawaii—enacted a law (since repealed) mandating that a woman adopt her husband's name upon marriage. Elizabeth F. Emens, *Changing Name Chang-*

ing: Framing Rules and the Future of Marital Names, 74 U. Chi. L. Rev. 761, 771–773 (2007). In traditional Latino culture, individuals are referred to by a combination of two surnames, one from each parent. When a woman marries, she retains her father's surname and adds her husband's father's last name to create her own surname. The couple's children are then given each parent's current surnames, hyphenated, free-standing, or separated by the letter "y," meaning "and," to create their surnames. Yvonne M. Cherena Pacheco, *Latino Surnames: Formal and Informal Forces in the United States Affecting the Retention and Use of the Maternal Surname,* 18 T. Marshall L. Rev. 1 (1992).

In contemporary America, most jurisdictions permit people to change any part of their names at will, provided the change does not defraud, misrepresent, or interfere with the rights of others. Most states allow a woman either to maintain her name or to accept her husband's last name, but other alternatives are not as easily accessible. In 2007, California enacted the Name Equality Act, which allows parties in a marriage or domestic partnership to choose their own names through an application for a marriage license or a domestic partnership certificate. Seven other states have statutes allowing a husband to take his wife's surname. In other states, however, if a couple chooses to adopt an entirely new name, they may be faced with the costs of a filing fee, running upwards of $100, an appearance in court, running between $200 and $500, and the expense of publishing a legal notice in the newspaper to inform creditors of this name change. These costs can deter many couples from exploring such options.

Notwithstanding the financial cost and the traditional expectation that a woman adopt her husband's last name at the time of marriage, some contemporary couples are making different choices. Among these options are the following:

    a.   Wife hyphenates her name and husband's last name;

    b.   Wife and husband both hyphenate their surnames, each adding the other's surname;

    c.   Husband takes wife's name;

    d.   Wife uses birth name as middle name;

    e.   Wife and husband each take the other's last names as their middle names; or

    f.   Wife takes husband's name socially, but keeps her name professionally; or

    g.   Wife and husband jointly select a new name that may use both of their birth surnames or be completely different.

The change of surname, even in the traditional case of a woman adopting her husband's family name, is not automatic upon marriage, and while a name change may not be financially costly, it can be time consuming. After obtaining a marriage certificate, a woman must then take affirmative steps to change her driver's license, Social Security card, passport, and voter's registration, each of which requires official documentation of the name change. Also, written notice of the name change must be given to banks, employment offices, insurance companies, hospitals, credit card administrators, utility offices, the post office, property records, creditors, and other such organizations. Once the proper documentation is received, the name changes will be made without cost.

Despite expectations that the number of women choosing to retain their birth names would increase, some evidence appears to indicate the contrary. Rich Lowry, *Ms. Goes Mrs.*, Nat'l Rev. Online, Aug. 6, 2004, http://www. nationalreview.com/ lowry/ lowry200408060855.asp. A study of married Harvard alumnae, for example, found that while 44% of the class of 1980 retained their birth names, the percentage fell to only 32% of the married alumnae in the class of 1990. *Id.* In addition, according to Massachusetts records, the percentage of "surname keepers" among college graduates in that state has steadily dropped from 23% in 1990, to 20% in 1995, and to 17% in 2000. *Id.* Approximately 10% of all married women in the United States have names other than their husband's surname; while there is less information concerning same-sex unions, it appears far less common for gay and lesbian couples to assume common names. Emens, *supra*, at 785–790.

NOTES AND QUESTIONS

1. *Children's surnames.* A couple's surname decision may become complicated when it seeks to establish its children's surnames. Some married couples give children of one sex the mother's last name and children of the other sex the father's last name. Mississippi law requires that the child receive the father's surname when both parents file a petition for the child's legitimization. Miss. Code Ann. S93–9–9(3) (2008). Children's surnames receive attention in other countries as well. In France, until 2005, a couple was required to give a baby the father's last name; in Germany, where married women have been able to give their names to their children, about 1% of women do so. Elaine Sciolino, *Blow to French Patriarchs: Babies May Get Her Name*, N.Y. Times, Jan. 20, 2005, at A3.

2. *Disagreement between parents about children's surnames.* Children's surnames become more complicated when parents differ on the proper last name for their children. When parents disagree about the surname for their marital or nonmarital child, court resolutions of the disputes offer interesting insights into the changing social and economic status of women. Most courts attempt to determine whether a name change is in the child's best interests.

In an initial naming dispute in which the father sought a hyphenated last name for his child, the Alaska Supreme Court held that there was no preference in favor of either parent's choice of a surname; the sole issue was which name was in the child's best interests. *In re Change of Name for A.C.S.*, 171 P.3d 1148 (Alaska 2007).

3. *Best-interests standard for child's surname change.* When courts apply a "best interests" standard in change-of-surname cases, the child's best

interests may not be clear. In *Huffman v. Fisher*, 38 S.W.3d 327 (Ark. 2001), for example, the court determined that it was in the best interests of the child, Jacob, to assume the nonmarital father's name, even though the mother, Ms. Huffman, maintained custody of the child:

> Ms. Huffman argues that the chancellor erred in finding that Jacob might suffer harassment or embarrassment if his name is not changed * * *. Both parties presented the testimony of expert witnesses. The two experts agreed that Jacob might suffer ridicule at the hands of his peers and the community as a result of not having his father's surname. According to [the father's expert] it is typical in [the town in which the child lives] for children to take the paternal surname, and a child who does not bear his father's surname may be stigmatized as illegitimate. * * *

> Ms. Huffman asserts that the chancellor's determination regarding the potential for ridicule and embarrassment was based solely on evidence of the "norm in the locale" with regard to a child taking his father's surname. * * * [E]vidence of what is normal in a particular locale may be relevant in determining whether a child may experience difficulties, harassment, or embarrassment from bearing a particular surname. * * * [The father's expert], a primary school principal, when asked whether she had seen significant problems with ridicule in the primary school setting, testified, "We might have teasing, like, 'Who's your daddy? Why don't you have a daddy?'" * * *

> The evidence supports the chancellor's conclusion that Jacob may suffer difficulties, harassment, or embarrassment if he were to retain his maternal surname.

Id. at 333–34.

In another case, a nonmarital father sought unsuccessfully to change his son's name based on "the societal tradition of children's retaining their father's last name." A Virginia court conceded that the tradition "has both social value in our culture at large and evidentiary weight in our courts," but held that the tradition was insufficient to warrant a name change in the child's best interests, because the mother was the child's sole physical and legal custodian. *In re* Byrd, 56 Va. Cir. 540 (2001). The Virginia Supreme Court has held that there is no legal presumption that it is in the child's best interests to have the father's last name, and that every case must be considered on its own facts. *See Spero v. Heath*, 593 S.E.2d 239 (Va. 2004).

A best interests principle was also applied in *Ronan v. Adely*, 861 A.2d 822 (N.J. 2004). Kathleen Ronan and Peter Adely, Jr. were never married, but they named their son, Brendan Peter Adely. The parents separated, and the mother became Brendan's primary caretaker. When Brendan was two years old, she requested that Ronan be added as his last name. The trial court refused to change Brendan's name because he was already two, but the New Jersey Supreme Court remanded for reconsideration in light of a "presumption in favor of the primary caretaker that the name selected is in the best interests of the child." *Id.* at 827.

PROBLEM 4–1

The Columbia state legislature is concerned about the custom of name changing, in which the vast majority of women continue to adopt their husbands' names upon marriage. It is also concerned about the lack of name commonality in families in which one partner's name does not change. It is considering legislation that would require all married and civil unioned couples to do one of the following: 1) to hyphenate their names; 2) to choose one partner's name as the name for all members of the family; or 3) to choose a new name to apply to all members of the family. What are the arguments on both sides of this issue? How would each of these options affect public perceptions of the couple and of each individual?

SECTION 2: DOMESTIC ROLES

A. INTRODUCTION

Notwithstanding increases in men's participation in the home, domestic work remains primarily women's responsibility. Although a significant portion of women have always worked for wages—including single mothers, women from low-income families and women of color—there is an ongoing debate in contemporary culture over whether mothers should work outside the home at all, or whether they should stay home with their young children. Many Americans remain ambivalent about whether women with young children should work outside the home. Indeed, when working mothers were asked whether they respected mothers who worked full-time outside the home, or mothers who stayed at home full-time with their pre-school children, 44% of working women stated they respected the stay-at-home mothers more, while only 24% were more respectful of mothers who worked full-time. Naomi Cahn, *The Power of Caretaking*, 12 Yale J.L. & Feminism 177, 192 (2000). Moreover, more than 50% of Americans believe that a pre-school child is likely to suffer when her mother works. *Id.*

In the past generation, the law has facilitated women's participation in the workplace. The Family and Medical Leave Act of 1993 ("FMLA") recognized the importance of having both mothers and fathers care for children. The Act's advocates hoped to promote a more gender-neutral allocation of work and family roles between parents, based on a belief that the law can and does significantly affect families by helping change gender expectations within the home. This Section discusses allocation of domestic work within the family, and then provides various perspectives on the balance between work and family, focusing on both child care and elder care.

ARLIE RUSSELL HOCHSCHILD WITH ANNE MACHUNG

The Second Shift.
3–4, 7–9 (Penguin Group 1989).

* * * What should a man and woman contribute to the family? How appreciated does each feel? How does each respond to subtle changes in the balance of marital power? How does each develop an unconscious "gender strategy" for coping with the work at home, with marriage, and, indeed, with life itself? These were the underlying issues.

* * * Adding together the time it takes to do a paid job and to do housework and childcare, I averaged estimates from the major studies on time use done in the 1960s and 1970s, and discovered that women worked roughly fifteen hours longer each week than men. Over a year, they worked an *extra month of twenty-four-hour days*. Over a dozen years, it was an extra year of twenty-four-hour days. Most women without children spend much more time than men on housework; with children, they devote more time to both housework and child care. Just as there is a wage gap between men and women in the workplace, there is a "leisure gap" between them at home. Most women work one shift at the office or factory and a "second shift" at home.

* * *

It was a woman who first proposed to me the metaphor, borrowed from industrial life, of the "second shift." She strongly resisted the *idea* that homemaking was a "shift." Her family was her life and she didn't want it reduced to a job. But as she put it, "You're on duty at work. You come home, and you're on duty. Then you go back to work and you're on duty." After eight hours of adjusting insurance claims, she came home to put on the rice for dinner, care for her children, and wash laundry. Despite her resistance, her home life *felt* like a second shift. That was the real story and that was the real problem.

Men who shared the load at home seemed just as pressed for time as their wives, and as torn between the demands of career and small children * * *. But the majority of men did not share the load at home. Some refused outright. Others refused more passively, often offering a loving shoulder to lean on, an understanding ear as their working wife faced the conflict they both saw as hers. At first it seemed to me that the problem of the second shift was hers. But I came to realize that those husbands who helped very little at home were often indirectly just as deeply affected as their wives by the need to do that work, through the resentment their wives feel toward them, and through their need to steel themselves against that resentment. * * * One way or another, most men I talked with do suffer the severe repercussions of what I think is a transitional phase in American family life.

One reason women took a deeper interest than men in the problems of juggling work with family life is that even when husbands happily shared the hours of work, their wives felt more *responsible* for home and children. More women kept track of doctors' appointments and arranged for playmates to come over. More mothers than fathers worried about the tail on a child's Halloween costume or a birthday present for a school friend. They were more likely to think about their children while at work and to check in by phone with the baby-sitter.

Partly because of this, more women felt torn between one sense of urgency and another, between the need to soothe a child's fear of being left at day-care, and the need to show the boss she's "serious" at work. * * *

* * * Even when couples share more equitably in the work at home, women do two-thirds of the *daily* jobs at home, like cooking and cleaning up—jobs that fix them into a rigid routine. Most women cook dinner and most men change the oil in the family car. But, as one mother pointed out, dinner needs to be prepared every evening around six o'clock, whereas the car oil needs to be changed every six months, any day around that time, any time that day. Women do more child care than men, and men repair more household appliances. A child needs to be tended daily while the repair of household appliances can often wait "until I have time." Men thus have more control over *when* they make their contributions than women do. * * *

* * * [W]omen more often juggle three spheres—job, children, and housework—while most men juggle two—job and children. For women, two activities compete with their time with children, not just one.

* * *

B.   THE LAW

Two federal laws, the Family and Medical Leave Act and the Pregnancy Discrimination Act, are designed to eliminate discrimination based on family-related issues. Each is discussed in this section.

1.   THE FAMILY AND MEDICAL LEAVE ACT, *29 U.S.C. § 2601 (2006)*

Congress enacted the Family and Medical Leave Act (FMLA) in 1993. It entitles eligible employees to take up to 12 weeks of unpaid leave from work for medical reasons related to a spouse, child, or parent. The FMLA is often used for maternity or parental leave, but it also can be used for leave to care for a sick family member. Eligibility is defined partly by whether the Act covers the individual's employer. The Act does not reach private employers with less than 50 employees at any one workplace, but does apply to all public agencies, and to both public and private elementary and secondary schools.

The following Department of Labor regulations summarize the scope and purposes of the Family and Medical Leave Act.

DEPARTMENT OF LABOR

Coverage Under the Family and Medical Leave Act.
29 CFR §§ 825.100—113. (2009).

825.100   The Family and Medical Leave Act

(a) The Family and Medical Leave Act of 1993 (FMLA or Act) allows "eligible" employees of a covered employer to take job-protected, unpaid leave, or to substitute appropriate paid leave if the employee has earned or accrued it, for up to a total of 12 workweeks in any 12 months [to engage in specified family caretaking]* * * In certain cases, this leave may be taken on an intermittent basis rather than all at once, or the employee may work a part-time schedule.

(b) An employee on FMLA leave is also entitled to have health benefits maintained while on leave as if the employee had continued to work instead of taking the leave. * * *

(c) An employee generally has a right to return to the same position or an equivalent position with equivalent pay, benefits and working conditions at the conclusion of the leave. The taking of FMLA leave cannot result in the loss of any benefit that accrued prior to the start of the leave. * * *

825.101   What is the purpose of the Act?

(a) FMLA is intended to allow employees to balance their work and family life by taking reasonable unpaid leave for medical reasons, for the birth or adoption of a child, and for the care of a child, spouse, or parent who has a serious health condition. The Act is intended to balance the demands of the workplace with the needs of families, to promote the stability and economic security of families, and to promote national interests in preserving family integrity. It was intended that the Act accomplish these purposes in a manner that accommodates the legitimate interests of employers, and in a manner consistent with the Equal Protection Clause of the Fourteenth Amendment in minimizing the potential for employment discrimination on the basis of sex, while promoting equal employment opportunity for men and women.

(b) The enactment of FMLA was predicated on two fundamental concerns—the needs of the American workforce, and the development of high-performance organizations. Increasingly, America's children and elderly are dependent upon family members who must spend long hours at work. When a family emergency arises, requiring workers to attend to seriously-ill children or parents, or to newly-born or adopted infants, or even to their own serious illness, workers need reassurance that they will not be asked to choose between continuing their employment, and meeting their personal and family obligations or tending to vital needs at home.

(c) The FMLA is both intended and expected to benefit employers as well as their employees. A direct correlation exists between stability in the family and productivity in the workplace. FMLA will encourage the development of high-performance organizations. When workers can count on durable links to their workplace they are able to make their own full commitments to their jobs. The record of hearings on family and medical leave indicate the powerful productive advantages of stable workplace relationships, and the comparatively small costs of guaranteeing that those relationships will not be dissolved while workers attend to pressing family health obligations or their own serious illness.

* * *

§ 825.113   What do "spouse," "parent," and "son or daughter" mean for purposes of an employee qualifying to take FMLA leave?

(a) Spouse means a husband or wife as defined or recognized under State law for purposes of marriage in the State where the employee resides, including common law marriage in States where it is recognized.

(b) Parent means a biological parent or an individual who stands or stood in loco parentis to an employee when the employee was a son or daughter as defined in (c) below. This term does not include parents "in law".

(c) Son or daughter means a biological, adopted, or foster child, a stepchild, a legal ward* * *

NOTES AND QUESTIONS

1.   *Limitations of the FMLA.* The FMLA is designed to protect individuals dealing with family illness or child care, but many limitations prevent a large percentage of employees from invoking its benefits. Employees are eligible only if they have already worked for the employer for a full year, and only if the employer employs at least 50 employees within one general worksite. What kinds of common worksites might not be covered? In addition, the employee must prove that he or she, or a family member, suffers from a serious medical condition (other than in situations of birth and adoption). The leave is unpaid, so taking time off can severely strain a family in need of support, and many covered persons cannot afford to take time off from work. Slightly more than 60% of employees are actually covered by the FMLA. Request for Information on the Family and Medical Leave Act, 71 Fed. Reg. 69504, 68511 (Dec. 1, 2006). Does the FMLA cover same-sex partners?

2.   *Leave-taking.* By 2000 (the last year in which the federal government collected comprehensive data on FMLA usage), more than 35 million employees (roughly 12% of the U.S. civilian workforce) had taken leave under the FMLA. The median length of leave was 10 days, with 80% of the 35 million taking 40 days or less off of work. Fifty-eight percent of leave takers were women and 42% were men. While 49% of women took time off because they themselves were sick, 58% of men took leave because of their own illness and not to care for another. Even though the FMLA does not require compensated leave, 66% of leave-takers received some compensation during their time away from work. Highlights of the U.S. Department of Labor Report—Balancing the Needs of Families and Employers: Family and Medical Leave Surveys 2–5 (Nicole Casta ed., Nat'l P'ship for Women & Families 2000).

3.   *The international perspective.* While the United States offers at most 12 weeks of guaranteed unpaid family medical leave, many European countries provide far greater support to employees. Sweden offers one of the

longest packages, providing 480 days of parental leave to be allocated between the parents. Annie Pelletier, *Comment: The Family Medical Leave Act of 1993—Why Does Parental Leave in the United States Fall so Far Behind Europe?*, 42 Gonz. L. Rev. 547, 570–71 (2006–2007). That time period includes 60 days that must be taken by the father, or else it is lost. According to Sweden's parental leave act of 1995, an employer may not fire or reassign an employee who chooses to take up to 18 months of leave. Parental Leave Act (Svensk författningssamling [SFS] 1995:584) (Swed.)

4. *Race and the FMLA.* Title VII can present a dilemma for minority women. The statute provides that an employee may allege either race or gender discrimination, but not both. In *Degraffenreid v. General Motors Assembly Div.*, 413 F.Supp. 142 (E.D. Mo. 1976), "the court refused to recognize the possibility of compound discrimination against black women and analyzed their claim using the employment of white women as the historical base." Kimberle Crenshaw, *Demarginalizing the Intersection of Race and Sex: A Black Feminist Critique of Antidiscrimination Doctrine, Feminist Theory and Anti-racist Politics*, 1989 U. Chi. Legal F. 139, 148.

2. THE PREGNANCY DISCRIMINATION ACT (PDA)

In 1978, Congress amended Title VII of the Civil Rights Act of 1964 to add the Pregnancy Discrimination Act ("PDA"). The PDA, 42 U.S.C. § 2000e(k), provides:

> The terms "because of sex" or "on the basis of sex" include, but are not limited to, because of or on the basis of pregnancy, childbirth, or related medical conditions; and women affected by pregnancy, childbirth, or related medical conditions shall be treated the same for all employment-related purposes, including receipt of benefits under fringe benefit programs * * *. This subsection shall not require an employer to pay for health insurance benefits for abortion, except where the life of the mother would be endangered if the fetus were carried to term, or except where medical complications have arisen from an abortion * * *.

The PDA prohibits employers from treating pregnant employees differently from non-pregnant employees. If, for example, an employer provides temporary disability benefits, those benefits must be available for pregnancy.

PROBLEM 4–2

Ace Employer offers neither temporary disability benefits nor a parental leave program. Amy is a pregnant employee who has sued Ace alleging that it must provide her with disability benefits for pregnancy and then 16 weeks of leave once the baby is born. You are counsel to Ace. What advice do you give about the lawsuit and policies? Does the Act mandate that an employer which does not otherwise offer temporary disability benefits make them available for pregnancy?

C. PERSPECTIVES ON THE BALANCE BETWEEN FAMILY AND WORK

The following articles offer a variety of perspectives on the issues that men and women face in balancing family and work. These issues involve child and elder care, and implicate financial issues within the household. Family-work balance issues are not new; poor and African–American women have historically participated in the labor market at far higher rates than have white, middle class women, and have confronted the family-work dilemma throughout their working lives. *See* Naomi Cahn & Michael Selmi, *The Class Ceiling*, 65 Md. L. Rev. 435 (2006). For example, in 1900, 26% of married black women were in the labor force, compared to 3.2% of comparable white women. Evelyn Nakano Glenn, *Cleaning Up/ Kept Down: A Historical Perspective on Racial Inequality in "Women's Work,"* 43 Stan. L. Rev. 1333, 1337 (1991).

1. THE MATERNAL WALL

JOAN WILLIAMS & NANCY SEGAL
Beyond the Maternal Wall: Relief for Family Caregivers
Who are Discriminated Against on the Job.
26 Harv. Women's L.J. 77, 90–98, 100–01 (2003).

A number of different researchers have studied stereotypes that are relevant to the experience of family caregivers in the workplace. * * *

The most striking set of studies plot stereotypes on a graph: one axis is "competence"; the other is "warmth." In a controlled setting, subjects rated "career women" as low in warmth but high in competence, similar to "career men" and "millionaires." In sharp contrast, "housewives" were rated as high in warmth but low in competence, close to (to quote the study's stigmatized terms) the "blind," "disabled," "retarded," and "elderly."

These studies have important implications for the care-work debate. Once a woman's status as a mother becomes salient—either because she gets pregnant, takes maternity leave, or adopts a flexible work arrangement—she may begin to be perceived as a low-competence caregiver rather than as a high-competence business woman. Thus, women who did not have problems at work before having children may find their competence questioned after they become mothers. For example, a lawyer found that once she announced her pregnancy, she began to encounter negative performance evaluations and other problems. * * *

The business woman/housewife studies need to be juxtaposed with an earlier study of stereotypes associated with part-time work. * * * [W]omen employed part-time are viewed as more similar to homemakers than to women employed full time. * * *

Another important strand of literature comes from business school studies that suggest that employers may make business-irrational decisions about competence and commitment tied to gender-based assumptions. * * * [M]anagers systematically confuse "face time" with commitment. * * *

* * *

The shifting standards studies also have implications for fathers. As [Martin] Malin has documented, fathers who insist on engaging in family care-giving often experience workplace hostility. Malin argues that male caregivers may be experiencing behavior that violates the Family and Medical Leave Act. * * *

* * *

These studies also provide insight as to why, given the business case for family-friendly policies, many employers have been unable to implement such policies effectively. Often, even well-intentioned attempts to shift toward a new workplace paradigm may be subverted by unexamined gender stereotypes.

* * *

Another pattern is what social scientists call benevolent stereotyping. Employers who think they are just being solicitous of mothers' new responsibilities, for example, may fail to consider mothers for jobs that require travel. In contrast to hostile stereotyping, benevolent stereotyping entails employers who may see themselves as "just being thoughtful" or "considerate" of a new mother's responsibilities.

Regardless of whether stereotyping is hostile or benevolent, it strips the decision-making power about how to interpret the responsibilities of motherhood away from the mother herself, in favor of an assumption that she will (or should) follow traditionalist patterns. In one instance, after a husband and wife who worked for the same employer had a baby, the wife was sent home at 5:30 P.M., with the solicitous sentiment that she should be at home with the child. In sharp contrast, the husband was given extra work and was expected to stay late. The additional work was meant to be helpful, for the husband now had a family to support. The employer effectively created workplace pressures that pushed the family into traditionalist gender roles; the decision about how to distribute family caretaking responsibilities was taken out of the hands of the family itself.

A third, subtler pattern of bias occurs when prescriptions about how mothers ought to behave transmute into descriptions of what mothers want. In *Trezza v. The Hartford, Inc.* [S.D. N.Y. 1998], when plaintiff Joann Trezza "asked why she had not been considered for [a particular] job, the Managing Attorneys . . . told plaintiff that because she had a family they assumed she would not be interested in the position." Such comments reveal how normative judgments—such as beliefs that mothers should have unlimited time to devote to family needs—translate into descriptions of what mothers want, e.g., that they are "not interested" in desirable jobs.

* * *

Stereotypes also influence the way ambiguous events are interpreted. For example, * * * when two parents arrived late for an early morning meeting, their co-workers assumed that the woman, but not the man, was having childcare problems (although, in fact, the man was having childcare problems while the woman's train was late).

Stereotypes also influence memory. "People are likely to 'remember' events that did not actually occur that are stereotype consistent[,] as well as to selectively remember actions and events that are stereotype consistent rather than stereotype inconsistent." Thus, once a woman becomes a mother or adopts a FWA [flexible work arrangement], her co-workers may begin to remember every time she leaves early, whereas they may forget when she stays late.

Finally, where there is no relevant information, people tend to infer characteristics about individuals that are consistent with relevant stereotypes. For example, even today, women sometimes are advised to remove their wedding rings when they interview for employment, presumably to avoid the inference that they will have children and not be serious about their careers.

* * *

Maternal wall problems may hit mothers particularly hard when they also are disadvantaged by problems associated with the glass ceiling. * * *

* * *

The masculine gendering of many high-status jobs means that "the same competence that is applauded in men [may be] regarded as unattractive in women." Women who live up to the ideals of the "go-getter"— women who are assertive, analytical, and commanding—may well find themselves viewed in a negative light.

* * *

* * * [W]omen often are separated into one group composed of traditionally feminine women, who are liked but not respected, and another group with more masculine traits, who are respected but disliked. * * * [I]f women act in traditionally feminine ways, they are likely to be considered unqualified for promotion because they are not "go-getters." Yet, if women act in traditionally masculine ways, they may trigger dislike that disqualifies them for promotion when compatibility with co-workers is deemed essential.

Each of these forms of glass ceiling discrimination may exacerbate a mother's experience of maternal wall discrimination. For example, if a mother has already been disadvantaged * * *, the mother in question may well find that she has little goodwill upon which to call when she becomes pregnant, returns from maternity leave, or seeks a FWA [flexible work arrangement]. * * *

* * *

A final interaction of the glass ceiling and the maternal wall may occur when a mother tries to counter the negative impact of maternal wall stereotyping. For example, when a woman working part-time encounters the assumption that "part-time" means "part-competent" and "part-committed," and responds by highlighting her accomplishments, she may face yet another pattern of discrimination: what is considered in a man to be a healthy sense of his own worth may be viewed as unseemly self-promotion in a woman.

* * *

2. SPIRITUAL AND MENIAL HOUSEWORK

DOROTHY E. ROBERTS

Spiritual and Menial Housework.
9 Yale J.L. & Feminism 51, 55, 59, 61, 63, 70, 73, 79 (1997).

Women's domestic labor is divided into two categories—spiritual and menial housework. This division exists within the context of the public/private split and also facilitates it. The ideological dichotomy between home and work incorporated a belief in women's spiritual nature. In this ideal division of labor, marriage constituted an exchange of the husband's economic sustenance for the wife's spiritual succor. The mother dispensed moral guidance to her family while the husband provided its primary financial support. The separate spheres ideology gave women a place, a role, and importance in the home, while preserving male dominance over women. The "cult of domesticity" legitimized the confinement of women to the private sphere by defining women as suited for motherhood (and unsuited for public life) because of their moral or spiritual nature. Thus, the very idealization of women's spirituality bolstered the opposition between maternal nurturing in the home and masculine work in the cutthroat marketplace.

Household labor, however, is not all spiritual. It involves nasty, tedious physical tasks—standing over a hot stove, cleaning toilets, scrubbing stains off of floors and out of shirts, changing diapers and bedpans. The notion of a purely spiritual domesticity could only be maintained by cleansing housework of its menial parts. The ideological separation of home from market, then, dictated the separation of spiritual and menial housework. Housework's undesirable tasks had to be separated physically and ideologically from the moral aspects of family life.

* * *

Although household work was the most common occupation for all women before 1900, a racial disparity emerged after the turn of the century. The ethnic background of menial houseworkers varied by region, but they were almost invariably immigrant and/or non-white women. * * * In addition to the overrepresentation of women of color in paid housework, there developed a racial hierarchy within domestic service. White servants were reserved for more respected positions such as housekeeper; Blacks and Latinas were relegated to cooking and laundering.

* * *

A corollary to the transferal of menial housework to less privileged women was the disregarding of the housework they performed in their own homes. In addition to devaluing their servants' capacity for spiritual domesticity, white employers generally assumed that Black women had a special ability to handle their own menial duties. * * * White mistresses rarely inquired about the childcare arrangements of the domestic help, and this pattern persists in the present day. One contemporary West Indian employee noted that her employers shared this view of her home life: "It's O.K. for them to ask me to stay extra time because they have their family together, but what about me? They don't think that I have my family waiting for me."

* * *

In addition to the ideological forces that distinguish between menial and spiritual domestic workers, government policies also reinforce the racialized division of housework. * * * American labor and welfare policy have been geared toward ensuring a ready supply of menial houseworkers from the ranks of minority and immigrant women. Paid household workers have been excluded from both paternalistic legislation designed to protect women workers as well as social insurance programs designed to protect male workers. At the turn of the century, for example, state legislatures passed laws limiting the hours women could work out of concern that dangerous working conditions threatened women's ability to bear and raise healthy children. These protective laws were reserved for white women considered to be moral mothers; they did not apply to domestics, who were primarily Black and poor white women. Today, domestics are also exempted from coverage under basic labor laws, including the National Labor Relations Act, Occupational Safety and Health Act regulations, and workers' compensation protection in most states.

* * *

Private employers often help to exclude household workers from social insurance programs by failing to pay their employees' Social Security, Medicare, and unemployment taxes, as well as other benefits. Even after the Zoe Baird controversy brought "nanny-tax" fraud to national attention [when President Clinton nominated her for the position of Attorney General in 1993], it has been observed that the compliance rate remains very low. The fact that household work is located in private homes has hindered workers' ability to organize, as well as government efforts to enforce employee rights.

* * *

* * * [The] division of women's labor privileges white, affluent women both materially and ideologically, and it perpetuates the devaluation and deprivation of women of color. Affluent white women, however, bear a terrible cost for their support of this hierarchy. Rather than increase the value of white women's domestic labor, the spiritual/menial split works to depress the value of all women's housework. Spiritual housework is by definition unpaid and unsupported. As Robin West writes, "Wherever intimacy is, there is no compensation." Spiritual housework is the aspect of domestic labor that is most foreign to the marketplace. It cannot be evaluated by the currency of the market economy. It can only be performed by women. Menial housework, on the other hand, can be delegated to others, commodified, and traded on the market. It is performed by women of subordinated classes for the cheapest wages. Moreover, the spiritual/menial split mischaracterizes the housework that all women do. This dichotomy is false. The truth is that housework usually involves both menial and spiritual aspects; women view many of their household and childcare tasks as an inseparable combination of manual labor and social nurturing. Fragmenting this experience robs it of its full meaning to women and value to society.

* * *

3. ELDER CARE, GENDER, AND WORK: THE WORK–FAMILY ISSUE OF THE 21st CENTURY

PEGGIE R. SMITH

Elder Care, Gender, and Work: The Work–Family Issue of the 21st Century.
25 Berkeley J. Emp. & Lab. L. 352–53, 360, 370, 379, 382, 386 (2004).

* * *

Presently, individuals 65 and older represent 12 percent of the total United States population, up from 4 percent in 1900. By 2030, the figure is expected to increase to 20 percent. The aging of the population has prompted predictions that caregiving for the elderly will equal, if not surpass, child care as the work-family concern of the twenty-first century. Estimates indicate that 22.5 million people in the United States currently care for an elderly person and 64 percent of them work for wages outside the home. By 2020, forty percent of the workforce expects to care for an elderly relative. In view of these transformations, it is critical that work-family discussions expand so as to allow for the multitude of ways in which employees care. * * *

* * *

The professional [toll] that elder care exerts on employees includes increased absenteeism, tardiness, a reduction in work hours, unavailability for overtime work, a shift from full-time to part-time work, and in some instances, early retirement or prolonged departures from the work force. * * *

* * *

Attempts to justify employer support for elder care reveal a central limitation on thinking about work-family policies largely from the perspective of child care. A frequent argument advanced in support of greater employer accommodation of work-family conflicts centers on expected future benefits that employers will reap once children become adults. As one commentator writes, "there is no business in the next generation unless businesses make it their responsibility to invest in that next generation." By providing child care, "employers will ensure that the workers of tomorrow are better prepared than their present day counterparts." To quote another commentator, employers should assist in helping workers with child care because they "profit from access to skilled, disciplined, and cooperative workers." The limits of such future-oriented arguments become readily apparent when applied to elder care.

A more convincing approach arguably rests in persuading employers that support for elder care, similar to support for child care, is good for their bottom line. * * *

* * *

* * * [W]hile employers are becoming more alert to the reality of elder care as a workplace issue, those that offer voluntary elder care benefits remain the exception rather than the rule. In its 2003 survey, the Society for Human Resource Management found that only 25 percent of all respondents provided elder care benefits. Absent specific employer initiatives, employees caring for aging family members and friends depend upon the FMLA. Because flexibility is the benefit that employed elder caregivers say they need most, the FMLA stands as an important vehicle to reduce work-family incompatibilities that center on elder care.

* * *

Although key illnesses and disabilities that confront the elderly qualify as a serious health condition [for purposes of FMLA leave], employed elder care providers may find some of the FMLA's limitations particularly frustrating. As noted, the FMLA only provides 12 weeks of unpaid leave. Yet, illnesses such as Alzheimer's and Parkinson's are long-term degenerative illnesses. Rarely is there a light at the end of the tunnel. Care, which is often prolonged and protracted, most often ceases when the care recipient dies. On the one hand, this reality illuminates the need for a leave policy that increases the limited 12–week provision that currently exists in the FMLA. On the other hand, it raises a real concern about the ability of the business community to accommodate the growing demand among workers to take care of aging relatives and family members.

* * *

NOTES AND QUESTIONS

1. *Should employers be responsible for child care?* Some commentators have questioned whether the workplace should bear the burden of child care obligations. Professor Mary Anne Case states:

* * * I want to put up some resistance, or at least begin to ask some preliminary, tough, critical questions about what it might mean, who might be benefited and who burdened, and how, if we looked in various alternative ways to employers or to the state to ease the burden of caring for children. This is by far the most difficult essay I have yet written as a legal academic. It is difficult not to sound churlish when raising these questions, particularly when one has chosen to have no children of one's own. After all, who but the selfish and heartless could oppose more benefits from employers or the state for mothers and their children? * * *

* * *

These sorts of concerns incline me to believe that, whether at the level of the employer or the state, having a child should on no account be simply a ticket to a benefit. This means at least two things. First, many benefits should also be available to those without children. Having a child should rarely, if ever, be the only way to get a benefit. Second, those few benefits that are limited to persons with children should have monitoring designed to ensure that the benefit actually goes to the child. * * *

Mary Anne Case, *How High the Apple Pie? A Few Troubling Questions About Where, Why, and How the Burden of Care for Children Should be Shifted*, 76 Chi.–Kent L. Rev. 1753, 1754–55, 1765–66 (2001).

Professor Martha McCluskey responds, briefly summarizing the debate:

As the conventional economic wisdom asks, why should people with a proclivity for the high-cost project of raising children deserve public support any more than those with a personal penchant for driving fancy cars?

Many feminists have responded to this standard "Porsche Preference" argument, as Martha Fineman terms it, by distinguishing child care as a source of public economic benefit—regardless of the personal consumption value children also may have to their parents or other caretakers. Some argue that child care is a "public good" deserving of public support, rather than a private asset or liability, because the productive benefits of child care spill over to society as a whole. For example, well-raised children are likely to grow up to be workers who will pay social security taxes that fund both nonparents' and parents' retirement benefits. In this view, the public should share in the costs as well as the gains of the child care that will produce future workers.

Martha McCluskey, *Caring for Workers*, 55 Me. L. Rev. 313, 321 (2003).

2. *Additional protections for working parents?* In 2007, the federal Equal Employment Opportunity Commission issued an Enforcement Guidance on

"Unlawful Disparate Treatment of Workers with Caregiving Responsibilities". It specifies some of the situations under which family caregivers may experience discrimination, such as asking female job applicants about their marital or caregiving responsibilities, but not asking men the same questions. Enforcement Guidance: Unlawful Disparate Treatment of Workers with Caregiving Responsibilities, 2 EEOC Compl. Man. (BNA) § 615 (May 23, 2007). Some states explicitly provide protection from discrimination for family caregivers. Professor Joan Williams suggests that these statutes would make it "easier for plaintiffs who have experienced discrimination to proceed under a statute specifically designed to address their concerns." Joan C. Williams & Holly Cohen Cooper, *The Public Policy of Motherhood*, 60 J. Soc. Issues 849, 859 (2004). Would you support such a statute? Why?

SECTION 3: MEDICAL DECISIONMAKING FOR ONE'S SPOUSE

Most spouses consult each other about major medical decisions, and may be asked in emergencies to make medical decisions for each other. The Notes following the lead case in this Section will explore a variety of issues concerning assumptions about who makes medical decisions within family units.

A. THE RIGHT OF MARRIED WOMEN TO CONTROL THEIR PREGNANCIES

The Supreme Court considered the extent to which spouses maintain separate identities and discrete privacy interests in the context of abortion in the following case.

PLANNED PARENTHOOD OF SOUTHEASTERN PENNSYLVANIA v. CASEY

Supreme Court of the United States, 1992.
505 U.S. 833.

JUSTICE O'CONNOR, JUSTICE KENNEDY, and JUSTICE SOUTER announced the judgment of the Court and delivered the opinion of the Court with respect to Parts I, II, III, V–A, [and] V–C * * *.

I

* * *

At issue in these cases are five provisions of the Pennsylvania Abortion Control Act * * *. The Act requires * * * [that] a married woman seeking an abortion must sign a statement indicating that she has notified her husband of her intended abortion. § 3209. The Act exempts compliance * * * in the event of a "medical emergency," which is defined in § 3203 of the Act. * * *

Before any of these provisions took effect, the petitioners, who are five abortion clinics and one physician representing himself as well as a class of physicians who provide abortion services, brought this suit seeking declaratory and injunctive relief. Each provision was challenged as unconstitutional on its face. The District Court entered a preliminary injunction against the enforcement of the regulations, and, after a 3–day bench trial, held all the provisions at issue here unconstitutional, entering a permanent injunction against Pennsylvania's enforcement of them. The Court of Appeals for the Third Circuit affirmed in part and reversed in part, upholding all of the regulations except for the husband notification requirement. We granted certiorari.

* * *

II

* * *

Our law affords constitutional protection to personal decisions relating to marriage, procreation, contraception, family relationships, child rearing, and education. *Carey v. Population Servs. Int'l,* 431 U.S. [678, 685 (1977)]. Our cases recognize "the right of the *individual,* married or single, to be free from unwarranted governmental intrusion into matters so fundamentally affecting a person as the decision whether to bear or beget a child." *Eisenstadt v. Baird,* 405 U.S. 438, 453 (1972) (emphasis in original). Our precedents "have respected the private realm of family life which the state cannot enter." *Prince v. Massachusetts,* 321 U.S. 158, 166 (1944). These matters, involving the most intimate and personal choices a person may make in a lifetime, choices central to personal dignity and autonomy, are central to the liberty protected by the Fourteenth Amendment. At the heart of liberty is the right to define one's own concept of existence, of meaning, of the universe, and of the mystery of human life. Beliefs about these matters could not define the attributes of personhood were they formed under compulsion of the State.

These considerations begin our analysis of the woman's interest in terminating her pregnancy but cannot end it, for this reason: though the abortion decision may originate within the zone of conscience and belief, it is more than a philosophic exercise. Abortion is a unique act. It is an act fraught with consequences for others: for the woman who must live with the implications of her decision; for the persons who perform and assist in the procedure; for the spouse, family, and society which must confront the knowledge that these procedures exist, procedures some deem nothing short of an act of violence against innocent human life; and, depending on one's beliefs, for the life or potential life that is aborted. Though abortion is conduct, it does not follow that the State is entitled to proscribe it in all instances. That is because the liberty of the woman is at stake in a sense unique to the human condition and so unique to the law. The mother who carries a child to full term is subject to anxieties, to physical constraints, to pain that only she must bear. That these sacrifices have from the beginning of the human race been endured by woman with a pride that ennobles her in the eyes of others and gives to the infant a bond of love cannot alone be grounds for the State to insist she make the sacrifice. Her suffering is too intimate and personal for the State to insist, without more, upon its own vision of the woman's role, however dominant that vision has been in the course of our history and our culture. The destiny of the woman must be shaped to a large extent on her own conception of her spiritual imperatives and her place in society.

* * *

V

* * *

C

Section 3209 of Pennsylvania's abortion law provides, except in cases of medical emergency, that no physician shall perform an abortion on a married woman without receiving a signed statement from the woman that she has notified her spouse that she is about to undergo an abortion. The woman has the option of providing an alternative signed statement certifying that her husband is not the man who impregnated her; that her husband could not be located; that the pregnancy is the result of spousal sexual assault which she has reported; or that the woman believes that notifying her husband will cause him or someone else to inflict bodily injury upon her. A physician who performs an abortion on a married woman without receiving the appropriate signed statement will have his or her license revoked, and is liable to the husband for damages.

The District Court heard the testimony of numerous expert witnesses, and made detailed findings of fact regarding the effect of this statute. These included:

> "273. The vast majority of women consult their husbands prior to deciding to terminate their pregnancy. . . .

* * *

> "279. The 'bodily injury' exception could not be invoked by a married woman whose husband, if notified, would, in her reasonable belief, threaten to (a) publicize her intent to have an abortion to family, friends or acquaintances; (b) retaliate against her in future child custody or divorce proceedings; (c) inflict psychological intimidation or emotional harm upon her, her children or other persons; (d) inflict bodily harm on other persons such as children, family members or other loved ones; or (e) use his control over finances to deprive [her] of necessary monies for herself or her children. . . .

* * *

> "281. Studies reveal that family violence occurs in two million families in the United States. This figure, however, is a conservative one that substantially understates * * * the actual number of families

affected by domestic violence. In fact, researchers estimate that one of every two women will be battered at some time in their life. . . .

* * *

"289.   Mere notification of pregnancy is frequently a flashpoint for battering and violence within the family. The number of battering incidents is high during the pregnancy and often the worst abuse can be associated with pregnancy. . . . The battering husband may deny parentage and use the pregnancy as an excuse for abuse. . . .

* * *

* * * The vast majority of women notify their male partners of their decision to obtain an abortion. In many cases in which married women do not notify their husbands, the pregnancy is the result of an extramarital affair. Where the husband is the father, the primary reason women do not notify their husbands is that the husband and wife are experiencing marital difficulties, often accompanied by incidents of violence.

* * * the District Court's findings reinforce what common sense would suggest. In well-functioning marriages, spouses discuss important intimate decisions such as whether to bear a child. But there are millions of women in this country who are the victims of regular physical and psychological abuse at the hands of their husbands. Should these women become pregnant, they may have very good reasons for not wishing to inform their husbands of their decision to obtain an abortion. * * *

The spousal notification requirement is thus likely to prevent a significant number of women from obtaining an abortion. It does not merely make abortions a little more difficult or expensive to obtain; for many women, it will impose a substantial obstacle. We must not blind ourselves to the fact that the significant number of women who fear for their safety and the safety of their children are likely to be deterred from procuring an abortion as surely as if the Commonwealth had outlawed abortion in all cases.

Respondents attempt to avoid the conclusion that § 3209 is invalid by pointing out that it imposes almost no burden at all for the vast majority of women seeking abortions. They begin by noting that only about 20 percent of the women who obtain abortions are married. They then note that of these women about 95 percent notify their husbands of their own volition. Thus, respondents argue, the effects of § 3209 are felt by only one percent of the women who obtain abortions. Respondents argue that since some of these women will be able to notify their husbands without adverse consequences or will qualify for one of the exceptions, the statute affects fewer than one percent of women seeking abortions. For this reason, it is asserted, the statute cannot be invalid on its face. We disagree with respondents' basic method of analysis.

The analysis does not end with the one percent of women upon whom the statute operates; it begins there. Legislation is measured for consistency with the Constitution by its impact on those whose conduct it affects. * * * The proper focus of constitutional inquiry is the group for whom the law is a restriction, not the group for whom the law is irrelevant.

Respondents' argument itself gives implicit recognition to this principle, at one of its critical points. Respondents speak of the one percent of women seeking abortions who are married and would choose not to notify their husbands of their plans. By selecting as the controlling class women who wish to obtain abortions, rather than all women or all pregnant women, respondents in effect concede that § 3209 must be judged by reference to those for whom it is an actual rather than an irrelevant restriction. Of course, as we have said, § 3209's real target is narrower even than the class of women seeking abortions identified by the State: it is married women seeking abortions who do not wish to notify their husbands of their intentions and who do not qualify for one of the statutory exceptions to the notice requirement. * * * [Section] 3209 * * * will operate as a substantial obstacle to a woman's choice to undergo an abortion. It is an undue burden, and therefore invalid.

This conclusion is in no way inconsistent with our decisions upholding parental notification or consent requirements [for minors]. Those enactments, and our judgment that they are constitutional, are based on the quite reasonable assumption that minors will benefit from consultation with their parents and that children will often not realize that their parents have their best interests at heart. We cannot adopt a parallel assumption about adult women.

We recognize that a husband has a "deep and proper concern and interest . . . in his wife's pregnancy and in the growth and development of the fetus she is carrying." *Planned Parenthood of Central Mo. v. Danforth*, 428 U.S. 52, 74 (1976). With regard to the children he has fathered and raised, the Court has recognized his "cognizable and substantial" interest in their custody. *Stanley v. Illinois*, 405 U.S. 645 (1972). If these cases concerned a State's ability to require the mother to notify the father before taking some action with respect to a living child raised by both, therefore, it would be reasonable to conclude as a general matter that the father's interest in the welfare of the child and the mother's interest are equal.

Before birth, however, the issue takes on a very different cast. It is an inescapable biological fact that state regulation with respect to the child a woman is carrying will have a far greater impact on the mother's liberty than on the father's. The effect of state regulation on a woman's protected liberty is doubly deserving of scrutiny in such a case, as the State has touched not only upon the private sphere of the family but upon the very bodily integrity of the pregnant woman. The Court has held that "when the wife and the husband disagree on this decision, the view of only one of the two marriage partners can prevail. Inasmuch as it is the woman who physically bears the child and who is the more directly and immediately affected by the pregnancy, as between the two, the balance weighs in her favor." *Planned Parenthood of Central Mo. v. Danforth*, 428 U.S. 52, 74 (1976). This conclusion rests upon the basic nature of marriage and the nature of our Constitution: "The marital couple is not an independent entity with a mind and heart of its own, but an association of two individuals each with a separate intellectual and emotional makeup. If the right of privacy means anything, it is the right of the *individual*, married or single, to be free from unwarranted governmental intrusion into matters so fundamentally affecting a person as the decision whether to bear or beget a child." *Eisenstadt v. Baird*, 405 U.S. at 453 (emphasis in original). The Constitution protects individuals, men and women alike, from unjustified state interference, even when that interference is enacted into law for the benefit of their spouses.

There was a time, not so long ago, when a different understanding of the family and of the Constitution prevailed. In *Bradwell v. State,* 16 Wall. 130 (1873), three Members of this Court reaffirmed the common-law principle that "a woman had no legal existence separate from her husband, who was regarded as her head and representative in the social state; and, notwithstanding some recent modifications of this civil status, many of the special rules of law flowing from and dependent upon this cardinal principle still exist in full force in most States." *Id.* at 141 (BRADLEY, J., joined by SWAYNE and FIELD, JJ., concurring in judgment). Only one generation has passed since this Court observed that "woman is still regarded as the center of home and family life," with attendant "special responsibilities" that precluded full and independent legal status under the Constitution. *Hoyt v. Florida*, 368 U.S. 57, 62 (1961). These views, of course, are no longer consistent with our understanding of the family, the individual, or the Constitution.

In keeping with our rejection of the common-law understanding of a woman's role within the family, the Court held in *Danforth* that the Constitution does not permit a State to require a married woman to obtain her husband's consent before undergoing an abortion. The principles that guided the Court in *Danforth* should be our guides today. For the great many women who are victims of abuse inflicted by their husbands, or whose children are the victims of such abuse, a spousal notice requirement enables the husband to wield an effective veto over his wife's decision. * * * the notice requirement will often be tantamount to the veto found unconstitutional in *Danforth*. The women most affected by this law—those who most reasonably fear the consequences of notifying their husbands that they are pregnant—are in the gravest danger.

The husband's interest in the life of the child his wife is carrying does not permit the State to empower him with this troubling degree of authority over his wife. The contrary view leads to consequences reminiscent of the common law. A husband has no enforceable right to require a wife to advise him before she exercises her personal choices. If a husband's interest in the potential life of the child outweighs a wife's liberty, the State could require a married woman to notify her husband before she uses a postfertilization contraceptive. Perhaps next in line would be a statute requiring pregnant married women to notify their husbands before engaging in conduct causing risks to the fetus. After all, if the husband's interest in the fetus' safety is a sufficient predicate for state regulation, the State could reasonably conclude that pregnant wives should notify their husbands before drinking alcohol or smoking. Perhaps married women should notify their husbands before using contraceptives or before undergoing any type of surgery that may have complications affecting the husband's interest in his wife's reproductive organs. And if a husband's interest justifies notice in any of these cases, one might reasonably argue that it justifies exactly what the *Danforth* Court held it did not justify—a requirement of the husband's consent as well. A State may not give to a man the kind of dominion over his wife that parents exercise over their children.

Section 3209 embodies a view of marriage consonant with the common-law status of married women but repugnant to our present understanding of marriage and of the nature of the rights secured by the Constitution. Women do not lose their constitutionally protected liberty when they marry. The Constitution protects all individuals, male or female, married or unmarried, from the abuse of governmental power, even where that power is employed for the supposed benefit of a member of the individual's family. These considerations confirm our conclusion that § 3209 is invalid.

* * *

[The opinion of STEVENS, J., concurring in part and dissenting in part, is omitted.]

JUSTICE BLACKMUN, concurring in part, concurring in the judgment in part, and dissenting in part.

I join Parts I, II, * * * , V–A, [and] V–C * * * of the joint opinion of JUSTICES O'CONNOR, KENNEDY, and SOUTER.

* * *

A State's restrictions on a woman's right to terminate her pregnancy also implicate constitutional guarantees of gender equality. State restrictions on abortion compel women to continue pregnancies they otherwise might terminate. By restricting the right to terminate pregnancies, the State conscripts women's bodies into its service, forcing women to continue their pregnancies, suffer the pains of childbirth, and in most instances, provide years of maternal care. The State does not compensate women for their services; instead, it assumes that they owe this duty as a matter of course. This assumption—that women can simply be forced to accept the "natural" status and incidents of motherhood—appears to rest upon a conception of women's role that has triggered the protection of the Equal Protection Clause. The joint opinion recognizes that these assumptions about women's place in society "are no longer consistent with our understanding of the family, the individual, or the Constitution."

* * *

* * * If there is much reason to applaud the advances made by the joint opinion today, there is far more to fear from THE CHIEF JUSTICE [REHNQUIST]'s opinion.

* * *

Even more shocking than THE CHIEF JUSTICE's cramped notion of individual liberty is his complete omission of any discussion of the effects that compelled childbirth and motherhood have on women's lives. The only expression of concern with women's health is purely instrumental— for THE CHIEF JUSTICE, only women's *psychological* health is a concern, and only to the extent that he assumes that every woman who decides to have an abortion does so without serious consideration of the moral implications of her decision. In short, THE CHIEF JUSTICE's view of the State's compelling interest in maternal health has less to do with health than it does with compelling women to be maternal.

Nor does THE CHIEF JUSTICE give any serious consideration to the doctrine of *stare decisis*. For THE CHIEF JUSTICE, the facts that gave rise to *Roe* are surprisingly simple: "women become pregnant, there is a point somewhere, depending on medical technology, where a fetus becomes viable, and women give birth to children." This characterization of the issue thus allows THE CHIEF JUSTICE quickly to discard the joint opinion's reliance argument by asserting that "reproductive planning could take virtually immediate account of" a decision overruling *Roe*.

* * *

But, we are reassured, there is always the protection of the democratic process. While there is much to be praised about our democracy, our country since its founding has recognized that there are certain fundamental liberties that are not to be left to the whims of an election. A woman's right to reproductive choice is one of those fundamental liberties. Accordingly, that liberty need not seek refuge at the ballot box.

* * *

CHIEF JUSTICE REHNQUIST, with whom JUSTICE WHITE, JUSTICE SCALIA, and JUSTICE THOMAS join, concurring in the judgment in part and dissenting in part.

* * *

We first emphasize that Pennsylvania has not imposed a spousal *consent* requirement of the type the Court struck down in *Danforth*, 428 U.S. at 67–72. Missouri's spousal consent provision was invalidated in that case because of the Court's view that it unconstitutionally granted to the husband "a veto power exercisable for any reason whatsoever or for no reason at all." *Id.* at 71. But the provision here involves a much less intrusive requirement of spousal *notification*, not consent. Such a law requiring only notice to the husband "does not give any third party the legal right to make the [woman's] decision for her, or to prevent her from obtaining an abortion should she choose to have one performed." *Hodgson* *v. Minnesota*, 497 U.S. 417, 496 (1990) (KENNEDY, J., concurring in judgment in part and dissenting in part). * * * Petitioners * * * argue that the real effect of such a notice requirement is to give the power to husbands to veto a woman's abortion choice. The District Court indeed found that the notification provision created a risk that some woman who would otherwise have an abortion will be prevented from having one. For example, petitioners argue, many notified husbands will prevent abortions through physical force, psychological coercion, and other types of threats. But Pennsylvania has incorporated exceptions in the notice provision in an attempt to deal with these problems. For instance, a woman need not notify her husband if the pregnancy is the result of a reported sexual assault, or if she has reason to believe that she would suffer bodily injury as a result of the notification. * * *

The question before us is therefore whether the spousal notification requirement rationally furthers any legitimate state interests. We conclude that it does. First, a husband's interests in procreation within marriage and in the potential life of his unborn child are certainly substantial ones. The State itself has legitimate interests both in protecting these interests of the father and in protecting the potential life of the fetus, and the spousal notification requirement is reasonably related to advancing those state interests. By providing that a husband will usually know of his spouse's intent to have an abortion, the provision makes it more likely that the husband will participate in deciding the fate of his unborn child, a possibility that might otherwise have been denied him. * * *

The State also has a legitimate interest in promoting "the integrity of the marital relationship." 18 Pa. Cons. Stat. § 3209(a) (1990). This Court has previously recognized "the importance of the marital relationship in our society." *Danforth*, [428 U.S.] at 69. In our view, the spousal notice requirement is a rational attempt by the State to improve truthful communication between spouses and encourage collaborative decisionmaking, and thereby fosters marital integrity. * * * The Pennsylvania Legislature was in a position to weigh the likely benefits of the provision against its likely adverse effects, and presumably concluded, on balance, that the provision would be beneficial. Whether this was a wise decision or not, we cannot say that it was irrational. We therefore conclude that the spousal notice provision comports with the Constitution.

* * *

[The opinion of SCALIA, J., concurring in part and dissenting in part, is omitted.]

NOTES AND QUESTIONS

1. *Understanding* Casey. Why did Pennsylvania seek to require that only married women, and not single women, notify the man most interested in the pregnancy?

2. *Autonomy for teenage girls. Casey* defended its holding against antici- pated arguments that it was inconsistent with the Court's earlier decisions upholding statutes that require parental notice or consent before a pregnant minor may have an abortion. In *Bellotti v. Baird*, 443 U.S. 622 (1979) (plurality opinion), for example, the plurality stated three factors that have traditionally justified "distinguishing the rights of minors from those of adults: (i) the 'peculiar vulnerability' of children; (ii) their presumed 'inability to make critical decisions in an informed, mature manner'; and (iii) the significance of the 'parental role in child rearing.'" Catherine J. Ross, *An Emerging Right for Mature Minors to Receive Information*, 2 U. Pa. J. Const. L. 223, 245–46 (1999).

Despite these distinguishing factors, *Bellotti* found that deference to parental authority is not always appropriate in the abortion context: "[T]he unique nature and consequences of the abortion decision make it inappropri- ate 'to give a third party an absolute, and possibly arbitrary, veto over the decision of the physician and his patient to terminate the patient's pregnancy, regardless of the reason for withholding the consent.'" *Bellotti*, 443 U.S. at 643 (citing *Planned Parenthood of Central Missouri v. Danforth*, 428 U.S. 52, 74 (1976)). *Bellotti* thus held that to protect pregnant minors from such absolute and arbitrary vetoes, parental consent and notification statutes must provide for a judicial bypass procedure—a procedure enabling the pregnant minor to go directly to court to obtain permission for an abortion without first consulting with or notifying her parents. If the minor can persuade the court that she is "mature enough and well enough informed to make her abortion decision, in consultation with her physician, independently of her parents' wishes," or that an abortion would be in her best interests, the court must authorize the operation. *Bellotti*, 443 U.S. at 643–44.

Bellotti raises interesting questions: (a) When a court solicits the views of a minor who wishes to obtain an abortion without her parents' consent, what factors would determine the child's maturity? (b) If an unmarried child becomes pregnant, she is likely a statutory rape victim. Statutory rape statutes conclusively presume that an underage victim is incapable of giving consent. If the victim, as a matter of law, is too immature to give consent to sex, why must the court make a fact-specific determination whether she is mature enough to request an abortion without her parents' consent? (c) Since abortion is a woman's constitutional right, why should a pregnant minor sometimes have to secure a parent's consent before the procedure may be performed? (d) A girl under eighteen is sufficiently mature, as a matter of law, to decide whether to keep and raise the child she delivers; why, then, may a court make a fact-specific determination that she is not sufficiently mature to decide whether to have an abortion? *See* Richard F. Storrow & Sandra Martinez, *"Special Weight" for Best–Interests: Minors in the New Era of Parental Autonomy*, 2003 Wis. L. Rev. 789.

Casey noted that "the vast majority of women consult their husbands prior to deciding to terminate their pregnancy." 505 U.S. at 888. So too, the majority of pregnant minors consult with their parents upon learning they are pregnant. For some adolescents, however, such consultation "simply is not a reasonable option." *Am. Acad. of Pediatrics v. Lungren*, 32 Cal.Rptr.2d 546, 561 (Ct. App. 1994), *rev'd*, 912 P.2d 1148 (Cal. 1996). Judicial bypass procedures are extremely important safeguards for minors who, because of an abusive home life or other reasons, cannot discuss their pregnancy with their parents without endangering themselves.

B. CASEY'S *VITALITY*

In 2006, the Supreme Court declined to revisit its abortion precedents in the context of a New Hampshire parental notification statute. *Ayotte* v. *Planned Parenthood of Northern New England*, 546 U.S. 320 (2006). *Ayotte* emphasized that "we have long upheld state parental involvement statutes," and that such statutes must provide for the "very small percentage of cases, [in which] pregnant minors, like adult women, need immediate abortions to avert serious and often irreversible damage to their health." *Id.* at 326–28. This statement reiterated the Court's position in *Stenberg* v. *Carhart,* 530 U.S. 914, 930, 937 (2000), which "expressly held that a statute banning intact D & E [sometimes labeled "partial birth abortion"] was unconstitutional in part because it lacked a health exception." *Gonzales* v. *Carhart*, 550 U.S. 124 (2007).

In 2003, a few years after *Stenberg*, Congress passed the Partial–Birth Abortion Ban of 2003, 18 U.S.C. § 1531 (2006) (the "Act")—without an exception for women's health. The Supreme Court considered the constitutionality of the Act in *Gonzales* v. *Carhart*, 550 U.S. 124 (2007). The Act barred a particular method of abortion which is a variation on the standard dilation and evacuation ("D & E") used in most abortions performed during the second trimester of pregnancy, which Congress labeled "partial-birth" abortion. The Court upheld the Act by a 5–4 vote, even though the Act did not provide an exception where necessary to save the life of the pregnant woman, a requirement the Court had reiterated the previous year in *Ayotte*.

Justice Kennedy's opinion for the majority in *Gonzales* stated at the outset that the majority was bound by *Casey* and was following *Casey's* precepts: " * * * Whatever one's views concerning the *Casey* joint opinion, it is evident a premise central to its conclusion—that the government has a legitimate and substantial interest in preserving and promoting fetal life—would be repudiated were the Court now to [strike down the Act]." *Casey*, Justice Kennedy explained, "struck a balance" which the Court would apply, using a "rational basis" analysis. *Id.* at. 1626–27.

The majority opinion discussed how women as a group respond to motherhood and to the termination of pregnancies:

> Respect for human life finds an ultimate expression in the bond of love the mother has for her child. * * *. Whether to have an abortion requires a difficult and painful moral decision. * * * While we find no reliable data to measure the phenomenon, it seems unexceptionable to conclude some women come to regret their choice to abort the infant life they once created and sustained.* * *

In a decision so fraught with emotional consequence some doctors may prefer not to disclose precise details of the means that will be used, confining themselves to the required statement of risks the procedure entails. * * *

It is, however, precisely this lack of information concerning the way in which the fetus will be killed that is of legitimate concern to the State. * * * The State has an interest in ensuring so grave a choice is well informed. It is self-evident that a mother who comes to regret her choice to abort must struggle with grief more anguished and sorrow more profound when she learns, only after the event, what she once did not know: that she allowed a doctor to pierce the skull and vacuum the fast-developing brain of her unborn child, a child assuming the human form.

It is a reasonable inference that a necessary effect of the regulation and the knowledge it conveys will be to encourage some women to carry the infant to full term, thus reducing the absolute number of late-term abortions. * * *

Justices Thomas and Scalia, who joined Justice Kennedy's opinion, wrote separately to underscore their "view that the Court's abortion jurisprudence, including *Casey* and *Roe* v. *Wade*, has no basis in the Constitution."

Dissenting, Justice Ginsburg (joined by Justices Stevens, Souter and Breyer), took issue with the majority's view of women and its treatment of *Casey*. Justice Ginsberg, who you will recall helped to craft the litigation strategy in *VMI*, wrote, in part:

Today's decision is alarming. It refuses to take *Casey* [] seriously. It tolerates, indeed applauds, federal intervention to ban nationwide a procedure found necessary and proper in certain cases by the American College of Obstetricians and Gynecologists (ACOG). * * * And, for the first time since *Roe*, the Court blesses a prohibition with no exception safeguarding a woman's health.

* * *

As *Casey* comprehended, at stake in cases challenging abortion restrictions is a woman's "control over her [own] destiny." 505 U.S., at 869 (plurality opinion). "There was a time, not so long ago," when women were "regarded as the center of home and family life, with attendant special responsibilities that precluded full and independent legal status under the Constitution. Those views, this Court made clear in *Casey*, "are no longer consistent with our understanding of the family, the individual, or the Constitution." Women, it is now acknowledged, have the talent, capacity, and right "to participate equally in the economic and social life of the Nation." *Id*. at 856, Their ability to realize their full potential, the Court recognized, is intimately connected to "their ability to control their reproductive lives." *Ibid*. Thus, legal challenges to undue restrictions on abortion procedures do not seek to vindicate some generalized notion of privacy; rather, they center on a woman's autonomy to determine her life's course, and thus to enjoy equal citizenship stature.

* * *

The Court offers flimsy and transparent justifications for upholding a nationwide ban on intact D & E *sans* any exception to safeguard a women's health. Today's ruling, the Court declares, advances "a premise central to [*Casey's*] conclusion"—*i.e.*, the Government's "legitimate and substantial interest in preserving and promoting fetal life." * * * . But the Act scarcely furthers that interest: The law saves not a single fetus from destruction, for it targets only a *method* of performing abortion. See *Stenberg*, 530 U.S. at 930.* * *

* * *

Ultimately, the Court admits that "moral concerns" are at work, concerns that could yield prohibitions on any abortion. * * *

Revealing in this regard, the Court invokes an antiabortion shibboleth for which it concededly has no reliable evidence: Women who have abortions come to regret their choices, and consequently suffer from "severe depression and loss of esteem."[7] Because of women's fragile emotional state and because of the "bond of love the mother has for her child," the Court worries, doctors may withhold information about the nature of the intact D & E procedure.[8] The solution the Court approves, then, is *not* to require doctors to inform women, accurately and adequately, of the different procedures and their attendant risks. Cf. *Casey*.[9]

This way of thinking reflects ancient notions about women's place in the family and under the Constitution—ideas that have long since been discredited. Compare, *e.g.*, *Muller* v. *Oregon* (1908) ("protective" legislation imposing hours-of-work limitations on women only held permissible in view of women's "physical structure and a proper discharge of her maternal function"); *Bradwell* v. *State* (1873) (Bradley, J., concurring) ("Man is, or should be, woman's protector and defender. The natural and proper timidity and delicacy which belongs to the female sex evidently unfits it for many of the occupations of civil life * * * . The paramount destiny and mission of woman are to fulfill the noble and benign offices of wife and mother."), with *United*

---

7. The Court is surely correct that, for most women, abortion is a painfully difficult decision. See *ante*, at 28. But "neither the weight of the scientific evidence to date nor the observable reality of 33 years of legal abortion in the United States comports with the idea that having an abortion is any more dangerous to a woman's long-term mental health than delivering and parenting a child that she did not intend to have [ ]."

8. Notwithstanding the "bond of love" women often have with their children, * * * not all pregnancies, this Court has recognized, are wanted, or even the product of consensual activity. See *Casey*, ("[O]n an average day in the United States, nearly 11,000 women are severely assaulted by their male partners. Many of these incidents involve sexual assault").

9. Eliminating or reducing women's reproductive choices is manifestly *not* a means of protecting them. When safe abortion procedures cease to be an option, many women seek other means to end unwanted or coerced pregnancies.

States v. *Virginia* (1996) (State may not rely on "overbroad generalizations" about the "talents, capacities, or preferences" of women; "such judgments have * * * impeded * * * women's progress toward full citizenship stature throughout our Nation's history") * * *

* * * this Court has repeatedly confirmed that "the destiny of the woman must be shaped * * * on her own conception of her spiritual imperatives and her place in society." *Casey.*

* * *

* * * The Court's hostility to the right *Roe* and *Casey* secured is not concealed. * * * Instead of the heightened scrutiny we have previously applied, the Court determines that a "rational" ground is enough to uphold the Act * * *

QUESTION

1. What are the views of women in the majority opinion and the Ginsburg dissent? How do those views compare with the views expressed in *Casey*?

C. THE DELEGATION OF MEDICAL DECISION-MAKING FOR INCOMPETENT ADULTS

A variety of circumstances arise in which once-competent adults become unable to make or express their own decisions about medical care due to temporary or permanent incapacity. These situations may involve terminal illnesses, emergencies or other crises. At such times, another adult who is close to the patient generally has legal power to make decisions on the patient's behalf, with the presumption that the surrogate decisionmaker is likely to be aware of the individual's values and preferences. This Section considers the default legal presumptions about the hierarchy of relationships—such as spouse, parent or domestic partner—that lead to a presumption that one person should make decisions on behalf of another. The Section also discusses the legal requirements for designating one's own surrogate decision-maker.

1. *End-of-life decisionmaking.* Because advancing medical technology frequently enables doctors to save patients who in the past certainly would not have survived, disputes over end-of-life decision-making have become more common. Michael P. Allen, *Life, Death, and Advocacy: Rules of Procedure in the Contested End-of-Life Case*, 34 Stetson L. Rev. 55, 56 (2004). Such disputes can often lead to bitter feuds and costly litigation involving the incapacitated person's parents, spouse, children, doctors, and even the government. *See, e.g., In re Guardianship of Schiavo*, 792 So.2d 551, 554–58 (Fla. Dist. Ct. App. 2001).

Florida law, like that of many other states, provides that when a person is incapacitated, his or her spouse is the default medical decision-maker, unless the person previously designated an alternative surrogate.

Fla. Stat. § 765.401 (2005). The case of Terri Schiavo, a young Florida woman who had spent 15 years in a persistent vegetative state, attracted national attention when her husband sought to remove her feeding tube over her parents' objections. The initial guardianship appointment of her husband, Michael, had been undisputed in the trial court. Jay Wolfson, Guardian ad litem *for Theresa Schiavo, A Report to Governor Jeb Bush and the Sixth Judicial Circuit in the Matter of Theresa Marie Schiavo*, at 8 (Dec. 1, 2003) *available at* http:// abstractappeal.com/ schiavo/ WolfsonReport.pdf. Later, as the Florida District Court of Appeal observed, her parents, the Schindlers, "attempted to bring suit as the 'natural guardians' * * * even though they kn[e]w she [was] an adult, married daughter with an appointed legal guardian [her husband] and a pending guardianship proceeding." *Schiavo*, 792 So.2d at 555. Michael asked that the trial court judge be substituted as surrogate decision-maker. *Id.* at 557.

The conflicting claims of parents, *qua* parents, and spouses on behalf of incapacitated adults never became the focus of legal arguments in the *Schiavo* case, but the issue raises intriguing questions. If you were a trial court judge in a state that made no default provision, what factors might you consider in deciding whether an incapacitated adult's spouse or the parents should make decisions on the patient's behalf?

2.   *The importance of written advance directives.* The highly-publicized *Schiavo* case and other cases involving intra-family disputes over medical decision-making highlight the importance of executing advance medical directives, including living wills and health care proxies. A living will is a written document that states a person's wishes regarding life-sustaining medical care in the event that he or she becomes incompetent. In a living will, a person may, for example, direct that she not be given life-sustaining artificial nutrition and hydration in the event that she is in a persistent vegetative state with no reasonable expectation of recovery. Links to sample living wills for each state can be found at http://www. uslivingwillregistry.com/. A health care proxy, or health care power of attorney, is a written document appointing another person to make health care decisions for the signer in the event that the signer becomes incapacitated. *See, e.g.*, Catherine J. Jones, *Decisionmaking at the End of Life*, 63 Am. Jur. Trials § 32 (2004). It is the responsibility of the appointed decision-maker (called a "proxy" or a "surrogate") to implement the patient's wishes as reflected in a living will or through "prior expressions or other indicia of the patient's values and preferences regarding end-of-life decisions." Norman L. Cantor, *Twenty–Five Years After Quinlan: A Review of the Jurisprudence of Death and Dying*, 29 J.L. Med. & Ethics 182, 189 (2001).

Despite the importance of living wills and health care proxies, less than 30% of Americans have executed these documents. Manny Fernandez & Paul Duggan, *End of Bitter Life-and-Death Fight Prods Many to End-of-Life Decisions*, Wash. Post, Apr. 1, 2005, at A11. Why? According to some scholars, people may be reluctant to prepare such documents because the process conjures up the basic human fear of confronting one's own mortality. *Id.* The publicity surrounding Terri Schiavo's life and death, however, sparked a national dialogue on end-of-life decision-making and the importance of executing advance medical directives. *Id.* In the week preceding her death, 27,000 people downloaded living wills and related forms from the Office of the Maryland Attorney General's web site, compared to just over 600 during a one-week period two months earlier. Eric Rich, *Before Schiavo, 1991 Case Led to Landmark Md. Law*, Wash. Post, Mar. 30, 2005, at B1. Even when the patient has executed a living will, family members or doctors may disagree about how to apply it under a given set of facts. Some medical centers are beginning to use alternative dispute resolution techniques to assist in decision-making in such cases, and even include specialists in bioethics in the discussions. John Schwartz, *For the End of Life, Hospital Pairs Ethics and Medicine: A Team Effort to Resolve Family Bedside Conflicts*, N.Y. Times, July 4, 2005, at B1.

3. *Who makes medical decisions for an incapacitated person who has not executed a health care proxy?* As of 2004, nearly 40 states had "family consent laws," which set forth a hierarchical scheme of default health care decision-makers, usually family members. *See* Catherine A. West, Comment, *Gay and Lesbian Partners Are Family Too: Why Wisconsin Should Adopt a Family Consent Law*, 19 Wis. Women's L.J. 119, 124 (2004). Under these statutes, spouses normally are the default decision-makers, usually followed in descending order of priority by the patient's adult children, parents, adult siblings, and other blood relatives. Some states recognize the possibility that "close friends" may serve as surrogate decision-makers, but these individuals are generally placed at or near the bottom of the hierarchy. *See, e.g.*, N.Y. Pub. Health L. § 2965(2) (McKinney 2008); Fla. Stat. § 765.401 (2008). Courts may appoint specific guardians in contested cases.

Of course, a default provision is only that. For example, in a state that provides for spouses to be default decision-makers, a married person may still execute an advance directive appointing someone other than the spouse to make decisions in the event of incapacity. Consider the case of a woman who regularly seeks medical care but is married to an observant Christian Scientist who will not seek medical assistance under any circumstances. If she came to consult you as an attorney to ask whether she and her husband should execute health care proxies, what factors might you advise her to consider?

4. *Where do same-sex partners fall in the hierarchy?* A limited number of states confer medical decision-making powers on same-sex couples who enter into legally recognized relationships. In the handful of states in which same-sex couples may legally marry as of 2008, same-sex spouses have the same medical decision-making rights as married heterosexual individuals. The jurisdictions that provide civil unions or registered domestic partnerships in 2008 also grant medical decision-making rights to same-sex partners.[6] In addition, a few states have family consent laws

---

6. These include the District of Columbia, Maine, New Hampshire, New Jersey, Oregon, Vermont and Washington. See http://www.hrc.org/issues/7935.htm.

that expressly recognize other gay and lesbian relationships in the medical decision-making hierarchy. *See* N.M. Stat. Ann. § 24–7A–5(B)(2) (2006); Me. Rev. Stat. Ann. tit. 18–A § 5–805(b)(1–A) (2008). New Mexico's family consent law, for example, places same-sex partners in the second highest hierarchical position—above the patient's adult children, parents, siblings, and grandparents. N.M. Stat. Ann. § 24–7A–5(B)(2).

Because the remaining states (40 as we go to press) do not legally recognize same-sex relationships for purposes of medical decisions, decision-making powers are presumptively assigned to the incapacitated patient's blood relatives, without consideration of whether they are estranged from or have disowned the incapacitated individual. *See, e.g.,* Ellen D. B. Riggle et al., *The Execution of Legal Documents by Sexual Minority Individuals,* 11 Psychol. Pub. Pol'y & L. 138, 149 (2005). Nineteen states have statutes providing that a "close friend" (who may be a same sex partner) may be recognized as the person who makes medical decisions for an incapacitated person, but usually only where persons who come earlier in the hierarchy are unavailable. *See, e.g.,* Illl. Comp. Stat. 40/25 (2007) (same sex partner is a "close friend" who may serve only if six other categories are unavailable); Miss. Code Ann.§ 41–41–211 (2007) (recognizing a person "who has exhibited special care and concern for the patient, who is familiar with the patient's values * * * ", but only after four categories of relatives). The remaining states have no statutory provisions that would recognize a same-sex partner as a medical decision-maker in the absence of a signed directive from the patient. Therefore, if individuals in a same-sex relationship would like their partners, as opposed to their blood relatives, to have medical decision-making powers in case of incapacitation, it is imperative that they execute health care proxies naming their partners as their agents.

Sometimes executing advance medical directives still does not provide sufficient legal protection to same-sex couples during health care crises. In February of 2002, Lambda Legal Defense Fund sued the University of Maryland Medical System over an incident involving a patient, Robert Daniel, and his partner of five years. Bill Flanigan. Joan M. Burda, Estate Planning for Same–Sex Couples 16 (2004) (discussing *Flanigan v. Univ. of Md. Med. Sys.,* which was argued before the Circuit Court of Baltimore City, Maryland). In that case, Daniel had fallen seriously ill and was admitted to the medical system's Shock Trauma Center. The hospital staff knew that Flanigan was Daniel's legal medical decision-making proxy, but they refused to allow him to see Daniel or confer with doctors about Daniel's health care wishes. The hospital told Flanigan that only family members are allowed to see patients and that "partners" did not qualify. Only after Daniel's mother and sister arrived four hours later was Flanigan provided information about Daniel's status and allowed to see him. By that point, Daniel was already unconscious; he died without regaining consciousness. At trial, a jury found for the hospital, rejecting Flanigan's claims of negligence and intentional infliction of emotional distress. Other states have addressed this problem by statute. Virginia law, for example, expressly protects a domestic partner's right to visit a patient in the hospital, but does not recognize a partner as a default decisionmaker. Va. Code Ann. § 54.1–2986 (2005).

5. *For the purposes of medical decision-making, should the law treat couples who cannot legally marry differently than couples who can, but choose not to?* New Jersey's Domestic Partnership Act, for example, offers domestic partnerships to same-sex couples and to opposite-sex couples over the age of 62. Should this make a difference?

SECTION 4: INTERSPOUSAL SUPPORT OBLIGATIONS

As you read the following materials, consider the nature of the reciprocal obligations of husband and wife.

A. THE GENERAL SUPPORT OBLIGATION

At common law, the husband was required to support the wife, and he had the corresponding right to her "domestic services." To enforce the support obligation, a wife might seek to force her husband to provide her with money or might use the "necessaries doctrine" to induce third parties to extend credit to her.

1. THE TRADITIONAL VIEW OF SUPPORT OBLIGATIONS

This classic case shows how courts interpreted the support duty.

McGUIRE v. McGUIRE

Supreme Court of Nebraska, 1953.
59 N.W.2d 336.

Opinion by MESSMORE, JUSTICE.

The plaintiff, Lydia McGuire, brought this action in equity in the district court for Wayne County against Charles W. McGuire, her husband, as defendant, to recover suitable maintenance and support money, and for costs and attorney's fees. Trial was had to the court and a decree was rendered in favor of the plaintiff.

The district court decreed that the plaintiff was legally entitled to use the credit of the defendant and obligate him to pay for certain items in the nature of improvements and repairs, furniture, and appliances for the household in the amount of several thousand dollars; required the defendant to purchase a new automobile with an effective heater within 30 days; ordered him to pay travel expenses of the plaintiff for a visit to each of her daughters at least once a year; that the plaintiff be entitled in the future to pledge the credit of the defendant for what may constitute necessaries of life; awarded a personal allowance to the plaintiff in the sum of $50 a month; awarded $800 for services for the plaintiff's attorney;

and as an alternative to part of the award so made, defendant was permitted, in agreement with plaintiff, to purchase a modern home elsewhere.

[The defendant appealed.]

* * *

The record shows that the plaintiff and defendant were married in Wayne, Nebraska, on August 11, 1919. At the time of the marriage the defendant was a bachelor 46 or 47 years of age and had a reputation for more than ordinary frugality, of which the plaintiff was aware. She had visited in his home and had known him for about 3 years prior to the marriage. After the marriage the couple went to live on a farm of 160 acres located in Leslie precinct, Wayne County, owned by the defendant and upon which he had lived and farmed since 1905. The parties have lived on this place ever since. The plaintiff had been previously married. Her first husband died in October 1914 * * *. * * *

* * *

The plaintiff testified that she was a dutiful and obedient wife, worked and saved, and cohabited with the defendant until the last 2 or 3 years. She worked in the fields, did outside chores, cooked, and attended to her household duties such as cleaning the house and doing the washing. For a number of years she raised as high as 300 chickens, sold poultry and eggs, and used the money to buy clothing, things she wanted, and for groceries. She further testified that the defendant was the boss of the house and his word was law; that he would not tolerate any charge accounts and would not inform her as to his finances or business; and that he was a poor companion. The defendant did not complain of her work, but left the impression to her that she had not done enough. On several occasions the plaintiff asked the defendant for money. He would give her very small amounts, and for the last 3 or 4 years he had not given her any money nor provided her with clothing, except a coat about 4 years previous. The defendant had purchased the groceries the last 3 or 4 years, and permitted her to buy groceries, but he paid for them by check. * * * For the past 4 years or more, the defendant had not given the plaintiff money to purchase furniture or other household necessities. Three years ago he did purchase an electric, wood-and-cob combination stove which was installed in the kitchen, also linoleum floor covering for the kitchen. The plaintiff further testified that the house is not equipped with a bathroom, bathing facilities, or inside toilet. The kitchen is not modern. She does not have a kitchen sink. * * * The plaintiff has had three abdominal operations for which the defendant has paid. She selected her own doctor, and there were no restrictions placed in that respect. When she has requested various things for the home or personal effects, defendant has informed her on many occasions that he did not have the money to pay for the same. She would like to have a new car. * * * The plaintiff further testified that she had very little funds, possibly $1,500 in the bank which was chicken money and money which her father furnished her * * *. * * *

It appears that the defendant owned 398 acres of land with 2 acres deeded to a church, the land being of the value of $83,960; that he has bank deposits in the sum of $12,786.81 and government bonds in the amount of $104,500; and that his income, including interest on the bonds and rental for his real estate, is $8,000 or $9,000 a year. * * *

* * *

The defendant assigns as error that the decree is not supported by sufficient evidence; that the decree is contrary to law; that the decree is an unwarranted usurpation and invasion of defendant's fundamental and constitutional rights; * * *. * * *

* * *

In the case of *Earle v. Earle*, 43 N.W. 118 [Neb. 1889], the plaintiff's petition alleged, in substance, the marriage of the parties, that one child was born of the marriage, and that the defendant sent his wife away from him, did not permit her to return, contributed to her support and maintenance separate and apart from him, and later refused and ceased to provide for her support and the support of his child. The court stated that it was a well-established rule of law that it is the duty of the husband to provide his family with support and means of living—the style of support, requisite lodging, food, clothing, etc., to be such as fit his means, position, and station in life—and for this purpose the wife has generally the right to use his credit for the purchase of necessaries. The court held that if a wife is abandoned by her husband, without means of support, a bill in equity will lie to compel the husband to support the wife without asking for a decree of divorce.

* * *

In the case of *Polster v. Polster*, 123 S.W. 81 [Mo. App. 1909], the evidence disclosed that the husband drank considerably, came home under the influence of intoxicating liquor, abused his wife, and struck her with his fist several times, on occasion blacking one of her eyes. He became enamored of another woman and went with her frequently, telling persons he was a single man and intended to marry her. He spent money entertaining her and gave her presents. The evidence was held sufficient to render his wife's condition in life intolerable. The court said where the husband's conduct is such as to render the wife's condition unendurable in his home she may leave the home without forfeiting her right to maintain an action for maintenance against him under a statute which was in existence in the State of Missouri. The court went on to say that where the husband has been guilty both of maltreatment of his wife and refusal to support her, the wife does not forfeit her right of action for maintenance merely because she lives under the same roof with her husband, if she lives separate and apart from him; and that while there may not be an abandonment of the wife by the husband from a physical point of view, there is an abandonment of the obligation resting upon the husband to provide for the support of the wife. * * *

* * *

It becomes apparent that there are no cases cited by the plaintiff and relied upon by her from this jurisdiction or other jurisdictions that will sustain the action such as she has instituted in the instant case. * * *

There are also several cases, under statutes of various states, in which separate maintenance was refused the wife, where the husband and wife were living in the same house. These cases are to the effect that it is an indispensable requirement of a maintenance statute that the wife should be living separate and apart from her husband without her fault, and that therefore, a wife living in the same house with her husband, occupying a different room and eating at a different time, was not entitled to separate maintenance.

* * *

In the instant case the marital relation has continued for more than 33 years, and the wife has been supported in the same manner during this time without complaint on her part. The parties have not been separated or living apart from each other at any time. In the light of the cited cases it is clear, especially so in this jurisdiction, that to maintain an action such as the one at bar, the parties must be separated or living apart from each other.

The living standards of a family are a matter of concern to the household, and not for the courts to determine, even though the husband's attitude toward his wife, according to his wealth and circumstances, leaves little to be said in his behalf. As long as the home is maintained and the parties are living as husband and wife it may be said that the husband is legally supporting his wife and the purpose of the marriage relation is being carried out. Public policy requires such a holding. It appears that the plaintiff is not devoid of money in her own right. She has a fair-sized bank account and is entitled to use the rent from the 80 acres of land left by her first husband, if she so chooses.

* * *

For the reasons given in this opinion, the judgment rendered by the district court is reversed and the cause remanded with directions to dismiss the cause.

Reversed and remanded with directions to dismiss.

YEAGER, JUSTICE, dissenting.

I respectfully dissent. * * *

* * *

At the time of the marriage plaintiff had a one-third interest in 80 acres of land left by her former husband. Later this interest was transferred to her two daughters. At the time of trial she had a bank account jointly with one of her daughters in the amount of $5,960.22.

* * *

As long as she was able plaintiff made a garden, raised chickens, did outside chores, and worked in the fields. From the sale of chickens and eggs she provided groceries, household necessities, and her own clothing. These things she is no longer able to do, but notwithstanding this the defendant does no more than to buy groceries. He buys her no clothing and does not give her any money at all to spend for her needs or desires. Only one incident is mentioned in the record of defendant ever buying plaintiff any clothing. He bought her a coat over 3 years before the trial.

* * *

There is and can be no doubt that, independent of statutes relating to divorce, alimony, and separate maintenance, if this plaintiff were living apart from the defendant she could in equity and on the facts as outlined in the record be awarded appropriate relief.

* * *

If relief is to be denied to plaintiff under this principle it must be denied because of the fact that she is not living separate and apart from the defendant and is not seeking separation.

In the light of what the decisions declare to be the basis of the right to maintain an action for support, is there any less reason for extending the right to a wife who is denied the right to maintenance in a home occupied with her husband than to one who has chosen to occupy a separate abode?

If the right is to be extended only to one who is separated from the husband equity and effective justice would be denied where a wealthy husband refused proper support and maintenance to a wife physically or mentally incapable of putting herself in a position where the rule could become available to her.

* * *

I think however that the court was without proper power to make any of the awards contained in the decree for the support and maintenance of the plaintiff except the one of $50 a month.

From the cases cited herein it is clear that a husband has the obligation to furnish to his wife the necessaries of life. These decisions make clear that for failure to furnish them the wife may seek allowances for her support and maintenance. However neither these decisions nor any others cited or found support the view contended for by plaintiff that the court may go beyond this and impose obligations other than that of payment of money for the proper support and maintenance of the wife.

* * *

NOTES AND QUESTIONS

1. *The husband's rights and obligations.* In return for assuming the "burden" of financially supporting his wife, the husband at common law had the right to control his wife and all their marital assets. "Once the parties 'merged,' the woman's separate existence as a legal entity was annihilated in the eyes of the law and her personal and economic rights were controlled and represented by her husband, the legal representative of the merged unit." Mechele Dickerson, *To Love, to Honor, and (Oh!) Pay: Should Spouses be Forced to Pay Each Other's Debts?* 78 B.U. L. Rev. 961, 970–71 (1998).

2. *The domestic curtain.* If courts fail to intervene to enforce one spouse's obligation to support the other, whose authority does this failure enhance? How meaningful was the wife's entitlement to "support"? Could a wife easily leave the marital household, a prerequisite for invoking the necessaries doctrine? What collateral consequences might she suffer if she left? Why were courts reluctant to intervene? Professor Twila Perry notes that in intact marriages even today, "the expectation is that each married couple will work out the definition of 'support' in their own marriage. * * * There is a strong belief that judicial intervention into disputes of such nature would violate principles of marital autonomy [and] hopelessly entangle the courts in the day-to-day marital relationship." Twila Perry, *The Essentials of Marriage: Reconsidering the Duty of Support and Services*, 15 Yale J.L. & Feminism 1, 14 (2003). A divorce filing shatters this expectation and raises the prospect of intrusive judicial scrutiny of the family's finances, matters treated in Chapters 9–11.

2. THE NECESSARIES DOCTRINE

To compensate for the wife's legal disabilities during marriage, the "necessaries doctrine" allowed her to buy necessities from a third party using her husband's credit. If the husband refused to pay, the creditor could sue the husband for the debt. The traditional necessaries doctrine provided merchants and other creditors with a guarantee that they could collect payment for goods or services purchased by a wife. Theoretically, this doctrine would help induce merchants to sell to women on credit, confident that the law implied a contract between the husband and the merchant even if the husband refused to pay. However, many merchants were unwilling to extend credit to women because.this logic broke down in practice. First, the definition of what constituted a "necessary" depended on "the family's social position and [was] limited by the husband's ability to pay." Note, *The Unnecessary Doctrine of Necessaries*, 82 Mich. L. Rev. 1767, 1773–75 (1984). Second, "the wife had to be cohabiting with her spouse or living apart through no fault of her own when the sale occurred, and the creditor had to rely on the husband's, not the wife's, credit—it was very difficult to know, before going to court, whether the doctrine of necessaries would apply." *Id.* In addition, a "merchant could collect for necessaries from a recalcitrant husband only if the merchant sued the husband and won. Litigation would be costly, and the doctrine of necessaries gave merchants no guarantee of success." Jill Elaine Hasday, *The Canon of Family Law*, 57 Stan. L. Rev. 825, 846 (2004).

NOTES AND QUESTIONS

1. *Current status of the husband's obligation to support his wife.* Some courts and legislatures have abolished the necessaries doctrine, explaining that the common law notion that a husband must provide for his wife's needs is no longer warranted. Nonetheless, most states retain the doctrine in some form. *See id.* at 847. A few states continue to place primary support obligations on the husband. For example, in Nevada, "[i]f the husband neglects to make adequate provision for the support of his wife, any other person may in good faith supply her with articles necessary for her support, and recover the reasonable value thereof from the husband." However, "the wife must support the husband out of her separate property when he has no separate property and they have no community property and he, from infirmity, is not able or competent to support himself." Nev. Rev. Stat. Ann. §§ 123.090, 123.110 (2008).

In *Marshfield Clinic v. Discher*, 314 N.W.2d 326 (Wis. 1982), the court held that husbands were primarily liable for the debts of either spouse and said that this approach satisfied the intermediate level of equal protection scrutiny because women generally earn less than men. This approach was subsequently modified by statute. W.S.A. § 765.001(2) (2006).

2. *Gender neutrality and the necessaries doctrine.* Most of the more than 30 states that have retained the doctrine have made it gender neutral. Generally, these gender neutral policies have developed only within the last several decades because many courts previously hesitated to abandon preconceived stereotypes. These states have adopted two different approaches.

The first approach is to make one spouse primarily responsible for payment of his or her own debts for necessaries before seeking reimbursement from the other spouse. In *Cheshire Med. Ctr. v. Holbrook*, 663 A.2d 1344 (N.H. 1995), the court modified the traditional common law doctrine instead of abolishing it. Although the state continues to recognize the necessaries doctrine, it must be applied in a gender-neutral manner; moreover, the medical provider was required to seek payment from the individual who incurred the debt before pursuing payment from the spouse.

As a variation of the first approach, Pennsylvania requires that "where debts are contracted for necessaries by either spouse for the support and maintenance of the family, it shall be lawful for the creditor in this case to institute suit against the husband and wife for the price of such necessaries and, after obtaining a judgment, have an execution against the spouse contracting the debt alone; and, if no property of that spouse is found, execution may be levied upon and satisfied out of the separate property of the other spouse." 23 Pa. Cons. Stat. Ann. § 4102 (West 2007).

The second approach makes the spouses jointly and severally liable for each other's debts for necessaries. In Illinois, the "expenses of the family and of the education of the children shall be chargeable upon the property of both husband and wife, or of either of them, in favor of creditors therefor, and in relation thereto they may be sued jointly or separately." 750 Ill.Comp.Stat. 65/15(a)(1) (2009). As discussed in the next note, there is extremely little intervention in the intact family when it comes to supporting children.

Which approach to the necessaries doctrine seems fairer? Why?

3. *Contemporary hurdles.* Even where the necessaries doctrine is gender neutral today, uncertainty about whether a particular purchase involves necessities may inhibit practical application of the doctrine. A layperson might expect that courts would find food, clothing and shelter to be quintessential necessities. No such bright line rule exists, however.

4. Child *support obligations in intact families.* When parties divorce or have a nonmarital child, the court is involved in a close, sometimes highly intrusive, inquiry into the parents' financial condition in order to determine child support obligations. (These obligations are discussed in Chapter 11.) This close inquiry contrasts starkly with the law's hands-off attitude concerning child support while the family remains intact.

"In an intact family, the law assumes that parents will provide for the children as well as they can." *Kiken v. Kiken,* 694 A.2d 557, 560 (N.J. 1997). The assumption, grounded in constitutional family privacy and autonomy doctrines, prevails as long as the parents provide at least a minimal level of child support sufficient to defeat a neglect petition in the juvenile or family court. This minimal level may be considerably lower than what the child support guidelines would require based on parental income and the child's needs and what observers would regard as adequate support. The tolerated level may also stem from recognition that the remedies available for neglect— which may include the child's temporary or permanent removal from the home for foster placement or other state custody—would not necessarily help the child if the bar were set higher. Concerning neglect generally, *see* Douglas E. Abrams & Sarah H. Ramsey, Children and the Law—Doctrine, Policy and Practice, ch. 4 (3d ed. 2007).

PROBLEM 4–3

Sam and Irene have been married for 25 years, and have one child in high school who lives at home, and another in college in a different state. Sam recently bought five shirts that he needs for both work and social events, two ties for business meetings, a convertible, and a brand new, top of the line computer. When he finds himself without enough money to cover all these expenses, who is responsible for any parts of Sam's debt under Nevada law? Under Illinois law?

B. SPOUSAL PROPERTY DISTRIBUTION UPON DEATH

When people write wills, they typically leave their assets to family members, generally to spouses. In community property states, regardless of what the will provides, the surviving spouse is entitled to one-half of the property accumulated during the marriage. But in common law states, the surviving spouse may be entirely left out of the will. The traditional protection for the surviving spouse in these states was either dower, under which a widow was entitled to a life interest in one-third of her husband's real property, or curtesy, through which a widower acquired a life interest in all of his wife's real property if children were born into the marriage.

Dower and curtesy no longer exist in most jurisdictions, but virtually all non-community property states have replaced them with the statutory elective share, which generally allows a surviving spouse to elect to receive one-third or, depending on the state, one-half of the estate of the deceased spouse. Unlike dower and curtesy, the elective share typically applies to all property, not just real estate; it is gender neutral; and it provides for full ownership, not just a life estate.

NOTES AND QUESTIONS

1. *Wills and the protection of spouses.* Professor Lawrence Waggoner questions whether the elective share provides sufficient protection:

> Elective share law protects a decedent's surviving spouse against disinheritance, but the theory behind traditional elective share law has not until recently been carefully developed, perhaps because the idea of granting such protection seems so intuitive. One plausible theory of the elective share is the marital sharing theory. Under that theory, marriage is viewed as an economic partnership, a view that imports a goal of equalizing the marital assets. Another plausible theory is the support theory, that the elective share is a means of continuing the decedent's duty of support beyond the grave. The traditional elective share statute implements neither theory. A fixed fraction of the decedent's estate, whether it be one-third or one-half, is not coordinated with the partnership or support theories. Regarding the partnership theory, one-third or one-half of the decedent's estate might be significantly less than the amount necessary to equalize the marital assets when those assets are disproportionately titled in the decedent's name and considerably in excess of the amount necessary to do so when those assets are already titled equally or are disproportionately titled in the survivor's name. Regarding the support theory, one-third or one-half might be significantly less than the amount necessary to satisfy the survivor's support needs in a smaller estate and considerably in excess of those needs in a larger estate.

Lawrence A. Waggoner, *The Uniform Probate Code's Elective Share: Time for a Reassessment*, 37 U. Mich. J.L. Reform 1, 3 (2003). Indeed, outside of the community property states, a surviving spouse may receive less protection at death than does a divorcing spouse under the property distribution and spousal maintenance statutes of those same states. *See* Laura A. Rosenbury, *Two Ways to End a Marriage: Divorce or Death*, 2005 Utah L. Rev. 1227. Does any theory convince you that the elective share is justified?

2. *Wills and protection of children.* Except in Louisiana, a parent can disinherit his or her marital or nonmarital child for any reason or no reason at all, no matter how young the child and no matter how much the child needs continued support. This majority rule is contrary to the rule that prevails in most other developed nations.

In *L.W.K. v. E.R.C.*, 735 N.E.2d 359 (Mass. 2000), the divorced father died in 1994, survived by an adult daughter from his only marriage and a four-year-old nonmarital daughter. He paid court-ordered support for the four-year-old daughter until his death. The father's will disinherited the younger daughter and left the bulk of the estate to an *inter vivos* trust whose sole beneficiaries were the father's sister and the older daughter.

L.W.K. applied the majority rules applicable when a parent dies testate (leaving a valid will): (1) A parent may disinherit a minor or adult child for no reason, no matter how young the child is, and even if disinheritance leaves the child with no means of support; (2) like the testator's other financial obligations, a legally enforceable obligation to pay child support must be satisfied before distribution of assets under the will; and (3) a child support order survives the parent's death and is not extinguished by it. *L.W.K.* held that the underlying child support order, which ordered the father to pay $100 per week "until further order of the Court," survived the parent's death.

Louisiana follows the civil law rule, which prohibits parents from disinheriting their minor or adult children, except in narrow circumstances that establish "just cause" for disinheritance. "Just cause" is established where the child attempted to murder or committed an act of violence against the parent, refused after reaching majority to contact the parent for two years, married while a minor without the parent's consent, or was convicted of a crime carrying the death penalty or life imprisonment. *See* La. Civ. Code Ann. art. 1621 (2006). Even in Louisiana, however, children over the age of 23 do not have the right to inherit. La. Civ. Code Ann. art. 1493 (2006).

Should the law permit parents to disinherit their children and leave the children without visible means of support? Should children, especially if they are minors when their parent dies, receive an elective share? Why have states not protected children in the same way as spouses?

3. *What if there is no will?* If the spouse dies without a will, intestacy law typically provides that the surviving spouse shares the estate equally with any descendants. Although state intestacy laws generally apply only to a spouse, several states, including Vermont, and Hawaii, grant intestacy succession rights to the surviving members of same-sex couples who have another legally-recognized status, such as a civil union or domestic partnership. *See* T.P. Gallanis, *Inheritance Rights for Domestic Partners*, 79 Tul. L. Rev. 55, 63–64 (2004).

When it comes to descendants, equal protection requires equal treatment of marital and nonmarital children, at least where a court entered a filiation order concerning the nonmarital child during the father's lifetime. *See Lalli v. Lalli*, 439 U.S. 259 (1978); *Trimble v. Gordon,* 430 U.S. 762 (1977). Intestacy laws provide that the children take equally, without regard to their age or other condition. Under what circumstances might this "sibling parity" cause hardship to minor children? How might a parent avoid this hardship?

SECTION 5: FAMILIAL EVIDENTIARY PRIVILEGES

The law's evolving conception of marriage and the status of spouses has affected a broad range of American law. The next decision provides one example of how legal and social change can produce ripple effects.

TRAMMEL v. UNITED STATES

Supreme Court of the United States, 1980.
445 U.S. 40.

CHIEF JUSTICE BURGER delivered the opinion of the Court.

We granted certiorari to consider whether an accused may invoke the privilege against adverse spousal testimony so as to exclude the voluntary testimony of his wife. This calls for a re-examination of *Hawkins v. United States*, 358 U.S. 74 (1958).

I

On March 10, 1976, petitioner Otis Trammel was indicted with two others, Edwin Lee Roberts and Joseph Freeman, for importing heroin into the United States from Thailand and the Philippine Islands and for conspiracy to import heroin * * *. The indictment also named six unindicted co-conspirators, including petitioner's wife Elizabeth Ann Trammel.

According to the indictment, petitioner and his wife flew from the Philippines to California in August 1975, carrying with them a quantity of heroin. Freeman and Roberts assisted them in its distribution. Elizabeth Trammel then traveled to Thailand where she purchased another supply of the drug. On November 3, 1975, with four ounces of heroin on her person, she boarded a plane for the United States. During a routine customs search in Hawaii, she was searched, the heroin was discovered, and she was arrested. After discussions with Drug Enforcement Administration agents, she agreed to cooperate with the Government.

Prior to trial on this indictment, petitioner moved to sever his case from that of Roberts and Freeman. He advised the court that the Government intended to call his wife as an adverse witness and asserted his claim to a privilege to prevent her from testifying against him. At a hearing on the motion, Mrs. Trammel was called as a Government witness under a grant of use immunity. She testified that she and petitioner were married in May 1975 and that they remained married.[1] She explained that her cooperation with the Government was based on assurances that she would be given lenient treatment.[2] She then described, in considerable detail, her role and that of her husband in the heroin distribution conspiracy.

After hearing this testimony, the District Court ruled that Mrs. Trammel could testify in support of the Government's case to any act she observed during the marriage and to any communication "made in the presence of a third person"; however, confidential communications between petitioner and his wife were held to be privileged and inadmissible. The motion to sever was denied.

At trial, Elizabeth Trammel testified within the limits of the court's pretrial ruling; her testimony, as the Government concedes, constituted virtually its entire case against petitioner. He was found guilty on both the substantive and conspiracy charges and sentenced to an indeterminate term of years * * *.

In the Court of Appeals petitioner's only claim of error was that the admission of the adverse testimony of his wife, over his objection, contravened this Court's teaching in *Hawkins v. United States*, and therefore constituted reversible error. The Court of Appeals rejected this contention. It concluded that *Hawkins* did not prohibit "the voluntary testimony of a spouse who appears as an unindicted co-conspirator under grant of immunity from the Government in return for her testimony."

II

The privilege claimed by petitioner has ancient roots. Writing in 1628, Lord Coke observed that "it hath been resolved by the Justices that a wife cannot be produced either against or for her husband." This spousal disqualification sprang from two canons of medieval jurisprudence: first, the rule that an accused was not permitted to testify in his own behalf because of his interest in the proceeding; second, the concept that husband and wife were one, and that since the woman had no recognized separate legal existence, the husband was that one. From those two now long-abandoned doctrines, it followed that what was inadmissible from the lips of the defendant-husband was also inadmissible from his wife.

Despite its medieval origins, this rule of spousal disqualification remained intact in most common-law jurisdictions well into the 19th century. It was applied by this Court in *Stein v. Bowman,* 13 Pet. 209, 220–23 (1839), in *Graves v. United States*, 150 U.S. 118 (1893), and again in *Jin Fuey Moy v. United States*, 254 U.S. 189, 195 (1920), where it was deemed so well established a proposition as to "hardly [require] mention." Indeed, it was not until 1933, in *Funk v. United States*, 290 U.S. 371, that this Court abolished the testimonial disqualification in the federal courts,

---

1. In response to the question whether divorce was contemplated, Mrs. Trammel testified that her husband had said that "I would go my way and he would go his."

2. The Government represents to the Court that Elizabeth Trammel has not been prosecuted for her role in the conspiracy.

so as to permit the spouse of a defendant to testify in the defendant's behalf. *Funk*, however, left undisturbed the rule that either spouse could prevent the other from giving adverse testimony. The rule thus evolved into one of privilege rather than one of absolute disqualification.

The modern justification for this privilege against adverse spousal testimony is its perceived role in fostering the harmony and sanctity of the marriage relationship. Notwithstanding this benign purpose, the rule was sharply criticized. Professor Wigmore termed it "the merest anachronism in legal theory and an indefensible obstruction to truth in practice." 8 Wigmore § 2228, at 221. The Committee on Improvements in the Law of Evidence of the American Bar Association called for its abolition [in 1938]. In its place, Wigmore and others suggested a privilege protecting only private marital communications, modeled on the privilege between priest and penitent, attorney and client, and physician and patient.[5]

These criticisms influenced the American Law Institute, which, in its 1942 Model Code of Evidence, advocated a privilege for marital confidences, but expressly rejected a rule vesting in the defendant the right to exclude all adverse testimony of his spouse. In 1953 the Uniform Rules of Evidence, drafted by the National Conference of Commissioners on Uniform State Laws, followed a similar course; it limited the privilege to confidential communications and "[abolished] the rule, still existing in some states, and largely a sentimental relic, of not requiring one spouse to testify against the other in a criminal action." See Rule 23(2) and comments. Several state legislatures enacted similarly patterned provisions into law.

In *Hawkins v. United States*, 358 U.S. 74, this Court considered the continued vitality of the privilege against adverse spousal testimony in the federal courts. There the District Court had permitted petitioner's wife, over his objection, to testify against him. With one questioning concurring opinion, the Court held the wife's testimony inadmissible; it took note of the critical comments that the common-law rule had engendered, but chose not to abandon it. Also rejected was the Government's suggestion that the Court modify the privilege by vesting it in the witness-spouse, with freedom to testify or not independent of the defendant's control. The Court viewed this proposed modification as antithetical to the widespread belief, evidenced in the rules then in effect in a majority of the States and in England, "that the law should not force or encourage testimony which might alienate husband and wife, or further inflame existing domestic differences." *Id.* at 79.

Hawkins, then, left the federal privilege for adverse spousal testimony where it found it, continuing "a rule which bars the testimony of one

---

5. This Court recognized just such a confidential marital communications privilege in *Wolfle v. United States*, 291 U.S. 7 (1934), and in *Blau v. United States*, 340 U.S. 332 (1951). In neither case, however, did the Court adopt the Wigmore view that the communications privilege be substituted *in place of* the privilege against adverse spousal testimony. The privilege as to confidential marital communications is not at issue in the instant case; accordingly, our holding today does not disturb *Wolfle* and *Blau*.

spouse against the other unless both consent." *Id*. at 78. Accord, *Wyatt v. United States*, 362 U.S. 525, 528 (1960).[7] However, in so doing, the Court made clear that its decision was not meant to "foreclose whatever changes in the rule may eventually be dictated by 'reason and experience.'" *Hawkins*, 358 U.S. at 79.

III

A

The Federal Rules of Evidence acknowledge the authority of the federal courts to continue the evolutionary development of testimonial privileges in federal criminal trials "governed by the principles of the common law as they may be interpreted . . . in the light of reason and experience." Fed. R. Evid. 501. The general mandate of Rule 501 was substituted by the Congress for a set of privilege rules drafted by the Judicial Conference Advisory Committee on Rules of Evidence and approved by the Judicial Conference of the United States and by this Court. That proposal defined nine specific privileges, including a husband-wife privilege which would have codified the *Hawkins* rule and eliminated the privilege for confidential marital communications. In rejecting the proposed Rules and enacting Rule 501, Congress manifested an affirmative intention not to freeze the law of privilege. Its purpose rather was to "provide the courts with the flexibility to develop rules of privilege on a case-by-case basis," 120 Cong. Rec. 40891 (1974) (statement of Rep. Hungate), and to leave the door open to change.

Although Rule 501 confirms the authority of the federal courts to reconsider the continued validity of the *Hawkins* rule, the long history of the privilege suggests that it ought not to be casually cast aside. That the privilege is one affecting marriage, home, and family relationships— already subject to much erosion in our day—also counsels caution. At the same time, we cannot escape the reality that the law on occasion adheres to doctrinal concepts long after the reasons which gave them birth have disappeared and after experience suggests the need for change. * * *

B

Since 1958, when *Hawkins* was decided, support for the privilege against adverse spousal testimony has been eroded further. Thirty-one jurisdictions, including Alaska and Hawaii, then allowed an accused a privilege to prevent adverse spousal testimony. The number has now declined to 24.[9] In 1974, the National Conference on Uniform State Laws

---

7. The decision in *Wyatt* recognized an exception to *Hawkins* for cases in which one spouse commits a crime against the other. *Wyatt v. United States*, 362 U.S. 525, 526 (1960). This exception, placed on the ground of necessity, was a longstanding one at common law. See *Lord Audley's Case*, 123 Eng. Rep. 1140 (1631); 8 Wigmore § 2239. It has been expanded since then to include crimes against the spouse's property, see *Herman v. United States*, 220 F.2d 219, 226 (CA4 1955), and in recent years crimes against children of either spouse, *United States v. Allery*, 526 F.2d 1362 (CA8 1975). Similar exceptions have been found to the confidential marital communications privilege.

9. Eight States provide that one spouse is incompetent to testify against the other in a criminal proceeding. Sixteen States provide a privilege against adverse spousal testimony and vest

revised its Uniform Rules of Evidence, but again rejected the *Hawkins* rule in favor of a limited privilege for confidential communications. See Uniform Rules of Evidence, Rule 504. That proposed rule has been enacted in Arkansas, North Dakota, and Oklahoma—each of which in 1958 permitted an accused to exclude adverse spousal testimony. The trend in state law toward divesting the accused of the privilege to bar adverse spousal testimony has special relevance because the laws of marriage and domestic relations are concerns traditionally reserved to the states. Scholarly criticism of the *Hawkins* rule has also continued unabated.

C

Testimonial exclusionary rules and privileges contravene the fundamental principle that " 'the public . . . has a right to every man's evidence.' "*United States v. Bryan*, 339 U.S. 323, 331 (1950). As such, they must be strictly construed and accepted "only to the very limited extent that permitting a refusal to testify or excluding relevant evidence has a public good transcending the normally predominant principle of utilizing all rational means for ascertaining truth." *Elkins v. United States*, 364 U.S. 206, 234 (1960) (FRANKFURTER, J., dissenting). Here we must decide whether the privilege against adverse spousal testimony promotes sufficiently important interests to outweigh the need for probative evidence in the administration of criminal justice.

It is essential to remember that the *Hawkins* privilege is not needed to protect information privately disclosed between husband and wife in the confidence of the marital relationship—once described by this Court as "the best solace of human existence." *Stein v. Bowman,* 13 Pet. at 223. Those confidences are privileged under the independent rule protecting confidential marital communications. The *Hawkins* privilege is invoked, not to exclude private marital communications, but rather to exclude evidence of criminal acts and of communications made in the presence of third persons.

No other testimonial privilege sweeps so broadly. The privileges between priest and penitent, attorney and client, and physician and patient limit protection to private communications. These privileges are rooted in the imperative need for confidence and trust. The priest-penitent privilege recognizes the human need to disclose to a spiritual counselor, in total and absolute confidence, what are believed to be flawed acts or thoughts and to receive priestly consolation and guidance in return. The lawyer-client privilege rests on the need for the advocate and counselor to know all that relates to the client's reasons for seeking representation if the professional mission is to be carried out. Similarly, the physician must know all that a patient can articulate in order to identify and to treat disease; barriers to full disclosure would impair diagnosis and treatment.

---

the privilege in both spouses or in the defendant-spouse alone. Nine states entitle the witness-spouse alone to assert a privilege against adverse spousal testimony. The remaining 17 states have abolished the privilege in criminal cases. * * *

The *Hawkins* rule stands in marked contrast to these three privileges. Its protection is not limited to confidential communications; rather it permits an accused to exclude all adverse spousal testimony. As Jeremy Bentham observed more than a century and a half ago, such a privilege goes far beyond making "every man's house his castle," and permits a person to convert his house into "a den of thieves." 5 Rationale of Judicial Evidence 349 (1827). It "secures, to every man, one safe and unquestionable and ever ready accomplice for every imaginable crime." *Id.* at 338.

The ancient foundations for so sweeping a privilege have long since disappeared. Nowhere in the common-law world—indeed in any modern society—is a woman regarded as chattel or demeaned by denial of a separate legal identity and the dignity associated with recognition as a whole human being. Chip by chip, over the years those archaic notions have been cast aside so that "[no] longer is the female destined solely for the home and the rearing of the family, and only the male for the marketplace and the world of ideas." *Stanton v. Stanton*, 421 U.S. 7, 14–15 (1975).

The contemporary justification for affording an accused such a privilege is also unpersuasive. When one spouse is willing to testify against the other in a criminal proceeding—whatever the motivation—their relationship is almost certainly in disrepair; there is probably little in the way of marital harmony for the privilege to preserve. In these circumstances, a rule of evidence that permits an accused to prevent adverse spousal testimony seems far more likely to frustrate justice than to foster family peace.[12] Indeed, there is reason to believe that vesting the privilege in the accused could actually undermine the marital relationship. For example, in a case such as this, the Government is unlikely to offer a wife immunity and lenient treatment if it knows that her husband can prevent her from giving adverse testimony. If the Government is dissuaded from making such an offer, the privilege can have the untoward effect of permitting one spouse to escape justice at the expense of the other. It hardly seems conducive to the preservation of the marital relation to place a wife in jeopardy solely by virtue of her husband's control over her testimony.

IV

Our consideration of the foundations for the privilege and its history satisfy us that "reason and experience" no longer justify so sweeping a rule as that found acceptable by the Court in *Hawkins*. Accordingly, we conclude that the existing rule should be modified so that the witness-spouse alone has a privilege to refuse to testify adversely; the witness may be neither compelled to testify nor foreclosed from testifying. This modification—vesting the privilege in the witness-spouse—furthers the impor-

---

12. It is argued that abolishing the privilege will permit the Government to come between husband and wife, pitting one against the other. That, too, misses the mark. Neither *Hawkins*, nor any other privilege, prevents the Government from enlisting one spouse to give information concerning the other or to aid in the other's apprehension. It is only the spouse's testimony in the courtroom that is prohibited.

tant public interest in marital harmony without unduly burdening legitimate law enforcement needs.

Here, petitioner's spouse chose to testify against him. That she did so after a grant of immunity and assurances of lenient treatment does not render her testimony involuntary. Accordingly, the District Court and the Court of Appeals were correct in rejecting petitioner's claim of privilege, and the judgment of the Court of Appeals is

Affirmed.

MR. JUSTICE STEWART, concurring in the judgment.

Although agreeing with much of what the Court has to say, I cannot join an opinion that implies that "reason and experience" have worked a vast change since the *Hawkins* case was decided in 1958. In that case the Court upheld the privilege of a defendant in a criminal case to prevent adverse spousal testimony, in an all-but-unanimous opinion by Mr. Justice Black. Today the Court, in another all-but-unanimous opinion, obliterates that privilege because of the purported change in perception that "reason and experience" have wrought.

The fact of the matter is that the Court in this case simply accepts the very same arguments that the Court rejected when the Government first made them in the *Hawkins* case in 1958. I thought those arguments were valid then, and I think so now.

The Court is correct when it says that "[the] ancient foundations for so sweeping a privilege have long since disappeared." But those foundations had disappeared well before 1958; their disappearance certainly did not occur in the few years that have elapsed between the *Hawkins* decision and this one. To paraphrase what Mr. Justice Jackson once said in another context, there is reason to believe that today's opinion of the Court will be of greater interest to students of human psychology than to students of law.

NOTES AND QUESTIONS

1. *From absolute disqualification to privilege.* As *Trammel* notes, rules limiting spousal testimony in criminal cases have evolved over time as conceptions of marriage have evolved. Early "spousal disqualification" rules forbidding a woman from testifying for or against her husband in criminal cases were grounded in the law's conception that a married woman lacked a legal identity separate from her husband. An accused was prohibited from testifying in his own behalf, so it necessarily followed that his wife—"one" with her husband in the eyes of the law—was also prohibited from testifying. This rule survived in the federal courts until 1933, when the Supreme Court abolished testimonial disqualification in favor of spousal privilege, which originally allowed either spouse to prevent the other from giving adverse testimony without regard to the nature or source of the spouse's information. *See Funk v. United States*, 290 U.S. 371, 373 (1933).

2. *Does the spousal privilege post–*Trammel *serve the social policy goals the privilege seeks to achieve?* Trammel preserved the adverse testimonial

privilege where both spouses asserted it, and also left the privilege covering confidential marital communications intact. Catherine J. Ross, *Implementing Constitutional Rights for Juveniles: The Parent–Child Privilege in Context*, 14 Stan. L. & Pol'y Rev. 85, 90 (2003). The Court, however, restricted the scope of the long-recognized common law spousal privilege by holding that a wife could voluntarily testify against her husband in a criminal trial despite his express assertion of the privilege. The Court reasoned that by the time one spouse is prepared to turn on the other in the witness box, "there is probably little in the way of marital harmony for the privilege to preserve." Do you agree with the Court's reasoning? Is testimony truly voluntary when, as in Elizabeth Trammel's case, one must choose between incriminating one's spouse and incarceration? For an insightful discussion of the spousal privilege, see Milton C. Regan, Jr., *Spousal Privilege and the Meanings of Marriage*, 81 Va. L. Rev. 2045 (1995) (examining cultural perspectives on marriage to explain why the communications privilege is widely accepted but the adverse testimony privilege is widely criticized).

3. *Comparative law on the scope of intrafamily privilege.* Compare the American approach to spousal testimony with that of European civil law countries, including France, Sweden, and Germany, where communications among a broad group of family members are protected from compelled testimony. *In re Grand Jury*, 103 F.3d 1140, 1162 (3d Cir. 1997) (Mansmann, J., dissenting). In France, any recipient of a subpoena may refuse to testify if related "by blood or by marriage in the direct line of one of the parties or his [or her] spouse, even though divorced." Ross, *supra* note 2, at 91. Similarly, German law provides extensive safeguards against compulsory testimony by family members. The right to refuse to testify in either civil or criminal matters begins with a couple's engagement to marry and continues after divorce, reaching relatives by blood and marriage "to the third degree." *Id.*

A parent-child testimonial privilege can be traced back to ancient Jewish law and Roman law, which "entirely barred family members from testifying against one another based on a desire to promote the solidarity and trust that support the family unit." *Grand Jury*, 103 F.3d at 1162. While there appears to be no express prohibition against a parent-child privilege in the American common law, most federal and state courts that have considered recognizing such a privilege have declined to do so. Furthermore, the Supreme Court has never granted review of a case involving an asserted parent-child privilege. Given the ancient roots of the parent-child privilege, why do you think American courts have consistently refused to recognize such a privilege, particularly in light of the status of the spousal privilege?

Professor Ross argues that courts have failed to distinguish among three kinds of confidences: (1) testimony concerning confidences from a minor child to a parent; (2) testimony concerning confidences from adult children to parents; (3) testimony concerning confidences from parents to their children; and have failed to distinguish all three from testimony not based on confidences at all. Ross, *supra* note 2, at 86, 93, 94. She argues that recognition of what she calls the "essential parent-child privilege," covering confidential communications from a minor child to a parent, is necessary before minors can meaningfully exercise their established constitutional rights, including the right to counsel and the right to be silent in the face of interrogation. *Id.* at

102. Parental advice and mediation may be the most effective means of preserving these rights or guaranteeing that any waiver by a minor is truly informed and intelligent. *Id.* at 107.

4. *Evidentiary privilege for same-sex partners.* Should the spousal privilege be confined to married couples, or should the privilege be extended to protect the confidential communications of same-sex couples? Consider Vermont's Civil Unions Act, which recites a list of legal benefits and protections held by parties to a civil union. Vt. Stat. Ann. tit. 15, § 1204 (2004). The Act explicitly includes application of "laws relating to immunity from compelled testimony and the marital communication privilege." *Id.* § 1204(e)(15); *see* Elizabeth Kimberly Penfil, *In the Light of Reason and Experience: Should Federal Evidence Law Protect Confidential Communications Between Same-Sex Partners?*, 88 Marq. L. Rev. 815, 834 (2005). Given the limited opportunities same-sex couples have to obtain legal recognition of their relationships, what alternative criteria could courts use to determine whether a same-sex couple is in a "marriage-like" relationship for the purpose of claiming a testimonial privilege?

5. *Effect of divorce on the spousal privilege: Wigmore on Evidence.* Wigmore asks whether the testimonial privilege continues after divorce: "After the grave cause for dissolution—adultery, desertion, crime or the like—has come to pass, and the parties have been * * * solemnly freed, by judicial decree, * * * is there any longer, either in fact or in policy, a marital peace which must be kept inviolable?" 8 J. Wigmore, Evidence § 2237, at 238 (McNaughton rev. ed. 1961). As Professor Wigmore suggests, the modern justification for the spousal privilege—the preservation of marital harmony—cannot be said to apply after divorce under common law. Some states, however, have enacted statutes that preserve the privilege for confidential communications even after the end of the marriage. *See e.g.*, Mich. Comp. Laws. § 600.2162 (4) (2000 & Supp. 2008) (the privilege covers "a married person or a person that has been previously married"). What policy considerations might justify preserving the privilege after divorce?

PROBLEM 4–4

Assume that you are a state legislator serving on a committee that is drafting an evidentiary standard covering the marital privilege in your state. Attention has turned to the status of the privilege following dissolution of a marriage. What is your view of the following questions, bearing in mind the purported policy functions of the spousal privilege:

1.   Should confidential communications and adverse testimony be treated the same after a marriage dissolves?

2.   To whom should the privilege belong and why?

3.   If your committee decides that the privilege should terminate upon the dissolution of the marriage, when should the privilege end (upon separation, legal divorce?) and should it be terminated retrospectively or prospectively (in other words, should communications made before the bright line date remain confidential)? Should observations? Why?

4. What would the impact of different choices be on existing marital relationships?

SECTION 6: FEDERAL LAW AND FAMILY FINANCES

Many families in the United States are on thin ice financially, especially families with children. According to figures released by the federal government, the cost of raising a child born in 2005 in a family earning more than $74,900 (in 2006 dollars) is at least $279,000. U.S. Dep't of Agric., Expenditures on Children by Families, 2006 (2007). Most observers believe that $16,000 a year is a very conservative estimate. The *Wall Street Journal* calculated the cost at about $800,000 to age 17. Eileen Daspin & Ellen Gamerman, *Family: The Million Dollar Kid*, Wall St. J., Mar. 3, 2007, at P–1. Although the government reports that housing is the biggest component of the cost of raising children, the government omits the cost of moving to a more expensive neighborhood with high property taxes in order to gain access to good public schools, buying a computer, tutoring services, piano lessons, sports equipment or such items as family trips designed to broaden a child's perspective. *Id*. This is because the study is designed to measure "how much money families with children must be compensated to bring the parents to the same utility level * * * of couples without children," not to find out how much money parents spend on their children. U.S. Dep't of Agric. *supra*, at 5. Add in the extras listed earlier (not to mention a nanny or a television for the child's room) and the costs climb steeply. Remember, these estimates are for one child, and economies of scale are not particularly effective for many of these items (except the good school district). *Id*. at iv. The federal income tax form allows a deduction of $3,500 for each child, but that is useful only to those who earn enough money to owe income taxes. 26 U.S.C. § 151 (2006). Families in the lowest income bracket—earning less than $44,500 with a mean income of $27,800—spend about $7,580 a year per child under the age of two, and about $8,500 for each teenager, according to government estimates, adding up to almost $144,00 by age 17. U.S. Dep't of Agric. *supra*, at ii. The majority of single-parent households are in the lowest income group. *Id*. at iv.

The next excerpt discusses some of the other economic pressures on the American family today, and the real decline in the family's purchasing power and level of financial security in the last thirty-five years.

ELIZABETH WARREN

The New Economics of the American Family.
12 Am. Bankr. Inst. L. Rev. 1, 14–16, 19–20 (2004).

The balance sheet for a family of four has undergone a profound transformation in just one generation. In 1973, a typical two-parent, two-child family would have had an annual income of $38,700—median wages for a fully employed male. (To make the comparisons easy, all figures are adjusted for inflation) * * *. * * * Once all the taxes, mortgage payments, and other fixed expenses are paid, the typical one-earner family would be left with $17,834 in discretionary income (inflation adjusted), or about 46 percent of their pretax paycheck. They were not rich, but they had nearly $1,500 a month to cover food, clothing, utilities, and anything else they might need.

Compare those numbers with the typical family of 2000. The husband's wages are $39,000 in 2000—not even 1 percent more than his counterpart of a generation ago. But there is one big difference: Thanks to the wife's full-time salary, the family's combined income is $67,800—a whopping 75 percent higher than the household income for the one-income family of 1973. * * *

* * * Like their 1973 counterparts, the two-income family bought an average home, but today that three-bedroom-two-bath ranch costs a lot more. Even with lower interest rates and frenetic refinancing, their annual mortgage payments are nearly $9,000. The older child still goes to the public elementary school, but after school and during summer vacations he goes to day care, at an average yearly cost of $4,350. The younger child attends a full-time preschool/day care program, which costs the family $5,320 a year. With both parents at work, a second car is essential, so the family spends more than $8,000 a year on its two vehicles. Health insurance is another essential, and even for a family lucky enough to have an employer pick up a big share of the cost, insurance now takes $1,650 from the couple's paychecks. Taxes also take their toll. Thanks in part to their higher income, the modern family has been bumped into a higher bracket, and the government takes 33 percent of the family's money. So where does that leave the family of 2000 after these basic expenses are deducted? With $17,045—about $800 *less* than the one-income family of a generation ago.

* * *

It is important to note that this shift in the family balance sheet cannot be corrected by the decision of one parent to stay home. Larger economic forces have overtaken these families. * * * [I]f they tried to live a normal, middle-class life in other ways—buy an average home, send their younger child to preschool, purchase health insurance, and so forth—they would be left with only $6,720 a year to cover all their other expenses. They would have to find a way to buy food, clothing, utilities, life insurance, furniture, appliances, and so on with less than $600 a month. The modern single-earner family that tries to keep up an average lifestyle faces a *60 percent* drop in discretionary income compared with its one-income counterpart of a generation ago. The increase in basic, fixed expenses leaves the family trying to get by on one median income with little chance to remain in the middle class.

* * *

* * * Today's family has no leeway to cut back if one earner's hours are cut or if one of them gets laid off. There is no room in the budget if someone needs to take a few months off work to care for Grandma or if a child becomes seriously ill. The modern American family is walking on a high wire without a net; parents pray there won't be any wind. If all goes well, they will make it across safely, their children will grow up and finish college, their own elderly parents will need no care, and they will move on to their own retirements. But if anything—anything at all—goes wrong, then today's two-income family is in big trouble.

* * *

NOTES

1. *Marriage penalty/bonus.* While there is substantial social pressure to marry, many couples may also consider the economic implications when they decide whether to marry or remain single. Most other countries, including Canada, Australia, Japan and Sweden, require each person to file taxes as an individual. In the United States, however, the tax code treats married people differently than single people, regardless of whether they file separately or jointly. *See, e.g.,* Ann F. Thomas, *Marriage and the Income Tax Yesterday, Today, and Tomorrow: A Primer and Legislative Scorecard*, 16 N.Y.L. Sch. J. Hum. Rts. 1, 11–12 (1999).

Persons who are legally married have the option to file their federal income tax returns jointly or separately. Depending on a number of factors, the option chosen will produce a marriage "bonus" or a marriage "penalty." A married person may not file as an unmarried person, but must file as "married-filing singly," which triggers a different, generally disadvantageous calculation of taxes owed. As a result, well over ninety percent of married couples choose to file joint federal income tax returns. *See* Boris Bittker, *Federal Income Taxation and the Family*, 27 Stan. L. Rev. 1389, 1409 n.55 (1975) (calling joint returns an offer "that could not be refused"). A marriage penalty results whenever a couple pays higher federal income taxes as a result of their marital status than they would if they had remained single and each filed individually. *See, e.g.,* Leslie A. Whittington & James Alm, *Tax Reductions, Tax Changes, and the Marriage Penalty*, 54 Nat'l Tax J. 455 (2001). Penalties are highest when two wage-earners earn roughly equal incomes. A marriage bonus, on the other hand, occurs whenever a married couple pays lower federal income taxes than would two unmarried individuals each filing separately. Bonuses are highest when only one spouse is in the paid labor market and earns all the household income. Thus, couples in "traditional" marriages, with one primary breadwinner (usually the husband), reap the most benefits under the current system.

Both Democrats and Republicans in Congress have expressed concern about the marriage penalty and made various attempts to alleviate the financial burden it imposes on married taxpayers. Lawrence Zelenak, *Doing Something About Marriage Penalties: A Guide for the Perplexed*, 54 Tax L. Rev. 1, 2 (2000). The Working Families Tax Relief Act of 2004 extends until 2010 several popular tax breaks from the 2001 and 2003 tax acts. Dustin

Stamper, *Bush Signs Tax Break Extension Bill*, 105 Tax Notes 146, 146 (Oct. 11, 2004). These reforms, however, have not fully eliminated the marriage penalty/bonus for high income earners. 2005 TNT 108–16 [Part 1 of 5] n. 1.

The classic formulation of the marriage penalty/bonus has no effect on low wage earners. These taxpayers are affected by another part of the Internal Revenue Code, the Earned Income Tax Credit ("EITC"), an antipoverty program that provides a sliding scale tax rate depending on income and the number of persons in a family. The EITC is available regardless of marital status, focusing instead on the number of children in the family unit, with a two-child ceiling. Lawrence Zelenak, *Redesigning the Earned Income Tax Credit as a Family–Size Adjustment to the Minimum Wage*, 57 Tax L. Rev. 301 (2004). However, when two low-wage earners marry, they may find that their combined income eliminates their eligibility for the EITC, creating a different sort of marriage penalty.

2. *The "innocent spouse" doctrine.* Filing a joint income tax return exposes each spouse to joint and several liability for the other's tax deficiencies. Joint and several liability means that the Internal Revenue Service can collect from one spouse any tax deficiency that is subsequently determined, even if the deficiency was caused entirely by the other spouse. *See, e.g.,* Amy C. Christian, *Lurking Marriage Penalty*, Nat'l L.J., Aug. 23, 1999, at A14. The agency may collect the entire amount of the deficiency from either spouse, but it will often choose to pursue one spouse over the other "because prospects of recovering from the other spouse are poor (e.g., the other spouse is judgment-proof, has no attachable income stream or the other spouse's whereabouts are unknown)." Lily Kahng, *Innocent Spouses: A Critique of the New Tax Laws Governing Joint and Several Tax Liability*, 49 Vill. L. Rev. 261, 264 (2004).

The "innocent spouse" doctrine creates an exception—although a very limited one—to the seemingly harsh joint and several liability regime. I.R.C. § 6015(b)–(c), (f) (2000). Relief from the consequences of joint return liability under § 6015(b) is available only in a small number of cases, and innocent spouses must prove: (1) that they neither knew nor had reason to know of the understatement of tax on the return; and (2) that when all the facts and circumstances are taken into account, it would be inequitable to hold them liable for the unpaid taxes, interest, and penalties. In evaluating the equities, courts generally examine whether the innocent spouse significantly benefited from the understatement of tax. To gain relief under § 6015(b), innocent spouses must prove every element, an often onerous task.

For taxpayers who are divorced, legally separated, or no longer living together, § 6015(c) provides an alternate form of relief from joint and several liability—"proportionate relief." Kahng, *supra*, at 267. Spouses seeking proportionate relief elect to limit their liability to their allocable share of the tax deficiency. *Id.* Proportionate relief is not available if the I.R.S. can demonstrate that the "innocent spouse" had actual knowledge of the understatement at the time he or she signed the joint return. *Id.* at 268–69. Innocent spouses who cannot gain relief under § 6015(b) or (c) may seek "equitable relief" under § 6015(f), if "taking into account all the facts and circumstances, it is inequitable to hold the individual liable for any unpaid tax or any deficiency (or any portion of either)."

3. *Bankruptcy*. Money is a frequent source of marital discord, and financial instability is often linked to marital instability. Families with children experience a great deal of financial pressure and often have little discretionary disposable income. Elizabeth Warren and Amelia Warren–Tyagi argue that "having a child is the single best predictor that a woman will end up in financial collapse." Elizabeth Warren & Amelia Warren–Tyagi, The Two–Income Trap: Why Middle Class Parents Are Going Broke 6 (2004). People struggling with crushing rates of debt often file for bankruptcy. The authors found that married couples with children are more than twice as likely to file for bankruptcy as childless couples, and a divorced woman raising a child is nearly three times as likely to file for bankruptcy as a woman who never had children. Indeed, in 2003, more people filed for bankruptcy than received a diagnosis of cancer, graduated from college or filed for divorce. According to the Federal Reserve, in 2008 the average household debt amounted to 120 percent of annual income (in addition to any mortgage debt). Peter S. Goodman, *On Every Front, Anxious Questions and Uncomfortable Answers*, N.Y. Times July 19, 2008, at p. A–10.

The decline in housing prices after 2005 "landed like a bomb" as millions of homeowners defaulted on their mortgages, often when the value of the home was less than the outstanding debt on the property. *Id*. According to RealtyTrac, foreclosures were up 81% in 2008 from 2007, and up 225% from 2006. http://www.realtytrac.com/Content management/pressrelease.aspx?

Bankruptcy affects husbands and wives in intact marriages differently. Men continue to be three times more likely to manage the family finances generally, but the pattern shifts when families are in financial trouble. In three-quarters of families that sought credit counseling or bankruptcy, the wives were in charge of trying to salvage the family finances. Their husbands often felt that their failure to be a "good provider" undermined their "identities as husbands, as fathers, as men." Warren and Warren–Tyagi, at 11; *see* Jessie Barnard, *The Good Provider Role: Its Rise and Fall*, 36 Am. Psych. 2 (Jan. 1981). The impact on the former spouse of post-divorce filing for bankruptcy will be discussed in Chapter 9.

4. *Joint liability for debt*. Spouses are fully liable for joint debts contracted during the marriage, and the liability continues both during marriage and after a marriage ends. During an intact marriage, many couples co-sign for loans, have jointly held credit cards, or establish lines-of-credit tied to the family home. If one spouse runs up bills based on credit that was established jointly, each spouse is individually liable for the entire amount. *See* Margaret M. Mahoney, *Debts, Divorce, and Disarray in Bankruptcy*, 73 UMKC L. Rev. 83, 87 (2004). The division of marital debt upon divorce will be discussed in Chapter 9.

CHAPTER 5

NONMARITAL FAMILIES

■ ■ ■

Nonmarital cohabitation is a major concern for policymakers and lawyers active in the domestic relations field. In 2005, the U.S. Census Bureau reported that unmarried couples made up 9.75% of the approximately 61 million coupled households in the United States. Unmarried–Partner Households and Household Type by Sex of Partner, 2005 American Community Survey, http://www.census.gov/compendia/statab/tables/08 s0062.xls. The nation's almost six million unmarried couple households included approximately 5.2 million opposite-sex couples and 777,000 same-sex couples.[1] These numbers marked an approximate 8% increase in nonmarital cohabitation from the 5.5 million cohabiting couples reported in the 2000 census. *Id.*

Couples may choose to cohabit, temporarily or permanently, rather than marry, for various reasons. Couples often use cohabitation as a prelude or trial period before marriage. Indeed, most marriages and remarriages now begin with cohabitation. Pamela J. Smock & Wendy D. Manning, Population Studies Ctr., Univ. of Mich., No. 04–555, Living Together Unmarried in the United States: Demographic Perspectives and Implications for Family Policy 2 (2004), *available at* http://www/psc.isr.umich.edu/pubs. Couples may also prefer cohabitation because they fear divorce, or because they have ethical or other personal objections to the institution of marriage. Divorced and widowed individuals also often choose cohabitation as a prelude or alternative to marriage. Finally, same-sex couples may choose cohabitation because their states prohibit them to marry.

Studies show that couples who cohabit before marrying are more likely to separate after marriage than couples who do not. More than 50% of cohabitation relationships, whether or not they culminate in marriage, end in separation within five years. *Id.* at 3. Comparatively, only 20% of married couples who did not previously cohabit separate within that same time period. *Id.* Researchers have found that individuals who do not consider marriage an important goal are more likely to cohabit than to marry; that individuals who prefer cohabitation are looking for intimacy,

---

1. These couples identified themselves as living in close quarters and having a close personal relationship, as opposed to roommates or housemates.

but not the commitment associated with marriage; and that cohabitants do not feel the same sense of obligation toward their partner that married couples feel, and are less likely to make joint investments, such as opening a joint bank account or investing together in a house. Renata Forste, *Prelude to Marriage or Alternative to Marriage? A Social Demographic Look at Cohabitation in the U.S.*, 4 J.L. Fam. Stud. 91, 93 (2002).

Over the last 40 years, there has been a significant increase in the number of unmarried cohabiting couples because cohabitation has become more acceptable as an alternative to marriage. Laws concerning cohabitation have changed markedly in recent years, reflecting society's growing acknowledgement of its frequency.

Despite increasing social acceptance, there is no uniformity between states on cohabitation issues. Some states still criminalize cohabitation, though these statutes are seldom enforced. On the other hand, some jurisdictions now have domestic partnership statutes and adjudicate property disputes between unmarried cohabiting couples.

This Chapter surveys various issues concerning the rights and relationships of nonmarital cohabitants, beginning with the different means of establishing legal obligations between nonmarital partners, before turning to specific issues that distinguish married and unmarried relationships. Because maternity and paternity determinations have historically depended on marriage, the Chapter also discusses establishment of maternity and paternity outside marriage.

SECTION 1: COHABITATION

Unlike marriage, which has established spousal rights pursuant to a set of status-based laws, there are comparatively few laws governing the rights of cohabitants during their relationships or upon the ending of their relationships. In the absence of settled law, cohabitants have pursued various theories to establish their claims against each other, and states have developed laws according rights to nonmarital relationships. As discussed later in the chapter, some jurisdictions have established mechanisms, such as civil unions or domestic partnerships, that allow cohabitants to obtain legal recognition of their relationships while they are ongoing.

A. INTENT (CONTRACT–BASED AGREEMENTS)

When relationships between cohabitants end, the parties must disentangle their formerly intertwined lives. This process may involve determining rights to property accumulated during the relationship. The next decisions illustrate courts' differing approaches to these claims. *Marvin*, set out below, was one of the earliest cases to recognize legal property and support rights arising from cohabitation, sometimes informally called "palimony," and it has been recognized as a landmark opinion. As you read *Marvin* and the cases that follow, consider how courts handle the termination of a cohabiting relationship and the availability of various remedies.

MARVIN v. MARVIN

Supreme Court of California, 1976.
557 P.2d 106.

Opinion by TOBRINER, JUSTICE.

During the past 15 years, there has been a substantial increase in the number of couples living together without marrying.[1] Such nonmarital relationships lead to legal controversy when one partner dies or the couple separates. * * *

We conclude: (1) The provisions of the Family Law Act [which apply to divorcing couples] do not govern the distribution of property acquired during a nonmarital relationship; such a relationship remains subject solely to judicial decision. (2) The courts should enforce express contracts between nonmarital partners except to the extent that the contract is explicitly founded on the consideration of meretricious sexual services. (3) In the absence of an express contract, the courts should inquire into the conduct of the parties to determine whether that conduct demonstrates an implied contract, agreement of partnership or joint venture, or some other tacit understanding between the parties. The courts may also employ the doctrine of *quantum meruit*, or equitable remedies such as constructive or resulting trust, when warranted by the facts of the case.

* * *

1. *The factual setting of this appeal.*

* * *

Plaintiff avers that in October of 1964 she and defendant "entered into an oral agreement" that while "the parties lived together they would combine their efforts and earnings and would share equally any and all property accumulated as a result of their efforts whether individual or combined." Furthermore, they agreed to "hold themselves out to the general public as husband and wife" and that "plaintiff would further render her services as a companion, homemaker, housekeeper and cook to ... defendant."

Shortly thereafter plaintiff agreed to "give up her lucrative career as an entertainer [and] singer" in order to "devote her full time to defendant ... as a companion, homemaker, housekeeper and cook;" in return defendant agreed to "provide for all of plaintiff's financial support and needs for the rest of her life."

---

1. "The 1970 census figures indicate that today perhaps eight times as many couples are living together without being married as cohabited ten years ago." (Comment, *In re Cary*: A *Judicial Recognition of Illicit Cohabitation*, 25 Hastings L.J. 1226 (1974)).

Plaintiff alleges that she lived with defendant from October of 1964 through May of 1970 and fulfilled her obligations under the agreement. During this period the parties as a result of their efforts and earnings acquired in defendant's name substantial real and personal property, including motion picture rights worth over $1 million. In May of 1970, however, defendant compelled plaintiff to leave his household. He continued to support plaintiff until November of 1971, but thereafter refused to provide further support.

On the basis of these allegations plaintiff asserts two causes of action. The first, for declaratory relief, asks the court to determine her contract and property rights; the second seeks to impose a constructive trust upon one half of the property acquired during the course of the relationship.

* * * Since the parties had stipulated that defendant's marriage to Betty Marvin did not terminate until the filing of a final decree of divorce in January 1967, the trial court treated defendant's motion as one for judgment on the pleadings augmented by the stipulation.

After hearing argument the court granted defendant's motion and entered judgment for defendant. * * * [Plaintiff appealed].

2. *Plaintiff's complaint states a cause of action for breach of an express contract.*

[Defendant offers various theories to sustain the ruling.]

* * *

Defendant first and principally relies on the contention that the alleged contract is so closely related to the supposed "immoral" character of the relationship between plaintiff and himself that the enforcement of the contract would violate public policy. He points to cases asserting that a contract between nonmarital partners is unenforceable if it is "involved in" an illicit relationship. A review of the numerous California decisions concerning contracts between nonmarital partners, however, reveals that the courts have not employed such broad and uncertain standards to strike down contracts. The decisions instead disclose a narrower and more precise standard: a contract between nonmarital partners is unenforceable only *to the extent* that it *explicitly* rests upon the immoral and illicit consideration of meretricious sexual services.

* * *

Although the past decisions hover over the issue in the somewhat wispy form of the figures of a Chagall painting, we can abstract from those decisions a clear and simple rule. The fact that a man and woman live together without marriage, and engage in a sexual relationship, does not in itself invalidate agreements between them relating to their earnings, property, or expenses. Neither is such an agreement invalid merely because the parties may have contemplated the creation or continuation of a nonmarital relationship when they entered into it. Agreements between nonmarital partners fail only to the extent that they rest upon a consideration of meretricious sexual services. Thus the rule asserted by defendant, that a contract fails if it is "involved in" or made "in contemplation" of a nonmarital relationship, cannot be reconciled with the decisions.

[All case law cited by defendant] involved consideration that *was* expressly founded upon [ ] illicit sexual services. In *Hill v. Estate of Westbrook*, [213 P.2d 727 (Cal. Ct. App. 1950)], the woman promised to keep house for the man, to live with him as man and wife, and to bear his children; the man promised to provide for her in his will, but died without doing so. Reversing a judgment for the woman based on the reasonable value of her services, the Court of Appeal stated that the action is predicated upon a claim which seeks, among other things, the reasonable value of living with decedent in meretricious relationship and bearing him two children * * *. * * *

* * *

* * * [A] contract between nonmarital partners, even if expressly made in contemplation of a common living arrangement, is invalid only if sexual acts form an inseparable part of the consideration for the agreement. In sum, a court will not enforce a contract for the pooling of property and earnings if it is explicitly and inseparably based upon services as a paramour. The Court of Appeal opinion in *Hill*, however, indicates that even if sexual services are part of the contractual consideration, any *severable* portion of the contract supported by independent consideration will still be enforced.

The principle that a contract between nonmarital partners will be enforced unless expressly and inseparably based upon an illicit consideration of sexual services not only represents the distillation of the decisional law, but also offers a far more precise and workable standard than that advocated by defendant. * * *

* * * [I]n the present case a standard which inquires whether an agreement is "involved" in or "contemplates" a nonmarital relationship is vague and unworkable. Virtually all agreements between nonmarital partners can be said to be "involved" in some sense in the fact of their mutual sexual relationship, or to "contemplate" the existence of that relationship. Thus defendant's proposed standards, if taken literally, might invalidate all agreements between nonmarital partners, a result no one favors. Moreover, those standards offer no basis to distinguish between valid and invalid agreements. By looking not to such uncertain tests, but only to the consideration underlying the agreement, we provide the parties and the courts with a practical guide to determine when an agreement between nonmarital partners should be enforced.

* * *

In summary, we base our opinion on the principle that adults who voluntarily live together and engage in sexual relations are nonetheless as competent as any other persons to contract respecting their earnings and property rights. Of course, they cannot lawfully contract to pay for the performance of sexual services, for such a contract is, in essence, an agreement for prostitution and unlawful for that reason. But they may agree to pool their earnings and to hold all property acquired during the relationship in accord with the law governing community property; conversely they may agree that each partner's earnings and the property acquired from those earnings remains the separate property of the earning partner. So long as the agreement does not rest upon illicit meretricious consideration, the parties may order their economic affairs as they choose, and no policy precludes the courts from enforcing such agreements.

In the present instance, plaintiff alleges that the parties agreed to pool their earnings, that they contracted to share equally in all property acquired, and that defendant agreed to support plaintiff. The terms of the contract as alleged do not rest upon any unlawful consideration. We therefore conclude that the complaint furnishes a suitable basis upon which the trial court can render declaratory relief. The trial court consequently erred in granting defendant's motion for judgment on the pleadings.

* * *

* * * We have examined the reasons advanced to justify this denial of relief, and find that none have merit.

First, we note that [prior] cases denying relief do not rest their refusal upon any theory of "punishing" a "guilty" partner. Indeed, to the extent that denial of relief "punishes" one partner, it necessarily rewards the other by permitting him to retain a disproportionate amount of the property. Concepts of "guilt" thus cannot justify an unequal division of property between two equally "guilty" persons.

Other reasons advanced in the decisions fare no better. The principal argument seems to be that "[e]quitable considerations arising from the reasonable expectation of . . . benefits attending the status of marriage . . . are not present [in a nonmarital relationship]" *Vallera v. Vallera*, [134 P.2d 761, 763 (Cal. 1943)]. But, although parties to a nonmarital relationship obviously cannot have based any expectations upon the belief that they were married, other expectations and equitable considerations remain. The parties may well expect that property will be divided in accord with the parties' own tacit understanding and that in the absence of such understanding the courts will fairly apportion property accumulated through mutual effort. We need not treat nonmarital partners as putatively married persons in order to apply principles of implied contract, or extend equitable remedies; we need to treat them only as we do any other unmarried persons.

The remaining arguments advanced from time to time to deny remedies to the nonmarital partners are of less moment. There is no more reason to presume that services are contributed as a gift than to presume that funds are contributed as a gift; in any event the better approach is to presume, as Justice Peters suggested, "that the parties intend to deal fairly with each other." *Keene*, [371 P.2d 329 at 339 (Peters, J., dissenting)].

The argument that granting remedies to the nonmarital partners would discourage marriage must fail; as *Cary* pointed out "with equal or greater force the point might be that the pre–1970 rule was calculated to cause the income-producing partner to avoid marriage and thus retain the benefit of all of his or her accumulated earnings." Although we recognize the well-established public policy to foster and promote the institution of marriage, perpetuation of judicial rules which result in an inequitable distribution of property accumulated during a nonmarital relationship is neither a just nor an effective way of carrying out that policy.

In summary, we believe that the prevalence of nonmarital relationships in modern society and the social acceptance of them, marks this as a time when our courts should by no means apply the doctrine of the unlawfulness of the so-called meretricious relationship to the instant case. As we have explained, the nonenforceability of agreements expressly providing for meretricious conduct rested upon the fact that such conduct, as the word suggests, pertained to and encompassed prostitution. To equate the nonmarital relationship of today to such a subject matter is to do violence to an accepted and wholly different practice.

* * *

The mores of the society have indeed changed so radically in regard to cohabitation that we cannot impose a standard based on alleged moral considerations that have apparently been so widely abandoned by so many. Lest we be misunderstood, however, we take this occasion to point out that the structure of society itself largely depends upon the institution of marriage, and nothing we have said in this opinion should be taken to derogate from that institution. The joining of the man and woman in marriage is at once the most socially productive and individually fulfilling relationship that one can enjoy in the course of a lifetime.

We conclude that the judicial barriers that may stand in the way of a policy based upon the fulfillment of the reasonable expectations of the parties to a nonmarital relationship should be removed. As we have explained, the courts now hold that express agreements will be enforced unless they rest on an unlawful meretricious consideration. We add that in the absence of an express agreement, the courts may look to a variety of other remedies in order to protect the parties' lawful expectations.

The courts may inquire into the conduct of the parties to determine whether that conduct demonstrates an implied contract or implied agreement of partnership or joint venture or some other tacit understanding between the parties. The courts may, when appropriate, employ principles of constructive trust or resulting trust. Finally, a nonmarital partner may recover in *quantum meruit* for the reasonable value of household services rendered less the reasonable value of support received if he can show that he rendered services with the expectation of monetary reward.[25]

[Concurring and dissenting opinion by CLARK, J., is omitted.]

NOTES AND QUESTIONS

1. *"Palimony." Marvin v. Marvin* dominated the headlines because it involved a high-profile defendant, movie star Lee Marvin, who was best known for his Academy Award-winning role in *Cat Ballou* (1965). Marvin was at the height of his popularity when he separated from wife Betty Marvin and began living with Michelle Triola. After Triola moved out and filed suit, *Newsweek* interviewed her high-profile attorney, Marvin Mitchelson, and coined the term "palimony" for her claims. The case drew so much media attention that comedian Dan Aykroyd parodied it on *Saturday Night Live*, calling Triola " 'a screeching, squealing, rapacious swamp sow.' " Mark K. Moller, *Almost Like Being Married*, Legal Times, Apr. 5, 2004, at 60.

2. *Marvin's ending.* On remand in 1979, the trial court ruled that Marvin and Triola had not executed an express contract. The court also dismissed the plaintiff's *quantum meruit* causes of action, and found that the parties' conduct did not demonstrate an implied contract. The trial court nonetheless awarded the plaintiff $104,000 for "rehabilitation purposes so that she may have the economic means to re-educate herself and to learn new, employable skills or to refurbish those utilized ... so that she may return from her status as companion of a motion picture star to a separate, independent but perhaps more prosaic existence." *Marvin v. Marvin*, No. C233303, 5 Fam. L. Rep. (BNA) 3077 (Cal. App. 1979). Two years later, the California appellate court reversed, finding that the trial court's $104,000 award was based on the plaintiff's need and the defendant's wealth, and was not rooted in a "recognized underlying obligation in law or in equity." *Marvin v. Marvin*, 176 Cal.Rptr. 555, 559 (Cal. Ct. App. 1981). At the end of a cohabiting relationship, just as at the end of a marriage, the household incomes of women in a cohabiting relationship typically decline by approximately one-third. Sarah Avellar and Pamela J. Smock, *The Economic Consequences of the Dissolution of Cohabiting Unions*, 67 *J. Marr. & Fam.* 315 (2005).

3. *Contract-based remedies.* Cohabiting couples may assert various contract-related claims against each other. A party may allege breach of an express contract, that is, that the other party has violated an agreement whose terms the parties have explicitly set out. An implied-in-fact contract is an agreement the parties presumably intended to make, either by tacit understanding or by their assumptions. An implied-in-law contract is an obligation imposed by law because of the parties' conduct, because of some special relationship between them, or because one of them would be otherwise unjustly enriched.

---

25. Our opinion does not preclude the evolution of additional equitable remedies to protect the expectations of the parties to a nonmarital relationship in cases in which existing remedies prove inadequate; the suitability of such remedies may be determined in later cases in light of the factual setting in which they arise.

Where the court finds and enforces an express or implied cohabitation contract, does the court necessarily express approval for the parties' lifestyle?

4. *Contract enforceability.* If the consideration is not based on sexual services, then most states continue to enforce express contracts between cohabitants in the same manner as they enforce other contracts between competent adults. Minnesota and Texas, however, have amended their statutes of frauds to require that contracts between cohabitants be in writing. Minn. Stat. § 513.075 (2008); Tex. Bus & Com. Code Ann. § 26.01 (Vernon 2007).

If you represented a cohabitant and wanted to ensure an express cohabitation agreement would not be held unenforceable for lack of valid consideration, what would your draft agreement say?

5. *Equitable remedies.* As *Marvin* recognizes, cohabitants may assert claims against one another based on theories other than contract law. Parties often seek judgments based on restitution, or unjust enrichment, through several methods. For instance, a constructive trust is an equitable remedy intended to prevent a person who has obtained property through actual or constructive fraud from benefiting at the expense of another person; a constructive trust might be imposed when one party has contributed consideration or time and labor to the other party's acquisition of property. Similarly, some jurisdictions allow parties to recover through a resulting trust, which a court can impose as a means of transferring title when circumstances indicate that the parties actually intended for the defendant to hold property on behalf of ("in trust for") the plaintiff. A resulting trust arises, for example, where the defendant holds title, but the plaintiff provided some of all the money used to purchase the property. *See* Kristine L. Tungol, *Cause of Action by Same–Sex or Heterosexual Unmarried Cohabitant to Enforce Agreement or Understanding Regarding Support or Division of Property*, 35 Causes of Action 2d 295 §§ 15–16 (2007). A *quantum meruit* suit allows an unmarried cohabitant to seek the value of services rendered or benefits conferred upon the other cohabitant.

The next case shows how, almost 30 years after *Marvin*, courts still struggle with palimony claims.

DEVANEY v. L'ESPERANCE

Supreme Court of New Jersey, 2008.
949 A.2d 743.

JUSTICE WALLACE, JR., delivered the opinion of the Court.

In this appeal, we determine whether cohabitation is an indispensable element of a cause of action for palimony. Plaintiff and defendant were involved in an intimate relationship. During the course of their twenty-year relationship, defendant, who was married, continued to live with his wife and never cohabited with plaintiff. However, he promised to divorce his wife, marry plaintiff, and have a child with her. Defendant's promises were not fulfilled and his relationship with plaintiff eventually ended.

Plaintiff filed a palimony complaint against defendant, asserting a breach of a promise to support her for life. The trial court denied relief because the parties essentially had a dating relationship rather than a marital-type relationship that was needed to support a palimony claim. The Appellate Division affirmed solely because the parties never cohabited. We granted certification to address whether a party may prove a cause of action for palimony absent cohabitation.

We hold that cohabitation is not an essential requirement for a cause of action for palimony, but a marital-type relationship is required. Because there was sufficient evidence for the trial court to conclude that the parties' relationship was not a marital-type relationship to support a palimony action, we affirm the judgment.

I.

The following evidence was presented at trial. In 1983, plaintiff, Helen Devaney, then twenty-three years old, began working for defendant, Francis L'Esperance, Jr., as a receptionist for his ophthalmology medical practice. At that time, defendant was fifty-one years old and had been married to his current wife for approximately twenty years. Plaintiff and defendant embarked on a romantic relationship. Although plaintiff was aware that defendant was married, she believed that he would divorce his wife.

In the beginning of their relationship, plaintiff lived in a variety of places, all of which were rented in her own name and mostly self-financed. At some point, defendant began paying plaintiff's telephone bill and gave her money for various other things. Plaintiff, however, remained largely self-sufficient during this period of their relationship. She continued working for defendant in various capacities, at first full-time, and then part-time.

For about ten years, plaintiff and defendant saw each other regularly and would spend vacations together. However, when the parties were not traveling, they rarely stayed overnight together. Defendant frequently had dinner at plaintiff's house, but he invariably returned home to his wife.

Plaintiff testified that defendant repeatedly told her that he would divorce his wife and marry her. In 1993, plaintiff terminated her employment with defendant and pursued educational opportunities. Shortly thereafter, plaintiff moved * * *. * * *

In 1997, defendant asked plaintiff to return to the East Coast. Plaintiff testified that defendant promised that he would "make things right" by divorcing his wife, marrying plaintiff, and having a baby with her. She testified that she agreed to move back after defendant showed her a separation agreement that was signed by both defendant and his wife. Plaintiff also testified that defendant promised to buy her a home.

Plaintiff returned to New Jersey in 1997, and moved into a North Bergen condominium that defendant leased for her. In 1999, defendant purchased the condominium unit and plaintiff continued to reside there. Defendant also purchased a car that plaintiff used; gave her money for various expenses; and paid for her undergraduate and graduate education. Plaintiff ultimately received a Master's degree.

Despite the increased support that defendant provided to plaintiff, the parties saw each other no more than two or three evenings at the condominium for dinner each week and sometimes one day on the weekend. During the seven years that plaintiff lived in the condominium, defendant spent only six or seven nights there.

In 2003, the parties considered having a child together. However, at some point, plaintiff learned that she would have difficulty conceiving a child. Defendant also changed his mind about wanting to have another child in August 2003 and conveyed that to plaintiff.

Finally, defendant told plaintiff that he wanted to discontinue the relationship. Plaintiff continued to live in the North Bergen condominium, and in December 2003, she began a relationship with another man. In February 2004, defendant attempted to visit the condominium when plaintiff's new boyfriend was present, but defendant was denied entrance by plaintiff.

Shortly thereafter, defendant sought to remove plaintiff from the condominium and filed an action for ejectment. Eventually, the trial court granted defendant possession of the condominium and the judgment was affirmed on appeal.

Plaintiff filed a complaint for palimony in October 2004, and defendant filed an answer. Following discovery, a bench trial was held. The Family Part judge issued an oral opinion in which she denied plaintiff's complaint for palimony. The judge found that defendant had made "general promises" to plaintiff that he would take care of her and that "things would work out," and that plaintiff used those promises to sustain her belief that they would eventually live together. Further, although over the years plaintiff became financially dependent on defendant, defendant never promised to provide plaintiff with lifetime financial support.

The trial judge rejected plaintiff's contention that the parties entered into an implied agreement for support, and citing *In re Estate of Roccamonte*, 174 *N.J.* 381, 808 *A.2d* 838 (2002), found that such an agreement requires that the parties have entered into a "marital-type" relationship. The judge cited several factors that contributed to her conclusion that the parties' relationship was not akin to a marriage. The judge considered that the parties had not cohabited, had not spent significant periods of time together, and had not demonstrated an intention to commingle property. The judge also found that although defendant did visit with plaintiff's family, the parties did not hold themselves out to the public as husband and wife and plaintiff did not attend social gatherings with defendant's friends, family, or colleagues.

In addition, the judge found that plaintiff's contributions to the relationship were not similar to those a wife would make in a marriage. Although plaintiff provided defendant with companionship and helped with some of his personal and business matters, the judge found no evidence that those actions were more than a typical dating relationship. Finally, the judge denied plaintiff's request for counsel fees because the equities weighed against such an award.

* * *

II.

Plaintiff argues that the Appellate Division erroneously held that cohabitation is an indispensable element of a palimony cause of action. * * * In contrast, defendant argues that * * * the law is "settled" that cohabitation is a prerequisite to a claim for palimony, and the fact that he was married and living with his wife during the entire course of the parties' relationship weighs against the finding of a marital-type relationship. * * *

III.

Preliminarily, we trace our history of a cause of action for palimony, which in general terms is a claim for support between unmarried persons. We first recognized such a cause of action in *Kozlowski v. Kozlowski*, 80 *N.J.* 378, 403 *A.*2d 902 (1979). Prior to that decision, our courts would not enforce support agreements between unmarried individuals or married persons who lived together with someone other than their spouses because they were considered meretricious.

* * *

The Court recognized that such an agreement may be expressed or implied because the "[p]arties entering this type of relationship usually do not record their understanding in specific legalese." *Id.* at 384, 403 *A.*2d 902. The Court concluded that "an agreement between adult parties living together is enforceable to the extent it is not based on a relationship proscribed by law, or on a promise to marry." *Id.* at 387, 403 *A.*2d 902.

* * *

Importantly, the Court defined a capable marital-type relationship as one

> in which people commit to each other, foregoing other liaisons and opportunities,doing for each other whatever each is capable of doing, providing companionship, and fulfilling each other's needs, financial, emotional, physical, and social, as best as they are able. And each couple defines its way of life and each partner's expected contribution to it in its own way. Whatever other consideration may be involved, the entry into such a relationship and then conducting oneself in accordance with its unique character is consideration in full measure.

* * *

We turn now to the present case. The question we have not previously addressed is whether the parties may have a marital-type relationship, which is the underpinning of the consideration needed to support a claim for palimony, when they have not cohabited. The panel below and several other published Appellate Division opinions have interpreted our jurisprudence to require cohabitation as an indispensable element of a palimony action. * * *

We do not read our jurisprudence as being so confining to make cohabitation a necessary requirement to a successful claim for palimony. Rather we opt for a more flexible approach that seeks to achieve substantial justice in light of the realities of the relationship. It is the promise to support, expressed or implied, coupled with a marital-type relationship, that are the indispensable elements to support a valid claim for palimony.

Indeed, whether the parties cohabited is a relevant factor in the analysis of whether a marital-type relationship exists, and in most successful palimony cases, cohabitation will be present. We recognize, however, that palimony cases present highly personal arrangements and the facts surrounding the relationship will determine whether it is a marital-type relationship that is essential to support a cause of action for palimony. There may be circumstances where a couple may hold themselves out to others as if they were married and yet not cohabit (i.e., couples who are separated due to employment, military, or educational opportunities and who do not cohabit). The trier of fact must consider the realities of the relationship in the quest to achieve substantial justice. Therefore, in addressing a cause of action for palimony, the trial judge should consider the *entirety* of the relationship and, if a marital-type relationship is otherwise proven, it should not be rejected solely because cohabitation is not present.

* * *

* * * In concluding that the parties did not enjoy a marital-type relationship, the [trial] judge found that the parties did not live together; they did not spend significant periods of time together; they did not commingle their property or share living expenses; and they did not hold themselves out to the public as husband and wife. The trial judge correctly considered the lack of cohabitation as a factor in reaching its determination and appropriately analyzed all of the factors of the highly personalized relationship between the parties, including the fact that defendant continued to live with his wife. Consequently, in rejecting plaintiff's argument of an implied contract to support her for life, the judge concluded that the marital-type relationship that informs the basis of a valid contract was lacking. As the trial judge so aptly phrased it, "the parties' relationship was best characterized as a dating relationship."

In summary, we hold that cohabitation is one of the many factors a trial judge should consider in determining whether a plaintiff has proven a marital-type relationship to support a cause of action for palimony. In these highly personalized cases, it is conceivable that a plaintiff, even in the absence of cohabitation, may establish a marital-type relationship and prove a cause of action for palimony. In the present case, however, there was sufficient credible evidence for the trial judge to reject plaintiff's palimony claim.

* * *

V.

As modified, the judgment of the Appellate Division affirming the trial court's rejection of plaintiff's claim for palimony is affirmed.

JUSTICE LONG, concurring.

I write separately to express my view that although the Court's opinion is an entirely correct paradigm in an implied contract case like the one before us, it should not be read in the future as applicable to an express contract.

* * * To be enforceable, a contract must be supported by valuable consideration which involves a detriment incurred by a promisee or a benefit received by a promisor, at the promisor's request. The nature and sufficiency of the consideration is not a factor so long as it has been bargained for. Even where those requirements are satisfied, however, today, as at common law, certain contracts cannot be enforced, for example, contracts that are illegal or violative of public policy. * * *

At common law, that bar applied where promises were based in whole or in part on sexual intercourse outside of the marriage relationship. 15 *Corbin on Contracts* § 81.4 (Perillo ed., rev. ed. 2003). Indeed, in a broad sweep, courts tended to view any contract arising from such a relationship as "meretricious" and unenforceable even if the relationship was not an express part of the bargain. *Ibid.*

* * *

The point is that, under our established case law, like every other person, a participant in a non-marital romantic relationship may recover in contract if she can show that she incurred a detriment in reliance on an express promise of support, that that promise was breached, and that she was damaged thereby. * * *

To be sure, to succeed on a claim of an express promise for lifetime support will be difficult because those kinds of representations are rarely made in the presence of witnesses and are usually denied by the putative promisor when the relationship breaks down. Nevertheless, in a case in which a plaintiff in fact proves an express promise of lifetime support, and that she provided the agreed upon consideration, she should not be barred from recovery based on the absence of a marital-type relationship.

For example, had the trial judge in this case credited Ms. Devaney's claim of an express promise of lifetime support by Dr. L'Esperance, the only questions for disposition would be the nature of the agreed upon consideration for the promise and whether Ms. Devaney fully performed her part of the bargain. Any other approach would confound our contract law and render a so-called palimony case an independent cause of action based upon the nature of the parties' relationship. * * *

* * *

JUSTICE RIVERA–SOTO, concurring in the result.

* * * [F]rom its inception, a cause of action for palimony, even if valid, always has required—at a bare minimum—objective proof of cohabitation. That requirement, and the rationale that undergirds it, require that the majority's reasoning be rejected. * * *

* * *

* * * [T]his Court indeed has recognized a cause of action for palimony. That recognition, however, is not without controversy. The majority does not mention, much less discuss, the objective fact that the overwhelming weight of authority nationwide rejects a claim for palimony—a post-nonmarital relationship support or alimony obligation—and instead limits recovery to what a cohabitant has contributed to the relationship.

As a threshold matter, Alabama, Idaho, Oklahoma, South Carolina and Utah recognize common law marriages, and, for that reason, do not allow palimony claims. * * *

The vast majority of states that do not acknowledge common law marriages also have rejected a cause of action for palimony, although most have allowed parties to recoup either assets brought into the relationship or the value of the services they have provided to the relationship. * * *

NOTES AND QUESTIONS

1. *Implications of* Devaney. How does *Devaney* extend *Marvin*? What is the relationship between a "marital-type relationship" and cohabitation? Do you think cohabitation should be a requirement? How should cohabitation be defined?

2. *No rights.* As Justice Rivera–Soto notes, notwithstanding *Marvin* and *Devaney*, some jurisdictions have refused to recognize marriage-like property or support rights between unmarried cohabitants for reasons of public policy. For example, in *Hewitt v. Hewitt*, 394 N.E.2d 1204 (Ill. 1979), the Illinois Supreme Court refused to allow *Marvin*-type remedies in Illinois, claiming that to do so would grant "legal status to a private arrangement substituting for the institution of marriage" and might undercut the state's goal of promoting marriage. The Illinois court criticized *Marvin*'s assumption that sexual relations do not form part of the consideration underlying contracts for mutual support between cohabitants. "[I]t would seem more candid to acknowledge the return of varying forms of common law marriage," *Hewitt* reasoned, "than to continue displaying the naiveté we believe involved in the assertion that there are involved in these relationships contracts separate and apart from the sexual activity * * *." *Id.* at 60. Indeed, following *Hewitt*, Illinois further limited the rights of cohabitants by ruling that cohabitation

may constitute grounds for removing children from the custody of their cohabiting parents, *Jarrett v. Jarrett*, 400 N.E.2d 421, 423 (Ill. 1979); for rejecting loss of consortium claims, *Medley v. Strong*, 558 N.E.2d 244, 248 (Ill. App. Ct. 1990); and for disallowing the award of an equitable interest of shared property, *Ayala v. Fox*, 564 N.E.2d 920, 922 (Ill. App. Ct. 1990).

Should speculation about the effect on the institution of marriage affect the court's decision whether to enforce a cohabitation agreement between competent adults? Will refusal to enforce cohabitation agreements likely lead many or most cohabitants to marry? If the court refuses to enforce a cohabitation agreement concerning a fifteen-year relationship as was true in *Hewitt*, does the decision benefit or hurt minor dependent children born during the parties' relationship? Should a state's abolition of common law marriage affect the willingness of the state courts to enforce cohabitation agreements between competent adults? Which approach is better, that of *Marvin* or *Hewitt*?

Currently, courts in several other states have chosen not to follow *Marvin*. In addition to *Hewitt*, see *Long v. Marino*, 441 S.E.2d 475 (Ga. Ct. App. 1994); *Schwegmann v. Schwegmann*, 441 So.2d 316 (La. Ct. App. 1983). These decisions have held that legislatures, not courts, should determine the rights and obligations of unmarried cohabitants. Although some of these decisions are decades old, courts have not changed their approach to the issues.

In *Davis v. Davis*, 643 So.2d 931, 936 (Miss. 1994), Elvis Davis and Travis Davis cohabited for thirteen years and were the natural parents of a daughter. Elvis declined to marry Travis, but she began using Travis's surname during their relationship. Travis also referred to Elvis as his wife in his will, set up a marital trust for her, and listed Elvis as his wife on his tax forms. The couple separated after Travis announced he was marrying his secretary. After the separation, he bought Elvis a new house, car, furniture, and appliances. The Mississippi Supreme Court considered whether Elvis was entitled to share in the more than $5 million Travis accumulated during their thirteen-year cohabitation. Elvis contended that under the equitable distribution doctrine, she was entitled to any property accumulated as the result of their joint efforts. Travis argued that there was no enforceable agreement between the parties, and that neither a partnership nor a joint venture relationship existed between them that would warrant equitable distribution of property. The court found that Elvis had not played an active role in building Travis' business empire, and granted her no relief, stating it was the legislature's role to create such an obligation:

> When opportunity knocks, one must answer its call. Elvis Davis failed to do so and thus her claim is all for naught. Our legislature has not extended the rights enjoyed by married people to those who choose merely to cohabit. To the contrary, cohabitation is still prohibited by statute. Elvis was well-compensated during and after the relationship. We see no reason to advocate any form of "palimony" when the legislature has not so spoken.

Davis, 643 So.2d at 936. A decade later, the Mississippi Supreme Court affirmed that if "a man and woman cohabit without the benefit of marriage, they do so at their own peril." *Nichols v. Funderburk*, 883 So.2d 554, 558 (Miss. 2004). On what bases do decisions like *Davis* and *Nichols* determine that cohabitants may not sue each other?

B. DETERMINING PROPERTY RIGHTS IN THE ABSENCE OF AN AGREEMENT

When a marriage ends, the spouses have claims against each other based on their status and, unlike the *Marvin* line of cases, need not plead the existence of a contract or an equitable claim. When a nonmarital cohabitation relationship ends, what rights, if any, should the cohabitants have in the absence of an enforceable agreement or other equitable claim? The American Law Institute (ALI), an organization composed of American judges, attorneys, and teachers, recommends that where unmarried couples have cohabited for a substantial period, the law should treat them in the same way that it treats married couples upon termination of the relationship. In its *Principles of the Law of Family Dissolution* (Principles), the ALI sets out model rules for "domestic partners" that are designed to govern financial claims between parties in a nonmarital relationship.

AMERICAN LAW INSTITUTE

Principles of the Law of Family Dissolution: Analysis and Recommendations.
(2002).

§ 6.03   Determination That Persons Are Domestic Partners

(1) For the purpose of defining relationships to which this Chapter applies, domestic partners are two persons of the same or opposite sex, not married to one another, who for a significant period of time share a primary residence and a life together as a couple.

(2) Persons are domestic partners when they have maintained a common household, as defined in Paragraph (4), with their common child, as defined in Paragraph (5), for a continuous period that equals or exceeds a duration, called the *cohabitation parenting period,* set in a rule of statewide application.

(3) Persons not related by blood or adoption are presumed to be domestic partners when they have maintained a common household, as defined in Paragraph (4), for a continuous period that equals or exceeds a duration * * * set in a rule of statewide application. * * *

* * *

(4) Persons *maintain a common household* when they share a primary residence only with each other and family members; or when, if they share a household with other unrelated persons, they act jointly, rather than as individuals, with respect to management of the household.

* * *

(6) When the requirements of Paragraph (2) or (3) are not satisfied, a person asserting a claim under this Chapter bears the burden of proving that for a significant period of time the parties shared a primary residence and a life together as a couple, as defined in Paragraph (7). Whether a period of time is significant is determined in light of all the Paragraph (7) circumstances of the parties' relationship and, particularly, the extent to which those circumstances wrought change in the life of one or both parties.

(7) Whether persons share a life together as a couple is determined by reference to all the circumstances, including:

(a) the oral or written statements or promises made to one another, or representations jointly made to third parties, regarding their relationship;

(b) the extent to which the parties intermingled their finances;

(c) the extent to which their relationship fostered the parties' economic interdependence, or the economic dependence of one party upon the other;

(d) the extent to which the parties engaged in conduct and assumed specialized or collaborative roles in furtherance of their life together;

(e) the extent to which the relationship wrought change in the life of either or both parties;

(f) the extent to which the parties acknowledged responsibilities to each other, as by naming the other the beneficiary of life insurance or of a testamentary instrument, or as eligible to receive benefits under an employee benefit plan;

* * *

(h) the emotional or physical intimacy of the parties' relationship;

(i) the parties' community reputation as a couple;

(j) the parties' participation in a commitment ceremony or registration as a domestic partnership;

* * *

(l) the parties' procreation of, adoption of, or joint assumption of parental functions toward a child; [and]

(m) the parties' maintenance of a common household, as defined by Paragraph (4).

§ 6.04   Domestic–Partnership Property Defined

(1) Except as [otherwise] provided in * * * this section, property is domestic-partnership property if it would be marital property * * * had the domestic partners been married to one another during the domestic-partnership period.

(2) The domestic-partnership period

    (a) starts when the domestic partners began sharing a primary residence, unless either partner shows that the parties did not begin sharing life together as a couple until a later date, in which case the domestic-partnership period starts on that later date, and

    (b) ends when the parties ceased sharing a primary residence.

For the purpose of this Paragraph, parties who are the biological parents of a common child began sharing life together as a couple no later than the date on which their common child was conceived.

* * *

NOTES AND QUESTIONS

1. *Critiques of the Principles.* Are the Principles too limited? Should they grant all of the incidents of marriage to cohabiting couples? Should a partnership be easier to prove? Professor Cynthia Grant Bowman suggests that cohabiting couples should be legally presumed to have a marital-type relationship if they have cohabited for two years or live together for any period of time and then have a child together.

> [The ALI Principles] provides only divorce-style remedies upon dissolution of the relationship. . . . [M]y proposal extends far beyond the divorce remedies that may be of use only to relatively well-off couples, those who have property or income to share after separating their households. It treats the couple as though they were married, thus entitling them, among other things, to the right to inheritance, rights against third parties (such as suits for negligent infliction of emotional distress and for loss of consortium), rights against the government (such as social security survivors benefits, workers compensation, and taxation as a coupled unit), and rights in the private sphere (such as eligibility for family health insurance, next-of-kin status in hospitals, and the like).

Cynthia Grant Bowman, *Social Science and Legal Policy: The Case of Heterosexual Cohabitation*, 9 J.L. Fam. Stud. 1, 45–46 (2007). Do you agree with her proposal? Should it apply to same-sex couples as well? Should there be any requirement of a showing of mutual interdependence? See Margaret F. Brinig, *Domestic Partnership: Missing the Target?*, 4 J.L. Fam. Stud. 19, 28–29 (2002).

2. *Model legislation?* If you were a state legislator, would you vote for a provision modeled on § 6.03? If not, what changes might lead you to vote for such a provision? Would § 6.03 hurt the institution of marriage, or would it provide worthwhile security for parties to a cohabitation relationship?

While the ALI Principles envision a statutory approach to the issue of cohabitants' rights, some courts have modified the common law in the absence of legislative guidance, and have created rights when they have found a "meretricious relationship." As *Marvin* and *Devaney* both suggest, the term "meretricious relationship" traditionally was used to denote an illicit sexual relationship. In Washington state law, however, the term came to describe more benignly an informal, marriage-like relationship giving rise to legal property and support rights regardless of the existence of any type of contract or other type of equitable claim. In 2007, the Washington Supreme Court, recognizing the term's traditional "negative connotations," substituted the term "committed intimate relationship" for "meretricious relationship." *See Olver v. Fowler*, 168 P.3d 348, 657 & n.1 (Wash. 2007). The next case in this chapter (decided before *Olver* and so still using the term "meretricious relationship") illustrates Washington's approach.

FLEMING v. SPENCER

Court of Appeals of Washington, 2002.
110 Wash. App. 1017.

PER CURIAM.

Norman Spencer appeals the trial court's decision to award certain real property to Sheila Fleming, his companion for many years. He argues that a meretricious relationship did not exist between them and that the trial court erred in distributing the property to her at the end of their relationship. Because we conclude that they had a meretricious relationship and that the trial court did not abuse its discretion in awarding the property to Fleming, we affirm.

FACTS

Spencer and Fleming met and became intimate in 1982, while Spencer was separated but not yet divorced from his wife. He moved into Fleming's cottage in the summer of 1983. That same year, he purchased real property in Sultan with borrowed money for the down payment and the balance carried on a real estate contract. * * * When Spencer and his wife formally divorced in July 1985, he received the Sultan property in the decree. According to the trial court's findings, however, Spencer 'paid off' the property entirely by the joint earnings of [Fleming and Spencer].

From 1984 to 1991, Spencer and Fleming lived at the Sultan property without interruption. In 1991, however, Spencer went to work in Alaska for about a year. He returned in 1992 and lived with Fleming at the property until 1995, when he went back to Alaska for work purposes. By 1996 or 1997, he returned to live at the property with Fleming. * * * [Fleming] enrolled in the Thomas Cooley Law School for one year between 1996 to 1997 and lived in Michigan during that time. During law school, she accumulated $27,000 in student loans. She returned to Sultan and worked at her sister's child care business until opening her own child care business on the Sultan property in 1999. Spencer and Fleming remodeled the property for this purpose. The couple filed joint income tax returns throughout the 1990s, and in 1994, named each other executor and heir to any property remaining after specific bequests. In October 1994, Spencer quitclaimed the Sultan property to Fleming to shelter it from a potential lawsuit. Over six years later [sic], however, Spencer had Fleming quitclaim the property back to him in December 1998.

As stated many times in the record, the parties ceased being intimate in 1997. They continued to live together, but in separate parts of the house. According to Fleming, Spencer had become religious and felt that he was still married to his first wife. * * * Yet, they continued to file joint income tax returns until 1999.

In the summer of 1999, Spencer would not let Fleming clear a field on the Sultan property for horses and a garden. A few months later, Fleming sought out her attorney. She sued Spencer for dissolution of their meretricious relationship. * * *

* * *

After the trial, the court found that Spencer and Fleming maintained a meretricious relationship from 1983 to 1997 and distributed the property acquired during that time frame. Spencer appeals.

DISCUSSION

I. Meretricious Relationship

Spencer first argues that there was no meretricious relationship. Determining whether a meretricious relationship exists is a mixed question of law and fact. *In re Marriage of Pennington*, 142 Wn.2d 592, 603, 14 P.3d 764 (2000). We accord deference to the trial court's findings of fact and review legal conclusions de novo. * * *

A meretricious relationship is a stable, marital-like relationship in which both parties cohabit knowing that a lawful marriage does not exist. * * * To determine whether such a relationship exists, courts look at five factors: (1) continuous cohabitation; (2) duration of the relationship; (3) purpose of the relationship; (4) pooling of resources; and (5) intent of the parties. * * * These factors are neither exclusive nor hypertechnical but merely a means to examine all relevant evidence. *Pennington*, 142 Wn.2d at 602. Ultimately, a court decides whether a meretricious relationship exists on a case-by-case basis. *Pennington*, 142 Wn.2d at 602.

Continuous Cohabitation: The trial court found that Spencer and Fleming commenced living together in 1983 when Spencer moved into Fleming's cottage after separating from his wife. In the winter of 1984, however, Spencer moved to the Sultan property. Fleming followed and permanently resided with Spencer, at about the same time Spencer formally divorced his wife. They lived together until 1991, when Spencer went to work in Alaska for about a year. He returned to the Sultan property in 1992 but went back to Alaska in 1995 to work for a short while. Meanwhile, from 1996 to 1997, Fleming attended Thomas Cooley Law School in Lansing, Michigan. After she returned to Sultan in 1997, they ceased being intimate and began living in separate rooms of the house. Based on these facts, it appears that except for career-related absences, they continuously cohabited from 1985 to 1997.

Duration of the Relationship: Spencer and Fleming met and became intimate in 1982. Their intimacy lasted until 1997. During this 15–year period, they remained apart from each other only for work and school related reasons. There is no evidence in the record that they dated other people while in this relationship. We conclude that the duration of their relationship was sufficiently long enough to support a stable, marital-like relationship.

Purpose of the Relationship: It is reasonable to infer from the trial court's findings that the purpose of the parties' relationship included friendship, companionship, intimacy, and mutual support. Such a purpose is marital-like.

Pooling of Resources: The pooling of resources and services for joint projects demonstrates a marital-like commitment also. According to the trial court's findings, Spencer and Fleming maintained joint bank accounts, commingled their earnings, and paid bills together. They even submitted joint income tax returns. With respect to the Sultan property, they paid off the real estate contract with joint earnings and remodeled the house three times, the latest remodel for the child care business. We conclude that they sufficiently pooled resources to imitate a marital-like relationship.

Intent of the Parties: Finally, a mutual intent to form a meretricious relationship is another factor to support the existence of such a relationship. As late as January 1994, Spencer and Fleming signed wills naming each other executor and heir to any remaining property after specific bequests. In October 1994, Spencer granted a quitclaim deed for the Sultan property to Fleming to shelter it from a potential lawsuit arising out of a construction job. Six years later [sic], in December 1998, Fleming quitclaimed the property back to Spencer. Granted, they discussed marriage three times to no avail. Nonetheless, the above facts demonstrate that the parties had a mutual intent to form a stable, marital-like relationship based on trust. Viewing the above factors as a whole, we must conclude that the parties had a meretricious relationship between 1983 and 1997. Spencer argues, however, that a meretricious relationship cannot commence when one party is married to another person.

* * * [T]he Supreme Court made it clear that equitable claims based on a meretricious relationship do not depend on whether the parties can legally marry each other. * * * This is so because comparing a meretricious relationship to marriage is a mere analogy and to literally define it as equivalent to marriage would result in a common law marriage, contrary to precedent. * * * In fact, this court has distributed property based on a meretricious relationship even when the parties purchased such property while one party was still married to a former spouse. * * * Therefore, Spencer and Fleming could have commenced a meretricious relationship before he obtained a formal divorce.

After determining that a meretricious relationship exists, the trial court evaluates the interest each party has in the property acquired during the relationship. * * * We review the trial court's decision on this matter under the abuse of discretion standard. * * * There is a rebuttable presumption that property acquired during such a relationship belongs to both parties. * * * A party may rebut this presumption with evidence demonstrating that he acquired the property in question with funds that would otherwise be characterized as separate property if he was married. * * * Although a party may have taken sole title to the property, that fact alone does not rebut the presumption of common ownership. * * *

Spencer argues that the trial court did not have authority to award the Sultan property to Fleming because he acquired it before the meretricious relationship and because a quitclaim deed from Fleming granted title to the Sultan property to him after the relationship ended. Based upon the analysis above, however, we have already determined that the parties commenced their meretricious relationship in 1983, before acquiring the Sultan property. Furthermore, title alone does not rebut the presumption of common ownership * * *. We conclude that the trial court did not abuse its discretion in finding that the Sultan property was subject to distribution at the end of the parties' meretricious relationship.

* * *

Spencer assigns error to the trial court's distribution of the property, indicating that it was not just and equitable. An appellate court reviews the trial court's distribution of property at the end of a meretricious relationship under the abuse of discretion standard. * * * In making the distribution, the trial court should prevent one party from being unjustly enriched and may look to the dissolution statute * * * for guidance. * * * [W]e cannot say that the trial court abused its discretion.

* * *

In summary, we conclude that Spencer and Fleming did have a meretricious relationship commencing in 1983. The trial court did not abuse its discretion by including the Sultan property in the distribution and eventually awarding it to Fleming with an equalizing payment to Spencer.

* * *

NOTES AND QUESTIONS

1. *Cohabitant rights surviving death.* In 2007, the Washington Supreme Court held that the property rights acquired by partners to a "meretricious" or "committed intimate relationship" survive the death of one or both partners. In *Olver v. Fowler*, 168 P.3d 348 (Wash. 2007), a man and woman who had been in a "committed intimate relationship" for 14 years died together in a traffic accident. The court held that the woman's estate was entitled to assert the same rights as a spouse to the property of her deceased partner. "By analogy to community property law, [the woman] had an undivided interest in the couple's jointly acquired property, even though it was titled in [her partner's] name," the court held. Although the couple's surviving son would ultimately inherit both parents' property, recognizing the

mother's own rights could potentially shield some of the property from a potential tort judgment against the father's estate.

2. *The Canadian approach.* In *M. v. H.*, the Canadian Supreme Court considered whether it was discriminatory to grant the right to seek spousal support to unmarried opposite-sex cohabitants but not to unmarried same-sex cohabitants. *M. v. H.*, [1999] 2 S.C.R. 3 (Can.), *available at* http://scc.lexum. umontreal.ca/en/1999/1999rcs2–3/1999rcs2–3.html. M and H were a lesbian couple who separated after ten years. M subsequently sought a court order for partition of the house and business they shared, as well as spousal support. She also alleged that the Ontario Family Law Act's definition of "spouse," which did not include individual members of cohabiting same-sex couples, violated Section 15 of the Charter of Rights and Freedoms (Canada's equivalent to the U.S. Constitution's Equal Protection Clause).

To support its decision that the Act violated the "human dignity of individuals in same-sex relationships," the court cited several factors, including the Act's different treatment of same-sex couples seeking access to the court-enforced support system, the Act's failure to consider the claimant's actual circumstances, and the cultural significance of uniformly excluding individuals of same-sex relationships from seeking support. After the decision, Ontario amended the Act to comply with the decision, and Canada's federal government began to offer various federal benefits to unmarried couples, regardless of sexual orientation, who had cohabited for more than a year. Modernization of Benefits & Obligations Act, 2000 S.C., ch. 12 (Can.), *available at* http://laws.justice.gc.ca/en/M–8.6/83436.html.

3. *Status or commitment?* Does § 6.03 of the Principles *or Fleming* require any particular form of commitment between the parties? Might property acquired during any cohabiting relationships become subject to distribution? Professor Marsha Garrison argues that commitment should be legally significant:

> Marital commitment explains why married couples have legal obligations to each other when unmarried couples do not. Unmarried couples, like their married counterparts, may establish a home, family, and life together; they may be sexually faithful to each other and may share the expectation that their relationship will endure. But they have not publicly and mutually agreed to assume the legally binding obligations of marriage. Indeed, they have decided not to publicly assume those obligations.

> * * * [C]ourts and legislatures in a number of other industrialized nations [are] fashioning a "conscriptive" model that bases cohabitant obligation on status. The conscriptive model imposes on the cohabiting couple that has chosen to avoid marriage some or all of the obligations the couple would have incurred had they chosen to marry. Several Canadian provinces, for example, now impose a support obligation on cohabitants who have lived together for periods ranging from one to three years. All of the Australian states have adopted legislation that extends marital property rights to cohabitants who have a common child or have lived together for at least two years. * * *

> Only one American high court has thus far adopted a conscriptive approach to cohabitant obligation, but the American Law Institute has

recently urged the states to abandon contract in favor of the conscriptive alternative.

Marsha Garrison, *Is Consent Necessary? An Evaluation of the Emerging Law of Cohabitant Obligation*, 52 UCLA L. Rev. 815, 817–19 (2005). Do you agree with Professor Garrison's characterization of the ALI and Washington approach to enforcing cohabitation agreements? In the absence of some form of commitment either through marriage or contract, why should cohabitants be entitled to any form of property distribution or support from one another after they are no longer cohabiting?

PROBLEM 5–1

Katherine and Richard began living together as unmarried lovers in 2000 in a house that Richard owned. In 2001, they moved to a new home, which Richard put in his own name, telling Katherine that "it was easier to place [the house] in his name because he had equity in another house and because they were not married." Katherine did not contribute funds for the house, but she helped plan, build and improve the house and the grounds. While they cohabited, Katherine made about $250,000, which she turned over to Richard. Richard, in turn, gave her an allowance for groceries, personal, and household expenses. The couple agreed that Katherine would be responsible for all the shopping, cooking and landscaping, while Richard would run his automotive business. After their cohabitation ended in 2009, Katherine sued Richard to obtain one half of the property and money they accumulated while living together from 2000–2009. What result in a jurisdiction following *Marvin*? In a jurisdiction following *Hewitt* and similar cases? In a jurisdiction that has adopted the ALI Principles?

C. OTHER INCIDENTS OF NONMARITAL COHABITATION

1. *Criminal prohibitions.* At the beginning of the 21st century, a minority of states (including Idaho, Illinois, Massachusetts, Mississippi, North Carolina, North Dakota, South Carolina, Utah, Virginia and West Virginia) still criminalized fornication between unmarried couples, and at least two states (Florida and Michigan) criminalized cohabitation. *See* Melanie C. Falco, *The Road Not Taken: Using the Eighth Amendment to Strike Down Criminal Prosecution for Engaging in Consensual Sexual Acts*, 82 N.C. L. Rev. 723, 738 (2004). Some long-standing state laws criminalizing cohabitation have been repealed or struck down by courts, but other states keep these laws on the books. For example, in January 2005, the North Dakota House of Representatives defeated a bill to repeal a law making nonmarital cohabitation a misdemeanor sex crime. While legislators and legal commentators alike have suggested that it is difficult to enforce such laws, in March 2004, a North Carolina woman was told she would have to quit her job as a sheriff's dispatcher because she would not marry her live-in boyfriend. Are such laws constitutional after *Lawrence*? *See ACLU Wins Challenge to North Carolina's Cohabitation Ban*,

July   20,   2006,   http://www.aclu.org/womensrights/discrim/26197prs
20060720.html; *Martin v. Ziherl*, 607 S.E.2d 367 (Va. 2005) (considering
an anti-fornication statute).

2. *Tax treatment.* Nonmarital cohabitants may not file joint federal
tax returns; each person must file as a single person. *Cf. Sullivan v.
Commissioner*, 256 F.2d 664, 666 (4th Cir. 1958) (holding that a legal
separation prevents parties from filing jointly). The Internal Revenue
Code does not specifically address the status or rights of unmarried
cohabitants. Under I.R.C. § 6013(a), however, only a couple deemed to be
married under applicable law can file a joint tax return. A cohabitant
cannot generally be claimed as a dependent, although a partner may
qualify as a dependent if that person receives at least half of his or her
support from the partner, lives in the partner's household, and is not a
party to a relationship that is illegal under local law. *See* Frank S. Berall,
Tax Consequences of Unmarried Cohabitants, 23 Quinnipiac L. Rev. 395,
399, 401 (2004). The tax treatment of married and divorcing couples is
discussed in Chapters 4 and 9.

D.   DOMESTIC PARTNERSHIPS
AND CIVIL UNIONS

Domestic partnerships and civil unions are each a relatively new
status that grants unmarried cohabiting couples some or most of the
benefits and rights of marriage. In 1997, Hawaii became the first state to
enact comprehensive domestic partnership legislation, in response to a
Hawaii Supreme Court decision suggesting that the state's ban on same-
sex marriages might violate the state constitution. *See Baehr v. Lewin*,
852 P.2d 44 (Haw. 1993); Haw. Rev. Stat. Ann. § 572C–4 (1999). The
legislation allows same-sex couples, as well as other couples legally prohibited from marrying one another, to register as "reciprocal beneficiaries."
This new system gives the couples eligibility for such benefits as health
insurance, inheritance rights, and retirement benefits.

Some states and local governments (including California, the District
of Columbia, Maine, Oregon and Washington) presently have domestic
partnership registries similar to Hawaii's "reciprocal beneficiaries" law.
Domestic partnership registries provide unmarried couples an official
means to record their commitment to each other in the absence of
marriage. Domestic partnership ordinances provide varying degrees of
protection and benefits for unmarried couples; some states and municipal-
ities offer a limited number of benefits while others are more expansive.
These rights include the right to make health care decisions, and the
rights to workers' compensation, family leave, and state tax deductions.

In California, registered domestic partners are treated like spouses for
virtually all state-law purposes. *See In re Marriage Cases*, 183 P.3d 384,
413–17 (Cal. 2008). Similarly, the Oregon Family Fairness Act, which
went into effect in 2008, grants same-sex couples who enter into domestic
partnerships the same rights and privileges, within the state of Oregon, as

married couples. *See* Janine Robben, *New Families New Laws: Understanding Oregon's Family Fairness Act*, 68 Or. St. B. Bull. 21, 23 (2007). Domestic partners in Oregon will be able to file joint state tax returns, but will have to file separate federal tax returns because the federal government will not recognize the domestic partnership. *See id* at 26. This could create some confusion in Oregon, because state taxes are based in part on federal tax returns. *Id.*

Vermont, Connecticut, New Jersey and New Hampshire offer same-sex couples the option of entering civil unions, which entitle them to all rights and responsibilities that the state confers on opposite-sex married couples. *See, e.g.*, Vt. Stat. Ann. tit. 15, § 1201 (2008). Civil unions in these four states are limited to same-sex couples only. *See, e.g.*, Vt. Stat. Ann. tit. 15, § 1202 (2008). This may be because the states do not want opposite-sex couples, who have the option of marriage, to be allowed to choose civil unions rather than marriage. *See* Mark Strasser, *The Future of Marriage*, 21 J. Am. Acad. Matrimonial Law. 87, 104 (2008).

In the public sector, ten state governments and the District of Columbia, and approximately 130 city and local governments, offer health benefits for domestic partners of public employees. A.B.A. Section of Family Law, *A White Paper: An Analysis of the Law Regarding Same Sex Marriage, Civil Unions and Domestic Partnerships*, 38 Fam. L. Q. 339, 348 (2004). Numerous private companies and colleges and universities provide health insurance for employees' domestic partners. Employers may provide benefits to domestic partners in an effort to enhance recruitment, raise morale, and to keep them competitive. As of 2007 more than 50% of Fortune 500 companies offered health insurance benefits for domestic partners. *See* The Human Rights Campaign Found., *The State of the Workplace for Lesbian, Gay, Bisexual and Transgender Americans 2006–2007*, at 26 (2007).

NOTES AND QUESTIONS

1. *Impact of domestic partnership provisions.* Critics argue that domestic partnership legislation has had a limited impact on couples involved in nonmarital cohabitation relationships. Nancy G. Maxwell, *Opening Civil Marriage to Same–Gender Couples: A Netherlands–United States Comparison*, 18 Ariz. J. Int'l & Comp. L. 141, 198 (2001). For instance, as of November 2006, only 1,284 reciprocal relationships were recorded in Hawaii, which has a population of almost 1.3 million. *See* Hawaii Family Forum, Reciprocal Beneficiaries, http://www.hawaiifamilyforum.org/issues/Reciprocal BeneficiariesHAWAII.htm.

2. *Discrimination against heterosexual cohabitants.* In *Irizarry v. Board of Educ.*, 251 F.3d 604 (7th Cir. 2001), the court rejected a city employee's argument that an ordinance extending spousal benefits only to same-sex domestic partners of school system employees denied the employee due process and equal protection. The Court of Appeals held that the ordinance had a rational basis because it attracted homosexual teachers to the system

who could serve as role models and provide support to gay and lesbian students. The plaintiff argued that all children of unmarried couples should enjoy equal opportunity to mentoring and role-modeling by teachers who lived in the same way as their unmarried parents. Judge Richard Posner responded:

> Cost considerations to one side, the argument collides with a nationwide policy in favor of marriage. True, it is no longer widely popular to try to pressure homosexuals to marry persons of the opposite sex. But so far as heterosexuals are concerned, the evidence [is] that on average married couples live longer, are healthier, earn more, have lower rates of substance abuse and mental illness, are less likely to commit suicide, and report higher levels of happiness—that marriage civilizes young males, confers economies of scale and of joint consumption, minimizes sexually transmitted disease, and provides a stable and nourishing framework for child rearing.... The Chicago Board of Education cannot be faulted, therefore, for not wishing to encourage heterosexual cohabitation; and, though we need not decide the point, the refusal to extend domestic-partner benefits to heterosexual cohabitators could be justified on the basis of the policy favoring marriage for heterosexuals quite apart from the reasons for wanting to extend the spousal fringe benefits to homosexual couples.

Id. at 607–08. Does Judge Posner make a valid point? Is favoring marriage, rather than cohabitation, between heterosexuals a justifiable reason for the classification created by the Chicago ordinance? Would your answer be different if the school board policy sought to discourage homosexual cohabitation? Why?

PROBLEM 5–2

Edward, an architect, is a widower with three children. He dated Lila, a teacher, for a year and then asked her to move in with him and his family. Edward and Lila decided that she would save him the cost of child care by quitting her job as a teacher and taking care of the three children. After cohabiting for two years, the couple separate and Lila moves out. Lila wishes to assert a property interest in the assets acquired by Edward during their two years together. The jurisdiction's domestic partnership statute sets the minimum cohabitation period at three years. Under the ALI Principles, what would be the result?

PROBLEM 5–3

Nadia and Monique have been in a stable relationship for three years. Nadia is a surgeon, and Monique works as a part-time artist while completing her graduate degree. The couple has recently decided to move in together. Presently, Nadia is in the midst of purchasing a house, in which she and Monique plan to live. Since Nadia has used her savings for the down payment, Monique has agreed to pay the monthly mortgage, using money from a trust fund her deceased parents left her. Although the women have made an oral agreement with each other, Nadia comes to you, separately, and asks whether drafting a cohabitation agreement would be prudent. What questions would you ask Nadia? Based on her answers, what advice would you give her?

PROBLEM 5–4

In May 2005, Shawna moved in with her boyfriend Don, who was separated from his wife, Prudence, and had initiated divorce proceedings. In January 2007, Shawna broke up with Don and began an affair with Tom, with whom she moved in. By May 2008, Shawna's affair with Tom had fizzled, and she had moved back in with Don, whose divorce from Prudence had become final.

Because Prudence had received the marital home in the divorce settlement, Don bought a new condo so that he and Shawna could live in it. They often had parties at the condo, and during these, Don told their friends that he would never marry again. In July 2008, Don presented Shawna with a new car, although it was titled solely in his name. In addition, Don gave Shawna a monthly allowance of $2,000. In return, Shawna performed all of the housekeeping and took care of Don's ten-year-old Dalmation and his fifteen-year-old Siamese cat. In November 2008, Shawna and Don broke up again and Shawna moved out of the condo. She sued for property obtained during the relationship. On what basis might Shawna be able to recover from Don? How should Don respond to her claims?

SECTION 2: ESTABLISHING PARENTHOOD

At common law, a married husband and wife were presumed to be the father and mother of children born into the marriage. Lord Mansfield's Rule, expounded in *Goodright v. Moss*, 98 Eng. Rep. 1257, 1258 (K.B. 1777), stated that "it is a rule, founded in decency, morality, and policy, that [the spouses] ... shall not be permitted to say after marriage, that they have had no connection, and therefore that the offspring is spurious." The rule effectively barred either spouse from testifying that the husband was not the child's father. The marital presumption rule appears to pre-date *Goodright,* and to be drawn from Roman law, which presumed that marriage established the identity of the father. *See* Jane C. Murphy, *Legal Images of Fatherhood: Welfare Reform, Child Support Enforcement, and Fatherless Children*, 81 Notre Dame L. Rev. 325, 331 (2005). Marriage guaranteed parental rights to the husband, and his paternity was virtually irrebuttable, absent proof of impotence, sterility, or his non-access to his wife for the relevant time period.

When the biological parents were not married to each other, the law differed with respect to the bundle of rights that accompanied parenthood, and to the individuals who were accorded parental status. At English common law and in colonial America, nonmarital children had no legally recognized relationship with either biological parent, and the parents had no recognized familial relationship with the child. Not until the end of the nineteenth century did most states enact laws recognizing that "illegitimate" children were part of their mothers' families. Slave children were treated like "illegitimate" children because their social status derived from their mothers, and their fathers had no parental rights. Children of a white male and black female were "illegitimate" because miscegenation was illegal, and because the infant received its social status from the mother. If both parents were slaves, their offspring were illegitimate, since marriage between slaves was not legally binding. It is likely that black fathers had no parental rights over their offspring, as they could do nothing when their "wives" were beaten and raped by white men. *See* Deborah Gray White, entry on slavery, *Reader's Companion to Women's History*, http://college.hmco.com/history/readerscomp/women/html/wh_034400_slavery.htm.

Similarly, courts refused to apply the marital presumption when a child with African–American features was born to a white couple. Evidence, such as the white husband's impotence or imprisonment during the child's conception, could be admitted to rebut the presumption. The purpose of admission was to prevent the court's having to recognize an African–American child as a "legitimate" offspring of a white male. *See* Mary Louise Fellows, *The Law of Legitimacy: An Instrument of Procreative Power*, 3 Colum. J. Gender & L. 495, 500 (1993).

Until the Supreme Court's 1972 decision in *Stanley v. Illinois*, 405 U.S. 645 (1972), most states granted fathers of nonmarital children few rights with respect to custody or consent to adoption (although they did have support obligations). Unless they had "legitimated" their children, fathers could not exercise parental powers and, in effect, were defined as nonparents.

The marital presumption exists in some form in virtually all states today, but the husband, the wife, and the biological father have the opportunity to rebut the presumption in most states. Professor Baker explains:

> A husband who has cause to believe that a child might not be biologically related to him, but who fails to question biological paternity once he has reason to, can be held responsible for child support. Comparably, a man who knew that he was the likely biological father, but failed to bring an action in time, can be barred from claiming any parental rights he might want to establish.

Katharine Baker, *Bargaining or Biology? The History and Future of Paternity Law and Parental Status*, 14 Cornell J.L. Pub. Pol'y 1, 12–13 (2004).

A. DETERMINING PATERNITY

In the absence of the marital presumption, state laws establish how nonmarital fathers can establish their paternity. In a line of cases culminating in the 1989 decision of *Michael H. v. Gerald D.*, 491 U.S. 110 (1989), the Supreme Court considered the rights of putative fathers. In *Stanley v. Illinois*, 405 U.S. 645, 652 (1972), the Court struck down an

Illinois statute that made children of unwed fathers wards of the state following the death of the mother. Petitioner Stanley sought the right to raise his three children following the death of their mother, Joan, with whom he had lived on and off for 18 years. Illinois argued it had an interest in the "moral, emotional, mental, and physical welfare of the minor and the best interest of the community." The Court disagreed with the State, and struck down the statute as violative of the Fourteenth Amendment's due process and equal protection clauses, finding that Illinois had incorrectly presumed that all unwed fathers were unfit. *Stanley* requires only that nonmarital fathers receive procedural justice concerning their parental rights.

The rights of a putative father were defined more clearly in *Quilloin v. Walcott*, 434 U.S. 246 (1978). A mother had raised her nonmarital child without the presence of the biological father. When her husband, the child's stepfather, attempted to adopt the child, the biological father, Quilloin, attempted to block it. The Georgia statute required that only the nonmarital child's mother approve the adoption. The Supreme Court held that *Stanley* did not require Georgia to grant Quilloin a veto because he had not shouldered significant responsibility for the child's upbringing.

The Supreme Court reached a different result in *Caban v. Mohammed*, 441 U.S. 380 (1979), in which the father, Abdiel Caban, had lived with and had a relationship with his two illegitimate children prior to the ending of his relationship with the children's mother, Maria Mohammed. The Court held that Caban could block the adoption by the children's new stepfather and struck down a New York statute that, like the *Quilloin* statute, required only the mother's consent for adoption of a nonmarital child. The Court held that the statute violated equal protection because Caban's "substantial relationship" with his children was different from Quilloin's "failure to act as a father." *Id.* at 389 n.7 (1979).

In *Lehr v. Robertson*, 463 U.S. 248 (1983), the nonmarital father challenged his daughter's adoption by the mother's new husband. In January 1979, Lehr filed an action for visitation, determination of paternity, support and reasonable visitation rights. He was informed that the girl's stepfather had adopted her a month earlier. On his motion to vacate the adoption, he argued that the statute deprived him of his Fourteenth Amendment due process liberty interest in a potential relationship with his child. The Supreme Court held that the biological relationship between a father and child does not warrant constitutional protection unless the father had developed a substantial relationship with the child. Because Lehr had not provided support or lived with the child, the state's interest in protecting the child outweighed the putative father's interest in blocking the adoption. The Court stated:

> The difference between the developed parent-child relationship that was implicated in *Stanley* and *Caban* * * * is both clear and significant. When an unwed father demonstrates a full commitment to the responsibilities of parenthood by "com[ing] forward to participate in

the rearing of his child," *Caban,* 441 U.S. at 392, his interest in personal contact with his child acquires substantial protection under the due process clause. At that point it may be said that he "act[s] as a father toward his children." *Id.* at 389, n.7. But the mere existence of a biological link does not merit equivalent constitutional protection. The actions of judges neither create nor sever genetic bonds. "[T]he importance of the familial relationship, to the individuals involved and to the society, stems from the emotional attachments that derive from the intimacy of daily association, and from the role it plays in 'promot[ing] a way of life' through the instruction of children as well as from the fact of blood relationship." *Smith v. Org. of Foster Families for Equal. & Reform,* 431 U.S. 816, 844 (quoting *Wisconsin v. Yoder,* 406 U.S. 205, 231–33 (1972)).

The significance of the biological connection is that it offers the natural father an opportunity that no other male possesses to develop a relationship with his offspring. If he grasps that opportunity and accepts some measure of responsibility for the child's future, he may enjoy the blessings of the parent-child relationship and make uniquely valuable contributions to the child's development. If he fails to do so, the Federal Constitution will not automatically compel a state to listen to his opinion of where the child's best interests lie.

Lehr, 463 U.S. at 261–62. Dissenting Justices White, Marshall, and Blackmun characterized the putative father's rights quite differently. They noted that Lehr had attempted to establish a relationship with his child but that the mother had concealed her location from him, thereby thwarting him in his efforts to visit. *Id.* at 268–69 (White, J. dissenting).

A "mere biological relationship" is not as unimportant in determining the nature of liberty interests as the majority suggests.

* * * The "biological connection" is itself a relationship that creates a protected interest. * * *

Lehr was entitled to due process, and the right to be heard is one of the fundamentals of that right, which "has little reality or worth unless one is informed that the matter is pending and can choose for himself whether to appear or default, acquiesce or contest." *Schroeder v. City of New York,* 371 U.S. 208, 212 (1962).

* * *

No state interest is substantially served by denying Lehr adequate notice and a hearing. * * *

* * * [I]n my view the failure to provide Lehr with notice and an opportunity to be heard violated rights guaranteed him by the Due Process Clause. * * *

Id. at 271–72, 275–76.

These decisions provided the framework for the Supreme Court's consideration of the following case.

1. CONSTITUTIONAL FRAMEWORK

MICHAEL H. v. GERALD D.

Supreme Court of the United States, 1989.
491 U.S. 110.

JUSTICE SCALIA announced the judgment of the Court and delivered an opinion, in which THE CHIEF JUSTICE joins, and in all but footnote 6 of which JUSTICE O'CONNOR and JUSTICE KENNEDY join.

Under California law, a child born to a married woman living with her husband is presumed to be a child of the marriage. Cal. Evid. Code Ann. § 621 (West Supp. 1989). The presumption of legitimacy may be rebutted only by the husband or wife, and then only in limited circumstances. The instant appeal presents the claim that this presumption infringes upon the due process rights of a man who wishes to establish his paternity of a child born to the wife of another man, and the claim that it infringes upon the constitutional right of the child to maintain a relationship with her natural father.

I

The facts of this case are, we must hope, extraordinary. On May 9, 1976, in Las Vegas, Nevada, Carole D., an international model, and Gerald D., a top executive in a French oil company, were married. The couple established a home in Playa del Rey, California, in which they resided as husband and wife when one or the other was not out of the country on business. In the summer of 1978, Carole became involved in an adulterous affair with a neighbor, Michael H. In September 1980, she conceived a child, Victoria D., who was born on May 11, 1981. Gerald was listed as father on the birth certificate and has always held Victoria out to the world as his daughter. Soon after delivery of the child, however, Carole informed Michael that she believed he might be the father.

In the first three years of her life, Victoria remained always with Carole, but found herself within a variety of quasi-family units. In October 1981, Gerald moved to New York City to pursue his business interests, but Carole chose to remain in California. At the end of that month, Carole and Michael had blood tests of themselves and Victoria, which showed a 98.07% probability that Michael was Victoria's father. In January 1982, Carole visited Michael in St. Thomas, where his primary business interests were based. There Michael held Victoria out as his child. In March, however, Carole left Michael and returned to California, where she took up residence with yet another man, Scott K. Later that spring, and again in the summer, Carole and Victoria spent time with Gerald in New York City, as well as on vacation in Europe. In the fall, they returned to Scott in California.

In November 1982, rebuffed in his attempts to visit Victoria, Michael filed a filiation action in California Superior Court to establish his paternity and right to visitation. In March 1983, the court appointed an attorney and guardian *ad litem* to represent Victoria's interests. Victoria then filed a cross-complaint asserting that if she had more than one psychological or *de facto* father, she was entitled to maintain her filial relationship, with all of the attendant rights, duties, and obligations, with both. In May 1983, Carole filed a motion for summary judgment. During this period, from March through July 1983, Carole was again living with Gerald in New York. In August, however, she returned to California, became involved once again with Michael, and instructed her attorneys to remove the summary judgment motion from the calendar.

For the ensuing eight months, when Michael was not in St. Thomas he lived with Carole and Victoria in Carole's apartment in Los Angeles and held Victoria out as his daughter. In April 1984, Carole and Michael signed a stipulation that Michael was Victoria's natural father. Carole left Michael the next month, however, and instructed her attorneys not to file the stipulation. In June 1984, Carole reconciled with Gerald and joined him in New York, where they now live with Victoria and two other children since born into the marriage.

In May 1984, Michael and Victoria, through her guardian *ad litem*, sought visitation rights for Michael *pendente lite*. To assist in determining whether visitation would be in Victoria's best interests, the Superior Court appointed a psychologist to evaluate Victoria, Gerald, Michael, and Carole. The psychologist recommended that Carole retain sole custody, but that Michael be allowed continued contact with Victoria pursuant to a restricted visitation schedule. The court concurred and ordered that Michael be provided with limited visitation privileges *pendente lite*.

On October 19, 1984, Gerald, who had intervened in the action, moved for summary judgment on the ground that under Cal. Evid. Code § 621 there were no triable issues of fact as to Victoria's paternity. This law provides that "the issue of a wife cohabiting with her husband, who is not impotent or sterile, is conclusively presumed to be a child of the marriage." Cal. Evid. Code Ann. § 621(a) (West Supp. 1989). The presumption may be rebutted by blood tests, but only if a motion for such tests is made, within two years from the date of the child's birth, either by the husband or, if the natural father has filed an affidavit acknowledging paternity, by the wife.

On January 28, 1985, having found that affidavits submitted by Carole and Gerald sufficed to demonstrate that the two were cohabiting at conception and birth and that Gerald was neither sterile nor impotent, the Superior Court granted Gerald's motion for summary judgment, rejecting Michael's and Victoria's challenges to the constitutionality of § 621. The court also denied their motions for continued visitation pending the appeal under Cal. Civ. Code § 4601, which provides that a court may, in its discretion, grant "reasonable visitation rights ... to any ... person having an interest in the welfare of the child." It found that allowing such visitation would "violat[e] the intention of the Legislature by impugning the integrity of the family unit."

On appeal, Michael asserted, *inter alia*, that the Superior Court's application of § 621 had violated his procedural and substantive due process rights. Victoria also raised a due process challenge to the statute, seeking to preserve her *de facto* relationship with Michael as well as with Gerald. She contended, in addition, that as § 621 allows the husband and, at least to a limited extent, the mother, but not the child, to rebut the presumption of legitimacy, it violates the child's right to equal protection. Finally, she asserted a right to continued visitation with Michael under § 4601. After submission of briefs and a hearing, the California Court of Appeal affirmed the judgment of the Superior Court and upheld the constitutionality of the statute. It interpreted that judgment, moreover, as having denied permanent visitation rights under § 4601 * * *.

* * * Michael and Victoria both raise equal protection and due process challenges. We do not reach Michael's equal protection claim, however, as it was neither raised nor passed upon below.

II

The California statute that is the subject of this litigation is, in substance, more than a century old. * * * In their present form, the substantive provisions of the statute are as follows:

"§ 621. Child of the marriage; notice of motion for blood tests

"(a) Except as provided in subdivision (b), the issue of a wife cohabiting with her husband, who is not impotent or sterile, is conclusively presumed to be a child of the marriage.

"(b) Notwithstanding the provisions of subdivision (a), if the court finds that the conclusions of all the experts, as disclosed by the evidence based upon blood tests performed pursuant to Chapter 2 (commencing with Section 890) of Division 7 are that the husband is not the father of the child, the question of paternity of the husband shall be resolved accordingly.

"(c) The notice of motion for blood tests under subdivision (b) may be raised by the husband not later than two years from the child's date of birth.

"(d) The notice of motion for blood tests under subdivision (b) may be raised by the mother of the child not later than two years from the child's date of birth if the child's biological father has filed an affidavit with the court acknowledging paternity of the child.["]

* * *

III

We address first the claims of Michael. At the outset, it is necessary to clarify what he sought and what he was denied. California law, like nature itself, makes no provision for dual fatherhood. Michael was seeking to be declared *the* father of Victoria. The immediate benefit he evidently sought to obtain from that status was visitation rights. See Cal. Civ. Code Ann.

§ 4601 (West 1983) (parent has statutory right to visitation "unless it is shown that such visitation would be detrimental to the best interests of the child"). But if Michael were successful in being declared the father, other rights would follow–most importantly, the right to be considered as the parent who should have custody, a status which "embrace[s] the sum of parental rights with respect to the rearing of a child, including the child's care; the right to the child's services and earnings; the right to direct the child's activities; the right to make decisions regarding the control, education, and health of the child; and the right, as well as the duty, to prepare the child for additional obligations, which includes the teaching of moral standards, religious beliefs, and elements of good citizenship." 4 [Cal. Fam.] Law § 60.02[1][b] (C. Markey ed. 1987) (footnotes omitted). All parental rights, including visitation, were automatically denied by denying Michael status as the father. While Cal. Civ. Code Ann. § 4601 places it within the discretionary power of a court to award visitation rights to a nonparent, the Superior Court here, affirmed by the Court of Appeal, held that California law denies visitation, against the wishes of the mother, to a putative father who has been prevented by § 621 from establishing his paternity.

Michael raises two related challenges to the constitutionality of § 621. First, he asserts that requirements of procedural due process prevent the State from terminating his liberty interest in his relationship with his child without affording him an opportunity to demonstrate his paternity in an evidentiary hearing. We believe this claim derives from a fundamental misconception of the nature of the California statute. While § 621 is phrased in terms of a presumption, that rule of evidence is the implementation of a substantive rule of law. California declares it to be, except in limited circumstances, *irrelevant* for paternity purposes whether a child conceived during, and born into, an existing marriage was begotten by someone other than the husband and had a prior relationship with him. * * * [T]he conclusive presumption not only expresses the State's substantive policy but also furthers it, excluding inquiries into the child's paternity that would be destructive of family integrity and privacy.

* * *

Michael contends as a matter of substantive due process that, because he has established a parental relationship with Victoria, protection of Gerald's and Carole's marital union is an insufficient state interest to support termination of that relationship. This argument is, of course, predicated on the assertion that Michael has a constitutionally protected liberty interest in his relationship with Victoria.

It is an established part of our constitutional jurisprudence that the term "liberty" in the Due Process Clause extends beyond freedom from physical restraint. See, *e.g., Pierce v. Society of Sisters,* 268 U.S. 510 (1925); *Meyer v. Nebraska,* 262 U.S. 390 (1923). * * * In an attempt to limit and guide interpretation of the Clause, we have insisted not merely that the interest denominated as a "liberty" be "fundamental" (a concept that, in isolation, is hard to objectify), but also that it be an interest traditionally protected by our society.[2] As we have put it, the Due Process Clause affords only those protections "so rooted in the traditions and conscience of our people as to be ranked as fundamental." *Snyder v. Massachusetts*, 291 U.S. 97, 105 (CARDOZO, J.). * * *

* * * Michael reads the landmark case of *Stanley v. Illinois,* 405 U.S. 645 (1972), and * * * subsequent cases * * * as establishing that a liberty interest is created by biological fatherhood plus an established parental relationship—factors that exist in the present case as well. We think that distorts the rationale of those cases. As we view them, they rest not upon such isolated factors but upon the historic respect—indeed, sanctity would not be too strong a term—traditionally accorded to the relationships that develop within the unitary family.[3] In *Stanley,* for example, we forbade the destruction of such a family when, upon the death of the mother, the State had sought to remove children from the custody of a father who had lived with and supported them and their mother for 18 years. As Justice Powell stated for the plurality in *Moore v. East Cleveland*, 431 U.S. 494, 503 (1977): "Our decisions establish that the Constitution protects the sanctity of the family precisely because the institution of the family is deeply rooted in this Nation's history and tradition."

Thus, the legal issue in the present case reduces to whether the relationship between persons in the situation of Michael and Victoria has been treated as a protected family unit under the historic practices of our society, or whether on any other basis it has been accorded special protection. We think it impossible to find that it has. In fact, quite to the contrary, our traditions have protected the marital family (Gerald, Carole, and the child they acknowledge to be theirs) against the sort of claim Michael asserts.

The presumption of legitimacy was a fundamental principle of the common law. Traditionally, that presumption could be rebutted only by proof that a husband was incapable of procreation or had had no access to his wife during the relevant period. As explained by Blackstone, nonaccess could only be proved "if the husband be out of the kingdom of England

---

2. We do not understand what Justice BRENNAN has in mind by an interest "that society traditionally has thought important ... without protecting it." The protection need not take the form of an explicit constitutional provision or statutory guarantee, but it must at least exclude (all that is necessary to decide the present case) a societal tradition of enacting laws *denying* the interest. Nor do we understand why our practice of limiting the Due Process Clause to traditionally protected interests turns the Clause "into a redundancy[.]" Its purpose is to prevent future generations from lightly casting aside important traditional values—not to enable this Court to invent new ones.

3. Justice BRENNAN asserts that only a "pinched conception of 'the family'" would exclude Michael, Carole, and Victoria from protection. We disagree. The family unit accorded traditional respect in our society, which we have referred to as the "unitary family," is typified, of course, by the marital family, but also includes the household of unmarried parents and their children. Perhaps the concept can be expanded even beyond this, but it will bear no resemblance to traditionally respected relationships—and will thus cease to have any constitutional significance—if it is stretched so far as to include the relationship established between a married woman, her lover, and their child, during a 3–month sojourn in St. Thomas, or during a subsequent 8–month period when, if he happened to be in Los Angeles, he stayed with her and the child.

(or, as the law somewhat loosely phrases it, *extra quatuor maria* [beyond the four seas]) for above nine months. . . ." 1 Blackstone's Commentaries 456 (J. Chitty ed. 1826). And, under the common law both in England and here, "neither husband nor wife [could] be a witness to prove access or nonaccess." [James] Schouler, [A Treatise on the] Law of the Domestic Relations § 225, [at] 306 (3 ed. 1882); A Century of Family Law: 1857–1957, at 158 ([R.H. Graveson & F.R. Crane eds.,] 1957). The primary policy rationale underlying the common law's severe restrictions on rebuttal of the presumption appears to have been an aversion to declaring children illegitimate, thereby depriving them of rights of inheritance and succession, and likely making them wards of the state. A secondary policy concern was the interest in promoting the "peace and tranquility of States and families," Schouler, *supra* § 225, at 304, a goal that is obviously impaired by facilitating suits against husband and wife asserting that their children are illegitimate. Even though, as bastardy laws became less harsh, "[j]udges in both [England and the United States] gradually widened the acceptable range of evidence that could be offered by spouses, and placed restraints on the 'four seas rule' . . . [,] the law retained a strong bias against ruling the children of married women illegitimate." [Michael Grossberg, Governing the Hearth: Law and the Family in Nineteenth Century America] 202 (1985).

We have found nothing in the older sources, nor in the older cases, addressing specifically the power of the natural father to assert parental rights over a child born into a woman's existing marriage with another man. Since it is Michael's burden to establish that such a power (at least where the natural father has established a relationship with the child) is so deeply embedded within our traditions as to be a fundamental right, the lack of evidence alone might defeat his case. But the evidence shows that even in modern times—when, as we have noted, the rigid protection of the marital family has in other respects been relaxed—the ability of a person in Michael's position to claim paternity has not been generally acknowledged. * * *

Moreover, even if it were clear that one in Michael's position generally possesses, and has generally always possessed, standing to challenge the marital child's legitimacy, that would still not establish Michael's case. As noted earlier, what is at issue here is not entitlement to a state pronouncement that Victoria was begotten by Michael. It is no conceivable denial of constitutional right for a State to decline to declare facts unless some legal consequence hinges upon the requested declaration. What Michael asserts here is a right to have himself declared the natural father *and thereby to obtain parental prerogatives.* * * * What counts is whether the States in fact award substantive parental rights to the natural father of a child conceived within, and born into, an extant marital union that wishes to embrace the child. We are not aware of a single case, old or new, that has done so. This is not the stuff of which fundamental rights qualifying as liberty interests are made.[6]

* * *

In *Lehr v. Robertson,* a case involving a natural father's attempt to block his child's adoption by the unwed mother's new husband, we observed that "[t]he significance of the biological connection is that it offers the natural father an opportunity that no other male possesses to develop a relationship with his offspring," 463 U.S. at 262, and we assumed that the Constitution might require some protection of that opportunity, *id.,* at 262–65. Where, however, the child is born into an extant marital family, the natural father's unique opportunity conflicts with the similarly unique opportunity of the husband of the marriage; and it is not unconstitutional for the State to give categorical preference to the latter. * * *

* * *

IV

We have never had occasion to decide whether a child has a liberty interest, symmetrical with that of her parent, in maintaining her filial relationship. We need not do so here because, even assuming that such a right exists, Victoria's claim must fail. Victoria's due process challenge is, if anything, weaker than Michael's. Her basic claim is not that California has erred in preventing her from establishing that Michael, not Gerald, should stand as her legal father. Rather, she claims a due process right to maintain filial relationships with both Michael and Gerald. This assertion merits little discussion, for, whatever the merits of the guardian *ad litem*'s belief that such an arrangement can be of great psychological benefit to a child, the claim that a State must recognize multiple fatherhood has no support in the history or traditions of this country. Moreover, even if we

---

6. Justice BRENNAN criticizes our methodology in using historical traditions specifically relating to the rights of an adulterous natural father, rather than inquiring more generally "whether parenthood is an interest that historically has received our attention and protection." There seems to us no basis for the contention that this methodology is "nove[l.]" For example, in *Bowers v. Hardwick*, 478 U.S. 186 (1986), we noted that at the time the Fourteenth Amendment was ratified all but 5 of the 37 States had criminal sodomy laws, that all 50 of the States had such laws prior to 1961, and that 24 States and the District of Columbia continued to have them; and we concluded from that record, regarding that very specific aspect of sexual conduct, that "to claim that a right to engage in such conduct is 'deeply rooted in this Nation's history and tradition' or 'implicit in the concept of ordered liberty' is, at best, facetious." [*Id.*] at 194. In *Roe v. Wade,* 410 U.S. 113 (1973), we spent about a fifth of our opinion negating the proposition that there was a longstanding tradition of laws proscribing abortion. [*Id.*] at 129–41.

We do not understand why, having rejected our focus upon the societal tradition regarding the natural father's rights vis-à-vis a child whose mother is married to another man, Justice BRENNAN would choose to focus instead upon "parenthood." Why should the relevant category not be even more general—perhaps "family relationships"; or "personal relationships"; or even "emotional attachments in general"? Though the dissent has no basis for the level of generality it would select, we do: We refer to the most specific level at which a relevant tradition protecting, or denying protection to, the asserted right can be identified. If, for example, there were no societal tradition, either way, regarding the rights of the natural father of a child adulterously conceived, we would have to consult, and (if possible) reason from, the traditions regarding natural fathers in general. But there is such a more specific tradition, and it unqualifiedly denies protection to such a parent.

were to construe Victoria's argument as forwarding the lesser proposition that, whatever her status vis-à-vis Gerald, she has a liberty interest in maintaining a filial relationship with her natural father, Michael, we find that, at best, her claim is the obverse of Michael's and fails for the same reasons.

* * *

The judgment of the California Court of Appeal is *Affirmed.*

JUSTICE O'CONNOR, with whom JUSTICE KENNEDY joins, concurring in part.

I concur in all but footnote 6 of Justice SCALIA's opinion. This footnote sketches a mode of historical analysis to be used when identifying liberty interests protected by the Due Process Clause of the Fourteenth Amendment that may be somewhat inconsistent with our past decisions in this area. * * *

JUSTICE STEVENS, concurring, in the judgment.

* * *

Under the circumstances of the case before us, Michael was given a fair opportunity to show that he is Victoria's natural father, that he had developed a relationship with her, and that her interests would be served by granting him visitation rights. On the other hand, the record also shows that after its rather shaky start, the marriage between Carole and Gerald developed a stability that now provides Victoria with a loving and harmonious family home. In the circumstances of this case, I find nothing fundamentally unfair about the exercise of a judge's discretion that, in the end, allows the mother to decide whether her child's best interests would be served by allowing the natural father visitation privileges. Because I am convinced that the trial judge had the authority under state law both to hear Michael's plea for visitation rights and to grant him such rights if Victoria's best interests so warranted, I am satisfied that the California statutory scheme is consistent with the Due Process Clause of the Fourteenth Amendment.

I therefore concur in the Court's judgment of affirmance.

JUSTICE BRENNAN, with whom JUSTICE MARSHALL and JUSTICE BLACKMUN join, dissenting.

In a case that has yielded so many opinions as has this one, it is fruitful to begin by emphasizing the common ground shared by a majority of this Court. Five Members of the Court refuse to foreclose "the possibility that a natural father might ever have a constitutionally protected interest in his relationship with a child whose mother was married to, and cohabiting with, another man at the time of the child's conception and birth." Five Justices agree that the flaw inhering in a conclusive presumption that terminates a constitutionally protected interest without any hearing whatsoever is a *procedural* one. Four Members of the Court agree that Michael H. has a liberty interest in his relationship with Victoria, and one assumes for purposes of this case that he does.

In contrast, only one other Member of the Court fully endorses Mr. Justice SCALIA's view of the proper method of analyzing questions arising under the Due Process Clause. Nevertheless, because the plurality opinion's exclusively historical analysis portends a significant and unfortunate departure from our prior cases and from sound constitutional decisionmaking, I devote a substantial portion of my discussion to it.

I

Once we recognized that the "liberty" protected by the Due Process Clause of the Fourteenth Amendment encompasses more than freedom from bodily restraint, today's plurality opinion emphasizes, the concept was cut loose from one natural limitation on its meaning. This innovation paved the way, so the plurality hints, for judges to substitute their own preferences for those of elected officials. Dissatisfied with this supposedly unbridled and uncertain state of affairs, the plurality casts about for another limitation on the concept of liberty.

It finds this limitation in "tradition." Apparently oblivious to the fact that this concept can be as malleable and as elusive as "liberty" itself, the plurality pretends that tradition places a discernible border around the Constitution. The pretense is seductive; it would be comforting to believe that a search for "tradition" involves nothing more idiosyncratic or complicated than poring through dusty volumes on American history. * * * Because reasonable people can disagree about the content of particular traditions, and because they can disagree even about which traditions are relevant to the definition of "liberty," the plurality has not found the objective boundary that it seeks.

Even if we could agree, moreover, on the content and significance of particular traditions, we still would be forced to identify the point at which a tradition becomes firm enough to be relevant to our definition of liberty and the moment at which it becomes too obsolete to be relevant any longer. The plurality supplies no objective means by which we might make these determinations. Indeed, as soon as the plurality sees signs that the tradition upon which it bases its decision (the laws denying putative fathers like Michael standing to assert paternity) is crumbling, it shifts ground and says that the case has nothing to do with that tradition, after all. "[W]hat is at issue here," the plurality asserts after canvassing the law on paternity suits, "is not entitlement to a state pronouncement that Victoria was begotten by Michael." But that is precisely what is at issue here, and the plurality's last-minute denial of this fact dramatically illustrates the subjectivity of its own analysis.

It is ironic that an approach so utterly dependent on tradition is so indifferent to our precedents. Citing barely a handful of this Court's numerous decisions defining the scope of the liberty protected by the Due Process Clause to support its reliance on tradition, the plurality acts as though English legal treatises and the American Law Reports always have provided the sole source for our constitutional principles. They have not. Just as common-law notions no longer define the "property" that the Constitution protects, neither do they circumscribe the "liberty" that it guarantees * * *.

It is not that tradition has been irrelevant to our prior decisions. Throughout our decisionmaking in this important area runs the theme that certain interests and practices—freedom from physical restraint, marriage, childbearing, childrearing, and others—form the core of our definition of "liberty." Our solicitude for these interests is partly the result of the fact that the Due Process Clause would seem an empty promise if it did not protect them, and partly the result of the historical and traditional importance of these interests in our society. In deciding cases arising under the Due Process Clause, therefore, we have considered whether the concrete limitation under consideration impermissibly impinges upon one of these more generalized interests.

Today's plurality, however, does not ask whether parenthood is an interest that historically has received our attention and protection; the answer to that question is too clear for dispute. Instead, the plurality asks whether the specific variety of parenthood under consideration—a natural father's relationship with a child whose mother is married to another man—has enjoyed such protection.

If we had looked to tradition with such specificity in past cases, many a decision would have reached a different result. Surely the use of contraceptives by unmarried couples, or even by married couples * * * and even the right to raise one's natural but illegitimate children, were not "interest[s] traditionally protected by our society," at the time of their consideration by this Court. * * *

* * * In the plurality's constitutional universe, we may not take notice of the fact that the original reasons for the conclusive presumption of paternity are out of place in a world in which blood tests can prove virtually beyond a shadow of a doubt who sired a particular child and in which the fact of illegitimacy no longer plays the burdensome and stigmatizing role it once did. Nor, in the plurality's world, may we deny "tradition" its full scope by pointing out that the rationale for the conventional rule has changed over the years, as has the rationale for Cal. Evid. Code Ann. § 621; instead, our task is simply to identify a rule denying the asserted interest and not to ask whether the basis for that rule—which is the true reflection of the values undergirding it—has changed too often or too recently to call the rule embodying that rationale a "tradition." Moreover, by describing the decisive question as whether Michael's and Victoria's interest is one that has been "traditionally *protected by* our society," (emphasis added), rather than one that society traditionally has thought important (with or without protecting it), and by suggesting that our sole function is to "*discern* the society's views," (emphasis added), the plurality acts as if the only purpose of the Due

Process Clause is to confirm the importance of interests already protected by a majority of the States. Transforming the protection afforded by the Due Process Clause into a redundancy mocks those who, with care and purpose, wrote the Fourteenth Amendment.

In construing the Fourteenth Amendment to offer shelter only to those interests specifically protected by historical practice, moreover, the plurality ignores the kind of society in which our Constitution exists. We are not an assimilative, homogeneous society, but a facilitative, pluralistic one, in which we must be willing to abide someone else's unfamiliar or even repellent practice because the same tolerant impulse protects our own idiosyncrasies. Even if we can agree, therefore, that "family" and "parenthood" are part of the good life, it is absurd to assume that we can agree on the content of those terms and destructive to pretend that we do. In a community such as ours, "liberty" must include the freedom not to conform. The plurality today squashes this freedom by requiring specific approval from history before protecting anything in the name of liberty.

* * *

II

The plurality's reworking of our interpretive approach is all the more troubling because it is unnecessary. This is not a case in which we face a "new" kind of interest, one that requires us to consider for the first time whether the Constitution protects it. On the contrary, we confront an interest—that of a parent and child in their relationship with each other—that was among the first that this Court acknowledged in its cases defining the "liberty" protected by the Constitution, see, *e.g., Meyer v. Nebraska,* 262 U.S. 390, 399 (1923); *Skinner v. Oklahoma,* 316 U.S. 535, 541 (1942); *Prince v. Massachusetts,* 321 U.S. 158, 166 (1944), and I think I am safe in saying that no one doubts the wisdom or validity of those decisions. Where the interest under consideration is a parent-child relationship, we need not ask, over and over again, whether that interest is one that society traditionally protects.

Thus, to describe the issue in this case as whether the relationship existing between Michael and Victoria "has been treated as a protected family unit under the historic practices of our society, or whether on any other basis it has been accorded special protection," is to reinvent the wheel. The better approach—indeed, the one commanded by our prior cases and by common sense—is to ask whether the specific parent-child relationship under consideration is close enough to the interests that we already have protected to be deemed an aspect of "liberty" as well. On the facts before us, therefore, the question is not what "level of generality" should be used to describe the relationship between Michael and Victoria, but whether the relationship under consideration is sufficiently substantial to qualify as a liberty interest under our prior cases.

On four prior occasions, we have considered whether unwed fathers have a constitutionally protected interest in their relationships with their children. *See Stanley v. Illinois,* 405 U.S. 645 (1972); *Quilloin v. Walcott,* 434 U.S. 246 (1978); *Caban v. Mohammed,* 441 U.S. 380 (1979); and *Lehr v. Robertson,* 463 U.S. 248 (1983). Though different in factual and legal circumstances, these cases have produced a unifying theme: although an unwed father's biological link to his child does not, in and of itself, guarantee him a constitutional stake in his relationship with that child, such a link combined with a substantial parent-child relationship will do so. "When an unwed father demonstrates a full commitment to the responsibilities of parenthood by 'com[ing] forward to participate in the rearing of his child,' ... his interest in personal contact with his child acquires substantial protection under the Due Process Clause. At that point it may be said that he 'act[s] as a father toward his children.' " *Lehr,* [463 U.S.] at 261. This commitment is why Mr. Stanley and Mr. Caban won; why Mr. Quilloin and Mr. Lehr lost; and why Michael H. should prevail today. Michael H. is almost certainly Victoria D.'s natural father, has lived with her as her father, has contributed to her support, and has from the beginning sought to strengthen and maintain his relationship with her.

Claiming that the intent of these cases was to protect the "unitary family," the plurality waves *Stanley, Quilloin, Caban,* and *Lehr* aside. In evaluating the plurality's dismissal of these precedents, it is essential to identify its conception of the "unitary family." If, by acknowledging that *Stanley* et al. sought to protect "the relationships that develop within the unitary family," the plurality meant only to describe the kinds of relationships that develop when parents and children live together (formally or informally) as a family, then the plurality's vision of these cases would be correct. But that is not the plurality's message. Though it pays lipservice to the idea that marriage is not the crucial fact in denying constitutional protection to the relationship between Michael and Victoria, the plurality cannot mean what it says.

The evidence is undisputed that Michael, Victoria, and Carole did live together as a family; that is, they shared the same household, Victoria called Michael "Daddy," Michael contributed to Victoria's support, and he is eager to continue his relationship with her. Yet they are not, in the plurality's view, a "unitary family," whereas Gerald, Carole, and Victoria do compose such a family. The only difference between these two sets of relationships, however, is the fact of marriage. The plurality, indeed, expressly recognizes that marriage is the critical fact in denying Michael a constitutionally protected stake in his relationship with Victoria: no fewer than six times, the plurality refers to Michael as the *"adulterous* natural father" (emphasis added) or the like. However, the very premise of *Stanley* and the cases following it is that marriage is not decisive in answering the question whether the Constitution protects the parental relationship under consideration. These cases are, after all, important precisely because they involve the rights of *unwed* fathers. It is important to remember, moreover, that in *Quilloin, Caban,* and *Lehr,* the putative father's demands would have disrupted a "unitary family" as the plurality defines it; in each case, the husband of the child's mother sought to adopt the child over the objections of the natural father. Significantly, our decisions in those cases in no way relied on the need to protect the marital family. Hence the plurality's claim that *Stanley, Quilloin, Caban,* and *Lehr* were about the "unitary family," as that family is defined by today's plurality, is surprising indeed.

The plurality's exclusive rather than inclusive definition of the "unitary family" is out of step with other decisions as well. This pinched conception of "the family," crucial as it is in rejecting Michael's and Victoria's claims of a liberty interest, is jarring in light of our many cases preventing the States from denying important interests or statuses to those whose situations do not fit the government's narrow view of the family. * * *

* * *

IV

The atmosphere surrounding today's decision is one of make-believe. Beginning with the suggestion that the situation confronting us here does not repeat itself every day in every corner of the country, moving on to the claim that it is tradition alone that supplies the details of the liberty that the Constitution protects, and passing finally to the notion that the Court always has recognized a cramped vision of "the family," today's decision lets stand California's pronouncement that Michael—whom blood tests show to a 98 percent probability to be Victoria's father—is not Victoria's father. When and if the Court awakes to reality, it will find a world very different from the one it expects.

JUSTICE WHITE, with whom JUSTICE BRENNAN joins, dissenting.

California law, as the plurality describes it, tells us that, except in limited circumstances, California declares it to be "*irrelevant* for paternity purposes whether a child conceived during, and born into, an existing marriage was begotten by someone other than the husband" (emphasis in original). This I do not accept, for the fact that Michael H. is the biological father of Victoria is to me highly relevant to whether he has rights, as a father or otherwise, with respect to the child. Because I believe that Michael H. has a liberty interest that cannot be denied without due process of the law, I must dissent.

I

Like JUSTICES BRENNAN, MARSHALL, BLACKMUN, AND STEVENS, I do not agree with the plurality opinion's conclusion that a natural father can never "have a constitutionally protected interest in his relationship with a child whose mother was married to, and cohabiting with, another man at the time of the child's conception and birth." Prior cases here have recognized the liberty interest of a father in his relationship with his child. In none of these cases did we indicate that the father's rights were dependent on the marital status of the mother or biological father. The basic principle enunciated in the Court's unwed father cases is that an unwed father who has demonstrated a sufficient commitment to his paternity by way of personal, financial, or custodial responsibilities has a protected liberty interest in a relationship with his child.

* * *

In the case now before us, Michael H. is not a father unwilling to assume his responsibilities as a parent. To the contrary, he is a father who has asserted his interests in raising and providing for his child since the very time of the child's birth. In contrast to the father in *Lehr,* Michael had begun to develop a relationship with his daughter. There is no dispute on this point. Michael contributed to the child's support. Michael and Victoria lived together (albeit intermittently, given Carole's itinerant lifestyle). There is a personal and emotional relationship between Michael and Victoria, who grew up calling him "Daddy." Michael held Victoria out as his daughter and contributed to the child's financial support. (Even appellee concedes that Michael has "made greater efforts and had more success in establishing a father-child relationship" than did Mr. Lehr.) The mother has never denied, and indeed has admitted, that Michael is Victoria's father. * * *

* * *

II

* * *

As the Court has said: "The significance of the biological connection is that it offers the natural father an opportunity that no other male possesses to develop a relationship with his offspring. If he grasps that opportunity and accepts some measure of responsibility for the child's future, he may enjoy the blessings of the parent-child relationship and make uniquely valuable contributions to the child's development." *Lehr,* 463 U.S. at 262. It is as if this passage was addressed to Michael. Yet the plurality today recants. Michael eagerly grasped the opportunity to have a relationship with his daughter (he lived with her; he declared her to be his child; he provided financial support for her) and still, with today's opinion, his opportunity has vanished. He has been rendered a stranger to his child.

* * *

NOTES AND QUESTIONS

1. *Conflicting rights.* In *Michael H.,* Justice Brennan argued that the Court should determine whether a liberty interest exists without reference to the facts that Carole was married to someone else when Victoria was conceived, and that Carole and Gerald wished to raise Victoria as their own. Is this position reasonable? Is Justice Scalia's response that this position "leads to the conclusion that if Michael had begotten Victoria by rape, that fact

would in no way affect his possession of a liberty interest in his relationship with her" persuasive? Consider the following:

> Perhaps the most controversial aspect of the decision was the plurality's effort to define the liberty clause in terms of those rights (whether of the parent or the child) which have historically received protection. Scalia's opinion repeatedly refers to Michael as the "adulterous natural father" and reiterates that it is the adultery part that has never been protected. The dissent treats Scalia's reliance on marriage as anachronistic and inconsistent with precedent given the line of Supreme Court cases extending constitutional recognition to the rights of unmarried fathers. If the Supreme Court is to rely on the historical status of institutions such as marriage for resolving paternity, however, what happens when the significance of such institutions evolve with time?

June Carbone & Naomi Cahn, *Which Ties Bind? Redefining the Parent–Child Relationship in an Age of Genetic Certainty*, 11 Wm. & Mary Bill Rts. J. 1011, 1042 (2003).

2. *Protecting a nonmarital father's rights.* Professor Janet L. Dolgin goes a step further, arguing that after *Michael H.*, "[a] biological father does protect his paternity by developing a social relationship with his child, but this step demands the creation of a family, a step itself depending upon an appropriate relationship between the man and his child's mother." The father must have established a marriage or marriage-like relationship with the mother. Janet L. Dolgin, *Just a Gene: Judicial Assumptions About Parenthood*, 40 UCLA L. Rev. 637, 650, 671 (1993). Indeed, a few state statutes confer rights only on nonmarital fathers who develop a relationship with both the child and the mother. *See, e.g.*, Kan. Stat. Ann. § 59–2136(h)(D)–(E) (2008); Wis. Stat. Ann. § 48.415(6)(a)–(b) (West 2008). Why do you think Michael fought so hard to establish a parental relationship with Victoria?

3. *Strains on constitutional law.* From *Stanley* to *Michael H.*, the Supreme Court's unwed-father decisions concerned children who were at least a few years old when the dispute arose, and children whose existence and whereabouts the fathers had known about since birth. The decisions do not explicitly answer two recurring questions:

(a) *Newborn adoptions.* Many transfers of children to nonrelative adoptive parents occur at birth or within days (but not years) thereafter. What are the unwed father's constitutional rights to veto an adoption at the child's birth, when the unwed father will have had no opportunity yet to "develop a relationship" with the child?

(b) *The "thwarted" nonmarital father.* What are the nonmarital father's constitutional rights where the biological mother, seeking to thwart his efforts to develop the requisite relationship with the child, places the child for adoption at birth or shortly afterwards after hiding the child from the father, after untruthfully asserting that she does not know the father's identity or whereabouts, after refusing to name the father, after forging his signature on consent documents, or after knowingly naming the wrong man? *See* David D. Meyer, *Family Ties: Solving the Constitutional Dilemma of the Faultless Father*, 41 Ariz. L. Rev. 753 (1999).

4. *Children's interests in identifying their biological father.* Beyond the possibility of additional financial resources, is paternity determination in the child's best interests? A child might have several interests at stake. First, knowing the identity of the father helps the child obtain information about medical history and genetic heritage. Second, it might benefit the child to establish a parental relationship. Moreover, *society* may have interests in ensuring that children receive adequate financial resources from their fathers, thereby decreasing their need for public assistance. Some suggest that societal interests might also favor fathers playing a parenting role in their children's lives. *See* Donald C. Hubin, *Daddy Dilemmas: Untangling the Puzzles of Paternity*, 13 Cornell L.J. & Pub. Pol'y 29 (2003).

5. *Paternity testing.* Prior to the advent of blood tests, paternity was sometimes determined by family resemblance. Beginning in the 1980s, the Human Leukocyte Antigen (HLA) blood-test system, which detects antigens on white blood cells, was used in conjunction with red-blood-cell tests to disprove paternity. Today, DNA testing can establish or disestablish paternity at a greater than 99% accuracy rate. June Carbone, *The Legal Definition of Parenthood: Uncertainty at the Core of Family Identity*, 65 La. L. Rev. 1295, 1314 (2005). Does the statutory presumption that decided *Michael H.* make sense now that paternity can be established with virtual certainty? California has since amended the marital presumption and allows the presumed father or the child's guardian *ad litem* to file a paternity action within two years of the child's birth. Cal. Fam. Code § 7541(b) (2008). What arguments do you see for the two-year limitation?

6. *Dual paternity.* Should the law ever recognize that a child could have two fathers? This is the Louisiana dual paternity solution. Louisiana recognizes that a child may have both a biological and a "legal" father. *See Smith v. Cole*, 553 So.2d 847, 854 (La. 1989). Moreover, having several fathers is "a social reality but not a legal category," given "our knowledge of the existence of multiple fathers, whether birthfathers, stepfathers, psychological fathers or other categories." Nancy E. Dowd, *Multiple Parents/Multiple Fathers*, 9 J. L. Fam. Stud. 231, 231 (2007). Should the law accord legal rights to all of these individuals?

2. PUTATIVE FATHER REGISTRIES

A number of states created putative father registries after *Lehr* upheld their general constitutionality. Where a man believes he is or may be a child's father, registry statutes place the burden on him to register (usually with the state department of health or similar agency) if he wishes to claim paternity and receive notice of a prospective adoption. Once the man receives notice, he may seek to establish paternity and assert his right to veto the adoption.

The New York registry statute at issue in *Lehr* established no time limit within which the putative father must register to preserve his claim of right. In some states, however, the statute requires him to register before the child is born or within a specified short period after birth. *See, e.g.*, Ariz. Rev. Stat. § 8–106.01B (2008) (any time before the child's birth but not later than 30 days after birth). Failure to register within the specified period may constitute waiver not only of the right of notice but also of the right to contest the adoption. *See, e.g., id.* § 8–106.01E.

Registries have not proved as effective as their proponents had hoped because most men never learn of the registry's existence. Most unwed fathers are not lawyers, and it is not normal practice to consult a lawyer about childbirth. A few states have amended their registry statutes to maximize publicity in places likely to be frequented by unwed fathers, such as hospitals, local health departments and other such health facilities, motor vehicle department offices, and schools and universities. Regardless of the extent of publicity, however, the putative father's lack of knowledge of the registry's existence does not excuse noncompliance with the registration provisions. Noncompliance is likewise not excused because the unwed father asserts he did not know about the pregnancy or the birth. The rationale is that men "are aware that sexual intercourse may result in pregnancy, and of the potential opportunity to establish a family." *In re Clausen*, 502 N.W.2d 649, 687 (Mich. 1993) (Levin, J., dissenting). In 2008, an Illinois court found that a father's failure to register with the Putative Father Registry did not preclude his parentage claim, and ordered that he be reinstated as a party in the contested adoption proceedings. *J.S.A. v. M.H.*, 893 N.E.2d 682, 688 (Ill. App. Ct. 2008).

Another problem is that, even if men know about the registries, they may not know where to register. Each state has enacted its own registry procedures, without reach or effect in other states. Assume two teenagers conceive a child while on summer vacation in state A, and then return to their homes in states B and C respectively. With the help of her parents, the teenage mother in state C then places the child for adoption in state D, asserting that she does not know the father's identity or whereabouts. If each of these states has a putative father registry, where should the father register? What if the father has no idea that adoption proceedings are pending in state D? What are the chances that registration will provide him notice of the adoption proceedings? Would a system of interstate cooperation, which would enable putative fathers to search the registries of all states after registering in their own state, help provide actual notice to men who truly want to assert their parental rights? Should Congress create a national or federal putative father registry to enhance and connect state registries? *See, e.g.*, Mary Beck, *Toward a National Putative Father Registry Database*, 25 Harv. J.L. & Pub. Pol'y 1031 (2002).

PROBLEM 5–5

You are a state legislator. In light of *Lehr* and *Michael H.*, would you vote to enact the following statutory provision?

In an adoption case, the juvenile court may terminate the rights of a child's unmarried father if it finds that termination is in the best interests of the child and when it appears by clear and convincing evidence that: the child's unmarried mother has voluntarily terminated her rights and the child's father, knowing he is the child's father, has provided no financial or emotional support to the mother during the pregnancy or at the birth of the child.

PROBLEM 5–6

After you complete the Family Law course, a friend confides that she has had intercourse with a man, that she is now pregnant, and does not intend to marry the man. Your friend asks whether she should encourage the man to register with the putative father registry, and what the legal consequences would be if he did register. What advice would you provide to her?

3. THE UNIFORM PARENTAGE ACT

In 1973, the National Conference of Commissioners on Uniform State Laws promulgated the Uniform Parentage Act (UPA), a then-revolutionary set of laws for determining parentage, paternity and child custody. It was adopted by 19 states. Michael Morgan, *The New Uniform Parentage Act*, 25 Fam. Adv. 11 (2002). The UPA reflected Supreme Court rulings that banned discrimination based on illegitimacy in a variety of circumstances. The UPA was substantially revised in 2002, and now reflects scientific developments in parentage law, including advances in genetic testing.

* * *

SECTION 201. ESTABLISHMENT OF PARENT–CHILD RELATIONSHIP.

(a) The mother-child relationship is established between a woman and a child by:

(1) the woman's having given birth to the child * * *;

(2) an adjudication of the woman's maternity;

(3) adoption of the child by the woman; or

(4) an adjudication confirming the woman as a parent of a child born to a gestational mother * * *.

(b) The father-child relationship is established between a man and a child by:

(1) an unrebutted presumption of the man's paternity of the child under [the marital presumption];

(2) an effective acknowledgment of paternity by the man * * *;

(3) an adjudication of the man's paternity;

(4) adoption of the child by the man; [or]

(5) the man's having consented to assisted reproduction by a woman * * *

* * *

[The revised Uniform Parentage Act includes a marital presumption, but allows it to be rebutted on the following basis under Section 607]

SECTION 607. LIMITATION: CHILD HAVING PRESUMED FATHER

(a) Except as otherwise provided in subsection (b), a proceeding brought by a presumed father [a presumed father is a man subject to the marital presumption], the mother, or another individual to adjudicate the parentage of a child having a presumed father must be commenced not later than two years after the birth of the child.

(b) A proceeding seeking to disprove the father-child relationship between a child and the child's presumed father may be maintained at any time if the court determines that:

(1) the presumed father and the mother of the child neither cohabited nor engaged in sexual intercourse with each other during the probable time of conception; and

(2) the presumed father never openly held out the child as his own.

Uniform Parentage Act (2002), *available at* http://www.law.upenn.edu/bll/ulc/upa/final2002.htm.

B. DETERMINING MATERNITY

The woman who gives birth to a child has been presumed to be the mother. But the legal issues with establishing maternity have become more complex as artificial reproductive technologies (ART) have enabled several women to contribute to maternity and as same-sex partners engage in mothering functions together. See Laura Oren, *Honor Thy Mother?: The Supreme Court's Jurisprudence of Motherhood*, 17 Hastings Woman's L.J. 187 (2006). The next decisions explore these complications, and Chapter 17 explores ART in great detail.

JOHNSON v. CALVERT

Supreme Court of California, 1993.
851 P.2d 776.

PANELLI, JUSTICE.

In this case we address several of the legal questions raised by recent advances in reproductive technology. When, pursuant to a surrogacy agreement, a zygote[1] formed of the gametes[2] of a husband and wife is implanted in the uterus of another woman, who carries the resulting fetus to term and gives birth to a child not genetically related to her, who is the child's "natural mother" under California law? Does a determination that

---

1. An organism produced by the union of two gametes. (McGraw–Hill Dict. of Scientific and Technical Terms (4th ed. 1989) p. 783.)

2. A cell that participates in fertilization and development of a new organism, also known as a germ cell or sex cell. (McGraw–Hill Dict. of Scientific and Technical Terms, *supra*, p. 2087.)

the wife is the child's natural mother work a deprivation of the gestating woman's constitutional rights? And is such an agreement barred by any public policy of this state?

* * *

FACTS

Mark and Crispina Calvert are a married couple who desired to have a child. Crispina was forced to undergo a hysterectomy in 1984. Her ovaries remained capable of producing eggs, however, and the couple eventually considered surrogacy. In 1989 Anna Johnson heard about Crispina's plight from a coworker and offered to serve as a surrogate for the Calverts.

On January 15, 1990, Mark, Crispina, and Anna signed a contract providing that an embryo created by the sperm of Mark and the egg of Crispina would be implanted in Anna and the child born would be taken into Mark and Crispina's home "as their child." Anna agreed she would relinquish "all parental rights" to the child in favor of Mark and Crispina. In return, Mark and Crispina would pay Anna $10,000 in a series of installments, the last to be paid six weeks after the child's birth. Mark and Crispina were also to pay for a $200,000 life insurance policy on Anna's life.[4]

The zygote was implanted on January 19, 1990. Less than a month later, an ultrasound test confirmed Anna was pregnant.

Unfortunately, relations deteriorated between the two sides. * * *

* * *

The child was born on September 19, 1990, and blood samples were obtained from both Anna and the child for analysis. The blood test results excluded Anna as the genetic mother. The parties agreed to a court order providing that the child would remain with Mark and Crispina on a temporary basis with visits by Anna.

At trial in October 1990, the parties stipulated that Mark and Crispina were the child's genetic parents. After hearing evidence and arguments, the trial court ruled that Mark and Crispina were the child's "genetic, biological and natural" father and mother, that Anna had no "parental" rights to the child, and that the surrogacy contract was legal and enforceable against Anna's claims. The court also terminated the order allowing visitation. * * *

DISCUSSION

Determining Maternity Under the Uniform Parentage Act

* * *

[The Uniform Parentage Act, enacted in 1975] replace[ed] the distinction between legitimate and illegitimate children with the concept of the

---

4. At the time of the agreement, Anna already had a daughter, Erica, born in 1987.

"parent and child relationship." The "parent and child relationship" means "the legal relationship existing between a child and his natural or adoptive parents incident to which the law confers or imposes rights, privileges, duties, and obligations. It includes the mother and child relationship and the father and child relationship." ([former Cal.] Civ. Code, § 7001.) "The parent and child relationship extends equally to every child and to every parent, regardless of the marital status of the parents." ([former Cal.] Civ. Code, § 7002.) The "parent and child relationship" is thus a legal relationship encompassing two kinds of parents, "natural" and "adoptive."

Passage of the Act clearly was not motivated by the need to resolve surrogacy disputes, which were virtually unknown in 1975. Yet it facially applies to *any* parentage determination, including the rare case in which a child's maternity is in issue. * * * [T]he Act offers a mechanism to resolve this dispute, albeit one not specifically tooled for it. We therefore proceed to analyze the parties' contentions within the Act's framework.

* * *

* * * [W]e are left with the undisputed evidence that Anna, not Crispina, gave birth to the child and that Crispina, not Anna, is genetically related to him. Both women thus have adduced evidence of a mother and child relationship as contemplated by the Act. Yet for any child California law recognizes only one natural mother, despite advances in reproductive technology rendering a different outcome biologically possible.[8]

* * *

Because two women each have presented acceptable proof of maternity, we do not believe this case can be decided without inquiring into the parties' intentions as manifested in the surrogacy agreement. Mark and Crispina are a couple who desired to have a child of their own genetic stock but are physically unable to do so without the help of reproductive technology. They affirmatively intended the birth of the child, and took the steps necessary to effect in vitro fertilization. But for their acted-on intention, the child would not exist. Anna agreed to facilitate the procreation of Mark's and Crispina's child. The parties' aim was to bring Mark's and Crispina's child into the world, not for Mark and Crispina to donate a zygote to Anna. Crispina from the outset intended to be the child's mother. Although the gestative function Anna performed was necessary to bring about the child's birth, it is safe to say that Anna would not have been given the opportunity to gestate or deliver the child had she, prior to implantation of the zygote, manifested her own intent to be the child's

---

8. We decline to accept the contention of amicus curiae the American Civil Liberties Union (ACLU) that we should find the child has two mothers. Even though rising divorce rates have made multiple parent arrangements common in our society, we see no compelling reason to recognize such a situation here. The Calverts are the genetic and intending parents of their son and have provided him, by all accounts, with a stable, intact, and nurturing home. To recognize parental rights in a third party with whom the Calvert family has had little contact since shortly after the child's birth would diminish Crispina's role as mother.

mother. No reason appears why Anna's later change of heart should vitiate the determination that Crispina is the child's natural mother.

We conclude that although the Act recognizes both genetic consanguinity and giving birth as means of establishing a mother and child relationship, when the two means do not coincide in one woman, she who intended to procreate the child—that is, she who intended to bring about the birth of a child that she intended to raise as her own—is the natural mother under California law.[10]

* * *

Constitutionality of the Determination That Anna Johnson is Not the Natural Mother

Anna argues at length that her right to the continued companionship of the child is protected under the federal Constitution.

First, we note the constitutional rights that are *not* implicated here.

There is no issue of procedural due process: although Anna broadly contends that the procedures prescribed for adoptions should be followed in the situation of a gestational surrogate's relinquishment to the genetic parents of the child she has carried and delivered, she cites no specific deficiency in the notice or hearing this matter received.

* * *

Anna relies mainly on theories of substantive due process, privacy, and procreative freedom, citing a number of decisions recognizing the fundamental liberty interest of natural parents in the custody and care of their children. * * *

Anna's argument depends on a prior determination that she is indeed the child's mother. Since Crispina is the child's mother under California law because she, not Anna, provided the ovum for the in vitro fertilization procedure, intending to raise the child as her own, it follows that any constitutional interests Anna possesses in this situation are something less than those of a mother. As counsel for the minor points out, the issue in this case is not whether Anna's asserted rights as a natural mother

---

10. Thus, under our analysis, in a true "egg donation" situation, where a woman gestates and gives birth to a child formed from the egg of another woman with the intent to raise the child as her own, the birth mother is the natural mother under California law.

The dissent would decide *parentage* based on the best interests of the child. Such an approach raises the repugnant specter of governmental interference in matters implicating our most fundamental notions of privacy, and confuses concepts of parentage and custody. Logically, the determination of parentage must precede, and should not be dictated by, eventual custody decisions. The implicit assumption of the dissent is that a recognition of the genetic intending mother as the natural mother may sometimes harm the child. This assumption overlooks California's dependency laws, which are designed to protect *all* children irrespective of the manner of birth or conception. Moreover, the best interests standard poorly serves the child in the present situation: it fosters instability during litigation and, if applied to recognize the gestator as the natural mother, results in a split of custody between the natural father and the gestator, an outcome not likely to benefit the child. Further, it may be argued that, by voluntarily contracting away any rights to the child, the gestator has, in effect, conceded the best interest of the child is not with her.

were unconstitutionally violated, but rather whether the determination that she is not the legal natural mother at all is constitutional.

Anna relies principally on the decision of the United States Supreme Court in *Michael H. v. Gerald D.*, 491 U.S. 110 (1989), to support her claim to a constitutionally protected liberty interest in the companionship of the child, based on her status as "birth mother." In that case, a plurality of the court held that a state may constitutionally deny a man parental rights with respect to a child he fathered during a liaison with the wife of another man, since it is the marital family that traditionally has been accorded a protected liberty interest, as reflected in the historic presumption of legitimacy of a child born into such a family. The reasoning of the plurality in *Michael H.* does not assist Anna. Society has not traditionally protected the right of a woman who gestates and delivers a baby pursuant to an agreement with a couple who supply the zygote from which the baby develops and who intend to raise the child as their own; such arrangements are of too recent an origin to claim the protection of tradition. To the extent that tradition has a bearing on the present case, we believe it supports the claim of the couple who exercise their right to procreate in order to form a family of their own, albeit through novel medical procedures.

* * *

DISPOSITION

The judgment of the Court of Appeal is affirmed.

[Concurring opinion by ARABIAN, J., omitted].

KENNARD, J., dissenting.

* * *

* * * [I]n California the existing statutory law applicable to this case is the Uniform Parentage Act, which was never designed to govern the new reproductive technology of gestational surrogacy. Under the UPA, both the genetic mother and the gestational mother have an equal right to be the child's natural mother. But the UPA allows one natural mother for each child, and thus this court is required to make a choice. To break this "tie" between the genetic mother and the gestational mother, the majority uses the legal concept of intent. In so doing, the majority has articulated a rationale for using the concept of intent that is grounded in principles of tort, intellectual property and commercial contract law.

But, as I have pointed out, we are not deciding a case involving the commission of a tort, the ownership of intellectual property, or the delivery of goods under a commercial contract; we are deciding the fate of a child. In the absence of legislation that is designed to address the unique problems of gestational surrogacy, this court should look not to tort, property or contract law, but to family law, as the governing paradigm and source of a rule of decision.

The allocation of parental rights and responsibilities necessarily impacts the welfare of a minor child. And in issues of child welfare, the standard that courts frequently apply is the best interests of the child. Indeed, it is highly significant that the UPA itself looks to a child's best interests in deciding another question of parental rights. This "best interests" standard serves to assure that in the judicial resolution of disputes affecting a child's well-being, protection of the minor child is the foremost consideration. Consequently, I would apply "the best interests of the child" standard to determine who can best assume the social and legal responsibilities of motherhood for a child born of a gestational surrogacy arrangement.

* * *

NOTES AND QUESTIONS

1. *Race matters*. In *Johnson*, Ms. Johnson was an African–American single mother, while Mark Calvert was white, and Crispina Calvert was Filipina. Did race factor into the court's decision? One scholar suggests that the decision reflects the position of African–American women who are hired to care for white children. "African–American women are expected to care for and love white children without any expectation of legal and social recognition of these relationships. In *Johnson*, the Black woman was allowed (and expected) to love and 'mother' the white child as long as she claimed no real power." April L. Cherry, *Nurturing in the Service of White Culture; Racial Subordination. Gestational Surrogacy, and the Ideology of Motherhood*, 10 Tex. J. Women & L. 83, 127 (2001). How persuasive is this argument? Would the court's decision have been different if Ms. Johnson had been a single white woman, and the Calverts had been African–American? Do you think the majority pays sufficient attention to the issue of exploitation of low-income women? Do you think the court disregards the issue of "commodification," that is, the treatment of the female reproductive capacity and the children born of gestational surrogacy arrangements as commodities that can be bought and sold?

2. *Defining parenthood*. The law has multiple potential bases for determining parenthood, including contract, intent, marriage, or biology, or a standard that considers only the child's best interests. Which did the court choose in *Johnson v. Calvert*? Should the bases for defining parenthood be the same for mothers and fathers?

3. *Two mothers*. Just as Louisiana has dual paternity, *see supra*, p. 302, note 6, Section 2.A(1), there are arguments that, in some circumstances, it is appropriate to recognize two mothers. Recognition would allow multiple adults to be entitled to the bundle of rights associated with parental status. *See* Melanie B. Jacobs, *Applying Intent–Based Parentage Principles to Nonlegal Lesbian Coparents*, 25 N. Ill. L. Rev. 433 (2005); Nancy D. Polikoff, *This Child Does Have Two Mothers: Redefining Parenthood to Meet the Needs of Children in Lesbian–Mother and Other Nontraditional Families*, 78 Geo. L.J. 459 (1990); Richard F. Storrow, *Parenthood by Pure Intention: Assisted Reproduction and the Functional Approach to Parentage*, 53 Hastings L.J. 597

(2002). Such a solution builds on the intent, biology, and contract approaches to determining parenthood. Given the complexities of adoption and surrogacy, and of alternative family forms, the reality of families may involve multiple adults providing significant caretaking for a child. Why did the court reject dual maternity in *Johnson v. Calvert*?

Issues involving the recognition of two mothers reappear in the following case, one of three involving lesbian custody disputes that the California Supreme Court decided on the same day in 2005.

K.M. v. E.G.

Supreme Court of California, 2005.
117 P.3d 673.

MORENO, JUSTICE.

* * *

In the present case, we must decide whether a woman who provided ova to her lesbian partner so that the partner could bear children by means of in vitro fertilization is a parent of those children. For the reasons that follow, we conclude that Family Code section 7613, subdivision (b), which provides that a man is not a father if he provides semen to a physician to inseminate a woman who is not his wife, does not apply when a woman provides her ova to impregnate her partner in a lesbian relationship in order to produce children who will be raised in their joint home. Accordingly, when partners in a lesbian relationship decide to produce children in this manner, both the woman who provides her ova and her partner who bears the children are the children's parents.

FACTS

On March 6, 2001, petitioner K.M. filed a petition to establish a parental relationship with twin five-year-old girls born to respondent E.G., her former lesbian partner. K.M. alleged that she "is the biological parent of the minor children" because "[s]he donated her egg to respondent, the gestational mother of the children." E.G. moved to dismiss the petition on the grounds that, although K.M. and E.G. "were lesbian partners who lived together until this action was filed," K.M. "explicitly donated her ovum under a clear written agreement by which she relinquished any claim to offspring born of her donation."

On April 18, 2001, K.M. filed a motion for custody of and visitation with the twins.

A hearing was held at which E.G. testified that she first considered raising a child before she met K.M., at a time when she did not have a partner. She met K.M. in October, 1992 and they became romantically involved in June 1993. * * *

* * *

* * * [After numerous attempts to become pregnant,] E.G. then asked K.M. to donate her ova, explaining that she would accept the ova only if K.M. "would really be a donor" and E.G. would "be the mother of any child," adding that she would not even consider permitting K.M. to adopt the child "for at least five years until [she] felt the relationship was stable and would endure." E.G. told K.M. that she "had seen too many lesbian relationships end quickly, and [she] did not want to be in a custody battle." E.G. and K.M. agreed they would not tell anyone that K.M. was the ova donor.

K.M. acknowledged that she agreed not to disclose to anyone that she was the ova donor, but insisted that she only agreed to provide her ova because she and E.G. had agreed to raise the child together. K.M. and E.G. selected the sperm donor together. K.M. denied that E.G. had said she wanted to be a single parent and insisted that she would not have donated her ova had she known E.G. intended to be the sole parent.

On March 8, 1995, K.M. signed a four-page form on UCSF letterhead entitled "Consent Form for Ovum Donor (Known)." The form states that K.M. agrees "to have eggs taken from my ovaries, in order that they may be donated to another woman." After explaining the medical procedures involved, the form states on the third page: "It is understood that I waive any right and relinquish any claim to the donated eggs or any pregnancy or offspring that might result from them. I agree that the recipient may regard the donated eggs and any offspring resulting therefrom as her own children." The following appears on page 4 of the form, above K.M.'s signature and the signature of a witness: "I specifically disclaim and waive any right in or any child that may be conceived as a result of the use of any ovum or egg of mine, and I agree not to attempt to discover the identity of the recipient thereof." E.G. signed a form entitled "Consent Form for Ovum Recipient" that stated, in part: "I acknowledge that the child or children produced by the IVF procedure is and shall be my own legitimate child or children and the heir or heirs of my body with all rights and privileges accompanying such status."

E.G. testified she received these two forms in a letter from UCSF dated February 2, 1995, and discussed the consent forms with K.M. during February and March. E.G. stated she would not have accepted K.M.'s ova if K.M. had not signed the consent form, because E.G. wanted to have a child on her own and believed the consent form "protected" her in this regard.

K.M. testified to the contrary that she first saw the ovum donation consent form 10 minutes before she signed it on March 8, 1995. K.M. admitted reading the form, but thought parts of the form were "odd" and did not pertain to her, such as the part stating that the donor promised not to discover the identity of the recipient. She did not intend to relinquish her rights and only signed the form so that "we could have children." Despite having signed the form, K.M. "thought [she] was going to be a parent."

* * * [E.G. gave birth to twins.] The twins' birth certificates listed E.G. as their mother and did not reflect a father's name. As they had agreed, neither E.G. nor K.M. told anyone K.M. had donated the ova, including their friends, family and the twins' pediatrician. Soon after the twins were born, E.G. asked K.M. to marry her, and on Christmas Day, the couple exchanged rings.

Within a month of their birth, E.G. added the twins to her health insurance policy, named them as her beneficiary for all employment benefits, and increased her life insurance with the twins as the beneficiary. K.M. did not do the same.

E.G. referred to her mother, as well as K.M.'s parents, as the twins' grandparents and referred to K.M.'s sister and brother as the twins' aunt and uncle, and K.M.'s nieces as their cousins. Two school forms listed both K.M. and respondent as the twins' parents. The children's nanny testified that both K.M. and E.G. "were the babies' mother."

The relationship between K.M. and E.G. ended in March, 2001 and K.M. filed the present action. In September, 2001, E.G. and the twins moved to Massachusetts to live with E.G.'s mother.

* * *

[The superior court granted the motion to dismiss. In a statement of decision, it found:]

" ... By voluntarily signing the ovum donation form, [K.M.] was donating genetic material. Her position was analogous to that of a sperm donor, who is treated as a legal stranger to a child if he donates sperm through a licensed physician and surgeon under Family Code section 7613[, subdivision] (b). The Court finds no reason to treat ovum donors as having greater claims to parentage than sperm donors ... * * *."

[The appellate court affirmed, and the California Supreme Court granted review.]

DISCUSSION

K.M. asserts that she is a parent of the twins because she supplied the ova that were fertilized in vitro and implanted in her lesbian partner, resulting in the birth of the twins. As we will explain, we agree that K.M. is a parent of the twins because she supplied the ova that produced the children, and Family Code section 7613(b), which provides that a man is not a father if he provides semen to a physician to inseminate a woman who is not his wife, does not apply because K.M. supplied her ova to impregnate her lesbian partner in order to produce children who would be raised in their joint home.[3]

* * *

---

3. Justice Werdegar's dissent asserts that our decision "inappropriately confers rights and imposes disabilities on persons because of their sexual orientation." We do not. We decide only

In *Johnson v. Calvert,* 851 P.2d 776 (1993), we determined that a wife whose ovum was fertilized in vitro by her husband's sperm and implanted in a surrogate mother was the "natural mother" of the child thus produced. We noted that the UPA [Uniform Parentage Act] states that provisions applicable to determining a father and child relationship shall be used to determine a mother and child relationship "insofar as practicable." We relied, therefore, on the provisions in the UPA regarding presumptions of paternity and concluded that "genetic consanguinity" could be the basis for a finding of maternity just as it is for paternity. Under this authority, K.M.'s genetic relationship to the children in the present case constitutes "evidence of a mother and child relationship as contemplated by the Act."

The Court of Appeal in the present case concluded, however, that K.M. was not a parent of the twins, despite her genetic relationship to them, because she had the same status as a sperm donor. Section 7613(b) states: "The donor of semen provided to a licensed physician and surgeon for use in artificial insemination of a woman other than the donor's wife is treated in law as if he were not the natural father of a child thereby conceived." * * * We held that the statute did not apply under the circumstances in *Johnson,* because the husband and wife in *Johnson* did not intend to "donate" their sperm and ova to the surrogate mother, but rather "intended to procreate a child genetically related to them by the only available means."

The circumstances of the present case are not identical to those in *Johnson,* but they are similar in a crucial respect; both the couple in *Johnson* and the couple in the present case intended to produce a child that would be raised in their own home. In *Johnson,* it was clear that the married couple did not intend to "donate" their semen and ova to the surrogate mother, but rather permitted their semen and ova to be used to impregnate the surrogate mother in order to produce a child to be raised by them. In the present case, K.M. contends that she did not intend to donate her ova, but rather provided her ova so that E.G. could give birth to a child to be raised jointly by K.M. and E.G. E.G. hotly contests this, asserting that K.M. donated her ova to E.G., agreeing that E.G. would be the sole parent. It is undisputed, however, that the couple lived together and that they both intended to bring the child into their joint home. Thus, even accepting as true E.G.'s version of the facts (which the superior court did), the present case, like *Johnson,* does not present a "true 'egg donation' "situation. K.M. did not intend to simply donate her ova to E.G., but rather provided her ova to her lesbian partner with whom she was living so that E.G. could give birth to a child that would be raised in their joint home. Even if we assume that the provisions of section 7613(b) apply

the case before us, which involves a lesbian couple who registered as domestic partners. We express no view regarding the rights of others and, of course, our "opinion is not authority for a proposition not therein considered."

to women who donate ova, the statute does not apply under the circumstances of the present case. * * *

* * *

As noted *ante*, K.M.'s genetic relationship with the twins constitutes evidence of a mother and child relationship under the UPA and, as explained *ante*, section 7613(b) does not apply to exclude K.M. as a parent of the twins. The circumstance that E.G. gave birth to the twins also constitutes evidence of a mother and child relationship. Thus, both K.M. and E.G. are mothers of the twins under the UPA.

It is true we said in *Johnson* that "for any child California law recognizes only one natural mother." But * * * this statement in *Johnson* must be understood in light of the issue presented in that case; "our decision in *Johnson* does not preclude a child from having two parents both of whom are women." *Elisa B. v. Super. Ct.*, 117 P.3d 660, 666–67 (Cal. 2005).

* * * Thus, this case differs from *Johnson* in that both K.M. and E.G. can be the children's mothers. Unlike in *Johnson*, their parental claims are not mutually exclusive. K.M. acknowledges that E.G. is the twins' mother. K.M. does not claim to be the twins' mother *instead of* E.G., but *in addition to* E.G., so we need not consider their intent in order to decide between them. Rather, the parentage of the twins is determined by application of the UPA. E.G. is the twins' mother because she gave birth to them and K.M. also is the twins' mother because she provided the ova from which they were produced.

* * * We simply hold that section 7613(b), which creates an exception to the usual rules governing parentage that applies when a man donates semen to inseminate a woman who is not his wife, does not apply under the circumstances of this case in which K.M. supplied ova to impregnate her lesbian partner in order to produce children who would be raised in their joint home. Because the exception provided in section 7613(b) does not apply, K.M.'s parentage is determined by the usual provisions of the UPA. As noted above, under the UPA, K.M.'s genetic relationship to the twins constitutes "evidence of a mother and child relationship."

* * *

DISPOSITION

The judgment of the Court of Appeal is reversed.

Dissenting opinion by KENNARD, J.

Unlike the majority, I would apply the controlling statutes as written. The statutory scheme for determining parentage contains two provisions that resolve K.M.'s claim to be a parent of the twins born to E.G. Under one provision, a man who donates sperm for physician-assisted artificial insemination of a woman to whom he is not married is not the father of the resulting child. Under the other provision, rules for determining fatherhood are to be used for determining motherhood "[i]nsofar as practical." Because K.M. donated her ova for physician-assisted artificial insemination and implantation in another woman, and knowingly and voluntarily signed a document declaring her intention *not* to become a parent of any resulting children, she is not a parent of the twins. * * *

Dissenting opinion by WERDEGAR, J.

The majority determines that the twins who developed from the ova K.M. donated to E.G. have two mothers rather than one. While I disagree, as I shall explain, with that ultimate conclusion, I agree with the majority's premise that a child can have two mothers. Our previous holding that "for any child California law recognizes only one natural mother" [*Johnson*, 851 P.2d at 781] must be understood in the context in which it arose—a married couple who intended to become parents and provided their fertilized ova to a gestational surrogate who did not intend to become a parent—and, thus understood, may properly be limited to cases in which to recognize a second mother would inject an unwanted third parent into an existing family. When, in contrast to *Johnson*, no natural or adoptive father exists, two women who intend to become mothers of the same child may do so either through adoption or because both qualify as natural mothers under the Uniform Parentage Act (Fam. Code, § 7600 et seq.) (UPA), one having donated the ovum and the other having given birth.

While scientific advances in reproductive technology now afford individuals previously unimagined opportunities to become parents, the same advances have also created novel, sometimes heartbreaking issues concerning the identification of the resulting children's legal parents. Declarations of parentage in this context implicate complex and delicate biological, personal, legal and social policy considerations. For these reasons, courts have sought above all to avoid foreseeable disputes over parentage with rules that provide predictability by permitting the various persons who must cooperate to bring children into the world through assisted reproduction to determine in advance who will and will not be parents, based on their expressed and voluntarily chosen intentions.

Precisely because predictability in this area is so important, I cannot agree with the majority that the children in this case do in fact have two mothers. Until today, when one woman has provided the ova and another has given birth, the established rule for determining disputed claims to motherhood was clear: we looked to the intent of the parties. "[I]n a true 'egg donation' situation, where a woman gestates and gives birth to a child formed from the egg of another woman with the intent to raise the child as her own, the birth mother is the natural mother under California law." [*Johnson*, 851 P.2d at 782.] Contrary to the majority's apparent assumption, to limit *Johnson*'s holding that a child can have only one mother to cases involving existing two-parent families does not require us to abandon *Johnson*'s intent test as the method for determining disputed claims of motherhood arising from the use of reproductive technology. * * *

* * * [T]he majority [displaces] *Johnson*'s intent test—at least for the purposes of this case—with the following new rule: a woman who has "supplied her ova to impregnate her lesbian partner in order to produce children who would be raised in their joint home" is a mother of the resulting children regardless of any preconception manifestations of intent to the contrary.

* * *

The new rule the majority substitutes for the intent test entails serious problems. First, the rule inappropriately confers rights and imposes disabilities on persons because of their sexual orientation. In a standard ovum donation agreement, such as the agreement between K.M. and E.G., the donor confirms her intention to assist another woman to become a parent without the donor becoming a parent herself. The majority's rule vitiates such agreements when its conditions are satisfied—conditions that include the fact the parties to the agreement are lesbian. * * * I see no rational basis—and the majority articulates none—for permitting the enforceability of an ovum donation agreement to depend on the sexual orientation of the parties. Indeed, lacking a rational basis, the rule may well violate equal protection. Why should a lesbian not have the same right as other women to donate ova without becoming a mother, or to accept a donation of ova without accepting the donor as a coparent, even if the donor and recipient live together and both plan to help raise the child?

* * *

Perhaps the most serious problem with the majority's new rule is that it threatens to destabilize ovum donation and gestational surrogacy agreements. One important function of *Johnson*'s intent test was to permit persons who made use of reproductive technology to create, before conception, settled and enforceable expectations about who would and would not become parents. *Johnson* thus gave E.G. a right at the time she conceived to expect that she alone would be the parent of her children—a right the majority now retrospectively abrogates. E.G.'s expectation has a constitutional dimension. We cannot recognize K.M. as a parent without diminishing E.G.'s existing parental rights. In light of the majority's abrogation of *Johnson* and apparent willingness to ignore preconception manifestations of intent, at least in some cases, women who wish to donate ova without becoming mothers, serve as gestational surrogates without becoming mothers, or accept ovum donations without also accepting the donor as a coparent would be well advised to proceed with the most extreme caution. While the majority purports to limit its holding to cohabiting lesbians, and possibly only to those cohabiting lesbians who are also domestic partners, these limitations, as I have explained, rest on questionable legal grounds and may well not stand the test of time. * * *

Perhaps the best way to understand today's decision is that we appear to be moving in cases of assisted reproduction from a categorical determination of parentage based on formal, preconception manifestations of intent to a case-by-case approach implicitly motivated at least in part by our intuitions about the children's best interests. We expressly eschewed a best interests approach in *Johnson,* explaining that it "raises the repugnant specter of governmental interference in matters implicating our most fundamental notions of privacy, and confuses concepts of parentage and custody." [*Johnson,* 851 P.2d at 782, n.10.] This case, in which the majority compels E.G. to accept K.M. as an unintended parent to E.G.'s children, in part because of E.G.'s and K.M.'s sexual orientation and the character of their private relationship, shows that *Johnson*'s warning was prescient. Only legislation defining parentage in the context of assisted reproduction is likely to restore predictability and prevent further lapses into the disorder of ad hoc adjudication.

NOTES AND QUESTIONS

1. *The intent test. Johnson* used an intent test to determine the parents. *K.M.* explained that the intent test should be limited to the *Johnson* situation because "whether there is evidence of a parent and child relationship under the UPA does not depend upon the intent of the parent. For example, a man who engages in sexual intercourse with a woman who assures him, falsely, that she is incapable of conceiving children is the father of a resulting child, despite his lack of intent to become a father." [117 P.3d at 682.] Is this a convincing distinction? Do you think that K.M. would have been able to donate under either California law or the clinic regulations without signing the agreement?

2. *Two mothers. Johnson* explicitly rejected the proposition that a child could have two mothers. In its discussion of this issue, the court cites *Elisa B. v. Super. Ct.,* 117 P.3d 660 (Cal. 2005), decided the same day. That case involved a lesbian partner who did not want the responsibilities of motherhood. The court held that a child could have two mothers, even if one was not biologically related to the children. Is this reasoning persuasive? Would another state be required to recognize their dual parenthood? *See* Deborah L. Forman, *Interstate Recognition of Same–Sex Parents in the Wake of Gay Marriage, Civil Unions, and Domestic Partnerships,* 46 B.C.L. Rev. 1 (2004).

3. *Legislative role.* Dissenting Justice Werdegar asserts that it is the role of the legislature to enact appropriate statutes defining parenthood in cases involving new reproductive technologies. What provisions should be included? What are the difficulties in drafting such a statute?

4. *Pre-birth parental declarations.* On the same day that it decided *K.M.,* the California Supreme Court granted parental status to a woman who had stipulated to a pre-birth court judgment that she was the "second mother/parent" of her female partners. *Kristine H v. Lisa R.,* 33 Cal.Rptr.3d 81 (2005).

C. DISESTABLISHING PATERNITY

In many of the other parenthood cases in this chapter, individuals were fighting over the right to become a parent. In some cases, however, an individual does not want to become a parent. As you read the following case and notes, consider the circumstances in which an individual who is biologically related to a child should, nonetheless, not be deemed a legal parent. Compare these outcomes to *Michael H.*

WALLIS v. SMITH
Court of Appeals of New Mexico, 2001.
22 P.3d 682.

BOSSON, CHIEF JUDGE.

Peter Wallis and Kellie Rae Smith were partners in a consensual sexual relationship. Allegedly, Smith misrepresented that she was practicing birth control when she was not, and Wallis unknowingly fathered her child. Wallis sued Smith for money damages, asserting four causes of action—fraud, breach of contract, conversion, and prima facie tort—that the district court dismissed for failure to state a claim upon which relief may be granted. Wallis appeals that dismissal * * *. We affirm the dismissal, holding that under these facts, the causes of action are not cognizable in New Mexico because they contravene the public policy of this state. * * *

* * *

Wallis and Smith began an intimate, sexual relationship some time before April 1997. They discussed contraceptive techniques and agreed that Smith would use birth control pills. Wallis and Smith further agreed that their sexual intimacy would last only as long as Smith continued to take birth control pills because Wallis made it clear that he did not want to father a child. Wallis participated in contraception only passively; he relied on Smith to use birth control and took no precautions himself.

As time went by, Smith changed her mind. She chose to stop taking birth control pills, but never informed Wallis of her decision. Wallis continued their intimate relationship, and Smith became pregnant. Smith carried the fetus to term and gave birth to a normal, healthy girl on November 27, 1998.

Wallis alleges that he has suffered, and will continue to suffer, substantial economic injury as a proximate result of his unintended fatherhood because New Mexico law requires him to pay child support for the next eighteen years. Due to his statutory obligations, Wallis asserts that he has been injured by Smith's conduct, and requests compensatory and punitive damages from her. The district court determined that public policy prohibited the relief sought by Wallis, and dismissed the case with prejudice.

CONTRACEPTIVE FRAUD
* * *

At the onset of our discussion it is important to distinguish the factual allegations of this case from other kinds of related lawsuits, and thus underscore the limited reach of this opinion. Wallis's complaint is not about sexually-transmitted disease, nor does it concern the damages arising from an unwanted pregnancy that led to an abortion, or an undesired pregnancy resulting in medical complications. This case is not even brought to recover the expense of giving birth. Wallis's complaint is limited to compensatory damages for the "economic injury" of supporting a normal, healthy child.

Although Wallis insists that he is not attempting to circumvent his child support obligations, we cannot agree. It is self-evident that he seeks to recover for the very financial loss caused him by the statutory obligation to pay child support. * * *

Our legislature has spoken to the public policy that governs the economic consequences of sexual relationships that produce children, and that policy is reflected in New Mexico child support laws. In 1986, our legislature adopted, with minor revisions, the Uniform Parentage Act (UPA), which outlines the legal procedure to establish a parent-child relationship and the corresponding obligation of child support. The UPA imposes a form of strict liability for child support, without regard to which parent bears the greater responsibility for the child's being.

Making each parent financially responsible for the conception and birth of children also illuminates a strong public policy that makes paramount the interests of the child. Our jurisprudence has abandoned the notion that the father of an "illegitimate" child could decline to accept the financial responsibility of raising that child. Currently, the state exercises its *parens patriae* authority to protect the best interests of all children by ensuring that the parents provide "an adequate standard of support." N.M. Stat. Ann. § 40–4–11.1(B)(1) (West 1995). Placing a duty of support on each parent has the added benefit of insulating the state from the possibility of bearing the financial burden for a child. In our view, it is difficult to harmonize the legislative concern for the child, reflected in the immutable duty of parental support, with Wallis's effort in this lawsuit to shift financial responsibility for his child solely to the mother.

New Mexico is not alone in its view of parental responsibility and the conflict created by lawsuits such as this. *See Welzenbach v. Powers*, 660 A.2d 1133, 1136 (N.H. 1995) (holding that the public policy behind the right of child support "does not favor the extension of tort liability as the plaintiff suggests, but rather stands firmly against it"); *Douglas R. v. Suzanne M.*, 487 N.Y.S.2d 244, 245 (N.Y. Sup. Ct. 1985) (holding that fraud and deceit actions would render support obligations "nugatory"). To our knowledge, no jurisdiction recognizes contraceptive fraud or breach of promise to practice birth control as a ground for adjusting a natural parent's obligation to pay child support. * * *

Some courts have dismissed contraceptive fraud cases on the ground that the claims tread too far into the realm of an individual's privacy interests. We agree that individuals are entitled a sphere of privacy into which courts should not tread. A person's choice whether or not to use contraceptives understandably fits into this sphere. *See Eisenstadt v. Baird*, 405 U.S. 438 (1972); *Griswold v. Connecticut*, 381 U.S. 479 (1965). We also believe that the "privacy interests involved ... require a cautious approach," and therefore we elect to rely primarily on the prevailing public policy of child support, while at the same time recognizing the serious privacy concerns implicated and threatened by the underlying lawsuit. *Douglas R.*, 487 N.Y.S.2d at 245.[1]

Wallis's attempt to apply traditional contract and tort principles to his contraceptive agreement is unconvincing and, in the end, futile. The contract analogy fails because children, the persons for whose benefit child support guidelines are enacted, have the same needs regardless of whether their conception violated a promise between the parents. Further, a parent being sued for causing the conception and birth of a child is no ordinary tortfeasor; a defendant under these circumstances is legally entitled to collect financial support on behalf of the child. We will not re-enter the jurisprudence of illegitimacy by allowing a parent to opt out of the financial consequences of his or her sexual relationships just because they were unintended. Nor will we recognize a cause of action that trivializes one's personal responsibility in sexual relationships. Indeed, permitting "such actions while simultaneously encouraging paternity actions for support flies in the face of all reason." *Welzenbach*, 660 A.2d at 1136. We also observe that if Wallis did not desire children, he was free and able to practice contraceptive techniques on his own.

Wallis tries to make the basis for liability not so much the birth of the child, but the fact that Smith lied, and perpetrated a fraud on him. But not all misrepresentations are actionable. Equally problematic for Wallis is that it is impossible to calculate damages without considering the birth of the child. Because the legislature has declared the public policy governing the sexual relationships of adults in our child support laws, any claim that undermines that legislative policy cannot go forward.

Finally, Wallis argues that our courts have recognized tort claims which measure damages by the economic injury of supporting an unwanted child. *See Lovelace Med. Ctr. v. Mendez*, 805 P.2d 603, 612 (N.M. 1991). However, *Lovelace* does not stand for the proposition that one parent can sue the other for the costs of raising a child. *Lovelace* held that a doctor has a duty to inform a couple that a surgical procedure to render one partner sterile was not successful, and the court determined the extent to which damages flow from the breach of that duty resulting in the birth of a healthy child. [*Id.* at 609.] The court in *Lovelace* also held that a couple who sought to protect their financial resources by limiting the size of their family through sterilization could sue for economic damages measured by

---

1. Although we embrace the rationale of the special concurrence, we want to clarify that by focusing on damages we do not mean to suggest, in the words of the special concurrence, that "we accept Wallis's argument that Smith's alleged commitment to practice birth control gave rise to legally-enforceable rights." We elect to rely primarily on the public policy of child support, and its message of personal responsibility. By choosing to focus on privacy, the special concurrence invokes rights of constitutional magnitude. *Griswold*, 381 U.S. at 485. Historically, we decide cases, if we can, by avoiding constitutional questions.

the cost of raising an additional child to the age of majority. [*Id.* at 612–13.] The damages sought compensated parents for what they were expending to support their child by identifying fault in a third party, not in each other. Therefore, *Lovelace* does not implicate the public policy of individual responsibility and liability illustrated in the UPA and our child support statutes. Because *Lovelace* does not speak to the issue of inter-parental liability, which is the crux of Wallis's appeal, it has no bearing on our decision.

Accordingly, we hold that the actions asserted here cannot be used to recoup the financial obligations of raising a child. We emphasize that this holding is gender neutral insofar as it precludes a monetary reimbursement for child support.

* * *

ALARID, JUDGE (specially concurring).

While I agree with the majority that the trial court should be affirmed, I am concerned that the majority opinion, by focusing on the issue of damages, may suggest to the reader that we accept Wallis' argument that Smith's alleged commitment to practice birth control gave rise to legally-enforceable rights. I write separately to emphasize my concern that the causes of action proposed by Wallis intrude on fundamental privacy interests.

In recent years, New Mexico courts have given substantial weight to privacy interests when confronted with arguments urging the extension of existing causes of action to intimate interpersonal behavior. These authorities suggest to me that causes of action which purport to regulate intimate interpersonal relationships are disfavored by New Mexico courts and that causes of action that intrude on the right of privacy must be supported by compelling countervailing considerations.

If we recognize a claim based on intentional misrepresentation, we have started down the road towards establishing standards of conduct in reproductive relationships-one of the most important and private forms of interpersonal relations. In the absence of a clear balance favoring the imposition of legal duties of disclosure in reproductive relations between competent adult sex partners, candor in reproductive matters should be left to the ethics of the participants.

* * *

Today, the Court establishes the principle that contraception is a non-delegable duty in New Mexico. I see nothing unfair in applying this rule to Wallis. Had Wallis bothered to investigate the state of the law prior to beginning a sexual relationship with Smith in April 1997, he would have learned that the overwhelming majority of jurisdictions considering the issue have refused to recognize a cause of action for economic damages stemming from contraceptive fraud/breach of promise to practice birth control. The lesson of these cases is that sex partners are strictly liable for the support of any child they engender by voluntarily engaging in sexual activity. Thus, even accepting Wallis' allegations that he extracted from Smith a commitment to practice birth control, Wallis would not have had a reasonable expectation that Smith's statements about her use of contraceptives gave rise to legally-enforceable rights.

* * *

NOTES AND QUESTIONS

1. *Tricked fatherhood.* The "tricked fatherhood" cases generally are brought under one of two factual scenarios. In the first, as in *Wallis*, the father alleges that the mother misrepresented her use of birth control. The second scenario, which happens with increasing frequency, occurs when a husband learns during divorce proceedings that he may not be the biological father. *See* Melanie B. Jacobs, *When Daddy Doesn't Want to Be Daddy Anymore: An Argument Against Paternity Fraud Claims*, 16 Yale J.L. & Femin. 193–94 (2004) (noting trend). In *Libro v. Walls*, 746 P.2d 632, 634 (Nev. 1987), the Nevada Supreme Court held that a wife's failure to disclose that a child conceived during the marriage may not be her husband's offspring was "extrinsic fraud." ("Extrinsic fraud" is wrongful conduct practiced outside of an adversary trial, such as keeping a party away from court or denying a party knowledge of the suit, that affects the manner in which a judgment is procured.) The husband claimed that he should not be liable for child support because he was not the biological father. Because the wife's deception prevented her husband from litigating the issue of paternity during their subsequent divorce proceedings, the appellate court reversed a trial court decision that had awarded her child support arrearages. *Id.* A tricked father's child support obligations are discussed further in Chapter 11.

2. *Emotional distress?* In February 2005, an Illinois appeals court allowed a man to pursue his emotional distress suit against a woman who used his sperm to have a baby. Dr. Richard Phillips accused his former lover, Dr. Sharon Irons, of secretly keeping his sperm after oral sex and then using the sperm to become pregnant. Phillips learned that he was the father of Irons' baby in 2003 when she filed a paternity suit, seeking child support (which he was subsequently ordered to pay). Phillips claimed that Irons caused him "nausea, inability to eat, difficulty in concentrating and sleeping" and "feelings of being trapped in a nightmare." The court upheld dismissal of Phillips' theft and fraud claims, stating that once he "delivered" the sperm, it was a gift—a transfer of property that contained no agreement that the original deposit be returned. However, the appellate court reversed the lower court's dismissal of the emotional distress claim, ruling that if the alleged facts were true, Irons had "deceitfully engaged in sexual acts, which no reasonable person would expect could result in pregnancy, to use plaintiff's sperm in an unorthodox, unanticipated manner yielding extreme consequences." Associated Press, *Sperm: The Gift That Keeps On Giving*, Feb. 24, 2005, *available at* http://msnbc.msn.com/id/ 7024930/(last visited Dec. 31, 2005); *see also* Melanie B. Jacobs, *My Two Dads: Disaggregating Biological and Social Paternity*, 38 Ariz. St. L. J. 809, 821 (2006).

In January 2004, a jury awarded a man the amount that he would have to pay in child support, as well as an additional $10,000 for emotional distress, after a Boston IVF clinic impregnated his estranged wife without his consent. The clinic used a frozen embryo from a previous procedure that the father had consented to, but did not inform him or get his consent before using it for the additional procedure. Thanassis Cambanis, *Father Wins Case Against Fertility Clinic*, Boston Globe, Jan. 31, 2004, http://www.boston.com/news/local/articles/2004/01/31/father_wins_case_against_fertility_clinic/. Does this seem like a more appropriate result?

3. *Parental estoppel.* In the 1990s, Congress passed child support legislation reflecting the advancement in scientific technologies. New laws required states to provide for genetic testing of all parties in contested paternity actions upon request. Congress also granted federal child support enforcement agencies the power to order genetic tests. *See* 42 U.S.C. 666(a) (2008). States are also required to implement a process in which parents can sign a voluntary acknowledgment of paternity, which becomes a binding legal document. *See* 42 U.S.C. § 666(a)(5)(D)(ii)(2008). Several states, including Georgia, Maryland, Ohio, and Virginia, have passed legislation allowing men to introduce genetic test evidence of biological exclusion in order to defeat child support orders.

States disagree, however, about whether genetic evidence trumps such child support orders where the presumed father was married to the child's mother. Some states follow the Pennsylvania model, which allows courts to exclude genetic evidence disproving paternity in favor of invoking the doctrine of parental estoppel. Paternity by estoppel bars a married man from denying legitimacy of a child born to his marriage where he represented the child as his own to the world; developed an emotional relationship with child and provided financial support; or prevented the child from knowing the biological father. This model penalizes the husband to avoid penalizing the child, who was an innocent victim.

The Massachusetts model rejects paternal estoppel as a basis for excluding genetic evidence because it may discourage husbands from voluntarily raising their stepchildren for fear of becoming permanently obligated to support the child. Finally, the New York model considers both the genetic evidence and parental estoppel, and the biological father's role, and makes a case-by-case determination based on the best interest of the child. Diane S. Kaplan, *Why Truth is Not a Defense in Paternity Actions*, 10 Tex. J. Women & L. 69, 73–80 (2000). Which approach best protects all interests involved?

4. *Parental contracts.* Seven years after *Wallis*, a New Mexico appellate court considered whether a man who provided sperm to a lesbian couple should have parental responsibilities. The parties had agreed that Kevin Zoernig would serve as a male role model, but would not be responsible for child support. The court applied an earlier version of the Uniform Parentage Act, which provided that donors who provided sperm for use by a licensed physician would have no parental rights. In this case, however, the parties had not used a licensed physician (the mother inseminated herself), so that section of the statute was inapplicable. Zoernig had "held out" the children as his own and established a relationship with them, so he was the legal father,

and obligated to pay child support. *Mintz v. Zoernig,* 198 P.3d 861 (N.M. Ct. App. 2008).

By contrast, in a Kansas case, the court upheld a statute providing that a man who provided sperm to a licensed physician would have no paternal rights "unless agreed to in writing." *In re K.M.H.,* 169 P.3d 1025 (Kan. 2007). The man sought to establish his paternal rights, including custody and visitation, but was precluded from doing so.

Should the establishment of parenthood turn on whether sperm has been provided to a licensed physician, as required by the 1982 UPA? Should individuals be able to determine, by contract, whether they must assume parental rights? These issues are discussed further in Chapter 11 on Child Support.

5. *Mothers choosing fathers.* Professor Katharine Baker has suggested that mothers should be able to enter into binding contracts with men concerning their parental support obligations, making fatherhood, unlike motherhood, a voluntary status. Katharine Baker, *Bargaining or Biology? The History and Future of Paternity Law and Parental Status,* 14 Cornell J.L. Pub. Pol'y 1 (2004). Does such a proposal seem warranted by existing case law? Does it recognize the realities of parenting?

PROBLEM 5–7

Molly Simmons has consulted you. She recently gave birth to a healthy daughter, Susan. Her pregnancy, however, was utterly unexpected. She had begun a relationship with Richard Prentice. Before engaging in sexual intercourse, they had extensively discussed birth control options because Molly did not want to get pregnant. Richard told her that he had had a vasectomy, so pregnancy should not be a concern. Based on that representation, they entered into a sexual relationship.

She did not find out that she was pregnant until her fourth month. She was unwilling to have an abortion after her first trimester, so she carried the child to term. What options does she have against Richard? How might a court rule?

CHAPTER 6

CIVIL AND CRIMINAL CONTROLS ON DOMESTIC VIOLENCE

■ ■ ■

Before the late twentieth century, the legal system did little to regulate violence between intimate partners. In early nineteenth century America, husbands had a legally-recognized right to chastise their wives, so long as they did so moderately. For example, in 1864, a North Carolina court upheld a husband's use of force against his wife, clarifying that the "husband is responsible for the acts of his wife, and he is required to govern his household, and for that purpose the law permits him to use towards his wife such a degree of force as is necessary to control an unruly temper and make her behave herself * * * unless some permanent injury be inflicted, or there be an excess of violence, or such a degree of cruelty as shows that it is inflicted to gratify his own bad passions * * *." *State v. Black*, 1 Win. 266, 266 (N.C. 1864). The court explained that the traditional refusal to intervene in cases of domestic violence stemmed partly from a belief that the law should not "invade the domestic forum or go behind the curtain" of home and family.

In 1871, Alabama became one of the first states to hold that a husband's "privilege, ancient though it be, to beat [his wife] with a stick, to pull her hair, choke her, spit in her face or kick her about the floor, or to inflict upon her like indignities, is not now acknowledged by our law." *Fulgham v. State*, 46 Ala. 143, 146–47 (1871). By the end of the nineteenth century, courts had generally repudiated a husband's chastisement right, but violence in the home continued.

Litigation, legislation, activism, and social services for battered women have proliferated over the last 40 years. Society has moved from virtual denial of the existence of domestic violence to an acknowledgment that it is a pervasive problem with profound legal, sociological, and psychological dimensions for the battered individual and other family members. Fundamental changes in civil and criminal law and practice have made battered women more visible throughout the legal system: protective restraining orders in the civil justice system are now available in every state; many states have amended their custody statutes to make domestic violence a significant factor in custody decisions; policies requiring police officers to arrest batterers are increasingly common; prosecutors' offices have become increasingly likely to prosecute domestic violence cases; and attorneys have developed a greater understanding of the effects of battering on their clients and their cases, particularly when battered women are defendants.

This Chapter focuses on domestic violence between adult spouses or partners. The Chapter only briefly discusses child abuse and neglect, which is frequently covered in detail in a second family law course. The Chapter begins by providing information about the occurrence of domestic violence before turning to civil and criminal approaches to counter it. As you review the materials in this Chapter and the remainder of this book, consider the relationship between domestic violence and various other aspects of family law. For example, under traditional divorce law, domestic violence appeared under the fault ground of cruelty; today, with the advent of no-fault divorce, domestic violence appears in separate actions based on that violence, such as civil protection orders, torts (discussed in Chapter Seven), and criminal prosecutions. Domestic violence may also affect property distribution, maintenance, and child custody actions.

SECTION 1: WHAT IS DOMESTIC VIOLENCE?

Domestic violence can be broadly defined as a pattern of attempts to exercise coercive control over an intimate partner, such as a current or former spouse, boyfriend, or girlfriend. Physical violence, including sexual violence, is often accompanied by emotionally or economically abusive behavior. Domestic violence victims are also called survivors to call attention to their ability to withstand the violence and attempt to protect themselves, rather than to experience it helplessly.

In 2006, according to U.S. Department of Justice statistics, 740,090 nonfatal violent victimizations, or more than 26% of all nonfatal violent crimes in the U.S., were committed by the victim's current or former spouse, boyfriend, or girlfriend. Michael Rand and Shannan M. Catalano, Bureau of Justice Statistics, Publ'n No. NCJ 219413, Criminal Victimization, 2006, at 5 (2008), http://www.ojp.usdoj.gov/bjs/pub/pdf/cv06.pdf. Women were victims in approximately 80% of these reported crimes (an estimated 595,740 victimizations), while men were victims in approximately 20% of these crimes (144,350 cases). *Id.* Estimates from the annual National Crime Victimization Survey (NCVS)[1] indicate that the number of crimes of intimate violence has been declining over the past decade.

Because domestic violence is underrerported, an accurate assessment of its prevalence is somewhat difficult. In general, however, it is a statistical fact that intimate partner violence is primarily a crime against

---

1. The National Crime Victimization Survey (NCVS) is conducted annually by the Bureau of Justice Statistics of the U.S. Department of Justice and is the primary source of information on criminal victimization in the United States. U.S. Dep't of Justice, *Crime and Victims Statistics*, http://www.ojp. usdoj.gov/ bjs/ cvict.htm. Since 1973, data are obtained each year from a nationally representative sample of 42,000 households (approximately 76,000 people) on the frequency, characteristics and consequences of reported and unreported criminal victimization. *Id.*

women. Empirical research from the NCVS and other sources provide extensive data on violence by intimates:

(a) In 2005, intimate partner violence made up 18.1% of nonfatal violent crimes against females 12 or older, but only 2.6% of nonfatal violent crimes against men. http://www.ojp.usdoj.gov/bjs/pub/pdf/cvus/current/cv0543a.pdf. Criminal Victimization in the United States 2005, Statistical tables, Table 43a (2006).

(b) In 2005, 1,170 women and 328 men were killed by an intimate partner. U.S. Department of Justice Office of Justice Programs Bureau of Justice Statistics, Homicide trends in the U.S. Intimate homicide. http://www.ojp.usdoj.gov/bjs/homicide/tables/intgendertab.htm.

(c) In 2005, an intimate killed about 33% of all female murder victims and 2.5% of all male murder victims. *Id.*

(d) Conservative estimates suggest that, in at least 30% of all intimate partner victimizations, the abusers also abuse their children. Colorado Coalition Against Domestic Violence, Law Enforcement Training Manual § 1:4 (2d ed. 2003), http://www. ccadv.org/ publications/ law_enforcement_manual_11–03.pdf.

(e) Nearly one in every three women will experience at least one physical assault by a partner during adulthood. Joseph R. Biden, Jr., Sen. Subcomm. on Crime, Corr. & Victims' Rights, Ten Years of Extraordinary Progress: The Violence Against Women Act 32 (2004), http:// biden.senate.gov/ documents/VAWA_Report.pdf.

Domestic violence survivors may face an increased risk of violence at the point when they attempt to leave the abusive relationship. According to statistics collected by the Department of Justice, "divorced or separated persons were subject to the highest rates of intimate partner victimization." Callie Marie Rennison & Sarah Welchans, Bureau of Justice Statistics, Publ'n No. NCJ 178247, Intimate Partner Violence 5 (2003), http:// www.ojp.usdoj.gov/bjs/pub/pdf/ipv.pdf. Studies have also shown that women are often murdered shortly after they attempt to leave, or soon after they have actually separated from, their batterer. Carol E. Jordan, *Intimate Partner Violence and the Justice System: An Examination of the Interface*, 19 J. Interpersonal Violence 1412, 1415–16 (2004). Scholars explain that because domestic violence entails a pattern of coercive control by the abuser, the risk of abuse increases when a victim tries to escape this control because the batterer may become increasingly possessive in his effort to retain power over the victim. Deborah M. Goelman, *Shelter from the Storm: Using Jurisdictional Statutes to Protect Victims of Domestic Violence After the Violence Against Women Act of 2000*, 13 Colum. J. Gender & L. 101, 107 (2004). Appreciating the complexities of this power dynamic helps in understanding the answer to the oft-repeated question: "Why doesn't she leave?" She may be well aware of the risk of further violence when she attempts to separate.

Despite the perception that men rarely become victims of domestic violence, the 2006 NCVS indicates that approximately 20% of all domestic violence occurs against men. Domestic violence against men is underreported because battered men historically have been ignored, ridiculed, or chastised because of negative gender stereotyping. *See* Philip W. Cook, Abused Men: The Hidden Side of Domestic Violence 84–85 (1997). Moreover, if men are battered in same-sex relationships, there may be further stigma in reporting this victimization.

NOTES AND QUESTIONS

1. *Domestic violence in the workplace.* The phrase "workplace domestic violence" includes not just violent acts that occur on the job, but also the effects on the workplace when the violence has occurred elsewhere. The predictable hours and location of a victim's employment allow abusers to find their victims readily. Between 1993 and 1999, intimate partners committed an average of 19,187 violent acts (or 1.1% of all workplace victimizations) each year in the United States against persons at work or on duty. Detis T. Duhart, Bureau of Justice Statistics, Publ'n No. NCJ190076, Violence in the Workplace, 1993–99, at 1–2, 8 (2001), http://www.ojp.usdoj.gov/bjs/pub/pdf/vw99.pdf.

2. *The effect of domestic violence on the workforce.* Domestic violence is a significant obstacle to victims remaining in the workforce. Because of domestic violence, victims in the United States miss more than eight million days of work each year, which is comparable to thirty-two thousand full time jobs. The average female domestic violence victim will lose almost four weeks of work per year because of incapacitating or humiliating injuries, a partner who won't let her leave the home, or her use of working hours to begin the process of leaving the abuser. Indeed, "—it is common for victims to lose their jobs due to absences, workplace disruptions, performance problems—or simple prejudice against victims." Deborah A. Widiss, *Domestic Violence and the Workplace: The Explosion of State Legislation and the Need for a Comprehensive Strategy*, 35 Fla. St. L. Rev. 669, 677 (2008).

Discriminating against battered women may expose employers to liability. In 2001, New York City enacted the first law in the country to prohibit this type of discrimination. California, Hawaii, Illinois, New York and Tennessee have considered similar statutes to create civil rights remedies for battered women who are fired or otherwise discriminated against at work because they are in an abusive relationship. Julie Goldscheid, *Advancing Equality in Domestic Violence Law Reform*, 11 Am. U.J. Gender Soc. Pol'y & L. 417, 425 (2003).

3. *Race and domestic violence.* Battered women of color may face special issues in both the civil and criminal justice systems because of their race and ethnicity.

For many victims of color, family and community take precedence as a means of addressing domestic violence concerns ... The criminal justice system's racial bias has discouraged many battered women of color and made them reluctant to call the police for help. Overall, a history of judicial unresponsiveness and racial bias has generated a deep-seated general distrust of the justice system by people of color. This sentiment is exacerbated by the history of hostility [by police].

Phyliss Craig–Taylor, *Lifting the Veil: The Intersectionality of Ethics, Culture, and Gender Bias in Domestic Violence Cases,* 32 Rutgers L. Rec. 31, 46 (2008). Indeed, "[f]eminist scholars of color have explained that the politics of racial identity in America cause some victims of color to feel they must choose between their race and gender. Not surprisingly, race wins * * *. For many victims of color, family and community must take precedence". Sarah Buel, *Effective Assistance of Counsel for Battered Women Defendants: A Normative Construct,* 26 Harv. Women's L.J. 217, 238 (2003). Consequently, many battered women of color may feel additional pressures to remain in their relationships.

4. *Immigrant victims.* Immigrant women who experience violence and are not legally in the United States must consider the additional risk of being deported if they decide to seek help. Immigrant women are especially vulnerable to domestic violence because many of them depend on their partners for information regarding their legal status. There may also be language barriers which serve to limit the opportunities for immigrant women who do not speak English to take advantage of existing support services, including shelters. In a survey of Latina immigrants in Washington, D.C., the researchers found that 21.7% of the battered immigrant women remained in abusive relationships because of their fears of being reported to immigration authorities if they left. Leslye E. Orloff & Janice V. Kaguyutan, *Offering a Helping Hand: Legal Protections for Battered Immigrant Women: A History of Legislative Responses,* 10 Am. U.J. Gender Soc. Pol'y & L. 95, 98 (2001).

Section 360 of the Illegal Immigration Reform and Immigrant Responsibility Act of 1996 makes domestic violence, stalking, sexual violence, child abuse, and violation of a civil protection order into offenses for which an alien risks deportation. 8 U.S.C. § 1227(a)(2)(E) (2008). Although the provision was designed to protect battered immigrant women, it may also create problems for them. For example, if a battered woman's report results in her partner being deported, then she will probably lose any economic help, such as child support, that he has been providing her. Leigh Goodmark, *The Legal Response to Domestic Violence: Problems and Possibilities, Law Is the Answer? Do We Know That for Sure?: Questioning the Efficacy of Legal Interventions for Battered Women,* 23 St. Louis U. Pub. L. Rev. 7, 37 (2004). There are special provisions of the Violence Against Women Act, discussed at the end of this Chapter, that protect battered immigrant women.

5. *Mandatory reporting.* In the early 1990s, the American Medical Association (AMA) called intimate violence against women a "public health problem that has reached epidemic proportions." AMA, Diagnostic & Treatment Guidelines on Domestic Violence 4 (1992), http://www.amaassn.org/ama1/pub/upload/mm/386/domesticviolence.pdf. A U.S. Department of Justice study on violence-related injuries reported that 17% of all women treated in hospital emergency rooms for violence-related injuries had been harmed by their former or current intimate partners. Michael R. Rand, Bureau of Justice Statistics, Publ'n No. NCJ 156921, Violence–Related Injuries Treated in

Hospital Emergency Departments 5 (1997), http://www.ojp.usdoj.gov/bjs/pub/ pdf/vrithed.pdf. Virtually all states require physicians to report to law enforcement officials some injuries that appear to have resulted from a criminal act. By contrast, few states have mandatory reporting laws that apply specifically to injuries resulting from domestic abuse, although they may shield physicians from liability for making such reports. Stephanie A. Wolfson, *Screening for Violence and Abuse through the Lens of Medical Ethics*, 11 DePaul J. Health Care L. 1, 5 (2007). Domestic violence advocates and health care workers are uncertain about the advisability of mandatory reporting, because they worry that such laws might not best ensure the safety of autonomous adult victims. Opposition to mandatory reporting laws also stems from concerns that it would not assure victims' safety; victims might avoid seeking health care because they fear that their injuries will be reported to the police, which, if it results in the batterer's arrest, might result in increased risk of violence and injury to them. At least six states do have mandatory reporting laws for domestic violence that apply to some categories of health workers, and researchers have found that a majority of domestic violence victim in hospital emergency rooms support these laws. Laura G. Iavicoli, *Mandatory Reporting of Domestic Violence: The Law, Friend or Foe?*, 72 Mt. Sinai J. Med. 228, 229– 30 (2005). As with other mandatory policies in the domestic violence area, consider the impact of this policy on victim autonomy.

SECTION 2: CIVIL PROTECTION ORDERS

Civil protection orders (CPOs), which became a tool in domestic violence cases in the 1970s, are court orders that bar an individual who has committed an act of intrafamilial violence from further harmful contact with the victim. By 1989, all 50 states and the District of Columbia had enacted statutes providing civil remedies for battered persons via protection orders. These civil statutes offer options for relief that may be more comprehensive than what would be available through the criminal justice system, and provide the victim with more control over the process. Victims generally may petition the court for various forms of injunctive relief, including orders that prohibit abusers from continuing to assault, threaten, harass, or physically abuse them, and require that the abusers stay away from their homes, workplaces, or other commonly visited areas, such as their children's schools. Unlike criminal sanctions, CPOs are prospective and regulate the batterer's future behavior.

A. OBTAINING A CIVIL PROTECTION ORDER

The specific procedures used to obtain a CPO vary throughout the country, but most states allow the victims first to seek a temporary *ex parte* order. These orders, which can be obtained without notice to the batterer, provide emergency injunctive relief restraining the batterer from inflicting further violence on the victim. They are effective for only a short period of time. Longer term, "permanent orders" are entered only after the abuser has had notice and an opportunity to be heard, and the court has found cause to issue the order. Depending on the state, a permanent order can last anywhere from several weeks to a year or longer.

1.   STATUTORY GUIDELINES

The following Florida statutes typify legislative directives for seeking protection against domestic violence:

a.   Domestic Violence Definitions

Section 741.28 of the Florida Statutes

* * *

(2) "Domestic violence" means any assault, aggravated assault, battery, aggravated battery, sexual assault, sexual battery, stalking, aggravated stalking, kidnapping, false imprisonment, or any criminal offense resulting in physical injury or death of one family or household member by another family or household member.

(3) "Family or household member" means spouses, former spouses, persons related by blood or marriage, persons who are presently residing together as if a family or who have resided together in the past as if a family, and persons who are parents of a child in common regardless of whether they have been married. With the exception of persons who have a child in common, the family or household members must be currently residing or have in the past resided together in the same single dwelling unit.

* * *

Fla. Stat. § 741.28 (2008).

b.   Injunctive Powers and Duties of the Court

Section 741.30 of the Florida Statutes

(1) There is created a cause of action for an injunction for protection against domestic violence.

(a) Any person described in paragraph (e), who is either the victim of domestic violence as defined in § 741.28 or has reasonable cause to believe he or she is in imminent danger of becoming the victim of any act of domestic violence, has standing in the circuit court to file a sworn petition for an injunction for protection against domestic violence.

* * *

(d) A person's right to petition for an injunction shall not be affected by such person having left a residence or household to avoid domestic violence.

(e) This cause of action for an injunction may be sought by family or household members. No person shall be precluded from seeking injunctive relief pursuant to this chapter solely on the basis that such person is not a spouse.

* * *

(i) The court is prohibited from issuing mutual orders of protection. This does not preclude the court from issuing separate injunctions for protection against domestic violence where each party has complied with the provisions of this section. Compliance with the provisions of this section cannot be waived.

(j) * * * [A] petition for an injunction for protection against domestic violence may be filed in the circuit where the petitioner currently or temporarily resides, where the respondent resides, or where the domestic violence occurred. * * *

* * *

(4) Upon the filing of the petition, the court shall set a hearing to be held at the earliest possible time. The respondent shall be personally served with a copy of the petition, financial affidavit, Uniform Child Custody Jurisdiction and Enforcement Act affidavit, if any, notice of hearing, and temporary injunction, if any, prior to the hearing.

(5) (a) When it appears to the court that an immediate and present danger of domestic violence exists, the court may grant a temporary injunction ex parte, pending a full hearing, and may grant such relief as the court deems proper, including an injunction:

1. Restraining the respondent from committing any acts of domestic violence.

2. Awarding to the petitioner the temporary exclusive use and possession of the dwelling that the parties share or excluding the respondent from the residence of the petitioner.

3. * * * [G]ranting to the petitioner temporary custody of a minor child. * * *

(b) In a hearing ex parte for the purpose of obtaining such ex parte temporary injunction, no evidence other than verified pleadings or affidavits shall be used as evidence, unless the respondent appears at the hearing or has received reasonable notice of the hearing. A denial of a petition for an ex parte injunction shall be by written order noting the legal grounds for denial. * * *

(c) Any such *ex parte* temporary injunction shall be effective for a fixed period not to exceed 15 days. A full hearing, as provided by this section, shall be set for a date no later than the date when the temporary injunction ceases to be effective. * * *

(6) (a) Upon notice and hearing, when it appears to the court that the petitioner is either the victim of domestic violence as defined by § 741.28 or has reasonable cause to believe he or she is in imminent danger of

becoming a victim of domestic violence, the court may grant such relief as the court deems proper, including an injunction:

1. Restraining the respondent from committing any acts of domestic violence.

2. Awarding to the petitioner the exclusive use and possession of the dwelling that the parties share or excluding the respondent from the residence of the petitioner.

3. * * * [A]warding temporary custody of, or temporary visitation rights with regard to, a minor child or children of the parties. * * *

4. * * * [E]stablishing temporary support for a minor child or children or the petitioner. * * *

5. Ordering the respondent to participate in treatment, intervention, or counseling services to be paid for by the respondent. * * *

6. Referring a petitioner to a certified domestic violence center. * * *

7. Ordering such other relief as the court deems necessary for the protection of a victim of domestic violence, including injunctions or directives to law enforcement agencies, as provided in this section.

(b) In determining whether a petitioner has reasonable cause to believe he or she is in imminent danger of becoming a victim of domestic violence, the court shall consider and evaluate all relevant factors alleged in the petition, including, but not limited to:

1. The history between the petitioner and the respondent, including threats, harassment, stalking, and physical abuse.

2. Whether the respondent has attempted to harm the petitioner or family members or individuals closely associated with the petitioner.

3. Whether the respondent has threatened to conceal, kidnap, or harm the petitioner's child or children.

4. Whether the respondent has intentionally injured or killed a family pet.

5. Whether the respondent has used, or has threatened to use, against the petitioner any weapons such as guns or knives.

6. Whether the respondent has physically restrained the petitioner from leaving the home or calling law enforcement.

7. Whether the respondent has a criminal history involving violence or the threat of violence.

8. The existence of a verifiable order of protection issued previously or from another jurisdiction.

9. Whether the respondent has destroyed personal property, including, but not limited to, telephones or other communications equipment, clothing, or other items belonging to the petitioner.

* * *

(g) A final judgment on injunction for protection against domestic violence entered pursuant to this section must, on its face, indicate that it is * * * a first degree misdemeanor, for the respondent to have in his or her care, custody, possession, or control any firearm or ammunition.

* * *

(9) (a) The court may enforce a violation of an injunction for protection against domestic violence through a civil or criminal contempt proceeding, or the state attorney may prosecute it as a criminal violation * * *. The court may enforce the respondent's compliance with the injunction through any appropriate civil and criminal remedies, including, but not limited to, a monetary assessment or a fine. * * *

Id. § 741.30.

    c. 24–Hour Availability for Temporary Relief

Section 26.20 of the Florida Statutes

* * * [A]t least one * * * judge[ ] shall be available as nearly as possible at all times to hold and conduct hearings in chambers. In each circuit [court], there must be at least one judge available on Saturdays, Sundays, holidays, and after hours on weekdays to hear motions for a temporary injunction ex parte in domestic violence cases. * * *

Id. § 26.20.

NOTES AND QUESTIONS

1. *Standard for issuing long-term protective orders.* What is the standard for issuance of a long-term protective order under the Florida statute? The standard varies among states. For example, Maryland requires a finding "by clear and convincing evidence" that at least one act of alleged abuse has occurred. Md. Code Ann., Fam. Law § 4–506(c)(ii) (2008). "Abuse" is defined as: "(i) an act that causes serious bodily harm; (ii) an act that places a person eligible for relief in fear of imminent serious bodily harm; (iii) assault in any degree; (iv) rape[,] sexual offense * * * or attempted rape or sexual offense in any degree; (v) false imprisonment; or (vi) stalking * * *." *Id.* § 4–501(b)(1).

In *Katsenelenbogen v. Katsenelenbogen*, 775 A.2d 1249, 1259 (Md. 2001), the court held that "when the abuse triggering a protective order is the commission of an act that places the victim 'in fear of imminent serious bodily harm,'" the standard for reasonableness of the fear is a subjective standard. The court explained that someone who has experienced violence may well be sensitive to nonverbal signals or code words which have proved threatening in the past to that victim but which someone else, not having that experience, would not perceive to be threatening. The victim's reasonable fears "must be viewed from the perspective of the particular victim. Any special vulnerability or dependence by the victim, by virtue of physical, mental, or emotional condition or impairment, also must be taken into account." *Id.* at 1259–60.

2. *Nature of relationship and protection orders.* All 50 states allow victims to seek domestic violence protection orders against individuals related to them by blood or marriage. Forty-nine states protect parents of a common child. (Louisiana provides protection only if the two parents of the opposite sex cohabit.) Forty-seven states protect cohabitants, two other states protect cohabitants only when they are dating, while New York is the only state without any protection for cohabitants unrelated by blood or marriage. In addition, 36 states provide protection to individuals in some form of dating relationship, whether or not the parties are cohabiting. Judith A. Smith, *Battered Non–Wives and Unequal Protection–Order Coverage: A Call for Reform*, 23 Yale L. & Pol'y Rev. 93, 102–07 (2005). Why do nearly all states provide some protections that extend beyond blood or marital relationships?

3. *Judicial availability as a first line of victims' defense.* A number of states have attempted to provide immediate judicial availability to address domestic violence emergencies. As you saw, Florida guarantees that in its larger communities, a circuit or county judge will be available 24 hours a day, seven days a week, to issue temporary injunctions. Fla. Stat. § 26.20 (2008). Maryland has either 24–hour commissioner stations or an "on-call" commissioner in every county to issue interim protective orders, which last either two days or until a judge holds an *ex parte* temporary hearing. Md. Code Ann., Fam. Law. § 4–504.1 (2008); *see* Maryland Judiciary, *Domestic Violence, How To Obtain Relief from Abusive Individuals*, http://www.courts.state.md.us/domesticviolence/courts.html.

4. *Types of Harms.* Should civil protection orders be available for financial harms that do not involve physical violence or direct threats, such as refusing to provide money for groceries or other necessaries? See Margaret Johnson, *Redefining Harm, Reimagining Remedies and Reclaiming Domestic Violence Law,* ___ U.C. Davis L. Rev. ___ (2009).

PROBLEM 6–1

Susan Brown had been dating Jack Thompson for three years. The couple maintained separate residences in the same city, although they had overnight visits at least three times a week. One day, Jack and Susan had an argument that resulted in Jack hitting Susan so hard that she had a black eye. Susan sought a protective order in Florida. According to the Florida statute, § 741.30, would Susan be able to obtain this protective order? As Susan's lawyer, what arguments would you make that Susan is protected under the statute? What arguments would you expect Jack to make in response?

PROBLEM 6–2

Mary Walsh and her brother Tom were in an intense fight. Tom became enraged and hit Mary. Mary and Tom had not resided in the same house for more than 40 years. As this was not the first time that Tom became violent with Mary, she filed for a protective order in Florida. According to the Florida domestic violence statute, § 741.30, can a court grant Mary this protective order? If you were Mary's lawyer, what arguments would you make? What arguments would Tom's lawyer make in response?

PROBLEM 6–3

Katherine Johnson, a resident of Florida, seeks a civil protection order against her former partner, Ann Smith. Ann has repeatedly beaten Katherine over the past three years of their relationship. The parties previously lived in a house together, but Katherine recently moved out in an attempt to escape the violence. Can Katherine obtain a civil protection order against her same-sex partner according to the Florida statute, § 741.30? If you were Katherine's lawyer, what arguments would you make on her behalf? What arguments would you expect Ann's lawyer to make?

2. ISSUING A CIVIL PROTECTION ORDER

TONS v. BLEY

Indiana Court of Appeals, 2004.
815 N.E.2d 508.

RATLIFF, SENIOR JUDGE.

* * *

THE ISSUE

Here we are presented with the issue of whether there was sufficient evidence presented to warrant the issuance, pursuant to the Indiana Civil Protection Order Act, of a protective order as to Barbara Bley and Brian Bley [her current husband] * * *.

FACTS

[Joseph E.] Tons and Barbara Bley formerly were married and are the parents of Travis Tons, their thirteen year old son. Tons and Barbara were divorced in 1996. They have shared joint custody of Travis, although at the time of the incident leading to the filing of Barbara's petition for a protective order Travis was living with Barbara. Travis has not done well in school, which has been a matter of concern and the underlying cause of some of the problems involved in this matter. The controversy here arose because Travis wished to attend a rodeo and participate in bull riding. Tons had forbidden Travis from attending the rodeo until he improved his grades. Although he had been provided with tutors in the past, improvement of his grades had not occurred. Despite Tons objections, Travis did attend the rodeo. In a telephone conversation with Barbara, Tons told her that if she took Travis to see any counselors, tutors, or attorneys that he would come over and beat Travis black and blue. This led to the filing of the petition in this case. There also was evidence that Tons had physically struck Travis in November of 2002 and on other occasions. Barbara testified that Tons had not threatened her, although she did relate that there had been some violence towards her by Tons during their marriage, and she expressed a fear of him. There was no evidence of any threats or acts of violence against Brian Bley, nor was there any evidence of any use or threats by firearms by Tons.

DISCUSSION AND DECISION

Under the applicable statute, a court may issue a protective order upon a showing, by a preponderance of the evidence, of domestic violence. The statute provides that "[a] finding that domestic or family violence has occurred sufficient to justify the issuance of an order under this section means that a respondent represents a credible threat to the safety of the petitioner or a member of the petitioner's household." The order issued in this case prohibited Tons from committing or threatening to commit acts of domestic or family violence against Barbara, Brian, or Travis, and prohibited Tons from harassing, annoying, telephoning, contacting, or directly or indirectly communicating with Barbara. The order further prohibited Tons from using or possessing a firearm, ammunition, or deadly weapon.

The Civil Protective Order Act provides for the granting of relief necessary to bring about a cessation of the violence or threat of violence. Issuance of the types of injunctive relief granted by the order in this case is within the kinds of relief authorized by the Act. The Act further provides that the relief may include an order directing the respondent to surrender to a law enforcement officer or agency all firearms, ammunition, and deadly weapons in the control, ownership, or possession of the respondent, or of another person on respondent's behalf.

* * *

[T]he evidence is sufficient to sustain the issuance of the protective order insofar as it applies to Travis. Tons does not challenge that portion of the order, and we affirm that part of the trial court's judgment.

The protective orders pertaining to Barbara and Brian present a serious problem. There is no evidence that Tons ever threatened Barbara, and she admitted that he did not. Any acts of violence by Tons against Barbara occurred during their marriage that ended in 1996. While the court may not deny the petition solely by reason of the lapse of time between the act of violence and the filing of the petition, we may consider remoteness in determining whether a sufficient threat exists to warrant the issuance of a protective order. We believe that unspecified acts of violence occurring eight years previously are a not sufficient basis for the issuance of a protective order. Therefore, we must reverse the protective order as it pertains to Barbara. Likewise there is absolutely no evidence of any acts of violence, or threats, by Tons toward Brian. The protective order as to Brian is reversed.

* * *

BARNES, JUDGE, dissenting.

I respectfully dissent. I believe the Civil Protection Order Act was enacted by the General Assembly to provide the umbrella of protection that the trial court extended here.

Here, there is evidence in the record that Tons has in the past violently disciplined his son Travis, including punching him in the head with his fist and throwing him down a flight of stairs. Additionally, there was evidence of violence during the marriage between Barbara Bley and Tons. One may reasonably infer that Tons' threat to beat Travis "black and blue" implicitly extended to anyone who might interfere with that mission, including Barbara and her current husband, Brian Bley. I believe, as with any factual determination by a trial court, that we should defer to the court's conclusion here that not just Travis, but also Barbara and Brian, should fall under the scope of the protective order it issued.

I also note that under [the relevant statute], a protective order may be ordered to apply not only with respect to the person petitioning for the order, but also with respect to "each designated family or household member." I believe this is tacit recognition by the General Assembly that when a respondent has threatened a petitioner with harm, other persons living with the petitioner who may not have been directly threatened are nevertheless at risk of harm by the respondent. I also conclude that the statute permits a protective order to be issued for the benefit of persons living with a threatened person, even if the respondent did not directly threaten those other persons.

* * *

I would affirm the trial court's order in its entirety.

NOTES AND QUESTIONS

1. *Issuance of a protective order.* Do you agree with the *Tons* dissent or the majority? Should a protective order be available to anyone in the household, or only to the person against whom a threat is made? What is the practical result of the distinction? What is the emotional result of the distinction (particularly for the victim)? Must the court hear evidence of a threat to all family members before it may issue a protective order to extend to all? Does the Indiana statute authorize the court to err on the side of protection? Should it? If you were a state legislator concerned about this decision, what amendments to the adult abuse statute would you recommend?

2. *The Violence Against Women Act and guns.* Congress enacted the Violence Against Women Act (VAWA) of 1994 to help states, tribes, and local governments develop and strengthen law enforcement, prosecutorial, and judicial strategies to combat violent crimes against women. Pub. L. No. 103–322, 108 Stat. 1902 (codified as amended in scattered sections of 8, 16, 18, 28 & 42 U.S.C.). Title VI of that Act, an amendment to the Gun Control Act of 1968, makes it a federal crime for a person to possess a firearm or ammunition while the person is subject to a qualifying court order restraining that

person from harassing, stalking or threatening an intimate partner, or committing acts that would place that partner in reasonable fear of bodily injury. 18 U.S.C. § 922(g)(8) (2003). To qualify, the protection order must also state that the person presents a credible threat to the victim's physical safety or it must prohibit the person from using force that would reasonably be expected to cause injury to the victim, and it must have been issued following a hearing at which the person had notice and opportunity to be heard. *Id.* Under this provision, a person is not barred from possessing a firearm following an *ex parte* temporary protection or restraining order hearing.

In 1996, Congress passed another significant amendment to the Gun Control Act of 1968, the Lautenberg Amendment, which prohibits gun possession by anyone with a domestic violence misdemeanor conviction. *Id.* § 922(g)(9). This provision applies regardless of whether there is a civil protection order underlying the conviction. The Gun Control Act already prohibited anyone convicted of a crime that is punishable by imprisonment of longer than a year from owning a gun.

3. *Statistics on guns and domestic violence.* In recent years, about one-third of female murder victims and about 3% of male murder victims were killed by an intimate. More than two-thirds of the murders of spouses or ex-spouses involved use of a gun. James Alan Fox & Marianne W. Zawitz, Bureau of Justice Statistics, *Homicide Trends in the U.S., Intimate Homicide* (2007), http://www.ojp.usdoj.gov/bjs/homicide/intimates.htm. Furthermore, a 1997 study found that when one or more guns were in the home, women were 7.2 times more likely to be victims of intimate homicide. Violence Policy Center, *Facts on Firearms and Domestic Violence* (*citing* James E. Bailey, *Risk Factors for Violence Death of Women in the Home*, 7 Archives of Internal Medicine 157, 777–82 (1997)), http://www.vpc.org/fact_sht/domviofs.htm.

B. ENFORCING A CIVIL PROTECTION ORDER

While civil protection orders are extremely helpful remedies for battered victims, the batterer does not always comply with the order's terms. In the following case, the Supreme Court considered enforcement issues in connection with the violations of a civil protection order.

CASTLE ROCK v. GONZALES

Supreme Court of the United States, 2005.
545 U.S. 748.

JUSTICE SCALIA delivered the opinion of the Court.

We decide in this case whether an individual who has obtained a state-law restraining order has a constitutionally protected property interest in having the police enforce the restraining order when they have probable cause to believe it has been violated.

I

* * * Respondent alleges that petitioner, the town of Castle Rock, Colorado, violated the Due Process Clause of the Fourteenth Amendment

to the United States Constitution when its police officers, acting pursuant to official policy or custom, failed to respond properly to her repeated reports that her estranged husband was violating the terms of a restraining order.

The restraining order had been issued by a state trial court several weeks earlier in conjunction with respondent's divorce proceedings. The original form order, issued on May 21, 1999, and served on respondent's husband on June 4, 1999, commanded him not to "molest or disturb the peace of [respondent] or of any child," and to remain at least 100 yards from the family home at all times. * * * The preprinted text on the back of the form included the following "**WARNING**":

> "**A KNOWING VIOLATION OF A RESTRAINING ORDER IS A CRIME**.... A VIOLATION WILL ALSO CONSTITUTE CONTEMPT OF COURT. **YOU MAY BE ARRESTED** WITHOUT NOTICE IF A LAW ENFORCEMENT OFFICER HAS PROBABLE CAUSE TO BELIEVE THAT YOU HAVE KNOWINGLY VIOLATED THIS ORDER."

The preprinted text on the back of the form also included a "**NOTICE TO LAW ENFORCEMENT OFFICIALS**," which read in part:

> "YOU SHALL USE EVERY REASONABLE MEANS TO ENFORCE THIS RESTRAINING ORDER. YOU SHALL ARREST, OR, IF AN ARREST WOULD BE IMPRACTICAL UNDER THE CIRCUMSTANCES, SEEK A WARRANT FOR THE ARREST OF THE RESTRAINED PERSON WHEN YOU HAVE INFORMATION AMOUNTING TO PROBABLE CAUSE THAT THE RESTRAINED PERSON HAS VIOLATED OR ATTEMPTED TO VIOLATE ANY PROVISION OF THIS ORDER AND THE RESTRAINED PERSON HAS BEEN PROPERLY SERVED WITH A COPY OF THIS ORDER OR HAS RECEIVED ACTUAL NOTICE OF THE EXISTENCE OF THIS ORDER."

* * *

According to the complaint, at about 5 or 5:30 p.m. on Tuesday, June 22, 1999, respondent's husband took the three daughters while they were playing outside the family home. No advance arrangements had been made for him to see the daughters that evening. When respondent noticed the children were missing, she suspected her husband had taken them. At about 7:30 p.m., she called the Castle Rock Police Department, which dispatched two officers. The complaint continues: "When [the officers] arrived ..., she showed them a copy of the TRO and requested that it be enforced and the three children be returned to her immediately. [The officers] stated that there was nothing they could do about the TRO and suggested that [respondent] call the Police Department again if the three children did not return home by 10:00 p.m."

At approximately 8:30 p.m., respondent talked to her husband on his cellular telephone. He told her "he had the three children [at an] amusement park in Denver." She called the police again and asked them to "have someone check for" her husband or his vehicle at the amusement park and "put out an [all points bulletin]" for her husband, but the officer with whom she spoke "refused to do so," again telling her to "wait until 10:00 p.m. and see if" her husband returned the girls.

At approximately 10:10 p.m., respondent called the police and said her children were still missing, but she was now told to wait until midnight. She called at midnight and told the dispatcher her children were still missing. She went to her husband's apartment and, finding nobody there, called the police at 12:10 a.m.; she was told to wait for an officer to arrive. When none came, she went to the police station at 12:50 a.m. and submitted an incident report. The officer who took the report "made no reasonable effort to enforce the TRO or locate the three children. Instead, he went to dinner."

At approximately 3:20 a.m., respondent's husband arrived at the police station and opened fire with a semiautomatic handgun he had purchased earlier that evening. Police shot back, killing him. Inside the cab of his pickup truck, they found the bodies of all three daughters, whom he had already murdered.

On the basis of the foregoing factual allegations, respondent brought an action under Rev. Stat. § 1979, 42 U.S.C. § 1983, claiming that the town violated the Due Process Clause because its police department had "an official policy or custom of failing to respond properly to complaints of restraining order violations" and "tolerate[d] the non-enforcement of restraining orders by its police officers." The complaint also alleged that the town's actions "were taken either willfully, recklessly or with such gross negligence as to indicate wanton disregard and deliberate indifference to" respondent's civil rights.

* * *

[The district court dismissed the complaint.]

A panel of the Court of Appeals affirmed the rejection of a substantive due process claim, but found that respondent had alleged a cognizable procedural due process claim. On rehearing en banc, a divided court reached the same disposition, concluding that respondent had a "protected property interest in the enforcement of the terms of her restraining order" and that the town had deprived her of due process because "the police never 'heard' nor seriously entertained her request to enforce and protect her interests in the restraining order." We granted certiorari.

II

The Fourteenth Amendment to the United States Constitution provides that a State shall not "deprive any person of life, liberty, or property, without due process of law." In 42 U.S.C. § 1983, Congress has created a federal cause of action for "the deprivation of any rights, privileges, or immunities secured by the Constitution and laws." Respondent claims the benefit of this provision on the ground that she had a property interest in police enforcement of the restraining order against her husband; and that the town deprived her of this property without due process by having a policy that tolerated nonenforcement of restraining orders.

As the Court of Appeals recognized, we left a similar question unanswered in *DeShaney v. Winnebago County Dep't of Soc. Servs.*, 489 U.S. 189 (1989), another case with "undeniably tragic" facts: Local child-protection officials had failed to protect a young boy from beatings by his father that left him severely brain damaged. We held that the so-called "substantive" component of the Due Process Clause does not "require[e] the State to protect the life, liberty, and property of its citizens against invasion by private actors." We noted, however, that the petitioner had not properly preserved the argument that—and we thus "decline[d] to consider" whether—state "child protection statutes gave [him] an 'entitlement' to receive protective services in accordance with the terms of the statute, an entitlement which would enjoy due process protection."

The procedural component of the Due Process Clause does not protect everything that might be described as a "benefit": "To have a property interest in a benefit, a person clearly must have more than an abstract need or desire" and "more than a unilateral expectation of it. He must, instead, have a legitimate claim of entitlement to it." *Bd. of Regents of State Colleges v. Roth*, 408 U.S. 564, 577 (1972). Such entitlements are " 'of course, . . . not created by the Constitution. Rather, they are created and their dimensions are defined by existing rules or understandings that stem from an independent source such as state law.' " *Paul v. Davis*, 424 U.S. 693, 709 (1976). * * *

* * *

B

The critical language in the restraining order came not from any part of the order itself (which was signed by the state-court trial judge and directed to the restrained party, respondent's husband), but from the preprinted notice to law-enforcement personnel that appeared on the back of the order. That notice effectively restated the statutory provision describing "peace officers' duties" related to the crime of violation of a restraining order. At the time of the conduct at issue in this case, that provision read as follows:

"(a) Whenever a restraining order is issued, the protected person shall be provided with a copy of such order. *A peace officer shall use every reasonable means to enforce a restraining order.*

"(b) *A peace officer shall arrest, or, if an arrest would be impractical under the circumstances, seek a warrant for the arrest of a restrained person* when the peace officer has information amounting to probable cause that:

"(I) The restrained person has violated or attempted to violate any provision of a restraining order; and

"(II) The restrained person has been properly served with a copy of the restraining order or the restrained person has received actual notice of the existence and substance of such order.

"(c) In making the probable cause determination described in paragraph (b) of this subsection (3), a peace officer shall assume that the information received from the registry is accurate. *A peace officer shall enforce a valid restraining order whether or not there is a record of the restraining order in the registry.*"

Colo. Rev. Stat. § 18–6–803.5(3) (1999) (emphases added). The Court of Appeals concluded that this statutory provision—especially taken in conjunction with a statement from its legislative history, and with another statute restricting criminal and civil liability for officers making arrests—established the Colorado Legislature's clear intent "to alter the fact that the police were not enforcing domestic abuse retraining orders," and thus its intent "that the recipient of a domestic abuse restraining order have an entitlement to its enforcement." Any other result, it said, "would render domestic abuse restraining orders utterly valueless." * * *

This last statement is sheer hyperbole. Whether or not respondent had a right to enforce the restraining order, it rendered certain otherwise lawful conduct by her husband both criminal and in contempt of court. The creation of grounds on which he could be arrested, criminally prosecuted, and held in contempt was hardly "valueless"—even if the prospect of those sanctions ultimately failed to prevent him from committing three murders and a suicide.

We do not believe that these provisions of Colorado law truly made enforcement of restraining orders *mandatory*. A well established tradition of police discretion has long coexisted with apparently mandatory arrest statutes.

* * *

The deep-rooted nature of law-enforcement discretion, even in the presence of seemingly mandatory legislative commands, is illustrated by *Chicago v. Morales,* 527 U.S. 41 (1999), which involved an ordinance that said a police officer " 'shall order' "persons to disperse in certain circumstances. *Id.* at 47 n.2. This Court rejected out of hand the possibility that "the mandatory language of the ordinance ... afford[ed] the police *no* discretion." *Id.* at 62 n.32. It is, the Court proclaimed, simply "common sense that *all* police officers must use some discretion in deciding when and where to enforce city ordinances." *Id.* (emphasis added).

Against that backdrop, a true mandate of police action would require some stronger indication from the Colorado Legislature than "shall use every reasonable means to enforce a restraining order" (or even "shall arrest ... or ... seek a warrant"). Colo. Rev. Stat. § 18–6–803.5(3)(a)–(b). That language is not perceptibly more mandatory than the Colorado statute which has long told municipal chiefs of police that they "shall pursue and arrest any person fleeing from justice in any part of the state" and that they "shall apprehend any person in the act of committing any offense . . . and, forthwith and without any warrant, bring such person before a . . . competent authority for examination and trial." It is hard to imagine that a Colorado peace officer would not have some discretion to determine that—despite probable cause to believe a restraining order has been violated—the circumstances of the violation or the competing duties of that officer or his agency counsel decisively against enforcement in a particular instance. The practical necessity for discretion is particularly apparent in a case such as this one, where the suspected violator is not actually present and his whereabouts are unknown. * * *

The dissent correctly points out that, in the specific context of domestic violence, mandatory-arrest statutes have been found in some States to be more mandatory than traditional mandatory-arrest statutes. The Colorado statute mandating arrest for a domestic-violence offense is different from but related to the one at issue here, and it includes similar though not identical phrasing. *See* [*id.*] § 18–6–803.6(1) ("When a peace officer determines that there is probable cause to believe that a crime or offense involving domestic violence . . . has been committed, the officer shall, without undue delay, arrest the person suspected of its commission . . .). Even in the domestic-violence context, however, it is unclear how the mandatory-arrest paradigm applies to cases in which the offender is not present to be arrested. As the dissent explains, much of the impetus for mandatory-arrest statutes and policies derived from the idea that it is better for police officers to arrest the aggressor in a domestic-violence incident than to attempt to mediate the dispute or merely to ask the offender to leave the scene. Those other options are only available, of course, when the offender is present at the scene.

* * *

Respondent does not specify the precise means of enforcement that the Colorado restraining-order statute assertedly mandated—whether her interest lay in having police arrest her husband, having them seek a warrant for his arrest, or having them "use every reasonable means, up to and including arrest, to enforce the order's terms." Such indeterminacy is not the hallmark of a duty that is mandatory. Nor can someone be safely deemed "entitled" to something when the identity of the alleged entitlement is vague. The dissent, after suggesting various formulations of the entitlement in question, ultimately contends that the obligations under the statute were quite precise: either make an arrest or (if that is impractical) seek an arrest warrant. The problem with this is that the seeking of an arrest warrant would be an entitlement to nothing but procedure * * *. After the warrant is sought, it remains within the discretion of a judge whether to grant it, and after it is granted, it remains within the discretion of the police whether and when to execute it.[11]

---

11. The dissent asserts that the police would lack discretion in the execution of this warrant, but cites no statute mandating immediate execution. The general Colorado statute governing arrest provides that police "may arrest" when they possess a warrant "commanding" arrest.

Respondent would have been assured nothing but the seeking of a warrant. This is not the sort of "entitlement" out of which a property interest is created.

Even if the statute could be said to have made enforcement of restraining orders "mandatory" because of the domestic-violence context of the underlying statute, that would not necessarily mean that state law gave *respondent* an entitlement to *enforcement* of the mandate. Making the actions of government employees obligatory can serve various legitimate ends other than the conferral of a benefit on a specific class of people. The serving of public rather than private ends is the normal course of the criminal law because criminal acts, "besides the injury [they do] to individuals, . . . strike at the very being of society; which cannot possibly subsist, where actions of this sort are suffered to escape with impunity." This principle underlies, for example, a Colorado district attorney's discretion to prosecute a domestic assault, even though the victim withdraws her charge.

Respondent's alleged interest stems only from a State's *statutory* scheme—from a restraining order that was authorized by and tracked precisely the statute on which the Court of Appeals relied. She does not assert that she has any common-law or contractual entitlement to enforcement. If she was given a statutory entitlement, we would expect to see some indication of that in the statute itself. * * *

* * *

III

We conclude, therefore, that respondent did not, for purposes of the Due Process Clause, have a property interest in police enforcement of the restraining order against her husband. It is accordingly unnecessary to address the Court of Appeals' determination that the town's custom or policy prevented the police from giving her due process when they deprived her of that alleged interest.[14]

In light of today's decision and that in *DeShaney,* the benefit that a third party may receive from having someone else arrested for a crime generally does not trigger protections under the Due Process Clause, neither in its procedural nor in its "substantive" manifestations. This result reflects our continuing reluctance to treat the Fourteenth Amendment as " 'a font of tort law,' " but it does not mean States are powerless to provide victims with personally enforceable remedies. Although the framers of the Fourteenth Amendment and the Civil Rights Act of 1871, 17 Stat. 13 (the original source of § 1983), did not create a system by which police departments are generally held financially accountable for crimes that better policing might have prevented, the people of Colorado are free to craft such a system under state law.

---

14. Because we simply do not address whether the process would have been adequate if respondent had had a property interest, the dissent is correct to note that we do not "contest" the point. Of course we do not *accept* it either.

The judgment of the Court of Appeals is *Reversed.*

JUSTICE SOUTER, with whom JUSTICE BREYER joins, concurring.

I agree with the Court that Jessica Gonzales has shown no violation of an interest protected by the Fourteenth Amendment's Due Process Clause, and I join the Court's opinion. The Court emphasizes the traditional public focus of law enforcement as reason to doubt that these particular legal requirements to provide police services, however unconditional their form, presuppose enforceable individual rights to a certain level of police protection. The Court also notes that the terms of the Colorado statute involved here recognize and preserve the traditional discretion afforded law enforcement officers. Gonzales's claim of a property right thus runs up against police discretion in the face of an individual demand to enforce, and discretion to ignore an individual instruction not to enforce (because, say, of a domestic reconciliation); no one would argue that the beneficiary of a Colorado order like the one here would be authorized to control a court's contempt power or order the police to refrain from arresting. These considerations argue against inferring any guarantee of a level of protection or safety that could be understood as the object of a "legitimate claim of entitlement," in the nature of property arising under Colorado law. Consequently, the classic predicate for federal due process protection of interests under state law is missing.

* * *

JUSTICE STEVENS, with whom JUSTICE GINSBURG joins, dissenting.

The issue presented to us is much narrower than is suggested by the far-ranging arguments of the parties and their *amici.* Neither the tragic facts of the case, nor the importance of according proper deference to law enforcement professionals, should divert our attention from that issue. That issue is whether the restraining order entered by the Colorado trial court on June 4, 1999, created a "property" interest that is protected from arbitrary deprivation by the Due Process Clause of the Fourteenth Amendment.

It is perfectly clear, on the one hand, that neither the Federal Constitution itself, nor any federal statute, granted respondent or her children any individual entitlement to police protection. See *DeShaney v. Winnebago County Dep't of Soc. Servs.,* 489 U.S. 189 (1989). Nor, I assume, does any Colorado statute create any such entitlement for the ordinary citizen. On the other hand, it is equally clear that federal law imposes no impediment to the creation of such an entitlement by Colorado law. Respondent certainly could have entered into a contract with a private security firm, obligating the firm to provide protection to respondent's family; respondent's interest in such a contract would unquestionably constitute "property" within the meaning of the Due Process Clause. If a Colorado statute enacted for her benefit, or a valid order entered by a Colorado judge, created the functional equivalent of such a private contract by granting respondent an entitlement to mandatory individual protection by the local police force, that state-created right would also qualify as "property" entitled to constitutional protection.

I do not understand the majority to rule out the foregoing propositions, although it does express doubts. ("[I]t is by no means clear that an individual entitlement to enforcement of a restraining order could constitute a 'property' interest".) Moreover, the majority does not contest, that if respondent did have a cognizable property interest in this case, the deprivation of that interest violated due process. As the Court notes, respondent has alleged that she presented the police with a copy of the restraining order issued by the Colorado court and requested that it be enforced. In response, she contends, the officers effectively ignored her. If these allegations are true, a federal statute, 42 USC § 1983, provides her with a remedy against the petitioner, even if Colorado law does not.

The central question in this case is therefore whether, as a matter of Colorado law, respondent had a right to police assistance comparable to the right she would have possessed to any other service the government or a private firm might have undertaken to provide. See *Bd. of Regents of State Colleges v. Roth*, 408 U.S. 564, 577 (1972) ("Property interests, of course, are not created by the Constitution. Rather, they are created and their dimensions are defined by existing rules or understandings that stem from an independent source such as state law—rules or understandings that secure certain benefits and that support claims of entitlement to those benefits").

* * *

III

Three flaws in the Court's rather superficial analysis of the merits highlight the unwisdom of its decision to answer the state-law question *de novo*. First, the Court places undue weight on the various statutes throughout the country that seemingly mandate police enforcement but are generally understood to preserve police discretion. As a result, the Court gives short shrift to the unique case of "mandatory arrest" statutes in the domestic violence context; States passed a wave of these statutes in the 1980's and 1990's with the unmistakable goal of eliminating police discretion in this area. Second, the Court's formalistic analysis fails to take seriously the fact that the Colorado statute at issue in this case was enacted for the benefit of the narrow class of persons who are beneficiaries of domestic restraining orders, and that the order at issue in this case was specifically intended to provide protection to respondent and her children. Finally, the Court is simply wrong to assert that a citizen's interest in the government's commitment to provide police enforcement in certain defined circumstances does not resemble any "traditional conception of property"; in fact, a citizen's property interest in such a commitment is just as concrete and worthy of protection as her interest in any other important service the government or a private firm has undertaken to provide.

In 1994, the Colorado General Assembly passed omnibus legislation targeting domestic violence. The part of the legislation at issue in this case mandates enforcement of a domestic restraining order upon probable cause of a violation, § 18–6–803.5(3), while another part directs that police officers "shall, without undue delay, arrest" a suspect upon "probable cause to believe that a crime or offense of domestic violence has been committed," § 18–6–803.6(1). In adopting this legislation, the Colorado General Assembly joined a nationwide movement of States that took aim at the crisis of police underenforcement in the domestic violence sphere by implementing "mandatory arrest" statutes. The crisis of underenforcement had various causes, not least of which was the perception by police departments and police officers that domestic violence was a private, "family" matter and that arrest was to be used as a last resort. In response to these realities, and emboldened by a well-known 1984 experiment by the Minneapolis police department, "many states enacted mandatory arrest statutes under which a police officer must arrest an abuser when the officer has probable cause to believe that a domestic assault has occurred or that a protection order has been violated." The purpose of these statutes was precisely to "counter police resistance to arrests in domestic violence cases by removing or restricting police officer discretion; mandatory arrest policies would increase police response and reduce batterer recidivism."

Thus, when Colorado passed its statute in 1994, it joined the ranks of 15 States that mandated arrest for domestic violence offenses and 19 States that mandated arrest for domestic restraining order violations.

Given the specific purpose of these statutes, there can be no doubt that the Colorado Legislature used the term "shall" advisedly in its domestic restraining order statute. While "shall" is probably best read to mean "may" in other Colorado statutes that seemingly mandate enforcement, cf. Colo. Rev. Stat. § 31–4–112 (2004) (police "*shall suppress* all riots, disturbances or breaches of the peace, *shall apprehend* all disorderly persons in the city ..." (emphases added)), it is clear that the elimination of police discretion was integral to Colorado and its fellow States' solution to the problem of underenforcement in domestic violence cases. Since the text of Colorado's statute perfectly captures this legislative purpose, it is hard to imagine what the Court has in mind when it insists on "some stronger indication from the Colorado Legislature."

While Colorado case law does not speak to the question, it is instructive that other state courts interpreting their analogous statutes have not only held that they eliminate the police's traditional discretion to refuse enforcement, but have also recognized that they create rights enforceable against the police under state law. * * *

Indeed, the Court fails to come to terms with the wave of domestic violence statutes that provides the crucial context for understanding Colorado's law. The Court concedes that, "in the specific context of domestic violence, mandatory-arrest statutes have been found in some

States to be more mandatory than traditional mandatory-arrest statutes,'' but that is a serious understatement. The difference is not a matter of degree, but of kind. Before this wave of statutes, the legal rule was one of discretion; as the Court shows, the "traditional," general mandatory arrest statutes have always been understood to be "mandatory" in name only. The innovation of the domestic violence statutes was to make police enforcement, not "more mandatory," but simply *mandatory*. If, as the Court says, the existence of a protected "entitlement" turns on whether "government officials may grant or deny it in their discretion," the new mandatory statutes undeniably create an entitlement to police enforcement of restraining orders.

* * *

Because the statute's guarantee of police enforcement is triggered by, and operates only in reference to, a judge's granting of a restraining order in favor of an identified " 'protected person,' " there is simply no room to suggest that such a person has received merely an " 'incidental' " or " 'indirect' " benefit. As one state court put it, domestic restraining order statutes "identify with precision when, to whom, and under what circumstances police protection must be afforded. The legislative purpose in requiring the police to enforce individual restraining orders clearly is to protect the named persons for whose protection the order is issued, not to protect the community at large by general law enforcement activity." Not only does the Court's doubt about whether Colorado's statute created an entitlement in a protected person fail to take seriously the purpose and nature of restraining orders, but it fails to account for the decisions by other state courts, that recognize that such statutes and restraining orders create individual rights to police action.

IV

* * *

Police enforcement of a restraining order is a government service that is no less concrete and no less valuable than other government services, such as education. The relative novelty of recognizing this type of property interest is explained by the relative novelty of the domestic violence statutes creating a mandatory arrest duty; before this innovation, the unfettered discretion that characterized police enforcement defeated any citizen's "legitimate claim of entitlement" to this service. Novel or not, respondent's claim finds strong support in the principles that underlie our due process jurisprudence. In this case, Colorado law *guaranteed* the provision of a certain service, in certain defined circumstances, to a certain class of beneficiaries, and respondent reasonably relied on that guarantee. As we observed in *Roth*, "[i]t is a purpose of the ancient institution of property to protect those claims upon which people rely in their daily lives, reliance that must not be arbitrarily undermined." 408 U.S. at 577. Surely, if respondent had contracted with a private security firm to provide her and her daughters with protection from her husband, it would be apparent that she possessed a property interest in such a contract. Here, Colorado undertook a comparable obligation, and respondent—with restraining order in hand—justifiably relied on that undertaking. Respondent's claim of entitlement to this promised service is no less legitimate than the other claims our cases have upheld, and no less concrete than a hypothetical agreement with a private firm. The fact that it is based on a statutory enactment and a judicial order entered for her special protection, rather than on a formal contract, does not provide a principled basis for refusing to consider it "property" worthy of constitutional protection.

* * *

V

Because respondent had a property interest in the enforcement of the restraining order, state officials could not deprive her of that interest without observing fair procedures. Her description of the police behavior in this case and the department's callous policy of failing to respond properly to reports of restraining order violations clearly alleges a due process violation. At the very least, due process requires that the relevant state decisionmaker *listen* to the claimant and then *apply the relevant criteria* in reaching his decision. The failure to observe these minimal procedural safeguards creates an unacceptable risk of arbitrary and "erroneous deprivation[s]."

* * *

NOTES AND QUESTIONS

1. *The Supreme Court and Domestic Violence.* Notwithstanding its decision in *Castle Rock*, the Supreme Court has repeatedly referred to the difficulties facing battered women, including in *Casey*, which was discussed in Chapter 4. In 2008, the Court considered the admissibility of a call for police help made by a battered woman who was subsequently killed by her batterer. In the course of considering the batterer's Confrontation Clause rights, the Court noted that "[d]omestic violence is an intolerable offense" and that "[a]cts of domestic violence often are intended to dissuade a victim from resorting to outside help." *Giles v. California*, 554 U.S. ___, 128 S.Ct. 2678, 2693 (2008).

2. *Effectiveness of CPOs.* A study published in the Journal of the American Medical Association found that battered women who obtained permanent protective orders experienced an 80% reduction in police-reported physical violence in the year following a violent episode. Victoria Holt et al., *Civil Protection Orders and Risk of Subsequent Police–Reported Violence*, 288 J. Am. Med. Ass'n 589, 593 (2002). Civil protection orders can perform a variety of functions, ranging from temporary financial assistance to physical protection; studies show that most battered women are satisfied with the entry of an order, and that they generally feel safer with the order. Sally F. Goldfarb, *Reconceiving Civil Protection Orders for Domestic Violence: Can*

Law Help End the Abuse Without Ending the Relationship? 29 Cardozo L. Rev. 1487, 1510 (2008). Batterers' compliance with orders varies. For example, batterers with prior criminal records are more likely than batters without criminal records to commit abuse. *Id.* at 1512–13.

3. *Enforcing a civil protective order.* Although civil protective orders can inhibit future violence when properly issued and enforced, a 2002 study commissioned by the U.S. Department of Justice found that many domestic violence victims believed that protective orders were not entirely effective safety measure because of lack of enforcement. Institute for Law and Justice, National Evaluation of the Grants to Encourage Arrest Policies Program, Final Report 97 (2002), http://www.ilj.org/publications/arrestpolicies.pdf.

Today, all 50 states and the District of Columbia have statutes that criminalize civil protective order violations. Most states treat violations as misdemeanors, and the remaining minority treat violations as felonies. Additionally, 38 states and the District of Columbia provide for criminal contempt charges against individuals who violate civil protective orders. Deborah Epstein, *Procedural Justice: Tempering the State's Response to Domestic Violence*, 43 Wm. & Mary L. Rev. 1843, 1859–60 (2002).

For a protective order to be effective, the battered woman must have a copy of the protective order with her and be willing to call the police should her abuser attempt to violate the order. If you were an attorney for a woman with a civil protective order, what would you advise her to do to enforce the protective order? What plans should she make to use the protective order to its full extent and how can she use it to protect herself?

4. *The victim's role in dissolving a protective order.* In *Stevenson v. Stevenson*, 714 A.2d 986 (N.J. Super. Ct. Ch. Div. 1998), the court held that it could deny a plaintiff's request to dissolve a final restraining order. The case began in November 1997, when the court found by a preponderance of evidence that the defendant was guilty of attempted criminal homicide, aggravated assault, terroristic threats, criminal restraint and burglary. Uncontroverted evidence established a "brutal, sadistic and prolonged attack by defendant on his wife" during which time "defendant beat and tortured his wife so severely that she was critically injured." *Id.* at 988. The court order prohibited any further acts of domestic violence, and barred the defendant from any contact or communication with the plaintiff and from harassing or stalking her.

In March 1998, the plaintiff asked the court to dissolve the final restraining order because she had reconsidered her relationship with the defendant and wanted him to be involved in their son's life. The court noted the public policy considerations that *"the official response to domestic violence * * * shall communicate the attitude that domestic violent behavior will not be excused or tolerated; and that it is the responsibility of the courts to protect victims of domestic violence by ordering those remedies and sanctions that are available to assure the safety of the victims and the public." Id.* at 992 (emphasis by the court). Even in cases of reconciliation, the court generally must make an independent finding that continued protection is unnecessary before vacating a restraining order. *Stevenson* held that "given the uncontroverted evidence of defendant's brutality against his wife, his history of violence both within and without the domestic arena, his alcohol abuse and uncontrolled assaultive behavior when under the influence, * * * a real threat of recurrence of domestic violence by defendant upon his battered wife will exist, if the Final Restraining Order is dissolved." *Id.* at 995.

Do you agree with *Stevenson*? Should courts permit battered wives to make decisions regarding their own safety and the safety of their families by dissolving a protective order? Must CPOs include stay-away orders? See Goldfarb, *supra*.

COMMENT ON BATTERED WOMAN'S SYNDROME

Battered Woman's Syndrome (BWS) has become a well-recognized term to describe what is commonly characterized as a three-phase cycle of an abusive relationship: (1) a tension-building phase, when the batterer commits relatively minor abusive acts and the victim attempts to placate the batterer to prevent further violence; (2) an acute-battering phase, when the batterer's violence escalates and the victim may be severely beaten; and (3) a loving-contrition phase, during which the batterer becomes remorseful, pleads for forgiveness, and typically promises that he will never again abuse the victim. Lenore E. Walker, The Battered Woman 55–70 (1979).

Stevenson noted that the plaintiff's dissolution request was consistent with phase three of BWS. The cycle theory of BWS often figures in cases in which battering victims are accused of striking back against their abusers. If a battering victim's resort to violence is not contemporaneous with fending off an abusive attack, traditional legal principles made a self-defense claim tenuous by insisting on an objective standard of reasonableness. For example, in *State v. Norman*, 378 S.E.2d 8 (N.C. 1989), the court refused to allow a jury instruction on self-defense for a battered woman who had killed her husband. The court held that the state's self-defense doctrine required proof that the defendant felt an imminent threat, and that "a defendant's subjective belief of what might be 'inevitable' at some indefinite point in the future does not equate to what she believes to be 'imminent.' " *Id.* at 14.

When allowed, BWS can be an effective mechanism to explain why battered women believe that they are in imminent danger and must use deadly force against their batterers. It emphasizes the importance of past threats and the severity of the anticipated future harm in understanding how domestic violence affects the victim, with the goal of explaining to courts and juries the reasonableness of the defendant's belief in the need to engage in self-defense and the reasons why retreat was not possible. Most courts today allow expert testimony about BWS in domestic violence-related homicide cases. *See* Leigh Goodmark, *When is a Battered Woman Not a Battered Woman? When She Fights Back*, 20 Yale J. L. & Feminism 75, 84 (2008).

Professor Elizabeth M. Schneider has argued that in accepting expert testimony on BWS, courts are acknowledging the following: "first, that women act in self-defense under different circumstances and in different ways than men; second, that the law of self-defense incorporates sex bias; and third, that sex-based stereotypes of women generally, and battered or raped women specifically, interfere with jurors' determinations of their claims." Elizabeth M. Schneider, Battered Women & Feminist Lawmaking 132 (2000).

Many states that allow expert testimony regarding BWS have developed gender-neutral terms for the syndrome, such as "Battering and Its Effects" or "Battered Spouse Syndrome." Some of these states recognize the gender-neutral term through statute, some through case law. For example, Nevada allows the admission of "evidence of domestic violence and expert testimony concerning the effect of domestic violence, including, without limitation, the effect of physical, emotional or mental abuse, on the beliefs, behavior and perception of the alleged victim of the domestic violence" in any criminal proceeding. Nev. Rev. Stat. § 48.061 (2008). While the gender-neutral terms include men who have experienced the impact of battering on their lives, it has been criticized because it omits any analysis of "the gendered experiences of women as a result of sexism, subordination, and stereotypical juror misperceptions." Gena Rachel Hatcher, Note, *The Gendered Nature of the Battered Woman Syndrome: Why Gender Neutrality Does Not Mean Equality*, 59 N.Y.U. Ann. Surv. Am. L. 21, 29–30, 40 (2003). Other states continue to allow testimony on the classic form of BWS, including issues of stereotyping and subordination of women in self-defense analysis.

In analyzing the utility of BWS, consider the reasons that courts would allow in evidence of it. Why might courts be hostile to BWS? As an attorney for battered women, what special challenges would arise from working with a client with BWS? How could BWS affect the attorney-client relationship? How might this affect the case? What stereotypes about battered women does BWS challenge, and which ones does it reinforce? See Goodmark, *supra*.

SECTION 3: CRIMINAL JUSTICE RESPONSE

A. ARREST

Police departments receive more calls reporting domestic violence than any other type of crime, and responses to these calls account for up to one-third of all police time. Yet, historically police departments have been reluctant to intervene by making arrests for domestic violence. For example, a 1984 study found that the typical police response to these calls was to do nothing but talk to the batterer; a similar study in 1985 reported that, even in incidents where the victim had been severely injured, 50% of the officers interviewed would not arrest the abuser. Catherine Popham Durant, Note, *When to Arrest: What Influences Police Determination to Arrest When There is a Report of Domestic Violence?*, 12 S. Cal. Rev. L. & Women's Stud. 301, 305–06 (2003). Reacting to pressure from battered women's advocates and to many civil lawsuits successfully challenging police policies and conduct, several jurisdictions by the 1980s started to enact legislation requiring changes in arrest policies for domestic violence offenses.

One of the earlier, and most significant, cases involving a civil challenge to a police domestic violence policy was *Thurman v. City of Torrington*, 595 F.Supp. 1521 (D. Conn. 1984). Between early October

1982 and June 1983, the police department ignored Thurman's repeated requests for its help in protecting her from her husband's threats against both her and her child. At one point, a police officer watched as her husband kicked her in the head, twice. Not until he approached her while she was lying on a stretcher did the police arrest him. In her lawsuit, she claimed that her constitutional rights had been violated by the "nonperformance or malperformance of official duties by the defendant police officers" and the city. *Id.* at 1524. The court held that "[a] man is not allowed to physically abuse or endanger a woman merely because he is her husband," and that a police officer may not " 'automatically decline to make an arrest simply because the assaulter and his victim are married to each other.' " *Id.* at 1528 (internal citation omitted). The jury awarded Thurman approximately $2.3 million for the police department's failure to respond to her repeated requests for assistance.

Thurman established that "the police policy of treating women and children abused by male relatives or friends differently from persons assaulted by strangers constituted sex discrimination under the Equal Protection Clause." Emily J. Sack, *Battered Women and the State: The Struggle for the Future of Domestic Violence Policy*, 2004 Wis. L. Rev. 1657, 1668 (2004). After additional lawsuits were brought around the country and as a result of direct pressure from women's advocates, many police departments and legislatures developed new arrest policies for domestic violence offenses. The movement for increased domestic violence enforcement was also supported by the publication of the results of the "Minneapolis Experiment" in 1984. The Minneapolis Experiment, a comprehensive study conducted by the Minneapolis Police Department with support from the National Institute of Justice, evaluated the effectiveness of different types of police responses to domestic violence cases. Police were randomly assigned to deal with domestic violence offenders in one of three ways: by arresting the offender, by mediating the dispute, or by requiring the offender to vacate the house for eight hours. To compare the relative success of the differing police responses, the researchers measured the frequency and seriousness of subsequent violence for the six months following the police intervention. The Experiment was limited with respect to the types of cases it included, and involved only misdemeanor domestic assaults where both the offender and the victim were present when the police arrived. It excluded cases where there were life-threatening or severe injuries.

The results from the Experiment showed that arresting the batterer had a significantly greater impact on reducing future incidents of domestic violence than did the other two police responses. According to the follow-up police reports, 10% of the arrested suspects, 19% of the mediated suspects, and 24% of the suspects removed for eight hours committed at least one repeat incident. The victims were also interviewed to determine their perceptions of repeat violence. The victims' reports showed that arrest was even more successful than indicated by the official police reports: according to their reports, 19% of the arrested suspects, 33% of the suspects sent away, and 37% of the advised suspects perpetrated at least one repeat attack during the follow-up period. Arrest was the most effective response according to both victims and police reports, and the U.S. Attorney General recommended that police departments make arrest their response to domestic violence cases. Lawrence W. Sherman, *The Influence of Criminology on Criminal Law: Evaluating Arrests for Misdemeanor Domestic Violence*, 83 J. Crim. L. & Criminology 1, 2, 16–20 (1992).

Consequently, jurisdictions have adopted policies of either "mandatory" arrest, which requires an arrest if the police have probable cause to believe that there has been an offense; or "preferred" arrest, which specifies that arrest is the "preferred" action where there is probable cause to believe that an offense has occurred. The data show that having either of these arrest policies in effect results in higher rates of arrest than in states without either policy. David Hirschel, Eve Buzawa, April Pattavina, Don Faggiani, *Domestic Violence and Mandatory Arrest Laws: To What Extent Do They Influence Police Arrest Decisions?* 98 J. Crim. L. & Criminology 255. 265, 296 (2007).

The Minneapolis Experiment's findings concerning the impact of arrest were somewhat controversial, and the study was replicated in five different cities across the country. The results of these studies qualified the initial findings in two ways. First, arrests for misdemeanor domestic assault varied in their effectiveness in different cities, and second, arrest affected the recidivism rates of abusers differently, based on factors such as whether the arrested person was employed. If the abuser was employed, then arrest served as more of a deterrent than if he were not working. Sherman, *supra*, at 25–30. Lawrence Sherman, one of the Minneapolis Experiment researchers, explained that "[w]hat may ultimately be acceptable * * * is different police policies or practices for different neighborhoods[,]" and that a "local option approach, informed by research on the specific deterrent effects of arrest in different communities, might be the best way to develop a workable policy from the findings." *Id.* at 43–44. Ultimately, "[t]he deterrent value of arrest is equivocal at best." C. Kristian Miccio, *A House Divided: Mandatory Arrest, Domestic Violence, and the Conservatization of the Battered Women's Movement,* 42 Hous. L. Rev. 237, 294 (2005).

In addition to its effects on recidivism, mandatory arrest may also "send a message to potential offenders, victims, and the community in general that domestic violence would be treated seriously as a crime by the justice system." Sack, *supra*, at 1678.

NOTES AND QUESTIONS

1. *Mandatory arrest.* Approximately 15–20 states and the District of Columbia have enacted mandatory arrest legislation. Studies have shown that mandatory arrest policies have significantly increased the number of arrests of batterers for domestic violence crimes. In Washington, D.C., for example,

the police arrested in 5% of domestic violence cases in 1990, but shortly after enactment of mandatory arrest legislation, the arrest rate increased to "41% of all domestic violence calls. In New York City, from 1993, the time the mandatory arrest policy was instituted, to 1999, felony domestic violence arrests increased 33%, misdemeanor domestic violence arrests rose 114%, and arrests for violation of orders of protection were up 76%." Sack, *supra*, at 1671–72.

2. *Conflicting opinions on mandatory arrest.* Advocates of mandatory arrest laws assert that arresting the batterer provides him a warning that he has committed criminal acts, and that the state will sanction him for the violence. For the victim, mandatory arrest laws provide support by letting her know that domestic violence is not her fault, but is instead part of a larger problem for which the state will take responsibility. Finally, because mandatory arrest—at least temporarily—removes the batterer and calls into play broader systems of social support, it can provide the victim with a temporary respite from the abusive relationship so that she can seek counseling, develop a safety plan, and think about possibilities for leaving the abuser. Nichole Miras Mordini, Note, *Mandatory State Interventions for Domestic Abuse Cases: An Examination of the Effects on Victim Safety and Autonomy*, 52 Drake L. Rev. 295, 315–16 (2004). On the other hand, opponents of mandatory arrest statutes suggest that police should defer to the victims' wishes and respect their ability to make their own choices. In addition, a victim may not want the abuser arrested for a variety of reasons, such as because she is economically dependent on him. *Id.* at 316. Moreover, criminalization is "insufficient public policy" * * * [because it] does not address battered women's need for housing and economic or emotional support." Miccio, *supra*, at 295.

Do you think mandatory arrest is a good policy? Lawrence W. Sherman, one of the Minneapolis Experiment researchers, argued that instead of mandatory arrest, police should adopt arrest as a preferred policy (depending on further research). Sherman, *supra*, at 21–22. Is that a better approach?

B. PROSECUTION

Once mandatory arrest laws were put in place, many domestic violence advocates addressed a second part of the criminal justice problem: the practices of prosecutors. Depending on the jurisdiction, prosecutors dismissed between 50% and 80% of domestic violence cases. However, as the numbers of domestic violence arrests have increased, many prosecutors have begun to endorse "no-drop" policies. Deborah Epstein, Margaret E. Bell, and Lisa A. Goodman, *Transforming Aggressive Prosecution Policies: Prioritizing Victims' Long–Term Safety in the Prosecution of Domestic Violence Cases*, 11 Am. U. J. Gender Soc. Pol'y & L. 465, 466 (2003). A no-drop policy means that it is the prosecutor's decision, not the victim's, of whether to proceed with prosecution of a domestic violence case. Hard no-drop jurisdictions require prosecutors to pursue the cases regardless of the victims' wishes and may also require victims to testify, even if they must be subpoenaed. Soft no-drop jurisdictions encourage victims to participate but provide prosecutors with discretion to drop, depending on the extent of the victims' participation.

Many prosecutors' offices have also adopted a "vertical prosecution" approach, pursuant to which one prosecutor is assigned to handle a case from beginning to end. Such an approach can ensure that information is not lost if a file is transferred between prosecutors, that the victim deals with only one primary person, and may promote consistency. Sack, *supra*, at 1673. Additionally, some states require creation of special prosecution units that handle only domestic violence cases. For example, the Florida statute provides: "Each state attorney shall develop special units or assign prosecutors to specialize in the prosecution of domestic violence cases * * *. These prosecutors, specializing in domestic violence cases, and their support staff shall receive training in domestic violence issues." Fla. Stat. § 741.2901 (2008).

NOTES AND QUESTIONS

1. *Supporters of no-drop policies.* The competing arguments for no-drop policies are similar to those for mandatory arrest. Proponents claim that domestic violence is a public issue, and that the state—not victims—should be responsible for holding batterers accountable for their actions; that it may be difficult for victims to appreciate fully the reasons for prosecuting; and that aggressive no-drop policies take the burden of going forward off the victim because, unlike in civil actions, she is not the "plaintiff." Mordini, *supra*, at 317–20.

2. *Opponents of no-drop policies.* By contrast, opponents of no-drop policies argue that the policies deprive a victim of her right to autonomous decisionmaking and may actually place her in further danger because the batterer will blame the victim for the prosecution. Opponents also argue that no-drop policies force the victim into a situation where she feels that she has no control, and that, consequently, she may be reluctant to call the police for help in jurisdictions that have instituted no-drop policies. *Id.*

Do you think that no-drop policies do more harm or good? Should victims be required to participate in prosecuting their batterer? Should the focus be on what is best for society or for the individual victim, or is there no conflict?

A domestic violence victim may be seeking different results from criminal justice intervention than other crime victims. She may simply be seeking an end to ongoing violence, rather than punishment for past violence. Mordini, *supra*, at 319. According to Linda G. Mills, mandatory prosecution does not necessarily protect the victim from abuse; instead, the effect may be to "align the battered woman with her batterer, to protect him, and to further entrench her in the abusive relationship." Linda G. Mills, *Intuition and Insight: A New Job Description for the Battered Woman's Prosecutor and Other More Modest Proposals*, 7 UCLA Women's L.J. 183, 191 (1997).

3. *No-contact orders.* Courts often issue criminal no-contact orders barring a criminal domestic violence defendant from contact with the victim. These orders, which may be issued in addition to the civil orders discussed above, are often a condition of pre-trial release or a condition of sentencing. No-contact orders can prohibit the defendant from returning to the home, or from being in the victim's presence at other places such as where the victim

works. Most jurisdictions do not require that these orders be issued, although they are quite common. As of 2002, five states (Alaska, Rhode Island, Colorado, South Dakota, and Utah) mandated issuance of no-contact orders in intimate violence cases. Deborah Epstein, *Procedural Justice: Tempering the State's Response to Domestic Violence*, 43 Wm. & Mary L. Rev. 1843, 1858 (2002). For example, the Rhode Island statute states: "Because of the likelihood of repeated violence directed at those who have been victims of domestic violence in the past, when a person is charged with or arrested for a crime involving domestic violence, * * * [the court] shall issue a no-contact order prohibiting the person charged or arrested from having contact with the victim." R.I. Gen. Laws § 12–29–4(a)(1) (2004).

Not all abused woman, however, wish to end their relationship with their batterer. These men can be their partners, providers, the fathers of their children and their security. Women may also view leaving a relationship, especially a marriage, as a disgrace or a sign of failure. Additionally, many women do not wish to see their partner punished for the abusive acts. They are not out for retribution, but peace. These women want the relationship to continue but the violence to stop. Other stay-away or no-contact orders exist which prohibit violence, but allow contact between the parties to continue. According to Sally F. Goldfarb, "...the law's response to domestic violence should support, rather than undermine, women's role as autonomous decision-makers." Sally F. Goldfarb, *Reconceiving Civil Protection Orders for Domestic Violence: Can Law Help End the Abuse Without Ending the Relationship?*, 29 Card. L. Rev. 1487, 1489 (2008). These stay-away orders put the power back in the hands of victim and arguably allow for the woman to control her own relationship.

4. *Batterer intervention programs.* Batterer intervention programs were established in the late 1970s as a tool to end domestic violence. These programs focus on changing the perpetrators' behavior and attitudes. They are often court-mandated and usually defer trial, conviction or sentencing of a batterer pending participation in the treatment program. Approximately half of the states have developed guidelines for batterer intervention programs.

There are numerous types of programs for batterers, but they are generally based on three distinct approaches to domestic violence: (1) the psychotherapeutic approach focuses on the abuser and holds that life experiences influence some people to commit violence; (2) the family systems approach regards the violence as a symptom of a problematic family and blames both partners in the relationship; and (3) the feminist approach focuses on the batterer's cultural conditioning concerning male dominance. Amanda Dekki, Note, *Punishment or Rehabilitation? The Case for State–Mandated Guidelines for Batterer Intervention Programs in Domestic Violence Cases*, 18 St. John's J. Legal Comment. 549, 566–68 & nn. 66–68 (2004). The feminist approach has been praised for not treating victims as complicit participants, but it has also been criticized for emphasizing socio-cultural factors rather than individual characteristics. *Id*. at 567–68 & n.68.

Many batterer intervention programs are based on a model developed by the Domestic Abuse Intervention Project of Duluth, Minnesota. *Id*. at 568. The programs typically involve classes designed to teach batterers various means of interaction. Often, the classes are taught by one female and one male counselor who are supposed to model healthy behaviour in intimate relationships. In addition, the programs contemplate court-designated probation officers whose role is to monitor and report on the batterers' program compliance. If the batterer successfully completes the program, charges are generally dismissed. *Id*. at 572. Counselors also familiarize victims with the goals and methods of the program, and victims are informed of their abuser's progress. *Id*. at 571.

Research on the impact of batterer intervention programs shows that they may be effective in helping men change their behaviors, but the programs' effectiveness in preventing recidivism remain unclear. Goldfarb, *supra*, at 1549. Some studies have found significant reductions—more than 50%—in the amount of physical abuse perpetrated by batterers after their participation in these programs, with long-term programs more effective than short-term programs. However, research is limited concerning which components of batterers' treatment programs are most effective. Dekki, *supra*, at 573–74. Moreover, critics of the programs argue that these programs lull victims into believing that the batterer has been cured, when this may not be accurate. On the other hand, because victims often return to their batterers even if they did not enter a treatment program, then at least abuser attendance provides some protection for some victims. *Id*. at 575–76.

5. *Specialized domestic violence court programs*. Many state courts have adopted special domestic violence court programs to address domestic violence issues more effectively. Most of the courts employ an interdisciplinary system of handling domestic violence. For example, in New York City and Washington, D.C., courts have combined the civil and criminal aspects of the court docket. Often these programs provide for the coordination of police departments, prosecutors, and courts. Another improvement to judicial approaches is the additional and specialized training of court personnel who are responsible for handling domestic violence cases. *See* Jennifer Thompson, Comment, *Who's Afraid of Judicial Activism? Reconceptualizing a Traditional Paradigm in the Context of Specialized Domestic Violence Court Programs*, 56 Me. L. Rev. 407 (2004).

SECTION 4:   OTHER ASPECTS OF ABUSE

A.   DOMESTIC VIOLENCE AND CHILD CUSTODY

Domestic violence has significant implications for child custody, an issue discussed further in Chapter 12. In 40% to 60% of domestic violence cases where children are in the home, batterers who abuse their partners also abuse the children. Research shows that, as a result of simply witnessing domestic violence in the home, children may suffer emotional, behavioral, and developmental difficulties. Many children in these homes experience anxiety and depression, perform poorly in school, and may behave aggressively toward others. Deborah M. Goelman, *Shelter from the Storm: Using Jurisdictional Statutes to Protect Victims of Domestic Violence After the Violence Against Women Act of 2000*, 13 Colum. J. Gender & L. 101, 108–10 (2004).

Indeed, every year, "between three and ten million children are forced to witness the emotional devastation of one parent abusing or killing the other. Many children are injured in the 'crossfire' while trying to protect the assaulted parent." Donna Wills, *Domestic Violence: The Case for Aggressive Prosecution*, 7 UCLA Women's L.J. 173, 175 (1997).

In deciding between parents, virtually all states now have statutes permitting or requiring that courts consider domestic violence as one factor in a custody award. Other statutes also recognize the interrelationship between domestic violence and custody determinations. The custody-oriented legislation can be divided into three categories. First, some statutes require courts to consider domestic violence before awarding joint or sole custody. For example, the Indiana statute directs courts to consider a series of factors in deciding child custody, including "[e]vidence of a pattern of domestic or family violence by either parent." Ind. Code Ann. § 31–17–2–8 (7) (West 2008).

Second, some statutes create a presumption against awarding custody to a batterer. For example, Massachusetts provides that a "court's finding, by a preponderance of the evidence, that a pattern or serious incident of abuse has occurred shall create a rebuttable presumption that it is not in the best interests of the child to be placed in sole custody, shared legal custody or shared physical custody with the abusive parent." M.G.L.A. 208, § 31A (West 2008).

A third set of statutes direct courts to take domestic violence into account when making other decisions, such as determining whether a parent has abandoned her children by fleeing domestic violence, or when establishing visitation arrangements. For example, Rhode Island's custody statute permits courts to condition visitation or custody on a domestic violence perpetrator's completion of a batterer's program; where the court has made a finding of domestic violence, the court must "consider as primary the safety and well-being of the child and of the parent who is the victim of domestic or family violence." R.I. Gen. Laws § 15–5–16 (g)(2) (2008). Alabama legislation specifies that the rebuttable presumption against relocation of the custodial parent and the children does not apply where the court finds that the party objecting to the relocation has committed domestic violence. Ala. Code 1975 § 30–3–169.4 (2008).

Because parents are presumed fit to raise their children, the law presumes that their custodial rights trump those of all third parties. Only a few states have statutes that, as a matter of law, prevent an abusive parent who has killed the other parent from prevailing in a custody battle against a third party such as the grandparents. Notwithstanding the increased sensitivity to domestic violence, Professor Joan Meier has concluded that trial courts are granting custody to batterers "more often than not." Joan S. Meier, *Domestic Violence, Child Custody, and Child Protection: Understanding Judicial Resistance and Imagining the Solutions*, 11 Am. U.J. Gender Soc. Pol'y & L. 657, 662 (2003).

Note and Question

In most states, it is difficult to deny visitation completely to the noncusto-dial parent absent extraordinary circumstances, an issue discussed further in Chapters 12 and 13. Proof of violence between the adults is rarely a sufficient basis. Nonetheless, because of the potential for abuse inherent in transferring children between parents, many courts consider mandating supervised visita-tion or imposing other conditions on visitation. Courts hearing testimony on a custodial parent's fear of further violence may order restrictions on visitation to ensure the safety of the child and the victim, regardless of whether the jurisdiction has explicit legislative directives.

What conditions might a court want to impose on visitation in cases involving domestic violence? Which conditions would protect the victim? Which conditions would protect the child?

B. DOMESTIC VIOLENCE AND MEDIATION

As Chapter 15 discusses, family court systems often encourage or require mediation before parties may proceed to court in divorce cases and other domestic disputes. In 1981, California became the first state to mandate mediation in domestic disputes, including those in which domes-tic violence is alleged. California does not exempt domestic violence victims from mandated mediation under any circumstances. California does, however, allow the mediator to meet with the parties separately, and allows the abused party to bring a "support person" into mediation. Ten other states mandate family mediation, but allow exceptions in domestic violence cases. For example, Colorado courts may not order mediation where one party claims prior physical or psychological abuse. Legislation in 43 states and the District of Columbia regulates family mediation in some form. *See* Alana Dunnigan, Comment, *Restoring Power to the Power-less: The Need to Reform California's Mandatory Mediation for Victims of Domestic Violence*, 37 U.S.F. L. Rev. 1031, 1034–37 (2003). Some jurisdic-tions permit the parties themselves to decide whether mediation is appro-priate, while others require that the court decide. For example, in Dela-ware, if there has been a court order concerning domestic violence, then custody and visitation disputes are excluded from mediation unless the victim and her lawyer request otherwise. Del. Code tit. 13, § 711A (2008).

Battered women's advocates disagree about whether the law should mandate—or even permit—mediation in domestic disputes in which one party alleges domestic violence. Many advocates contend that domestic violence undermines the voluntary participation, equal bargaining power and confidentiality that mark mediation. For example, opponents claim that mandatory mediation reinforces the victim's lack of power and control. *See* Dunnigan, *supra*, at 1041. They also argue that mandatory mediation places the victim at risk for additional abuse, and may result in agreements that do not adequately protect the victim. She may be unable to articulate her own needs because she is so intimidated by the abuser or because she may fear retaliation.

On the other hand, some commentators contend that mediation may be suited for divorce and child custody disputes even where domestic violence is present. They claim that mediation requires parties to take responsibility for their past and to set boundaries for their future. Victims might also take a passive role in an adversary system, but mediation forces both parties to take an active role and cooperate. "[B]y serving as a model of effective communication, mediation assists batterers and victims change their behavioral patterns which in turn decreases the risk of future violence." Holly Joyce, *Mediation and Domestic Violence: Legislative Responses*, 14 J. Am. Acad. Matrim. L. 447, 456 (1997).

Chapter 15 further discusses domestic violence and other gender-related issues that may affect the advisability and conduct of family mediation.

QUESTIONS

If you were representing a victim of domestic violence in divorce, would you suggest that the case be mediated? What factors would affect your recommendation?

If you did choose to go to mediation, what steps would you take to ensure your client's comfort? How would you prepare her for mediation?

SECTION 5: SAME–SEX PARTNER ABUSE

While male-to-female abuse is the most common form of domestic violence, gay men and lesbians also experience partner abuse in their relationships. The National Coalition of Anti–Violence Programs documented a record 3,534 reported incidents of same-sex domestic violence in 2006. This was a 15% decrease in the number of cases reported by the same organization from 2005. In the 2006 cases, there appeared to be equal incidents of domestic violence among both gay and lesbian relationships. *Lesbian, Gay, Bisexual and Transgender Domestic Violence In The United States in 2006*. A Report of the National Coalition of Anti–Violence Programs.   http://www.ncavp.org/common/document_files/Reports/2006 NationalDVReport(Final).pdf.

Despite the statistics, same-sex domestic violence has received comparatively little attention from the gay and lesbian and domestic violence communities. The gay and lesbian communities have been reluctant to confront the problem because domestic violence risks reinforcing negative stereotypes as they seek to secure legal recognition of other rights. According to Nancy Knauer, the domestic violence movement has given same-sex violence less attention because "the existence of domestic violence in the absence of gender differences presents a direct challenge to the feminist construction of domestic violence as a gender-specific deployment of power and violence." Nancy Knauer, *Same–Sex Domestic Violence: Claiming a Domestic Sphere While Risking Negative Stereotypes*, 8 Temp. Pol. & Civ. Rts. L. Rev. 325, 328 (1999).

Notwithstanding the lack of attention to same-sex domestic violence, the vast majority of protective order statutes are written in gender-neutral language and thus are available to victims of same-sex domestic violence. For example, Colorado extends protection to victims with whom the batterer "is living or has lived in the same domicile," or with whom the batterer is "involved or has been involved in an intimate relationship." Colo. Rev. Stat. § 13–14–101(2) (2008). A few states, including Hawaii, Illinois, Kentucky, New Jersey, Ohio and Pennsylvania, have made domestic violence protection explicitly available to victims of same-sex domestic violence. A few states (Delaware, Louisiana, North Carolina, and South Carolina) have statutes that narrowly define the class of people who can obtain a protective order and exclude individuals in same-sex relationships. Ruth Colker, *Marriage Mimicry: The Law of Domestic Violence*, 47 Wm. & Mary L. Rev. 1841, 1858 (2006).

With the enactment of statutes barring gay marriage that are discussed further in Chapter 3, states have considered the ongoing applicability of domestic violence protections to same-sex relationships. In 2006, the Virginia Attorney General issued an advisory opinion on the effect of legislative proposals banning same-sex marriages or comparable relationships on domestic violence protection for same-sex partners. The existing domestic violence criminal statute prohibited acts against someone defined as a "family or household member," which was, in turn, defined as a spouse or a cohabitant. The Attorney General opined that applying the statute would not give a cohabitant the same status or rights as a spouse, and that the legislature had recognized that cohabitants deserved domestic violence protection. He concluded: "Passage of the amendment, therefore, would not prevent prosecution of an individual cohabiting in a same-sex or other unmarried relationship for assault and battery of the other individual." Commonwealth of Virginia Office of the Attorney General, *Official Advisory Opinion* 11–12 (Sept. 14, 2006), available at http://www.vaag.com/OPINIONS/2006opns/06–003Newmanetal.pdf.

NOTES AND QUESTIONS

1. *Same-sex abuse, gender, and domestic violence.* Does same-sex partner abuse challenge conventional images of domestic violence? Professor Elizabeth M. Schneider has argued for a comprehensive redefinition of battering relationships, pointing out that the traditional model explaining domestic violence in terms of "patriarchal control" fails when "the violent partner is a woman, or the victim is a man." Elizabeth M. Schneider, *Particularity and Generality: Challenges of Feminist Theory and Practice in Work on Woman–Abuse*, 67 N.Y.U. L. Rev. 520, 543 (1992). However, other legal scholars have pointed out that states have broadened their laws to include same-sex domestic violence by simply removing gender references from their statutes. Such a change has, according to some critics, had the unintended effect of removing the focus of domestic violence laws from patriarchy. Additionally, this method does not typically address the unique needs of victims of domestic violence in same-sex relationships, because the abuse may take different forms. Shannon

Little, Note, *Challenging Changing Legal Definitions of Family in Same–Sex Domestic Violence*, 19 Hastings Women's L.J. 259 (2008).

2. *Mimicking marriage.* Professor Ruth Colker has alleged that domestic violence laws are premised on protecting only those in a marital-type relationship "in that they are characterized by two people who have financial interdependence, share an intimate relationship, live in the same household, and have a long-term commitment to the relationship." Colker, *supra*, at 1845. Such a model may be difficult to apply in same-sex relationships, as well as in a series of other situations, such as a woman who is intimately involved with a man but does not live with him (perhaps because he is married to someone else), or victims in other family-type relationships, like stepmothers. *Id.* at 1870, 1881. Are there other groups who are left out by existing statutes? Should these groups be covered?

SECTION 6: MARITAL ASSAULT AND RAPE

Since the seventeenth century, the marital rape exemption has provided that a man is legally incapable of raping his wife. Various explanations have been offered for the affirmative defense. English common law defined rape as *unlawful* intercourse with a female without her consent. It has been suggested that the marital rape exemption is derived from this definition because intercourse between husband and wife is not unlawful. Some commentators have also theorized that the exemption originates from the traditional belief that marriage constitutes blanket consent to sexual intercourse by both spouses. Others have claimed that marital immunity comes from the traditional notion that a wife is merely a possession of her husband, or that marriage is a unity in the name of the husband, and the husband cannot rape himself.

Justifications for the English common law exemption originated in Sir Mathew Hale's *The History of the Pleas of the Crown*, which was first published in England in 1736. Hale, who was a Chief Justice of the Court of King's Bench, wrote a treatise that became extraordinarily influential to American legal commentaries. Hale stated, " 'the husband cannot be guilty of a rape committed by himself upon his lawful wife, for by their mutual matrimonial consent and contract the wife hath given up herself in this kind to her husband, which she cannot retract.' " Theresa Fus, Note, *Criminalizing Marital Rape: A Comparison of Judicial and Legislative Approaches*, 39 Vand. J. Transnat'l L. 481, 483 (2006). Hale's assertion that a husband is entitled to sexual intercourse, and his theories on marital rape, were generally accepted as law in English courts and later in American courts.

The Model Penal Code preserves this traditional marital exemption. Section 213.1 defines the act of "rape" as sexual intercourse between a male and a "female not his wife," and section 213.4 defines sexual assault as sexual contact between a person and another "not his spouse." The 1962 Commentary to the exemption mirrors Hale's analysis on unending consent: "[M]arriage ... while not amounting to a legal waiver of the woman's right to say 'no,' does imply a kind of generalized consent.... The relationship itself creates a presumption of consent, valid until revoked." Model Penal Code § 213.1 cmt. 8(c)(Proposed Official Draft 1962 & Revised Comments 1980).

In the last several decades, states have widely reconsidered their approaches to the marital rape exemption. In 1984, the New York Court of Appeals abolished the marital rape exemption in that state. *See People v. Liberta*, 474 N.E.2d 567 (N.Y. 1984). (Ironically, the opinion was written by Judge Sol Wachtler, who later went to prison for stalking a woman.) Mr. Liberta and his wife were legally separated, were not cohabiting, and were subject to a protective order issued by the court. The lower court dismissed the indictment based on the marital rape exemption. The Court of Appeals (the state's highest court) held that the spousal exemption violated the Fourteenth Amendment's Equal Protection Clause. The court stated that the exemption demonstrated no rational basis for distinguishing between marital and nonmarital rape. *Liberta* marked the beginning of judicial attentiveness to this spousal immunity, and many other states have abolished the traditional spousal exemptions by decision or statute.

NOTES AND QUESTIONS

1. *Current approaches.* As of 2003, 24 states and the District of Columbia had abolished marital immunity for sexual offenses. Marital immunity is still retained in 26 states in some form. In many of these states, there is no marital immunity for forcible rape, but marital immunity for other sexual offenses is preserved. For instance, 20 states allow marital immunity for sex with a partner who is incapacitated or unconscious, and cannot consent. In 15 states marital immunity is granted unless specific requirements such as prompt complaint, extra force, separation, or divorce are met. Michelle J. Anderson, *Marital Immunity, Intimate Relationships, and Improper Inferences: A New Law on Sexual Offenses by Intimates*, 54 Hastings L.J. 1465, 1468–73 (2003).

Arizona and South Carolina statutes explicitly distinguished rape or sexual assault committed by spouses from rape or sexual assault committed by strangers. *Id.* at 1490. These states mandated lesser penalties for spousal rape than for other rapes, regardless of the force used or injury caused. For example, in Arizona, it is a defense to certain sexual offenses that the defendant and the victim were married. Ariz. Rev. Stat. § 13–1407 D (2008).

Additionally, many states have imposed more stringent requirements for proving the elements of rape when it occurs within a marriage. In Oklahoma, for example, rape only exists within marriage if the offender uses or threatens to use force or violence. 21 Okla. Stat. 1111 (2008). Tennessee amended its law to treat marital rape like other forms of rape only in 2005.

Overall, although marital rape exemptions are slowly diminishing, and are being replaced by laws with no distinction between marital or non-marital rape, many states continue to include some form of marital rape immunity within their penal systems. Some proponents of treating marital rape differently argue that "spousal sexual offenses are not as harmful as other rapes, so they do not warrant harsh criminal sanctions ... [and] the exemption promotes marital reconciliation and the resumption of normal marital relations ... and ... there is a need to prevent vindictive wives from pursuing false charges." Morgan Lee Woolley, *Marital Rape: A Unique Blend of Domestic Violence and Non–Marital Rape Issues*, 18 Hastings Women's L.J. 269, 280–281 (2007).

If you were a state legislator, which approach would you support?

2. *Marital rape in practice.* As in any other forcible rape case, the prosecution in a marital rape case must prove that the intercourse that gave rise to the charge was not consensual. Even where spouses have separated, defense counsel may successfully raise doubt in the jurors' minds about consent when the couple considered reconciling.

SECTION 7:   THE FEDERAL VIOLENCE AGAINST WOMEN ACT

In 1994, Congress enacted the Violence Against Women Act (VAWA) to provide women a legal remedy for violence motivated by gender. Pub. L. No. 103–322, 108 Stat. 1902. The goals of the Act included enhancing the justice system's protection for battered women and expanding collaboration and cooperation between support services for battered women and the criminal and civil justice systems. VAWA provides funds for many services within and outside of the legal system, including police, prosecutors, battered women service providers, and state domestic violence coalitions. For example, Title II of VAWA, as amended in 2000, provides for legal assistance, shelter services, and transitional housing assistance for victims of domestic violence and their children. Pub. L. No. 106–386, 1201–1300, 114 Stat. 1491, 1504–09 (2000) (codified as amended in scattered sections of 42 U.S.C.). This Title also authorizes a national domestic violence hotline, federal counselors for victims, and provides funding "[t]o develop policies, educational programs, and training in police departments to improve tracking of cases involving domestic violence and dating violence." 42 U.S.C. § 3796hh(b)(2) (2008). The legislation requires that full faith and credit be accorded civil protection orders issued in another state. 18 U.S.C. § 2265 (2008). VAWA was again reauthorized by Congress in December 2005 and was signed into law by President George W. Bush on January 5, 2006.

During the four years of hearings leading to the original enactment of VAWA, supporters emphasized the need to change the country's tolerance for violence against women. When an early version of VAWA was being considered, the Judiciary Committee report stated:

> Our country has an unfortunate blind spot when it comes to certain crimes against women. Historically, crimes against women have been perceived as anything but crime—as a "family" problem, as a "private" matter, as sexual "miscommunication." * * * Until we name a problem, we cannot hope to see it for what it is. And until we name all

violence against women as crime, it will be seen neither as violence nor as crime.

S. Rep. No. 102–97, at 37 (1991) (Conf. Rep.).

Since VAWA was signed into law in 1994, it has made a critical difference in the lives of women. More than $1.5 billion in funds have supported victim advocates, social service professionals, and the work of prosecutors in support of domestic violence victims. Deborah M. Goelman, *Shelter from the Storm: Using Jurisdictional Statutes to Protect Victims of Domestic Violence after the Violence Against Women Act of 2000*, 13 Colum. J. Gender & L. 101, 148 (2004).

NOTES AND QUESTIONS

1. *VAWA's broad scope.* VAWA includes many provisions aimed at mitigating the impact of domestic violence on citizens and immigrant women. The statute also created new federal crimes and criminal penalties for perpetrators, and a private civil rights cause of action for gender-motivated crimes of violence.

In 2000, the Supreme Court struck down VAWA's civil remedy for gender-motivated crimes of violence. In *United States v. Morrison*, 529 U.S. 598 (2000), the Court held that Congress exceeded its Commerce Clause powers because gender-motivated violence was not an economic activity. The Supreme Court also held that the provision exceeded Congress's Enforcement Clause power under Section Five of the Fourteenth Amendment, stating that the Clause does not give Congress authority to create a cause of action against a private actor to remedy state discrimination. For a critique of the Court's decision, see Sally F. Goldfarb, *The Supreme Court, the Violence Against Women Act, and the Use and Abuse of Federalism*, 71 Fordham L. Rev. 57 (2002). It is important to note that *Morrison* overturned only one VAWA provision, the private federal civil remedy for gender-motivated crimes of violence.

Lower courts have rejected constitutional challenges to VAWA's criminal remedies. For example, VAWA makes it a crime for a person to travel across a state line: (1) "with intent to kill, injure, harass, or intimidate a spouse or intimate partner" and, in the course of travel, "commit[ ] or attempt[ ] to commit a crime of violence;" or (2) to cause a spouse or intimate partner to cross a state line by "force, coercion, duress, or fraud" that results in the person committing or attempting to commit a crime of violence. 18 U.S.C. § 2261(a)(1)-(2) (2003). Notwithstanding *Morrison*, several lower courts have upheld this provision because it regulates channels of interstate commerce used to facilitate domestic violence. *See, e.g., United States v. Al–Zubaidy*, 283 F.3d 804, 812 (6th Cir. 2002).

2. *VAWA 2000.* On October 28, 2000, Congress enacted the Violence Against Women Act of 2000, which renewed and amended many of VAWA's provisions. Pub L. No. 106–386, Div. B, 114 Stat. 1491 (2000) (codified as amended in scattered sections of 8, 20, 28 & 42 U.S.C.).

Among other changes, Title IV establishes a federal Domestic Violence Task Force, and allocates funds for education and training efforts designed to end domestic violence against women with disabilities. 42 U.S.C. § 3796gg–97(a) (2003). This Title also funds training for judges and court personnel that includes coverage of "the extent to which addressing domestic violence and victim safety contributes to the efficient administration of justice." *Id.* §§ 13991, 13992(22) (2003).

3. *Battered Immigrant Women Protection Act of 2000.* Title V of VAWA 2000 attempted to remedy problems with implementation of VAWA's provisions relating to immigrants; the statute was supplemented with yet additional remedies in 2005. The 1994 act had provided that immigrant women could apply for legal residency without support from their batterers so long as certain conditions were met. Subsequent enactments of VAWA have attempted to ameliorate some of the barriers in this process and have tried to limit an abuser's ability to interfere with a victim's citizenship application. *See* Kerry Abrams, *Immigration Law and the Regulation of Marriage*, 91 Minn. L. Rev. 1625, 1695–96 (2007). For example, VAWA now provides protection for a domestic violence victim "who demonstrates a connection between the legal termination of the marriage within the past 2 years and battering or extreme cruelty by the United States citizen spouse." 8 U.S.C.A. § 1154(a)(1)(A)(iii)(II)(aa)(CC) (2008).

SECTION 8: CHILD ABUSE AND NEGLECT

Domestic violence against an adult may be accompanied by abuse or neglect of one or more of the children in the household. The parental conduct may take the form of physical abuse, such as beating or punching, sexual abuse, emotional abuse, or neglect of their children's needs. Civil protection orders may protect children, but it is the government's abuse and neglect system that focuses on protecting children from harmful parental conduct.

Abuse or neglect of children is the primary cause of state inquiry into the privacy of family life outside the inquiries that may accompany family dissolution.

Three major systems regulate families when child abuse or neglect is suspected. The first is the criminal law, which, throughout most of our country's history, has prosecuted parents who abuse or neglect their children. The second is the child welfare system, which intervenes in poor families and which may work with the other systems. The third major system of regulation is the civil child protection system, which may provide services to abused or neglected children while they remain in their homes, or may remove children from their homes. These three systems are governed by local, state, and federal laws.

States have four types of laws dealing with abuse and neglect:

(a) *Reporting statutes* require specific people (such as physicians, teachers and law enforcement officials) to report suspected child abuse and neglect to the appropriate authorities, and permit other persons to make such reports;

(b) *Child protective statutes* provide services for children in families with suspected abuse and neglect, and govern possible removal of abused children from their homes on an emergency or long-term basis;

(c) *Criminal statutes* specify the circumstances when persons may be prosecuted for child abuse and neglect; and

(d) *Social services statutes* provide appropriate services for abused and neglected children.

Once the juvenile or family court has adjudicated a child abused or neglected, the court may remove the child from the home for placement in foster care, and also may require the family to participate in mandated services, including treatment that addresses safety and domestic violence.

The federally funded foster care system provides funding to care for children whose parents are unable or unwilling to care for them. Approximately one-half million children are currently in the foster care system. Children enter foster care when the state removes them based on abuse or neglect, or when parents voluntarily place their children in the system. Foster care is supposed to offer temporary out-of-home care in a family-like setting. And, yet, as Maxine Eichner observes, "[t]he difficulty that states have had administering and monitoring the foster care system means that children who enter it are far from assured a benign experience." Maxine Eichner, *Children, Parents, and the State: Rethinking Relationships in the Child Welfare System*, 12 Va. J. Soc. Pol'y & L. 448, 453 (2005).

Foster care has a long history. Traditionally, older children in Western culture entered out-of-home placement through indenture to learn a craft, work as a servant, or learn appropriate demeanor. In colonial Massachusetts, laws expressly empowered the Selectmen to place poor children with families other than their own. After indenture ceased to be a normal part of growing up for children of all social classes, placement in the presumptively worthy families of non-relatives remained a dominant option for the care of impoverished children. For about 100 years, beginning in the mid–19th century, philanthropic organizations or state and local governments arranged such out-of-home placements.

The Social Security Act of 1935, which provided for Aid to Dependent Children in their own homes, did not provide direct subsidies for the care of children not living with family members or close relatives. Beginning in 1961, the federal government authorized the use of federal funds to subsidize foster families. Over the past several decades, Congress has enacted two major pieces of legislation that have firmly established federal oversight of the foster care system.

Federal financial and regulatory involvement in state-run foster care systems expanded in 1980 with the passage of the Adoption Assistance and Child Welfare Act (AACWA). Pub. L. 96–272, 94 Stat. 500 (1980) (codified as amended at 42 U.S.C. §§ 620 to 628b, 670 to 679b (2008)). The AACWA attempted to federalize state foster care programs to some extent by establishing comprehensive standards for foster care systems. It also regularized federal reimbursements for state-approved foster care.

In 1997, Congress again enacted major legislation, the Adoption and Safe Families Act (ASFA), which confirmed federal government control over foster care. Pub. L. 105–89, 111 Stat. 2115 (1997) (codified as amended in scattered sections of 42 U.S.C.). The primary purpose of ASFA was to increase the number of children adopted from the foster care system; indeed, legislators named the bill the "Adoption Promotion Act" when it passed the House of Representatives. ASFA emphasizes the temporary nature of foster care. ASFA reiterates previous law in requiring states to make reasonable efforts to preserve and reunify existing families but places new emphasis on permanency planning and adoption. Rather than the previous focus on pursuing reunification before adoption, the new legislation allows for simultaneous pursuit of "reasonable efforts to place a child for adoption or with a legal guardian [and] reasonable efforts [to reunify families]." Pub. L. 105–89, 101, 111 Stat. 2115, 2117 (1997) (codified at 42 U.S.C. 671(a)(15) (2008)).

NATIONAL CLEARINGHOUSE ON CHILD ABUSE AND NEGLECT INFORMATION, U.S. DEP'T OF HEALTH AND HUMAN SERVS.

Definitions of Child Abuse and Neglect State Statute Series, 2007.
http://www.childwelfare.gov/systemwide/laws_policies/statutes/defineall.pdf.

* * *

Child abuse and neglect are defined by Federal and State law. The Child Abuse Prevention and Treatment Act (CAPTA) is the Federal legislation that provides minimum standards that States must incorporate in their statutory definitions of child abuse and neglect. The CAPTA definition of "child abuse and neglect" refers to:

> Any recent act or failure to act on the part of a parent or caretaker, which results in death, serious physical or emotional harm, sexual abuse, or exploitation, or an act or failure to act which presents an imminent risk of serious harm.

The CAPTA definition of "sexual abuse" includes:

> The employment, use, persuasion, inducement, enticement, or coercion of any child to engage in, or assist any other person to engage in, any sexually explicit conduct or simulation of such conduct for the purpose of producing a visual depiction of such conduct; or

> The rape, and in cases of caretaker or interfamilial relationships, statutory rape, molestation, prostitution, or other form of sexual exploitation of children, or incest with children.

Types of Abuse

All States, the District of Columbia, American Samoa, Guam, the Northern Mariana Islands, Puerto Rico, and the Virgin Islands provide definitions of child abuse and neglect in statute. As applied to reporting statutes, these definitions determine the grounds for State intervention in the protection of a child's well-being. States recognize the different types of abuse in their definitions, including physical abuse, neglect, sexual abuse, and emotional abuse. Some States also provide definitions in statute for parental substance abuse and/or for abandonment as child abuse.

Physical Abuse

Physical abuse is generally defined as "any nonaccidental physical injury to the child," and can include striking, kicking, burning, or biting the child, or any action that results in a physical impairment of the child. In approximately 36 States and American Samoa, Guam, the Northern Mariana Islands, Puerto Rico, and the Virgin Islands, the definition of abuse also includes acts or circumstances that threaten the child with harm or create a substantial risk of harm to the child's health or welfare.

Neglect

Neglect is frequently defined in terms of deprivation of adequate food, clothing, shelter, medical care, or supervision. Approximately 21 States and American Samoa, Puerto Rico, and the Virgin Islands include failure to educate the child as required by law in their definition of neglect. Seven States further define medical neglect as failing to provide any special medical treatment or mental health care needed by the child. In addition, four States define as medical neglect the withholding of medical treatment or nutrition from disabled infants with life-threatening conditions.

Sexual Abuse/Exploitation

All States include sexual abuse in their definitions. Some States refer in general terms to sexual abuse, while others specify various acts as sexual abuse. Sexual exploitation is an element of the definition of sexual abuse in most jurisdictions. Sexual exploitation includes allowing the child to engage in prostitution or in the production of child pornography.

Emotional Abuse

All States and territories except Georgia and Washington include emotional maltreatment as part of their definitions of abuse or neglect. Approximately 22 States, the District of Columbia, the Northern Mariana Islands, and Puerto Rico provide specific definitions of emotional abuse or mental injury to a child. Typical language used in these definitions is "injury to the psychological capacity or emotional stability of the child as evidenced by an observable or substantial change in behavior, emotional response, or cognition," or as evidenced by "anxiety, depression, withdrawal, or aggressive behavior."

Parental Substance Abuse

Parental substance abuse is an element of the definition of child abuse or neglect in some States. Circumstances that can be considered abuse or neglect include:

Prenatal exposure of a child to harm due to the mother's use of an illegal drug or other substance.

Manufacture of a controlled substance in the presence of child or on the premises occupied by a child

Allowing a child to be present where the chemicals or equipment for the manufacture of controlled substances are used or stored

Selling, distributing, or giving drugs or alcohol to a child

Use of a controlled substance by a caregiver that impairs the caregiver's ability to adequately care for the child

Abandonment

Many States and territories now provide definitions for child abandonment in their reporting laws. Approximately 18 States and the District of Columbia include abandonment in their definition of neglect. Approximately 13 States, Guam, Puerto Rico, and the Virgin Islands provide separate definitions for establishing abandonment. In general, it is considered abandonment of the child when the parent's identity or whereabouts are unknown, the child has been left by the parent in circumstances where the child suffers serious harm, or the parent has failed to maintain contact with the child or to provide reasonable support for a specified period of time.

Standards for Reporting

The standard for what constitutes an abusive act varies among the States. Many States define abuse in terms of harm or threatened harm to a child's health or welfare. Other standards commonly seen include "acts or omissions," "recklessly fails or refuses to act," "willfully causes or permits," and "failure to provide." These standards guide mandatory reporters in their decision on whether to make a report to child protective services.

* * *

Exceptions

A number of States provide exceptions in their reporting laws, which exempt certain acts or omissions from their statutory definitions of child abuse and neglect. For instance, in 11 States and the District of Columbia, financial inability to provide for a child is exempted from the definition of neglect. In 14 States, the District of Columbia, American Samoa, and the Northern Mariana Islands, physical discipline of a child, as long as it is reasonable and causes no bodily injury to the child, is an exception to the definition of abuse.

* * *

NOTES AND QUESTIONS

1. *Definitions.* If you were drafting a family violence statute, how would you define abuse and neglect? What exceptions would you include? Would you define partner abuse and child abuse differently? Should financial inability to provide for a child provide the basis for a neglect charge?

2. *Emotional abuse.* Committing domestic violence in the presence of a child can be the basis for a finding of emotional abuse. As discussed earlier, many children who witness domestic violence inflicted on a parent suffer profoundly adverse effects, including severe emotional and behavioral problems. Studies have shown that girls who witness domestic violence are more likely to be abused as adults, and that boys who witness the violence are more likely themselves to become abusers as adults. *See, e.g.,* Lois A. Weithorn, *Protecting Children from Exposure to Domestic Violence: The Use and Abuse of Child Maltreatment*, 53 Hastings L.J. 1 (2001).

Some states also criminalize "committing domestic violence in the presence of a child," *e.g.,* Idaho Code Ann. § 18–918(4) (2008), or permit prosecution under criminal child endangerment statutes, *see, e.g., People v. Johnson*, 740 N.E.2d 1075 (N.Y. 2000). Given other sanctions for domestic violence, should committing this violence while a child is present constitute a separate crime?

CHAPTER 7

TORT LAW

■ ■ ■

The preceding Chapter considered various "public law" responses, including criminal sanctions and orders of protection, to problems of domestic violence and abuse. This Chapter examines the availability of "private law" remedies through tort law for injury to family members and relationships. Just as public law affecting the family has been transformed in recent decades, with historic criminal immunities yielding to new social attitudes favoring intervention against family violence, tort law has moved—somewhat more haltingly—in the same direction.

Historically, courts barred almost all tort actions within the family. If a husband battered his wife or injured his children by negligently driving the family car, intra-family immunities precluded any tort remedy. At the same time, however, courts entertained a menagerie of tort actions against third parties for injuries to family-type relationships—including so-called "heart balm" actions for seduction, breach of promise to marry and alienation of affections. Today, the situation is almost reversed. Courts and legislatures have widely abolished the traditional "heart balm" torts against third parties, out of a sense that it is misguided or futile to provide legal redress for such intimate misconduct. At the same time, they have peeled away common-law immunities to permit a wide range of tort litigation between family members. Practical barriers, such as exclusions in insurance coverage, continue to deter some suits, but spouses and often parents and children are now generally permitted to sue one another for negligence, battery, infliction of emotional distress and other torts.

Notwithstanding the clear trend expanding tort law's reach into the family, abrogation of wholesale tort immunity has led to a number of subsidiary dilemmas. Tort law—like criminal law—continues to struggle with the need to balance society's interests in curbing harmful conduct with its respect for pluralism and family privacy. Thus, while opening the door to private remedies through tort law, courts and legislatures have suggested that conduct between family members should sometimes be judged by different and more forgiving standards than conduct between people with no familial relationship. What constitutes actionable "outrage" between strangers, for instance, may not trigger liability between family members; the usual "reasonableness" standard that governs negligence liability may not apply to childrearing judgments by parents.

Even if workable standards of family misconduct can be discerned, it is debatable whether the expansion of tort litigation within the family is consistent with policies favoring "no fault" divorce. Much of the divorce reform of the 1970s and 1980s sought to suppress judicial inquiries into marital fault as incompetent, counter-productive or wasteful, as discussed in Chapter 8. Allowing tort recovery for marital misbehavior may simply reintroduce the same inquiries in a new courtroom—or perhaps even the very same proceeding if the tort suit is joined with the divorce.

Finally, growing diversity in family life has forced courts and legislatures to decide whether to extend tort rules governing "family" to nontraditional relationships. Many states have been willing to extend domestic violence laws to protect nonmarital partners, but courts so far have been more reluctant to expand the boundaries of tort liability by providing recovery for injuries to cohabiting and other informal intimate relationships.

This Chapter surveys these and other issues. Section 1 describes the collapse of common-law intrafamilial tort immunities and identifies the pockets of immunity that remain in some jurisdictions. Section 2 considers the modern availability of tort recovery within the family. These actions often raise challenging questions of both substantive tort law—for instance, whether tort law should tolerate a larger measure of hurtful conduct between spouses than between strangers—and procedure—for instance, whether tort claims should be tried separately from or together with an action for divorce. Finally, Section 3 examines the modern availability of tort recovery against third parties for injuries to family-type relationships, exploring opposing developments in the law governing "heart balm" recovery (where liability is shrinking) and loss of consortium (where there are new calls to expand liability to cover non-traditional family relationships).

SECTION 1: THE RETREAT OF
FAMILY TORT IMMUNITIES

Traditionally, the common law barred one spouse from suing the other in tort. This immunity was rooted in the English common law rule, introduced in Chapter 4, that regarded husbands and wives as a single legal entity. In a world in which wives had to rely on their husbands to bring suit on their behalf, and in which husbands controlled their wives' property, the idea of a wife suing her husband seemed preposterous. The Married Women's Property Acts enacted throughout the United States in the nineteenth century, partially restoring to wives an independent legal identity and control over their own property, largely destroyed the original justification for interspousal immunity. Yet the immunity doctrine lived on for many more decades, based on new policy concerns such as the impact of tort litigation on family harmony and judicial resources and the danger of collusive actions designed to defraud insurance companies.

In addition to interspousal immunity, many jurisdictions have also recognized a parallel tort immunity shielding parents for injuries caused to their children. The historical roots of parent-child immunity are more recent, dating back to court decisions in the late 1800s. Beyond arguments based on family harmony, immunity in this context was further justified by respect for the authority of parents and a reluctance to second-guess their childrearing judgments.

In recent decades, courts have grown more skeptical about the rationales for family tort immunities and have incrementally cut back on their scope. Early decisions—a few dating as far back as 1917—chipped away at traditional immunities by allowing recovery in cases of domestic violence. *See Prosser v. Prosser*, 102 S.E. 787 (S.C. 1920); *Johnson v. Johnson*, 77 So. 335 (Ala. 1917). Additional cracks in immunity doctrine came later in negligence actions involving automobile accidents. Allowing such actions, courts reasoned, posed relatively little threat to family harmony because any recovery was almost certain to come from an insurance company rather than a loved one's pocket. *See, e.g., Transamerica Ins. Co. v. Royle*, 656 P.2d 820, 823–24 (Mont. 1983); *see also* Carl Tobias, *Interspousal Tort Immunity in America*, 23 Ga. L. Rev. 359 (1989). From there, tort liability was extended to other claims of negligent and intentional injury. As a result, interspousal tort immunity has now been all but extinguished. Parent-child immunity has proved somewhat more resilient, but it, too, has been scaled back significantly in many states.

A. INTERSPOUSAL TORT IMMUNITY

In the following case, Maryland's highest court considered whether to lift immunity in a husband's malicious-prosecution action against his wife. He alleged, in a suit filed during the couple's divorce, that she had falsely accused him of stalking and harassing her, resulting in his incarceration on five occasions. Prior decisions in the state had abolished interspousal immunity in actions alleging negligence and intentional torts involving "outrage," but had not done so for other intentional tort claims.

BOZMAN v. BOZMAN

Maryland Court of Appeals, 2003.
830 A.2d 450.

BELL, CHIEF JUDGE.

* * *

III.

The doctrine of interspousal immunity in tort cases is a rule of law existing in the common law of Maryland. In *Boblitz* [*v. Boblitz*, 462 A.2d

506, 507 (Md. 1983) (abrogating interspousal immunity in negligence suits)], we noted that it is a rule of "ancient origin" and created "exclusively from judicial decisions." * * *

The rationale underlying the interspousal immunity rule has been discussed in our cases. In *David* [*v. David*, 157 A. 755, 756 (Md. 1932)], the Court stated: "The reason usually given for that rule is the presumed legal identity of the husband and wife." A more complete statement of the rationale was provided in *Lusby* [*v. Lusby*, 390 A.2d 77, 78–79 (Md. 1978) (abrogating immunity in suits alleging intentional torts involving "outrage")], with attribution to Blackstone:

> " 'By marriage, the husband and wife are one person in the law: that is, the very being of legal existence of the woman is suspended during the marriage, or at least is incorporated and consolidated into that of the husband: under whose wing, protection, and cover, she performs everything * * *.'

> "He adds, in discussing the consequences of this union of husband and wife, 'If the wife be injured in her person or her property, she can bring no action for redress without her husband's concurrence, and in his name, as well as her own: neither can she be sued without making the husband a defendant.' "

[(quoting 1 Commentaries *442–43).] * * * The *Boblitz* Court, too, commented on the effect of the doctrine on women:

> "Application of the words interspousal immunity to this ancient rule of law borders on mockery. It would more aptly be called a 'rule in derogation of married women.' Under it the person or property of a woman upon marriage came under the 'protection and influence' of her husband—for good or ill. She became subservient to his will and fitted with a distasteful yoke of servitude and compelled obeisance that was galling at best and crushing at worst."

462 A.2d at 507.

Our laws pertaining to the rights of married women were completely revised in 1898, with the enactment of the Married Women's Act. [Among other things, the Act recognized the separate legal identity of married women and their independent authority to bring lawsuits. Nevertheless, this Court] * * * concluded that the Maryland Act "g[a]ve the wife a remedy, by her suit alone, for actionable wrongs which could not theretofore be thus independently redressed," and did not "create, as between husband and wife, personal causes of action which did not exist before the act." [*Furstenburg v. Furstenburg*, 136 A. 534, 536 (Md. 1927).]

That the Court uniformly applied the doctrine, without exception, did not mean that it did not recognize its flaws. * * * [In 1932, the Court described the "fiction of identity" between husband and wife as a "technical and artificial" rationale for interspousal immunity.] The Court in *Gregg* [*v. Gregg*, 87 A.2d 581, 583 (Md. 1952)], labeled the domestic tranquility rationale for the interspousal immunity doctrine "as artificial as" the unity of husband and wife rationale. Expounding on that theme, it pointed out:

"It applies to a post-bellum situation a theory which is clearly only applicable to conditions prior to the difficulty which caused the bringing of the legal action. After discord, suspicion and distrust have entered the home, it is idle to say that one of the parties shall not be allowed to sue the other because of fear of bringing in what is already there."

Id. at 583. * * *

Our reluctance to change the common law and, thus, our continued adherence to the interspousal immunity doctrine, was in deference to the Legislature.

The first breach of the interspousal immunity doctrine in Maryland occurred with our decision in *Lusby.* There, the wife brought a tort action against her husband for damages. As reported by the Court,

"She alleged that while she was operating her motor vehicle on a public highway the husband 'pulled alongside of [her] in his pick-up truck and pointed a highpowered rifle at her.' She attempted to flee by increasing the speed of her car. [However, her husband and two unknown accomplices in a separate vehicle forced her car off the road, sexually assaulted her, and threatened to kill her if she reported the attack.] * * *"

390 A.2d at 77–78. * * *

* * *

The *Lusby* Court concluded:

"We can conceive of no sound public policy in the latter half of the 20th-century which would prevent one spouse from recovering from another for the outrageous conduct here alleged. There certainly can be no domestic tranquility to be preserved in the face of allegations such as we have before us[.]"

[*Id.* at 88.] * * *

* * *

Merely five years after *Lusby,* we were asked "to reexamine the interspousal immunity rule ... and to declare that rule to be no longer viable in tort cases involving personal injury to a spouse resulting from the negligence of the other spouse." *Boblitz,* 462 A.2d at 506. In that case, a wife sued her husband for injuries she sustained almost a year before the marriage, as a result, she alleged, of his negligence in the operation of an automobile. * * * [Abrogating interspousal immunity for negligence in *Boblitz,* we] explained:

"We share the view now held by the vast majority of American States that the interspousal immunity rule is unsound in the circumstances of modern life in such cases as the subject. It is a vestige of the past.

We are persuaded that the reasons asserted for its retention do not survive careful scrutiny. * * * "

Id. at 521.

* * *

[After canvassing decisions from other states, most of which had abrogated spousal immunity in whole or in part, *Boblitz* identified six primary reasons cited in favor of immunity:]

"1.   The unity of husband and wife;

"2.   Interspousal tort actions will destroy the harmony of the marital relationship;

"3.   Retention of the doctrine will prevent collusive and fraudulent claims;

"4.   Retention of the doctrine will guard against an increase in trivial claims;

"5.   Divorce and criminal courts furnish adequate redress;

"6.   Change is solely within the purview of the Legislature.["]

[*Boblitz*, 462 A.2d at 513.]

* * * [W]ith respect to the first four reasons advanced for retaining the doctrine of interspousal immunity, the Court discussed the decision of the Supreme Court of Pennsylvania [in *Hack v. Hack*, 433 A.2d 859 (Pa. 1981),] abrogating the doctrine completely:

* * *

"As to (1), the Court stated that the very purpose of Married Women's Acts was to abolish this concept of law; as to (2) the Court expressed the belief that an action in tort for negligence would be less likely to disturb family harmony than permitted causes of action for breach of contract or conversion that typically involve intentional wrongdoing; as to (3), the Court adopted the reasoning of the Court in *Immer v. Risko*, 267 A.2d 481, 488 (N.J. 1970) that 'it seems unjust to deny the claims of the many because of the potentiality for fraud by the few'; and as to (4), the Court declared that the suggested avoidance of trivial claims is subject to the same analytical weakness as the argument regarding collusion. * * * "

Boblitz, 462 A.2d at 519.

As an example of the response to the argument that there are alternative remedies to allowing interspousal tort actions, the Court [agreed with the Supreme Court of New Jersey, in *Merenoff v. Merenoff*, 388 A.2d 951, 962 (N.J. 1978), that] * * *

" * * * no court in this day and age subscribes seriously to the view that the abrogation of marital immunity for tortious injury is 'unnecessary' because redress for the wrong can be obtained through other means. * * * The criminal law may vindicate society's interest in punishing a wrongdoer but it cannot compensate an injured spouse for her or his suffering and damages. Divorce or separation provide escape from tortious abuse but can hardly be equated with a civil right to redress and compensation for personal injuries."

Id. at 518 (citations omitted).

Finally, as to the sixth rationale for retaining the doctrine, namely, that it is a job for the Legislature, the Court [stated] * * * :

* * *

" 'In recent years, * * * we have forcefully stated that in matters of torts involving the marital relationship we cannot 'stubbornly, hollowly and anachronistically' stay bound by the 'shackles' of the 'formalism' of the common law. * * * ' "

Id. at 517 [(quoting) *MacDonald v. MacDonald*, 412 A.2d 71, 74 (Me. 1980)].

* * *

* * * [Nevertheless, *Boblitz* stopped short of abrogating interspousal immunity altogether and limited its ruling to negligence actions.] The question to be answered, therefore, * * * is whether those torts * * * that fall in the gap created by *Lusby* and *Boblitz* should be subject to the immunity defense or whether, on the contrary, the time has come to bridge that gap. * * *

* * * In the twenty-years since *Boblitz,* the trend in favor of abrogation and away from the doctrine has not abated. Now, nine of the twelve States that recognized the doctrine in 1983 have completely abrogated the doctrine by court decision. Another of those states, Hawaii, has done so by statute. The remaining two states have abrogated the doctrine in part.

* * * By our count, therefore, no less than forty-six States have abrogated the doctrine, either fully or partially, leaving only four States still retaining it.

* * *

The respondent argues that alternative remedies, already provided by the courts, are adequate for "garden-variety intentional torts between spouses" that do not fit within our *Boblitz* and *Lusby* holdings. In particular, the respondent emphasizes that Maryland is a marital property State, in which equity, rather than title controls property distribution. She also notes that the statutory scheme provides for the consideration of eleven factors when the equities and rights of the parties are being adjusted, and asserts that tortious conduct may be considered in granting alimony or making a monetary award. In addition, the respondent points to the domestic violence provisions of the Family Law Article, noting that they permit * * * the court to order custody, exclusive use and possession of the family home, spousal support, etc., for up to one year. Finally, the respondent states that the aggrieved spouse has the benefit of the criminal law; he or she may charge the offender and seek restitution for any medical treatment required.

This argument has been rejected * * *. * * * [W]hile divorce dissolves the marriage, thereby preventing future tortious abuse, that is not the same as civil redress or compensation for personal injuries and * * * the criminal law's vindication of society's interest in punishing wrongdoers does not compensate a spouse for injuries and suffering. The "remedies" the respondent proffers are, in the same sense, not compensation for tort damages.

* * *

The overwhelming weight of authority supports the petitioner's argument that the interspousal immunity doctrine should be abrogated. Joining the many of our sister States that have already done so, we abrogate the interspousal immunity rule, a vestige of the past, whose time has come and gone, as to all cases alleging an intentional tort. * * *

NOTES AND QUESTIONS

1. *Lingering remnants of interspousal immunity.* As *Bozman* recounts, rejection of interspousal immunity in recent years has been nearly total. *See, e.g., Ellis v. Estate of Ellis*, 169 P.3d 441 (Utah 2007) (abrogating interspousal immunity for all tort claims in case arising from fatal accident on couple's honeymoon). Immunity survives in reduced form in only a small handful of jurisdictions. *See, e.g., Gates v. Gates*, 587 S.E.2d 32 (Ga. 2003).

2. *Policy concerns supporting immunity.* Scholars have mostly ridiculed the traditional rationales for interspousal immunity. Reviewing a list of rationales substantially similar to the list collected in *Bozman*, Professor Homer Clark opined that "[t]he kindest thing to be said about the first five of these policy arguments is that they are frivolous." Homer H. Clark, Jr., The Law of Domestic Relations in the United States 371 (2d ed. 1988). But, assuming that the tort recovery will be paid by the spouses' homeowner or automobile insurance policy, might there be validity to the fear of manufactured claims? Even if the disputed injury is entirely genuine, should courts be concerned that a judgment paid by an insurance policy will inure partly to the benefit of the tortfeasor where the couple remains married? Professor Clark considered this concern to "make[] a little more sense in terms of the traditional view of tort law as turning on the fault of the defendant and the freedom from fault of the plaintiff." *Id.* at 372.

B. PARENT–CHILD TORT IMMUNITY

HERZFELD v. HERZFELD

Supreme Court of Florida, 2001.
781 So.2d 1070.

ANSTEAD, J.

* * * At issue in this case is whether the public policies served by the parental immunity doctrine continue to support its valid application to claims of sexual abuse by a parent against a child. * * *

* * * The facts underlying the alleged abuse by the parent against the child are summarized [by the lower court] as follows:

> The plaintiff [minor child] was placed in the defendant's care as a foster child in 1988. The defendant adopted the plaintiff three years later when the plaintiff was sixteen years old. [Almost six years later, the son alleged that his father had sexually abused him and sought recovery under several intentional tort theories.] * * *

The minor child appealed the trial court's orders granting his adoptive father's motions to dismiss and for summary judgment [on the basis of parental tort immunity]. * * * [T]he Third District reversed and held that because family harmony is already destroyed in sexual abuse cases, "the parental immunity doctrine does not bar the action by the minor child against his parent for damages arising from sexual abuse." *Id.* Notwithstanding, the court acknowledged that its ruling was in direct conflict with *Richards v. Richards,* 599 So.2d 135 (Fla. [Dist. Ct. App.] 1992), which held that parental immunity barred a similar intentional tort suit by a child against his father predicated upon the father's alleged sexual assaults. We approve * * * the decision of the Third District.

FAMILY MEMBERS' IMMUNITY

* * * Legal commentators note that the rule granting parents legal immunity from tort actions brought by their children does not have its origins or any long roots in the English common law, but appears, rather, to have been created by American state courts. Commentators trace the rule's origin to an opinion of the Mississippi Supreme Court decided in 1891. The case involved a young married woman, separated from her husband at the time, who sued her mother for wrongfully confining her to an insane asylum when she was a minor. *See Hewellette v. George,* 9 So. 885 (Miss. 1891). In reviewing the young woman's claim, the court noted that "so long as the parent is under obligation to care for, guide, and control, and the child is under reciprocal obligation to aid and comfort and obey, no such action as this can be maintained." The court explained its rationale:

> The peace of society, and of the families composing society, and a sound public policy, designed to subserve the repose of families and the best interests of society, forbid to the minor child a right to appear in court in the assertion of a claim to civil redress for personal injuries suffered at the hands of the parent. The state, through its criminal laws, will give the minor child protection from parental violence and wrong-doing, and this is all the child can be heard to demand.

Id. [at 887.] * * *

In *McKelvey* [*v. McKelvey*, 77 S.W. 664 (Tenn. 1903)], the Tennessee Supreme Court [further] reasoned that allowing a minor's suit would interfere with public policy supporting discretionary parental control and discipline. * * *

RECENT TRENDS

Although the majority of states in this country initially adopted the parental immunity doctrine in varying degrees, many have now either abrogated the doctrine completely or have established significant exceptions to its application [such as allowing negligence claims covered by liability insurance or certain intentional tort claims]. * * *

* * *

Abrogation of the parental immunity doctrine in accident cases has been largely based on the prevalence of liability insurance. Importantly, the courts have emphasized that the domestic harmony policy concern is diminished under these circumstances because the injured child's dispute is actually with the financially responsible insurance carrier rather than with the parents. The courts have also noted that allowing recovery against an insurance fund would not impact family assets. Similarly, claims that fraud would increase in such cases have been rejected either outright as no greater than concerns about fraud in any litigation, or as insufficiently demonstrated.

* * *

INTENTIONAL SEXUAL TORTS

After carefully evaluating the policies behind the parental immunity doctrine, the national trends, and our own prior case law, we conclude that the district court was correct in holding that the policies relied upon to support the doctrine are insufficient to continue application of the doctrine to bar intentional sexual tort claims by a child against a parent. We agree with the district court that the fear of disrupting the fabric and nucleus of families by allowing actions based upon intentional sexual abuse simply appears to be without merit. If indeed the principal reason for the parental immunity doctrine is to preserve family harmony, then it appears that the immunity can have no justification in such cases of intentional and malicious sexual abuse, for in those cases the inescapable conclusion is that the family fabric has already been tragically disrupted by the serious misconduct alleged. We agree that the mere additional stress of a lawsuit in such circumstances is an insufficient reason by itself to bar a claim for that misconduct.

Further, while we have genuine concerns that some may abuse the judicial system through false claims in domestic relations cases as well as tort cases, we believe the protections available in the judicial process are adequate to address the issue of false or fraudulent claims in this context as well as others. We find the depletion of family resources argument unpersuasive as well. As was noted by the court below, it is apparent that the depletion of family resources by itself cannot justify the parental immunity theory, since "any time a person is sued for actions not covered by liability insurance, his or her family's resources are threatened."

* * *

Accordingly, because we find that the policies behind the parental immunity doctrine are insufficient to justify barring a minor from recovering for intentional sexual abuse perpetrated by a parent, we approve the opinion and decision below and disapprove *Richards.*

It is so ordered.

[The concurring opinion of HARDING, J., joined by ANSTEAD, PARIENTE and LEWIS, JJ., is omitted.]

WELLS, C.J., dissenting.

* * *

I am concerned that this decision will be used to foster litigation involving children in stances in which the real battle is between the two parents. Although I certainly agree with dealing harshly with parents who abuse their children—sexually, physically, mentally, or emotionally—I find a great deal of wisdom in Judge Cobb's opinion in *Richards:*

> Recovery against a parent by an individual child for an intentional tort, where insurance is not available, decreases the assets available for the support of other family members who may also be in need of assistance. Moreover, the majority of any punitive damage recovery by the child/plaintiff would pass to the state, further depleting family assets.

> We also note that opening the doors to tort actions for damages by children against parents would avail an unscrupulous parent of the opportunity to manipulate a minor child and the legal system by bringing frivolous actions against the other parent. The criminal court, rather than the civil court, is better equipped to process charges such as those leveled in the instant case. As succinctly pointed out in the appellee's brief:

>> The benefits to be gained by a child's intentional tort action against a parent do not justify abrogating the parent/child immunity doctrine. If a parent abuses a minor child, the parent is already obligated by law to provide the minor child with all necessary care, including medical and psychological care. The law also recognizes the child's right to enforce this obligation. It is not necessary that the child be given the right to sue a parent for intentional tort for the obligation to be enforced. The parent's obligation to provide for the child also continues beyond the age of majority if the child is unable to provide for himself or herself as a result of a physical or psychological disability. * * *

Richards v. Richards, 599 So. 2d at 136–37.

NOTES AND QUESTIONS

1. *Tort actions by parents against their children.* Parent-child immunity normally operates to immunize a parent for tortious injuries caused to a child, and is premised at least partly on the need to leave room for parental judgment in childrearing. Should a parallel immunity bar parents from suing their children for tortious injuries? The scenario is not often presented, but "[t]he principle that a parent may not prosecute a tort action against his or her unemancipated minor child is a recognized corollary to parental immunity." *Bentley v. Bentley,* 172 S.W.3d 375, 377 (Ky. 2005); *see also Mauk v. Mauk,* 466 N.E.2d 166, 167 (Ohio 1984). A number of these courts, however, have cut back tort immunity for children in step with abrogation of immunity for parents. *See, e.g., Bentley,* 172 S.W.3d at 377–78 (abolishing parent-child immunity except for claims arising from "commonplace incidents in family life").

2. *Claim-specific immunity. Herzfeld* abrogates parent-child immunity specifically for intentional torts arising from sexual abuse. An earlier Florida decision, *Ard v. Ard,* 414 So.2d 1066 (Fla. 1982), had abrogated parent-child immunity only for negligence claims covered by an insurance policy. *Herzfeld* expressly declined to extend abrogation to other tort claims against parents. *See* 781 So.2d at 1079 n.17. Does reshaping immunity in this way make sense? Is it appropriate to allow a tort remedy for sexual abuse while denying one for other forms of physical or emotional abuse? *See Newman v. Cole,* 872 So.2d 138, 140 (Ala. 2003) (extending immunity exception for sexual abuse claims, Alabama's sole exception to parent-child immunity, to cover other instances "where it is shown by clear and convincing evidence that a parent's willful and intentional injury caused the death of his or her child").

3. *Claims of negligent parent supervision. Herzfeld* notes that one rationale for parental immunity is that tort regulation of childrearing decisions "would interfere with public policy supporting discretionary parental control and discipline." 781 So.2d at 1072. In fact, the Supreme Court has held that parenting decisions about how to raise children are entitled to heightened protection from judicial oversight as a fundamental constitutional right. *See, e.g., Troxel v. Granville,* 530 U.S. 57, 65–66 (2000) (discussed as lead case in Chapter 13). Accordingly, courts often hesitate to find "abuse" or "neglect" that would authorize intrusive state intervention based merely on ordinary parental carelessness, insisting instead on a showing of more culpable misconduct. *E.g., State v. Wilder,* 748 A.2d 444, 456 (Me. 2000) (in prosecuting a parent for unreasonable use of corporal punishment, state must show that the parent's judgment was "grossly deviant from what a reasonable and prudent parent would believe necessary in the same situation").

To avoid excessive intrusion on parental discretion in the context of private tort actions, some jurisdictions have similarly retained a qualified immunity against negligence actions premised on a parent's childrearing judgment. A number of courts, for instance, have generally abolished parental tort immunity "except in the two following situations: (1) where the negligent act relied on for a recovery involves the reasonable exercise of parental authority over the child, and (2) where the alleged negligent act involves the exercise of ordinary parental discretion with respect to provisions for the care and necessities of the child." *Bentley*, 172 S.W.3d at 377 (quoting *Rigdon v. Rigdon*, 465 S.W.2d 921, 923 (Ky. 1970)). Thus, a parent might be sued for negligently driving the family car in which the child was a passenger, but not for negligently maintaining the family home or entrusting the child to the care of an incompetent babysitter. *See Cates v. Cates*, 619 N.E.2d 715, 729 (Ill. 1993).

The New Jersey Supreme Court offered this rationale for immunizing parenting judgments:

> There are certain areas of activities within the family sphere involving parental discipline, care, and control that should and must remain free from judicial intrusion. Parents should be free to determine how the physical, moral, emotional, and intellectual growth of their children can best be promoted. That is both their duty and their privilege. Indeed, every parent has a unique philosophy of the rearing of children. That philosophy is an outgrowth of the parent's own economic, educational, cultural, ethical, and religious background, all of which affect the parent's judgment on how his or her children should be prepared for the responsibilities of adulthood. Such philosophical considerations come directly to the fore in matters of parental supervision.

Buono v. Scalia, 843 A.2d 1120, 1123 (N.J. 2004) (quoting *Foldi v. Jeffries*, 461 A.2d 1145, 1152 (N.J. 1983)). Do the concerns raised in these decisions support immunizing parenting judgment from judicial review in tort, or do they simply call for recognizing a broad range of what should qualify as "reasonable" parenting?

Some jurisdictions refuse to recognize parental immunity for "negligent supervision" and simply subject all parenting decisions to negligence review under a straightforward " 'reasonable parent test,' in which a parent's conduct is judged by whether [it] * * * comported with that of a reasonable and prudent parent in a similar situation." *Broadbent v. Broadbent*, 907 P.2d 43, 50 (Ariz. 1995); *see also Gibson v. Gibson*, 479 P.2d 648, 652–53 (Cal. 1971). Is it desirable to allow judges or juries to impose their own judgment of "reasonable" parenting through tort law? Is it *constitutional*, given the Constitution's special respect for parenting authority?

4. *Immunity for stepparents.* Many courts have permitted stepparents to claim parental immunity—but some jurisdictions limit immunity to stepparents who can prove that they fully assumed parental responsibility for their stepchildren by providing financial support and "educating, instructing, and caring for the child's general welfare." *Zellmer v. Zellmer*, 188 P.3d 497, 506 (Wash. 2008).

5. *Parental immunity to third parties.* If public policy favors barring a tort suit brought by a child against his parent for negligent parenting, should it also bar similar actions brought by persons outside the family? The New Jersey Supreme Court answered yes in *Buono, supra.* There a woman sought to recover against her neighbor for his negligent failure to supervise his child at a neighborhood block party; the man had allowed his five-year-old son to ride his bicycle near others and the child had collided with the plaintiff's toddler, seriously injuring her. The court held that the same immunity

considerations precluded the neighbor's suit premised on negligent parenting supervision. *See Buono*, 843 A.2d at 1126. Do you agree? Compare, for example, section 316 of the Restatement (Second) of Torts (1965):

> A parent is under a duty to exercise reasonable care so to control his minor child as to prevent it from intentionally harming others or from so conducting itself as to create an unreasonable risk of bodily harm to them, if the parent (a) knows or has reason to know that he has the ability to control his child, and (b) knows or should know of the necessity and opportunity for exercising such control.

SECTION 2: INTRA–FAMILY TORTS

A substantial share of tort actions within the family involve straightforward negligence actions, often arising from careless operation of the family car. As *Herzfeld* suggests, the chief reason for abandoning immunity in these actions was that any judgments were likely to be paid by insurers. As one court explained, "[t]he existence of liability insurance prevents family discord and depletion of family assets in automobile [and other] negligence cases." *Transamerica Ins. Co. v. Royle*, 656 P.2d 820, 823 (Mont. 1983). Indeed, one prominent torts scholar has asserted that "the judges who abolished interspousal immunity did so not for genuine negligence-oriented reasons but instead in order to give one member of the family access to the other member's liability insurance policy." Gary T. Schwartz, *The Beginning and the Possible End of the Rise of Modern American Tort Law*, 26 Ga. L. Rev. 601, 644–45 (1992). Insurance companies responded by modifying their policies to exclude liability for intra-family torts, but some courts have held these "family exclusion clauses" to be partially or wholly unenforceable on grounds of public policy. *See, e.g., American Standard Ins. Co. v. Hargrave*, 34 S.W.3d 88 (Mo. 2000); *Transamerica, supra*. In some states, family exclusion clauses are void in automobile insurance coverage but enforceable in other insurance policies. *See, e.g., State Farm Mut. Auto. Ins. Co. v. Marley*, 151 S.W.3d 33 (Ky. 2004). As a result, the practical feasibility of intra-family tort recovery today often hinges more directly on public policies mandating insurance coverage than on the remnants of common-law immunity.

Notwithstanding the broad retreat of interspousal and parent-child immunities, many courts continue to believe that conduct within the family should be judged by tort standards different from those governing harms caused by strangers. As one court observed in the context of an interspousal tort suit, "the abolition of immunity does not mean that the existence of the marriage must be ignored in determining the scope of liability." *Hakkila v. Hakkila*, 812 P.2d 1320, 1323 (N.M. Ct. App. 1991) (discussed as a lead case, *infra*, p. 395). Thus, in a real sense, the abrogation of immunities has simply reformed legal concern for family privacy from a categorical barrier to tort regulation into a more case-by-case (or perhaps tort-by-tort) search for the proper balance.

When the claim relates to driving a car, the spousal relationship may have no particular bearing on the negligence determination. *E.g.*, *Ellis v. Estate of Ellis*, 169 P.3d 441 (Utah 2007) (husband negligently lost control of car on honeymoon trip, killing himself and injuring his wife). But what if the negligence claim rests on something more "domestic," such as the way the house was maintained? *See, e.g.*, *Nelson v. Nelson*, 50 P.3d 139 (Mont. 2002) (wife permitted to sue husband for negligently exposing her to pesticides on family ranch); *Brown v. Brown*, 409 N.E.2d 717 (Mass. 1980) (wife could recover for husband's negligence in failing to remove snow and ice from steps and walkways). Should the fact that the litigants are married or otherwise related affect the assessment of the "wrongfulness" of their conduct, and if so how? The answers are not always clear. Professors Ira Ellman and Stephen Sugarman write:

> On one hand, the marital relation implies for most people an enhanced moral duty to one's spouse, suggesting that a finding of unreasonable conduct might arise from behavior that would not violate one's obligation to others. It is surely worse to ignore a spouse's birthday than a friend's. Yet, at the same time, love implies a mutual indulgence and tolerance for the shortcomings of one's spouse, including even his or her unreliability in these very matters. Hence, an incident of spousal insensitivity may be at the same time negligent and excusable. Heightened moral obligation and special privilege, so to speak, seem to go hand in hand.

Ira Mark Ellman & Stephen D. Sugarman, *Spousal Emotional Abuse as a Tort?*, 55 Md. L. Rev. 1268, 1302 (1996).

Some matters are relatively uncontroversial. Few would disagree today, for instance, that a husband who savagely beats his wife should be liable for battery. *See Cater v. Cater*, 846 S.W.2d 173 (Ark. 1993) (upholding award of $20,000 in compensatory damages and $350,000 in punitive damages in such a case). And courts have applied the usual definition of battery—an intentional harmful or offensive bodily contact—without modification in cases between spouses. *E.g.*, *Plath v. Plath*, 428 N.W.2d 392 (Minn. 1988) (finding that husband's act of pushing his wife away, causing her to fall and break her hip, constituted intentional offensive touching and, therefore, a battery); *McPherson v. McPherson*, 712 A.2d 1043 (Me. 1998) (holding that husband's unwitting transmission of a sexually transmitted disease to his wife was not a battery because the wife consented to intercourse, though ignorant of his infidelity).

Despite the analytical suitability of traditional battery law to provide legal redress, relatively few domestic violence victims actually pursue tort claims. Indeed, Professor Jennifer Wriggins "reviewed thousands of cases on Westlaw in the summer of 2003 and found only thirty-four tort cases dealing with domestic violence." Jennifer B. Wriggins, *Toward a Feminist Revision of Torts*, 13 Am. U. J. Gender Soc. Pol'y & L. 139, 155 (2005). What factors might explain such a low "claims rate" for domestic violence injuries? Professor Wriggins points chiefly to the difficulty of collecting a judgment from batterers. Given the limited financial assets of many batterers, she contends that the common practice of denying insurance coverage for such torts through family exclusion clauses means that *"de facto* interspousal tort immunity persists in the form of insurance exclusions."* Jennifer B. Wriggins, *Interspousal Tort Immunity and Insurance "Family Member Exclusions": Shared Assumptions, Relational and Liberal Feminist Challenges,* 17 Wis. Women's L.J. 251, 252 (2002). Accordingly, she urges reforming the law to require universal insurance coverage through a "Domestic Violence Torts Insurance Plan." Jennifer B. Wriggins, *Domestic Violence Torts,* 75 S. Cal. L. Rev. 121, 152–57 (2001). Other scholars point to additional barriers to spousal battery claimants which may be harder to eliminate, including fears of physical or legal retaliation, feelings of shame or culpability in the victimization, and expectation that the legal system will be hostile or indifferent to their claims. *See* Sarah M. Buel, *Access to Meaningful Remedy: Overcoming Doctrinal Obstacles in Tort Litigation Against Domestic Violence Offenders,* 83 Or. L. Rev. 945, 953–55 (2004); Ellman & Sugarman, *supra,* at 1293. Many of these same barriers obstruct victims' use of legal protections outside tort law and are discussed in Chapter 5.

Permitting spouses to sue one another for emotional distress is potentially more vexing. Withdrawal of interspousal tort immunity coincided roughly with recognition in many states of a new tort remedy for intentional infliction of emotional distress (often called IIED). States have differed, however, in their willingness to allow spouses to bring IIED claims for marital cruelty. Some courts have not hesitated to permit married persons to seek redress for a spouse's infliction of emotional distress, while others have been more wary of the encroachment of tort law on marital relations, particularly in divorce actions where a party may use tort claims for bargaining advantage. What differences do you see in the approaches taken in the two decisions that follow?

FELTMEIER v. FELTMEIER

Supreme Court of Illinois, 2003.
798 N.E.2d 75.

JUSTICE RARICK delivered the opinion of the court:

Plaintiff, Lynn Feltmeier, and defendant, Robert Feltmeier, were married on October 11, 1986, and divorced on December 16, 1997. * * * On August 25, 1999, Lynn sued Robert for the intentional infliction of emotional distress. According to the allegations contained in the complaint, Robert engaged in a pattern of domestic abuse, both physical and mental in nature, which began shortly after the marriage and did not cease even after its dissolution.

* * *

[The trial court denied Robert's motion to dismiss but, recognizing the novelty of Lynn's claim under state law, authorized an interlocutory appeal. The intermediate appellate court affirmed, and the state supreme court granted leave to appeal.]

The first matter before us for review is whether Lynn's complaint states a cause of action for intentional infliction of emotional distress. * * *

According to the allegations contained in Lynn's complaint, since the parties' marriage in October 1986, and continuing for over a year after the December 1997 dissolution of their marriage:

"[Robert] entered into a continuous and outrageous course of conduct toward [Lynn] with either the intent to cause emotional distress to [Lynn] or with reckless disregard as to whether such conduct would cause emotional distress to [Lynn], said continuing course of conduct, including but not limited to, the following:

A. On repeated occasions, [Robert] has battered [Lynn] by striking, kicking, shoving, pulling hair and bending and twisting her limbs and toes.

* * *

B. On repeated occasions, [Robert] has prevented [Lynn] from leaving the house to escape the abuse.

* * *

C. On repeated occasions, [Robert] has yelled insulting and demeaning epithets at [Lynn]. Further, [Robert] has engaged in verbal abuse which included threats and constant criticism of [Lynn] in such a way as to demean, humiliate, and degrade [Lynn].

* * *

D. On repeated occasions, [Robert] threw items at [Lynn] with the intent to cause her harm.

* * *

E. On repeated occasions, [Robert] attempted to isolate [Lynn] from her family and friends and would get very upset if [Lynn] would show the marks and bruises resulting from [Robert's] abuse to others.

* * *

F. On repeated occasions since the divorce, [Robert] has engaged in stalking behavior.

* * *

G. On at least one occasion, [Robert] has attempted to interfere with [Lynn's] employment by confiscating her computer. Additionally, [Robert] broke into [Lynn's] locked drug cabinet for work on or about March 23, 1997."

The complaint further alleged, as examples of conduct within the categories set forth above, dozens of episodes of abusive behavior, including specific details and time frames for the various physical and emotional attacks.

In *McGrath v. Fahey*, 533 N.E.2d 806 (Ill. 1988), this court set forth the three elements necessary to state a cause of action for intentional infliction of emotional distress, stating:

> "First, the conduct involved must be truly extreme and outrageous. Second, the actor must either *intend* that his conduct inflict severe emotional distress, or know that there is at least a high probability that his conduct will cause severe emotional distress. Third, the conduct must in fact cause *severe* emotional distress."

In the case at bar, Robert first contends that the allegations of Lynn's complaint do not sufficiently set forth conduct which was extreme and outrageous when considered "[i]n the context of the subjective and fluctuating nature of the marital relationship." In support of this contention, Robert cites several cases from other jurisdictions that have addressed the policy ramifications of allowing a spouse to maintain an action for intentional infliction of emotional distress based upon acts occurring during the marriage. In *Pickering v. Pickering,* 434 N.W.2d 758, 761 (S.D. 1989), the Supreme Court of South Dakota held that the tort of intentional infliction of emotional distress should be unavailable as a matter of public policy when predicated on conduct which leads to the dissolution of a marriage.
* * *

* * * Robert cites a Texas case, *Villasenor v. Villasenor,* 911 S.W.2d 411, 415 n.2 (Tex. Civ. App. 1995), wherein the court, in *dicta,* noted that because the marital relationship " 'is highly subjective and constituted by mutual understandings and interchanges which are constantly in flux[,]' * * * [f]or purposes of determining outrageous conduct, the insults, indignities, threats, annoyances, petty oppressions, or other trivialities associated with marriage and divorce must be considered upon the individual facts of each case." However, Illinois case law makes clear that under no circumstances would " 'mere insults, indignities, threats, annoyances, petty oppressions, or other trivialities' " qualify as outrageous conduct. *McGrath*, [533 N.E.2d at 809], quoting Restatement (Second) of Torts § 46, Comment *d,* at 73 (1965). Rather, the nature of the defendant's conduct must be so extreme as to go beyond all possible bounds of decency and to be regarded as intolerable in a civilized community. Thus, while we agree that special caution is required in dealing with actions for intentional infliction of emotional distress arising from conduct occurring within the marital setting, our examination of both the law of this state and the most commonly raised policy concerns leads us to conclude that no valid reason exists to restrict such actions or to require a heightened threshold for outrageousness in this context.

One policy concern that has been advanced is the need to recognize the "mutual concessions implicit in marriage," and the desire to preserve marital harmony. *See Henriksen v. Cameron,* 622 A.2d 1135, 1138–39 (Me. 1993). However, in this case, brought after the parties were divorced, "there is clearly no marital harmony remaining to be preserved." *Id.* at 1139. Moreover, we agree with the Supreme Judicial Court of Maine that "behavior that is 'utterly intolerable in a civilized society' and is intended to cause severe emotional distress is not behavior that should be protected in order to promote marital harmony and peace." [*Id.*]

Indeed, the Illinois legislature, in creating the Illinois Domestic Violence Act of 1986, has recognized that domestic violence is "a serious crime against the individual and society" and that "the legal system has ineffectively dealt with family violence in the past, allowing abusers to escape effective prosecution or financial liability." 750 [Ill. Comp. Stat. Ann.] 60/102(1), (3) (West 2002). * * * Thus, it would seem that the public policy of this state would be furthered by recognition of the action at issue.

A second policy concern is the threat of excessive and frivolous litigation if the tort is extended to acts occurring in the marital setting. Admittedly, the likelihood of vindictive litigation is of particular concern following a dissolution of marriage, because "the events leading to most divorces involve some level of emotional distress." *Henriksen,* 622 A.2d at 1139. However, we believe that the showing required of a plaintiff in order to recover damages for intentional infliction of emotional distress provides a built-in safeguard against excessive and frivolous litigation. As the appellate court herein stated: "When conduct is truly extreme and outrageous, it is more likely that severe emotional distress suffered by the victim was actually caused by that conduct."

Another policy consideration which has been raised is that a tort action for compensation would be redundant. * * * [However, an] action for dissolution of marriage * * * provides no compensatory relief for domestic abuse. In Illinois, as in most other states, courts are not allowed to consider marital misconduct in the distribution of property when dissolving a marriage.

* * *

* * * Illinois cases in which the tort of intentional infliction of emotional distress has been sufficiently alleged have very frequently involved a defendant who stood in a position of power or authority relative to the plaintiff. While these past cases have generally involved abuses of power by employers, creditors, or financial institutions, we see no reason to exclude the defendant at issue here, a spouse/former spouse, from the many types of individuals who may be positioned to exercise power over a plaintiff.

Therefore, we conclude that neither the policy considerations commonly raised nor the law of this state support a conclusion that an action for intentional infliction of emotional distress based upon conduct occurring in the marital setting should be barred or subject to any heightened threshold for establishing outrageousness. With this background in mind, we now examine the allegations set forth in Lynn's complaint to determine whether Robert's conduct satisfies the "outrageousness" requirement.

* * *

In the instant case, we must agree with the appellate court that, when the above-summarized allegations of the complaint are viewed in their entirety, they show a type of domestic abuse that is extreme enough to be actionable:

> "It combines more than a decade of verbal insults and humiliations with episodes where freedom of movement was deprived and where physical injury was often inflicted. The alleged pattern of abuse, combined with its duration, worked a humiliation and loss of self-esteem. Regardless of the form in which it arrived, violence was certain to erupt, and when seasons of spousal abuse turn to years that span the course of a decade, we are unwilling to dismiss it on grounds that it is unworthy of outrage."

Therefore, where we find that a reasonable trier of fact could easily conclude that Robert's conduct was so outrageous as to be regarded as intolerable in a civilized community, we reject his contention that the complaint fails to sufficiently allege this element.

It is equally clear * * * that Lynn's complaint adequately pleads the second element necessary to state a cause of action for intentional infliction of emotional distress, *i.e.*, that Robert either intended to inflict, or knew that his conduct was likely to inflict, severe emotional distress upon Lynn. However, Robert does contest the adequacy of the complaint as to the third necessary element, that his conduct in fact caused severe emotional distress. * * *

Lynn's complaint specifically alleges that, "[a]s a direct and proximate result of the entirety of [Robert's] course of conduct, [she] has sustained severe emotional distress including, but not limited to[,] loss of self-esteem and difficulty in forming other relationships, and a form of Post Traumatic Stress Disorder sustained by battered and abused women as a result of being repeatedly physically and verbally abused and harassed over a long period of time." The complaint also alleges that Lynn has suffered depression and a "fear of being with other men," and that her enjoyment of life has been substantially curtailed. Finally, it is alleged that Lynn has incurred, and will continue to incur, medical and psychological expenses in an effort to become cured or relieved from the effects of her mental distress.

* * * Here, we find that Lynn has sufficiently alleged that as a result of enduring Robert's physical and psychological abuse for the duration of their 11–year marriage and beyond, she suffered severe emotional distress. Therefore, where the complaint sets forth sufficient facts which, if proven, could entitle Lynn to relief, we conclude that she has stated a cause of action for intentional infliction of emotional distress. * * *

* * *

Affirmed.

NOTE AND QUESTIONS

Varying tolerance for marital misconduct. Feltmeier relied partly on the duration of the parties' marriage in finding the husband's conduct sufficiently outrageous to trigger tort liability. Would the husband's conduct have been tortious in a shorter marriage? Is it appropriate for courts to vary their assessment of "outrage" according to the individual circumstances of the parties' marriage? In defining what qualifies as a ground for divorce, the South Dakota Supreme Court has held:

> Any definition of extreme cruelty in a marital setting must necessarily differ according to the personalities of the parties involved. What might be acceptable and even commonplace in the relationship between rather stolid individuals could well be extraordinary and highly unacceptable in the lives of more sensitive or high-strung husbands and wives. Family traditions, ethnic and religious backgrounds, local customs and standards and other cultural differences all come into play when trying to determine what should fall within the parameters of a workable marital relationship and what will not.

Hybertson v. Hybertson, 582 N.W.2d 402, 404–05 (S.D. 1998) (quoting *Pochop v. Pochop,* 233 N.W.2d 806, 807 (S.D. 1975)). Should courts consider such variables in defining the boundaries of tort liability within a marriage? How would the *Hybertson* court, or the *Feltmeier* court, assess the sufficiency of the tort claim in the following case?

HAKKILA v. HAKKILA

Court of Appeals of New Mexico, 1991.
812 P.2d 1320.

HARTZ, JUDGE.

In response to the petition of E. Arnold Hakkila (husband) for dissolution of marriage, Peggy J. Hakkila (wife) counter-petitioned for damages arising from alleged intentional infliction of emotional distress. Husband appeals from the judgment entered against him on the tort claim and from the award of attorney's fees in the divorce proceeding. We reverse the damage award and remand for further proceedings with respect to the award of attorney's fees.

I. FACTS

Husband and wife were married on October 29, 1975. Each had been married before. They permanently separated in February 1985. Husband filed his petition for dissolution of marriage the following month. Husband, who holds a Ph.D. in chemistry, had been employed at Los Alamos National Laboratory throughout the marriage. Wife, a high school graduate with credit hours toward a baccalaureate degree in chemistry and a vocational degree as a chemical technician, had been employed at the laboratory as a secretary for seven years and as a chemical technician for about seven and one-half years. She voluntarily terminated her employment in December 1979.

The district court found that "[wife's] emotional and mental health, especially since the parties' separation, has been shown to have been characterized by acute depression and one psychotic episode." * * * Apparently all the experts agreed that wife was temporarily emotionally disabled at the time of the hearing.

Finding No. 22 summarized husband's intentional misconduct:

The manner in which [husband] treated [wife] during the marriage and which resulted in her disability and impairment is as follows. [Husband] on occasions throughout the marriage and continuing until the separation[:]

a. assaulted and battered [wife],

b. insulted [wife] in the presence of guests, friends, relatives, and foreign dignitaries,

c. screamed at [wife] at home and in the presence of others,

d. on one occasion locked [wife] out of the residence over night in the dead of winter while she had nothing on but a robe,

e. made repeated demeaning remarks regarding [wife's] sexuality,

f. continuously stated to [wife] that she was crazy, insane, and incompetent,

g. refused to allow [wife] to pursue schooling and hobbies,

h. refused to participate in normal marital relationship with [wife] which ultimately resulted in only having sexual relations with [wife] on four occasions in the last three years of the marriage, [and]

i. blamed his sexual inadequacies upon [wife].

* * *

* * * [Evidence in the record shows, among other acts,] several incidents of assault and battery. In late 1984 when wife was pushing her finger in husband's chest, he grabbed her wrist and twisted it severely. In 1981 during an argument in their home husband grabbed wife and threw her face down across the room, into a pot full of dirt. In 1978 when wife was putting groceries in the camper, husband slammed part of the camper shell down on her head and the trunk lid on her hands. * * *

* * *

II.   Should We Recognize the Tort of Intentional Infliction of Emotional Distress in the Marital Context?

* * *

* * * [In other contexts, New Mexico law has allowed recovery for intentional infliction of emotional distress.] Wife contends that we must recognize the tort when committed by one spouse against the other because New Mexico has abandoned immunity for interspousal torts. Yet the abolition of immunity does not mean that the existence of the marriage must be ignored in determining the scope of liability. * * *

* * * [T]he family relationship can be an important consideration in analyzing intrafamilial torts, both negligent and intentional. * * *

* * *

Considerations that justify limiting liability for intentional infliction of emotional distress to only outrageous conduct also suggest a very limited scope for the tort in the marital context.

Conduct intentionally or recklessly causing emotional distress to one's spouse is prevalent in our society. This is unfortunate but perhaps not surprising, given the length and intensity of the marital relationship. Yet even when the conduct of feuding spouses is not particularly unusual, high emotions can readily cause an offended spouse to view the other's misconduct as "extreme and outrageous." Thus, if the tort of outrage is construed loosely or broadly, claims of outrage may be tacked on in typical marital disputes, taxing judicial resources.

In addition, a spouse's most distressing conduct is likely to be privileged. Partners who are pledged to live together for a lifetime have a right to criticize each other's behavior. * * * "You look awful" or even "I don't love you" can be very wounding, but these statements cannot justify liability.

Not only should intramarital activity ordinarily not be the basis for tort liability, it should also be protected against disclosure in tort litigation. * * * Any litigation of a claim is certain to require exposure of the intimacies of married life. This feature of the tort distinguishes it from intramarital torts already recognized in New Mexico. For example, a suit by one spouse against another arising out of an automobile accident poses no such risk. Nor does one ordinarily think of exposure of an incident of battery as implicating legitimate privacy interests. In contrast, in this case the judge found that it was extreme and outrageous conduct for husband to refuse sexual relations with wife. Should we really use this tort as a basis for inquiry into a matter of such intimacy? In determining the scope of the tort of outrage in the marital context, it is necessary to consider the privacy interests of the accused spouse.

* * *

A cautious approach to the tort of intramarital outrage also finds support in the public policy of New Mexico to avoid inquiry into what went wrong in a marriage. New Mexico was the first state to provide for no-fault divorce on the ground of incompatibility. New Mexico apportions community property without regard to fault, and grants alimony without consideration of punishment to either spouse.

* * *

Consequently, in determining when the tort of outrage should be recognized in the marital setting, the threshold of outrageousness should be set high enough—or the circumstances in which the tort is recognized should be described precisely enough, *e.g.*, child snatching—that the social good from recognizing the tort will not be outweighed by unseemly and invasive litigation of meritless claims.

* * *

III.   DID WIFE PROVE OUTRAGE?

We now move to the specifics of the case before us. The merits of wife's claim can be disposed of summarily. Husband's insults and outbursts fail to meet the legal standard of outrageousness. He was privileged to refrain from intercourse. There was no evidence that the other conduct caused severe emotional distress, as opposed to transient pain or discomfort.

Indeed, this case illustrates the risk of opening the door too wide to claims of this nature. Despite the claim's lack of merit, husband was subjected to a six-day trial, to say nothing of discovery and other preparation, surveying the rights and wrongs of a ten-year marriage. Motions for summary judgment should be viewed sympathetically in similar cases. If the potential harms from this kind of litigation are too frequently realized, it may be necessary to reconsider husband's suggestion that the tort of outrage be denied in the interspousal context.

We reverse the decision in favor of wife on her claim of intentional infliction of emotional distress.

* * *

IT IS SO ORDERED.

DONNELLY, JUDGE (specially concurring).

* * *

This case raises a troublesome issue of first impression. Husband argues on appeal that public policy considerations should preclude a spouse from initiating a cause of action for intentional infliction of emotional distress predicated upon conduct arising during the marriage of the parties and from raising the tort claim in the divorce proceeding.

* * *

* * * [I]n *Simmons v. Simmons*, 773 P.2d 602 (Colo. Ct. App. 1988), the Colorado Court of Appeals observed that considerations of fault or

misconduct are inappropriate in proceedings for dissolution of marriage, noting that divorce actions are primarily equitable in nature. The *Simmons* court held:

> [W]e adopt the reasoning of the Utah and Arizona courts, and hold that the efficient administration of dissolution cases requires their insulation from the peculiarities of matters at law. The joinder of marriage dissolution actions with claims sounding in tort or, for instance, contract would require our trial courts to address many extraneous issues, including trial by jury, and the difference between the "amicable settlement of disputes that have arisen between parties to a marriage," and the adversarial nature of other types of civil cases. Moreover, such would create tension between the acceptance of contingent fees in tort claims and our strong and longstanding public policy against contingent fees in domestic cases. We conclude that sound policy considerations preclude either permissive or compulsory joinder of interspousal tort claims, or non-related contract claims, with dissolution of marriage proceedings.

Id. at 604–05.

* * *

* * * Because emotional distress, and at times severe emotional distress, is a concomitant factor accompanying the dissolution of many marriages, litigation of a tort claim for intentional infliction of emotional distress at the same time the court is hearing an action for dissolution of marriage improperly injects issues of fault into no-fault divorce proceedings and is destructive of efforts of the trial court to mediate custody and property disputes or to achieve an equitable resolution of the issues between the parties. * * * The better procedure for the trial judge to follow where a tort claim for outrage is joined with an action for dissolution of marriage is to bifurcate the tort claim from the trial of the divorce proceedings so that the tort claim may be tried separately.

* * *

NOTES AND QUESTIONS

1. *"Outrageous conduct" in marriage.* Like most courts that have permitted spouses to sue for intentional infliction of emotional distress, *Feltmeier* adopts the standard definition of the tort without any special modifications for the marital context. The usual tort standard requires "conduct * * * so outrageous in character, and so extreme in degree, as to go beyond all possible bounds of decency, and to be regarded as atrocious, and utterly intolerable in a civilized community." Restatement (2d) of Torts § 46, *cmt. d* (1965); *see also Moyer v. Moyer*, 2005 WL 2043823 (Tex. Ct. App. Aug. 26, 2005) (approving use of standard jury instruction patterned after this Restatement language in a spousal IIED case); *McCulloh v. Drake*, 24 P.3d 1162, 1170 (Wyo. 2001) (adopting this standard in spousal IIED case).

Should an even higher standard of atrocity be required to permit tort recovery against a spouse, as *Hakkila* suggests? In what way exactly should the fact that the parties are married affect our judgment about their conduct? *Hakkila* suggests that the law should anticipate and privilege a certain amount of hurtful conduct that might be actionable between strangers. On the other hand, should the intimacy and emotional vulnerability of the marital relationship make us judge deliberate cruelties *more* harshly?

Professors Ellman and Sugarman take the position that *Hakkila* did not go far enough in raising the bar against spousal IIED claims. They acknowledge that some cases are extreme enough to warrant tort recovery between spouses, but worry that even *Hakkila*'s "heightened" standard will do little to limit judicial intervention to the truly exceptional cases:

> * * * [W]e remain concerned about how the *Hakkila* vision actually will play out. * * * For example, in *Koepke v. Koepke*, [556 N.E.2d 1198 (Ohio Ct. App. 1989),] a husband sued his wife for IIED when she revealed that her child was not his. The Ohio appeals court, overturning the trial court's dismissal, remanded the case to have the jury decide whether the wife's conduct was outrageous. In *Whelan v. Whelan*, [588 A.2d 251 (Conn. Super. Ct. 1991),] a wife sued her husband claiming that he had falsely told her that he had tested positive for AIDS and that she should go away with their son so that he would not have to watch his father die. The wife complained of suffering additional distress when she later learned that her husband had lied to her and did not have AIDS after all. Although this case arose on the pleadings, the Connecticut court made it clear that so far as it was concerned, if the allegations were proven the husband's behavior would meet the "outrageousness" standard.

> Although we do not condone the lies the defendant spouses allegedly told in these two cases, they seem to us to be just the sort of lies that commonly lead to marital break-ups. The conduct does not seem to us to be meaningfully different from that in *Hakkila* * * *, nor does it seem to meet the "high threshold" discussed in *Hakkila*. Yet given the reactions of the appeals courts in these two cases, we have little doubt that even with *Hakkila*'s admonitions, some juries would find for the plaintiffs— and in large amounts.

* * *

> In the end, then, we conclude that it is probably a mistake for the courts to make tort law available for claims between divorcing spouses, apart from cases in which the abusive conduct is criminal. This would bar most, if not all, claims for IIED or invasion of privacy [or misrepresentation], while allowing claims for physical violence and the like.

Ira Mark Ellman & Stephen D. Sugarman, *Spousal Emotional Abuse as a Tort?*, 55 Md. L. Rev. 1268, 1328–29, 1343 (1996). Does this proposal set the bar too high? Not high enough? *See Chen v. Fischer*, 810 N.Y.S.2d 96, 98 n.2 (2005) (holding that "New York does not recognize a cause of action to recover damages for intentional infliction of emotional distress between spouses") (internal quotation omitted). Would you favor liability in either of the misrepresentation cases mentioned above, even if no criminal conduct occurred?

2. *Tortious misrepresentation of paternity.* Professors Ellman and Sugarman criticize *Koepke* for leaving open the possibility of tort recovery where a wife deliberately misleads her husband into believing that he is the biological father of her child. A later Ohio decision denied recovery on these facts, concluding that the wife's concealment that the child was conceived during an extramarital affair was not "extreme and outrageous." *Bailey v. Searles–Bailey*, 746 N.E.2d 1159, 1166 (Ohio Ct. App. 2000). Some other courts have held even more broadly that any tort recovery for misrepresenting paternity would be against public policy. *See Day v. Heller*, 653 N.W.2d 475 (Neb. 2002); *Doe v. Doe*, 747 A.2d 617 (Md. 2000); *Pickering v. Pickering*, 434 N.W.2d 758 (S.D. 1989). Certainly, recognizing a legal duty on the part of pregnant wives to notify their husbands about possible non-paternity might destabilize marriages that otherwise would survive in ignorant "bliss." But should tort recovery be denied after divorce when there is no longer any marriage to be saved? *Cf. Koelle v. Zwiren*, 672 N.E.2d 868, 875 (Ill. App. Ct. 1996) (allowing IIED claim where parties were never married). What other policy concerns might remain? If one party tricks the other into conceiving a child, such as by lying about use of birth control, does the tricked parent have a tort action against the other? *See Wallis v. Smith*, 22 P.3d 682 (N.M. Ct. App. 2001) (rejecting tort liability on public policy grounds). *Wallis* appears as a lead case in Chapter 5; a tricked father's child support obligations are discussed further in Chapter 11.

3. *Tortious transmission of disease.* Courts have held that a spouse who knows or should know that he carries a sexually transmitted disease has a duty to disclose the disease to the other spouse before engaging in sexual relations. *E.g., Ray v. Wisdom*, 166 S.W.3d 592 (Mo. Ct. App. 2005); *San Pedro v. San Pedro*, 910 So.2d 426 (Fla. Ct. App. 2005); *Dubovsky v. Dubovsky*, 725 N.Y.S.2d 832 (Sup. Ct. 2001); *see generally* Deana A. Pollard, *Sex Torts*, 91 Minn. L. Rev. 769 (2007). Should a similar duty be extended to any spouse who has engaged in extramarital relations, on the theory that the affair *might* have exposed him or her to infection? *See In re Marriage of J.T.*, 891 P.2d 729, 732 (Wash. Ct. App. 1995) (holding that "Washington law does not recognize a legal duty to disclose extramarital sexual relations to one's spouse"). Why or why not?

4. *Compatibility with policy of no-fault divorce.* As *Hakkila* acknowledges, allowing interspousal tort recovery arguably undermines the policy goals of no-fault divorce. As explained more fully in Chapter 8, all states now allow some form of no-fault divorce, although in most states divorce on traditional fault grounds remains an option. In many jurisdictions, moreover, courts are not permitted to consider marital fault in decisions concerning alimony or property distribution. No state permits consideration of marital fault in determining child support amounts; marital fault may be considered in custody and visitation decisions only where the misconduct affects the best interests of the child. Professor Robert Spector suggests that the very unavailability of divorce as a forum for vindicating fault claims helped fuel interest in interspousal tort litigation. "The use of a tort suit is a method of vindicating the moral innocence of one spouse and, at the same time, indicating the moral blame of the other." Robert G. Spector, *Marital Torts: The Current Legal Landscape*, 33 Fam. L.Q. 745, 746 (1999). Yet, a leading rationale for the shift

to no-fault divorce was a conviction that judicial assignment of blame for marriage failure is often futile or socially destructive. Does this conviction suggest the need to limit the sort of tort claims spouses may litigate? Professor Harry Krause contends that returning considerations of marital fault to "the financial aftermath of marriage through tort law will reintroduce to the end of marriage more and worse acrimony than no-fault divorce ever eliminated." Harry D. Krause, *On the Danger of Allowing Marital Fault To Re–Emerge in the Guise of Torts,* 73 Notre Dame L. Rev. 1355, 1364 (1998).

5. *The problem of double recovery.* In jurisdictions that permit consideration of marital fault in alimony or marital property awards, a tort judgment might duplicate compensation the party has already received through the division of marital assets in divorce. For example, in one Texas case, a wife obtained a divorce from her husband for cruelty and requested a disproportionate share of the marital assets based partly on the husband's "fault in the breakup of the marriage." In the same action, the wife sought tort damages for the husband's intentional infliction of emotional distress, claiming that he had engaged in a long pattern of physically and emotionally abusive behavior. She prevailed in both her requests: The trial court awarded her 60% of the marital assets plus $150,000 in tort damages, more than wiping out the husband's share of the property division. *See Ross v. Ross,* 2004 WL 792317 (Tex. Ct. App. Apr. 15, 2004). All agree that when "a tort action is tried with the divorce, the court must avoid awarding a double recovery," *id.* at *2, but avoidance can sometimes be difficult. The court of appeals sustained both awards for the wife in *Ross,* holding that the disproportionate property award to her could have been properly based on factors other than the husband's cruelty during the marriage, such as his greater earning capacity. *Id.* at *12. South Dakota has attempted to solve the problem by holding that "the tort of intentional infliction of emotional distress should be unavailable as a matter of public policy when it is predicated on conduct which leads to the dissolution of a marriage." *Pickering v. Pickering,* 434 N.W.2d 758, 761 (S.D. 1989). Even so, the state supreme court later upheld an IIED award in a divorce action, reasoning that the tort judgment compensated solely for outrageous conduct during the pendency of the divorce proceeding, while other, earlier cruelty provided a sufficient ground for the divorce itself. *See Christians v. Christians,* 637 N.W.2d 377, 381–83 (S.D. 2001).

6. *Questions of joinder and procedure.* As Judge Donnelly's concurring opinion in *Hakkila* suggests, availability of tort remedies between spouses raises complex procedural questions. Should the tort claims be joined with the divorce action itself? Should the failure to raise a tort claim at the time of the divorce preclude raising the claim later in a separate action? Or, to the contrary, should parties be required to litigate torts claims separately from the divorce? The courts are sharply divided on all of these questions. *See* Barbara Glesner Fines, *Joinder of Tort Claims in Divorce Actions,* 12 J. Am. Acad. Matrimonial Law. 285 (1994).

As in *Hakkila,* many jurisdictions permit spouses to litigate tort claims in the divorce action itself, and some actually *require* joinder. *See, e.g., Brennan v. Orban,* 678 A.2d 667 (N.J. 1996) (joinder is ordinarily mandatory, but trial judge retains discretion to sever divorce and tort claims); *San Pedro v. San Pedro,* 910 So.2d 426 (Fla. Ct. App. 2005) (permissive joinder); *Twyman v.*

Twyman, 855 S.W.2d 619 (Tex. 1993) (joinder encouraged but not required). Some jurisdictions disallow or discourage joinder, so parties must litigate sequentially, as in *Feltmeier*. E.g., *McCulloh v. Drake*, 24 P.3d 1162 (Wyo. 2001) (joinder not allowed). In a number of jurisdictions, trial judges may exercise discretion in deciding whether to allow joinder on the facts of each case, depending on factors such as whether the tort claimant has demanded a jury trial or whether the divorce is sought on no-fault grounds. *See Christians v. Christians*, 637 N.W.2d 377, 386–87 (S.D. 2001) (Konenkamp, J., specially concurring). Combining the actions is likely to minimize overall court time and litigation expense, but it raises other complications. In rejecting a rule requiring joinder, the New York Court of Appeals summarized the prevailing concerns:

> [P]ersonal injury tort actions and divorce actions do not constitute a convenient trial unit. * * * They seek different types of relief and require different types of proof. Moreover, a personal injury action is usually tried by a jury, in contrast to a matrimonial action, which is typically decided by a judge when the issue of fault is not contested. Further, personal injury attorneys are compensated by contingency fee, whereas matrimonial attorneys are prohibited from entering into fee arrangements that are contingent upon the granting of a divorce or a particular property settlement or distributive award.
>
> * * *
>
> * * * To require joinder of interspousal personal injury claims with the matrimonial action would complicate and prolong the divorce proceeding. This would be contrary to the goal of expediting these proceedings and minimizing the emotional damage to the parties and their families. Delaying resolution of vital matters such as child support and custody or the distribution of assets to await the outcome of a personal injury action could result in extreme hardship and injustice to the families involved, especially for victims of domestic violence.

Chen v. Fischer, 810 N.Y.S.2d 96, 98–99 (2005).

Where joinder is allowed, principles of res judicata may bar a claimant from bringing subsequently a tort claim that could have been raised in the divorce. *See Horwitz v. Horwitz*, 16 S.W.3d 599, 604–05 (Mo. Ct. App. 2000). Res judicata is ordinarily no barrier where joinder is prohibited or where the factual basis for the tort claim is independent of the ground for divorce. *See McCulloh*, 24 P.3d at 1171; *Christians,* 637 N.W.2d at 387 (Konenkamp, J., specially concurring); *Cater v. Cater*, 846 S.W.2d 173 (Ark. 1993). In New York, failure to join tort claims in a dissolution proceeding will bar a subsequent suit only "if fault allegations are actually litigated in a matrimonial action." *Chen*, 810 N.Y.S.2d at 102. For a helpful analysis, see Andrew Schepard, *Divorce, Interspousal Torts, and Res Judicata*, 24 Fam. L.Q. 127 (1990). An additional pitfall for tort claimants may be found in a settlement agreement filed in connection with the divorce. An agreement broadly claiming to resolve "all claims" between the divorcing parties may be found to preclude future tort claims. *See, e.g., Cerniglia v. Cerniglia*, 679 So.2d 1160 (Fla. 1996).

SECTION 3:　TORT RECOVERY AGAINST THIRD PARTIES

Even when interspousal tort immunity was the norm, courts entertained several different kinds of family-related tort litigation against defendants outside the intact family. First, courts allowed *aspirants* to marriage—not yet within the scope of interspousal immunity—to sue for "breach of promise to marry" and a host of other "heart balm" torts (so called because legal damages were meant to provide balm for the wounded heart). Second, in addition to permitting recovery for intentional invasions of family interests, plaintiffs were permitted to recover for damage to family relationships—"loss of consortium"—occasioned by negligent injury to a loved one.

Courts and legislatures have comprehensively reexamined these tort actions in recent decades. For one thing, many of these actions were once gender-specific and patently patriarchal. Loss of consortium claims were originally available only to husbands—not wives—because only wives were obligated to provide services in the marriage; the actions of criminal conversation and seduction originally protected only the interests of husbands and fathers in the chastity of their wives and daughters. (An 1872 California statute, for instance, recognized an action for "[t]he seduction of a wife, daughter, orphan sister, or servant." Cal. Civ. Code Ann. § 49 historical note (West 1982).) Changing social attitudes, as well as modern understandings of the Equal Protection Clause, plainly made these gender boundaries untenable. Many jurisdictions now provide gender equality by extending a right of action to wives and mothers, while other jurisdictions have simply eliminated the causes of action altogether.

Beyond specific concerns over gender discrimination, most jurisdictions have more generally reconsidered the utility of providing legal redress for broken hearts. While most jurisdictions continue to provide recovery for loss of consortium—and some have even expanded liability to cover additional family relationships—the trend is now strongly against "heart balm" recovery for intimate injuries. This Section examines both developments, starting with the growing hostility to "heart balm" remedies and then turning to the continuing allowance for "consortium" damages. As you read these materials, consider whether the two lines of doctrine are in tension.

A.　HEART BALM TORTS

At common law, a host of tort causes of action protected interests in family relations against intentional disruption by outsiders. A jilted fiancée could recover for "breach of promise to marry." A spouse whose partner had been led astray could sue the paramour for "alienation of affections." Many courts recognized a parallel action for parents who claimed that a third party—a counselor or coach, for example—had turned a child against the parents. Other actions provided tort recovery directly for wrongful sexual intercourse: "Criminal conversation" created liability for having intercourse with a partner married to another; "seduction" provided recovery for deceitful courting to a parent or, in some states, the target of the seduction.

In recent decades, the tide has turned against these torts. Many states have enacted "heart balm" statutes abolishing the amatory torts. Where the common law torts persist, courts now construe them narrowly or limit the available remedy. Even so, as the following decisions suggest, plaintiffs continue to turn to the courts, sometimes attempting to recast their complaints in more modern forms.

BROWN v. STRUM

U.S. District Court for the District of Connecticut, 2004.
350 F. Supp. 2d 346.

ARTERTON, DISTRICT JUDGE.

Plaintiff Cleveland Brown brings a personal injury lawsuit against Adam Strum, alleging fraud and intentional infliction of emotional distress after the termination of their two-month romantic relationship. * * * The complaint invokes this Court's diversity jurisdiction under 28 U.S.C. § 1332. Defendant now moves to dismiss the complaint for failure to state a claim upon which relief may be granted, under Fed. R. Civ. P. 12(b)(6). For the reasons that follow, Defendant's Motion to Dismiss is GRANTED.

I. FACTUAL BACKGROUND

The following facts are alleged in the complaint. Brown and Strum were members of an online dating service known as Match.Com. On September 17, 2002, Strum read the plaintiff's online profile and emailed her through the Match.Com service. Brown viewed Strum's online profile, which indicated that Strum was divorced, and then answered his email. On September 24, 2002, the parties spoke over the phone, and Strum again, in answer to a question from Brown, represented that he was divorced and looking to remarry and have more children.

Over the next few weeks, Brown and Strum met in person several times. The complaint does not specify where the parties met; the plaintiff is from Stamford, Connecticut and the defendant from Mt. Kisco, New York. The parties also spoke on the telephone "almost daily" during this time. On the weekend of October 4, 2002, Strum and Brown went to Puerto Rico together. They saw each other several times over the next few weeks, and "engaged in sexual relations on most occasions."

Brown alleges that throughout this time, Strum "kept reinforcing [her] belief that he was divorced and interested in marrying her." * * *

* * *

III. DISCUSSION

Plaintiff argues that Defendant's conduct amounts to fraud because he induced her to enter a romantic relationship and to engage in sexual relations upon the false representation that he was unmarried. She further alleges that the defendant's conduct amounted to intentional infliction of emotional distress because he knew that she was particularly vulnerable and took advantage of her sensitivities. The defendant counters that plaintiff's complaint is no more than an attempt to circumvent statutes in Connecticut and New York that eliminated so-called "heart balm" causes of action, including seduction, breach of promise to marry, criminal conversation, and alienation of affections.

A. *Choice of Law*

* * *

The outcome-determinative legal issue in this case is whether there exists a cause of action for seduction or breach of promise to marry. Connecticut and New York laws are identical in this regard. * * * Thus there is no need to perform a choice of law analysis, and the rules common to both Connecticut and New York will be applied.

B. *Common Law "Heart Balm" Actions*

At common law, a plaintiff could bring a variety of damages actions arising in the context of romantic relationships. These included causes of action for alienation of affections, criminal conversation, seduction, and breach of promise to marry. Only a spouse could bring an action for alienation of affections or criminal conversation; the former tort action provided redress against a third party who won the love of the plaintiff's spouse, while the latter involved sexual intercourse with the plaintiff's spouse. Because no spousal relationship is alleged, these two tort actions are inapplicable here.

At common law in Connecticut, a cause of action for seduction belonged to the parent of a dependant child who was seduced, and allowed the parent to recover damages for, *e.g.*, loss of the child's services or the expense of delivering an out-of-wedlock baby. In Connecticut, a woman could not maintain a cause of action for her own seduction, absent an allegation of forcible rape. Thus Brown's action could not have been maintained on her own behalf as a seduction claim in Connecticut. New York common law, however, allowed a woman to maintain an action for seduction on her own behalf.

Under both Connecticut and New York common law, there existed a tort action for breach of a promise to marry. This action could be maintained by an unmarried plaintiff who received and relied on the defendant's promise to marry him/her, which the defendant broke. Commonly, such tort actions were brought when a fiancé "enter[ed] into and [broke] off a sexual relationship by means of allegedly false promises" to marry the plaintiff. *Sanders v. Rosen*, 605 N.Y.S.2d 805, 811 (Sup. Ct. 1993).

Both Connecticut and New York have statutorily abolished the cause of action for breach of promise to marry. Conn. Gen. Stat. § 52–572b, N.Y. Civ. Rights L. § 80–a. New York also abolished its common law cause of action for seduction, and even criminalized the filing of any lawsuit alleging any abolished heart balm claim. N.Y. Civ. Rights L. §§ 81, 83.

The Connecticut Supreme Court explained its legislature's reasoning in barring heart balm actions as follows:

> . . . [T]he Act was designed to do away with excessive claims for damages, claims coercive by their very nature and, all too frequently, fraudulent in character; the purpose was to prevent the recovery of damages based upon contused feelings, sentimental bruises, blighted affections, wounded pride, mental anguish and social humiliation; for impairment of health, for expenditures made in anticipation of the wedding, for the deprivation of other opportunities to marry and for the loss of the pecuniary and social advantages which the marriage offered.

Piccininni v. Hajus, 429 A.2d 886, 888 (Conn. 1980). The New York legislature was motivated by similar concerns, namely avoiding "grave abuses, causing extreme annoyance, embarrassment, humiliation and pecuniary damage" that were attendant to seduction and breach of promise to marry actions. *Tuck v. Tuck,* 238 N.Y.S.2d 317 (App. Div. 1963).

C.   *Emotional Distress and Fraud*

Courts of both states have held that a plaintiff may not circumvent the statutory prohibition on heart balm actions by recharacterizing them as emotional distress or fraud claims. To determine whether a plaintiff has a bona fide claim or is simply using an emotional distress claim to evade the anti-heart balm statute, courts look to the underlying factual allegations of the complaint. * * *

* * * The plaintiff in *Bouchard* [*v. Sundberg,* 834 A.2d 744 (Conn. App. Ct. 2003)], for example, attempted to bring a claim for emotional distress based upon his ex-wife's alleged attempts to alienate his children from him after a divorce. Because Connecticut had barred damages actions for alienation of affection, the plaintiff's claim was not cognizable even when framed as a claim for infliction of emotional distress. In reaching this conclusion, the court examined the factual basis for the plaintiff's claim, which included the ex-wife encouraging the children not to communicate with him, and stated that any action "stemming from the alienation activities" would be barred by statute.

* * *

The Connecticut Supreme Court has also made clear that an action for fraud may not be maintained as a method of circumventing § 52–572b. *Piccininni,* 429 A.2d at 888. A fraud action relating to a promise to marry only may be maintained in Connecticut for "restitution of specific property or money transferred in reliance on various false and fraudulent representations, apart from any promise to marry, as to their intended use." *Id.* at 888–89. Thus, a plaintiff was permitted to maintain an action where he sued to recover money spent renovating the defendant's house in reliance on defendant's promise that she would marry him and allow him to move in with her. However, the Supreme Court carefully distinguished an action to regain property from one "to recover for the breach [of a promise to marry] itself." *Id.* at 889.

* * *

Plaintiff Brown has not made any equivalent allegations in the instant case triggering any exception. * * *

* * *

"The conduct described in the complaint is dishonorable, but this court is powerless to provide plaintiff the relief she seeks." *Manko* [*v. Volynsky,* No. 95–CIV–2585 (MBM), 1996 WL 243238, at *1 (S.D.N.Y. May 10, 1996)]. Plaintiff may not circumvent clear statutory directives by reframing her claims as fraud or infliction of emotional distress.

IV.   CONCLUSION

For the foregoing reasons, the complaint fails to state a claim upon which relief may be granted, and Defendant's Motion to Dismiss must be GRANTED * * * .

* * *

NOTE

Brown is an unusual foray by a federal court into the fields of tort and family law based on the parties' diversity of citizenship. The decision bars emotional distress claims arising from intimate misconduct in dating, based on the legislature's desire to preclude recovery for mere " 'contused feelings [and] sentimental bruises.' " In contrast, *Feltmeier* refused to bar emotional distress claims between spouses, noting that the usual IIED standard of "outrageous conduct" sets a high enough bar to avoid imposing liability for " 'mere insults, indignities, threats, annoyances, petty oppressions, or other trivialities.' " 798 N.E.2d at 80. Consider whether *Brown* could similarly have relied on the standard IIED elements to screen out insubstantial claims of injury. The contrasting results in *Brown* and *Feltmeier* arguably turn the traditional common-law rule on its head: recovery for intimate injury is allowed *within* marriage, but denied *outside* marriage. In evaluating the outcome in *Brown,* consider also the Missouri Supreme Court's decision in the following case.

HELSEL v. NOELLSCH

Supreme Court of Missouri, 2003.
107 S.W.3d 231.

RICHARD B. TEITELMAN, JUDGE.

Katherine and David Helsel divorced in January 2001. In March 2001, [Katherine] Helsel filed suit against Sivi Noellsch for alienation of affection, alleging that Noellsch intentionally interfered with the marriage and caused it to fail.[1] A jury returned a verdict in favor of Helsel. Noellsch filed post-trial motions in the trial court to abolish the tort of alienation of affection. The trial court declined. The issue before this Court is whether the common law tort of alienation of affection remains a viable cause of action in Missouri. Because alienation of affection is premised upon antiquated concepts, faulty assumptions, and is inconsistent with precedent, the tort is abolished in Missouri. The judgment is reversed.

I.   HISTORY OF THE TORT

In order to ensure pure bloodlines and discourage adultery, the early Germanic tribes provided that men were entitled to payment from the wife's lover so that the husband could purchase a new spouse. As successors to the Germanic tradition, the Anglo–Saxons also provided a cause of action for men to recover for another's interference with the marital relationship. The basis for this cause of action was that wives were viewed as valuable servants to their husband. Later, early English common law established two causes of action, enticement and seduction, which are the precursors to the modern day torts of alienation of affection and criminal conversation. The purpose underlying both causes of action was to vindicate the husband's property rights in his wife.

Beginning with New York in 1864, almost every state in this country eventually established a cause of action for alienation of affection in which men, but not women, could vindicate their rights in the marital relationship. In the late nineteenth and early twentieth centuries, most states, including Missouri, acted to equalize the legal status of wives by allowing them to sue in their own names. Therefore, the original justification for the tort, that husbands had a property right in their wives, was undermined. Nonetheless, the tort persisted, but with a new rationale. Modern courts came to justify suits for alienation of affection as a means of preserving marriage and the family.

II.   ABOLITION

There are many persuasive reasons for abolishing the tort of alienation of affection. * * *

* * *

---

1.   In Missouri, a claim of alienation of affection requires proof that 1) the defendant engaged in wrongful conduct; 2) the plaintiff lost the affections or consortium of his or her spouse; and, 3) there was a causal connection between the defendant's conduct and the plaintiff's loss.

Even though the original property concepts remain inextricably bound to the tort, some still argue that suits for alienation of affection must be retained as a useful means of preserving marriages and protecting families. While these are laudable goals, it is unlikely that suits for alienation of affection actually serve this purpose. To the contrary, the opposite is likely true.

First, suits for alienation of affection are almost exclusively brought after the marriage is either legally dissolved or irretrievably broken. Revenge, not reconciliation, is often the primary motive.

Second, by filing suit, the plaintiff is publicly acknowledging the intimate details that led to the breakdown of the marriage. The necessarily adversarial positions taken in litigation over intensely personal and private matters does not serve as a useful means of preserving the marriage.

* * *

In *Thomas v. Siddiqui*, [869 S.W.2d 740 (Mo. 1994),] this Court abolished the closely related common law tort of criminal conversation. The only difference between alienation of affection and criminal conversation is that criminal conversation requires proof of an adulterous sexual relationship. However, this difference in the elements of the torts does not provide a good basis [for] distinguishing alienation of affection from criminal conversation because both torts simply represent different ways of interfering with the same relational interests. Moreover, in reality, criminal conversation and alienation of affection are typically alleged concurrently as the conduct at issue almost always involves adultery. If a spouse cannot recover because of an adulterous affair under a criminal conversation theory, a spouse should likewise be barred from recovery by simply attaching the moniker of "alienation of affection" to the petition. Consistency demands that the tort of alienation of affection be abolished as was the tort of criminal conversation.

III. CONCLUSION

When the reason for a rule of law disappears, so to[o] should the rule. * * * The tort of alienation of affection is abolished in Missouri.[3]

The judgment is reversed.

DUANE BENTON, JUDGE, dissenting.

The common law consistently compensates for interference with the marriage relation—"loss of consortium." Loss of consortium is the second of three elements in an alienation of affection claim. "The foundation of a cause of action for alienation of affection is the loss of consortium." *Kraus v. Kraus*, 693 S.W.2d 869, 873 (Mo. App. 1985).

---

3. This holding brings Missouri in line with the overwhelming majority of jurisdictions that have already abolished alienation of affection. Prior to this decision, thirty-four states have abolished the tort by statute and six have abolished it through the courts. Louisiana and Alaska never recognized the tort.

In tort cases where a spouse is injured, the other spouse often has a separate claim for loss of consortium. Most of these losses are caused by a defendant's negligence. In alienation of affection—an intentional tort—a defendant's intentional conduct causes the loss. It is inconsistent that the law compensates for negligent conduct causing a loss of consortium, but (after this opinion) does not compensate for intentional conduct causing the same loss.

The Restatement (Second) of Torts classifies loss of consortium as an "Indirect Interference with Marriage Relation." Restatement (Second) of Torts, section 693 (1977). The Restatement classifies alienation of affection as a "Direct Interference with Marriage Relation." [*Id.* § 683]. It is inconsistent that the law compensates for indirect interference with the marriage relation, but (after this opinion) not for direct interference.

The first reason the majority advances is the "antiquated property concepts" that originally justified alienation of affection. The original justification for loss of consortium was to compensate (only) a husband for his losses from an injury to his wife. *Novak v. Kansas City Transit, Inc.,* 365 S.W.2d 539, 543 (Mo. banc 1963). If the origin of a cause of action is decisive, consistency dictates abolishing loss of consortium claims.

The majority's second reason is "faulty assumptions." The majority expresses concern that suits for alienation of affection are brought after a marriage is dissolved or broken. This does not justify abolishing the tort, because claims for loss of consortium may be brought after the marriage relation ends. *See Bridges v. Van Enterprises,* 992 S.W.2d 322, 325 (Mo. Ct. App. 1999); *Wyatt v. R.D. Werner Co.,* 524 N.W.2d 579, 580–81 (N.D. 1994); Restatement (Second) of Torts, § 693, cmt. f (1977).

The majority intends to prevent public acknowledgment of the "intimate details" of the marriage and its breakdown. Again, this concern applies equally to loss of consortium claims.

> The most common explanation for allowing recovery for loss of consortium by a spouse ... is the impairment or destruction of the sexual life of a married couple by a tort-feasor as an element of damage in the spouse's consortium action.... [But] there are other elements, such as love, affection, care and companionship....

Powell [*v. American Motor Corp.*, 834 S.W.2d 184, 188 (Mo. 1992)].

The third reason advanced to abolish alienation of affection is "consistency" with abolition of the tort of criminal conversation nine years ago in *Thomas v. Siddiqui,* 869 S.W.2d 740 (Mo. banc 1994). To the contrary, a rationale for abolishing criminal conversation was that the tort of alienation of affection would still compensate for interference with the marriage relation. *Id.* at 741.

The *Thomas* case recognized that—contrary to the majority's assertion—there is a difference between the torts. Criminal conversation had only two elements: 1) an actual marriage, and 2) defendant had sexual intercourse with plaintiff's spouse. The only defense to criminal conversation was consent by the plaintiff. Damages were presumed.

Alienation of affection has three elements: 1) defendant's wrongful conduct; 2) plaintiff's loss of consortium; and, 3) a causal connection between defendant's conduct and plaintiff's loss. There are various defenses to alienation of affection, including causation, and the lack of wrongful conduct. Damages must be proved.

* * *

I would continue to recognize the tort of alienation of affection, like seven other states—Illinois, Hawaii, Mississippi, New Mexico, North Carolina, South Dakota, and Utah. True, six states have previously abolished alienation of affection by judicial decision. However, three Supreme Courts—having abolished criminal conversation—recently refused to abolish alienation of affection. *Bland v. Hill*, 735 So. 2d 414 (Miss. 1999); *Veeder v. Kennedy*, 589 N.W.2d 610 (S.D. 1999); *Norton v. Macfarlane*, 818 P.2d 8 (Utah 1991).

Because I would leave further action to the General Assembly, I dissent.

NOTES AND QUESTIONS

1. *Reframing amatory tort claims.* As *Brown* and *Helsel* illustrate, most states in recent decades have barred tort recovery for soured romance, even when plaintiffs attempt to frame their claims in other terms. *E.g., Marmelstein v. Kehillat New Hempstead*, 892 N.E.2d 375 (N.Y. 2008) (barring fraud and breach of fiduciary duty claims premised on religious leader's affair with plaintiff); *Bailey v. Faulkner*, 940 So.2d 247 (Ala. 2006) (barring claim of "negligent marital counseling" premised on the defendant's affair with the plaintiff's then-wife); *Jones v. Henderson*, 2004 WL 1936496 (Tenn. Ct. App. Aug. 30, 2004) (barring IIED claim against wife's paramour). But, as Judge Benton's dissent points out, the traditional tort actions linger on in some form in a handful of jurisdictions, sometimes recast as intentional infliction of emotional distress or some other cause of action. New Mexico, for example, permits IIED actions against paramours for disrupting a marriage but, following *Hakkila*, requires plaintiffs to "demonstrate the same high standard of extreme and outrageous conduct" that would apply in an action between spouses. *Padwa v. Hadley*, 981 P.2d 1234, 1239 (N.M. Ct. App. 1999). That standard is high indeed. *Padwa* found no cause of action against a one-time friend who allegedly set out to have sexual relationships with the plaintiff's wife, former wife, and former fiancée, causing a divorce and considerable torment for the plaintiff. In *Jones, supra*, the court found that the discovery of the defendant-paramour hiding naked in the closet of the marital bedroom while the wife's minor children slept in an adjacent room was not sufficiently "outrageous" to support recovery for IIED. *See Jones, supra,* at *3 (concluding that defendant's behavior was not "so atrocious as to go beyond the bounds of decency").

2. *Adultery torts.* In recent years, some academic commentators have suggested that courts and legislatures have gone too far in eliminating liability for interference with marital relations. Some of these critics have urged a revival of tort protection to promote society's important interests in marriage stability. *See* Nehal A. Patel, Note, *The State's Perpetual Protection of Adultery: Examining* Koestler v. Pollard *and Wisconsin's Faded Adultery Torts,* 2003 Wis. L. Rev. 1013, 1037. Professor William Corbett writes:

> Why do the laws of most states not permit you to sue your spouse's partner? If you are willing to forego killing her or him (which past civilizations assumed you would do) why can you not sue the marital interloper? If instead of engaging in sex with your spouse, the other person had walked up to you and taken a swing at you and hit you, you would have had a tort action for battery (and probably assault). If the person had taken a swing at you and missed, you probably would have had a tort action for assault. The person has sex with your spouse, and you have no tort action against that person. What does it say about contemporary American tort law and society that you cannot sue one who interferes in, and perhaps destroys, your marriage by engaging in sexual relations with your spouse?

William R. Corbett, *A Somewhat Modest Proposal To Prevent Adultery and Save Families: Two Old Torts Looking for a New Career,* 33 Ariz. St. L.J. 985, 988–89 (2001). Does Professor Corbett have a point? Isn't the pain caused by the breakup of a marriage likely to be far more significant than a simple (and plainly actionable) punch in the nose? Given the courts' recurring acknowledgment of society's powerful interests in marriage stability, shouldn't the law seek to deter adultery through tort? On the other hand, if one spouse strays from the marriage, is the third party likely to be the source of the problem?

3. *A modern role for the tort of seduction?* What about tort protection for sexual misconduct outside of marriage? Some jurisdictions continue to recognize a "tort of 'seduction of a person under the age of legal consent,' " although little modern case law applies the tort. *Donaldson v. Dep't of Real Estate,* 36 Cal.Rptr.3d 577, 589 (Ct. App. 2005); *see also* Wash. Rev. Code Ann. § 4.24.020 (West 2005) (providing that "[a] father or mother[ ] may maintain an action as plaintiff for the seduction of a child"); *D.L.S. v. Maybin,* 121 P.3d 1210 (Wash. Ct. App. 2005) (holding that seduction and other claims brought by father alleging that assistant manager of McDonald's restaurant had introduced his 15–year-old daughter, a restaurant employee, to "drugs and sex" could not be sustained against McDonald's parent corporation, but must be brought directly against assistant manager and franchise operator); *L.N.K. v. St. Mary's Med. Ctr.,* 785 N.E.2d 303 (Ind. Ct. App. 2003).

Is there any place for a modern tort of seduction involving only adults? A few jurisdictions have yet to abolish the tort. *E.g., Hodges v. Howell,* 4 P.3d 803, 805–06 (Utah Ct. App. 2000) (allowing husband to sue wife's paramour for alienation of affections and acknowledging continued existence of tort of seduction). Some commentators have defended a continuing role for a seduction tort from a feminist perspective. Professor Jane Larson has proposed reviving and revising the tort of seduction as one for "sexual fraud":

Sexual fraud, as I have named the tort for modern purposes, is an act of intentional, harmful misrepresentation made for the purpose of gaining another's consent to sexual relations. * * * I use the term "fraud" in this precise legal sense, not as the term is sometimes loosely used to refer to other, vaguely wrongful behavior. My purpose is to craft a legal vehicle that will address the physical and emotional injuries caused by deceptive inducement into sex. I begin from the premise that sexual fraud leads to nonconsensual sex because it deprives the victim of control over her body and denies her meaningful sexual choice. Like other sexual acts that are not fully consensual, sex induced by fraud has the potential to cause grave physical and emotional injury.

Jane E. Larson, *"Women Understand So Little, They Call My Good Nature 'Deceit' ": A Feminist Rethinking of Seduction,* 93 Colum. L. Rev. 374, 379–80 (1993). Does Professor Larson's emphasis on fraudulent inducement adequately overcome the concerns that have led most jurisdictions to reject tort recovery for seduction?

4. *Breach of promise to marry—and to divorce?* A few jurisdictions continue to recognize an action for breach of promise to marry, but lawsuits are rare. *E.g., In re Marriage of Witten,* 672 N.W.2d 768, 781 & n.3 (Iowa 2003); *Phillips v. Blankenship,* 554 S.E.2d 231 (Ga. Ct. App. 2001). In 2008, a Georgia jury awarded a would-be bride $150,000 in damages after her fiancé left a note in their bathroom breaking off the engagement. *See* Stephen M. Silverman, *Jury Awards Jilted Bride $150K,* People, July 25, 2008. Some jurisdictions limit damages to out-of-pocket losses. 740 Ill. Comp. Stat. Ann. § 15/2 (West 2002).

What about a breach of promise to *divorce*? In *Norton v. McOsker,* 407 F.3d 501 (1st Cir. 2005), the "other woman" in a 23–year adulterous relationship sued her lover for breaching an alleged promise to "divorce his wife, marry [the plaintiff] and take care of her for the rest of her life." Applying Rhode Island law, the First Circuit held that legal enforcement of a promise to divorce would be against public policy. The court went on, however, to analyze whether the plaintiff might vindicate her expectation of lifetime support from the husband under promissory estoppel. The court ultimately denied relief on the grounds that any promise made by the husband was too vague and that the plaintiff's claimed reliance was unreasonable. *Id.* at 506–08; *see also M.N. v. D.S.,* 616 N.W.2d 284, 288 (Minn. Ct. App. 2000) (female paramour's suit to recover for husband's misrepresentations about "his intentions to leave his wife, marry her, and have children in the future" was implicitly barred by state's "heart balm" statute abolishing the torts of seduction and breach of promise to marry). What public policy might be offended by compensating a broken promise to divorce? If it is a policy against destabilizing marriage, will enforcing a promise of financial support to an extramarital lover pose any less threat? Is a policy against destabilizing marriage forceful in a nation whose annual divorce rate under no-fault regimes hovers around 50%? Could such cases be brought instead as claims between cohabitants?

B. LOSS OF CONSORTIUM

The action for "loss of consortium" compensates family members for impairment of their intimate relationship with a tortiously injured loved one. Spouses are permitted to recover for the loss of the services, companionship, or society of a wrongfully injured or deceased spouse. And many courts recognize a similar claim for damage to the intimate relationship between parents and children. Thus, for example, a motorist who negligently collides with another driver may be held liable not only to the injured driver for the physical injuries directly caused, but also to the driver's spouse or children for any impairment of their relationship to their injured loved one. *E.g.*, *Peters v. Williams*, 917 So.2d 702 (La. Ct. App. 2005).

"The compensable elements of a claim of loss of consortium of a spouse include loss of love and affection, loss of companionship, loss of material services, loss of support, loss of aid and assistance, and loss of felicity. The elements of the child's claim [or a parent's] are the same except for any component of sexual relations." *Id.* at 712. Thus, where a defendant negligently injured a husband and father in a traffic accident, the accident victim's wife and daughter could recover for their losses:

> "Jackie [the wife] testified, without contradiction, that after this accident, Peters became withdrawn and alienated from his family; he is no longer intimate with her, and they physically separated in August 2003. Raisa testified that her dad is no longer available to talk about her problems, help her keep her animals or go fishing."

Id.

Some jurisdictions, while permitting recovery for spousal loss of consortium, do not allow similar claims on behalf of parents and children. *See, e.g.*, *Robinson v. Hartzell Propeller Inc.*, 276 F. Supp. 2d 412, 415 (E.D. Pa. 2003) (applying Pennsylvania law); *Roberts v. Williamson*, 111 S.W.3d 113 (Tex. 2003); *Mendillo v. Bd. of Educ. of East Haddam*, 717 A.2d 1177 (Conn. 1998). In these jurisdictions, a parent may recover for "loss of services of a child upon a proper showing of the value of lost services," but may not recover damages for the emotional injuries occasioned by lost love and companionship. *See Santoro v. Donnelly*, 340 F. Supp. 2d 464, 492–93 (S.D.N.Y. 2004) (applying New York law). At the other end of the spectrum, a few jurisdictions have been willing to allow loss-of-consortium damages to the parents of even an adult child, *see, e.g.*, *Hern v. Safeco Ins. Co.*, 125 P.3d 597, 607–08 (Mont. 2005) (recovery allowed where parents and adult child had "an extraordinarily close and interdependent relationship"), or to grandparents for injury to a grandchild, *see Fernandez v. Walgreen Hastings Co.*, 968 P.2d 774 (N.M. 1998) (grandparent may recover "where the plaintiff was a family caretaker and provider of parental affection to the deceased").

NOTES AND QUESTIONS

1. *Relationship to "heart balm" torts.* Is Judge Benton, dissenting in *Helsel*, correct that it is inconsistent to allow recovery for loss of consortium while denying recovery for alienation of affections and other heart balm torts?

2. *Consortium in non-traditional families.* Increasingly in recent years, plaintiffs have sought to recover for loss of consortium in the absence of a formal, legally recognized family relationship. The Massachusetts Supreme Judicial Court offered the following rationale for refusing to allow recovery by an unmarried female cohabitant after her male partner of more than 10 years was severely injured:

> A loss of consortium claim presupposes a legal right to consortium of the injured person. While [the two partners] * * * well may have a "stable, significant romantic relationship," * * * they chose not to marry and, consequently, have neither the obligation nor the "benefit of the rules of law that govern property, financial, and other matters in a marital relationship." To recognize a right to recover for loss of consortium by a person who could have but has declined to accept the correlative responsibilities of marriage undermines the "deep interest" that the Commonwealth has that the integrity of marriage "is not jeopardized."

Fitzsimmons v. Mini Coach of Boston, Inc., 799 N.E.2d 1256, 1257 (Mass. 2003). Other jurisdictions have widely agreed. *See, e.g., Milberger v. KBHL, Inc.*, 486 F. Supp. 2d 1156, 1160–65 (D. Haw. 2007) (applying Hawaii law); *Cramer v. Archdiocese of Cincinnati*, 814 N.E.2d 97, 103 (Ohio Ct. App. 2004); *Robinson*, 276 F. Supp. 2d at 413–14.

Would recognizing the relational injury to longterm cohabitants really undermine the state's interest in the integrity of marriage? Are there other reasons to deny recovery? What if the claimants had been prevented from legally marrying at the time of the injury? In 2008, the Massachusetts Supreme Judicial Court refused to allow a woman's consortium claim for injury to her same-sex partner; the couple had married as soon as the option became available after *Goodridge v. Department of Public Health*, 798 N.E.2d 941 (Mass. 2003), but the injury occurred earlier when they were living together as committed partners. Chief Justice Margaret Marshall, author of the court's opinion in *Goodridge*, expressed sympathy but emphasized the need for a clear rule:

> [T]he relief the plaintiff seeks ... would erase the bright line between civil marriage and other forms of relationship that has heretofore been carefully preserved by the Legislature and our prior decisions, including *Goodridge*. Granting such relief would create in effect a common-law or de facto quasi marital status that would promote litigation, permit judges to select from among marital benefits to which quasi marital couples might or might not be entitled, create uncertainty in the private as well as the public sphere about who is (or was) quasi married and for what purpose, and undercut the Legislature's role in defining the qualifications and characteristics of civil marriage.

Charron v. Amaral, 889 N.E.2d 946, 952–53 (Mass. 2008) (Marshall, C.J., concurring) (footnotes omitted); *accord Rettig v. Town of Woodbridge*, 2008 WL 2345145 (Conn. Super. Ct. May 14, 2008).

Are these concerns persuasive of the need to bar all such claims? At least one jurisdiction recently has allowed loss-of-consortium claims involving co-habiting partners who share "an intimate familial relationship." *Lozoya v. Sanchez*, 66 P.3d 948 (N.M. 2003); *see also* Barbara J. Cox, *Alternative Families: Obtaining Traditional Family Benefits Through Litigation, Legislation and Collective Bargaining*, 15 Wis. Women's L.J. 93, 133–37 (2000); John G. Culhane, *A "Clanging Silence": Same–Sex Couples and Tort Law*, 89 Ky. L.J. 911 (2000–2001).

3. *Wrongful birth.* Parents may ordinarily recover for the wrongful death of a minor child. Thus, where a child is killed through tortious misconduct, "the surviving parent, or parents, may recover for loss of affection and companionship that would have been derived from such child during its minority, in addition to all other elements of the damage usually recoverable in a wrongful death action." Ky. Rev. Stat. § 411.135 (Michie 1992). There is somewhat more controversy, however, over whether they should be able to recover in tort for the "wrongful birth" of a disabled child. Some courts permit recovery against doctors who negligently failed to diagnose a congenital defect or other medical abnormality in a fetus prior to birth, on the rationale that the negligence deprived the parents of an opportunity to make an informed decision about whether to go forward with the pregnancy. *See, e.g., Draper v. Jasionowski*, 858 A.2d 1141 (N.J. Super. Ct. App. Div. 2004); *Kush v. Lloyd*, 616 So.2d 415 (Fla. 1992). Other jurisdictions, however, have rejected such liability, contending that it would violate public policy to recognize the birth of an unwanted child as a compensable legal injury. The South Carolina Supreme Court, joining other jurisdictions in rejecting recovery for "wrongful birth," recently counted "[t]wenty-seven states, by judicial opinion, statute, or both, [that] have either refused to recognize or limited a wrongful life action" and "[t]hree states [that] * * * have allowed such a cause of action." *Willis v. Wu*, 607 S.E.2d 63, 68 (S.C. 2004); *see also* Philip G. Peters, Jr., *Rethinking Wrongful Life: Bridging the Boundary Between Tort and Family Law*, 67 Tul. L. Rev. 397 (1992); Mark Strasser, *Wrongful Life, Wrongful Birth, Wrongful Death and the Right To Refuse Treatment: Can Reasonable Jurisdictions Recognize All But One?*, 64 Mo. L. Rev. 29 (1999).

CHAPTER 8

DIVORCE

■ ■ ■

The preceding chapters have focused primarily upon legal regulation of the intact family or attempts to establish families through marriage, cohabitation, or parenthood. This Chapter commences an extended and regrettably necessary study of the laws of family dissolution. This Chapter focuses on the grounds for exiting marriage through divorce. Chapters 9 through 13 will explore the major ramifications of that exit, including property distribution, alimony, and child support, custody and visitation.

Public discussions of divorce often paint a bleak picture. Divorce is sometimes described as epidemic in the United States, a condition assertedly traceable largely to the "no-fault revolution" of the 1970s. Newspaper editorials grimly (and accurately) advise that the United States suffers from one of the world's highest divorce rates, and that U.S. marriages have barely a fifty-fifty chance of success. Estimates suggest that more than one million divorces occur each year in the United States. Given all this, it is perhaps hard to believe that the U.S. wedding industry continues to rake in an estimated $72–80 billion a year!

As with most popular accounts, the doomsday portrait of American marriage is partly true and partly false. There is no denying that divorce imposes genuine economic and emotional hardships on many families. (The effects of divorce on children are described in greater detail in Chapter 12.) It is also true, of course, that divorce has become commonplace in our society, with the divorce rate doubling since 1960. *See* Nat'l Marriage Project, The State of Our Unions 2007: The Social Health of Marriage in America 18 (2007), http://marriage.rutgers.edu/Publications/SOOU/SOOU2007.pdf.

But these statistics can also give an exaggerated impression of the risk of divorce. For starters, although the United States has one of the world's highest divorce rates (3.6 divorces per 1,000 population in 2005), it also has one of the world's highest marriage rates (7.5 marriages per 1,000 population in 2005). Paul D. Sutton & Martha L. Munson, U.S. Dep't of Health & Hum. Servs., *Births, Marriages, Divorces, and Deaths: Provisional Data for 2005*, 54 Nat'l Vital Stat. Rep. 15 (2006), http://www.cdc.gov/nchs/data/nvsr/nvsr54/nvsr54_15.pdf. Also, fair or not, the risk of marriage failure is not evenly distributed across the population. The risk of divorce is higher for second and subsequent marriages, and is further correlated with the spouses' age at marriage, income, educational attainment, religious affiliation, and family history of divorce. One study, for example, suggests that the risk of marriage failure is 30 percent lower for couples with an annual income over $50,000 than for those making less than $25,000; marrying after age 25 (versus under age 18) lowers the risk by 24%. *See* Nat'l Marriage Project, *supra*, at 20. Divorce is also disproportionately concentrated in the early years of marriage—half of all divorces occur within the first seven years of marriage—so that the risk of dissolution diminishes over time.

The divorce rate has actually been edging downward since peaking in the early 1980s. Nevertheless, the trend is "described by many experts as 'leveling off at a high level.' " *Id.* at 18. Given that domestic relations cases are said to constitute one-third of the civil dockets of the state courts, *see Developments in the Law—Unified Family Courts and the Child Protection Dilemma*, 116 Harv. L. Rev. 2099, 2099 (2003), divorce is necessarily an important focus of family law.

The limited data available suggest that most divorces are initiated by women. *See* E. Mavis Hetherington & John Kelly, For Better or For Worse: Divorce Reconsidered 8 (2002) (noting that in a comprehensive study of 1,400 families, "two out of every three marriages ended because the wife walked out"); Margaret F. Brinig & Douglas W. Allen, *"These Boots Are Made for Walking": Why Most Divorce Filers Are Women*, 2 Am. L. & Econ. Rev. 126 (2000). This might seem surprising given that women are more likely to bear the brunt of divorce's economic dislocation and are less likely to remarry. Yet, studies also show that men and women tend to experience and benefit from marriage differently. For men, marriage generally brings larger earning capacity and better physical and mental health; for women, the benefits of marriage more often dependant on its emotional quality. *See* Margaret F. Brinig, *In Search of Prince Charming*, 4 J. Gender, Race & Just. 321, 326–28 (2001). Professor Brinig writes:

> Since the emotional success of the marriage has little to do with the man's payoff and a great deal to do with his wife's, it is not surprising that she will frequently be the one to end the relationship in an unhappy marriage even if it has produced material rewards. Accordingly, the wife usually files for divorce or seeks separation, particularly if she can obtain custody of the children. Although she is less likely than he to repeat the marriage experience, she will be happier outside marriage than in an emotionally unsatisfying one.

Id. at 331–32.

SECTION 1: DIVORCE IN HISTORICAL CONTEXT

Divorce is very much a current topic of debate, but it is an ancient institution. For example, under Athenian law, a husband or wife needed only to file a notice with a magistrate to end all marital ties. Sarah B. Pomeroy, Goddesses, Whores, Wives, and Slaves: Women in Classical Antiquity 64–65 (1975). The divorce process was also relatively easy in early Egypt. Either the wife or husband could initiate a divorce, but only women were required to show cause, typically physical cruelty. Barbara Watterson, Women in Ancient Egypt 70–72 (1991). Divorce was permitted under Roman law and, in early modern Europe, under both Anglo–Saxon and Germanic law. It was, however, forbidden under the doctrine of the Roman Catholic Church and accordingly was prohibited in parts of Europe, such as France and Italy, closely identified with Catholicism.

The Reformation brought new interest in Protestant Europe in reforming divorce. The Protestant reformers favored the availability of divorce, but their notions of its proper boundaries were as shaped by religious ideas as was the Catholic Church's rejection of divorce through the doctrine of indissolubility:

> Protestant reformers considered that the dissolution of marriage was not to be seen "as a remedy for marriage breakdown as such but as punishment for matrimonial crime and as a relief for the victim of the crime." Therefore the petitioner had to be demonstrably innocent and many divorce laws only permitted remarriage for the innocent spouse. The guilty spouse had to be severely punished "if not by death, then by banishment or imprisonment or fine." * * * The introduction of divorce into the Reformed countries was therefore by no means a recognition of the individual's liberty to escape from an unhappy marriage. Divorce, irrespective of the competent authority (state or ecclesiastical), was strictly regulated and extremely difficult to obtain.

Masha Antokolskaia, Convergence of Divorce Laws in Europe 3–4 (unpublished paper), http://www.law2.byu.edu/ISFL/saltlakeconference/papers/isflpdfs/Antokolskaia.pdf.

Even this limited allowance of divorce, however, was too liberal for England. Before 1857, the ecclesiastical courts, which followed canon law, had exclusive jurisdiction over marriage. These courts were empowered to grant legal separation (*"divorce a mensa et thoro"*) or annulment where a religious impediment had already rendered the attempted marriage defective, but could not grant absolute divorce. Professor Homer Clark provides this summary of divorce practice in the ecclesiastical courts:

> (a) True divorce in the modern sense of the term could never be granted for any reason. (b) Divorce a mensa et thoro, or limited divorce, without a right of remarriage, could be granted for adultery or cruelty. (c) Annulments sometimes confusingly referred to as divorces *a vinculo*, were granted freely for impediments existing at the time of the marriage. The impediments most commonly relied upon were affinity, consanguinity, and prior informal marriage, and since the Church held very remote degrees of relationship to be objectionable, annulments on these grounds became useful devices for evading the prohibition on divorce.

Homer H. Clark, Jr., The Law of Domestic Relations in the United States § 12.1, at 406 (2d ed. 1988); *see also* Roderick Phillips, Putting Asunder: A History of Divorce in Western Society (1988). The power of the ecclesiastical courts ended in 1857 when Parliament established the Court of Divorce and Matrimonial Causes, which had jurisdiction to grant absolute divorces and related relief by judicial decree.

Divorce was more freely available in America and was a matter for the civil courts from the earliest days of the colonies. Yet, though the United States shunned the use of religious courts, the nation accepted in broad outline the religiously grounded premises of *fault-based* divorce. Under this system, divorce was available only to an innocent party victimized by the spouse's serious misconduct. A party who was unable to prove the spouse's serious misconduct was barred from obtaining a divorce; likewise, a party whose own misconduct offset the spouse's could be barred from obtaining a divorce. Such rules made sense from a perspective that viewed divorce law as a mechanism for punishing moral wrongs rather than for redressing family conflict. But the rules could be cruel to those whose family conflicts led them into court.

A fitting illustration is provided by an 1890 California case, in which a Los Angeles woman sought a divorce after her husband defied a premarital pledge to give up excessive drinking and took to verbally abusing her whenever he was drunk. *See Waldron v. Waldron*, 85 Cal. 251 (1890). A trial court granted her a divorce, but the California Supreme Court reversed because, in effect, she had not suffered enough. The husband's "defamatory, obscene, and profane language . . . was wholly unjustified, inexcusable, and unmanly," the court agreed, but it could not justify divorce absent proof that it had resulted in bodily harm to his wife. *Id.* at 265. The court explained:

> The grave remedy of divorce is disproportioned to the petty marital wrongs and annoyances whose injurious effect upon the body or health cannot be shown * * *. Many of such wrongs and annoyances, productive of more or less unhappiness, must be borne, if they cannot be justly remedied or avoided by the parties themselves.

Id. at 257. The court's parting advice to the unhappy wife was to avoid nagging her husband about his misbehavior and to try to melt his heart through "uniform kindness" instead. *Id.* at 265.

Until the advent of no-fault divorce provided more systematic relief, litigants and judges managed to make traditional fault-based divorce somewhat more tolerable through a serious of innovations and artifices. First, judges and legislators over time added more malleable offenses— "mental cruelty," for example—to the list of traditional fault grounds, making it easier for litigants to generate a claim of misconduct. Second, judges regularly looked the other way when litigants gamed the system by colluding to manufacture artificial fault grounds or bury legitimate defenses. And, finally, resourceful litigants could often circumvent legal barriers to divorce in one state by migrating to another jurisdiction with shorter residency requirements and looser conceptions of fault. The system was not a source of pride for anyone, but such devices made it tolerable until the arrival of "no-fault" divorce in the 1970s.

SECTION 2: MODERN GROUNDS FOR DIVORCE

American divorce was quite suddenly transformed within the span of little more than a decade starting in 1969. Dissatisfaction with traditional fault divorce had been building for decades. Many had come to see the system, with its attendant prying, perjury and collusion, as corrupt and inhumane, as "rotting from within." Lawrence M. Friedman, *A Dead Language: Divorce Law and Practice Before No–Fault*, 86 Va. L. Rev. 1497, 1498 (2000). In 1969, Governor Ronald Reagan of California signed into law the nation's first statute providing for "no-fault" divorce. In 1970, a draft of the Uniform Marriage and Divorce Act also recommended no-fault divorce and the idea spread rapidly across the country. *See* Herma Hill Kay, *"Making Marriage and Divorce Safe for Women" Revisited*, 32 Hofstra L. Rev. 71, 74–75 (2003); Robert J. Levy, *A Reminiscence About the Uniform Marriage and Divorce Act—and Some Reflections About Its Critics and Policies*, 1991 BYU L. Rev. 43, 44. By the mid–1980s, every state had adopted some form of no-fault system for divorce.

No-fault divorce laws vary in their language describing the new grounds for divorce, but they share a simple and important premise. Instead of seeking to identify the victimization of one spouse by the other, no-fault laws look simply to the fact of marital breakdown. Depending on the legislative directive, if a court finds that a marriage has suffered an "irretrievable breakdown," that the spouses have stopped cohabitating for a statutorily set time, or that the spouses have "irreconcilable differences," it is empowered to dissolve the marriage, without assigning a specific cause for the collapse or blame between the parties.

Arrival of no-fault divorce reshaped divorce practice everywhere in the United States, but it did not altogether supplant the traditional fault-based system of divorce. In fact, most states simply added no-fault as an alternative route to divorce, while retaining the old fault-based system. As a result, "thirty-five years after the so-called no-fault divorce 'revolution,' only a small minority of states [and the District of Columbia]—about fifteen—are 'true' no-fault jurisdictions." Peter Nash Swisher, *Marriage and Some Troubling Issues with No–Fault Divorce*, 17 Regent U.L. Rev. 243, 258 (2004–05); *see also* Linda D. Elrod & Robert G. Spector, *Review of the Year in Family Law, 2006–2007: Judges Try To Find Answers to Complex Questions*, 41 Fam. L.Q. 661, 713 (2008) (Chart 4).

No-fault divorce dispenses with the need to prove fault, but often requires the spouses to live separately for a specified period before a divorce may be granted. And, regardless of whether divorce is sought on fault or no-fault grounds, most states require that divorce petitioners establish their residency in the state for a specified period. These time periods vary from jurisdiction to jurisdiction. For instance, in Kentucky, a party may obtain a no-fault divorce by claiming in the petition state residency of at least 180 days and 60 days of living separate and apart from the other spouse. Some states, such as Oregon, have no waiting period and a short residency requirement for a no-fault divorce. Rhode Island, Texas and Utah have the longest separation requirement (three years), with residency requirements of one year, six months, and 90 days, respectively. *See* Elrod & Spector, *supra*, at 713 (Chart 4). The required duration of separation often varies depending on whether both spouses, or only one, desire divorce. For example, in the District of Columbia, a voluntary separation by the parties requires six months of living apart prior to filing for divorce, while an involuntary separation requires a full year's separation. D.C. Code § 16–904(a) (2006).

Why would a spouse ever choose to seek a fault-based divorce when no-fault divorce is available? First, obtaining a divorce is sometimes faster under the fault system. While no-fault divorce typically requires a waiting period during which the parties live apart, proof of a fault ground ordinarily permits immediate divorce, subject only to the pace of the court docket. Second, litigating fault can have financial implications in states that permit consideration of marital fault in shaping property and alimony awards. And, finally, some spouses genuinely desire a forum in which they can win formal acknowledgment of their sense of victimization and force a resented spouse to incur a measure of public accountability.

Thus, although fault-based divorce law no longer stands as a serious obstacle to those wishing to end a marriage, it continues to be used by many divorcing couples today. Some critics of no-fault divorce, moreover, have called recently for a revitalization of fault principles in divorce. Accordingly, understanding modern divorce law requires careful attention to both fault and no-fault grounds. The next section of this Chapter surveys the modern law of fault-based divorce. The following section then describes prevailing no-fault laws, and the concluding section of the Chapter assesses recent calls to counter the so-called "no-fault revolution" by making divorce, once again, harder to obtain.

SECTION 3: FAULT–BASED DIVORCE

Originally, the fault grounds sufficient to permit divorce were very few. Adultery was universally recognized as a ground for divorce—until 1967, it was the only ground for divorce in New York—and many states added desertion. Some states went farther and allowed divorce based on physical cruelty. Beyond these basic grounds, there was considerable state-by-state variation, with the southern states generally having the most restrictive divorce laws. Over time, additional and often more contestable fault grounds were added to the lists, including mental cruelty and "indignities." The defenses allowed against divorce actions underscored that the ultimate aim of divorce law in this period was, like early tort law, to vindicate the righteous and punish the wicked. The material in this section briefly surveys the most common fault grounds and defenses. The recency of the decisions demonstrates that fault grounds survive in robust form in many states where legislative compromise prevented wholehearted embrace of no-fault divorce.

A. FAULT GROUNDS

1. PHYSICAL CRUELTY

Cruelty as a ground for divorce traces its roots directly to the English ecclesiastical courts, where it was recognized as a ground for divorce *a menso et thoro*, *i.e.*, legal separation. In its original form, "cruelty" required acts of bodily harm, or threats of bodily harm, substantial enough to be deemed reasonably intolerable. *See, e.g., Waldron v. Waldron*, 85 Cal. 251, 256–57 (1890). Reflecting the traditional view, one court explained that "not every occurrence of actual violence constitutes a ground for divorce. It is only actual violence, or threats inducing the reasonable apprehension of violence, of a degree attended with danger to life or health that is a ground for divorce." *Boldon v. Boldon,* 354 So.2d 275, 275–76 (Ala. Ct. Civ. App. 1978). As the decision below indicates, judicial conceptions of just what level of abuse should be considered "tolerable" have changed significantly in recent years.

DAS v. DAS

Court of Special Appeals of Maryland, 2000.
754 A.2d 441.

Tʜɪᴇᴍᴇ, Jᴜᴅɢᴇ.

* * *

The parties were married on August 13, 1978, in New Delhi, India. Two children were born of the marriage: Radha, on October 7, 1983, and Jaya, on October 3, 1985.

The parties separated in January 1998, following entry of a domestic violence protective order granted to Wife by the District Court of Montgomery County. The order granted the Wife custody of the children, who are minors. * * *

[Thereafter, the Husband fled the country, first to Japan and ultimately to India, taking Radha with him. A default judgment was entered against the Husband in the subsequent divorce action, granting the Wife a divorce on grounds of cruelty and excessively vicious conduct and awarding the Wife custody of both children. Through counsel in the United States, the Husband appealed.]

* * *

IV.

THE DIVORCE

* * * Husband asks if the trial court erred or abused its discretion in granting Wife an absolute divorce. He argues that the facts alleged by Wife at the August 11 hearing do not support grounds for divorce based on either cruelty or excessively vicious conduct because they * * * fail to reach the level of egregiousness described in some of our older cases. * * * We disagree.

Whether the events that bring a divorce complainant to court constitute cruelty or excessively vicious conduct has never been the stuff of which bright line rules are made, and even now our standards are shifting. Only recently, in 1998, did the legislature make cruelty and excessively vicious conduct grounds for absolute divorce in Maryland. Before that time, cruelty of treatment gave grounds for limited divorce only, a rule that originated in English ecclesiastical courts. Because divorce itself was disfavored by the church, the rule existed only to protect the victim-party from further and more serious physical harm. "The cruelty which entitles the injured party to a divorce ... consists in that sort of conduct which endangers the life or health of the complainant, and renders cohabitation unsafe." *Harris v. Harris,* 161 Eng. Rep. 697 (1813). Maryland adopted this English rule, as the Court of Appeals explained in *Scheinin v. Scheinin,* 89 A.2d 609 ([Md.] 1952) ("In 1851 Chancellor Johnson announced in the High Court of Chancery that the words 'cruelty of treatment' as contained in the Maryland divorce statute would be given the same interpretation as given to them by the English Ecclesiastical Courts.") (citations omitted). The English rule, as articulated in *Scheinin* and older cases, was for many years our gold standard, setting the parameters for what constituted cruelty:

> Ordinarily a single act of violence slight in character does not constitute cruelty of treatment as a cause for divorce. But it is now accepted in Maryland, as well as generally throughout the country, that a single act may be sufficient to constitute the basis for a divorce on the ground of cruelty, if it indicates an intention to do serious bodily harm or is of such a character as to threaten serious danger in the future.

Id. [at 612.]

The Court in *Scheinin,* however, went on to point out that the original definition of "cruelty" had grown more broad, to encompass mental as well as physical abuse:

> It is now accepted that cruelty as a cause for divorce includes any conduct on the part of the husband or wife which is calculated to seriously impair the health or permanently destroy the happiness of the other. Thus any misconduct of a husband that endangers, or creates a reasonable apprehension that it will endanger, the wife's safety or health to a degree rendering it physically or mentally

impracticable for her to properly discharge the marital duties constitutes cruelty within the meaning of the divorce statute.

Id. Even under this more modern definition, the cases for limited divorce on grounds of cruelty and excessively vicious conduct—there are no reported cases for absolute divorce on these grounds—show remarkable tolerance for abusive behavior. "[A] divorce cannot be granted on the ground of cruelty of treatment merely because the parties have lived together unhappily as a result of unruly tempers and marital wranglings. . . . [M]arital neglect, rudeness of manner, and the use of profane and abusive language do not constitute cruelty." *Id.*; *see also Harrison v. Harrison*, 164 A.2d 901 (Md. 1960) (where husband struck wife and gave her a black eye, a "single act of violence complained of by appellee does not measure up to what the law of this State requires for a showing of cruelty . . . [or justify] the wife's living apart from her husband"); *Bonwit v. Bonwit*, 181 A. 237 (Md. 1935) (husband's "violent outbursts of temper, accompanied in some instances by . . . slapping" wife did not constitute cruelty); *McKane v. McKane*, 137 A. 288 (Md. 1927) (husband's "spells," caused by drinking, during which he called wife vile names, implied unchastity on her part, cursed her, pouted, and refused to eat did not constitute cruelty). On the other hand, the Court of Appeals upheld a limited divorce on grounds of cruelty where it appeared that one party had been in significant peril, *e.g.*, incidents of drunken rage and physical abuse that required the wife to seek police intervention and seek refuge with relatives. *See Hilbert v. Hilbert*, 177 A. 914 (Md. 1935).

In reviewing these oft-cited cases on cruelty and excessively vicious conduct, we note that most are quite old and give victims little relief from their aggressive partners by modern standards. In part, we believe, the courts' reluctance to grant relief stems from the fact that cruelty and excessively vicious conduct were grounds for limited and not for absolute divorce, and Maryland courts have historically disfavored divorce from bed and board. *See, e.g., Bonwit,* [181 A. at 239] ("[T]he policy of the law of this state looks with disfavor upon divorces *a mensa et thoro.* . . . 'It is not the function of the courts . . . to arbitrate family quarrels, but to determine upon the evidence whether either of the parties has been guilty of such conduct as would make a continuance of the marital relation inconsistent with the health, self-respect, and reasonable comfort of the other.'"). Disapproval of limited divorce likely colored past analysis in the cases where cruelty or excessively vicious conduct was alleged.

In more recent years, however, a greater awareness and intolerance of domestic violence has shifted our public policy toward allowing the dissolution of marriages with a violence element. In the courts, we have responded to this trend by permitting absolute divorce on grounds of constructive desertion, a doctrine far friendlier to victims of violence in terms of the quality of proof required to grant freedom from the shackles of an abusive spouse. Likewise, the General Assembly responded in 1980 by enacting the domestic violence statute, which grants Maryland courts the power to issue civil protective orders and offers various forms of relief to victims. In 1998, as part of its continuing modernization of our family law, the legislature acknowledged that persons subject to domestic abuse should be entitled to seek absolute divorce immediately without a waiting period prior to the filing of a complaint. It thus expanded the grounds for absolute divorce to include cruelty and excessively vicious conduct.

In the courts, we are now left holding a stack of cases—all "good law"—dating from the 1920's that no longer square with our modern understanding of appropriate family interaction. Verbal and physical abuse may have been tolerated in another era, and our predecessors at bar may have placed the continuity of the marital bond above the well-being of individual participants, but our values are different today. * * *

Against this background, we turn to the instant case. Husband claims that his conduct toward Wife never "endangered her life, person, or health, or would have otherwise caused her to feel apprehension of bodily suffering," and, to be sure, during her brief time on the witness stand on August 11, Wife did not account for the particulars of specific violent incidents. Nevertheless, from Wife's direct testimony and in the pleadings, the court below learned that the history of violence between Husband and Wife justified entry of a one-year protective order in January 1998, after a particularly violent incident that was "one in several cases of domestic violence." Wife went on to testify that the parties' marriage was an arranged marriage, which "in our culture ... the way it is conducted is basically subservience." She spoke of ongoing cruelty, including "making me stay up all night in order to listen to him, isolating me from my friends and from my family, and not allowing contact as much as possible. . . . [H]itting, pinching, pulling hair, etc." Wife testified in some detail how Husband's controlling behavior harmed her previously close relationship with her family. She told the court how she has continuing health problems, including cardiac arrhythmia brought on by the "stress of the marriage and the tensions at home." Wife also spoke with fear of Husband's taunting questions about what she might do when the protective order expired. Although Wife's testimony did not track Husband's mistreatment of her in minute detail, it is clear from that testimony and the very existence of a protective order that Husband's conduct far exceeded mere "sallies of passion, harshness, [and] rudeness," *Short*, [135 A. at 176], and in fact threatened Wife's physical and emotional well-being. "[W]here violence has been inflicted and threats have been made," as in the instant case, "a Court of Equity should not hesitate to grant relief, especially where the facts indicate a probability that violence might be repeated." *Timanus v. Timanus*, 10 A.2d 322[, 325 (Md.] 1940).

* * *

Judgment Affirmed.

NOTES AND QUESTIONS

1. *Absolute vs. limited divorce.* Why might the Maryland courts have been more reluctant to find adequate grounds for a divorce *a menso et thoro* than to permit an absolute divorce? Are the courts not also forced to "arbitrate family quarrels" in deciding whether to grant an absolute divorce? Does the universal availability of no-fault divorce provide sufficient support for a national policy favoring relaxation of traditional fault grounds, found in decisions such as *Das*? What accounts for the court's decision to relax traditional requirements for divorce based on cruelty?

2. *Changing attitudes toward family violence.* *Das* recites several decisions reflecting the "old" tolerance of domestic violence. Many older decisions show an even more shocking tolerance. In *DeMott v. DeMott*, 92 S.E.2d 342, 345 (Va. 1956), for example, the court found insufficient evidence of cruelty in an attack by a husband in which he "grabbed [his wife], threw her against the wall, and threatened her with a knife." Moreover, as legal historian William Nelson has observed, a double standard existed: "[C]ases held that one or two isolated acts of violence by a husband against his wife did not amount to cruel and inhuman treatment," yet "the courts were clear that a single violent act by a wife against her husband amounted to wrongdoing on her part." William E. Nelson, *Patriarchy or Equality: Family Values or Individuality,* 70 St. John's L. Rev. 435, 517 (1996).

2. MENTAL CRUELTY

As *Das* indicates, many jurisdictions eventually enlarged or supplemented the original divorce ground of physical cruelty to include mental cruelty as well. The addition of mental cruelty to the list of fault grounds was an important step toward liberalizing divorce law. Called "indignities" in some states, mental cruelty requires a showing of "habitual, continuous, permanent and plain manifestation of settled hate, alienation, and estrangement on the part of one spouse, sufficient to render the condition of the other intolerable." *Anderson v. Anderson*, 600 S.W.2d 438, 440 (Ark. Ct. App. 1980). Even with common statutory modifiers such as "extreme and repeated," the concept of psychological mistreatment was sufficiently vague and malleable to be of great utility. *See* James Herbie DiFonzo, Beneath the Fault Line: The Popular and Legal Culture of Divorce in Twentieth–Century America 51–55, 61 (1997).

As the *Spence* decision below illustrates, however, the concept is not limitless. Some courts hold that the quantum and quality of "cruelty" required to justify divorce is higher in a long marriage than in a shorter one. *See, e.g., C.P. v. G.P.*, 800 N.Y.S.2d 343 (N.Y. Sup. Ct. Mar. 3, 2005). Is such variability sensible? Should the definition of "cruelty" vary also depending upon the individual sensitivities of the couple at issue?

3. ADULTERY

This oldest of all fault grounds is straightforward. All forms of sexual contact between persons of any gender—not just intercourse—generally qualify as "adultery" justifying divorce. *See* N.Y. Dom. Rel. L. § 170(4) (West Supp. 2008) (defining adultery to include "sexual intercourse, oral sexual conduct or anal sexual conduct"); *Brown v. Brown*, 665 S.E.2d 174, 178 (S.C. App. 2008) (defining adultery to include all forms of "sexual intimacy," including kissing and fondling); *S.B. v. S.J.B.*, 609 A.2d 124, 127 (N.J. Super. Ct. 1992) ("find[ing] that adultery exists when one spouse rejects the other by entering into a personal intimate sexual relationship with any other person, irrespective of the specific sexual acts performed, the marital status, or the gender of the third party"). *But see In re Blanchflower*, 834 A.2d 1010, 1011–12 (N.H. 2003) (ruling that same-sex liaison does not count as "adultery" for divorce purposes). Instead of definitional problems, then, spouses wishing to rely on adultery as a ground for divorce more often encounter evidentiary issues. Because of the nature of the offense, direct proof is usually in short supply. Accordingly, divorce law has long permitted proof of adultery to be made through circumstantial evidence. Yet, as the following decision shows, even "[s]trongly suspicious circumstances" are often found insufficient, *Watts*, 581 S.E.2d at 226–27; instead, many jurisdictions require that the evidence effectively excludes any innocent explanation.

SPENCE v. SPENCE

Court of Appeals of Mississippi, 2005.
930 So.2d 415.

MYERS, J., for the Court.

This case arises from the Chancery Court of Lauderdale County where Donna Spence was granted a divorce from Charles Spence on the grounds of habitual, cruel and inhuman treatment and adultery. * * *

* * *

On December 29, 1981, Charles and Donna were married, and two children, Leah and Josh, were born of the marriage. * * *

At trial, Donna testified to several incidents which she contends constituted habitual, cruel and inhuman treatment. * * * Further, Donna argues that the circumstances surrounding the relationship between Charles and a neighbor, Gail Gullette, provides sufficient grounds for a finding of adultery.

* * *

DISCUSSION

Charles first argues that the chancellor erred in awarding Donna a divorce on the grounds of habitual, cruel and inhuman treatment and adultery. Charles argues each of these two grounds separately and we will address each ground in like fashion.

Adultery

In order to prevail on a claim of adultery, a party must prove his or her claim by clear and convincing evidence. This showing by clear and convincing evidence must demonstrate both an adulterous inclination and a reasonable opportunity to satisfy that inclination. Although circumstantial evidence may aid in proving such a claim, the proponent retains the burden of presenting satisfactory evidence which is sufficient to lead the trier of fact to a conclusion of guilty.

Charles argues that though there was evidence of affection between he and Gail, there was no evidence of a sexual relationship, and any proof of an adulterous relationship was circumstantial at best. Donna argues that due to this Court's highly deferential standard of review in examining the decision of a chancellor, * * * based upon the evidence presented, the decision must be affirmed.

In making the decision to grant a divorce on the ground of adultery, the chancellor was required to make a finding of fact. "Where chancellors make such findings of fact, this Court has consistently held that their decisions will not be set aside on appeal unless they are manifestly wrong." [*Dillon v. Dillon*, 498 So. 2d 328, 330 (Miss. 1986).]

The chancellor's opinion, when addressing the ground of adultery, focused on the testimony given regarding the relationship between Charles and Gail. The chancellor noted that the proof of an adulterous relationship was circumstantial in nature. In determining that such a relationship existed, the chancellor concentrated on Charles's testimony in which he admitted to having affection for Gail, admitted having hugged Gail, admitted having kissed Gail, and admitted that he loved her as a friend. The chancellor takes this a step further, reasoning that because the two parties communicate regularly and share a close friendship, that even though there is no direct evidence of a sexual relationship, only innuendo, "it is not a stretch to believe that this has developed over the time that they have spent together."

There are several instances of testimony which at first blush would lead one to believe that such a relationship was indeed present, but when viewing the testimony as a whole, it becomes readily apparent that such a determination was manifest error. * * *

Though Charles testified about his affections for Gail, he denied any type of romantic involvement or sexual relationship, and denied any plans of marriage. Gail testified in a similar manner. When asked about Charles's feelings towards her, she stated that he "[l]ove[s] me as a person. Maybe the person I am, you know. But as far as being in love with someone, you know—(witness shakes head in negative response)." Both parties' testimony stated that the two were not romantically involved, only that they had developed a strong friendship, as they both shared the experience of going through divorce.

* * *

The chancellor put a great amount of weight in the testimony of Charles and opined that due to the nature of their close relationship, that it was logical to conclude that the two had committed adultery. In buttressing this opinion, the chancellor relied on the testimony of Donna's cousin, Stacey. Stacey testified that she resided at the same apartment complex as Charles and Gail. She stated that she had seen Charles's and Gail's vehicles parked together in front of one or the other's apartment on two or three occasions and that the two vehicles had remained in place throughout the night. Further, Stacey testified that she had overheard Charles discussing his and Gail's plans to take off work to spend the day together. Finally, Stacey testified that she had witnessed Gail leave Charles's apartment clad in a robe and pants.

On cross-examination, Stacey admitted that when she witnessed Gail leaving Charles's apartment in a robe, it was approximately 8:00 or 9:00 o'clock on a Saturday morning in December and that she was unaware what other clothing she was wearing underneath the robe. Further, Stacey testified that she did not see Gail go into the apartment. When asked about his plans to take the day off from work to spend time with Gail, Stacey admitted that she was uncertain who Charles intended to spend the day with. Further testimony in the record negates Stacey's assertion that Charles's and Gail's vehicles were parked next to one another throughout the night. Gail testified that her neighbor's daughter owns the exact make, model, and color vehicle as Charles, and that she from time to time would park in front of Gail's apartment.

* * *

Further, the court focused on the lunches shared by Charles and Gail in which they meet at the park, feed the ducks, and eat peanut butter and jelly sandwiches while discussing life's problems. Though admittedly if taken at face value, such meetings *could* indicate a relationship of a different character, these lunches are also characteristic of the type of activity which can occur when a person is experiencing a troubling time and would need a friend's advice. When taking the testimony as a whole, Charles's alleged infidelity has not been proven by clear and convincing evidence. * * * As the Mississippi Supreme Court has previously held, when one alleges adulterous activity, "the burden of proof is a heavy one . . . because the evidence must be logical, tend to prove the facts charged, *and be inconsistent with a reasonable theory of innocence." Owen v. Gerity*, 422 So. 2d 284, 287 (Miss.1982). The facts upon which the chancellor relied are not clear and convincing in nature and are not inconsistent with a reasonable theory of innocence. As the Mississippi Supreme Court has previously stated: " 'Trifles light as air' may be sufficient to convince the jealous or the suspicious, but they do not impress the court with the same degree of credulity. Before accepting charges so seriously affecting the character of a person, the evidence must be clear and convincing." *Banks v. Banks*, 79 So. 841, 842 (Miss. 1918). As such, the evidence presented does not rise above mere suspicion of adultery. Therefore, the award of divorce to Donna on the ground of adultery is reversed.

Habitual, Cruel and Inhuman Treatment

Charles next contends that the chancellor erred by granting Donna a divorce based upon the ground of habitual, cruel and inhuman treatment. In support of his position, Charles argues that the evidence concerning this ground for divorce consisted of the uncorroborated testimony of Donna and that the events about which she testified were isolated incidents, failing to establish sufficient grounds for divorce.

In granting Donna a divorce on the ground of habitual, cruel and inhuman treatment, the chancellor again relies on the entire line of testimony favorable to Donna in regards to the alleged incidents of which she testified, while neglecting the unfavorable testimony given by Leah and Josh, which negated Donna's assertions. Donna testified that Charles belittled her, called her names, and manipulated the finances to the family's detriment. Portions of this testimony were corroborated by the children, as both Leah and Josh testified that their parents would often quarrel and that Charles had manipulated the finances on occasion, by decreasing the amount available to the household for the week's groceries.

* * *

The testimony established there were repeated arguments, though no evidence or testimony was presented which would corroborate Donna's assertion and support a finding of habitual, cruel and inhuman treatment. Leah testified that both parties would participate in these arguments. Other than quarrels between Donna and Charles, there was no evidence presented of any other occurrences which would make Charles's actions

> a course of conduct on the part of the offending spouse which was so unkind, unfeeling or brutal as to endanger or put one in reasonable apprehension of danger to life, limb or health, and further, that such course of conduct must be habitual, that is, done so often, or continued so long that it may reasonably be said a permanent condition.

Wilson v. Wilson, 547 So. 2d 803, 805 (Miss. 1989).

The burden of proof for habitual, cruel and inhuman treatment is of a less stringent standard than that of proving adultery. Habitual, cruel and inhuman treatment is to be proven by a preponderance of the credible evidence; yet, we find that granting a divorce in this instance was improper. The only evidence of bad circumstances in the marital home, which was corroborated, was that the spouses had arguments. The Mississippi Supreme Court has previously held, and it is well-established in our case law, that denial of a divorce based upon this ground may "[result] in rendering her unhappy and her marital bond irksome, but for that alone the law of this state does not sanction a divorce." *Russell v. Russell,* 128 So. 270, 272 (Miss. 1930).

* * *

Reversed.

NOTES AND QUESTIONS

1. *Heightened proof requirements.* As in *Spence*, many jurisdictions insist upon heightened proof of adultery, such as "clear and convincing evidence." *See, e.g., Marcotte v. Marcotte*, 886 So.2d 671, 679 (La. App. 2004); *Michael D.C. v. Wanda L.C.*, 497 S.E.2d 531, 535–36 (W. Va. 1997). Is there good reason to require a higher standard of proof to establish adultery than to establish that someone is guilty of "cruelty" or "indignities"? Are heightened standards likely to induce spouses to resort to private detectives and other more invasive evidence-gathering tactics?

2. *Circumstantial evidence of adultery.* Although courts often demand convincing proof of adultery, they do not insist upon direct evidence. As *Spence* acknowledges, parties may rely on circumstantial evidence showing "an adulterous inclination and a reasonable opportunity to satisfy that inclination." In *Curtis v. Curtis*, 796 So.2d 1044 (Miss. Ct. App. 2001), the court sustained a finding of adultery based upon evidence that the husband had lived off and on in the home of another woman in another city, including photographs taken by a private investigator showing the husband stringing Christmas lights at the woman's home and the husband's own testimony that he spent Christmas in the home. Although the investigator observed no expressions of affection or intimacy between the husband and the other woman—the husband insisted that he was merely renting a separate bedroom in the house while separated from his wife—the court held that the evidence reasonably supported an inference of adultery. *Id.* at 1049–51; *see also, e.g., Brown v. Brown*, 665 S.E.2d 174, 178–79 (S.C. Ct. App. 2008) (finding adultery based on evidence that wife had two dozen secretive meetings with alleged paramour in city parking lots, combined with "admissions to meeting for one-on-one lunches, calling each other frequently, kissing, and fondling"); *Popham v. Popham*, 607 S.E.2d 575, 576 (Ga. 2005) (wife permitted to introduce evidence of husband's prescription for Viagra). Do you agree that the evidence in *Spence* showed nothing more than a "mere suspicion" of adultery?

3. *Post-separation adultery. Curtis*, mentioned in the preceding note, rested its finding of adultery on conduct that commenced only after the spouses were separated and making plans for divorce. Courts granting divorces based on post-separation adultery point out that spouses remain married until a final divorce decree is entered and that infidelity while separated may destroy any prospect for reconciliation. *See Curtis*, 796 So.2d at 1051; *Barnett v. Barnett*, 908 So.2d 833, 836–37 (Miss. Ct. App. 2005); *Bushkar v. Bushkar*, 2005 WL 1812499 (Va. Cir. Ct. June 24, 2005). Some other courts, however, have been more reluctant to grant divorce based on post-separation adultery, at least where alternative grounds exist. *See Smith v. Smith*, 964 So.2d 663 (Ala. Ct. Civ. App. 2005) (upholding trial court's decision not to grant divorce based on adultery, where husband's extramarital relationship commenced after spouses had already separated due to their "acrimonious relationship"; divorce granted based on incompatibility instead).

4. *Virtual adultery?* In 1996, a New Jersey man filed for divorce based on adultery after discovering that his wife had been carrying on a torrid

"virtual" affair with a North Carolina man through online chat rooms. Although the wife never met her cyber-paramour in person, "the relationship began to permeate their lives" and she "began neglecting her job, family, and marriage." Christina Tavella Hall, Note, *Sex Online: Is This Adultery?*, 20 Hastings Comm. & Ent. L.J. 201, 202–03 (1997). A decision on the issue was avoided in the New Jersey case because the marital couple reconciled. Of course, if a spouse actually travels to meet an online partner in person, courts may infer adultery without much difficulty. *See Bower v. Bower*, 758 So.2d 405, 408 (Miss. 2000) (upholding finding of adultery where wife, among other acts, traveled to another city and spent the weekend at a motel with a man she met on the Internet). But what about "cybersex" conducted entirely online? In 2008, a British couple, both avid participants in "Second Life," a virtual reality in which participants interact through their online avatars, divorced after the wife discovered that her husband's avatar had engaged in sex with another avatar. *See Second Life Affair Ends in Divorce,* CNN.com, http://www.cnn.com/2008/WORLD/europe/11/14/second.life.divorce/index.html. Professor Brenda Cossman observes that evolving social understandings appear to embrace "an ever-expanding definition of infidelity," including "virtual" and other "non-sexual encounters, as the harm of adultery has been recast in some instances as a violation of *emotional* intimacy." Brenda Cossman, *The New Politics of Adultery*, 15 Colum. J. Gender & L. 274, 274–77 (2006) (emphasis in original). Should divorce law encompass this broader definition? *Cf. Maddox v. Maddox*, 553 So.2d 611, 612 (Ala. Ct. Civ. App. 1989) (exchange of love letters does not constitute or prove adultery).

5. *Interplay of fault considerations.* In *Spence*, the court appears to analyze the husband's suspicious conduct separately from his quarreling and manipulation of the family finances, finding each to be insufficient alone to provide a ground for divorce. Even if they are separately insufficient, should they be considered cumulatively sufficient? In *Evans v. Evans*, 610 S.E.2d 264 (N.C. Ct. App. 2005), the court found evidence of sufficiently intolerable "indignities" where a wife, in addition to slapping her husband 15 to 20 times over a period of four or five years and allowing the home to fall into a slovenly condition while he was away, sent sexually explicit e-mails to another man, carried condoms in her purse, and disappeared for several days at a time.

4. DESERTION

One of the most widely accepted grounds for divorce, desertion is typically defined as the willful abandonment of cohabitation for a sufficient period of time, usually lasting at least one year. *See, e.g.*, 23 Pa. Cons. Stat. Ann. § 3301 (West 2008) ("willful and malicious desertion, and absence from the habitation of the injured and innocent spouse, without a reasonable cause, for the period of one or more years"). The other requisite element is intent by the offending spouse to abandon. Desertion cases have raised a tangle of questions, not all of them clearly resolved. For instance, can a spouse abandon marital cohabitation without actually leaving the marital home? Most jurisdictions say no, but some have allowed desertion premised on the spouses living separately under the same roof and ceasing sexual relations. Which approach better serves sound policy considerations?

The concept of "constructive desertion" presents further complications. Like the concept of "constructive eviction" in landlord-tenant law, a party who has walked out on the marriage may be permitted to show that her spouse drove her to it by making life within the marital home reasonably intolerable. As you might expect, however, just what will be deemed fairly intolerable is not always clear. Although " 'nagging, rudeness, and abusive language, standing alone, will generally not justify one spouse in leaving the other,' ... the camel's back may nonetheless be broken" by a habitual pattern of abusive conduct or demands for " 'abnormal' sexual relations." *Lemley v. Lemley*, 649 A.2d 1119, 1123–28 (Md. Ct. Spec. App. 1994). Although the concepts of "constructive desertion" and "cruelty" may overlap when both are premised on acts of violence or other mistreatment, "constructive desertion" may be established with a smaller quantum of proof. *See Das v. Das*, 754 A.2d 441, 460 n.24 (Md. Ct. Spec. App. 2000). In *C.P. v. G.P.*, 800 N.Y.S.2d 343 (N.Y. Sup. Ct. Mar. 3, 2005), the court concluded that a husband's refusal for the last 12 years of a 33–year marriage to share a meal, attend family funerals, events, or holidays, engage in any but the briefest exchange of words, or sleep with his wife was insufficient to constitute cruelty, but did state a case of "constructive abandonment."

B.   FAULT–BASED BARS AND DEFENSES

Traditional divorce law matched the battery of fault grounds with an array of special bars and defenses capable of defeating the action for divorce. Like the fault grounds themselves, these defenses were borrowed from practice in the English ecclesiastical courts. In keeping with the premise that a fault-based divorce should be awarded only to an innocent party wronged by a blameworthy spouse, the bars and defenses each seek to determine whether the party seeking a divorce is guilty of some misconduct that should preclude relief.

1.   RECRIMINATION

Recrimination is an affirmative defense predicated on the claim that both spouses were guilty of off-setting faults. As Professor Clark sums it up, "[r]ecrimination is the outrageous legal principle which ordains that when both spouses have grounds for divorce, neither may have a decree." Homer H. Clark, Jr., The Law of Domestic Relations in the United States § 13.11, at 527 (2d ed. 1988). Denial of relief was nominally consistent with traditional equitable doctrines which deny relief to those with "unclean hands," and yet resulted in the rather strange policy of keeping two wrongdoers locked together in the unbreakable bonds of matrimony. For better or worse, recrimination came into even greater use as divorce law expanded fault to include softer grounds like mental cruelty, and it became easier for the respondent to assemble plausible "cross-claims" of fault. Because of recrimination's somewhat bizarre implications, courts have long disfavored the defense. Many jurisdictions have repealed it altogether; others have limited its application to specific claims (namely, adultery) or to cases in which the respondent and petitioner allegedly committed conduct establishing the same fault ground. Even when the defense is available on the books, courts often seem reluctant to apply it in specific cases. *See, e.g., Golub v. Ganz*, 802 N.Y.S.2d 526, 528–29 (App. Div. 2005) (finding insufficient evidence of adultery supporting a recrimination defense notwithstanding wife's admission that "she became 'romantically involved'" with another man and her invocation of her Fifth Amendment rights when asked if she had become sexually intimate). Some jurisdictions retain recrimination as a defense, but allow courts discretion in deciding whether to invoke it. *See, e.g., Ware v. Ware*, ___ So.2d ___, 2008 WL 1869547, at * 2 (Miss. Ct. App. Apr. 29, 2008) (upholding trial court's discretionary power to grant husband a divorce based on wife's adultery, notwithstanding husband's admission that he, too, had committed adultery).

2. PROVOCATION

The defense of provocation is available to a respondent who claims his own faulty conduct was reasonably provoked by the petitioner's. The petitioner's provoking conduct need not be so bad that it qualifies as a free-standing fault ground of its own. But it is necessary that the provoking conduct be bad enough to make the respondent's faulty reaction proportionate to the provocation.

3. CONNIVANCE

Like the entrapment defense in criminal law, connivance bars relief if the party seeking the divorce is found to have participated in manufacturing the fault upon which divorce is sought. The typical scenario is where one spouse engineers the other's adultery by arranging and encouraging a tryst with another partner. *See, e.g., Hollis v. Hollis*, 427 S.E.2d 233 (Va. Ct. App. 1993).

4. CONDONATION

The defense of condonation rests on the idea that the fault ground raised in the divorce has already been forgiven by the respondent and therefore cannot be invoked to dissolve the marriage. The rationale is that if the victim of the wrong had already generously wiped the slate clean, the victim should not be permitted to go back on her word—at least unless the wrongdoing spouse "revived" the prior wrong by committing another bad act. "Condonation" could be either express, as where the wronged spouse gives verbal dispensation, or implied, as where the wronged spouse signals forgiveness by resuming normal marital relations.

IN RE MARRIAGE OF HIGHTOWER

Appellate Court of Illinois, 2005.
830 N.E.2d 862.

JUSTICE GROMETER delivered the opinion of the court.

* * *

Petitioner first asserts that the trial court erred in denying her April 10, 2003, petition for dissolution of marriage on the ground of adultery. * * * In this case, it is undisputed that respondent was unfaithful to petitioner during the parties' marriage. However, respondent raised the affirmative defense of condonation.

"Condonation, in the law of divorce[,] is the forgiveness of an antecedent matrimonial offense on condition that it shall not be repeated and that the offender shall thereafter treat the forgiving party with conjugal kindness." *Quagliano v. Quagliano*, 236 N.E.2d 748 (Ill. App. Ct. 1968). Condonation is a question of intent and is to be shown by words and deeds that reflect full, free, and voluntary forgiveness. The burden is on the party raising the affirmative defense of condonation to prove by a preponderance of the evidence that the wronged party intended to forgive the matrimonial offenses of his or her spouse. Whether an injured spouse intended to forgive the marital offense is a question of fact which turns on appraising the credibility of the witnesses and weighing their testimony. * * *

In determining whether a party intended to forgive his or her spouse's behavior, courts look to a combination of factors, including an expression of forgiveness, the fact of cohabitation, the length of time the parties cohabited after the injured spouse learned of the matrimonial offense, whether the cohabitation was the result of necessity, and whether the parties continued to have sexual relations. In this case, petitioner admitted that she learned of petitioner's infidelity between 1995 and 1997 while the parties were undergoing counseling. Respondent testified that petitioner forgave him for his conduct. The parties continued to live together for several years following respondent's admission, and there was no evidence that this living arrangement was continued out of necessity. Moreover, respondent testified that he and petitioner shared the same room, shared domestic duties, and continued sexual relations until petitioner filed for divorce in May 2001. Based on this evidence, we conclude that the trial court's finding on the issue of condonation is not against the manifest weight of the evidence.

* * *

NOTES AND QUESTIONS

1. *Revival of fault following condonation.* Generally, "[c]ondonation is conditioned on the offending spouse's continued good behavior." *Brewer v. Brewer*, 919 So.2d 135, 139 (Miss. Ct. App. 2005). Thus, prior fault, even if

initially forgiven, may be "revived" as a ground for divorce if the errant spouse reoffends. In *Brewer*, for example, the court held that a wife's prior adultery was not condoned, despite her husband's resumption of marital relations with knowledge of her affair, because she committed additional acts of adultery during a later separation. Although *Brewer* involved repeated acts of adultery, the misconduct reviving prior fault need not itself qualify as a new fault ground for divorce; lesser offenses will suffice as long as they " 'amount to more than slight acts of coldness, unkindness, or mere quarreling, and [are] . . . so pronounced as to raise a reasonable probability that if the marriage relation is continued a new cause for divorce will arise.' " *Tigert v. Tigert*, 595 P.2d 815, 819–20 (Okla. Ct. App. 1979).

2. *Effect of condonation defense on marital reconciliation.* "The rationale behind allowing the [condonation] defense is that reconciliations will be encouraged and society's interest in the continuation of marital relationships furthered by allowing the errant spouse some protection under the law." *Tigert*, 595 P.2d at 820. Do you agree that condonation will promote reconciliation? Might the condonation defense discourage reconciliation by treating forgiveness as a legal waiver?

5. COLLUSION

Collusion exists when the spouses conspire to manufacture grounds for a divorce. Fault-based divorce, of course, did not allow divorces founded on the parties' mere consent. If parties sought to circumvent that rule by offering evidence of a phony fault ground, or by agreeing to suppress truthful evidence of an available defense, their collusion (if discovered) would bar a divorce. This rule posed a potential challenge for spouses who were negotiating the terms of their divorce: if one agreed, for example, not to defend in exchange for some promise relating to property or alimony—the normal stuff of settlement negotiations—their agreement might be considered collusion. Other defenses might be forfeited if not asserted by the defending spouse, but collusion is a bar to fault-based divorce which the court may raise on its own because collusion implicates the court's subject matter jurisdiction.

It must be acknowledged, however, that the bar against collusive divorce existed within a legal system that, by universal understanding, was rife with collusion. *See* Lawrence M. Friedman, *A Dead Language: Divorce Law and Practice Before No–Fault*, 86 Va. L. Rev. 1497, 1504–07 (2000). From interests of both efficiency and humanity, judges did not generally police the collusion bar aggressively and often cooperated by entering default judgments in uncontested divorces. As Professor DiFonzo writes, "[t]he Michigan divorce judge who opened morning hearings in uncontested cases by intoning 'Let the perjury begin,' understood the strictly symbolic character of the courtroom rituals." James Herbie DiFonzo, Beneath the Fault Line: The Popular and Legal Culture of Divorce in Twentieth–Century America 90 (1997). Nevertheless, the bar remained at the ready and sometimes reared up to deny relief. *See* Friedman, *supra*, at 1507.

PROBLEM 8–1

In April, three years into their marriage, Rachael confronted her husband, Tom, with suspicions that he was having an affair with a co-worker, Phoebe. Tom admitted having dinner and drinks with Phoebe after work on four or five occasions, and socializing with Phoebe on two weekends when Rachael was away on business trips, but insisted that he was only trying to give her emotional support while Phoebe was separating from her husband. Tom denied having an affair but promised to stop socializing with Phoebe in the future, and Rachael relented. Tom and Rachael enjoyed relative marital harmony for the next four months, until one afternoon in August when Rachael happened to spot Tom's car leaving the parking lot of a local motel. Driving closer, Rachael saw that Tom was driving and Phoebe was in the passenger seat. Furious, Rachael pulled her car alongside Tom's. When Tom sped up to avoid her, Rachael gave chase and ultimately rammed Tom's rear bumper twice before her own car spun into a ditch. No one was injured in the incident, but Tom and Phoebe were greatly frightened and alarmed. Later that day, Tom moved out of the marital home and has not returned. Tom has admitted that he and Phoebe rented a room in the motel during their lunch hour, but insists they did so only to have a private, quiet place to talk about issues relating to Phoebe's impending divorce. He and Phoebe both deny having a sexual relationship.

What advice would you give Rachael about her prospects for obtaining an immediate divorce? What advice would you give Tom if he wished to file for divorce? If the parties were both amenable, could they simply stipulate to the necessary grounds?

SECTION 4:   NO–FAULT DIVORCE

As mentioned in Section 2, dissatisfaction with the corruption and hardships of traditional fault-based divorce led to the enactment of no-fault divorce in California in 1969 and to its rapid acceptance in other states over the next 15 years. As the materials in this section explain, "no-fault" divorce in most jurisdictions requires a judicial finding that the marriage is "irretrievably broken" and the satisfaction of a waiting period while living "separate and apart." In most states, no-fault divorce is merely an alternative to fault-based divorce; in 18 states and the District of Columbia, however, divorce may be obtained only on no-fault grounds. *See* Elrod & Spector, *supra*, at 713 (Chart 4).

The statutory excerpts that follow illustrate two typical no-fault regimes, the first in a jurisdiction that recognizes only no-fault grounds for divorce and the second in a jurisdiction that simply added no-fault grounds as a supplement to the pre-existing fault-based regime.

A. EXCLUSIVE NO–FAULT REGIMES

The approach recommended by the Uniform Marriage and Divorce Act in 1970 makes "irretrievable breakdown" of the marriage the exclusive ground for divorce. The UMDA approach is implemented in the statutory excerpts below, adopted by Kentucky in 1972. It remains, however, the minority rule nationwide. As you read the excerpt, consider how the stated purposes of the exclusive no-fault statute differ from the underlying objectives of traditional fault-based divorce.

Chapter 403 of the Kentucky Revised Statutes Dissolution of Marriage

403.110   Purpose of chapter

This chapter shall be liberally construed and applied to promote its underlying purposes, which are to:

(1) Strengthen and preserve the integrity of marriage and safeguard family relationships;

(2) Promote the amicable settlement of disputes that have arisen between parties to a marriage;

(3) Mitigate the potential harm to the spouses and their children caused by the process of legal dissolution of marriage;

(4) Make reasonable provision for spouse and minor children during and after litigation; and

(5) Make the law of legal dissolution of marriage effective for dealing with the realities of matrimonial experience by making irretrievable breakdown of the marriage relationship the sole basis for its dissolution.

403.140   Marriage–Court may enter decree of dissolution or separation

(1) The Circuit Court shall enter a decree of dissolution of marriage if:

[the petitioner satisfies the jurisdiction and conciliation requirements of the statute and]:

* * *

(c) The court finds that the marriage is irretrievably broken * * *.

* * *

403.170   Marriage; irretrievable breakdown

(1) If both of the parties by petition or otherwise have stated under oath or affirmation that the marriage is irretrievably broken, or one of the parties has so stated and the other has not denied it, the court, after hearing, shall make a finding whether the mar-

riage is irretrievably broken. No decree shall be entered until the parties have lived apart for 60 days. Living apart shall include living under the same roof without sexual cohabitation. The court may order a conciliation conference as a part of the hearing.

(2) If one of the parties has denied under oath or affirmation that the marriage is irretrievably broken, the court shall consider all relevant factors, including the circumstances that gave rise to filing the petition and the prospect of reconciliation, and shall:

(a) Make a finding whether the marriage is irretrievably broken; or

(b) Continue the matter for further hearing not fewer than 30 nor more than 60 days later, or as soon thereafter as the matter may be reached on the court's calendar, and may suggest to the parties that they seek counseling.

The court, at the request of either party shall, or on its own motion may, order a conciliation conference. At the adjourned hearing the court shall make a finding whether the marriage is irretrievably broken.

(3) A finding of irretrievable breakdown is a determination that there is no reasonable prospect of reconciliation.

Ky. Rev. Stat. Ann. §§ 403.110, .140, .170 (West 2008).

B. MIXED FAULT/NO–FAULT REGIMES

A minority of jurisdictions followed the UMDA's suggestion and abandoned fault-based divorce in favor of no-fault, but most simply added no-fault provisions to supplement their existing fault laws. In these jurisdictions, illustrated by the Pennsylvania statute below, a party seeking a divorce may elect whether to proceed on fault or no-fault grounds.

Title 23, Section 3301 of the Pennsylvania Consolidated Statutes

§ 3301. Grounds for divorce

(a) Fault.—The court may grant a divorce to the innocent and injured spouse whenever it is judged that the other spouse has:

(1) Committed willful and malicious desertion, and absence from the habitation of the injured and innocent spouse, without a reasonable cause, for the period of one or more years.

(2) Committed adultery.

(3) By cruel and barbarous treatment, endangered the life or health of the injured and innocent spouse.

(4) Knowingly entered into a bigamous marriage while a former marriage is still subsisting.

(5) Been sentenced to imprisonment for a term of two or more years upon conviction of having committed a crime.

(6) Offered such indignities to the innocent and injured spouse as to render that spouse's condition intolerable and life burdensome.

(b) Institutionalization.—The court may grant a divorce from a spouse upon the ground that insanity or serious mental disorder has resulted in confinement in a mental institution for at least 18 months immediately before the commencement of an action under this part and where there is no reasonable prospect that the spouse will be discharged from inpatient care during the 18 months subsequent to the commencement of the action. * * *

(c) Mutual consent.—The court may grant a divorce where it is alleged that the marriage is irretrievably broken and 90 days have elapsed from the date of commencement of an action under this part and an affidavit has been filed by each of the parties evidencing that each of the parties consents to the divorce.

(d) Irretrievable breakdown.—

(1) The court may grant a divorce where a complaint has been filed alleging that the marriage is irretrievably broken and an affidavit has been filed alleging that the parties have lived separate and apart for a period of at least two years and that the marriage is irretrievably broken and the defendant either:

(i) Does not deny the allegations set forth in the affidavit.

(ii) Denies one or more of the allegations set forth in the affidavit but, after notice and hearing, the court determines that the parties have lived separate and apart for a period of at least two years and that the marriage is irretrievably broken.

(2) If a hearing has been held pursuant to paragraph (1)(ii) and the court determines that there is a reasonable prospect of reconciliation, then the court shall continue the matter for a period not less than 90 days nor more than 120 days unless the parties agree to a period in excess of 120 days. During this period, the court shall require counseling as provided in section 3302 (relating to counseling). If the parties have not reconciled at the expiration of the time period and one party states under oath that the marriage is irretrievably broken, the court shall determine whether the marriage is irretrievably broken. If the court determines that the marriage is irretrievably broken, the court shall grant the divorce. Otherwise, the court shall deny the divorce.

* * *

23 Pa. Cons. Stat. Ann. § 3301 (West 2008).

C. LIVING SEPARATE AND APART

In its original form, the UMDA did not require any separation period and allowed divorce solely on a finding that the marriage was "irretrievably broken." After a few years, the UMDA was revised to permit no-fault divorce, in section 302(a)(2), only where "the court finds that the marriage is irretrievably broken, if the finding is supported by evidence that (i) the parties have lived separate and apart for a period of more than 180 days next preceding the commencement of the proceeding, or (ii) there is serious marital discord adversely affecting the attitude of one or both of the parties toward the marriage." 9A U.L.A. 200 (1998).

Some states have embraced the UMDA's approach without modification, permitting divorce without any waiting period on a showing of "serious marital discord." But most states, including Kentucky and Pennsylvania, have added a mandatory separation period to their no-fault laws. Kentucky requires a relatively short wait of 60 days (*see* Ky. Rev. Stat. Ann. § 403.170(1), quoted above). Pennsylvania mandates a two-year separation period, except where both spouses consent to the divorce (*see* the Pennsylvania statute, quoted above). What purpose is served by requiring the parties to endure a separation period before granting a divorce? Why shorten the wait when both spouses agree? Are the purposes different for couples with minor dependent children than for other couples?

No matter what length is prescribed for the required separation, disputes may arise over whether the parties have genuinely lived "separate and apart" for the statutory period. Disputes sometimes center on whether the parties may live "separately" within the same dwelling; other times, parties may disagree about the date on which their separation began. The following decision presents both questions. As you read it, consider whether the purposes of the statutory separation period were satisfied by the manner in which these spouses lived "separate and apart."

FREY v. FREY

Superior Court of Pennsylvania, 2003.
821 A.2d 623.

STEVENS, J.

This is an appeal from the May 10, 2002 order entered in the Court of Common Pleas of Fayette County issuing a final decree in divorce * * *.

[Wife "oppos[ed] the entry of a divorce decree on the grounds that the parties had not lived separate and apart for at least two years and the marriage was not irretrievably broken." The trial court accepted Husband's contention that the parties' separation commenced on August 6, 1999, and granted a no-fault divorce.]

* * *

* * * On direct examination, Husband testified that he filed a complaint in divorce on August 6, 1999, and when he filed the complaint, he and Wife were living in the same residence with their daughter. Husband testified that, prior to this time, he occasionally ate meals with Wife and his daughter, but he and Wife had not slept together in the same bed since March 23, 1998. * * * Husband indicated that he refused to move because he had no other house, he had built the house, his daughter lived in the house, and his lumber company was located next to the house. * * * Husband admitted that, following the filing of the divorce complaint, he, Wife, and their daughter went on vacations to Walt Disney World and Myrtle Beach. However, Husband testified that he and Wife did not sleep together while on vacation, and the sole purpose for the trips was to benefit their daughter. * * *

On cross-examination, Husband admitted that in December 1999, Wife attended the lumber company's Christmas party, and on December 31, 1999, he and Wife hosted a party at their house. Husband testified that he stayed at home on New Year's Eve so that he could be with his daughter. Husband further admitted that he and Wife saw a marriage counselor in March and August of 2000, and during the summer of 2000, Husband coached his daughter's t-ball team, with Wife being present. Husband also took Wife and their daughter to a concert at the local fair during the summer of 2000 because he had been given the tickets as a gift, and they went again in September 2001. * * * Husband testified that in May 2001, he, Wife, and their daughter went to Monroeville, Pennsylvania for a weekend of shopping. Husband indicated that he did this solely for his daughter because he had promised that he would take her. * * *

* * *

Wife testified that she believes the parties separated in October 2001 because that is when she and Husband first met with attorneys and Wife came to realize that the parties would not reconcile. Wife testified that from 1999 to October 2001, she, Husband, and their daughter attended school activities and holidays, went to the movies and dinner, and went on vacations together. Wife admitted that Husband generally eats with his mother, but she indicated that she washed all of his clothes, with the exception of his shirts. Wife testified that from 1999 to 2001 she and Husband had sexual intercourse on a regular basis, and the last time they had sexual intercourse was the weekend of October 28, 2001. * * *

* * *

Wife first contends that the trial court erred in concluding that the parties' date of separation was August 6, 1999, and not October 2001, and, therefore, the statutory period for a no-fault divorce was not met. * * *

* * * Subsection 3301(d)(1) provides that the court may grant a no-fault divorce where a complaint has been filed alleging that the marriage is irretrievably broken and an affidavit has been filed alleging that the parties have lived separate and apart for a period of at least two years.

When considering a challenge to the trial court's determination of the date of separation, we have applied the following standard:

> The Divorce Code defines "separate and apart" as follows: "Complete cessation of any and all cohabitation, whether living in the same residence or not." 23 Pa. [Cons. Stat. Ann.] § 3103. In *Thomas v. Thomas*, 483 A.2d 945 (Pa. Super. Ct. 1984), this [C]ourt held that "cohabitation" means "the mutual assumption of those rights and duties attendant to the relationship of husband and wife." Thus, the gravamen of the phrase "separate and apart" becomes the existence of separate lives not separate roofs. * * *

Wellner v. Wellner, 699 A.2d 1278, 1281 (Pa. Super. Ct. 1997) (citations and quotations omitted). * * *

Applying the foregoing, we conclude that the trial court did not err when it determined the date of separation to be August 6, 1999, as the date is supported by sufficient, credible evidence. For example, Husband testified that, as of August 6, 1999 to the time of the hearing, he did not sleep in the same room as Wife, and, in fact, he used the marital residence for sleeping purposes only. Husband testified that he remained in the house for reasons other than those relating to Wife. As for the eating of meals, Husband testified that, after August 6, 1999, he usually ate meals at his mother's house and that, when he did eat at the marital residence, it was with his daughter only. Husband testified that Wife washes his work jeans sometimes, but he takes all of his shirts to his mother and he sometimes washes his own jeans. With regard to vacations and other outings, Husband admitted that he went on vacations and other outings with Wife and his daughter after August 6, 1999; however, Husband specifically testified that such activities were for the benefit of his daughter only and Wife was aware of this fact. Husband did not engage in sexual intercourse or sleep in the same bed as Wife during the vacations, and as Husband testified, he and Wife gave the appearance that everything was fine for the sake of their daughter. Based on the aforementioned, we conclude that the evidence supported the August 6, 1999 separation date.

We specifically disagree with Wife's contention that the fact she attended the lumber company's 1999 Christmas party, the parties sought counseling twice in 2000, and the parties had dinner together in October 2001 requires a finding that the date of separation should be after August 6, 1999. This Court has held that isolated attempts at reconciliation do not begin running anew the marital relationship. Moreover, the fact Wife's testimony differed from Husband's in many respects is not determinative in this case. Husband testified that, after August 6, 1999, he and Wife did not have sexual relations[;] however, Wife testified that they regularly had sexual relations. Apparently finding neither spouse to be totally forthcoming, the trial court concluded that occasional sexual relations occurred between Husband and Wife following August 6, 1999.[1] The trial court was

---

1. We note that the trial court properly found that occasional sexual contact between Husband and Wife after August 6, 1999 did not require a conclusion that the parties were cohabiting.

free to make its credibility determination, and we will not disturb this determination on appeal.

In sum, the evidence in this case reveals that Husband and Wife led separate lives, even though the parties generally slept under the same roof, and their activities together were knowingly performed solely for the benefit of their daughter. Husband should not be penalized for attempting to make life for his daughter more pleasurable and his isolated, unsuccessful attempts at reconciliation. We believe that "cohabitation" contemplates more of a martial relationship than what occurred in this case after August 6, 1999. As such, we conclude that the trial court did not err in this regard.

* * *

Affirmed.

NOTES AND QUESTIONS

1. *Sharing the same dwelling.* Most states agree that parties to a no-fault divorce should be required to satisfy a period of separation, but the states disagree on precisely what it means for two spouses to live "separate and apart." Some states agree with *Frey* that parties may satisfy the requisite separation period while living in the same house, so long as they are effectively living separate lives. *See, e.g.,* Ky. Rev. Stat. Ann. § 403.170(1) (West 2008), quoted above; *In re Marriage of A.J.H.*, 2002 WL 31454020, at *1 n.1 (Del. Fam. Ct. May 1, 2002). But other jurisdictions require the parties to live in separate dwellings. *See, e.g., Viator v. Miller*, 900 So.2d 1135, 1138 n.1 (La. Ct. App. 2005); *In re Marriage of Norviel*, 126 Cal.Rptr.2d 148 (Ct. App. 2002). What concerns might affect the choice between these two positions?

2. *Intention to end the marriage.* Even where the parties indisputably live "apart," they may not be considered "separated" unless their removal is accompanied by a subjective intention to dissolve their marriage. "The separation must be 'coupled with an intention on the part of at least one of the parties to live separate and apart permanently, and [this] intention must be shown to have been present at the beginning' of the separation period." *Pearson v. Vanlowe*, 2005 WL 524597, at *4 (Va. Ct. App. Mar. 8, 2005). Thus, if the parties are separated by one spouse's military duty or incarceration, the absence will not count as "living separate and apart" unless at least one party makes clear an intent never to resume cohabitation. *See Sinha v. Sinha*, 526 A.2d 765, 767–68 (Pa. 1987).

3. *Factors in determining intention of parties to separate.* As *Frey* illustrates, "[d]etermination of whether and when the parties have 'lived separate and apart without cohabitation' is a fact-based inquiry, requiring examination of all the circumstances before the court." *Bchara v. Bchara*, 563 S.E.2d 398, 402 (Va. Ct. App. 2002). Particularly where the parties claim to have lived separately while sharing the same home, the outcome often turns on careful attention to their interaction, such as whether they "continued to attend social outings together, or continued to act jointly in financial matters." *In re*

Marriage of Shaughnessy, 2004 WL 1759260, at *3 (Cal. Ct. App. Aug. 6, 2004).

Bchara, found that the parties satisfied Virginia's one-year separation period. After discovering a videotape of her husband having sex with another woman, the wife moved all of his possessions out of the master bedroom and into a guest bedroom. In addition,

> Wife testified in deposition that she stopped depositing money into their joint account after discovering the videotape. She also stopped going to church with husband and stopped attending his family's functions after the discovery. She admitted buying groceries, doing laundry, and cooking food that husband ate. She also accepted flowers from husband, given to her in their son's name on Mother's Day of 2000.

563 S.E.2d at 402. This demonstrated the wife's intention to live "separate and apart" from her husband. "Continuing to share food and keep a clean house are not behaviors that, as a matter of law, require a finding that the parties were living together." *Id.*

By contrast, in *Catalano v. Catalano,* 2005 WL 1154251 (Va. Ct. App. Apr. 28, 2005), the wife moved into a guest bedroom after discovering that her husband had divided a shared bank account. They ceased all intimate relations but "agreed that they would stay together for the sake of the kids until the end of the school year," *id.* at *2, and continued to share some activities together as a family:

> Although Mr. Catalano expressed to coworkers and some family members that he was separated from his wife, he continued to host and attend family gatherings with his wife, as well as to attend various church services and numerous and varied other social functions with her until he moved out of the marital home. In short, the parties continued to hold themselves out as a couple. The parties continued to take some meals together, and the family went out to dinner once a week. Throughout the period, Ms. Catalano continued to do the cooking and shopping for the family, cleaning of the dishes, house and laundry. Mr. Catalano continued to support financially the family activities.

Id. The court concluded that "although the parties slept in separate bedrooms, they did not live physically separate and apart, without cohabitation, while they remained under one roof." *Id.* If you represented a party who wished a no-fault divorce based on living separate and apart, what steps would you suggest the client take to make clear the intent and the fact of separation?

4. *Effect of reconciliation attempts on separation period.* If separated spouses reconcile and resume cohabiting, their reconciliation may effectively reset the clock on their separation period for purposes of a later divorce. As in *Frey,* however, courts distinguish between brief overtures toward reconciliation (which will not terminate the separation period) and intentional resumption of the marital relationship (which will). In *Pearson, supra,* for example, a couple initially separated in October 1997 and remained apart for more than the one-year separation period required for a no-fault divorce. In May 1999, however, they reconciled and lived together until October 1999, when they

again parted ways. The court held that their separation began in October 1999, and continued uninterrupted for the statutory period, despite the fact that the parties began "a dating relationship" six months into their second separation, including a resumption of occasional sexual relations and an exchange of "affectionate correspondence" raising the possibility of reconciliation. *See Pearson, supra*, at *2. The appellate court agreed with the trial court that "wife's references to marriage counseling and reconciliation were attempts to improve communications with husband, indicating her intent 'to ease the hardship of getting out of the marriage on everybody,' and 'not an intent to resume the marriage.' " *Id.* "Mere casual cohabitation between the parties, after the separation, unaccompanied by resumption of normal married life . . . is not sufficient to show a reconciliation or an agreement to live and cohabit together again on a permanent basis as husband and wife." *Id.* at *4 (internal citation omitted). Why might courts decline to treat reconciliation attempts as terminating a separation? In *Pearson*, should the parties' initial separation between 1997 and 1999 have provided a sufficient basis for a no-fault divorce in October 1999? Why or why not?

5. *Role of separation agreements.* Parties often negotiate formal agreements at the time of their separation. These can prove highly useful for several purposes. First, parties may use an agreement to make unambiguous their intention to live "separate and apart." For example, *Catalano*, found no intent to separate, partly because the wife "specifically rejected the idea of entering into a proposed property settlement agreement to establish a date of separation." *Catalano, supra*, at *2. In New York, a written separation agreement is statutorily required for no-fault divorce. N.Y. Dom. Rel. L. § 170(6) (West Supp. 2008). Beyond establishing no-fault grounds for divorce, separation agreements commonly play a dominant role in determining the financial and other consequences of dissolution. As discussed in detail in Chapter 14, parties may specify how their property is to be divided at divorce, the terms of any spousal support, and custody arrangements for their children, and courts will normally defer, often incorporating the parties' agreement as part of the divorce decree. In some states, parties may enforce the terms of a separation agreement to divide their property even before the divorce, allowing for an earlier severance of economic entanglements. *See, e.g., Grider v. Grider,* 968 S.W.2d 653, 654–55 (Ark. Ct. App. 1998).

D.   IRRETRIEVABLE BREAKDOWN

"Irretrievable breakdown of the marriage" has been defined to mean that "either or both of the spouses are unable or unwilling to cohabit and there are no prospects for reconciliation." *Caffyn v. Caffyn,* 806 N.E.2d 415, 419 n.6 (Mass. 2004). What if one spouse wants to end the marriage but the other is convinced that their conflicts can be overcome or resolved through counseling or other intervention? Do you agree with the way the following court resolved this dilemma?

RICHTER v. RICHTER

Court of Appeals of Minnesota, 2001.
625 N.W.2d 490.

SHUMAKER, JUDGE.

* * *

The parties married in 1983 and wife petitioned to dissolve the marriage in September 1999. Husband opposed wife's attempts to dissolve the marriage. * * * On April 25, husband, pro se, moved to dismiss the proceeding, alleging, among other things, that (a) there was no irretrievable breakdown of the marriage; (b) marriage is a contract; and (c) the statutes allowing dissolution of a marriage infringed on the constitutional right to contract. * * *

[The district court denied the husband's motion to dismiss and a later motion for a continuance. The husband then declined to participate in the hearing on the divorce petition and the court granted the wife's request for divorce after hearing her testimony.]

* * *

Minnesota allows marriages to be dissolved if there has been an "irretrievable breakdown of the marriage relationship." Minn. Stat. § 518.06, subd. 1 (2000). While husband denies challenging the constitutionality of * * * Minnesota's dissolution statute, he argues that to be constitutional, the statute cannot be construed to allow "divorce on demand" because that would interfere with his right to contract. *See* U.S. Const. art. I, § 10 (prohibiting laws "impairing the obligation of contracts"); Minn. Const. art. I, § 11 (same). * * * Such an argument assumes that the Minnesota dissolution statutes allow "divorce on demand" and that marriage is a contract. Both assumptions are incorrect.

I.

In Minnesota, if there is a dispute about whether a marriage is irretrievably broken, "the court shall consider all relevant factors" and find whether the marriage is irretrievably broken. Minn. Stat. § 518.13, subd. 2 (2000). "Irretrievable breakdown" occurs when "there is no reasonable prospect of reconciliation." *Id.* To find irretrievable breakdown of a marriage in a case where the existence of such a breakdown is contested,

> [t]he finding [of irretrievable breakdown] must be supported by evidence that (i) the parties have lived separate and apart for a period of not less than 180 days immediately preceding the commencement of the proceeding, or (ii) there is serious marital discord adversely affecting the attitude of one or both of the parties.

Id. Here, the parties had been separated, but not for 180 days, before wife petitioned to dissolve the marriage. The district court, however, believed wife's testimony about the state of the parties' marriage and found an irretrievable breakdown of the marriage. A party's testimony is a sufficient basis for a finding of irretrievable breakdown of a marriage. *See Hagerty v. Hagerty*, 281 N.W.2d 386, 388 (Minn. 1979) (stating irretrievable breakdown "can also be shown by evidence of only one party's belief that it is the existing state, particularly where the parties have been living apart"); *Hollander v. Hollander*, 359 N.W.2d 55, 56–57 (Minn. App. 1984) (affirming finding of irretrievable breakdown [and] noting that, among other things, it was supported by wife's testimony). A statute that requires proof of "no reasonable prospect of reconciliation" and "serious marital discord adversely affecting the attitude of one or both of the parties" before a marriage can be dissolved does not allow "divorce on demand." Moreover, husband's withdrawal from the courtroom means he neither entered evidence contrary to wife's assertions on this point nor cross-examined her regarding the state of the marriage. Thus, the only evidence regarding the state of the parties' marriage was wife's uncontradicted testimony.

II.

Marriage, "so far as its validity in law is concerned," is a contract. Minn. Stat. § 517.01 (2000). That marriage is a contract for determining its *validity* does *not* mean marriage is a contract in the usual sense of that term. * * *

Any doubt * * * was eliminated in *Maynard v. Hill*, 125 U.S. 190 (1888). There, a husband moved away from his wife and to the Oregon Territory. Once there, he, without the knowledge or consent of his wife, procured a divorce. Later, he died. In the resulting litigation involving his estate, the validity of the divorce was questioned. The Supreme Court stated:

> * * * Assuming that the prohibition of the federal constitution against the impairment of contracts by state legislation applies equally, as would seem to be the opinion of the supreme court of the territory, to legislation by territorial legislatures, *we are clear that marriage is not a contract within the meaning of the prohibition.* As was said by Chief Justice Marshall in the *Dartmouth College Case* * * * : "The provision of the constitution never has been understood to embrace other contracts than those which respect property or some object of value, and confer rights which may be asserted in a court of justice. It never has been understood to restrict the general right of the legislature to legislate on the subject of divorces."

Maynard, 125 U.S. at 210 (emphasis added).

* * *

The Minnesota dissolution statutes do not allow "divorce on demand," marriage is not a contract for purposes of the Contract Clauses of the United States and Minnesota Constitutions, and husband has not shown that the district court abused its discretion in denying his request for a continuance [or committed clear error in finding that the marriage was irretrievably broken]. Therefore, we affirm the district court.

Affirmed.

NOTES AND QUESTIONS

1. *Unilateral divorce.* Even in cases of mutual consent, no-fault statutes generally require a judicial determination that the marriage is, in fact, "irretrievably broken." Yet courts have widely considered that one partner's resolute wish to leave the marriage conclusively establishes breakdown. Should irretrievable breakdown mean something different in consent cases than where one spouse opposes the divorce? *Richter* upheld the district court's finding of irretrievable breakdown partly based on the husband's failure to cross-examine his wife concerning the state of their marriage, but could any cross-examination have convinced the court that the marriage was sound? Does the court convincingly demonstrate that the Minnesota law (taken from the current UMDA) does not provide for "divorce on demand"? Should government care whether the parties' marriage might be saved? Should the public interest depend, at least partly, on whether the parties have minor dependent children? If the government should not care, why demand pleading and proof of irretrievable breakdown? If the government should care, why not order reasonable efforts to repair a marriage?

Many states now require divorcing parents to attend short counseling sessions or programs addressing the impact of divorce on children, but courts and legislators mostly remain wary of getting involved in other efforts at marriage repair. In *Hagerty v. Hagerty*, 281 N.W.2d 386 (Minn. 1979), mentioned in *Richter*, the court rebuffed a wife's suggestion that her marriage could be saved if the court would only order her husband to seek treatment for his alcoholism. If states are willing to compel counseling or educational programs as part of the process of divorce, why not compel treatment for the underlying causes of marital discord in order to avoid divorce?

2. *Withholding divorce.* There are very exceptional cases in which courts decline to find an "irretrievable breakdown." Consider *In re Estate of Carlisle*, 653 N.W.2d 368 (Iowa 2002):

> Francis and Dorthy Carlisle had been married for sixty-five years when, in 1998, Dorthy fell and broke her hip. She wanted to install a bathroom on the first floor of their home to accommodate her resulting disability. Francis refused because it would be too expensive to cut into the limestone walls of their home. Dorthy moved in with her daughter. On August 16, 1999, she filed a petition for legal separation and maintenance. Francis answered and counterclaimed for a decree of dissolution. Francis acknowledged that his wife "has been a wonderful lady and this action should never have happened." Nevertheless, he wanted a dissolution because he did not want Dorthy to request more property from him.

> On May 23, 2000, the district court entered a decree of separate maintenance. The court's opinion stated that, "There has *not* been a breakdown in the marital relationship to the extent that the legitimate objects of matrimony have been destroyed."

Id. at 368–69. Are the facts of *Carlisle* really distinguishable from those of *Richter*? What "legitimate objects of matrimony" might remain in the Carlisle marriage?

3. *Consent divorce.* Under many no-fault divorce laws, including Pennsylvania's (*see* Pennsylvania statute excerpted *supra*, at pp. 441–42), divorce is made easier if both parties consent, by shortening the required separation or waiting period. In a few states, however, most prominently New York, no-fault divorce is permitted *only* if both spouses consent. *See* N.Y. Dom. Rel. L. § 170(6) (West Supp. 2008) (permitting divorce based on one year's separation "pursuant to a written agreement of separation" filed with the county clerk). In 2006, after a comprehensive two-year study of the state's divorce law, a special Matrimonial Commission appointed by the state's Chief Judge recommended that New York adopt a broader no-fault law without endorsing any particular legislative approach. N.Y. State Comm'n to Promote Public Confidence in Judicial Elections, Final Report to the Chief Judge of the State of New York 18–19 (2006), http://law.fordham.edu/commission/judicialelections/images/jud-finreport.pdf. If you were a New York legislator, would you support abandoning the requirement of mutual consent for a no-fault divorce?

4. *California summary dissolution.* California law permits some couples with relatively few entanglements to obtain a divorce through a summary legal process. To qualify for summary dissolution, the couple must both desire a divorce, have been married no more than five years, have no children and only modest financial assets (and no real estate), waive any claim to spousal support and agree on the disposition of community property. Couples who qualify can then file a joint petition for dissolution, which will be granted in due course by a court following a six-month waiting period. *See* Cal. Fam. Code §§ 2400–2406 (West 2008).

5. *Other constitutional attacks on no-fault divorce.* For many spouses who married at a time when divorce was available only for fault, the introduction of no-fault divorce came as a shock and effectively stripped them of the ability to deny a divorce to a wrongdoing spouse. As in *Richter*, many spouses resisted application of no-fault laws on constitutional grounds. These efforts uniformly failed. *See, e.g., In re Marriage of Walton*, 104 Cal.Rptr. 472 (Ct. App. 1972) (rejecting Due Process and Contract Clause arguments); *Gluck v. Gluck*, 435 A.2d 35 (Conn. 1980) (rejecting claim of unconstitutional vagueness); *Buchholz v. Buchholz*, 248 N.W.2d 21 (Neb. 1976) (rejecting Equal Protection and Due Process arguments).

PROBLEM 8–2

Ruth and Kenneth separated after 10 years of marriage in March 2006, because of disputes over debts and spending. They sold the marital home, divided the proceeds, and moved into separate residences until April 2008. During that month, the parties discussed a possible reconciliation; and in May of the same year, Kenneth moved into Ruth's residence. During the next two months, Ruth and Kenneth shared the same bedroom and resumed sexual relations, shared household chores, opened a joint checking account, and had a social life as husband and wife. The parties' attempt at reconciliation failed in July 2008. Kenneth moved out and immediately filed for divorce. In his petition, he asserted that the marriage had suffered an "irretrievable breakdown" and that the parties had lived "separate and apart" for two years, as required by the state's no-fault divorce law. Ruth contests the divorce on the grounds that their differences over money could be bridged through financial counseling and that they have not satisfied the state's separation period for no-fault divorce. What advice would you give Ruth about her prospects for resisting divorce? Would your advice be any different as a family law practitioner in Minnesota rather than Pennsylvania?

SECTION 5: QUESTIONING NO–FAULT DIVORCE

No-fault divorce won remarkably rapid and widespread acceptance in U.S. law after its introduction in 1969, but it remains controversial. Since its introduction, no-fault divorce has faced a wide range of criticisms, including that it has increased the divorce rate, reduced the economic security of women and children, condoned misconduct within marriage, and encouraged hasty entry into marriage by ensuring easy exit. The controversy has not faded in the nearly four decades since its arrival. *See, e.g.*, James Herbie DiFonzo, Beneath the Fault Line: The Popular and Legal Culture of Divorce in Twentieth Century America (1997); Allen M. Parkman, *Reforming Divorce Reform*, 41 Santa Clara L. Rev. 379 (2001). Indeed, recent calls to repeal or reform no-fault divorce have generated considerable attention. *See* Lynn D. Wardle, *Divorce Reform at the Turn of the Millennium: Certainties and Possibilities*, 33 Fam. L.Q. 783 (1999). Bills to limit the availability of no-fault divorce—by reintroducing fault grounds, requiring mutual consent, or mandating counseling or longer waiting periods—have been introduced throughout the country.

Many of the basic issues in the controversy are outlined in the following classic pair of essays debating the topic written by two prominent social critics.

END NO–FAULT DIVORCE?

75 First Things 24 (1997).

YES: Maggie Gallagher

* * *

What have we gotten in exchange for [no-fault's] sweeping abandonment of the idea that marriage is a public, legal commitment, and not merely a private exchange of sentimental wishes? When in the 1970s and early 1980s no-fault divorce swept through state legislatures, its advocates promised us two great benefits: (1) no-fault would reduce conflict, as spouses would no longer be forced to assign legal blame for the marriage's end, and (2) no-fault would enhance respect for the law, as couples longing for a divorce would no longer have to commit perjury, lodge false accusations of adultery, to get one.

* * *

In reality no-fault divorce laws did something decidedly * * * revolutionary. Rather than transferring to the couple the right to decide when a divorce is justified, no-fault laws transferred that right to the individual. No-fault is thus something of a misnomer; a more accurate term would be unilateral divorce on demand.

The idea that couples who wish to divorce should be able to do so without making false accusations is now uncontroversial. Even the most aggressive of the new divorce reforms to restore fault recently proposed in Michigan permits couples to dissolve their marriages quietly and amicably, by mutual consent. * * *

What the current no-fault debate revolves around is the lesser question: Is marriage less than a legal contract between two people? Is the marriage contract enforceable, and if so how? When we marry, are we making a binding commitment or a fully revocable one (if "revocable commitment" is not an oxymoron)? If the latter, what is the difference, morally and legally, between getting married and living together? Why have a legal institution dedicated to making a public promise the law considers too burdensome to enforce?

As for no-fault's second promise—to lower the conflict around divorce—I defy anyone but a lawyer to come to that conclusion. Lawyers like no-fault divorce because it moves much nasty human conflict out of their sight. When a wife comes crying that her husband is leaving her for the new blonde in sales, the lawyer's job is now simply to interrupt and say, "Get over it." That is no longer a legally relevant fact. No-fault divorce may have lowered the status of marriage, but at least it improved the working conditions of divorce lawyers.

Meanwhile our social landscape is littered with the cruelties, large and small, divorcing partners inflict on each other under the purest of no-fault statutes. * * *

* * *

The theory that the anger and hurt generated by divorce is somehow the product of what happens for a few days in the courtroom is based on a remarkably shallow, improbable reading of the human heart. If anything, no-fault divorce shifted the long-drawn-out legal battles from fault grounds to custody, which is surely to no child's advantage.

* * *

Despite the large logical gaps in the argument, the fear that reforming no-fault divorce might somehow endanger abused women is widely shared. * * *

But the more one learns about the crime of domestic violence, the less likely it seems that the formal mechanisms of divorce law have much influence one way or another in helping women escape their batterers. For one thing, most batterers are not husbands. * * * Cohabitating women, according to one review of the literature, are four times more likely to suffer severe violence than married women.

It is not a marriage license that gives batterers their hold over their victims; men willing to exert brutal physical control over women don't depend on the fine print of divorce laws for their power. * * *

Could there be any relationship between the embrace of no-fault and the rise in divorce? Until recently, academic researchers said not. "Nearly every study of divorce and the law has concluded that legal changes have little or no impact upon the rate of marital dissolutions," wrote social historian Elaine Tyler May in *Great Expectations: Marriage and Divorce in Post–Victorian America* (1989), repeating the conventional scholarly wisdom. But evaluating the effect of law on divorce rates turned out to be tricky. * * *

Several recent studies, however, confirm what common sense suggests: Changes in divorce law did increase the divorce rate. No-fault divorce laws may account for somewhere between 15 and 25 percent of the increase in divorce that took place in the seventies.

In other words, while there are many social and economic factors conspiring to weaken our marriages, no-fault divorce laws have pushed us over the edge from being a society in which the majority of marriages succeed to one in which (according to demographers' estimates) a majority of new marriages will fail. When divorce is made quicker and nonjudgmental, more marriages fail. And the story about marriage contained in the law—of marriage as a temporary bond sustained by mutual emotion alone—is becoming the dominant story we tell about marriage in America, eclipsing older narratives about stubborn faith and commitment, "till death do us part."

* * *

NO: Barbara Dafoe Whitehead

As a critic of contemporary divorce, I am eager to find ways to curb the American appetite for divorce. * * *

Even so, I do not favor legislation to restore fault to the divorce process. To be sure, no-fault divorce law is nothing to brag about. Intended to simplify the administration of divorce, it has unintentionally led to a legal system of divorce on demand. Nonetheless, it does not follow that the repeal or reform of no-fault divorce will be effective as a deterrent to divorce in general. Indeed, at this moment in time, I believe a fault requirement would do more harm than good.

In the short term, the obligation to establish a legal finding of fault may deter some divorces, encouraging couples who are wavering over a decision to divorce to work out their marital difficulties. But the deterrent effect is likely to be weak. Most people do not contemplate divorce until their marriage is in very bad shape; by then, clergy and therapists say, it is very difficult to salvage the marriage. The fault barrier comes too late in the divorcing process. Moreover, the deterrent effect of a fault requirement would also be indiscriminate. Some marriages will be preserved that probably should end, including those that involve physical violence and abuse. * * *

Fault law invites litigiousness as well, and thus intensifies and prolongs conflict. * * * Requiring fault would be bound to hurt the children who will be caught in the crossfire. If we have learned anything from thirty years of high divorce, it is this: When divorcing parents have legal incentives to fight, they will. And fault gives them yet another incentive. * * *

Moreover, establishing fault in contested cases would require more aggressive and time-consuming litigation and thus more billable hours from lawyers, therapists, private investigators, pension specialists, expert witnesses, and all the others in the divorce industry. * * * Marital assets will be squandered and dissipated in fault battles, leaving fewer resources for the maintenance and care of the children after the divorce.

Over the long term, proponents of fault argue, higher barriers to divorce will increase commitment to marriage. If divorce is harder to get, couples will try to maintain high-quality marriages from the outset. This argument is appealing in the abstract. But it is less persuasive in the concrete, especially when we consider the cohort that will probably be most deeply influenced by the reintroduction of fault: young adults approaching marriage for the first time.

One of the most disastrous consequences of the divorce revolution often goes unacknowledged. Today's young adults, many the children of divorce, are more ignorant and wary of marriage than any earlier generation in the nation's history. * * *

For a generation so worried and confused, the impact of fault law is more likely to discourage marriage than encourage it. * * *

There is a yet larger problem posed by fault law. It seeks to reassert institutional authority over marriage in a society where that authority has broken down elsewhere. This is an understandable response to our current plight. But the single-minded focus on fault law is misplaced. It misidentifies (and underestimates) the nature of the problem—which is not the breakdown of legal authority over marriage and divorce, but something that lies outside the domain of the law.

The divorce revolution was a cultural rather than legal phenomenon. It grew out of a historic transformation in ideas and practices regarding sex, marriage, and parenthood. This transformation involved a complex set of social, economic, and cultural factors, but a key element was the introduction of a new psychotherapeutic ethic governing family life. According to this ethic, individuals had a primary obligation to pursue their own emotional well-being in family relationships and especially marriage. Accordingly, a good marriage was one that promoted individual emotional well-being and a bad marriage was one that at least one spouse deemed unsuccessful in achieving this goal. * * *

No-fault divorce laws lagged nearly a decade behind these cultural changes. The states adopted no-fault divorce laws in the 1970s in an effort to bring legal norms into closer conformity with the more permissive extralegal norms. * * *

The point is this: There is a close and dynamic interplay between legal and extralegal norms governing marriage and divorce. Although they are not identical, they work in a complementary way to support a commonly shared set of values, ideas, and practices. Legal sanctions will not curb divorce in a culture where extralegal permissions remain in full play. Consequently, we must be skeptical of the claim that more restrictive fault law will join together what the larger culture has so relentlessly put asunder.

* * *

NOTES AND QUESTIONS

1. *No-fault divorce and the divorce rate.* As Maggie Gallagher notes, the precise cause-and-effect relationship between no-fault divorce and the rise in the divorce rate has been hotly debated. Some researchers have concluded that no-fault did, in fact, contribute to the rise in divorce, at least in some states. *Compare* Paul A. Nakonezny et al., *The Effect of No–Fault Divorce Law on the Divorce Rate Across the 50 States and Its Relation to Income, Education, and Religiosity*, 57 J. Marriage & Fam. 477 (1995), *with* Stephen J. Bahr, *Social Science Research on Family Dissolution*, 4 J.L. & Fam. Stud. 5, 7–8 (2002) (citing Leora Friedberg, *Did Unilateral Divorce Raise Divorce Rates? Evidence from Panel Data*, 88 Amer. Econ. Rev. 608 (1998)). Even if no-fault divorce has increased the number of divorces, is that a sufficient reason to curtail it?

2. *No-fault divorce and a culture of "radical autonomy."* Some critics have blamed no-fault divorce for broadly undermining important social values of service and commitment. Professor J. Herbie DiFonzo writes:

> No-fault enshrined in statute and practice what American culture had been only idly drifting toward in other aspects of life: a predilection for formal and radical autonomy. The reification of divorce on demand intensified the development of what Milton C. Regan, Jr., has aptly termed the *"acontextual self,"* a creature "who stands apart from any social relationship in which he or she is involved." The marital relationship has exhibited no immunity from this legal virus. The "happiness principle embedded in the no-fault ground has dealt a devastating blow to the durability of marriages." And the dethronement of mutual consent in divorce has fostered a loss of mutuality throughout American society.

J. Herbie DiFonzo, Beneath the Fault Line: The Popular and Legal Culture of Divorce in Twentieth–Century America 172–73 (1997); *see also* Carl E. Schneider, *Marriage, Morals, and the Law: No–Fault Divorce and Moral Discourse*, 1994 Utah L. Rev. 503. Does no-fault divorce send a message approving selfish individualism? Would restricting the availability of divorce encourage social norms of commitment and respect for others?

3. *No-fault divorce and the interests of women.* Much of the debate over no-fault divorce has centered on its impact on women. "[I]t is quite well settled now that men do somewhat better financially than their former wives, at least without taking into account tax consequences," even though "[b]oth men and women seem to suffer financially from loss of economies of scale relative to couples that stay together." Margaret F. Brinig, *Empirical Work in Family Law*, 2002 U. Ill. L. Rev. 1083, 1099–1100; *see also* E. Mavis Hetherington & John Kelly, For Better or for Worse: Divorce Reconsidered 48–49 (2002). Some critics have contended that unilateral no-fault divorce has aggravated the financial blow of divorce to women by eliminating any need for husbands to bargain for their consent. *See, e.g.*, Allen Parkman, No–Fault Divorce: What Went Wrong? 1–6, 44–46, 76–87 (1992). Other scholars, however, have disagreed. Comparing divorces in New York (where no-fault divorce remains available only by mutual consent) with other jurisdictions, Professor Marsha Garrison found no clear economic advantage for New York wives. *See* Marsha Garrison, *The Economics of Divorce: Changing Rules, Changing Results*, in Divorce Reform at the Crossroads 75, 90 (Stephen D. Sugarman & Herma Hill Kay eds. 1990). Accordingly, she found it "unlikely that the adoption of no-fault grounds for divorce has played the dominant role in producing reduced awards to divorced wives." *Id.* at 100. In addition, given that most divorces are initiated by wives, creating new barriers to divorce may frustrate more women than men. *See, e.g.*, Hetherington & Kelly, *supra*, at 8; Margaret F. Brinig & Douglas W. Allen, *"These Boots Are Made for Walking": Why Most Divorce Filers Are Women*, 2 Am. L. & Econ. Rev. 126 (2000).

4. *No-fault divorce and the interests of children.* The contested evidence concerning the impact of divorce on children is discussed in Chapters 12 and 13, which concern custody and visitation disputes. To the extent that no-fault divorce has increased the incidence of divorce, some critics have charged that it has harmed children. Reviewing Mavis Hetherington's 2002 book, *For Better or For Worse: Divorce Reconsidered*, Professor William Galston wrote:

> What about the children of divorce? * * * Even after we screen out other background variables, divorce has an independent, significant, and negative effect on children's cognitive, emotional, and social development. First-rate researchers who doubted this a decade ago have changed their minds in response to new and better evidence. Hetherington agrees. Her work shows that 20 to 25 percent of young people from divorced families have experienced serious problems, compared to only 10 percent from non-divorced families. In a *New York Times* interview, she acknowledged that this two-fold increase in risk is larger than the association between smoking and cancer.
>
> In this context, the framing and presentation of her findings is nothing short of astonishing. The crucial chapter is, "Mostly Happy:

Children of Divorce as Young Adults." The crucial finding is as follows: "The big headline in my data is that *80 percent of children from divorced homes eventually are able to adapt to their new life and become reasonably well adjusted.*" * * *

But what of it? A thought-experiment, if you will: Imagine a new smoking study entitled "Mostly Healthy," which emphasized that the overwhelming majority of smokers do not contract cancer and *enjoy reasonably full and healthy lives*. It would be true, statistically, but beside the point. Why does Hetherington think divorce presents a different case? * * *

* * * Hetherington seems to suggest that when we take into account the positive as well as negative consequences of divorce, the doubling of risk for children, though obviously undesirable, is acceptable as part of the total package—like a military assessment of collateral damage to civilians. If I wanted to put her argument in the worst possible light, I would summarize it as follows: Relative to the status quo in 1970, the current divorce regime is (on average, though not in all cases) bad for men, bad for children, and good for women. And therefore, we should ignore the naysayers and regard the changes of the past 30 years as, on balance, positive. * * *

William A. Galston, *What About the Children?*, Blueprint Mag. (Democratic Leadership Council, Washington, D.C.), May 21, 2002, http://www.dlc.org/ndol_ci.cfm?kaid=114 & subid=144 & contentid=250506. Legislation has been proposed in several states to make divorce harder for couples with children, either by requiring a finding of fault or by insisting upon mutual consent of the spouses. *See* DiFonzo, *supra*, at 927–28. Would you support such a measure?

Can some other reform measure, short of reinstituting fault-based divorce, mitigate the harm to children from divorce? A significant number of jurisdictions in recent years have implemented mandatory programs to educate divorcing parents about how to help their children cope with the dissolution. *See* Linda D. Elrod, Child Custody Practice & Procedure § 1:14 (Supp. 2005). Research shows that parenting styles after divorce do significantly affect children's welfare. *See* Hetherington & Kelly, *supra*, at 126–40, 229–30. In 2004, Michigan Governor Jennifer Granholm vetoed legislation that would have mandated counseling for divorcing parents, explaining that "the decisions men and women make about marriage are private decisions" and that "[s]tate government should not expand its role into such private matters." *See* Brad Knickerbocker, *More States Stir Against Ease of 'No Fault' Divorce*, Christian Sci. Mon., Feb. 1, 2005, at 1. Do you agree?

5. *Longer waiting periods.* The Gallagher–Whitehead debate above focuses on proposals to reintroduce fault as a requirement for divorce. Many states, however, have considered less drastic measures to reduce the ease of no-fault divorce. One strategy has been to lengthen the required separation period for a no-fault divorce. Opinions continue to differ, however, on how long the wait should be. Legislation proposed in Georgia would extend the waiting period for an uncontested divorce from 30 days to four months. *See* Sonji Jacobs, *Bill Extends Wait Time for Divorce*, Atlanta J. Const., Jan. 20,

2006, at 1D. Professor Galston, on the other hand, has proposed requiring couples with children to satisfy a five-year waiting period for a no-fault divorce. *See* William Galston, *Braking Divorce for the Sake of Children*, Am. Enterprise, May–June 1996, at 36. Would children necessarily benefit from longer separation periods?

6. *Covenant marriage.* In 1997, Louisiana amended its marriage laws to give couples the choice of entering into a standard marriage with the usual no-fault divorce rules, or a "covenant marriage" subject to a different and more restrictive set of rules for dissolution. Dissolution of a covenant marriage requires proof of specific fault grounds (from a narrow list of serious offenses) or satisfaction of an extended separation period (two years or, if there are minor children, three and a half years). La. Rev. Stat. §§ 9:272 to 9:276 (West 2008). Arizona and Arkansas have followed Louisiana's example, and legislation along these lines is introduced annually in many other states. Ariz. Rev. Stat. §§ 25–901 to 25–906 (West 2007); Ark. Code Ann. §§ 9–11–801 to 9–11–811 (2008). So far, fewer than three percent of couples have opted for covenant marriage in Louisiana, Arizona, and Arkansas. *See* Katherine Shaw Spaht, *Covenant Marriage Seven Years Later: Its As Yet Unfulfilled Promise*, 65 La. L. Rev. 605 (2005). Given the limited use of covenant marriage where it is available, is it likely to have any significant impact? Given that it simply gives couples more options, is there any reason for legislators to oppose it?

One recent study concluded that covenant marriage does, in fact, seem to produce stronger and happier marriages than "standard form" marriage. *See* Margaret F. Brinig & Steven L. Nock, *What Does Covenant Mean for Relationships?*, 18 Notre Dame J. L. Ethics & Pub. Pol'y 137, 159–60 (2004) (discussing unpublished study by Steven L. Nock, Laura Sanchez, Julia C. Wilson & James D. Wright, *Intimate Equity: The Early Years of Covenant and Standard Marriages*). After controlling for some of the variables that might steer some couples toward covenant marriage (such as political ideology, religious background, education, and income), the study found that couples who opted for covenant marriage reported more marital satisfaction and stability and experienced faster income growth after two years of marriage than their counterparts who opted for standard marriages. *See id.* at 158–60. If the study is correct that the covenant marriage form helps to produce stronger and more satisfying marital bonds than standard marriage, should state laws aggressively encourage (or even require) couples to choose covenant marriage?

Professors John Witte and Joel Nichols suggest another benefit of covenant marriage. Apart from discouraging married couples from divorcing, it may screen out poorly matched couples from marrying in the first instance, both by requiring pre-marital counseling and by forcing couples to discuss their expectations. "Having [a] choice [of marriage form] encourages inaptly matched couples to discover their incompatibility before marriage, rather than after it," they contend. "If one engaged party wants a contract marriage and the other a covenant marriage, the disparity in prospective commitment should, for many couples, be too plain to ignore." John Witte, Jr. & Joel A. Nichols, *More Than a Mere Contract: Marriage as Contract and Covenant in Law and Theology*, 5 U. St. Thomas L.J. 595, 598 (2008).

A state senator has asked for your advice about whether to support any of three divorce-reform bills pending before the state legislature:

(1) The first would allow "summary divorce" to any couple without children who agreed on all financial and property issues relating to their dissolution. Such couples would be automatically granted a divorce upon the filing of a joint petition and a written agreement setting out the agreed terms of their property distribution and any support obligations.

(2) The second would continue to allow couples without children to obtain a no-fault divorce upon satisfaction of a six-month separation period, but would permit divorce between couples with minor, dependent children only if a family court determined that divorce would be in the children's "best interests." The bill would also provide for the appointment of independent counsel to represent the children in the proceeding.

(3) The third would adopt a version of "covenant marriage," asking marrying couples to choose between a standard-form marriage (with the usual no-fault grounds for divorce) and a covenant marriage, in which divorce would be possible only upon proof of traditional fault grounds or the satisfaction of a five-year separation period.

In addition to providing your views on these proposals, the senator has invited you to suggest any reform ideas of your own.

SECTION 6: ANNULMENT

With a spate of recent annulments involving celebrities such as Britney Spears and Renée Zellweger, readers of supermarket tabloids might understandably have the impression that annulments are simply divorces for quickly regretted marriages. In fact, a decree of annulment is something quite different (or at least is supposed to be): a declaration recognizing that the marriage attempted by the parties never came into existence at all because of a fatal impediment at the time of formation. This rationale allowed the English ecclesiastical courts, though allowing no divorce, to permit exit from some failed marriages with the possibility of "remarriage." This distinctive nature of annulment was carried over into civil law in the United States, where it remains available in cases of marriages deemed to have been void or voidable from the start. However, as statutes and case law have intervened to provide for property and support rights in cases of annulment, annulment is coming increasingly to resemble divorce for most practical purposes.

A. GROUNDS FOR ANNULMENT

To obtain an annulment, a petitioner must show that the marriage suffers from a serious defect dating back to its inception rendering it "void" or "voidable." As discussed in Chapter 3, void marriages are those that violate core marriage prohibitions, defined in most states to include bigamous, incestuous and same-sex marriages. *See, e.g.*, Alaska Stat. §§ 25.05.013, 25.05.021 (2006); D.C. Code Ann. § 46–401 (2006); Minn. Stat. Ann. § 517.03 (West Supp. 2008). Voidable marriages offend somewhat less stringent public policies, typically including the prohibitions involving persons who marry too young, without the proper mental or physical capacity, or under the inducement of fraud. *See* Alaska Stat. § 25.05.031 (2006); D.C. Code Ann. § 46–403 (2006).

B. EFFECTS OF ANNULMENT

Given the theory upon which annulment is premised—that a legal impediment rendered the marriage defective from the very beginning—an annulment clears the way for the parties to marry other persons, but traditionally could also result in very harsh consequences. If the marriage was deemed never to have existed, early law saw no basis for affording either party the economic or social protections that come with marriage. Thus, even a destitute and defrauded wife would have no claim for alimony, *see, e.g.*, *Knott v. Knott*, 51 A. 15 (N.J. Ch. 1902), and a child born during the putative marriage was retroactively deemed "illegitimate," *see, e.g.*, *Eisenberg v. Eisenberg*, 160 A. 228, 230 (Pa. Super. Ct. 1932).

The obvious injustice of this legal regime generated strong pressure for change. Many states adopted statutes providing that children born during a later-annulled marriage retain their status as "legitimate." And some courts early on resorted to equitable devices, such as estoppel or constructive trust, to justify some economic provision in annulment for unwitting participants in a void marriage. *See, e.g.*, *Speiss v. Speiss*, 183 N.W. 822, 824 (Minn. 1921). Even today, some states having no other legal framework for relief rely on the Putative Spouse Doctrine (discussed in Chapter 3) to mitigate the economic hardships that can attend annulment. *See Williams v. Williams*, 97 P.3d 1124 (Nev. 2004). Over the years, however, many states have regularized relief by enacting statutes that expressly authorize courts to provide alimony or property distribution in cases of annulment. Minnesota's statute, for instance, borrowing language taken from section 208(e) of the UMDA, 9A U.L.A. 186–87 (1998), provides simply that the statutory "provisions * * * relating to property rights of the spouses, maintenance, support and custody of children on dissolution of marriage are applicable to proceedings for annulment." Minn. Stat. § 518.03 (2006). As the following decision shows, some courts have arrived at the same result even when the governing statutes are much less explicit.

SPLAWN v. SPLAWN

Supreme Court of South Carolina, 1993.
429 S.E.2d 805.

CHANDLER, JUSTICE:

The sole issue in this domestic matter is whether Family Court has subject-matter jurisdiction to equitably distribute property of a bigamous marriage.

We hold that it does and, accordingly, affirm.

FACTS

The parties, Nathaniel and Louvenia Splawn (Husband and Wife), were "married" in April, 1961. Unbeknownst to either, Husband had not been divorced from a first marriage which occurred in 1955.[1]

Husband and Wife continued the marriage until their separation in 1990, at which time Wife instituted divorce proceedings on the ground of physical cruelty. The divorce was denied for failure of proof; Family Court, however, ordered that the property of the parties be equitably distributed, 60% to Wife and 40% to Husband.

Husband subsequently instituted this action for divorce on the ground of one year's continuous separation; his Complaint sought enforcement of the previous equitable distribution Order. In her Answer, Wife alleged recent discovery of Husband's prior, undissolved marriage. She contended (a) that their marriage was void, (b) that Husband was not entitled to a divorce, and (c) that since the marriage was void, Family Court was without jurisdiction to equitably distribute the property.

Family Court found that the parties' marriage was "not legal" but, nevertheless, ordered Wife to comply with the Order of Equitable Distribution. Wife appeals.

DISCUSSION

This case is controlled by our opinion in *White v. White*, 323 S.E.2d 521 (S.C. 1984). In *White*, the Husband was granted an annulment based upon his discovery that, at the time of his marriage to Wife, she was married to another man. Husband contended that "once the decision to annul is reached, Family Court jurisdiction ends absolutely." We rejected this contention and held that S.C. Code Ann. § 20–7–420(6) (1985) vests Family Court with jurisdiction to consider and rule upon *all* matters in annulment actions.

There is no legal distinction between a marriage which is annulled and one terminated by reason of bigamy. Legally, they are both void *ab initio,* "from the inception."

Wife contends that the public policy of this State will be violated by rewarding one who may *willfully* commit bigamy with the protections and

---

1. Husband testified that he had retained an attorney to obtain a divorce. For reasons unknown, a decree of divorce was never finalized.

benefits of the equitable distribution statute. We disagree. The statute accords Family Courts discretion to consider misconduct, fault, and "such other relevant factors" as it deems appropriate. Accordingly, where a spouse knowingly commits bigamy, the Family Court shall consider such bad conduct in determining the equitable distribution.

AFFIRMED.

NOTES AND QUESTIONS

1. *The convergence of annulment and divorce.* The South Carolina statute upon which the court relied, S.C. Code Ann. § 20–7–420 (1985 & West Supp. 2007), did not specifically authorize courts to divide property and award alimony in cases of annulment. Rather, it provided that the family court shall have exclusive jurisdiction over all family law matters (including annulment) and, in a later subsection, also over all questions relating to family support or property rights. *Id.* § 20–7–420(6) & (30). The court's willingness to construe the statute to authorize the recognition of support and property rights within void marriages reflects the convergence of the laws of annulment and divorce in recent years. If the legal consequences of marriage in terms of alimony and property attach to void marriages, are these marriages "void" in any real sense?

2. *Revival of alimony following annulment.* One possible continuing distinction between annulment and divorce concerns the legal consequences for parties outside the putative marriage. In some states, the ex-spouse's alimony obligation, previously terminated because of the recipient's remarriage, may be "revived" if the recipient's remarriage is later annulled. Revival is available even in some states, like South Carolina, that would permit the recipient to seek alimony from the second "spouse" incident to the annulment. In some jurisdictions, alimony revival depends on whether the subsequent marriage is classified as "void" or "voidable." If void, the obligor's duty is revived on the theory that the second marriage never came into existence; if the later marriage is merely voidable, the duty is not revived on the theory that the marriage was legally valid until annulled. *See, e.g., Watts v. Watts,* 547 N.W.2d 466 (Neb. 1996). In some other states, the matter is simply decided case-by-case according to general considerations of equity. *See, e.g., Joye v. Yon,* 586 S.E.2d 131 (S.C. 2003) (holding that courts should look to general equitable considerations in deciding whether an earlier alimony obligation should be revived). The UMDA similarly takes the position that in deciding whether to give full retroactive effect to an annulment decree, courts should be permitted to consider the interests of third parties and all other "relevant circumstances." *See* UMDA § 208(e), 9A U.L.A. 186–87 (1998). If retroactive effect is withheld, there may be no meaningful legal difference between an annulment and a divorce.

3. *Religious versus civil annulments.* Annulment carries religious significance for adherents of certain faiths. Roman Catholics, for example, must annul a marriage before they marry again in the Church. Annulments for these purposes are granted under religious law by religious authorities. Although the civil law of annulment has roots in ecclesiastical law, it is now a purely secular matter. Canonical annulments have no legal effect on the validity of a civil marriage, and religious authorities of course retain autono-

my to decide for themselves whether to give effect to civil judgments concerning annulment or divorce.

SECTION 7: LEGAL SEPARATION

The English ecclesiastical courts did not allow absolute divorce, but they did permit spouses to effect a formal legal separation through divorce *a mensa et thoro*, or divorce from bed and board. In U.S. law, this remedy, sometimes called "limited divorce," was carried over and offered as an alternative to divorce. In some states today, divorce from bed and board has been supplanted by, or exists alongside, the action for "separate maintenance." Both actions are essentially similar in that they seek to formalize marital property and support rights where a married couple intends to remain married while living separate and apart. There are, however, some significant distinctions between them.

The following Maryland statutes exemplify the distinctions between the grounds and requirements for an absolute divorce and legal separation:

Section 7–103 of the Maryland Code

Absolute divorce

(a) Grounds for absolute divorce.—The court may decree an absolute divorce on the following grounds:

(1) adultery;

(2) desertion, if:

    (i) the desertion has continued for 12 months without interruption before the filing of the application for divorce;

    (ii) the desertion is deliberate and final; and

    (iii) there is no reasonable expectation of reconciliation;

(3) voluntary separation, if:

    (i) the parties voluntarily have lived separate and apart without cohabitation for 12 months without interruption before the filing of the application for divorce; and

    (ii) there is no reasonable expectation of reconciliation;

(4) conviction of a felony or misdemeanor * * *;

(5) 2–year separation, when the parties have lived separate and apart without cohabitation for 2 years without interruption before the filing of the application for divorce;

(6) insanity * * *;

(7) cruelty of treatment toward the complaining party or a minor child of the complaining party, if there is no reasonable expectation of reconciliation; or

(8) excessively vicious conduct toward the complaining party or a minor child of the complaining party, if there is no reasonable expectation of reconciliation.

* * *

Md. Code Ann., Fam. Law § 7–103(a) (2006).

Section 7–102 of the Maryland Code

Limited divorce

(a) Grounds for limited divorce.—The court may decree a limited divorce on the following grounds:

(1) cruelty of treatment of the complaining party or of a minor child of the complaining party;

(2) excessively vicious conduct to the complaining party or to a minor child of the complaining party;

(3) desertion; or

(4) voluntary separation, if:

(i) the parties are living separate and apart without cohabitation; and

(ii) there is no reasonable expectation of reconciliation.

(e) Decree of limited divorce on prayer for absolute divorce.—If an absolute divorce is prayed and the evidence is sufficient to entitle the parties to a limited divorce, but not to an absolute divorce, the court may decree a limited divorce.

Id. § 7–102(a), (e).

* * *

A divorce from bed and board generally requires proof of a ground that would justify absolute divorce. In some states, the grounds are somewhat narrower than for absolute divorce. *See, e.g.*, N.C. Gen. Stat. § 50–7 (2007) (listing only fault grounds); Va. Code Ann. § 20–95 (2008) (requiring proof of "cruelty, reasonable apprehension of bodily hurt, willful desertion or abandonment"). In other states, the grounds are somewhat broader. *See, e.g.*, R.I. Gen. Laws § 15–5–9 (2003) (stating that divorce from bed and board "may be granted for any of the causes for which by law a divorce from the bond of marriage may be decreed, *and for other causes which may seem to require a divorce from bed and board*") (emphasis added). Once an adequate ground is shown, the court may then enter a decree dividing the couple's property and ordering payment of support while the couple lives apart.

An order of separate maintenance, by contrast, is available in some states without proof of a traditional divorce ground, simply on a showing that the parties intend to live separate and apart. While a separate maintenance decree can fix the parties' support obligations and specify which party shall occupy the marital home or hold other marital property, the decree typically does not—and, in some states, cannot—actually divide legal ownership of marital property. *See Grider v. Grider*, 968 S.W.2d 653, 655 (Ark. Ct. App. 1998). Accordingly, marital property rights may continue to accrue after the entry of an order of separate maintenance, whereas these rights ordinarily do not continue in cases of divorce from bed and board. *See In re Estate of Carlisle*, 653 N.W.2d 368 (Iowa 2002) (wife qualified as a "surviving spouse" entitled to an elective share of her husband's estate, notwithstanding prior entry of decree of separate maintenance).

In recent years, statutes in some states have simplified matters by eliminating the need to draw such distinctions. These statutes authorize courts to enter a decree of "legal separation" for separating spouses on terms basically identical to those possible for no-fault divorce. *See, e.g.*, Ala. Code § 30–2–40 (Michie 1998); Alaska Stat. § 25.24.410 (2006); Ariz. Rev. Stat. § 25–313 (West 2007). Even here, however, state laws continue to vary on whether a divorce ground or mutual consent of the spouses is required.

Why might spouses, who otherwise have grounds for divorce, desire a legal separation instead? There are several possible reasons. Legal separation may be the best option for those who still hope for reconciliation, who have religious or other objections to divorce, or who wish to retain the legal or other benefits of marriage without actually sharing life together as a married couple. In *D.L.J. v. B.R.J.*, 887 So.2d 242 (Ala. Ct. Civ. App. 2003), for example, a wife who had been diagnosed with brain cancer substituted a petition for legal separation for her earlier request for divorce in order to maintain health insurance through her husband.

CHAPTER 9

DIVISION OF MARITAL PROPERTY
AT DISSOLUTION

■ ■ ■

As you learned in Chapter 5 regarding nonmarital cohabitation, marriage has traditionally provided a bright line for determining who is entitled to share property with a significant other if and when it comes time to break up. This Chapter discusses the disposition of marital property when a marriage dissolves. Chapter 10 will cover alimony.

The division of marital property and alimony are frequently considered together by textbooks as well as courts, but they have different rationales and raise distinctive problems. Division of marital property is premised on the principle that marriage is a partnership that must be unwound fully and fairly when it terminates. Because marriage is a collaboration, contemporary law assumes that both parties have earned their respective shares of the marital assets, a concept that will be discussed more fully below. In contrast, continuing maintenance payments respond to the need of a former spouse "who is unable to support him or herself through appropriate employment * * *." *Schenk v. Schenk*, 880 A.2d 633, 640 n.7 (Pa. Super. Ct. 2005).

News coverage of celebrity divorces suggests that divorce battles always rage over how to split up the riches. In reality, however, most families facing divorce have few, if any, valuable assets. The median net worth of all married couples in the United States in 2002 (the most recent data available) was $101,975—a figure that includes home equity; when home equity is excluded the median net worth of married households is reduced to $24,950. Alfred O. Gottschalk, U.S. Census Bureau, Publ'n No. P70–115, U.S. Census Current Population Reports, *Net Worth and Asset Ownership of Households: 2002*, at 15 (2008), *available at* www.census. gov/prod/2008pubs/p70–115.pdf. In Chapter 8, you learned that divorce is more likely when people marry at a younger age. The median net worth of households headed by someone under the age of 35 is only $2,446, exclusive of home equity. *Id.* at 11. For persons between 35 and 44, median net worth hovers at $9,512. *Id.* Even in the highest quintile of U.S. households, the median net worth is roughly $188,000, $10,000 less than for the same quintile in 2000. *Id.* at 7; *see also* Shawna Orzechowski & Peter Sepielli, U.S. Census Bureau, Publ'n No. P70–88, U.S. Census

Current Population Reports, *Net Worth and Asset Ownership of House-holds: 1998 and 2000, at* 13, 15 (2003), *available at* www.census.gov/prod/2003pubs/p70–88.pdf. Families with a typical net worth will not normally be inclined to litigate the division of assets, nor can they easily afford to do so. The most recent census data on net worth were collected in 2002 and therefore do not reflect the downward trend in the price of real estate. Beginning in 2006 and continuing through at least 2008, real estate values declined significantly. As of 2008 (when this volume went to press) it is estimated that about 10 million families (about one in five of all home-owners with mortgages and nearly half of the 22 million Americans who bought homes between 2005 and 2007) have mortgages that exceed the current value of their homes. Martin Feldstein, *A Home Price Firewall*, Wash. Post, June 19, 2008, at A–19; Paul Krugman, *Home Not–So–Sweet Home,* N.Y. Times, June 23, 2008, at A–21. Instead of being an asset, the home may be a financial liability.

Although most people do not have substantial assets to divide upon divorce, it is essential for lawyers to understand the default rules that govern marriage and property. Knowing the rules may help many individuals avoid unpleasant surprises. In the following sections, you will learn about the types of property regimes that various states impose during marriage and at dissolution, what counts as property, how to decide whether property belongs to the marriage or to the individual spouse, and what principles govern the division of the property that is subject to distribution at divorce.

SECTION 1: PROPERTY REGIMES DURING MARRIAGE

State residency determines the regime that governs marital property during the marriage and property disposition at divorce. Most states apply different rules to property ownership during marriage and at dissolution.

The first part of this Section introduces the two basic property regimes that apply during marriage: title theory and community property. The next Section will describe the regimes that govern division of property at divorce. Some community property regimes continue to apply community property principles at divorce. However, all states that use a title regime during marriage currently require that marital property be subjected to "equitable distribution" in the event that the marriage dissolves.

A. TITLE THEORY

The title theory, or "separate property," system emerged from British and American common law. Under this approach, the spouse who holds title to each asset retains ownership of it. As discussed in Chapter 4, under the common law theory of coverture, husbands owned all property acquired during marriage. Even after the mid-nineteenth century—when many states enacted married women's property statutes, allowing married women to retain separate property during the marriage and at divorce—courts in title states "continued to adhere to the common law rules based on title when confronted with the task of dividing marital property upon divorce. The allocation of marital property to the party who held title thereto tended to reward the spouse directly responsible for its acquisition, while overlooking the contribution of the homemaking spouse." *White v. White*, 324 S.E.2d 829, 831 (N.C. 1985).

The common law title system for divorce "at times resulted in unjust distributions, especially [in] cases of a traditional family where most property was titled in the husband * * *." *Ferguson v. Ferguson*, 639 So.2d 921, 926 (Miss. 1994). Although most states continue to apply the title system during the course of a marriage, in 1994 Mississippi became the last state to abandon the title system for dividing marital assets when a marriage dissolves. *Id.* at 926–27. All remaining title theory states limit its application to the life of the marriage. In these separate property states, the person who holds the title to property has no legal obligation to consult with his or her spouse regarding the use or disposition of the property during the marriage.

As you may recall from your Property course, three forms of title may be used to record shared ownership of real property: joint tenancy, tenancy by the entirety, and tenancy in common. In joint tenancy, each tenant is the owner of the whole estate and of an undivided part of the estate. After the death of one joint tenant, the surviving tenant or tenants continue as owners of the whole estate. As applied to spouses, the surviving spouse becomes the owner of the whole without any need for probate or estate taxes. The form of tenancy by the entirety is reserved for married couples, as it requires "unity of person." As with joint tenancy, the surviving tenant receives ownership of the entire estate. The major difference between the joint tenancy and tenancy by the entirety is that a tenancy in the entirety is protected from partition except by mutual consent or operation of law. A third form of joint ownership is tenancy in common, in which each tenant has an equal right to possession, but no right of survivorship. This form of ownership is generally not recommended for married couples because a spouse could bequeath his or her share to a third party. The forms of title summarized here only apply if the spouses share ownership of real property. Remember that under the title system, the primary wage earner often held title in his own name. As you will see later in this Chapter the form of title may have continuing relevance at divorce.

B. COMMUNITY PROPERTY

Community property systems developed from Spanish and French law, initially imported from Mexico to California before it became a U.S. territory, and to Louisiana under the influence of French-based civil law. *See Spreckels v. Spreckels*, 48 P. 228, 230 (Cal. 1897); *Bender v. Pfaff*, 282

U.S. 127 (1930). Eight states are community property states today.[1] Under the community property regime, each spouse has a present, vested one-half interest in all property acquired during the marriage. At divorce, three community property states require division of all community property into equal shares.[2]

During the marriage, community property is distinguished from "separate property." Separate property usually includes property acquired by either spouse before the marriage, or during the marriage by gift, bequest or devise. Community property regimes sometimes refer to the marriage itself as a community or "partnership." *Bender*, 282 U.S. at 131. Therefore, during the marriage, neither spouse may dispose of community property without the consent of his or her spouse. This was not always the case. Consistent with theories of coverture discussed in Chapter 4, husbands in California "had exclusive management and control of the spouses' community property prior to 1975" when the legislature amended the code "to give the wife joint management and control of community property * * *." *In Re Marriage of Ashodian*, 157 Cal.Rptr. 555, 558 (Cal. Ct. App. 1979).

SECTION 2: DIVISION OF MARITAL PROPERTY

At one time, it mattered a great deal whether or not a couple lived in a community property state. Before reforms designed to accomplish equitable distribution of marital property became effective in the last decades of the twentieth century, the primary wage earner (almost always the husband) normally held title to most or all of the family's property, and at divorce the title holder was considered the sole owner of the property titled in his name. This meant that any property awarded at divorce to the non-title-holding spouse was seen as a distribution from her husband's property not as a share of property she already owned in partnership with her husband. Because the wife did not have a "right" to a share of the property as a co-owner she often received very little at divorce. As you will see later in this Chapter, contributions to the family's well-being that did not generate monetary compensation were ignored under the common law title system.

Under contemporary law, the differences between property regimes are more significant during a marriage than at dissolution. Today, the two regimes that govern property distribution at divorce—equitable distribution and community property—lead to virtually indistinguishable results.

---

1. Arizona, California, Idaho, Louisiana, Nevada, New Mexico, Texas and Washington. Wisconsin is a community property state during marriage and a "kitchen sink" regime at divorce. (The term is explained on page 474. *See Gerczak v. Estate of Gerczak*, 702 N.W.2d 72 (Wis. Ct. App. 2005); *Wierman v. Wierman*, 387 N.W.2d 744 (Wis. 1986).

2. California, Louisiana and New Mexico. ALI, Principles of the Law of Family Dissolution: Analysis and Recommendations 22 n.31 (2002). Five community property states require an equitable rather than an equal division of property at divorce. J. Thomas Oldham, Divorce, Separation and the Distribution of Property § 3.03 (2005).

Moreover, most community property states require equitable rather than equal division of assets at divorce.

"Equitable distribution reflects the idea that marriage is a partnership enterprise to which both spouses make valuable contributions," entitling each spouse to a fair share of the property acquired during the marriage, regardless of how it is titled. *White*, 324 S.E.2d at 832. In this respect, equitable distribution jurisdictions resemble community property jurisdictions. Today, 42 states and the District of Columbia are equitable distribution jurisdictions at divorce, but apply title theory during the course of the marriage. In other words, spouses in those states may own property in their own names during a marriage, regardless of when or how they obtained it.

Although specific provisions and nuances may vary by jurisdiction, the overall approach at divorce is similar in each equitable distribution state. Most jurisdictions provide some guidance to trial courts through a list of relevant factors to be considered. The factors tend to illustrate "two basic but conflicting principles: Property should be allocated in proportion to the spousal contributions to its acquisition, and property should be allocated according to relative spousal need." ALI, Principles of the Law of Family Dissolution: Analysis and Recommendations § 4.09 cmt. a (2002). As in community property regimes, the division requires a court to determine whether each asset is marital or separate. Equitable distribution states generally characterize property acquired before marriage, or through gift or inheritance bestowed upon only one spouse, as separate.

A. PROPERTY REGIMES AT DIVORCE

During divorce, the process of dividing the property that the couple shares by virtue of being married requires three steps: (1) identifying and characterizing each asset as marital or separate; (2) valuing each asset that is marital; and (3) distributing all divisible assets equitably or equally, or, in the alternative, ordering a monetary award from one spouse to another to adjust their financial positions in accordance with the court's decision. In most jurisdictions, whether they apply common law or community property rules, courts may divide only marital property at divorce. A minority of states authorize courts to divide all property owned by the couple or by either member, regardless of when or how it was acquired. In those jurisdictions, courts do not need to characterize the property, they only need to identify all of the property available for distribution.

Each of the four approaches to marital and separate property presented below shares a common principle: the labor and contributions of both spouses during marriage create a body of mutual assets. The approaches differ in their views of what constitutes a contribution, what constitutes compensation for labor, and whether and to what extent assets acquired without the contribution of either spouse are divisible.

1. A SAMPLE EQUITABLE DISTRIBUTION REGIME

Title 23, Section 3501 of the Pennsylvania Consolidated Statutes

(a) General rule—As used in this chapter, "marital property" means all property acquired by either party during the marriage and the increase in value of any nonmarital property acquired pursuant to paragraphs (1) and (3) * * *. However, marital property does not include:

(1) Property acquired prior to marriage or property acquired in exchange for property acquired prior to the marriage.

(2) Property excluded by valid agreement of the parties entered into before, during or after the marriage,

(3) Property acquired by gift, except between spouses, bequest, devise or descent or property acquired in exchange for such property.

(4) Property acquired after final separation until the date of divorce, except for property acquired in exchange for marital assets.

(5) Property which a party has sold, granted, conveyed or otherwise disposed of in good faith and for value prior to the date of final separation.

(6) Veterans' benefits exempt from attachment, levy or seizure pursuant to the act of September 2, 1958 (Public Law 85–857, 72 Stat. 1229), as amended, except for those benefits received by a veteran where the veteran has waived a portion of his military retirement pay in order to receive veterans' compensation.

(7) Property to the extent to which the property has been mortgaged or otherwise encumbered in good faith for value prior to the date of final separation.

(8) Any payment received as a result of an award or settlement for any cause of action or claim which accrued prior to the marriage or after the date of final separation regardless of when the payment was received.

* * *

(b) Presumption—All real or personal property acquired by either party during the marriage is presumed to be marital property regardless of whether title is held individually or by the parties in some form of co-ownership such as joint tenancy, tenancy in common or tenancy by the entirety. The presumption of marital property is overcome by a showing that the property was acquired by a method listed in subsection (a).

23 Pa. Cons. Stat. Ann. § 3501 (West 2001 & 2008 Supp.).

2. A SAMPLE COMMUNITY PROPERTY REGIME

Article 1, Section 21 of the California Constitution

Property owned before marriage or acquired during marriage by gift, will, or inheritance is separate property.

Cal. Const. Art. 1, § 21.

Section 760 of the California Family Code

Except as otherwise provided by statute, all property, real or personal, wherever situated, acquired by a married person during the marriage while domiciled in this state is community property.

Cal. Fam. Code § 760 (West 2004).

Section 770 of the California Family Code

§ 770. (a) Separate property of a married person includes all of the following:

(1) All property owned by the person before marriage.

(2) All property acquired by the person after marriage by gift, bequest, devise, or descent.

(3) The rents, issues, and profits of the property described in this section.

(b) A married person may, without the consent of the person's spouse, convey the person's separate property.

Id. § 770.

3. HOTCHPOT, OR "KITCHEN SINK," JURISDICTIONS

Fourteen states follow some variation of the model set forth in the Uniform Marriage and Divorce Act, which permits a court to consider and "divide all property owned by either or both spouses, regardless of how or when it was acquired." J. Thomas Oldham, Divorce, Separation and the Distribution of Property § 3.03[2] (2005).[3] This approach is sometimes called the "all-property" method. The terms "hotchpot" and "kitchen sink" capture the idea—all assets belonging to either spouse separately or to both spouses jointly are thrown into the pot and are up for grabs. The hotchpot approach eliminates legal disputes over the characterization of assets as marital or separate (what goes in the pot), but may exacerbate disputes over how to distribute the assets equitably. Proponents of the hotchpot approach argue that it makes equity easier to achieve after a long marriage in which the spouses have very different resources at their disposal. ALI, Principles of the Law of Family Dissolution: Analysis and Recommendations § 4.03 cmt. a (2002). The Connecticut statute provides a simple example.

Section 46b–81 of the Connecticut General Statutes

Assignment of property and transfer of title.

---

3. The states include Connecticut, Hawaii, Indiana, Kansas, Massachusetts, Michigan, Mississippi, Montana, New Hampshire, North Dakota, Oregon, South Dakota, Vermont and Wyoming. Oldham, § 3.03.

(a) At the time of entering a decree * * * dissolving a marriage * * *, the * * * court may assign to either the husband or wife all or any part of the estate of the other. * * *

Conn. Gen. Stat. § 46b–81 (West 2004).

4. PROPOSAL FOR REFORM: THE ALI PRINCIPLES

AMERICAN LAW INSTITUTE

Principles of the Law of Family Dissolution:
Analysis and Recommendations (2002).

§ 4.03　Definition of Marital and Separate Property

(1) Property acquired during marriage is marital property, except as otherwise expressly provided * * *.

(2) Inheritances, including bequests and devises, and gifts from third parties, are the separate property of the acquiring spouse even if acquired during marriage.

(3) Property received in exchange for separate property is separate property even if acquired during the marriage.

* * *

§ 4.06　Property Acquired in Exchange for Marital or Separate Property

* * *

(3) Property acquired on credit before marriage is presumed to be the separate property of the acquiring spouse, except that the acquired property is marital property to the extent the principal balance of the loan is reduced with payments made from marital property.

* * *

§ 4.08　Deferred or Contingent Earnings and Wage Substitutes

(1) Property earned by labor performed during marriage is marital property whether received before, during, or after the marriage. * * *

* * *

Notes and Questions

1. *Compare the approaches.* In what respects does the ALI proposal resemble each of the other regimes? What does it add that is completely new? As you read the cases presented in this Chapter, consider which regime governs each case, and whether the results would have been different if the parties had appeared in a jurisdiction that used another approach to dividing marital property.

2. *"Personal" property.* Property we all think of as "personal"—such as clothing and art—is marital property if purchased with marital funds, and therefore is subject to division. Personal property should not be confused with

"separate" property, which belongs solely to one spouse. Gifts received from a spouse may or may not be considered separate property, depending on such factors as the source of the funds used to acquire the gift and the donor's intent. Is a valuable diamond cocktail ring a husband purchased with marital funds for the couple's anniversary the wife's "separate" property for purposes of valuing the couple's total marital assets? Or is the ring merely "personal," but marital and thus subject to division? Would it matter whether the husband told his wife at the time he gave her the ring, "I know it is a big indulgence, but we can always sell it if we hit hard times," or, alternatively, "now, no matter what the future holds for us, you will always be provided for"?

B. MODELS AND UNDERSTANDINGS OF THE MARITAL RELATIONSHIP AS THEY RELATE TO DISTRIBUTION OF ASSETS

Societal expectations about the structure and meaning of marriage are reflected in the laws that govern distribution of property at divorce. This Chapter presents the default rules. Parties to a marriage are largely free to opt out of the state's rules by entering into private agreements before or during the marriage. (Private ordering through pre-nuptial and separation agreements is the subject of Chapter 14). In reading this Chapter, bear in mind that litigation reflects the parties' failure to reach an agreement they can present to the court for approval. As Chapter 14 explains more fully, negotiation of an antenuptial, postnuptial or separation agreement will be informed by the default rules that establish what the participant would likely be entitled to receive in the absence of an agreement.

Day-to-day decisions about the division of marital responsibilities may also come into play when courts assess the equities at the end of any marriage. These decisions, in turn, may reflect societal expectations incorporated into divorce law. The following selections reflect different scholarly approaches to the interaction of social norms, private choices and division of property.

BARBARA STARK

Marriage Proposals: From One–Size–Fits–All to Postmodern Marriage Law.
89 Cal. L. Rev. 1479, 1483–86 (2001).

* * *

There are innumerable marriages * * * and most of them go through different phases. The law ignores this, however, until and unless the marriage ends in divorce * * *. Then its characterization becomes critical. In order to divide property * * * the courts must decide what kind of marriage it was. Was it a breadwinner/breadmaker relationship, an economic partnership between two wage earners, an arrangement in which the parties' roles changed over time, or none of the above?

As marriages become increasingly diverse, this analysis becomes increasingly strained. Where is the certainty, the predictability, that law is supposed to assure? * * *

* * *

After the marriage, the parameters of the divorce settlement depend as much on the state in which the parties find themselves at the time and the judge before whom they appear as on their expectations before marriage or their experience during marriage. * * *

ELIZABETH S. SCOTT & ROBERT E. SCOTT
Marriage as Relational Contract.
84 Va. L. Rev. 1225, 1230–32, 1301 (1998).

* * * Under the no-fault regime, the law does not enforce the explicit promises of the marriage partners (the wedding vows); nor does it enforce promises about conduct during the marriage. On the other hand, when the relationship terminates, the law purports to enforce the implicit understandings of the couple regarding investment in the joint venture, understandings that often have never been expressly articulated.

Relational contract theory largely resolves this puzzle. The marriage vows express the couple's emotional commitment and use hortatory language to emphasize the seriousness of the undertaking. * * * But emotional commitments are difficult to translate into quantifiable standards of performance * * *. * * * Thus, legal enforcement is limited to policing massive defections from the cooperative norm and to resolving economic and parental claims upon termination of the marriage (when the extralegal incentives to cooperate are greatly diminished). * * *

* * *

* * * [The problem] is the failure of contemporary legal rules governing divorce to protect marital investment adequately and to discourage opportunistic defection. * * *

* * *

* * * [M]ost modern legal doctrines regulating divorce are best understood and analyzed as majoritarian default rules. * * *

* * * A central normative implication of our analysis is that important default rules governing divorce fail adequately to protect marital investments. * * *

CAROLYN J. FRANTZ & HANOCH DAGAN
Properties of Marriage.
104 Colum. L. Rev. 75, 76–77, 103–06 (2004).

* * * The law governing the division of property upon divorce operates on ongoing marriages because possibilities upon divorce give spouses reasons to act in ways better or worse for their individual marriages. * * *

[G]overnance rules operate during marriage * * * to shape spouses' expectations and behavior with respect to marital property. * * *

* * *

* * * [We argue] that certain conceptions of community, autonomy, and equality can * * * complement each other under one vision of marriage: marriage as an egalitarian liberal community. * * *

* * *

* * * [W]e propose a justification for the equal division rule based on the ideal of marriage as an egalitarian liberal community. First, equal division * * * stands against investigation into the interior functioning of the marital community to determine individual desert, and best demonstrates that no party is any more entitled to marital resources than any other. Equal division also decreases parties' incentives to view their marriages individualistically. A fifty percent rule ensures there is no advantage to keeping an accounting of individual investments in and returns from the marital relationship. The party who shows up in divorce court with a stack of receipts tracing back to the beginning of the marriage has clearly not signed on to a communal understanding of the institution. * * * Moreover, equal division makes it easier for spouses to engage in sharing behavior—investing in relationship-specific goods, specializing, and making individual sacrifices for the overall good of the community. * * *

* * *

Contribution-based rules should * * * be rejected because they threaten to reinforce problematic gender roles. Due to (unjustified) differences in market earning power, in most marriages it is efficient for the woman to work less in the market and more inside the home. * * * Equal division * * * spreads the risks of spouses' own sharing choices without aiming to encourage any particular choice. * * *

* * * Division of existing marital assets sends a powerful message of ownership—that the award is not a social welfare handout, but rather an entitlement. Unlike alimony, which carries the stigma of dependency and weakness, equal division promotes spouses' sense of personal dignity by signaling equal ownership of all marital property.

C. CHARACTERIZING ASSETS AS MARITAL OR SEPARATE

As the statutes presented earlier in this Chapter make clear, in both community property and common law property jurisdictions, it is crucial to determine whether each asset is marital or separate property. Characterization is a threshold issue because outside of kitchen sink jurisdictions the courts must award all separate property to the individual to whom it belongs. The court must characterize each asset independently as separate or marital because the balance of factors may tilt differently depending on the history of the particular asset. The court then divides marital assets between the parties, either equitably or equally, depending on the jurisdiction. In equitable distribution jurisdictions, knowing the value of the separate property assigned to each spouse may affect the court's assessment of how to divide the marital assets in a fair manner. The question of what constitutes an equitable result will be discussed in greater detail later in this Chapter.

An asset's initial character as either separate or marital may change over the course of a marriage. At one extreme, one spouse may expressly make a gift of her own property to the marital union. Assets may also change character by more subtle means, as described more fully below. A spouse who seeks to show that property that appears to be separate should be treated as marital bears the burden to show that its characterization has shifted so that the separate property comes within the applicable statute's definition of marital property. *Keyt* v. *Keyt* , 244 S.W.3d 321, 328 (Tenn. 2007). The Supreme Court of Tennessee has described how a spouse's separate property may become marital property by either "commingling" or "transmutation":

> [s]eparate property becomes marital property [by commingling] if inextricably mingled with marital property or with the separate property of the other spouse. If the separate property continues to be segregated or can be traced into its product, commingling does not occur * * * [Transmutation] occurs when separate property is treated in such a way as to give evidence of an intention that it become marital property * * * [T]hese doctrines create[] a rebuttable presumption of a gift to the marital estate.

Langschmidt v. *Langschmidt*, 81 S.W.3d 741, 747 (Tenn. 2002).

The following decision, from a common law, equitable distribution jurisdiction, demonstrates how the characterization of property can change, or be "transmuted," during a marriage. The following case also illustrates that though concepts may appear simple at first glance, they may turn out to have many complexities upon closer examination. Among the issues you will want to consider while reading the case are the potential for title to remain important at divorce, and the evidentiary issues that arise when a court tries to determine the intentions of spouses and their relatives after the fact. You will recall that the statutory regime governing division of property at dissolution is a default rule. In this case, the spouses executed a valid pre-nuptial agreement that listed their separate assets before they entered the marriage and that specified their intention not to create marital property. As you read the case, consider how the issues that appear to have been governed by the couple's agreement might have come out in the absence of the prenuptial agreement, and think about how the court treated the agreement.

NACK v. EDWARDS NACK

Virginia Court of Appeals, 2007.
2007 WL 2592902, unpublished opinion.

HUMPHREYS, J.

Steven Douglas Nack ("husband") appeals from a final divorce decree entered August 11, 2006. Husband argues that the trial court erred by classifying: (1) a Legg Mason investment portfolio; (2) a 1987 Mercedes–Benz; and (3) a 1993 Lexus, buffalo, and assorted farm equipment as marital property.[1] * * * For the following reasons, we reverse the trial court regarding the classification of the Mercedes–Benz and the Lexus, and affirm the trial court regarding the investment portfolio, buffalo, and farm equipment. * * *

ANALYSIS

Husband contends that the trial court erred by failing to retrace the separate funds that husband contributed to the Legg Mason account, and by classifying the two automobiles, buffalo, and farm equipment as marital property.

* * *

A.   Legg Mason

Husband first argues that the trial court erred in failing to retrace the separate funds he contributed to the joint Legg Mason account. Because the Cornerstone account, which later became the Legg Mason account, and the National Life annuity were created around the same time, under nearly identical circumstances, husband reasons the trial court erred in classifying them differently. We disagree.

Code § 20–107.3(A)(2)(i) defines marital property as "all property titled in the names of both parties, whether as joint tenants, tenants by the entirety or otherwise, except as provided by [Code § 20–107.3(A)(3)]," which recognizes the concept of part marital and part separate, or "hybrid" property. *See Rahbaran v. Rahbaran*, 494 S.E.2d 135, 140 (1997). Code § 20–107.3(A)(3) "presupposes that separate property has not been segregated but, rather, combined with marital property." *Id.* at 141. When such assets are combined by the contribution of one to another,

> resulting in the loss of identity of the contributed property, the classification of the contributed property shall be transmuted to the category of property receiving the contribution. However, to the extent the contributed property is retraceable by a preponderance of the evidence and was not a gift, such contributed property shall retain its original classification.

---

1.   The farm equipment included a John Deere tractor, a Kawasaki mule farm utility vehicle, water jugs, a palpation cage, and a "buffalo squeeze chute."

"In order to trace the separate portion of hybrid property, a party must prove that the claimed separate portion is identifiably derived from a separate asset. Whether a transmuted asset can be traced back to a separate property interest is determined by the circumstances of each case[.]" *Asgari v. Asgari*, 533 S.E.2d 643, 648 (2000). However, "if a party 'chooses to commingle marital and non-marital funds to the point that direct tracing is impossible,' the claimed separate property loses its separate status." *Rahbaran*, 494 S.E.2d at 141 (quoting *Melrod v. Melrod*, 83 Md. App. 180, 574 A.2d 1, 5 (Md. App. 1990)). "Even if a party can prove that some part of an asset is separate, if the court cannot determine the separate amount, the 'unknown amount contributed from the separate source transmutes by commingling and becomes marital property.' " *Id.* at 141 (quoting Brett R. Turner, *Equitable Distribution of Property* 268 (1994)).

Here, husband deposited his separate assets from White City[a] and his Fidelity account into the parties' joint checking account, thereby commingling separate and marital assets.[3] The parties continuously deposited and withdrew unspecified sums of marital funds from the account. Husband provided no account balances, deposit slips, cancelled checks, or any other documentation that would have enabled the court to retrace his separate assets.[4] Thus, in late 1997 and early 1998, when husband and wife withdrew funds from their joint checking account to acquire their joint Cornerstone account, which later became the Legg Mason account, "the identity of husband's separate funds had been lost in countless unspecified transactions involving marital funds, resulting in the irreversible transmutation of separate into marital property."

The distinction between the Legg Mason portfolio and the National Life annuity is readily apparent. The Legg Mason accounts were jointly titled, yet the National Life annuity was titled only in husband's name. The trial court could thus retrace husband's White City funds, which husband deposited into the parties' joint checking account, but later reemerged as distinctly separate assets when husband used them to

---

a. "White City" refers to money the husband received from the sale of stock in White City Electric company which he owned before the marriage and sold during the marriage

3. The dissent notes that "[h]usband insists that the parties maintained separate finances and that the accounts at both First Virginia and Cornerstone were his accounts, set up as joint accounts purely for convenience." This assertion is of no moment, because wife testified to the contrary at trial, the trial court implicitly accepted wife's testimony over husband's, and our standard of review compels us to view the facts in the light most favorable to wife as the party who prevailed below. *Black v. Powers*, 628 S.E.2d 546, 549 (2006).

4. In reasoning that the Cornerstone account "included part marital, part separate and part hybrid property," the dissent notes two checks to husband from his parents totaling $10,464.73, deposited into the joint checking account on the same day as the first payment to Cornerstone, and submitted into evidence by wife. In citing these checks as evidence by which the trial court could have retraced a portion of husband's assets, the dissent ignores wife's testimony that these checks represented gifts "put into [their] joint account [and] used for anything." Thus, viewing the evidence most favorably to wife, these checks represent joint gifts made from husband's parents to both husband and wife as a couple, and therefore the checks from husband's parents to husband are not evidence from which the trial court could retrace husband's separate assets. Furthermore, wife testified that these checks were not deposited into the joint account specifically to fund the Cornerstone account.

purchase the separate annuity. Because the Legg Mason accounts were jointly titled, husband was unable to prove that his White City and Fidelity funds regained any separate identity in the Legg Mason accounts, and thus the trial court was unable to retrace these funds as husband's separate assets. The trial court, therefore, did not abuse its discretion by classifying the Legg Mason portfolio as marital property, and we affirm the trial court on this issue.

B. The 1987 Mercedes and the 1993 Lexus

Husband next argues that the trial court erred in classifying the 1987 Mercedes as marital property, because it was his separate property prior to the marriage, remained titled in his name, and was not a gift [to his wife or to the marital estate]. He also argues that the Lexus is his separate property pursuant to the prenuptial agreement. We agree with husband that both automobiles remain his separate property.

Property acquired by either party before the marriage is presumed to remain separate property. As stated above, however, [the] Code * * * provides:

> When marital property and separate property are commingled by contributing one category of property to another, resulting in the loss of identity of the contributed property, the classification of the contributed property shall be transmuted to the category of property receiving the contribution. However, to the extent the contributed property is retraceable by a preponderance of the evidence and was not a gift, such contributed property shall retain its original classification.

1. The Mercedes

In this case, the commissioner recommended the classification of the Mercedes as marital property. In her report, the commissioner noted that around 1999 or 2000, wife began to drive the 1987 Mercedes SL, a vehicle that had previously "sat in the garage for 10 or 12 years and 'rotted.' From that point on, [wife] was the primary driver of the Mercedes SL until the parties' separation. Joint funds were used to … pay for the upkeep and maintenance of the … Mercedes." The classification of the Mercedes as marital property solely on this basis was an abuse of discretion by the trial court, and we reverse that decision.

Here, wife made payments for upkeep and maintenance of the Mercedes, thereby contributing marital property to husband's separate property. Wife's payments therefore transmuted to separate property, the category of property receiving the contribution, and the burden then falls upon wife to retrace her payments. Under this statute, wife's payments for the upkeep of the Mercedes make the Mercedes hybrid property at best. However, the prenuptial agreement, * * * provides that the Mercedes, listed in the prenuptial agreement as husband's separate property acquired prior to the marriage, remain separate property in any event, regardless of wife's financial contributions towards the vehicle's upkeep. Thus, the Mercedes remains husband's separate property, and the trial court erred in classifying the Mercedes as marital property. Accordingly, we reverse the trial court's classification of the Mercedes.

2. The Lexus

Husband next argues that the Lexus is titled in his name and, thus, remains his separate property under the agreement.

"The owner of an automobile is the party who has legal title to it." *McDuffie v. Commonwealth*, 638 S.E.2d 139, 141 (2006); *see also* Code § 46.2–100. * * *

Husband had sole legal title to the Lexus. Husband is thus the vehicle's owner, and as a result, the Lexus is his separate property. Pursuant to the prenuptial agreement, wife forfeited any interest she may have had in the Lexus by virtue of her financial contributions towards the vehicle. The Lexus remains husband's separate property, and the trial court abused its discretion in classifying it as marital property. Thus, we reverse the judgment of the trial court in this regard as well.

C. The Buffalo and Farm Equipment

Husband's final contention on appeal is that the trial court erred in classifying the buffalo and assorted farm equipment as marital, because the prenuptial agreement prohibited the creation of marital property. We affirm the trial court's classification of the buffalo and farm equipment as marital property.

"Property acquired during the marriage is presumptively marital, unless shown to be separate property." *Robinson v. Robinson*, 621 S.E.2d 147, 152 (2005); Code § 20–107.3(A)(2)(iii). Husband concedes that the parties used their joint checking account to purchase all of these items during the marriage. However, as noted above, husband argues that the parties' joint First Virginia checking account was only for convenience and that the parties intended to keep their money separate. Thus, husband reasons that the joint checking account was his "de facto" separate account. Accordingly, husband concludes that the buffalo and farm equipment were all purchased from separate funds and, therefore, remain his separate property under the relinquishment of claims section of the prenuptial agreement. However, the only evidence husband presented that the First Virginia account was, in fact, intended to be his separate property was his own testimony. As stated above, wife disputed the testimony, and the chancellor implicitly rejected husband's testimony. In fact, wife testified that she deposited a portion of her paycheck into the First Virginia account, and offered into evidence several checks from husband's parents made to her as gifts of their estate that were deposited into the account.

Viewing the evidence in the light most favorable to wife, we reject husband's assertion that the First Virginia account was comprised solely of husband's separate property. Because husband and wife purchased the farm equipment and buffalo with marital property, and because husband did not meet his burden of retracing his separate funds from these purchases, we affirm the trial court's classification of this property as marital.

* * *

CONCLUSION

For the reasons stated therein, we affirm the trial court's classification of the Legg Mason account, buffalo, and farm equipment as marital property, and reverse the trial court's classification of the Mercedes and Lexus as marital property. * * * We remand the case for further proceedings consistent with this opinion.

Affirmed in part, reversed in part, and remanded.

* * *

HALEY, J., concurring, in part, and dissenting, in part.

I respectfully dissent only as to the majority's conclusion regarding the Legg Mason account.

The parties entered into a prenuptial agreement on September 4, 1992. Attached to that agreement was a schedule of their respective separate property. Husband's separate property included stock in White City Electric Company (White City Electric) and an account at Fidelity Investments (Fidelity). The majority concludes that husband failed to trace this separate property into Legg Mason. I disagree.

The Legg Mason account at issue was funded in February 1999, by transfer from husband and wife's joint investment account with Cornerstone Capital Management (Cornerstone). The source of funds in the Cornerstone account, therefore, is critical to our evaluation of this cause. In 1997, husband received a distribution in the amount of $273,146 for his ownership of White City Electric stock, listed as husband's separate property in the prenuptial agreement. Husband deposited the White City Electric distribution in a joint checking account at First Virginia Bank. In addition to his salary and other income, the First Virginia Bank also included money received from husband's Fidelity account (listed as his separate property in the prenuptial agreement) and money given by husband's parents to both parties as tax-free gifts from their estate.[8]

---

8. Both husband and his father argue that the gifts were intended to be for husband. Nevertheless, husband's parents wrote several checks to wife for the purpose of passing their estate tax-free to the parties. * * * [eds. note: Each individual is allowed to make an unlimited number of annual gifts without incurring tax consequences. People who anticipate that their estates will be subject to taxation after they die often use this provision of the Internal Revenue Code to transfer assets to their children while they are alive. The Code, however, limits the amount of each annual tax-free gift to a particular individual. The wealthy can, however, double the amount of the annual transfer by writing checks to their children and to the spouses of their children. The intent of the donor in transferring funds to those spouses commonly becomes an issue at divorce.]

On September 7, 1997, husband and wife * * * open[ed] a joint account [at Cornerstone], for the purpose of funding their retirement 10 to 15 years later. To finance the Cornerstone account, husband and wife wrote three checks. First, * * * wife wrote a check to Cornerstone in the amount of $20,000, drawn on the parties' joint checking account at First Virginia.[9] [Later] * * * wife wrote a second check from that account in the amount of $77,500. Shortly thereafter, husband wrote a check to Cornerstone from the same First Virginia account in the amount of $155,000.

Husband argues that the trial court erred in classifying the parties' joint Legg Mason account as marital property. Because the Legg Mason account was financed with both separate and marital assets, the statutory guidelines for classification of commingled property necessarily apply. Code § 20–107.3(A) provides, in pertinent part:

(3) The court shall classify property as part marital property and part separate property as follows:

* * *

(d) When marital property and separate property are commingled by contributing one category of property to another, resulting in the loss of identity of the contributed property, the classification of the contributed property shall be transmuted to the category of property receiving the contribution. However, to the extent the contributed property is retraceable by a preponderance of the evidence and was not a gift, such contributed property shall retain its original classification.

(e) When marital property and separate property are commingled into newly acquired property resulting in the loss of identity of the contributing properties, the commingled property shall be deemed transmuted to marital property. However, to the extent the contributed property is retraceable by a preponderance of the evidence and was not a gift, the contributed property shall retain its original classification.

* * * [H]usband may retain his separate property if he can show the property "is retraceable by a preponderance of the evidence and was not a gift." [The] Code * * * states, "No presumption of gift shall arise under this section where (i) separate property is commingled with jointly owned property; (ii) newly acquired property is conveyed into joint ownership; or (iii) existing property is conveyed or retitled into joint ownership."

In *Rahbaran v. Rahbaran*, 494 S.E.2d 135, 141 (1997), this Court held:

---

9. Wife offered evidence, in the form of a check register, to show that the parties deposited $20,038.73 into their First Virginia account to cover the first check written to Cornerstone on September 26, 1997. The checks deposited include: 1) $9,500 to husband from his mother; 2) $9,500 to wife from husband's parents; 3) $73 to husband and wife from the Commonwealth of Virginia Department of Taxation; and, 4) $964.73 to husband from his parents.

In order to trace the separate portion of hybrid property, a party must prove that the claimed separate portion is identifiably derived from a separate asset. This process involves two steps: a party must (1) establish the identity of a portion of hybrid property and (2) directly trace that portion to a separate asset.

"When a party satisfies this test, and by a preponderance of the evidence traces his or her separate contributions to commingled property, the code states that the contributed separate property 'shall retain its original classification.'" *Hart v. Hart*, 497 S.E.2d 496, 506 (1998). Husband can prevail, therefore, by sufficiently tracing the source of the Legg Mason funds to his separate property.

The Legg Mason account was initiated by a transfer of funds from the parties' joint account at Cornerstone. Therefore, we must look to the source of the Cornerstone funds to determine whether husband's separate property financed the Legg Mason account.

[Judge Haley then provides a detailed analysis of how the White City funds and funds from the husband's Fidelity account made their way to the Cornerstone account, and then to Legg Mason, to show that the funds are traceable to the husband's separate property. The dissent notes that the wife corroborated this history of how the funds moved from one account to another. The dissent continues:].

* * *

* * * In the parties' prenuptial agreement, the Fidelity account was listed as husband's separate property. However, * * * husband testified that, since the parties were married, "roughly $20,000" of wife's money (gifts received from husband's parents) had been deposited into the Fidelity account.

* * * [O]n the same day that wife wrote a $20,000 check to Cornerstone, a deposit was made to the parties' joint account at First Virginia in the amount of $20,038.73, ostensibly to cover the check to Cornerstone. That deposit included a check from husband's parents to wife for $9,500. * * *

The evidence overwhelmingly suggests, therefore, that the Cornerstone account included part marital, part separate, and part hybrid property. * * * [T]he total equity contributed to the Cornerstone account by the parties equaled $252,500. Of this amount, however, husband withdrew $55,000 to purchase an annuity in his name. Therefore, the total contributed equity that was later transferred to the Legg Mason account equaled the difference, $197,500. At least a portion of that balance necessarily came from husband's separate property.

* * *

* * * I would hold that husband traced those contributions of separate property into Legg Mason, that Legg Mason was part wife's separate property, part husband's separate property, and part marital property, and thus remand to the trial court to apportion the same. * * *

NOTES AND QUESTIONS

1. *The level of proof required.* Once a showing of transmutation or commingling has been made, the spouse who argues that marital property is really separate property bears the burden of proof to provide evidence demonstrating an intent to keep the property separate, or evidence tracing the contested property back to separate property. The evidentiary standard varies depending on the jurisdiction. In some jurisdictions the evidentiary standard remains unclear. In California, for example, some courts impose a requirement of "clear and convincing" proof to overcome the presumption that property is marital, while others use the lesser common civil standard, a "preponderance of the evidence." *In re the Marriage of Ettefagh*, 59 Cal. Rptr.3d 419 (Ct. App. 2007) (reviewing inconsistencies and concluding that only a preponderance of the evidence is required because the spouses have "inverse but equal" interests at stake).

2. *The date of acquisition.* In *Isbell v. Willoughby*, 2005 WL 1744468 (Cal. Ct. App. July 26, 2005) (unpublished opinion), the wife appealed the trial court's holding that the couple's beagle was the husband's separate property. The court analyzed the problem by asking when the beagle was acquired. The husband had purchased the beagle in May 1994, shortly before the couple moved in together and more than a year before they married. The beagle was, and remained, separate property, even though the parties shared the dog during the marriage, and the husband had left the dog in the wife's care after executing the separation agreement while he was away completing job training.

To what extent did the timing of the acquisition of the Legg Mason account, the buffalo and the farm equipment influence the *Nack* court's characterization of these properties as marital? What other factors did the court weigh in each instance? Was the majority correct in finding the creation of marital property notwithstanding the apparent intent of the prenuptial agreement, whose validity and enforceability was not directly challenged by either party? What policy considerations may have been in play?

3. *Tracing.* As *Nack* demonstrates, when a divorcing party claims that commingled property remains separate, one crucial inquiry is whether the separate property is traceable. "The commingling of separate property with other property of any type does not destroy the identity of the property as separate property, except when the separate property is not traceable." Ohio Rev. Code Ann. § 3105.171(A)(6)(b) (Anderson 2003). In Virginia, assets that have not been maintained as separate cannot be awarded to the individual owner unless the assets can be traced back from their current use directly to the separate source. The party asserting that the assets remain separate bears the burden of showing by a preponderance of the evidence that the retitled property can be traced back to separate assets. *Robinson v. Robinson*, 613 S.E.2d 484, 490 (Va. Ct. App. 2005).

While this burden may seem high, it is possible to trace even liquid assets, such as cash, back to separate property. Do you think that the majority or the dissent in *Nack* was more convincing in its treatment of the Legg Mason account? Why?

In some jurisdictions, such as Florida, courts reject efforts to trace the source of commingled funds. *Pfrengle* v. *Pfrengle*, 976 So.2d 1134, 1136 (Fla. Dist. Ct. App. 2008) ("Money is fungible, and once commingled it loses its separate character" as do all funds in the commingled account).

The length of time the assets are commingled may matter. In *In re Marriage of Wojcik*, 838 N.E.2d 282 (Ill. App. Ct. 2005), each spouse argued that a means of transport was separate property. Paul Wojcik argued that his motorcycle, purchased with funds inherited from his father after the funds had been deposited in the parties' joint checking account for several months, was his separate property. His wife Karen, in turn, argued that her Mercury Sable, purchased with money her brother had given her as a gift that she deposited in the couple's checking account for one day, was her separate property. The court distinguished the two sets of transactions, holding that Karen's car was her separate property, but that Paul's motorcycle was a marital asset subject to distribution. In dividing up the marital property, however, the court distributed the motorcycle to Paul.

4. *What constitutes a gift?* The husband in *Nack* denied that he intended to make a gift of any of his property to the marital estate. Commingling and transmutation share the underlying rationale that merging separate property into joint property " 'creates a rebuttable presumption of a gift to the marital estate.' " *Ferguson* v. *Ferguson*, 2008 WL 425945, at *4 (Tenn. Ct. App. 2008). The fact that property can be traced back to separate property does not prevent its recharacterization where donative intent or retitling render it divisible. *Steinmann* v. *Steinmann*, 749 N.W.2d 145 (Wis. 2008). " 'Donative intent is presumed where property is transferred, or transmuted, from non-divisible property to joint tenancy subject to division.' " *Id.* at 155.

Nack also involves an undeveloped dispute over whether the gifts the wife received from her in-laws were her separate property. Donative intent has three elements: " 'an intention on the part of the donor to make an immediate gift of property, delivery of the property to the donee, and acceptance of the gift by the donee.' " *Jackson* v. *Jackson*, 2008 WL 836015, at *8 (Ohio Ct. App. 2008). Courts may consider whether the donor intended a gift or inheritance to go directly to a child's spouse. *See, e.g., In re Marriage of Francis–Hoyle*, 753 N.W.2d 18 (Iowa Ct. App. 2008). How did the *Nack* court treat the checks the wife received from her in-laws?

5. *How to avoid commingling.* Before her marriage, Jean Johnson found land she wanted to purchase, but she did not close the deal until a month after her wedding. The mortgage, note and title on the property were all in her maiden name as were her signatures on those documents. Jean made the down payment with a check from her mother's mutual funds, and made the monthly mortgage payments either from joint accounts she shared with her son from an earlier marriage or with her mother, or from proceeds from the sale of her mother's house. Finally, Jean paid the taxes on the property from a separate account she maintained in her own name. The court rebuffed the

husband's claim that the property was marital because it was acquired during the marriage. *Johnson* v. *Johnson*, 979 So.2d 350 (Fla. Dist. Ct. App. 2008). In contrast, in *Patel* v. *Patel*, 2006 WL 2594179 (Va. Ct. App. 2006), as in *Nack*, separate property was transmuted when husband "conducted hundreds of inter-account transactions" among accounts in his name and joint accounts with his wife, his father and his daughter.

6. *Does title still matter?* The *Nack* court states that the title to the Lexus is dispositive—showing that the car was the husband's separate property. Similarly, the court recognized the annuity titled in the husband's name as his separate property because it was purchased with traceable funds. Just a year earlier, however, the same court had found the lack of donative intent overcame joint title in property purchased with separate funds. *Lesesne* v. *Zablocki*, 2007 WL 49651 (Va. Ct. App. 2007). Other jurisdictions have attempted to bolster predictability by using "a more bright-line approach that classified real property as marital if it were held in joint ownership during the marriage," ignoring intent and motivation. *Hedges* v. *Pitcher*, 942 A.2d 1217, 1221 (Me. 2008).

7. *Contributions and reimbursement.* As the rule cited in *Nack* indicates, transmutation can work in either direction—from separate to marital or marital to separate. In *Nack*, the majority notes that the wife contributed marital property to the upkeep and maintenance of the husband's Mercedes, thus transmuting marital property to separate property, or "at best" hybrid property, that is, part separate and part marital. What would the characterization of the Mercedes and the Lexus have been in the absence of the prenuptial agreement?

Where the spouse who contributed property to a marital acquisition can document the contribution, he or she may be entitled to reimbursement. For example, if one spouse contributes separate funds to the down payment for a house, and can trace those funds, then reimbursement is appropriate. *In re Marriage of Weaver*, 26 Cal.Rptr.3d 121 (Ct. App. 2005).

8. *The family home.* Disagreements sometimes center on the characterization of the family home, especially where one party acquired the home before marriage but marital funds and labor subsequently contributed to the mortgage and upkeep. Special rules may govern the treatment of the marital home where there are minor children of the marriage, regardless of its characterization.

Where the divorcing couple has minor children, courts often try to award the family home to the parent who receives physical custody where it is economically feasible to do so. The current doctrine urges parents and courts to avoid abrupt changes to the child's environment. Sandra Morgan Little, 2 Child Custody and Visitation Law and Practice § 10.09 (2004). This was not always the case. In her pivotal work on the impoverishment of women and children following divorce, Lenore Weitzman argued that California's community property regime often meant that the home had to be sold in order to divide the marital assets; sale of the marital home forced custodial mothers and their children to move to smaller residences in less desirable neighborhoods that were in different school districts. These dislocations exacerbated the child's sense of loss following divorce. Lenore J. Weitzman, The Divorce

Revolution: The Unexpected Social and Economic Consequences for Women and Children in America 31, 369 (1985).

The law in Maryland exemplifies the contemporary approach. The preamble to the Maryland marital property statute instructs courts to pay *"particular and favorable attention"* to the needs of minor children when adjusting the property interests of their parents in a dissolution proceeding. *Maness* v. *Sawyer*, 950 A.2d 830, 838 (Md. Ct. Spec. App. 2008). The legislature further instructs the courts to award the family home to the parent who receives primary custody of the children so that the children may " 'live in an environment and community which is familiar to them.' " *Id.* For that reason, the court may even specify that when it is time for the custodial parent to move out of the family home, the move must be delayed until the after the end of the school year. *Id.* at 835. The Maryland court notes that this approach is not only what the law requires, it is "the right thing to do." *Id.*

Creative arrangements allowing for delay in the sale of the family home until a triggering event, such as the year the youngest child enters or graduates from college, are common. The goal of preserving the child's residence generally favors custodial parents (not necessarily the mother). *See, e.g., Kjelland v. Kjelland*, 609 N.W.2d 100 (N.D. 2000) (affirming award of custody to father where, among other things, mother had run a small business and rented an apartment in another city and the children wanted to stay in their home); *Schmidt v. Schmidt*, 660 N.W.2d 196 (N.D. 2003) (affirming award of custody to the father where the family lived on a farm that had been in the father's family, near extended family with whom the children had a close bond).

9. *ALI Proposals for reform.* The American Law Institute's Principles of Family Dissolution propose two reforms that would affect the treatment of separate and marital property. Section 4.12 of the Principles provides for gradual recharacterization of separate property as marital in marriages of long duration. To address the common circumstance that couples purchase property together before they marry, such as a residence that becomes the marital home, Section 403(b) provides that property "acquired during a relationship between the spouses that immediately preceded their marriage, and which was a domestic-partner relationship * * * as defined [in another section], is treated as if it were acquired during the marriage."

D. APPRECIATION OF SEPARATE PROPERTY DURING THE MARRIAGE

Most states distinguish between ownership of separate property and ownership of any appreciation in the value of the separate property during the marriage.

This issue is considered in greater detail in the next decision, involving a stockyard in which the husband and his brother were partners before and during the marriage.

MIDDENDORF v. MIDDENDORF

Supreme Court of Ohio, 1998.
696 N.E.2d 575.

LUNDBERG STRATTON, JUSTICE.

In this case, we examine the legal standards for determining when appreciation in separate property becomes marital property for purposes of the division of property in a domestic relations case under R.C. 3105.171. Max asserts that in order for a court to determine that an increase in separate property is marital property, the court must find that *both* spouses have expended significant marital funds or labor directly contributing to the increase or that the non-owning spouse must contribute substantial work to improvement and maintenance of the separate property. We disagree.

* * *

* * * R.C. 3105.171(A)(3)(a), as amended, states:

" 'Marital property' means * * * all of the following:

" * * *

"(iii) * * * all income and appreciation on separate property, due to the labor, monetary, or in-kind contribution of *either or both of the spouses* that occurred during the marriage." (Emphasis added.) 144 Ohio Laws, Part I, 1754–1755.

R.C. 3105.171(A)(6)(a) states:

" 'Separate property' means all real and personal property and any interest in real or personal property that is found by the court to be any of the following:

" * * *

"(iii) Passive income and appreciation acquired from separate property by one spouse during the marriage."

Finally, R.C. 3105.171(A)(4) states:

" 'Passive income' means income acquired other than as a result of the labor, monetary, or in-kind contribution of either spouse."

* * *

The plain language of R.C. 3105.171(A)(3)(a)(iii) unambiguously mandates that when *either* spouse makes a labor, money, or in-kind contribution that *causes* an increase in the value of separate property, that increase in value is deemed marital property.

* * * Accordingly, the appellate court did not err in affirming the trial court's interpretation of R.C. 3105.171, that an increase in the value of separate property due to *either* spouse's efforts is marital property.

We must now determine if there was sufficient evidence to support the trial court's determination that there was an increase in the value of the stockyard during Max and Pat's marriage and that the increase was *due to* the labor, money, or in-kind contributions made by Max. If the evidence indicates that the appreciation of the separate property is *not due* to the input of Max's (or Pat's) labor, money, or in-kind contributions, the increase in the value of the stockyard is passive appreciation and remains separate property.

A trial court has broad discretion in making divisions of property in domestic cases. A trial court's decision will be upheld absent an abuse of discretion. "Abuse of discretion" is more than an error of law or judgment; it implies that the court acted in an unreasonable, arbitrary, or unconscionable fashion. If there is some competent, credible evidence to support the trial court's decision, there is no abuse of discretion. Therefore, if there is some competent, credible evidence that there was an increase in the value of the stockyard during the marriage and that the increase in the valuation was due to labor, money, or in-kind contributions of either Max or Pat, or both, the increase in valuation is classified as marital property and subject to division.

On remand from the court of appeals, the magistrate hired Philip Brandt as an independent expert to value the stockyard. Brandt testified that the value of the stockyard when the Middendorfs were married was $201,389 and the value in December 1992, the stipulated date for purposes of determining value, was $309,930. Thus, the increase was $108,541. Both the magistrate and the court rejected the defense expert's testimony and found the court-appointed expert more credible. This testimony provided credible evidence of an increase in the value of the stockyard during the Middendorfs' marriage.

The second issue upon which we must determine if credible evidence has been submitted is whether this increase in value of the stockyard was *due to* labor, monetary, or in-kind contribution by Max.

The stockyard business primarily involves buying hogs from farmers and then reselling them to the slaughterhouse. As a sideline, the stockyard would contract with farmers to feed the hogs until the hogs reached a marketable size, whereupon they would be sold to a meatpacking company. * * *

Max argues that there is no evidence that the increase in the stockyard's value was due to his funds or labor. Max asserts that the increase was due solely to passive appreciation from "market changes." However, Max's position fails to take into account all of the other factors contributing to the increase.

Passive forces such as market conditions may influence the profitability of a business. However, it is the employees and their labor input that make a company productive. In today's business environment, executives and managers figure heavily in the success or failure of a company, and in the attendant risks (*e.g.*, termination, demotion) and rewards (*e.g.*, bonuses, stock options) that go with the respective position. These individuals are the persons responsible for making pivotal decisions that result in the success or failure of the company. There is no reason that these factors should not likewise be relevant in determining a spouse's input into the success of a business.

* * * [M]onitoring market prices in order to make timely purchases and sales, deciding the numbers of hogs purchased, and deciding whether to contract with farmers to care for hogs are a few of the calculated decisions made by the stockyard management that also affect profitability. Thus, no matter how high hog prices went, the business would not operate, let alone increase in value, without the necessary ingredients of labor and leadership from the owners and management. Making these calculated decisions was part of Max's responsibilities as a livestock buyer and co-owner of the stockyard. Max testified that he spent long hours working there * * *.

* * * The trial court found that "the increase in value of Middendorf Stockyard Company was the direct result of the pivotal role which [Max] played in the management of the company during the course of the marriage." The appeals court found that [ ] Max "played a vital role in the management of the Stockyards. * * * " * * *

Although we note that Pat contributed substantial efforts to the family relationship that freed Max of the responsibilities of the home and children and enabled him to devote more time to the business, we need not reach the issue of the value of her contributions. Because Max's efforts contributed to the appreciation of the Middendorf Stockyards, the requirements of R.C. 3105.171(A)(3)(a)(iii) are met, as the statute requires the contribution of only one spouse. Thus, we find some competent, credible evidence that Max's interest in the stockyard increased in value by $108,541, during Max and Pat's marriage, due to Max's labor. Therefore, the trial court did not abuse its discretion in finding that the $108,541 appreciation of the stockyard was a marital asset to be divided between Max and Pat. Accordingly, we affirm the judgment of the court of appeals.

NOTES AND QUESTIONS

1. *More on* Middendorf. The Middendorfs married in 1986 and divorced in 1993. During the marriage, Max's three children from a prior marriage lived in the couple's home. No children were born to the marriage. Before the marriage, Pat worked as an interior designer. She gave decorating advice on the improvements to the marital residence, which had been Max's home prior to the marriage. Because her advice was professional in nature, Pat received a share of the appreciation on the marital residence. The house was located on, and adjacent to, farmland that came from Max's family. In an earlier proceeding, an appellate court reversed the award of a portion of the appreciation of the land to the wife, holding that the crop land appreciated over time without any contribution from either party. *Middendorf v. Middendorf*, 1996 WL 740968 (Ohio Ct. App. Dec. 17, 1996).

2. *How do states treat the appreciation in value of a separate asset?* Many courts have held that if either spouse puts resources or effort into the appreciation, then the value of the increase is marital property. For example, in *Mitchell v. Mitchell*, 841 So.2d 564 (Fla. Ct. App. 2003), the trial court classified the increase in value of unimproved separate real estate as marital property, but the Court of Appeals reversed, since the improvement was solely due to passive inflation rather than to any effort of the parties. The California statute provides that all income and profit from separate property remains separate. Cal. Fam. Code § 770(a)(3) (West 2004). Some other states, however, treat the appreciation of a marital asset as marital, regardless of whether either of the spouses contributed to the appreciation. *See, e.g.,* Or. Rev. Stat. Ann. § 107.105(1)(f) (West 2005); 23 Pa. Stat. Ann. § 3501(a)(1) (West 2001).

3. *When does marriage end for purposes of property distribution?* Marital property accumulates only during the marriage. All jurisdictions agree that a marriage begins on the day the legal ceremony takes place. Jurisdictions differ, however, about when the marriage ends for purposes of continuing to acquire marital property. Two separate but related issues arise: First, how long does property acquired by one spouse continue to be counted as marital? Second, at what point should marital property be valued for purposes of distribution? Some jurisdictions regard as separate all property (and increases in value) acquired after the date of legal separation. *See, e.g.,* Cal. Fam. Code § 771 (West 2004); Wash Rev. Code Ann. § 26.09.080 (West 2005). Others continue to count as marital all property acquired until the date on which one party files for divorce, the trial is held, or the divorce is granted. *See, e.g., Koeth v. Koeth*, 765 N.Y.S.2d 640 (App. Div. 2003) (counting as marital property accumulated until commencement of the action for divorce); *Fitzwater v. Fitzwater*, 151 S.W.3d 135 (Mo. Ct. App. 2004) (the date for determining and valuing marital assets is the date of trial); *Schumacher v. Schumacher*, 986 S.W.2d 883 (Ark. Ct. App. 1999) (property acquired after separation but before absolute divorce is considered marital property).

Which approach seems more equitable? Which approach seems more amenable to manipulation by a sophisticated spouse?

4. *Non-monetary contributions that do not add value.* What if a woman works very hard to improve the value of a house her husband owned before the marriage, but the appraiser concludes that the improvements did not significantly enhance its value because a prospective buyer might "raze the house and build a new one on the site"? *See Quinn v. Quinn*, 689 N.W.2d 605, 612 (Neb. Ct. App. 2004). What if a declining real estate market means that despite the improvements, the house is worth less than when she moved in?

A NOTE ON THE TIMING AND METHOD OF VALUATION

Valuation poses a number of interrelated issues. First, what should the date of valuation be? It is crucial to distinguish the date of valuation from how long accumulation continues to be treated as marital, discussed *supra* note 3. The dates may be different. In other words, a state may treat all property acquired after the legal separation as separate, but may value the marital estate as of the date of the divorce decree.

States vary in which dates they use for valuation. Some use the date of separation, others the date of trial, and still others the date on which the decree issues, or even the date of the final decree in the event of remand. J. Thomas Oldham, Divorce, Separation and the Distribution of Property § 13.03 (2005). At least one state uses the date of filing of the divorce complaint or commencement of the marital litigation. *Hatfield v. Van Epps*, 594 S.E.2d 526 (S.C. Ct. App. 2004). Some states leave the date of valuation up to the discretion of the court. *See Macci v. Macci*, 904 So.2d 517 (Fla. Dist. Ct. App. 2005); *Wallop v. Wallop*, 88 P.3d 1022 (Wyo. 2004).

Due to appreciation and fluctuation, the date on which marital property is valued may prove quite significant and equitable considerations may enter into the decision. For example, in *In re Marriage of Wojcik*, 838 N.E.2d 282 (Ill. App. Ct. 2005), the appellate court held that the trial court erred by using the value the parties had assigned to the husband's retirement account when they executed a stipulation, where undisputed evidence showed that the account had later declined in value due to market conditions.

A second question is how a judge assigns a value to any particular asset if the parties cannot agree on valuation. Normally, judges rely on appraisals and other expert opinions if the parties are unwilling to stipulate to the value of an asset that cannot easily be measured. Experts, in turn, rely on a number of methodologies in valuing assets, and some individual experts themselves offer competing models and results for the judge's consideration. *See, e.g., Collins v. Collins*, 104 P.3d 1059, 1063 (Mont. 2004) (affirming the decision below where the wife's expert "testified to three different methods used when valuing a business" and the court chose one of them). The trial court's decision on valuation will be sustained as "long as the court's findings are grounded in the evidence, even if substantial contrary evidence exists." *Wade v. Wade*, 878 A.2d 303, 310 (Vt. 2005). As one court summarized the broad discretion accorded to the trial court: "In determining the value of marital property, the court is free to accept all, part or none of the evidence as to the true and correct value of the property." *Baker v. Baker*, 861 A.2d 298, 302 (Pa. Super. Ct. 2004).

Provided the trial court states that it has estimated the value of all of the marital assets before distributing them, the court need not determine the exact value of the marital estate, a task which may be impossible before assets are sold. *In re Marriage of Hayes*, 60 P.3d 431 (Mont. 2002) (the trial court is not required to state the values it assigned to each marital asset, but only that it assigned values).

E. THE CONTRIBUTIONS OF HOMEMAKERS

The *Middendorf* court noted that it did not have to evaluate the extent to which Pat's contribution as a homemaker freed Max to run the stockyards, because the statute required that only one of them have contributed to the increase in the value of the business. Under the common law title system courts regularly failed to accord credit to homemakers for their contributions. As Mississippi's highest court explained in announcing that it would no longer apply the title system: "to allow a system of property division to ignore non-financial contributions is to create a likelihood of unjust division of property." *Ferguson* v. *Ferguson*, 639 So.2d 921, 926 (Miss. 1994). The court explained that "[o]ur separate property system at times resulted in unjust distributions, especially involving cases of a traditional family where most property was titled in the husband, leaving a traditional housewife and mother with nothing but a claim for alimony, which often proved unenforceable. In a family where both spouses worked, but the husband's resources were devoted to investments while the wife's earnings were devoted to paying the family expenses or vice versa, the same unfair results ensued. The flaw of the separate property system, however, is not merely that it will occasionally ignore the financial contributions of the non-titleholding spouse. The system ... is also unable to take account of a spouse's non-financial contribution. In the case of many traditional housewives such non-financial contributions are often considerable." *Id.*

Today, equitable distribution of all marital assets in title jurisdictions is the primary acknowledgement of homemaker contributions to the marital estate. The homemaker spouse is entitled to a fair share of the assets, the argument goes, because she contributed to the accumulation of those assets even if she did not earn a wage.

Assigning a dollar value to the contributions of homemakers proves more difficult. Courts often struggle to calculate the value of a homemaker's services:

> * * * This value can be determined using at least three different calculations: the cost of replacing a homemaker's services with market labor; the lost opportunity costs borne by the homemaker by virtue of devoting her time to homemaking instead of market labor; and econometric models based on economic theory and statistical analysis. While the lost opportunity cost model is popular * * *, it also has been criticized by feminists for its focus on the costs borne by homemakers and failure to account for the benefits primary wage earners enjoy as a result of gendered divisions of domestic labor. Specifically, primary homemakers make it possible for primary wage earners to achieve "ideal-worker" status * * * largely unhindered by child care or other domestic responsibilities.

Martha M. Ertman, *Commercializing Marriage: A Proposal for Valuing Women's Work Through Premarital Security Agreements*, 77 Tex. L. Rev. 17, 21–22 (1998).

Estimates of a homemaker's value by economists and other experts vary wildly. One study calculated the market value of a mother's services based on job titles "ranging from housekeeper and day care center teacher to van driver, psychologist and chief executive" at nearly $117,000 a year for a full time "stay-at-home mom" and just over $68,000 a year for a part timer who also has an "outside job." AP, *Their Labor of Love*, Newsday, May 10, 2008, at A–6 (citing a study by Salary.com). The salary estimate included substantial overtime pay since the survey of 18,000 mothers revealed that full-time mothers worked about 94.4 hours each week. *Id.* The part-time mothers also earned hypothetical overtime: they worked an average of 54.6 hours a week as moms. *Id.* A comparable study in Great Britain reported that the average "mum" worked almost nine hours a day every day of the year, and that it would cost about £ 30,000 a year (roughly $60,000 in 2008) to replace a mother's services. *Housewife 'would be paid £30,000'*, BBC.co.uk, Feb. 19, 2008, http://new.bbc.co.uk/2/hi/business/7252504.stm.

Other studies, as well as insurance companies, place the economic value of homemakers much lower when homemakers die or are incapacitated. In the real world, families do not replace all of the functions a homemaker performs with paid labor, and the employees they hire are paid on average between $10 and $15 an hour. Liz Pulliam Weston, *What's a Homemaker Worth? The shocking truth*, MSN Money, May 4, 2003, http://moneycentral.msn.com/content/CollegeandFamily/P46800.asp (citing an economist). For this reason the lifetime economic value assigned to a woman homemaker who dies at age 30 is around $300,000 as compared to a 30–year–old worker making just under $20 an hour, currently valued at over $1 million. *Id.* This low value is reflected in statutes that govern the insurance industry. *See, e.g.,* Minn. Stat. Ann. § 65B.44 subdiv. 5 (West 2005) (benefits for loss of full-time homemaker "shall be subject to a maximum of $200 per week" in Minnesota).

Courts, in contrast, increasingly recognize the complex interaction of the spousal roles. The modern approach to determining "a spouse's contribution which justifies equitable distribution" is to look "not only at cash contributions and assistance in the spouse's workplace or business, but also to domestic work in the home such as caring for children, cooking meals, cleaning house, and washing and ironing clothes. 'The persistent attempts made to put a monetary value on a homemaker's contributions are likely to undervalue the magnitude of such contributions.' The spouse who is accumulating the monetary assets will have more time to accumulate more assets if someone is taking care of all of the domestic responsibilities." *Haney v. Haney,* 907 So.2d 948, 955 (Miss. 2005) (internal citations omitted).

Wives of very successful executives often argue that they make special contributions as "corporate wives" who, in addition to managing the usual domestic duties, contribute to their husband's careers by extensive work-related entertainment and travel. *Wendt v. Wendt,* 757 A.2d 1225, 1230 (Conn. App. Ct. 2000). They demand a fair share of the resulting wealth and lifestyle. *Id.* Lorna Wendt, who successfully appealed from a trial court's award of ten percent of the marital property accumulated during her marriage to a successful CEO, asserts: "My case was never about the money. It was about someone implying I was a ten percent participant in my partnership. In reality, I always gave 100 percent, putting my career on hold to raise the children, manage the household and support him in his business endeavors." Equality in Marriage Institute, Lorna Wendt, http://www.equalityinmarriage.org/lorna.html (archived page).

Homemakers of every social class still run the risk that their contributions to the family and to their spouses' careers will not receive adequate recognition in the form of property distribution in the event the marriage dissolves. They also assume significant opportunity costs, including declining future employment prospects and loss of retirement savings and other benefits that may leave them disadvantaged after divorce. *See* Pamela Laufer–Ukeles, *Selective Recognition of Gender Difference in the Law: Revaluing the Caretaker Role*, 31 Harv. J. L. & Gender 1 (2008).

QUESTIONS

1. Does it matter what economic value is assigned to a homemaker's services if he or she receives an equitable share of marital assets at divorce? In other words, is equitable distribution a sufficient compensation for full-time homemaking?

2. When spouses decide that one of them should be a full-time homemaker, is their choice of which spouse should stay at home truly a joint personal plan or is the choice largely predetermined by larger societal expectations and the preferences of employers?

3. Martha Fineman has argued that caretaking is a societal function that should be compensated by society. Martha Fineman, The Autonomy Myth: A Theory of Dependency (2005). What are the pros and cons of a government payment to an adult who takes care of dependent children or adults at home? Would such a payment be likely to affect the distribution of responsibilities in families or the economic repercussions of family dissolution?

PROBLEM 9–1

Gordon and Ellen married in 2001 and separated two years later. No children were born of the marriage. Neither party was employed during the marriage. Their sole source of income was approximately $50,000 a month, after taxes, which Gordon received as a beneficiary of a family trust valued at nearly $60 million. Gordon is one of several beneficiaries, does not control the trust, and cannot invade the principal.

During the marriage the couple established joint checking and savings accounts. The trust payments were electronically deposited into the joint checking account every month, and used to pay virtually all of their expenses. They used the funds, among other things, to make a down payment and mortgage payments on a home known as "Bleak House" in which they held joint title. They also purchased two late model luxury cars, furnished their home, and added a swimming pool and basketball court. At the date of separation the checking account contained nearly $70,000.

Ellen took primary responsibility for paying the bills, and urged her husband to curb his spendthrift ways. Each month Ellen took responsibility for transferring funds to the savings account, which contained $244,000 when they separated. She also took care of the home and cooking. Gordon did the grocery shopping and maintained the exterior of their home.

You are the trial judge in an equitable distribution jurisdiction, and are hearing Ellen's petition for divorce. Ellen argues that all of the parties' assets should be equitably distributed because Gordon's use of his trust fund indicated his desire to make a gift to her. Gordon argues that it was simply more convenient to have joint accounts and joint titles, and that no intent to transfer ownership should be inferred. Ellen also argues that the savings account would never have been funded absent her efforts.

What assets are subject to distribution? Why? How would you distribute the assets? Would the result differ in a "kitchen sink" jurisdiction?

F. DEBTS

Liabilities accumulated during a marriage are also marital property subject to division. Liabilities include indebtedness created through borrowing (such as the mortgage on a house or a car loan), business debts, and obligations under contracts or judgments. The following decision discusses the extent to which each spouse may be held responsible for joint debts after a marriage dissolves.

SUNKIDD VENTURE, INC. v. SNYDER–ENTEL

Court of Appeals of Washington, 1997.
941 P.2d 16.

SCHULTHEIS, ACTING CHIEF JUDGE.

We are asked to decide whether a wife is separately bound as a tenant to a lease agreement signed only by her husband. The Spokane County Superior Court affirmed a district court decision to dismiss Sunkidd Venture, Inc.'s complaint against Shannon Snyder–Entel for damages due to breach of a lease agreement. * * * Sunkidd contends the district court erred as a matter of law in holding that the lease was not a community obligation and that Ms. Snyder–Entel was not separately liable for breach. We reverse and remand:

In March 1988, William Entel entered into a lease for a term that expired in August 1988. The landlord was * * * Wieber Pacific Management, Inc. A provision in the lease states that the rental is to be occupied only "by Tenants with the ability to contract whose signatures are affixed hereto, consisting of one adult and no children. . . ." Occupancy by any other people was declared a breach of the agreement.

After Mr. Entel married Ms. Snyder–Entel in June 1988, the couple lived together in the apartment. Beginning in early August 1988, Wieber sent three notices to the apartment, addressed to Mr. Entel, informing him he had three days to quit the premises or pay rent. The third notice included a form that allowed Mr. Entel to check a box and extend the lease for a year, "with all other terms and conditions remaining the same." Mr. Entel signed the lease extension and sent it to Wieber. His wife did not sign, but she later testified she remembered receiving the third notice and understanding that the landlord intended to terminate the tenancy at the end of the month. She also testified her husband told her he had extended the lease and she assumed they would live there another year.

During their tenancy, Ms. Snyder–Entel usually wrote the rent checks from a joint account and occasionally complained to Wieber about maintenance problems. The couple continued to live in the apartment until October 1988, when Ms. Snyder–Entel sent notice that they intended to vacate by the end of the month. Wieber sent Mr. Entel a "Tenant Deposit Closing Statement" in November charging him $3,770 for cleaning, rent through the term of the lease, average utilities for that period and advertising for new tenants. Ms. Snyder–Entel responded, denying liability for those expenses and contending Wieber broke the lease because it did not fix the maintenance problems. Sometime in 1988 or 1989, Wieber assigned the debt to Sunkidd/American Bonded for collection.

In May 1991, Sunkidd filed a complaint in district court against Ms. Snyder–Entel as "individually liable" for the accounts due on the lease abandonment. This amount had been reduced to $1,444, because Wieber had been able to rent the apartment within two months. The Entels separated in September 1992 and divorced in April 1993. In June 1994, Ms. Snyder–Entel answered the complaint, denying any contractual relationship with Wieber or any duty to pay an obligation of her former spouse. * * *

[At trial in 1995, the district court] * * * found that the lease extension was not Ms. Snyder–Entel's separate obligation because she did not sign it and had no notice of it before its execution. Although the judge recognized that in some cases debts for "family expenses" may be recovered from a spouse's separate property, she held that such expenses were limited to urgent, immediate needs, like medical expenses. She also held that equitable principles of fundamental fairness obliged her to deny the claim while allowing Sunkidd to refile against Mr. Entel, the signatory on the lease.

* * *

The primary issue on appeal is whether Ms. Snyder–Entel is separately bound by the lease extension agreement signed only by her husband. Sunkidd contends the lease extension, signed while the married couple was living in the apartment, was a community obligation. Sunkidd also asserts Ms. Snyder–Entel is separately liable on the lease, first because she participated in the transaction by acquiescing in it, and second because the lease was an expense of the family pursuant to RCW 26.16.205.

We review the decision of a district court to determine whether it committed errors of law. The district court's factual determinations will be accepted if they are supported by substantial evidence in the record.

We begin with the general presumption that a debt incurred by either spouse during marriage is a community debt. This presumption may be rebutted by clear and convincing evidence that the debt was not contracted for community benefit. The key test is whether, at the time the obligation was entered into, there was a reasonable expectation the community would receive a material benefit from it. Actual benefit to the community is not required as long as there was an expectation of community benefit.

At the time Mr. Entel signed the lease extension, he was undeniably entering into the agreement for the benefit of the marital community. We must presume he reasonably expected that he and his wife would live together in the apartment. As a result, he created a community debt. Usually, when a spouse's act creates a community liability, it is enforceable only against the community property and the acting spouse's separate property. If the obligation is for a family expense, however, it can be enforced against the separate property of one spouse even though the other spouse alone incurred the liability. RCW 26.16.205.[6]

Family expenses * * * are synonymous with a family's "necessaries," those items required for the sustenance, support and ordinary requirements of a family. *Smith v. Dalton*, 795 P.2d 706 (Wash. Ct. App. 1990); *Bush & Lane Piano Co. v. Woodard*, 175 P. 329 (Wash. 1918). Rental of the family residence is a recognized family expense that subjects the spouses to both community and separate liability.

* * * Mr. Entel's agreement to a one-year extension was necessary to ensure housing for the community. Accordingly, the lease obligation was incurred as a family expense. The district court erred as a matter of law in concluding otherwise.[7] Although the marital community has been dissolved, the liabilities of its members continue and Sunkidd may proceed against the former spouses either individually or collectively. * * *

* * *

Reversed and remanded to the district court.

* * *

THOMPSON, JUDGE (concurring in part, dissenting in part).

The alleged lease liability in this case clearly is a community debt. The general rule is that upon dissolution of the marriage, the former spouses are individually liable for the former community's debt, but only as to "property held by either spouse which was formerly the couple's community property and which is otherwise subject to execution." Howev-

---

6. "The expenses of the family and the education of the children, including stepchildren, are chargeable upon the property of both husband and wife, or either of them, and they may be sued jointly or separately." RCW 26.16.205.

7. The district court also misapplied the statute of limitations found in Washington's "marital bankruptcy" statute, RCW 26.16.200. This statute provides that any separately incurred antenuptial debt must be reduced to judgment within three years of the marriage of the parties. The lease extension here was signed after the parties were married and does not come under the classification of an antenuptial debt.

er, a creditor's recovery in this circumstance "is limited to the net community equity at the time of dissolution of the marriage."

In this case, since the community has been dissolved, the creditor sought to hold Ms. Snyder–Entel liable *individually*. The creditor hopes to satisfy the judgment against Ms. Snyder–Entel's individual property that was not a part of the former community's net equity at the time of the dissolution, such as her current earnings.

As noted in the majority opinion, a former spouse may be liable individually under * * * the family expense doctrine. Under this statute, a community debt for a family expense may be enforced against the separate property of either spouse, even if that spouse did not individually incur the debt. Rent of the family's residence is a family expense.

* * * No cases in Washington have addressed the issue presented in this case: expenses for a dwelling after the family has moved.

Lease liability in these circumstances should not be a family expense. After moving from the apartment the Entel family certainly resided elsewhere; thus, under the majority opinion, the costs of maintaining *two* dwellings would be family expenses * * *, even though the family did not actually reside in one of the dwellings during the period at issue. Rental expense for a dwelling in which the family did not reside should not be a family expense.

Here the alleged liability is purely contractual, based on an agreement Ms. Snyder–Entel did not sign. As the creditor points out, both spouses are competent to manage and control the community's property. Therefore, the community is liable for the contractual debts incurred by either spouse on behalf of the community. However, the liability in this circumstance is to the *community*, not to the individual spouse. * * * [T]he creditor's judgment should be limited to the former community's net equity at the time of the dissolution.

I agree the case must be remanded, but I would not permit the creditor to obtain a judgment against Ms. Snyder–Entel's current assets that were not part of the former community's net equity at the time of the dissolution.

NOTES AND QUESTIONS

1. *Should separate property be available to pay marital obligations after the marriage ends?* In most jurisdictions, each spouse's obligation for debts incurred by the other or jointly during marriage is limited to the extent of former marital property; only the spouse who incurred the liability may be forced to pay an obligation from separate funds. *In re Marriage of Jorgenson*, 143 P.3d 1169, 1172 (Colo. Ct. App. 2006).

2. *May marital funds be used to pay joint obligations undertaken with respect to separate property?* If the marriage has benefited from the separate property, it is appropriate to use marital funds to repay joint debts connected

to the property. For example, in *In re Marriage of Crook*, 813 N.E.2d 198 (Ill. 2004), throughout their 33–year marriage, the couple lived in a house on a farm that the wife had inherited from her family and the husband farmed the land. They jointly took out a bank loan to improve the building in which they stored farm equipment. When the husband stopped farming and they sold farm equipment, they placed about $50,000 of the proceeds in their joint bank account. After the husband filed for divorce, the wife used $40,000 of the funds in the joint account to pay down the bank loan. The trial court awarded the farm to the wife as her separate property and ordered her to repay the marital estate the $40,000. The Supreme Court of Illinois, however, held that the wife was not required to repay the money to the marital estate. It reasoned that the funds had been used to pay a *"marital* debt" since the marital estate had "reaped the benefit of [the wife's] nonmarital contributions in providing the marital estate with a home, free of rent or mortgage payments, and the buildings necessary to sustain a successful farming operation for most of the marriage." *Id.* at 207.

G. THE NEW PROPERTY

Traditionally, parties to a divorce claimed only tangible property, following Blackstone's definition of property ownership as the "definite right of use, control and disposition which one may lawfully exercise over particular things or objects." William Blackstone, 2 Commentaries *2. Today, according to Professor J. Thomas Oldham:

> There is great confusion in family law regarding the appropriate analysis for determining the existence of property. * * *

> The confusion * * * stems from the dramatic changes that have occurred in the types of rights that are valuable.

> * * *

> * * * [A]n increasing number of the valuable rights held by middle class individuals relate to things other than tangible property. For example, a person's career * * *[is] quite valuable to that person. * * * Other examples [include] * * * certain fringe benefits relating to a job, such as seniority rights, stock options, pension rights, union membership, and paid vacation and sick leave time.

> These rights are all valuable, but does that mean they are all 'property' which should be valued and divided at divorce? Few state divorce statutes define what property means in this context. * * *

> Many divorce courts have been reluctant to expand the scope of 'property' to include intangible rights. * * *

> * * *

> [Some] states have developed a broader concept of what constitutes divisible property. * * * For example, courts have concluded that increased earning capacity, a possible future inheritance, a contingent

trust interest, a professional degree, a professional license, and professional goodwill all are divisible property. * * *

Other states have accepted by statute a broader definition of property. For example, the West Virginia statute provides that "marital property" includes "every valuable right and interest, corporeal or incorporeal, tangible or intangible."

J. Thomas Oldham, Divorce, Separation and the Distribution of Property § 5.02 (2005).

Valuation of the new property may prove particularly complicated, especially when the value of the property received in compensation for work performed during the marriage may not become clear until sometime in the future. Stock options, discussed in the notes following the next case, are a classic example. Because the resolution of all issues related to distribution is final and not subject to modification after the divorce is granted, the parties and the court must engage in a delicate balancing act to neither overstate nor understate the future potential of such holdings in a manner that would be unjust to either party.

The next case illustrates the importance of what social scientists call "human capital," which includes the combination of education, opportunity and enhanced earning potential.

1. PROFESSIONAL LICENSES, PROFESSIONAL DEGREES AND FUTURE EARNING CAPACITY

In 1985, New York's highest court became the first in the nation to treat a professional license as a marital asset. *O'Brien* v. *O'Brien*, 489 N.E.2d 712 (N.Y. 1985). In *Holterman*, the case excerpted below, the highest court in New York revisits the *O'Brien* doctrine. As the dissent notes, although *O'Brien* received a lot of attention, not a single other state followed New York's lead. As you read *Holterman*, consider whether New York's approach or the approach taken by other states seems more equitable, and whether there may be other ways to reach similar results.

HOLTERMAN v. HOLTERMAN

Court of Appeals of New York, 2004.
814 N.E.2d 765.

GRAFFEO, J.

* * *

I.

Plaintiff Amy Holterman (wife) and defendant Robert Holterman (husband) were married in 1981. At the time of the parties' marriage, husband was a third-year student at a medical school in Philadelphia. Wife, who had a Master's degree in business administration, was employed full time as a program analyst and her income contributed to the support of the household. Husband graduated from medical school in 1983 and obtained his license to practice medicine the following year. The parties then moved to another locale in Pennsylvania where husband began a three-year medical residency program. Shortly thereafter, wife began experiencing significant health problems and was eventually diagnosed with chronic fatigue syndrome and fibromyalgia. The parties agreed that wife would become a homemaker due, in part, to her chronic health problems. Their first child was born in 1985 and a second child was born in 1991.

Husband continued to advance his professional credentials, becoming board-certified in emergency medicine in 1987. From 1986 to 1990 he was employed as an attending staff physician at a hospital. Once husband received his license to practice medicine in New York, the family moved to Albany. Since that time, husband has been an emergency room physician at a hospital, earning a salary of $181,837 in 2000.

After 19 years of marriage, wife commenced an action for divorce in September 2000. * * * [T]he parties entered into a stipulation of joint custody of their two children with wife having primary physical custody. Following the bench trial of this action, * * * [t]he court dissolved the marriage based on husband's constructive abandonment of wife; awarded wife maintenance of $35,000 per year for five years and $20,000 per year thereafter for the remainder of her life; determined that wife was entitled to $214,200 as her equitable share of husband's enhanced earnings premised on his medical license; ordered husband to pay child support for their two children in the amount of $34,875.65 annually; distributed the marital property, including equally dividing $242,815.39 in retirement and investment accounts; gave wife title and possession of the marital residence and set husband's half share of the parties' equity in the marital home at $29,268.48; obligated wife to pay the mortgage, home equity loan payments and taxes on the residence (totaling about $26,500 per year); required husband to maintain certain health and life insurance policies for the benefit of wife and the children; divided equally a tax refund check and a mortgage escrow refund check; ordered husband to reimburse wife for certain expenses pertaining to the children; and directed husband to contribute $20,894 toward wife's counsel and expert fees.

The Appellate Division affirmed * * * [and modified the husband's obligation to maintain life insurance policies with his wife as beneficiary.]

II.

On appeal, husband raises several challenges relating to the equitable distribution of the value of his medical license * * *. Supreme Court and the Appellate Division determined that the marital portion of husband's medical license had a present-day value of $612,000 in accordance with testimony presented by wife's expert, a certified public accountant. Husband did not challenge the methodology employed by the expert or the economic value of the license itself. In fact, he did not present any expert testimony. The court determined that wife was entitled to 35% of the value of husband's enhanced earning capacity as a licensed physician, which amounted to $214,200. The court then deducted $29,268.48 from that figure, representing the credit due husband for the conveyance of his interest in the marital residence, thereby establishing a net distributive award of $184,931.52 owed to wife. Husband was directed to pay the award in monthly installments over a 15–year period, at six percent interest per annum from the date of commencement of the action, resulting in annual payments of $21,288. Husband contends that Supreme Court abused its discretion by awarding wife 35% of the marital portion of the enhanced earning capacity derived from his medical license and asserts that her share should be reduced to no more than 10%. We disagree.

In recognizing marriage as an economic partnership, the Domestic Relations Law mandates that the equitable distribution of marital assets be based on the circumstances of the particular case and directs the trial court to consider a number of statutory factors listed in Domestic Relations Law § 236. These factors encompass the income and property of each party at the time of marriage and at the time of commencement of the divorce action, the duration of the marriage, the age and health of the parties, any maintenance award, and the non-titled spouse's direct or indirect contributions to the marriage, including "services as a spouse, parent, wage earner and homemaker."

As this Court declared in *O'Brien v. O'Brien,* 489 N.E.2d 712 [(N.Y. 1985)], these considerations are particularly relevant when evaluating the parties' respective contributions to the attainment of a professional license by one spouse. In *O'Brien,* we held that a professional license is marital property subject to equitable distribution. In the 19 years since we adopted the *O'Brien* rule, we have adhered to the principle that both parties in a matrimonial action are entitled to fundamental fairness in the allocation of marital assets, and that the economic and noneconomic contributions of each spouse are to be taken into account. Trial courts that examine the statutory factors are granted substantial discretion in determining the extent to which the distribution of marital property, including enhanced earnings attributable to a professional license, will be equitable. Absent an abuse of discretion, this Court may not disturb the trial court's award.

Here, Supreme Court issued a careful, comprehensive decision addressing all relevant factors, including the parties' 19–year marriage, wife's employment and monetary contributions during husband's final two years of medical school, the parties' mutual decision that wife would forgo her career to take care of the children and home, the gross disparity in the parties' current and probable future incomes, the fact that husband was 44 years of age and wife was 46 years of age at the time of trial and husband's good health in contrast to wife's chronic health difficulties. In light of these considerations, particularly wife's economic and noneconomic contributions to husband's acquisition of his medical license and subsequent career, the termination of wife's career to raise the parties' two children and maintain the marital household, wife's absence from the job market for more than 17 years, the length of the marriage and wife's long-term health problems, we cannot conclude that Supreme Court abused its discretion in awarding wife 35% as her marital portion of husband's enhanced earning capacity as a physician practicing medicine in New York.

* * *

Accordingly, the order of the Appellate Division should be affirmed, with costs.

R.S. SMITH, J. (dissenting).

I think the decision of Supreme Court, which the Appellate Division affirmed, is flawed * * *. * * * [I]t applies our decision in *O'Brien v. O'Brien,* on facts totally opposite, in material respects, to the facts of *O'Brien* itself * * *. * * * I dissent from the majority's decision to affirm.

* * *

* * * [T]his is not a case where one party made sacrifices to put the other through school, but was prevented by divorce from enjoying the resulting benefits. The benefits of the sacrifices both parties made have been enjoyed by both of them for more than a decade, and are fully reflected in defendant's current income.

Supreme Court nevertheless felt compelled to apply our decision in *O'Brien,* which held that a medical license is an "asset" subject to equitable distribution. It did this by dividing defendant's $180,000 income into an "asset" portion and an "income" portion, and awarding plaintiff a percentage of both. In principle, this was a largely useless but harmless exercise. * * * [W]e should hold that the application of *O'Brien* is restricted to cases where its application produces some significant benefit.

The prototype of such a case is *O'Brien* itself. Michael and Loretta O'Brien were married for nine years. At the beginning of the marriage, he had not yet obtained his bachelor's degree. During the marriage, he obtained that degree, took premedical courses, went to medical school, completed his internship and obtained a license to practice medicine. His wife helped him to become a doctor by giving up her own opportunity to obtain a professional certification, working in various jobs and contributing her earnings to their joint expenses. Two months after getting his license, he began an action for a divorce. While his income at that moment was apparently meager, his medical license had created sufficient "enhanced earning potential" that an expert was able to value the license at $472,000.

O'Brien, in short, presented what the Appellate Division in that case called "the classical 'student-spouse, working-spouse' syndrome"—a situation which,* * * had been called "almost a cliché." This is a situation with which courts and commentators have struggled both before and since the *O'Brien* decision. Our solution in *O'Brien* was to hold that the medical license constituted "marital property," and that a portion of its value could be paid to Loretta O'Brien as a distributive award.

In *O'Brien* we became the first state court of last resort to hold that a professional license is marital property, though the Supreme Court of Iowa had previously come close to doing so (*In re Marriage of Horstmann,* 263 N.W.2d 885 [(Iowa 1978)]). Some may have hoped that *O'Brien* would begin a trend; if so, those hopes have been disappointed. In 19 years, not one other state has adopted the *O'Brien* rule, and Iowa seems to have backed away (*In re Marriage of Francis,* 442 N.W.2d 59 [(Iowa 1989)]). In the other 49 states, a professional license is not itself an asset subject to equitable distribution, although in many states the enhanced earning capacity reflected by a license may be considered in awarding alimony or maintenance, or in distributing other assets.

* * *

* * * I do not suggest that we should now overrule *O'Brien*. The potential for injustice in the "student-spouse/working-spouse" syndrome is very real, and *O'Brien* is an attempt to remedy it; it is an imperfect remedy, but no remedy would be perfect. I make now the more modest suggestion that *O'Brien* be applied only in those situations where there is a problem for *O'Brien* to remedy * * *.

* * *

[In addition,] a multiyear equitable distribution under *O'Brien,* unlike an award of maintenance, does not cease at the recipient's death or remarriage. * * * In this case, for example, if the parties had remained married, and plaintiff had happened to predecease defendant, her estate would have had no claim on his medical license, or the income derived from it. I do not see why divorce should change that. * * *

Finally, it may be said that in characterizing annual payments to an ex-spouse as maintenance rather than a distributive award, the courts deny the recipient's status as "partner." The theory is that, to use this case as an example, plaintiff's contributions to defendant's attainment of his medical license make her equitably a 35% partner in the marital portion of that asset, and thus it is symbolically wrong to award her 35% of his income only as maintenance, rather than as something she owns. What is theoretically right or wrong in this area is a difficult, almost a metaphysical, question. * * *

For all these reasons, I believe that *O'Brien* should be limited to cases involving the "student-spouse/working-spouse" syndrome, or some reasonably analogous situation. *O'Brien* should not be used where, as here, the enhanced earning capacity associated with the professional license is already fully reflected in the license holder's earnings.

* * *

NOTES AND QUESTIONS

1. *Enhanced earning capacity.* No other state has fully followed New York's lead in the arena of professional education and licenses. However, a few states will consider the enhanced earning capacity that flows from professional training. For example, the California statute expressly provides that professional education, training and earning capacity are separate property but that statute also allows reimbursement of community funds used to support that education. Enhanced earning capacity may also be considered in awarding alimony. The California code further instructs trial courts to consider whether the standard of living of the marital estate has already benefited from one spouse's professional training. Cal. Fam. Code § 2641 (West 2004).

2. *Other approaches designed to serve similar goals.* Oregon law provides that the present value of enhanced earning capacity arising during the marriage may be divided at dissolution if the other spouse contributed substantially to the enhancement. Or. Rev. Stat. Ann. § 107.105(1)(f) (West 2005). Pennsylvania courts use the concept of "equitable reimbursement" to compensate "a spouse for his or her contribution to the marriage where the marital assets are insufficient to do so," often through monthly installment payments that are distinguishable from alimony. *See, e.g., Schenk v. Schenk,* 880 A.2d 633, 640 (Pa. Super. Ct. 2005). The concept is appropriately applied where one spouse supports the other through graduate training that enhances earning capacity and the couple separates before jointly reaping the benefits of the degree. *Id.*

3. *Tax implications.* Since the goal in an equitable distribution regime is equity between the two spouses, the governing law contemplates that divorcing parties will take tax consequences into account when structuring the division of assets. The *Holterman* dissent notes that whether a payment is described as distribution or maintenance (discussed in Chapter 10) may have serious financial implications. The spouse who owes money to the other is normally the higher earner, and is in a higher tax bracket. Distribution of assets does not appear as a transfer on either spouse's tax return, because the property already belongs to both of them. The sole exception is that where assets must be sold to effect the division of marital property, the proceeds of the sale may be subject to capital gains tax, or may even be treated as income if the couple has not owned the property long enough to treat the increase in value as a capital gain. In contrast, maintenance payments may be deducted from the payor's gross income, and count as income to the recipient for tax purposes.

4. *Attorney's fees—who pays?* The court ordered Dr. Holterman to pay a portion of his wife's attorney's fees. In civil litigation, each party generally is liable for his or her own attorney's fees. *See, e.g., In re Marriage of Michel,* 142 S.W.3d 912 (Mo. Ct. App. 2004). But in divorce actions courts have equitable powers to order that one party pay the spouse's attorney's fees. The trial court will not be reversed except for abuse of discretion. In *Yount v. Yount,* 91 S.W.3d 777 (Tenn. Ct. App. 2002), the court of appeals upheld the trial court's order requiring the husband to pay the wife's legal bills. The court reasoned that such orders are:

* * * considered most appropriate where the final decree of divorce does not provide the obligee spouse with a source of funds, such as from property division or alimony in solido, with which to pay his or her attorney. * * *

In the present case, there was no award of alimony * * * and Mr. Yount disposed of most of the marital property prior to the divorce. While it appears that Ms. Yount would not find it easy to pay her attorney, Mr. Yount has demonstrated that he has the ability to produce considerable sums of money when he is sufficiently motivated. * * *

Id. at 783.

An award of attorney's fees is entrusted to the discretion of the trial court, but the court must determine whether the fees requested are reasonable. *Arnal v. Arnal*, 609 S.E.2d 821 (S.C. Ct. App. 2005). Many states provide for awards of attorney's fees by statute in limited circumstances. *E.g.,* Tex. Fam. Code Ann. § 106.002 (Vernon 2004 & 2008 Supp.); Fla. Stat. Ann. § 61.16 (West 2005). These awards are predominantly made to ensure that each party has equitable access to counsel. *See, e.g., Levy v. Levy*, 900 So.2d 737 (Fla. Dist. Ct. App. 2005).

In practice, at separation many affluent couples negotiate an agreement that the party with greater access to assets will pay the other party's attorney's fees. The other party's lawyer may accept or continue the representation, and accept such payment, only where the lawyer "determines that there will be no interference with the lawyer's independent professional judgment and there is informed consent from the client." Model Rules of Prof'l Conduct, R. 1.8(f), cmt. 11 (2002); *see also* Model Rules of Prof'l Conduct, R. 5.4(c) (2002) ("A lawyer shall not permit a person who * * * pays the lawyer to render legal services for another to direct or regulate the lawyer's professional judgment in rendering such legal services.").

5. *Life insurance.* Courts have the equitable power in marital cases to order obligors to guarantee satisfaction of their obligations by retaining or procuring life insurance. Courts tend to issue such orders where transfer of assets is structured to take place gradually, or where there is reason to suspect that the former spouse will prove recalcitrant. In *Holterman*, for example, the court required the husband to maintain a $500,000 life insurance policy with his wife as primary beneficiary until his obligations to pay the distributive award, maintenance and child support were satisfied in full or until the existing 20–year term life insurance policy expired, whichever occurred first. The court further ordered Dr. Holterman to maintain $300,000 in life insurance through his employer until he had completed his payment obligations to his wife.

6. *Mechanics and structure of distribution.* As *Holterman* illustrates, when large sums of money are redistributed at divorce, parties may agree to, or the court may order, a payment schedule that stretches out over a number of years. Courts may be very specific when ordering such schedules. In *In re Hayes*, 60 P.3d 431 (Mont. 2002), for example, the court upheld a disproportionate distribution of the marital estate in which the disabled husband received the bulk of the marital assets. The trial court specifically ordered:

the immediate sale of various assets, including [two real properties consisting of commercial real estate even though neither party had requested that the properties be sold], and certain life insurance policies. The Order also provided that, in the event the parties could not agree on a reasonable sales price for the properties, the [court] would set a price which would be reduced 5 percent monthly until they sold. The court ordered that the net proceeds from the sale of these assets be placed into an account and applied against the marital estate's debts. * * * [A]fter the marital debts were satisfied, [the wife] was to receive a $100,000 cash payment 'as partial adjustment for the property distributed to [the husband after which the wife would receive 75% of whatever remained].'

Id. at 433. The reviewing court not only upheld the detailed order, but expressly found that it was not an abuse of discretion for the trial court to ensure that the party in ill health received his share of the distribution as soon as possible, and that the healthy, self-supporting spouse received hers after all other financial matters were resolved. *Id.* at 435.

When distribution is to be paid in installments, it is essential that the obligation be secured. In *Winters v. Patel*, 2005 WL 3046536 (3d Cir. Nov. 14, 2005), the Third Circuit affirmed a jury verdict finding that an attorney committed malpractice when he failed to take the necessary steps to secure a former husband's obligations to his ex-wife, the attorney's client. The parties had agreed, and the court had ordered, that the husband would transfer $143,000 in marital assets to his wife after the divorce in four installments. The parties' agreement contemplated that the husband's retirement plan would secure the obligation, and that the husband would maintain a life insurance policy for the benefit of his ex-wife until he had completed the payments. The wife's attorney never perfected either of the guarantees. When the former husband died unexpectedly without having completed his payments, his current wife successfully claimed both his life insurance benefits and the proceeds of his pension plan. A jury ordered the former wife's attorney to pay her nearly $300,000 in compensatory damages, including attorney's fees for the malpractice action.

A NOTE ON OTHER COMMON FORMS OF "NEW PROPERTY"

Spouses make claims on many forms of "new property", and jurisdictions differ on the treatment of some of them. At divorce many couples and courts consider claims to property that the law once uniformly deemed separate, including pension rights, stock options, and business goodwill. Lottery winnings also arise in a surprising number of cases, given the odds against winning a substantial sum. *See* ALI, Principles of the Law of Family Dissolution: Analysis and Recommendations § 4.03 (2002).

a. *Pension plans.* Next to the marital home, a pension plan is generally a couple's most valuable asset. Every jurisdiction treats an employer-sponsored retirement plan as a marital asset. *See, e.g., Coggin v. Coggin*, 837 So.2d 772, 775 (Miss. Ct. App. 2003). However, only 52% of all American families have a retirement account of any sort. Elizabeth Warren & Amelia Warren Tiyagi, The Two–Income Trap: Why Middle–Class Parents Are Going Broke 208 n.122 (2005).

Most traditional pension plans raise complex valuation issues because their future value is normally not easy to predict from their present value. For example, the pension may or may not have vested or matured at the date of dissolution. "Vesting" means that the employee is entitled to retain plan benefits even if employment is terminated. Pension plans "mature" when the employee reaches retirement age and can reap the benefits. Even if a plan has neither vested nor matured, it is subject to valuation and distribution. Sometimes pension plans decline in value due to market fluctuation over time. *See Grecian v. Grecian*, 97 P.3d 468 (Idaho Ct. App. 2004) (holding that where the divorce decree awarded wife 50% of the value of the husband's 401K plan on the date of divorce, husband bore the entire loss when the account declined in value). Some retirement plans are "defined benefit" pension plans, in which the monthly benefits payable to an employee at retirement are generally based on a formula that reflects factors including the length of the employee's service and his or her salary level. Whether the retirement plan is a "defined contribution" plan, based on individual contributions (like a 401(k) plan), or is a defined benefit plan, the ultimate value of the retirement package may change based on choices the employed spouse makes after divorce.

Federal law protects the claims of former spouses to the proportion of the private pension awarded to them under the divorce decree. The Employment Retirement Income Security Act of 1974 (ERISA), 29 U.S.C. §§ 1001–1461 (2006), regulates most private employer-sponsored retirement plans. ERISA permits state courts to divide pension benefits along with other marital assets at divorce and facilitates enforcement by creating qualified domestic relations orders (QDROs), which recognize the rights of a person other than the plan beneficiary, often called an "alternate payee," to receive benefits under the plan " 'if and when the benefits are actually received.' " *Sampson v. Sampson*, 816 N.E.2d 999, 1005 n.12 (Mass. App. Ct. 2004) (internal citations omitted). A QDRO authorizes the pension administrator either to segregate a portion of the participant's account into a separate account exclusively for the former spouse or to pay a percentage or lump-sum portion of the benefits directly to the recipient former spouse; without a court-approved QDRO, the administrator cannot divide the participant's interest. The failure to submit properly prepared and executed QDROs first to the court and then to the plan administrator creates frequent segregation, distribution and enforcement problems.

Federal retirement benefits are treated under separate legislation, but also allow assignment of a proportion of the benefit pursuant to a divorce decree. *See, e.g.*, 5 U.S.C. § 8445 (2006) (providing rights to former spouses under the Federal Employees' Retirement System); 10 U.S.C. § 1408 (2006) (military retirement pensions); 45 U.S.C. § 231a (2000) (amending the Railroad Retirement Act).

Social Security benefits, however, may not be assigned. 42 U.S.C. § 407(a) (2000). Courts are divided as to whether a spouse's expectations of Social Security benefits may be taken into account when crafting an equitable distribution. *See In re Marriage of Crook*, 813 N.E.2d 198, 202, 205 (Ill. 2004) (summarizing the split and holding that Social Security benefits may not be used to offset unequal marital distribution because " '[c]alling a duck a horse does not change the fact that it is still a duck' ").

b. *Stock options.* Stock options (an employee's right to purchase shares of the employer's stock in the future at a price designated today) are an increasingly important part of many compensation packages. *See* Tracy A. Thomas, *The New Marital Property of Employee Stock Options*, 35 Fam. L.Q. 497 (2001) (observing that stock options are "[o]ne of the most valuable assets in a dissolution case today"). Stock options are marital property to the extent that they constitute deferred compensation for work performed during the marriage. *Fisher v. Fisher*, 769 A.2d 1165, 1168 (Pa. 2001). Like pension plans, the present value of stock options that have not yet matured is hard to estimate and calls for expert calculations. *See* David S. Rosettenstein, *Options on Divorce: Taxation, Compensation Accountability, and the Need for Holistic Solutions*, 37 Fam. L.Q. 203 (2003). A stock option is a mere expectancy, because if the stock price declines, the employee may decline to exercise his or her option to purchase the stock. Nonetheless, several valuation methods are possible, including calculation of a present value, deferred distribution, or transfer of the options themselves if the employer permits such transfer. In *In re Marriage of Langham*, 106 P.3d 212 (Wash. 2005), the court held that the husband's unauthorized sale of Microsoft stock options reserved for the wife in the dissolution order at a lower price than she might have received at a later date wrongfully deprived the wife of her property. The court ordered the husband to compensate his former wife by paying her the difference between the value of the stock on the date he first exercised his options and the lower value on the date of sale.

c. *Business goodwill and other small business issues.* The difficulty of valuing a closely held business is one of the most intractable problems concerning property in divorce cases. *Sampson v. Sampson*, 816 N.E.2d 999, 1006 n.14 (Mass. App. Ct. 2004). Closely held businesses may depend primarily on the principals' abilities, and therefore may be worth far more than their book value. This gap between book value and actual value is known as "goodwill."

Business goodwill is generally regarded as a divisible marital asset, but it is difficult to measure with any precision. "In valuing the business, the trial court must consider whether goodwill that is included within the total value of a business enterprise is personal to one spouse. * * * [W]e distinguish between enterprise goodwill, which is divisible property, and personal goodwill, which is excluded from the marital estate. Enterprise goodwill is based on the intangible, but generally marketable, existence in a business of established relations with employees, customers and suppliers, and may include factors such as * * * reputation. * * * On the other hand, personal goodwill is goodwill that is based on the personal attributes of the individual." *DeSalle v. Gentry*, 818 N.E.2d 40, 47 (Ind. Ct. App. 2004). The two concepts are frequently entwined. For example, in *Gentry*, the couple owned and jointly operated an antique toy business, which they promoted at toy show venues across the country. The couple owned the business in corporate form, with the wife holding 51% of the stock. When the trial court divided the company as a marital asset, it awarded the wife exclusive rights to the most profitable toy show venues. An appellate court reversed, reasoning that access to the venues amounted to "rights in future earnings" which are not marital property subject to division, but personal to the individual. *Id.*

Owners of small businesses frequently use the businesses to acquire property for personal use, creating additional valuation problems. For example, in *Gohl v. Gohl*, 700 N.W.2d 625 (Neb. Ct. App. 2005), the couple owned Golight, a small business which had recently won a patent infringement suit against Wal–Mart. Because Wal–Mart was appealing that decision at the time of the divorce hearing, the ultimate value of Golight hinged on the still-unknown outcome of the litigation. After the couple separated, Golight provided the husband with a car and housing. The husband was also a partner in a second business, Gohl Brothers, engaged in farming and oil leases. Gohl Brothers owned the marital home. Gohl Brothers obviously was not a party to the divorce litigation, and thus was beyond the court's jurisdiction. The court awarded the marital home to the wife and ordered the husband to convince the partnership to deliver the marital home to the wife or to pay her an additional sum equal to the value of the home. The partnership ultimately "consent[ed]" to transfer the home to the wife. *Id.* at 628–30.

Adding to the complexity, Golight owned a bed-and-breakfast property known as Waterfjord House valued at $700,000, which had produced an income of only $16,000 in its most profitable year. After the separation, the husband spent hundreds of thousands of dollars of Golight funds renovating Waterfjord House. Describing Waterfjord House as "a voracious consumer of Golight's capital," an appellate court remanded for consideration of "whether the expenditures in the Waterfjord House were merely a sham to obscure the financial status of Golight by artificially and unreasonably inflating its debt load, and thereby obscuring its profitability and valuation." *Id.* at 637.

d. *Shares in closely-held corporations.* Many small businesses are formed as corporations order to receive tax advantages and protect the owners from personal liability in the event of law suits. When the owners of shares in these corporations divorce, their spouses frequently claim a right to a portion of the company's value, especially where the corporation is owned by the shareholder's family. In a typical case, Theresa Joynt appealed the trial court's decision to treat as separate property the accumulated but undistributed profits of a family-held corporation in which her husband Michael, the corporation's president, owned 33% of the shares. The court affirmed the treatment of the property as separate because Michael did not own a controlling interest (though he would after his father's death) and did not have the unilateral power to distribute the profits. Michael received a salary and annual bonuses for serving as president, compensation which benefited the marital unit. The retained earnings were deemed part of the company's assets, not property which partially belonged to Michael personally. *In re Marriage of Joynt*, 874 N.E.2d 916 (Ill. App. Ct. 2007). How important is it that the court determine whether the compensation Michael received met industry standards? What if the family owned a controlling share of a publicly-traded company?

e. *Personal injury: disability pensions and tort recoveries.* Whether recoveries for personal injuries are considered marital property depends on how the recoveries are characterized. To the extent that the award is for pain and suffering, it is the personal property of the individual who suffered the injury.

See Shearer v. Shearer, 700 N.W.2d 580 (Neb. 2005). However, an award for economic losses becomes marital property. Awards and compensation for loss of consortium are generally found to be the separate property of the uninjured spouse. In *Conrad v. Conrad*, 612 S.E.2d 772 (W. Va. 2005), the court analyzed various approaches to disability insurance benefits. Many states, it found, consider the benefits marital, absent a statute to the contrary.[4] Other states regard private disability benefits as marital if the policy premiums were purchased with marital funds or the benefits were obtained as compensation for past services as part of employment benefits. Still other jurisdictions regard all disability payments as separate property because the payments are intended to replace future earnings. *Conrad* declined to adopt a *per se* rule, but held that treatment should be based on evidence of the parties' intent and other case-by-case factual determinations. *Id.* at 776–77 (following *Metz v. Metz*, 61 P.3d 383 (Wyo. 2003)).

f. *Lotteries.* It is settled law that "a lottery prize won during a marriage is generally considered property acquired during a marriage subject to equitable distribution * * *." *Parker v. Parker*, 773 N.Y.S.2d 518, 521 (Sup. Ct. 2003). However, courts may engage in the same sort of analysis that applies to other kinds of property. For example, they may examine whether the ticket was purchased with marital or separate funds, whether the proceeds were acquired actively or passively, and what would be "equitable." *See, e.g., Noel v. Noel*, 884 So.2d 615 (La. Ct. App. 2004); *Ware v. Ware*, 748 A.2d 1031 (Md. Ct. Spec. App. 2000).

PROBLEM 9–2

Tom and Nancy married in 1987, and live in an equitable distribution state. They separated in 1989, but never filed for divorce. They continued to have intermittent contact with one another, but generally lived separate lives, with neither spouse contributing financially to the other. In 2001, Tom filed for divorce, but before the divorce was finalized, he won $2.9 million in the lottery. At the divorce hearing, Nancy argues that the winnings are marital property and should be shared equally. You are the judge. How will you analyze Nancy's claim? How will you rule?

SECTION 3: WHAT DISTRIBUTION IS EQUITABLE?

During the era when only fault-based grounds justified divorce, fault was also the key to distributing assets and awarding alimony. That is no longer the case. When the National Conference of Commissioners of Uniform State Laws (NCCUSL) was established in 1892, it identified the law of marriage and divorce as one of two areas clearly appropriate for development of uniform laws. However, NCCUSL did not issue a report on marriage and divorce until 1970. When it did so, it advocated reform of the entire conceptual culture from fault to no-fault, and urged that states

---

4. The primary statute is 38 U.S.C. § 5301 (2000), which provides that disability benefits to veterans shall not be assignable.

make all of the ancillary changes such rethinking required. To that end, the committee that drafted the Uniform Marriage and Divorce Act (UMDA) concluded that the "distribution of property upon the termination of a marriage should be treated, as nearly as possible, like the distribution of assets incident to the dissolution of a partnership." UMDA prefatory note, 9A U.L.A. (1973). As you have observed in your readings for this course, the UMDA is the basis for much contemporary family law. The UMDA expressly states that one of its purposes is to "make reasonable provision for spouse and minor children during and after litigation." *Id.* § 102(5), 9A U.L.A. (1998).

By statute or common law, each state provides a list of factors for trial courts to consider when dividing property at divorce. The factors are not assigned weight, and some factors may conflict with others in particular cases. For example, a court may be required to evaluate each spouse's need for post-marital support as well as each spouse's contribution to the marital estate. One spouse may have great need for support, but may not have made any contribution to the marital estate. Which factor is more important? One expert has concluded that legislatures intentionally enact "vague and ambiguous" property division statutes "because it is impossible to set forth one definite set of property division principles that should be applied to all marriages." J. Thomas Oldham, Divorce, Separation, and the Distribution of Property § 13.02[1] (2005).

The theory behind the award of maintenance differs from the partnership notion that supports equitable distribution of property, but courts are generally instructed to consider the relationship between property distribution and the need for continuing maintenance. *See, e.g.*, Vt. Stat. Ann. tit. 15, § 751(b) (2002). "The two forms of relief are simply separate but closely intertwined ways of getting to the same result." *Ware v. Ware*, 748 A.2d 1031, 1048 (Md. Ct. Spec. App. 2000). "All awards to a spouse must be considered together to decide if they are equitable and fair." *Coggin v. Coggin*, 837 So.2d 772, 775 (Miss. Ct. App. 2003).

Reliance on property distribution is favored because decisions regarding distribution, unlike alimony, are final and eliminate the need for continuing interaction between former spouses. *In re Marriage of Selinger*, 814 N.E.2d 152 (Ill. App. Ct. 2004). As discussed in the beginning of this Chapter, approaches to distribution include "equal" division under a few community property regimes, and "equitable distribution" in the common law states. Some equitable distribution states require a fair and equitable distribution, while others mandate equal division or instruct courts to begin with a rebuttable assumption that property should be distributed equally.

Pennsylvania's equitable distribution statute, which follows, is representative.

Title 23, Section 3502 of the Pennsylvania Consolidated Statutes

(a) General rule.—Upon the request of either party in an action for divorce or annulment, the court shall equitably divide, distribute or assign, in kind or otherwise, the marital property between the parties without regard to marital misconduct in such percentages and in such manner as the court deems just, after considering all relevant factors. The court may consider each marital asset or group of assets independently and apply a different percentage to each marital asset or group of assets. Factors which are relevant to the equitable division of marital property include the following:

(1) The length of the marriage.

(2) Any prior marriage of either party.

(3) The age, health, station, amount and sources of income, vocational skills, employability, estate, liabilities and needs of each of the parties.

(4) The contribution by one party to the education, training or increased earning power of the other party.

(5) The opportunity of each party for future acquisitions of capital assets and income.

(6) The sources of income of both parties, including, but not limited to, medical, retirement, insurance or other benefits.

(7) The contribution or dissipation of each party in the acquisition, preservation, depreciation or appreciation of the marital property, including the contribution of a party as homemaker.

(8) The value of the property set apart to each party.

(9) The standard of living of the parties established during the marriage.

(10) The economic circumstances of each party, including Federal, State and local tax ramifications, at the time the division of property is to become effective.

(10.1) The Federal, State and local tax ramifications associated with each asset to be divided, distributed or assigned, which ramifications needs not be immediate or and certain.

(10.2) The expense of sale, transfer or liquidation associated with a particular asset, which expense need not be immediate and certain.

(11) Whether the party will be serving as the custodian of any dependent minor children.

23 Pa. Cons. Stat. Ann. § 3502(a) (West 2001 & 2008 Supp.).

The following opinion considers whether an uneven division of marital assets is equitable. Massachusetts is a common law, kitchen sink jurisdiction that requires the court to reach an equitable result in distributing property. In reading the opinion below, consider how much discretion the trial court has in crafting an equitable distribution, the extent to which the court considered whether property was marital notwithstanding the kitchen sink statute, and what factors seem to have influenced the trial court in dividing the assets.

KETTERLE v. KETTERLE

Appeals Court of Massachusetts, 2004.
814 N.E.2d 385.

KAFKER, J.

Central to this dispute about the division of marital assets is the husband's 2001 Nobel Prize for Physics.[1] The judge found that winning the Nobel Prize identified the husband as a superstar in the scientific and academic universe, and she projected his having substantial ability to acquire future income and assets. Relying heavily on this factor, she assigned the wife a greater percentage of the existing marital assets.

The husband has appealed, claiming (1) the wife received a disproportionate share of the assets, (2) the $83,000 the judge assigned to the husband out of the 2001 Nobel Prize proceeds, which was his share after taxes and his gift to his mentor of one-half of the prize money,[2] was illusory, and (3) the judge prematurely assigned to him the cost of his three children's college education.

We conclude that (1) the judge did not abuse her discretion in her overall division of assets, including her consideration of the Nobel Prize's impact on his ability to acquire future income and assets, (2) the judge's crediting of the husband with $83,000 in Nobel Prize proceeds was not clearly erroneous, and (3) the judge did not err in ordering the husband to pay the imminent college costs of the oldest child, but did err in ordering the husband to pay the future college costs of the two younger children.

Facts. The plaintiff, Gabriele Ketterle (wife) and the defendant, Wolfgang Ketterle (husband), were married on September 20, 1985, in Germany. This seventeen-year marriage was the first for both parties. They had three children, born March 6, 1986, October 25, 1988, and September 28, 1992.

As found by the judge, the husband was a tenured full professor at the Massachusetts Institute of Technology (MIT), whose total wages from MIT were $179,160.98 in 2001. His health was also excellent. The wife worked part-time as a teacher's aide earning $7,317.98 in 2001. Although

---

1. The husband won the Nobel Prize for Physics for his work on Bose–Einstein condensates. "Bose–Einstein condensation has been described as making atoms behave like the photons in a laser beam," rather than move about in their normal state, where they "flit around randomly." 2001 Nobel Prizes, MIT Technology Review, March, 2002, at 15. The condensates have near and long-term applications: "One technological application that promises to bear fruit in the near term is using the condensates to create super-accurate atomic clocks or to make ultra-precise measurements of forces like rotation and gravity. Even further down the road are possible applications in quantum computing and nanotechnology." *Ibid.*

2. In about 1990, the husband and his mentor, David Pritchard, started working together at the Massachusetts Institute of Technology (MIT) on Bose–Einstein condensation. In 1993, in order to keep the husband at MIT, Pritchard took the "extraordinary" step of turning the entire project—"equipment, students and grants"—over to the husband. 2001 Nobel Prizes, MIT Technology Review, March, 2002, at 15.

her physical health was fine, her mental health was "fragile." In August, 2001, she was committed for a time to McLean Hospital because of a suicide attempt and severe depression. She continued to be maintained on three kinds of antidepressants.

The judge found "much to admire in the conduct of both [parties] as spouses and as parents." The husband's brilliance and hard work made the family financially secure. "The wife's total commitment to child rearing and tending to the home permitted the husband to pursue his career," which involved "very long hours at his laboratory." The wife also came to the United States from Germany to enhance her husband's career despite her "lack of fluency in English and . . . familiarity with . . . American culture."

The judge identified five basic marital assets: the former marital home in Brookline (equity of $578,000), the husband's new home (equity of $70,000), the after-tax proceeds from the Nobel Prize (this totaled either $83,000 or $166,000 depending on whether the mentor's share is included or excluded), the husband's retirement/pension funds (approximately $183,000[3]), and the wife's bank account ($54,000).

The judge awarded the marital home to the wife, and the retirement/pension funds and the after-tax Nobel Prize proceeds to the husband.[4] The judge also permitted the husband to give away one-half of his Nobel Prize money to his mentor as she was "fully persuaded that the husband's motivation is admirable and honorable, and in . . . keeping with the lofty, humanitarian, and generous values embodied by the rich history and tradition of the Nobel Prize." The judge made this ruling, however, "hand-in-glove" with her ruling that the wife not be required, as the husband requested, to refinance the marital home to provide him with cash that would permit him to take, as he argued, "his half." She also rejected his contention that he was "cash-poor."

According to the judge's calculations, she gave the wife either sixty-eight percent or sixty-two percent of the assets, depending on how the mentor's share of the award is considered. In explaining her division of assets, the judge relied "heavily" upon the statutory factor of the "ability of the parties to acquire future income and assets." The judge concluded that the husband's ability is excellent, as he retains a retirement asset in which his employer "matches his future contributions dollar for dollar," and his "receipt of the Nobel [P]rize opens wide new horizons for his income potential." The wife's future prospects were found to be "paltry and stagnant by comparison." The judge found that the wife had "no

---

3. The husband's retirement assets consist of a 401k account and a defined benefit pension plan. At the time of the divorce, there was $109,401.92 in the 401k plan, in which MIT matched the husband's contribution dollar for dollar. The husband's interest in the defined benefit plan was $73,649.89 at the time of the divorce. The projected worth of the defined benefit plan by the year 2023, when the husband becomes 65 years old, was $684,409.

4. The judge carved out for purposes of division the equity in the husband's new home and the wife's bank account, treating them as essentially a wash. This was because the parties earlier had equally divided a joint bank account, each taking $97,000. The husband used his share mostly to purchase and furnish his new home and the wife saved most of her share in her bank account.

likelihood of acquiring significant future assets or increasing her earned income."

The parties were given joint legal custody of the three children with, as the parties agreed, the oldest and youngest children residing primarily with the wife and the middle child residing with the husband. The husband was ordered to pay monthly child support of $2,500 to the wife and monthly alimony of $2,000.

* * *

Discussion. The husband objects to the "disproportionate" division of marital assets. Nevertheless, "an equitable, rather than an equal, division of property is the ultimate goal of [the relevant statute on alimony and assignment of property]." *Williams v. Massa*, [728 N.E.2d 932, 939] ([Mass.] 2000). As provided by statute, the trial judge has "broad discretion to 'assign to either the husband or the wife all or any part of the estate of the other,' after consideration of the factors enumerated in the statute. . . . A division of marital property which is supported by findings as to the required factors will not be disturbed on appeal unless 'plainly wrong and excessive.' " *Passemato v. Passemato*, [691 N.E.2d 549, 553] ([Mass.] 1998).

There is no question that the judge here expressly considered all the appropriate factors. She also exercised her discretion to give more weight to some factors than others, particularly the ability to acquire future income and assets.[7] The husband contends that the judge's heavy reliance on this factor was misplaced because the judge erroneously found (1) that the husband's future income and assets would be enhanced as a result of his receipt of the Nobel Prize; and (2) the wife would be unable to increase her earning capacity.

The judge's findings on the wife's inability to acquire future income and assets are well-supported, given the wife's limited vocational skills and mental illness. In regard to the husband, the judge emphasized not only the Nobel Prize but also the husband's lucrative retirement plan. There is no dispute regarding the valuation of the retirement plan. We also discern no error in the judge's determination that the Nobel Prize, in combination with the husband's brilliance, work ethic, good health, and relative youth (he was forty-four years old at the time of the trial), will provide him with significant future income and assets given the extraordinary nature of his scientific breakthrough, its worldwide recognition, and its projected near and long-term technological applications. The husband's and wife's ability to acquire future income and assets are therefore strikingly different and justify the judge's heavy reliance on this factor. See Kindregan & Inker, Family Law and Practice § 40:18, at 45 (3d ed. 2002) ("If the evidence demonstrates that one party has little or no ability to produce income and little prospect of obtaining assets by other means

---

7. The husband's argument that the judge did not properly consider the husband's contribution to the marriage is without support in the record. She just weighed his contribution differently than he did.

[such as inheritance], and the other party has a history of producing income, then a strong case exists for property assignment and/or alimony in favor of the party with minimal economic prospects'').

The husband also contends that the judge created a seventy-six—twenty-four split of assets, not the sixty-eight—thirty-two split that she intended. He argues that there were only two assets: the house and the retirement plan, because all of the Nobel Prize money was offset by his liabilities. We conclude, however, that the judge's crediting him with $83,000 out of the Nobel Prize proceeds was not clearly erroneous, as the prize proceeds have remained under his exclusive control since their receipt, and even when the taxes and the mentor's share are subtracted, $83,000 remains.

The husband was also awarded the right to give $83,000 of the Nobel Prize proceeds to his mentor. The judge correctly treated this commitment as a professional or moral obligation and not a legal debt. Although the wife has not appealed, and therefore this issue is waived, the $83,000 promised to the mentor should have been included in the marital estate. * * * [W]e conclude that the judge did not allow the husband's generosity to his mentor to prejudice his wife,[11] but the asset split she devised was actually sixty-two—thirty-eight, not the sixty-eight—thirty-two split the judge describes, or the seventy-six—twenty-four split the husband claims. In sum, the husband has no basis for arguing that he was shortchanged $83,000.

* * *

Conclusion. * * * [T]he judgment is affirmed. * * *

[The concurring opinion by LENK, J. is omitted.]

NOTES AND QUESTIONS

1. *How uneven may the division be and still be "equitable"?* In *Wade v. Wade*, 878 A.2d 303 (Vt. 2005), the court upheld an order awarding 90% of the marital assets to the wife as equitable. The court found that the trial judge had not abused his discretion because the family lived in a house the wife had purchased before the marriage and had used gifts from the wife's mother and the wife's earnings from the nursery school she ran to pay the mortgage and household expenses; the husband worked sporadically by choice, did not serve as a homemaker and ran up substantial credit card debt for his personal expenses. The court rejected the husband's argument that he was entitled to more property or to alimony because the marriage lasted twelve years, he lacked a college degree, and he needed more money to provide "a proper home" for their 14–year–old daughter when she spent the night with him under the parenting agreement.

2. *The "prodigious earner."* The equities are particularly controversial where the marital estate is so substantial that the lower-earning spouse can

---

11. She makes this clear when she allows the transfer only "hand in glove" with her assignment of the house to the wife, and when she rejects the husband's claims that he is "cash-poor."

maintain his or her accustomed life style without receiving an "equal" share. In such circumstances, many courts award the phenomenally successful earner, or so-called "prodigious spouse," a disproportionate share of the marital assets. Debra DiMaggio, *The "Prodigious Spouse": Equitable Distribution and Wealthy Wage Earner*, 91 Ill. B.J. 460 (2003). High earners, who have accumulated high-asset marital estates, argue that they should be compensated for the demanding nature of their jobs outside the home. *Id.* For marital estates valued at over three million dollars, one critical factor in determining whether the award is equitable is whether it provides the dependent spouse sufficient assets to generate income that will support substantially the same life style as prevailed during the marriage. David N. Hofstein et al., *The Big Case: Issues in High Income/High Asset Cases*, 17 J. Am. Acad. of Matrimonial Law 307, 342–44 (2001). Any larger share of the assets may be regarded as exceeding the value of the dependent spouse's contribution.

Despite the informal "cap" that may be imposed on the dependent spouse's share of lavish marital assets, wealthy dependent spouses are likely to receive far more in the United States than in many other countries. In England, for example, the standard divorce awards the wife one-third of the total capital assets and, if needed, maintenance payments that will bring her post-divorce income up to one-third of the couple's previous joint income. Karey Burkholder, Note, *Darting to England: A Comparison of the United States' and England's Divorce Laws*, 13 Temp. Int'l & Comp. L. J. 163, 176 (1999). Moreover, a wealthy spouse who agrees to a settlement that will meet the dependent spouse's "reasonable requirements" is relieved of the obligation to disclose all of his assets fully. *Id.* at 166. "Reasonable requirements" prove "elastic," and may overlook the possibility that "the reasonable needs of the very wealthy can be * * * different from those of ordinary people." *Id.* at 169, 183.

3. *When will an appellate court find a distribution inequitable?* "[A] disproportionate division must be supported by some reasonable basis." *Smith v. Smith*, 143 S.W.3d 206, 214 (Tex. App. 2004). Because distributions will be reversed only for abuse of discretion, the single most important cause of reversal is the trial court's failure to state that it has examined and applied the relevant factors, or to state reasons for disproportionate divisions. *See, e.g., Gohl v. Gohl*, 700 N.W.2d 625, 638 (Neb. Ct. App. 2005) (discussed in note c at p. 514, *supra*) (remanding a case presenting complex issues in which the trial court set "arbitrary time limitations" for presentation of evidence creating an "incomplete and inadequate" record); *Moses v. Moses*, 879 So.2d 1043 (Miss. Ct. App. 2004) (finding "capricious" and "casual" mention of the factors insufficient where the trial court's opinion failed to state reasons for giving the husband possession of the marital home, and finding the trial court committed error by failing to ascertain the value of the home or the indebtedness on the home).

4. *Fault-related factors.* The Pennsylvania statute, reproduced above, specifically bars consideration of marital misconduct in establishing distribution awards, but a significant number of states—including pure no-fault jurisdictions—allow the court to consider contributions to marital breakdown as a factor in equitable distribution. J. Thomas Oldham, Divorce, Separation

and the Distribution of Property § 13.02[1][a] (2005) (listing 19 of these jurisdictions).

In crafting equitable distribution orders, courts in all jurisdictions weigh economic fault. Economic fault includes dissipation of marital assets and attempts to hide assets or otherwise mislead the court.

Some jurisdictions regard dissipation of the marital estate as "a spouse's expenditures for his or her own personal enjoyment at a time when the marriage is apparently coming to an end * * *." *Kittredge v. Kittredge*, 803 N.E.2d 306, 313 (Mass. 2004) (concluding that whether to treat large gambling losses as dissipation of assets depends on case-specific timing and circumstances, including whether sufficient assets remain). For example, in *Sequeira v. Sequeira*, 888 So.2d 1097 (La. Ct. App. 2004), the court held that the cost of LASIK corrective eye surgery performed on the husband just two weeks before the divorce decree and charged to the couple's credit card did not "benefit or enhance the community." *Id*. at 1101. Payments to a paramour from marital funds generally constitute dissipation. *Gray v. Gray*, 909 So.2d 108 (Miss. Ct. App. 2005). However, the impact on a trial judge who knows about gifts to a paramour may be difficult to distinguish from a ruling that takes marital misconduct into account. Other examples of dissipation include running up significant credit card bills, destroying a spouse's credit rating, and inability to account for post-separation expenses.

In *Field v. Field*, No. FA9969449S, 2001 WL 1561067 (Conn. Super. Ct. Nov. 20, 2001), the court found that an unemployed husband dissipated the marital assets following the parties' initial appearance by, among other things, hiring a driver at a cost of $1,000 a month after losing his license, transferring $58,000 to a friend, and living an extravagant lifestyle that included a luxury vehicle and a $6,700 hot tub. The court held that the husband's lack of malicious intent was irrelevant. Even though the husband acted based on his expectations of future success that would match his earlier achievements, the court wanted "to preserve marital assets for distribution at the time of dissolution." *Id*. at *3. Because the husband was living so well while reporting no income, the court further ordered that "[i]f either party has failed to disclose any assets at the time of * * * judgment, that party shall pay 65% of the value of that asset [at judgment] to the other party," plus 10% interest from the date of judgment to the date of discovery. *Id*. at *4.

Bad behavior does not necessarily constitute dissipation. In *Walter v. Walter*, 561 S.E.2d 571 (N.C. Ct. App. 2002), the wife removed several truckloads of property from the marital home after the couple separated. When the husband returned from a fishing trip, he found "[s]he took basically everything. Everything [is] gone." *Id*. at 573. In awarding the husband more than half of the marital estate, the trial court considered the wife's acts "in wasting, neglecting, and converting marital property between the date of separation and the trial," including the assets she removed from the home valued at $190,000. *Id*. at 574. The appellate court reversed because the wife's misconduct did not cause the value of the marital estate to decline after the date of separation. She still possessed the property, which was subject to equitable distribution.

Parties to contentious divorce proceedings commonly attempt to hide assets by using offshore accounts, structuring holdings so that personal funds look like business accounts, and so forth. Extrinsic fraud provides grounds for revisiting a distribution order, but it is frequently necessary to retain experts to identify hidden funds. Sometimes the approach is less sophisticated. In *In re Marriage of Rossi*, 108 Cal.Rptr.2d 270 (Ct. App. 2001), for example, the wife won the California lottery as part of an office pool while the couple was still married, but did not inform her husband of her good fortune. Instead, unhappy in her marriage, she consulted the Lottery Commission, where an employee told her to file for divorce before they issued the first check. The wife did so, and began collecting her winnings payable at $66,800 a year for 20 years. The parties divided their assets pursuant to a settlement agreement, which contained a disclosure clause. After the agreement had been executed, the husband discovered that his wife had won the lottery. He moved to set aside the settlement agreement as fraudulent, and was awarded the entire amount of the lottery winnings.

5. *Assigning assets to marital children.* Where evidence shows that marital assets were deposited in a separately titled asset to benefit the children by providing for their college education, courts generally treat the asset as marital and reserve it for the benefit of the children. *Barnett v. Barnett*, 908 So.2d 833 (Miss. Ct. App. 2005). But courts lack the power to order affluent families to provide for their children beyond the amounts required for child support. (This point will be covered in greater detail in Chapter 11.) On the other hand, many wealthy families achieve this goal through settlement agreements that set up trust funds or savings accounts for the children.

In one atypical example, when media magnate Rupert Murdoch divorced Anna, his wife of 30 years, in 1999, to marry 31–year–old Wendi Deng, Anna voluntarily gave up many of the millions to which she would have been entitled under California law. Instead, Anna negotiated to ensure that her three grown children from the marriage would eventually control Murdoch's News Corp holdings, which include the Fox television network and Fox News. The settlement agreement between Rupert and Anna specified that their three children, along with a daughter from Rupert's first marriage, would retain control of the publicly traded corporation. Subsequently, Rupert had two more children with Wendi. In 2005, Rupert requested a modification to the trust holding the family's 28.5% stake in News Corp that would provide equal treatment for his young children with Wendi. The four adult children, third party beneficiaries of his agreement with Anna, agreed to share the money (estimated at more than six billion dollars) but would not relinquish voting control. Richard Siklos & Geraldine Fabrikant, *An Issue of Trust for Murdochs; Talk of Giving Control to 2 Youngest Children Adds to Friction*, Int'l Herald Trib., Aug. 3, 2005, at F3.

PROBLEM 9–3

You are an appellate judge in Pennsylvania considering a wife's appeal of the property division in her divorce. The couple married in 2000 and separated in 2003. They have one child born in 2001. When they separated, the wife remained in the family residence, a doublewide mobile home that the couple purchased in 2000, for approximately $15,000. The down payment came from a loan taken from the husband's retirement plan.

The wife, 26–years–old, has a junior college degree, and worked part-time at minimum wage jobs when the marriage began. She stayed at home during most of the marriage to care for the couple's child. After they separated, the wife paid all of the monthly costs on the home, which included lot fees, utilities and loan payments, using her sole source of income—temporary monthly maintenance payments from her husband. The husband is 28, in good health, and holds a technical degree that enables him to work consistently at skilled jobs. The couple paid off the husband's educational loans in full during the marriage. The husband's retirement funds are currently valued at roughly $6,000.

The trial court awarded one-third of the couple's assets to the wife, and the remaining two-thirds, including the home and the retirement account, to the husband. The wife's share amounted to $3,349. The distribution was largely based on the judge's conclusion that the mobile home had zero equity based on outstanding obligations for loans and other carrying expenses. The wife sought $2,500 as her share of the value of the home. The husband, who had leased an apartment after the couple separated and therefore could not move back into the marital home, argued that if he had to sell the home the sales price might not cover the outstanding loan amount. In fact, after the wife moved out the husband's parents moved into the mobile home as renters, with an agreement that ownership would be transferred to them as soon as the loan was repaid in full.

The wife claims that she did not receive any recognition for her contributions to the marriage, for the use of marital funds to pay for the husband's education, or for the payments made on the home. The wife will not receive any maintenance payments once the divorce is final, following determination of her appeal. It is undisputed that the wife is currently barely making ends meet while the husband enjoys a better standard of living.

Bearing in mind that the statutory goal is "effectuating economic justice between the parties and achieving a just determination of their property rights," what factors would you apply from the Pennsylvania statute? How would you weigh them and why? How would you rule?

SECTION 4:   HOW EQUITABLE IS EQUITABLE DISTRIBUTION?

Few families have sufficient resources to maintain two households at the same standard of living enjoyed by the marital household, regardless of where that standard falls. Despite high expectations, equitable distribution has not resolved the economic hardships that divorce imposes. The following excerpts offer some reflections on the disappointing results under equitable distribution as well as suggestions for reform.

PENELOPE E. BRYAN

Reasking the Woman Question at Divorce.
75 Chi.–Kent L. Rev. 713, 713–20 (2000).

The assertion that many divorced women and their dependent children suffer financial hardship no longer sparks controversy. Many feminists and others have done much to expose and establish that the standards of living of many women decline precipitously at divorce. * * *

Discrimination against women in the workplace helps explain women's financial vulnerability at divorce, but many other factors contribute as well. * * * At divorce, a time when wives have little access to their husbands' earnings, many wives cannot afford, and proceed without, adequate legal representation. * * *

* * *

* * * Typically, wives continue to receive fewer of the marital assets than do their husbands.

* * *

The ideology of formal equality currently pervades divorce law and ignores the wife's financial dependence upon her husband that stems from her marginal workforce participation and her responsibilities for family care. Encouraged to perceive wives as the formal equals of their husbands, judges and lawyers fashion outcomes that fail to address the wife's financial needs at divorce.

ALICIA BROKARS KELLY

The Marital Partnership Pretense and Career Assets: The
Ascendency of Self Over the Marital Community.
81 B.U. L. Rev. 59, 61–63 (2001).

* * * The view of marriage as a partnership, both economic and emotional, pervades * * * the law of marriage and divorce.

Despite continued and repeated adherence to the rhetoric of a marital community, * * * in important ways legal decision makers do not actually believe the tale they so often tell. Instead, another view of marriage—almost always obscured by other rationales, but unmistakably present—often drives outcomes upon divorce. * * * [I]n many cases, the ascendant value is solitary individualism. On this view, although there may be a specific exchange of resources that needs to be accounted for upon divorce, both spouses enter and depart marriage as separate individuals who have had relatively minimal influence on one another. Sovereign identity is treated as fundamental and untransformed by marriage.

The primacy of individualism over the competing partnership ideal is manifest in both the results and the reasoning of many judicial opinions that address whether and how to allocate the economic advantages of a spouse's career that were enhanced during marriage. * * *

This rejection of partnership ideology has important consequences. * * *

* * *

* * * [R]epudiation of the sharing principles embraced in the partnership model evokes a portrait of marriage that many would find unsatisfying. Although individualism is surely a valuable component of marriage, alone, it is an incomplete account. * * *

These two depictions, one of community, and one of individualism, are extreme. Real life and marital law, of course, reflect aspects of each. The challenge in marital law is to reconcile these competing visions. * * *

LAURA A. ROSENBURY

Two Ways to End a Marriage: Divorce or Death.
2005 Utah L. Rev. 1227, 1274–75, 1282–84, 1289.

* * *

In most states, the way a marriage ends—divorce or death—greatly affects how the property of a marriage will be distributed under the states' default rules. If the marriage ends by divorce, in every state the court is required to make either an equal or equitable distribution of most of the property * * * in accordance with a partnership theory of marriage. If the marriage ends by the death of a spouse, in most states * * * there is no concept of marital property or community property * * *. Instead, when a spouse dies without a will, intestacy laws give the surviving spouse the right to a share of only [certain] assets titled in the deceased spouse's name [with the remainder going to children and other blood relatives]. And if the deceased spouse attempted to disinherit the surviving spouse through the execution of a will, most elective share laws give the surviving spouse the right to less than one-half of those assets. * * *

* * *

* * * While the partnership theory [at divorce] obscures wifely sacrifice, it does not eliminate such sacrifice and may, in fact, reinforce it. * * *

* * *

[T]he underlying premise of the partnership theory * * * most increases the material well-being of those wives who forego market work in order to do care work. Indeed, these women would own no property but for the partnership theory of marriage. * * *

In addition, * * * wives who forego market work receive half of every dollar earned by their husbands. Therefore, the more money earned by the husband, the more the wife benefits from the partnership theory of marriage. The partnership theory of marriage thus most benefits * * * women who are married to wealthy men.

* * * [W]omen who both work outside of the home and do the bulk of the care work within the home may not benefit from the partnership theory of marriage and may even be harmed by it. For example, the intangible contributions of a wife who earns as much as her husband yet also does most of the housework and child-care coordination * * * will be completely unvalued pursuant to the partnership theory of marriage. * * *

* * *

[A]lthough the partnership theory of marriage may have been a useful interim tool for ensuring that women were not left destitute after the introduction of no-fault divorce, it * * * reinforc[es] traditional gender expectations, including the expectation of wifely sacrifice. * * *

ALLEN M. PARKMAN

Bringing Consistency to the Financial Arrangements at Divorce.
87 Ky. L.J. 51, 70, 75–76 (1999).

* * *

The financial obligations at divorce should be based on debts incurred during marriage. People make choices due to their being married, and some of these choices result in debts, which are obligations of one person to pay or compensate another. * * *

* * *

* * * When people marry, they sacrifice the opportunity to marry someone else. The couple may choose to have children recognizing the future time, money, and emotional costs that the children will require. The spouses may sacrifice current consumption to save, thereby accumulating marital property. To accommodate their spouse and children, spouses may limit their career [or finance a spouse's education].

All of these sacrifices should be viewed as potentially creating debts * * *.

PROBLEM 9–4

You are chief counsel to the state legislature's family law committee. The chairperson of the committee has asked you to advise her about whether the state needs to reform its equitable distribution statute, which resembles those you have seen in this Chapter. To prepare for the hearings, you review the materials in this Chapter in light of the arguments presented above by Professors Bryan, Kelly, Rosenburg and Parkman, as well as the excerpts from other scholars in Section II.B of the Chapter.

What would you advise the committee chairperson about the need for reform? If you think reform is needed, what should the focus of the reform be?

The chairperson also asks you to advise her about the advantages and limits of the following language adapted from Section 4.09 of the ALI Principles:

Division of Marital Property

(1) Except as provided in Paragraph (2) of this section, marital property and marital debts are divided at dissolution so that the spouses receive net shares equal in value, although not necessarily identical in kind.

(2) The spouses are allocated net shares of the marital property or debts that are unequal in value if, and only if, one or more of the following is true:

(a) the court compensates one spouse in whole or in part for a loss created by contribution to the other spouse's education or training.

(b) the court grants one spouse an enhanced share because the other spouse improperly disposed of some portion of the marital property.

(c) marital debts exceed marital assets and it is equitable to assign the debt unequally because of a significant disparity in the spouse's financial capacity, their contribution to the decision to incur the debt, or their consumption of the goods for which the debt was used.

(d) Debt incurred to finance one spouse's education shall be treated as the separate obligation of the spouse who received the education.

* * *

What recommendation will you give your boss?

SECTION 5: THE IMPACT OF POST-DIVORCE BANKRUPTCY FILING

Sunkidd Venture v. *Snyder–Entel* demonstrated that a debt undertaken during marriage is marital debt for which both spouses remain responsible after divorce. When too many debts accumulate, people are entitled to file for bankruptcy. Some spouses file for bankruptcy together before divorce, or as part of the structure of their marital settlement. It is estimated that divorce triggers about one in four of all bankruptcy filings. Shayna M. Steinfeld & Bruce R. Steinfeld,: The Family Lawyer's Guide To Bankruptcy Forms, Tips And Strategies 2 (2d ed. 2008). You will recall that most divorcing couples have very few assets. After divorce, two households generally need to live on roughly the same amount of money that previously supported one household—meaning two instead of one rent or mortgage payments, perhaps a second car and so forth. In addition, problems with financial implications, such as loss of one spouse's job, or business or medical expenses, may be among the stressors that contribute to divorce. What happens to obligations imposed by the court or a settlement agreement pursuant to a divorce when one of the parties subsequently files for bankruptcy relief?

Before the Bankruptcy Reform Act of 2005, post-divorce payments to settle the distribution of marital property were fully dischargeable in bankruptcy. This meant that the former spouse who was obligated to transfer funds over a period of years could avoid the payments by declaring bankruptcy. When Congress reformed the bankruptcy law in 2005, it intended to rein in "abusive" filings, a label applied to cases in which a petitioner for bankruptcy succeeded in unraveling the requirements imposed by a final divorce decree. In many cases, the petitioner had gone on a "shopping spree" after the divorce, kept everything he or she had purchased (including a new home and/or car), and, as a result of bankruptcy, was relieved of debts to his or her former spouse pursuant to the property distribution order. These abusive filings were estimated to comprise about four percent of all bankruptcy petitions. Shayna M. Steinfeld & Bruce R. Steinfeld, The Family Lawyer's Guide to Bankruptcy: Forms, Tips and Strategies 1 (2d ed. 2008). The former spouse who was deprived of payments owed pursuant to an order that provided future satisfaction of amounts owned to complete the distribution of marital property had no recourse because the orders regarding property distribution are final.

Obligations for ongoing living expenses (child support and alimony) were normally not dischargeable debts before 2005. The labels attached to financial obligations in divorce agreements and court orders did not, however, always accurately reflect the function of the payments. Federal bankruptcy courts frequently confronted the question whether a post-divorce payment was in fact alimony (only rarely dischargeable), or whether it was a term-payment owed as part of equitable distribution (fully dischargeable in bankruptcy). In such cases, the obligor would argue that payments labeled as alimony were really designed to accomplish equitable distribution of marital property and should be discharged (forgiven) in bankruptcy.

As of October 2005, federal law provides that "domestic support obligations" (defined as, among other things, "debts owed to or recoverable by * * * a spouse, former spouse * * * in the nature of alimony * * * or * * * established * * * by reason of * * * a separation agreement, divorce decree, or property settlement agreement") "shall not be dischargeable in bankruptcy." 11 U.S.C. §§ 101(14A), 523(a)(5) (2006); *see* William Houston Brown, *Taking Exception to a Debtor's Discharge: The 2005 Bankruptcy Amendments Make It Easier*, 79 Am. Bankr. L. J. 419 (2005). As the statutory language indicates, Congress contemplated that the distinction between payments to complete the division of property and payments for on-going support would no longer be significant in bankruptcy cases.

This distinction has disappeared for all bankruptcy filings under Chapter 7 of the 2005 Bankruptcy Act, and for what are known as "hardship" cases under Chapter 13: in both instances no divorce-related obligations are dischargeable in bankruptcy. They must be paid. Some individuals, however, earn too much to file under Chapter 7, and must file under Chapter 13, the terms of which are generally less favorable to petitioners.[3] If the bankrupt party files under Chapter 13, only domestic support obligations are automatically nondischargeable. The federal bank-

---

3. The distinctions between the Chapters of the Bankruptcy Act and the reasons for filing under one or the other are beyond the scope of this course.

ruptcy court may therefore still need to determine if payments have been correctly characterized as domestic support (maintenance or child support) and remain binding or are owed pursuant to property distribution, in which case they may be discharged in bankruptcy. Note that these issues arise in a federal bankruptcy court, not a state court, and apply federal bankruptcy law, not state law governing the dissolution of marriages.

Although one goal of the Bankruptcy Reform Act was to protect women and children after divorce by allowing them to collect funds owed under a divorce decree despite the bankruptcy of the obligor, a second provision of the Act frequently interferes with collection efforts by former spouses. The Act provides special protection for obligations owed to credit card companies; in bankruptcy proceedings, credit card debts are payable before debts accrued pursuant to divorce or child support obligations. *See* Hatty Yip, *Double Whammy: How the New Credit Card Nondischargeability Provision and the New Means Test Hit Single Mothers Over the Head*, 15 Buff. Women's L. J. 33 (2006–2007).

The following case—although decided under the bankruptcy statute in effect in 2002—illustrates the way that courts analyze the characterization of divorce-related payments in bankruptcy cases. The analysis remains useful under the new Act.

CLINE v. CLINE

U.S. Court of Appeals for the Tenth Circuit, 2008.
259 Fed. Appx. 127.

TACHA, CHIEF CIRCUIT JUDGE

Appellant Richard A. Cline appeals from a decision of the Bankruptcy Appellate Panel of the Tenth Circuit (BAP) affirming a decision of the United States Bankruptcy Court for the Western District of Oklahoma. The bankruptcy court ruled that a $250,000 divorce-related debt Mr. Cline owed to his ex-wife, appellee Donna Cline (the $250,000 obligation), was in the nature of spousal support and therefore could not be discharged in his Chapter 7 bankruptcy. Mr. Cline argued that the $250,000 debt was not support and was susceptible to discharge as part of a property settlement. On appeal by both parties, the BAP affirmed the bankruptcy court's decision. * * * Mr. Cline filed a motion for rehearing in which he argued * * * that the bankruptcy court error was related not to its reading of the provisions of the divorce decree and settlement agreement-which expressly stated that the $250,000 obligation was part of a property settlement-but instead to the court's determination that the parties intended the $250,000 obligation to function as support despite the agreement's express statements to the contrary. Mr. Cline's motion for reconsideration was denied by the BAP and he filed his notice of appeal in this court.

On appeal, Mr. Cline argues * * * that the bankruptcy court erred in finding that the $250,000 obligation was in the nature of support * * *.

ANALYSIS

The parties agree that this case is controlled by *Sampson v. Sampson (In re Sampson)*, 997 F.2d 717 (10th Cir. 1993). As in *Sampson,* we are faced with application of 11 U.S.C. § 523(a)(5). That statute provides that debts to a "former spouse ... for alimony to, maintenance for, or support of such spouse" may not be discharged in Chapter 7 bankruptcy proceedings provided that "such liability is actually in the nature of alimony, maintenance, or support,". 11 U.S.C. 523(a)(5) (2002). "Whether an obligation to a former spouse is actually in the nature of support is a factual question subject to a clearly erroneous standard of review." *Sampson,* 997 F.2d at 721. * * * We have also held that "[t]he bankruptcy court's findings should not be disturbed absent the 'most cogent reasons in the record.' " *In re Goin,* 808 F.2d 1391, 1393 (10th Cir. 1987) (per curiam) (quotation omitted).

* * * Consequently, we must independently review the record on appeal and determine whether reversal is appropriate.

* * *

* * *

Under *Sampson,*

> whether an obligation is nondischargeable under § 523(a)(5) is a dual inquiry into both the parties'[ ] intent and the substance of the obligation. The party seeking to hold the debt nondischargeable has the burden of proving by a preponderance of the evidence [(1)] that the parties intended the obligation as support and [(2)] that the obligation was, in substance, support.

997 F.2d at 723. Mr. Cline argues that the bankruptcy court erred in finding that the parties intended the $250,000 obligation as support, claiming that the bankruptcy court based its decision solely on the parties' intent without inquiring into whether the obligation was, in substance, support. We disagree.

"The parties' intent is the 'initial inquiry' to determine whether a debtor's obligation to his or her former spouse is actually in the nature of alimony, maintenance or support." *Id.* (quoting *In re Yeates,* 807 F.2d 874, 878 (10th Cir. 1986)). " 'A written agreement between the parties is persuasive evidence of intent.' " *Id.* (quoting *Yeates,* 807 F.2d at 878).

According to the bankruptcy court the settlement agreement provided that:

> husband will pay the wife $250,000 within 12 months of the divorce decree and, upon receipt of the payment she will then transfer certain real property to him. The obligation to pay the $250,000 is unconditional and is not dependent upon success in recovery on the business claims.

* * * . [I]t is clear from the bankruptcy court's decision that the settlement agreement specified that the $250,000 obligation was to be consid-

ered part of the property settlement and that the settlement agreement also contained an express waiver of alimony by Mrs. Cline.[9] Mr. Cline does not dispute these findings as to the contents of the provisions in the settlement agreement.

How the obligation is treated in the settlement agreement, however, is only *persuasive evidence* of the parties' intent, and we held in *Sampson* that "§ 523(a)(5) requires federal courts to look beyond the label which the parties attach to an obligation." 997 F.2d at 722. In *Yeates* this court held that the determination of the parties' intent "must be made by looking at the substance of the agreement viewed in the crucible of surrounding circumstances." 807 F.2d at 878 (quotation omitted). In the case of *In re Goin* we set forth four factors to be considered when determining intent:

> (1) if the agreement fails to provide explicitly for spousal support, the court may presume that the property settlement is intended for support if it appears under the circumstances that the spouse needs support; (2) when there are minor children and an imbalance of income, the payments are likely to be in the nature of support; (3) support or maintenance is indicated when the payments are made directly to the recipient and are paid in installments over a substantial period of time; and (4) an obligation that terminates on remarriage or death is indicative of an agreement for support.

808 F.2d at 1392–93. Similarly, in *Sampson*, we held that a "Plaintiff's obvious need for support at the time of the divorce is enough to presume that the obligation was intended as support even when it is otherwise identified in an agreement between the parties as property settlement." *Id.* at 725. "[S]uch a presumption [as to intent] is proper regardless of the label attached to the obligation either in the settlement agreement or in the parties' own minds," since " 'the crucial issue is the function the award was intended to serve.' " *Id.* (quoting *In re Williams,* 703 F.2d 1055, 1057 (8th Cir. 1983)).

As to Mrs. Cline's need for support at the time of the divorce, we hold that the bankruptcy court did not commit clear error when it found that Mrs. Cline "had no significant employment prospects, at least such as would allow her to continue her standard of living, she had a meager education, no independent income and she most likely had a need for support at the time the divorce was decreed." Aplt. App. at 192. Mr. Cline's argument is basically that it was clear error to rule that despite the clear wording of the settlement agreement the parties intended the $250,000 obligation to be in the nature of support because Mrs. Cline was "in good health and apparently had no impediment to seeking employ-

---

9. The bankruptcy court also acknowledged that this provision was found in a section of the settlement agreement entitled "SETTLEMENT OF ANTICIPATED REVENUES FROM CORPORATE ENTITIES," and that testimony indicated that the husband's businesses had claims against other entities that both parties believed that the $250,000 would probably be paid from the substantial recovery that was anticipated from these claims. As noted above, however, the obligation was unconditional and was not made dependent on success in recovery on the business claims.

ment," Br. of Aplt. at 15, and that under the terms of the settlement agreement she was to have few debts or expense.[10]

This is not enough to find clear error. The parties had been married for approximately twelve years and the marriage produced three children. Mrs. Cline had only a high school education with short university experience, had been employed in "some clerical and secretarial jobs" prior to the marriage but had no meaningful employment after the marriage, and had received a meager inheritance from her father but had no other independent means of supporting herself. She had stayed home and cared for the children after they were born, which Mr. Cline wished her to do. Mr. Cline on the other hand earned approximately $13,000 per month in the oil and gas business and ran at least two companies engaged in this business. One of the factors that may be considered under *Goin,* is: "if the agreement fails to provide explicitly for spousal support, the court may presume that the property settlement is intended for support if it appears under the circumstances that the spouse needs support." *In re Goin,* 808 F.2d 1391, 1392 (10th Cir. 1987). Here it was clear that Mrs. Cline needed support and we are not left with "the definite and firm conviction" that the court made a mistake in ruling that the $250,000 obligation was intended to provide that support. *Miniscribe Corp.,* 309 F. 3d at 1240.

As for Mr. Cline's argument that the bankruptcy court failed to proceed to the second step of the *Sampson* test and find that the $250,000 obligation was "in substance" support, and that such a finding could not be proper without evidence of Mrs. Cline's monthly expenses, we find no reversible error. Here, the court found Mrs. Cline's need of support was so obvious as to indicate that the parties intended for the provision in question to constitute support, despite the settlement agreement's specific language to the contrary. All of the court's findings as to Mrs. Cline's need for support would apply with equal weight to the second step of *Sampson*. While the better practice would have been for the bankruptcy court to have acknowledged the fact that it also considered $250,000 obligation to be "in substance" support, it would be a waste of judicial resources to reverse simply for the finding to be made. * * *

* * *

* * * "The determination of whether an obligation arising out of a divorce settlement is in the nature of alimony, maintenance, or support [, however,] is a matter of federal bankruptcy law." Consequently, the state divorce decree, and the settlement agreement calling the $250,000 obligation a property settlement, did not "decide" the issue of whether the

---

10. According to the bankruptcy court, under the agreement Mrs. Cline was to have a home provided by Mr. Cline free and clear of any liens. The settlement agreement further provided "for division of certain personal property, and for payment of health insurance premiums by the husband. It goes on to obligate the husband to pay various debts, particularly credit card statements and provides that [the parties] will each have certain horses." The settlement agreement also provided that Mr. Cline would pay support for the minor children and also dealt "with college funds for the children, waiver of any claim to retirement annuities, and other miscellaneous provisions."

obligation was in the nature of support for the purposes of bankruptcy.
* * *

The judgment of the bankruptcy court is AFFIRMED.

O'BRIEN, dissenting:

Because the majority decision is contrary to our precedent and the clearly expressed intent of both parties at the time they entered into their divorce decree and settlement agreement, I must respectfully dissent. "[T]he critical inquiry is the *shared* intent of the parties at the time the obligation arose." *Sampson v. Sampson, (In re Sampson),* 997 F.2d 717, 723 (10th Cir. 1993) (*citing Tilley v. Jessee,* 789 F.2d 1074, 1078 (4th Cir. 1986)) (emphasis added). Both the settlement agreement and the circumstances point but one way, Mrs. Cline agreed with Mr. Cline to waive spousal support in exchange for a debt-free new beginning, a one-time property settlement payment, and substantial child support payments. Although a discharge of the settlement payment in Mr. Cline's bankruptcy substantially changes Mrs. Cline's payoff, it does not change the parties' intent at the time of the settlement agreement.

We "begin with the assumption that dischargeability is favored under the Code." *Tilley,* 789 F.2d at 1077. Mrs. Cline must prove by a preponderance of the evidence that (1) she *and Mr. Cline* "intended the obligation as support *and* [2] that the obligation was, in substance, support." *Sampson,* 997 F.2d at 723 (emphasis added). While we look to both the parties' agreement and the surrounding circumstances, our inquiry "does not turn on one party's post hoc explanation as to his or her state of mind at the time of the agreement, even if uncontradicted." *Id.*

* * * In this case, there can be no doubt regarding the parties' written intent.

The testimony at Mr. Cline's bankruptcy hearing revealed a carefully drafted settlement agreement listing the $250,000.00 payment under the Property Settlement section. The settlement agreement clearly states the payment was intended to distribute a potential award in a lawsuit. Child support was addressed in a separate section. And importantly, yet another section clearly and affirmatively waived both parties' rights to spousal support.[1] Even the bankruptcy court recognized the affirmative waiver of alimony contained in the settlement agreement "couldn't be more definitive." (R. App. at 190). Thus, under our own precedent, there is no question the settlement agreement supplies compelling evidence that the mutual intent of the parties creates a "substantial obstacle" to the success of Mrs. Cline's claim.

The surrounding circumstances do not overcome this compelling evidence of intent. *Goin v. Goin (In re Goin),* 808 F.2d 1391, 1392–93 (10th Cir. 1987). According to *Goin,* we first look to whether the agree-

---

1. Research has revealed no case law finding a support obligation when there is an express waiver of alimony and no specific language providing the property settlement is in lieu of alimony or spousal support.

ment provides "explicitly for spousal support." *Id.* at 1392. If it does not, we "may presume that the property settlement is intended for support *if it appears under the circumstances that the spouse needs support.*" *Id.* (emphasis added). The majority concludes there was no explicit provision for spousal support. Contrary to the majority's assessment, however, the agreement specifically and explicitly provided for spousal support; it was waived, *i.e.* $0. It is important to recognize Mrs. Cline agreed to this provision only after seeking advice from two attorneys—her attorney and a well-known bankruptcy attorney—in anticipation of her husband's bankruptcy filing. This is yet another reason to give weight to the written agreement in that we look to the surrounding circumstances primarily because "it is likely that neither the parties nor the divorce court contemplated the effect of a subsequent bankruptcy when the obligation arose." *Gianakas v. Gianakas (In re Gianakas),* 917 F.2d 759, 762 (3d Cir. 1990) (quotations omitted). The bankruptcy was clearly contemplated at the time of the settlement agreement. * * *

As to the second *Goin* factor—the presence of minor children and an imbalance of income—there was no determination in this case that the child support was inadequate to support the family * * *. Neither was there "evidence that payment of the debt is necessary in order for the plaintiff to maintain daily necessities such as food, housing and transportation" * * * ("Provisions to pay expenditures for the necessities and ordinary staples of everyday life may reflect a support function.") (quotations omitted) * * *

The third and fourth factors—installment payments terminating on remarriage of death—are equally inapplicable in this case. The payment was intended to be a one time event and the obligation did not terminate should Mrs. Cline remarry or die. * * *

Nonetheless, the majority presumes the payment is support because Mrs. Cline did not have the education or experience to secure a job which paid sufficiently to maintain her lifestyle. However, without inquiry into her resources, that is pure speculation—hardly a reliable basis for a decision. What we know is, with the assistance of divorce counsel and bankruptcy counsel, Mrs. Cline agreed to waive exactly what she now seeks. Competent adults must be left with the consequences of their decisions, particularly when those decisions involve the evaluation of uncertain events. When events turn out differently than anticipated, the law does not allow one contracting party to choose another course of action at the expense of the other. * * *

With the benefit of 20/20 hindsight, the bankruptcy judge probably reached a fair result. It is one I would embrace if it were not contrary to law. However, in the face of the settlement agreement it is not enough to merely say Mrs. Cline needed support. Mr. Cline was not required to prove the obligation was as labeled, a property settlement. Instead, it was Mrs. Cline's burden to show the parties' intended the payment, in effect, to be support. She did not do so. Under our case law, I see nothing that overcomes the substantial obstacle created by the compelling evidence of the parties' mutual intent as evidenced by the settlement agreement. * * * I would reverse the decision of the bankruptcy court and remand for further proceedings.

NOTES

1. *To what extent may bankruptcy courts consider the equities in determining the nature of post-divorce payments?* As *Cline* suggests, bankruptcy courts had considerable discretion to try to structure an equitable result even under the old statute. For example, in *In re Duffy*, 331 B.R. 137 (S.D.N.Y. 2005), Dr. Duffy agreed to a court-ordered settlement under which he would pay his ex-wife $2,000 a month for ten years as compensation for her interest in his medical practice established during the marriage. After Dr. Duffy had paid $165,000 of his $240,000 obligation, he suffered extreme mental health disorders, including depression and obsessive compulsive disorder, which contributed to the loss of his medical license. He was alternately unemployed and working at very low level jobs when the family court threatened to jail him for contempt because he was so far in arrears on his alimony and child support payments. The federal bankruptcy court held that the payments the family court had designated as alimony had been so labeled to make them deductible from Dr. Duffy's then-high income, and were in fact disguised equitable distribution payments. The court discharged him from further payments. The equities were clearly on Dr. Duffy's side, as his wife had left him for another man whom she subsequently married and was quite comfortable.

In other instances, however, reclassification of payments during bankruptcy hearings resulted in serious hardship. In *Hilsen v. Hilsen*, 122 B.R. 10 (S.D.N.Y. 1991), the bankruptcy court held that payments designated spousal maintenance were actually equitable distribution payments for the wife's share of a co-op apartment. After the court relieved Dr. Hilsen of his obligation, his ex-wife and three children found themselves in a homeless shelter. Because the doctor, a psychotherapist who had once managed the rock group Kiss, remained in arrears on his child support obligations and fled the country, the case dragged on for 17 years. Alan Feuer, *Kiss's Therapist Ex–Manager Buys His Freedom*, N.Y. Times, Nov. 1, 2005, at B1.

2. *The interaction between on-going proceedings for divorce and bankruptcy.* As one federal bankruptcy court explained, " * * * complications often arise regarding the division of property between divorcing spouses when one spouse has filed for bankruptcy" but the divorce has not yet been finalized. *In re Sauro*, 2008 WL 2237036, at *2 (Bankr. D.N.J. 2008). "The interplay of bankruptcy law and state family law presents complicated issues for both the federal and state courts * * *. As these areas have become increasingly intertwined" the tension between the federal requirement to give the debtor a fresh start and the state court's exclusive jurisdiction over dissolution has mounted. *Id.* In *Sauro*, the bankruptcy trustee for the debtor wife, with the husband's consent, sold the marital residence held by the couple as tenants-in-the-entirety, and used half of the proceeds to satisfy the wife's creditors. The trustee kept the remaining proceeds of the sale in trust as part of the

bankruptcy proceeding. The bankruptcy court ordered the trustee to distribute the husband's share of the proceeds from the sale of the home to him immediately, holding that neither the trustee nor the creditors have any right to the non-debtor's money. The court further held that if the state court distributed any portion of the husband's proceeds to the wife as part of equitable distribution, such funds would remain outside the reach of the bankruptcy court because more than 180 days had passed since the wife filed for bankruptcy and in accordance with federal law any funds received by the debtor after that time are not part of the bankrupt estate. Courts remain alert to the possibility that post-separation transfers between spouses may be intended to protect assets after one spouse has filed for bankruptcy, which would constitute fraud.

CHAPTER 10

ALIMONY

■ ■ ■

SECTION 1: OVERVIEW

Post-divorce financial arrangements between spouses typically address property division and alimony. This casebook treats the two forms of post-divorce support in separate chapters, although the decisions and commentary in both chapters show the complicated relationship between the two. Property division concerns assets and debts the parties acquired during the marriage, and alimony (also called maintenance or spousal support) concerns ongoing payments after the marriage ends. Nonetheless, courts often consider the two forms of post-divorce financial allocations together.

Because of historical assumptions about roles within marriage, alimony was usually available only to the wife, and it was meant to provide her with the support she would have continued to receive had she remained married. Alimony also served as a form of supplemental compensation to the wife because, under a title-based property distribution system, the husband received almost all of the couple's marital property. Notwithstanding these rationales, courts awarded alimony only infrequently; for example, studies have shown that between 1887 and 1922, fewer than 16% of divorcing wives received alimony. Jana Singer, *Alimony and Efficiency: The Gendered Costs and Benefits of the Economic Justification for Alimony*, 82 Geo. L.J. 2423, 2424 n.5 (1994). In the era of fault divorce, courts generally awarded alimony to the "innocent" spouse based on the other spouse's breach of the marital obligation. However, because of the need to prove cause to secure a divorce, the dependent spouse, who often had the greater desire for divorce (and thus the greater need for proof), was forced to negotiate and agree to the financially secure spouse's terms. The support system was intended to protect the "innocent" spouse, but, in reality, the "guilty" spouse often held the power to manipulate the terms of the divorce.

Traditional justifications for alimony no longer prevail in light of the growth of no-fault divorce and equitable distribution of marital property, the increasing equality of women, and other changes in the family. Alimony is now often viewed as an earned award, not an expected entitlement. Even with these profound changes, however, studies show that the number of alimony awards has not decreased and that fewer than 20% of divorces involve alimony today. On the other hand, the nature of the award may have changed, with more temporary, rather than life-time, awards. *See* Cynthia Lee Starnes, *One More Time: Alimony, Intuition, and the Remarriage–Termination Rule*, 81 Ind. L.J. 971, 989 (2006).

A. THE HISTORY OF ALIMONY

The current status of alimony derives from its complex past. The following article provides an initial diagnosis of what is wrong with contemporary alimony awards before reviewing the history and efforts to develop a rationale for this form of ongoing, post-dissolution support.

MARY KAY KISTHARDT
Re–Thinking Alimony: The AAML's Considerations for Calculating
Alimony, Spousal Support or Maintenance.
21 J. Am. Acad. Matrim. Law. 61, 62, 65–73 (2008).

* * *

[A Commission of the American Academy of Matrimonial Lawyers, a national organization of family law attorneys] concluded that there are two significant and related problems associated with the [contemporary] setting of spousal support. The first is a lack of consistency resulting in a perception of unfairness. From this flows the second problem, which is an inability to accurately predict an outcome in any given case. This lack of consistency and predictability undermines confidence in the judicial system and further acts as an impediment to the settlement of cases, because without a reliable method of prediction clients are in a quandary and lawyers can only offer forecasts based on experiential, rather than empirical, backing. * * *

* * *

The initial rationale for alimony or support had its origins in the English common law system. Historically there were two remedies from the bonds of marriage. Although an absolute divorce was theoretically possible, it required an act of Parliament and was therefore hardly ever used. More commonly a plea was made for a separation from bed and board (mensa et thoro). This action available from the ecclesiastical courts constituted a legal separation as absolute divorce was prohibited under canon law. A husband who secured such a divorce retained the right to control his wife's property and the corresponding duty to support his wife. Even after Parliament authorized the courts to grant absolute divorces, the concept of alimony remained. The initial rationale appeared be premised on the fact that women gave up their property rights at marriage and after the marriage ended they were without the means to support themselves. The original award of alimony was similar to the wife's claim of dower, and courts used the traditional one-third of the property standard so instead of one-third of the estate at the husband's death she would receive one-third of the income of her husband at the time of the divorce. The concept of alimony came across the Atlantic with the founding of the colonies but seemingly without a corresponding rationale.

The introduction of the Married Women's Property Acts changed the ability of women to retain property, but alimony remained. It appears that at least one rationale was based on contract theories because, for many courts, the role of fault played a significant role. Alimony then became damages for breach of the marital contract reflected in the fact that in most states it was only available to the innocent and injured spouse. The measure of damages often approximated the standard of living the wife would have enjoyed but for her husband's breach. Alternatively it represented compensatory damages for tortious conduct.

B.   The Beginning of the "Modern Era"

In the 1970's the economic picture of spouses at divorce began to change. Many states adopted principles of equitable distribution allowing for property acquired during the marriage to be divided between the spouses regardless of how it was titled. This allowed economically dependent spouses to retain assets that were previously unavailable to them. Property division was used to address the inequities. These statutes resulted in decreasing spousal support awards.

In addition, women, who were historically the economically dependent spouses, joined the workforce in increasing numbers. The previous assumption that women would be unable to support themselves through employment gave way to the idea that dependence could no longer be used as a rationale for alimony. However, the practical reality of women's financial dependency remained in many marriages.

With the advent of no-fault divorce, alimony also lost its punitive rationale. The Uniform Marriage and Divorce Act (UMDA) changed the character of these awards to one that was almost exclusively needs based and at the same time gave spousal support a new name: maintenance. Maintenance was only available to the spouse who had an inability to meet his or her reasonable needs through appropriate employment. The marital standard of living was only one of six factors relied upon in making awards under the UMDA, where the focus was now on "self-support" even if it was at a substantially lower level than existed during the marriage. In addition, when awards were made they were generally only for a short term, sufficient to allow the dependent spouse to become "self-supporting." This spousal support reform often left wives, who were frequently the financially dependent spouses in long term marriages, without permanent support.

Maintenance was sometimes awarded for "rehabilitative" purposes such as providing income for the time it takes the recipient to acquire skills or education necessary to become self-supporting. Short term transitional awards were used to make a spouse economically self sufficient as soon as possible.

C.   1990's Reforms

In response to the denial of long term awards for those most in need of them, the "second wave" of reform took place in the 1990's and expanded the factors justifying an award beyond "need." This new legislation encouraged courts to base awards more on the unique facts of a case and less on broad assumptions about need and the obligation to become self-supporting in spite of the loss of earning capacity that often occurs in long term marriages. The use of vocational experts to measure earning capacity became more widespread and there were attempts to quantify the value of various aspects of homemaker services as part of a support award.

As a result of the frustration in developing a cohesive theory of alimony that would in turn lead to more consistent awards, many commentators turned to an analysis premised on compensation for loss of human capital by virtue of non-market work engaged in by the claimant during the marriage. In the human capital view, a claim for post-divorce support is based on an economic analysis that assumes that during a marriage the parties are engaged in a search for economic efficiency. These models assume that in addition to income generation, the parties also value child-rearing, and the development of income producing skills and abilities. Rational economic decisionmaking guides the parties in choices that will maximize the ability of the partnership to realize the largest gains. In most instances since women are less likely to command as high a wage in the job market, the efficiency model would lead to a decision that the non-market tasks be assumed by her. While this results in an economically satisfactory arrangement during the marriage, it often means that at divorce the non-market spouse will be disadvantaged if there is insufficient compensation for the efforts that were devoted to the partnership.

* * *

In response to the problems highlighted above, the ALI [American Law Institute] in its Principles recommends the setting of presumptions or guidelines. The ALI focuses on spousal payments as compensation for economic losses that one of the spouses incurred as a result of the marriage. The ALI guidelines are premised on the assumption that when a marriage is dissolved there are usually losses associated with it such as lost employment opportunities or opportunities to acquire education or training that lead to disparities in post-divorce earning capacities. The ALI takes the position that these losses, to the extent they are reflected in a difference in incomes at the time of dissolution, should be shared by the partners. The Principles assume a loss of earning capacity when one parent has been the primary caregiver of the children. They also make provisions for compensation for losses in short term marriages where sacrifices by one spouse leave that spouse with a lower standard of living than he or she enjoyed prior to the marriage. Finally, under the Principles, compensation could be awarded based on a loss of a return on an investment in human capital (where one spouse has supported the other through school). This would be most important in the vast majority of states that do not recognize enhanced earning capacity or a degree or license as a divisible marital partnership asset. In setting the amount and duration, the ALI recommends a formula that is based on a specified percentage of the difference in the spouses' post-divorce income for a period of time that is dependent on the length of the marriage.

E. Guidelines

While the ALI chose to focus on both the substantive rationale for alimony as well as a guideline approach to ensuring some predictability, increasing numbers of jurisdictions have chosen to focus primarily on the prediction problem by turning to mathematical formulas or guidelines. In almost all instances n63 these guidelines are intended to be used as a starting point for discussion and do not constitute a presumption. * * *

NOTES AND QUESTIONS

1. *What now?* Professor Kisthardt offers a succinct diagnosis of the problems with contemporary alimony. As you review the other materials in the chapter, consider what rationale provides the most compelling basis for requiring that one former spouse continue to transfer money to the other after the marriage has ended.

2. *Alimony and gender.* For most of our history, many state alimony statutes explicitly excluded men as potential recipients. This gender-based regime changed entirely with *Orr v. Orr*, 440 U.S. 268 (1979). *Orr* struck down Alabama's alimony statute, which explicitly provided that courts could order only husbands to pay. The Court stated:

> Appellant views the Alabama alimony statutes as effectively announcing the State's preference for an allocation of family responsibilities under which the wife plays a dependent role, and as seeking for their objective the reinforcement of that model among the State's citizens. We agree, as he urges, that prior cases settle that this purpose cannot sustain the statutes. * * * If the statute is to survive constitutional attack, therefore, it must be validated on some other basis.

> The opinion of the Alabama Court of Civil Appeals suggests other purposes that the statute may serve. Its opinion states that the Alabama statutes were "designed" for "the wife of a broken marriage who needs financial assistance." This may be read as asserting either of two legislative objectives. One is a legislative purpose to provide help for needy spouses, using sex as a proxy for need. The other is a goal of compensating women for past discrimination during marriage, which assertedly has left them unprepared to fend for themselves in the working world following divorce. We concede, of course, that assisting needy spouses is a legitimate and important governmental objective. We have also recognized "[r]eduction of the disparity in economic condition between men and women caused by the long history of discrimination against women * * * as * * * an important governmental objective." *Califano v. Webster*, 430 U.S. 313, 317 (1977). * * *

* * *

But in this case, even if sex were a reliable proxy for need, and even if the institution of marriage did discriminate against women, these factors still would "not adequately justify the salient features of" Alabama's statutory scheme, *Craig v. Boren*, [429 U.S. at 202–03]. Under the statute, individualized hearings at which the parties' relative financial circumstances are considered *already* occur. There is no reason, therefore, to use sex as a proxy for need. Needy males could be helped along with needy females with little if any additional burden on the State. * * *

Moreover, use of a gender classification actually produces perverse results in this case. As compared to a gender-neutral law placing alimony obligations on the spouse able to pay, the present Alabama statutes give an advantage only to the financially secure wife whose husband is in need. Although such a wife might have to pay alimony under a gender-neutral statute, the present statutes exempt her from that obligation. Thus, "[t]he [wives] who benefit from the disparate treatment are those who were ... nondependent on their husbands," *Califano v. Goldfarb*, 430 U.S. 199, 221 (1977) (STEVENS, J., concurring in judgment). They are precisely those who are not "needy spouses" and who are "least likely to have been victims of ... discrimination," [*id.*], by the institution of marriage. A gender-based classification which, as compared to a gender-neutral one, generates additional benefits only for those it has no reason to prefer cannot survive equal protection scrutiny.

3. *Gender neutrality.* Today, all states have gender neutral alimony statutes that permit either the husband or wife to receive an award. The law in practice, however, does not always reflect the law on the books. "[M]en seldom receive alimony, in part because they seldom request it and perhaps in part because judges may continue to harbor prejudices against awarding alimony to men." Timothy Garrison, Orr v. Orr, 14 J. Contemp. Legal Issues 137, 142 n.21 (2004). From 2001–2006, the percentage of alimony awards going to men was 3.6%, a number that presumably will increase as the number of wives who earn more than their husbands increases. Anita Raghaven, *Men Receiving Alimony Want a Little Respect*, Wall St. J., April 1, 2008, p. A1. Of course, even when a spouse can support one household independently, there may still be concerns about an ability to completely fund two households.

4. *Women's post-divorce economic status.* Alimony may help equalize some disparate impacts of divorce. In 1985, Lenore Weitzman created great publicity for this issue with her book, The Divorce Revolution: The Unexpected Social and Economic Consequences for Women and Children in America (1985). Weitzman's study of California divorces suggested that the economic effects of divorce had significantly different impacts on men and women. She found that men experienced a 42% gain in their standards of living after divorce, but that women experienced a 73% decrease in their standards of living. *Id.* at 323. These statistics do not, Professor Weitzman explained, necessarily reflect changes in salaries; instead, they are based on the increase in expenses relative to income for female-headed households with children,

and on the decrease in expenses for male-headed households without children. *Id*. at 340–42.

Scholars have questioned the accuracy of Weitzman's data and the magnitude of the differences between men's and women's standards of living post-divorce, but subsequent studies confirm her general conclusion. For example, another study documented the gap between men's and women's incomes, and found that women experience closer to a 30% decrease in standard of living upon divorce. *See* Jennifer L. McCoy, *Spousal Support Disorder: An Overview of Problems in Current Alimony Law*, 33 Fla. St. U. L. Rev. 501 (2005).

Few have questioned Weitzman's conclusion that men's standards of living generally increase while women's standards of living generally decrease after divorce. It is estimated that for the average divorced woman, family income was approximately 1.6 times the poverty level, but would have been 3.5 times the poverty level if she had remained married. Robert I. Lerman, *Marriage and the Economic Well–Being of Families with Children: A Review of the Literature* 25 (July 2002), http://www.urban.org/UploadedPDF/410541_LitReview.pdf. Though not quite as attention grabbing as Weitzman's finding of 73%, these numbers still constitute a considerable deterioration from the marital standard of living.

5. *Alimony, race and class.* Because alimony awards involve ongoing transfers of money, they are available to only a small percentage of divorcing couples, usually relatively affluent ones. As a result, use of alimony is subject to some criticism:

> Whereas historically many white women have been able to enhance their standards of living by "marrying well," this has seldom been the case for Black women. Because Black men typically earn less than white men, for most Black families, having the mother in the workforce has always been a necessity. Black women are less likely than white women to have the option of choosing part-time work in order to spend more time with their children, and, obviously, Black women are less likely than white women to be confronted with the "dilemma" of having to decide whether to leave a promising job to follow a husband whose company has transferred him or who has found a job opportunity elsewhere.

* * *

> Feminists must, however, recognize that the search for a theory of alimony also reinforces privilege—or at least the image of privilege—in a group that is predominately white and middle or upper-middle class, in a world where women of color and other poor women often live lives of economic desperation. To the extent that alimony reinforces the subordination of poor and minority women, it fuels a divisiveness that undermines and weakens the women's movement. Feminists must also recognize that to the extent women are protected when they play the role of full-time homemaker they will continue to see it as a viable option. The result is continued economic dependence on men. * * *

Twila L. Perry, *Alimony: Race, Privilege, and Dependency in the Search for Theory*, 82 Geo. L.J. 2481, 2489–90, 2519 (1994). Indeed, approximately 90%

of the population receiving alimony in 2000 was white. A. Michele Dickerson, *Race Matters in Bankruptcy*, 61 Wash. & Lee L. Rev. 1725, 1749 (2004).

Do you agree with Professor Perry that the availability of alimony perpetuates the breadwinner/homemaker family model? Do Professor Perry's arguments apply to poor families as well as black families? *See* Keith L. Shoji, *Alimony: Race, Privilege, and Dependency in the Search for Theory*, 11 J. Contemp. Legal Issues 309 (2000).

B. THE UNIFORM MARRIAGE AND DIVORCE ACT

As Professor Kisthardt notes, the 1970 Uniform Marriage and Divorce Act (UMDA) established a standard for alimony or maintenance awards that focused on spousal need, rather than fault. Once a spouse established need, the Act directed the court to consider several factors in deciding on the award's amount and length.

UNIFORM MARRIAGE AND DIVORCE ACT

9A U.L.A. 446 (1998).

§ 308. Maintenance

(a) In a proceeding for dissolution of marriage, legal separation, or maintenance * * * the court may grant a maintenance order for either spouse only if it finds that the spouse seeking maintenance:

> (1) lacks sufficient property to provide for his reasonable needs; and
>
> (2) is unable to support himself through appropriate employment or is the custodian of a child whose condition or circumstances make it appropriate that the custodian not be required to seek employment outside the home.

(b) The maintenance order shall be in amounts and for periods of time the court deems just, without regard to marital misconduct, and after considering all relevant factors, including:

> (1) the financial resources of the party seeking maintenance, including marital property apportioned to him, his ability to meet his needs independently, and to the extent to which a provision for support of a child living with the party includes a sum for that party as custodian;
>
> (2) the time necessary to acquire sufficient education or training to enable the party seeking maintenance to find appropriate employment;
>
> (3) the standard of living during the marriage;
>
> (4) the duration of the marriage;
>
> (5) the age and the physical and emotional condition of the spouse seeking maintenance; and

(6) the ability of the spouse from whom maintenance is sought to meet his needs while meeting those of the spouse seeking maintenance.

NOTES AND QUESTIONS

1. *Interpreting the Uniform Marriage and Divorce Act.* In *Otis v. Otis*, 299 N.W.2d 114 (Minn. 1980), the court narrowly construed the meaning of "reasonable needs" under the UMDA when it awarded the wife alimony for four years. Although the husband's annual salary was approximately $120,000, the court expected that the wife, who had not worked for the last 23 years of the 25–year marriage, would be able to earn $12,000 to $18,000 as a secretary, "with some additional training." Many other courts had an aggressive commitment to "self support," which sometimes resulted in difficulties for dependent spouses. In evaluating the UMDA and the other approaches to alimony discussed in this chapter, consider the impact of the various policies on the recipient spouse.

2. *Rate of alimony awards.* Despite the extensive discussion of alimony indicated by the initial material in this chapter, very few spouses actually receive it today. Although estimates of the rate of awards vary, alimony is awarded in only about twenty percent of divorce cases. *See* Karen Turnage Boyd, *The Tale of Two Systems: How Integrated Divorce Laws Can Remedy the Unintended Effects of Pure No–Fault Divorce,* 12 Cardozo J.L. & Gender 609, 622 (2006). "Although one study found that 80 percent of women assume they will be able to get alimony if they need it, in fact few women are awarded alimony today (about 8 percent), or have ever been," awards remain low, and "two thirds of alimony awards are temporary." Joan Williams, Unbending Gender: Why Family and Work Conflict and What to Do About It 122 (2000).

Why is there such a dramatic difference between a spouse's expectation of alimony and the actual award rate?

SECTION 2:　JUSTIFICATIONS FOR ALIMONY

This section considers the rationale for alimony awards, while the next section examines how courts use various rationales when they make alimony awards. Justifications for alimony have evolved over the years. Until the mid-twentieth century, alimony under the fault-based divorce system was typically available in limited circumstances and was awarded only to an "innocent" wife. Moreover, most states divided property between the divorcing spouses based on a "title system," which awarded each spouse only the property titled in his or her name. However "if, as was generally the case, the title system left a wife without sufficient property or earning potential to support herself after divorce, courts awarded her permanent alimony." Deborah H. Bell, *Family Law at the Turn of the Century*, 71 Miss. L.J. 781, 791 (2002). Because awards were based on need or fault, courts provided little explanation for their underlying theoretical basis or for their amount. With the development of the no-fault divorce system, the old gender-based rationale based on "innocence" or "guilt" no longer provided a principled basis for alimony awards. Regardless of the form that alimony takes, the fundamental issue today is why one spouse must support the other once a marriage has ended and marital property has been distributed equitably.

A. JUSTIFICATIONS FOR ALIMONY AWARDS

As you learned at the beginning of the Chapter, alimony awards lack consistency from state to state. Some inconsistencies may result from difficulties in identifying a justification for such ongoing support payments in a world of no-fault divorce, where marriages may be of limited duration, and where, at least sometimes, both spouses contribute financially to the household during the marriage. Courts, legislatures and commentators have identified various rationales for alimony, but each justification raises its own set of issues. Alimony might be awarded based on theories of providing compensation, addressing needs, rewarding expectations, or dissolving a partnership. As you review these justifications, consider how they relate to, and overlap with, the types of alimony discussed in this Chapter.

1. THE "FAULT–BASED" JUSTIFICATION

Even with no-fault divorce, the traditional rationale for alimony may retain some validity. The UMDA removed fault from the guidelines for determining entitlement to alimony, but commentators have begun suggesting that fault should be reinserted into the calculation, and some states retain fault-based alimony. For example, a South Carolina court "may not award alimony to a spouse who commits adultery before the earliest of (1) the formal signing of a written property or marital settlement agreement or (2) entry of a permanent order of separate maintenance and support." S.C. Code Ann. § 20–3–130(A) (2008). Other states allow courts to consider adultery or other fault as one factor in establishing the award. Marriages with domestic violence may be particularly sympathetic candidates for fault-based awards.

Considering fault in the alimony determination, however, can produce problems. First, a determination of fault may require the type of "dirty laundry" factfinding that no-fault divorce was designed, in part, to prevent. Second, in some states (such as South Dakota), the court is required to determine "relative fault." Such a determination may be quite complex, because both parties often share responsibility for the breakdown of the marriage. Finally, to the extent that fault-based alimony "rewards" innocence, it may diminish the importance of other factors that may be significant to alimony, such as the spouses' reasonable expectations or needs. Can you think of other problems with an alimony calculus that permits consideration of fault?

2. THE "NEED–BASED" JUSTIFICATION

This justification for alimony examines the dependent spouse's needs. As the ALI explains, one "spouse frequently seems in need at the conclusion of a marriage because its dissolution imposes a particularly severe loss on him or her. The intuition that the former spouse has an obligation to meet that need arises from the perception that the need results from the unfair allocation of the financial losses arising from the marital failure." ALI, Principles of the Law of Family Dissolution: Analysis and Recommendations § 5.02, cmt. a (2002). After spouses have been married for some time, it seems reasonable that they would expect to maintain (to the extent possible) their same standard of living post-divorce.

However, the definition of "need" depends on each judge's exercise of discretion. Some judges believe that "need" means an award that maintains the same standard of living as the parties enjoyed during the marriage, but other judges define need in a more limited manner, perhaps to cover only the parties' minimal necessaries. Moreover, need is a conclusory basis for alimony, and does not provide a justification for why one party should be required to support the other once the marriage ends. Invocation of need as a justification highlights "the law's historic inability to provide any consistent principle for determining when, and to what extent, a former spouse is 'in need'. We cannot choose among the many possible definitions of need if we do not know the reason for imposing the obligation to meet it." Ira Mark Ellman, *Do Americans Play Football?*, 19 Intl. J.L. Pol'y & Fam. 257, 260–61 (2005).

3.　THE "CONTRACT" JUSTIFICATION

This justification for alimony analogizes marriage to a contractual relationship between the parties. As in any other contract, the parties enter into a written agreement, i.e., the marriage certificate, to engage in a joint enterprise. The exact parameters of each party's obligations are not spelled out, but it is generally assumed that each party is willing to make some sacrifices as "consideration" for the benefits that party will receive from performance of the marriage agreement.

Yet this justification also raises problems because the contract analogy requires a court to examine how a contract was breached:

> One might of course ask why courts require one spouse to meet the other's needs after divorce. A contractual theory would answer: as damages for breach of contract. If that were the correct answer, then alimony would always be awarded to the spouse in compliance with the contract, who showed his or her former mate to be in breach, and never awarded to the spouse in breach. Yet that is not the law or the practice, in either fault or no-fault states. Most obviously, awards of alimony are made in many dissolutions in which the court finds neither spouse at fault—a large proportion of cases even in those states that allow the court to consider fault in making alimony awards. Moreover, no state awards alimony to an "innocent" but financially more secure spouse, against a financially weaker one at fault, even egregious fault. So, for example, the housewife who shoots

her high-earning husband would never be ordered to pay him alimony, so long as he continued to earn more than she. Clearly "breach" cannot be the main story of alimony * * *.

Ira Mark Ellman & Sharon Lohr, *Marriage as Contract, Opportunistic Violence, and Other Bad Arguments for Fault Divorce*, 1997 U. Ill. L. Rev. 719, 743.

4. THE "PARTNERSHIP" JUSTIFICATION

This justification of alimony views marriage as analogous to a partnership, with is an agreement to share profits, assets and debts. Similar to the contract rationale, this view suggests that spouses have an implied agreement to work for the joint venture's benefit rather than for the individual's. Upon divorce, alimony also assures that each spouse takes responsibility for the burden for the failed partnership. *See* Ira Mark Ellman, *The Theory of Alimony*, 77 Cal. L. Rev. 1, 33 (1989). This approach might require that

> a spouse whose earnings disproportionately increase during marriage in relation to those of his partner should be required to buy out her interest at divorce. This marital exit price resembles the buyout required of a fixed-term partnership that continues to operate after dissociation of a partner. The principle underlying buyout is simple: when partnership contributions generate value, i.e., enhance the ability of the partnership to generate future income, a departing partner is entitled to a share of that value. Partners who elect to continue what was once a shared effort are thus required to compensate a departing partner.

Cynthia Lee Starnes, *Mothers as Suckers: Pity, Partnership, and Divorce Discourse*, 90 Iowa L. Rev. 1513, 1543 (2005).

However, partnership law's normal standards are difficult to apply to a marriage because partnership and marriage are drastically different. The central purpose of a business partnership is an economic goal, but a marriage is expected to be centered on companionship and love, rather than economic advancement. A married couple expects a lifelong intimate commitment rather than a temporary, or even long term, business deal. For this reason, one spouse might sacrifice economic advancement, such as by leaving the work force to raise a family, despite the fact that the decision is not economically rational. Marriage creates "far more economic interdependency, division of labor, and lost opportunities than business relationships ever contemplate." Katharine K. Baker, *Contracting for Security: Paying Married Women What They've Earned*, 55 U. Chi. L. Rev. 1193, 1198 (1988). Because the market does not adequately value the economic benefits of a spouse's contribution to homemaking, a partnership analogy makes it difficult to measure and adequately evaluate the terms of alimony.

5. THE "RESTITUTION" JUSTIFICATION

Courts have suggested that an agreement-based justification is flawed because spouses do not explicitly agree to an exchange of services. Restitution, however, provides an alternative basis for alimony because it requires repayment for the benefits of a quasi-contract, even if the parties did not directly discuss such an agreement when they married. Restitution is based on the concept that when one spouse confers a benefit on the other, the benefit is conferred at the first spouse's expense. Consequently, the other spouse's continuing enjoyment of the benefit without compensation is unjust. A homemaker who works without pay to advance her husband's career goals, for example, may argue for restitution-based alimony because she has conferred the benefit of support, lost her wage earning capacity and will suffer unjustly if she does not receive compensation for her contributions. Such a theory relies on the court's ability to recognize the value of the claimant's contributions to the marriage.

The real problem with a restitution rationale lies in determining whether the payee can actually establish the elements of the claim. Both parties may acknowledge that the payor was enriched at the payee's expense, but did the benefit constitute *unjust* enrichment? A spouse claiming alimony may perform family duties under the expectation that he or she would benefit, at least to some extent, from the other spouse's actions, but still may have difficulty proving that performance occurred with assumption of a monetary benefit. Moreover, if restitution requires proof that a spouse has lost wage-earning capacity, then the court must determine that spouse's career possibilities, which may result in a relatively minimal award (depending on the type of wages that the spouse might have earned).

6. THE "REIMBURSEMENT" JUSTIFICATION

Reimbursement alimony describes both a form and a justification for a time-limited award. In contrast to most permanent or other forms of temporary alimony awards, reimbursement alimony does not terminate upon remarriage or other cohabitation. Reimbursement alimony is designed to compensate one spouse for enhancing the other's earning capacity, typically through support for graduate or professional school. Based on the acknowledgement that both spouses worked toward attaining the degree, the law recognizes that both should be entitled to claim some of the benefits.

Determining when to award reimbursement alimony and the appropriate amount may be difficult. For example, the New Jersey court which introduced the concept of reimbursement alimony explained that it "should cover all financial contributions towards the former spouse's education, including household expenses, educational costs, school travel expenses and any other contributions used by the supported spouse in obtaining his or her degree or license." However, not "every spouse who contributes toward his or her partner's education or professional training is entitled to reimbursement alimony. Only monetary contributions made with the mutual and shared expectation that both parties to the marriage will derive increased income and material benefits should be a basis for such an award." *Mahoney v. Mahoney*, 453 A.2d 527, 535 (N.J. 1982). The New Jersey statute, which is set out in the next section, was amended in 1999 to authorize the award of reimbursement alimony "under circumstances in which one party supported the other through an advanced education, anticipating participation in the fruits of the earning capacity generated by that education." N.J. Stat. Ann. § 2A:34–23(e) (West 2008).

What factors should be considered in measuring the price of support while a spouse pursues an advanced education? Should compensation be in the form of alimony or periodic payments in satisfaction of equitable distribution? Does it make any difference?

NOTES AND QUESTIONS

1. *Clarity about the rationale and type of award.* Courts setting alimony awards may use various theories depending on the result they reach. In *Bertolino v. Bertolino*, 2004 WL 2757564 (Conn. Super. Ct. Nov. 2, 2004) (unpublished opinion), the wife provided free labor to her husband's struggling bookstore and coffee shop. The court extensively analyzed the inequality of the relationship and the husband's unjust treatment of his wife. However, the court explained that the alimony award was simply for temporary maintenance and rehabilitation, rather than to reimburse the wife's unpaid service to her husband. The husband was initially required to pay temporary alimony, but stopped paying after a limited period. On appeal, the court required the husband to pay rehabilitative alimony totaling $16,500. What rationale do you think provides a basis for the court's decision?

2. *Self-sufficiency.* Does a spouse deserve support based simply on her inability to achieve self sufficiency after divorce? Should an alimony award depend on whether a specified level of difference exists between the respective incomes of the husband and wife?

B. THE ALI APPROACH: COMPENSATION FOR LOSS

The American Law Institute Principles of the Law of Family Dissolution recommend and articulate the concept of "compensatory payments" to support the spouse who has incurred a loss in earning capacity during the marriage based on the greater responsibilities for the family. ALI Principles of the Law of Family Dissolution: Analysis and Recommendations § 5.03 (2002). The primary justification for these payments is to provide a just allocation of the financial losses resulting from divorce. To determine which spouse needs support, the Principles abolish any mention of fault and instead focus on the difference in the spouses' financial standing.

1. THE PRINCIPLES

AMERICAN LAW INSTITUTE PRINCIPLES OF THE LAW OF FAMILY DISSOLUTION: ANALYSIS AND RECOMMENDATIONS (2002)

§ 5.04   Compensation for Loss of Marital Living Standard

(1) A person married to someone with significantly greater wealth or earning capacity is entitled at dissolution to compensation for a portion of the loss in the standard of living he or she would otherwise experience, when the marriage was of sufficient duration that equity requires that some portion of the loss be treated as the spouses' joint responsibility.

(2) Entitlement to an award under this section should be determined by a rule of statewide application under which a presumption of entitlement arises in marriages of specified duration and spousal-income disparity.

(3) The value of the award made under this section should be determined by a rule of statewide application that sets a presumptive award of periodic payments calculated by applying a specified percentage to the difference between the incomes the spouses are expected to have after dissolution. This percentage is referred to in this Chapter as the *durational factor*, and should increase with the duration of the marriage until it reaches a maximum value set by the rule.

(4) The presumptions established under this section should govern unless there are facts, set forth in written findings of the trial court, establishing that the presumption's application to the case before the court would yield a substantial injustice. An award may be made under this section in cases where no presumption of entitlement arises, if facts not present at the dissolution of most marriages of similar duration and income levels establish that a substantial injustice will result if there is no compensation, and those facts are set forth in written findings of the trial court.

* * *

§ 5.05   Compensation for Primary Caretaker's Residual Loss in Earning Capacity

(1) A spouse should be entitled at dissolution to compensation for the earning-capacity loss arising from his or her disproportionate share during marriage of the care of the marital children, or of the children of either spouse.

(2) Entitlement to an award under this section should be determined by a rule of statewide application under which a presumption of entitlement arises at the dissolution of a marriage in which

(a) there are or have been marital children, or children of either spouse;

(b) while under the age of majority the children have lived with the claimant (or with both spouses, when the claim is against the stepparent of the children), for a minimum period specified in the rule; and

(c) the claimant's earning capacity at dissolution is substantially less than that of the other spouse.

(3) A presumption of entitlement governs in the absence of a determination by the trial court that the claimant did not provide substantially more than half of the total care that both spouses together provided for the children.

(4) The value of an award under this section should be determined by a rule of statewide application under which a presumption arises that the award shall require a set of periodic payments in an amount calculated by applying a percentage, called the *child-care durational factor*, to the difference between the incomes the spouses are expected to have at dissolution.

(a) The rule of statewide application should specify a value for the child-care durational factor that increases with the duration of the *child-care period*, which is the period during which the claimant provided significantly more than half of the total care that both spouses together provided for the children. * * *

(5) A claimant may be entitled to both an award under this section and an award under § 5.04, but in no case shall the combined value of the child-care durational factor, and the durational factor employed to determine the presumed award under § 5.04, exceed the maximum value allowed for the durational factor alone.

(6) The presumed value of the award, as set under Paragraph (4), should govern unless there are facts, set forth in the written findings of the trial court, establishing that the presumption's application to the case before the court would yield a substantial injustice.

NOTES AND QUESTIONS

1. *Justifying compensation for loss.* In critiquing the Uniform Marriage and Divorce Act's reliance on need, and in justifying a standard based on compensation for loss, the Principles explain:

> There is first the failure to provide any satisfactory explanation for placing the obligation to support needy individuals on their former spouses rather than on their parents, their children, their friends, or society in general. The absence of any explanation for requiring an individual to meet the needs of a former spouse leads inevitably to the second problem, the law's historical inability to provide any consistent principle for determining when, and to what extent, a former spouse is 'in need.' * * *

> A spouse frequently seems in need at the conclusion of a marriage because its dissolution imposes a particularly severe loss on him or her.

The intuition that the former spouse has an obligation to meet that need arises from the perception that the need results from the unfair allocation of the financial losses arising from the marital failure. * * *

Principles, § 5.02 cmt. a.

Is this explanation persuasive? Do reasons other than unfair allocation of losses during the marriage justify why one former spouse might have a continuing obligation to support the other?

2. *Fault.* Like the laws in many jurisdictions, the Principles eschew consideration of fault, the traditional basis for alimony awards. Should fault have a role in alimony?

2.   COMMENTS AND CRITICISM OF THE PRINCIPLES

Some scholars have criticized the Principles' approach to alimony. The following two commentaries point to areas for possible future revisions:

JUNE CARBONE

The Futility of Coherence: The ALI's Principles of the Law of
Family Dissolution, Compensatory Spousal Payments.
4 J.L. Fam. Stud. 43, 77–78 (2002).

If coherence is not necessarily an appropriate measure of the ALI's success, persuasiveness may nonetheless be an important component [of] the ALI's ability to ensure adoption and consistent interpretation of its proposals. Could the precepts set forth in the *Principles* [have] been set forth more clearly—and more persuasively? I believe that the ALI could take a few measures that would put the principles on a stronger footing.

First, the ALI could acknowledge the substantive grounds for rejecting fault. Fault rested historically on the nature of marriage as a lifelong commitment made by the couple not only to each other, but to God and community. Herma Hill Kay describes modern marriage as a joint venture undertaken for limited purposes and dissolvable by either party at will. The ALI's efforts to provide greater protection for completed exchanges than executory ones are consistent with Kay's vision. Recognizing the changed legal basis for marriage would provide a stronger framework for the ALI approach than the conclusion that the otherwise relevant consideration of fault is simply too difficult to define.

Second, the ALI should have stayed with the Reporter's initial inclination to make restitution for lost career opportunities and other marital contributions the primary basis for compensatory awards. The majority of marriages produce children, and childcare almost always entails some sacrifice of career opportunities that extend beyond the end of the marriage. * * *.

Third, the ALI should explore the different nature of marital assets. Acknowledging that meteoric success in the rap industry might merit different treatment of the family car would allow the creation of more flexible categories. Most marriages do involve career interests that become increasingly commingled. If the ALI is to recognize merging interests, it should provide greater flexibility in recognizing the respective contributions to those interests over time.

Finally, the ALI should explicitly acknowledge the continuing role of public as well as private rationales for the financial resolutions made at divorce.* * * The public policy reasons for recognizing long-term homemakers may be stronger than the private justifications that the ALI invokes.

LARA LENZOTTI KAPALLA

Some Assembly Required: Why States Should Not Adopt the ALI's
System of Presumptive Alimony Awards in Its Current Form.
2004 Mich. St. L. Rev. 207, 234–35.

* * * [T]he Chief Reporter of the Principles, Ira Mark Ellman, * * * posits that alimony is "an entitlement earned through marital investment," and thus should not compensate spouses who "invested little" in the relationship. As he uses the term, "investment" means making a choice that, while benefiting the couple as a whole, would be of detriment to one spouse if the relationship did not last. It entails making a decision that a spouse would not otherwise make, if acting only in self-interest and not for the good of the marriage. Examples of such investment include supporting the other spouse through a degree or training program, providing domestic services that allow the other spouse to increase his or her earning capacity, and raising the couple's children. Not surprisingly, these examples of investment are also scenarios under which the Principles recognize alimony awards.

It follows then, that a "substantial injustice" can be limited to an instance in which a spouse who was otherwise entitled to an award had not invested in the relationship. For example, this standard would encompass situations where the couple never contemplated sharing the loss or benefits of the relationship, or had long ceased to do so. Under such a scenario, both spouses would have acted in their own financial self-interest during the marriage. If they did not rely on one another for financial support during the marriage, an award upon the dissolution of the marriage would not be appropriate.

Similarly, section 5.05's requirement that a claimant perform "substantially more than half" of the total care given to the children apparently exists to ensure that the claimant had invested in this activity. Because it could potentially reduce an alimony hearing to arguments over how time spent at little league should rate against an equivalent amount of time spent in a doctor's office, or what should be done in a situation where one spouse provided fifty-one percent of the child care and the other spouse provided forty-nine percent, this term should be replaced. Again, the concept of investment seems relevant. If, in order to take care of children, the claimant spouse has made decisions that negatively impact her earning capacity, she should be compensated for this investment. This is true regardless of whether the investment resulted in her providing twenty percent of the overall parenting responsibility, or eighty percent of the responsibility. * * *

* * *

NOTES AND QUESTIONS

1. *Substantial injustice.* How would you define "substantial injustice"? Should the Principles be based on return on investment rather than compensation for loss?

2. *Gender issues.* Feminists have criticized the ALI's approach to alimony for perpetuating gender inequality. They say that by using gender neutral language while also promoting specialization based on earning capacity, the alimony proposal forces women to remain in the domestic role of the marriage. Do the two excerpts clarify these issues?

PROBLEM 10–1

You are a member of the ALI task force responsible for revising the ALI approach. What revisions will you suggest?

SECTION 3: HOW SHOULD COURTS AWARD ALIMONY?

Courts must consider numerous factors in deciding alimony claims during divorce proceedings. The parties may have large or small incomes, may include a caretaking parent, or may be ending a long or a short marriage. If a court determines that an alimony award is appropriate, then the court must then decide its form and amount. This Section examines the various types of alimony and the means for awarding it. As you read about the different forms of awards, think about how they relate to the justifications discussed in the previous section.

A. THE FORM OF ALIMONY

As explained above, most divorces involve no alimony awards. If the parties agree to alimony or if a court awards it, alimony payments can generally be classified according to their duration and purpose:

1. TYPES OF ALIMONY

(1) **Temporary alimony (alimony *pendente lite)*—The dependent spouse receives support while the parties are litigating to determine their respective rights and obligations arising out of the marriage. Alimony *pendente lite* is different from other types of alimony because it is overwhelming based on financial *need*, so

that the dependent spouse will have a means of support during the divorce proceedings. Courts generally award temporary alimony based on the dependent spouse's reasonable need and the other spouse's ability to pay.

(2) **Final awards**—A primary social policy underlying contemporary alimony awards is the need to rehabilitate, if possible, the dependent spouse to become economically self-sufficient. However, many states recognize that the dependent spouse would sometimes find it impractical or impossible to achieve financial independence, or that an unjust disparity between the parties' standards of living would result unless alimony is awarded. Consequently, alimony statutes reflect the goal of rehabilitation, but also allow awards for other reasons. Numerous variations remain among states concerning the availability of various types of alimony:

(a) **Rehabilitative alimony** (also known as "transitional" or "short term" alimony)—Support is provided for a definite period while the recipient seeks to become "self supporting." The period varies, depending on the type of "rehabilitation" the recipient needs, such as education or training. For example, South Carolina's statute specifies that a court may award rehabilitative alimony in appropriate circumstances, but that the court must "provide modifiable ending dates coinciding with events considered appropriate by the court such as the completion of job training or education and the like," and must "require rehabilitative efforts by the supported spouse." S.C. Code § 20–3–130(B)(3)(2008).

(b) **Reimbursement alimony**—With this type of alimony, the spouse whose financial contributions during the marriage directly enhanced the other spouse's earning capacity is awarded compensation. The New Jersey statute set out later in this Section explicitly provides that reimbursement alimony is available only where "one party supported the other through an advanced education, anticipating participation in the fruits of the earning capacity generated by that education." N.J.S.A. § 2A:34–23(e).

(c) **Bridge-the-gap (or limited-duration) alimony**—This type of alimony, recognized by a few states, "provides necessary funds to 'bridge the gap' between married and single status—that is, to meet identifiable, short-term support needs that are not expressly rehabilitative in nature." Brett R. Turner, *Spousal Support in Chaos*, 25 Fam. Advoc. 14, 14 (2003). New Mexico courts, for example, may award "transitional spousal support to supplement the income of the receiving spouse for a limited period of time; provided that the period shall be clearly stated in the court's final order." N.M. S. A. § 40–4–7(B)(1)(b) (2008).

(d) **Permanent, indefinite or periodic alimony**—The spouse receives support for an undefined duration, awarded in periodic installments, to take effect from the final order of dissolution until either party's death or the recipient's remarriage. Courts award this type of payment after determining that the dependent spouse, because of age, illness or disability, "cannot reasonably be expected" to become self-supporting, or the resulting differences in the parties' respective standards of living would be "unconscionably disparate." Md. Code Ann., Fam. Law § 11–106(c) (2008). An award of permanent alimony is the exception, not the rule.

(3) **"Lump sum" alimony**—This form of alimony is a single payment not subject to modification. In nonlitigious divorces, a lump sum alimony payment is often an attractive option, permitting immediate financial settlement. Courts commonly make lump-sum awards only when periodic payments cannot be implemented for some specific reason, such as where the payor has a substance abuse problem or is an habitual spendthrift. Other courts make a rehabilitative lump-sum award when rehabilitation expenses are all due immediately (e.g., tuition for a final year of schooling), or when periodic rehabilitative support cannot be awarded for some other reason. Lump-sum alimony is generally awarded in one payment, though some courts have allowed for installment payments when necessary. This type of award was at issue in *Russell*, set out on p. 561.

2. STATUTORY AUTHORIZATION

As an example of one state's approach to alimony, the New Jersey statute includes a list of nonexclusive factors for the court to consider, and carefully sets out the different kinds of alimony that can be awarded. The statute applies to any divorce proceeding as well as to civil union dissolution proceedings.

N.J. S.A. § 2A:34–23 (2008)

§ 2A:34–23. Alimony, maintenance

* * *

b. In all actions brought for divorce, dissolution of a civil union, divorce from bed and board, legal separation from a partner in a civil union couple or nullity the court may award one or more of the following types of alimony: permanent alimony; rehabilitative alimony; limited duration alimony or reimbursement alimony to either party. In so doing the court shall consider, but not be limited to, the following factors:

(1) The actual need and ability of the parties to pay;

(2) The duration of the marriage or civil union;

(3) The age, physical and emotional health of the parties;

(4) The standard of living established in the marriage or civil union and the likelihood that each party can maintain a reasonably comparable standard of living;

(5) The earning capacities, educational levels, vocational skills, and employability of the parties;

(6) The length of absence from the job market of the party seeking maintenance;

(7) The parental responsibilities for the children;

(8) The time and expense necessary to acquire sufficient education or training to enable the party seeking maintenance to find appropriate employment, the availability of the training and employment, and the opportunity for future acquisitions of capital assets and income;

(9) The history of the financial or non-financial contributions to the marriage or civil union by each party including contributions to the care and education of the children and interruption of personal careers or educational opportunities;

(10) The equitable distribution of property ordered and any payouts on equitable distribution, directly or indirectly, out of current income, to the extent this consideration is reasonable, just and fair;

(11) The income available to either party through investment of any assets held by that party;

(12) The tax treatment and consequences to both parties of any alimony award, including the designation of all or a portion of the payment as a non-taxable payment; and

(13) Any other factors which the court may deem relevant. * * *

In determining the length of the term, the court shall consider the length of time it would reasonably take for the recipient to improve his or her earning capacity to a level where limited duration alimony is no longer appropriate.

d. Rehabilitative alimony shall be awarded based upon a plan in which the payee shows the scope of rehabilitation, the steps to be taken, and the time frame, including a period of employment during which rehabilitation will occur. An award of rehabilitative alimony may be modified based either upon changed circumstances, or upon the nonoccurrence of circumstances that the court found would occur at the time of the rehabilitative award.

This section is not intended to preclude a court from modifying permanent alimony awards based upon the law.

e. Reimbursement alimony may be awarded under circumstances in which one party supported the other through an advanced education, anticipating participation in the fruits of the earning capacity generated by that education.

NOTES AND QUESTIONS

1. *Forms.* Unlike New Jersey, other states have not adopted statutes that explicitly explain the types of alimony that might be awarded. Is the New Jersey approach appropriate, or is it an excessive limit on the court's discretion?

2. *Factors.* Must a New Jersey court consider each of the listed factors? Are there other factors that the court should consider? Later in this section, you will see a Delaware court applying a list of factors to the determination of an alimony award.

3. CASE LAW

In the next case, the court struggles with the form of alimony that can be awarded within the constraints of the Florida alimony statute, which provides:

> In a proceeding for dissolution of marriage, the court may grant alimony to either party, which alimony may be rehabilitative or permanent in nature. In any award of alimony, the court may order periodic payments or payments in lump sum or both. The court may consider the adultery of either spouse and the circumstances thereof in determining the amount of alimony, if any, to be awarded. In all dissolution actions, the court shall include findings of fact relative to the [statutory] factors * * *.

F.S.A. § 61.08(1) (2008),

RUSSELL v. RUSSELL

District Court of Appeals of Florida, 2004.
890 So.2d 1148.

KLEIN, J.

* * *

This is an appeal from a dissolution judgment in which the husband asserts that the court erred in awarding the wife lump sum alimony in the form of the husband's interest in the marital home. We affirm.

Both parties, who were married in 1985, once worked for the wife's father. The husband left that employment in 1989 and currently earns around $350,000 a year as a business broker. The wife has remained with her father's company and earns about $95,000 a year.

During the marriage the wife's parents gave the wife and husband $20,000 each annually, a total of $560,000. At the time of the dissolution the family had been living in a $2.5 million dollar home paid for partially with a one-time gift of $450,000 from the wife's parents. Subtracting the mortgage on the home leaves a net equity of about $1.5 million dollars. The wife has borrowed about $700,000 from her parents to pay for living expenses and professional fees. In all, the couple had $2.4 million in assets after deducting liabilities.

The court adopted the equal marital distribution suggested by the husband's CPA under which, as to the home, each party was awarded one-half of the equity and responsible for one-half of the mortgage.

At the time they separated, the parties, who were married for fifteen years, had lived in the home for only one year, but by the time the judgment was entered they had been there four years. The court awarded the wife a reduced amount of permanent periodic alimony, $5,000 a month, and lump sum alimony of $625,000, to be paid from the husband's one-half interest in the equity in the home, which was about $750,000. The wife was required to assume the $953,000 mortgage. The court explained the lump sum award as follows:

> Based on all of the foregoing factors, permanent periodic alimony is appropriate. Moreover, a lump sum alimony award would also be beneficial in providing stability for the Wife and minor children and maintaining the marital residence for the Wife and children. An award of lump sum alimony is appropriate to aid the Court not only for purposes of support, but also in order to achieve equitable distribution. Although the Court rejects the unequal distribution urged by the Wife, the Court does find, given the source of the parties' accumulation of wealth over the years having been derived from the Wife's parents, that it is appropriate to eliminate the Husband's interest in the marital residence so that the Wife and children may remain there. This will provide the parties with as clean a break as possible, and enable them to maintain a lifestyle that both parties can enjoy, and to maintain the most stability possible for the minor children. Should the Wife ultimately be required to sell the marital home at some point (i.e., in the event that the Wife's parents' financial assistance is insufficient or not forthcoming in the future) this award keeps a subsequent sale from being an issue between the parties at a later time.

* * *

The husband argues that the court erred in the lump sum alimony award pointing out that it left him with only one-fourth of the marital assets. * * *

Under section 61.08 [of the Florida Statutes] (2002), which governs both lump sum and periodic alimony, the court "shall consider all relevant economic factors," including the following, which we find particularly applicable: standard of living, financial resources of each party, contribution of each party to the marriage and any other factor necessary to do equity and justice.

We conclude that, under the unusual facts in this case, the award of lump sum alimony, combined with a substantially reduced periodic alimony award, was not an abuse of discretion. The court found that it was important for the wife and children to be able to remain in the house, that they would only be able to afford to do so with the continued generosity of the wife's parents, and that using lump sum as a substitute for a higher periodic alimony award would be the best way to accomplish that. In addition the court found that the husband was understating his income.

We find the remaining issues raised by the husband to be without merit. Affirmed.

WARNER, J., concurring specially.

I concur in the majority's opinion, however not all of its reasoning. The award of most of the husband's equity to the wife as lump sum alimony is really justified as an equitable distribution of property not as a substitute for support. * * *

* * *

Under the circumstances, there is justification that comports with logic and reason as to why the wife should receive the marital home as equitable distribution, making the parties' share of marital assets unequal. The equity in the marital property was due largely to the contributions by the wife's parents, much of which the wife has agreed to repay. The husband is repaid through their contribution to his education, which has increased his earning capacity.

* * *

NOTES AND QUESTIONS

1. *The governing Florida statute.* What assumptions concerning alimony underlie the statute? Florida law presumes that property distribution should be equal, unless the circumstances justify otherwise. F.S.A. § 61.075(1)(2009). Did this provision affect the court's award in *Russell*?

In *Posner v. Posner*, a Florida appellate court refused to uphold a divorce financial award because "the husband's income is nearly exhausted on obligations imposed" by the judgment, which "leave him in a hole." 988 So.2d 128, 130 (2008). The husband was a hedge fund manager, the wife stayed home to care for the parties' triplets, and the couple had been married for four years. In addition to the property distribution award, the court ordered the husband to pay lump-sum alimony of more than $90,000, leaving him with -$64,000 in net marital assets. Moreover, the husband's net monthly income was $4,134, and the alimony and child support-related awards totaled $4,109. Why might the trial judge have made this award?

2. *The UMDA's continuing influence.* Approximately 11 states reflect the UMDA philosophy and provide for alimony only where property division is insufficient to support the potential recipient's needs and where other conditions are satisfied. In these jurisdictions, courts "do not have discretion to consider whether a spouse has sacrificed his or her earning capacity for the benefit of the marriage" and, consequently, whether the spouse could "suffer permanent damage to earning capacity." Mary Frances Lyle & Jeffrey L. Levy, *From Riches to Rags: Does Rehabilitative Alimony Need to be Rehabili-*

tated?, 38 Fam. L.Q. 3, 15 (2004). Should there ever be a presumption for alimony?

B. DETERMINING ALIMONY AWARDS

Once a court decides that alimony will be awarded, the trial judge must then determine the amount and duration of the award. States have developed different approaches to guide courts' decisions in this area, often establishing a set of factors by statutes, as you saw in the New Jersey statute set out earlier. Some jurisdictions have also developed presumptions or guidelines to help courts exercise their discretion. The next decision shows a court applying a list of statutory factors.

1. CONSIDERATION OF STATUTORY FACTORS

S.A.T. v. K.D.T.

Delaware Family Court.
2004 WL 2334330 (Apr. 27, 2004).[1]

WASERSTEIN, J.

* * *

The Court now turns to the merits of Husband's claim for alimony. According to [Del. Code Ann. tit. 13, § 1512]:

> (b) A party may be awarded alimony only if he or she is a dependent party after consideration of all relevant factors contained in subsection (c) of this section in that he or she:
>
> > (1) Is dependent upon the other party for support and the other party is not contractually or otherwise obligated to provide that support after the entry of a decree of divorce or annulment;
> >
> > (2) Lacks sufficient property, including any award of marital property made by the Court, to provide for his or her reasonable needs; and
> >
> > (3) Is unable to support himself or herself through appropriate employment or is the custodian of a child whose condition or circumstances make it appropriate that he or she not be required to seek employment.

In determining the amount of alimony a party may receive, the Court must consider the [following] factors enumerated in [§ 1512(c)]:

> *(1) The financial resources of the party seeking alimony, including the marital or separate property apportioned to him or her, and his or her ability to meet all or part of his or her reasonable needs independently;*

---

1. Unpublished opinion.

A. HUSBAND'S INCOME

Husband worked for G–P in Port of Wilmington for twenty-three years, serving as a supervisor during the last three, until 1999. When the parties' children left home in 1999, Husband became depressed in April, suicidal in May, and currently receives treatment for clinical depression and bipolar disorder. Following the suicide attempt, his company placed Husband on disability for eighteen months. According to Husband's Social Security statement, his taxed Social Security earnings totaled $51,997, six months of which, Husband testified, was sick pay.

* * *

Husband contends that his mental health status prevents his employment, and yet Husband has held a number of positions that came to an end for reasons other than Husband's termination. While the Court recognizes that Husband's stated inability to concentrate limits his earning potential, it is equitable to attribute to Husband income at the rate of $10 per hour, the amount he earned while working for Caldwell and only one dollar more than his earnings at Food Lion. Husband's attributed annual income therefore totals $20,800. This interim attribution is not a final finding of ability to work, since no evidence involving medical or vocational analysis of Husband was presented to the Court.

B. HUSBAND'S EXPENSES

At trial, Husband presented total monthly expenses in the amount of $1,680, not including any health insurance cost to himself. In light of Husband's listed expenses and the associated explanations at trial, in considering his reasonable needs, Husband is attributed with the following reasonable monthly expenses totaling $1,428.

* * *

(2) The time necessary and expense required to acquire sufficient education or training to enable the party seeking alimony to find appropriate employment;

This factor is not applicable.

(3) The standard of living established during the marriage;

There was no direct evidence presented relating to this factor, though the standard of living is inherently taken into account in approximating the monthly expenses of the parties.

(4) The duration of the marriage;

The parties married on February 21, 1976 and separated on or about January 21, 2003. Wife filed a Petition for Divorce on May 22, 2003 which was scheduled to be heard on May 13, 2004. The parties separated after nearly twenty-seven years of marriage.

(5) The age, physical and emotional condition of both parties;

Wife is age 44 and in fair health. She suffers from migraine headaches and stomach problems, both requiring medication, and has recently lost sixty pounds, leaving her underweight. According to her testimony, these conditions are likely stress-related.

Husband suffers from bi-polar disorder and clinical depression, for which he takes three medications and visits a psychiatrist at least nine times per year. He stated that he has problems with concentration and rational thinking.

(6) Any financial or other contribution made by either party to the education, training, vocational skills, career or earning capacity of the other party;

This factor is not applicable.

(7) The ability of the other party to meet his or her needs while paying alimony;

A. WIFE'S INCOME

Wife's salary for 2004 is $55,000 for her service as a coordinator for MBNA, where she has been employed for fifteen years. Wife may receive a bonus, depending on her performance and the performance of the company as a whole.

Wife's father resides with her in the former marital home. He suffers from heart problems and has recently suffered the loss of spouse [sic], Wife's father contributes $700 per month to the household expenses.

B. WIFE'S EXPENSES

In light of Wife's expenses and their explanations in her deposition, for the purposes of Husband's alimony claim, Wife is attributed with the following reasonable monthly expenses totaling $2,597.

* * *

(8) Tax consequences;

Any alimony paid by Husband to Wife would be a tax deduction to him and taxable income to her.

(9) Whether either party has foregone or postponed economic, education or other employment opportunities during the course of the marriage; and

This factor is not applicable.

(10) Any other factor which the Court expressly finds is just and appropriate to consider.

The Court did not consider any other factors.

Based on the [financial plan prepared by the trial judge], Wife shall pay to Husband $505 in monthly interim alimony, beginning on May 5, 2004 and payable on the 15th of every month thereafter.

IT IS SO ORDERED.

NOTES AND QUESTIONS

1. *Weighing the factors.* What did you think of the way the court applied the statutory factors? How much discretion did the court exercise?

2. *Which factors?* In most states (39), a statutory list of factors helps guide alimony decisions. Twenty-three states do not enumerate marital fault as a factor. Forty-three jurisdictions consider standard of living as a determinative factor in calculating the amount of alimony to award, and 29 states consider the payee's status as a custodial parent. *Charts,* 41 Fam. L.Q. 709 (2008).

3. *Alimony based on the recipient's health.* Alimony can be allocated to provide not only the money to continue the accustomed standard of living, but also the cost of additional care based on each party's physical and mental health. In *Moore v. Moore,* 858 So.2d 1168 (Fla. Dist. Ct. App. 2003), for example, the wife requested alimony based partly on her diagnosis of Crohn's Disease. The husband argued that the trial court improperly considered the wife's medical condition because her illness was under control at the time of trial and she could support herself. The appellate court affirmed the award on the ground that while alimony may not anticipate a future illness, an alimony award that considered the wife's current medical condition was appropriate in light of the parties' physical and emotional health during marriage, the disparity in their incomes, their lifestyle and the duration of the marriage.

4. *The relationship between property distribution and alimony.* In *McKee v. McKee,* 664 S.E.2d 505 (Va. Ct. App. 2008), the husband transferred his interest in the marital home to the wife, who agreed to become responsible for all remaining mortgage payments. The court of appeals upheld the trial court's consideration of the wife's mortgage payments when determining the amount of spousal support.

2. INCOME EQUALIZATION

When an economically dominant spouse and an economically dependent spouse separate, one foreseeable consequence is that the dependent spouse's standard of living will fall. Post-divorce disparity of income is another factor courts must consider in alimony determinations. The following decision sets forth some of the considerations involved in determining whether the award should take the form of income equalization.

IN RE MARRIAGE OF REYNARD

Illinois Appellate Court, 2003.
801 N.E.2d 591.

JUSTICE COOK delivered the opinion of the court:

Petitioner, Mary Anne Reynard, appeals the December 31, 2002, order of the Coles County circuit court dissolving Mary Anne's marriage to respondent, Charles G. Reynard, and awarding Mary Anne maintenance in the amount of $1,600 per month until the first to occur of the following contingencies: (1) the death of either party; (2) Mary Anne's remarriage; (3) Mary Anne's cohabitation with another person on a resident, continuing, conjugal basis; or (4) completion of the January 1, 2013, payment. We affirm.

I. BACKGROUND

Mary Anne and Charles were married on January 29, 1969. They had two children: Rachel born in 1977 and Meghan born in 1982. On March 6, 2001, Mary Anne filed a petition for dissolution of marriage. On December 31, 2002, the trial court entered a judgment of dissolution of marriage and an order that addressed maintenance and the division of assets.

Both Mary Anne and Charles earned college degrees. Mary Anne earned her degree in English and took all of the required undergraduate teaching classes. After graduation from college, Mary Anne and Charles accepted teaching positions. Charles also attended law school at night. Upon graduation from law school in May 1974, Charles became a McLean County assistant State's Attorney. The new job required the parties to move from Chicago to Bloomington/Normal, Illinois. * * *

Mary Anne became a homemaker in 1977 after the birth of the parties' first child, Rachel. In 1978, Charles entered the private practice of law. In 1979, Charles unsuccessfully ran for McLean County State's Attorney. Mary Anne managed Charles's campaign and cared for Rachel. To lend help financially, Mary Anne also became a part-time employee at the Regional Office of Education.

* * *

After losing the 1979 election, Charles returned to private practice. In 1987, Charles was appointed as the McLean County State's Attorney. He ran for election in 1988 and for re-election in 1992 and 1996. Mary Anne assisted in all three campaigns by setting appointments, distributing materials, and holding campaign meetings in the home.

Mary Anne testified her responsibilities for the care of the parties' children did not allow for full-time employment. Charles acknowledged that in addition to being his most significant volunteer in political campaigns, Mary Anne was a good mother, helped out family finances through part-time employment, and had stuck with him through difficult times.

At the time of hearing, Meghan was a first-semester sophomore in college. Charles paid between $2,900 and $3,400 per month to Wellesley for Meghan's schooling. This figure does not include other expenses such as medical and travel. Mary Anne was 54 years old and in good health. She did receive psychotherapy and massages for fibromyalgia. Mary Anne worked as the coordinator of volunteers and college interns at the McLean County Museum of History. She began the position in May 1999 and earned $29,819 per year. * * * Charles was 56 years old and also in good health. He had recently won an election for circuit court judge of McLean County. His projected earnings were $136,546 per year.

* * *

When fashioning the maintenance award, the trial court considered the parties' financial-affairs affidavits. Mary Anne's affidavit indicated her average monthly expenses were $4,527. * * * The court adjusted Mary Anne's projected expenses for gardening, snow removal, household help, replacement of appliances, food, clothing, psychotherapy, lunch money, vacations, retirement plan, Internal Revenue Service, and America On–Line. The court determined a more realistic estimate of Mary Anne's expenses at the time of hearing was $3,060 per month.

Charles's financial-affairs affidavit indicates his monthly net income from all sources, including interest and dividend payments is $7,973. His total average monthly expenses are $8,542.38, including expenses for Meghan but not including a maintenance payment.

* * *

At hearing, Mary Anne called [her financial expert] to present calculations of each party's net disposable, after-tax income at varying rates of maintenance. [The expert] testified that to equalize the parties' net disposable incomes, the trial court should award maintenance somewhere between $3,700 per month and $3,800 per month. * * * [The court noted the expert's analysis failed to consider the statutory factors, including contributions toward one child's] college educational expenses. The court awarded Mary Anne maintenance in the amount of $1,600 per month * * *.

The trial court found Mary Anne's monthly net income, including the $1,600–per-month maintenance award, to be $3,040. In addition to this income, at the time of trial, Mary Anne received $300 per month from a boarder and a $3,547 federal income tax refund for the year 2001.

Notably, the trial court found:

"Charles['s] [f]inancial [a]ffairs [a]ffidavit seems to demonstrate an inability to pay maintenance in the court-ordered amount. Nevertheless, Charles has income-producing assets and a borrowing ability that will enable him to meet this obligation. A higher maintenance obligation would adversely affect his ability to meet his own needs, resulting in a greater sacrifice by Charles in his standard of living than by Mary Anne in hers. The $1,600 maintenance award affects the lifestyles of both parties, but avoids creating a substantial lifestyle deficit for either of them."

II. ANALYSIS

On appeal, Mary Anne argues she is entitled to a maintenance award of $3,750 a month to equalize the parties' net disposable incomes.

"Maintenance issues are presented in a great number of factual situations and resist a simple analysis." *In re Marriage of Mayhall*, 725 N.E.2d 22, 25 (Ill. App. Ct. 2000). The trial court has discretion to determine the propriety, amount, and duration of a maintenance award. * * * [The statutory] factors the [trial] court must consider * * * include the income and present and future earning capacity of the parties; the needs of each party; any impairment of earning capacity due to devoting time to domestic duties or having forgone or delayed opportunities due to the marriage; the time necessary to acquire appropriate education, training, and employment; the ability of the party to support himself or herself; the standard of living established during the marriage; the duration of the marriage; the age and physical and emotional condition of the parties; contributions and services by the party seeking maintenance to the education, training, or career of the other spouse; and any other factor the court expressly finds to be just and equitable. [750 Ill. Comp. Stat. 5/504(a)] (West 2000). The court is not required to give the factors equal weight and has broad discretion to "grant a temporary or permanent maintenance award for either spouse in amounts and for periods of time as the court deems just." *Id.*

* * * [The current Illinois divorce statutes] "enable a formerly dependant spouse to acquire financial independence for the future." *Mayhall*, 725 N.E.2d at 24. * * * "[A]lthough the 1993 [statutory] amendments made it easier for maintenance to be awarded, the amendments did not change the underlying approach that maintenance should only be awarded when necessary. Maintenance is not the absolute right of every party to a marriage." *Id.*

* * *

Mary Anne argues she is entitled to a maintenance award that equalizes the parties' net disposable incomes. Neither the [Illinois statutes] nor Illinois case law requires the equalization of incomes. * * *

Equalization of the parties' incomes may be appropriate in some cases. Marriage is a moral and financial partnership of coequals. It is inequitable upon dissolution to saddle a party with the burden of her reduced earning potential and to allow the other party to continue in the advantageous position he reached through their joint efforts.

Mary Anne made a significant contribution to the family during the parties' 33 years of marriage by working part-time, raising the parties' children, and managing Charles's election campaigns. Mary Anne gave up her employment in Chicago to move to Bloomington/Normal for Charles's job as an assistant State's Attorney. * * *.

Despite Mary Anne's significant sacrifices and contributions, we cannot say the trial court abused its discretion by awarding Mary Anne maintenance in the amount of $1,600 per month. The facts of this case do not rise to the level necessary to equalize the parties' net disposable incomes.

* * *

The parties do have disparate earning capacities. * * * "[W]hen former spouses have grossly disparate earning potentials, the goal of financial independence may not be achievable because of the dependent former spouse's inability to maintain the standard of living shared during the marriage." *In re Marriage of Charles*, 672 N.E.2d 57, 64 (1996). Mary Anne, however, has the ability to become self-supporting. * * * Mary Anne worked part-time during the majority of 33 years of the parties' marriage. * * *

A higher maintenance award would adversely affect Charles's ability to meet his own needs. Charles indicated in his affidavit that his monthly expenses are $8,542.38 and his monthly income is $7,973. The trial court found Charles's affidavit demonstrates he has income-producing assets and a borrowing ability that will enable him to meet a maintenance obligation of $1,600 per month. The court was concerned, however, with Charles's ability to pay more maintenance than the court ordered. Both parties' expenses exceed their incomes. Mary Anne, however, has no house or car payment and was assigned no debt. Charles must pay two mortgages, a car payment, college expenses for Meghan, and a $12,000 premarital campaign loan.

* * *

JUSTICE MCCULLOUGH, specially concurring:

* * *

* * * The dissent points to the present college expenses paid for Meghan's education and the ex-husband's substantial income in working and retirement years and concludes that maintenance should be set now at $3,750 per month and the ex-wife should be required to pay one-half of the college expenses. To do this, we would simply be the trier of fact.

JUSTICE MYERSCOUGH, dissenting.

I respectfully dissent. I would reverse the trial court's award of maintenance as an abuse of discretion. Mary Anne was clearly entitled to additional maintenance. She contributed and sacrificed 33 years of her life as wife, mother, and campaign worker. She now has a much lower present and future earning capacity, unmet needs, greater age, lesser physical and emotional capabilities, and lowered standard of living. Moreover, she has clearly made a good-faith effort to support herself.

The trial court erroneously criticized Mary Anne's expenditures and cast a blind eye on Charles's affidavit and testimony. Mary Anne's estimates were just as realistic as Charles's. The court refused to require Charles to sell assets but required Mary Anne to do so.

* * *

Although Illinois law does not require an equalization of net disposable income in large-income cases, the needs of the parties must still be met where possible. While this couple did not live an extravagant lifestyle so they could afford to send their children to college, they enjoyed substantial income, which should not be retained in large part by Charles, especially where, here, it was because of Mary Anne's sacrifices and significant contributions to the family during the parties' long marriage that Charles is able to have a greater earning capacity than does Mary Anne. As the majority points out "it is inequitable upon dissolution to saddle a party with the burden of her reduced earning potential and to allow the other party to continue in the advantageous position he reached through their joint efforts" and that is what the trial court did in this case.

Notes and Questions

1. *Support for income equalization.* Professor Joan Williams argues:

An asset [such as salary] produced by two adults should not be unilaterally awarded to only one of them. * * *

* * * A divorced husband may not have to share his income if no children were born of the marriage. But once they are, typically the children's mother will do the child rearing and other family work that allows her husband *both* to perform as an ideal worker *and* to have his children raised according to the norm of parental care after *divorce* as well as before.

* * *

In most families, ownership of accumulated property is not the most important issue. We live in a cash-flow society where most people's primary asset is their human capital, their ability to earn a wage. Very few divorcing families have substantial property because most have invested instead in the ideal-worker's wage. One study found that the average family had only $3,400 in savings upon divorce. This is why income sharing is the key to ending the postdivorce impoverishment of women and children.

Joan Williams, Unbending Gender: Why Work and Family Conflict and What to Do About It 116, 126, 129 (2000). Is the rationale for income sharing more convincing than the rationales for more traditional forms of alimony?

2. *Methods for calculating income equalization.* Professor Jane Rutherford suggests adding the incomes of the former spouses, dividing the amount by the number of family members who need support, and then allocating the money, with each member receiving an equal share. Jane Rutherford, *Duty in Divorce: Shared Income as a Path to Equality*, 58 Fordham L. Rev. 539 (1990). Does this adequately recognize the interests of the primary caretaker once the children have left home? Professor Jana Singer has suggested that income equalization should occur for a period equal to one-half of the duration of the marriage. Jana Singer, *Alimony and Efficiency: The Gendered Costs and Benefits of the Economic Justification for Alimony*, 82 Geo. L.J. 2423 (1994).

3. *Imputation of income and self-support.* How realistic are courts' assumptions about the ability of a homemaking spouse to become self-sufficient? In *Welch v. Welch*, 951 So.2d 1017 (Fla. Dist. Ct. App. 2007), the wife, who had been a registered nurse, stayed home during the marriage to home school the parties' four children. Upon divorce, she explained that she could not resume working because of her home schooling responsibilities, and the trial court awarded her alimony. An appellate court reversed, noting that "the former wife's goal of home schooling her children is laudable, [but] many

things change as a result of a marriage ending, and this may be one of them."
Id. at 1019.

PROBLEM 10–2

You are a trial court judge assigned to the family law docket. The following four cases are part of your current calendar. Your jurisdiction provides for award of alimony in an amount "based on the judge's discretion, considering the circumstances of the parties." How will you decide these four cases, each of which concerns the first marriage for both spouses? Will you award alimony in all four? If you would, what type, how much and for how long? If not, then why not?

a.   Sally and Bob marry in 2005, after both have finished college. They move to a different city so Bob can work as a manager at a large corporation. Sally takes an entry level position as a sales clerk, expecting to leave the workforce in the next few years to start a family. However, Sally does not become pregnant and after four years of marriage, the couple is seeking a divorce based on irreconcilable differences.

b.   Susan and Bernard marry in 2005, after both have finished college. They move to a different city so Bernard can work as a manager at a large corporation. Susan takes an entry level position as a sales clerk, expecting to leave the workforce in the next few years to start a family. Susan becomes pregnant after three years of marriage, and quits work when she nears the end of her pregnancy. Within the first year after the birth of their child, the couple decides to divorce.

c.   Jim and Nancy marry in 1998, when both are in their late twenties. Jim has built up a solid career as a car salesman, and Nancy spent her years after college working in secretarial positions. After they marry, Nancy returns to law school and within the next five years, obtains a position at a law firm, substantially exceeding Jim's salary in the car business. After ten years of marriage, the couple divorces.

d.   Sam and Jill marry in 1984. While married, Jill returns to graduate school to receive a Ph.D, and Sam returns to law school for a J.D. Initially, Sam works as a government lawyer and Jill works as a college professor. After a few years, though, the couple has five children, and Jill decides to teach part time until the children reach high school. The couple divorces after 25 years of marriage, with two children still in elementary school.

3.   ESTABLISHING ALIMONY GUIDELINES

Given the various and differing factors that courts consider in alimony determinations and the trial judge's broad discretion, awards vary widely from state to state, family court to family court, and even from trial judge to trial judge. In response to this unpredictability and inconsistency, several states and local court systems have promulgated formulas to help courts determine the amount and duration of alimony awards. These guidelines are designed to facilitate a more consistent and predictable framework for assessing the appropriate amount of an alimony award. Such predictability may also provide more background information for spouses as they negotiate divorce settlement agreements. Virginia R. Dugan & Jon A. Feder, *Alimony Guidelines: Do They Work?*, 25 Fam. Advoc. 20, 20–23 (Spring 2003). The American Law Institute's Principles of Family Dissolution, discussed earlier in the Chapter, similarly advocate guidelines.

The following list summarizes the alimony guideline practices already used by some state court systems. These practices vary, from mathematical formulas to limits based on length of marriage or amount of obligor's income.

a. Arizona—To help minimize the unpredictability of alimony awards, the Maricopa County court system adopted guidelines for application in conjunction with a list of statutory factors. *Cullum v. Cullum*, 160 P.3d 231 (Ariz. Ct. App. 2007). The award amount is based on a "duration factor," which increases with the length of the marriage. This factor is then multiplied by the difference between the spouses' salaries. The length of the marriage is also significant in determining the duration of the alimony obligation. If the marriage has lasted longer than 20 years and the recipient spouse is at least 50 years old, the duration is indefinite.

b. California—The state's alimony statute recites a list of factors to be used in determining the alimony award, but many counties have established guidelines that apply to temporary support. For example, Santa Clara County court rules calculate an alimony award by taking 40% of the payor's net income, and then subtracting 50% of the payee's net income, adjusted for tax consequences. *Family Rules*, Superior Court for the State of California, County of Santa Clara, *available at* http://www.sccsuperiorcourt.org/rules/PDFs/final.7.05/Family.pdf. Marin County applies a similar guideline. *Family Law Rules*, Marin County Superior Court, *available at* http://www.co.marin.ca.us/courts/PDFs-localrules/6 Family.pdf.

c. Maine—In Maine, courts apply rebuttable presumptions that general support "may not be awarded if the parties were married for less than 10 years * * * [and] that general support may not be awarded for a term exceeding ½ the length of the marriage if the parties were married for at least 10 years but not more than 20 years as of the date of the filing of the action for divorce." The presumptions do not apply to other forms of alimony, such as reimbursement or pendent lite. 19–A M.R.S.A. § 951–A(2)(A)(1) (2008).

d. Texas—For a spouse to be eligible for alimony, the marriage must have lasted at least 10 years. Support may not exceed the lesser of $2,500 or 20% of the obligor's gross monthly income, and is limited to no more than three years, with exceptions for few specified circumstances, including where the recipient spouse is mentally or physically disabled or is the caretaker of a young child. *See* V.T.C.A., Family Code §§ 8.051–.055 (2008).

1. *Are guidelines and duration parameters useful?* Do these alimony guidelines account for the variations in roles, responsibilities and earning capacities within different marriages? Do they provide models for consistent awards?

2. *Model guidelines?* If you were a state legislator reviewing alimony statutes, which model would you choose? Would you implement guidelines or presumptions? If so, on what would they be based? If you were a judge, which approach would you prefer? A litigant?

SECTION 4: ENFORCEMENT OF ALIMONY AWARDS

A. METHODS FOR ENFORCING ALIMONY AWARDS

Once the court determines that a spouse is entitled to alimony, issues remain concerning enforcement of the ongoing alimony obligation. Divorced spouses sometimes pay early installments, but then fail to continue payment.

1. MEANS OF ENFORCEMENT

To enforce the alimony award, the recipient spouse may need to bring another lawsuit. Courts may retain jurisdiction over divorce decrees, which then become enforceable through contempt proceedings.

In *Schneider v. Schneider*, 644 A.2d 510 (Md. 1994), the court enforced an alimony award even though the spouses lied about the husband's behavior to procure a speedier divorce. During their 24 years of marriage, the husband, Mark, dominated the wife, Janet. In 1990, Mark moved out of the marital home. A year later, mistakenly believing that the statutory waiting period for a voluntary divorce was two years (when in fact, it is 12 months), Mark told Janet that he did not want to wait the full statutory waiting period for a no-fault absolute divorce and that he would promise to pay spousal support if she filed for a fast divorce based on adultery. Janet was granted alimony on this basis. Mark initially paid as promised, but stopped after the first two payments.

The trial court dismissed Janet's two enforcement actions as punishment for her perjury during the divorce proceedings. However, the state's highest court recognized that the dismissals harmed only Janet, while allowing Mark to benefit from this "scheme." Furthermore, the court wished to enforce Mark's initial promise to provide spousal support to achieve a divorce. The court explained that dismissing the case would simply reward the economically superior spouse for his perjury, while punishing the wife by denying her alimony. Thus, despite the parties' lack of truth to obtain their divorce, the court ordered enforcement of their alimony agreement.

2. PRIVATE ENFORCEMENT METHODS

As alternatives to a judicial enforcement action, there may be other creative means for securing the payment of alimony. Two of the most common methods involve establishing a separate trust for alimony awards, or requiring the payor spouse to obtain life insurance. In *Gilfillin v. Gilfillin*, 512 S.E.2d 534, 536 (S.C. Ct. App. 1999), the court rejected the wife's request for a lump-sum alimony award, but granted her $3,200 per month, with the requirement that the husband establish a trust to ensure alimony payments if he predeceased her.

As noted in Chapter 9, life insurance may similarly ensure protection of the payee spouse's interest or help recover any unpaid alimony obligations. *See, e.g., Sobelman v. Sobelman*, 541 So.2d 1153 (Fla. 1989). However, a payor spouse may be required to obtain life insurance only when special circumstances demonstrate need for this precaution. In *Levy v. Levy*, 900 So.2d 737 (Fla. Dist. Ct. App. 2005), for example, the court denied the former wife's request for an order that her husband purchase life insurance to secure her permanent alimony award. The court held that the wife had failed to produce " 'evidence of the payor's insurability, the cost of the proposed insurance, and the payor's ability to afford the insurance.' " *Id.* at 745.

3. ENFORCEMENT FOR MILITARY PERSONNEL

The Uniformed Services Former Spouses Protection Act allows state courts to distribute a military service member's retirement pay to former spouses, under the Defense Department's enforcement authority. A portion can be paid directly to a former spouse in accordance with a court's alimony award. The Act applies only if the parties have been married for at least ten years, and if the payor spouse performed at least ten years of military service during the marriage. The spouse is entitled to no more than 50% of the payor's disposable retirement pay. Not all former spouses will automatically receive a portion of the retirement benefits. Former spouses cannot collect for past due payments, but the Act provides an important procedure for guaranteeing collection of future alimony. 10 U.S.C. § 1408 (2008); Military Pay: Garnishment, Child Support and Alimony Q & A, *available at* http://www.dfas.mil/militarypay/garnishment/supp-qa.html.

But where alimony proceedings involve a spouse who is serving in the military, the Servicemembers Civil Relief Act, 50 U.S.C.S App. § 521–527 (2008), may make it difficult for the other spouse to enforce an alimony award. This law allows for the temporary suspension of all civil proceedings against servicemembers while they are on active duty.

4. ATTACHMENT OF WAGES

Courts may also enforce an alimony award by attaching a portion of the payor's earnings. Like the procedure for payments by former military personnel, this attachment removes a portion of the payor's earnings from his or her paycheck. The payor's employer receives a notice of wage attachment, instructing the employer to pay over a portion of the payor's salary to a levying officer. If the employer fails to comply, it will be liable for contempt and may be forced to repay the withheld balance.

5. INCARCERATION

Some statutes make failure to pay court-ordered alimony an act of contempt of court subject to imprisonment or other sanction. In Louisiana, for example, contempt arising from nonpayment of court-ordered spousal support is punishable by up to three months in jail as well as a $500 fine. La. Rev. Stat. Ann. § 13:4611(1)(d)(2008).

B. BANKRUPTCY AND ALIMONY ENFORCEMENT

For many years, bankruptcy provided ex-spouses a basis for terminating an alimony obligation. Because alimony was a debt dischargeable in bankruptcy, the obligor spouse could file for bankruptcy and emerge free of any alimony claims.

In 1994, Congress expanded the list of obligations which are not dischargeable upon bankruptcy to include alimony and other forms of prospective, ongoing spousal support. As initially enacted, however, payment was excused if the debtor did not have the ability to pay the debt from income or property reasonably expended to cover the debt. *See* 11 U.S.C. § 523(a)(15)(A)(2008). Additionally, the court was required to balance the benefit to the debtor from discharging the debt against the detriment to the other spouse if denied alimony or support payments. *See* 11 U.S.C. § 523(a)(15)(B). A bankrupt spouse could still find excuses to avoid paying alimony.

In 2005, Congress amended 11 U.S.C. § 523 to reaffirm the non-dischargeability of alimony, and to remove the court's discretion to order discharge support obligations in alimony. Most significantly, this change eliminates the balancing test.

As a result of this amendment, "alimony, maintenance, support and property settlement debts have been given new status as 'domestic support obligations[.]' * * * In addition, the rules relating to the discharge of alimony, maintenance, support and property settlement obligations have been streamlined." Peter C. Alexander, *"Herstory Repeats: The Bankruptcy Code Harms Women and Children*, 13 Am. Bankr. Inst. L. Rev. 571, 578 (2005).

SECTION 5:   MODIFICATION AND TERMINATION OF ALIMONY

Unless an alimony order prevents modification, the obligor or obligee spouse may normally petition the court to increase or decrease alimony due to an unexpected and substantial change in circumstances. Such a change requires the court to examine both spouses' changed financial circumstances, and whether similar changes in circumstances have produced modification in prior cases. Courts then consider several factors, including the effects of modification on the other party, the length of the marriage itself, each party's current health, the purpose of the alimony originally awarded and other relevant factors. Courts also evaluate whether the changes are self-induced, or whether they are based on factors beyond the control of the payor or payee. *See* Mark R. Soboslai, *Three Steps to Modification: Responding to a Change in Circumstances*, 25–SPG Fam. Advoc. 35 (2003). In deciding whether to modify an alimony award, courts have considerable discretion.

An order may specify the conditions on which it can be terminated, and state statutes establish standards for termination.

A. MODIFICATION

Courts recognize the need for modification, but they also make clear that changes in financial situation or physical health do not by themselves guarantee a right to modification.

MARTINDALE v. MARTINDALE

Tennessee Court of Appeals, 2005.
2005 WL 94366 (Aug. 22, 2005).[1]

HOLLY M. KIRBY, J.

This is a post-divorce alimony case. The parties were divorced in 1995 and the mother was awarded rehabilitative alimony for seven years. In 2003, the trial court extended the rehabilitative alimony until the youngest of the parties' four children graduated from high school. The extension of alimony was based on the demands of being the primary residential parent for the parties' four young sons, two of whom were found to have learning disabilities. The father appealed the extension of rehabilitative alimony. We affirm.

Plaintiff/Appellant Michael Lynn Martindale, M.D., ("Father") and Defendant/Appellee Margo Miller Martindale ("Mother") were divorced on March 31, 1995. At the time of the divorce, the parties had four minor children: Michael Rand Martindale, born September 11, 1988, Miles Thomas Martindale, born February 8, 1990, Austin Edward Martindale, born December 12, 1991, and Miller Christian Martindale, born April 24, 1993. Mother worked teaching school while Father was in medical school. When the parties' first child was born, Mother became a full-time homemaker. Father's medical practice was with Jackson Clinic.

At the time of the divorce, the parties entered into a Marital Dissolution Agreement ("MDA"), which was incorporated into the final divorce

---

1. Unpublished opinion.

decree. Under the final decree, Mother was awarded sole physical and legal custody of the children * * *.

Under the final decree, Father agreed to pay wife $5,000.00 per month as rehabilitative alimony. The alimony was to continue until two and one-half years after the youngest child entered the first grade. This resulted in monthly alimony payments to Mother for seven years, scheduled to end on February 15, 2002.

On February 8, 2002, prior to the termination of the alimony payments, Mother filed a Motion * * * to Modify Final Order. In this petition, Mother sought * * * to continue the rehabilitative alimony, and to award alimony *in futuro*.

A hearing on the issues was held on April 24, 2002. Both parties testified extensively regarding child support, alimony, and financial issues. Father testified that when the parties divorced, he made approximately $292,000, and that since 1997 he had made in excess of $400,000 per year. Mother worked at a medical clinic for $15.00 per hour. She worked part-time so that she could be available for the children's activities after school, and to assist their two learning-disabled sons with their school work. * * *

* * *

* * * At the end of the hearing, the trial court found that Mother ha[d] not been able to rehabilitate herself as contemplated in the MDA * * * due to the demands of being custodian and primary care parent for four young sons, whose demands on her times and energy [have] increased every year. And the Court finds this will probably continue to [be] so.

The trial court also noted that the learning problems of two of the sons could not have been contemplated when the parties entered into the MDA. As a result, the trial court continued the $5,000 monthly rehabilitative alimony until the youngest child graduates from high school. * * *

[Father appealed.]

* * *

Modification of an alimony award is factually driven, calling for a careful balance of many factors. The trial court is given wide latitude, and its decision will not be disturbed unless it is "not supported by the evidence or is contrary to the public policies reflected in the applicable statutes." *Bogan v. Bogan*, 60 S.W.3d 721, 727 (Tenn. 2001). * * *

* * *

* * * Father asserts that the evidence showed that Mother had rehabilitated herself, and therefore the trial court erred in extending Mother's rehabilitative alimony. The record shows that Mother became recertified to teach school, and that Mother was employed part-time in a medical clinic. However, Mother also offered substantial testimony on the amount of time needed to care for the four children, due to their extensive

extracurricular activities and the learning disabilities of two of the children. Mother testified that the children's demands on her time prevent her from working a forty-hour work week. Based on this testimony, the trial court found that Mother was not fully rehabilitated and would be unable to fully rehabilitate herself until the children graduate from high school. After a full review of the record, we cannot say that the evidence preponderates against this finding.

Father further asserts that the evidence did not show that Mother's alleged inability to rehabilitate herself was due to unforeseen circumstances. Father argues that an award of alimony can only be modified "upon a showing of a substantial and material change" as provided in Tennessee Code Annotated § 36–5–101. Father argues that there has been no material change in circumstances and that Mother's current situation is exactly what the parties contemplated when the MDA was signed. The trial court, however, found that the learning disabilities of the parties' two sons could not have been contemplated when the parties signed the MDA, and that it adversely impacted Mother's ability to work full-time and to rehabilitate herself. From our review of the record, the evidence does not preponderate against this finding.

Finally, Father asserts that if Mother is not rehabilitated, it is because she did not make a reasonable attempt to rehabilitate herself. Father argues that Mother knew that she had seven years of rehabilitative alimony but did not use this time [to] further her education or prepare for a new career. After hearing the evidence, the trial court found that Mother "has not been able to rehabilitate herself as contemplated in the MDA ... due to the demands of being custodian and primary care parent for four young sons." Again, the evidence in the record does not preponderate against this finding.

Mother argues on appeal that the award of rehabilitative alimony should be converted to alimony *in futuro*, and that the trial court erred in refusing to do so. She notes that she will be 51 years old when the younger child graduates from high school, and contends that, in view of the disparity in income between the parties, rehabilitation is not possible. The trial court found that Mother could not be fully rehabilitated until the youngest son graduates from high school. The trial court did not find that Mother cannot be rehabilitated, and declined to convert the award to alimony *in futuro* at that time. After reviewing the record, we cannot find that the trial court erred in declining Mother's request.

* * *

NOTES AND QUESTIONS

1. *Legitimate changes in the parties' income.* In *Rosen v. Rosen*, 2002 WL 31440782 (Conn. Super. Ct. Oct. 20, 2002) (unpublished opinion), the court had initially ordered the husband to pay alimony of $4,583.33 per month, based on his salary as the chief executive officer at the International

Center for Disabilities in New York. However, one year after the divorce, the husband was terminated from his position unexpectedly and involuntarily. His position was highly specialized, and he had very few opportunities to use his skills. Mr. Rosen ultimately secured a job teaching, but his new annual salary was more than $60,000 lower. The court reduced the alimony payments to $1,000 a month, explaining that modification was acceptable because the payor had made reasonable efforts to secure employment but that his earning capacity was limited by circumstances beyond his control. However, the court was quick to note that this was only a temporary solution until Mr. Rosen could secure other employment.

A Mississippi court refused to modify a husband's spousal support obligation when his wife, a stay-at-home mother during the marriage, returned to work. The court found that, even with her work income, the wife's standard of living did not exceed her husband's, and that her net income was much less than her husband's. *Dix v. Dix*, 941 So.2d 913, 917–918 (Miss. Ct. App. 2006).

2. *Putting alimony agreements into the parties' hands.* Initial alimony agreements are enforced until the court orders modification. In *Eldridge v. Eldridge*, 710 A.2d 757 (Conn. 1998), the husband decided to stop alimony payments upon ascertaining that his former wife had reached an adequate level of self sufficiency. The initial alimony agreement entitled him to a reduction in payments after an increase in the wife's earning, but the court held that the husband must move for modification rather than engage in "self-help." Moreover, the alimony award could not be modified retroactively. The court held the husband in contempt for failing to pay the alimony.

A man who self-modified an alimony order by terminating spousal support payments in 1994 after his former wife began cohabiting with another man breached the parties' separation agreement, which required him to pay support until 1997. He was responsible for the past amount due together with interest, even though the former wife did not commence her action until 2004. *Rivers v. Rivers*, 826 N.Y.S.2d 347 (App. Div. 2006).

3. *Providing for modification.* If you were drafting an alimony order, which factors would you deem acceptable as bases for modification? Would your order recite any situations in which alimony should not be modifiable?

B.   TERMINATION

Most states provide that alimony ends upon either party's death, upon the recipient's remarriage, or, in many states, cohabitation, unless a court order or an agreement between the parties provides otherwise. *See, e.g.,* Utah Code Ann. § 30–3–5(9) (2008); Cal. Fam. Code § 4337 (2008). The next decision considers the meaning of cohabitation for purposes of alimony termination.

GARCIA v. GARCIA

Utah Court of Appeals, 2002.
60 P.3d 1174.

JACKSON, PRESIDING JUDGE:

Appellant Amado Garcia appeals the district court's denial of his motion for summary judgment, which sought termination of alimony to his ex-wife, Appellee Diane Garcia. We reverse and remand.

BACKGROUND

On March 2, 1999, Amado filed a Verified Petition to Modify Decree of Divorce. Diane filed an Answer to the petition, but failed to respond to Amado's Request for Admissions. Thus, pursuant to rule 36(a) of the Utah Rules of Civil Procedure, Diane admitted the following facts: (1) that "she was acquainted with Kimberly Ellis"; (2) "[t]hat she and Ellis lived together at an address in Seaside, Oregon, from September 19, 1997, to December 1998"; (3) "that she and Ellis shared a bedroom, bed, and had sexual contact at that residence during that period of time"; (4) that she "and Ellis shared the living expenses at that residence during that period of time"; (5) that she "and Ellis shared an address in Cannon Beach, Oregon, from December 1998 to March 1999"; (6) "that she and Ellis shared a bedroom, bed, and had sexual contact at that residence during that period of time"; and (7) that she "and Ellis shared the living expenses at that residence during that period of time."

Based on these facts, Amado filed a motion for summary judgment, contending "that Petitioner has admitted a relationship constituting cohabitation, and therefore, the [district court should have] enter[ed] an [o]rder terminating alimony payments as of August 1997 on the grounds that [Diane] entered into a cohabitation relationship on or about that date." The district court denied Amado's motion for summary judgment. It ruled that had Ellis and Diane been of the opposite sex, their conduct would have clearly been viewed as cohabitation sufficient to terminate alimony. However, the court concluded "that the plain meaning of 'cohabitation' requires a sexual relationship between members of the opposite sex." Amado appeals the district court's denial of his motion for summary judgment.

* * *

ANALYSIS

Utah Code Ann. § 30–30–5(9) (1998) provides: "Any order of the court that a party pay alimony to a former spouse terminates upon establishment by the party paying alimony that the former spouse is cohabitating with another person." In *Pendleton v. Pendleton*, 918 P.2d 159 (Utah Ct. App. 1996), we ruled that "cohabitation is comprised of . . . two elements: (1) common residency and (2) sexual contact evidencing a conjugal association." *Id.* at 160, n.1 (citing *Haddow v. Haddow*, 707 P.2d 669, 672 (Utah 1985)). The trial court acknowledged that Diane and Kimberly Ellis met the residency requirement. That conclusion is not challenged on appeal.

Regarding the second element, the trial court concluded that Diane's " 'same sex' relationship cannot, as a matter of law, amount to 'cohabitation.' " We disagree. According to the plain language of the statute, alimony terminates "upon establishment by the party paying alimony that the former spouse is cohabitating *with another person*." Utah Code Ann. § 30–30–5(9) (emphasis added). The plain language of the statute requires only that the alimony payee cohabit "with another person," and contains no requirement that the other person be a member of the opposite sex. * * *

Thus, we conclude that Diane's admission "that she and Ellis shared a bedroom, bed, and had sexual contact" meets the second element necessary to establish cohabitation. Accordingly, the trial court erroneously concluded "that the plain meaning of 'cohabitation' requires a sexual relationship between members of the opposite sex."

* * *

CONCLUSION

* * * Thus, we reverse the trial court's denial of Amado's motion for summary judgment and remand for proceedings consistent with this opinion.

NOTES AND QUESTIONS

1. *Cohabitation with whom?* Despite disagreement about statutory interpretation, *Garcia* arises under a gender neutral alimony termination statute. However, other statutes specifically state that modification is available only for cohabitation with a member of the opposite sex. *See, e.g.*, Ala. Code 1975 § 30–2–55 (2008). In Oklahoma, "voluntary cohabitation of a former spouse with a member of the opposite sex shall be a ground to modify provisions of a final judgment or order for alimony as support." 43 Okl.St.Ann. 43, § 134(C) (2008). Connecticut has adopted a different approach, allowing for modification of an alimony award where the recipient "is living with another person under circumstances which the court finds should result in the modification, suspension, reduction or termination of alimony because the living arrangements cause such a change of circumstances as to alter the financial needs of that party." Conn. Gen. Stat. § 46b–86(b)(2008).

2. *What is cohabitation? What is marriage?* S.A.T. *v.* K.D.T., discussed earlier in this Chapter, also addressed termination of alimony for "cohabitation." The husband spent a portion of his time at the home of his girlfriend, whom he called his "possible future bride." 2004 WL 2334330, at *1 (Del. Fam. Ct. Apr. 27, 2004) (unpublished opinion). However, the court concluded that the husband was motivated by his need for a place to stay while in her area for work-related purposes. *Id.* Because the husband stayed with the

girlfriend only while he was in town for business and never for a weekend visit, the court found that this arrangement did not satisfy the definition of cohabitation, which was "regular residence with another adult." *Id.*

What if the applicable statute provides that remarriage terminates a spousal support order, but the remarriage is void? A California court refused to terminate a support order based on the wife's void remarriage. *In re Marriage of Campbell*, 136 Cal.App.4th 502 (2006). And, in another California case, a man challenged his obligation to pay alimony to his former wife, who had registered as a domestic partner with another woman. Maura Dolan, *Same–Sex Union Test: Alimony*, L.A. Times, July 22, 2007, at A1. The issue is under what circumstances a legally-recognized domestic partnership is the same as marriage. Should a civil union or domestic partnership terminate the obligation to pay alimony?

3. *Why terminate alimony?* Why should cohabitation or remarriage result in modification or termination of an alimony award? Professor Cynthia Starnes found no "coherent rationale for the remarriage-termination rule consistent with contemporary understandings of alimony." Cynthia Lee Starnes, *One More Time: Alimony, Intuition, and the Remarriage–Termination Rule*, 81 Ind. L.J. 971, 976 (2006). Instead, the strong intuition supporting the rule remains rooted "in archaic principles of coverture, which cast a wife not as a marital partner, but rather as a man's burden, dependent on her husband for protection and survival until the next man comes along to relieve him of the task." *Id.* at 999. Do you agree? Is there no better justification for the rule?

In Oregon, remarriage and cohabitation are analyzed in the same manner as any other change in circumstances, and do not, by themselves, constitute bases for termination. A court refused to terminate the ex-husband's obligation to pay $3500/month to his ex-wife indefinitely even after she married a lawyer whose monthly income was more than $7,000/month. *In re Marriage of Lenhart*, 162 P.3d 292 (Or. Ct. App. 2007).

SECTION 6: TAXATION OF ALIMONY

Alimony is generally deducted from the payor's gross income for federal tax purposes, and taxed to the recipient, although the parties may agree otherwise. Classification of a payment as alimony benefits the higher income payor by reducing his or her taxable income, and results in lower taxes being paid on the amount transferred from the higher to the lower income former spouse. Thus, post-dissolution payments raise complicated tax questions concerning when a financial transfer between former spouses is properly treated as alimony, child support, or property distribution

In 1984, Congress clarified the standards for classifying post-divorce financial transfers. Alimony payments must generally meet specified criteria, including these:

(1) Payments must be received under an order of a divorce or "separation instrument," which includes written separation agreements as well as court decrees of support;

(2) Payments must be made in cash or the equivalent (i.e., alimony does not include a property award);

(3) Payments must end at the payor's death;

(4) The parties cannot file a joint tax return; and

(5) Payments cannot include child support.

I.R.C. § 71 (2008).

Moreover, the Internal Revenue Service (IRS) has developed stringent rules to prevent taxpayers from disguising property distribution or child support as alimony. First, a "recapture rule," designed to prevent front-loading of alimony payments, applies when payments in the first year exceed payments in subsequent years by a specific statutory amount ($15,000). The rule requires "a recalculation and inclusion in income by the payor and deduction by the payee of previously paid alimony to the extent that the amount of such payments * * * falls short of the amount of payments during a prior year by" the specified amount. 26 C.F.R. § 1.71–1T(d) (2008). Second, rules prevent spouses from disguising child support as alimony. If a payment characterized as alimony is reduced upon the occurrence of "a contingency relating to a child of the payor," such as a child's reaching a certain age, marrying, or leaving school, then the payment will be treated as child support. Id. § 1.71–1T(c). The following excerpt from the federal regulations provides some guidance on the approach of the IRS.

26 C.F.R. § 1.71–1T (2008)

* * *

Q–6 May payments of cash to a third party on behalf of a spouse qualify as alimony or separate maintenance payments if the payments are pursuant to the terms of a divorce or separation instrument?

A–6 Yes. Assuming all other requirements are satisfied, a payment of cash by the payor spouse to a third party under the terms of the divorce or separation instrument will qualify as a payment of cash which is received "on behalf of a spouse." For example, cash payments of rent, mortgage, tax, or tuition liabilities of the payee spouse made under the terms of the divorce or separation instrument will qualify as alimony or separate maintenance payments. * * *

* * *

Q–8 How may spouses designate that payments otherwise qualifying as alimony or separate maintenance payments shall be excludible from the gross income of the payee and nondeductible by the payor?

A–8 The spouses may designate that payments otherwise qualifying as alimony or separate maintenance payments shall be nondeductible by the payor and excludible from gross income by the payee by so providing in a divorce or separation instrument (as defined in [the tax code]). * * *

* * *

Notwithstanding the seeming clarity of the IRS guidance, the lines between alimony, child support, and property may not be as simple as they seem, "where 'equitable distribution' statutes now blend property rights with support payments in an inextricably mixed payment stream." Deborah A. Geier, *Simplifying and Rationalizing the Federal Income Tax Law Applicable to Transfers in Divorce*, 55 Tax Law. 363, 433 (2002). Instead, Professor Geier notes that, "in this dot-com world in which we live, when stock options increasingly are used to compensate workers, family law courts are now arguing that stock options awarded after a divorce" are not property, but are a form of income that should more appropriately be included in determining alimony awards. *Id.* at 434.

NOTES AND QUESTIONS

1. *Theory of alimony.* Which of the possible justifications for alimony discussed in this Chapter does the tax treatment of alimony support? According to Professor Patricia Cain, the tax treatment of alimony suggests an "underlying principle * * * that the now-divided family will only be taxed once on the income that is used to support its prior members. This principle is consistent with the notion that the spousal unit is a single economic unit for federal tax purposes." Patricia Cain, *Taxing Families Fairly*, 48 Santa Clara L. Rev 805, 828 (2008). By contrast, transfers between former nonmarital partners are not entitled to the same favorable treatment. *Id.* at 830. Does this seem equitable?

2. *Tax brackets.* Under our graduated income tax system, the percentage of income paid as tax increases as income increases. Consequently, a lower income spouse is subject to lower taxes than his or her partner. When one party pays alimony to a former spouse who earns substantially less, the total tax burden is reduced by the transfer of funds from one spouse to the other. Consider this example:

> Assume a husband and wife are about to be divorced. Before payment of alimony, the wife has a taxable income of $10,000 and the husband has a taxable income of $70,000. If they each were to pay taxes on these amounts, their combined tax liability would be $17,991. (The husband would pay $16,487; the wife would pay $1,504, applying the 1999 federal tax tables).

> If the husband were to pay the wife $20,000 per year in alimony, his taxable income would drop to $50,000, and the wife's taxable income would increase to $30,000. Their combined federal income tax payments then would be $15,720 ($10,660 by husband and $5,060 by wife). The savings on their combined tax bills would be $2,271 over what would be paid if the alimony payments were taxable to the husband.

> The wife's tax bills have gone up, but so has her income.

A.B.A., Guide to Family Law 7 (1996), *available at* http://www.abanet.org/publiced/practical/books/family.

Should the tax code encourage this type of bargaining for higher alimony payments?

CHAPTER 11

CHILD SUPPORT

■ ■ ■

SECTION 1: THE NATURE OF THE CHILD SUPPORT OBLIGATION

Child support—payments for children who do not live with both of their parents—presents some of the thorniest, yet most important, questions in family law. The numbers underscore the centrality of financial support to the lives of America's marital and nonmarital children. According to some estimates, as many as half of this generation's children will live in a single-parent household at some time during their childhood and adolescence. In 2005, nearly a quarter (23%) of children lived with only their mothers, 5% lived with only their fathers, and 5% lived with neither parent. Most of these children (more than 21 million) were entitled to support from the noncustodial parent until they reach majority and sometimes longer. U.S. Census Bureau, *The Living Arrangements of Children in 2005*, at 1 (2008).

The divorce rate has hovered near 50% for the past generation, and the median age at first divorce has been quite young, 31.5 years for men and 29.4 years for women in 2001. Rose M. Krieder, U.S. Census Bureau, Publ'n No. P70–97, U.S. Census Current Population Reports, *Number, Timing, and Duration of Marriages and Divorces: 2001*, at 8 tbls. 4–5 (2005), http://www.census.gov/prod/2005pubs/p70–97.pdf. Periods of separation frequently precede divorce. Young separating and divorcing parties typically have minor dependent children, and divorces each year involve more than one million children, who find themselves temporarily or permanently in single-parent households. *Id.*

In recent years, the birth rate outside marriage has remained slightly above 33% of all live births annually. In 2006, 38% of all births in the United States were to unmarried women, many of whom will raise their children without ever marrying the other biological parent. *See* Federal Interagency Forum on Child and Family Statistics, America's Children in Brief: Key National Indicators of Well–Being, 2008, at 4.

This Chapter begins by exploring the nature of the child support obligation, and then discusses how support is determined, modified and enforced. As you study the Chapter, consider how the law balances the interests of custodial and noncustodial parents with the child's right to support from both. As you learn the law of child support, consider too what the law should be. What reforms, if any, would you advocate if you served on a law revision commission or similar body charged with ongoing examination and development?

A.　THE SOURCE OF THE OBLIGATION

STATE EX REL. HERMESMANN v. SEYER

Supreme Court of Kansas, 1993.
847 P.2d 1273.

HOLMES, C.J.

* * *

Colleen Hermesmann routinely provided care for Shane Seyer as a baby sitter or day care provider during 1987 and 1988. The two began a sexual relationship at a time when Colleen was 16 years old and Shane was only 12. The relationship continued over a period of several months and the parties engaged in sexual intercourse on an average of a couple of times a week. As a result, a daughter, Melanie, was born to Colleen on May 30, 1989. At the time of the conception of the child, Shane was 13 years old and Colleen was 17. Colleen applied for and received financial assistance through the Aid to Families with Dependent Children program (ADC) from SRS.[1]

On January 15, 1991, the district attorney's office of Shawnee County filed a petition requesting that Colleen Hermesmann be adjudicated as a juvenile offender for engaging in the act of sexual intercourse with a child under the age of 16, Shanandoah (Shane) Seyer, to whom she was not married * * *. Thereafter, Colleen Hermesmann entered into a plea agreement with the district attorney's office, wherein she agreed to stipulate to the lesser offense of contributing to a child's misconduct. On September 11, 1991, the juvenile court accepted the stipulation, and adjudicated Colleen Hermesmann to be a juvenile offender.

On March 8, 1991, SRS filed a petition on behalf of Colleen Hermesmann, alleging that Shane Seyer was the father of Colleen's minor daughter, Melanie. The petition also alleged that SRS had provided benefits through the ADC program to Colleen on behalf of the child and that Colleen had assigned support rights due herself and her child to SRS. The petition requested that the court determine paternity and order Shane to reimburse SRS for all assistance expended by SRS on Melanie's behalf. * * *

* * *

* * * The court found that the issue of Shane's consent was irrelevant and ordered Shane to pay child support of $50 per month. The court

---

1.　SRS is the acronym for the Kansas Department of Social and Rehabilitation Services.

also granted SRS a joint and several judgment against Shane and Colleen in the amount of $7,068, for assistance provided by the ADC program on behalf of Melanie through February 1992. The judgment included medical and other birthing expenses as well as assistance paid after Melanie's birth. * * *

* * *

* * * Shane asserts as his first issue that, because he was a minor under the age of 16 at the time of conception, he was legally incapable of consenting to sexual intercourse and therefore cannot be held legally responsible for the birth of his child. * * *

* * *

The Kansas Parentage Act specifically contemplates minors as fathers and makes no exception for minor parents regarding their duty to support and educate their child. * * *

* * *

* * * Shane does not contest that he is the biological father of the child. As a father, he has a common-law duty, as well as a statutory duty, to support his minor child. This duty applies equally to parents of children born out of wedlock.

Under the statutory and common law of this state, Shane owes a duty to support his minor child. * * * We conclude that the issue of consent to sexual activity under the criminal statutes is irrelevant in a civil action to determine paternity and for support of the minor child of such activity. * * *

For Shane's next issue, he asserts that it is not sound public policy for a court to order a youth to pay child support for a child conceived during the crime of indecent liberties with a child when the victim was unable to consent to the sexual intercourse. * * *

* * *

This State's interest in requiring minor parents to support their children overrides the State's competing interest in protecting juveniles from improvident acts, even when such acts may include criminal activity on the part of the other parent. Considering the three persons directly involved, Shane, Colleen, and Melanie, the interests of Melanie are superior, as a matter of public policy, to those of either or both of her parents. This minor child, the only truly innocent party, is entitled to support from both her parents regardless of their ages.

As his third issue, Shane asserts that the district court erred in finding he and Colleen were jointly and severally liable for the child support. He argues that, as Colleen was the perpetrator of the crime of statutory rape, she alone should be held responsible for the consequences of the act. * * *

* * *

* * * Nowhere does the law in this state suggest that the mother's "wrongdoing" can operate as a setoff or bar to a father's liability for child support. Under the facts as presented to this court, the district court properly held that Shane owes a duty of support to Melanie and properly ordered that Shane and Colleen were jointly and severally liable for the monies previously paid by SRS.

* * *

* * * The judgment of the district court is affirmed.

NOTES AND QUESTIONS

1. *The contours of the child support obligation. Hermesmann* nicely demonstrates that the parental child support obligation is grounded in biology, not marriage. This obligation was recognized even before it was embodied in law:

> The duty of parents to provide for the maintenance of their children is a principle of natural law; an obligation * * * laid on them not only by nature herself, but by their own proper act, in bringing them into the world; for they would be in the highest manner injurious to their issue, if they only gave their children life that they might afterwards see them perish. By begetting them, therefore, they have entered into a voluntary obligation, to endeavor, as far as in them lies, that the life which they have bestowed shall be supported and preserved.

William Blackstone, 1 Commentaries *447. Both biological parents assume the child support obligation regardless of whether they were ever married to one another, whether they were together only once to conceive the child, or whether they were minors at the time of conception. For an explanation of the moral foundations of the parental obligation, see Gregory A. Loken, *Gratitude and the Map of Moral Duties Toward Children*, 31 Ariz. St. L.J. 1121 (1999).

Hermesmann also demonstrates the strength of the parental support obligation in contemporary American law. Thirteen-year-old Shane Seyer was a sex-crime victim. Statutory rape and similar crimes seek to protect children from sexual abuse, one of the strongest child-protective policies known to the law. The Kansas Supreme Court acknowledged the strength of this child-protective policy, but—like other courts that have decided the question—held that the policy yields to the paramount policy entitling children to support from both parents.

Hermesmann concerned a child conceived during "statutory rape" (that is, non-forcible sexual activity with a victim under the age of consent) perpetrated by another juvenile. In the absence of force, courts have likewise uniformly imposed child support obligations on minors who conceive children with adult perpetrators, who the law might assume have particular influence over less experienced juveniles. *See, e.g., County of San Luis Obispo v.*

Nathaniel J., 57 Cal.Rptr.2d 843 (Ct. App. 1996) (15–year–old boy and 34–year–old woman). Should the law impose similar strict liability on the victim of a forcible rape to support the child thus conceived?

2. *Questions about* Hermesmann. (a) Why should an underage sex abuse victim, who the criminal law deems incapable of consent to intercourse because of immaturity, ever have a child support obligation imposed by civil law? (b) Should an underage parent be excused from a child support obligation where the other parent, like Colleen Hermesmann, is convicted of a crime arising from conception? (c) Will three-year-old Melanie, whom the court labeled "the only truly innocent party," necessarily receive any of the financial support collected from Shane as a result of this lawsuit, at least in the immediate future? (d) In light of relaxed contemporary sexual mores, should a non-custodial parent, whether a child like 13–year–old Shane Seyer or an adult, be saddled for years with an obligation to support a child conceived during a "one-night stand" or similarly brief sexual encounter? Who may end up supporting the child if an adult parent or minor parent who engaged in "recreational sex" does not? (e) What advice would *Hermesmann* lead you to impart to teenagers?

3. *Trickery and intent.* Where one parent tricks the other into conceiving the child, such as by lying about use of birth control, the tricked parent must nonetheless pay child support. In *N.E. v. Hedges*, 391 F.3d 832, 834 (6th Cir. 2004), the father alleged that "the mother of the child 'fraudulently induced' sexual intercourse, claiming that her birth control pills would prevent pregnancy, then left the state, [and] married another man." He argued that as applied to him, support statutes violate sexual and procreative privacy rights recognized by the Supreme Court. The Sixth Circuit affirmed the support obligation and noted that child support "has long been a tax fathers have had to pay in Western civilization." *Id.* at 836.

In *L. Pamela P. v. Frank S.*, 449 N.E.2d 713 (N.Y. 1983), the unwed father (Frank Serpico, the New York City police officer who gained fame for his testimony about police corruption) alleged that the mother deliberately misrepresented that she had used contraception before the child was conceived. The court held that despite any fraud, the father must support the child because support depends on the child's needs and the parents' ability to pay, without regard to parental fault. *Frank S.* suggested that the father might have a civil fraud claim against the mother, but parents allegedly defrauded into conception have found such actions difficult to win.

4. *Nonmarital children.* In *Gomez v. Perez*, 409 U.S. 535, 538 (1973), the Court held that "once a state posits a judicially enforceable right on behalf of children to needed support from their biological fathers there is no constitutionally sufficient justification for denying such an essential right to a child simply because the biological father has not married its mother." The decision has come to mean that equal protection bars state discrimination against nonmarital children in setting the amount or terms of child support. *See, e.g.*, *People ex rel. B.W.*, 17 P.3d 199, 201 (Colo. Ct. App. 2000).

5. *The commencement of the child support obligation.* The child support obligation begins at the marital or nonmarital child's birth, even if the obligor

parent did not know of the child or the birth, or even if paternity is not established until later.

Where a court does not enter a child support order until the child is older, however, this rule does not necessarily guarantee an order retroactive to the child's birth. If the court enters the support order when the parties divorce, the order dates from separation or divorce because "[i]n an intact family, the law assumes that parents will provide for the children as well as they can." *Kiken v. Kiken*, 694 A.2d 557, 560 (N.J. 1997). The assumption, grounded in constitutional family privacy and autonomy doctrines, prevails during an intact marriage as long as the parents provide at least a minimal level of support sufficient to defeat a neglect petition in the juvenile or family court.

If the child was born outside marriage but the parents lived together for some period after the child's birth, the law may similarly presume that both parents supported the child while they lived together. *See, e.g., Kochinsky v. Moore*, 729 So.2d 407, 408 (Fla. Dist. Ct. App. 1999).

Where unmarried parents have not lived together since the child's birth, most decisions enter orders retroactive to the date of birth. *See, e.g., Skinner v. Hagberg*, 183 P.3d 486 (Alaska 2008). Some courts apply a rebuttable presumption in favor of such retroactive awards in this circumstance. *See, e.g., Ellison v. Walter ex rel. Walter*, 834 P.2d 680 (Wyo. 1992). Retroactivity to the date of birth is generally ordered even where the mother has concealed the nonmarital child from the father. *See, e.g., In re State ex rel. Reitenour*, 807 A.2d 1259 (N.H. 2002) (ordering support retroactive to birth in paternity action brought when the child was fourteen). Where the court does not enter a support order until the child is older, an award retroactive to the child's birth can instantly saddle the obligor parent with significant "arrears" (support payments that came due before the court enters the support order), including interest.

Where unmarried parents have not lived together, some courts have entered orders retroactive only to some date after birth, such as the date the paternity or support action is filed. *See, e.g., Rodgers v. Diederichsen*, 820 So.2d 362 (Fla. Dist. Ct. App. 2002). On the facts of particular cases, other courts have rejected retroactivity on such equitable grounds as waiver, estoppel or laches. *See, e.g., Chitwood v. Chitwood*, 211 S.W.3d 547 (Ark. Ct. App. 2005) (equitable estoppel barred custodial mother from collecting child support arrears); *Webb v. Menix*, 90 P.3d 989, 991–92 (N.M. Ct. App. 2004) (custodial mother waived claim to retroactive child support for 12–year–old child by actively denying the father's paternity and not seeking child support from him for 12 years, though she knew she was entitled to it).

"[L]aches and estoppel are not favored defenses in the context of child support." *Tovsland v. Reub*, 686 N.W.2d 392, 402 (S.D. 2004). The same can be said about waiver. Why the disfavor?

6. *Gender neutrality*. Today the vast majority of non-custodial child support obligors are men. The parental support obligation is gender neutral, however, with each parent liable in accordance with his or her respective means. Gender neutrality also governs the duration of the child support obligation. For much of our history, the obligation ended earlier for girls than for boys. The rationale was that girls should be married (and thus supported

by their husbands) at a younger age than boys were ready to support themselves. Equal protection now requires that the maximum support age be the same for boys and girls. *See Stanton v. Stanton*, 421 U.S. 7 (1975).

7. *Emancipation.* Emancipation is the process by which a minor attains rights and obligations of adulthood before (or sometimes after) reaching the age of majority.

The grounds for emancipation differ from state to state. A discrete event, such as the minor's marriage or entry into active military service, may produce emancipation as a matter of law. *See, e.g., Porath v. McVey*, 884 S.W.2d 692 (Mo. Ct. App. 1994) (terminating the father's obligation to support his minor son who entered U.S. Military Academy at West Point while still a minor; the statute provided for termination when the child "[e]nters active duty in the military," and federal law provides that West Point cadets are part of the regular Army). On a case-by-case basis, the court may also order emancipation in the best interests of the child. Courts generally order best-interests emancipation only where a child near the age of majority can fend for himself emotionally and financially. *See, e.g., Edmonds v. Edmonds*, 935 So.2d 980 (Miss. 2006) (divorced father must continue to support his 14–year-old son, who was convicted of murder as an adult and sentenced to life imprisonment; continued support would help pay for the boy's appeal and provide him minimal expenses in prison).

The importance of best-interests emancipation has diminished since most states lowered the general age of majority from 21 to 18 in the early 1970s, but emancipation petitions still appear in the nation's courts. Whether based on a discrete event or on a best-interests analysis, emancipation typically ends the parents' obligation to pay future support unless the parent has agreed to pay post-emancipation support. Emancipation, however, typically does not relieve the parents' obligation to pay arrears. In their study of California emancipation cases, Professors Sanger and Willemsen found that parents sometimes sought emancipation in an effort to avoid future support obligations. *See* Carol Sanger & Eleanor Willemsen, *Minor Changes: Emancipating Children in Modern Times*, 25 U. Mich. J. L. Ref. 239, 299–300 (1992). Where a child support obligation has been terminated by a child's emancipation, it may be revived if the child reverts to unemancipated status. *See State ex rel. Dep't of Econ. Security v. Demetz*, 130 P.3d 986 (Ariz. Ct. App. 2006) (father's obligation to support his 17–year-old daughter reinstated after her one-year marriage was annulled for fraudulent inducement).

8. *The non-role of parental misconduct.* Only about half the states follow the Uniform Marriage and Divorce Act approach that property distribution and spousal maintenance awards are to be made "without regard to marital misconduct." UMDA §§ 307–08, 9A U.L.A. 288 (1998). No state, however, factors parental fault into the initial child support award or later modifications. Does *Hermesmann* provide any clues about why parental fault is irrelevant to a child support award? BI of Child!

9. *The child's obligations.* In return for support, parents at common law were entitled to their children's earnings, a parental right seldom invoked today but still recognized in many states, often by statute. In Missouri, for example, parents living apart "are entitled to an adjudication * * * as to their

powers, rights and duties in respect to the * * * earnings and management of the property of their unmarried minor children"; before the adjudication, the custodial parent has the sole right to the child's earnings. *See, e.g.,* Mo. Rev. Stat. § 452.150 (2008). In California, on the other hand, "[t]he parent, as such, has no control over the property of the child." *See* Cal. Fam. Code § 7502 (2008).

The child's right to support also carried a common law obligation to obey the parents:

> The rights of parents result from their duties. As they are bound to maintain and educate their children, the law has given them a right to such authority; and in the support of that authority, a right to the exercise of such discipline as may be requisite for the discharge of their sacred trust. * * * The duties that are enjoined upon children to their parents, are obedience and assistance during their own minority, and gratitude and reverence during the rest of their lives.

2 James Kent, Commentaries on American Law *202, 206 (3d ed. 1836).

Today, breach of the duty to obey may be a ground for terminating the support obligation where a child capable of financial and emotional independence wrongfully repudiates or abandons the parent, as sometimes happens following a contentious divorce. The parent's conduct determines whether such "self-emancipation" has occurred. *See, e.g., Labanowski v. Labanowski,* 857 N.Y.S.2d 737 (App. Div. 2008) (child may forfeit the right to support by refusing, without cause, all contact and visitation with the noncustodial parent; however, a child does not forfeit the right by refusal justified by a parent's malfeasance, misconduct, neglect or abuse). Some states do not recognize repudiation or abandonment by the child as a ground for terminating support, finding that any loss of financial support contradicts the best interests of the child standard. *E.g., Holston v. Holston,* 473 A.2d 459, 463 (Md. Ct. Spec. App. 1984) ("The amount of money that the noncustodial parent is required to pay for the support of his minor children should not be determined by the amount of love the children show toward that parent. The proper inquiry * * * is what is in the best interest of the child.").

As you will learn from reading the *Usack* decision in Chapter 13, in states that recognize abandonment by the child, its effect may depend on the extent of the noncustodial parent's efforts to maintain the relationship. *Compare Usack v. Usack,* 793 N.Y.S.2d 223 (App. Div. 2005) (suspending noncustodial mother's support obligation because father frustrated nearly all contact between children and mother for over four years, despite mother's repeated efforts), *with Jaffee v. Jaffee,* 608 N.Y.S.2d 649 (App. Div. 1994) (son's refusal to see his father did not warrant termination of support obligation because the father had made only a minimal effort to maintain a relationship with him).

Should courts recognize repudiation or abandonment by the child as a ground for suspending or terminating support? Should the child's age affect the answer? Why is parental fault determinative in this context but immaterial in *Hermesmann*? Chapter 13 fully explores these questions.

NOTES ON SUPPORT OBLIGATIONS OF PERSONS OTHER THAN BIOLOGICAL PARENTS

a. *Stepparents' support for their stepchildren.* A stepparent is usually defined as a person who is married to one of the child's biological parents, but who has not adopted the child. Adoption is possible only where the court has terminated the parental rights of the child's other biological parent by consent or in a contested proceeding. The metes and bounds of the stepparent support obligation vitally affect the younger generation because about one in five children under eighteen lives in a stepfamily, and as many as one in three may live in a stepfamily for some time during childhood or adolescence. *See* John C. Mayoue, *Stepping In To Parent*, 25 Fam. Advoc. 36 (Fall 2002). Some stepchildren receive little or none of the support that the law obligates the noncustodial legal parent to pay.

For much of our history, life expectancy was much lower than today and most stepfamilies were created after a biological parent's death. Once states began enacting adoption statutes in the second half of the nineteenth century, the stepparent's adoption of a "half-orphan" child might follow a biological parent's death. In recent years, the percentage of stepfamilies has risen dramatically not primarily from death, but from high rates of divorce and remarriage, and from the tendency of young single mothers to keep their babies and then marry someone other than the child's biological father. Where both biological parents remarry after divorce, a child has two stepparents.

Most wage-earning stepparents probably contribute to a stepchild's day-to-day support while they are married to the custodial parent and living with the child, without concern for (or perhaps even knowledge of) what the law requires. This moral or social obligation, however, is not grounded in the law, which generally confers parental rights, and imposes parental obligations, only on biological parents and adoptive parents. The common law imposes no general obligation on a stepparent to support a stepchild merely because of marriage to the child's biological parent. The *in loco parentis* or estoppel doctrines may impose the obligation in circumstances discussed in "b" below, and courts have also enforced stepparents' agreements to support their stepchildren. *See, e.g., Dewey v. Dewey*, 886 P.2d 623, 625 (Alaska 1994).

Some states, however, have statutes requiring stepparents to support stepchildren living in their households, though the support obligation is usually more limited than the obligation the law imposes on biological or adoptive parents. The stepparent's obligation may be only secondary, or may be imposed only where the stepchild would otherwise be a public charge. *See, e.g.*, Ky. Rev. Stat. § 205.310 (2008). The stepparent may be able to recover from the noncustodial parent the amounts provided in support. *See, e.g.*, Mo. Rev. Stat. § 453.400 (2008). The support obligation may terminate when the stepparent and biological parent divorce or when the biological parent dies, even where termination would be harsh on the dependent child. A few states continue the obligation after the end of the marriage, but only where the stepparent has received the stepchild into the stepparent's household and the stepchild continues to reside there. *See, e.g.*, N.D. Cent. Code § 14–09–09 (2008).

Even where the law does not obligate stepparents to support children directly, major public assistance programs have considered stepparents' income in determining a child's welfare eligibility and grant amount, thus making stepparents indirectly responsible for support. The income of a wage-earner who marries a welfare recipient with children, for example, may be deemed available to support the children, resulting in reduction or loss of the welfare grant. Stepparents can also be indirectly responsible for supporting stepchildren when their income is considered in determining the financial resources of their spouses (the biological parents) in child support determinations. *See* Sarah H. Ramsey, *Stepparents and the Law, in* Stepparenting: Issues in Theory, Research and Practice (Kay Pasley & Marilyn Ihinger–Tallman eds., 1994). The stepparent's income may also affect the availability and amount of need-based higher education scholarships.

b. *Persons* in loco parentis *and parents by estoppel.* The *in loco parentis* ("in the place of the parent") doctrine, under which a person who assumes parental obligations is treated as a parent for some purposes, "has wide application in the area of child support." Margaret M. Mahoney, *Stepparents as Third Parties in Relation to Their Stepchildren*, 40 Fam. L.Q. 81, 100 (2006). Courts applying the doctrine examine the person's conduct and statements to determine whether he or she intentionally assumed parental obligations, including the child support obligation. *See, e.g., Zellmer v. Zellmer*, 188 P.3d 497 (Wash. 2008) ("a stepparent is not subject to the family support statute unless he or she has established a loco parentis relationship with a child, which requires more than merely taking a child into one's home or exercising temporary custody and control"). Because *in loco parentis* relationships can be terminated at will, however, a stepparent or other adult in the household typically can avoid continued financial responsibility when the marriage ends by simply declaring that the relationship no longer exists. The *in loco parentis* doctrine thus tends to be relevant only to prior support, and to claims by third parties. For example, a court could deny a stepparent's claim for reimbursement for expenses related to the child if the stepparent was *in loco parentis* when the expenses were incurred.

Promissory estoppel or equitable estoppel may also impose a support obligation on persons who promise support, treat the child as their own, or discourage contact between the noncustodial biological parent and the child. *See, e.g., J.R. v. L.R.*, 902 A.2d 261, 265–66 (N.J. Super. Ct. App. Div. 2006). Because courts reserve estoppel and other equitable doctrines for particularly compelling cases, however, sympathetic facts do not always produce a support obligation. *See, e.g., In re Glaude*, 855 A.2d 494, 495 (N.H. 2004) (refusing to apply equitable estoppel against stepfather who received physical custody of his stepson when he and the biological mother divorced, and supported the boy for nine years until the biological mother resumed custody).

Should states enact statutes imposing support obligations on all residential stepparents, or should the law apply the *in loco parentis* or estoppel doctrines on a case-by-case basis? Which approach is more child-protective? Which approach better reflects the settled expectations of most adults in stepfamilies? Why might a court be reluctant to impose a continuing support obligation on stepparents merely for nurturing stepchildren who live in their households?

c. *Adoptive parents*. Adoption, a focus of Chapter 17, is "the legal equivalent of biological parenthood." *Smith v. OFFER*, 431 U.S. 816, 844 n.51 (1977). Where a biological parent consents to the child's adoption, the parent generally must continue paying child support until the court enters the adoption decree. *See Greene County Dep't of Soc. Servs. v. Ward*, 870 N.E.2d 1132, 1133 (N.Y. 2007). The decree terminates the birth parent's future obligation to support the child, and the adoptive parents assume that obligation.

d. *Grandparents' support obligations*. At common law, a grandparent has no obligation to support a grandchild simply because of the grandparent-grandchild relationship. A support obligation may arise only where the grandparent is the child's legal guardian or custodian, where the *in loco parentis* or estoppel doctrines would support the obligation, or where the grandparent has agreed to provide support.

By statute, however, more than a dozen states impose a support obligation on grandparents whose unemancipated minor children become parents. The obligation usually continues until the unemancipated minor parents reach majority. *See, e.g.*, Mo. Rev. Stat. § 210.847.1 (2008). In California, however, "[a] parent does not have the duty to support a child of the parent's child." Cal. Fam. Code § 3930 (2008). Which approach represents sounder public policy?

e. *Children's support for their parents*. Adult children must support their elderly parents only where a "filial responsibility" statute imposes the obligation, though adult children often informally provide financial support and personal care. These statutes have attracted renewed attention in recent decades because medical advances have produced longer life expectancies, which in turn have increased the prospect that adults will suffer diminished capacity, illness and perhaps prolonged disability in their advancing years. The hefty divorce rate has also left growing numbers of the elderly without spousal support. Social Security and other public support programs have not kept pace with costs of living and rising health care costs.

Filial responsibility statutes have had a checkered history. Early English common law imposed no duty on children to support their elderly parents. The duty derives from the Elizabethan Poor Laws, which imposed on children an obligation to support elderly parents who had supported them during their minority, thus creating a private "safety net" designed to relieve the state of the support burden. *See* Seymour Moskowitz, *Filial Responsibility Statutes: Legal and Policy Considerations*, 9 J.L. & Pol'y 709, 710–13 (2001).

The American colonies imported the Elizabethan Poor Laws (and the policy choice to substitute private for public support), and filial responsibility statutes remained on the books throughout the eighteenth and nineteenth centuries. About thirty states have filial responsibility statutes today. *See* Shannon Frank Edelstone, *Filial Responsibility: Can the Legal Duty to Support Our Parents Be Effectively Enforced?*, 36 Fam. L.Q. 501, 502 (2002).

Filial responsibility statutes typically impose obligations much lower than parents' obligations to support their minor children. Many destitute parents have children in dire financial straits themselves, and children are charged with a support obligation only where they have sufficient money after providing first for their own spouse and children. South Dakota's statute, for example, provides that "[a]ny adult child, having the financial ability to do so shall provide necessary food, clothing, shelter, or medical attendance for a parent who is unable to provide for oneself." S.D. Codified Laws § 25–7–27 (2008).

Filial responsibility statutes remain quite unpopular in many quarters, but have survived constitutional scrutiny. *See, e.g., Americana Healthcare Ctr. v. Randall,* 513 N.W.2d 566, 571–73 (S.D. 1994) (rejecting an equal protection challenge (1) because the indigent parent's support and care of the child during minority provided a rational basis for imposing a duty on the child to support the parent once the child reached adulthood, and (2) because the state has a legitimate interest in providing for the welfare and care of the elderly).

[handwritten margin note: rationale 4 filial obligation]

Parents may enforce filial responsibility statutes in private support actions, though such actions are rare, perhaps because of parents' general reluctance to burden their children. Depending on the state, civil enforcement may also be pursued by government agencies or (as in *Randall*) by hospitals, nursing homes and other private providers that care for the parent. Some states also impose criminal liability on children for nonsupport of their parents, though prosecutions are scarce. In a number of states, civil and criminal filial responsibility laws on the books for decades have apparently never been invoked. *See* Ann Britton, *America's Best Kept Secret: An Adult Child's Duty to Support Aged Parents,* 26 Cal. W. L. Rev. 351, 365–66 (1990).

PROBLEM 11–1

You are a newly elected member of the state House of Representatives, and you have just been assigned to the Children, Youth and Families Committee. The committee is considering whether to report the following bill favorably to the full House:

Sec. 1. A stepparent shall support his or her stepchild to the same extent that a biological or adoptive parent is required to support his or her child so long as the stepchild is living in the same home as the stepparent. However, nothing in this section shall be construed as abrogating or in any way diminishing the duty a parent otherwise would have to provide child support, and no court shall consider the income of a stepparent, or the amount actually provided for a stepchild by a stepparent, in determining the amount of child support to be paid by a biological or adoptive parent.

Sec. 2. A biological or adoptive parent shall be liable to a stepparent for the sum of money expended by a stepparent for the support of a stepchild when that sum of money was expended because of the neglect or refusal of the biological or adoptive parent to pay any part of or all of the court-ordered amount of support.

Sec. 3. This statute shall not abrogate or diminish the common law right that a stepparent may possess to recover from a biological or adoptive parent the expense of providing necessaries for a stepchild in the absence of a court order for child support determining the amount of support to be paid by a biological or adoptive parent.

* * *

How would you vote? If you favor the concept of the bill, would you recommend any changes to it during committee deliberations?

PROBLEM 11–2

You are an influential state senator. The following bill has cleared committee and will soon be debated by the full senate:

In any action to determine child support needs and obligations for a child whose alleged father is less than 18 years old, the parents of the alleged father and the parents of the mother, if the mother is also less than 18 years old, shall be made joint parties and may be jointly liable for the support ordered by the court to the child until both the father and the mother reach the age of 18 years.

How would you vote on this bill? What amendments, if any, would you suggest? As you prepare for floor debate, what policy considerations weigh in favor of, or against, the bill? If you were informed that parents control grandparents' access to their grandchildren, would this information affect your thinking? *See Troxel v. Granville*, 530 U.S. 57 (2000), a principal case in Chapter 13.

PROBLEM 11–3

You are a state legislator considering a bill that would require children to support their elderly parents. What policy considerations would you weigh in deciding how to vote? If you favor such a bill, what should the standard of support be?

B. EXTENDING THE OBLIGATION PAST MINORITY

With many children saddled with substantial housing costs or higher education debts, parents today may informally support their children well into their twenties. Stories abound of children moving back home into the parents' formerly "empty nest." *See, e.g.*, Nisha Ramachandran, *The Parent Trap: Boomerang Kids*, U.S. News & World Rep., Dec. 12, 2005, at 64. But does the law ever compel parents to provide post-majority support?

1. SUPPORT DURING POST–SECONDARY EDUCATION

Until the early 1970s, the general age of majority was 21. Shortly after approval of the Twenty–Sixth Amendment (lowering the minimum voting age to 18 in federal and state elections), most states lowered the age of majority to 18.

The lower age creates tension with the parental support obligation. At 21, most children have completed high school and many have nearly completed college. Children are likely either to have entered, or to be on the verge of entering, a trade or occupation. At 18, on the other hand, a child might not even have completed high school and may be facing the most costly period of life, arising from financing higher education.

The common law imposed no general obligation on parents to support their children's pursuit of higher education past majority. Any such general obligation would have been out of place for much of our nation's early history, when children were not even required to attend elementary and secondary school, and when college and university education was available only to a select few. In *Middlebury College v. Chandler,* 16 Vt. 683, 683 (1844), for example, the court held that the father was not obligated to pay for his son's college education because the evidence did not show "wealth, or station in society, or that [the son] exhibited peculiar indications of genius or talent, which would suggest the fitness and expediency of a college education for him, more than for the generality of youth in community."

In recent generations, however, higher education has become more essential than ever before to career entry and advancement. The cost of higher education has outpaced inflation almost every year for at least the past three decades, threatening to place advanced study beyond the reach of many high school graduates without some measure of support from their parents.

As discussed more fully in Chapter 14, marital settlement agreements and child support and visitation agreements often recite the parents' respective obligations to support the children's higher education. Even in the absence of an agreement to pay, at least 20 states have statutes authorizing courts to order that parents provide children support until graduation from high school and for at least some part of higher education completed within a few years thereafter. *See, e.g.,* Mo. Rev. Stat. § 452.340 (2008) (until completion of high school or age 21, whichever occurs first; until completion of higher education or age 22, whichever occurs first). It has been held that these statutes reach not only children enrolled in public or private elementary or secondary schools when the court enters the order, but also home-schooled children. *See, e.g., Davis v. Davis,* 873 N.E.2d 1305 (Ohio 2007). Some states specify that an educational support order may be based directly on the costs of tuition, books and expenses. *See, e.g.,* Conn. Gen. Stat. § 46b–56c(f) (2008).

Where no statute authorizes support beyond age 18, some courts have exercised equitable authority to order post-majority support for higher education. *See, e.g., Ex parte Bayliss,* 550 So.2d 986 (Ala. 1989). The general approach is to authorize imposition of post-majority support on only the non-custodial parent, perhaps on the rationale that the custodial parent will be more likely to provide support voluntarily. *See, e.g.,* William V. Fabricius et al., *Divorced Parents' Financial Support of their Children's College Expenses,* 41 Fam. Ct. Rev. 224, 224–25 (2003).

Statutes imposing post-majority educational support obligations on parents of divorced or nonmarital children, but not on parents in intact families, raise ticklish questions. In *Curtis v. Kline,* 666 A.2d 265, 269 (Pa.

1995), the court held that the post-majority educational support statute violated equal protection because the state has no authority to "selectively * * * empower only [children] from non-intact families to compel" their parents to help finance their higher education. *Curtis* expresses the minority view, and most jurisdictions have followed the approach expressed in *In re Marriage of Kohring*, 999 S.W.2d 228, 233 (Mo. 1999). *Kohring* rejected the equal protection challenge on the ground that the state has a legitimate interest in securing higher education opportunities for children from broken homes, and that the statute rationally advanced that interest by requiring financially capable parents to support their children's higher education.

2. SUPPORT FOR DISABLED ADULT CHILDREN

HASTINGS v. HASTINGS

Third District Court of Appeal of Florida, 2003.
841 So.2d 484.

FLETCHER, JUDGE.

In 1953 Jean Audrey Hastings, n/k/a Jean Audrey Shepard [mother] and Lawrence Vaeth Hastings [father] divorced. The father was ordered to pay child support until their son reached the age of 21.[1] In 2001 the father filed a declaratory action, seeking to have determined whether he has an obligation to pay support for his 50–year–old son, who has an autism-related, chronic condition (Asperger's syndrome) for which he began receiving treatment at age 8.[2] The mother and the son counter-petitioned for the establishment of support for the son under Section 743.07(2), Florida Statutes, a savings clause enacted when the disability of nonage was removed for persons 18 years of age and over. Section 743.07(2) reads in pertinent part:

> This section shall not prohibit any court of competent jurisdiction from requiring support for a dependent person beyond the age of 18 years when such dependency is because of a mental or physical incapacity which began prior to such person reaching majority . . .

By this enactment the legislature did not create a right or a cause of action, but "saved" any common law right or cause of action from extinction by section 743.07(1).

The trial court granted summary judgment for the father, apparently concluding that after the passage of many years it is now too late for the support action to be brought. We disagree.

" * * * [T]here is no doubt that the son has a common law right of support from his parents. * * *

---

1. The age of majority at that time.

2. The mother supported the parties' dependent son by herself from the time the son was 21 until recently when she became unable to continue doing so.

In summary, the right to support belongs to the mentally or physically disabled adult child whose disability began prior to her or his majority, and the duty of support lies with both parents, throughout their lives. Thus the issue of support is not totally resolved in divorce actions wherein the mother and father allocate (or have allocated for them) the support payments for their dependent child as such a dependent person can bring an action in accordance with the rule establishing appropriate parties in actions involving legal incompetents. * * *

Reversed and remanded for further proceedings consistent herewith.

COPE, J., concurs.

[The dissenting opinion of LEVY, J., is omitted.]

NOTES AND QUESTION

1. *State variations*. "States differ radically in their answer to the question of whether parents should be subject to an ongoing legal duty to support adult children whose disabilities prevent them from supporting themselves. Nine recognize no such duty. Twenty-four recognize such a duty only if the child becomes disabled prior to majority or emancipation. The remaining eighteen, plus the District of Columbia, impose a duty of support regardless of when disability occurs." Sande L. Buhai, *Parental Support of Adult Children with Disabilities*, 91 Minn. L. Rev. 710, 775 (2007).

As *Hastings* demonstrates, Florida falls within the second category. In the second-category and third-category states, the continuing obligation may last for the lifetimes of the parent or child. What policy considerations underlie imposition of the continuing obligation?

2. *When does the disability occur?* Sometimes the date on which the disability begins is not difficult to establish. In *Lueckenotte v. Lueckenotte*, 34 S.W.3d 387 (Mo. 2001), for example, the boy suffered a brain virus diagnosed when he was 13. In *Riggs v. Riggs*, 578 S.E.2d 3 (S.C. 2003), however, the court imposed a support obligation on the divorced father of a girl who was diagnosed with a degenerative metabolic disease after she had reached majority. The court credited expert medical testimony that the disease was a "genetic error of metabolism," and thus had existed since birth.

SECTION 2: DETERMINING THE CHILD SUPPORT AMOUNT

A. THE NEED FOR GUIDELINES

Well into the 1970s, courts considering child support requests received little guidance from statutes that imposed the support obligation but provided no criteria for determining awards. A few states enacted section 309 of the Uniform Marriage and Divorce Act which, as promulgated in 1970 and amended in 1973, required courts to consider all relevant factors, including the child's financial resources, the custodial parent's financial resources, the standard of living the child would have enjoyed had the marriage not been dissolved, the child's physical and emotional condition and educational needs, and the non-custodial parent's financial resources and needs. UMDA § 309, 9A U.L.A. 167 (1979), *amended by* UMDA § 309, 9A U.L.A. 573 (1998).

By the early 1970s, Congress grew concerned that broad trial court discretion in setting child support awards (subject to only deferential appellate review under the abuse-of-discretion standard, if appeal was taken at all) imposed few constraints and left many children with awards "pathetically low by any standard." Sylvia Law, *Access to Justice: The Social Responsibility of Lawyers: Families and Federalism*, 4 Wash. U. J.L. & Pol'y 175, 187–88 (2000). Children similarly situated often received dissimilar awards based on a judge's own notions about the parents, the child and the role of support itself. Some observers argued that evidently standardless decisions encouraged evasion and discouraged payment by inviting resentment from custodial and noncustodial parents alike. Not only did unduly low awards sometimes consign children to single-parent households below the federal poverty line; such awards also frequently cast the lion's share of the cost of child-rearing on the custodial parent, usually the mother.

To produce greater horizontal uniformity within particular states and to remedy the inconsistent case-by-case approach, the federal Child Support Enforcement Amendments of 1984 required states, among other things, to establish discretionary numerical guidelines to assist courts and agencies in determining child support awards. Pub. L. No. 98–378, 98 Stat. 1305 (codified as amended in scattered sections of 26 & 42 U.S.C. (2003)). The federal Family Support Act of 1988 went a significant step further, mandating that states promulgate mandatory presumptive child support guidelines by 1994. Pub. L. No. 100–485, 102 Stat. 2343 (1988). All states now have such guidelines, whose formulas can be quite intricate.

The 1988 Act, grounded in Congress' spending power, made designated child welfare funds available only to states that developed written rebuttable guidelines for calculating child support obligations. *See* 42 U.S.C. § 667(a), (b)(2). Federal regulations today require that state guidelines (1) consider all the nonresidential parent's earnings and income, (2) base awards on specific descriptive and numeric criteria and result in computation of the support obligation, and (3) provide for the child's health care needs through health insurance or other means. 45 C.F.R. § 302.56 (2008).

States must also (1) establish criteria for determining when the presumptive award amount would be unjust or inappropriate in a particular case, and (2) reexamine and revise their guidelines at least once every four years "to ensure that their application results in the determination of appropriate child support awards." The four-year review must consider "economic data on the cost of raising children," and must "analyze case data, gathered through sampling or other methods, on the application of, and deviations from, the guidelines." *Id*. § 302.56(e), (h).

The intricate guidelines demonstrate more clearly than ever before that diminished family privacy is an inevitable consequence of divorce. "While a family is intact, the parents' choice of employment, child care, and standard of living are left to the parties, as long as the child's basic needs are met. Upon divorce, however, courts are plunged into the divorced parents' personal lives to ensure that the interests of minor children are protected." *Chen v. Warner*, 695 N.W.2d 758, 769 (Wis. 2005).

B. GUIDELINE METHODS

Because Congress did not mandate any particular guideline method, states remain free to create their own methods by statute, administrative regulation or court rule. Three general guideline methods have emerged: the "income shares model" (which about two-thirds of the states use), the "percentage of the obligor's income" model (which about 13 states use), and the "Melson formula" (which Delaware, Hawaii and Montana use). In addition, Massachusetts and the District of Columbia have alternative methods to calculate child support, which are basically "hybrids" of the Melson formula and percentage of the obligor's income models. Jane C. Venohr & Robert G. Williams, *The Implementation and Periodic Review of Child Support Guidelines*, 33 Fam. L.Q. 7, 10 (1999).

The *Income Shares* model is grounded in two principles: (1) that both parents living apart have a legal obligation to support the child in accordance with their respective means; and (2) that the child should receive the same percentage of joint parental income the child would receive in an intact family. This method first combines both parents' incomes, as if the household were intact. More than half of Income Shares states use gross (pre-tax) income, and other states use net (after-tax) income. A support amount is assigned to that income, reflecting a percentage of what the parents would spend on the child if the household were intact, and excluding average amounts for health insurance, child care and the child's extraordinary medical expenses. In most Income Shares model jurisdictions, the percentage of income that must be paid in child support decreases as parental income increases, and a straight calculation of income shares does not apply for parents with high combined income levels. *E.g.*, North Carolina Court System, Schedule of Basic Child Support Obligations, http://www.nccourts.org/Forms/Documents/981.pdf. The child support obligation is then apportioned to each parent in proportion to his or her relative income. A portion or prorated share of child care and medical expenses is then factored into each parent's basic support obligation. *E.g.*, Tenn. Dep't of Human Services, Child Support Worksheet, http://www.state.tn.us/sos/rules/1240/1240–02/1240–02–04.pdf. Other adjustments may apply for shared physical custody, other dependents, any imputed income, other existing child support, educational expenses, and transportation expenses related to visitation. *Compare* Maryland Judiciary, Form No. DR34, Child Support Guidelines Worksheet A (Primary Physical Custody), http://www.courts.state.md.us/family/forms/dr34.pdf, *with* Form No. 35, Worksheet B (Shared Physical Custody), http://www. courts.state.md.us/family/forms/dr35.pdf. The noncustodial parent must pay his or her percentage, and the guidelines assume the custodial parent will pay the remainder without court order.

The *Percentage of the Obligor's Income* model, the simplest guideline method, is based on only the noncustodial parent's income and determines that parent's support obligation based on the number of children to be supported. *E.g.*, Arkansas Judiciary, Monthly Family Support Chart, http://courts.state.ar.us/pdf/child_support_monthlychart.pdf. The assumption is that even without a court order, the custodial parent will support the child living under her roof. The noncustodial parent's obligation is a fixed percentage of his income, though some states assign lower percentages to low-income parents than to higher-income parents. Some states use gross income with appropriate deductions and adjustments, and other states use net income. Where the obligor's income is higher than the maximum guidelines, the guidelines may not apply and the court may award a higher amount than the maximum guideline amount.

The *Melson Formula,* named after Delaware Family Court Judge Elwood F. Melson, Jr., who created it for use in his courtroom, has three steps:

(1) The *"primary support allowance."* Each parent's net income is determined, and the minimum amount each parent needs for his or own subsistence (the "primary support allowance") is subtracted from that amount. If the net income is less than the primary support allowance, the parent owes no child support.

(2) *Providing for the child's primary support needs.* If a parent's net income is greater than the primary support allowance, the "excess income" is assigned to that parent. If only one parent has excess income, that parent must pay all the child's basic support needs, up to the amount of the excess income. If both parents have excess income, they share the basic support obligation in accordance with the relative amounts of their excess incomes.

(3) The *"standard of living allowance."* If a parent still has income left after satisfying the parent's and the child's primary support needs, the parent must pay an additional percentage of his or her income to child support.

E.g., Delaware State Court, Form No. 509, Child Support Calculation, http://courts.delaware.gov/forms/download.aspx?id=268.

As often happens, the devil is in the details because "no two states have identical guidelines, even when their underlying models are similar." Jo Michelle Beld & Len Biernat, *Federal Intent For State Child Support Guidelines: Income Shares, Cost Shares, and the Realities of Shared Parenting*, 37 Fam. L.Q. 165, 166 (2003). "State guidelines vary with respect to the income basis for the determination of support; the estimates of spending on children upon which the guidelines are based; the treatment of child care costs; the treatment of medical insurance and out-of-pocket expenditures for medical care; provisions for other children to whom the parent owes a duty of support; adjustments for parenting time; and provisions for adjusting support when the obligor is low-income." *Id.* With these variations in mind, the remainder of this Section examines how the guidelines operate.

C. WHAT IS "INCOME"?

1. THE GUIDELINES DEFINITION

Guidelines begin calculation of child support by defining parental "income." Regardless of the guideline method the state uses, "income" is defined broadly before any of the adjustments discussed above are made.

Section 403.212 of the Kentucky Revised Statutes

(2) For the purposes of the child support guidelines:

(a) "Income" means actual gross income of the parent if employed to full capacity or potential income if unemployed or underemployed.

(b) "Gross income" includes income from any source, except as excluded in this subsection, and includes but is not limited to income from salaries, wages, retirement and pension funds, commissions, bonuses, dividends, severance pay, pensions, interest, trust income, annuities, capital gains, Social Security benefits, workers' compensation benefits, unemployment insurance benefits, disability insurance benefits, Supplemental Security Income (SSI), gifts, prizes, and alimony or maintenance received. Specifically excluded are benefits received from means-tested public assistance programs, including but not limited to public assistance as defined under Title IV–A of the Federal Social Security Act, and food stamps.

(c) For income from self-employment, rent, royalties, proprietorship of a business, or joint ownership of a partnership or closely held corporation, "gross income" means gross receipts minus ordinary and necessary expenses required for self-employment or business operation. * * * Expense reimbursement or in-kind payments received by a parent in the course of employment, self-employment, or operation of a business or personal use of business property or payments of expenses by a business, shall be counted as income if they are significant and reduce personal living expenses such as a company or business car, free housing, reimbursed meals, or club dues.

(d) If a parent is voluntarily unemployed or underemployed, child support shall be calculated based on a determination of potential income, except that a determination of potential income shall not be made for a parent who is physically or mentally incapacitated or is caring for a very young child, age three (3) or younger, for whom the parents owe a joint legal responsibility. Potential income shall be determined based upon employment potential and probable earnings level based on the obligor's or obligee's recent work history, occupational qualifications, and prevailing job opportunities and earnings levels in the community. A court may find a parent to be voluntarily unemployed or underemployed without finding that the parent intended to avoid or reduce the child support obligation.

(e) "Imputed child support obligation" means the amount of child support the parent would be required to pay from application of the child support guidelines.

* * *

Ky. Rev. Stat. Ann. § 403.212(2) (West 2008).

2. IMPUTING INCOME

[handwritten: Pretty much always to non custodial parent]

The court may impute income to a parent who voluntarily remains unemployed or underemployed. *See, e.g., id.* § 403.212(2)(d). In determining whether to impute income, courts decide whether the obligor acted in good faith, or whether the obligor's diminished income resulted from efforts to shirk obligations to the child, or from other wrongdoing. "Shirking is an employment decision to reduce or forgo income that is both voluntary and unreasonable under the circumstances." *Chen v. Warner*, 683 N.W.2d 468, 470 (Wis. Ct. App. 2004), *aff'd*, 695 N.W.2d 758 (Wis. 2005). The court may find shirking where the parent voluntarily fails to earn to his or her full capacity to avoid paying child support, or where the parent makes a voluntary and unreasonable decision resulting in a lowered income. 683 N.W.2d at 470 n.2.

Imputation decisions are quite fact-specific. On the one hand, divorce should not force parents to "make their career decisions based strictly upon the size of potential paychecks." *Adams v. Adams*, 873 N.E.2d 1094, 1099 (Ind. Ct. App. 2007). Like other adults, child support obligors should retain the opportunity to make reasonable career choices and other lifestyle decisions, even where the decision results in loss of income at least temporarily. On the other hand, divorce does not dissolve the parents' obligations to support their children.

Once the court decides to impute income for unemployment or underemployment, the court must determine how much to impute. The determination turns on the obligor's earning capacity. " 'Earning capacity is composed of (1) the ability to work, including such factors as age, occupation, skills, education, health, background, work experience and qualifications; (2) the willingness to work exemplified through good faith efforts, due diligence and meaningful attempts to secure employment; and (3) an opportunity to work which means an employer who is willing to hire.' " *In re Marriage of Henry*, 23 Cal.Rptr.3d 707, 713 n.3 (Ct. App. 2005).

This Chapter covers imputed income in greater detail in Section 3, beginning at page 635 below.

3. SEEK–WORK ORDERS

Before imputing income for unemployment or underemployment, courts sometimes issue a seek-work order directing the obligor parent to search for employment to produce or add to income. Violation of a seek-work order can expose the obligor to citation for contempt of court.

In *In re Marriage of Dennis*, 344 N.W.2d 128 (Wis. 1984), for example, the divorced father of three never earned more than $3500 per year in his auto repair business. During and after the marriage, the parents remained below the poverty line and received public assistance. After reducing Mr. Dennis' monthly child support obligation from $15 to $5 per child, the court ordered him to "use his good faith efforts to apply for other work at least in ten places per month, and be in a position to show such compliance and efforts made." *Id.* at 129. The order did not direct him to accept any particular employment offer.

Dennis testified that because of his limited income and his monthly expenses, he could not afford to apply for ten jobs a month. For failing to make the required applications or to pay the $15 monthly child support and arrears, the trial court found him in contempt and ordered him imprisoned. The state supreme court upheld the seek-work order: "Until the defendant and the judge know what other work and income is available, there is no way the judge can determine, except by suspicion, that the defendant can do no better and there is no way, except by way of inference, to determine that the defendant is satisfied with his own lot in life and is willing to allow society to support his children." *Id.* at 132.

PROBLEM 11–4

When Mike and Julie Brown divorced, the court awarded the 46–year–old wife $200 monthly in rehabilitative alimony for two years. She had a high school education and, during the couple's 13–year marriage, was a homemaker who cared for the two children. The husband was an engineer earning more than $63,000 annually, plus stock options and other fringe benefits. During the two-year rehabilitative period, Julie became a full-time student pursuing a nursing degree. Should the court impute income to her during that two-year period? Would a seek-work order be appropriate?

PROBLEM 11–5

When John and Jean Smith of Lexington, Kentucky divorced after a 10–year marriage, John received primary physical custody of their two children. Eight years earlier, Jean earned an annual salary of $33,000 in her last full-time job, which she left so she could stay home and raise the children. Since then, she has earned a masters degree in electrical engineering, but has not reentered the work force. In the divorce proceeding, the trial court imputed an annual income of $66,000 after taking judicial notice of the U.S. Department of Labor's Bureau of Labor Statistics Report, which placed the national median annual earnings for electrical engineers at $64,910.00. Applying the Kentucky statute quoted above, did the trial court decide correctly? Does the statute's imputation provision properly weigh the interests of both parents and the two children?

D. DEVIATING FROM THE GUIDELINES AMOUNT

By congressional mandate, states must apply a rebuttable presumption that the guidelines amount is the correct amount of child support payable by an obligor parent. A court may deviate or depart from (or "adjust" or "vary") the guidelines amount, either upward or downward. The court may do so, however, only on a written or specific finding on the record that the guidelines amount would be unjust or inappropriate in a particular case, as determined under criteria established by the state. To insure the guidelines' integrity, states are left to determine the showing required to rebut.

Section 403.211 of the Kentucky Revised Statutes

* * *

(3) A written finding or specific finding on the record that the application of the guidelines would be unjust or inappropriate in a particular case shall be sufficient to rebut the presumption and allow for an appropriate adjustment of the guideline award if based upon one (1) or more of the following criteria:

(a) A child's extraordinary medical or dental needs;

(b) A child's extraordinary educational, job training, or special needs;

(c) Either parent's own extraordinary needs, such as medical expenses;

(d) The independent financial resources, if any, of the child or children;

(e) Combined monthly adjusted parental gross income in excess of the Kentucky child support guidelines;

(f) The parents of the child, having demonstrated knowledge of the amount of child support established by the Kentucky child support guidelines, have agreed to child support different from the guideline amount. However, no such agreement shall be the basis of any deviation if public assistance is being paid on behalf of a child under the provisions of Part D of Title IV of the Federal Social Security Act; and

(g) Any similar factor of an extraordinary nature specifically identified by the court which would make application of the guidelines inappropriate.

(4) "Extraordinary" as used in this section shall be determined by the court in its discretion.

* * *

Ky. Rev. Stat. Ann. § 403.211(3)–(4) (West 2008).

NOTES AND QUESTIONS

1. *The required showing.* Because deviation is meant to be the exception rather than the rule, only a compelling showing rebuts the presumption, at least where deviation is sought for "extraordinary" circumstances not specifically enumerated in the applicable statute or rule. Where the guidelines recite an exclusive enumeration of the grounds the court may consider, the court commits reversible error if it deviates on an unenumerated ground. *See, e.g., Khaldy v. Khaldy,* 892 P.2d 584, 585–86 (Nev. 1995).

The propriety of deviation may depend on the guidelines' method for calculating the support obligation in the first place. In *In re Marriage of Beecher,* 582 N.W.2d 510, 514 (Iowa 1998), for example, the court denied downward deviation for the child's medical expenses, which the guidelines had already considered in determining the parent's net income. *Beecher* held that downward deviation based on these expenses would give the noncustodial parent, in effect, a double deduction.

2. *"Parenting time."* Initially many states based their child support guidelines on the model that prevailed in most divided households—one parent with sole physical custody of the children, and the other parent with reasonable visitation. The schedule presumed a custodial parent with direct ongoing expenses while the child was living under her roof, and a noncustodial parent who would contribute with support payments. "Visitation" normally reflected the expectation that the child would not live with the noncustodial parent for more than a modest period each year. Courts could consider unusual custody arrangements as grounds for deviating from the presumed guidelines amount.

Since the early 1980s, however, more and more divided families have been marked by custody and visitation arrangements ("parenting plans") that depart from the traditional model. During their periodic reviews of the guidelines, states have wrestled with contentions that the guidelines unfairly burden noncustodial parents (typically fathers) whose children live with them for periods longer than the modest period that marks traditional visitation. These parents, it is claimed, are victims of "double-dipping" because they shoulder greater direct support costs during these longer periods while also paying support under guidelines that calculate support based on circumstances that traditionally marked divided families.

Many courts have responded by deviating from the guidelines where the noncustodial parent enjoys extended overnight visitation, typically more than 30% of overnights. Because frequent exercise of such judicial discretion might threaten congressional intent to achieve regularity in child support awards, however, some state guidelines have created formulas for extended-visitation cases.

The guidelines formula may combine mandate with discretion. Florida, for example, requires the court to adjust a child support award "[w]henever a particular shared parental arrangement provides that each child spend a substantial amount of time with each parent." Fla. Stat. § 61.30(11)(b) (2008). A "substantial amount of time" means that "the non-custodial parent exercises visitation at least 40 percent of the overnights of the year." *Id.* § 61.30(11)(b)(10). The court retains discretion to order adjustment "[w]here the child spends a significant amount of time, but less than 40% of the overnights, with the noncustodial parent." *Id.* § 61.30(11)(a)(10). Where a parent fails to take advantage of court-ordered visitation of 40% or more of the overnights, the other parent may seek modification of the support order for substantially changed circumstances. *Id.* § 61.30(11)(c). The court must take evidence concerning the child's residential patterns. *See, e.g., Cheverie v. Cheverie*, 898 So.2d 1028 (Fla. Dist. Ct. App. 2005) (father entitled to adjustment because child stayed with him more than 40% of overnights); *Karimi v. Karimi*, 867 So.2d 471 (Fla. Dist. Ct. App. 2004) (father not entitled to adjustment because children spent about 33% of overnights with him).

Formulas that reduce support payments for the time the child spends with the nonresidential parent may introduce new inequities because direct expenses borne by that parent do not necessarily reduce the residential parent's expenses, such as housing and utility costs. Professor Marygold S. Melli notes other problems with reliance on formulas:

> First, it rewards nonresidential parents disproportionately for spending small amounts of extra time with their children. Consequently, it may encourage a nonresidential parent to seek small amounts of shared time over the threshold amount to obtain a substantial decrease in child support. Second, if ordinary visitation has already been factored in and the basic child support award has already been discounted for the expenditures by the nonresidential parent on ordinary visitation, a formula based on a strict proportional time with the child doubles the discounts for ordinary visitation.

Marygold S. Melli, *Guideline Review: Child Support and Time Sharing By Parents*, 33 Fam. L.Q. 219, 228 (1999).

Critics have also contended that some disputes about parenting time might actually be disguised disputes about child support itself. In an effort to reduce the child support obligation, for example, the nonresidential parent might seek increased time with the child when nothing indicates the child would benefit from an increase. *See* Robert Scott Merlin, *The New Line 11 Visitation Credit: The Non–Custodial Parent Wins While the Child Loses*, 55 Wash. U. J. Urb. & Contemp. L. 317, 342–43 (1999). By the same token, the residential parent seeking to avoid lower support payments might deny the nonresidential parent increased visitation time, even when the extra time would be in the best interests of the child.

3. *The child's resources.* Some state guidelines permit or require the court to consider the child's financial resources in determining the parent's basic support obligation. *See, e.g.,* Mo. Rev. Stat. § 452.340.1(1) (2008). In other states, such as Kentucky, quoted *supra* page 607, the child's financial resources do not affect that determination, but may be a basis for downward

deviation on the ground that the guideline amount is unjust or inappropriate. Ky. Rev. Stat. Ann. § 403.212(2) (West 2008).

The child's resources may include Social Security, which provides more benefits to children than any other government social program. Most Americans are familiar with Social Security as a retirement insurance program. Social Security, however, is also a family insurance program for workers, spouses and children, providing income support to disabled workers and their families, and to survivors of workers who die. More than three million children benefit from Social Security after a parent has died, retired or become disabled; nearly one million children benefit from Social Security because the child has a specified disability such as Down syndrome. *See* Nancy K. Cauthen, *Why Social Security Matters to Children and Families* 1–2 (2005). In some states, Social Security benefits to the child for any of these reasons remain the child's property and do not diminish the parental support obligation. *See, e.g., Luongo v. Luongo*, 856 N.Y.S.2d 636, 637 (App. Div. 2008). In other states, the parent is entitled to a credit in the amount of such benefits received for any reason. *See, e.g., In re State & Estate of Crabtree*, 926 A.2d 825, 830 (N.H. 2007). In still other states, Social Security benefits paid because of the parent's disability or retirement may, in the court's discretion, diminish the support obligation after considering the child's needs. *See, e.g., Thompson v. Thompson*, 868 N.E.2d 862 (Ind. Ct. App. 2007).

In determining the effect of the child's Social Security benefits, why might a state treat a child with a deceased parent differently from a child with a disability? Why might the court treat a child with a disabled parent differently?

Where the child is the beneficiary of trust income, the question whether such income reduces the parent's obligation or justifies a downward deviation may depend on the child's needs, or on the settlor's intent expressed in the trust. The child's tort recovery may reduce, without extinguishing, the parents' support obligation. In *In re B.S.R.*, 965 S.W.2d 444 (Mo. Ct. App. 1998), for example, the 10–day–old boy was seriously injured in an automobile accident that killed his mother and left him permanently disabled. The lawsuit against the other driver resulted in a $380,000 settlement paid to the boy's conservator estate, plus an annuity that would pay the estate $6430 a month for the rest of the boy's life or twenty years, whichever was longer. *B.S.R.* held that the father had abandoned the child by providing him no support for more than six months. The court rejected the father's contention that there had been no abandonment because the child was being supported by the conservator fund. "The fact that a child has resources of his own to provide for his or her support does not relieve a parent of his or her obligation to financially support the child; rather, it is simply a factor in determining the appropriate amount of support a parent should pay." *Id.* at 449.

4. *Parental agreement.* Parents frequently reach an agreement concerning the amount of child support one or both will pay. The law views these agreements as "legitimate incidents of parental authority and control * * * entitled to serious consideration by a court," but the agreements remain subject to court approval. The test is whether the agreement is in the best interests of the children. "Although, as a rule, it is not in the best interest of

the children when their parents agree to an amount of child support below the Guidelines, no one can convincingly argue that the best interests of the children are not served when their parents agree to support in excess of the amount established by the Guidelines." *Pursley v. Pursley*, 144 S.W.3d 820, 825 (Ky. 2004).

The court's inquiry is likely to be particularly searching where the parents' agreement stipulates an amount lower than the guidelines amount. A lower amount may be appropriate, for example, where the non-custodial parent has assumed financial obligations not considered in the guidelines, such as promises in the marital settlement agreement to pay for extracurricular activities, summer camps or lessons, or where the parenting plan provides for visitation with the obligor parent for periods that are substantial, but less than would trigger automatic reduction under extensive visitation deviation guidelines. *E.g.*, *Kammueller v. Kammueller*, 672 N.W.2d 594, 596 (Minn. Ct. App. 2003). These issues are discussed further in Chapter 14, Privatizing the Ramifications of Marriage and Divorce.

Where a divorcing parent agrees to support a child for a period longer than the support statute requires, the court enforces the agreement under ordinary contract law principles. *See, e.g.*, *Shands v. Shands*, 237 S.W.3d 597 (Mo. Ct. App. 2007).

E. HIGH–INCOME OBLIGORS

SMITH v. STEWART

Supreme Court of Vermont, 1996.
684 A.2d 265.

DOOLEY, JUSTICE.

Defendant, Potter Stewart, Jr., appeals the decision of the Windham Family Court awarding increased child support for 1993 and 1994 to his former wife, plaintiff Judith Smith. He argues that the court erred by awarding support beyond the guideline maximum, by extrapolating from the guidelines, by not basing the guideline calculation on shared custody, and by awarding attorney's fees to plaintiff. We affirm the court's grant of attorney's fees and refusal to apply the shared custody guidelines, but reverse the child support award and remand for recalculation consistent with this opinion.

The parties were married in 1971 and divorced in 1991. They have two sons whose physical custody was awarded to plaintiff but who are frequently with defendant when not in school. This case involves calculation of support for the children for 1993 and 1994 in accordance with the 1991 divorce order. The order, which was based on a stipulation of the parties, provides:

> The Defendant shall pay to the Plaintiff child support in accordance with the Vermont Child Support Guidelines. Said support shall be recalculated annually on January 1 or as soon thereafter as possible. Each party shall provide the other with income and tax information

necessary to recalculate said support amount. The amount recalculated shall be retroactive to January 1 of the relevant year. * * *

The parties agreed to this arrangement to accommodate defendant's fluctuating salary. * * *

* * *

Defendant's income in 1991 was approximately $146,000. In 1992, it rose to $299,951. In 1993, it fell to $180,523. In February 1994, defendant left his law firm and started his own practice. He estimated that he would earn approximately $75,000 in 1994 from this practice. Plaintiff's income in 1992 was $36,952, including the maintenance payments; in 1993, it dropped to $29,480.

In 1992, defendant paid child support in the amount of $337 per week, based on his 1991 income. Defendant filed his 1992 income tax return in April 1993, but did not give plaintiff a copy until July 1993. He continued the preexisting child support amount until July 16, when he raised it to $434 per week. During 1993, defendant paid $19,949 in child support.

In 1994, defendant lowered his child support payment when he left his firm to start his own practice. Since January he has been paying $128 per week. He provided his 1993 income tax returns in May 1994.

On January 12, 1994, defendant * * * requested that the court determine the proper amount of child support pursuant to the 1991 order. On January 26, 1994, plaintiff responded by moving to enforce the 1991 order with respect to child support for the years 1993 and 1994.

* * *

A

Defendant first argues that the court erred by awarding child support in an amount greater than the guideline maximum. He claims that the court may award support beyond the guideline maximum only if it finds that the needs of the children have not been met, and that no such finding was or could have been made here. This argument requires us to revisit the purposes and policies of our child support system.

In 1986, the Legislature adopted a new child support system which established guidelines for determining the financial support obligations of parents in most cases. The guideline system has three main purposes: to ensure children receive the same proportion of parental income after separation or divorce as they would have received if the parents had never separated, to eliminate discrepancies in awards between children in similar circumstances and to improve the efficiency of child support adjudication. The central component of the system is a set of tables which reflect "the percent of combined available income which parents living in the same household in Vermont ordinarily spend on their children." The table amounts are expressed in dollars and are "presumed to be the total support obligation of parents." When the events in this case took place, the tables covered combined available incomes up to $11,575 per month. When the combined available income of the parents exceeds the "upper-most levels of the support guideline," the "court may use its discretion in determining child support."

* * *

We conclude that the family court acted reasonably and was correct in its approach. The 1991 order specifies defendant would pay support "in accordance with the Vermont Child Support Guidelines." Defendant inter-prets these words to mean that he is required to pay no higher than the maximum amount provided for in the tables irrespective of his income. This is an unreasonable interpretation of the language. The guideline maximum is not a cap on child support to be paid. Instead it represents the highest income for which tables are useful or appropriate. When the 1991 agreement and order determined support in accordance with the guidelines, it necessarily included the full guideline system, including the power of the court to set amounts above the tables when the income of the parties exceeds the guideline maximum. Thus, the family court was enforcing the 1991 order according to its terms and not modifying it.

No matter how the action is characterized, defendant acknowledges that the statute gives the trial court discretion to set a support level above that provided for at the highest income of the guidelines. He argues, however, that this discretion may be exercised only when there is demon-strated need for the children to receive the additional amount. We dis-agree that the sole criterion for determining the support amount for above-guideline-income cases is the need of the child. The children are entitled to share in family income if it grows after the parents separate. Thus, the children are entitled to a part of the "fruits of one parent's good fortune after a divorce."

Moreover, the term "need" must be used broadly to reflect the general standard of living of the family. Children are not expected to live at a minimal level of comfort while one or more parents enjoy a luxury lifestyle. A child's needs "increase proportionally with their opportunity to participate in educational, cultural, and recreational activities." The fact that the basic needs of defendant's children are met does not mean that they do not have needs that should be addressed by a further increase in child support.

We are also concerned that defendant's position would actually re-ward the noncustodial parent for having failed to share his increase in income. It would be unreasonable to expect plaintiff to spend more money on the children in anticipation of its coerced receipt from defendant. We could require the custodial parent to present lists of items she would purchase for the children if the additional support were received. Howev-er, while such a list might be helpful to the trial court, we would not rely on it as the sole basis for determining a support amount.

Much of defendant's argument is based on his claim that any additional support will simply go to plaintiff as disguised additional maintenance. There is nothing in the family court decision to suggest that the increased support was intended to be used by plaintiff and not for the support of the children. Although increased child support necessarily has an incidental benefit for the custodial parent, the real beneficiaries are the children. There is no evidence to suggest they would not benefit from the order issued here.

Thus, we reject defendant's argument that, based on the evidence, the court was required to issue an order in an amount no higher than that reflecting the highest income covered by the guidelines. * * * [T]he family court had discretion to consider an award above the maximum guideline amount based on the factors in 15 V.S.A. § 659(a) [which are nearly verbatim the factors stated in section 309 of the UMDA, *supra* page 603— eds.].

B

Next, defendant argues that the family court erred by calculating support based on an extrapolation from the highest income reflected in the guidelines. Although the actual calculation was different from defendant's characterization, as discussed below, we agree in part with defendant's argument and remand for a redetermination of the support obligation.

The guidelines establish "the percent of combined available income which parents living in the same household in Vermont ordinarily spend on their children." They are stated as dollars per month and are broken down by combined available income, in increments of $50 per month, and number of children. Reflecting the spending pattern of intact families, the percentage of income spent on children decreases as income rises. At the low end income of $575 per month, parents have been found to spend 38.2% of their income on support of two children. At the high end income of $11,575 per month, the percentage is 19.0.

When first created, the guidelines determined the support obligation based on gross income. In 1990, the Legislature amended the applicable statutes to base the guidelines on available income, which is defined as gross income, less the amount of certain deductions, including FICA taxes and state and federal income taxes.

Defendant argues that the statutory scheme should be read to prohibit extrapolation from the guidelines to set support amounts for incomes above the maximum provided for in the guideline tables. By extrapolation, we mean "[t]he process of estimating an unknown number outside the range of known numbers." In this case, the "process" with which defendant takes issue is to calculate the presumptive support level using the percentage of income at the high end of the guidelines—that is, 19% for two children.

Defendant relies on decisions from other courts that have held that extrapolation from the guidelines is prohibited under the applicable statutory scheme. Other courts have given trial courts more discretion in computing support obligations for high-income parents without prohibiting any particular methodology. We are not persuaded by those decisions that prohibit extrapolation based on the percentage of income for child support at the guideline maximum. We see nothing in our statutory scheme that prohibits this approach in the proper case.

* * *

In *Ainsworth* [*v. Ainsworth*, 574 A.2d 772 (Vt. 1990)], we held that when a court deviates from the guidelines because application of the guidelines would be unfair to a party or to the child, "the trial court's findings and conclusions must show it considered the factors specified in § 659(a) as well as other relevant factors and must show the reasons for the deviation from the guidelines and the amount of support ordered." These requirements apply when a court is determining the level of support * * * for a noncustodial parent with income above the guidelines. As long as the court considers the statutory factors, makes adequate findings and explains its reasoning in determining the support obligation, its discretion is not limited to adopt or avoid a particular methodology. The only additional requirement is that its decision must reflect the principles behind the guidelines.

[The court remanded because the trial court's brief statement did not indicate whether it had considered the Section 659 factors.]

Didn't neccesarily agree * * * *w/ D, but trial ct. didn't explain reasoning!*

NOTES AND QUESTIONS

1. *High-income obligors.* The vast majority of state guidelines cap annual parental incomes between $70,000 and $180,000, so it is not unusual to find parents (like Mr. Stewart, the son of the former Supreme Court Justice) with incomes "off the schedule" at the high end. The National Conference of State Legislatures periodically summarizes treatment by all states and the District of Columbia of high incomes that are in excess of the cap of the state's child support guidelines. NCSL, *States Treatment of High Income*, http://www.ncsl.org/programs/cyf/incomehi.htm.

Because typically no explicit statutory directive governs treatment of high-income obligors, courts differ in their treatment even within the same state. In a significant number of jurisdictions, courts "extrapolate" the guidelines upward, as the court did in *Stewart*. These courts have concluded that the guidelines establish percentages generally applicable regardless of the parent's income. Under an extrapolation, high-income parents pay the percentage assigned to the uppermost level of incomes stated on the schedule, even though their incomes are higher than that level; the support amount is subject to any deviation according to criteria stated in the applicable statute or rule. The generally applicable percentages may depend on the number of children to whom the parent owes support. *See, e.g.*, 750 Ill. Comp. Stat. Ann. § 5/505(a)(1) (2008) (ranging from 20% for one child, to 50% for six or more children).

Some states presume that the guidelines' highest award amount is the proper amount in high-income-obligor cases, but permit courts to deviate from that amount based on the parties' standard of living and the child's needs. The court denied upward deviation in *State v. Hall*, 418 N.W.2d 187 (Minn. Ct. App. 1988), which affirmed a $1000 monthly child support award entered against entertainer Daryl Hall in favor of his son. Hall and the mother "have never been married to each other, nor have they ever resided together. Their relationship consisted of a single sexual encounter." *Id.* at 187. Hall's net income was about $1.4 million a year, or $116,000 per month. The mother's monthly income consisted of about $437 in AFDC payments and an average of $120 in food stamps.

The $1000 monthly award entered against Hall was the presumptive guideline amount for payors earning $4000 or more per month, the highest income amount on the schedule at that time. The schedule thus stopped at a relatively low maximum amount and vested discretion in the trial court to deviate in appropriate cases. *Hall* rejected the mother's contention that the court abused its discretion by declining to deviate based on Hall's standard of living. "[T]he legislature has effectively declared that a child's needs are normally not higher than $1000 per month. * * * The maximum appropriate award under the guidelines effectively suggests a normal 'cap' on the use of support to upgrade a child's standard of living." *Id.* at 190.

For the portion of the parent's income that is "off the schedule" at the high end, some states determine the child support obligation by applying common law standards, such as those codified in Section 309 of the Uniform Marriage and Divorce Act, *supra* page 603, which consider generally the child's needs and the parent's ability to pay. The guidelines themselves create no formula or presumption for that portion of income. *See, e.g., Zaleski v. Zaleski*, 432 S.E.2d 538 (W. Va. 1993).

Stewart states Vermont's view that for the amount of the obligor's income that is "off the schedule," the court may extrapolate from the percentage applicable to the schedule's highest income figure, or may determine generally the child's needs and the parent's ability to pay.

Stewart concerned the child support obligations of a parent whose high income placed him "off the schedule" at the high end. Poverty may place a parent "off the schedule" at the guidelines' low end, a matter discussed below at page 665.

2. *A high-income obligor case from the headlines.* In 2002, 36–year–old Lisa Bonder Kerkorian sought child support of $320,000 a month for her three-year-old daughter from her ex-husband, 85–year–old billionaire investor Kirk Kerkorian, one of the world's richest men and the head of Metro–Goldwyn–Mayer Studios. The couple was married for only a month, and Kerkorian was not even the girl's biological father. (Lisa Kerkorian admitted that she had faked the DNA paternity test by using saliva from Kerkorian's adult daughter, but Kerkorian said he would support the girl anyway because he had grown attached to her.)

Ms. Kerkorian initially claimed the girl needed monthly stipends of $150,000 for jet travel; $3,900 for clothes; $14,000 for parties and play dates; $7,000 for charity; $11,000 for meals; $2,500 for movies and other outings; $1,400 for laundry and cleaning; $1,000 for toys, books and videos; and $436 for the care of her bunny and other pets. During the trial, the mother had increased her request to $1.5 million per month, to which she argued she was entitled under California's child support guidelines. Finding the request "incredible" and "a disguised form of spousal support," the court awarded the girl support of $50,316 per month. After the decision, Lisa (described as "visibly upset" by the Los Angeles Times) said the judge "severely underestimated the cost it takes to maintain our daughter in a lifestyle he created for her." *See Kerkorian to Pay $50,316 Per Month*, L.A. Times, Sept. 14, 2002, at 4. In 2008, Mr. Kerkorian's lawyer and a Hollywood private investigator were convicted of conspiracy to wiretap Ms. Kerkorian's telephone conversations during the child support dispute. *See* Victoria Kim, *Attorney, Pellicano Guilty of Snooping*, L.A. Times, Aug. 30, 2008, at B1.

3. *Income fluctuation.* Notice that Mr. Stewart's income fluctuated from year to year. Where annual income fluctuates significantly without wrongdoing by the parent, the guidelines in many states permit the court to enter a support order based on an average of the parent's recent annual income, usually for the immediately prior three to five years. *See, e.g., Gress v. Gress*, 743 N.W.2d 67, 74–75 (Neb. 2007).

4. *Tensions between child support and spousal maintenance.* Mr. Stewart complained that any "off the schedule" child support would go to his ex-wife as "disguised additional maintenance." The same issue lurked in the Hall and Kerkorian proceedings described in notes 1 and 2. Should it matter that a larger support payment from the non-custodial parent will inevitably benefit not only the child but also the custodial parent? Can such incidental benefit to the custodial parent be avoided?

The tension between child support and spousal maintenance is not confined to high-income obligor cases. Child support is a right held by the child, but the obligor parent pays installments to the custodial parent, either directly or through the court. Courts have sometimes likened custodial parents to constructive trustees or fiduciaries who hold support payments for the child's use and benefit. *See, e.g., Vagenas v. Vagenas*, 879 N.E.2d 1155, 1158 (Ind. Ct. App. 2008) (constructive trustee). As a general matter, however, the custodial parent generally controls discretionary spending. Many states have statutes authorizing the court to order the custodial parent to account for the spending, and the court may hold the custodial parent responsible for spending as the child's fiduciary in an extraordinary case. *See, e.g.,* Mo. Rev. Stat. § 452.342 (2008). Courts, however, have generally not been receptive to obligors' accusations that the custodial parent spends some or all of the money on herself and not on the child.

In *State v. Campbell*, 931 P.2d 416 (Alaska 1997), for example, the court rejected the obligor mother's claim for child support credits for amounts she had paid for clothing for the children in excess of her support payments. She contended that the custodial father had been spending her child support payments on himself rather than the children. The state supreme court acknowledged that "special considerations of an equitable nature may justify a court in crediting" an obligor's voluntary expenditures in excess of court ordered support, but the court imposed "strict limitations" on judicial authority to grant such credits: "In those few cases in which credit has been granted, it is for payments made at the request of the parent or guardian with custody or for cash gifts used for child support, the disbursement of which was controlled by the parent or guardian with custody." *Id*. at 420. *Campbell* applied the general rule: "Since the father has custody, it is the father's prerogative here to decide how to spend the support money on the children. If he is not fulfilling his parental role responsibly, then [the non-custodial mother] may petition for custody or take other measures to insure that the children are provided for. But a non-custodial parent should not be allowed to make the decisions that are by law entrusted to the custodial parent." *Id*.

Questions about discretionary spending of child support monies frequently arise where a high-income obligor pays significant sums. In *Smith v. Freeman*, 814 A.2d 65 (Md. Ct. Spec. App. 2002), for example, the custodial mother moved for upward modification of support for the five-year-old non-marital child of a professional football player who earned about $1.2 million a year when the parties signed their initial support agreement, and about $3.2 million a year by the time the mother filed her motion. The father was already paying child support of $42,000 per year, plus other amounts such as private school tuition and all attendant costs, health insurance, and all uncovered health costs. In addition, Freeman had established a college fund of at least $100,000, and had secured a $500,000 life insurance policy for the minor. The trial court denied the motion to increase child support, stating that the child's needs had not changed and expressing concern that a higher support award would personally benefit the mother.

The Court of Special Appeals (Maryland's intermediate appellate court) vacated the judgment and remanded the case. "A custodial parent of a child whose noncustodial parent is extremely wealthy will inevitably reap some benefits," the panel reasoned, citing *Stewart*. "[I]f the wealth of the father justifies the child's residence in a well appointed home in an upscale neighborhood, with a large screen television and a playroom, as well as luxurious vacations, the child obviously cannot live in the house alone or travel by herself." *Id*. at 84.

Do you think the trial court was correct to deny the motion, or do you agree with the appellate decision? In 2004, Antonio Freeman retired from professional football. Should he be able seek a reduction in child support based on his current income? What other factors should the trial court *all assets!* consider in determining reasonable and fair support in high-income cases?

5. *Nonmarital children*. Where the parents were not married to one another, determining the high-income obligor's support obligation may be difficult where the court retains discretion concerning income "off the schedule" at the high end. As another ground for denying upward modification in *Smith v. Freeman*, the trial court concluded that the child had not grown accustomed to her father's wealth because the unmarried parents never resided in a single household. Again, the intermediate appellate court vacated the judgment:

> Regardless of whether a child is born out-of-wedlock or to parents whose marriage ended in divorce, every child is entitled to a level of support commensurate with the parents' economic position. A system that rewards those children whose parents were once married to each other, or who had at least lived together, would contravene the objective of the Guidelines "to achieve equity and consistency in child support awards."

Smith, 814 A.2d at 84. Is this approach consistent with the approach taken in *State v. Hall, supra* note 1?

6. *Determining the child's "needs."* *Stewart* makes much of the child's "needs," one factor that (together with the parent's ability to pay) is central under the child support guidelines. In the ordinary case, the guidelines themselves address the "needs" question by assigning a presumptive support amount based on parental income and permitted adjustments. But how does the court determine the child's needs when (as in *Stewart*) some amount of the income of one or both parents is "off the schedule" at the high end and the court has discretion about how much support to assign from that amount?

One might say that "needs" (as opposed to "wants") consist of only the bare essentials of life—modest food, clothing and shelter. Blackstone described a support obligation that did not extend beyond these essentials. William Blackstone, 1 Commentaries on the Laws of England *447. American courts determining child support awards, however, have long held that the "child's need is measured by the parents' current station in life," and thus that a child of wealthy parents "is entitled to, and therefore 'needs' something more than the bare necessities of life." *In re Marriage of Williams*, 58 Cal.Rptr.3d 877, 890 (Ct. App. 2007).

F. CRITIQUING THE GUIDELINES

Child support guidelines have doubtless reined in judicial discretion and lent a measure of coherence and predictability to child support awards, but have the guidelines played a meaningful role in improving the lot of America's children? Consider this critique:

> In application, child support guidelines in most states have not increased the size of child support awards as much as expected and so have not contributed as much as hoped to the reduction of poverty among children. But, as critics of existing guidelines have pointed out, there was no particular reason to expect that the guidelines would produce awards that satisfy the needs of the child(ren) because they do not take into account the actual economic conditions in the household in which the child(ren) actually live. They are, instead, based on a hypothetical situation in which the income of both the child(ren)'s parents supports only the parents and the child(ren) in only one household. In fact, the income of the child(ren)'s residential parent may be significantly different from (and often is significantly lower than) that of the non-residential parent, and either or both households may have additional members. Thus, the standards of living in the two households may be very different from each other and from that of the hypothetical intact household.

Leslie Joan Harris, *The ALI Child Support Principles: Incremental Changes to Improve the Lot of Children and Residential Parents*, 8 Duke J. Gender L. & Pol'y 245, 247–48 (2001).

NOTE

Federal law requires that in its four-year reviews of the support guidelines, "a State must consider economic data on the cost of raising children." 45 C.F.R. § 302.56(h) (2008). The efficacy of a state's guidelines depends in some measure on whether they reflect actual patterns of parental expenditures on childrearing, which some guidelines reflect better than others. Consider this description of the intricacies of parental spending on their children:

> Rearing children requires expenditures of both time and money. Money expenditures consist of out-of-pocket direct maintenance expenditures for items such as food, clothing, shelter, medical care, education, and other categories. Time or opportunity expenditures refer to the opportunities foregone by the time spent with children. These opportunity expenditures are perhaps less tangible, but no less important, and are often measured by the income the mother gives up by reducing her labor force participation below what it would be without children.

* * *

Persons wanting to know how much couples spend on their children often ask, "How much does it cost to raise a child?" * * * [A]sking only about the *cost* of raising a child is unsatisfactory, not only because it invites answers that focus on some minimum level required for biological subsistence but also because the question implies a single answer when in fact a range of answers is possible. The following example clarifies the latter point. Suppose one asked, "What does it cost to own a car today?" Obviously, the answer depends on what kind of car one owns—old model versus new model, the cost of car insurance, the car's repair record, gas mileage, and the like. Thus * * * we distinguish between the concepts of cost and expenditure. * * * [W]e are estimating parental expenditures on children, not the cost of raising them. * * *

Examining dollar expenditures on children does not by itself paint the whole picture of the economic responsibilities of parenthood because parents' ability to pay also varies. Perhaps a more complete view emerges when the percentage of total family consumption that represents expenditure on the children is analyzed. Our results show that this fraction varies remarkably little with a family's socioeconomic status but depends significantly on the number of children. Families with one child can expect to commit about 30 percent of total family expenditures on their child; in families with two children the proportion rises to between 40 and 45 percent; and in families with three children nearly 50 percent of total family spending is for the children.

* * *

As children age they tend to become more expensive. * * * [I]n general we find that approximately 26 percent of total child-related expenditures to age 18 arise at ages 0–5, and roughly equal amounts occur at ages 6–11 (36 percent) and 12–17 (38 percent). These age-group shares tend to vary with the birth order of the child in the family. Because the economies of scale related to having more than one child are concentrated under age 6, the second child's expenses in a two-child family are more heavily weighted toward the older years. When all 18 years are combined, we find that despite the existence of economies of scale in childrearing, they are not large; savings of 5 to 10 percent of expenditures on the previous child are usually identified with each additional child. * * *

Thomas J. Espenshade, Investing in Children: New Estimates of Parental Expenditures 1–4 (Urban Inst. 1984).

SECTION 3: MODIFICATION OF CHILD SUPPORT ORDERS

A child support order defines only the parent's "present obligations." *Crews v. Crews*, 751 A.2d 524, 531 (N.J. 2000). The order may remain in force for nearly two decades or more, unless a parent seeks modification based on changes over time in the child's needs or the parent's ability to pay. A parent may seek downward modification of the amount he or she must pay, or upward modification of the amount the other parent must pay.

By permitting courts to modify existing child support orders, states have created an exception to the common law claim preclusion doctrine, which provides for the finality of claims that the parties litigated, or could have litigated, in the first suit. *See, e.g., In re Marriage of Krieman*, 571 N.W.2d 425 (Wis. Ct. App. 1997). A child custody judgment is conclusive of the facts and the parties' rights at the time of entry, but remains modifiable for sufficiently changed circumstances. *See, e.g., Howard v. Howard*, 968 So.2d 961, 972 (Miss. Ct. App. 2007). Parents' agreements purporting to oust the court of its continuing jurisdiction, or otherwise to prohibit modification of support orders, are unenforceable as contrary to the public policy of protecting children. *See, e.g., Larson v. Larson*, 694 N.W.2d 13, 16 (N.D. 2005).

A. THE STRICTEST STANDARD

Compare the UMDA proposal to a typical state statute governing when a court may modify a child support order.

UNIFORM MARRIAGE AND DIVORCE ACT
9A U.L.A. 102 (1998).

§ 316(a).

* * * [T]he provisions of any decree respecting maintenance or [child] support may be modified * * * only upon a showing of changed circum-

stances so substantial and continuing as to make the terms unconscionable.

Section 598.21C of the Iowa Code

1.   * * * [T]he court may subsequently modify child * * * support orders when there is a substantial change of circumstances.

Iowa Code Ann. § 598.21C (2008).

NOTE AND QUESTIONS

An arrangement is "unconscionable" when it "affronts the sense of decency." Joseph M. Perillo, Calamari and Perillo on Contracts 388 (5th ed. 2003). In what way is the UMDA test stricter than Iowa's? What policies underlie strict tests for modification of outstanding child support orders?

B.   APPLYING THE GENERAL "CHANGE OF CIRCUMSTANCES" STANDARD

Most states permit modification of child support on showings short of unconscionability. The required showing varies from state to state, but remains strict everywhere. Iowa and many other states, for example, require that the movant demonstrate a substantial (or material) change of circumstances in the child's needs or the parent's ability to provide support. A material change is "the occurrence of something which, had it been known to the dissolution court at the time of the initial decree, would have persuaded the court to decree differently." *Collett v. Collett*, 707 N.W.2d 769, 773 (Neb. 2005). Where the court knew of the condition before entry of the divorce decree, the condition may not be a predicate for modification. *See, e.g.*, *Murphy v. Holman*, 945 P.2d 1193, 1195 (Wyo. 1997) (noncustodial mother moved for modification on the ground that her asthma left her unable to work, but the court denied the motion because the mother had received treatment for asthma before the divorce).

1.   STATUTORY GUIDELINES

The following Iowa statute typifies legislative statements of the criteria courts must consider in deciding motions to modify child support orders:

Section 598.21C of the Iowa Code

598.21C.   Modification of child * * * support orders.

1.   * * * In determining whether there is a substantial change in circumstances, the court shall consider the following:

    a.   Changes in the employment, earning capacity, income, or resources of a party.

    b.   Receipt by a party of an inheritance, pension, or other gift.

    c.   Changes in the medical expenses of a party.

    d.   Changes in the number or needs of dependents of a party.

    e.   Changes in the physical, mental, or emotional health of a party.

    f.   Changes in the residence of a party.

    g.   Remarriage of a party.

    h.   Possible support of a party by another person.

    i.   Changes in the physical, emotional, or educational needs of a child whose support is governed by the order.

* * *

    l.   Other factors the court determines to be relevant in an individual case.

* * *

Iowa Code § 598.21C (2008).

2. DETERMINING WHETHER THE CHANGE IN CIRCUMSTANCES IS SUBSTANTIAL

Modification statutes often provide no more than skeletal outlines of factors to consider, which leave much to the discretion of the reviewing court.

IN RE MARRIAGE OF NELSON

Supreme Court of Iowa, 1997.
570 N.W.2d 103.

HARRIS, JUSTICE.

* * *

Respondent-appellant Scott J. Nelson appeals from a district court ruling modifying and increasing his child support obligations for two children from $425 per month to $695 per month. * * *

Jane and Scott, married in 1984, are parents to two children: Reann, born May 30, 1983, and Jessica, born July 12, 1985. Their marriage was dissolved in September 1989. At that time, Scott was a law student. The parties agreed his completion of law school would be a substantial change in circumstances justifying a review of child support. The original decree ordered Scott to pay $137.50 per month per child in child support. In March 1993, Jane filed a modification action requesting an increase in Scott's child support payments. Jane had remarried. The district court increased Scott's child support payments for both children to a total of $425 per month.

On August 30, 1995, Jane filed a second modification action seeking an increase in child support payments. At trial, Jane offered evidence Scott's income had increased from $15,000 per year in 1991 to $38,524 in

1994. Jane testified her second husband is a farmer, but that she worked part-time at the Manning hospital earning $5.20 per hour as a cook. She has two children from her second marriage. Scott argued that excluding the bonus he received in 1994 his net annual income increased only $408 from what he earned in 1993. He also argued Jane and her new husband's net worth had increased $70,000 since 1992 while his had stayed the same. The district court found Scott's income had increased and accordingly increased his child support obligations to $695 per month.

* * *

* * * When justice clearly demands it, the guidelines provide for a modicum of flexibility. Special circumstances can call for an adjustment up or down when necessary to do justice between the parties. Any request for variation should however be viewed with great caution. It must be remembered that impetus for the guidelines came from the federal and state legislatures and the amounts were fixed only after exhaustive study of suggestions invited from all known public and private interests. The guidelines must therefore be respected as carefully considered social determinations.

Scott nevertheless contends the special circumstances of this case qualify for a deviation from the guidelines and that the trial court's failure to adjust his obligation downward was error. He claims the modification order, which requires him to pay $695 per month, leaves him seven percent of his net income to cover his own living expenses, therefore impoverishing him and causing an undue financial burden. He argues his law school loan payments—totaling $417 per month—constitute a special circumstance. * * *

Scott submitted a financial affidavit in November 1995. He listed his net income at $1950 and his total monthly expenses at $2150. Scott's expenses were calculated using the prior child support payments of $425, but did not list the $181 he pays in health insurance to his children. Considering the 1995 modification, Scott's monthly expenses equal $2358 with only $1846 in monthly net income. He does make car payments of $358 a month for a vehicle he needs in his work. He lives modestly and it would be very difficult to decrease his expenses.

There is nothing startling or even unusual about Scott's bleak financial position. It is typical of the financial dilemmas routinely presented in domestic court disputes. With very rare exceptions, involving persons of affluence, child support payments are more than the obligor can readily afford—and much less than reasonably needed for the child or children involved. The guidelines were drafted with full appreciation of this dismal reality and specify the priorities to be considered in fixing support orders. In yielding to the guidelines, we are not insensitive to the difficult financial bind in which Scott is placed. But yield we must.

Retirement of indebtedness is expressly made a lower priority than the needs of children. In common with many persons obliged to pay child support payments, Scott faces most of all a burdensome indebtedness. In Scott's case two obligations—for student loans ($417.34 per month) and car payments ($358.60 per month)—represent $775.94 of the $2150.94 he lists as monthly expenses. It was obviously reasonable—and perhaps to the children's eventual benefit—for Scott to complete his legal education. Jane subscribed to the plan by agreeing to reduced support while he finished his studies, though she did not agree to reduced support during all the years it takes to retire the student loans. For a ten-year period this would amount to more than half of the usual child support period. Notwithstanding Scott's financial bind, the guidelines clearly and expressly render the reduction of debt a priority status inferior to the needs of his children. The guidelines presuppose that debts can be refinanced, but that childhood cannot be postponed.

[The court affirmed the modification order.]

* * *

NOTES AND QUESTIONS

1. *The parent's lost or changed employment.* In an era marked by corporate downsizing and outsourcing of jobs overseas, parents may lose employment for reasons beyond their control. Courts may grant downward modification of child support obligations, at least temporarily, while the affected parent seeks reemployment. *See, e.g., Brewer v. Brewer*, 898 So.2d 986, 987 (Fla. Dist. Ct. App. 2005) (granting downward modification motion by father who lost his job as an insurance company's in-house counsel and was currently opening his own law office). The court may deny downward modification, however, where the obligor parent's criminal behavior or other wrongdoing leads to unemployment. In *Lambert v. Lambert*, 617 N.W.2d 645 (Neb. Ct. App. 2000), for example, the court denied the father's downward modification motion because he lost his job for failing a drug test and refused to accept treatment from the employer. The father's changed financial situation was "due to fault or voluntary wastage of his talents and assets." *Id.* at 648–49.

2. *Lottery winnings.* In *In re Marriage of Bohn*, 8 P.3d 539 (Colo. Ct. App. 2000), the 1996 divorce decree ordered the father to pay $352 per month in child support, based on his $2,472 monthly gross income. In 1998, the father won $1.2 million gross in the state lottery. After taxes were withheld, he received a one-time lump sum payment of $816,000. The trial court held that the entire $1.2 million was gross income for the 1998 calendar year, and thus that the father's monthly gross income for that year was $104,743.17. The court ordered him to pay child support of $4,208 per month for that year. Because the child support statute specified application of gross monthly income, *Bohn* rejected the father's contention that his modified child support amount for 1998 should be based on his net lottery winnings because he would never have access to the portion withheld for taxes.

Are lottery winnings "income" under Ky. Rev. Stat. Ann. § 403.212(2) (West 2008), *supra* page 607? Under Iowa's statutes quoted above, would receipt of lottery winnings be a predicate for modifying a child support obligation?

3. *Personal injury recoveries.* In *In re Jerome*, 843 A.2d 325, 328–30 (N.H. 2004), the court held that the non-custodial mother's $560,000 annuity, received to settle a personal injury claim, constituted "income" under New Hampshire's child support guidelines, which define "income" to include "all income from any source" and specifically include "annuities." The court rejected the mother's contention that the annuity was designed to make her whole and not to compensate for lost income. The state supreme court affirmed upward modification of her child support obligation.

Where the parent receives a lump sum recovery, rather than an annuity, in a civil settlement or after trial, the outcome turns on the guidelines' definition of "income." In *In re State ex rel. Taylor*, 904 A.2d 619, 623 (N.H. 2006), the court held that a lump sum tort recovery constituted income under the state's comprehensive definition because, after *Jerome*, a contrary holding "might encourage litigants to structure personal injury settlements as lump sum settlements rather than annuities to avoid child support obligations." In *Department of Human Services v. Monty*, 704 A.2d 401, 402–03 (Me. 1998), however, the court excluded the parent's lump sum settlement of a personal injury suit because the statute reached only income from "ongoing sources."

Is a personal injury recovery "income" under the Kentucky statute quoted at page 607? Under Iowa's statutes quoted above, would receipt of such a recovery be a predicate for modifying a child support obligation?

4. *"In-kind" payments.* Company cars, free housing and other non-cash, in-kind benefits received by the obligor parent may count as "income." In *In re Marriage of Long*, 921 P.2d 67 (Colo. Ct. App. 1996), for example, the non-custodial father, a member of the U.S. Air Force, elected to receive free housing and utilities on the military base instead of a $513 monthly allowance for living expenses. The court held that the free housing and utilities constituted "income," which the state child support guidelines defined to include "[e]xpense reimbursements or in-kind payments received by a parent in the course of employment * * * if they are significant and reduce personal living expenses."

In *In re Clark*, 910 A.2d 1198 (N.H. 2006), however, the court held that housing and an employer-provided vehicle did not constitute gross income because, unlike the items specifically enumerated in the statutory definition of that term, they were not paid in money. The statutory definition of "gross income" did not specifically include in-kind benefits. Even if the definition does not include in-kind benefits, may the trial court ever consider the value of such benefits in determining or modifying a child support order?

Are in-kind payments "income" under the Kentucky statute quoted at page 607? Under Iowa's statutes quoted above, would receipt of such payments be a predicate for modifying a child support obligation?

5. *Inheritance.* Where a parent inherits property after entry of a support order, the inheritance may be a basis for upward modification of the initial child support award. Even where the guidelines definition of "income" does not recite "inheritances," the definition usually recites "gifts." Courts consid-

er inheritances to be gifts and "discern no appreciable difference between one who receives property by an *inter vivos* gift and one who receives the same or similar property by testamentary transfer." *Gardner v. Yrttima*, 743 N.E.2d 353, 358 (Ind. Ct. App. 2001).

In some states, "income" for child support purposes (1) excludes one-time lump-sum inheritances, but includes (2) interest, rents, dividends and other income actually earned from inherited property, or (3) amounts the court may, in its discretion, impute based on income the inheritance could have earned if invested. *See, e.g., Crayton v. Crayton*, 944 P.2d 487, 490 (Alaska 1997).

Is receipt of an inheritance "income" under the Kentucky statute quoted at page 607? Under Iowa's statute quoted above, would receipt of an inheritance be a predicate for modifying a child support obligation?

6. Inter vivos *gifts.* In *In re Fulton*, 910 A.2d 1180 (N.H. 2006), the ex-husband moved for downward modification of his child support obligation because his unemployed ex-wife's family was regularly providing her money, which he and the court characterized as gifts. The child support guidelines defined "income" as "all income from any source, whether earned or un-earned, including, but not limited to" several specifically enumerated sources. The enumeration did not specify "gifts." *Fulton* denied modification on the ground that gifts did not constitute income because (1) all the enumerated sources involved payments in the form of money, and a gift may be non-monetary, and (2) the recipient generally has a legally enforceable right to all the enumerated sources and may recover them by court order if withheld. *Id.* at 1183–84. Even if "gross income" does not include *inter vivos* gifts, may the trial court ever consider the value of such gifts in determining or modifying a child support order?

Is receipt of an *inter vivos* gift "income" under the Kentucky statute quoted at page 607? Under Iowa's statute quoted above, would receipt of such a gift be a predicate for modifying a child support obligation?

7. *Commissions, overtime pay, and other remuneration from employment.* In *Markey v. Carney*, 705 N.W.2d 13, 19–20 (Iowa 2005), the court held that a support obligor's commissions and overtime pay constitute "income," unless the obligor demonstrates that they are uncertain or speculative. In the absence of this showing when the court enters the support order, the obligor may later move for downward modification if he or she believes the circumstances warrant. Bonuses received from an employer may similarly constitute "income." *See, e.g., Krepps v. Krepps*, 234 S.W.3d 605, 617–18 (Mo. Ct. App. 2007).

In *Walker v. Walker*, 868 A.2d 887 (Me. 2005), the court held that a lump sum severance payment the ex-husband received from his employer constituted income that would be an appropriate basis for upward modification of his child support obligation. The child support statute provided that "[g]ross income includes income from an ongoing source, including, but not limited to * * * severance pay * * *." *Id.* at 889. The court rejected the ex-husband's contention that his severance pay was not from an "ongoing source" because his employment had terminated. The court held that the legislature intended gross income to include all payments a parent receives in the scope of employment. *Id*. at 890.

Is receipt of commissions, overtime pay or severance pay "income" under the Kentucky statute quoted at page 607? Under Iowa's statute quoted above, would receipt of any of these payments be a predicate for modifying a child support obligation?

8. *The parent's remarriage or other obligations to a new household.* After entry of a child support order, divorced parents may remarry and unwed parents may marry for the first time. Well into the 1960s, courts held that, as a matter of law, a remarried parent's support obligations to children of the first family took precedence over obligations to children of the second family. *See, e.g., Beddoes v. Beddoes*, 393 P.2d 1 (Colo. 1964).

Today, courts disagree about whether, and if so how, a parent's obligations to children of a new family may affect the support entitlement of children of an earlier family. "First in time, first in right" decisions create a preference for children of the first family. *See, e.g., In re Marriage of Pollard*, 991 P.2d 1201 (Wash. Ct. App. 2000) (discussed in detail above). In *Pohlmann v. Pohlmann*, 703 So.2d 1121, 1125 (Fla. Dist. Ct. App. 1997), for example, the majority found a rational basis for preferring children subject to an existing support order because the state has a legitimate interest in assuring support for these children. The *Pohlmann* dissenter called the preference "state-mandated, court-enforced child abuse" because "the state has no business discriminating between children based solely on the fact of a divorce." *Id*. at 1128 (Harris, J., dissenting).

Other decisions, however, hold that obligations to children of a new family may work a change in the obligor's financial situation sufficient to warrant modification of an order relating to children of the first family. In *Martinez v. Martinez*, 660 A.2d 13, 17 (N.J. Super. Ct. 1995), for example, the court held that equal protection guarantees children of the second family equal treatment under the child support guidelines because "[a] child's right to be adequately fed, clothed, housed and educated should not primarily depend on the date of his or her birth, the family in which he or she is born."

The ability of the current spouse or partner of the obligor or obligee to help support their respective families' children may affect the propriety of modification. In *In re Marriage of Ladely*, 469 N.W.2d 663 (Iowa 1991), for example, the court denied downward modification of the existing child support order because the obligor's current wife had a modest income that could help support the family, and because insurance met the second family's health costs.

Should courts favor children of the first family, or should support be apportioned among children of both families? Do decisions requiring division of support among children of each family discourage noncustodial parents (usually fathers) from starting second families, or at least from marrying single parents with children? Or do these decisions unfairly diminish the reasonable expectations of the earlier family's children? If a high-income obligor's later family lives a much more affluent lifestyle than the first family, would upward modification be warranted? Why or why not?

9. *The parent's health or other special medical needs*. The obligor parent's health or special medical needs may support downward modification of a child support order. *See, e.g., Macauley v. Duffy*, 747 N.Y.S.2d 246, 246–47 (App. Div. 2002) (granting father's downward modification motion because of his serious medical condition, but requiring payment of arrears that accrued before the filing).

10. *The child's health or other special medical needs*. The child's unanticipated health or other special needs may support upward modification of the support award. In *Doherty v. De Angelo*, 645 N.Y.S.2d 345, 346 (App. Div. 1996), for example, the court found that the child's hearing loss at age ten after contracting spinal meningitis was an unanticipated change of circumstances that warranted upward modification of the father's child support obligation established in the parents' earlier separation agreement. In *Miller v. Jacobsen*, 714 N.W.2d 69 (S.D. 2006), the court increased the father's support obligation for his 15–year–old son, who was born with cerebral palsy and a seizure disorder and needed a specially-equipped van and professional caregivers as he grew older.

11. *Incarceration*. On June 30, 2007, federal and state prisons and local jails held nearly 2.3 million prisoners, the highest inmate population in the nation's history. An estimated 2.4 million children have a parent behind bars. The average age of these children is just eight, and more than 20% are under five; most reside in low-income homes in which the incarcerated parent's pre-arrest monthly income was less than $1,000. An estimated 10 million children, or about one of every eight children in America, have experienced parental incarceration at some time during their childhood or adolescence. *See* Bureau of Justice Statistics, *Prison Statistics*, http://www.ojp.usdoj.gov/bjs/prisons.htm (2008); Nancy G. La Vigne et al., Broken Bonds: Understanding and Addressing the Needs of Children with Incarcerated Parents 2 (Urban Inst. 2008); U.S. Dep't of Health and Human Servs., *Incarceration, Reentry and Child Support Issues: National and State Research Overview* (2006); Jeremy Travis et al., Families Left Behind: The Hidden Costs of Incarceration and Reentry (Urban Inst. 2005).

Continued child support can help ease the child's trauma when a parent is incarcerated, but only about 7% of inmates are employed in prison industries. The pay is nominal (perhaps no more than $350 a year), and generally insufficient to permit the prisoner to pay meaningful support to children on the outside. During their incarceration and immediately after release, prisoners typically receive money from their families, not the other way around. *See* Jessica Pearson & Lanae Davis, *Serving Fathers Who Leave Prison*, 41 Fam. Ct. Rev. 307, 307 (2003); The Challenges of Prisoner Reentry: Facts and Figures (Urban Inst. 2008).

Parents who retain their parental rights during incarceration often move to modify downward an existing support order on the ground that they cannot pay the full amount while they are behind bars. More than a dozen states, as a matter of law, prohibit or restrict downward modification of child support obligations during incarceration. *See, e.g., In re A.M.S. ex rel. Farthing v. Stoppleworth*, 694 N.W.2d 8, 9 (N.D. 2005) (state imputes federal minimum-wage income to incarcerated obligors and, as a matter of law, obligors may not reduce these payments by showing lack of financial resources due to imprisonment). Support payments accrue while the parent is imprisoned, and the released parent remains liable for arrears in amounts he cannot pay.

Because an inflexible rule precluding downward modification during incarceration often "would build a high arrearage burdening * * * reentry into the community upon * * * release," other states permit courts to order downward modification where support would otherwise accrue in amounts the prisoner cannot pay. *See, e.g., Clark v. Clark*, 887 N.E.2d 1021 (Ind. Ct. App. 2008) (modifying downward the $53 weekly child support obligation of the incarcerated father who earned $21 per month in his prison job assignment). Incarceration does not extinguish the child support obligation unless the court terminates the prisoner's parental rights, but disposition of the prisoner's motion for downward modification may depend on whether the parent has pre-incarceration assets or the prospect of some minimal income from prison work. *See, e.g., Adkins v. Adkins*, 656 S.E.2d 47, 54 (W. Va. 2007).

Should the state continue the child support obligation while the parent is in prison?

12. *The "clean hands" doctrine*. The doctrine—derived from the maxim that a party who seeks equity "must come with clean hands"—permits the court to deny equitable relief to a claimant or defending party who intentionally committed inequitable or wrongful conduct concerning the matter or transaction before the court. Courts occasionally invoke the doctrine against a parent who, having failed to pay past-due support, now seeks downward modification of future obligations. *See, e.g., Seeley v. Stafford*, 840 So.2d 111, 114 (Miss. Ct. App. 2003) (denying downward modification motion by non-custodial father who had intentionally failed to pay over $35,000 in past-due child support). The parent's fraudulent transfer of assets or other misconduct to avoid payment may also lead to invocation of the doctrine. *See, e.g., Richardson v. Anderson*, 604 N.W.2d 427, 434–35 (Neb. Ct. App. 2000) (fraudulent transfer of assets).

Application of the clean hands doctrine in *Seeley* benefited the child by maintaining a higher support amount than modification would have provided. Should a court invoke the doctrine when invocation would result in a lower child support amount, that is, where the wrongdoing parent seeks upward modification of the other parent's obligation?

13. *The effects of inflation*. Inflation may erode the real purchasing power of a child support award that remains unmodified for a significant period. In an effort to avoid the time and expense of future modification motions based on this erosion, parties may agree to inclusion of cost of living adjustments (COLAs) in the initial order. Courts are generally receptive to these agreements, which are designed to maintain the status quo over time. *See, e.g., Fishler v. Fishler*, 769 N.Y.S.2d 273, 275 (App. Div. 2003). Because an obligor's ability to pay support may not increase with inflation (and indeed may decrease), however, the court may retain authority to approve any adjustments as consistent with statutory and guidelines criteria.

14. *"Rules-of-thumb."* For a custodial parent with fresh memories of the divorce, and perhaps also of frustrated efforts to secure compliance with the initial support order, thoughts of seeking upward or downward modification

may conjure images of a new emotional roller coaster not worth riding. To produce household stability, reduce uncertainty, and thus limit the burdens on parents and child support enforcement agencies, states have enacted statutes establishing entitlement to modification when the existing child support amount varies by more than a specified percentage or dollar amount above or below the amount that would be due currently under the guidelines. *See, e.g.,* Iowa Code § 598.21C(2)(a) (2008) (10% or more). Some states apply the rule-of-thumb only after passage of a specified number of years from the prior support order. *See, e.g.,* Ind. Code Ann. § 31–16–8–1(b)(2)(A) (2008) (more than 20% after at least one year). Where a parent purports to waive the prospective ability to move for upward modification in the event a child support obligation varies from the guideline amount by more than the specified percentage, should the court enforce the waiver?

15. *Parental agreements concerning modification.* Parents, who may agree on initial support amounts, may also agree later on modification. The restrictions on the parents' power to agree initially, discussed on page 613, also apply to modification agreements. *See, e.g., Rosen v. Rosen,* 167 P.3d 692, 695 (Alaska 2007) (parents may agree to modification to a greater amount than the child support guidelines presumptively establish, but ordinarily may not agree to modification to a lesser amount). Because parents may not bargain away their children's right to support, their modification agreement becomes effective only when the court approves it as consistent with the best interests of the children. *See, e.g., Babcock v. Martinez,* 857 N.E.2d 911, 921 (Ill. App. Ct. 2006).

Where the parents initially agree to a support amount lower than the amount prescribed by the guidelines and the court approves the agreement, the court on either parent's motion may later modify the amount upward in the best interests of the child without a showing of changed circumstances. Where a parent, however, agrees to pay child support greater than the amount prescribed by the guidelines, or for a period longer than that mandated by the support statute, the parent is held to the bargain and may not later obtain downward modification by showing variance greater than the percentage set forth in the statutory rule-of-thumb discussed in note 14. *See, e.g., Reik v. Bowden,* 872 N.E.2d 1253, 1259 (Ohio Ct. App. 2007).

PROBLEM 11–6

As a legislator, would you vote to enact Section 3.19(1) of the ALI Principles of the Law of Family Dissolution, which provides:

> A child-support award should be subject to review at least once every three years in order to reassess the child-support award in light of the parents' current economic circumstances. The review should include reapplication of the child-support formula * * *. The periodic review * * * should be automatic, without a petition by either parent. The review should be performed by an agency designated by the court or legislature.

ALI, Principles of the Law of Family Dissolution: Analysis and Recommendations § 3.19(1) (2002).

C. IMPUTING INCOME ON MODIFICATION

IN RE MARRIAGE OF POLLARD

Court of Appeals of Washington, 2000.
991 P.2d 1201.

SCHULTHEIS, J.

A parent may not avoid a child support obligation by voluntarily remaining unemployed or underemployed. Joan Pollard Brookins's petition for modification of a child support order was granted, decreasing the amount she paid to her ex-husband, Martin Pollard, for support of the couple's two children. Mr. Pollard appeals, contending the trial court erred in failing to impute income to Ms. Brookins, who quit working full time to care for the two children of her new marriage. We reverse and remand for recalculation of child support.

The Pollards were divorced in Washington in October 1989. The support order entered at that time provided that Ms. Pollard would pay Mr. Pollard, as custodial parent, $217 per month for the couple's two children, born in 1983 and 1984.

In January 1997, Ms. Pollard, now Ms. Brookins, petitioned in Lincoln County for modification of the child support order, claiming change in income. Both Mr. Pollard and Ms. Brookins had been in active military service while married. After remarriage and the birth of two additional children, Ms. Brookins had left military service and now worked part time for the military while working full time as a mother and homemaker. She lived in Norfolk, Virginia. Mr. Pollard had also remarried and moved from the state, and was now living in Astoria, Oregon. He, too, had left the military and was attempting to find full-time work in the private sector.

Affidavits from the parties indicate that during 1997 Mr. Pollard earned approximately $31,000 as an electrician. During the last year of her full-time military employment, Ms. Brookins earned approximately $22,150. By January 1998, Ms. Brookins was a full-time mother and homemaker, making approximately $323 per month in her part-time work for the military. She requested reduction of her support obligation to $58 per month ($29 per child), effective from the date she filed the petition in January 1997.

In April 1998, the trial court modified the support order, reducing Ms. Brookins's obligation to $85 per month ($42.50 per child), with a starting date of February 1, 1997. * * * In the findings and conclusions entered on the modification, the court indicated the original order had been modified because Ms. Brookins's income had been substantially reduced. The court concluded that "[t]he mother is not voluntarily underemployed with an intent to avoid child support but is working as a mother in the home full time raising children." * * *

MODIFICATION OF CHILD SUPPORT

Mr. Pollard argues on appeal that the trial court erred in failing to impute income to Ms. Brookins, a career woman who voluntarily quit working full time to work part time and care for the two children of her new marriage.

* * * In setting child support, the trial court must take into consideration all factors bearing upon the needs of the children and the parents' ability to pay. Overall, the child support order should meet each child's basic needs and should provide any "additional child support commensurate with the parents' income, resources, and standard of living." To facilitate these goals, the Legislature directs that the child support obligation should be "equitably apportioned between the parents."

In proceedings to modify child support, the trial court applies the uniform child support schedule, basing the support obligation on the combined monthly incomes of both parents. Voluntary unemployment or underemployment will not allow a parent to avoid his or her financial obligation to the children who are the subjects of the support order. When assessing the income and resources of each household, the court must impute income to a parent when that parent is voluntarily unemployed or voluntarily underemployed. The court determines whether to impute income by evaluating the parent's work history, education, health, age and any other relevant factor. If the court decides the parent is "gainfully employed on a full-time basis," but also underemployed, the court makes a further determination whether the parent is purposely underemployed to reduce his or her support obligation.

In this case, the trial court found that Ms. Brookins was "working as a mother in the home full time raising children" and refused to impute income because it found that she was "not voluntarily underemployed with an intent to avoid child support[.]" This finding is open to two interpretations. One, the court may have meant that Ms. Brookins was a full-time worker, voluntarily underemployed, but not with an intent to avoid child support. Pursuant to RCW 26.19.071(6), however, an underemployed parent may not escape imputation of income unless he or she is *gainfully* employed on a full-time basis and is not underemployed to reduce the support obligation. Because Ms. Brookins's full-time work as a mother and homemaker is not "gainful," she does not come within this provision of RCW 26.19.071(6).

Two, the court may have meant that Ms. Brookins was *not* voluntarily underemployed. The facts do not support this interpretation. Clearly Ms. Brookins's choice to leave the military and her former salary of over $22,000 per year (based on a 1995 W–2 form) was voluntary, motivated by her desire to raise the two young children of her new family. * * * While laudable, these actions cannot adversely affect her obligation to the two older children she had with Mr. Pollard. * * * "[B]y choosing not to allow a parent to escape child support obligations because of the existence of a new family we are recognizing the needs of children to the love, support, and sacrifice of both parents." If the shoe were on the other foot, and a noncustodial father sought to reduce his child support obligation because he chose to stay home with his children from a new marriage, most courts would impute income to such a voluntarily unemployed or underemployed parent. * * * The mother should be held to a like standard. * * *.

Under either interpretation of the findings, the trial court abused its discretion in finding that Ms. Brookins was not voluntarily underemployed and in failing to impute income to her. Accordingly, we reverse the order of child support modification for abuse of discretion. Remand is necessary to recalculate child support.

* * *

NOTES AND QUESTIONS

1. *Questions about* Pollard. (a) In common parlance, are homemaking and child care "gainful" activities akin to employment for wages or salary? (b) Should the court consider homemaking and child care to be "gainful" employment when it decides whether to impute income? (c) Do you agree with the commentator who writes that "[t]o conclude that a parent who chooses to stay at home with children is 'voluntarily unemployed or underemployed,' a court must implicitly find a parent's work in the home to be of lesser worth than employment in the marketplace, or that it is not work at all"? Karl A.W. DeMarce, Note, *Devaluing Caregiving in Child Support Calculations: Imputing Income to Custodial Parents Who Stay Home With Children*, 61 Mo. L. Rev. 429, 466 (1996). Or does imputation for uncompensated child care simply recognize, in appropriate cases, that both spouses often suffer diminished standards of living following divorce, perhaps making employment outside the home necessary even if placing the child in day care or other substitute care is the likely alternative? (d) Ms. Pollard remarried and had two more children with her new husband. Should income be imputed to an ex-spouse who remarries or begins cohabiting with a partner?

2. *A contrary view.* The West Virginia Supreme Court of Appeals has held that income may not be imputed to an unemployed or underemployed parent who "has chosen to devote time to care for children (including those who are above pre-school age or those to whom the parties do not owe a joint legal responsibility for support) under circumstances in which a reasonable, similarly-situated parent would have devoted time to care for the children had the family remained intact or, in cases involving a non-marital birth, had a household been formed." *State ex rel. W. Va. Dep't of Health & Human Resources v. Gibson*, 535 S.E.2d 193, 200 (W. Va. 2000). In the final analysis, who determines reasonableness?

3. On motions to modify child support orders, courts have considered imputing income to obligors in a variety of circumstances, including these:

a. *Further education.* In *Kelly v. Hougham*, 504 N.W.2d 440, 444 (Wis. Ct. App. 1993), the court declined to impute income to an ex-husband who left a well-paying job to return to school. The court found that the husband acted reasonably because he delayed returning to school until his former wife finished law school and secured a well-paying job, continued to work part-time "at a respectable wage" while attending school, and expected that further schooling would substantially increase his income and thus benefit the children before too long.

In *Marriage of Doerr*, 525 N.W.2d 745, 752 (Wis. Ct. App. 1994), however, the court imputed income to a husband who quit his carpentry business and enrolled in art school when he was served with divorce papers. The trial court found the husband's decision unreasonable because it was "not related to any desire to increase [his] future earning power," and because the husband "is a skilled carpenter and enjoys a reputation as a reliable and diligent worker [who] needs incentives to maximize his earnings in order that he might contribute his fair share to the support of his children."

b. *Relocation*. In *Abouhalkah v. Sharps*, 795 N.E.2d 488 (Ind. Ct. App. 2003), the court declined to impute income to a father whose earnings fell after he left his previous employer, which was moving the father's department to Minnesota. The court found that the father acted reasonably because he left the employer not to avoid paying child support, but to avoid relocating out-of-state a few hundred miles away from his children.

In *In re Marriage of McKenzie*, 709 N.W.2d 528 (Iowa 2006), however, the ex-husband's annual income fell from $45,260 (with a company that had employed him for 22 years) to $21,199 when he relocated from Iowa to South Carolina to be with his girlfriend. The trial court imputed income to him at the higher figure because his "desire for self-fulfillment is outweighed by the pre-existing duty he had to his former spouse to provide adequate support for his minor child." *Id*. at 534.

In general, what factors should the court consider in determining the reasonableness of an obligor parent's decision to relocate?

c. *Early retirement*. In *Bassette v. Bartolucci*, 652 N.E.2d 623 (Mass. App. Ct. 1995), the father took early retirement from his position as a letter carrier for the U.S. Postal Service because he and his second wife wanted to do missionary work in Jamaica. Because Jamaican authorities would not allow them to take paid employment, their only source of income was his small retirement pension, considerably lower than his previous salary. *Bassette* applied the child support guidelines to the father's pre-retirement salary. The court found no evidence that the father retired and turned to missionary work in an effort to avoid his child support obligations, but held that early retirement was an unreasonable voluntary decision.

In *Dunn v. Dunn*, 307 N.W.2d 424 (Mich. Ct. App. 1981), however, the court held that where the father retired and joined a religious order and took a vow of poverty, his child support obligation would be based on his actual income rather than his earning capacity because he had acted reasonably without trying to avoid obligations to his children.

d. *New spouse's income*. In *Miller v. Clough*, 165 P.3d 594, 599–601 (Alaska 2007), the issue was whether the income of the ex-wife's wealthy new husband should be considered in calculating her child support obligation. Because the imputation statute directed the court to consider only the obligor's "work history, qualifications, and job opportunities," the court held that imputed income may not be based on a later spouse's financial circumstances.

e. *Voluntary change of employment.* When parents in intact families accept reduced income from employment changes, the law presumes that the parents have weighed family members' needs. Following dissolution, however, the court may impute income to an obligor whose income falls, at least temporarily, when he or she accepts a new position. In *Auman v. Auman*, 464 S.E.2d 154 (Va. Ct. App. 1995), for example, the divorced father was a clothing salesman whose income fell during the parties' separation when he voluntarily left a salaried position for a job paying a lower salary, and then fell again a few months later when he took a job providing compensation only on commission. The Virginia Court of Appeals affirmed imputation of income based on the initial position's salary because a divorced parent "is not free to make career decisions that disregard the needs of his dependents and his potential obligation to them." *Id.* at 156.

The Indiana Court of Appeals reached a different result in *In re Paternity of E.M.P.*, 722 N.E.2d 349 (Ind. Ct. App. 2000). In 1998, the father earned a gross salary of $46,680 as a sanitation worker. In 1999, eight days before the evidentiary hearing on the mother's petition for upward modification of his child support obligation, he quit his job and began working for a telephone company for $12.10 an hour, or $25,168 annually. The Court of Appeals found no basis for imputing income to the father, who testified that he had been pursuing this job change for three years, lifted twenty to twenty-four tons of garbage for six to seven and a half hours a day, left work tired and wanting only to go to sleep, had bad knees and other health concerns from his employment, and did not want this regimen to continue for the next forty years. He also testified that the new position had better benefits and that his salary would increase over time.

f. *Parental fault.* In *Maya v. Maya*, 1996 WL 8270 (Va. Ct. App. Jan. 11, 1996) (unpublished opinion), the court imputed income to a non-custodial father who was employed as a waiter for $2.13 an hour after being jailed for forgery. He had earned $21,700 a year as an accounts billing clerk, but had been laid off shortly before his arrest. The court found him voluntarily underemployed because imprisonment reduced his opportunities for renewed employment in positions of trust.

g. *Self-employment.* Self-employment does not produce wages or salaries established by a third party. Where a parent seeks to impute income to a self-employed ex-spouse for underemployment, the determinative question is whether self-employment income is "significantly less than prevailing amounts earned in the community by persons with similar work history and occupational qualifications." N.D. Admin. Code § 75–02–04.1–07(1)(b) (2008).

4. *Transferring assets or receiving support by another.* The court may impute income to an obligor parent who transfers assets to a third person in an effort to reduce or eliminate income. Imputing may also be appropriate where the parent, asserting low income or no income, is supported by a relative or other person or lives above his purported means.

In *Phelps v. La Point*, 725 N.Y.S.2d 461 (App. Div. 2001), the noncustodial father sought downward modification of his support obligations to his two sons, from whose mother he had been divorced since 1989. The father had a decade-long history of evasiveness known to the court. In 1990, the court had found "preposterous" his argument that he should pay only $25 a month (the minimum guideline amount for a parent with income below the federal poverty line) to support his infant daughter by another woman, even though he had earned $900,000 the preceding year as a pitcher for the New York Yankees. The father was retired from major league baseball by the time the family court decided the 1990 action, but the court found that he had the capacity to earn $40,000 annually and set support for the girl accordingly.

By the time of his motion for downward modification of support for his two sons, La Point had surrendered his daughter for adoption and thus was no longer responsible for her support. He claimed that he was essentially unemployed (and thus unable to pay any support for the two boys), with an earning capacity of only $24,000 as a salaried manager of a sports bar wholly owned by his current wife. She had recently received $200,000 in "collusion" funds from the Major League Baseball Players Association, a sum La Point had assigned to her in a postnuptial agreement. It was anticipated that she would receive $575,000 in these collusion funds by the end of 1998, plus additional future payments of at least $400,000. The hearing examiner also heard testimony about the couple's comfortable lifestyle, nice home, new vehicle, country club membership, tens of thousands of dollars in annual credit card charges, and golf vacations.

The hearing examiner found the testimony of La Point and his current wife "patently incredible." *Id.* at 464. The appellate court criticized the ex-pitcher's "strategy of delay, obfuscation, concealment and duplicity," denied his downward modification motion, and affirmed the order imputing an annual earning capacity of $40,000, the same amount imputed in the earlier support action relating to his daughter. *Id.* at 465.

PROBLEM 11–7

John and Mary Jones married in 1988 and divorced in 2002, when their two children were eleven and eight years old. At the time of the divorce, John was a staff psychologist at a local community hospital. Two years later, he sought new employment after the hospital notified him that the terms of his employment and salary would be changed dramatically. He became a psychologist in a nearby public school system at a salary of $44,000, more than $20,000 less than his former hospital salary. John now receives his salary from the school district in 12 monthly installments, but he has a nine-month contract, with duties during the district's three-month summer recess. John pays about $1000 per month in child support for the two children. The summer recess consists of seven weeks.

You are the trial judge hearing John's motion to reduce his child support obligation on the ground that he has had a substantial and involuntary decrease in his salary. Mary moves to increase John's support obligation by imputing income to him for the summer recess. How would you rule on Mary's motion? Would your answer be different if John has primary physical custody of the children for three of the seven weeks? What if John had no school district duties, and no primary custody of his children, during the seven-week summer recess?

PROBLEM 11–8

When David and Cindy Smith were divorced in 2002, Cindy received physical custody of the couple's only child. The court ordered David, a machinist and shop steward earning $19.50 an hour at a local tractor assembly plant, to pay $120 per week in child support. Earlier this week, David moved for downward modification of the child support amount on the ground that he is no longer able to pursue his regular occupation because his union went out on strike against the employer three days earlier. David has belonged to the union for 20 years, and he supports the strike. In his motion papers, David asserted that the strike's purpose is "to protect our jobs, our families' future." He denied taking part in the strike to avoid paying child support to his former wife.

If you were David's lawyer, what arguments would you make in support of the motion? If you were Cindy's lawyer, what arguments would you make in opposition? If you were the judge hearing the modification motion, what factors would you consider in deciding whether to grant the motion? If you were inclined to grant the motion, would you grant permanent downward modification?

A NOTE ABOUT THE BRADLEY AMENDMENT

In 1986, Congress enacted the Bradley Amendment, which mandates that states provide that "any payment or installment of support under any child support order * * * is (on and after the date it is due) * * * not subject to retroactive modification." 42 U.S.C. § 666(a)(9) (2003). Why do you think Congress felt the Bradley Amendment was necessary?

By treating each child support installment as a vested judgment entitled to full faith and credit when it becomes due, the Bradley Amendment can hurt good-faith obligors who delay or avoid seeking downward modification by court order, and instead reach an informal arrangement with the parent, custodian or other recipient of support. Parents without ready access to legal representation, who may be unaware of the Amendment and without means to move for modification, are particularly likely to opt for informality (typically with the recipient's tacit approval or acquiescence). The Amendment means, however, that after a lengthy period of informal adjustment, the full support bill is already past due (in most states, with interest at the statutory rate) as soon as the custodian seeks enforcement and perhaps a contempt order. One commentator calls the Bradley Amendment "a classic example of the unanticipated consequences of federal overkill." Ronald K. Henry, *Child Support at a Crossroads: When the Real World Intrudes Upon Academics and Advocates*, 33 Fam. L.Q. 235, 246 (1999).

In *Houser v. Houser*, 535 N.W.2d 882 (S.D. 1995), ex-husband Bob Houser became his children's *de facto* custodial parent for long periods and thus directly provided them food, clothing and shelter while also remaining obligated to pay child support as the "non-custodial" parent. The court required him to pay ten years' worth of arrears amounting to nearly $32,000, even though he was probably the children's primary source of support when they lived with him for long periods as the arrears mounted.

The Bradley Amendment can also work hardship on non-custodial parents who make "nonconforming" child support payments—significant sums spent informally on the children, for gifts and clothes and the like—in addition to (or instead of) making support payments in the manner prescribed in the child support order. Informal support does not excuse payments mandated by the order or create entitlement to a credit for these payments. *See, e.g., Vander Woude v. Vander Woude*, 501 N.W.2d 361 (S.D. 1993).

The Bradley Amendment's mandate is not airtight. For one thing, because the Amendment is child-protective legislation, it permits retroactive upward modification of support arrears. *See, e.g., Carey v. Carey*, 2006 WL 700961 (N.J. Super. Ct. App. Div. Mar. 21, 2006). For another, the Amendment does not bar a parent current on all support obligations from seeking a correction for prior overpayments. *See, e.g., Miller v. Jacobsen*, 714 N.W.2d 69, 80 (S.D. 2006). Because the Amendment prohibits only retroactive modification of arrears that accrued under a prior support order, the Amendment also does not affect the court's authority to enter the first support order relating to a child, and to make the order retroactive to the child's birth. This authority is discussed above at page 592, note 5.

Some courts have invoked waiver or estoppel to grant the obligor a credit for payments previously made in a manner not conforming with the outstanding order. *See, e.g., In re Marriage of Winters*, 87 P.3d 1005 (Mont. 2004) (estoppel). Courts may also order retroactive modification of child support arrears where the recipient secured the support order through fraud, or where another ground for reopening a civil judgment appears under general civil procedure rules. *See, e.g., Richards v. Richards*, 2007 WL 2685201, at *3 (Alaska Sept. 12, 2007) (retroactive modification permissible where support amount was miscalculated because of clerical error).

Because the Bradley Amendment provides that each child support installment is a vested judgment on the date it is due, collection actions are subject to the statute of limitations, and installments in most states are subject to laws that impose interest on civil money judgments. Limitations periods generally range from six to ten years after the debt has been reduced to judgment, though the period may be longer. In some states, the limitations period is tolled during the child's minority. *See, e.g.*, Ind. Code Ann. § 34–11–2–10 (2008). Subject to the statute of limitations, the recipient parent may sue for the vested arrears even where the child has reached majority. *See, e.g., Lichtenwalter v. Lichtenwalter*, 229 S.W.3d 690, 693 (Tenn. 2007).

SECTION 4: CHILD SUPPORT ENFORCEMENT

A. FEDERAL AND STATE ENFORCEMENT

1. HISTORICAL DEVELOPMENT

Before the women's movement began advocating gender equity in the 1960s, the law perceived child support as generally a private matter between divorcing or nonmarital parents. Courts lacked authority to initiate enforcement proceedings, and many mothers lacked the resources to pursue fathers who failed to meet their obligations. "Even if a child support obligation was legally established, the absent father could all but choose not to pay. The obligation was rarely enforced effectively—especially across state lines." Harry D. Krause, *Child Support Reassessed: Limits of Private Responsibility and the Public Interest*, 24 Fam. L.Q. 1, 4–5 (1990).

For custodial mothers able to afford counsel or willing to proceed *pro se*, enforcement against recalcitrant non-custodial fathers usually meant suing in state court to secure or enforce a support order. Many custodial mothers entitled to child support never made it to court, and even fewer persevered to final judgment and collection. Even for a custodial mother who managed to locate and serve the father (insurmountable hurdles for many mothers, particularly if the father had moved out of state or changed jobs or addresses), civil docket pressures often meant long delays between filing and final judgment. Many judges were unresponsive or unsympathetic to claims for past-due child support. Proceedings were time-consuming, expensive and emotionally draining for single parents chasing a former spouse or partner. These costs often exceeded the likely value of a judgment, which would still need to be enforced.

2. CIVIL ENFORCEMENT

The states' failure to enforce child support obligations led Congress to enact the Family Support Act in 1974, codified as Title IV–D of the Social Security Act. Pub. L. No. 93–647, 88 Stat. 2351, 2351–58 (1974) (codified as amended at 42 U.S.C. § 651–60 (2003)). The new section created the Child Support Enforcement Program, a federal-state partnership under which each participating state would designate an agency (known as a "IV–D agency") to help custodial parents locate nonresident parents, establish paternity where necessary, and establish, enforce and modify child support obligations. The IV–D agencies would not handle property settlement, custody or visitation matters. *See* 42 U.S.C. § 652(a)(1)-(2). Congress created the Office of Child Support Enforcement (OCSE), a division of what is now the Department of Health and Human Services, to facilitate and fund interstate and intrastate child support enforcement efforts and state enforcement programs. *See* Office of Child Support Enforcement, U.S. Dep't of Health & Human Services, Handbook on Child Support Enforcement (2005), http://www.acf.hhs.gov/programs/cse/pubs/2005/handbook_on_cse.pdf.

The state's IV–D agency could be a newly created agency or a separate division of an existing agency. To reduce federally funded welfare payments to poor custodial mothers, the IV–D agencies initially served only welfare parents, who were required to cooperate with the agencies' collection efforts as a condition of receiving public assistance. In 1984, Congress extended agency services to other custodial parents, who would pay a nominal fee. As a result, much of child support establishment and enforcement has now moved from state courts to the state administrative arena.

Despite the IV–D agencies, a federal commission concluded in 1992 that "millions of children in the United States fail[ed] to receive the financial support they are owed" because the enforcement system was still "complicated and slow * * *, unable to efficiently collect" support. U.S. Comm'n on Interstate Child Support, Supporting Our Children: A Blueprint For Reform xii, 298 (1992). The commission report led to sweeping changes enacted in the major 1996 welfare legislation, the Personal Responsibility and Work Opportunity Reconciliation Act of 1996 (PRWORA). Pub. L. 104, 110 Stat. 2105 (1996) (codified as amended in scattered sections of 42 U.S.C.).

PRWORA made headlines for replacing the potentially open-ended Aid to Families With Dependent Children (AFDC) entitlement with the Temporary Assistance to Needy Families program (TANF), which places a time limit on a family's entitlement to public assistance. Less noticed were comprehensive PRWORA mandates designed to strengthen child support enforcement and secure payments from nonresidential parents anywhere in the nation.

For example, PRWORA requires states to provide that a signed voluntary acknowledgment of paternity (which a father frequently signs at the hospital when the child is born) establishes paternity without need for further judicial or administrative action after a short period for rescission. States must also provide for speedy genetic testing of alleged fathers, which generally produces admissions without need for court action where the test indicates paternity. Public assistance programs must require women to name the father of each child and to cooperate with the IV–D agency in its collection efforts. If the agency collects money from the father, the state is entitled to the amount it previously paid and that amount does not necessarily increase the income available to the child. Establishing paternity has proved essential to child support enforcement efforts because nearly two-thirds of children in the federal child support enforcement system are born outside marriage. *See* Heather Koball & Ayana Douglas–Hall, *State Policy Choices: Child Support* (Nat'l Center for Children in Poverty 2004).

In recent years, wage withholding (where the employer deducts child support payments from the noncustodial parent's wages and sends them to the appropriate state agency for distribution) has been the most effective way to collect child support payments. In 2006, for example, about 69% of child support payments were collected through wage withholding. *See* U.S. Gov't Accountability Office, Bankruptcy and Child Support Enforcement: Improved Information Sharing Possible Without Routine Data Matching 9 (2008). To help effectuate wage withholding from obligors who move across state lines and change employment, PRWORA creates a national directory to report new hires. States must also enact the Uniform Interstate Family Support Act (UIFSA), which creates procedures for interstate enforcement of child support orders. (UIFSA is discussed in Chapter 16.)

PRWORA seeks to enhance mass case processing through computerized matching of available state records and expedited procedures for handling routine cases. PRWORA mandates that states must give these agencies access to public state records (such as ones relating to vital statistics, tax payments, business and real property ownership and professional licensing), and some private records (such as ones maintained by public utilities and cable television companies). Regardless of whether the obligee parent is receiving public assistance, the state must seek to induce payment by establishing procedures authorizing revocation or suspension of the obligor's drivers, professional, recreational and occupational licenses (including law licenses). 42 U.S.C. § 666(a)(1) (2003). Does it make sense to suspend these licenses held by a noncustodial parent in arrears?

Today custodial parents receiving financial assistance through TANF, Medicaid or federally assisted foster care programs may receive free services from the state's IV–D agency. Most custodial parents seeking IV–D services today, however, are not receiving public assistance; these parents may have to pay a fee of not more than $25.00, though some states pay all or part of the cost. When the custodial parent contacts the agency, a caseworker is assigned. The caseworker will try to locate the other parent through the Federal or State Parent Locator Service or, if the other parent lives in another state, through UIFSA. When the noncustodial parent is found, the agency will notify him or her that the custodial parent seeks child support and will take action to secure it. Where necessary, the agency will take steps to establish paternity. *See* Office of Child Support Enforcement, *supra*, at 13–17.

The IV–D agencies have not supplanted the private bar. About two-thirds of custodial parents seeking to establish or enforce child support orders opt for the IV–D program because private enforcement remains costly, particularly when the parties live in different states. But IV–D agencies are still most likely to serve lower- and middle-income custodial parents, and the IV–D program "simply does not have the resources to provide effective services for the families already in its caseload, let alone those outside the caseload." Laura Wish Morgan, *Child Support Enforcement in the United States and the Role of the Private Bar*, SupportGuidelines.com, http://www.childsupportguidelines.com/articles/art200009.html.

NOTES AND QUESTIONS

1. *PRWORA's effects*. In 2003, about 60% of custodial parents had some type of agreement or court award to receive child support from the noncustodial parent, an increase of 7.4% from 1994. Most of these agreements were established by a court or agency, and only a relatively few stemmed from informal agreements or understandings. About 64.2% custodial mothers and 39.8% of custodial fathers had child support agreements or awards. About three-quarters (76.5%) of custodial parents received at least some child support payments directly from the noncustodial parent. Only about 45.3% of custodial parents received every payment due. Of the 1.7 million custodial

parents below the poverty line and due child support, 68.7% received at least some payments (35.2% received the full amount and 33.5% received less than the full amount). In all, custodial parents reported receiving about 68.6% of child support due that year (about $25.4 billion of $37 billion). *See* Timothy S. Grall, *Current Population Reports: Custodial Mothers and Fathers and Their Child Support: 2003*, at 4–9 (U.S. Census Bureau 2006).

Discussing the PRWORA child support enforcement provisions in light of the remaining problems, one commentator writes that "[t]he only possible stronger measures would be turning the entire enforcement process over to the federal government." Linda D. Elrod, *Child Support Reassessed: Federalization of Enforcement Nears Completion*, 1997 U. Ill. L. Rev. 695, 703. Wholesale federalization does not appear on the horizon. Because the rate of federal taxpayer compliance is considerably higher than the rate of compliance with child support orders, however, some observers have recommended that the Internal Revenue Service collect child support payments in the first instance (supported by income withholding) and then disburse the payments to custodial parents or state public assistance agencies. *See, e.g.,* Adam Clymer, *Child–Support Collection Net Usually Fails*, N.Y. Times, July 17, 1997, at A16.

"Child support is highly relevant to children who receive it, especially poor children not on cash assistance." Elaine Sorensen & Chava Zibman, To What Extent Do Children Benefit From Child Support? 5–6 (Urban Inst. 2000). Among custodial mothers below the federal poverty level who received any child support payments in 2003, for example, the average child support received represented nearly half (49.5%) their average income. *See* Grall, *supra*, at 4–9. Regardless of a household's economic circumstances, payment of support due is also normally seen to serve the child's emotional wellbeing by avoiding resentment at the non-custodial parent's perceived abandonment and lack of concern. *See, e.g.,* Monica Hof Wallace, *Child Support Savings Accounts*, 85 N.C. L. Rev. 1155, 1168–70 (2007).

The economic importance of child support to poor families is likely to grow, not only because PRWORA has instituted the time-limited TANF program, but also because Congress has "shifted its primary focus from reimbursing the government's welfare program to maximizing the amount of support passed on to the family." U.S. Dep't of Health & Hum. Servs., Office of Child Support Enforcement, *FY 2005 Annual Report to Congress* 2 (2008). The decision that opened this chapter, *State ex rel. Hermesmann v. Seyer*, demonstrated than as a condition for receiving TANF (or previously AFDC) assistance, the custodial parent must assign the right to receive that support to the government as reimbursement for public assistance payments made. States may choose to "pass through" collected child support to the family, but most states elected not to do so before 2005. In 2004, for example, states collected about $635 million in child support on behalf of TANF families, but distributed only about 27% to the families.

The Deficit Reduction Act of 2005, Pub. L. No. 109–171, 120 Stat. 4 (2006), however, gives states greater incentives to pass through more child support to TANF families. Beginning October 1, 2008, states may pass through up to $100 per month to families with one child and up to $200 month to families with two or more children without having to reimburse the federal government for its share of child support collected. In 2004, families receiving TANF assistance had an average annual income of $14,829 (or $20,627, when other means-tested benefits were added); the $100/$200 pass-through would have increased average family income by $488, or 3.3%. Laura Wheaton & Elaine Sorensen, The Potential Impact of Increasing Child Support Payments to TANF Families 1–2 (Urban Inst. 2007). The Urban Institute concludes that "[m]ost TANF families are highly disadvantaged and cannot count on any form of private-sector income, so even modest increases in child support can be very beneficial." *Id.* at 5.

2. *Custodial mothers who do not seek child support awards.* Federal law requires custodial mothers receiving public assistance to cooperate in good faith with the state in paternity determination and collection efforts unless "good cause" for non-cooperation is established. In the absence of good cause, about thirty states terminate TANF benefits of mothers who refuse to cooperate with state authorities. Other states reduce benefits for noncooperation. PRWORA leaves it to individual states to define good cause justifying non-cooperation, but most states have embraced the prior federal agency definition, which stated that good cause existed (1) when securing support was contrary to the best interest of the child, for example because cooperation risked physical or emotional harm to the parent or child (domestic violence), or (2) when the child was conceived by rape or incest.

Forgoing child support has been an option for custodial mothers who are not on public assistance. Aside from a history of domestic violence in the household, why might a custodial mother choose not to seek child support payments from the child's father? For some answers, see Tonya L. Brito, *The Welfarization of Family Law*, 48 U. Kan. L. Rev. 229, 265–66 (2000).

3. *State compliance with federal mandates.* "[F]ederal authority is relatively weak. When it comes to family matters, federal officials must rely on incentives and moral persuasion to move states in the direction they would have them go. Hence, at any point in time, there is enormous variation across the states with respect to their political will and their capacity (both financial and managerial) to enforce child support obligations." Irwin Garfinkel et al., *Introduction,* Fathers Under Fire 3 (Irwin Garfinkel et al., eds. 1998). In *Blessing v. Freestone*, 520 U.S. 329 (1997), the Court held that Title IV–D does not grant parents a private right of action to sue the state child support enforcement agency or its personnel for alleged non-compliance with the Title's requirements.

4. *Bonds.* Under federal law, states must have procedures for using bonds to secure child support payments in appropriate cases. Bonds can be important to secure the flow of money to the children of obligors whose income fluctuates or who are paid irregularly, such as seasonally-paid farmers, salespersons who work on commissions or bonuses, and self-employed workers. Because risk of loss has created a scarcity of underwriters, however, most states have not routinely used bonds in child support cases. *See* U.S. Comm'n on Interstate Child Support, Supporting Our Children: A Blueprint For Reform 162 (1992).

5. *Civil contempt.* Courts may use their civil contempt power to jail a parent for willful failure to pay child support in violation of a court order. *See, e.g., In re Marriage of Deike,* 887 N.E.2d 628 (Ill. App. Ct. 2008). In a civil contempt proceeding, state law may presume that a parent can pay child support, placing the burden on the obligor to rebut the presumption. *See Hicks v. Feiock,* 485 U.S. 624 (1988). The obligor must be released if he satisfies the burden. *See, e.g., Gallaher v. Breaux,* 650 S.E.2d 313, 315–16 (Ga. Ct. App. 2007).

Contempt is available only where the nonpayor has a legal, rather than merely a contractual or moral, support obligation. In *Brown v. Brown,* 412 A.2d 396 (Md. 1980), for example, the court applied contract law to enforce the stepfather's agreement to pay $30 per week support for the stepchild until majority. The court held that because the stepfather had no underlying legal duty of support, his jailing for contempt for nonpayment constituted imprisonment for debt in violation of the state constitution. The stepfather's obligation was merely a "contractual" debt because state law recognized no general stepparent support obligation.

6. *Involuntary servitude and imprisonment for debt.* Incarceration for willful failure to pay child support does not offend state constitutional provisions prohibiting imprisonment for debt because child support is not a debt, but rather a duty that biological or adoptive parents owe to their dependent children and society. *See, e.g., Wetmore v. Markoe,* 196 U.S. 68, 76 (1904); *In re Bielefeld,* 143 S.W.3d 924, 928 (Tex. Ct. App. 2004).

Nor does imprisoning a parent for willful nonpayment of child support violate the Thirteenth Amendment's ban on slavery or involuntary servitude because "the relationship between parent and child is much more than the ordinary relationship between debtor and creditor. The parent is responsible for bringing the child into the world and in so doing assumes a moral obligation to provide the child with the necessities of life, and to ensure the child's welfare until it is emancipated and able to provide for itself. When parents neglect their children, this raises more than a private legal dispute. It is a matter of vital importance to the community." *United States v. Ballek,* 170 F.3d 871, 874 (9th Cir. 1999).

7. *Privatizing child support collection.* Several states have privatized some or all child support collection efforts, statewide or locally, by contracting with private firms to supplement or replace services otherwise provided by public IV–D agencies. Depending on the jurisdiction, the private firms may collect past-due support, and may also perform other functions such as processing payments, establishing paternity and support orders, and locating parents. *See* U.S. Gen. Accounting Office, Child Support Enforcement: States and Localities Move to Privatized Services (Nov. 1995). PRWORA expressly permits states to privatize child support enforcement "through contracts with charitable, religious, or private organizations." 42 U.S.C. § 604(a) (2003).

When state efforts to locate obligors and collect child support have failed, some custodial parents themselves have engaged private, for-profit collection agencies, which the media sometimes call "bounty hunters." These private collection agencies, which sometimes charge parents as much as one-third of amounts recovered, ignite controversy. One critic charged that when the private agencies "take 33 percent of the money that's supposed to feed the children, what are they taking? Breakfast, lunch or dinner?" Other custodial parents, however, conclude that "66 percent of something is more than 100 percent of nothing." These parents note too that when a parent hires a lawyer to seek private collection, the lawyer typically charges a substantial fee, regardless of whether collection efforts succeed. *See* Tamar Lewin, *Private Firms Help Single Parents Get What's Due*, N.Y. Times, May 21, 1994, at 1.

8. *Innovative efforts to collect child support.* States have resorted to novel child support collection methods. An early Wisconsin innovation was struck down in *Zablocki v. Redhail*, 434 U.S. 374 (1978) (discussed *supra* Chapter 3). Other methods, however, have passed constitutional muster. Many states disseminate "Most Wanted" posters featuring photos of non-paying parents. *See, e.g.*, http://www.oag.state.tx.us/evaders/poster.pdf ("Texas' Top 10 Most Wanted Child Support Evaders"). Some states seize obligors' lottery winnings. In 2002, Virginia became the first state to use "booting" against nonpaying obligor parents. The parent's automobile is immobilized by attaching a heavy locking device—the "boot"—to a tire until the parent agrees to a payment plan. Pink boots for daughters and blue boots for sons are placed on the vehicles, together with bright fluorescent window stickers explaining the reason for booting. Law enforcement officials attach the boot and have the key to release it. *See* Drew A. Swank, *Das Boot! A National Survey of Booting Programs' Impact on Child Support Compliance*, 4 J. L. & Fam. Stud. 265, 268–70 (2002). In 2005, Virginia also began issuing subpoenas to cell phone companies in an effort to learn the numbers of nonpayors. *See Governor Kaine Announces National Honor For Virginia's Child Support Program*, States News Serv. (Nov. 20, 2007). Do measures that smack of shaming necessarily serve the best interests of the children who are owed support?

Where the U.S. Department of Health and Human Services (HHS) certifies to the U.S. State Department that a parent owes child support payments in excess of $2,500, the parent is ineligible to receive a U.S. passport. 22 C.F.R. § 51.70(a)(8) (2008). The passport will not be issued until the appropriate state agency certifies to HHS that acceptable payment arrangements have been made, and HHS removes the parent's name from the electronic list it gives the State Department. *See* Child Support Payments and Getting a U.S. Passport, http://travel.state.gov/passport/ppi/family/family_863. html. The Passport Denial Program has new teeth now that passports are required to travel to Canada, Mexico and the Caribbean.

9. *Child support and bankruptcy.* The Bankruptcy Abuse and Prevention and Consumer Protection Act of 2005, Pub. L. No. 109–8, 119 Stat 23 (2005), included provisions designed to help insure that obligors filing for bankruptcy continue paying child support, and that child support obligations receive high priority in bankruptcy:

> * * * One of these provisions clarifies that proceedings to establish or modify a domestic support obligation (e.g., child support) owed to a governmental unit (e.g., state CSE agencies) are exempt from the automatic stay. An automatic stay bars creditors from taking measures to collect a debt pending resolution of the bankruptcy proceeding. Another

provision allows for the continued operation of wage withholding for domestic support obligations (e.g., child support). Further, the Bankruptcy Reform Act, for example, requires that noncustodial parents filing for Chapter 13 bankruptcy [under which filers submit a repayment plan to the court agreeing to pay part or all of their debts over time, usually three to five years] must be current on their child support obligations to confirm a repayment plan. In addition, the Bankruptcy Reform Act provides child support with the first priority for payment of unsecured claims, up from a seventh-level priority under previous Bankruptcy Code provisions.

U.S. Gov't Accountability Office, Bankruptcy and Child Support Enforcement: Improved Information Sharing Possible Without Routine Data Matching 7, 9 (2008).

3. CRIMINAL ENFORCEMENT

Most child support establishment and enforcement is done through the civil process, but the criminal law also plays a role at the federal and state levels.

With state criminal jurisdiction over out-of-state obligors unclear, federal criminal enforcement made its debut in 1992, when about 30% of support cases involved obligor parents not living in the same state as the child. A federal commission concluded that besides eliminating jurisdictional hurdles, federal legislation would be "a powerful deterrent[,] * * * a statement that America believes nonsupport to be a serious enough crime to warrant federal attention." U.S. Comm'n on Interstate Child Support, Supporting Our Children: A Blueprint For Reform xxvi, 178 (1992).

Enacted at the commission's request, the Child Support Recovery Act of 1992 (CSRA), 18 U.S.C. § 228 (2003), makes it a federal crime (1) to willfully fail to pay support to a child who resides in another state, where the obligation has remained unpaid for more than a year or is greater than $5,000, or (2) to travel in interstate or foreign commerce with intent to evade a support obligation. The statute provides greater punishment for second or later offenses, or where the obligation has remained unpaid for longer than two years or is greater than $10,000. The Deadbeat Parents Punishment Act of 1998 amended the CSRA to increase the punishments and create a rebuttable presumption that the parent in arrears had the ability to pay the obligations due. The presumption shifts the burden of proof to the nonpaying parent. In CSRA prosecutions, federal courts have uniformly refused to relitigate issues previously determined by state child-support orders. *See, e.g., United States v. Johnson*, 114 F.3d 476, 482 (4th Cir. 1997). Eleven U.S. courts of appeals have upheld the CSRA as a proper exercise of Congress' Commerce Clause power. *See, e.g., United States v. Kukafka*, 478 F.3d 531, 534–35 (3d Cir. 2007) (citing decisions).

The CSRA covered an estimated four million non-custodial parents who were behind in their support payments to children living in other states, but this volume of prosecutions has not happened because U.S.

Attorneys prosecute less than 60,000 persons a year for all federal crimes, and the Federal Bureau of Investigation (which has primary investigative jurisdiction over the CSRA) handles only about 10,000 cases of all types annually. The U.S. Justice Department has confined CSRA prosecutions to a modest number of egregious cases. *See* U.S. Dep't of Justice, Prosecutive Guidelines and Procedures for the Child Support Recovery Act of 1992, http://www.usdoj.gov/ag/readingroom/childspt2.htm.

Most criminal child support enforcement arises under state laws that authorize imprisonment for willful non-payment. The next decision provides an illustration.

STATE v. OAKLEY

Supreme Court of Wisconsin, 2001.
629 N.W.2d 200.
Reconsideration denied and opinion clarified, 635 N.W.2d 760.

JON P. WILCOX, J.

* * * [W]e must decide whether as a condition of probation, a father of nine children, who has intentionally refused to pay child support, can be required to avoid having another child, unless he shows that he can support that child and his current children. We conclude that in light of Oakley's ongoing victimization of his nine children and extraordinarily troubling record manifesting his disregard for the law, this anomalous condition—imposed on a convicted felon facing the far more restrictive and punitive sanction of prison—is not overly broad and is reasonably related to Oakley's rehabilitation. Simply put, because Oakley was convicted of intentionally refusing to pay child support—a felony in Wisconsin—and could have been imprisoned for six years, which would have eliminated his right to procreate altogether during those six years, this probation condition, which infringes on his right to procreate during his term of probation, is not invalid under these facts. Accordingly, we hold that the circuit court did not erroneously exercise its discretion.

* * *

I

David Oakley (Oakley), the petitioner, was initially charged with intentionally refusing to pay child support for his nine children he has fathered with four different women. The State subsequently charged Oakley with seven counts of intentionally refusing to provide child support as a repeat offender. His repeat offender status stemmed from intimidating two witnesses in a child abuse case—where one of the victims was his own child. * * *

* * *

* * * The State noted that during the relevant time period, Oakley had paid no child support and that there were arrears in excess of $25,000.

* * *

After taking into account Oakley's ability to work and his consistent disregard of the law and his obligations to his children, Judge Hazlewood observed that "if Mr. Oakley had paid something, had made an earnest effort to pay anything within his remote ability to pay, we wouldn't be sitting here," nor would the State argue for six years in prison. But Judge Hazlewood also recognized that "if Mr. Oakley goes to prison, he's not going to be in a position to pay any meaningful support for these children." Therefore, even though Judge Hazlewood acknowledged that Oakley's "defaults, are obvious, consistent, and inexcusable," he decided against sentencing Oakley to six years in prison consecutive to his three-year sentence in Sheboygan County, as the State had advocated. Instead, Judge Hazlewood sentenced Oakley to three years in prison on the first count, imposed and stayed an eight-year term on the two other counts, and imposed a five-year term of probation consecutive to his incarceration. Judge Hazlewood then imposed the condition at issue here: while on probation, Oakley cannot have any more children unless he demonstrates that he had the ability to support them and that he is supporting the children he already had. * * * [The court of appeals affirmed.]

* * *

II

* * *

The effects of the nonpayment of child support on our children are particularly troubling. In addition to engendering long-term consequences such as poor health, behavioral problems, delinquency and low educational attainment, inadequate child support is a direct contributor to childhood poverty. And childhood poverty is all too pervasive in our society. * * * Although payment of child support alone may not end childhood poverty, it could reduce current levels and raise childhood standards of living. Child support—when paid—on average amounts to over one-quarter of a poor child's family income. There is little doubt that the payment of child support benefits poverty-stricken children the most. * * *

* * *

In the present case, the record indicates that Judge Hazlewood was familiar with Oakley's abysmal history prior to sentencing. The record reveals that Judge Hazlewood knew that Oakley had a number of support orders entered for his nine children, but he nevertheless continually refused to support them. He was aware that Oakley's probation for intimidating two witnesses in a child abuse case—where one of the witnesses was his own child and the victim—was in the process of being revoked. Judge Hazlewood was also apprised that Oakley had promised in the past to support his children, but those promises had failed to translate into the needed support. Moreover, he knew that Oakley had been employed and had no impediment preventing him from working. * * *

* * * Judge Hazlewood asserted that some prison time coupled with conditional probation might convince Oakley to stop victimizing his children. With probation, Judge Hazlewood sought to rehabilitate Oakley while protecting society and potential victims—Oakley's own children—from future wrongdoing. The conditions were designed to assist Oakley in conforming his conduct to the law. * * * Here, the judge fashioned a condition that was tailored to that particular crime, but avoided the more severe punitive alternative of the full statutory prison term through the rehabilitative tool of probation. At the same time, Judge Hazlewood sought to protect the victims of Oakley's crimes—Oakley's nine children.

But Oakley argues that the condition imposed by Judge Hazlewood violates his constitutional right to procreate. This court, in accord with the United States Supreme Court, has previously recognized the fundamental liberty interest of a citizen to choose whether or not to procreate. *Eberhardy v. Circuit Court for Wood County*, 307 N.W.2d 881 (1981); *Skinner v. Oklahoma ex rel. Williamson*, 316 U.S. 535, 541 (1942) (recognizing the right to procreate as "one of the basic civil rights of man"). Accordingly, Oakley argues that the condition here warrants strict scrutiny.[23] That is, it must be narrowly tailored to serve a compelling state interest. *See Zablocki v. Redhail*, 434 U.S. 374, 388 (1978). Although Oakley concedes, as he must, that the State's interest in requiring parents to support their children is compelling, he argues that the means employed here is not narrowly tailored to serve that compelling interest because Oakley's "right to procreate is not restricted but in fact eliminated." According to Oakley, his right to procreate is eliminated because he "probably never will have the ability to support" his children. Therefore, if he exercises his fundamental right to procreate while on probation, his probation will be revoked and he will face the stayed term of eight years in prison.

While Oakley's argument might well carry the day if he had not intentionally refused to pay child support, it is well-established that convicted individuals do not enjoy the same degree of liberty as citizens who have not violated the law. We emphatically reject the novel idea that Oakley, who was convicted of intentionally failing to pay child support, has an absolute right to refuse to support his current nine children and any future children that he procreates, thereby adding more child victims to the list. * * *

---

23. While the condition here survives strict scrutiny, we note that probation conditions—like prison regulations—are not subject to strict scrutiny analysis, contrary to the unwarranted assumptions in the arguments of both Oakley and Justice Bradley. * * *

* * * Justice Sykes identifies the correct test. However, Justice Sykes missteps by failing to apply that test and, in relying on *Zablocki v. Redhail*, 434 U.S. 374, 376, she utilizes strict scrutiny, like Justice Bradley. Although it may be that the facts of *Zablocki* are interesting because it was a Wisconsin case, its holding is not implicated here for the simple reason that the test in *Zablocki* was ?[w]hen a statutory classification significantly interferes with the exercise of a fundamental right, it cannot be upheld unless it is supported by sufficiently important state interests and is closely tailored to effectuate only those interests,? a.k.a., strict scrutiny. 434 U.S. at 388. * * *

* * * [W]e believe that in light of Oakley's troubling record of child witness intimidation and intentional refusal to pay child support, denying his nine children assistance for their basic needs, the condition here will provide his child victims and any future child victims with some measure of protection from any of Oakley's future acts that may violate the law.

Furthermore, Oakley fails to note that incarceration, by its very nature, deprives a convicted individual of the fundamental right to be free from physical restraint, which in turn encompasses and restricts other fundamental rights, such as the right to procreate. Therefore, given that a convicted felon does not stand in the same position as someone who has not been convicted of a crime, we have previously stated that "conditions of probation may impinge upon constitutional rights as long as they are not overly broad and are reasonably related to the person's rehabilitation."[27] * * *

Applying the relevant standard here, we find that the condition is not overly broad because it does not eliminate Oakley's ability to exercise his constitutional right to procreate. He can satisfy the condition of probation by making efforts to support his children as required by law. Judge Hazlewood placed no limit on the number of children Oakley could have. Instead, the requirement is that Oakley acknowledge the requirements of the law and support his present and any future children. If Oakley decides to continue his present course of conduct—intentionally refusing to pay child support—he will face eight years in prison regardless of how many children he has. Furthermore, this condition will expire at the end of his term of probation. He may then decide to have more children, but of course, if he continues to intentionally refuse to support his children, the State could charge him again under § 948.22(2).[a] Rather, because Oakley can satisfy this condition by not intentionally refusing to support his current nine children and any future children as required by the law, we find that the condition is narrowly tailored to serve the State's compelling interest of having parents support their children. It is also narrowly tailored to serve the State's compelling interest in rehabilitating Oakley through probation rather than prison. The alternative to probation with conditions—incarceration for eight years—would have further victimized his children. And it is undoubtedly much broader than this conditional impingement on his procreative freedom for it would deprive him of his fundamental right to be free from physical restraint. Simply stated, Judge Hazlewood preserved much of Oakley's liberty by imposing probation with conditions rather than the more punitive option of imprisonment.

---

27. * * * Accordingly, in light of the weight of authority indicating that strict scrutiny does not apply when a probation condition infringes upon a fundamental right and the dearth of authority to the contrary, we are convinced that the reasonability standard is the constitutionally valid approach to evaluate a probation condition that infringes upon a fundamental right. * * *

a. This provision of the statute provides, in pertinent part, that "[a]ny person who intentionally fails for 120 or more consecutive days to provide spousal, grandchild or child support which the person knows or reasonably should know the person is legally obligated to provide is guilty of a Class I felony." Wis. Stat. § 948.22 (2003–04). [eds.]

Moreover, the condition is reasonably related to the goal of rehabilitation. * * * Here, Oakley was convicted of intentionally refusing to support his children. The condition at bar will prevent him from adding victims if he continues to intentionally refuse to support his children. As the State argues, the condition essentially bans Oakley from violating the law again. Future violations of the law would be detrimental to Oakley's rehabilitation, which necessitates preventing him from continuing to disregard its dictates. Accordingly, this condition is reasonably related to his rehabilitation because it will assist Oakley in conforming his conduct to the law.

* * *

The decision of the court of appeals is affirmed.

WILLIAM A. BABLITCH, J. (concurring) [joined by JON P. WILCOX and N. PATRICK CROOKS, JJ.]

* * *

* * * As long as the defendant continues to intentionally refuse to pay support, the alternatives posed by the dissents will end up with incarceration—which of course accomplishes indirectly what the dissents say the state cannot do directly.

* * *

I conclude that the harm to others who cannot protect themselves is so overwhelmingly apparent and egregious here that there is no room for question. Here is a man who has shown himself time and again to be totally and completely irresponsible. He lives only for himself and the moment, with no regard to the consequences of his actions and taking no responsibility for them. He intentionally refuses to pay support and has been convicted of that felony. The harm that he has done to his nine living children by failing to support them is patent and egregious. He has abused at least one of them. Under certain conditions, it is overwhelmingly obvious that any child he fathers in the future is doomed to a future of neglect, abuse, or worse. That as yet unborn child is a victim from the day it is born.

I am not happy with this result, but can discern no other. And the dissents provide none. Accordingly, I join the majority opinion.

[The concurring opinion of N. PATRICK CROOKS, J., is omitted.]

ANN WALSH BRADLEY, J. (dissenting) [joined by SHIRLEY S. ABRAHAMSON, C.J., and DIANE S. SYKES, J.]

I begin by emphasizing the right that is at issue: the right to have children. The majority acknowledges this right, but certainly does not convey its significance and preeminence. The right to have children is a basic human right and an aspect of the fundamental liberty which the Constitution jealously guards for all Americans. *See Skinner v. Oklahoma ex rel. Williamson,* 316 U.S. 535, 536 (1942).

* * * The majority's decision allows, for the first time in our state's history, the birth of a child to carry criminal sanctions. * * * Ultimately, the majority's decision may affect the rights of every citizen of this state, man or woman, rich or poor.

* * *

The circuit court's order forbidding Oakley from having another child until he first establishes his ability to support all his children is unconstitutional. Even the circuit court judge who imposed the condition acknowledged that Oakley will be unable to meet this condition. The probation condition is not narrowly drawn to serve the governmental interest at stake. Additionally, aside from the constitutional infirmities, such a condition of probation entails practical problems and carries unacceptable collateral consequences.

I

* * *

* * * The right [to have children] is embodied in the sphere of personal privacy protected from unjustified governmental intrusion by the Due Process Clause of the Fourteenth Amendment. *Eisenstadt v. Baird*, 405 U.S. 438, 453 (1972). * * *

Because the right implicated by the condition of probation in this case is one that is central to the concept of fundamental liberty, the state action infringing upon that right is subject to heightened scrutiny. In *Edwards v. State*, 246 N.W.2d 109 (1976), we explained that conditions of probation may impinge upon constitutional rights so long as they are "not overly broad" and are reasonably related to the probationer's rehabilitation. In the non-probation context, any state action infringing upon a fundamental liberty interest can be justified only by a compelling state interest and must be "narrowly drawn" to express only the legitimate state interests at stake. *Carey v. Population Servs. Int'l*, 431 U.S. 678, 688–89 (1977). Because of the heightened importance of the liberty interest at stake, whether one chooses to frame the means-end inquiry in a case involving the right to procreate while on probation as "not overly broad" or as "narrowly drawn," I believe the essence of the inquiry is the same.

* * * Ordinarily, where a state action infringes upon a liberty interest that is deemed fundamental under the Fourteenth Amendment, it is " 'presumptively unconstitutional.' " The State must justify its action by establishing that it is narrowly drawn in light of the governmental interest at stake.

It is important to bear in mind exactly what the circuit court order proscribed. The circuit court order forbids Oakley from fathering another child until he can first establish the financial ability to support his children. Oakley is not prohibited from having intercourse, either indiscriminately or irresponsibly. Rather, the condition of probation is not triggered until Oakley's next child is born.

* * *

While on its face the order leaves room for the slight possibility that Oakley may establish the financial means to support his children, the order is essentially a prohibition on the right to have children. Oakley readily admits that unless he wins the lottery, he will likely never be able to establish that ability. The circuit court understood the impossibility of Oakley satisfying this financial requirement when it imposed the condition. The court explained that "it would always be a struggle to support these children and in truth [Oakley] could not reasonably be expected to fully support them." * * *

In light of the circuit court's recognition of Oakley's inability to meet the condition of probation, the prohibition cannot be considered a narrowly drawn means of advancing the state's interest in ensuring support for Oakley's children.

In a similar context, the United States Supreme Court has explained that a statutory prohibition on the right to marry, a right closely aligned with the right at issue, was not a justifiable means of advancing the state's interest in providing support for children. *Zablocki v. Redhail*, 434 U.S. 374, 388–90 (1978). The *Zablocki* court addressed a Wisconsin statute that prohibited people from marrying until they established that their child support obligations had been met. The Court, in finding the statute unconstitutional, explained that Wisconsin law provided other available means of advancing the state's interest that did not infringe upon the liberty interest at stake * * *.

Rather than juxtapose the means chosen in the instant case with the alternatives suggested in *Zablocki*, the majority compares the infringement of Oakley's reproductive liberty with the loss of liberty he would suffer had the circuit court chosen to imprison him. It is true that if Oakley were imprisoned he would suffer an incidental inability to exercise his procreative rights. However, the fact of the matter is that Oakley has not been imprisoned. He is a probationer and has retained a degree of his liberty, including "a significant degree of privacy under the Fourth, Fifth and Fourteenth Amendments." While the State has chosen not to exercise control over Oakley's body by depriving him of the freedom from restraint, it does not necessarily follow that the State may opt to exercise unlimited control over his right to procreate.

The narrowly drawn means described by the Supreme Court in *Zablocki* still exist today and are appropriate means of advancing the state's interest in a manner that does not impair the fundamental right to procreate. *See, e.g.*, Wis. Stat. § 767.265 (garnishment/wage assignment); § 767.30 (lien on personal property); § 785.03 (civil contempt). These means, as well as other conditions of probation or criminal penalties, are available in the present case.[3]

In light of these alternative means of advancing the compelling state interest at issue, the State has failed to justify that the elimination, or at best qualification, of the right to procreate is narrowly drawn, or in the words of *Edwards*, that it is "not overly broad." The State, and the majority, can do little more than "infer" that these "less drastic methods" will be ineffective in the case of David Oakley. Such an inference does not a constitutional justification make. In the absence of such a justification, the state action limiting Oakley's right to procreate is unconstitutional.

II

In addition to the obvious constitutional infirmities of the majority's decision, upholding a term of probation that prohibits a probationer from fathering a child without first establishing the financial wherewithal to support his children carries unacceptable collateral consequences and practical problems.

First, prohibiting a person from having children as a condition of probation has been described as "coercive of abortion." * * * In *People v. Pointer*, 199 Cal. Rptr. 357 [(Cal. Ct. App. 1984)], the court concluded that a condition of probation prohibiting a female probationer from becoming pregnant was unconstitutional. It advanced that such a condition fosters state-coerced abortion. * * *

If the tables are turned to the present case where the probationer is a man, a similar risk arises. Because the condition is triggered only upon the birth of a child, the risk of imprisonment creates a strong incentive for a man in Oakley's position to demand from the woman the termination of her pregnancy. It places the woman in an untenable position: have an abortion or be responsible for Oakley going to prison for eight years. Creating an incentive to procure an abortion in order to comply with conditions of probation is a result that I am not prepared to foster.

Second, by allowing the right to procreate to be subjected to financial qualifications, the majority imbues a fundamental liberty interest with a sliding scale of wealth. Men and women in America are free to have children, as many as they desire. They may do so without the means to support the children and may later suffer legal consequences as a result of the inability to provide support. However, the right to have a child has never been rationed on the basis of wealth.

---

3. I do not set forth a list of other available conditions of probation or penalties, because they are too numerous to list. However, as the majority acknowledges, at sentencing Oakley requested an opportunity to maintain full employment, provide for his children, and make serious payments towards his child support arrearages. Given Oakley's ability to work, an alternative approach could have been as follows: sentence Oakley to eight years in prison; stay the sentence and place him on probation; a condition of probation is that he serve a substantial amount of time in jail with work release privileges; after getting work release hours extended, another condition of probation is that he maintain two full-time jobs, working a minimum of 70 hours per week; conditions of probation also include parenting classes and alcohol and drug assessment/counseling if deemed appropriate. * * *

Nevertheless, the majority has essentially authorized a judicially-imposed "credit check" on the right to bear and beget children. Thus begins our descent down the proverbial slippery slope. While the majority describes this case as "anomalous" and comprised of "atypical facts," the cases in which such a principle might be applied are not uncommon. The majority's own statistical data regarding non-payment of support belies its contention that this case is truly exceptional.

Third, the condition of probation is unworkable. David Oakley is not restrained, and realistically cannot be stopped, from having intercourse—protected or otherwise. The condition of probation will not be violated until the woman with whom he has sexual relations carries her pregnancy to term. Then, Oakley will be imprisoned, and another child will go unsupported. * * *

* * *

Let there be no question that I agree with the majority that David Oakley's conduct cannot be condoned. It is irresponsible and criminal. However, we must keep in mind what is really at stake in this case. The fundamental right to have children, shared by us all, is damaged by today's decision. Because I will not join in the majority's disregard of that right, I dissent.

* * *

DIANE S. SYKES, J. (dissenting).

* * *

While I sympathize with the circuit court's understandable exasperation with this chronic "deadbeat dad," I cannot agree that this probation condition survives constitutional scrutiny. It is basically a compulsory, state-sponsored, court-enforced financial test for future parenthood.

* * *

While I recognize that the constitutional tests are somewhat different, *Zablocki* is otherwise closely analogous to this case. Here, as in *Zablocki*, there are less restrictive means available to achieve the State's objectives short of encumbering what everyone agrees is a fundamental human right. As noted by Justice Bradley in her dissent, the circuit court can order Oakley to maintain full-time employment—or even two jobs—as a condition of probation, and to execute a wage assignment to pay off his child support arrearages and satisfy his ongoing support obligations. His tax refunds can be intercepted annually. Liens can be placed on his personal property, and he can be found in civil contempt. He can be criminally prosecuted for any additional intentional failures to support his children, present or future. His probation can be revoked if he fails to maintain employment and make support payments. Granted, Oakley's arrearages are so great, and his history so troublesome, that these means may not ultimately be completely successful in achieving the State's objective of collecting child support. But the same was true in *Zablocki*, and the Supreme Court nevertheless found the statute in that case unconstitutional. I reach the same conclusion here.

* * * Conditioning the right to procreate upon proof of financial or other fitness may appear on the surface to be an appropriate solution in extreme cases such as this, but it is unprecedented in this country, and for good reason. * * * I know of no authority for the proposition that the State can order that a child not be conceived or born, even to an abysmally irresponsible parent, unless the State first grants its consent.

* * *

NOTES AND QUESTIONS

1. *Questions about* Oakley. (a) Do you think the aggravating factors that *Oakley's* majority recites differ much from the aggravating factors in many other criminal child support prosecutions? (b) Must the state tolerate a parent who begets nearly a dozen children, without evident intent or ability to support any of them? (c) Will the court's decision likely help the conditions of any of Oakley's children? Would the children have been better off if the trial court had ordered their father to complete a job training program?

2. Zablocki *redux.* Did *Oakley's* majority adequately distinguish *Zablocki v. Redhail* (discussed in Chapter 3)? If Wisconsin's earlier effort violated Mr. Redhail's fundamental right to marry, why did the condition imposed on Mr. Oakley not violate his fundamental right to procreate?

3. *Understanding the trial court decision. Oakley's* seven Justices disagreed about whether the trial court's probation condition required the defendant to make only partial support payments within his capabilities, or whether the order required full payment of arrears before he could father more children. The majority said the trial judge "recogni[zed] that Oakley might not be able to earn large amounts of money in the future, but that he would be expected to provide support based on his ability to earn and pay." 629 N.W.2d at 207 n.21. Justice Bablitch concluded that "[r]ead in the context of the entire record, * * * if Oakley were to show the court a good faith effort to support his children, the order would be amended." *Id.* at 214 n.1 (Bablitch, J., concurring). Dissenting Justice Bradley, however, called the trial court order "essentially a prohibition on the right to have children" by forbidding Oakley to have further children while on probation (in the words of the order) "unless it can be shown to the Court that he is meeting the needs of his other children and can meet the needs of this one." *Id.* at 217 (Bradley, J., dissenting). If you were a Justice sitting in *Oakley,* would the meaning of the trial court order have affected your decision about the constitutionality of the probation condition?

4. *A "slippery slope"?* The state supreme court decided *Oakley* by a four-to-three vote. The four-Justice majority were men, and the three dissenters were women. All three dissenters joined fully in the two dissenting opinions. Do the dissenters provide any clues about the questions that concerned them?

Dissenting Justice Bradley chides the majority for "allowing the right to procreate to be subjected to financial qualifications," imposing "a sliding scale of wealth" on childbearing, rationing the right to have a child based on wealth, and "essentially authoriz[ing] a judicially-imposed 'credit check' on the right to bear and beget children" because *Oakley's* facts are not uncommon. Is she right that *Oakley* is a first step on the "descent down the proverbial slippery slope"? Does the slope lead beyond criminal prosecution into the civil arena?

One newspaper speculated that *Oakley's* rationale might justify "the arrest of moms for giving birth or even the forced sterilization of women." *A Perilous Ruling for American Dads*, N.W. Florida Daily News, July 17, 2001, at A6. Indeed, some state measures designed to limit the fertility of women on public assistance have already met with court approval. *See, e.g., Sojourner A. v. New Jersey Dep't of Human Services*, 828 A.2d 306 (N.J. 2003) (upholding the constitutionality of the Work First New Jersey Act, which caps a family's cash assistance at the level set when the family enters into the state welfare system, and prohibits increases in cash assistance for any child born more than ten months after the family initially applies for and obtains these benefits).

5. *David Oakley*. Sometimes a court decision assumes greater meaning when a litigant assumes a human face rather than merely paragraphs in the reports. Consider this profile of Mr. Oakley:

> He was born in 1966 in the Taycheedah Correctional Institution, a women's prison in Fond du Lac, Wisconsin. Sharon Oakley, his mother, remained incarcerated until 1974, but authorities, of course, removed Oakley from the prison. After a period in state care, he was raised primarily by his maternal grandparents. Run-ins with law enforcement officials marked his youth, and while in his teens Oakley was sent to Lincoln Hills School, a home for delinquent boys located near Wausau, Wisconsin. * * * According to Cheri Pasdo, mother of a boy Oakley fathered, "He always used to say his life was doomed from the day he was born."

> After completing his sentences in juvenile facilities, Oakley lived largely in an area on the western shore of Lake Michigan in central Wisconsin. To say he "settled" there would perhaps convey the wrong impression because, like many of the poor, he moved frequently from one home to another. Most of his residences were in or near Sheboygan and Manitowoc, Wisconsin * * * [which] have significant unemployment.

> * * *

> With a limited formal education and virtually no skills, Oakley was unable to find or hold meaningful jobs. He worked for a while as a sandblaster, but his absenteeism became an issue. After four formal warnings, Musical Paint Finishers LLC released him. Oakley also worked for Manpower Temporary services, but the company eventually stopped placing him because he was unreliable. As with many of the poor, Oakley's ability to find and get to work was limited by his lack of a motor vehicle. * * *

Oakley's lengthy criminal record also without doubt made him less than an ideal hire in the minds of some employers. By the time of the Wisconsin Supreme Court's decision in 2001, Oakley had amassed nearly 200 formal contacts with the Manitowoc Police and Manitowoc County Sheriff's Department. He had been convicted of disorderly conduct, receiving stolen property, illegal possession of a firearm, and intimidating a witness. * * *

The mothers of Oakley's children, themselves among Manitowoc County's poor, do not unanimously condemn Oakley. * * *

* * * Lucretia Thompson–Smith and Rachel Ward remain sympathetic to Oakley. Thompson–Smith, mother of Oakley's fourteen year-old daughter, does not see much difference between Oakley and the two other fathers of her children when it comes to paying child support faithfully. Even if Oakley had a minimum-wage job, his child support would eat it up. "How could he live?" she asked. "They don't pay very much in Manitowoc County." * * *

David Ray Papke, State v. Oakley, *Deadbeat Dads, and American Poverty*, 26 W. New Eng. L. Rev. 9, 10–13 (2004).

PROBLEM 11–9

You are the newly elected county prosecutor, and you have been invited to appear at a public forum on child support enforcement. The other panelists will include child advocates, representatives from fathers' rights groups, social workers, and academics. You have been asked to speak about the factors a prosecutor should consider in deciding whether to indict a parent for willful non-support, or whether to leave support enforcement to civil authorities. You understand that the decision whether to convict and imprison a parent in arrears presents complex issues for prosecutors and courts. What will you say at the forum?

The panel's moderator is intrigued by *Oakley*, and she asks you to talk about the decision. Would you have opted for prosecution or civil enforcement if you were the state official charged with making the decision? Would your decision have been influenced, in one way or the other, by the financial condition of Mr. Oakley or the children's households?

B. WHO DOES NOT PAY?

"Of those everyone loves to hate, few can compete with the deadbeat dad for longevity." Kathleen Parker, *Beating Up On Fathers Once Again*, Baltimore Sun, May 5, 2008, at 9A. Much of the fury unleashed by courts, legislatures and the public, however, is misdirected because men hold no monopoly on shirking. In 2002, for example, custodial mothers received child support more often than did custodial fathers (64% compared with 43%). On average, custodial mothers also received greater amounts of child support than custodial fathers ($1720 compared with $430). Among custodial parents with child support orders, 81% of custodial mothers but only 61% of custodial fathers received child support. *See* Liliana Sousa & Elaine Sorenson, *The Economic Reality of Nonresident Mothers and Their Children* 4 (Urban Inst. 2006). With the performance of both some noncustodial mothers and some noncustodial fathers leaving much to be desired, what might explain the media's continuing primary focus on noncustodial fathers?

In 1999, an estimated 2.5 million nonresident fathers with incomes below the federal poverty level did not pay child support. But one million poor nonresident fathers did pay some or all of what they owed. More than a quarter of these fathers spent 50% or more of their personal income on child support, while only 2% of non-poor fathers spent that much. *See* Elaine Sorensen & Helen Oliver, Policy Reforms are Needed to Increase Child Support from Poor Fathers 4–5 (Urban Inst. 2002).

After prosecuting and collecting child support from thousands of nonresident fathers for more than a decade, an Oklahoma prosecutor wrote that "[t]he real deadbeat dad is seldom a model citizen, but he is even more seldom the mythical monster described by politicians. Most deadbeat dads are frightened, angry, and depressed men." Bruce Walker, *Deadbeat Dads? Look Closer*, Christian Sci. Mon., Aug. 16, 1996, at 18. Many parents behind in their child support payments are poor, unemployed, undereducated, abusers of drugs or alcohol, or saddled with criminal records that impede a job search. Some are disabled or suffer bad health. Others lack English skills or are saddled with transportation barriers, lack of access to a telephone, or housing instability. Some work only intermittently or can hold only minimum-wage jobs, making the most effective means of support collection—wage withholding—largely ineffective. Many poor nonpayors are remarried with obligations to second families, are assisting their children's mother informally, or remain liable for support even after they assume custody of the children. A substantial number of poor nonresident fathers who do not pay child support are in prison. Others are dead, but the child support system has not caught up with record keeping. *See* Elaine Sorensen & Chava Zibman, A Look At Poor Dads Who Don't Pay Child Support 5 (Urban Inst. 2000).

"People who work in the child support loop know that the biggest barrier to child support payment is unemployment, yet this message seldom seems to get through." Parker, *supra*. In 2007, an in-depth Urban Institute study of child support arrears in nine large states found that "70% of the arrears were owed by obligors who had either no reported income or reported income of $10,000 a year or less." Elaine Sorenson et al., *Assessing Child Support Arrears in Nine Large States and the Nation* 3 (Urban Inst. 2007), http://aspe.hhs.gov/hsp/07/assessing-CS-debt/. Some support obligors with little or no reported income may have unreported income or assets, but "the group as a whole appears less able to pay child support than other groups of obligors." *Id*. at 4–5. The study predicted that less than half of arrears owed "will be collected over 10 years * * * because so much of the arrears are owed by obligors with no or low reported income." *Id*. at 7. In light of these numbers, did it make sense for

Congress in the Deadbeat Parents Punishment Act of 1998 to create a rebuttable presumption that a parent, prosecuted for nonpayment under the Child Support Recovery Act, can pay the obligations due? Is the presumption consistent with the policy considerations that normally underlie enactment of statutory presumptions?

To be sure, the landscape is dotted with noncustodial parents who seek to evade child support obligations they can clearly afford. Consider, for example, *Phelps v. La Point*, 725 N.Y.S.2d 461 (App. Div. 2001), discussed above on page 639. Professor Harry D. Krause, however, finds that the realities of child support enforcement differ from common perceptions. "While very impressive progress in child-support collection from absent parents has been made, that very progress has led us to overestimate, and consequently overemphasize, the financial support that can be obtained from absent parents." Harry D. Krause, *Child Support Reassessed: Limits of Private Responsibility and the Public Interest*, 24 Fam. L.Q. 1, 34 (1990).

Many commentators urge enforcement authorities to treat poor fathers not as "deadbeat dads" but as "dead-broke dads." *See, e.g.*, Solangel Maldonado, *Deadbeat or Deadbroke: Redefining Child Support for Poor Fathers*, 39 U.C. Davis L. Rev. 119 (2006). Poor custodial mothers and poor noncustodial fathers face similar employment barriers, but "society devotes considerably more resources to helping poor mothers succeed in the labor market than it does to helping poor fathers do so." Elaine Sorenson & Chava Zibman, *Poor Dads Who Don't Pay Child Support: Deadbeats or Disadvantaged?*, No. B–30, New Federalism: National Survey of America's Families 1 (Urban Inst. 2001), http://www.urban.org/ UploadedPDF/anf_b30.pdf. The Urban Institute recommends that states and localities provide poor fathers job training and other employment services, as well as health insurance (which about half of them lack) and food stamps so they can meet their own nutritional and health needs while paying child support. Elaine Sorensen & Helen Oliver, Policy Reforms Are Needed to Increase Child Support from Poor Fathers 15–17 (Urban Inst. 2002). PRWORA permits states and localities to use some federal funding under the Act to provide noncustodial fathers such services, and a number of jurisdictions report greater child support payment rates when they have done so. *See, e.g.*, DC Appleseed Center for Law and Justice, Taking Care of the District's Children 17–18 (2007).

NOTES AND QUESTIONS

1. *Is the playing field level?* "Whereas middle- and upper-income fathers usually negotiate their child support agreements in private and with the services of a lawyer who represents their interests, poor fathers often find themselves without counsel and confronted by public officials who represent the interests of the state." Irwin Garfinkel et al., *Introduction* to Fathers Under Fire 6–7 (Irwin Garfinkel et al., eds. 1998). The initial child support order may be based on imputed income, that is, what a person of the obligor's

age and general skill level could earn, rather than what the unemployed or underemployed obligor actually earns. Arrears may quickly mount, increased by accumulating interest, with the person effectively unable to navigate the system or secure periodic review and adjustment. As a result, "[p]oor fathers often face child support orders that are set at levels they cannot pay; their orders are rarely modified during periods of unemployment, and they accrue unrealistic levels of debt. This may motivate fathers to lose contact with their families and evade the child support system." Karin Martinson & Demetra Nightingale, *Key Findings From Responsible Fatherhood Initiatives* 3, 7 (2008). Courts have nonetheless rejected contentions that the IV–D agency violates equal protection when it represents custodial parents and leaves non-custodial parents to fend for themselves in enforcement proceedings. *See, e.g., Clark v. Clark*, 638 A.2d 667, 671–72 (D.C. 1994).

2. *Interest.* "The primary factor that has caused arrears to grow so dramatically has been the assessment of interest on a routine basis." Elaine Sorenson et al., Assessing Child Support Arrears in Nine Large States and the Nation (Urban Inst. 2007). As a general matter, why do most states charge interest on child support arrears, and what hardships might interest charges cause?

3. *Low-income obligors and the guidelines.* Federal law specifies that state child support guidelines apply to all parents, including poor parents. 45 C.F.R. § 302.56 (2008). A poor non-custodial parent may be unemployed and without much or any income, or his income may consist solely of means-tested public assistance benefits. (A benefit is "means-tested" if eligibility for the benefit, or its amount, is based on the recipient's income or resources.)

States differ about the support obligations of low-income obligors whose poverty is not caused by voluntary unemployment or underemployment. Some state guidelines specify that means-tested public assistance benefits do not constitute income at all; a child support award of $0 would be warranted where the parent has no non-benefit income. *See, e.g., Becker County Human Services v. Peppel*, 493 N.W.2d 573 (Minn. Ct. App. 1992). Some states leave indigent parents' support obligations to judicial discretion, without stating any presumed or absolute amount the parent must pay. Other states create a rebuttable presumption that a poor noncustodial parent must pay the lowest support amount recited on the guidelines schedule; the presumption may be rebutted where the amount would be unjust or inappropriate, though the state may also limit the amount of arrears that may accumulate against a poor parent. *See, e.g.*, N.Y. Fam. Ct. Act § 413(1)(g) (2005) (not more than $500). Still other states mandate an irrebuttable minimum support amount, regardless of the payor's income; the irrebuttable minimum may be quite low, but downward deviation is unavailable. *See, e.g.*, Ky. Rev. Stat. Ann. § 403.212(4), (6) (2004) ($60 per month).

In *Rose v. Moody*, 629 N.E.2d 378 (N.Y. 1993), the court held that New York's then-effective $25 irrebuttable monthly minimum was preempted by the 1988 federal mandate that child support awards carry only a rebuttable presumption that the guideline amount is just and appropriate under the circumstances. Moody, the indigent non-custodial mother of two children, subsisted on Social Services financial aid. The state conceded that the $25 award was uncollectible, but argued that the mandatory minimum award sent a "public policy message." *Id.* at 380. *Rose* found the mandatory minimum rebutted and affirmed an award of $0 per month. "Since [the mother] has nothing, she can pay nothing. * * * [A] perfunctory, legally noncollectible judicial order of support * * * would degrade the value and integrity of the judicial decree, and it would unjustly and unaccountably brand the respondent parent a deadbeat." *Id.* at 381.

What policies are vindicated when a court imposes a token child support obligation (which will not make much difference to the child's economic well-being) on a poor noncustodial parent in an amount the parent can pay? Is justice done when the court imposes a support obligation in an amount a poor parent concededly cannot pay? Does a court do justice when it imposes a child support obligation on a parent whose sole source of income is public assistance?

PROBLEM 11–10

You have practiced family law for more than a decade and are a leading member of the state bar association's family law committee. You have agreed to speak at a bar-sponsored continuing legal education program next month, "Child Support Enforcement: Yesterday, Today and Tomorrow." Other family lawyers will address the history of state and federal child support enforcement efforts, and will provide an overview and critique of present efforts. You will present recommendations for improving rates of child support payment by avoiding accumulation of arrears, particularly among obligors who are unemployed or otherwise report little or no income. What will you recommend?

CHAPTER 12

CHILD CUSTODY

■ ■ ■

Child custody decisions are among the most divisive for parents, the most difficult for judges, and the most critical for the children themselves. Most parents agree about initial custody and visitation arrangements, but many others litigate the issues, both at the time of divorce and afterwards. The stakes are high—and emotions run high too. This Chapter considers how courts make initial child custody decisions when the parents cannot reach an agreement. Chapter 13 will look at some custody and visitation issues that are commonly the subjects of prolonged, repeated litigation after dissolution of the parents' relationship.

Every year more than one million children experience their parents' divorce. Children's Defense Fund, *The State of Children in America's Union: A 2002 Action Guide to Leave No Child Behind* 13, 49 (2002), http://www.childrensdefense.org/data/minigreenbook.pdf. In addition, about a third of all children born each year are born to unmarried parents (including 34.6% of children born in 2002), and many of these children will also be the subjects of custody and visitation decisions. Brady E. Hamilton, et al., U.S. Dep't of Health & Human Servs., *Births: Preliminary Data for 2003*, 53 Nat'l Vital Stat. Rep. 9 (2004), http://www.cdc.gov/nchs/data/nvsr/nvsr53/nvsr5309.pdf. Still other children live with two unmarried adults who may not remain together permanently. In March 2002, for example, 15% of all children under 15 living with a single mother or a single father were living in households with two cohabiting but unmarried adults, at least one of whom was their biological parent. Jason Fields, U.S. Census Bureau, Publ'n No. P20–547, U.S. Census Current Population Reports, *Children's Living Arrangements and Characteristics: March 2002*, at 2, 4 (2003), http://www.census.gov/prod/2003pubs/p20–547.pdf.

The combination of a high divorce rate and high percentages of children born outside of marriage means that only an estimated one-quarter to one-half of children born at the turn of the twenty-first century will live with both parents throughout their entire childhood and adolescence. A. Leon Higginbotham, Jr. & Catherine J. Ross, *Introduction* to A.B.A. Presidential Working Group on the Unmet Legal Needs of Children and Their Families, America's Children at Risk: A National Agenda for

Legal Action vi (1993). A substantial portion of the children of divorcing, single and cohabiting parents will be the subject of custody disputes or agreements at some point before reaching majority. *See* Matthew D. Bramlett & William D. Mosher, Nat'l Center for Health Stat., U.S. Dep't of Health & Human Servs., *Cohabitation, Marriage, Divorce, and Remarriage in the United States*, 23 Vital & Health Stat. 22 (2002), http://www.cdc.gov/nchs/data/series/sr_23/sr23_022.pdf. Census data do not permit us to distinguish households in which both adults are the child's biological parents from households in which a child lives with one biological parent and that parent's significant other. But regardless of the marital or parental status of the adults with whom they live, all children are likely to suffer some degree of dislocation and trauma from dissolution of the household they live in.

Several factors help children adapt successfully to their parents' divorce and the custody arrangements that follow. Early social science studies forecasted catastrophic effects for children of divorce, but a large body of empirical research has since provided a more balanced albeit complex understanding of the impact of divorce on children. Despite a number of limitations, including the samples, the time frame, and questions concerning causality, the research reveals several consistent themes. Divorce is very stressful for all children, but the long-term effects on an individual child correlate with the child's individual resilience and support systems. E. Mavis Hetherington & John Kelly, For Better or Worse: Divorce Reconsidered 7–8 (2002). The three most important factors contributing to a child's healthy adjustment to divorce are the reduction of parental conflict, the presence of a well-functioning custodial parent, and regular contact with the non-custodial parent. Schepard, Children, Courts, and Custody, *supra* at 36–37.

Most parents reach custodial agreements without judicial intervention, often without any outside assistance and sometimes using alternative dispute resolution techniques such as those discussed in Chapter 15. Family law practitioners often encourage their clients to reduce stress on their children by pursuing conciliatory methods of resolving their custody and visitation disputes, and many parents are able to do so. A smaller number of parents pursue litigation to decide and modify custody and visitation, perpetuating a torrent of high-level conflicts that can linger in the court system for years, often until the child reaches majority. Experts consider these long-term, unresolved conflicts to be the most harmful aspect of family breakup for children. Michael E. Lamb et al., *The Effects of Divorce and Custody Arrangements on Children's Behavior, Development, and Adjustment*, 35 Fam. & Conciliation Cts. Rev. 393, 396 (1997). Chapter 13 will address these ongoing struggles.

Even when parents dissolving their relationship reach a private agreement concerning child custody and visitation, the agreement does not become effective until a court approves it. This Chapter examines the standards courts apply and the factors courts consider when, as a last resort, they are called upon to impose custody and visitation decisions on a family. As with decisions about how to divide a family's material assets, discussed in Chapter 9, private bargaining takes place in the shadow of the participants' predictions about the resolution the courts would likely otherwise impose.

The first Section of this Chapter explains the contemporary understanding of the constitutional rights of fit parents to the care, custody, and nurture of their children. The Chapter continues with a review of presumptions that once determined the outcome of custody disputes between parents: the paternal rights doctrine and the tender years doctrine. The Chapter then focuses on the meaning of the "best interests of the child" standard, on the factors that courts often weigh in determining custody disputes, and on some alternatives that have been suggested, including various ways of learning what the children themselves want. Finally, you will learn about ongoing controversies involving shared parenting time.

SECTION 1: CONSTITUTIONAL CONSIDERATIONS

Chapter 1 introduced *Meyer* and *Pierce*, the Supreme Court decisions that established a parent's Fourteenth Amendment substantive due process liberty interest in the care, custody and nurture of his or her children. These decisions presumed a model of married parents who agreed about major family decisions. Custody disputes are grounded in constitutional law emanating from the *Meyer–Pierce* line of decisions, but parental discord can strain the classic model. Other complex issues arise when a custody dispute pits a biological parent against a non-parent. A custody dispute between a child's father and maternal grandparents gave rise to the following custody decision that examines the evolution of the parental rights doctrine.

McDERMOTT v. DOUGHERTY

Court of Appeals of Maryland, 2005.
869 A.2d 751.

Cathell, J.

This appeal arises as an outgrowth of the lengthy and unfortunately acrimonious dispute over custody of Patrick Michael McDermott * * *, the minor son of petitioner Charles David McDermott * * *, between Mr. McDermott and respondents, Hugh and Marjorie Dougherty, the child's maternal grandparents * * *.[1]

* * * The circuit court issued its decision on September 8, 2003, awarding the maternal grandparents sole legal and physical custody of the child based upon that court's finding that Ms. Dougherty was "unfit,"

---

1. There has also been litigation between petitioner and Laura A. Dougherty * * *, the child's natural mother and petitioner's former wife. The conflicts between them are not at issue in the present case.

and, *although not finding Mr. McDermott an "unfit"* parent, the court found that his employment in the merchant marine, requiring him to spend months-long intervals at sea, constituted "exceptional circumstances" as that term was defined in *Ross v. Hoffman*, 372 A.2d 582, 593 (1977), and the "best interest of the child" and need for a stable living situation thus warranted that custody be placed with the Doughertys. * * *

[The intermediate court affirmed the lower court's decision.]

* * *

We hold that in disputed custody cases where private third parties are attempting to gain custody of children from their natural parents, the trial court must first find that both natural parents are unfit to have custody of their children or that extraordinary circumstances exist which are significantly detrimental to the child remaining in the custody of the parent or parents, before a trial court should consider the "best interests of the child" standard as a means of deciding the dispute.

We further hold that under circumstances in which there is no finding of parental unfitness, the requirements of a parent's employment, such that he is required to be away at sea, or otherwise appropriately absent from the State for a period of time, and for which time he or she made appropriate arrangements for the care of the child, do not constitute "extraordinary or exceptional circumstances" to support the awarding of custody to a third party.

Accordingly, we shall reverse and direct the lower courts to grant custody of Patrick to petitioner. Although we find the declaration, announced by the plurality opinion in *Troxel* [*v. Granville*], affirming "the fundamental right of parents to make decisions concerning the care, custody, and control of their children," 530 U.S. 57, 66 (2000), to be instructive, our determination also rests upon the potential for absurd results that might result from a holding that denies custody to a fit and willing parent on the basis that the means by which he or she supports himself or herself and his or her family calls for his or her periodic absence from the State although having arranged suitable and safe alternative care for the child, or based upon the fact that the child, in a particular case, might be "better raised" by grandparents. * * *

I. Facts

By the time of the current dispute there had been a lengthy series of events in the dispute over the custody of Patrick Michael McDermott, born April 30, 1995, to Charles David McDermott and Laura A. Dougherty, who were married on November 26, 1994 * * *. * * * [T]he spouses separated shortly after Patrick's birth. * * * [In] the action to which the instant appeal can be most directly traced, various parties, whether represented by counsel or proceeding [*pro se*], utilized the full measure of the court's resources in their filings of petitions and motions in regard to support and custody of Patrick.

[Ms. Dougherty, who had a history of alcohol abuse, was incarcerated after her fourth conviction for drunk driving. Just before beginning her jail term in 2002, Ms. Dougherty, who had residential custody of Patrick, signed a power of attorney entrusting Patrick to the care of her parents. At about the same time, McDermott filed for a modification of custody under which he would share custody with the child's maternal grandparents. Just before filing his petition, McDermott signed on for six months of employment at sea.

While McDermott was at sea, his relationship with his former wife's parents deteriorated. In February 2002, the Doughertys filed for third-party custody of Patrick by *ex parte* order, requesting McDermott's parents share joint legal custody with them. At an *ex parte* hearing, the court ordered temporary joint legal custody to the Doughertys and McDermott's parents, with residential custody to the Doughertys. When McDermott returned from sea, the Doughertys allowed Patrick to return to his father "to mollify the child's sustained entreaties and crying that he wanted to be with his father." McDermott filed a petition seeking permanent legal and physical custody of Patrick; his parents supported the petition, but the Doughertys filed an opposition.

In December 2002, McDermott retained an attorney, and went to sea again in early 2003 "in order to 'make the money to pay'" the attorney who was handling his custody case. During a two-week break in March 2003, McDermott returned to Maryland to see his son.

The court ultimately found the mother, Ms. Dougherty, to be unfit to have custody of Patrick.

The merits trial on McDermott's custody petition and the Dougherty[s'] opposition took place in July 2003. The maternal grandparents argued that by this time they had provided a stable home for Patrick for four years. The parties continued to jostle for custody while the ruling remained pending. In September 2003, the trial court granted sole legal and physical custody to the Doughertys. McDermott appealed.]

II. Discussion

A. Fundamental Constitutional Parental Right to Raise One's Children

One of the earlier United States Supreme Court cases in respect to parental rights, and one that has been described in subsequent cases as seminal, is the case of *Meyer v. Nebraska*, 262 U.S. 390 (1923) * * *. It is important primarily for its language, which stressed the importance of family in our society. * * *

* * *

One of the early cases citing to *Meyer* was *Pierce v. Society of Sisters of the Holy Names of Jesus and Mary*, 268 U.S. 510, 530 (1925) * * *. The Court [relied on *Meyer* for the proposition that: "The child is not the mere creature of the state; those who nurture him and direct his destiny have the right, coupled with the high duty, to recognize and prepare him for additional obligations.''][

* * *

In the 1970's the United States Supreme Court wrestled with a series of cases that, although not always directly concerning custody issues, continued to recognize the importance of the rights of parents.

In *Stanley v. Illinois*, 405 U.S. 645, 651–58 (1972) * * * [t]he Court said:

* * *

"The private interest here, that of a man in the children he has sired and raised, undeniably warrants deference and, absent a powerful countervailing interest, protection. It is plain that the interest of a parent in the companionship, care, custody, and management of his or her children 'come[s] to this Court with a momentum for respect lacking when appeal is made to liberties which derive merely from shifting economic arrangements.'

"The Court has frequently emphasized the importance of family. The rights to conceive and raise one's children have been deemed 'essential,' *Meyer v. Nebraska*, 'basic civil rights of man,' *Skinner v. Oklahoma*, 316 U.S. 535, 541 (1942), and '[r]ights far more precious . . . than property rights,' *May v. Anderson*, 345 U.S. 528, 533 (1953). 'It is cardinal with us that the custody, care and nurture of the child reside first in the parents, whose primary function and freedom include preparation for obligations the state can neither supply nor hinder.' *Prince v. Massachusetts*, 321 U.S. 158, 166 (1944). The integrity of the family unit has found protection in the Due Process Clause of the Fourteenth Amendment, the Equal Protection Clause of the Fourteenth Amendment, and the Ninth Amendment, *Griswold v. Connecticut*, 381 U.S. 479, 496 (1965) (GOLDBERG, J., concurring).

* * *

Wisconsin v. Yoder, 406 U.S. 205, 214–42 (1972) * * * was also based in part on the fundamental rights of parents to raise their children. The Court stated:

* * *

" * * * [T]his case involves the fundamental interest of parents, as contrasted with that of the State, to guide the religious future and education of their children * * *. Th[e] *primary* role of the parents in the upbringing of their children is now established *beyond debate* as an enduring American tradition. [The Court then cited to *Pierce* and *Meyer*].''

In the exclusionary zoning case of *Moore v. City of East Cleveland*, 431 U.S. 494, 499–508 (1977) [*Ed.'s note*: Chapter 1 of this book] * * *, the Court noted:

" * * * 'This Court has long recognized that freedom of personal choice in matters of marriage and family life is one of the liberties protected by the Due Process Clause of the Fourteenth Amendment.' A host of cases, tracing their lineage to *Meyer* ... have consistently acknowledged a 'private realm of family life which the state cannot enter.' Of course, the family is not beyond regulation. But when the government intrudes on choices concerning family living arrangements, this Court must examine carefully the importance of the governmental interests advanced and the extent to which they are served by the challenged regulation.['']

* * *

Quilloin v. Walcott, 434 U.S. 246 (1978), was a factually unusual case, and is one of, if not the only, case in which the Supreme Court upheld the sole use of the "best interests" standard in regard to the third-party placement of children, although at the same time it opined that *if a parent were fit* it would generally be constitutionally prohibited to take custody from that parent on the basis of the "best interest of the child." * * *

* * *

"We have little doubt that the Due Process Clause would be offended '[i]f a State were to attempt to force the breakup of a natural family, over the objections of the parents and their children, *without some showing of unfitness and for the sole reason that to do so was thought to be in the children's best interest.'* But this is not a case in which the unwed father at any time had, or sought, actual or legal custody of his child. * * *['']

[*Id.*] at 254–55 (emphasis added).

* * *

Even in *Lassiter v. Department of Social Services of Durham County*, 452 U.S. 18, 27 (1981), a case in which the Supreme Court upheld the denial of legal representation for indigent parents in state generated termination cases, the Court nevertheless, recognized the fundamental and constitutional rights of parents to raise their children:

"This Court's decisions have by now made plain beyond the need for multiple citation that a parent's desire for and right to 'the companionship, care, custody and management of his or her children' is an important interest that 'undeniably warrants deference and, absent a powerful countervailing interest, protection.' * * *['']

* * *

In *M.L.B. v. S.L.J.*, 519 U.S. 102, 116 (1996) [*Ed.'s note*: an appeal by a biological mother whose parental rights had been terminated to free her child for a step-parent adoption], the Court reversed a Mississippi case which had upheld a state statute that required certain fees to be paid before an appeal could be taken. * * * The Court found for the mother. Justice Ginsburg writing for the Court stated that:

> "Choices about marriage, family life, and the upbringing of children are among associational rights this Court has ranked as 'of basic importance in our society,' rights sheltered by the Fourteenth Amendment against the State's unwarranted usurpation, disregard, or disrespect. * * *

* * *

> " * * * [T]he Court was unanimously of the view that 'the interest of parents in their relationship with their children is sufficiently fundamental to come within the finite class of liberty interests protected by the Fourteenth Amendment.' It was also the Court's unanimous view that '[f]ew consequences of judicial action are so grave as the severance of natural family ties.' "

In the recent case of *Troxel v. Granville*, 530 U.S. 57 (2000), the Court reaffirmed its principles, in a challenge to a third-party visitation statute in the state of Washington. * * *

In *Troxel,* a mother desired to limit her children's visitation with the parents of their deceased father, a man to whom she had never been married. The paternal grandparents invoked a Washington statute that permitted any person to petition the superior court for visitation rights of any child at any time, and gave discretion to the court to grant visitation when in the best interest of the children, without regard to any change in circumstances. * * * In criticizing the trial court's "slender findings" in support of its visitation order, the United States Supreme Court faulted the statute's failure to accord sufficient deference to the parent's interests * * *. In addition, *Troxel* observed that the trial court did not order non-parental visitation based upon "any special factors [*i.e.,* exceptional circumstances] that might justify the State's interference with [the mother's] fundamental right to make decisions concerning the rearing of her [children]" [*Id.*] at 68 (alterations added).

* * *

> * * * [T]he *Troxel* decision affirmed the Washington Supreme Court's invalidation of a state statute because the Due Process Clause does not permit a State to "infringe on the fundamental right of parents to make child rearing decisions simply because a state judge believes a 'better' decision could be made." [*Id.*] at 72–73. Accordingly, *Troxel* is further instructive as to this case insofar as it recognizes the parent's fundamental right to direct his or her children's care, custody and control, and it impliedly rejects the substitution of a judge's opinion that a particular child would be better raised in a situation a trial judge prefers.[13] [*Ed.'s note: Troxel* is covered in Chapter 13 of this book.]

* * *

***

13. Every child might be "better" in a different situation in the opinion of one judge or another. The "best interest" standard is not a rule to be used to take children away from fit

The circumstances of the case *sub judice* illuminate a complexity in the "best interests of the child" standard that governs, *inter alia,* custody disputes between parents. In a situation in which both parents seek custody, each parent proceeds in possession, so to speak, of a constitutionally-protected fundamental parental right. Neither parent has a superior claim to the exercise of this right to provide "care, custody, and control" of the children. *See* Md. Code [Ann., Fam. Law] § 5–203 (d)(2) [2004].[14] Effectively, then, each fit parent's constitutional right neutralizes the other parent's constitutional right, leaving, generally, the best interests of the child as the *sole standard* to apply to these types of custody decisions. Thus, in evaluating each parent's request for custody, the parents commence as presumptive equals and a trial court undertakes a balancing of each parent's relative merits to serve as the primary custodial parent; the child's best interests tips the scale in favor of an award of custody to one parent or the other.

Where the dispute is between a fit parent and a private third party, however, both parties do not begin on equal footing in respect to rights to "care, custody, and control" of the children. The parent is asserting a fundamental constitutional right. The third party is not. A private third party has no fundamental constitutional right to raise the children of others. Generally, absent a constitutional statute, the non-governmental third party has no rights, constitutional or otherwise, to raise someone else's child.

B. Best Interests of the Child in the Absence of Parental Unfitness and Extraordinary or Exceptional Circumstances

The arguments and outcome of the instant case in no way alter the "best interests of the child" standard that governs courts' assessments of disputes *between fit parents* involving visitation or custody. We have frequently and repeatedly emphasized that in situations where it applies, it is the central consideration. So critical is the best interests standard that it has garnered superlative language in the many cases in which the concept appears: This Court labeled it "of transcendent importance" in *Dietrich v. Anderson*, 43 A.2d 186, 191 (Md. 1945), as the "ultimate test" in *Fanning v. Warfield*, 248 A.2d 890, 894 (Md. 1969), and as the "controlling factor" in *In re Adoption/Guardianship No. 10941*, 642 A.2d 201, 208 (Md. 1994). Although the child's well-being remains the focus of a court's analysis in disputes between fit parents, "[t]he best interests standard does not ignore the interests of the parents and their importance to the child. We recognize that in almost all cases, it is in the best

---

parents and give them to third parties because a judge believes the child will be better off with richer, better educated, more stable, third parties. If that were so, no parent would be safe from having his or her children given to others to raise. The phrase "best interests of the child" is not synonymous with "with whomever the child would be better off." Children are born into different circumstances. They are dealt different hands. The vast majority of them cope. Some from humble origins and upbringing even end up on state supreme courts. It is simply the way life is.

14. Md. Code [Ann., Fam. Law] § 5–203 (d)(2) [2004] states, "Neither parent is presumed to have any right to custody that is superior to the right of the other parent."

interests of the child to have reasonable maximum opportunity to develop a close and loving relationship with each parent." *Boswell v. Boswell*, 721 A.2d 662, 669 (Md. 1998).

C.   Standards for Custody Determination

When considering the application of the "best interests of the child" standard it is essential to frame the different situations in which it is attempted to be applied. First, and certainly the most important application of the standard, is in disputes between fit natural parents, each of whom has equal constitutional rights to parent. In those cases the dispute can be resolved best if not solely, by an application of the "best interests of the child" standard. This situation most often arises in marriage dissolution issues between natural parents and it is necessary to resolve the matters of custody and visitation between two constitutionally equally qualified parents. * * *

The second most frequent situation in which that standard has been applied is, we believe, in the various types of state proceedings in which the states are injecting themselves into the parenting situation in the exercise of their generally recognized power to protect the child. * * *

This category is generically referred to as "third-party" custody disputes, *i.e.*, persons other than natural parents or the State attempting, directly or indirectly, to gain or maintain custody or visitation in respect to the children of natural parents. * * *

Even within the third-party subset of custody actions there are further differences. Some states have conceptualized the idea of * * * third parties who have, in effect, become parents and thus, the case is considered according to the standards that apply between natural parents. This further reduces the number of pure third-party cases. The pure third-party cases are further narrowed in some jurisdictions by "failure of adoption" cases, in which, upon the "failure of adoption," a "best interest" standard may be applied. In still other pure third-party cases, in respect to the standard to be used, all parties seeking custody of children are designated as third parties. In that situation there are no constitutional rights involved (although in some cases constitutional claims are made using terms such as "psychological parent" and the like) and the "best interest" standard is generally applied. * * *

* * *

D.   Holding

The best interests of the child standard is, axiomatically, of a different nature than a parent's fundamental constitutional right. Moreover, the best interests of the child standard in third-party cases is not simply an adding of the "pluses" offered by one party over another. Were that so, any third party who offered a better neighborhood, better schooling, more financial capability, or more stability would consistently prevail in obtaining custody in spite of a fit natural parent's constitutional right to parent.

Our case law does not allow for such a result that dilutes a parent's constitutional right to rear his or her child based merely upon such considerations. Quite simply, the non-constitutional best interests of the child standard, absent extraordinary (*i.e.,* exceptional) circumstances, does not override a parent's fundamental constitutional right to raise his or her child when the case is between a fit parent, to whom the fundamental parental right is inherent, and a third party who does not possess such constitutionally-protected parental rights. In cases *between fit natural parents* who both have the fundamental constitutional rights to parent, the best interests of the child will be the "ultimate, determinative factor." In respect to third-party custody disputes, we shall adopt for Maryland, if we have not already done so, the majority position. In the balancing of court-created or statutorily-created "standards," such as "the best interest of the child" test, with fundamental constitutional rights, in private custody actions involving private third-parties where the parents are fit, absent extraordinary (*i.e.,* exceptional) circumstances, the constitutional right is the ultimate determinative factor; and only if the parents are unfit or extraordinary circumstances exist is the "best interest of the child" test to be considered * * *.

E. Factors for a Finding of "Exceptional Circumstances"

* * * We stated in *Ross v. Hoffman*:

"The factors which emerge from our prior decisions which may be of probative value in determining the existence of exceptional circumstances include the [1] length of time the child has been away from the biological parent, [2] the age of the child when care was assumed by the third party, [3] the possible emotional effect on the child of a change of custody, [4] the period of time which elapsed before the parent sought to reclaim the child, [5] the nature and strength of the ties between the child and the third party custodian, [6] the intensity and genuineness of the parent's desire to have the child, [7] the stability and certainty as to the child's future in the custody of the parent."

[372 A.2d 582, 593 (1977)] (alterations added). * * *

The circuit court examined each of the *Hoffman* guidelines in turn, and, in its opinion, found Mr. McDermott's relationship with Patrick to be wanting, particularly in relation to his absences from the child's life while at sea. The circuit court presented the following summary in its September 2003 memorandum opinion, which stated, in relevant part:

* * *

6. *The intensity and genuineness of the parent's desire to have the child. It is clear from Mr. McDermott's testimony that he feels that Patrick's interests are served by being in his custody, that his care and custody would be superior to any other family member, and that he has a genuine interest in raising Patrick.* However, the court is unable to agree with the totality of Mr. McDermott's self-assessment. It has

appeared at various time[s] during these proceedings that Mr. McDermott's interest in having custody of Patrick was not strictly limited to his desire to care for Patrick, but also his desire to control Ms. Dougherty, and that he has used Patrick as a pawn in the ongoing engagement between Ms. Dougherty and himself. * * *

7. *The stability and certainty as to the child's future in the custody of the parent.* Mr. McDermott was initially awarded custody in this case. For the most part, custody was changed first to Ms. Dougherty and then to the Doughertys because of Mr. McDermott's lengthy periods of absence from the State due to his employment as a merchant seaman. It would appear that Mr. McDermott's periodic absences and relinquishment of custody [have] had adverse effects on Patrick. For example, shortly after Ms. Dougherty's arrest and subsequent incarceration in early 2002, Mr. McDermott signed onto ship going to Africa and not expected to return until summer 2002.... It is self-evident that a revolving door of custodians would not be in Patrick's best interest, now or in the future."

We conclude that the circuit court inappropriately found that the absences inherent in Mr. McDermott's job requirements constituted "exceptional circumstances."

First, we note that, although the [circuit court] expressed some reservation as to Mr. McDermott's ability to provide a "consistent and stable environment for his child," it failed to find Mr. McDermott to be an unfit parent and it is presumed that fit parents act in the best interests of their children. * * *

Mr. McDermott's parental fitness having been established, or more precisely, not adjudged to be lacking, the inquiry, according to *Hoffman,* shifts to examining whether any "exceptional circumstances" exist that might overcome the presumption favoring a fit parent's rearing of his child * * *. It is in this latter phase of the inquiry that the circuit court erred by inappropriately equating "exceptional circumstances" with the absences occasioned by Mr. McDermott's merchant marine work. By finding that the dictates of Mr. McDermott's employment voided his right to be a custodial parent, the circuit court overlooked its own lack of a finding of unfitness and failed to accord petitioner with the presumptive benefits of a natural parent, especially a fit natural parent.

* * * [T]his Court [has previously] explained the requisite showing to overcome the presumption that a child's best interests are served by the child's remaining in the custody of the parent:

"Where parents claim the custody of a child, there is a *prima facie* presumption that the child's welfare will be best subserved in the care and custody of its parents rather than in the custody of others, and the burden is then cast upon the parties opposing them to show the contrary." * * * **44** * * *

F. Father's Employment in the Merchant Marine

Mr. McDermott is a graduate of the United States Merchant Marine Academy and a licensed ship Captain in the Merchant Marine. Many of his previous jobs have involved maritime work. Prior to his marriage he worked aboard ships but upon his marriage he ceased ocean-going and worked primarily in the Port of Baltimore. Following his divorce from Ms. Dougherty, petitioner accepted periodic jobs which took him to sea for several months at a time. Such is the nature of much maritime work, and the attendant required time commitments also are not uncommon in other lines of work including military deployments, ground transportation of goods, natural gas and oil production, offshore commercial fishing, sport fishing, etc.

Mr. McDermott's job duties do not involve work that is illegal, untoward, or otherwise injurious. Nor is there evidence in this case of any illegal conduct on his part. * * * This Court recognizes Maryland's tradition as a maritime State * * * and going to sea is but one of many occupations which require the worker to depart the State and absent himself or herself for months at a time. We would be loathe to reach a holding that jeopardizes a fit parent's right to custody of his child, by the change of custody to third parties, simply because the source of what is his livelihood and his means to support himself and his family takes him from the State for months' long periods of time.

* * *

The absences inherent to Mr. McDermott's merchant marine work are not unlike those required of military personnel or others in occupations mandating periods of service away from one's home. Custody issues should be determined on a case-by-case basis. * * *

* * *

Although the Doughertys did not maintain Patrick in their home and raise the child from infancy, the relative regularity of their contribution as well as the positive contribution of all grandparents must be acknowledged. Nevertheless, their efforts on Patrick's behalf under the circumstances of this case cannot overcome the fundamental constitutional right of a fit parent to exercise care and custody of his child and the circuit court, clearly impressed with the grandparents' care, cannot invoke absences occasioned by the parent's proper employment in support of placing the child with the grandparents due to "exceptional circumstances."

* * *

---

44. * * *

Our courts over the years have found "exceptional circumstances" in awarding custody even to third parties, generally upon a parent's prolonged, non-work-related absence and the child's having been in the consistent care of a third party for a period of years. * * * *In the present case, the father's absences have not been computed in years' long periods, nor is there evidence that the child has failed to maintain bonds with him.*

* * *

III.   Conclusion

In this case there is no doubt that Patrick loves his father and Mr. McDermott loves his son. Petitioner has maintained his relationship with his son since the child's birth, even when the child was not domiciled with him. The results of myriad examinations, reports and testimony were insufficient to convince the circuit court that Mr. McDermott was an unfit parent, and clearly, Mr. McDermott's vigorous use of the family courts provides insight on his desire to have custody of Patrick. Courts cannot preempt the established and constitutionally-protected fundamental rights of a parent, who is not "unfit," simply because that parent's job takes him from the State for extended periods of time or merely because a child might be better off, in a particular judge's view, living elsewhere. The circuit court erred in invoking the dictates of Mr. McDermott's work as a merchant marine, insofar as the requirements of the job caused him to be absent from the state for several months-long periods of time, and arriving at the conclusion that application of the guidelines for "exceptional circumstances" warranted placing Patrick in the custody of his maternal grandparents.

We reverse the judgment of the Court of Special Appeals and remand to that court with instructions to reverse the decision of the circuit court. The case is ordered remanded to the circuit court in order for it to address the issue of counsel fees. All costs to be paid by respondents.[49]

Judgment of the court of special appeals reversed. Case remanded to that court * * *.

WILNER, J. concurs.

I concur in the judgment because it is clear to me that, under the standards that this Court has consistently applied since *Ross v. Hoffman,* 372 A.2d 582 (1977), the trial court erred in granting custody of Patrick to the Doughertys. * * * [I]t is not clear to me what the Court has really done in its 113–page slip opinion, other than to sow uncertainty and confusion in an area that demands clear and accessible guidelines.

In *Ross,* this Court, synthesizing earlier decisions, laid out a very clear standard for resolving custody disputes between a parent and a non-parent. We said:

> " * * * When the dispute is between a biological parent and a third party, it is presumed that the child's best interest is subserved by custody in the parent. That presumption is overcome and such custody will be denied if (a) the parent is unfit to have custody, or (b) if there are such exceptional circumstances as [to] make such custody detrimental to the best interest of the child."

Id., 372 A.2d at 587.

---

49. * * *

The Court has gone to great lengths to affirm that the present opinion is limited to the context of attempts by pure third parties to gain custody over the children of others.

We recognized in *Ross* that parents "have the natural right to the custody of their children," but regarded the strong presumption in favor of such custody as sufficient to protect that right. We made clear that "the ordinary entitlement of parents to the custody of their minor children" was not absolute and that it "would not be enforced inexorably, contrary to the best interest of the child, on the theory of an absolute legal right."

* * *

Only two years ago, in *Shurupoff v. Vockroth*, * * * we consciously and clearly confirmed what we said and held in *Ross*: "The court must always, necessarily, inquire into what is in the child's best interest, *for that is the ultimate, determinative factor*." [814 A.2d 543, 557 (2003)] (emphasis added). * * *

The Court today, in a 113–page slip opinion suggests, with its right hand, that the best interest of the child standard no longer applies in disputes between a parent and a non-parent—that the parent's Constitutional right to custody is predominant—but, with its left hand, seems to indicate that that is not the case at all, and that, in the end, courts must act in the child's best interest. Why the Court chooses to take such an unnecessarily convoluted path is a mystery to me.

* * *

In the end, even under the Court's new approach, the trial court will have to apply the best interest standard. The Court agrees that a parent's Constitutional right to raise his/her children is not absolute. It agrees that custody may be denied to a parent if the evidence shows that the parent is unfit, and it even continues to bless the alternative basis for denying parental custody—exceptional circumstances *which would made* [sic] *parental custody detrimental to the child's best interest*. That will necessarily require the court to examine and be governed by what is in the child's best interest. So why go through 113 pages of convolution to say, in the end, what has already been said, confirmed, and reconfirmed in a few clear simple paragraphs?

NOTES AND QUESTIONS

1. *Questions about* McDermott. (a) Patrick McDermott was 10 years old when the case reached the Court of Appeals, Maryland's highest court. Does the court give any indication that the trial court ever asked the boy what custodial arrangement he preferred? Should it have done so? (b) If the Court of Appeals had affirmed the decision below, would the holding have stood for the proposition that any single parent on active duty in the Merchant Marine could lose custody of his or her children to a relative? (c) Aside from the constitutional doctrine, why does the law presume that a child's best custodians are his or her parents? (d) What do you think the result in *McDermott* would have been if the father testified that he planned to take the child with him for months while he was aboard ship, thereby causing the boy to miss school? (e) How would you distinguish a divorce proceeding in which Patrick's

parents were both fit, both sought custody, and Mr. McDermott planned to remain in the Merchant Marine and at sea for months at a time?

2. *The risks of asking for help.* For many reasons, including illness or financial instability, a custodial parent may find it impossible to provide adequately for a child for some period of time. Parents in distress may choose to place their children temporarily with a relative or friend on the condition that they will regain custody once their problems have been resolved. If the temporary custodian bonds with the child, or comes to view the parent as unfit, however, the custodian may turn around and seek a judicial determination of custody.

Courts consider many factors in determining whether a parent may regain custody of a child once relinquished for temporary informal care, including: (1) the circumstances under which the parent relinquished custody; (2) proof that the parent is fit and will properly care for the child; (3) the amount of contact, in the form of visits or financial support, the parent had with the child during the period of separation; and (4) the degree of attachment between the child and the temporary custodian. George L. Blume, *Right of Parent to Regain Custody of Child after Temporary Conditional Relinquishment of Custody*, 6 A.L.R. 6th 229 (2005).

In accordance with *Meyer* and *Pierce*, parents have a *prima facie* right to custody of their children, but they may forfeit this right through their actions, no matter how fit they may be in other respects. Decisions turn on the facts. In *Willette v. Bannister*, 351 So.2d 605, 606 (Ala. Ct. Civ. App. 1977), for example, the court granted the maternal grandmother custody after her daughter had repeatedly left her five-year-old child with the grandmother for long periods.

3. *Distinguishing the nature of child custody disputes. McDermott* distinguishes among at least three kinds of child custody disputes: (1) disputes between two legal parents, (2) disputes between one or two parents on the one hand, and a third party on the other (the situation in *McDermott* itself), and (3) disputes in which the state challenges parental custody based on alleged abuse or neglect. What difference do these distinctions make in determining the standards the court applies and the strength of the parents' constitutional rights?

4. *Is child custody a zero-sum game?* Is it possible to weigh each parent's constitutional interest in his or her child equally, and at the same time make each child's best interests paramount to the custody decision? What are the obstacles to balancing each of these concerns with the others?

5. *What are "exceptional circumstances"? McDermott* states the majority rule, which protects the rights of fit parents to custody of their children in contests against third parties. Absent allegations of neglect or abuse, courts rarely find "exceptional circumstances" sufficient to deny custody to a biological or adoptive parent. For example, in a proceeding filed by the lesbian partner of an adoptive mother, the Maryland Court of Appeals, applying *McDermott,* declined to find exceptional circumstances sufficient to order visitation between the partner and the child she had helped raise for five years, from the moment of adoption. *Janice M.* v. *Margaret K.*, 948 A.2d 73 (Md. 2008).

One of the rare decisions to recognize exceptional circumstances is *Banks v. Banks*, 726 N.Y.S.2d 795 (App. Div. 2001), which followed guidelines similar to those set forth in *Ross v. Hoffman* (cited in *McDermott*). After the death of the children's father, *Banks* granted custody to the children's stepmother over their biological mother's objection. The court noted the poor relationship between the children and their biological mother, "as evidenced by their refusal to visit her on the weekends"; the special needs of the older child, who had behavioral problems and a history of drug and alcohol abuse; and the mother's own testimony that she was no longer involved in the children's school or extracurricular activities and visited the children only sporadically.

The court also found exceptional circumstances in *Parliament v. Harris*, 697 N.Y.S.2d 694 (App. Div. 1999), where a 15–year–old boy's biological father was incarcerated for sexually abusing his long-term girlfriend's daughter. The father had not abused his own son. The court granted custody to the father's girlfriend because the boy and his brother had lived in the woman's home for nine years, had a close and loving relationship with her, and expressed their desire to remain in her home.

What other circumstances do you think courts should consider as "exceptional"?

SECTION 2: HISTORICAL EVOLUTION OF PRESUMPTIONS GOVERNING CHILD CUSTODY

During the colonial period and the early republic, American jurisdictions followed English common law, which gave fathers absolute control of their children according to the doctrine of *pater familias*, a concept rooted in Roman law, which made the father "master" of the family, with authority over its members. Judges sometimes deviated from the rule, but their primary task was to determine whether a specific situation required deviation. By the 1820s, however, pressure from the women's movement led courts to shift their focus and consider whether mothers should be treated equally, or even receive preferential treatment. *See* Michael Grossberg, Governing the Hearth: Law and the Family in Nineteenth Century America 244–47 (1985).

A. THE TENDER YEARS DOCTRINE

Once courts had to choose between parents seeking custody, a number of presumptions evolved in many jurisdictions. By the late nineteenth century, one rule that emerged as a new orthodoxy was that children of "tender years"—that is, infants and very young children—should be placed with their mother, unless she was unfit to care for them.

Two feminist scholars have discussed the tender years doctrine in cultural and historical perspective. When the doctrine was in its prime, they explain:

Children who were beyond the "tender" age * * * [were placed] with the parent of the same sex. The practical effect * * * was to implement, as a legal norm, the placement of infants and older female children with their mothers, while fathers claimed the benefits of older male children whose labor could contribute to the fathers' economic well-being.

In fact, both the system that gave fathers absolute rights over their children, and the reform of that system which led to the formulation of the "best interest" test, were consistent with the dominant paternalistic rhetoric of the times. While patriarchy was initially challenged by the wave of domestic feminist ideology and the cult of womanhood, it easily met the challenge and absorbed the opposition.

It is important to note that the changes in the rules were consistent with the dominant ideology of the time and represented the setting apart of women from the world of work and market. Assigning women care of younger children in the home was consistent with the notion that women needed to be sheltered and protected so that they could fulfill their destiny and reproduce and nurture the species. Motherhood, in both its legal and social manifestations, was thus constructed in a manner which gave women more power or rights in regard to their children, both in marriage and at divorce, so long as they did not violate other patriarchal norms such as fidelity and temperance.

* * *

The ideology of equality, the discourse of women's liberation, and the father's rights movement with its corresponding backlash, have set the stage for an attack on the norm of mother custody. As the divorce rate has increased, the notion of awarding custody to the mother, based on the "tender years" doctrine, has increasingly come under attack as presenting an unfair advantage to women. Perhaps ironically, the attack has in part been fueled by twentieth century feminist attacks on the cultural norms that excluded women from the market and relegated them to the home and child care. Part of the battle that these feminists fought was to break this rigid deterministic view of the lot of women and to bring men into the houses, sharing the duties so that women would be free to expend their energies at work. The rhetorical effect of such endeavors was an attempt to redefine the expectations associated with motherhood, making them merely equally dividable components of the responsibilities of "parenthood."

Martha L. Fineman & Anne Opie, *The Uses of Social Science Data in Legal Policymaking: Custody Determinations at Divorce,* 1987 Wis. L. Rev. 107, 112–13.

Beginning in the 1970s and accelerating during the 1980s, state courts began to hold that the tender years doctrine violated emerging constitutional law concerning gender equality. See Lynn Marie Kohm, Tracing the Foundation of the Best Interests of the Child Standard in American Jurisprudence, 10 J. L. & Fam. Stud. 337 (2008). In 1973, New York's highest court held that the doctrine was inconsistent with recent statutory amendments providing that "there shall be no *prima facie* right to the custody of the child in either parent," and that the doctrine did not serve the determinative statutory standard—the best interests of the child. *Watts v. Watts*, 350 N.Y.S.2d 285, 287 (N.Y. 1973). *Watts* held that a persistent preference for mothers—revealed in the facts of the case before it, and in data showing that "in well over ninety percent of the cases adjudicated, the mother is awarded custody"—violated fathers' rights to equal treatment under the law. *Id.* at 286. *Watts'* constitutional underpinnings came from *Frontiero v. Richardson*, 411 U.S. 677 (1973), and other decisions discussed in Chapter 4 of this book.

Watts concluded that the tender years presumption amounted to a "blanket judicial finding of fact * * * based on outdated social stereotypes rather than rational and up-to-date consideration of the welfare of the children involved." 350 N.Y.S.2d at 287. On remand, the family court awarded custody to the father.

Today, all 50 states have rejected the tender years doctrine. Julie E. Artis, *Judging the Best Interests of the Child: Judges' Accounts of the Tender Years Doctrine*, 38 Law & Soc'y Rev. 769, 774 (2004). However, some theorists, judges, and lawyers continue to believe that mothers are more important than fathers in the early stages of child development. In *Copeland v. Copeland*, 904 So.2d 1066 (Miss. 2004), the court permitted consideration of whether a child is of tender years as one factor in child custody determinations. South Carolina still uses the doctrine as a tie-breaker. *Woodall v. Woodall*, 471 S.E.2d 154 (S.C. 1996). Some trial courts expressly continue to apply the tender years doctrine and may be reversed for doing so. *See Johnson v. Adair*, 884 So.2d 1169, 1171 (Fla. Dist. Ct. App. 2004) (holding that grant of custody to mother "based on the [tender] age of the child" was contrary to statutes designed "to override the court's persistence in applying this doctrine").

With which parent do children of divorce live today? Exact figures are hard to come by, but children who live with only one parent following divorce remain far more likely to live with their mothers than their fathers. Based on an empirical study of families at three junctures following divorce, Professors Robert Mnookin and Eleanor Maccoby concluded that about 70% of children reside primarily with their mothers. The typical father in those instances maintained contact with the children through one or two overnight visits bi-weekly, and some daytime visits. The father was the primary custodian in only about 10% of the families. Robert Mnookin & Eleanor Maccoby, *Facing the Dilemmas of Child Custody*, 10 Va. J. Soc. Pol'y & L. 54, 57 (2002).

Census data indicate that children who live in a single-parent household are four times more likely to live with a single mother than a single father. Jason Fields, U.S. Census Bureau, Publ'n No. P20–547, U.S. Census Current Population Reports, *Children's Living Arrangements and Characteristics: March 2002*, at 2 (2003), http://www.census.gov/prod/2003 pubs/p20–547.pdf. On the other hand, the proportion of children who live primarily with a father is much higher than it was 30 years ago. In 1970, just 1% of U.S. households were headed by a single father, compared to 6% in 2003. Jason Fields, U.S. Census Bureau, Publ'n No. 20–553, Current Population Reports, *America's Families and Living Arrangements: 2003*, at 8 (2004), http://www.census.gov/prod/2004pubs/p20–553.pdf. The proportion of households headed by a single mother grew from 12% to 26% during the same time period. *Id.*

B. THE BEST INTERESTS OF THE CHILD

By the beginning of the nineteenth century, the presumption favoring fathers began to yield to the rights of mothers and some courts began to balance the rights of both parents. Initially courts were likely to find the father's presumptive rights rebutted only where they found him egregiously immoral—where, for example, they found evidence of adultery, alcoholism or spousal abuse. By the 1830s and 1840s, some states had enacted legislation that authorized courts to determine child custody on a case-by-case basis, placing the mother and father on an equal footing because " 'the happiness and welfare of the child are to determine its care and custody.' " Michael Grossberg, Governing the Hearth: Law and the Family in Nineteenth Century America 241 (1985) (quoting a Massachusetts statute enacted in the 1840s). This approach came to be known as "the best interests of the child."

Courts and legislatures have long used the term "best interests of the child" to describe the standard that should govern child custody decisions. But many observers have asked whether the best interests standard is a euphemism for unfettered judicial discretion. The following classic decision illustrates the range of factors a court can use to assess a child's best interests, and the lack of guidance the best interests standard provides for assessing those factors.

When reading this decision, consider how it compares to the lower court's decision in *McDermott v. Dougherty*.

PAINTER v. BANNISTER

Supreme Court of Iowa, 1966.
140 N.W.2d 152.

STUART, JUSTICE.

We are here setting the course for Mark Wendell Painter's future. Our decision on the custody of this 7 year old boy will have a marked influence on his whole life. The fact that we are called upon many times a year to determine custody matters does not make the exercising of this awesome responsibility any less difficult. Legal training and experience are of little practical help in solving the complex problems of human relations. However, these problems do arise and under our system of government, the burden of rendering a final decision rests upon us. It is frustrating to know we can only resolve, not solve, these unfortunate situations.

The custody dispute before us in this habeas corpus action is between the father, Harold Painter, and the maternal grandparents, Dwight and Margaret Bannister. Mark's mother and younger sister were killed in an automobile accident on December 6, 1962, near Pullman, Washington. The father, after other arrangements for Mark's care had proved unsatisfactory, asked the Bannisters, to take care of Mark. They went to California and brought Mark to their farm home near Ames in July, 1963. Mr. Painter remarried in November, 1964 and about that time indicated he wanted to take Mark back. The Bannisters refused to let him leave and this action was filed in June, 1965. Since July 1965 he has continued to remain in the Bannister home under an order of this court staying execution of the judgment of the trial court awarding custody to the father until the matter could be determined on appeal. For reasons hereinafter stated, we conclude Mark's better interests will be served if he remains with the Bannisters.

Mark's parents came from highly contrasting backgrounds. His mother was born, raised and educated in rural Iowa. Her parents are college graduates. Her father is agricultural information editor for the Iowa State University Extension Service. The Bannister home is in the Gilbert Community and is well kept, roomy and comfortable. The Bannisters are highly respected members of the community. Mr. Bannister has served on the school board and regularly teaches a Sunday school class at the Gilbert Congregational Church. Mark's mother graduated from Grinnell College. She then went to work for a newspaper in Anchorage, Alaska, where she met Harold Painter.

Mark's father was born in California. When he was 2 1/2 years old, his parents were divorced and he was placed in a foster home. Although he has kept in contact with his natural parents, he considers his foster parents, the McNellys, as his family. He flunked out of a high school and a trade school because of a lack of interest in academic subjects, rather than any lack of ability. He joined the navy at 17. He did not like it. After receiving an honorable discharge, he took examinations and obtained his high school diploma. He lived with the McNelly's [sic] and went to college for 2 1/2 years under the G. I. bill. He quit college to take a job on a small newspaper in Ephrata, Washington in November 1955. In May 1956, he went to work for the newspaper in Anchorage which employed Jeanne Bannister.

Harold and Jeanne were married in April, 1957. Although there is a conflict in the evidence on the point, we are convinced the marriage, overall, was a happy one with many ups and downs as could be expected in the uniting of two such opposites.

We are not confronted with a situation where one of the contesting parties is not a fit or proper person. * * * It is obvious the Bannisters did not approve of their daughter's marriage to Harold Painter and do not want their grandchild raised under his guidance. The philosophies of life are entirely different. As stated by the psychiatrist who examined Mr. Painter at the request of Bannisters' attorneys: "It is evident that there exists a large difference in ways of life and value systems between the Bannisters and Mr. Painter, but in this case there is no evidence that psychiatric instability is involved. Rather, these divergent life patterns seem to represent alternative normal adaptations."

It is not our prerogative to determine custody upon our choice of one of two ways of life within normal and proper limits and we will not do so. * * *

The Bannister home provides Mark with a stable, dependable, conventional, middle-class, middlewest background and an opportunity for a college education and profession, if he desires it. It provides a solid foundation and secure atmosphere. In the Painter home Mark would have more freedom of conduct and thought with an opportunity to develop his individual talents. It would be more exciting and challenging in many respects, but romantic, impractical and unstable.

* * *

Our conclusion as to the type of home Mr. Painter would offer is based upon his Bohemian approach to finances and life in general. We feel there is much evidence which supports this conclusion. His main ambition is to be a freelance writer and photographer. He has had some articles and picture stories published, but the income from these efforts has been negligible. * * * In the 10 years since he left college, he has changed jobs seven times. He was asked to leave two of them; two he quit because he didn't like the work; two because he wanted to devote more time to writing and the rest for better pay. He was contemplating a move to Berkeley at the time of trial. * * *

* * *

There is general agreement that Mr. Painter needs help with his finances. Both Jeanne and Marilyn, his present wife, handled most of them. Purchases and sales of books, boats, photographic equipment and houses indicate poor financial judgment and an easy come easy go attitude. He dissipated his wife's estate of about $4300, most of which was a gift from her parents and which she had hoped would be used for the children's education.

* * *

The house in which Mr. Painter and his present wife live, compared with the well kept Bannister home, exemplifies the contrasting ways of life. In his words "it is a very old and beat up and lovely home * * * ". They live in the rear part. The interior is inexpensively but tastefully decorated. The large yard on a hill in the business district of Walnut Creek, California, is of uncut weeds and wild oats. The house "is not painted on the outside because I do not want it painted. I am very fond of the wood on the outside of the house."

* * *

Mr. Painter is either an agnostic or atheist and has no concern for formal religious training. He has read a lot of Zen Buddhism and "has been very much influenced by it". Mrs. Painter is Roman Catholic. They plan to send Mark to a Congregational Church near the Catholic Church, on an irregular schedule.

He is a political liberal and got into difficulty in a job at the University of Washington for his support of the activities of the American Civil Liberties Union in the university news bulletin.

There were "two funerals" for his wife. One in the basement of his home in which he alone was present. He conducted the service and wrote her a long letter. The second at a church in Pullman was for the gratification of her friends. He attended in a sport shirt and sweater.

These matters are not related as a criticism of Mr. Painter's conduct, way of life or sense of values. An individual is free to choose his own values, within bounds, which are not exceeded here. They do serve however to support our conclusion as to the kind of life Mark would be exposed to in the Painter household. We believe it would be unstable, unconventional, arty, Bohemian, and probably intellectually stimulating.

Were the question simply which household would be the most suitable in which to rear a child, we would have unhesitatingly chosen the Bannister home. We believe security and stability in the home are more important than intellectual stimulation in the proper development of a child. There are, however, several factors which have made us pause.

First, there is the presumption of parental preference, which, though weakened in the past several years, exists by statute. We have a great deal of sympathy for a father who, in the difficult period of adjustment following his wife's death, turns to the maternal grandparents for their help and then finds them unwilling to return the child. There is no merit in the Bannister claim that Mr. Painter permanently relinquished custody. It was intended to be a temporary arrangement. A father should be encouraged to look for help with the children, [sic] from those who love them without the risk of thereby losing the custody of the children permanently. This fact must receive consideration in cases of this kind. However, as always, the primary consideration is the best interest of the child and if the return of custody to the father is likely to have a seriously disrupting and disturbing effect upon the child's development, this fact must prevail.

Second, Jeanne's will named her husband guardian of her children and if he failed to qualify or ceased to act, named her mother. The parent's wishes are entitled to consideration.

Third, the Bannisters are 60 years old. By the time Mark graduates from high school they will be over 70 years old. Care of young children is a strain on grandparents and Mrs. Bannister's letters indicate as much.

We have considered all of these factors and have concluded that Mark's best interest demands that his custody remain with the Bannisters. Mark was five when he came to their home. The evidence clearly shows he was not well adjusted at that time. He did not distinguish fact from fiction and was inclined to tell "tall tales" emphasizing the big "I". He was very aggressive toward smaller children, cruel to animals, not liked by his classmates and did not seem to know what was acceptable conduct. As stated by one witness: "Mark knew where his freedom was and he didn't know where his boundaries were." In two years he made a great deal of improvement. He now appears to be well disciplined, happy, relatively secure and popular with his classmates, although still subject to more than normal anxiety.

* * *

Dr. Hawks is head of the Department of Child Development at Iowa State University. * * *

Between June 15th and the time of trial he spent approximately 25 hours acquiring information about Mark and the Bannisters, including appropriate testing of and "depth interviews" with Mark. Dr. Hawks' testimony covers 70 pages of the record and it is difficult to pinpoint any bit of testimony which precisely summarizes his opinion. He places great emphasis on the "father figure" and discounts the importance of the "biological father.". "The father figure is a figure that the child sees as an authority figure, as a helper, he is a nutrient figure, and one who typifies maleness and stands as maleness as far as the child is concerned."

His investigation revealed: " * * * the strength of the father figure before Mark came to the Bannisters is very unclear. Mark is confused about the father figure prior to his contact with Mr. Bannister." Now, "Mark used Mr. Bannister as his father figure. This is very evident. It shows up in the depth interview, and it shows up in the description of Mark's life given by Mark. He has a very warm feeling for Mr. Bannister."

Dr. Hawks concluded that it was not for Mark's best interest to be removed from the Bannister home. He is criticized for reaching this conclusion without investigating the Painter home or finding out more about Mr. Painter's character. He answered:

> I was most concerned about the welfare of the child, not the welfare of Mr. Painter, not about the welfare of the Bannisters. Inasmuch as Mark has already made an adjustment and sees the Bannisters as his parental figures in his psychological makeup, to me this is the most critical factor. Disruption at this point, I think, would be detrimental to the child even tho [sic] Mr. Painter might well be a paragon of virtue. I think this would be a kind of thing which would not be in the best interest of the child.* * *

* * * I am appalled at the tremendous task Mr. Painter would have if Mark were to return to him because he has got to build the relationship from scratch. There is essentially nothing on which to build at the present time. * * *

It was Dr. Hawks' opinion "the chances are very high (Mark) will go wrong if he is returned to his father." This is based on adoption studies which "establish that the majority of adoptions in children who are changed, from ages six to eight, will go bad, if they have had a prior history of instability, some history of prior movement. When I refer to instability I am referring to where there has been no attempt to establish a strong relationship." Although this is not an adoption, the analogy seems appropriate, for Mark who had a history of instability would be removed from the only home in which he has a clearly established "father figure" and placed with his natural father about whom his feelings are unclear.

* * *

Other items of Dr. Hawks' testimony which have a bearing on our decision follow. He did not consider the Bannisters' age anyway disqualifying. He was of the opinion that Mark could adjust to a change more easily later on, if one became necessary, when he would have better control over his environment.

* * *

Mark has established a father-son relationship with Mr. Bannister, which he apparently had never had with his natural father. He is happy, well adjusted and progressing nicely in his development. We do not believe it is for Mark's best interest to take him out of this stable atmosphere in the face of warnings of dire consequences from an eminent child psychologist and send him to an uncertain future in his father's home. Regardless of our appreciation of the father's love for his child and his desire to have him with him, we do not believe we have the moral right to gamble with this child's future. He should be encouraged in every way possible to know his father. We are sure there are many ways in which Mr. Painter can enrich Mark's life.

For the reasons stated, we reverse the trial court and remand the case for judgment in accordance herewith.

Reversed and remanded.

All Justices concur * * *.

NOTES AND QUESTIONS

1. *Epilogue.* In August 1968, the Associated Press reported:

Joy fills Painter home. The Harold Painter household was filled with joy today because 10–year–old Mark Painter's grandmother in Iowa has said he can stay here with his father and new mother. 'There's no way to tell you how happy this makes us all,' said Harold Painter, Mark's father, foreseeing the peaceful end to a long custody battle over the boy. * * * The Rev. Mr. Lumpkins visited with the Painters here last week to ask the boy whether he wanted to stay on with his father or return to his grandparents in Iowa. * * * This summer Mark came west to spend his usual vacation with his father. He said he liked it here, wanted to stay and didn't want to go back to Iowa.

Associated Press, *Joy Fills Painter House,* Wash. Post & Times–Herald (1959–1973), Aug. 19, 1968, at B6.

2. *Postscript by a psychoanalyst.* In 1968, Dr. Anna Freud commented on *Painter v. Bannister*, noting the similarities to many other cases confronting children's clinics and highlighting the differences between legal and clinical approaches to child custody resolutions following divorce. In the following passage, Dr. Freud explains how a clinical resolution of custody differs from a court's imposition of a legal solution on the parties to a child custody dispute and argues for a very different kind of expert consultation than the one the court received in *Painter*:

> Unlike the two courts, [psychoanalysts] are in the lucky position not to have to pronounce judgment. [Psychoanalysts] merely formulate advice. When doing so, [psychoanalysts] disregard or minimize the importance of some of the facts which swayed the courts.
>
> In disagreement with the trial judge, and in agreement with his expert, Dr. Hawks, we discount the importance of the "biological father" as such. The 'blood-ties' between parent and child as well as the alleged paternal and maternal 'instincts' are biological concepts which, only too often, prove vague and unreliable when transferred to the field of psychology. Psychologically speaking, the child's 'father' is the adult man to whom the child attaches a particular, psychologically distinctive set of feelings. When this type of emotional tie is disrupted, the child's feelings suffer. When such separations occur during phases of development in which the child is particularly vulnerable, the whole foundation of his personality may be shaken. The presence of or the reunion with a biological father to whom no such ties exist will not recompense the child for the loss which he has suffered. Conversely, the biological father's or mother's unselfish love for their child is by no means to be taken for granted. It happens often enough that biological parents fail in their duty to the child, while other adults who are less closely related to him, i.e., who have no 'instinctive' basis for their feeling, successfully take over the parental role.
>
> We place less emphasis than Mr. Justice Stuart on benefits such as a 'stable, dependable background' with educational and professional opportunities. Important as such external advantages are, [psychoanalysts] have seen too often that they can be wasted unless they are accompanied by the internal emotional constellations which enable the children to profit from them. Children are known to thrive in socially and financially unstable situations if they are firmly attached to their parents, and to come to grief under the best social conditions when such emotional security is missing.

We are in agreement with Mr. Justice Stuart concerning the inadvisability of gambling with a child's future. So long as development seems to proceed well, we—like he—feel reluctant to interfere. On the other hand, on the basis of clinical experience, we have learned that in this respect, as in many others, surface appearances may be misleading.

It is not possible at this point to foretell whether, after investigation, our advice will be in line with the judgment of the trial court or with Mr. Justice Stuart. We shall advise that Mark had better stay with his grandparents provided that the following facts be ascertained: that the transfer of his attachment from the parents to the grandparents is fairly complete and promises to be permanent during his childhood; that, given this attachment, a further change is not advisable; and that the grandparents, on their part, cherish Mark for his own sake, not only as a replacement for the daughter who was killed, nor as a pawn in the battle with their son-in-law.

Conversely, we shall advise that Mark had better be returned to his father if the following facts emerge: that Mr. Painter still retains his place as 'father' in Mark's mind and that in spite of separation and new experiences the child's feelings and fantasies continue to revolve around him; that anger about the 'desertion' (and perhaps blame for his mother's death) have not succeeded in turning this relationship into a predominantly hostile one; that the father cherishes Mark for his own sake; and that it can be shown that Mr. Painter's using the child for publicity purposes was not due to lack of paternal consideration on his part but happened owing to the bitterness and resentment caused by the fight for possession of his son.

Anna Freud, *Painter v. Bannister: Postscript by a Psychoanalyst*, 7 Writings of Anna Freud 247–55 (1967).

3. *Competing policy grounds.* A number of competing policy considerations are at stake in a case like the one involving Mark Painter. Society may generally want to encourage parents to rely on extended family in times of crisis without jeopardizing their parental rights. Therefore, it may be disconcerting that the grandparents refused to return Mark when asked, and thus accomplished their goal of entrenching him even further in their household while the litigation progressed. How should the courts weigh such concerns against the needs of a particular child whose fate is being determined in a custody dispute? How do you feel about the *Painter* court's addressing such factors as Harold Painter's "political liberalism," his religious beliefs, his financial standing, and his apparent desire to "move to Berkeley"? The court stated that Harold Painter was not morally unfit, but does the decision mean the court found him an unfit parent? Could the trial court have spared the boy further emotional turmoil by simply asking him for his custodial preference, and then by considering that preference? If Mrs. Painter had not died and the Painters had divorced, would she necessarily have been entitled to custody of Mark? The state supreme court says that "[i]t is not our prerogative to determine custody upon our choice of one of two ways of life," but did the court nonetheless hand down a "hometown decision" based on local values? Should a third party ever be able to defeat a fit legal parent's custody

claim? If Mr. Painter had never relinquished temporary custody of his son, would a court have been justified in granting the grandparents' custody petition?

4. *The vanished world of the Bannisters.* Legal scholars continue to probe the significance of *Painter* v. *Bannister.* Professor Carol Weisbrod proposes that the case exists "between two worlds": the judge presumed "a shared system of moral values throughout the country," even though that idealized uniformity may never have existed and was in any event "unquestionably gone by 1966." Carol Weisbrod, *Painter* v. *Bannister: Still,* 2006 Utah L. Rev. 135, 155. Do you think that similar divisions in world view are likely to affect custody decisions today? If so, can you identify some of them? Keep these issues in mind as you read the rest of the custody decisions in this book.

C. THE PSYCHOLOGICAL PARENT

The psychological parent, or primary caretaker, presumption has been one of the most important bases for decision-making in child custody cases over the past quarter-century.

1. INFLUENCE OF CHILD PSYCHOANALYSTS ON LEGAL THEORY

The primary caretaker presumption is based largely upon the "psychological parent" concept, which grew out of the work of Joseph Goldstein, Anna Freud and Albert Solnit, three child psychoanalysts, one of whom (Goldstein) was also a lawyer. More than a thousand child custody decisions have cited their writings.

Goldstein, Freud and Solnit—along with many other scholars and practitioners—criticized the "best interests of the child" standard for failing to provide sufficient guidance to courts, failing to achieve certainty of outcome, and failing to ensure that the child's needs remained in the forefront of the decision-making process. They drew on the psychological literature of "attachment theory," which emerged from studies of young children separated from their parents during the World War II bombing of England.

Goldstein, Freud and Solnit placed the child's needs and perceptions at the heart of the custody decision, a contribution that has persisted despite criticisms that have been leveled at their work in the divorce context. (Their work remains much more uniformly accepted in the context of the child welfare and foster care systems, where they cautioned against excessive intervention in families and argued that state intervention could itself be harmful.) Their work on custody emphasized four foundational principles:

1. The psychological parent model, which they acknowledged was difficult to define;

2. The child's need for continuity of "relationships, surrounding and environmental influence";

3. Emphasis on the child's sense of time, characterized by urgency and the need for quick resolution of legal disputes; and

4. Because of the limits of law as a predictor of future behavior and development, replacing the "best interests" standard with "the least detrimental alternative"—the "specific placement and procedure for placement which maximizes, in accord with the child's sense of time and on the basis of short-term predictions given the limitations of knowledge, his or her opportunity for being wanted and for maintaining on a continuous basis a relationship with at least one adult who is * * * his psychological parent."

Joseph Goldstein, Anna Freud & Albert J. Solnit, Beyond the Best Interests of the Child 53 (1973).

2. SELECTED WRITINGS FROM GOLDSTEIN, FREUD AND SOLNIT

* * * [P]rimitive and tenuous first attachments form the base from which any further relationships develop. What the child brings to them next are no longer only his needs for body comfort and gratification but his emotional demands for affection, companionship, and stimulating intimacy. Where these are answered reliably and regularly, the child-parent relationship becomes firm, with immensely productive effects on the child's intellectual and social development. * * * Where there are changes of parent figure or other hurtful interruptions, the child's vulnerability and the fragility of the relationship become evident. The child regresses along the whole line of his affections, skills, achievements, and social adaptation. It is only with the advance toward maturity that the emotional ties of the young will outgrow this vulnerability. The first relief in this respect is the formation of internal mental images of the parents which remain available even if the parents are absent. The next step is due to the identification with parental attitudes. Once these have become the child's own, they ensure stability within his inner structure.

As the prototype of true human relationship, the psychological child-parent relationship is not wholly positive but has its admixture of negative elements. Both partners bring to it the combination of loving and hostile feelings that characterize the emotional life of all human beings, whether mature or immature. The balance between positive and negative feelings fluctuates during the years. For children, this culminates in the inevitable and potentially constructive struggle with their parents during adolescence.

Whether any adult becomes the psychological parent of a child is based thus on day-to-day interaction, companionship, and shared experiences. The role can be fulfilled either by a biological parent or by an adoptive parent or by any other caring adult—but never by an absent, inactive adult, whatever his biological or legal relationship to the child may be.

Goldstein et al., Beyond the Best Interests of the Child 18–19 (1973).

* * * [T]he primary caretaker guidelines explicitly identify the factors to be considered in terms of their function—assuring continuity of care for the child. They enable judges and lawyers to achieve a degree of literacy in child development—to gain some understanding of the reasons for the preference. Unlike the early preferences for biological parents, the preference provides more than 'mere assertions of end results.' The new preference is no longer divorced from the ideas, concepts, and theories that need to be understood in order to recognize its purpose. The gender-related, the bloodtie, and the primary caregiving parent preferences are all meant to enable courts to identify who has been the most or who is most likely to be responsible for the child's care. But only the primary caregiver preference explicitly identifies the evidence essential for assuring that this function will be served. There is no presumption to overcome in order to harmonize a placement decision with its purpose.

Joseph Goldstein, Anna Freud & Albert J. Solnit, In the Best Interests of the Child 66–67 (1986).[2]

NOTES AND QUESTIONS

1. *West Virginia—a laboratory.* With the decline of the tender years doctrine, the primary caretaker presumption rose to prominence in child custody decisions across the United States. The seminal primary-caretaker decision is *Garska v. McCoy*, 278 S.E.2d 357 (W. Va. 1981), which reversed an order that had granted custody to a parent who had visited the child only briefly on a few occasions. *Garska* defined a primary caretaker (presumably entitled to custody) as the "natural or adoptive parent who, until the initiation of divorce proceedings, has been primarily responsible for the caring and nurturing of the child." *Id.* at 358.

The state supreme court reasoned that because the parent who has not spent as much time with the child may have greater economic resources than the other parent, courts should not grant custody based only upon whether a parent could provide for the child financially. To guide lower courts, the supreme court offered this non-exclusive list of caring and nurturing duties that would help determine which parent had been the child's "primary caretaker":

(1) preparing and planning of meals;

(2) bathing, grooming, and dressing;

(3) purchasing, cleaning, and care of clothes;

(4) medical care * * * ;

(5) arranging for social interaction among peers * * * ;

---

2. The complete Goldstein, Freud and Solnit trilogy, including Beyond The Best Interests of The Child (1973), and its successors Before the Best Interests of the Child (1979) and In the Best Interests of the Child (1986), have been published together in Joseph Goldstein, Anna Freud, Albert J. Solnit & Sonya Goldstein, The Best Interests Of The Child: The Least Detrimental Alternative (1996).

(6) arranging * * * babysitting, daycare, etc.;

(7) putting child to bed at night * * * ;

(8) disciplining * * * ;

(9) educating, i.e. religious, cultural, social, etc.; and

(10) teaching elementary skills, i.e., reading,, writing and arithmetic.

Id. at 363.

Garska also noted that parents might use custody improperly "as a coercive weapon" in divorce proceedings, that determining the relative fitness of two equally suited parents can be a near-impossible judicial task, and that the law needs a clear standard that couples can rely upon when negotiating a settlement. The West Virginia court considered settlements preferable to court proceedings, but expressed concern about the risks of Solomonic decision-making, in which the parent with a greater attachment to the children may sacrifice economic security to gain custody.

Effective in 2000, West Virginia adopted the pertinent custody provisions of the then-draft ALI Principles of Family Dissolution, discussed below at page 701. The current statute continues to scrutinize each parent's history as a caretaker, but favors shared parenting responsibilities rather than designating one parent as the primary caretaker. *See* W. Va. Code Ann. § 48–1–210 (LexisNexis 2004).

2. *Current approaches to the primary caretaker presumption.* Today no state expressly follows a primary caretaker presumption, but several states consider primary caretaking as a factor in child custody determinations. *See, e.g.*, Michigan Child Custody Act of 1970, Mich. Comp. Laws Ann. § 722.23 (West 2002) (*infra* at p. 704).

In some states, the primary caretaker inquiry remains a creature of common law. In *Kjelland v. Kjelland*, 609 N.W.2d 100 (N.D. 2000), for example, the court upheld the trial court's consideration of the primary caretaker in its child custody determination, despite the fact that the North Dakota statute, N.D. Cent. Code § 14–09–06.2(1) (2007), does not explicitly mention primary caretaking as a factor in its best interests test. In 2003, the same court explained that parent-child ties are "not about which parent fixes the most meals or washes the most clothes. This factor is about bonding." *Schmidt v. Schmidt*, 660 N.W.2d 196, 200 (N.D. 2003).

3. *To what extent does child psychology inform custody law?* Professor Lee Teitelbaum has considered the relationship between psychological theories and changing views of the legal doctrine governing child custody:

> * * * [C]hild psychology is a common source of content for determining a child's best interests. It would be right to say that judicial acceptance of the importance of continuity in child-raising, most famously (although not originally) set out in Goldstein, Freud, and Solnit's *Beyond the Best Interests of the Child*, has powerfully affected custodial practices in this country and abroad. * * * The weight given to continuity is found in the willingness of some courts to recognize for non-parent care givers who have formed a bond with a child claims nearly or fully equivalent to those

of biological parents, and in the widespread use of a presumption favoring custody in the parent who was the primary care giver before divorce.

* * *

* * * Adoption of the primary caretaker presumption was based * * * on the importance associated with continuity of child care. To my knowledge, no one has examined the importance of competing considerations. Divorced mothers commonly must find new or increased employment; fathers usually have greater financial resources, and remarriage by the father may make available care in the home. Likely his new wife would remain at home to care for her stepchild. Although these circumstances seem relevant on their face to custodial decisions, none-perhaps for policy as well as practical reasons has been explored. The preference for joint custody rested largely on studies of small and atypical populations until * * * and the [latest] research hardly points unambiguously toward the desirability of joint custody.

Lee E. Teitelbaum, *Rays of Light: Other Disciplines and Family Law*, 1 J.L. Fam. Stud. 1, 2, 10 (1999).

4. *The debates.* The advantages and drawbacks of the primary caretaker approach have been widely debated. Proponents of the presumption tout its facial gender-neutrality because regardless of gender, it will tilt the scales in favor of the parent who has performed the majority of the caretaking. Robert F. Cochran, Jr., *The Search for Guidance in Determining the Best Interests of the Child at Divorce: Reconciling the Primary Caretaker and Joint Custody Preferences*, 20 U. Richmond L. Rev. 1, 37 (1985). However, Professor David Chambers argues that the "weakest part of the case for the primary caretaker is not that it exaggerates the importance of attachment in general, but that it exaggerates the importance of the bond to the primary-caretaker parent in comparison to the bond with the other parent." David L. Chambers, *Rethinking the Substantive Rules for Custody Disputes in Divorce*, 83 Mich. L. Rev. 477, 533 (1984). He argues that research "indicates that although children have very different relationships with their secondary-caretaker fathers than with their mothers, they typically form strong attachments to both." *Id.* at 533–34.

Professor Mary Becker criticizes the contemporary primary caretaker presumption, which she believes disadvantages women. She argues that in addition to discounting women's work during childbearing and their later emotional caretaking, the presumption encourages courts to give disproportionate weight to a father's smaller contributions to childcare. Mary Becker, *Maternal Feelings: Myth, Taboo, and Child Custody*, 1 S. Cal. Rev. L. & Women's Stud. 133, 201–02 (1992).

Some proponents of the psychological parent presumption argue that it offers a bright line rule that reduces litigation, but Judge Gary Crippen claims that the presumption leads to more litigation, citing the experience in Minnesota. Gary Crippen, *Stumbling Beyond Best Interests of the Child: Reexamining Child Custody Standard–Setting in the Wake of Minnesota's Four Year Experiment in the Primary Caretaker Preference*, 75 Minn. L. Rev. 427, 461 (1990).

The question of which parent is the psychological parent is frequently litigated. If one parent is a homemaker and the other works for wages outside the home, is remunerative work outside the home a form of caretaking? In families with such arrangements, does the primary caretaker presumption resurrect the overtly gender-based tender years presumption by favoring the homemaker, usually the wife? Does the primary caretaker presumption work best when the parents' individual relationships with the children are so clearly different that no presumption is needed?

5. *The family network model.* Professor Peggy Cooper Davis questions the efficacy of the Goldstein, Freud and Solnit primary caregiver preference in child custody cases. Peggy Cooper Davis, *The Good Mother: A New Look at Psychological Parent Theory*, 22 N.Y.U. Rev. L. & Soc. Change 347, 347–48 (1996). Goldstein, Freud and Solnit advocate maintaining relationships between children and their "psychological parent"—the one adult who is most critically important to the child—and protecting children from any relationships or contact (such as court-ordered visitation) over that parent's objection. Professor Davis argues that children benefit from bonds with multiple family members and that "the inevitability of separations can be managed consciously and used constructively in the maturation process." *Id.* at 350. Thus, she advocates "abandon[ing] [the] single-minded focus on preserving a primary bond in favor of acknowledging—and allowing children to acknowledge—the full network of kin attachments." *Id.*

6. *Other family models.* Professor Jean Koh Peters concludes that:

[The] Goldstein, Freud, and Solnit psychological parenting model has captured the discourse and in many ways deepened lawyers' basic understanding of child developmental needs. The model has exhorted children's lawyers[1] to treat time as precious and to put their client's interests first.

Jean Koh Peters, Representing Children in Child Protective Proceedings: Ethical and Practical Dimensions 613–14 (2d ed. 2001). However, Professor Peters criticizes the Goldstein et al. approach for (1) failing to preserve the non-custodial parent's visitation rights unless the primary caretaker chooses to allow visits; (2) opposing shared decisionmaking once the parents separate; and (3) insisting that the child does not need an independent voice in custody hearings because the primary caretaker would adequately represent the child's interests.

PROBLEM 12–1

You are a law professor serving on a drafting committee for an interdisciplinary national panel charged with resolving the question:

Where the best interests of the child clearly point to one outcome in a custody case, and the rights of the parent or parents point toward a different solution, how should judges resolve the conflict?

The committee hears conflicting testimony. Mental health professionals urge that "when a child's best interests conflict with fairness for the interested adults, the child's best interests shall be paramount." Albert J. Solnit, et

---

1. And judges.

al., When Home Is No Haven: Child Placement Issues 12 (1992). A sitting appellate judge testifies that "while psychiatric considerations may very well be important, they must not be made determinative * * * because often times 'psychiatry and the law are not co-extensive.'" *T.B. v. L.R.M.*, 874 A.2d 34, 38 (Pa. Super. Ct. 2005).

You are asked to summarize the considerations that lawyers must weigh in determining the answer to the question the committee is charged with answering. Based on what you have read so far in this Chapter, what would you say?

D. CONTEMPORARY INTERPRETATIONS OF THE BEST INTERESTS OF THE CHILD

Commentators have proposed a number of approaches designed to impose more structure on child custody decisions. Two leading approaches are the ones presented by the Uniform Marriage and Divorce Act's definition of "best interest of the child," and by the American Law Institute's Principles of the Law of Family Dissolution. How much guidance would these provisions offer judges and parents trying to resolve a custody dispute?

1. UNIFORM MARRIAGE AND DIVORCE ACT

UNIFORM MARRIAGE AND DIVORCE ACT

9A U.L.A. 282 (1998).

§ 402. Best Interest of Child

The court shall determine custody in accordance with the best interest of the child. The court shall consider all relevant factors including:

(1) the wishes of the child's parent or parents as to his custody;

(2) the wishes of the child as to his custodian;

(3) the interaction and interrelationship of the child with his parent or parents, his siblings, and any other person who may significantly affect the child's best interest;

(4) the child's adjustment to his home, school, and community; and

(5) the mental and physical health of all individuals involved.

The court shall not consider conduct of a proposed custodian that does not affect his relationship to the child.

2.　THE ALI PRINCIPLES

AMERICAN LAW INSTITUTE

Principles of the Law of Family Dissolution: Analysis and Recommendations.
(2002).

§ 2.08　Allocation of Custodial Responsibility

(1) Unless otherwise resolved by agreement of the parents * * *, the court should allocate custodial responsibility so that the proportion of custodial time the child spends with each parent approximates the proportion of time each parent spent performing caretaking functions for the child prior to the parents' separation or, if the parents never lived together, before the filing of the action, except to the extent required under § 2.11[1] or necessary to achieve one or more of the following objectives:

　(a) to permit the child to have a relationship with each parent which, in the case of a legal parent or a parent by estoppel who has performed a reasonable share of parenting functions, should be not less than a presumptive amount of custodial time set by a uniform rule of statewide application;

　(b) to accommodate the firm and reasonable preferences of a child who has reached a specific age, set by a uniform rule of statewide application;

　(c) to keep siblings together when the court finds that doing so is necessary to their welfare;

　(d) to protect the child's welfare when the presumptive allocation under this section would harm the child because of a gross disparity in the quality of the emotional attachment between each parent and the child or in each parent's demonstrated ability or availability to meet the child's needs;

　(e) to take into account any prior agreement, other than one under § 2.06,[2] that would be appropriate to consider in light of the circumstances as a whole, including the reasonable expectations of the parties, the extent to which they could have reasonably anticipated the events that occurred and their significance, and the interests of the child;

　(f) to avoid an allocation of custodial responsibility that would be extremely impractical or that would interfere substantially with the child's need for stability in light of economic, physical, or other circumstances, including the distance between the parents' residences, the cost and difficulty of transporting the child, each parent's

---

　1.　Section 2.11 concerns parenting plans, detailed written description of each parents' rights and responsibilities.

　2.　Section 2.06 provides that "[t]he court should order provisions of a parenting plan agreed to by the parents, unless the agreement (a) is not knowing or voluntary, or (b) would be harmful to the child."

and the child's daily schedules, and the ability of the parents to cooperate in the arrangement;

(g) to apply the Principles set forth in § 2.17(4) [governing relocation by the custodial parent] one parent relocates or proposes to relocate at a distance that will impair the ability of a parent to exercise the presumptive amount of custodial responsibility under this section;

(h) to avoid substantial and almost certain harm to the child.

(2) In determining the proportion of caretaking functions each parent previously performed for the child under Paragraph (1), the court should not consider the division of functions arising from temporary arrangements after the parents' separation, whether those arrangements are consensual or by court order. The court may take into account information relating to the temporary arrangements in determining other issues under this section.

(3) If the court is unable to allocate custodial responsibility under Paragraph (1) because there is no history of past performance of caretaking functions, as in the case of a newborn, or because the history does not establish a sufficiently clear pattern of caretaking, the court should allocate custodial responsibility based on the child's best interests, taking into account the factors and considerations that are set forth in this Chapter, preserving to the extent possible this section's priority on the share of past caretaking functions each parent performed.

(4) In determining how to schedule the custodial time allocated to each parent, the court should take account of economic, physical, and other practical circumstances, such as those listed in Paragraph (1)(f).

NOTES AND QUESTIONS

1. *Origins of the ALI's approximation standard.* Professor Elizabeth S. Scott first advocated what she called an "approximation" standard for allocating child custody based partly on the positive correlation between past caretaking roles and the parents' preferences. Elizabeth S. Scott, *Pluralism, Parental Preference, and Child Custody*, 80 Cal. L. Rev. 615 (1992). Professor Scott argued that the optimal response to the current pluralism in family structure is a rule that seeks to replicate past parental roles within the particular family. She argued that the "approximation" standard ameliorates the destructive effects of bargaining at divorce by promoting continuity and stability for children and encouraging cooperative rather than adversarial resolution of custody. She also argued that this approach would encourage both parents to invest in parenting before and after divorce.

Professor Katharine T. Bartlett, who served as the reporter for Chapter 2 of the ALI Principles, relied heavily on Professor Scott's work. Katharine T. Bartlett, *Preference, Presumption, Predisposition, and Common Sense: From Traditional Custody Doctrines to the American Law Institute's Family Dissolution Project*, 36 Fam. L.Q. 11 (2002). Bartlett believes that "[t]he role of presumptions and preferences in refining rather than eliminating the best-interests standard is important to a greater general understanding of custody conflict." *Id.* at 16. She argues that the Principles will introduce greater predictability to custody disputes by bringing specificity to those generalized presumptions. *Id.* at 24; *see also* Elizabeth Barker Brandt, *Concerns at the Margins of Supervised Access to Children*, 9 J. L. & Fam. Stud. 201 (2007).

2. *Criticisms of the ALI's approximation standard.* Ironically, the principal criticism of the ALI approximation standard is that it fails to achieve gender equality because so many families continue to follow traditional gender roles. Critics worry about whether the ALI's approach to custody is fair to fathers. Professor Margaret Brinig finds it significant that the ALI Principles' custody chapter was drafted by a feminist reporter, who incorporated the ideas of a woman scholar. She urges that states adopting the ALI Principles consider how to protect the interests of fathers. Margaret F. Brinig, *Feminism and Child Custody Under Chapter Two of the American Legal Institute's Principles of The Law of Family Dissolution*, 8 Duke J. Gender L. & Pol'y 301 (2001).

Similarly, Professor Andrew Schepard expresses concern that the approximation standard would most likely allocate more of a child's post-dissolution time to the mother because "mothers do most of the pre-divorce work of caring for children." He argues that "men will likely perceive the approximation presumption as gender-biased and an incentive for women to file for divorce." He acknowledges that the ALI proposal rewards parents who spend more of their time caring for children, but argues that "[a] custody award to a parent * * * should not be a form of indirect compensation for time expended on child rearing." Instead, custody should be determined according to what a child needs, rather than what a parent deserves. Andrew I. Schepard, Children, Courts, and Custody: Interdisciplinary Models for Divorcing Families 167–69 (2004).

A second concern voiced about the approximation standard is that it fails to recognize the dynamic nature of marital relationships. Like Professor Teitelbaum, Professor Schepard criticizes the static quality of the approximation approach. Schepard argues that because the ALI standard is based on past performance, it "does not take into account the probability of post-divorce change in parenting roles. It is difficult to say with any degree of confidence that pre-divorce or separation caretaking arrangements in a particular family will remain stable after divorce or after separation. Many parents take new jobs and new partners after divorce. Some reduce their work loads to spend more time with their children." He concludes that the law should grant parents the flexibility to redefine their relationship to work, to their children, and to each other after divorce rather than rigidly continuing pre-divorce patterns. *Id.* at 169.

A psychologist critiqued the ALI Standards in 2007, concluding that they are no clearer than the best interests of the child approach and that they do not always accurately measure the parents' respective contributions. Richard A. Warshak, *Punching the Parenting Time Clock: The Approximation Rule, Social Science, and the Baseball Bat Kids*, 45 Fam. Ct. Rev. 600 (2007).

3. STATUTORY DEFINITIONS OF "BEST INTERESTS"

State statutes governing divorce give varying meanings to the term "best interests of the child." The following statutes demonstrate some of the different approaches state legislatures have enacted to guide judicial determinations of child custody.

Michigan Child Custody Act of 1970

Sec. 3. As used in this act, the "best interests of the child" means the sum total of the following factors to be considered, evaluated, and determined by the court:

(a) The love, affection, and other emotional ties existing between the parties involved and the child.

(b) The capacity and disposition of the parties involved to give the child love, affection, and guidance and to continue the education and raising of the child in his or her religion or creed, if any.

(c) The capacity and disposition of the parties involved to provide the child with food, clothing, medical care or other remedial care recognized and permitted under the laws of this state in place of medical care, and other material needs.

(d) The length of time the child has lived in a stable, satisfactory environment, and the desirability of maintaining continuity.

(e) The permanence, as a family unit, of the existing or proposed custodial home or homes.

(f) The moral fitness of the parties involved.

(g) The mental and physical health of the parties involved.

(h) The home, school, and community record of the child.

(i) The reasonable preference of the child, if the court considers the child to be of sufficient age to express preference.

(j) The willingness and ability of each of the parties to facilitate and encourage a close and continuing parent-child relationship between the child and the other parent or the child and the parents.

(k) Domestic violence, regardless of whether the violence was directed against or witnessed by the child.

(*l*) Any other factor considered by the court to be relevant to a particular child custody dispute.

Mich. Comp. Laws Ann. § 722.23 (West 2002).

Section 3011 of the California Family Code

Factors considered in determining best interest of child

In making a determination of the best interest of the child * * * the court shall, among any other factors it finds relevant, consider all of the following:

(a) The health, safety, and welfare of the child.

(b) Any history of abuse by one parent or any other person seeking custody against any of the following:

(1) Any child to whom he or she is related by blood or affinity or with whom he or she has had a caretaking relationship, no matter how temporary.

(2) The other parent.

(3) A parent, current spouse, or cohabitant, of the parent or person seeking custody, or a person with whom the parent or person seeking custody has a dating or engagement relationship. * * *

(c) The nature and amount of contact with both parents * * *.

(d) The habitual or continual illegal use of controlled substances or habitual or continual abuse of alcohol by either parent. * * *

(e) (1) Where allegations about a parent pursuant to subdivision (b) or (d) have been brought to the attention of the court in the current proceeding, and the court makes an order for sole or joint custody to that parent, the court shall state its reasons in writing or on the record. In these circumstances, the court shall ensure that any order regarding custody or visitation is specific as to time, day, place, and manner of transfer of the child as set forth in subdivision (b) of Section 6323.

(2) The provisions of this subdivision shall not apply if the parties stipulate in writing or on the record regarding custody or visitation.

Cal. Fam. Code § 3011 (West 2004).

NOTES AND QUESTIONS

1. *The totality of the circumstances.* The vast majority of states have specified factors for courts to consider in assessing child custody claims, but some states expressly rely on a "totality of the circumstances" test for determining the best interests of the child, acknowledging that while "principles certainly provide guidance, child custody disputes, by their very nature, must be analyzed on a case-by-case basis." *John A. v. Bridget M.*, 791 N.Y.S.2d 421, 429 (App. Div. 2005) (Sullivan, J., concurring); see also *id.* at 431 ("It is always necessary to consider the totality of the circumstances when determining custody") (Saxe, J., concurring). Thus New York courts hold that no one factor can be determinative, no matter how significant that factor may seem.

Would the Michigan and California formulations necessarily produce different outcomes than the sparser UMDA formulation quoted above on page 700?

2. *Abuse of controlled substances or alcohol.* The California statute expressly includes either parent's abuse of controlled substances or alcohol as

a factor to weigh in the best interests inquiry. Substance abuse problems regularly arise in child custody cases, both in contests between parents, and when the child welfare system alleges child abuse or neglect. There has been some controversy about whether abuse of illegal substances should be a *prima facie* justification for denying a parent custody. *Compare* Dorothy E. Roberts, *Punishing Drug Addicts Who Have Babies: Women of Color, Equality and the Right of Privacy*, 104 Harv. L. Rev. 1419 (1991) (arguing that prosecution of women who use crack cocaine during pregnancy illegally discriminates against poor, black women), *with* Elizabeth Bartholet, Nobody's Children: Abuse and Neglect, Foster Drift, and the Adoption Alternative, 67–80 (1999) (arguing that drug addiction "and cocaine addiction in particular are chronic, relapsing conditions," which "cause or exacerbate" child abuse and neglect, thus justifying removal).

Regardless of the weight assigned to substance abuse in custody decisions, Professor Catherine Ross says that it would be "misguided to ignore the pernicious effects that parental substance abuse may have on children, regardless of the precise substance of choice. Substance abuse can alter judgment, diminish impulse control, and stimulate aggression. At the core of the problem, substance abuse may make it impossible for a parent to perceive—much less respond to—a child's needs." Catherine J. Ross, *The Tyranny of Time: Vulnerable Children, "Bad" Mothers, and Statutory Deadlines in Parental Termination Proceedings*, 11 Va. J. Soc. Pol'y & L. 176, 210–11 (2004). The rise in the number of children actually or virtually abandoned by parents addicted to methamphetamine illustrates the problem. Kate Zernike, *A Drug Scourge Creates Its Own Form of Orphan*, N.Y. Times, July 11, 2005, at A1. Which approach should states adopt to protect children when the custody dispute is between two parents, one of whom is a substance abuser?

PROBLEM 12–2

In an effort to avoid custody determinations grounded in gender-based factors, your state's legislature recently amended the divorce act to provide that "no preference may be given to either parent in the awarding of custody because of that parent's gender, or because of the age or gender of the child." You are a trial court judge with a heavy divorce docket. This week you will hear two cases in which both parents have mounted strong claims for custody. The first case involves a four-month-old infant whom the mother is nursing. The second case involves a 14–year–old boy, and the father will present expert testimony that teenage boys thrive best when they live in a household with a strong father figure. What effect, if any, will the new statute likely have on your decision-making?

SECTION 3: FACTORS IN DETERMINING BEST INTERESTS

Depending on the jurisdiction, a court may apply the best interests balancing test, a contemporary statute that does not impose a presumption, or the totality-of-the-circumstances common law approach. Regardless of the specific approach, child custody cases by their very nature are intensely fact specific. The decisions in this Section illustrate how courts weigh various factors in determining "best interests" under statutes or common law; the decisions also illustrate the lingering impact of some considerations that the law has formally discarded.

A. GENDER ROLES/CAREERS

YOUNG v. HECTOR

District Court of Appeal of Florida, 1999.
740 So.2d 1153.

ON REHEARING EN BANC.

GREEN, J.

* * *

The former husband/father (Robert Young) appeals from the final judgment of dissolution of marriage. We affirm the trial court's decision designating the former wife/mother (Alice Hector) as the primary custodial parent of the two minor children * * *.

The father's main contention on this appeal is that the trial court abused its discretion when it awarded custody of the minor children to the mother. We do not agree. After laboriously reviewing all of the record evidence in this case, we conclude that there was substantial competent evidence to support the trial court's discretionary call in this regard. Thus, there is no basis for us to overturn the lower court's decision.

* * * The simple issue for our consideration is whether the trial court abused its discretion when it determined that the best interests of the two minor children dictated that their mother be designated their primary custodial parent. * * *

At the outset, it is important to emphasize that both the mother and father are very loving and capable parents. Nobody disputes this fact, which alone made the trial court's determination all the more difficult. What then tilted the scales in favor of awarding custody to the mother? The father suggests that it was gender bias. The record evidence, however, simply does not support this suggestion.

I

At the time of their marriage in 1982, both the father and mother were successful professionals in New Mexico. He was an architectural designer with his own home design firm as well as an entrepreneur with a publishing company. She was an attorney in private practice at her own firm. Their marriage was a second for both. He had no children from his first marriage. She had custody of her two minor children (now grown) from her first marriage which she successfully reared while simultaneously juggling the demands of her law practice.[1]

---

1. This certainly was a valid consideration which could have factored into the lower court's determination as to the custody of the minor children in this case.

Hector and Young became the parents of two daughters born in 1985 and 1988. After the birth of their children, both parents continued to work outside of the home and pursued their respective professional endeavors with the assistance of a live-in nanny, *au pair*, or housekeeper. As typical working parents, they would both arrive home between the hours of 5:30 and 6:00 each evening. Both contributed to and shared in the household expenditures at all times.

Sometime in late 1987, the father's business ventures began to suffer certain financial reversals and the mother became bored with her practice in New Mexico. Both parties agreed to relocate to Miami. Although there is a complete conflict in the record between the parties as to who broached the subject of the couple's relocation to Miami and the circumstances under which they would relocate in terms of their respective careers, it is significant that *neither* of these parties ever testified that they ever agreed or expected the mother to pursue her legal career while the father remained at home as the full-time caregiver to their minor children. To the contrary, the father actively pursued job leads in the Miami area prior to the couple's relocation.

In June 1989, the mother and her two minor daughters arrived in Miami first. During that summer, she studied for and took the Florida Bar exam and landed a position with a mid-sized law firm. The father stayed behind in New Mexico until October 1989 in order to complete the construction of a new house and to remodel the couple's New Mexico home in order to enhance its resale potential.

After the father's move to Miami in the fall of 1989, he studied for and passed the Florida contractor's examination. Thereafter, during the spring and summer of 1990, the father spent his time repairing the couple's first marital residence in Miami. Thereafter, he renovated the home which ultimately became the couple's second marital residence. It is significant to point out at this juncture, that it is undisputed that from the time the minor children were brought to Miami in 1989 until the fall of 1993, the needs of the minor children were attended to by a live-in housekeeper when they were not in school during the day and by the mother upon her arrival from work in the evenings.

After the father's renovations to the couple's second Miami residence were completed and the family moved in, the mother testified that she began to have serious discussions (which eventually escalated into arguments) about the father's need to find gainful employment. Although the mother was earning a very decent income as an attorney at the time, it was undisputed that this family was operating with a negative cash flow.

Rather than pursue gainful employment to financially assist the household and his minor children, the father turned his attentions elsewhere. During the remainder of 1990 through 1993, the father left the state and was frequently away from the mother and minor children for months at a time. * * * During this time, the father spent approximately fourteen months away from his family pursuing buried gold in New

Mexico on a treasure hunt. The minor children were continuously being cared for by the housekeeper/babysitter during the day and the mother after work. * * *

When the father finally returned to South Florida, in the fall of 1993, the mother had accepted a partnership position with a large Florida law firm at a salary of approximately $300,000 annually. Even with the mother's salary increase, the family remained steep in debt. At that time, the couple no longer had a live-in nanny or babysitter for the children. The children were in a public school full-time between the hours of 8:30 a.m. and 2:00–3:00 p.m. The mother had employed a housekeeper ("Hattie") who came to the house each weekday between the hours of noon and 8:00 p.m. to clean, pickup and babysit the children after school. The mother's time with the children during the weekdays consisted of her awakening, dressing, and having breakfast with them prior to transporting them to school, and spending the early evening hours with them prior to their bedtime. The mother engaged in activities with the children on a full-time basis on the weekends. When the children became ill or distressed during the middle of the night, the mother was always the parent they looked to for assistance or solace.[2]

Approximately one month after the father's return to the household in 1993, the mother asked the father for a divorce because of his continued refusal to seek gainful employment and due to his extramarital affair in New Mexico. It must be re-emphasized that at *no* time did the mother and father have any mutually expressed or tacit agreement for the father to remain unemployed. The father candidly conceded as much at trial. Consequently, this case simply did not involve the typical scenario where two spouses, by mutual agreement, agreed for one to remain at home to care for the children and the other spouse to work outside of the home.

Once the mother announced to the father that she wanted a divorce, the father began to spend less of his time away from Miami. Although he steadfastly refused to make any efforts to obtain employment, he did become more involved in the activities of his two daughters, who by that time, were 8 and 5. Since both girls were in school full-time at this time, the father's involvement with the girls' activities occurred primarily Mondays through Fridays between the hours of 3:00 p.m. and 6:30 p.m., prior to the mother's arrival from work. Upon the mother's arrival at the home, the father generally absented himself.[4]

---

2. The fact that the children deemed their mother to be the "go to" parent when they were ill or distressed during the night speaks volumes about which parent they deemed to have been their constant caregiver. Moreover, it supports the guardian ad litem's observation that the mother had been "the more constant factor throughout the entire relationship."

4. As the father testified:

[Q] In the evenings, when Alice comes home, do you pretty much absent yourself since the time that she's indicated that she wants this divorce?

[A] Yes and no. She, a lot of times, likes to sit down have a little time to herself and eat dinner and not be bothered. Then after that she will engage the kids. And I will either leave the house and leave her with the kids or I may go to my room or I may go to the study and close the door. I

The father nevertheless maintained that he was the "primary care-taker" or "Mr. Mom" of these two children in the three years preceding this dissolution proceeding. The trial court viewed this contention with some degree of skepticism as it was entitled. The trial court's skepticism or disbelief was not at all unreasonable, given the father's admission that the nanny, Hattie, had taken care of these children in large part during the afternoon hours until their mother's arrival at home. The father's concession is what prompted the court to ultimately make inquiry as to why the father did not seek employment or alternatively, why there was a need for a full-time nanny:

* * *

[The Court]: Is Hattie there five days a week?

[Father]: Yes sir. She comes at noon every day. She cleans the house in the afternoons. She prepares the dinners. The kids eat. We eat. I eat with the children every day typically at 6:30. She cleans up after that. She'll draw a bath for Avery and she leaves at eight o'clock in the evening five days a week.

[The Court]: Maybe I'm missing something. Why don't you get a job.

[Father]: Well, because my background is architecture. That's my degree, but when I graduated, they did not have computers. Today, it's computer dominated and I'm computer illiterate.

* * * Previously, because of the number of hours Ms. Hector worked, I filled in. Ms. Hector has a secretary that handles her whole life at the office and in a sense I was the secretary that handled her whole life at home and took care of the children.

[The Court]: But you've got a nanny doing that.

[Father]: No sir, I don't believe you can buy parents. Nannies can pick up. They can drop off.

[The Court]: Why [sic] do you need the nanny for, if you're there doing it?

[Father]: She cooks. She cleans. I could do a lot of that. Typically, people that have incomes of over a quarter of a million dollars or $300,000 can afford the luxury of having help, hired help.

I am not the kind of person that sits around and watches soap operas. I try to do meaningful, worthwhile things.

[The Court]: Go ahead, counsel.

Contrary to the father's suggestion on appeal, this inquiry by the court is not evidence of gender bias. Given the undisputed large financial indebted-

---

don't generally sit down next to her and say, "Let's all play this game together." Yes, I try to give her space with the kids, as I mentioned earlier. I don't compete with her, either.

[Q] Do you spend most evenings and some nights away from the home?

[A] Most evenings, I don't know. I spend, because of the situation, a good deal of time away after she comes home.

ness of this couple, the trial court's inquiry about the need to employ a full-time nanny was both logical and practical under these circumstances and certainly could have also been appropriately posed to the mother if she had been recalcitrant about seeking gainful employment to assist the family's financial situation.

II

Apart from this evidence, the court also had the report and recommendations of the guardian *ad litem* upon which to rely. In recommending that the mother be named the primary custodial parent, the guardian *ad litem* cited three factors, all of which we find are supported by competent substantial evidence in the record. First of all, the guardian noted that the mother had been the more economically stable of the two parents throughout the marriage. We do not believe that the guardian gave the mother the edge simply because she earned a large salary. We believe, that what the guardian was attempting to convey was that the mother had shown a proclivity to remain steadily employed, unlike the father who unilaterally removed himself from the job market, although he was employable and the family needed the additional income. The trial court concluded that the father was "where he is largely because of his own choice." The trial court was obviously not oblivious to the fact that the father was also a Florida licensed contractor who had built homes in New Mexico and renovated both of the parties' Florida marital residences. * * *

The second factor relied upon by the guardian *ad litem* in recommending that the mother be declared the primary custodial parent was the fact that the mother had been a constant factor and dominant influence in the children's lives and the father had not. The guardian *ad litem* observed:

> There have been times in the children's life [sic] when Bob has been, for whatever reasons, away from the home for substantial periods of time and Alice has been the dominant influence.
>
> More recently, while she has been working, he has been available at home more hours of the day than she has been, but over a continuum of time, I believe that her presence has been a more steady presence in the sense of available almost the same time for the kids throughout the relationship, whereas Bob has been intensely absent and intensely present.

In its determination as to the best interests of the minor children, the trial court obviously deemed it more important to assess the children's time spent with each of the parents throughout the course of the marriage and not merely focus on the years immediately preceding the announcement of the dissolution action. That is, the trial court, in an effort to maintain continuity, could have legitimately determined that the children's best interests dictate that they remain with the parent who had continuously been there to care for their needs throughout their young lives rather than the parent who had devoted a substantial amount of time with them perhaps only when it was convenient and/or opportunistic to do so. The record evidence clearly supports the trial court's conclusion that the mother had been the constant parent throughout the children's lives. Thus, there was no basis for the panel to overturn the trial court's finding in this regard.

The last factor cited by the guardian *ad litem*, which tilted the scale in favor of the mother, was the mother's superior ability to control her anger around the children. The guardian *ad litem* testified that he personally witnessed one of the father's outbursts of anger in the presence of the children. For that reason, the guardian, who is also a retired circuit court judge, went so far as to recommend that the father receive anger control counseling.

Given this substantial competent evidence in the record, we cannot conclude that the trial court abused its discretion when it awarded custody of the minor children to their mother. Nor can we conclude that the court's determination was impermissibly influenced by gender bias against the father.

Custody determinations are perhaps the most sensitive and delicate decisions that family court judges make. We recognize that at times, it can be a very difficult and agonizing call for the trial judge to make when both parents are as loving and caring as the mother and father are in this case. * * * [T]he trial court has the unique advantage of meeting both parents prior to making its decision. Thus, the trial court, unlike an appellate court, is entitled to rely, not only upon the record evidence presented, but upon its mental impressions formed about each of the parents and their respective parenting strengths and weaknesses. Moreover, trial judges sitting as triers of fact in these proceedings are not required to shed their common sense and life's experiences when they don their black robes to preside over these proceedings. As long as the trial court's decision is supported by substantial competent evidence and is not based upon legally impermissible factors such as gender bias, it must be affirmed on appeal. For this reason, we affirm the order awarding primary residential custody of the minor children to the mother. However, on remand, the trial court should grant the father liberal and frequent access to the children.

* * *

Affirmed in part and reversed and remanded in part.

* * *

SCHWARTZ, CHIEF JUDGE (dissenting).

I remain convinced by the panel decision and by the dissents of Judge Nesbitt and Judge Goderich that the trial court's "award" of the children's primary physical residence to the mother is unsupported by any cognizable, equitable consideration presented by the record. As the panel opinion, which has not in my view been successfully challenged by any of the contrary briefs or opinions,[1] demonstrates, the children's parents, who know and care most about their welfare, had themselves established an arrangement prior to the dissolution as a part of which, upon any fair assessment, the father was the primary caretaker. *See* A.L.I., Principles of the Law of Family Dissolution: Analysis and Recommendations (Am. Law Inst.1998) (Tentative Draft No. 3, Part I) § 2.03(6).[2] As everyone agrees, under that regime, if not because of it, their girls have turned out to be well-behaved, well-adjusted, and accomplished young women who love both their parents: just what we all devoutly wish for and from our children. There is simply no reason for a court to tamper with what has worked so well. * * * [T]he children are themselves entitled to stability in their lives and routine which would be compromised by any purposeless change in their caregiver. In many areas, the law properly recognizes the undesirability of disrupting the children's circumstances any more than is already necessarily required by their parents' separation and divorce. * * *

* * *

A.

In my opinion, there is no question whatever that the result below was dictated by the gender of the competing parties. It is usually extremely difficult to gauge the underlying motivations of any human being and one resists even more the assignment of an unworthy or impermissible reason to any judge's exercise of her judicial functions. This case, however, permits no other conclusion. I believe that this is shown by contemplating a situation in which the genders of the hard working and high earning

---

1. Much of the picking at the panel fallaciously assigns the "caretaking functions" of the housekeeper to the mother and relies upon a possible change in the circumstances of the parents which might follow the dissolution.

2. § 2.03 Definitions

(6) Caretaking functions are tasks that involve interaction with the child or direct the interaction and care provided by others. Caretaking functions include

(a) feeding, bedtime and wake-up routines, care of the child when sick or hurt, bathing, grooming, personal hygiene, dressing, recreation and play, physical safety, transportation, and other functions that meet the daily physical needs of the child;

(b) direction of the child's various developmental needs, including the acquisition of motor and language skills, toilet training, self-confidence, and maturation;

(c) discipline, instruction in manners, assignment and supervision of chores, and other tasks that attend to the child's needs for behavioral control and self-restraint;

(d) arrangements for the child's education, including remedial or special services appropriate to the child's needs and interests, communication with teachers and counselors, and supervision of homework;

(e) the development and maintenance of appropriate interpersonal relationships with peers, siblings, and adults;

(f) arrangements for health care, including making appointments, communication with health-care providers, medical follow-up, and home health care;

(g) moral guidance; and

(h) arrangement of alternative care by a family member, baby-sitter, or other childcare provider or facility, including investigation of alternatives, communication with providers, and supervision.

lawyer and the stay at home architect were reversed, but everything else remained the same. The male attorney's claim for custody would have been virtually laughed out of court, and there is no realistic possibility that the mother architect would have actually "lost her children."[7] (The fact, so heavily emphasized by members of the majority, that the hypothetical *mother* architect might have sought employment after the dissolution, as usually occurs, and that her time with the children would have therefore diminished, would have made no difference either.)[8] It is, at best, naive in the extreme to suggest, let alone find, that the result below was not dictated by the evil of gender bias.

B.

By rejecting the obvious but unacceptable in its search for a basis for the result below, the majority has, in my opinion, relied upon something even worse. In the end, after a meticulous inquiry into the father's long past and non-parental conduct which few mortals could withstand, it bases its determination that the discretion of the trial court was properly exercised upon the belief that the record shows (or that the trial court might have properly believed) that Mr. Young is less sincere, less well motivated, less admirable and generally a worse person and a worse parent than Ms. Hector. As I might do myself, one may agree with this assessment of the parties while profoundly disagreeing, as I certainly do, with the idea that any such consideration is a proper basis for decision-making in this field.

It is of course true, as the majority repeatedly emphasizes, that a "custody" decision is one within the discretion of the trial court. But judicial discretion may properly be exercised only on the basis of factors which are legally pertinent to the issue involved. In this area, that issue is the children's best interests. Its resolution, in turn, cannot be based on a subjective assessment of the worth of the contending parties so long as, as was conclusively demonstrated in this case, the conduct and character traits referred to have not impacted upon the children. We had, I thought, come a long way from the time when a parent could be denied her parental rights—or, more properly stated, when the children could be

---

7. That the issues have so often been put in these terms, which better describe a sports event than a dispassionate search for a result which most benefits the children is one of the most unfortunate aspects of this case. See *Mize v. Mize,* 621 So. 2d 417, 420 (Fla.1993) (Barkett, J., concurring) (expressing grave doubts as to wisdom of employing adversary process in resolving family issues). That it should be widely thought that a mother, and only a mother, is considered morally or maternally deficient if she is not granted custody, is a testament to the pervasiveness of sexual stereotyping in our supposedly gender-blind society. That the majority decision will likely serve to perpetuate both of these fallacies is disheartening.

8. That working fathers have almost never actually gained custody has not prevented the use of such claims or even the threat of bringing them as effective "bargaining chips"—meaning instruments of extortion—in settling the financial disputes which are usually the only real issues in these cases. Taking the majority at its word that the sex of the working parent makes no difference, the result in this case, which means that a non-caretaking father may actually succeed in "taking the children away" from the mother, will inevitably result in a great increase in the dollar value of this nefarious tactic, and in the involvement of the courts in the use of children as pawns in personal disputes between alienated spouses. Of all the many adverse consequences of today's decision, these may be the most serious.

deprived of *their* rights to having only *their* interests considered—merely because a judge may disapprove of her standards of conduct, much less of her character. Apparently, I was mistaken. Although only with the best of intentions, and fortunately in a case in which children will thrive in the care of either parent (or both of them), the majority has perhaps unwittingly provided that custody decisions are subject to the personal views of a particular judge, who sits as a Dostoevskian Grand Inquisitor, the effectuation of whose own notions of right and wrong are subject to objective review by no one on this earth. In a society of law and not persons, unknowable and unjudgable questions of character, personal worth, and even actual "misconduct," if irrelevant to the issue under consideration, should not govern decision making in this area or any other. * * *

NESBITT, J. (dissenting):

I respectfully dissent.

* * *

The record demonstrates that both the mother and the father of the children are completely and entirely fit and worthy (as the trial court found) to serve as primary residential parent. As the wife's law practice grew and prospered (she was working 11 and 12 hour days and was frequently gone overnight), she relied more and more upon the husband, who accepted the responsibility for the care and needs of the girls. The arrangement began in the fall of 1993 and continued until the 1996 dissolution proceeding which led to the husband's summary eviction from the marital home. Acquiescence to the child custody arrangement can and has been found to be an important factor of various aspects of child custody problems. This salient factor was wholly ignored by the trial court. Section 61.13(2)(b)1, Florida Statutes (1995), in part provides "the father of the child shall be given the same consideration as the mother in determining the primary residence of a child irrespective of the age or sex of the child."

* * *

In this proceeding the trial judge totally ignored the gender neutral policy. For example, at one point in the proceeding he asked the husband, "Maybe there's something I don't understand—why don't you get a job?" It is extremely unlikely that any circuit judge in Florida would have asked the same question of the mother of young children whose husband was then earning a substantial annual income.

Sub silentio, this court like the trial court continues to pillory the father because he is not the substantial bread winner in the family. But there is little or no correlation between being the money maker or between being wealthy or not[ ] in order to make one an effective parent.

By today's decision, the court remains aligned with the traditional view that a mother will not lose her entitlement to become the primary residential parent unless her unfitness is demonstrated; no matter how actively she is engaged outside of and away from the home, even though the other parent is fit and willing to serve in that capacity. Such holding necessarily implies that children therefore will be substantially or in part reared by a surrogate parent. It occurs to me that both the children and the societal interest are better served by placement with a natural parent who is available.

Given the parties' own conduct toward the care and rearing of these children it leaves no doubt that their best interests would be that they remain with their primary care giver; here their natural father. Where parents themselves have established an arrangement (which they do not either dispute, contradict or refute) which supports the children's best interests—there is no reason for the courts to interfere.

I therefore dissent * * *.

NOTES AND QUESTIONS

1. *Does working in a demanding job expose women to the risk of losing their children?* The lawyer who represented Alice Hector in the *en banc* proceedings has said that "[p]erhaps what is most disturbing about the *Young* panel decision is that it is neither an anomaly or a surprise. In the area of child custody, courts typically have not rewarded working women." Amy Ronner, *Women Who Dance on the Professional Track: Custody and the Red Shoes*, 23 Harv. Women's L. J. 173, 173 (2000). She argues that to the court of appeals panel, whose opinion the *en banc* court overturned, Ms. Hector was "a talented, ambitious, highly successful, and aggressive litigator, [who] personified a threat to male power." *Id*. at 176. Professor Ronner argues that Mr. Young's stance as a "Mr. Mom" was nothing more than a classic litigation strategy, developed in anticipation of a pending divorce. *Id*. at 212. She concludes that professional women are doubly jeopardized on divorce. Their custody claims are imperiled, but they do not command large divorce settlements or child support payments if they receive custody.

The mid–1990s saw a series of highly publicized cases involving professional women threatened with losing custody of their children, largely because of the demands of their jobs. "Combining work and motherhood has become treacherous * * *. In the 1990s, mothers, to be good parents (and fit the gender-based and now court-created stereotype), had to pick up their children from school, carpool children's activities, put children to bed, and organize family events." Jacquelyn H. Slotkin, *Should I Have Learned to Cook? Interviews with Women Lawyers Juggling Multiple Roles*, 13 Hastings Women's L.J. 147, 153 (2002). In *Prost v. Greene*, 652 A.2d 621 (D.C. 1995), the mother, who held a high pressure position as counsel for the Republicans on the U.S. Senate Judiciary Committee, lost custody of her two children to her frequently unemployed husband, also an attorney, who, according to the trial judge, had assumed more of the day-to-day responsibility for the children. Similarly, a Michigan trial judge shifted custody of a three-year-old child of teenage parents to the father when the mother enrolled in college and placed the child in day care. The judge reasoned that the father's mother would do a better job of watching the child than a "stranger." The decision was reversed on appeal, in litigation that attracted 61 amicus briefs on behalf of the mother. *Ireland v. Smith*, 542 N.W.2d 344 (Mich. Ct. App. 1995), *aff'd*, 547 N.W.2d 686 (Mich. 1996). The young mother ultimately gained custody of her child.

2. *Mr. Mom.* Mr. Young claimed that he was a "Mr. Mom" (a reference to several films including the Academy Award-winning 1979 film *Kramer v. Kramer* (Columbia Pictures 1979) and *Mr. Mom* (MGM, 1983), in which fathers received custody). Might fathers' rights advocates argue that if Mr. Young were a female stay-at-home parent, *h*e would have retained custody? How would you respond to those arguments?

3. *Women in military service.* In 2004, a Missouri court denied the appeal of a mother who had lost custody of her young daughter after she volunteered for overseas military duty, even though the mother had presented evidence that the father had used marijuana, had hit her once, and had viewed pornography. The mother argued that the trial court's decision precluded a woman in the military from having children. *Cooley v. Cooley*, 131 S.W.3d 901 (Mo. Ct. App. 2004). Is there anything unique about military service overseas? How might this case be distinguishable from *McDermott*?

B.   DOMESTIC VIOLENCE

WISSINK v. WISSINK

Supreme Court of New York, Appellate Division, 2002.
749 N.Y.S.2d 550.

S. MILLER, J.

This appeal presents a vexing custody dispute over a teenaged girl who has expressed a clear preference to live with her father. While both parents are seemingly fit custodians, the father has a history of domestic violence directed at the mother; yet he has never posed a direct threat to the child. Because of this circumstance, we hold that the Family Court erred in awarding custody to the father without first ordering comprehensive psychological evaluations to ensure that this award of custody was truly in the child's best interest.

The child in controversy, Andrea, born June 21, 1986, is the biological child of the mother and father; the mother also has a daughter, Karin, by a prior marriage. The parties have had a tumultuous relationship marked by numerous episodes of heated arguments, physical violence, police intervention and Family Court orders of protection. It is apparent that when it comes to his dealings with the mother, the father is a batterer whose temper gets the better of him. When it comes to Andrea, however, the father is the favored parent; he has never directly mistreated Andrea.

The parties have lived apart at various times during their marriage, and separated most recently in 1999 following yet another physical altercation. The mother commenced a family offense proceeding and a proceeding for custody of Andrea. The father cross-petitioned for custody. The

Family Court assigned a law guardian and ordered a mental health study which was clearly deficient. A hearing was held at which the parties, Karin, and other witnesses testified, and the court examined Andrea in camera; she downplayed the father's culpability and expressed her clear preference for living with him.

The order appealed from awarded custody to the father. In separate orders, the Family Court dismissed the mother's custody petition and sustained the mother's family offense petitions, directing, *inter alia*, that the father enter and complete a domestic violence program. We now reverse the order awarding custody to the father and remit for a new custody hearing following an in-depth forensic examination of the parties and child.

Andrea's preference for her father and her closely bonded relationship to him were confirmed by her law guardian and the "mental health professional" social worker who interviewed her. Indeed, putting aside the established fact of his abusive conduct toward her mother, Andrea's father appears a truly model parent. He is significantly involved in her school work and her extracurricular activities. They enjoy many pleasurable activities, including movies, shopping, building a barn, and horseback riding. He provides her with material benefits—a television set, clothing, a horse, a trip to Europe. He is loving and affectionate. She is his "princess," his "best girl." In contrast, Andrea's mother has not been significantly involved in her school work or her extracurricular activities, and Andrea does not enjoy her company or their relationship.

Were it not for the documented history of domestic violence confirmed by the court after a hearing, we would have unanimously affirmed the Family Court's award of custody to the father in accordance with Andrea's expressed preference and the evidence documenting their positive relationship. However, the fact of domestic violence should have been considered more than superficially, particularly in this case where Andrea expressed her unequivocal preference for the abuser, while denying the very existence of the domestic violence that the court found she witnessed.

The record is replete with incidents of domestic violence reported by the mother, and by evidence supporting her testimony. The earliest incident that the mother reported was perpetrated when Andrea was merely an infant in 1986. In a fit of anger the father hit and kicked the mother and pulled out chunks of her hair. In the course of the attack she heard him say, "Oh well, she's going to die." On Super Bowl Sunday in 1995, he attacked her, throwing her on the floor, kicking, hitting, and choking her. She sustained marks on her neck and a sore throat causing pain while speaking and inhibiting her ability to swallow.

In March 1995, she obtained an order of protection from the Village Court of Montgomery. In the fall of that year the father allegedly held a knife, approximately 8 to 10 inches long, to the mother's throat while Andrea, then nine, sat on her lap. In February 1996, the mother again obtained an order of protection from the Village Court of Montgomery.

In 1997, the father attacked the mother, hit and kicked her, resulting in her obtaining a permanent order of protection from the Orange County Family Court. The severity of her injuries are documented by a photograph, entered in evidence, showing a large black and blue bruise on her left hip.

In June 1999, the mother left the marital home with Andrea and moved into a shelter where they remained for five days. Upon their return home the father blocked her car in the driveway, yelled at the mother and punched her.

On June 24, 1999, a few days after her return from the shelter, during a dispute over tax returns, the father tried to wrest papers the mother held in her teeth by squeezing her face in his hands, leaving marks and even enlisting the assistance of Andrea; he allegedly directed the child to "hold [the mother's] nose so she can't breathe."

On December 20, 1999, while Andrea was at home, the father attacked the mother, choking her. She had marks on her neck for days.

The latter two incidents were the subjects of the mother's most recent Family Offense petition, which the court sustained. In doing so, the Family Court also noted that a final order of protection had been entered in 1997, stating "based upon the proceeding [of 1997] as well as the succeeding [incidents] ... Mr. Wissink is guilty of incidents of domestic violence occurring on June 24, [1999,] and December 20, [1999]."

Domestic Relations Law § 240 (1) provides that in any action concerning custody or visitation where domestic violence is alleged, "the court must consider" the effect of such domestic violence upon the best interest of the child, together with other factors and circumstances as the court deems relevant in making an award of custody. In this case the Family Court did not entirely ignore that legislative mandate, and specifically noted that it had considered the effect of domestic violence in rendering its custody determination. However, the "consideration" afforded the effect of domestic violence in this case was, in our view, sorely inadequate.

The court-ordered mental health evaluation consisted of the social worker's interview of Andrea on two occasions (about 45 minutes each) and each parent once (about one hour each). These interviews resulted in the social worker's clearly foreseeable conclusion that Andrea was far more comfortable and involved with her father than her mother, that she did not relate well to her mother, and that she preferred living with her father.

In a case such as this, where the record reveals years of domestic violence, which is denied by the child who witnessed it, and the child has expressed her preference to live with the abuser, the court should have ordered a comprehensive psychological evaluation. Such an evaluation would likely include a clinical evaluation, psychological testing, and review of records and information from collateral sources. The forensic evaluator would be concerned with such issues as the nature of the psychopathology of the abuser and of the victim; whether the child might be in danger of becoming a future victim, or a witness to the abuse of some other victim; the child's developmental needs given the fact that she has lived in the polluted environment of domestic violence all of her life and the remedial efforts that should be undertaken in regard to all parties concerned.

The devastating consequences of domestic violence have been recognized by our courts, by law enforcement, and by society as a whole. The effect of such violence on children exposed to it has also been established. There is overwhelming authority that a child living in a home where there has been abuse between the adults becomes a secondary victim and is likely to suffer psychological injury.

Moreover, that child learns a dangerous and morally depraved lesson that abusive behavior is not only acceptable, but may even be rewarded.

In many states a rebuttable presumption that perpetrators of domestic violence should not be eligible for legal or physical custody has been accepted and the courts of those states are required to specify why custody should be granted to an offender and how such an order is in the best interest of the child (see Philip M. Stahl, Complex Issues in Child Custody Evaluations, [36 (Sage 1999)]). We in New York have not gone that far, but the legislature, in enacting Domestic Relations Law § 240, has recognized that domestic violence is a factor which the court must consider among others in awarding custody or visitation.

Moreover, the court also erred in limiting the mother's inquiry regarding the father's failure to comply with child support obligations and in finding financial consideration "not relevant at all" to the custody proceeding. The Family Court was required to consider the parties' support obligations and their compliance with court orders and to evaluate each party's ability to support the child. If, as the mother alleged, the father violated the child support order, and if he terminated the telephone and electrical services in the marital residence after he had been ordered to stay away pursuant to an order of protection, these facts would clearly be relevant to the court's custody determination.

Only after considering the complex nature of the issues and the relative merits and deficiencies of the alternatives can the court attempt to determine the difficult issue of the best interest of the child in a case such as this.

For the above reasons we thus reverse the custody order and direct a new custody hearing to be conducted after completion of a comprehensive psychological evaluation of the parties and the child. However, we stay Andrea's return to her mother, permitting her continued residence with her father, pending a final custody determination.

We note that the foregoing is without prejudice to the mother renewing her petition for custody, which was dismissed by an order from which no appeal was taken.

* * *

ORDERED that pending the final custody determination, the father shall have temporary custody of the child, Andrea, with visitation to the mother pursuant to the terms of the order appealed from.

NOTES AND QUESTIONS

1. *How courts consider evidence of domestic violence.* In *Wissink*, the trial court's decision to award custody to a man who had abused his wife goes against the majority rule. Most states either include domestic violence as a factor in the best interests standard or provide that evidence of domestic violence creates a rebuttable presumption against awarding custody to the abusive parent Which approach makes better sense?. *See* Amy B. Levin, *Comment, Child Witnesses of Domestic Violence: How Should Judges Apply the Best Interests of the Child Standard in Custody and Visitation Cases Involving Domestic Violence*, 47 UCLA L. Rev. 813 (2000); *see also* Joan S. Meier, *Domestic Violence, Child Custody,and Child Protection: Understanding Judicial Resistance and Imagining the Solution*,11 Am. U. J. Gender Soc. Pol'y & L. 657 (2003)

2. *Domestic violence as a factor in custody determinations in New York.* A New York family court judge has pointed out the limits of that state's statutory reforms to date:

* * *

* * * In 1990, a joint resolution of Congress urged the states to adopt a legislative presumption that it is detrimental to a child when custody is awarded to an abusive spouse. The Model Code on Domestic and Family Violence, developed by the National Council of Juvenile and Family Court Judges in 1994, and a report by the American Bar Association ("ABA") adopted this Congressional recommendation.

New York was one of the last states to adopt the recommended legislation. Thus, before the New York amendment was adopted in 1996, thirty-eight states and the District of Columbia already had laws making domestic violence a relevant factor in custody and visitation determinations. By 1997, the number of states grew to forty-four and, according to the most recent information from the ABA, forty-six states currently require consideration of domestic violence before custody decisions are made.

The New York statute, adopted six years after the original national proposal, differs from the congressional proposal in one major respect. New York expressly declined to adopt a presumption against awarding custody to a battering parent and, instead, only mandated that domestic violence be considered by courts as a factor in making such awards. Further, the statutory mandate only applies when allegations of violence are contained in a sworn pleading. In this regard, the New York amendment reflects the tension between the strong public policy in favor of protecting children from the effects of a violent household and the concern that general, non-particularized claims of violence could be raised in order to gain an unfair advantage in a custody/visitation dispute.

* * *

In 1996, the [New York] state legislature amended *section 240 of the New York Domestic Relations Law* ("DRL") to provide that in connection with determining the 'best interests' of the child in custody and/or visitation disputes, the court is mandated to consider, if raised, the issue of domestic violence. Thus, section 240.1(a) of the DRL now provides in pertinent part:

> * * * [T]he court must consider the effect of such domestic violence upon the best interest of the child, together with such other facts and circumstances as the court deems relevant in making a direction pursuant to this section.

In 1998, the legislature amended [the code] to prohibit an award of custody or visitation to a person convicted of murdering the child's parent, except in very limited circumstances. * * *

* * * The 1996 amendment provides the only statutorily mandated factor * * * that the court must consider [in custody cases]. The 1998 amendment is even stronger because it eliminates judicial discretion and mandates a result in custody and visitation cases involving a murder conviction of the petitioning parent.

The 1996 amendment was adopted in response to a growing national concern about the effect of domestic violence on children. * * *

* * *

B. The Definition of Domestic Violence

The 1996 amendment does not define domestic violence. It would be reasonable, however, for courts to conclude that domestic violence includes the commission of those acts enumerated in [the criminal code] as family offenses that justify the grant of an order of protection. In at least one reported decision, the trial court broadly defined domestic violence to include psychological violence and not just overt acts leading to physical injury. The court's definition in that case drew upon the current mental health paradigm that refers to domestic violence as a pattern of behaviors designed to exercise control over the victim.

C. The Weight to Be Given a Finding of Domestic Violence

Once the trial court finds, by a preponderance of the evidence, that there is domestic violence, the court must go on to consider what effect, if any, the finding will have on its custody or visitation determination. Courts often look at domestic violence in the factual context of an entire case, considering the common law factors of 'best interests' as well. Courts may also consider mitigating factors, such as the parties' successful efforts at domestic violence counseling. Thus, domestic violence, while a significant consideration in custody and visitation disputes, is not necessarily dispositive of the outcome of the case.

While not dispositive, however, a finding that a parent is a batterer will weigh heavily against an award of custody to that parent. On the other hand, the same finding will not usually result in the court denying visitation. In order to deny visitation, the court must find that contact will have a detrimental effect on the child. * * *

D. The "Accused But Not Yet Convicted" Murderer Problem

* * * The 1998 amendment still leaves open to court discretion the question of where the child should reside after arrest, but prior to conviction. In general, before a court can consider the custody or visitation petition of a non-parent, 'extraordinary circumstances' must be established. The courts are divided over whether this threshold is met when one parent is accused of murdering the other * * *. Even when such extraordinary circumstances are present, the court must still determine where it would be in the child's 'best interest' to live. Custody cases necessarily require a prediction of future behavior based upon past history. * * *

Conclusion

Both the 1996 and 1998 amendments to the DRL focus attention on the serious, long-lasting, detrimental effect that domestic violence can have on children living in the household. They each recognize that children are psychologically damaged by such behaviors regardless of whether the child, or some other household member, is the actual victim. The amendments, however, provide little guidance for the courts and leave many unanswered questions. * * *

* * *

Judith J. Gische, *Domestic Violence as a Factor in Child Custody Determinations in New York*, 27 Fordham Urb. L. J. 937, 937–43 (2000).

3. *Teen wins fight for new parents, is adopted after "divorcing" father for killing mother.*

A teen who won a groundbreaking legal battle last summer to "divorce" his killer father walked out of court Thursday with new adoptive parents. "I don't think I'll ever be over it," Patrick Holland said of his mother's 1998 slaying by his father, "but it's a step forward. It's about the biggest step you can take at one time."

Patrick, 15, was adopted by Ron and Rita Lazisky; the pair have been his guardians and were close friends of the teen's mother. The Laziskys, of Sandown, N.H., have cared for Patrick since shortly after Daniel Holland fatally shot Liz Holland at the family's Quincy, Mass. home. Then 8, Patrick found his mother's body the following morning. Daniel Holland is serving life in prison without parole.

Patrick was one of the first children to initiate a parental-rights termination proceeding against one parent for killing the other. He argued

Daniel Holland forfeited any right to be his father the night he shot Liz Holland eight times.

* * *

After nearly three years of legal wrangling over whether a minor could sue to terminate parental rights—and whether the case belonged in Massachusetts or New Hampshire—Patrick got a hearing date. On the eve of the trial last July, Daniel Holland agreed to settle, signing away his parental rights in an agreement specifying Patrick was the sole heir to the slain woman's estate and clearing the way for the adoption.

Katharine Webster, Associated Press, *Adoption Final for Teen Who "Divorced" Killer Dad*, Charleston (W.Va.) Daily Mail, March 25, 2005, at P3C.

4. *Evidentiary problems.* Professors Jane Aiken and Jane Murphy address the evidentiary problems that stem from gender bias in domestic violence cases. They suggest that judges and juries often minimize or disbelieve reports of domestic violence. Jane H. Aiken & Jane C. Murphy, *Evidence Issues in Domestic Violence Civil Cases*, 34 Fam. L.Q. 43, 44–45 (2000). Statutes in several states, for example Arizona and California, attempt to address these problems. *See* Ariz. Rev. Stat. Ann. § 25–403.01(A) (West 2000) (joint custody shall not be awarded "if the court makes a finding of the existence of significant domestic violence * * * or if the court finds by a preponderance of the evidence that there has been a significant history of domestic violence"); Cal. Fam. Code § 3011 (West 2004 & Supp. 2008) (courts may require "substantial independent corroboration" before considering a history of abuse by one parent as a factor in determining the best interests of the child).

5. *A rebuttable presumption against perpetrators?* In *Heck v. Reed*, 529 N.W.2d 155 (N.D. 1995), the trial court found that although the father had perpetrated domestic violence against the mother, other factors rebutted the presumption that a perpetrator may not be awarded sole or joint custody of the children. The Supreme Court of North Dakota reversed, finding that the statutory presumption against awarding custody of the children to a perpetrator of domestic violence was not overcome:

> Domestic violence is "a pattern of assaulting and controlling behavior" committed by one household member against another. Domestic violence is not caused by stress in the perpetrator's life, alcohol consumption, or a particular victim's propensity to push a perpetrator's buttons. Rather, domestic violence is a learned pattern of behavior aimed at gaining a victim's compliance.

> Perpetrators can "unlearn" the pattern of domestic violence; however, this requires sufficient motivation for changing their violent behavior. The most recent episode of domestic violence by [the father] occurred less than two years prior to the custody hearing. [The father] introduced no evidence at the hearing that he had considered or participated in any form of treatment program or counseling related to domestic violence. Absent such proof of rehabilitation, it was clearly erroneous to conclude,

as the trial judge did here, that [the father] will no longer use domestic violence as a means of controlling his intimate partners.

* * *

[The applicable statute] reflects the public policy of our state that a perpetrator of domestic violence is generally not a proper person to have custody and the presumption against awarding that parent custody of the children may be overcome only by compelling circumstances, not present in this case.

Id. at 164–66 (alterations added).

6. *Another perspective on domestic violence.* Domestic violence presents a glass-half-empty/glass-half-full dilemma. Some psychologists have found that as many as 60% of the children whose parents were violent with one another were not themselves victims of physical abuse. This finding also means that 40% of these children, quite a hefty number, were victims. The findings suggest that decision-makers must assess the relationships with parents directly, without simply assuming that children must have been abused because their parents were violent with one another. Anne E. Appel & George W. Holden, *The Co–Occurrence of Spouse and Physical Child Abuse: A Review and Appraisal*, 12 J. Fam. Psychol. 578, 598–99 (1998). Do the numbers also suggest who should get the benefit of the doubt if proof of physical child abuse is equivocal? Appel and Holden argue that reports of parental conflict should not be allowed to have an undue influence on decisions about parent-child contact. Do you agree?

7. *Friendly-parent provisions.* "Friendly parent" provisions, which require courts "to consider which parent is more likely to encourage close contact with the other parent" were in place in twenty-two states in 1996. Frederica Lehrman, *Factoring Domestic Violence into Custody Cases*, Trial, Feb. 1996, at 32. These provisions pose special problems in families where a pattern of domestic violence exists:

> Violent parents often speak to their children and to the courts in glowing terms of shared parenting, promising a harmonious future despite past violence. If an abused parent strenuously objects to shared parenting, he or she may appear recalcitrant and unforgiving in court, while the violent parent presents an image of contrition and loving good will.

> The problem may be compounded when the abused parent has sought a civil protection order against the batterer. A person seeking safety by ending all contact with an abusive partner may run headlong into friendly parent provisions, which clash with the parent's need to be safe and endanger the parent's change of being awarded custody.

Id. at 34–35; *see also* Carol Bruch, *Parental Alienation Syndrome and Parental Alienation: Getting It Wrong in Child Custody Cases*, 35 Fam. L. Q. 527 (2001).

In 2001, a study of over 100 psychologists who regularly perform child custody evaluations for courts reported that "the friendly parent criterion was ranked by respondents as more significant" than the presence of domestic violence, "raising the concern that a * * * victim who is appropriately reluctant to encourage visitation between an abuser and the children may be penalized for this and may even lose custody." Nancy S. Erickson & Joan Zorza, *Evaluating the Handling of Domestic Violence Cases by Custody Evaluations*, 10 Domestic Violence Rep. 49, 49 (2005). Another survey found that the evaluators had recommended joint custody in an "astounding" 39% of the cases in which they believed the domestic violence allegations to be credible. *Id.* at 62.

8. *Domestic violence and visitation.* In 2000, the American Bar Association adopted a new policy concerning domestic violence and custody, and recommended that states and lawyers take action to provide for the safety of adult and child domestic violence victims during visitation and visitation exchanges. Linda D. Elrod & Robert G. Spector, *A Review of the Year in Family Law: Redefining Families, Reforming Custody Jurisdiction, and Refining Support Issues*, 34 Fam. L.Q. 607 (2001). For the text of the ABA policies, see ABA Comm'n on Domestic Violence, http://www.abanet.org/domviol/attorneys.html.

In 1998, the American Psychological Association (APA) reported that "an abusive man is more likely than a nonviolent father to seek sole physical custody of his children and may be just as likely (or even more likely) to be awarded custody as the mother." Am. Psychological Ass'n, Report of the American Psychological Association Presidential Task Force on Violence and the Family, Issues and Dilemmas in Family Violence, Issue 5 (1998), http://www.apa.org/pi/pii/familyvio/issue5.html. The APA Presidential Task Force also found that courts often minimize the harmful impact to a child who witnesses violence between parents. According to the APA, some courts ignore the advice of psychologists that "it may be better for children's development to restrict the father's access to them and avoid continued danger to both mothers and the children." *Id.*

A NOTE ON EXPERT OPINIONS

The decisions you have read in this Chapter demonstrate that courts hearing child custody cases frequently receive testimony from experts in fields such as psychology, psychiatry, and social work. In *McDermott v. Dougherty*, for example, the trial court heard testimony from experts regarding both parents' fitness during the divorce proceedings. In *Painter v. Bannister*, the court heard testimony from an expert who had known the grandparents for a long time, but who had never met Mark's father. You will continue to see references to expert testimony in many of the remaining decisions in this book.

The psychological parent/least detrimental alternative approach and the best interests approach to custody frequently require lawyers and judges to consider a range of issues beyond their legal expertise, much as might happen in complex products liability or antitrust cases. Several issues arise about the use of experts in child custody cases, including the conditions of the expert's appointment, the best methods for evaluating the child's needs and relationships, and the weight the court should accord to the expert's opinion. *See* Janet M. Bowermaster, *Legal Presumptions and the Role of Mental Health Professionals in Child Custody Proceedings*, 40 Duq. L. Rev. 265 (2002).

1. *Conditions of appointment.* A leader in forensic child psychiatry has stated "it is an egregious error for a clinician to be selected by one party, to perform a one-sided evaluation, or to offer an opinion based on interviews with only one of the parties." He cautions that "mental health professionals performing child custody evaluations should do so only if they have been court appointed or agreed to by all sides." Stephen P. Herman, *Child Custody Evaluations and the Need for Standards of Care and Peer Review*, 1 J. Center for Child. & Cts. 139, 141 (1999).

2. *Guidelines for conducting custody evaluations.* A high quality child custody consultation is extremely intensive. The best practices for court-ordered custody evaluations include interviews with each parent alone, and each parent together with the child or children. The evaluator should initially see the siblings together and then, if warranted, separately. Even young children can be interviewed alone if the interviewer relies on correct techniques, such as using dollhouses and dolls, or drawing a family portrait. *Id.* at 142. "Collateral interviews" may also be conducted with other family members, and with other people who know the family well, including teachers. *Id.* at 141. With the parents' permission, the clinician can examine school and other records pertaining to the child. Finally, the evaluator must write a clear, accessible and comprehensive report to the court explaining the reasoning behind each conclusion. *Id.* at 144.

Several professional guidelines apply to psychiatrists and psychologists who conduct child custody evaluations, which involve specialized skills. Evaluators need to be careful not to merge their role as a forensic expert with their more accustomed role as a therapist. Experts like Dr. Herman urge that the principles of confidentiality and protecting the patient from harm mitigate against a treating therapist's serving as a forensic consultant about the patient, but other experts have argued that the treating therapist knows more about the family than a consultant who has just arrived on the scene. *Compare* Herman, *supra* at 145, *with* Jean Koh Peters, Representing Children in Child Protective Proceedings: Ethical and Practical Dimensions 592–94 (2001).

Even if best practices are followed, do any risks accompany a decision to involve the children in their parents' custody dispute? How should lawyers discuss these risks with their clients?

C. SEXUAL BEHAVIOR

ZEPEDA v. ZEPEDA

Supreme Court of South Dakota, 2001.
632 N.W.2d 48.

KONENKAMP, JUSTICE.

* * *

A.

Jorge and Leslie Renee Zepeda (Renee) met in 1986 while they were both students at Louisiana State University. They married on November

27, 1987. Both eventually earned bachelor's degrees. Jorge graduated from LSU with a degree in electrical engineering. Renee received her degree from the University of Alabama, after accumulating college credit at various institutions. Before completing her degree, she gave birth to the couple's only child, Jorgito, born November 6, 1996. Renee cared for Jorgito "during the daytime when [Jorge] was at work." After obtaining her degree, Renee stayed home to provide full-time childcare.

In November 1998, Jorge accepted a position with Gateway Computer Company, and the couple moved to Dakota Dunes, South Dakota. This position provided a substantial salary increase. Renee continued to stay at home with Jorgito. In her words, she accepted the "woman's role in the house." She "took care of the majority of attending to Jorgito, his feeding, cleaning, dressing, shopping for clothes for him, [and] buying food for him." Jorge's brother, who lived with the couple for a short time, substantiated her rendition for the most part. Jorge recalled that he also spent a great deal of his free time playing with and educating Jorgito. Renee disputed Jorge's recollection, insisting that Jorge worked long hours and spent little time with his son either during the week or on the weekends.

After their move to South Dakota, marital difficulties began to emerge. According to Renee, Jorge was either "controlling" or he ignored her, choosing to "talk to his computer or the TV rather than [her]." For his part, Jorge became suspicious of Renee's activities on the Internet while he was at work. He installed software on their home computer to covertly monitor her keystrokes. What he discovered would become a focal point in the divorce proceedings. In trial, Renee admitted that from late July 1999 until sometime in October of that year she engaged in "highly erotic" discourse on Internet "chatrooms" with two different adult men. These communications occurred, in her estimate, perhaps "once a week."[3] She explained that "it was kind of enjoyable that someone was finding interest in me." But her infidelity was not confined to the Internet. Renee had sexual relations several times with another man in July 1999. On one occasion, after sharing a bottle of wine, the two engaged in sexual intercourse in Renee and Jorge's apartment while Jorgito was sleeping.

Jorge sued for divorce in September 1999. As the precipitating cause, he blamed Renee's sexual affair along with her "cybersex" conversations. He believed that Renee's Internet use had become an addiction. In her answer, Renee also requested a divorce. Both Jorge and Renee sought temporary custody of Jorgito. Before the interim hearing, the couple was evaluated by psychologist, Dr. Matt Stricherz. Stricherz opined that "while not appropriate for the marriage," Renee's Internet use was not an addiction. Stricherz also noted that "[n]either [parent] has issues in their

---

3. The parties disagree on the amount of time Renee spent engaging in these conversations. In his brief, Jorge asserts that "Renee ... began spending substantial hours nearly every day pursuing illicit relationships on the [I]nternet with adult men." Jorge fails to cite the record to support his statement.

past that would indicate an inability to provide adequate care for the child. The father has his strengths. The mother has her strengths."

Following the hearing, the court granted temporary custody to Renee, with visitation for Jorge. The court placed express conditions on Renee. First, she was not to have "any men in her apartment or in her presence while the child [was] present." Second, she was to refrain from consuming alcohol. Third, she could not use the Internet throughout the duration of the divorce and custody proceedings unless required by her employment.

In February 2000, Jorge accepted a position with Dell Computer Corporation in Austin, Texas. His benefits included a $10,000 per year pay increase and a more flexible schedule. The parties agreed to modify Jorge's visitation. Every other Wednesday Jorge flew back to South Dakota and kept Jorgito from Wednesday through Sunday. Renee in no way hindered Jorge's ability to visit his son.

The divorce trial was held in August 2000. Jorge offered computer log-on records from August 1 through October 22, 1999. They showed a substantial amount of Internet use in the household. For example, the computer was logged on for up to seven hours a day in August 1999. These records do not indicate, however, which member of the household used the Internet or whether the computer was simply left logged-on.

The court heard testimony from a licensed independent social worker, Judy Conner, who had visited with all three members of the family. She described Jorgito as a very active child who spoke very well even at age two. She observed that he "appeared to be very attached to both of his parents." Conner found Jorge and Renee "to be very caring parents." She saw nothing "that raised a red flag ... or any kind of alarm." Dr. Stricherz's opinions coincided with Conner's. He had re-evaluated Renee in July 2000 in an attempt to ascertain any behavioral changes since the temporary hearing. Stricherz reaffirmed that Renee had no Internet addiction and noted that his initial conclusion was supported by the absence of any substituted behaviors after her computer was taken away.[5] At trial, Jorge produced no evidence that Renee had engaged in any inappropriate conduct since the temporary hearing.

Jorgito has attended the same daycare facility since December 1999. One of the daycare providers confirmed Jorgito's strong attachment to his mother:

> When she brings him in every morning, he has his arms around her waist ... [a]nd he always hugs her goodbye and says goodbye.... She always turns back twice and waves goodbye, and he's always waiting for her to turn back again[.]

---

5. Jorge offered testimony from Dr. Scott Pribyl, a psychologist. Pribyl thought there was a "possibility" that Renee had an Internet addiction. He testified that it appeared "there were times ... that her use of the Internet was impacting her sleep patterns and perhaps her ability to attend to the child." In its bench ruling, the court found Stricherz and Conner to be the more credible witnesses because they had actually met with the family. Pribyl's opinion was based solely on his review of documentary evidence.

The same witness described Jorgito as "very intelligent" and "soft-hearted."

* * *

At the end of the trial, the court ruled from the bench, granting joint legal custody to the parents, with Renee retaining primary physical custody. Jorge was ordered to pay monthly child support of $899. * * * In its written findings of fact and conclusions of law, the court held that Renee was a "fit parent who provides a stable environment, with commensurate continuity of care as well." Jorge appeals the custody decision on his assertion that the trial court failed to adequately consider Renee's misconduct and Jorgito's need to maintain contact with both parents.

B.

Child Custody

To decide a custody dispute, a court must consider the child's temporal, mental, and moral welfare. No precise formula exists for making a custody determination, but the decision should be balanced and methodical. We recognize several "guiding principles" in weighing the evidence. These considerations include parental fitness; stability; primary caretaker; child's preference; harmful parental misconduct; and separation of siblings. A court is not bound to make a specific finding in each category; indeed, certain elements may have no application in some cases, and for other cases there may be additional relevant considerations. In the end, our brightest beacon remains the best interests of the child. A trial court is in a better position to evaluate the facts, and its conclusions on a child's best interests will stand unless we find an abuse of discretion.

* * *

Jorge contends that the circuit court "improperly concluded that Renee's behavior did not detract from her future ability to parent." Generally, marital misconduct alone is not a controlling consideration when making a custody determination. However, when misconduct results in some demonstrable harm to the child, parental fitness becomes an issue. Harm is self-evident when misconduct occurs in the presence of a child mature enough to perceive it.

The trial court found different categories of marital misconduct and examined each one. Regarding Renee's Internet usage, the court believed that Dr. Stricherz was the more credible expert. Stricherz discredited the suggestion that Renee suffered an Internet addiction. The court believed Renee's testimony that she had abstained from Internet usage and erotic discourse since the temporary custody hearing. Although the court labeled such conduct "potentially harmful" and "appalling," it found no "demonstrable effect on [Jorgito]." In discussing the instance of sexual intercourse in the home while Jorgito was sleeping, the court again emphasized that Renee's conduct was reprehensible. The court concluded, however, that the child was not in Renee's direct presence, that he was monitored with a baby monitor, and that the incident was an isolated one. Consequently, the court found no harmful effect on the child. The court discounted allegations of excessive drinking based on the lack of evidence. All Renee's misconduct occurred in a three month time span from July to October 1999.

We review findings of fact deferentially, applying the clearly erroneous standard. In Jorge's brief, he asserts that Renee was not candid with the trial court. In essence, he argues that the court erred when it failed to accept his version of the facts. It was obvious to the trial court, and it is obvious to us now, that Jorge is a dedicated and loving father. Indeed, the judge acknowledged that the custody decision was a close one. Yet, we are in no position to reweigh the evidence. Absent clear proof of error, we must defer to the judge's firsthand perception of the witnesses and the significance the judge gave to their testimony. Like the circuit court, we do not condone Renee's misconduct, but we cannot hold that the court was clearly erroneous when it ruled that the misconduct had no harmful effect on Jorgito. Finding no error or abuse of discretion, we affirm the circuit court's decision to award custody to Renee.

* * *

NOTES AND QUESTIONS

1. *The "nexus" test.* Zepeda applies the contemporary approach: to establish that a parent's immoral behavior warrants denial of custody, the other parent must demonstrate a nexus between that behavior and harm to the child. This focus on the relationship between parental misconduct and the child's best interest is a fairly recent development, and reflects a movement away from punishing the morally guilty parent. *See* Jane C. Murphy, *Rules, Responsibility and Commitment to Children: The New Language of Morality in Family Law*, 60 U. Pitt. L. Rev. 1111, 1187–88 (1999). Many jurisdictions use the nexus test, while others continue to apply a *per se* rule that parental immorality warrants loss of custody or at least a rebuttable presumption of loss.

2. *The argument that infidelity frequently harms children.* Professor Lynn Wardle argues that the contemporary refusal to admit or consider evidence of parental fault in custody hearings "tragically turns a blind eye to the significant harms that parental infidelity generally causes for children." Lynn D. Wardle, *Parental Infidelity and the "No–Harm" Rule in Custody Litigation*, 52 Cath. U. L. Rev. 81, 81 (2002). Professor Wardle notes that courts currently find harm where the parent's adultery has been outrageous rather than discreet, the infidelities have been numerous, the adultery "has been obsessive to the point of neglecting the child," or the child has witnessed adulterous acts. *Id.* at 89.

3. *Conditions for finding a "demonstrable effect" on a child.* At least one unreported custody decision has held polyamory (a family unit or sexual relationship among three or more adults of either sex or any sexual identity) against an offending spouse. Elizabeth F. Emens, *Monogamy's Law: Compul-*

sory Monogamy and Polyamorous Existence, 29 N.Y.U. Rev. L. & Soc. Change 277, 310–12 (2004). In *Gustaves v. Gustaves*, 57 P.3d 775 (Idaho 2002), the court affirmed a decision awarding custody to the father where the mother had engaged in a flagrant affair with a married family friend while continuing to live with her husband and two children. The trial court found her a "fit parent" in other respects, but concluded that the open and long-lasting affair caused the marital breakup, which in turn negatively affected the parties' seven-year-old, who became withdrawn, regressed and began to act out. *Id.* at 781–82.

4. *Sexual orientation.* In child custody disputes involving a biological parent who is gay, lesbian, bisexual or transgendered, courts generally use one of three approaches in arriving at a custody determination: (1) the nexus approach, (2) the *per se* approach, or (3) the middle ground or balancing approach. Jovana Vujovic, *Family Law Chapter: Child Custody and Visitation*, 5 Geo. J. Gender & L. 477, 491 (2004). All three approaches allow the court to consider a parent's sexual orientation as a factor in determining the best interests of the child, but they differ in how much weight to place on this factor. *Id.*

Under the nexus approach, the court may not deprive a parent of custody unless the parent's sexual orientation causes, or will cause, harm to the child. For a discussion of the trend toward application of the nexus approach see Nancy G. Maxwell and Richard Donner, *The Psychological Consequences of Judicially Imposed Closets in Custody and Visitation Disputes Involving Gay or Lesbian Parents*, 13 Wm. & Mary J. of Women & L. 305, 315–16 (2006); *see also, e.g., Berry v. Berry*, 2005 WL 1277847, 3 (Tenn. Ct. App.) ("a parent's sexual orientation can be a factor * * * but it does not control the outcome of the case absent evidence of its adverse effect on the child"). At least half the states and the District of Columbia follow this approach. Vujovic, *supra*, at 491–92.

The *per se* approach, adopted by a minority of jurisdictions, places much greater emphasis on sexual orientation by creating a presumption that a gay, lesbian, bisexual or transgendered parent should not have custody of a child. *Id.* at 492. The decision in *Roe v. Roe*, 324 S.E.2d 691, 694 (Va. 1985) represented the apex of the *per se* approach. The court held that although the child had lived with her father for six years, "the father's continuous exposure of the child to his immoral and illicit relationship renders him an unfit and improper custodian as a matter of law" and warranted a change of custody to the mother). Since then, Virginia courts have noted that the continued vitality of *Roe* has been at least partially undermined by *Lawrence v. Texas*, 539 U.S. 558 (2003), which decriminalized homosexual acts. *A.O.V. v. J.R.V.*, 2007 WL 581871, 4 (Va. Ct. App. 2007).

The aptly named middle ground approach lies somewhere between the nexus approach and the *per se* approach. The approach does not view a parent's sexual orientation as determinative, but may presume that a parent's homosexuality will adversely affect the child to some degree. *See, e.g., J.A.D. v. F.J.D.*, 978 S.W.2d 336, 339 (Mo. 1998) ("a homosexual parent is not *ipso facto* unfit for custody of his or her child," but a court may "consider the impact of homosexual or heterosexual misconduct upon the children in making a custody determination"). By the turn of the 21st century, several states that had previously followed the *per se* approach, including Missouri, North Carolina, Utah and Virginia, adopted the middle ground approach. Vujovic, *supra*, at 493.

D. HOME ENVIRONMENT AND HEALTH ISSUES

BLEVINS v. BARDWELL

Supreme Court of Mississippi, 2001.
784 So.2d 166.

PITTMAN, CHIEF JUSTICE, for the Court:

Adam L. Blevins appeals a chancery court judgment awarding the permanent paramount care, custody and control of his daughter Darby Colleen Blevins to her mother Dawn Elizabeth Bardwell (Funsch).

Facts and Proceedings Below

Adam Blevins and Dawn Bardwell (now Funsch) met in June of 1996 while both were stationed at Keesler Air Force base in Biloxi, Mississippi. After a period of friendship, they became romantically involved. This brief relationship temporarily ended just a few weeks before Dawn married her "high school sweetheart," Jason Singleton, that August. About a month later Dawn began treatment for stress and depression at the Keesler Mental Health Clinic. Despite Dawn's marriage, Adam and Dawn renewed their romance. While still married to Jason, Dawn discovered that she was pregnant and received an honorable discharge from the Air Force. She then moved in with Adam in January of 1997. From that time forward Adam and Dawn lived together and proclaimed themselves a couple.

Darby Colleen Blevins was born July 19, 1997. Over the following two weeks a DNA parentage test was administered; Dawn's divorce from Jason was finalized; and it was conclusively proven that Adam was Darby's biological father. Adam and Dawn continued to co-habitate un-married and care for their daughter, with Dawn being the primary care giver. During this time Adam worked full time, and Dawn held a part time job. Both admitted in testimony that it was their intention to marry at some point in the future.

Eventually Dawn decided to reenlist in the Air Force. Because the Air Force prohibits custodial single parents from enlisting, Dawn executed a "Order Approving Custody of Child" granting custody of Darby to Adam. At the time both believed they would marry at the conclusion of Dawn's technical training, or alternatively, once Dawn gained "permanent party" status, she would regain custody of Darby without jeopardizing her position in the Air Force. Adam and Dawn agree that they intended the change of custody to be a temporary arrangement.

Dawn left for technical training in July of 1998. Adam served as the primary care giver for Darby over the next 9 months. After Dawn came home on leave in September of 1998, relations became strained between the couple. By the end of her five-day leave Dawn and Adam had ended their relationship. Before leaving for her new assignment at Lackland Air Force Base in San Antonio, Texas, Dawn expressed her desire to take Darby with her since Dawn had successfully attained "permanent party" status. Adam refused to allow Dawn to take Darby citing his custody rights per the "Order Approving Custody of Child." Dawn and Adam have not lived together since.

A month after her arrival at Lackland Air Force Base, Dawn filed her Complaint in the Chancery Court of the Second Judicial District of Harrison County, Mississippi, for Change in Custody and Other Relief in the hope of regaining custody of Darby. While working at Lackland, Dawn met Anthony Funsch, whom she later married prior to the custody hearing. Dawn claims that in the months leading up to the custody hearing, while Darby was still in her father's custody, Adam was uncooperative in allowing visitation and promoting a close relationship between Dawn and Darby. Dawn also asserts that, on occasion, the chancery court was forced to implement visitation on behalf of Dawn, although there is nothing in the record to support this assertion. Prior to the court hearing in April of 1999 Adam and Darby moved to Melbourne, Kentucky, so that Adam could be with his father who was suffering from a number of serious illnesses.

After a four-day hearing, the chancellor issued the court's Memorandum Opinion and Judgment providing the following: 1) the prior order which awarded custody to Adam was a temporary, non-final adjudication of custody; 2) joint legal custody of Darby was awarded to both parties; 3) paramount care, custody and control of Darby was awarded to Dawn; 4) visitation was awarded to Adam, and 5) Adam was ordered to pay child support. From this judgment Adam appeals the award of paramount care, custody and control of Darby to Dawn.

Discussion

I. DID THE TRIAL COURT CORRECTLY DETERMINE THAT THE CUSTODY AGREEMENT WAS TEMPORARY?

* * *

At the time of their agreement regarding Darby's custody, Dawn and Adam intended to marry sometime after Dawn completed her training in the Air Force. Ultimately, they did not marry, and there was a need for the hearing below to determine permanent custody. It is undisputed that both parties voluntarily stipulated that the custody agreement made before Dawn's reentry into the Air Force was temporary in nature. Because single mothers with custody of children are not allowed to reenlist, the chancellor duly noted the pressure on Dawn to agree to the custody order so that she could return to the Air Force.

On its face, the "Order Approving Custody of Child" granting custody of Darby to Adam contains no language to indicate that it is anything but an order for permanent[1] custody. This Court gives great deference to the sanctity of orders made by chancellors and the belief that orders should be followed as they are written. *We are able to revisit this order because both parties agree that it was intended to be temporary.*

* * *

[O]f greatest importance as this is a child custody matter, we must defer to the polestar consideration in every child custody case, the best interests of the child.

Because of our determination that the custody order was, in fact, temporary, the chancellor was free to make a *de novo* original award of custody based on the factors in *Albright v. Albright*, 437 So. 2d 1003, 1005 (Miss. 1983). The chancellor did make such an analysis in awarding custody to Dawn and on every single factor where the chancellor favored one parent over the other, the chancellor concluded that custody with Dawn was favorable.

* * *

* * * Thus, there should be no reversal of the chancellor's finding that Dawn should have custody. Accordingly, the chancellor's decision should be affirmed.

II.   DID THE TRIAL COURT PROPERLY APPLY THE *ALBRIGHT* FACTORS TO THE EVIDENCE PRESENTED AT TRIAL?

This Court has stated that child custody matters are within the chancellor's discretion, and this Court will not reverse absent a finding that the chancellor was manifestly wrong, clearly erroneous, or applied an erroneous legal standard. * * * *Albright* clearly states that the primary consideration in all child custody cases is "the best interest and welfare of the child". *Id.* at 1005. *Albright* sets forth a number of factors which should be considered by a chancellor in a child custody case:

> We reaffirm the rule that the polestar consideration in child custody cases is the best interest and welfare of the child. The age of the child is subordinated to that rule and is but one factor to be considered. Age should carry no greater weight than other factors to be considered, such as: health, and sex of the child; a determination of the parent that has had the continuity of care prior to the separation; which has the best parenting skills and which has the willingness and capacity to provide primary child care; the employment of the parent and responsibilities of employment; physical and mental health and age of parents; emotional ties of parent and child; moral fitness of

---

1.   It is often said that no child custody order is permanent. Technically, this is correct because custody is always subject to modification in the best interest of the child. The terms "permanent" and "temporary" are used here because they are the terms chosen by the chancellor to distinguish between the chancery court award of custody arising out of the custody arrangement which Adam and Dawn temporarily entered into for the sole purpose of enabling Dawn to reenlist in the Air Force and a regular chancery court award of custody that is intended to continue indefinitely, until modified by order of the court.

parents; the home, school and community record of the child; the preference of the child at the age sufficient to express a preference by law; stability of home environment and employment of each parent, and other factors relevant to the parent-child relationship.

Id.

Adam claims that the Chancellor erred in the application of the following factors: A) age, B) health of parties, C) future religious example, D) home environment, and E) willingness and ability to provide primary care. Dawn contends that the Chancellor properly considered the *Albright* factors before rendering her decision.

* * *

B) Health of Parents

Adam claims that the Chancellor erred in giving an edge in health to Dawn because Adam smokes and, in addition, that Dawn's medical records were not properly considered when the Chancellor assessed the health of the parents. The records in question are from October, 1996, when Dawn received counseling from a military psychologist. The evaluations of the psychologist included statements that she suffered from an "adjustment disorder with depressed mood" and a provisional "schizoid personality disorder." These evaluations also mentioned the risk of potential suicide and that Dawn might be harmful to others. Dawn admitted at the trial that these records were accurate. Adam argues that the chancellor's conclusion is not a true reflection of the evidence that was presented before the court and that her conclusion was not supported by substantial evidence * * *.

Dawn addresses the health of the parents issue by pointing out that the Chancellor actually addressed physical and mental health in two separate subparagraphs, (g and h of the court's opinion). In the first subparagraph, (g), the chancellor states:

> Adam smokes, Dawn does not so the mother has somewhat of an edge in health.

In subparagraph (h) the chancellor stated:

> Much was attempted to be made of Dawn's medical records. The Court agrees with the testimony of the recruiting officer, there was nothing negative in her file. This is also proven by the fact that the Air Force took her back. If anything, the Court would hold Adam's failure to sign his medical waiver against him. His attorney's explanation that they hadn't presented them with one is unconvincing. This issue of medical waivers was fully discussed with the Court, when Dawn delivered hers, Adam certainly had the opportunity to deliver a signed waiver.

Dawn believes that the chancellor properly reviewed the medical records in question when coming to her decision regarding Dawn's mental health. Dawn relies on statements made by the Chancellor that show the records were properly considered. After Dawn's counsel objected to their admission into evidence, the chancellor stated,

> * * * I am going to look at these medical records knowing that they obtain hearsay, knowing that she has said under oath that she has never committed suicide, never attempted to commit suicide. That her diagnosis was stress-related to an adjustment for military. She has testified that she has absolutely no mental health problems now and I know what her testimony has been and I've noted all the objections for the record.

The Chancellor further states:

> * * * the reason I am letting the medical records in is I think * * * one of the factors in *Albright* is mental health. And I feel like I need to look at the record to make an informed decision.

Dawn contends that the Chancellor was free to give these medical records whatever weight she deemed proper and points out that the medical records being reviewed predated Darby's birth by almost a year. She also argues that if these medical records were so damaging then the Air Force would not have allowed her to reenlist. Testimony of Dawn's air force recruiter confirms that the records that he is required to review when she explored reenlisting did not contain any negative or derogatory information. Testimony does not clearly indicate whether the medical records in question were part of what the Air Force recruiter considered in Dawn's allowance to reenlist, but the recruiter did state that the military records he reviewed would contain any information that the Air Force considered ''negative or derogatory.''

* * *

The record clearly indicates that the Chancellor properly considered the mental and physical health of both parents and that her decision was based on the factors as outlined in *Albright*. Because of this, and the fact that Adam failed to request specific findings of fact and conclusions of law, this Court is hard pressed to find that the Chancellor's decision is manifestly wrong, clearly erroneous, or the result of the application of an erroneous legal standard. This Court has stated that child custody matters are solely within the Chancellor's discretion and we find that there was no abuse of this discretion in the Chancellor's determination of the health of the parents.

* * *

D) Home Environment

Adam argues that the Chancellor incorrectly focused on Adam's infirm father in making her determination regarding home environment and ignored many of the surrounding facts and circumstances that could have resulted in a different conclusion. Adam offers that a comparison of both homes reveals that Adam's was favorable over Dawn's at the time of the hearing. Adam was living in a house located on seven acres in

Kentucky while Dawn was in a one bedroom apartment. Adam's mother, aunt, grandmother and grandfather were all within twenty minutes of him while Dawn's parents were three hours from her.

Adam's father is an HIV positive hemophiliac and suffers from cancer. Adam's father also smokes three to four packs of cigarettes a day. The Chancellor considered these factors and stated * * *:

> The Court would like to make it perfectly clear that it is not penalizing Adam because he moved to take care of his critically ill father, it is commendable. Nor is the Court reacting to an irrational fear or prejudice of persons who are HIV positive. The Court does however, question if the home of a critically ill patient, regardless of the illness, is the best environment in which to raise a toddler. It also is not assuring to hear that the paternal grandfather smokes three to four packs of cigarettes a day, even if it is true he does not smoke when Darby is home. The atmosphere of the home would still have to be tainted with smoke. The Court finds the stability of the home environment should favor Dawn.

This Court does not see that the Chancellor abused her discretion in considering home environment in order to determine who received custody of Darby. It also cannot be said that the Chancellor's decision regarding home environment is manifestly wrong, clearly erroneous, or the result of the application of an erroneous legal standard.

* * *

CONCLUSION

Based on the foregoing analysis, we affirm the judgment of the Harrison County Chancery Court.

AFFIRMED.

NOTES AND QUESTIONS

1. *Custody disputes concerning children born outside of marriage.* Most states formerly heard custody disputes concerning children born outside of marriage in different courts and under different statutes than disputes concerning marital children. Today, however, all custody cases are generally heard in the same courts and decided under the same statutes regardless of the parents' marital status. *See, e.g., Wyatt v. White*, 626 So.2d 816 (La. Ct. App. 1993). Similarly, in *Gomez v. Perez*, 409 U.S. 535 (1973), the Court held that states violated the Equal Protection Clause when they distinguished between marital and nonmarital children in establishing the terms or amount of child support.

2. *Continuity.* Do the trial and appellate court decisions in *Blevins v. Bardwell* weigh continuity of care for Darby? Under the various standards and balancing tests you read about in the beginning of this Chapter, what outcome would be best for Darby? What concerns do you think the courts were balancing against concerns about continuity?

When parents separate, they often reach informal agreements regarding who will have physical custody of the children pending the court's ruling on the issue. One or both parents may intend these arrangements to be temporary, but courts, noting the children's need for continuity in their lives, may find the children's best interests served by awarding permanent physical custody to the residential parent. In *Moser v. Moser*, 343 N.W.2d 246 (Mich. Ct. App. 1983), the husband gave his wife an ultimatum: she could either move out of the marital residence so that the woman with whom he was having an extramarital affair could move in, or he would move out himself. Because the wife's income did not allow her to support their children and maintain the marital residence, the wife moved out, agreeing to leave the children with her husband until she established herself financially. Both parties testified that they intended the agreement to be temporary, with the wife regaining physical custody after one to two years. However, in what the wife characterized as "a case of custody by trick," the husband sought and received permanent physical custody of the children. *Id.* at 247. The trial court noted that the children had lived in a "stable, satisfactory environment" with their father for the 18 months leading up to trial. *Id*. The court of appeals affirmed on the ground that where an established custodial relationship exists, physical custody should not be changed absent clear and convincing evidence that change would be in the children's best interests.

Was *Moser* an egregious case of a mother whose husband took advantage of her, was it a tough case that illustrates that the custody test is "best interests of the child" and not best interests of the parents, or was it both? Considering that parental sexual behavior that harms the child may affect the custody decision, did the father's in-home affair harm the children?

In the end, do decisions like *Moser* end up harming the children by encouraging the parents to accelerate their custody fight? Faced with the risk of "temporary" agreements becoming permanent, a divorcing parent may understandably be reluctant to give the other parent custody, even temporarily. Acrimonious custody battles may begin well before the parents ever enter a courtroom. Unfortunately, this early race to create continuity of residence may quickly intensify an already hostile separation, exposing children to prolonged periods of discord and upheaval that outlast the divorce decree.

3. *Smoking by parents.* Courts in most, if not all, jurisdictions "recognize the mounting and virtually undisputed body of evidence that environmental tobacco smoke is harmful to children, but no court has held that smoking should control all other factors" in determining the best interests of the child. Harriet Dinegar Milks, Annotation, *Smoking as a Factor in Child Custody and Visitation Cases*, 36 A.L.R. 5th 377 (1996). In *Scott v. Steelman*, 953 S.W.2d 147 (Mo. Ct. App. 1997), both the mother and her new husband smoked inside their home despite the child's respiratory problems. The court awarded the non-smoking father physical custody of his daughter during the school year because he "made better choices involving [his daughter's] health." *Id*. at 150. *See also Pierce* v. *Pierce*, 860 N.E.2d 1087 (Ohio Ct. App. 2006) (holding that the trial court did not err in naming the father the residential parent where, all other factors being equal, the mother smoked and father did not). Courts have also held that a parent's smoking may be a

legitimate reason to limit visitation. *See, e.g., Badeaux* v. *Badeaux*, 541 So.2d 301, 302–03. (La. Ct. App. 1989).

4. *Care of elderly parents.* How should the court view Adam's decision to care for his dying father? Consider that some of the court's concerns about the appropriateness of Adam's home focused on the grandfather's smoking, his HIV status, and the fact that he was dying of cancer. Are any of these considerations appropriate? Are they distinguishable from one another? Would it matter if the source of the grandfather's HIV infection were not traceable to blood transfusions he received as a hemophiliac? Should the trial court have focused more clearly on the "commendable" aspects of Adam's commitment to taking care of his father's care? As a matter of social policy, what behavior should the law encourage for people in Adam's position? Does this ruling promote the most desirable social goals?

5. *Parents with disabilities.* In *Blevins v. Bardwell*, the issue of Dawn's mental health status was before the court but the evidence that she suffered from serious depression was not convincing. If the court had been convinced that she suffered from depression that was not being treated successfully, what would the next step in the court's analysis have been? In *KES v. CAT*, 107 P.3d 779 (Wyo. 2005), the court conditioned the mother's continued custody on her receiving treatment for bipolar disorder, including counseling and medication under stringent monitoring.

The Americans with Disabilities Act of 1990 (ADA) prohibits discrimination against persons with disabilities in many areas, including employment, public transportation, public accommodations, housing, and education, but the act does not apply to child custody cases. In custody cases, the court may consider a parent's physical and mental health when determining the "best interests of the child."

In the landmark decision of *In re Marriage of Carney*, 598 P.2d 36, 42 (Cal. 1979), the trial court awarded custody to the father after the mother relinquished custody of their two sons. The mother had virtually no contact with the children until five years later, when the father became a quadriplegic after a Jeep accident that occurred while he was serving in the military reserve. The trial court then granted the mother physical custody of the two children and permitted her to remove them from their father's California home to her New York home. The California Supreme Court reversed on the ground that the trial court had "premised its ruling on outdated stereotypes of both the parental role and the ability of the handicapped to fill that role." *Id.* at 37. The state supreme court discussed the "common knowledge that many persons with physical handicaps have demonstrated their ability to adequately support and control their children and to give them the benefits of stability and security through love and attention," and the public policy of integrating disabled persons "into the responsibilities and satisfactions of family life, cornerstone of our social system." *Id.* at 44–45.

Carney held that it was impermissible for a court to rely on a parent's disability "as *prima facie* evidence of the person's unfitness as a parent or of probable detriment to the child":

> [R]ather, in all cases the court must view the handicapped person as an individual and the family as a whole. To achieve this, the court should

inquire into the person's actual and potential physical capabilities, learn how he or she has adapted to the disability and manages its problems, consider how the other members of the household have adjusted thereto, and take into account the special contributions the person may make to the family despite—or even because of—the handicap. Weighing these and all relevant factors together, the court should then carefully determine whether the parent's condition will in fact have a substantial and lasting adverse effect on the best interests of the child.

Id. at 42.

When parents with disabilities seek judicial resolution of custody disputes, they may face procedural barriers in addition to substantive bias. In *Bednarski v. Bednarski*, 366 N.W.2d 69 (Mich. Ct. App. 1985), for example, the trial court awarded custody of two hearing children to their hearing paternal grandparents, citing concerns that the children, ages eight and three, would not be able to develop oral language skills if they remained with their mother, who was deaf and unable to speak. The Michigan Court of Appeals reversed the decision and remanded for a new trial, holding that the trial court had abused its discretion by not adhering to the statutory presumption that the best interests of the child are served by awarding custody to a biological parent unless there is clear and convincing evidence to the contrary.

The Court of Appeals also cited the trial court's numerous violations of, and indeed apparent unawareness of, the state's Deaf Persons' Interpreters Act. Contrary to the Act's mandates, only one interpreter was provided for the two deaf parties (the mother and father) and four deaf witnesses. When the sole interpreter was occupied with interpreting the witnesses' testimony, the mother was unable to ask questions or otherwise communicate with her counsel. Contrary to the statute's requirements, it appeared that the interpreter had not been available to assist the mother and her counsel during preparation for trial. *See* Megan Kirshbaum et al., *Issue Facing Family Courts: Parents with Disabilities: Problems in Family Court Practice*, 4 J. Center for Families, Child. & Cts. 27 (2003). Procedural irregularity frequently produces substantive error in American law; if the *Bednarski* trial court decision had become final without appeal after the court failed to heed the mother's procedural rights with the state's lawyers present in the courtroom, what is the likelihood that the trial court decision would have denied the mother her substantive custody rights?

The ADA also recognizes substance abuse as a disability for individuals who have stopped using illegal drugs. Courts frequently must resolve custody disputes in which one parent seeking custody has a history of drug abuse or is struggling with drug addiction. *See In re Marriage of Czapranski v. Czapranski*, 63 P.3d 499 (Mont. 2003) (upholding lower court's finding of sufficient evidence to support terminating joint custody because of mother's history of chemical dependence, need for inpatient care, and associated instability and risk to the child).

E. RACE

PALMORE v. SIDOTI

Supreme Court of the United States, 1984.
466 U.S. 429.

CHIEF JUSTICE BURGER delivered the opinion of the Court.

* * *

I

When petitioner Linda Sidoti Palmore and respondent Anthony J. Sidoti, both Caucasians, were divorced in May 1980 in Florida, the mother was awarded custody of their 3–year–old daughter.

In September 1981 the father sought custody of the child by filing a petition to modify the prior judgment because of changed conditions. The change was that the child's mother was then cohabiting with a Negro, Clarence Palmore, Jr., whom she married two months later. Additionally, the father made several allegations of instances in which the mother had not properly cared for the child.

After hearing testimony from both parties and considering a court counselor's investigative report, the court noted that the father had made allegations about the child's care, but the court made no findings with respect to these allegations. On the contrary, the court made a finding that "there is no issue as to either party's devotion to the child, adequacy of housing facilities, or respectability of the new spouse of either parent."

The court then addressed the recommendations of the court counselor, who had made an earlier report "in [another] case coming out of this circuit also involving the social consequences of an interracial marriage. *Niles v. Niles*, 299 So. 2d 162 [(Fla. Dist. Ct. App. 1974)]." From this vague reference to that earlier case, the court turned to the present case and noted the counselor's recommendation for a change in custody because "[t]he wife [petitioner] has chosen for herself, and for her child, a life-style unacceptable to the father *and to society* .... The child ... is, or at school age will be, subject to environmental pressures not of choice."

The court then concluded that the best interests of the child would be served by awarding custody to the father. The court's rationale is * * * [that]:

"The father's evident resentment of the mother's choice of a black partner is not sufficient to wrest custody from the mother. It is of some significance, however, that the mother did see fit to bring a man into her home and carry on a sexual relationship with him without being married to him. Such action tended to place gratification of her own desires ahead of her concern for the child's future welfare. *This Court feels that despite the strides that have been made in bettering relations between the races in this country, it is inevitable that Melanie will, if allowed to remain in her present situation and attains school age and thus more vulnerable to peer pressures, suffer from the social stigmatization that is sure to come."*

The Second District Court of Appeal affirmed without opinion, thus denying the Florida Supreme Court jurisdiction to review the case. We granted certiorari, and we reverse.

II

The judgment of a state court determining or reviewing a child custody decision is not ordinarily a likely candidate for review by this Court. However, the court's opinion, after stating that the "father's evident resentment of the mother's choice of a black partner is not sufficient" to deprive her of custody, then turns to what it regarded as the damaging impact on the child from remaining in a racially mixed household. This raises important federal concerns arising from the Constitution's commitment to eradicating discrimination based on race.

The Florida court did not focus directly on the parental qualifications of the natural mother or her present husband, or indeed on the father's qualifications to have custody of the child. The court found that "there is no issue as to either party's devotion to the child, adequacy of housing facilities, or respectability of the new spouse of either parent." This, taken with the absence of any negative finding as to the quality of the care provided by the mother, constitutes a rejection of any claim of petitioner's unfitness to continue the custody of her child.

The court correctly stated that the child's welfare was the controlling factor. But that court was entirely candid and made no effort to place its holding on any ground other than race. Taking the court's findings and rationale at face value, it is clear that the outcome would have been different had petitioner married a Caucasian male of similar respectability.

A core purpose of the Fourteenth Amendment was to do away with all governmentally imposed discrimination based on race. *See Strauder v. West Virginia,* 100 U.S. 303, 307–08, 310 (1880). Classifying persons according to their race is more likely to reflect racial prejudice than legitimate public concerns; the race, not the person, dictates the category. *See Personnel Administrator of Mass. v. Feeney,* 442 U.S. 256, 272 (1979). Such classifications are subject to the most exacting scrutiny; to pass constitutional muster, they must be justified by a compelling governmental interest and must be "necessary ... to the accomplishment" of their legitimate purpose, *McLaughlin v. Florida,* 379 U.S. 184, 196 (1964). *See Loving v. Virginia,* 388 U.S. 1, 11 (1967).

The State, of course, has a duty of the highest order to protect the interests of minor children, particularly those of tender years. In common with most states, Florida law mandates that custody determinations be made in the best interests of the children involved. The goal of granting custody based on the best interests of the child is indisputably a substantial governmental interest for purposes of the Equal Protection Clause.

It would ignore reality to suggest that racial and ethnic prejudices do not exist or that all manifestations of those prejudices have been eliminated. There is a risk that a child living with a stepparent of a different race may be subject to a variety of pressures and stresses not present if the child were living with parents of the same racial or ethnic origin.

The question, however, is whether the reality of private biases and the possible injury they might inflict are permissible considerations for removal of an infant child from the custody of its natural mother. We have little difficulty concluding that they are not. The Constitution cannot control such prejudices but neither can it tolerate them. Private biases may be outside the reach of the law, but the law cannot, directly or indirectly, give them effect. "Public officials sworn to uphold the Constitution may not avoid a constitutional duty by bowing to the hypothetical effects of private racial prejudice that they assume to be both widely and deeply held." *Palmer v. Thompson*, 403 U.S. 217, 260–61 (1971) (WHITE, J., dissenting).

This is by no means the first time that acknowledged racial prejudice has been invoked to justify racial classifications. In *Buchanan v. Warley*, 245 U.S. 60 (1917), for example, this Court invalidated a Kentucky law forbidding Negroes to buy homes in white neighborhoods.

> "It is urged that this proposed segregation will promote the public peace by preventing race conflicts. Desirable as this is, and important as is the preservation of the public peace, this aim cannot be accomplished by laws or ordinances which deny rights created or protected by the Federal Constitution."

Id. at 81. Whatever problems racially mixed households may pose for children in 1984 can no more support a denial of constitutional rights than could the stresses that residential integration was thought to entail in 1917. The effects of racial prejudice, however real, cannot justify a racial classification removing an infant child from the custody of its natural mother found to be an appropriate person to have such custody.

The judgment of the District Court of Appeal is reversed.

It is so ordered.

NOTES AND QUESTIONS

1. *Epilogue: Melanie's father retained custody.* Professor Randall Kennedy has commented that "there often exists a gap between formal rights declared on paper and the actual enjoyment of those rights":

> * * * This gap was vividly illustrated by the frustration faced by Linda Sidoti Palmore after her victory [in the Supreme Court]. Even though the Supreme Court had ruled in her favor, she did not regain custody of her daughter. During the pendency of the case, Anthony Sidoti had moved

Melanie and his new wife to a new home in Texas. After losing in the federal Supreme Court, he appealed for help to various state courts, which responded affirmatively. First, a Texas court issued a restraining order that barred Linda Palmore from taking custody of Melanie. Then, Judge Buck, in Florida [the judge who had issued the initial order removing Melanie from her mother's custody], granted Anthony Sidoti's request to transfer the case to judicial authorities in Texas. * * * The Florida court also rejected the argument that allowing Sidoti to retain custody of his child amounted to defiance of the Supreme Court's ruling. The Supreme Court, it noted, had not expressly ordered that custody of Melanie be awarded to Mrs. Palmore * * *. * * *

Randall Kennedy, Interracial Intimacies: Sex, Marriage, Identity and Adoption 384–85 (2003).

2. *The passage of time as a factor in determining best interests.* As suggested by the *Palmore* outcome, the emphasis on stability and continuity as critical aspects of the best interests evaluation often means that "possession is nine-tenths of the law."

Melanie was three years old when her father sought to remove her from her mother's custody. By the time the Supreme Court ruled on the case she was eight. When the Florida District Court of Appeals rejected Linda Palmore's appeal from the trial court's order transferring jurisdiction to Texas, it explained:

> * * * Under all the circumstances we cannot say that at this time it has been established to be in Melanie's best interests that she be ordered returned to her mother and that the trial court erred in not so ordering.

> The eight-year-old child appears to have had substantial upheavals of her life, and we find no compelling reason at this point to add a further upheaval. The record indicates that Melanie lived with both her parents until they separated when she was about two and one-half years old. She then lived with her mother for about two years until her father was awarded custody. After only two months with her father, Melanie was returned to her mother by court order. She stayed with her mother for about eight months, and then was ordered to her father's custody, where she has remained for about two and one-half years except for a ten-day visit with her mother in August 1984. We cannot disagree that it appears to be in the best interests of Melanie that she continue in the status quo at least for the time being until the custody issue is finally resolved.

Palmore v. Sidoti, 472 So.2d 843, 846–47 (Fla. Dist. Ct. App. 1985).

Did the outcome after remand serve society's interest in racial harmony by allowing Melanie to live with a parent who objected to her having an African–American stepfather?

1. *Race as a persistent factor in custody disputes.* In *Parker v. Parker*, 986 S.W.2d 557 (Tenn. 1999), the court upheld an award of custody to the child's father even though it held that the trial court erred in admitting "race-based testimony." The mother, who had always cared for her young son, worked as a nurse for an African–American doctor, with whom the husband insisted she was having an affair. The mother denied having a sexual

relationship with her employer, but she "conceded that they were good friends who occasionally would see one another outside of work." *Id.* at 559. The trial court admitted expert testimony from a family nurse practitioner, who said that in contrast to the situation in large cities, in this case "it may be harmful for a child 'to be raised in an interracial household because of small town views.'" *Id.* The trial court did not find the mother unfit, but found the father comparatively more fit because "it was wrong for anyone to have a relationship with her employer." *Id.*

The judge's statements at trial provided further basis for the mother's unsuccessful appeal. While there was no transcript of the trial, the mother averred that during cross-examination of the child's maternal grandmother, the judge commented that the grandmother "comes from the same school I do. She can't help the way she feels. Society today feels differently than the way we were brought up (this referred to the wife who is white, seeing Dr. Sidberry, who is black)." *Id.* at 560 (alterations in original). Later, the judge explained that he was not concerned with race, but about "shacking up. I am not referring to white or black. * * * No where did I ever make any comment * * * that the Court has some objection [to] interracial associations. I don't care whether they are black, white, red or what they are. * * * I probably made some kind of a statement in there about that." *Id.* (alterations in original).

The Tennessee Supreme Court was "troubled by the interjection of race-based testimony in these proceedings, which is so clearly prohibited in *Palmore*":

> The trial court allowed a nurse practitioner to testify as an expert regarding the alleged harmful effects upon a child from an interracial relationship. When counsel for Richard Parker made inquiries as to the racial issue in his cross-examination of Gail Scism, the trial judge remarked that he and Ms. Scism were 'from the same school' and that the views of society are different today. Although the trial judge later explained that his comments were aimed at unmarried people 'shacking up' or living together, there is no evidence in this record to show that Teri Parker and Dr. Sidberry lived together. Finally, we observe that as part of the final divorce judgment, the trial court ordered that the child was to have no contact with Dr. Sidberry—a condition that was not discussed or requested by any party to the case.

In applying the *Palmore* decision to the present case, however, it is apparent that there are differences. First, in *Palmore*, custody was granted to the natural mother and the father later filed for a change in custody. Second, the trial court's ruling in *Palmore* was solely based on race. In contrast, this case involves an initial custody hearing and a comparison of the fitness of the two parents where evidence of a racial factor was admitted. At the post-trial hearing on the statement of evidence, the trial court denied that he considered race while excluding comments alleged to reflect racial bias. He indicated that his concern was the presence of an extramarital affair that interfered with the well-being of the child.

As an appellate court, we recognize that the trial court must exercise broad discretion in child custody matters. We accept the trial court's statement that race did not play a part in its decision-making in awarding custody to the father.

Id. at 563.

Does *Parker* suggest that despite *Palmore*, a trial court hearing a hotly contested custody dispute can usually find another basis for a decision it wants to base on race? Was *Palmore* simply an "easy case" for the unanimous Supreme Court because the trial judge was entirely candid about what he was doing?

F. SIBLINGS AND RELIGION

ARTHUR v. ARTHUR

Court of Appeals of Ohio, 1998.
720 N.E.2d 176.

WILLIAM B. HOFFMAN, JUDGE.

Plaintiff-appellant/cross-appellee Cindy A. Arthur (hereinafter "wife") appeals the October 16, 1997 Judgment Entry/Decree of Divorce of the Fairfield County Court of Common Pleas, Domestic Relations Division, granting her a divorce from defendant-appellee/cross-appellant Michael J. Arthur (hereinafter "husband") and approving a shared parenting plan for the couple's four minor children. Husband appeals that decree as well as the March 31, 1998 Judgment Entry finding him in contempt of court.

Statement of the Facts and Case

Husband and wife were married in Vincennes, Indiana on August 15, 1981. Four children were born as issue of the marriage: Megan Jo * * *, Eric M. * * *, Jacob M. * * *, and Mary K. * * *.

Upon her graduation from high school in 1978, wife worked in a department store in the Vincennes, Indiana area. Following a brief marriage to another individual, wife met husband, who was working part-time in the same department store while attending Vincennes University. In 1983, husband completed an associates degree in computer science. While husband attended school, wife supported the couple. After wife gave birth to their first child, Megan, in 1983, the couple decided wife would remain at home full-time.

In 1987, husband accepted a job offer in the Columbus, Ohio area. Around the same time, wife began regularly watching the television ministry of the World Harvest Church (hereinafter "the Church"), which originates from Columbus. After the family moved to Ohio, they attended the Church. In November, 1987, husband accepted a position with the Church as the Director of Computer Operations.

The Church became the focal point of the family. Their lives centered around the Church, including worship, friendships, and activities. The children attended the World Harvest Christian Academy ("the Academy"), a church affiliated school. The children's contacts outside the Church were limited.

In 1994, husband left his position with the Church to accept a position with Cap Gemini America, Inc. Prior to leaving his employment with the Church, husband began to disassociate himself from the institution and its members.

In December, 1995 husband informed wife he desired a divorce. On or about December 24, 1995, husband moved out of the marital residence. On January 12, 1996, wife filed a complaint for divorce. * * *

* * * [On] March 26, 1996, the trial court entered temporary orders for a shared parenting arrangement. Pursuant to the temporary orders, wife was designated the residential parent and legal custodian of the four children for school purposes. Husband was granted possession of the children on weekends and for short weeknight visits, subject to timely notice. Throughout the proceedings, husband and wife contested the issues of custody and the children's enrollment at the Academy.

The matter proceeded to trial. At trial, Dr. John Mason, the court appointed psychologist, reiterated the concerns he voiced in his report to the trial court regarding the children's attendance at the Academy, which, he opined, shielded them from the real world. Mason testified, while in wife's custody, the children's outside contacts were limited to church members. Due to the lack of cooperation between husband and wife, Mason recommended shared parenting in order to avoid the development of a parental-alienation syndrome.

Mason met with the three oldest children on several occasions. During the initial visit, the children expressed a desire to stay with wife and continue their education at the Academy. Although the children expressed little interest in living with husband, they indicated their desire to visit him on a regular basis. When the children originally expressed these desires, they had not been visiting husband because * * * [he was co-habiting with another woman]. After visits with husband commenced, the three children told Mason they wanted to live with husband. The children reiterated this position over the course of their visits with Mason.

Mason testified that sports are paramount in the boys' lives. With husband, the boys became involved in organized, competitive sports leagues. When Megan originally saw Mason, she stated she considered living with husband because she did not want to attend Bible College for two years before she started regular college. During her last meeting with Mason, Megan told him wife informed her she could make the decision regarding her attendance at Bible College.

Regarding the children's continued enrollment at the Academy, Mason expressed his concerns regarding the cloistering aspect of the school and the limited social contact the children had outside of the Church environment. The testimony revealed that the Academy has below average class sizes, problems with staffing, teachers who lacked practical experience, and a lack of curriculum. The extra curricular activities available to the children were limited and included only noncompetitive activities. A substantial portion of the school day was devoted to bible studies. All of the text books used at the school had a religious emphasis.

* * *

After hearing all the evidence, the trial court entered findings of fact and conclusions of law on August 12, 1997. On October 16, 1997, the trial court filed the Judgment Entry/Decree of Divorce. Pursuant to the divorce decree, wife was named the residential parent for school purposes of Megan and Mary, and husband was named the residential parent for school purposes of Jacob and Eric. * * *

* * *

I

In her first assignment, wife maintains that the trial court abused its discretion in separating the four children by ordering a shared parenting plan.

The standard of review of an appellate court of a trial court's determination in a custody proceeding is abuse of discretion. In order to find an abuse of discretion, we must determine that the trial court's decision was unreasonable, arbitrary, or unconscionable and not merely an error of law or judgment. We must look to the totality of the circumstances in the case *sub judice* and determine whether the trial court acted unreasonably, arbitrarily, or unconscionably.

During a divorce proceeding, a trial court is required to allocate the parental rights and responsibilities for the care of the minor children pursuant to [the applicable statute]. The trial court has two options when allocating parental rights and responsibilities. The court may either designate one parent as the residential parent and legal custodian who bears the primary rights and responsibilities for the care of the children, or may issue a shared-parenting order requiring the parents to share all or some of the aspects of the physical and legal care of the children.

Despite the trial court's classification of the custody order as a shared-parenting plan and wife's attack on the same basis, the practical effect is a split custody order. Generally, this Court would not encourage a trial court to resolve a custody dispute in such a manner, however; under the facts of the case *sub judice*, we do not find the trial court abused its discretion in ordering split custody.

The testimony at trial revealed that the children, particularly the boys, had interests outside the activities available at the Church and the Academy. By designating husband as the residential parent of Eric and Jacob, the court gave the boys an opportunity to engage in organized sports, activities which were extremely important to them.

Although the trial court's custody determination results in a separation of the children, the record reveals that the order establishes an extensive visitation schedule for wife with the boys, for husband with the girls, and for the children together. Pursuant to the order, the children are together one hundred eighty-five whole days during the year, and seventy-two partial days during the year, resulting in only one hundred eight days of separation.

In support of her position, wife contends the trial court improperly considered her religious affiliation when the court determined she should not be designated the residential parent for all the children. Wife relies on *Pater v. Pater* (1992), 588 N.E.2d 794, in which the Ohio Supreme Court held:

> A parent may not be denied custody on the basis of his or her religious practices unless there is probative evidence that those practices will adversely effect the mental or physical health of the child. Evidence that the child will not be permitted to participate in certain social or patriotic activities is not sufficient to prove possible harm.

[*Id*. at 800.]

A review of the trial court's findings of fact and conclusions of law belies wife's argument that the trial court improperly considered wife's religious affiliation. In its findings of fact, the trial court stated its concerns about the education the children were receiving at the Academy, including the below average class sizes, the problems with teacher staffing, the lack of teacher experience, the lack of curriculum, and the sheltered life style. The trial court did not indicate any concerns regarding the religious philosophy of the Church. Rather, the trial court's concerns centered around the quality of education the children were receiving. The testimony regarding the Worthington Public School System revealed the public school the children would attend offered gifted programs and a wide curriculum.

We agree with *Pater*, that a parent may not be denied custody on the basis of his or her religious practices unless such practices adversely affect the mental or physical well-being of the child. We find that the trial court in the instant action did not deny wife custody of all the children based upon her affiliation with the Church. Rather, the trial court merely raised concerns about the education the children were receiving at a school that happens to be church affiliated.

Wife's first assignment of error is overruled.

* * *

NOTES AND QUESTIONS

1. *Should siblings always stay together after their parents split up?* Most jurisdictions acknowledge the strong connection that frequently exists among siblings and express a preference for keeping siblings together. *See, e.g.,*

Owens v. *Owens*, 950 So.2d 202 (Miss. Ct. App. 2006) (keeping siblings together is assumed to serve their best interests in the absence of a showing to the contrary). The ALI Principles propose that in allocating custody, one objective should be "to keep siblings together where the court finds that doing so is necessary to their welfare." A.L.I., Principles of the Law of Family Dissolution: Analysis and Recommendations § 2.08(c) (2002).

2.   *When is it appropriate to separate siblings?* The preference for keeping siblings together is consistent with the emphasis on maintaining continuity in children's lives and preserving family bonds after dissolution of the parents' marriage. Appellate courts, however, permit separation where the siblings have different needs. *See, e.g., Nomland v. Nomland,* 813 A.2d 850 (Pa. Super. Ct. 2002) (boys who were well-settled in school and thriving with their father had different needs than their sister, who chose to move to her mother's home after her father remarried). Other exceptions to the general no-separation rule can be found when (1) the siblings have never lived together or have been separated for a substantial amount of time; (2) the siblings express a strong preference to live with different parents; (3) the siblings do not get along well with one another; or (4) a significant age difference separates the siblings. ALI, Principles, § 2.08 cmt. g.

In determining whether to separate siblings, courts also consider the parents' respective capacities to care for their children and the parents' moral, mental or physical qualifications. *See, e.g.,* Jay M. Zitter, Annotation, *Child Custody: Separating Children by Custody Awards to Different Parents—Post–1975 Cases,* 67 A.L.R. 4th 354 (2005). In *Donahue v. Buisch,* 696 N.Y.S.2d 254 (App. Div. 1999), the court affirmed an order that split custody by awarding the older child to the mother and the younger child to the father. The older child had severe emotional problems and mental illness, and the mother was the only parent willing to seek professional psychological intervention. The younger child, on the other hand, had a close and loving relationship with her father, who the court noted was involved with and committed to her education. The lower court had mandated family counseling, individualized counseling for the older child, and extensive sibling visitation.

Unique issues arise in custodial disputes involving half-and step-siblings. Courts have "traditionally applied the policy of keeping siblings together in custody decisions only to children of the same marriage." *In re D.R.L.M.,* 84 S.W.3d 281, 303 (Tex. Ct. App. 2002). Accordingly, courts appear to order split custody more frequently for half-siblings than for siblings with the same biological parents. *See* ALI, Principles, § 2.08 cmt. g. Where the bond between the half-siblings is strong, however, courts prefer to keep them together. *Id.* Indeed, in *Michael G. B. v. Angela L. B.,* 642 N.Y.S.2d 452 (App. Div. 1996), the court held that the strong bond between the two half-siblings created extraordinary circumstances sufficient to justify awarding custody of both children to the father, who was not the older child's biological father.

Separation of siblings is also a serious issue in adoption and foster care. Separation in these settings offers potentially useful analogies for custody cases and is discussed in Chapter 17.

3.   *Religion as an element of best interests.* Some trial courts continue to consider a parent's piety or religious practices as a factor in determining best

interests. In a portion of the *Blevins v. Bardwell* opinion not reproduced in this casebook, the court held that it was not an abuse of discretion to consider each parent's likely "future religious example," and to determine that the mother was much more committed to her child's religious training. 784 So.2d 166, 176 (Miss. 2001). As a condition of the divorce decree, an Indiana trial court in 2005 ordered a couple practicing Wiccan, a form of paganism, not to expose their child to the non-mainstream religion's beliefs and rituals. *Jones v. Jones*, 832 N.E.2d 1057, 1061 (Ind. Ct. App. 2005). The appellate court held the decision to be an abuse of discretion and ordered that the limitation on "parental authority to determine the religious training" of the child be stricken from the decree. *Id.*

4. *Conflicting parental beliefs and First Amendment rights.* The First Amendment's religion clauses may limit the court's capacity to use religious practices and beliefs as a basis for choosing one parent over the other in a custody dispute. Most jurisdictions hold that each parent has a right to expose the child to the religious practices he or she observes, absent a clear showing of harm to the child. *See, e.g.,* Joanne Ross Wilder, *Religion and the Best Interests of Children*, 18 J. Am. Acad. Matrim. Law 211, 222 (2002).

In *Abbo v. Briskin*, 660 So.2d 1157 (Fla. Dist. Ct. App. 1995), for example, a man and a woman of different faiths met and fell in love. The woman converted to Judaism, but converted back to Catholicism shortly after their daughter's birth. They obtained a divorce when their daughter was 4–1/2 years old. The principal dispute at trial was the child's religion. The appellate court held that the courts may not decide "in favor of a specific religion over the objection of the other parent. As with married parents who share diverse religious beliefs, the question of a child's religion must be left to the parents even if they clash. A child's religion is no proper business of judges." The court held that when determining the best interests of the child, "[t]here is absolutely nothing in the statutory listing that expressly makes the religious training of the child a factor that the court should consider." *Id.* at 1159.

In other jurisdictions, spiritual or religious well-being is one of the statutory "best interests" factors for courts to consider. In *Zummo v. Zummo*, 574 A.2d 1130 (Pa. Super. Ct. 1990), for example, the court reversed an order that prohibited the father from taking his children to religious services "contrary to the Jewish faith" during periods of custody or visitation. *Zummo* held that courts may constitutionally restrict a parent's post-divorce rights to direct the child's religious upbringing, but set a very high standard for court intervention, requiring a showing that the parent's religious decisions demonstrated "substantial threat" of "physical or mental harm to the child." *Id.* at 1141 (quoting the standard set forth in *Wisconsin v. Yoder*, 406 U.S. 205, 230 (1972)). *Zummo* contrasted intact marriages and post-divorce families:

> * * * In intact families, parents are left to decide their children's 'best interests' on an *ad hoc* basis. Significantly, "a marital couple is not an independent entity with a mind and heart of its own, but an association of two individuals with a separate intellectual and emotional makeup." One parent may be a Republican the other a Democrat, one may be a Capitalist the other a Communist, or one may be a Christian and the other a Jew. Parents in healthy marriages may disagree about important

matters; and, despite serious, even irreconcilable, differences on important matters, the government could certainly not step in, choose sides, and impose an orthodox uniformity in such matters to protect judicially or bureaucratically determined "best interests" of the children of such parents. Rather, intervention is permitted only upon a showing of a substantial risk of harm to the child in absence of intervention, and that the intervention proposed is the least intrusive means adequate to prevent the harm.

* * *

Significantly, while divorce does not change the *standard* for legitimate government intervention in such matters, it may nonetheless lead to increased legitimate governmental intervention. Some divorced parents may conduct such religious upbringing disputes in a more acrimonious and injurious manner than parents who remain married, and thereby create greater risk of harm to their children in more such cases. * * *

Zummo, 574 A.2d at 1139–40 (quoting *Eisenstadt v. Baird*, 405 U.S. 438, 453 (1972)).

5. *Preserving choice for the child.* Where divorcing devout Hindu parents disagreed about whether to perform the Hindu ritual of Chudakarana on their three-year-old daughter, the trial court reserved performance of the ceremony "until the child is of sufficient age to make that determination herself, absent a written agreement between the parties." *Sagar v. Sagar*, 781 N.E.2d 54, 56 (Mass. App. Ct. 2003). Chudakarana is a ritual in which mantras are recited while a priest removes hair from five parts of the child's head, and the child's head is then shaved and an auspicious mark is placed on the child's forehead. The court concluded that since the parents had competing free exercise claims, it was unclear whether the ceremony was integral to the Hindu faith. The father seemed motivated at least in part by a wish to control family members, and he conceded that atonement could be made by later performance.

The child's religious upbringing often remains a source of conflict long after the dissolution of the parents' relationship. Such disputes will be the subject of additional discussion in Chapter 13.

6. *Pets.* Like siblings, pets may be an important source of solace, company and continuity to children. In addition, many adults are loathe to be separated from their pets upon dissolution of a relationship with a spouse or significant other, sometimes even to the point of litigating over "custody" of the pet. Traditionally, family law treated pets as personal property. In *Arrington v. Arrington*, 613 S.W.2d 565, 569 (Tex. Ct. Civ. App. 1981), the court held that because the dog was a gift to the wife, it was her separate property and the husband had no right to joint conservatorship. *Arrington* underscored the irony that while many divorcing parents use their children "as human ropes in a post-divorce tug-of-war * * * [d]ogs involved in divorce cases are luckier * * *. [T]hey do not have to be treated as humans." *Id*. The court concluded that "Bonnie Lou is a very fortunate little dog with two humans to shower upon her affections and genuine love frequently not received by human children from their divorced parents." *Id*.

Although custody statutes by their express terms apply only to "children," the contemporary trend is to treat pets as if they are members of the family. For example, in *Juelfs v. Gough*, 41 P.3d 593 (Alaska 2002), the parties' separation agreement, incorporated in the divorce decree, provided for shared ownership of the couple's dog. For a six-month period in 2000, the couple had reciprocal restraining orders against each other as a result of an altercation that occurred when the former husband attempted to regain custody of the dog after his former wife had taken the dog without his permission. "Arguing that 'a pet is not just a thing but occupies a special place somewhere in between a person and a piece of personal property,'" the former wife appealed after the trial court modified the divorce decree to award full custody of the chocolate Labrador retriever to her former husband. *Id.* at 594. The appellate court affirmed the modification because the shared custody arrangement was not working and "the parties were unable to share custody of ['Coho,' the dog] without severe contention." *Id.* at 597.

SECTION 4: THE CHILD'S PREFERENCE

Most states follow the Uniform Marriage and Divorce Act's approach of requiring courts to consider a sufficiently mature child's custody preference, but leave questions about maturity and the weight of the mature child's preference to judicial discretion. UMDA § 402, 9A U.L.A. 282 (1998). *See, e.g.*, Cal. Fam. Code § 3042(a); (West 2004 & Supp. 2008); Fla. Stat. Ann. § 61.13(3)(i) (West 1997 & Supp. 2006; *see also* ALI, Principles of the Law of Family Dissolution: Analysis and Recommendations § 2.08 Reporter's Notes to cmt. f (2002). A few states require deference to the wishes of children over a specified age (generally 12 to 14 years old). In all other states, the judge has discretion about whether to consider the child's preference and what weight to accord that preference. In all states, the younger the child, the less likely that his or her opinion will be solicited, much less taken seriously.

A. GALS, LAWYERS AND STANDARDS

The issue of how the child's wishes should be communicated to the court is the subject of much debate. Courts have traditionally used two primary methods of ascertaining a child's preferences: through an appointed guardian *ad litem* (GAL) or by interviewing the child *in camera*, usually promising the child confidentiality. A GAL is appointed by the court, and may be either a lawyer or a layperson. In most states, children do not hold an absolute right to have a GAL appointed for them in private custody disputes, at least unless abuse or neglect is alleged. Exceptions exist. The Oregon statute, for example, provides that a court hearing a custody case "shall appoint counsel for the child or children" if the children request an attorney. Or. Rev. Stat. Ann. § 107.425(6) (West 2005). All courts, however, have the equitable power to appoint GALs at their discretion. The same GAL is normally appointed to represent all siblings in the family, even though it is possible that the siblings may not all agree on what they want, as you saw in *Arthur*. The court may order one or both parents to pay the GAL.

The parameters of the GAL's job are not always clear, and may vary greatly depending on the judge and the jurisdiction. GALs may perform various roles, including fact-gatherer, advocate for the child's best interests, advocate for the child's views, or some combination of roles. The GAL may or may not be an attorney. Some GALs are Court Appointed Special Advocates (CASAs), lay persons who receive special training to serve as GALs. The proper role when the GAL is in fact an attorney is hotly debated, but it is generally agreed that the court should specify its expectations when it appoints a GAL so that all parties and the judge understand the GAL's role in the particular proceeding. Courts do not, however, always do so. It is not reversible error, for example, for a GAL to communicate the child's views to the court, while simultaneously serving as a quasi-special master who investigates the circumstances and formulates his or her own quite different opinion about the child's best interests. *Auclair* v. *Auclair*, 730 A.2d 1260 (Md. Ct. Spec. App. 1999).

The Supreme Court of South Carolina has expressly held that a GAL in a private custody dispute "functions as a representative of the court, appointed to assist the court in making its determination of custody by advocating for the best interest of the children and providing the court with an objective view." *Patel* v. *Patel*, 555 S.E.2d 386, 389 (S.C. 2001). *Patel* also set baseline standards for GALs, beginning with the responsibility to:

> conduct an *independent, balanced, and impartial* investigation to determine the facts relevant to the situation of the child and the family, which should include: reviewing relevant documents; meeting with and observing the child in the home setting and considering the child's wishes, if appropriate; and interviewing parents, caregivers, and others with knowledge relevant to the case * * *.

Id. at 390 (emphasis by the court). Other jurisdictions have emphasized that the court must ultimately make its own determination. *Bencomo* v. *Bencomo*, 147 P.3d 67, 72 (Haw. 2006) ("In a divorce case, the family court is not authorized * * * to delegate its decision-making authority to a guardian ad litem"). *See also Shugar* v. *Shugar*, 924 So.2d 941 (Fla. Dist. Ct. App. 2006).

The Supreme Court of Illinois has held that when a GAL functions as both fact-finder and an advocate for the child's preference, and where the court relies on the GAL's written report in its findings of fact, the parent holds the right to cross-examine the GAL as a witness. *In re Marriage of Bates*, 819 N.E.2d 714 (Ill. 2004). Where the parties have an opportunity to cross-examine the GAL, the GAL may rely on and transmit to the court the out-of-court statements of persons she interviewed without violating the rule against hearsay. *Bates–Brown* v. *Brown*, 2007 WL 2822596 (Ohio Ct. App. 2007).

Formal testimony by a GAL who is also a lawyer is, however, fraught with difficulties. The lawyer GAL who formally testifies as a sworn witness would appear to violate Model Rule 3.7 of the ABA Model Rules of Professional Conduct, which states that a "lawyer shall not act as an advocate at a trial in which the lawyer is likely to be a necessary witness * * *." Even if the lawyer GAL does not necessarily advocate for the position preferred by the child, the GAL arguably advocates for a position, namely, the GAL's own conclusion about the best interests of the child. The comments to the Model Rules focus on possible confusion or prejudice in the jurors' minds, but no exception appears for bench trials, the format in which courts decide child custody cases. Moreover, the GAL's formal testimony about the child's wishes is likely to be challenged as hearsay, *e.g.*, *In re Marriage of Bates*, 819 N.E.2d 714 (Ill. 2004), although it may meet an exception, similar to the exception in the Federal Rules of Evidence with respect to the speaker's present state of mind or then-existing mental or emotional condition. *See* Fed. R. Evid. 803(1)–(3).

The use of *in camera* interviews to learn the children's wishes concerning their custody, long considered the method of inquiry that best protects children's emotional interests, raises problems too, and has increasingly been the subject of due process challenges. In *Couch v. Couch*, 146 S.W.3d 923 (Ky. 2004), the court addressed a parent's ability to access *in camera* taped interviews with children in custody cases. The court stated:

> In an action concerning custody or visitation, any procedure whereby the trial court prohibits disclosure of the transcript of a child's interview to the parties raises significant due process questions. The parties are entitled to know what evidence is used or relied upon by the trial court, and have the right generally to present rebutting evidence or to cross-examine, unless such right is waived. If a trial court accepts and acts upon statements made by the child during the *in camera* interview, it is manifestly unfair not to record and disclose the contents of the interview in order to provide an opportunity for rebuttal.

Id. at 925. *Couch* upheld the trial court's discretion to conduct *in camera* interviews without the parties and counsel, but held that a record must be made so that the parties have the opportunity to determine and contradict the accuracy of child's statements and facts. *Id.*; *cf. KES v. CAT*, 107 P.3d 779 (Wyo. 2005) (holding that no *in camera* interviews with children should be conducted over a parent's objection because such interviews deprive the parent of the right to cross-examine witnesses).

Creating a record also facilitates appellate review. Some state courts have held that the due process rights of parents are preserved by allowing appellate courts to review the record without making it available to the parent. *Myers* v. *Myers*, 867 N.E.2d 848 (Ohio App. 2007). This approach allows the child to speak honestly and the trial judge to preserve confidences. In still other states appellate courts have not had a recent opportunity to consider these issues. *See Abbott* v. *Virusso*, 862 N.E.2d 52 (Mass. App. Ct. 2007) (summarizing some of the literature and noting that the issue has not been addressed in Massachusetts for more than a decade).

Professor Cynthia Starnes identifies three risks inherent in *in camera* interviews of children: "(1) process risks (a child's increased entanglement in custody conflict); (2) information risks (a custody decision based on a child's inaccurate statements and unreasonable preferences); and (3) outcome risks (a child's burdensome sense of responsibility for the custody choice)." Cynthia Starnes, *Swords in the Hands of Babes: Rethinking Custody Interviews After* Troxel, 2003 Wis. L. Rev. 115, 117. Starnes argues that these risks increase significantly when the judge interviews children *in camera* regarding their preferences, when the court makes children's preferences a dispositive factor, and when parents do not have an opportunity to challenge the veracity of the *in camera* statements (for example, where *in camera* interviews take place without the presence of a court reporter or attorneys for the parties).

Oregon's statutory scheme anticipates these concerns, and provides that in custody actions a court may elicit the child's views by retaining an expert witness to interview the child, appointing counsel for the child, or hearing directly from the child through testimony or in conference. The statute specifies that if the judge hears directly from the child, the court "may exclude from the conference the parents and other persons if the court finds that such action would be likely to be in the best interests of the child * * *. However, the court shall permit an attorney for each party to attend the conference and question the child, and the conference shall be reported." O.R.S. § 107.425 (2), (6) and (7) (2007).

Children may also testify under oath in open court. The Federal Rules of Evidence, adapted in whole or in part by many states, allow a child to testify under oath in any matter. To satisfy the requirement that witnesses testify on oath or affirmation, courts generally make a threshold inquiry into whether the child understands the difference between truth and falsehood. Roughly two-thirds of the states also require a preliminary inquiry into the competency of child witnesses below a specified age. Such hearings frequently emphasize the child's ability to understand questions and communicate responses to them, as well as the child's awareness of the duty to tell the truth. *See* Lucy S. McGough, Child Witnesses: Fragile Voices in the American Legal System 97–99 (1994). When a child testifies, he or she is subject to cross-examination and the testimony may be affected by the presence of both parents in the courtroom.

Professor Catherine J. Ross has argued that where children have attorneys, the attorneys should ensure that the children's voices are heard:

Where children are concerned * * * courts and commentators too frequently collapse the roles of attorneys and guardians *ad litem*. The differences in these roles should be stark. Attorneys are bound by professional standards that require them to pursue the wishes and objectives of the child where the child is capable of making considered decisions in his [or her] own interest. The guardian *ad litem*, in contrast, presents an independent voice in the litigation and is charged with protecting the child's best interest [as the guardian understands it] rather than the child's viewpoint.

Catherine J. Ross, *From Vulnerability to Voice: Appointing Counsel for Children in Civil Litigation*, 64 Fordham L. Rev. 1571, 1615 (1996) (internal quotation omitted). Professor Ross argues that the attorney's advocacy of the child's preference is only one factor in the judge's decision, which the judge will properly weigh against the other views presented. While most courts do not share this viewpoint, some do. For example, an appellate court in Ohio reversed a custody award where the attorney GAL's unsworn testimony urged the court to grant custody to one parent, while the 10–year–old child told the judge in camera and in a letter submitted to the court that she wanted to live with the other parent. The appellate court reversed because the court below failed to appoint a separate attorney to advocate for the child's preference. *In re Butler*, 2006 WL 2533010 (Ohio Ct. App. 2006) (dependency action involving the mother, but not the father who sought custody).

Some observers worry about allowing an attorney to advocate for the child's viewpoint when the attorney perceives that viewpoint to be wrong-headed. The bases for this concern include role identification with parents, distrust of children, and a sense that children are inherently less "rational" than adults, and do not always accurately identify their own best interests, much less act on them. Attorneys, however, may not be competent to substitute their own judgment for that of their clients. Attorneys may lack specialized training or expertise in assessing the variety of emotionally charged issues likely to come into play in litigation involving a child's life choices.

Professor Martin Guggenheim argues that the use of lawyers for children in divorce cases is a costly waste of resources on a number of grounds. First, children do not get to participate in the decision when parents choose to end their relationship, and where the parents are able to agree on custody without litigation, children have only the input their parents allow them. Second, Professor Guggenheim posits that the very lack of clarity about the role of lawyers for children undermines the claim that lawyers play a useful role: "If there are to be lawyers for children, there must be a clear definition of the lawyer's role. * * * It would be inconceivable for the legal profession to call for lawyers for adults without having first identified the purpose and role of the lawyer." Third, Professor Guggenheim maintains that "[p]rotecting children from being forced to choose where to live may, in the long run, best serve the interests of most children." Martin Guggenheim, What's Wrong with Children's Rights? 162–63 (2005). Professor Guggenheim argues that a custody dispute is almost always about parental rights. In most cases, both parents are adequate and judges should not lose sleep over the outcome for the child. *Id.* at 151.

As you can see, legal scholars disagree about how lawyers should relate to their child clients, and about the lawyer's ethical obligations to advocate for the child's wishes. Professor Katherine Hunt Federle, for example, argues that by emphasizing the child client's capacity, the law diminishes lawyers' ability to focus on children's rights, including the right to participate in decisions that affect them. Katherine Hunt Federle, *The Ethics of Empowerment: Rethinking the Role of Lawyers in Interviewing and Counseling the Child Client*, 64 Fordham L. Rev. 1655 (1996). Professor Emily Buss, in contrast, argues that young children cannot understand their lawyer's role, and that such limitations on child clients' cognitive capacities impair their ability to be truly empowered by legal representation. Emily Buss, *Confronting Developmental Barriers to the Empowerment of Child Clients*, 84 Cornell L. Rev. 895, 898 (1999). Professor James Dwyer argues many state statutes give short shrift to children's rights in decision-making regarding their most intimate relationships. *See* James G. Dwyer, *A Taxonomy of Children's Existing Rights in State Decision Making About Their Relationships*, 11 Wm. & Mary Bill Rts. J. 845, 907–26 (2003).

During the last decade a number of professional groups have issued standards for attorneys and guardians ad litem appointed to represent children in either private custody disputes or abuse and neglect proceedings brought by the state, a subject generally covered in another law school course. These include the American Academy of Matrimonial Lawyers (AAML), Standards for Attorneys and Guardians ad Litem in Custody or Visitation Proceedings, 13 J. Am. Acad. Matrim. Law. 1 (1995), the American Bar Association's Proposed Standards of Practice for Lawyers Who Represent Children in Abuse and Neglect Cases, 29 Fam. L. Q. 375 (1995), and the ABA's Standards of Practice for Lawyers Representing Children in Custody Cases, 37 Fam. L. Q. 131 (2003) (ABA Custody Standards). All of these standards remain aspirational unless incorporated in state law, but provide useful guidance to attorneys. The AAML's Standard 3.5, for example, directs GALs to "take appropriate measures to protect the child from harm that may be incurred as a result of the litigation by striving to expedite the proceedings and encouraging settlement in order to reduce trauma that can be caused by the litigation."

From 2003 to 2008, NCCUSL developed standards governing the representation of children. *The Uniform Representation of Children in Abuse, Neglect, and Custody Proceedings Act*, 42 Family L. Q. 1 (2008). Generally, the ABA's House of Delegates approves NCCUSL's proposed uniform acts before the Commissioners on Uniform State Laws "promulgate" them, or formally issue them for consideration by state legislatures. NCCUSL twice withdrew the standards governing representation of children from consideration by the ABA, most recently in February 2008, in the face of strong opposition from several ABA Sections concerned that the proposed uniform act did not protect a child's right to an attorney who would represent her views consistent with the Model Rules of Professional Conduct.

In the following article, which focuses on the NCCUSL Act, the Act's reporter describes the different positions several professional groups have adopted concerning the representation of children. The most controversial aspect of the Act was its reliance on three distinct categories of representatives: the "child's attorney"; the "best interests attorney," a lawyer who resembles a traditional GAL; and the non-lawyer "best interests advocate" who also resembles a traditional GAL. The first two types of representative build on the ABA Custody Standards, which had remained controversial even after adoption. Both the ABA Custody Standards and the NCCUSL Act abandon the term "guardian ad litem" because of the rampant confusion over the role of GALs, as explained below. Appointing a representative for the child in custody cases, regardless of how the representative is defined, would be discretionary under NCCUSL's proposal.

BARBARA ANN ATWOOD

The Uniform Representation of Children in Abuse, Neglect, and Custody Proceedings
Act: Bridging the Divide Between Pragmatism and Idealism.
42 Family Law Quarterly 63 (2008).

Over the last decade, standards governing the representation of children have received more attention from courts, legislators, and policymakers than ever before. * * *. The practice of child advocacy has become a specialization for which there is certification, and child advocacy clinics are now commonplace in law schools across the United States. * * *

The increased attention to child representation, however, has not produced a clear consensus about what children's representatives should do. Instead, statutory provisions and procedural rules for children's lawyers and guardians ad litem vary dramatically from state to state. Scholars debate such fundamental questions as whether a child's lawyer should function as a traditional client-directed lawyer or a best interests advocate, * * * whether courts should *ever* appoint lawyers for children in private divorce actions, and whether guardians ad litem are a help or a hindrance in protecting children's interests. * * *

* * *

The evolution of the Representation of Children Act * * * was a fluid (if sometimes contentious) process of vigorous discussion, deliberation, debate, and compromise. * * *. The controversy that surrounds the Act's approach to children's lawyers will undoubtedly continue * * *

II. Child Representation Today

* * *

In the context of private custody disputes, the statutory law of most states authorizes courts to appoint an attorney or a guardian ad litem for the child as a matter of discretion, but a few states require the appointment of a representative when custody is contested. Regardless of label, the representative's role typically is to assist the court in protecting the child's best interests rather than to advocate the child's wishes. Arizona became the first state to adopt the three categories of representatives * * * for family law disputes * * *. [A] few states have prescribed procedures for the potential conflict in private custody disputes that can arise when the child's preferences diverge from the attorney's perception of the child's interests. Most states, however, have simply left the potential conflict to be resolved by the representative on a case-by-case basis.

* * *

III. Competing Standards from Professional Groups

The standards for children's representatives that have emerged from professional groups, and their points of divergence, reveal some of the key debates in this area. * * * The impetus for each set of standards was the common recognition that the lack of clear guidance for children's representatives ultimately disserves children, but the approaches taken in the various models contrast sharply. The AAML has come down strongly in favor of client-directed lawyering and would strictly limit the functions of lawyers for children who are too young to direct counsel. The role of a lawyer under the AAML guidelines largely depends on whether the child is "impaired" or "unimpaired," and the guidelines recommend the use of a presumptive age demarcation. The role of a lawyer for an "unimpaired" child closely parallels the role of a lawyer for an unimpaired adult client-the lawyer must zealously pursue his client's objectives and otherwise maintain an ordinary lawyer-client [sic] relationship. The lawyer for the impaired child, in contrast, should not advocate a position on the outcome of the proceeding or on contested issues, but should merely develop facts for the decision-maker to consider. In the AAML's view, "[t]he most serious threat to the rule of law posed by the assignment of counsel for children is the introduction of an adult who is free to advocate his or her own preferred outcome in the name of the child's best interests."

To varying degrees, the recommended standards from other professional groups permit children's lawyers under certain circumstances to diverge from a child client's wishes or to engage in substituted judgment to arrive at a position the child has not formulated. * * *

* * *

IV. Key Provisions of the Representation of Children Act

Drawing on the *ABA Custody Standards*, the Act provides for two distinct lawyer roles-the child's attorney and the best interests attorney. The Act also endorses a lay representative, denominated "best interests advocate," and rejects the hybrid category of attorney/guardian ad litem. Like the *ABA Custody Standards*, the Act directs lawyers to remain within their professional role and bars them from functioning as witnesses. Conversely, the best interests advocate is not to function as a lawyer even if the individual appointed possesses a license to practice law. For all three categories, the Act seeks to improve the overall competence and professionalism of children's representatives. The Act requires that lawyers and best interests advocates be qualified by experience or training, and the commentary encourages states to adopt statewide standards of practice.

* * *

The child's attorney is the child's legal advocate in the proceeding and cannot refuse to advance the child's position based simply on a disagreement with the child's wishes. On the other hand, if a child takes a position that the attorney determines will seriously endanger the child, the attorney should counsel the child to reconsider his or her position. If the child adheres to the position despite the attorney's efforts to counsel the child to reconsider and the attorney determines that the child's goal will place the child "at risk of substantial harm," * * * [t]he attorney may continue to represent the child and request the appointment of a best interests advocate or a best interests attorney, or, alternatively, the attorney may withdraw from representation and request the appointment of a best interests attorney. * * *

The best interests attorney, in contrast, must advocate a position that will serve the child's best interests "according to criteria established by law and based on the circumstances and needs of the child and other facts relevant to the proceeding." * * * [T] he best interests attorney is not bound by the child's expressed objectives but must consider those objectives and give them due weight according to the underlying reasons and the child's developmental level. Although the best interest attorney's assessment of the child's interests may often coincide with the child's wishes, sometimes they will diverge. * * *.

The best interests attorney, like the child's attorney, may not reveal client confidences unless otherwise permitted by the rules of professional conduct. * * *. [However, the best interests attorney may use the child's confidences to develop admissible evidence even over the child's objections.]

The third category of representative under the Act is the "best interests advocate," an individual, not functioning as an attorney [even if she is one], appointed to assist the court in determining the best interests of the child. The definition of the best interests advocate includes volunteer advocates such as persons affiliated with Court Appointed Special Advocate (CASA) programs. The advocate's duties include many functions associated with guardians ad litem, but the Act avoids the "guardian ad litem" terminology because of the widespread disagreement and confusion about the meaning of that term. Under [the Act] * * * , the best interests advocate must meet with the child, determine the child's needs, circumstances, and views, and conduct a full investigation. Just as both categories of attorney must present the child's expressed objectives to the court, the advocate must also do so and must consider the child's goals in deciding what recommendations to make in the proceeding. * * *

* * *

Attorneys can employ the full range of their legal skills to identify and analyze legal issues affecting their child clients and protect their clients' procedural and substantive interests throughout the pendency of the case. The role of counsel may vary, but legal representation can ensure that decisions in a case are based on an accurate, informed, and sensitive assessment of the child's circumstances. * * *

* * *

Under the Act, the court determines the role of the attorney at the time of the appointment, based on information then available to it concerning the child and the child's circumstances. * * *. For practical purposes, judges * * * may need to use the child's age and developmental level as a rough measure for purposes of the initial designation of an attorney role. At the same time, the Act recognizes that a child's capacity to direct counsel is "contextual and incremental and is not simply a function of chronological age." * * * [A] court may revise the designation in light of new information or changed circumstances. Thus, if a best interests attorney determines that the child is capable of directing counsel and conveys that information to the court, [the Act] permits the court to redesignate the best interests attorney as a child's attorney or to add the appointment of a child's attorney where appropriate. Conversely, if a child's attorney determines that the child cannot or will not direct counsel, the attorney may ask the court to appoint a best interests attorney. By giving the court the power to designate the category of representative, the Act seeks to ensure that the appointee and the court will understand the nature of the role from the time of the initial appointment forward.

* * *

V.   Two Models of Lawyering

* * * [T] he approach taken in the Act has engendered considerable controversy among child advocates. In particular, critics have argued that the Act's endorsement of a "best interests attorney" alternative for children's counsel is a step back-ward in the field of children's advocacy. A curious disjuncture exists between the law governing children's representatives around the country, on the one hand, and the arguments of many child advocates about the ideal role for children's lawyers, on the other. In contrast to the models of representation that one sees in the statutes, procedural rules, and case law, many children's rights advocates today endorse an exclusively client-directed model for children capable of directing counsel. The recommendations that emerged from [two academic conferences] * * * oppose the concept of best interests lawyering. * * *

Although child advocates have been recommending stronger client-directed roles for lawyers for more than two decades, state legislatures have not moved consistently in that direction. Recent legislative changes in various states have endorsed * * * a best interests model of child representation as well as a client-directed model. * * *

Criticisms of the best interests attorney role can be loosely grouped into three kinds of concerns. First, critics contend that lawyers who engage in best interests representation are acting outside ethical boundaries since they are unmoored from the bedrock of client direction. Second, critics contend that lawyers lack expertise to determine children's interests. Legal training, it is said, does not prepare a person to make the nuanced and complex evaluations required in arriving at a position that is in the child's best interests, and lawyers who exercise unbridled discretion in determining children's interests may give effect to personal biases and prejudices. Third, child advocates argue that children, as possessors of basic human rights, are entitled to have their views advocated in proceedings affecting their interests. Children should be empowered as rights-bearers, rather than being viewed as vulnerable and the subject of paternalistic lawyering.

By providing guidelines for the best interests attorney, the new Act seeks to constrain the lawyer's discretion while also imposing affirmative duties on the lawyer that are consistent with a traditional attorney's role. The *ABA Model Rules* require that a lawyer remain in a traditional lawyer-client relationship "as far as reasonably possible." * * *. Moreover, under the Act the child's views must be made known to the court in every case, regardless of the category of representative, if the child so desires. * * *

The best interests lawyer diverges from the traditional duty of loyalty, however, in not being bound to follow the child's expressed wishes. The basis for that divergence is found in the nature of childhood—better viewed as a process of evolution, rather than as a status—during which the child is developing an identity, formulating viewpoints, and becoming less dependent on adults. Because of that immaturity, the child lacks legal decision-making power in most respects. Under traditional rules of professional conduct, lawyers have the authority to act on behalf of persons with diminished capacity to protect their interests. Model Rule 1.14 recognizes that the lawyer's role must change if the client's capacity to make "adequately considered decisions . . . is diminished." The commentary does not define "adequately considered decisions" but notes that when the client is a minor, "maintaining the ordinary client-lawyer relationship may not be possible in all respects." At the same time, the commentary emphasizes that even young children have opinions that are entitled to weight in court proceedings affecting their custody. * * *

Those who criticize best interests lawyering because lawyers lack expertise to make such determinations seem to envision a lawyer arriving at a litigation position in a vacuum, driven solely by personal bias or whim. Instead, the best interests lawyer must base his or her legal position on input from the child and the child's relatives, friends, teachers, treating physicians, and others closely affiliated with the child. * * *. The best interests lawyer is in a position to bring to the court's attention multiple sources of information bearing on the child's welfare. When doing so, the attorney's independent and informed interpretation of the evidence will necessarily shape the presentation, but the attorney's advocacy is constrained by the applicable law and the availability of evidence.

The risk that best interest lawyers may act with unconstrained discretion is a legitimate concern, one that the Act addresses through the provision of guidelines governing the lawyer's conduct. * * *. In short, the best interests lawyer who complies with the guidelines of the Act will have regular direct contact with the child and will keep the child's unique identity and needs at the center of the representation.

Moreover, other standards that emphasize the client-directed model nevertheless countenance the exercise of considerable discretion under the rubric of "substituted judgment." * * *. A lawyer's interpretation of what the child would have wanted were the child able to express a position may mask arbitrary value judgments more than would a transparent assessment of best interests.

* * *

If critics are animated in part by the fear of excessive judicial deference to children's lawyers, the remedy would seem to be in educating judges and reforming the substantive law, not in eliminating the advocacy function of lawyers. The court is the ultimate decision maker and should not rely exclusively on the position of a child's attorney, a best interests attorney, a best interests advocate, or an expert witness. * * *

Critics also fear that best interests lawyering disempowers children. In this respect, the debate about the role of children's lawyers may be the result of differing perceptions about children, lawyers, and the adversary system. Put simply, those who argue for the client-direction model view children as rights-bearers whose voices have too long been silenced, and they view best interests lawyers as dangerous players in the system whose biased determinations of children's interests and desires to be "heroes" have hurt children. As Professor Jane Spinak writes, the best interests attorney model permits a lawyer "to protect his or her client and not to represent them." In the view of the client-direction champions, the adversary system works best when each player, including the child, has a vigorous advocate. The judge's task is to determine the truth or, at a minimum, to reach a resolution that will best serve the child's interests. * * *

The concept of children's empowerment, however, is highly contextual. Even the staunchest of children's rights advocates do not argue for the issuance of drivers' licenses to ten year olds. Similarly, most children's rights champions do not urge that young children's wishes in custody disputes should be determinative. * * *. Children lack the legal capacity to make decisions for themselves in most circumstances and often lack the cognitive and emotional capacity to be fully, or consistently, self-determining. Children in the throes of a custody dispute * * * may be particularly vulnerable, and their expressed desires may be acutely unstable and unreliable. * * *. Moreover, because an increasing number of divorce litigants have no legal representation, the child's appointed lawyer in a custody dispute may be the only lawyer in the courtroom. * * *

* * *

NOTES AND QUESTIONS

1. *How should a judge decide?* If you were the divorce court judge and listened to the child express a wish to be in the physical custody of one parent rather than the other, what factors might help you determine how much weight to give to that expressed wish?

2. *An international perspective: The United Nations Convention on the Rights of the Child.* Every nation in the world, with the exception of the United States and Somalia, has ratified the United Nations Convention on the Rights of the Child, promulgated in 1989. The Convention recognizes that a child has separate interests from his or her parents in every legal proceeding and requires that all decisions affecting children be resolved based on the "best interests of the child." Arts. 12 and 3. Because the child's voice is often absent from hearings that will determine his or her home until majority, the failure to grant children representation in child custody cases, and the fact that the child's preference is only one in a long list of factors, would appear to violate Article 12, were it binding in the United States. *See* Mary Ann Mason, *The U.S. and the International Children's Rights Crusade: Leader or Laggard?*, 38 J. of Soc. Hist. 955 (2005). How do you think ratification by the United States would have altered the outcome of custody decisions you have read so far in which the children's preference played a role? Do you think the United States should adopt the Convention's approach to this issue? Why or why not?

3. *Comparing competing standards.* What are the major distinctions between the roles of the three kinds of representatives for children set out in the NCCUSL act? How does that Act differ from the AAML standards? Which approach to the representation of children in custody disputes do you find most persuasive? Why?

4. *May children who are the subjects of custody disputes be parties to their parents' divorce litigation?* Every state court that has considered this question has strongly rebuffed the children's claims that they needed to appear as party-intervenors to ensure that their views received adequate consideration. In *Auclair* v. *Auclair*, three of the Auclair children wanted the court to fire the GAL who disagreed with them, and to appoint an attorney who would represent their views, but they also wanted to intervene as parties. They lost on both counts. Similarly, in *Miller v. Miller*, 677 A.2d 64 (Me. 1996), the court held that minor children are not entitled to intervene in their parents' custody dispute. Trial courts in Maine hold statutory authority to

appoint a GAL for children in custody disputes. The *Miller* court noted, however, that no statute entitles children to an additional representative to advocate for their views. Both *Auclair* and *Miller* concluded that even though children have an interest in the outcome of their parents' custody litigation, denial of intervention did not violate their rights because the trial court and the GAL were obligated to act in the children's best interests and to consider their preferences for custody. *Miller* also concluded that the state had a substantial interest in not including children as parties represented by counsel, because intervention would complicate the proceedings and "result in a substantial additional financial burden on both the parties and [the] court system." *Id.* at 70; *see also, J.A.R.* v. *County of Maricopa*, 877 P.2d 1323 (Ariz. 1994).

In an ordinary civil proceeding, would adults and corporate entities necessarily be satisfied if they were denied the right to a lawyer, based on the court's appointment of a representative to argue for their best interests and the court's assurance that it too would watch out for those interests? In a custody battle, do you think the children meet the ordinary civil standard for intervention as of right or permissive intervention? *Cf.* Fed. R. Civ. P. 24.

5. *How long do a GAL or attorney's duties to the court and the child last?* The generally applicable rules governing attorneys indicate that the attorney continues to serve until the matter is completely resolved—that is, through any appeals. One Texas court, however, has ruled that where an attorney is appointed to " 'assist the [trial] court in protecting a child's best interests rather than to provide legal services to the child' ", that attorney lacks standing to file an appellate brief because the trial court is not a party to the appeal. *O'Connor* v. *O'Connor*, 245 S.W.3d 511, 515 (Tex. Ct. App. 2007).

PROBLEM 12–3

You have recently been appointed to represent a ten-year-old girl in a bitter custody dispute between her parents. During your career as a lawyer, you have never represented a minor before, and the judge has not given you any instructions. You ask the other attorneys in your office what your role should be, and the advice they give you is all over the place. What should you do?

SECTION 5: JOINT CUSTODY

Widespread support for joint custody developed during the last quarter of the twentieth century, reflecting a desire to bring gender and emotional equality to child custody decisions. "Joint *legal* custody" confers on both parents shared decision-making on important issues relating to the children's upbringing, such as education, medical care and religion. "Joint *physical* custody" generally confers on both parents shared day-to-day decision-making and responsibility for their children, and the right to have the children divide their time roughly equally between both homes. In jurisdictions that give a preference to joint custody, courts begin their child custody determinations with a presumption that both parents love their children and that the child will benefit from having a continuing custodial relationship with both parents. When the court orders joint custody, the order means that neither parent is considered better than the other, or a superior decision-maker for the child.

Professor Schepard summarizes the history and origins of the movement toward joint custody:

> Until the late 1970s and early 1980s, courts did not distinguish between joint legal and joint physical custody, and were hostile to the concept of joint custody in any form for essentially the same reasons Goldstein, Freud, and Solnit advanced in support of their "psychological parent" theory. Courts believed that ordering joint custody for conflicted parents created emotional instability * * * for the child that could be eliminated only by choosing one over the other. In 1934, in *McCann v. McCann*, 173 A. 7, 9 (Md. 1934), the Maryland Court of Appeals denounced joint custody as an arrangement "to be avoided, whenever possible, as an evil fruitful of the destruction of discipline, in the creation of distrust, and in the production of mental distress in the child." * * *

* * *

> * * * [C]ourts began to change their views of joint custody in the late 1970's and the early 1980's by beginning to award joint custody even over the opposition of one or both parents. Change came in two forms: (1) Under the influence of fathers' groups, a state legislature enacted a revised child custody statute that authorized a court to award joint custody in contested cases; (2) A court reinterpreted its state's current statute to the same effect, and the legislature later amended the statute to incorporate the court's rulings.

Andrew I. Schepard, Children, Courts, and Custody: Interdisciplinary Models for Divorcing Families 45–46 (2004).

Professor Robert Mnookin highlighted the limitations of the adjudicative process as a vehicle for identifying the preferred custodial parent, and argued that "[w]e would more frankly acknowledge both our ignorance and the presumed equality of the natural parents were we to flip a coin." Robert Mnookin, *Child–Custody Adjudication: Judicial Functions in the Face of Indeterminacy*, Law & Contemp. Probs., Summer 1975, at 226, 289. Mnookin himself acknowledged that the idea of using a coin toss to determine child custody appears "callous" or even "repulsive" to most observers. He argued, however, that our response to a custody lottery "may reflect an intuitive appreciation of the importance of the educational, participatory, and symbolic values of adjudication as a mode of dispute settlement." *Id.* at 291.

The prospect of not having to choose between parents at all, however, was even more attractive. Professor Mary Ann Mason has labeled joint or shared custody "the most politically attractive concept of the 1990s." Mary Ann Mason, The Custody Wars 40 (1999). The joint custody option proved popular among judges. "Joint custody * * * permits the court to escape an agonizing choice, to keep from wounding the self esteem of either parent and to avoid the appearance of discrimination between the sexes." *Id.* at 40 (citing *Dodd v. Dodd*, 403 N.Y.S.2d 401 (Sup. Ct. 1978)).

A. A JUDICIAL OVERVIEW: THE IOWA SUPREME COURT RECONSIDERS JOINT PHYSICAL CUSTODY

In 2001, Maine amended its law to encourage judges to award joint physical custody even if only one parent requests it, unless the judge can explain why the arrangement would not be in the best interests of the child. Me. Rev. Stat. Ann. tit. 19–A, § 1653 (West 1998 & Supp. 2008). California, which once led the way by establishing a presumption in favor of joint custody in all cases, currently presumes that a joint custody award is in the best interest of the child when both parents have agreed to share custody. Cal. Fam. Code § 3080 (West 2004).

Iowa also amended its code as of 2005 to provide that, so long as it is reasonable and in the best interest of the child, courts should make the custody award that will "assure the child the opportunity for the maximum continuing physical and emotional contact with both parents * * *." Iowa Code § 598.41 (2005). The statute, enacted in 2004, was widely thought to modify Iowa's longstanding disapproval of joint physical custody due to language favoring "continuing physical and emotional contact with both parents" so long as it is reasonable and in the interests of the child. *See* Abrams et al. Contemporary Family Law 757 (West 2006). In 2007 the Supreme Court of Iowa surveyed the most recent scholarship on the benefits and risks of joint physical custody in its first comment on the impact of reforms enacted by the state's legislature in 1997 and 2004. As you read its opinion, consider the arguments for and against joint physical custody, how and the extent to which it differs from assigning primary custody to one parent with liberal visitation to the other, and what kinds of families would seem to be the best candidates for joint physical custody.

IN RE THE MARRIAGE OF HANSEN
Supreme Court of Iowa, 2007.
733 N.W.2d 683.

In this case, we review physical care * * * issues related to the parties' dissolution of marriage. The district court granted joint legal custody and joint physical care of the two children to Lyle and Delores Hansen. * * * Delores appealed. * * * The court of appeals reversed the district court on the physical care issue, granting physical care of the children to Delores. * * *

With respect to the holdings of the court of appeals, we affirm the holding as modified in this opinion on the physical care issue * * *. The matter is remanded to the district court for further proceedings consistent with this opinion.

I. FACTUAL BACKGROUND.

Lyle and Delores were married on September 4, 1987. The marriage lasted approximately eighteen years. At the time of trial, Lyle was forty-five years of age and Delores was forty-six. Two children were born of the marriage, Miranda, who was twelve years old at the time of the district court proceedings, and Ethan, who was eight.

At all times prior to the filing of the divorce petition, Delores was the primary caregiver. Lyle * * * was the main breadwinner. For example, during the course of the marriage Delores attended parent teacher conferences on a regular basis, while Lyle did not. The vast majority of the time, it was Delores who helped the children with their homework. Lyle admits that she was better at it, particularly math. During the marriage, Lyle missed important childhood events because of social activities or work-related assignments. When the children were in infancy, Delores opened a day care center in their home. Later, when family finances became an issue, she held full-time employment outside the home. After the parties' separation, however, Lyle has become more involved in the lives of the children.

The record developed at trial reveals serious marital stress. The record demonstrates a history of recurrent arguments, excessive consumption of alcohol, allegations of infidelity and sexual misconduct, and allegations of domestic abuse. Unfortunately, at least some of these contretemps were in front of the children. It was not a pleasant proceeding. * * *

The record further reveals that Delores tended to acquiesce to Lyle when there were disagreements. For example, when Delores was pregnant with Miranda, she wanted to attend child-birthing classes, but Lyle stated that *he* had already undergone training and that, as a result, the classes were not needed. When Delores began operating a child care center out of their home, Lyle insisted on reviewing applicant backgrounds and controlled which children could utilize the service. He further demanded that parents or custodians pick up their children by 5:00 p.m. sharp. Delores did not agree with these practices, but felt she had no choice but to acquiesce. In addition, Delores asked Lyle if he would participate in marital counseling, but he refused, stating that he did not believe in counseling. Delores testified that she agreed to temporary joint physical care prior to trial only because she did not feel she could stand up to her husband. Delores expressed concern that if she disagrees with Lyle, he becomes angry and intimidating.

The parties appear to have different approaches to child rearing. Delores wants the children to be active in the Methodist church and other extracurricular activities. While not being overtly resistant, during the course of the marriage, Lyle did not encourage these kinds of activities. The parties also have different approaches to discipline. Lyle claims to have been the disciplinarian in the marital home. The record reveals that there are occasions when Lyle believed that discipline needed to be more severe than Delores was willing to impose. * * *. * * *

At trial, Lyle expressed concern that Delores will expose their children to her family, which he finds highly dysfunctional. Delores testified that her father abused her as a child, but they have reconciled sufficiently to maintain an ongoing relationship. Lyle's concern, however, extends beyond the father, as other members of Delores' family have been convicted of child endangerment and drug offenses. Delores counters that when the children visit her family, it is always under her supervision.

Prior to trial, the parties were apparently able to work out the scheduling issues inherent in a joint physical care arrangement. There was not always agreement, however, on matters related to the children. For instance, when one child experienced unexpected academic difficulties, Delores believed professional counseling would be of help. Lyle disagreed, once again stating that he did not believe in professional counseling. Delores acquiesced, and counseling was not obtained. On another occasion, the kids called their mother and asked to be picked up because Lyle was angry that they had not cleaned their rooms, and had slammed the kitchen door, breaking its glass pane. Moreover, Delores testified that Miranda told her she desired a more stable living arrangement with a home base.

While much of the record in this case is unattractive, it is clear that both Lyle and Delores love their children. They are both capable of making substantial contributions to their lives. The record further reveals that the children are bright and generally well-adjusted.

* * * [A]t the time of trial, Lyle was earning $46,300 per year as a detective for the City of Washington Police Department. Delores was employed as a bank teller, earning $18,900 per year. Delores has only a high school education and little prospect in Washington, Iowa, for substantial increase in income.

* * *

II. PRIOR PROCEEDINGS.

On November 15, 2004, Lyle filed a petition for dissolution of marriage. The district court entered an order on December 30, 2004 which granted temporary physical care and legal custody to both parents. The temporary order did not establish a physical care schedule. Lyle suggested a pattern of alternating care on a weekly basis, to which Delores acquiesced. The matter came to trial on November 2, 2005. Each party requested physical care. Only Lyle sought joint physical care as a secondary alternative. The district court did not require the parties to submit a joint physical care plan, and, as a result, none was provided to the court. The district court heard testimony from each party and several additional witnesses. On December 30, 2005, the district court entered findings of fact, conclusions of law, and a decree in the case.

The district court granted "joint legal custody" and "joint physical care" of the minor children to Lyle and Delores. The district court order, however, established a schedule where "physical care" would alternate between Lyle and Delores for six-month periods beginning on January 1, 2006, with liberal visitation for the spouse not currently having physical care.

The district court order nevertheless, recognized the parties' difficulty in making mutual decisions. For example, the court ordered that each parent "shall permit the child(ren) to continue the activities after a physical care change." Because Delores was awarded physical care for the first six-month period, the effect of the court order was that her choices of extracurricular activities would be binding on Lyle. The district court additionally ordered that Delores "shall select the church affiliation for the children." The district court ordered that Delores be present when the children visited her family. The court further ordered that if a party moved from the Washington School District, the nonmoving party shall become the physical custodian until further order of the court.

Lastly, the district court decision contained the following language in bold print:

> **This custody arrangement is predicated on the court's belief that the parties are able to communicate regarding the best interests of their children. Failure to communicate in a positive manner may constitute a basis for modification of this decree.**

* * *

The court of appeals agreed with Delores that the best interests of the children required that she should be awarded physical care. The court of appeals held that the alternating six-month schedule did not promote the legislature's goal of frequent contact with both parents. Further, the court of appeals specifically found that Delores was the primary caretaker and that the children had thrived under her parenting and were comfortable with her care. * * * [T]he court of appeals relied upon past history of caregiving and the desire for stability and continuity in awarding physical care to Delores.

* * *

IV. ANALYSIS.

A. Custody and Care Issues.

1. Legal Framework.

On appeal, no party contests the district court's award of joint legal custody. With respect to the children, Delores seeks to overturn the district court's ruling awarding joint physical care to both parties. She seeks physical care. Lyle, however, seeks physical care, but in the event this does not occur, is willing to accept joint physical care * * *.

At the outset, it is important to discuss the differences between joint legal custody and joint physical care. "Legal custody" carries with it certain rights and responsibilities, including but not limited to "decision-making affecting the child's legal status, medical care, education, extracurricular activities, and religious instruction." Iowa Code § 598.1(3), (5) (2005). When joint legal custody is awarded, "neither parent has legal custodial rights superior to those of the other parent." *Id.* A parent who is awarded legal custody has the ability to participate in fundamental decisions about the child's life.

On the other hand, "physical care" involves "the right and responsibility to maintain a home for the minor child and provide for routine care of the child." *Id.* If joint physical care is awarded, "both parents have rights to and responsibilities toward the child including, but not limited to, shared parenting time with the child, maintaining homes for the child, [and] providing routine care for the child. . . ." *Id.* The parent awarded physical care maintains the primary residence and has the right to determine the myriad of details associated with routine living, including such things as what clothes the children wear, when they go to bed, with whom they associate or date, etc.

If joint physical care is not warranted, the court must choose a primary caretaker who is solely responsible for decisions concerning the child's routine care. *Id.* Visitation rights are ordinarily afforded a parent who is not the primary caretaker.

2. Traditional Approach of Iowa Appellate Courts to Joint Physical Care.

For decades, Iowa appellate courts have disfavored joint physical care arrangements in dissolution cases as not in the best interest of children. In *In re Marriage of Burham*, 283 N.W.2d 269 (Iowa 1979), this court outlined reasons against "divided custody." Specifically, the court cited Iowa precedent for the proposition that divided custody is destructive of discipline, induces a feeling of not belonging to either parent, and in some instances can permit one parent to sow seeds of discontent concerning the other. *Id.* at 272. * * * [L]ater cases made it clear that the underlying rationale regarding the best interest of children applied to cases involving "joint physical care."

These cases have generally emphasized that the best interest of children is promoted by stability and continuity. Although a child's best interests will be served by associating with both parents, "an attempt to provide equal physical care may be harmfully disruptive in depriving a child of a necessary sense of stability." *In re Marriage of Muell*, 408 N.W.2d 774, 776 (Iowa Ct. App. 1987). As a result, Iowa appellate courts have stated divided physical care is "strongly disfavored" as not in the best interest of children except in the most unusual of circumstances.

3. Legislative Action Regarding Joint Physical Care.

The Iowa legislature has shown recent interest in joint physical care as a potential alternative in dissolution cases. In 1997 and again in 2004, the legislature amended the Iowa Code to mandate certain procedures regarding the request, award, and denial of joint physical care.

* * *

In 2004, the legislature [amended] * * * Iowa Code section 598.41(5) to read, in relevant part:

> If joint legal custody is awarded to both parents, the court may award joint physical care to both joint custodial parents upon the request of either parent. . . . If the court denies the request for joint physical care, the determination shall be accompanied by specific findings of fact and conclusions of law that the awarding of joint physical care is not in the best interest of the child.

(now codified at Iowa Code § 598.41(5) (2005)).

* * * [T]he 2004 amendment * * * simply provides that a party interested in joint physical care should request it from the court, and if the court denies joint physical care, it should make findings of fact and conclusions of law that such an alternative was not in the "best interest of the child," which is the traditional standard in child custody matters.

This court has not had occasion to consider the implication of the 1997 and 2004 amendments. * * *

* * * [T]he 1997 and 2004 legislation did not create a presumption in favor of joint physical care. There is simply nothing in the language of the amendments that supports such an assertion. Indeed, the Iowa legislative action in 1997 and 2004 is strikingly different from action in other states where presumptions in favor of joint physical care were enacted into law.

* * * With respect to legal joint custody, the legislature has declared that if the court does not grant joint custody, it shall "cite clear and convincing evidence" that joint custody is unreasonable and not in the best interests of a child. Iowa Code § 598.41(2)(b). No similar language appears in the joint physical care provisions of Iowa law.

* * * While the amendments clearly require that courts consider joint physical care at the request of any party and that it make specific findings when joint physical care is rejected, the legislation reiterates the traditional standard—the best interest of the child—which appellate courts in the past have found rarely served by joint physical care. The amendments only require the courts to consider and explain the basis of decisions to deny physical care.

4. Review of the Traditional Approach to Joint Physical Care.

While we find that the Iowa legislature has not overridden prior case law regarding joint physical care, we nonetheless believe that the notion that joint physical care is strongly disfavored except in exceptional circumstances is subject to reexamination in light of changing social conditions and ongoing legal and research developments. Increasingly in Iowa and across the nation, our family structures have become more diverse. While some families function along traditional lines with a primary breadwinner and primary caregiver, other families employ a more undifferentiated role for spouses or even reverse "traditional" roles. A one-size-fits-all approach in which joint physical care is universally disfavored is thus subject to serious question given current social realities.

In addition, the social science research related to child custody issues is now richer and more varied than it was in the past. In the past, many scholars and courts rejected joint physical care based on the influential writings of Joseph Goldstein, Anna Freud, and Albert J. Solnit. These scholars utilized attachment theory to emphasize the need to place children with a single "psychological parent" with whom the children had bonded. Joseph Goldstein, Anna Freud, & Albert J. Solnit, *Beyond the Best Interests of the Child* 98 (1979). Although the research upon which the "psychological parent" attachment theory was based rested upon studies of infants, it was also thought to apply throughout the life cycle of a child.

The psychological parent approach stressed the important role of a strong, caring parent-child dyad and embraced what is sometimes termed a monotropic view of infant-child bonding. * * * The "psychological parent" approach based on attachment theory seems to have influenced a number of courts.

Attachment theory that emphasizes primary relationships continues to have strong advocates. The validity of the parent-child dyad or monotropic view of attachments, however, has been subject to substantial question. Many scholars now view infants as capable of attaching to multiple caregivers and not simply one "psychological parent." * * * Further, a growing body of scholarship suggests that the continued presence and involvement of both parents is often beneficial to the lives of children and not necessarily detrimental as believed by many adherents of the "psychological parent" theory. [Some scholars document the] disadvantages of children growing up in fatherless families, including psychological adjustment, behavior and achievement at school, educational attainment, employment trajectories, and income generation * * * .

As a result, a substantial body of scholarly commentary now challenges the blanket application of the monotropic psychological parent attachment theory to avoid joint physical care. * * *

* * *

* * * Some academic observers suggest that joint physical care may be a way to encourage continued involvement of both spouses in the lives of the children. * * * They cite a wide range of studies to suggest that children may be better off with joint physical care than other arrangements.

The current social science research cited by advocates of joint custody or joint physical care, however, is not definitive on many key questions. To begin with, there are substantial questions of definition and methodology. Such criticisms include: samples that only examine parents who voluntarily choose joint custody, the use of small and homogenous groups, the skewing of samples toward middle class parents with higher incomes and education, the lack of control groups, and the lack of distinction between "joint custody" arrangements and traditional sole custody with visitation, and the failure to differentiate the effects of preexisting parental characteristics from the effects of custody type. * * *

Further, the data is conflicting or ambiguous. As noted by one recent academic observer, the research to date on the benefits of joint physical care is inconclusive and has produced mixed results. * * *

An exhaustive review commissioned by the Washington State Supreme Court Gender and Justice Commission and the Domestic Relations Commission [1999] examined the many studies related to child custody issues. The review concluded that the available research did not reveal any particular post-divorce residential schedule to be most beneficial to children. While the review concluded that the research did not demonstrate significant advantages to children of joint physical care, the research also did not show significant disadvantages.

While it seems clear that children often benefit from a continuing relationship with both parents after divorce, the research has not established the amount of contact necessary to maintain a "close relationship." Preeminent scholars have noted that "surprisingly, even a fairly small amount of close contact seemed sufficient to maintain close relationships, at least as these relationships were seen from the adolescents' perspective." Eleanor E. Maccoby, et al., *Postdivorce Roles of Mothers and Fathers in the Lives of Their Children*, 7 J. Fam. Psychol. 24, 24 (1993), * * *.

There is thus growing support for the notion that the quality, and not the quantity, of contacts with the non-custodial parent are the key to the wellbeing of children. Quality interaction with children can, of course, occur within the framework of traditional visitation and does not occur solely in situations involving joint physical care.

At present, the available empirical studies do not provide a firm basis for a dramatic shift that would endorse joint physical care as the norm in child custody cases. Nonetheless, in light of the changing nature of the structure of families and challenges to the sweeping application of psychological parent attachment theory, we believe the joint physical care issue must be examined in each case on the unique facts and not subject to cursory rejection based on a nearly irrebuttable presumption found in our prior cases. * * *

Any consideration of joint physical care, however, must still be based on Iowa's traditional and statutorily required child custody standard—the best interest of the child. Physical care issues are not to be resolved based upon perceived fairness to the *spouses,* but primarily upon what is best for the *child.* The objective of a physical care determination is to place the children in the environment most likely to bring them to health, both physically and mentally, and to social maturity.

We recognize that the "best interest" standard is subject to attack on the ground that it is no standard at all, that it has the potential of allowing gender bias to affect child custody determinations, and that its very unpredictability increases family law litigation. On the other hand, the advantage of the standard is that it provides the flexibility necessary to consider unique custody issues on a case-by-case basis. * * * We believe the best approach to determining difficult child custody matters involves a framework with some spine, but the sufficient flexibility to allow consideration of each case's unique facts.

In Iowa, the basic framework for determining the best interest of the child has long been in place. In the context of *custody decisions*, the legislature has established a nonexclusive list of factors to be considered. Iowa Code § 598.41(3) (citing nonexclusive factors * * *). Although Iowa Code section 598.41(3) does not directly apply to *physical care* decisions, we have held that the factors listed here as well as other facts and circumstances are relevant in determining whether joint physical care is in the best interest of the child.

In considering whether to award joint physical care where there are two suitable parents, stability and continuity of caregiving have traditionally been primary factors. Stability and continuity factors tend to favor a spouse who, prior to divorce, was primarily responsible for physical care.

We continue to believe that stability and continuity of caregiving are important factors that must be considered in custody and care decisions. * * *. While no post-divorce physical care arrangement will be identical to predissolution experience, preservation of the greatest amount of stability possible is a desirable goal. In contrast, imposing a new physical care arrangement on children that significantly contrasts from their past experience can be unsettling, cause serious emotional harm, and thus not be in the child's best interest.

As a result, the successful caregiving by one spouse in the past is a strong predictor that future care of the children will be of the same quality. Conversely, however, long-term, successful, joint care is a significant factor in considering the viability of joint physical care after divorce.

Stability and continuity concepts have been refined in the recent literature and expressed in terms of an approximation rule, namely, that the caregiving of parents in the post-divorce world should be in rough proportion to that which predated the dissolution. Recently, the American Law Institute's *Principles of Family Law*, published in 2000, adopted the general rule that custodial responsibility should be allocated "so that the proportion of custodial time the child spends with each parent approximates the proportion of time each parent spent performing caretaking functions for the child prior to the parents' separation...." *Principles* § 2:08, at 178. * * *

We do not, however, adopt the ALI approximation rule in its entirety. Iowa Code section 598.41(3) and our case law requires a multi-factored test where no one criterion is determinative. * * *

Nonetheless, we believe that the approximation principle is a factor to be considered by courts in determining whether to grant joint physical care. By focusing on historic patterns of caregiving, the approximation rule provides a relatively objective factor for the court to consider. The principle of approximation also rejects a "one-size-fits-all" approach and recognizes the diversity of family life. Finally, it tends to ensure that any decision to grant joint physical care is firmly rooted in the past practices of the individual family.

There may be circumstances, of course, that outweigh considerations of stability, continuity, and approximation. For example, if a primary caregiver has abandoned responsibilities or had not been adequately performing his or her responsibilities because of alcohol or substance abuse, there may be a strong case for changing the physical care relationship. In addition, the quality of the parent-child relationship is not always determined by hours spent together or solely upon past experience.

All other things being equal, however, we believe that joint physical care is most likely to be in the best interest of the child where both parents have historically contributed to physical care in roughly the same proportion. Conversely, where one spouse has been the primary caregiver, the likelihood that joint physical care may be disruptive on the emotional development of the children increases.

A second important factor to consider in determining whether joint physical care is in the child's best interest is the ability of spouses to communicate and show mutual respect. A lack of trust poses a significant impediment to effective co-parenting. Evidence of controlling behavior by a spouse may be an indicator of potential problems. Evidence of untreated domestic battering should be given considerable weight in determining custody and gives rise to a presumption against joint physical care.

Third, the degree of conflict between parents is an important factor in determining whether joint physical care is appropriate. Joint physical care requires substantial and regular interaction between divorced parents on a myriad of issues. Where the parties' marriage is stormy and has a history of charge and countercharge, the likelihood that joint physical care will provide a workable arrangement diminishes. It is, of course, possible that spouses may be able to put aside their past, strong differences in the interest of the children. Reality suggests, however, that this may not be the case.

In short, a stormy marriage and divorce presents a significant risk factor that must be considered in determining whether joint physical care is in the best interest of the children. The prospect for successful joint physical care is reduced when there is a bitter parental relationship and one party objects to the shared arrangement. * * * [T]here is evidence that high levels of child contact with a nonresidential father are beneficial to children in low conflict families, but harmful to children in high conflict families. * * *

Conflict, of course, is a continuum, but expressions of anger between parents can negatively affect children's emotions and behaviors. Even a low level of conflict can have significant repercussions for children. Courts must balance the marginal benefits obtained from the institution of a joint physical care regime as compared to other alternatives against the possibility that interparental conflict will be exacerbated by the arrangement, to the detriment of the children.

Because of the perceived detrimental impact of parental conflict on children, some commentators have urged that joint physical care should be encouraged only where both parents voluntarily agree to it. *See* Or.Rev. Stat. § 107.169(3) (2007) (joint custody only upon agreement of parents); Vt. Stat. Ann. tit 15, § 665(a) (2007) ("When parents cannot agree to divide or share parental rights and responsibilities, the court shall award parental rights and responsibilities primarily or solely to one parent."). Iowa Code section 598.41(5)(*a*), however, requires the court to consider joint physical care upon the request of either party. While we, therefore, reject the notion that one spouse has absolute veto power over whether the court grants joint physical custody, the lack of mutual acceptance can be an indicator of instability in the relationship that may impair the successful exercise of joint physical care. *See* Iowa Code § 598.41(3)(*g*) (court should consider whether one or both spouses agree or are opposed).

A fourth important factor in determining whether joint physical care is in the best interest of the children, particularly when there is a turbulent past relationship, is the degree to which the parents are in general agreement about their approach to daily matters. * * * . * * * [I]n order for joint physical care to work, the parents must generally be operating from the same page on a wide variety of routine matters. The greater the amount of agreement between the parents on child rearing issues, the lower the likelihood that ongoing bitterness will create a situation in which children are at risk of becoming pawns in continued post-dissolution marital strife.

While the above factors are often significant in determining the appropriateness of joint physical care, we do not mean to suggest that they are the exclusive factors or that these factors will always be determinative. This court has stated, despite application of a multi-factored test, that district courts must consider the total setting presented by each unique case. The above factors present important considerations, but no iron clad formula or inflexible system of legal presumptions.

Once it is decided that joint physical care is not in the best interest of the children, the court must next choose which caregiver should be awarded physical care. Iowa Code § 598.41(1)(*a*), (5). The parent awarded physical care is required to support the other parent's relationship with the child. * * * The court should be alert, however, to situations where the emotional bonds between children and a parent who has not been the primary caregiver are stronger than the bonds with the other parent.

In making decisions regarding joint physical care and, if joint physical care is not appropriate, in choosing a spouse for physical care, courts must avoid gender bias. There is no preference for mothers over fathers, or vice versa. * * *

In summary, we believe that statements in the case law indicating that joint physical care is strongly disfavored are overbroad. Factors often of importance in determining the viability of joint physical care include an overriding interest in stability and continuity, the degree of communication and mutual respect, the degree of discord and conflict prior to dissolution, and the extent to which the parties agree on matters involving routine care. While we believe that in many contested cases, the best interests of the child will not be advanced by joint physical care, the courts must examine each case based on the unique facts and circumstances presented to arrive at the best decision.

5.   Best Interests of Children in this Case.

In light of the above principles, and after our de novo review of the entire record, we agree with the court of appeals that joint physical care is not in the best interest of the children under the unique facts presented in this case. For most of the marriage, Delores has been the primary caregiver. * * *

The record also shows that the parties have significant difficulties in communication. * * *

The record also demonstrates differences in parenting styles. * * * . Over the long haul, we believe there is a high potential for conflict if joint physical care were to continue.

The district court recognized the problems in the relationship and attempted to address them in its order. For example, the court found it necessary to decide who would determine the children's religious affiliation and to include pointed language ensuring that extracurricular choices of each spouse would be honored. These are the kind of decisions that inhere in joint custody, not joint physical care. The fact that the district court found it necessary to include such provisions, and thereby raise the possibility of contempt in the event of violation, does not reflect a high degree of confidence in the ability of the parties to have a smooth, working relationship which is a prerequisite to a successful joint physical care arrangement.

The district court's order alternating physical custody on six-month intervals may have also been designed to lessen potential friction between the parties. There was no evidence in the record to suggest that the alternate six-month arrangement was designed to accommodate work schedules of the parties or was based on some other logistical factor. Like the court of appeals in this case, a number of appellate courts have invalidated similar arrangements. * * *

It is not necessary, however, for us to consider the validity of such an alternating physical care arrangement. * * * [W]e hold that this is not a case where joint physical care is in the best interest of the children * * *. We conclude that the best interest of the children will be advanced by awarding physical care to Delores rather than to award joint physical care.

* * *

At the same time, Lyle has an important role to play in his children's lives. No one questions his devotion to them and their need for his guidance and support. A responsible, committed, nonresident parent, with good parenting skills, has the potential to engage in a high-quality relationship with his or her child and to positively impact the child's adjustment. * * *

Because the district court ordered the parties to share joint legal custody, Lyle will continue to be involved in major decisionmaking for his children. In order to promote the desirable level of physical contact, on remand, the district court should establish liberal visitation for Lyle * * *. [The court sets out the details of a liberal visitation schedule]. * * *

* * *

DECISION OF THE COURT OF APPEALS AFFIRMED AS MODIFIED; DISTRICT COURT JUDGMENT AFFIRMED IN PART, REVERSED IN PART, AND CASE REMANDED WITH INSTRUCTIONS.

NOTES AND QUESTIONS

1. *Propriety of awarding joint custody.* Many courts have held (and experts agree) that the most important criteria for an award of joint custody are the parties' agreement and their ability to cooperate in reaching shared decisions in matters affecting the children's welfare. *See Aydani v. Wagner*, 2007 WL 603393 *3 (Ark. Ct. App. 2007) (*citing Gray v. Gray*, 239 S.W.3d 26 (2006)) ("An award of joint custody where cooperation is lacking is reversible error"); *In re Marriage of Seitzinger*, 775 N.E.2d 282, 286 (Ill. App. Ct. 2002) (when determining whether joint custody is in the best interests of the child, a court must consider "the ability of the parents to cooperate effectively and consistently in matters that directly affect the joint parenting of the child").

2. *The Iowa statute.* If you were a women's rights advocate, what criticisms might you have of the Iowa statute? If you were an advocate for a fathers' rights group, what would you say about the statute? How does the statute differ from other approaches to custody discussed in this Chapter? As a neutral observer, what concerns might you have about the statute's impact?

3. *Current status of joint custody in other states.* Joint custody remains controversial, but nearly all states allow it, some give it preference, and some, like Iowa, permit courts to impose joint custody even against the wishes of one or both parties. The District of Columbia statute codifies a rebuttable presumption that joint custody is in the best interest of the child. D.C. Code § 16–914(a)(2) (2001 & 2008 Supp.). But many of the 50 states are harder to categorize. It should not surprise you to learn that different commentators use different definitions of joint custody. As a result, there is no consensus regarding how many states in addition to the District of Columbia have

presumptions favoring joint custody. An American Bar Association study concluded in 2008 that twenty-two states and the District of Columbia have presumptions favoring joint legal custody. American Bar Association Commission on Domestic Violence, Child Custody and Domestic Violence by State, http://www.abanet.org/domviol/statutorysummarycharts.html. In contrast, a 2007 study reported that 37 states have some level of preference for joint custody. Melissa A. Tracy, *The Equally Shared Parenting Time Presumption–A Cure–All or a Quagmire for Tennessee Custody Law?*, 38 U. Mem.L.Rev. 153 m.69–74 (2007). *See also, e.g.,* Solangel Maldonado, *Beyond Economic Fatherhood: Encouraging Divorced Fathers to Parent*, 153 U. Pa. L. Rev. 921, 986 n.326 (2005) (finding presumptions or preferences for joint custody in 24 states); Minn. Stat. Ann. § 518.17 (West 2006) (creating a rebuttable presumption that joint custody is in the best interest of the child if either parent requests it). In many states, however, the preference or presumption applies only when both parents request joint custody. Maldonado, *supra*, at 986; *see, e.g.,* Ala. Code § 30–3–152(c) (1998 & 2008 Supp.) (joint custody presumed to be in the child's best interests if both parents request it); Mich. Comp. Laws Ann. § 722.26a(2) (2002) (if both parents agree on joint custody, then the court shall award it unless not in the best interest of the child). Virtually all other states expressly permit joint custody as an option at the court's discretion.

4. *Specific arrangements.* The *Hansen* court did not reach the question whether the trial court's order that joint custody be accomplished by moving the children every six months was an appropriate use of the court's powers or promoted the children's best interests. Other courts have noted the importance of minimizing disruption and instability and ensuring that school age children are in living arrangements that promote educational continuity. What would you want to know in order to decide whether splitting the year in half made sense? Do you think the trial court should have issued the order requiring the children to move every six months rather than integrating shared custody throughout the year?

5. *"Custody blackmail."* In an influential 1984 article, Chief Justice Richard Neely of the West Virginia Supreme Court of Appeals, formerly a practicing domestic relations lawyer, explained how a party may use "custody blackmail" to abuse joint custody claims during divorce negotiations:

> Divorce decrees are typically drafted for the parties after compromises reached through private negotiation. These compromises are then approved by a judge, who generally gives them only the most perfunctory sort of review. The result is that parties (usually husbands) are free to use whatever leverage is available to obtain a favorable settlement. In practice, this tends to mean that husbands will threaten custody fights, with all of the accompanying traumas and uncertainties * * * as a means of intimidating wives into accepting less child support and alimony than is sufficient to allow the mother to live and raise the children appropriately as a single parent. Because women are usually unwilling to accept even a minor risk of losing custody, such techniques are generally successful.

Richard Neely, *The Primary Caretaker Parent Rule: Child Custody and the Dynamics of Greed*, 3 Yale L. & Pol'y Rev. 168, 177 (1984).

If Chief Justice Neely is correct, how would a statute favoring joint custody—such as the Maine statute discussed at the beginning of this Section that allows a judge to grant joint physical custody upon the request of only one parent—likely affect divorce negotiations?

6. *A critique of joint custody.* Professors Jana Singer and William Reynolds have criticized judicially-imposed joint custody arrangements on a number of grounds, including the widespread confusion over the meaning of the term. They argue that:

> [P]roponents have failed to acknowledge that the vast majority of court-ordered joint custody decrees provide for equal parental *rights,* but impose vastly unequal parental *responsibilities.* Joint *legal* custody denotes parents' equal authority, or legal right, to make the vital decisions affecting a child's life. Joint *physical* custody refers to the approximately equal parental sharing of physical care and living time with the child—that is, to equal custodial responsibilities.

They point out that "virtually all court-imposed joint custody decrees involve joint *legal* custody only," so that:

> [t]he children in such arrangements live with and are primarily cared for by one parent—usually the mother. The nonresidential parent—generally the father—enjoys liberal visitation rights, just as he does in most traditional sole custody arrangements. The critical difference is that under joint legal custody the nonresidential father also enjoys equal legal authority to control the child's upbringing. This means that he must concur in—or at least not object to—all major decisions affecting the child's life. Thus, the nonresidential father has most of the privileges but few of the day-to-day responsibilities of raising a child. Conversely, the residential mother loses much of the decision-making authority generally enjoyed by other adults who assume the day-to-day responsibilities of caring for children.

Jana Singer & William Reynolds, *A Dissent on Joint Custody,* 47 Md. L. Rev. 497, 503–04 (1988).

Professors Singer and Reynolds also worry that joint custody may restrict the mobility of the primary residential caretaker, but not of the non-residential parent. (The problem of parental relocation will be addressed in Chapter 13). And they wonder whether joint custody orders—"particularly joint legal custody—guarantee continuing parental involvement." *Id.* at 506.

Distinguishing carefully between voluntary agreements to share custody and court-imposed joint custody, Singer and Reynolds concede that "joint custody can work well", if certain conditions are met:

> Motivated, caring, and wealthy parents can manage a true sharing of the children. That sharing, unaccompanied by strife, may even benefit the children. But those parents do not need a judicial order to achieve joint custody; such arrangements can be accommodated easily under the existing umbrella of sole custody *cum* liberal visitation rights.

Id. at 518.

But, they conclude, "joint custody, for the overwhelming majority of families, is a snare and a delusion." In their view:

> joint custody is all too likely to be another millstone around the neck of the real custodial parent, who will find she has to share rights (but not responsibilities) with a recalcitrant former spouse, yet who is likely to find lessened support payments the real payoff to her of the arrangement. The sincerity of many joint custody advocates cannot conceal the reality that joint custody creates many harmful effects, and that a court order cannot overcome the difficult problems presented by a disintegrating family.

Id.

7. *Domestic violence and joint custody.* The presence of a controlling spouse and the risk of domestic violence lay just under the surface in *Hansen.* The following commentary explains the risks of joint custody in such situations:

> Joint legal custody requires both parents to make decisions concerning the children's lives, including issues of school, home, medical care and religion. In acrimonious divorces between parents with no history of violence, joint custody can provide an angry parent with a channel through which he or she can emotionally abuse the other parent. Some suggest that in these cases sole custody awards may be preferable to joint custody awards.
>
> In cases involving domestic violence, joint custody awards can offer the violent parent a court-sanctioned opportunity to continue physical and emotional abuse against the other parent. In some states, a court may award joint custody even if only one parent requests it. A batterer often seeks joint custody as a means of continuing control over an abused person and as a means of significantly reducing child support payments.

Frederica Lehrman, *Factoring Domestic Violence into Custody Cases*, Trial, Feb. 1996, at 32, 34; *see also*, Judith G. Greenberg, *Domestic Violence and the Danger of Joint Custody Presumptions*, 25 N. Ill. L. Rev. 403 (2005).

8. *Paternal activism.* Joint custody had its genesis in the fathers' rights movement, and fathers in countries ranging from Great Britain to Israel and the United States continue to seek greater engagement in the lives of their children after divorce. An article in the *New York Times Magazine* described the political battle for equal custodial rights in the United States as of 2005:

> There are dozens of fathers' rights groups in the States, including the American Coalition for Fathers and Children, Dads Against Discrimination and the Alliance for Noncustodial Parents Rights. * * * [T]hey work quietly behind the scenes, pushing for custody laws like the ones Iowa and Maine have passed, lobbying Congress and generally doing what they can to improve not just the rights but also the image of divorced fathers. In this last task, oddly enough, these groups have benefited from federal initiatives designed to motivate divorced or never-wed fathers who care all too little about their kids, as publicly financed ad campaigns remind the public how indispensible [sic] fathers are. ("Fathers Matter," shouted ads on New York City buses last year.)

Fathers' groups also benefit from a more general recognition that fathers, at least in some socioeconomic circles, are now much more involved in their children's lives. Some of that involvement is born of necessity, given how many mothers work, but necessity also seems to have effected a cultural shift, ushering in the era of the newly devoted dad. The traditional custody arrangement, with Mom as sole custodian and Dad demoted to weekend visitor, may have been painful, but practical, in a family with a 50's-style division of labor; but to the father who knows every Wiggle by name, the pediatrician's number by heart and how to make a bump-free ponytail, such an arrangement could be perceived as an outrage, regardless of what might be more convenient or who is the primary caretaker.

On the other hand, divorced dads still face some serious image problems, a function of well-known statistics that are hard to spin. In the United States, in the period following divorce, one study has found, close to half of all children lose contact with their fathers, with that figure rising to more than two-thirds after 10 years. Although child-support payments have crept up in recent years, in 2001 only 52 percent of divorced mothers received their full child-support payments; among women who had children out of wedlock, the number was around 32 percent. Fathers' rights groups have a tall order explaining those statistics, convincing judges—and the country at large—that if fathers skip town, or refuse payment, it's a function of how unfairly family courts treat them rather than the very reason that the courts treat fathers the way they do. Kim Gandy, president of the National Organization for Women, told me that fathers' rights groups are "focused only on the rights of fathers, and not on the rights of children, and particularly, not on the obligations of fathers that should go with those rights."

* * *

* * * Fathers and Families, a Massachusetts organization committed to improving fathers' access to their children * * * reached a milestone [in 2004], when it managed to put a nonbinding question about shared custody on the ballot for the November elections; 86 percent of those who voted on the issue supported a presumption of joint physical and legal custody. * * *

* * *

Susan Dominus, *The Fathers' Crusade*, N.Y. Times Magazine, May 8, 2005 (Magazine), at 26.

9. *Fathers' rights or children's rights?* Critics, including children's rights groups, argue that the legal presumption that fathers' rights advocates seek to impose creates a "one-size-fits-all standard that only takes the focus off the children." Dee McAree, *Broad Campaign Aimed at Altering Custody Laws; Advocates Allege Bias, Opponents Warn of Taking Focus Off Children*, Nat'l L.J., Oct. 25, 2004, at 4. Do you agree? Does a legal presumption of joint custody favor parents' rights over the sometimes-incompatible needs of children?

PROBLEM 12–4

Martha and Frank have three children ages six, eight and ten. During the marriage Frank worked 10 to 12 hour days in his career, providing a comfortable life for the family. By mutual agreement, Martha was a stay-at-home parent who provided for most of the children's daily needs. Frank spent about three or four hours a week supervising the children, although he was at home most weekends. When the couple decides to divorce, Frank seeks equal parenting time. He estimates that his weekends at home amount to about 20% of the week based on past performance, but he says he is now at a stage in his career where he can cut back to four days a week and he plans to do so if awarded joint physical custody. Assuming that Martha and Frank have a cordial relationship and similar values, should the court award Frank joint physical custody of the children? What would the outcome be under: (a) the best interests standard; (b) the ALI Principles; and (c) the Iowa statute?

PROBLEM 12–5

Imagine a prime time television address by the President of the United States, who appears flanked by the majority and minority leaders of Congress. The President announces that the government is concerned about the number of fathers who disengage from their children after they separate from the children's mothers. He announces a major bi-partisan initiative which will help parents in intact and dissolving families handle parenting issues that arise, and plan for shared parenting after separation. The initiative includes generous funding to establish storefront parenting walk-in centers in communities all over the country. These centers will offer mediation, counseling and parent education among other services, to parents as well as grandparents and other involved caretakers.

What would it take for this scenario to become reality in the United States? What are the pros and cons of such a plan? Do you think such a center might help Martha and Frank (Problem 12–4) agree on and succeed at shared parenting?

CHAPTER 13

VISITATION AND POST-DISSOLUTION CUSTODY DISPUTES

■ ■ ■

After reading Chapter 12, you may agree with New York's highest court that the "only absolute in the law governing custody of children is that there are no absolutes." *Friederwitzer v. Friederwitzer*, 432 N.E.2d 765, 767 (N.Y. 1982). More recently, a Connecticut trial judge observed that a parent "can no more win" a bitter custody dispute "than win an earthquake." *Davidson* v. *Davidson*, 2008 WL 1799679 * 1 (Conn. Super. Ct. 2008) (unpublished opinion). These disputes, she said, have "no 'winner'" but only "tragic victims"—the children. *Id*. Consider these statements as you examine the varied and evolving interpretations of the law applied to disputes over custody and visitation that may continue to fester after the court's initial decree has determined the parties' rights and obligations.

This Chapter covers a range of issues that can involve parents in ongoing, acrimonious litigation after the initial custody decision. Only a small proportion of custody cases continue to be litigated after the court issues its initial decree, but judges commonly feel inundated with post-divorce litigation concerning enforcement of visitation rights, disagreements about child-rearing, and requests to modify custodial arrangements or the terms of parenting agreements.

According to a leading deskbook for judges, litigation produced by disputes over alleged violations of visitation orders is, "almost always hostile, highly emotional, expensive, and exhausting for the parties, their lawyers, and the judge." National Interdisciplinary Colloquium on Child Custody, Legal and Mental Health Perspectives on Child Custody Law: A Deskbook for Judges § 19:1 (Robert J. Levy, ed. 1998). The same holds true for other post-decretal litigation concerning childrearing.

Because of the importance, relative frequency, and difficulty of these seemingly endless disputes, this casebook devotes a separate chapter to post-dissolution disputes about custody and visitation. As you will see, many factors considered in the initial custody decision (discussed in Chapter 12) continue to fuel conflict between parents after dissolution:

religion, educational choices, the other parent's sexual behavior and morality, and so forth.

Disputes over visitation occur between parents and third parties as well as between two legal parents whose relationship with each other has ended. In exceptional cases, as you will see, a number of equitable doctrines permit courts in some states to award parental status to a third party who can then petition for custody and visitation.

In Chapter 12 you saw that parents sometimes ask courts to modify custody orders, and the material in this Chapter often centers on requests for modification. Toward the end of the Chapter you will learn about the grounds for modification of custody and visitation orders as well as the special doctrines governing requests for modification when a parent who has primary physical custody decides to move. Finally, you will read about parents who take the law into their own hands by absconding with their children.

In addition, third parties such as grandparents and stepparents, who were not and could not have been parties to the divorce, may make claims that affect a custodial parent's control of the children.

SECTION 1:   DISPUTES ABOUT MAJOR CHILDREARING DECISIONS

Perpetual disputes about custody, visitation and childrearing reflect a myriad of issues that often survive dissolution of the parents' relationship. These issues include each parent's conviction that he or she is the better parent who understands what is best for the child. The custodial parent (or both parents where physical custody is shared) often perceives that he or she is being forced to prolong a terminated relationship; the non-custodial parent in turn may resent that his or her interest in the child has been severely diminished because the child now "belongs" to the custodial parent. Finally, because struggles for control frequently lie at the heart of troubled marriages, hostility toward a former spouse (or lover) may be a defense mechanism against confronting the severity and finality of the lost relationship. Disputes with the other parent "provide the major route through which each spouse can continue to attempt to control, punish, and frustrate the other." Deskbook for Judges, *supra*, § 4:4.

A. COLLAPSE OF JOINT PARENTING

The following case provides an excellent, if extreme, example of the extent of animosity between some parents following divorce. The gulf dividing the parents gives rise to the kinds of issues that frequently become focal points in post-divorce disputes: disputes over religious up-bringing, relocation, educational choices, and access to the children's daily activities.

NICITA v. KITTREDGE

Superior Court of Connecticut, 2004.
2004 WL 2284292 (Sept. 22, 2004).

PRESTLEY, J.

* * *

This highly contentious case involves the filing of numerous post-judgment motions by both parents with respect to their two young children, Alec and Madison. After numerous days of hearing, testimony from many witnesses, including at least two experts and exhibits entered, this court makes the following findings.

FINDINGS

The parties' marriage was dissolved on June 6, 2001 by agreement. * * * [T]he parties agreed to joint legal custody of the minor children, primary residence with the defendant * * * [the mother, who] would be responsible for all day-to-day decisions regarding the children's care. The agreement noted that major decisions, as defined in the agreement, "shall be considered and discussed in depth by and agreed to by both parties to the greatest extent possible." Those major decisions were defined in the judgment. In entering this agreement, the parties recognized that their powers would not be exercised "for the purpose of frustrating, denying, or controlling in any manner the lifestyle of the other parent." Finally, the parties agreed that they would "exert their best efforts to work cooperatively in developing future plans consistent with the best interests of the children and in amicably resolving such disputes as may arise."

To suggest that the above provisions have been largely ignored would be an understatement. The court file is replete with no less than seventy-five motions having been filed by both parties, during the pendency of the dissolution action, within weeks of the date of dissolution, and over the past three years. Many of these motions were resolved by agreement or after hearing only to have new motions filed within a short period of time. Additional motions have been filed since the hearing closed and as recently as last week * * * . * * *

At least two and possibly three Guardians *Ad Litem* have been appointed to represent the children. The first withdrew because of alleged threats of litigation made by the defendant's family members. At one point an attorney was appointed to represent the GAL. There have been allegations made by the plaintiff of threats made against him by the defendant's attorneys.

This case has a long and tortured history of events that led up to the demise of the marriage and has continued since the dissolution. * * * [T]he stepfather * * * moved into the marital home within weeks of the plaintiff moving out. The children's religious upbringing has been the source of numerous motions and perhaps the most contentious topic of dispute between the parties.

The defendant is remarried and lives in Burlington, Connecticut with her husband and the two children. The plaintiff continues to reside in Farmington, Connecticut but works in the state of New York, has a girlfriend there and spends the majority of his time with his children there visiting his family, his girlfriend and her children as well.

* * *

Custody and Parenting Schedule

There have been a few modifications to the parenting plan since the date of dissolution. There is at present, no primary residential designation. The current custody and visitation arrangement allows for a traditional schedule but specifically also includes parenting time by the plaintiff every other weekend from Friday until Monday, mid-week access from Wednesday to Thursday and an additional 10 days access throughout the year. The plaintiff has also had access to the children on alternating Mondays overnight. The children are at the plaintiff's home a minimum of twelve nights per month. April vacation and Christmas vacation weeks and Easter Sunday are reserved to the plaintiff as are two non-consecutive weeks in the summertime. The children are happy with the current schedule.

There was ample evidence offered throughout the course of the protracted hearings that compel this court to conclude that both parties have taken actions that have undermined the other parent and have been detrimental to the children. They are hypercritical of one another on an unrelenting basis. The defendant has consistently taken unilateral action over the objection of or without seeking input from the plaintiff. The plaintiff is consistent in rigidly resisting any attempt or position offered by the defendant when she does seek his input.

* * * [T]hese issues have been recurring and have been the subject of motions in the past. While the number of examples of inappropriate conduct by the parties is too numerous to list, the following are a sample:

Religion

The parties were married by both a priest and a rabbi. During the course of their marriage, they celebrated both Christmas and Chanukah. When Alec was born, they had a Jewish baby naming ceremony but there was no Bris ceremony. It is clear to the court that the parties, individually and collectively, had not committed to raising their children as either Jewish or Christian by the date of the dissolution.

At some point after the dissolution, the defendant made the unilateral decision that the children would be raised in the Jewish faith. The plaintiff, who is Catholic, was upset about this unilateral decision for the reason that he did not agree to it. This issue became the subject of a series of motions with the plaintiff ultimately agreeing that the children would be raised in the Jewish faith. Alec was then signed up to attend Hebrew school, which takes place every Sunday morning during the school year from 3rd grade until he is 9 or 10 years old when the program becomes more intense in preparation for being Bas or Bar Mitzvah'd. * * * [The father] has refused to allow Alec to attend Hebrew school on his weekend time with his children. He has also begun to take the children to church on his weekends with them and has affirmatively given them mixed messages about their religion.

Relocation

At some point, the defendant made the unilateral decision that she and her new husband would move from Farmington, Connecticut where the plaintiff resides and the children attended school to Burlington, Connecticut and a new school district. She listed her house for sale without informing the plaintiff and he only learned of the impending move from a neighbor. Again, this unilateral decision resulted in a flurry of motions with the end result being that the plaintiff agreed to allow the children to make this move.

Therapy

Alec began having stomach problems with vomiting, quite possibly in response to the tension created by the animosity between the parties. There were discussions with his teacher and the school social worker about starting him in therapy. The defendant unilaterally began to bring Alec to a therapist without consulting the plaintiff, which in this case, the court finds was appropriate. The plaintiff did not take any action to oppose this in court but then the defendant changed the therapist, purportedly because the therapist was recommending that the children spend more time with the plaintiff. She did this without consulting the plaintiff and apparently gave short shrift to the fact that the new therapist was "out-of-network" and therefore not covered by the plaintiff's insurance. She then demanded that the plaintiff share in the expense of the out-of-network therapist.

* * *

Other Examples

* * *

In the course of signing up her children for activities, the defendant listed her current husband as "the father" on activities registration forms and her husband and her brother as emergency contacts as well. Nowhere was the plaintiff listed as the parent or as an emergency contact. As a consequence, on at least one occasion, the children's day camp administrators refused to send the plaintiff forms or information about their program.

The defendant unilaterally committed the children to activities on a regular basis and then would inform the plaintiff. Some of these activities impacted on the plaintiff's parenting schedule with the children. This was, in part, due to the plaintiff's unwillingness to respond to requests by the defendant for activity input in a timely fashion. This was especially true when the defendant needed to make a decision about summer day camp in order to secure a spot for each of the children. Despite her repeated attempts to get feedback from the plaintiff, he refused to select his summer vacation time until the very last moment as specified in the original judgment but well beyond the date needed to secure the children a place.

* * *

On at least one occasion, the plaintiff requested medication from the defendant for Alec's asthma, the defendant indicated that she was too busy and the stepfather replied "you'll get what she gives you."

The plaintiff does not want the stepfather at Alec's ball games and there have been several unpleasant encounters. * * *

Both the stepfather and the plaintiff's girlfriend seem to be entirely appropriate and very loving to the children. It is indeed unfortunate that these four individuals cannot be actively involved with the children without such involvement becoming unpleasant, confrontational and uncomfortable for the children.

THE CHILDREN

The children are beautiful, bright and articulate. Currently, Alec is in karate and baseball. Madison is in Daisy Scouts, soccer, dance and piano. The children also attend summer day camp at Camp Chase and Winding Trails. Since the decision was made to allow the children to be raised in the Jewish faith, they now identify themselves as Jews.

The children are happy to see the plaintiff and enjoy the time that they spend with him in New York, with his fiancée and her children, with the plaintiff's extended family, and at his home. Unfortunately, Alec is intensely aware of the tension, animosity, and belligerence that exists between his parents and he is very uncomfortable when he is in the presence of both his stepfather and his father. In fact, he indicated to the GAL that he must ask the parent he is with to speak to his other parent when they run into them. There is much that the children are not revealing to either parent about their feelings vis-à-vis the current untenable situation. Alec believes that there is a list of topics that he cannot discuss with either parent. All of this has manifested in Alec having physical symptoms of illness, necessitating therapy for this third grader.

Alec is told by the defendant that he is Jewish and by the plaintiff that he is Catholic and Jewish. He is very confused about his religious identity.

There is no question in the court's mind that each of these parties, individually, love these children and take excellent care of them when they are in their respective homes. * * * Individually, both the defendant and the plaintiff are very good parents.

Collectively, however, the parties' co-parenting of these children is a disaster. Their positions are so intractable that neither party is capable of compromise. * * * Mediation and the Peace Program do not seem to have assisted the parties in resolving differences. In fact it was during mediation that the defendant signed up the children for Hebrew school when the issue had not yet been resolved. The plaintiff calls the defendant derogatory names and speaks ill of the defendant in the presence of the children. The defendant retaliates in kind by being inflexible and by saying and doing things that she knows will "push the defendant's buttons."

The plaintiff retaliates in a similar fashion * * * . * * * The nasty, demeaning tone in the litany of email communications that the court reviewed speaks volumes about the parties' inability to civilly co-parent their two children. This court will also note that the defendant's attorneys have done little to defuse this litigious, escalating situation. There is no question that Alec and Madison have become victims of not only this parenting arrangement but of this legal case as well.

Based upon all of the above, it is clear to the court that the original orders in the judgment of dissolution must be modified in order to minimize contact between the parties and to minimize any opportunities the parties may have to continue to battle each other, all to the detriment of Alec and Madison.

ORDERS

1. The joint custody order shall remain in place. Except in the event of an emergency, all major decisions making shall be mutually agreed upon by the parties. Those decisions include but are not limited to non-routine medical treatment and relocation.

2. The defendant shall be primarily responsible for making the day-to-day decisions for the children including the scheduling of their activities. The defendant shall request input from the plaintiff before scheduling but may schedule the children in no more than two activities per child per season without the plaintiff's agreement. The defendant shall make her best efforts not to schedule activities that interfere with the plaintiff's parenting time. The plaintiff will make his best efforts to take the children to their activities on his parenting time. All information regarding the children's activities shall be provided to the plaintiff in a timely fashion.

3. This court is cognizant of the plaintiff's ties to the state of New York, the children's need to spend time with his extended family, and his need to parent autonomously. While continuity for the children would certainly be in their best interests, the plaintiff will have to decide whether to take the children to those activities that impact on his weekends with them. * * * The plaintiff shall not schedule the children

for any activities with any substantial time commitment without the agreement of the defendant.

4.   The defendant shall be authorized to make all decisions involving routine doctor's and dentist's appointments including the selection of those professionals so long as she seeks the plaintiff's input and bears the added expense of any out-of-network providers.

5.   The defendant shall provide the plaintiff's parent contact information on each and every application in the appropriate place for each and every activity and school that the children are engaged with. The plaintiff will have independent access to all of his children's activity providers regardless of whether he is paying the bill or not.

6.   Both parties are encouraged to participate in their children's education. The defendant shall be authorized to make the final day-to-day educational decisions for the children after seeking the plaintiff's input. The children are permitted to attend private school locally as long as the defendant bears the cost of this extraordinary expense.

7.   The plaintiff shall be permitted and encouraged to participate in the children's therapy as recommended by their therapist. Any out-of-network therapy expenses, including sessions involving participation by the plaintiff, above and beyond those in-network expenses that the plaintiff would have otherwise been responsible for under his insurance plan, shall be borne by the defendant.

8.   Other than in a true emergency situation, there shall be no telephone contact by either parent to the other's home. The children may enjoy unlimited telephone contact with the nonresidential parent as they wish. Those conversations shall take place with the children afforded some privacy. The parents will communicate only by email and in a civil, non-sarcastic manner.

9.   Each parent shall provide the other parent with all necessary medications for the child during his time at the other parent's home.

10.   * * * [The parents shall inform each other about their respective vacation plans by a set date.]

11.   The children shall continue to be formally raised in the Jewish faith as agreed upon by the parties. While it is hoped that the defendant at some point will participate in the Bar or Bas Mitzah [sic] events in the children's lives, he shall not be required to bring the children to Hebrew school on his weekends with them. * * * Any Hebrew School tutoring costs resulting from the defendant's decision to raise the children in the Jewish faith, the joint custodial arrangement and the plaintiff's reluctance to be involved in the children's religious education, shall be borne by the defendant.

12.   This court would have no problem with the plaintiff exposing the children to his religion if it was confident that the children would not be pressured to take part in rituals that might confuse them. Unfortunately, this issue has become yet another forum for contention and a source of

strife between the parties. Therefore, the children shall not attend church with the plaintiff except for those holidays which have a secular component to them such as Easter Sunday and Christmas, and any other celebrations such as baptism, funerals and weddings. They shall not take part in any sacrament events such as receiving communion or ashes nor shall they be encouraged to engage in any Christian rituals such as kneeling and making the sign of the cross.

13. The current parenting schedule shall be maintained with the formal inclusion of the alternating Monday overnights with the plaintiff. * * * Barring a *bona fide* emergency, pick up by the plaintiff shall be by 7:00 p.m. with 30 minutes of leeway to account for the plaintiff's commute. Drop-off by the plaintiff shall be at the defendant's home at 7:15 a.m. All pickups and drop-offs shall be at the defendant's residence curbside unless otherwise agreed upon.

14. The plaintiff shall have the first opportunity to coach his children's teams. There is nothing to preclude the stepfather's involvement as well but it is hoped that the stepfather will take into account the feelings of the children and the extraordinary sensitivities in this case in deciding his level of involvement.

15. Neither party shall speak in a derogatory fashion about the other party, the party's religion or the party's significant other.

* * *

NOTES AND QUESTIONS

1. *Is joint custody appropriate when parents express extreme animosity toward each other?* Courts have recognized that a joint custody award is appropriate only where the arrangement would be in the best interests of the child. Vitauts M. Gulbis, Annotation, *Propriety of Awarding Joint Custody of Children,* 17 A.L.R. 4th 1013 (2005). As you read in Chapter 12, "a cardinal criterion for an award of joint custody is the agreement of the parties and their mutual ability to co-operate in reaching shared decisions in matters affecting the child's welfare." *Id.* Even when the parents agree about custody and visitation arrangements, the court with jurisdiction over the child—based on its *parens patriae* authority to decide in the child's best interests—may modify provisions of a marital settlement agreement relating to care, custody and education. *E.g.*, Md. Code Ann., Fam. Law § 8–103 (2008).

In *McCauley v. Schenkel*, 977 S.W.2d 45, 46 (Mo. Ct. App. 1998), for example, the divorce decree awarded the parents joint physical and legal custody of their five-year-old daughter. The parents' animosity escalated until the trial court ordered all exchanges of physical custody (which occurred four times weekly) to take place on the steps of the local family courthouse. Both parents moved for termination of the joint custody arrangement and an award of primary physical and legal custody. Despite the parents' inability to cooperate as evidenced by major disputes over scheduling and educational decisions, the trial court found that joint legal and physical custody continued to be in the child's best interests. The Missouri Court of Appeals reversed and remanded, with instructions that the lower court award one parent sole legal custody and reconsider its award of joint physical custody. The Court of Appeals noted the "constant, ongoing, severe tension and bickering between the parties," the fact that the parents could not speak to each other civilly on the telephone and communicated only in writing, and an incident in which the child's admission to a private kindergarten was revoked after the school witnessed the parents' severe hostility toward one another. *Id.* at 51. Such problems are so pervasive that a divorced father started a website to help parents who do not live together to coordinate their children's schedules, pick up times and so forth without having to speak to each other; registered families may use tools such as a color-coded calendar that makes clear when the child is with each parent and what commitments the child has each day. www.ourfamilywizard.com.

In light of all the circumstances, do you think that the judge in *Nicita* crafted a solution that is likely to prove workable? Which, if any, of the court's orders in *Nicita* are enforceable? How can the court enforce them?

2. *Disagreements about educational decisions.* In *Nicita*, the mother apparently was considering enrolling the children in private schools. Why did the court specify that the children must attend "local" schools? Why did the court specify who should pay for the children's schooling?

Disputes often arise when children have special educational needs because of learning disabilities or severe disciplinary problems. Parents of these children may resort to the courts after failing to agree on the appropriate educational setting. In *Green v. Hahn*, 689 N.W.2d 657, 659 (Wis. Ct. App. 2004), for example, the parties had divorced in 1990, with physical custody of their two small children awarded to the mother. The parties shared joint legal custody. In 2003, when the children, Adam and Spencer, were 17 and 14 years old respectively, the father sought to modify the divorce judgment and moved for an order allowing him to enroll his sons in a military boarding school three hours away from their mother's home. Following the guardian *ad litem's* (GAL) recommendation, the trial court found that it was "in the best interests of the children that [their father] * * * be designated as the person responsible for determining Spencer's school enrollment, and that [their mother] * * * be the person responsible for determining Adam's school enrollment." A major factor in the GAL's recommendation was Adam's statement that, if sent to boarding school, he would drop out when he turned 18 in December. The trial court noted Adam's difficulties—drug use, criminal activity, and poor academic performance—and reasoned that "unless something changes, Spencer is going down the exact same path that Adam has already started.* * * As to Spencer, there is some time, there is some help. We can do something." The court of appeals affirmed the trial court's decision that the boys' behavioral problems constituted a substantial change in circumstances sufficient to warrant modification of the divorce judgment and award educational decision-making power to the father.

3. *Medical information and medications.* The dispute over medical bills and treatment in *Nicita* is fairly common among non-cooperating divorced and estranged parents. For example, in *Higginbotham v. Higginbotham*, 822 N.E.2d 609, 610 (Ind. Ct. App. 2004) the parents initially shared joint legal

custody and the mother had primary physical custody of their child. The father asked the court to modify custody to grant him two midweek overnight visits with his daughter each week. His ex-wife objected, testifying that during overnight visits the father had routinely failed to help the daughter with homework and had threatened not to provide her with prescribed medication. The trial court found that communication and cooperation had broken down between the parents and awarded full physical and legal custody to the mother. The court of appeals affirmed the modified judgment on the grounds that joint legal custody was not in the best interest of the daughter, and that visitation with father contributed to "scholastic and emotional difficulties." *Id.* at 610. *Higginbotham* demonstrates that where the evidence clearly indicates that restrictions are in the best interests of the child, the court may limit, and even deny, visitation, without ruling on the parent's fitness. Where a parent fails or refuses to share medical information or medications with the other parent who has visitation or custodial rights, would failure or refusal ever cross the line so that prosecution for child endangerment would be appropriate? What would be an appropriate penalty? Is it possible to promote continuity of care and achieve justice between feuding parents in such a situation?

4. *How long does parental acrimony last?* Parental conflicts over their children can last well into the child's adulthood. In 2005, the divorced parents of 28–year–old Staff Sergeant Jason Hendrix, who was killed in the Iraq war, fought over whether to bury him in the maternal or paternal family plot. The father won, based on the 1993 decree that awarded him custody and on the Army's internal rules for deciding such conflicts. The funeral was delayed for more than a month pending judicial resolution of the custody dispute. Matthew B. Stannard, *Burial–Rights Fight: Court Sides With Father In Clash Over Where Soldier Will Be Laid To Rest*, S.F. Chron., Mar. 24, 2005, at A1. The legal dispute continued even after Sgt. Hendrix was interred next to his paternal grandfather. Ken McLaughlin, *Battle Continues Over Soldier's Body*, Contra Costa Times (Walnut Creek, Cal.), Nov. 4, 2005, at Q4.

5. *What is P.E.A.C.E?* Judges often refer divorcing parents to the Parent Education and Custody Effectiveness program (P.E.A.C.E.), an educational program that informs parents about the legal and emotional issues surrounding divorce in an effort to reduce the emotional turmoil divorce causes for children. According to Professor Andrew Schepard, "[c]ourt-affiliated parent education programs [such as P.E.A.C.E.] are an integral part of the child custody dispute resolution in most states. Parent education programs inform disputing parents about the legal process, the emotional impact of divorce and separation on adults, and, most importantly, the impact on children and how parents can make their children's transitions during family reorganization easier." To avoid unrealistic expectations, however, divorcing parents should keep in mind that "P.E.A.C.E. is not [ ] a program of therapy or alternative dispute resolution. It is not designed to change parental behavior or facilitate a resolution of parental disputes." Andrew Schepard, *Evaluating P.E.A.C.E. (Parent Education and Custody Effectiveness)*, N.Y.L.J., May 11, 2000, at 3.

B.   TIE–BREAKING ARRANGEMENTS

Courts are justifiably reluctant to serve as continuing arbiters when parents sharing legal custody cannot resolve their disputes about major decisions or values. But if the alternative is to give one parent more weight in decision-making, what does it mean to be a legal custodian with a minority vote? The Supreme Court considered the ramifications of awarding tie-breaking powers to one parent in *Elk Grove Unified School District v. Newdow*, 542 U.S. 1 (2004). Michael Newdow, who shared custody of his daughter with her mother, sought a declaratory judgment that the words "under God" in the Pledge of Allegiance recited daily at his daughter's elementary school violated the Establishment Clause, as well as his right as an atheist and a parent to inculcate his beliefs in his daughter.

The Ninth Circuit held that Newdow had standing "as a parent to challenge a practice that interferes with his right to direct the religious education of his daughter." *Newdow v. U.S. Congress*, 292 F.3d 597, 602 (9th Cir. 2002) (*Newdow I*), and ruled in his favor. The Supreme Court granted certiorari to consider whether Newdow had standing as a non-custodial parent to challenge the school district's policy.

ELK GROVE UNIFIED SCHOOL DISTRICT v. NEWDOW

Supreme Court of the United States, 2004.
542 U.S. 1.

JUSTICE STEVENS delivered the opinion of the Court.

* * *

After the Court of Appeals' initial opinion was announced, Sandra Banning, the mother of Newdow's daughter, filed a motion for leave to intervene, or alternatively to dismiss the complaint. She declared that although she and Newdow shared "physical custody" of their daughter, a state-court order granted her "exclusive legal custody" of the child, "including the sole right to represent [the daughter's] legal interests and make all decision[s] about her education" and welfare. Banning further stated that her daughter is a Christian who believes in God and has no objection either to reciting or hearing others recite the Pledge of Allegiance, or to its reference to God. Banning expressed the belief that her daughter would be harmed if the litigation were permitted to proceed, because others might incorrectly perceive the child as sharing her father's atheist views. Banning accordingly concluded, as her daughter's sole legal custodian, that it was not in the child's interest to be a party to Newdow's lawsuit. On September 25, 2002, the California Superior Court entered an order enjoining Newdow from including his daughter as an unnamed party or suing as her "next friend." That order did not purport to answer the question of Newdow's Article III standing. *See Newdow v. U.S. Congress*, 313 F.3d 500, 502 (CA9 2002) (*Newdow II*).

In a second published opinion, the Court of Appeals reconsidered Newdow's standing in light of Banning's motion. The court noted that Newdow no longer claimed to represent his daughter, but unanimously concluded that "the grant of sole legal custody to Banning" did not deprive Newdow, "as a noncustodial parent, of Article III standing to object to unconstitutional government action affecting his child." The court held that under California law Newdow retains the right to expose his child to his particular religious views even if those views contradict the mother's, and that Banning's objections as sole legal custodian do not defeat Newdow's right to seek redress for an alleged injury to his own parental interests.

* * *

* * * [T]he extent of the standing problem raised by the domestic relations issues in this case was not apparent until * * * Banning filed her motion for leave to intervene or dismiss the complaint following the Court of Appeals' initial decision. At that time, the child's custody was governed by a February 6, 2002, order of the California Superior Court. That order provided that Banning had " '*sole* legal custody as to the rights and responsibilities to make decisions relating to the health, education and welfare of ' " her daughter. The order stated that the two parents should " 'consult with one another on substantial decisions relating to' " the child's " 'psychological and educational needs,' " but it authorized Banning to " 'exercise legal control' " if the parents could not reach " 'mutual agreement.' "

That family court order was the controlling document at the time of the Court of Appeals' standing decision. After the Court of Appeals ruled, however, the Superior Court held another conference regarding the child's custody. At a hearing on September 11, 2003, the Superior Court announced that the parents have "joint legal custody," but that Banning "makes the final decisions if the two . . . disagree."[6]

Newdow contends that despite Banning's final authority, he retains "an unrestricted right to inculcate in his daughter—free from governmental interference—the atheistic beliefs he finds persuasive." The difficulty with that argument is that Newdow's rights, as in many cases touching upon family relations, cannot be viewed in isolation. This case concerns not merely Newdow's interest in inculcating his child with his views on religion, but also the rights of the child's mother as a parent generally and under the Superior Court orders specifically. And most important, it implicates the interests of a young child who finds herself at the center of a highly public debate over her custody, the propriety of a widespread national ritual, and the meaning of our Constitution.

---

6. * * *

Despite the use of the term "joint legal custody" * * * Newdow has the right to consult on issues relating to the child's education, but Banning possesses what we understand amounts to a tiebreaking vote.

The interests of the affected persons in this case are in many respects antagonistic. Of course, legal disharmony in family relations is not uncommon, and in many instances that disharmony poses no bar to federal-court adjudication of proper federal questions. What makes this case different is that Newdow's standing derives entirely from his relationship with his daughter, but he lacks the right to litigate as her next friend. * * * [T]he interests of this parent and this child are not parallel and, indeed, are potentially in conflict.

Newdow's parental status is defined by California's domestic relations law. Our custom on questions of state law ordinarily is to defer to the interpretation of the Court of Appeals for the Circuit in which the State is located. In this case, the Court of Appeals, which possesses greater familiarity with California law, concluded that state law vests in Newdow a cognizable right to influence his daughter's religious upbringing. * * * Animated by a conception of "family privacy" that includes "not simply a policy of minimum state intervention but also a presumption of parental autonomy," the state cases create a zone of private authority within which each parent, whether custodial or noncustodial, remains free to impart to the child his or her religious perspective.

Nothing that either Banning or the School Board has done, however, impairs Newdow's right to instruct his daughter in his religious views. Instead, Newdow requests relief that is more ambitious * * *. He wishes to forestall his daughter's exposure to religious ideas that her mother, who wields a form of veto power, endorses, and to use his parental status to challenge the influences to which his daughter may be exposed in school when he and Banning disagree. The California cases simply do not stand for the proposition that Newdow has a right to dictate to others what they may and may not say to his child respecting religion. * * * The cases speak not at all to the problem of a parent seeking to reach outside the private parent-child sphere to restrain the acts of a third party. A next friend surely could exercise such a right, but the Superior Court's order has deprived Newdow of that status.

* * *

JUSTICE SCALIA took no part in the consideration or decision of this case.

CHIEF JUSTICE REHNQUIST, with whom JUSTICE O'CONNOR joins, and with whom JUSTICE THOMAS joins as to Part I, concurring in the judgment.

* * *

[*Ed.'s note*: In the first footnote to his concurrence, Chief Justice Rehnquist noted "that respondent contends that he has never been a 'noncustodial' parent and points out that under the state court's most recent order he enjoys joint legal custody."]

The Court does not take issue with the fact that, under California law, respondent retains a right to influence his daughter's religious upbringing and to expose her to his views. But it relies on Banning's view of the merits of this case to diminish respondent's interest, stating that the respondent "wishes to forestall his daughter's exposure to religious ideas that her mother, who wields a form of veto power, endorses, and to use his parental status to challenge the influences to which his daughter may be exposed in school when he and Banning disagree." As alleged by respondent and as recognized by the Court of Appeals, respondent wishes to enjoin the School District from endorsing a form of religion inconsistent with his own views because he has a right to expose his daughter to those views without the State's placing its *imprimatur* on a particular religion. Under the Court of Appeals' construction of California law, Banning's "veto power" does not override respondent's right to challenge the Pledge ceremony.

* * * Surely, under California case law and the current custody order, respondent may not tell Banning what she may say to their child respecting religion, and respondent does not seek to. Just as surely, respondent cannot name his daughter as a party to a lawsuit against Banning's wishes. But his claim is different: Respondent does not seek to tell just anyone what he or she may say to his daughter, and he does not seek to vindicate solely her rights.

Respondent asserts that the School District's Pledge ceremony infringes his right under California law to expose his daughter to his religious views. While she is intimately associated with the source of respondent's standing (the father-daughter relationship and respondent's rights thereunder), the daughter *is not the source* of respondent's standing; instead it is their relationship that provides respondent his standing, which is clear once respondent's interest is properly described.[2]

* * *

[The concurring opinions of O'CONNOR, J., and THOMAS, J., are omitted.]

NOTES AND QUESTIONS

1. *What does it mean for a parent to share legal custody after* Newdow? Because *Newdow* held that the father lacked standing to maintain the suit, the Court did not reach the merits. Many commentators feared that the decision would undermine the status of parents who have legal custody but not physical custody of their children, or even of parents who hold joint custody but less than equal "voting rights" in disputes. So far, however, state courts do not appear to have applied the doctrine more broadly in family law

---

2. * * * The same Superior Court that determined that respondent could not sue as next friend stated:

"'To the extent that by not naming her you have . . . an individual right as a parent to say that, "not only for all the children of the world but in—mine in particular, I believe that this child—my child is being harmed," but the child is . . . not actually part of the suit, I don't know that there's any way that this court could preclude that.'"

The California court did not reject Newdow's right as distinct from his daughter's, and we should not either.

disputes. In practical terms, what does it mean for a parent to hold joint legal or physical custody if the other parent holds a tie-breaking vote? Does the procedural right to have one's views considered by the ultimate decision-maker adequately preserve the other parent's rights to the "care, custody and nurture" of the children? In *Feldman v. Feldman*, 874 A.2d 606, 611 (N.J. Super. Ct. App. Div. 2005) a New Jersey court held that a custodial parent has the sole right to direct the child's religious upbringing even where the parents shared joint legal custody and that the custodial parent's choices may not be undermined during visitation. In *In re Marriage of McSoud*, 131 P.3d 1208, 1215 (Colo. Ct. App. 2006), however, a Colorado court held that a parent who does not have decision-making authority concerning the child's religion retains a constitutional right to educate the child in the parent's own religion absent a clear showing that doing so would substantially harm the child, If parents are unable to reach decisions jointly, should a court need to find one parent predominantly responsible for the breakdown in shared decision-making before denying that parent of an equal role in decision-making? What other alternative tie-breakers exist? Chapter 15 will discuss alternative dispute resolution, including post-divorce arbitration.

2. *The relationship between the parents' free exercise rights and the Establishment Clause in parental disputes over religious training.* As some decisions in the previous Chapter demonstrate, the Free Exercise Clause confers on parents both the individual right to practice their religion and the right to instill their religious beliefs in their children. Where a parent's own religious beliefs evolve over time, the Free Exercise Clause may bar courts from enforcing parental agreements about their children's religious upbringing *E.g., Abbo v. Briskin*, 660 So.2d 1157, 1158–59 (Fla. Dist. Ct. App. 1995). In addition, some courts have held that the Establishment Clause bars courts from examining the appropriateness of any religious practice or belief. *In re Ervin R. v. Phina R.*, 717 N.Y.S.2d 849, 852 (Fam. Ct. 2000). Nonetheless, a court may intervene where religious practices or disputes affect the best interests of the child. *Holder v. Holder*, 872 N.E.2d 1239, 1242–44 (Ohio Ct. App. 2007). As one Pennsylvania court summarized the doctrine in 2005:

> The vast majority of courts addressing th[e] issue [of the deleterious effects, if any, of exposing children to a competing religion after grounding them in the tenets of an earlier religion] have concluded that each parent must be free to provide religious exposure and instruction, as that parent sees fit, during any and all periods of legal custody or visitation without restrictions, unless the challenged beliefs or conduct of the parent are demonstrated to present a substantial threat of present or future, physical or emotional harm to the child in absence of the proposed restriction.

Hicks v. Hicks, 868 A.2d 1245, 1249 (Pa. Super. Ct. 2005) (quoting trial court opinion).

In *Boldt* v. *Boldt*, 176 P.3d 388 (Or. 2007), *cert. denied*, 129 S.Ct. 47 (2008), the custodial father converted to Judaism and sought to have the couple's 12–year–old son circumcised so that he could also convert. The mother petitioned for a change of custody (standards for modification of custody orders are discussed in Section 3 of this Chapter) or, in the alternative, an order barring circumcision. Given the boy's age, the Supreme Court of

Oregon remanded the case for an inquiry into the boy's views on the matter, directing the trial court to use any of the three methods of ascertaining children's preferences discussed in Chapter 12: interview by an expert, in camera interview by the judge, or appointment of an attorney for the child. *Id.* at 395, n.9. The court expressly noted that the state's statutes provide that a grant of sole custody to one parent does not deprive the non-custodial parent of certain "specific rights," including the right to review the child's medical records and consult with the child's medical providers. The court did not, however, reach the question of whether the noncustodial parent's rights are limited to those specified in the state code. *Id.* at 393–95.

SECTION 2: VISITATION

This Section discusses a non-custodial parent's right to have access to his or her child, and the extent to which grandparents and others may seek court intervention when parents frustrate visitation with them.

When one parent receives sole physical custody, the other parent normally receives liberal visitation with the child. Visitation is best conceptualized as temporary custody for a discrete period of time, regardless of whether the non-custodial parent shares legal custody with the custodial parent.

A. THE FIT NON–CUSTODIAL PARENT'S RIGHT TO VISITATION

Visitation is generally thought to be the right of any fit non-custodial parent, and is also believed to promote healthy child development. Parents generally have a right to visitation with their children unless visitation would be detrimental to the best interests of the child. The Uniform Marriage and Divorce Act (UMDA) provides:

§ 407. Visitation

(a) A parent not granted custody of a child is entitled to reasonable visitation rights unless the court finds, after a hearing, that visitation would endanger seriously the child's physical, mental, moral or emotional health.

(b) The court may modify an order granting or denying visitation rights whenever the modification would serve the best interests of the child; but the court shall not restrict a parent's visitation rights unless it finds that the visitation would endanger seriously the child's physical, mental, moral or emotional health.

9A U.L.A. 398 (1998). Note that the UMDA standard for denying visitation is much more restrictive than the "best interests" standard that applies to custody.

Consistent with its reform agenda, the American Law Institute abandoned the concept of visitation, which it regards as a form of "custodial responsibility." The ALI drafters note that several states "have moved away from the terminology of custody and visitation to alternative language more accommodating of a continuum of residential arrangements." ALI, Principles of the Law of Family Dissolution: Analysis and Recommendations § 2.03 cmts. e–f (2002) (citing Florida, Maine, Michigan, Montana, Ohio, Texas, Vermont, Washington and Wisconsin). Such alternative language includes "residential provisions," "parental rights and responsibilities," and "parental contact" or "parental time."

Problem 13–1

You are a family court judge. When you entered the divorce judgment for the Smiths, who have two children, ages 9 and 12, you gave the parents joint custody, but made mother the primary residential parent. Because the father had a history of abusing alcohol and illegal substances, including DUI convictions, the custody order specified that the father "shall not have any alcohol or illegal substances in his possession while the children are in his care in this State." The mother later moved to another state, but the children spend school vacations with the father in your jurisdiction.

While the children were visiting him last month, the father was arrested for driving while intoxicated and possession of marijuana. He pled guilty. The mother has moved to find the father in contempt of the custody order and seeks to discontinue visitation in this state. She is willing to allow the father to see the children if he travels to her home.

The father argues that he did not violate the order because the children were staying overnight at his mother's house when he was arrested.

Applying the UMDA, how would you resolve the following issues:

(1) Is the phrase "in his care" limited to times when the children are in the father's immediate presence?

(2) Should the court cite the father for contempt, and if so, what would be an appropriate penalty?

(3) Do the father's actions justify limiting or eliminating his visitation rights?

B. DENIAL OF VISITATION

Custodial parents and child development experts lament that the relationships between non-custodial parents and children are often so attenuated that parents and children become strangers for all practical purposes. But the fault cannot be attributed exclusively to the non-custodial parent whose visits and calls decline over time. Custodial parents frequently frustrate visitation with the non-custodial parent. Courts may find it difficult to sort out whether the custodial parent thwarts visits, or whether older children themselves are disinclined to pursue the relationship. As you read the following decision, consider whether an effective and equitable remedy exists even where the court concludes that the custodial parent has engineered a breakdown in the relationship between the non-custodial parent and the children.

USACK v. USACK

Supreme Court of New York, Appellate Division, 2005.
793 N.Y.S.2d 223.

SPAIN, J.

* * *

The parties were married for 20 years and had three children, a son born in 1983 and daughters born in 1986 and 1988. Plaintiff [husband] commenced this action for divorce in early 2002 and defendant moved out of the marital residence later that year and cross-claimed for divorce. After a nonjury trial, Supreme Court, among other things, awarded plaintiff a divorce upon the parties' stipulation, distributed their property, and granted plaintiff custody of the daughters and exclusive ownership and possession of the marital residence. The court ordered defendant to pay child support and a portion of the uninsured medical expenses for all three children.

Supreme Court [the trial court] issued a detailed written decision containing extensive findings of fact which accurately portrays the tragedy often visited upon children—even teenage children—who have been manipulated into parental estrangement. The court denied defendant's request that she be relieved, permanently or temporarily, of her child support obligations. That request was based upon, among other grounds, plaintiff's near complete frustration of any relationship, communication or contact between defendant and her children since December 2001, when plaintiff first learned of and told the children about defendant's relationship with another man. The court found that "plaintiff and [the] children have rejected every effort of defendant to demonstrate her continued devotion to her offspring with a vehemence which is remarkable for its undiminished intensity over a protracted period which still continues." The court also concluded that plaintiff had "encouraged" the children's "unbridled enmity" toward and "total exclus[ion]" of their mother through "a course of conduct calculated to inflict the most grievous emotional injury upon her." The court ultimately determined that there was insufficient circumstantial or professional evidence to attribute the children's uniform attitudes and behavior to plaintiff.

Defendant now appeals, contending that her child support obligation should have been suspended due to plaintiff's deliberate actions in alienating their children from her, a conclusion we find inescapable on this record and from Supreme Court's findings of fact, which we adopt.

A parent, of course, has a statutory duty to support a child until the age of 21. However, "where it can be established by the noncustodial parent that the custodial parent has unjustifiably frustrated the noncustodial parent's right of reasonable access, child support payments may be suspended". *Smith v. Bombard*, [741 N.Y.S.2d 336, 338 (2002)].

* * * The Law Guardian expressed to Supreme Court the children's wishes to remain with their father and control their own contact with their mother.[1] Plaintiff testified that while the marriage began to experience difficulties in early 2001, the family was "perfectly happy" and defendant enjoyed a close relationship with the children and was very involved in all of their activities until he revealed defendant's affair to them in December 2001. He claimed that, after that discovery, they unilaterally chose to completely ostracize defendant and reject all of her repeated efforts to communicate, to attend their sporting activities or to have any meaningful contact or relationship with her, although she continued to live in the family home. This ostracism and estrangement of defendant from the family continued for nine months, unabated, until September 2002, when defendant finally moved out, and it continued until the time of the trial. Plaintiff, whose credibility Supreme Court found to be "seriously impaired," denied actively discouraging or preventing the children's relationship with defendant. He did not address many of the specific incidents to which defendant thereafter testified, and failed to demonstrate any meaningful efforts on his part to facilitate the children's continued relationship with their mother.

The testimony of defendant, credited by Supreme Court and much of it unrefuted, detailed plaintiff's callous and insensitive conduct toward defendant prior to December 2001, which the court recognized as the probable inducement for defendant's affair. She also described plaintiff's relentless actions—following the discovery of her affair—in excluding defendant from the family entirely, vehemently rejecting any efforts on her part to have a meaningful relationship with her children or to continue any parental role and involvement. Her testimony established that plaintiff, among other things, often yelled at her to leave, disparaged her, locked her out, and told the children that defendant did not want to be—and was no longer—part of their family because she had chosen someone else. Plaintiff also used his immediate family members to care for the children and shield them from interaction with defendant at home in his absence and he did nothing to dissuade the children's public humiliation of defendant.

By his example, his actions and his inaction, plaintiff orchestrated and encouraged the estrangement of defendant from the children. He exploited their unhappiness toward her over the affair and the break-up of the family and manipulated their loyalty to him—and the exclusion of defendant—to punish her for her rejection of him. As Supreme Court noted in reducing defendant's child support arrears, the treatment of defendant was "needlessly vindictive" and, we find, a clear violation of plaintiff's responsibility "to assure meaningful contact between the children and the other parent". *Raybin v. Raybin*, [613 N.Y.S.2d 726, 729 (1994)]. Indeed,

---

1. * * * [I]t is not proper for a Law Guardian to make a "report" to a court. Here, the Law Guardian submitted—at Supreme Court's direction—a report containing her own unsworn observations regarding the parties, recounting personal interactions or opinions about them, all of which, we note, could have been explored and elicited by calling witnesses and upon cross-examination of the parties and other witnesses

plaintiff utterly failed in his duty to rise above his anger at defendant to affirmatively encourage the children to have contact and a relationship with their mother. Instead, he chose * * * to deprive them of the undeniable benefit and right of having two loving, supportive parents; he also denied defendant her right to a normal relationship with them. Most importantly, plaintiff never—at any time—suggested that defendant had been other than a dedicated, eager, involved, loving, willing and hard working mother who genuinely pursued a continued role in the lives of her children. Clearly, defendant's decision to engage in and pursue an extramarital affair while continuing to reside with plaintiff and the children resulted in turmoil in the children's lives. However, plaintiff did not demonstrate that defendant exposed the children to anything related to that affair * * * .

Thus, we find that defendant amply met her burden of demonstrating that plaintiff deliberately frustrated her relationship and visitation with the children. While alteration of defendant's child support obligations may be an imperfect remedy with which to address plaintiff's harmful, unfair conduct, there is no proof that suspending defendant's obligations temporarily would result in the children becoming public charges. Accordingly, defendant's support obligations are suspended pending further court order upon a showing that plaintiff has made good faith efforts to actively encourage and restore defendant's relationship with the children, and defendant's visitation with the children.

* * *

NOTES AND QUESTIONS

1. Usack *represents an exception to the general rule.* Usack noted that suspending child support was an "imperfect remedy"; moreover, the decision conflicts with settled law in most jurisdictions. As you learned in Chapter 11, it has long been established that the obligation to pay child support is generally distinct from the question of access to the child for visitation. *See, e.g., Sampson v. Johnson*, 846 A.2d 278, 287 (D.C. Ct. App. 2004) ("Public policy * * * requires the treatment of support of children and visitation rights as distinct problems * * * " (quoting *Mallinger v. Mallinger*, 175 A.2d 890, 892 (Pa. Super. Ct. 1961))); *see also Stancill v. Stancill*, 408 A.2d 1030, 1034 (Md. 1979). Similarly, "a substantial majority of the courts have held that while refusal to pay child support is reprehensible, a [non-custodial parent's] visitation rights cannot be conditioned upon compliance with a support order." *Sampson*, 846 A.2d at 287. Denial of visitation is generally rejected as a defense to an action for failure to pay support. What is the reasoning behind the general rule that support obligations survive despite denial of visitation? Most courts assume that "support payments are necessary for the child's welfare, and that terminating or suspending the obligation to make them would therefore be harmful to children." Ira Mark Ellman, *Should Visitation*

Denial Affect the Obligation to Pay Support?, 36 Ariz. St. L.J. 661, 664 (2004). Do you believe the *Usack* decision was in the best interests of the children?

Non-custodial parents resisting payment of child support sometimes complain that (1) the children do not benefit from the payments, which they believe are used to subsidize the custodial parent's standard of living, or that (2) the noncustodial parent has no control over the custodial parent's choices about how to spend the money if it is spent to benefit the children. To reduce friction between parents that might contribute to a breakdown of support payments and/or visitation, states authorize courts to order the custodial parent to provide periodic accountings showing how the child support money is spent. *See e.g.*, Mo. Rev. Stat. § 452.342 (2008).

2. *Other forms of interference.* Some custodial parents interfere with visitation by disrupting or entirely blocking telephone or Internet communication between the child and the non-custodial parent. *See In re Marriage of Almquist*, 704 N.E.2d 68, 72 (Ill. App. Ct. 1998) (imposing criminal contempt on mother, whose loud playing of audiotape during phone conversations constituted obnoxious interference). Courts may order teleconferencing by Internet in addition to in-person visits. *'Virtual' Visits For Divorced Parents Sought*, Chi. Sun–Times, July 11, 2005, at 28. In 2004, Utah became the first state to enact a law expressly authorizing courts to order virtual visitation. Utah Code Ann. § 30–3–35(2)(*o*) (2007). For an example of a virtual visitation information website, see http://www.internetvisitation.org.

3. *The wronged non-custodial parent.* Like the mother in *Usack*, many non-custodial parents feel that they are wrongly denied visitation by the custodial parent, and that they should not have to pay child support if their relationship with the child is frustrated. Should it matter whether the custodial parent is interfering with visits, or whether the child independently decides to discontinue visitation? How would a court determine which is true? How important is the child's age to such a determination?

In *In re Marriage of Kimbrell*, 119 P.3d 684 (Kan. Ct. App. 2005), the father appealed an order that modified "parenting time" with his 16–year–old son from a specific schedule of one midweek evening and one weekend day and overnight, to only time "as is mutually requested" by father and son. As a result of that order, the father had no parental contact with his son from late 2002 until 2005. The court agreed that the order "improperly impinged" on the father's statutory right to reasonable visitation absent a finding of unfitness or likely harm to the child. In addition, the court held that the "trial court erred in giving dispositive effect" to the son's preference. *Id*. at 423.

4. *Remedies and enforcement.* Non-custodial parents who believe that the custodial parent is interfering with their visitation rights may seek a variety of remedies in addition to reduction or tolling of child support obligations. The range of potential remedies includes modification of the visitation order or parenting agreement to provide a more detailed schedule and conditions for visitation, additional "make-up" visitation, contempt pro-

ceedings, and, in particularly egregious cases, civil damages for intentional infliction of emotional distress. *See, e.g., In re Marriage of Myers*, 99 P.3d 398, 401 (Wash. Ct. App. 2004) ("A parent who refuses to perform the duties imposed by a parenting plan is *per se* acting in bad faith."). What are the relative advantages and disadvantages of each of these remedies?

5. *Supervised visitation.* Where unsupervised visitation with a non-custodial parent would risk harm to the child, courts may order and oversee visitation supervised by third party. Courts may find the child at risk of harm where, for example, evidence supports a finding of physical or sexual abuse, or where the non-custodial parent suffers from mental illness or has a substance abuse problem. Supervised visits may occur at a variety of settings, including a designated visitation center run by a private or public agency; a therapist's office; a neutral public place such as a fast food restaurant or park; or a private home, including the home of the non-custodial parent or a relative of the parent. Supervisors may include professionals, such as licensed social workers, or friends or relatives. *See, e.g., Cummings v. Ames*, 2005 WL 2621447 (N.J. Super. Ct. App. Div. Oct. 17, 2005) (unpublished opinion) ("The monitor could be the parties' nanny, their 15–year–old eldest daughter (if and only if she was willing to serve in that role), or some other relative or third-party jointly agreed to by the parties."). Supervision by a private agency or professional is extremely expensive. In *Cummings*, the mother spent $7,000 for supervision in just four months, before the court allowed an alternative arrangement. The parties ultimately agreed to use the child's piano teacher as a supervisor every other week.

In *Cummings*, the appellate panel initially suggested that a teenage sibling might be an appropriate supervisor, if willing, but ultimately retracted that suggestion. *Id.* at *5. Why would it be inappropriate to designate one of the parties' older children as a supervisor for visits? Under what conditions, if any, would it be wise to use a relative as a supervisor?

In addition to deciding whether supervision is warranted, and what kind of supervision is needed, the family court must decide how long to continue supervision, whether to reduce the constraints on visits, and when, if ever, to allow unsupervised visitation. In some divorce cases, allegations of abuse result in long-term involvement with the family by the state's child protection agencies; other cases may never reach a public agency if the court concludes the allegations are unsubstantiated. *See Simburger v. Simburger*, 701 N.W.2d 880 (N.D. 2005); *S.B. v. J.P.*, 831 N.E.2d 959 (Mass. App. Ct. 2005).

6. *Domestic violence and visitation.* Sometimes supervised visitation or supervised transfers of the child are impossible or inappropriate because serious domestic violence requires the court to hide the custodial parent's location from the non-custodial parent. In abusive relationships, the period following separation "is a period of extreme volatility and increased risk," because "the abuser is forced to acknowledge his loss of control over his partner and his loss of the relationship itself, on which he may be profoundly dependent." Clare Dalton, *When Paradigms Collide: Protecting Battered Parents and Their Children in the Family Court System*, 37 Fam. & Concil. Cts. Rev. 273, 289 (1999).

In one publicized case, a Seattle woman and her two-year-old daughter were shot and killed by her estranged husband at Common Ground, a neutral pick-up and drop-off spot for parents with court-ordered custody and visitation plans. *See* Elaine Porterfield, *Suicide Note Says That Slain Wife 'Had it Coming' But Edwards Didn't Mean to Shoot Daughter*, Seattle Post–Intelligencer, Dec. 24, 1998, at A1. The mother had filed for divorce and had obtained a protective order against her husband, who had inflicted severe physical and verbal abusive during their marriage. The court granted her husband unsupervised overnight visitation with their daughter, with transfers of custody to occur at Common Ground. The mother moved with her daughter to a secret location, traded her old car in for one her husband would not recognize, and hired a private bodyguard, but the "neutral spot" proved to be the one place where her husband knew she would be. *See* Kim Barker, *Killer "Breathed" Wife's Terror—Edwards Was Tyrant, Observers Say*, Seattle Times, Dec. 23, 1998, at B1. While the outcome in this instance was extreme, the problem it illustrates is all too common. Courts must consider whether, and under what circumstances, visitation is appropriate in cases with a history of domestic violence, and must carefully craft any parenting plan to protect the victim from the abuser.

PROBLEM 13–2

You are an appellate judge considering the following case.

Mother appeals an order transferring custody of a four-year-old girl to her father. The parents were never married, but had a long relationship. The father, who was married and had several adult children, met the mother, an actress, during a business trip to New York City in 1998. In 1999, mother became pregnant. Father's wife discovered the affair and the pregnancy, and threatened divorce. Father and his wife urged mother to abort the fetus, but she did not and the child was born in September 1999. Father was listed on the child's birth certificate and DNA subsequently confirmed paternity, although the mother admitted involvement in another relationship.

Between the child's birth and the summer of 2002, the father made more than 70 visits to the child in New York, where he stayed with the mother and child, played with and "parented" the child, read to her and took her on outings. He also provided monthly child support. The mother testified that she provided day-to-day care and made all major decisions about the child.

In September 2002, after the relationship between mother and father had ended, father filed in New York for an order of filiation. Mother denied his paternity and demanded a second DNA test, meanwhile denying the father visitation. After a second round of testing confirmed the father's paternity, he filed suit in New York seeking visitation, and received limited visitation rights pending resolution.

During the proceedings, the mother accused the father of sexually molesting the child. She moved to terminate the temporary visitation. He responded by amending his petition to seek custody. The court continued visitation during the proceedings. The father and his wife agreed to move to New York if the father prevailed, so that the child could have regular visits with her mother. Father argued that mother (1) was fabricating the sexual abuse allegations and coaching the daughter to make false statements about her father, (2) was maliciously trying to frustrate the father's relationship with the child, and (3) was placing her own needs above the child's need for both parents. Both sides presented expert witnesses who supported their respective positions. The child's appointed representative supported transferring custody to the father, with liberal visitation to the mother.

Adequate evidence supported the trial court's findings that no sexual abuse had occurred, and that the mother, while a "good mother" as measured by the child's development, had turned the child into a pawn in her battle with the father. The court further found that the father was a good and devoted father capable of facilitating mother's continued relationship with their daughter if he received custody. The trial court awarded custody to the father, conditioned on his residence in New York, with supervised visitation to the mother.

Mother argues that the transfer of custody was not based on the best interests of the child, but was designed instead to punish her for her own behavior. She further argues that a transfer of custody is not in the child's best interests, which would be promoted by continuity of care with her primary caretaker.

How would you rule and why?

C. THIRD–PARTY VISITATION

In Chapter 12, you read about the efforts of grandparents to gain or retain custody of their grandchildren in *McDermott v. Dougherty* and *Painter v. Bannister*. Grandparents and other third parties frequently turn to the courts in an effort to gain or expand visitation despite the custodial parent's objections. The following Supreme Court decision considers the scope of the parent's right to control visitation.

TROXEL v. GRANVILLE

Supreme Court of the United States, 2000.
530 U.S. 57.

JUSTICE O'CONNOR announced the judgment of the Court and delivered an opinion, in which THE CHIEF JUSTICE, JUSTICE GINSBURG, and JUSTICE BREYER join.

Section 26.10.160(3) of the Revised Code of Washington permits "[a]ny person" to petition a superior court for visitation rights "at any time," and authorizes that court to grant such visitation rights whenever "visitation may serve the best interest of the child." Petitioners Jenifer and Gary Troxel petitioned a Washington Superior Court for the right to visit their grandchildren, Isabelle and Natalie Troxel. Respondent Tommie Granville, the mother of Isabelle and Natalie, opposed the petition. The case ultimately reached the Washington Supreme Court, which held that § 26.10.160(3) unconstitutionally interferes with the fundamental right of parents to rear their children.

I

Tommie Granville and Brad Troxel shared a relationship that ended in June 1991. The two never married, but they had two daughters, Isabelle and Natalie. Jenifer and Gary Troxel are Brad's parents, and thus the paternal grandparents of Isabelle and Natalie. After Tommie and Brad separated in 1991, Brad lived with his parents and regularly brought his daughters to his parents' home for weekend visitation. Brad committed suicide in May 1993. Although the Troxels at first continued to see Isabelle and Natalie on a regular basis after their son's death, Tommie Granville informed the Troxels in October 1993 that she wished to limit their visitation with her daughters to one short visit per month.

In December 1993, the Troxels commenced the present action by filing, * * * a petition to obtain visitation rights with Isabelle and Natalie. The Troxels filed their petition under * * * Section 2610.160(3) [which] provides: "Any person may petition the court for visitation rights at any time including, but not limited to, custody proceedings. The court may order visitation rights for any person when visitation may serve the best interest of the child whether or not there has been any change of circumstances." At trial, the Troxels requested two weekends of overnight visitation per month and two weeks of visitation each summer. Granville did not oppose visitation altogether, but instead asked the court to order one day of visitation per month with no overnight stay. In 1995, the Superior Court * * * entered a visitation decree ordering visitation one weekend per month, one week during the summer, and four hours on both of the petitioning grandparents' birthdays.

Granville appealed, during which time she married Kelly Wynn. * * * [T]he Washington Court of Appeals remanded the case to the Superior Court for entry of written findings of fact and conclusions of law. On remand, the Superior Court found that visitation was in Isabelle and Natalie's best interests:

> "The Petitioners [the Troxels] are part of a large, central, loving family, all located in this area, and the Petitioners can provide opportunities for the children in the areas of cousins and music.

> "... The court took into consideration all factors regarding the best interest of the children and considered all the testimony before it. The children would be benefited from spending quality time with the Petitioners, provided that that time is balanced with time with the childrens' [sic] nuclear family. The court finds that the childrens' [sic] best interests are served by spending time with their mother and stepfather's other six children."

Approximately nine months after the Superior Court entered its order on remand, Granville's husband formally adopted Isabelle and Natalie.

The Washington Court of Appeals reversed the lower court's visitation order * * * . * * *

The Washington Supreme Court granted the Troxels' petition for review and * * * affirmed. * * *

We granted certiorari, and now affirm the judgment.

II

The demographic changes of the past century make it difficult to speak of an average American family. The composition of families varies greatly from household to household. * * * In 1996, children living with only one parent accounted for 28 percent of all children under age 18 in the United States. Understandably, in these single-parent households, persons outside the nuclear family are called upon with increasing frequency to assist in the everyday tasks of child rearing. In many cases, grandparents play an important role. For example, in 1998, approximately 4 million children—or 5.6 percent of all children under age 18—lived in the household of their grandparents.

The nationwide enactment of nonparental visitation statutes is assuredly due, in some part, to the States' recognition of these changing realities of the American family. Because grandparents and other relatives undertake duties of a parental nature in many households, States have sought to ensure the welfare of the children therein by protecting the relationships those children form with such third parties. The States' nonparental visitation statutes are further supported by a recognition, which varies from State to State, that children should have the opportunity to benefit from relationships with statutorily specified persons—for example, their grandparents. The extension of statutory rights in this area to persons other than a child's parents, however, comes with an obvious cost. * * * [T]hese statutes can present questions of constitutional import. In this case, we are presented with just such a question. Specifically, we are asked to decide whether § 26.10.160(3), as applied to Tommie Granville and her family, violates the Federal Constitution.

The Fourteenth * * * Amendment's Due Process Clause * * * "provides heightened protection against government interference with certain fundamental rights and liberty interests." *Washington v. Glucksberg,* 521 U.S. 702, 720 (1997).

The liberty interest at issue in this case—the interest of parents in the care, custody, and control of their children—is perhaps the oldest of the fundamental liberty interests recognized by this Court. More than 75 years ago, in *Meyer v. Nebraska,* 262 U.S. 390, 399, 401 (1923), we held that the "liberty" protected by the Due Process Clause includes the right of parents to "establish a home and bring up children" and "to control the education of their own." Two years later, in *Pierce v. Society of Sisters,* 268 U.S. 510, 534–35 (1925), we again held that the "liberty of parents and guardians" includes the right "to direct the upbringing and education of children under their control." We explained in *Pierce* that "[t]he child is not the mere creature of the State; those who nurture him and direct his destiny have the right, coupled with the high duty, to recognize and prepare him for additional obligations." *Id.* at 535. We returned to the subject in *Prince v. Massachusetts,* 321 U.S. 158 (1944), and again confirmed that there is a constitutional dimension to the right of parents to direct the upbringing of their children. "It is cardinal with us that the custody, care and nurture of the child reside first in the parents, whose primary function and freedom include preparation for obligations the state can neither supply nor hinder." *Id.* at 166.

In subsequent cases also, we have recognized the fundamental right of parents to make decisions concerning the care, custody, and control of their children. In light of this extensive precedent, it cannot now be doubted that the Due Process Clause of the Fourteenth Amendment protects the fundamental right of parents to make decisions concerning the care, custody, and control of their children.

Section 26.10.160(3), as applied to Granville and her family in this case, unconstitutionally infringes on that fundamental parental right. The Washington nonparental visitation statute is breathtakingly broad. According to the statute's text, "*[a]ny person* may petition the court for visitation rights *at any time*," and the court may grant such visitation rights whenever "visitation may serve *the best interest of the child*." That language effectively permits any third party seeking visitation to subject any decision by a parent concerning visitation of the parent's children to state-court review. Once the visitation petition has been filed in court and the matter is placed before a judge, a parent's decision that visitation would not be in the child's best interest is accorded no deference. * * * Instead, the Washington statute places the best-interest determination solely in the hands of the judge. Should the judge disagree with the parent's estimation of the child's best interests, the judge's view necessarily prevails. Thus, in practical effect, in the State of Washington a court can disregard and overturn *any* decision by a fit custodial parent concerning visitation whenever a third party affected by the decision files a visitation petition, based solely on the judge's determination of the child's best interests. The Washington Supreme Court had the opportunity to give § 26.10.160(3) a narrower reading, but it declined to do so.

Turning to the facts of this case, the record reveals that the Superior Court's order was based on precisely the type of mere disagreement we have just described and nothing more. * * *

First, the Troxels did not allege, and no court has found, that Granville was an unfit parent. That aspect of the case is important, for there is a presumption that fit parents act in the best interests of their children. * * * Accordingly, so long as a parent adequately cares for his or her children (*i.e.,* is fit), there will normally be no reason for the State to inject itself into the private realm of the family to further question the ability of that parent to make the best decisions concerning the rearing of that parent's children.

The problem here is not that the Washington Superior Court intervened, but that when it did so, it gave no special weight at all to

Granville's determination of her daughters' best interests. More importantly, it appears that the Superior Court applied exactly the opposite presumption. In reciting its oral ruling * * * the Superior Court judge explained:

"* * * I think in most situations a commonsensical approach [is that] it is normally in the best interest of the children to spend quality time with the grandparent, unless the grandparent, [sic] there are some issues or problems involved wherein * * * their lifestyles are going to impact adversely upon the children. That certainly isn't the case here from what I can tell."

The judge's comments suggest that he presumed the grandparents' request should be granted unless the children would be "impact[ed] adversely." In effect, the judge placed on Granville, the fit custodial parent, the burden of *disproving* that visitation would be in the best interest of her daughters. * * *

The decisional framework employed by the Superior Court directly contravened the traditional presumption that a fit parent will act in the best interest of his or her child. In that respect, the court's presumption failed to provide any protection for Granville's fundamental constitutional right to make decisions concerning the rearing of her own daughters. In an ideal world, parents might always seek to cultivate the bonds between grandparents and their grandchildren. Needless to say, however, our world is far from perfect, and in it the decision whether such an intergenerational relationship would be beneficial in any specific case is for the parent to make in the first instance. And, if a fit parent's decision of the kind at issue here becomes subject to judicial review, the court must accord at least some special weight to the parent's own determination.

Finally, we note that there is no allegation that Granville ever sought to cut off visitation entirely. * * *

* * * [T]he visitation order in this case was an unconstitutional infringement on Granville's fundamental right to make decisions concerning the care, custody, and control of her two daughters. The Washington Superior Court failed to accord the determination of Granville, a fit custodial parent, any material weight. In fact, the Superior Court made only two formal findings in support of its visitation order. First, the Troxels "are part of a large, central, loving family, all located in this area, and the [Troxels] can provide opportunities for the children in the areas of cousins and music." Second, "[t]he children would be benefitted from spending quality time with the [Troxels], provided that that time is balanced with time with the childrens' [sic] nuclear family." These slender findings * * * show that this case involves nothing more than a simple disagreement between the Washington Superior Court and Granville concerning her children's best interests. The Superior Court's announced reason for ordering one week of visitation in the summer demonstrates our conclusion well: "I look back on some personal experiences.... We always spen[t] as kids a week with one set of grandparents and another

set of grandparents, [and] it happened to work out in our family that [it] turned out to be an enjoyable experience. Maybe that can, in this family, if that is how it works out." * * * [T]he Due Process Clause does not permit a State to infringe on the fundamental right of parents to make childrearing decisions simply because a state judge believes a "better" decision could be made. * * * Accordingly, we hold that § 26.10.160(3), as applied in this case, is unconstitutional.

Because we rest our decision on the sweeping breadth of § 26.10.160(3) and the application of that broad, unlimited power in this case, we do not consider the primary constitutional question passed on by the Washington Supreme Court—whether the Due Process Clause requires all nonparental visitation statutes to include a showing of harm or potential harm to the child as a condition precedent to granting visitation. We do not, and need not, define today the precise scope of the parental due process right in the visitation context. * * *

* * *

JUSTICE SOUTER, concurring in the judgment.

I concur in the judgment affirming the decision of the Supreme Court of Washington * * *. I would say no more. * * *

* * *

Our cases, it is true, have not set out exact metes and bounds to the protected interest of a parent in the relationship with his child, but *Meyer*'s repeatedly recognized right of upbringing would be a sham if it failed to encompass the right to be free of judicially compelled visitation by "any party" at "any time" a judge believed he "could make a 'better' decision" than the objecting parent had done. The strength of a parent's interest in controlling a child's associates is as obvious as the influence of personal associations on the development of the child's social and moral character. Whether for good or for ill, adults not only influence but may indoctrinate children, and a choice about a child's social companions is not essentially different from the designation of the adults who will influence the child in school. * * *

* * *

JUSTICE THOMAS, concurring in the judgment.

I write separately to note that neither party has argued that our substantive due process cases were wrongly decided and that the original understanding of the Due Process Clause precludes judicial enforcement of unenumerated rights under that constitutional provision. As a result, I express no view on the merits of this matter, and I understand the plurality as well to leave the resolution of that issue for another day.

* * *

JUSTICE STEVENS, dissenting.

The Court today wisely declines to endorse either the holding or the reasoning of the Supreme Court of Washington. In my opinion, the Court would have been even wiser to deny certiorari. Given the problematic character of the trial court's decision and the uniqueness of the Washington statute, there was no pressing need to review a State Supreme Court decision that merely requires the state legislature to draft a better statute.

* * *

* * * [A] key aspect of the Washington Supreme Court's holding—that the Federal Constitution requires a showing of actual or potential "harm" to the child before a court may order visitation continued over a parent's objections—finds no support in this Court's case law. While, as the Court recognizes, the Federal Constitution certainly protects the parent-child relationship from arbitrary impairment by the State, we have never held that the parent's liberty interest in this relationship is so inflexible as to establish a rigid constitutional shield, protecting every arbitrary parental decision from any challenge absent a threshold finding of harm.[7] The presumption that parental decisions generally serve the best interests of their children is sound, and clearly in the normal case the parent's interest is paramount. But even a fit parent is capable of treating a child like a mere possession.

Cases like this do not present a bipolar struggle between the parents and the State over who has final authority to determine what is in a child's best interests. There is at a minimum a third individual, whose interests are implicated in every case to which the statute applies—the child.

* * *

Despite this Court's repeated recognition of these significant parental liberty interests, these interests have never been seen to be without limits. * * *

* * *

While this Court has not yet had occasion to elucidate the nature of a child's liberty interests in preserving established familial or family-like bonds, it seems to me extremely likely that, to the extent parents and families have fundamental liberty interests in preserving such intimate relationships, so, too, do children have these interests, and so, too, must their interests be balanced in the equation. * * *

This is not, of course, to suggest that a child's liberty interest in maintaining contact with a particular individual is to be treated invariably

---

7. The suggestion by Justice THOMAS that this case may be resolved solely with reference to our decision in *Pierce v. Society of Sisters*, 268 U.S. 510, 535 (1925) is unpersuasive. *Pierce* involved a parent's choice whether to send a child to public or private school. While that case is a source of broad language about the scope of parents' due process rights with respect to their children, the constitutional principles and interests involved in the schooling context do not necessarily have parallel implications in this family law visitation context, in which multiple overlapping and competing prerogatives of various plausibly interested parties are at stake.

as on a par with that child's parents' contrary interests. Because our substantive due process case law includes a strong presumption that a parent will act in the best interest of her child, it would be necessary, were the state appellate courts actually to confront a challenge to the statute as applied, to consider whether the trial court's assessment of the "best interest of the child" incorporated that presumption. * * *

* * * The almost infinite variety of family relationships that pervade our ever-changing society strongly counsel against the creation by this Court of a constitutional rule that treats a biological parent's liberty interest in the care and supervision of her child as an isolated right that may be exercised arbitrarily. * * *

Accordingly, I respectfully dissent.

JUSTICE SCALIA, dissenting.

In my view, a right of parents to direct the upbringing of their children is among the "unalienable Rights" with which the Declaration of Independence proclaims "all Men . . . are endowed by their Creator." And in my view that right is also among the "othe[r] [rights] retained by the people" which the Ninth Amendment says the Constitution's enumeration of rights "shall not be construed to deny or disparage." The Declaration of Independence, however, is not a legal prescription conferring powers upon the courts; and the Constitution's refusal to "deny or disparage" other rights is far removed from affirming any one of them, and even farther removed from authorizing judges to identify what they might be, and to enforce the judges' list against laws duly enacted by the people. Consequently, while I would think it entirely compatible with the commitment to representative democracy set forth in the founding documents to argue, in legislative chambers or in electoral campaigns, that the State has *no power* to interfere with parents' authority over the rearing of their children, I do not believe that the power which the Constitution confers upon me *as a judge* entitles me to deny legal effect to laws that (in my view) infringe upon what is (in my view) that unenumerated right.

* * * The sheer diversity of today's opinions persuades me that the theory of unenumerated parental rights * * * has small claim to *stare decisis* protection. A legal principle that can be thought to produce such diverse outcomes in the relatively simple case before us here is not a legal principle that has induced substantial reliance. While I would not now overrule those earlier cases (that has not been urged), neither would I extend the theory upon which they rested to this new context.

* * *

For these reasons, I would reverse the judgment below.

JUSTICE KENNEDY, dissenting.

The Supreme Court of Washington has determined that petitioners Jenifer and Gary Troxel have standing under state law to seek court-ordered visitation with their grandchildren, notwithstanding the objections of the children's parent, respondent Tommie Granville. * * * After acknowledging this statutory right to sue for visitation, the State Supreme Court invalidated the statute as violative of the United States Constitution, because it interfered with a parent's right to raise his or her child free from unwarranted interference. * * * [T]he court invalidated the statute on its face, ruling it a nullity.

* * *

* * * I would remand the case to the state court for further proceedings. * * *

* * *

The State Supreme Court sought to give content to the parent's right by announcing a categorical rule that third parties who seek visitation must always prove the denial of visitation would harm the child. * * *

While it might be argued as an abstract matter that in some sense the child is always harmed if his or her best interests are not considered, the law of domestic relations, as it has evolved to this point, treats as distinct the two standards, one harm to the child and the other the best interests of the child. * * *

On the question whether one standard must always take precedence over the other in order to protect the right of the parent or parents, "[o]ur Nation's history, legal traditions, and practices" do not give us clear or definitive answers. *Washington v. Glucksberg*, 521 U.S. 702, 721 (1997). The consensus among courts and commentators is that at least through the 19th century there was no legal right of visitation; court-ordered visitation appears to be a 20th-century phenomenon. A case often cited as one of the earliest visitation decisions, *Succession of Reiss*, 15 So. 151, 152 (1894), explained that "the obligation ordinarily to visit grandparents is moral and not legal" * * * . * * *

To say that third parties have had no historical right to petition for visitation does not necessarily imply, as the Supreme Court of Washington concluded, that a parent has a constitutional right to prevent visitation in all cases not involving harm. * * *

My principal concern is that the holding seems to proceed from the assumption that the parent or parents who resist visitation have always been the child's primary caregivers and that the third parties who seek visitation have no legitimate and established relationship with the child. That idea, in turn, appears influenced by the concept that the conventional nuclear family ought to establish the visitation standard for every domestic relations case. As we all know, this is simply not the structure or prevailing condition in many households. * * *

Cases are sure to arise—perhaps a substantial number of cases—in which a third party, by acting in a caregiving role over a significant period of time, has developed a relationship with a child which is not necessarily subject to absolute parental veto. Some pre-existing relationships, then, serve to identify persons who have a strong attachment to the child with the concomitant motivation to act in a responsible way to ensure the child's welfare. * * *

* * * Since 1965 all 50 States have enacted a third-party visitation statute of some sort. Each of these statutes, save one, permits a court order to issue in certain cases if visitation is found to be in the best interests of the child. * * * Many States limit the identity of permissible petitioners by restricting visitation petitions to grandparents, or by requiring petitioners to show a substantial relationship with a child, or both. * * *

* * * [I]t would be more appropriate to conclude that the constitutionality of the application of the best interests standard depends on more specific factors. In short, a fit parent's right vis-à-vis a complete stranger is one thing; her right vis-à-vis another parent or a de facto parent may be another. * * *

It must be recognized, of course, that a domestic relations proceeding in and of itself can constitute state intervention that is so disruptive of the parent-child relationship that the constitutional right of a custodial parent to make certain basic determinations for the child's welfare becomes implicated. * * * If a single parent who is struggling to raise a child is faced with visitation demands from a third party, the attorney's fees alone might destroy her hopes and plans for the child's future. * * *

It should suffice in this case to reverse the holding of the State Supreme Court that the application of the best interests of the child standard is always unconstitutional in third-party visitation cases. * * *

* * *

NOTES AND QUESTIONS

1. *Exposure to music.* The trial court noted that the grandparents exposed the girls to music. Indeed, Gary Troxel, the plaintiff-grandfather, was the lead singer in the Fleetwoods, a pop music group that had a number of hit songs in the 1950s and early 1960s, including "Come Softly to Me" and "Mr. Blue." Their songs were featured in the soundtracks of several movies, including "Stand by Me," "Crossing Delancey," "Diner," "National Lampoon's Vacation," and "American Graffiti." *See* The Fleetwoods Home Page, http://www.thefleetwoods.com/fleetwoodsbio.html.

2. *Later developments.* When the Supreme Court decided *Troxel* in 2000, all 50 states had some form of grandparent visitation statute and the Court declined to hold that such statutes violate due process "as a *per se* matter." *Troxel,* 530 U.S. at 73. Five years after *Troxel,* the Supreme Court of Washington again addressed the issue of grandparent visitation in *In re Parentage of C.A.M.A.,* 109 P.3d 405 (Wash. 2005). In that case, the child's grandmother petitioned for visitation under the grandparent visitation statute governing a "pending dissolution, legal separation or modification of parenting plan proceeding," Wash. Rev. Code § 26.09.240 (1996), a different statute

from the broader third-party visitation statute at issue in *Troxel, id.* § 26.10.160. Subsection 5(a) of the statute held unconstitutional in *C.A.M.A.* states: "Visitation with a grandparent shall be presumed to be in the child's best interest when a significant relationship has been shown to exist. This presumption may be rebutted by a preponderance of evidence showing that visitation would endanger the child's physical, mental, or emotional health." The court struck down the statute for creating a presumption favoring grandparent visitation despite *Troxel's* command that courts "accord 'special weight' to the parent's own determination." 109 P.3d at 411.

3. *The rights of grandparents to visit with grandchildren after their own child's death.* As in *Troxel*, many grandparent visitation cases arise after one parent dies and the surviving parent limits or denies visitation by the deceased parent's own parents. In *Harrold v. Collier*, 836 N.E.2d 1165, 1169 (Ohio 2005), *cert. denied*, 547 U.S. 1004 (2006), the court unanimously upheld a statute aimed specifically at this contingency. Brittany Collier, the child of an unmarried mother, lived with her mother and her maternal grandparents for the first two years of her life. After Brittany's mother died of cancer, her maternal grandparents received temporary custody. But two years later, her biological father received custody and denied visitation to the maternal grandparents, leading to protracted litigation. Brittany did not move into her father's home until she was five.

Collier upheld a statute that expressly protects the visitation rights of grandparents of a child whose unmarried parent is deceased if a court finds visitation to be in the best interests of the child. *Id.* at 1169. The statute also extends to the deceased parent's other relatives. The court rejected the father's challenge to the statute under *Troxel*, as well as the intermediate appellate court's novel standard of proof that required petitioners seeking visitation to show "overwhelmingly clear circumstances" favoring visitation. The court further held that Ohio courts must "afford special weight to the wishes of parents of minor children when considering petitions for nonparental visitation," but that "nothing in *Troxel* suggests that a parent's wishes should be placed before a child's best interests." *Id.* at 1168, 1172. Do you agree with *Collier's* interpretation of *Troxel*?

4. *Do stepparents retain visitation rights? Troxel* has also been applied to stepparent visitation. In *In re Marriage of Engelkens*, 821 N.E.2d 799, 801 (Ill. App. Ct. 2004), for example, the child's biological father originally agreed to a temporary order allowing his ex-wife to visit twice a month with Jacob, her stepchild with whom she had lived with since the boy was four weeks old. The stepmother received custody of a second child born during the marriage. After the father learned that the child born during the marriage was not his biological child, and after the stepmother reported the father to authorities for abusing Jacob, the father petitioned to terminate the stepmother's right to visit with Jacob.

The Illinois statute permitted the court to grant visitation to a stepparent who satisfies certain conditions, where visitation would be in the best interests of the child. Citing *Troxel*, the Appellate Court of Illinois struck down this portion of the act for contravening the presumption that a custodial parent's decisions regarding visitation are in the child's best interests. The court held that common law confers no right to stepparent visitation, and the stepmother in *Engelkens* did not rely on the temporary agreement, which the court deemed "nothing more than a gratuitous undertaking." *Id.* at 806. Since the stepmother had cared for Jacob since he was an infant, do the principles of continuity of care discussed in Chapter 12 suggest that Jacob might suffer from loss of the relationship? Would it matter how old Jacob was by the time of the decision? (Jacob's age at the time of trial is not clear, though the boy lived with the stepmother before she and father married, the marriage lasted from 1995 to 1998, and visits between Jacob and his stepmother continued until 2003.)

An Indiana appellate court has also applied *Troxel* to the problem of whether stepparents have visitation rights. In *Schaffer v. Schaffer*, 884 N.E.2d 423 (Ind. Ct. App. 2008) the court opined that stepparents and grandparents should be treated similarly when courts craft initial visitation orders. As a threshold matter, under Indiana law, both must show that a custodial relationship exists with the child and that visits would be in the child's best interests. However, after the initial decree awarded visitation to a stepparent, and the parent implicitly consented by failing to appeal the order, it is not erroneous, the court held, for the trial court to decline parent's request to terminate visitation with the stepparent. The court reasoned that parental rights are " 'not akin to a property right, but [are] more in the nature of a trust which may be subject to the well-being of the child as perceived by the courts of this state.' " *Id.* at 428, *quoting Francis v. Francis*, 654 N.E.2d 4, 7 (Ind. App. 1995), a case decided before *Troxel*.

5. *Do separated siblings have a right to visit each other?* Where a child lives with a parent who has no right to visit the child's sibling, the child usually has no standing to seek visitation.

In *M.B.B. v. E.R.W.*, 100 P.3d 415, 418–20 (Wyo. 2004), the court held that because of the deference accorded to parental decisionmaking under both *Troxel* and the common law, only grandparents and primary caretakers—the two classes of non-parents identified in the relevant statute—have standing to seek visitation. Like other relatives and live-in lovers, siblings have no standing to seek visitation absent a statutory provision. *Id.* at 420. Pennsylvania courts agree. *See Frank v. Frank*, 833 A.2d 194 (Pa. Super. Ct. 2003). However, in the seminal Pennsylvania decision, *Ken R. ex rel. C.R. v. Arthur Z.*, 682 A.2d 1267 (Pa. 1996), the dissenting judge took the position that "a sibling who desires to maintain a relationship with his or her sibling(s) has a legal interest [in receiving a hearing to determine] * * * whether visitation is in the best interest of the children involved." *Id.* at 1274. The position adopted by the dissent was in line with decisions in some other jurisdictions. For example, in *L. v. G.*, 497 A.2d 215, 221 (N.J. Super. Ct. 1985), a New Jersey appellate court found that the right to visit a sibling is at least equal to "if not greater" than the right to visit one's grandchildren. Two years after *L. v. G.* was decided, the New Jersey legislature amended the state's third party visitation statute to place siblings on the same footing with grandparents in seeking visitation rights. N.J. S. A. 9:2–7.1 (1987). After *Troxel*, the state's highest court construed the statute to require that grandparents who seek visitation over the objection of a parent must show that the child would suffer harm absent visitation in order to justify the infringement on the parent's rights that a visitation order would entail. *Moriarty* v. *Bradt*, 177 N.J. 84 (2003), *cert. denied*, 540 U.S. 1177 (2004).

D. *DE FACTO* PARENTS

As indicated in the notes following *Troxel*, the constitutional right of legal parents to decide which adults spend time with their children bears directly on the claims of all third parties, including unmarried partners of a biological or adoptive parent. Both the ALI Principles and the Uniform Parentage Act urge states to recognize the role of a non-parent who has lived with the child since birth and, by agreement with the legal parent, helped raise the child and taken on "full parental responsibilities." ALI, § 2.03(b). (Excerpts from both are set forth in the notes following the main case in this section.) When unmarried couples together raise one partner's children, the children often regard both adults as their parents; in many states, however, only one adult has a legal claim to custody or visitation after the couple breaks up.

Recognition of a partner's parenthood claims can occur during an initial custody hearing, but many unmarried couples do not go to court when they split up. As illustrated in the next case, virtually all reported cases about the right of a parent's former partner to visit a child reach the courts only after an initial informal agreement to allow visits falls apart and the legal parent prohibits further contact between the former partner and the child. A key, and perhaps confusing, difference between the grandparents who sought visitation in *Troxel* and the former partner who seeks visitation is that the former partner usually must convince the court that she is not a third party at all, but a parent who deserves legal recognition.

V.C. v. M.J.B.

Supreme Court of New Jersey, 2000.
748 A.2d 539.

LONG, J.

In this case, we are called on to determine what legal standard applies to a third party's claim to joint custody and visitation of her former domestic partner's biological children, with whom she lived in a familial setting and in respect of whom she claims to have functioned as a psychological parent. Although the case arises in the context of a lesbian couple, the standard we enunciate is applicable to all persons who have willingly, and with the approval of the legal parent, undertaken the duties of a parent to a child not related by blood or adoption.[1]

I

The following facts were established at trial. V.C. and M.J.B., who are lesbians, met in 1992 and began dating on July 4, 1993. On July 9, 1993,

---

1. For the purpose of this opinion the term legal parent encompasses biological and adoptive parents.

M.J.B. went to see a fertility specialist to begin artificial insemination procedures. * * * According to M.J.B., she made the final decision to become pregnant independently and before beginning her relationship with V.C. * * *

According to V.C., early in their relationship, the two discussed having children. However, V.C. did not become aware of M.J.B.'s visits with the specialist and her decision to have a baby by artificial insemination until September 1993. * * *

Nonetheless, V.C. claimed that the parties jointly decided to have children and that she and M.J.B. jointly researched and decided which sperm donor they should use. M.J.B. acknowledged that she consulted V.C. on the issue but maintained that she individually made the final choice about which sperm donor to use.

* * * In December 1993, V.C. moved into M.J.B.'s apartment. Two months later, on February 7, 1994, the doctor informed M.J.B. that she was pregnant. M.J.B. called V.C. at work to tell her the good news. Eventually, M.J.B. was informed that she was having twins.

During M.J.B.'s pregnancy, both M.J.B. and V.C. prepared for the birth of the twins by attending pre-natal and Lamaze classes. In April 1994, the parties moved to a larger apartment to accommodate the pending births. * * *

The children were born on September 29, 1994. V.C. took M.J.B. to the hospital and she was present in the delivery room at the birth of the children. At the hospital, the nurses and staff treated V.C. as if she were a mother. Immediately following the birth, the nurses gave one child to M.J.B. to hold and the other to V.C., and took pictures of the four of them together. After the children were born, M.J.B. took a three-month maternity leave and V.C. took a three-week vacation.

The parties opened joint bank accounts for their household expenses, and prepared wills, powers of attorney, and named each other as the beneficiary for their respective life insurance policies. At some point, the parties also opened savings accounts for the children, and named V.C. as custodian for one account and M.J.B. as custodian for the other.

The parties also decided to have the children call M.J.B. "Mommy" and V.C. "Meema." M.J.B. conceded that she referred to V.C. as a "mother" of the children. In addition, M.J.B. supported the notion, both publicly and privately, that during the twenty-three months after the children were born, the parties and the children functioned as a family unit. * * * M.J.B. encouraged a relationship between V.C. and the children and sought to create a "happy, cohesive environment for the children." * * *

M.J.B. agreed that both parties cared for the children but insisted that she made substantive decisions regarding their lives. * * * V.C. countered that she was equally involved in all decision-making * * *. * * *

M.J.B. acknowledged that V.C. assumed substantial responsibility for the children, but maintained that V.C. was a mere helper and not a co-parent. However, according to V.C., she acted as a co-parent to the children and had equal parenting responsibility. Indeed, M.J.B. listed V.C. as the "other mother" on the children's pediatrician and day care registration forms. M.J.B. also gave V.C. medical power of attorney over the children.

* * *

Together the parties purchased a home in February 1995. Later that year, V.C. asked M.J.B. to marry her, and M.J.B. accepted. In July 1995, the parties held a commitment ceremony where they were "married." At the ceremony, V.C., M.J.B. and the twins were blessed as a "family."

* * *

Additionally, as a group, V.C., M.J.B. and the twins attended family functions, holidays, and birthdays. * * *

During their relationship, the couple discussed both changing the twins' surname to a hyphenated form of the women's names and the possibility of V.C. adopting the children. M.J.B. testified that the parties considered adoption and in June 1996 consulted an attorney on the subject. * * * The parties never actually attempted to * * * proceed with the adoption. * * *

Just two months later, in August 1996, M.J.B. ended the relationship. The parties then took turns living in the house with the children until November 1996. In December 1996, V.C. moved out. M.J.B. permitted V.C. to visit with the children until May 1997. During that time, V.C. spent approximately every other weekend with the children, and contributed money toward the household expenses.

In May 1997, * * * M.J.B. refused to continue V.C.'s visitation with the children, and at some point, M.J.B. stopped accepting V.C.'s money. M.J.B. asserted that she did not want to continue the children's contact with V.C. * * *. Both parties became involved with new partners after the dissolution of their relationship. Eventually, V.C. filed this complaint for joint legal custody.

At trial, expert witnesses appeared for both parties. Dr. Allwyn J. Levine testified on behalf of V.C., and Dr. David Brodzinsky testified on behalf of M.J.B. Both experts arrived at similar conclusions after having examined the women individually and with the children, and after examining the children separately.

Dr. Levine concluded that both children view V.C. as a maternal figure and that V.C. regards herself as one of the children's mothers. "[B]ecause the children were basically parented from birth" by V.C. and M.J.B. "until they physically separated," Dr. Levine concluded that the children view the parties "as inter-changeable maternal mothering objects" and "have established a maternal bond with both of the women."

* * * Dr. Levine explained that the children would benefit from continued contact with V.C. because they had a bonded relationship with her. * * *

Likewise, Dr. Brodzinsky concluded that V.C. and the children enjoyed a bonded relationship that benefitted both children. * * *

In contrast to Dr. Levine's opinion, Dr. Brodzinsky believed that the loss of V.C. was not akin to the loss of a parent in a heterosexual divorce. The doctor explained that societal views foster the expectation that a child and a parent will continue their relationship after a divorce, but that no similar expectation would exist for the children's relationship with V.C. Still, Dr. Brodzinsky testified that "[t]he ideal situation is that [M.J.B.] is allowed to get on with her life as she wants, but to the extent possible that . . . these children be able at times to have some contact with [V.C.] who's important to them." Assuming that the parties could maintain a reasonably amicable relationship, Dr. Brodzinsky felt that the children "would probably benefit from ongoing contact [with V.C.] as they would with any person with whom they have a good solid relationship that can nurture them."

The trial court denied V.C.'s applications for joint legal custody and visitation because it concluded that she failed to establish that the bonded relationship she enjoyed with the children had risen to the level of psychological or *de facto* parenthood. * * *

Finding that V.C. did not qualify as a psychological parent to the children, the trial court opined that it would "only be able to consider [V.C.'s] petition for custody if [she] was able [to] prove [M.J.B.] to be an unfit parent." Because V.C. did not allege that M.J.B. was an unfit parent, the trial court held that V.C. lacked standing to petition for joint legal custody. The court also denied V.C.'s application for visitation, determining that even a step-parent would not be granted such visitation except for equitable reasons, not present here. * * * Upon the entry of judgment, V.C. appealed.

On March 5, 1999, an Appellate Division panel decided the case in three separate opinions. * * * [T]he majority opinion * * * affirmed the denial of V.C.'s application for joint legal custody but reversed the denial of her petition for visitation. In so doing, the court concluded that V.C. had established a parent-like relationship and "stood in the shoes of a parent." The majority analyzed the case under the best interests of the child standard * * *. The trial court's judgment denying V.C.'s petition for joint custody was affirmed.

As to visitation, although recognizing that animosity between the parties is an important factor in the best interests test, the majority concluded that M.J.B. cannot deprive V.C. or the twins of visitation simply because M.J.B. harbors negative feelings toward V.C. Relying on the experts' testimony, the majority concluded that V.C.'s continued contact with the children is in their best interests; therefore, it reversed the judgment denying V.C.'s petition for visitation and remanded for proceedings to establish a visitation schedule.

* * *

An order for visitation was established on March 26, 1999. Both M.J.B. and V.C. appealed * * *. * * *

II

On appeal, M.J.B. argues that we lack subject matter jurisdiction to consider V.C.'s custody and visitation claims because the legislative scheme and the common law do not recognize her rights; that * * * V.C.'s application intrudes on M.J.B.'s basic liberty interest in raising her children as she sees fit; that protection of the children from serious harm is the only basis for governmental intervention into her private life with her children; that she has an absolute right to decide with whom her children will associate; that V.C. was the equivalent of a nanny whose status deserves no special acknowledgment; that she did not give consent to V.C.'s role as a "parent"; and finally that the Appellate Division erred in substituting its fact-finding for that of the trial court.

V.C. counters that she qualifies as a parent * * * ; that she is a psychological parent[3] of the twins thus justifying the invocation of the court's *parens patriae* power to sustain that relationship; that in such circumstances the best interests test applies; and, on her cross-appeal, that denial of joint legal custody was erroneous because of her status as a *de facto* parent.

* * *

III

We turn first to M.J.B.'s claim that we lack jurisdiction and that V.C. lacks standing to apply for joint custody and visitation because neither the statutes nor the common law acknowledge the existence of such a cause of action by a third party.

A

There are no statutes explicitly addressing whether a former unmarried domestic partner has standing to seek custody and visitation with her former partner's biological children. That is not to say, however, that the current statutory scheme dealing with issues of custody and visitation does not provide some guiding principles. * * *

* * * [T]he Legislature has expressed the view that children should not generally be denied continuing contact with parents after the relationship between the parties ends.

---

3. The terms psychological parent, *de facto* parent, and functional parent are used interchangeably in this opinion to reflect their use in the various cases, statutes, and articles cited. Psychological parent is the preferred term.

* * * M.J.B. argues that because V.C. is not a natural or adoptive parent, we lack jurisdiction to consider her claims. That is an incomplete interpretation of the Act. Although the statutory definition of parent focuses on natural and adoptive parents, it also includes the phrase, "when not otherwise described by the context." That language evinces a legislative intent to leave open the possibility that individuals other than natural or adoptive parents may qualify as "parents," depending on the circumstances.[4]

* * *

By including the words "when not otherwise described by the context" in the statute, the Legislature obviously envisioned a case where the specific relationship between a child and a person not specifically denominated by the statute would qualify as "parental" under the [statutory] scheme * * *. Although the Legislature may not have considered the precise case before us, it is hard to imagine what it could have had in mind in adding the "context" language other than a situation such as this, in which a person not related to a child by blood or adoption has stood in a parental role vis-a-vis the child. It is that contention by V.C. that brings this case before the court and affords us jurisdiction over V.C.'s complaint.

B

Separate and apart from the statute, M.J.B. contends that there is no legal precedent for this action by V.C. She asserts, correctly, that a legal parent has a fundamental right to the care, custody and nurturance of his or her child. Various constitutional provisions have been cited as the source of that right, which is deeply imbedded in our collective consciousness and traditions. In general, however, the right of a legal parent to the care and custody of his or her child derives from the notion of privacy. According to M.J.B., that right entitles her to absolute preference over V.C. in connection with custody and visitation of the twins. She argues that V.C., a stranger, has no standing to bring this action. We disagree.

The right of parents to the care and custody of their children is not absolute. For example, a legal parent's fundamental right to custody and control of a child may be infringed upon by the state if the parent

---

    4. We note that all fifty states, to one extent or another, grant statutory standing to third parties to petition for custody and/or visitation of the biological or adoptive children of others. Those statutes reveal a full spectrum of approaches. * * * .

    The more expansive statutes allow third parties, without regard to blood relationship, to seek both custody and visitation. Examples include: Conn. Gen. Stat. Ann. § 46b–57,—59 (West 1999) (allowing custody or visitation to "any interested third-party . . . upon such conditions and limitations as [the court] deems equitable"); Haw. Rev. Stat. Ann. § 571–46(2), (7) (West 1999) (granting standing to third persons for custody when in the best interests of child and granting *de facto* parent *prima facie* award of custody; visitation standing granted to "any person interested in the welfare of the child" in court's discretion); Mass. Gen. Laws Ann. ch. 208, § 28 (West 1999) (granting standing to any third party to petition for custody if court deems such award expedient or in child's best interest); Or. Rev. Stat. § 109.119(1)(granting standing to "[a]ny person . . . who has established emotional ties" for either custody or visitation); Va. Code Ann. § 16.1–241(A) (Michie 1999) (granting standing to "any party with a legitimate interest" to petition for visitation or custody of child).

endangers the health or safety of the child. Likewise, if there is a showing of unfitness, abandonment or gross misconduct, a parent's right to custody of her child may be usurped.

According to M.J.B., because there is no allegation by V.C. of unfitness, * * * there is no reason advanced to interfere with any of her constitutional prerogatives. What she elides from consideration, however, is the "exceptional circumstances" category * * * that has been recognized as an alternative basis for a third party to seek custody and visitation of another person's child. The "exceptional circumstances" category contemplates the intervention of the Court in the exercise of its *parens patriae* power to protect a child.

Subsumed within that category is the subset known as the psychological parent cases in which a third party has stepped in to assume the role of the legal parent who has been unable or unwilling to undertake the obligations of parenthood.

Cases in other jurisdictions have also recognized the psychological parent doctrine. * * * *Custody of H.S.H.–K.*, 533 N.W.2d 419, 421 (Wis. 1995) (outlining four prong test for establishing *de facto* parent relationship).

At the heart of the psychological parent cases is a recognition that children have a strong interest in maintaining the ties that connect them to adults who love and provide for them. That interest, for constitutional as well as social purposes, lies in the emotional bonds that develop between family members as a result of shared daily life. * * *

To be sure, prior cases * * * have arisen in the context of a third party taking over the role of an unwilling, absent or incapacitated parent. The question presented here is different; V.C. did not step into M.J.B.'s shoes, but labored alongside her in their family. However, because we view this issue as falling broadly within the contours we have previously described, and because V.C. invokes the "exceptional circumstances" doctrine based on her claim to be a psychological parent to the twins, she has standing to maintain this action separate and apart from the statute.

IV

The next issue we confront is how a party may establish that he or she has, in fact, become a psychological parent to the child of a fit and involved legal parent. That is a question which many of our sister states have attempted to answer. Some have enacted statutes to address the subject by deconstructing psychological parenthood to its fundamental elements, including: the substantial nature of the relationship between the third party and the child, *see, e.g.*, Ariz. Rev. Stat. Ann. § 25–415(G)(1) (West 2000); whether or not the third party and the child actually lived together, *see, e.g.*, Minn. Stat. Ann. § 257.022(2b) (West 1999); and whether the unrelated third party had previously provided financial support for the child, *see, e.g.*[,] 1999 Nev. Stat. 125A.330(3)(I).

Several state courts have attempted to refine the concept further.
* * *

* * *

The most thoughtful and inclusive definition of *de facto* parenthood is the test enunciated in *Custody of H.S.H.-K.*, 533 N.W.2d 419, 421 (Wis. 1995) * * *. It addresses the main fears and concerns both legislatures and courts have advanced when addressing the notion of psychological parenthood. Under that test,

> [t]o demonstrate the existence of the petitioner's parent-like relationship with the child, the petitioner must prove four elements: (1) that the biological or adoptive parent consented to, and fostered, the petitioner's formation and establishment of a parent-like relationship with the child; (2) that the petitioner and the child lived together in the same household; (3) that the petitioner assumed the obligations of parenthood by taking significant responsibility for the child's care, education and development, including contributing towards the child's support, without expectation of financial compensation [a petitioner's contribution to a child's support need not be monetary]; and (4) that the petitioner has been in a parental role for a length of time sufficient to have established with the child a bonded, dependent relationship parental in nature.

[*Id.*] (footnote omitted).

Recapping, the legal parent must consent to and foster the relationship between the third party and the child; the third party must have lived with the child; the third party must perform parental functions for the child to a significant degree; and most important, a parent-child bond must be forged. We are satisfied that that test provides a good framework for determining psychological parenthood in cases where the third party has lived for a substantial period with the legal parent and her child.[6]

Prong one is critical because it makes the biological or adoptive parent a participant in the creation of the psychological parent's relationship with the child. Without such a requirement, a paid nanny or babysitter could theoretically qualify for parental status. * * *

The requirement of cooperation by the legal parent is critical because it places control within his or her hands. That parent has the absolute ability to maintain a zone of autonomous privacy for herself and her child. However, if she wishes to maintain that zone of privacy she cannot invite a third party to function as a parent to her child and cannot cede over to that third party parental authority the exercise of which may create a profound bond with the child.

---

6. Obviously, the notion of consent will have different implications in different factual settings. For example, where a legal parent voluntarily absents herself physically or emotionally from her child or is incapable of performing her parental duties, those circumstances may constitute consent to the parental role of a third party who steps into her shoes relative to the child. As in all psychological parent cases, the outcome in such a case will depend on the full factual complex and the existence of the other factors contained in the test.

Two further points concerning the consent requirement need to be clarified. First, a psychological parent-child relationship that is voluntarily created by the legally recognized parent may not be unilaterally terminated after the relationship between the adults ends. Although the intent of the legally recognized parent is critical to the psychological parent analysis, the focus is on that party's intent during the formation and pendency of the parent-child relationship. The reason is that the ending of the relationship between the legal parent and the third party does not end the bond that the legal parent fostered and that actually developed between the child and the psychological parent. * * *

In practice, that may mean protecting those relationships despite the later, contrary wishes of the legal parent in order to advance the interests of the child. As long as the legal parent consents to the continuation of the relationship between another adult who is a psychological parent and the child after the termination of the adult parties' relationship, the courts need not be involved. Only when that consent is withdrawn are courts called on to protect the child's relationship with the psychological parent.

The second issue that needs to be clarified is that participation in the decision to have a child is not a prerequisite to a finding that one has become a psychological parent to the child. * * * Although joint participation in the family's decision to have a child is probative evidence of the legally recognized parent's intentions, not having participated in the decision does not preclude a finding of the third party's psychological parenthood. Such circumstances parallel the situation in which a woman, already pregnant or a mother, becomes involved with or marries a man who is not the biological or adoptive father of the child, but thereafter fully functions in every respect as a father. * * *

Concerning the remaining prongs of the *H.S.H.–K.* test, we accept Wisconsin's formulation with these additional comments. The third prong, a finding that a third party assumed the obligations of parenthood, is not contingent on financial contributions made by the third party. Financial contribution may be considered but should not be given inordinate weight when determining whether a third party has assumed the obligations of parenthood. * * *

Indeed, we can conceive of a case in which the third party is the stay-at-home mother or father who undertakes all of the daily domestic and child care activities in a household with preschool children while the legal parent is the breadwinner engaged in her occupation or profession. * * *

It bears repeating that the fourth prong is most important because it requires the existence of a parent-child bond. A necessary corollary is that the third party must have functioned as a parent for a long enough time that such a bond has developed. What is crucial here is not the amount of time but the nature of the relationship. * * * [A] determination will have to be made about the actuality and strength of the parent-child bond. Generally, that will require expert testimony.

The standards to which we have referred will govern all cases in which a third party asserts psychological parent status as a basis for a custody or visitation action regarding the child of a legal parent, with whom the third party has lived in a familial setting.

V

* * * What we have addressed here is a specific set of circumstances involving the volitional choice of a legal parent to cede a measure of parental authority to a third party; to allow that party to function as a parent in the day-to-day life of the child; and to foster the forging of a parental bond between the third party and the child. In such circumstances, the legal parent has created a family with the third party and the child, and has invited the third party into the otherwise inviolable realm of family privacy. By virtue of her own actions, the legal parent's expectation of autonomous privacy in her relationship with her child is necessarily reduced from that which would have been the case had she never invited the third party into their lives. Most important, where that invitation and its consequences have altered her child's life by essentially giving him or her another parent, the legal parent's options are constrained. It is the child's best interest that is preeminent as it would be if two legal parents were in a conflict over custody and visitation.

VI

Once a third party has been determined to be a psychological parent to a child, under the previously described standards, he or she stands in parity with the legal parent. Custody and visitation issues between them are to be determined on a best interests standard * * *.

* * *

* * * [U]nder ordinary circumstances when the evidence concerning the child's best interests (as between a legal parent and psychological parent) is in equipoise, custody will be awarded to the legal parent.

Visitation, however, will be the presumptive rule, * * * as would be the case if two natural parents were in conflict. * * * Once the parent-child bond is forged, the rights and duties of the parties should be crafted to reflect that reality.

VII

Ordinarily, when we announce a new standard, we remand the case to the trial court for reconsideration. That is not necessary here. * * * [W]e agree with the Appellate Division that V.C. is a psychological parent to the twins.

That said, the issue is whether V.C. should be granted joint legal custody and visitation. * * *

We note that V.C. is not seeking joint physical custody, but joint legal custody for decision making. However, due to the pendency of this case,

V.C. has not been involved in the decision-making for the twins for nearly four years. To interject her into the decisional realm at this point would be unnecessarily disruptive for all involved. We will not, therefore, order joint legal custody in this case.

Visitation, however, is another matter. V.C. and the twins have been visiting during nearly all of the four years since V.C. parted company from M.J.B. Continued visitation in those circumstances is presumed. Nothing suggests that V.C. should be precluded from continuing to see the children on a regular basis. Indeed, it is clear that continued regular visitation is in the twins' best interests because V.C. is their psychological parent. We thus affirm the judgment of the Appellate Division.

VIII

Third parties who live in familial circumstances with a child and his or her legal parent may achieve, with the consent of the legal parent, a psychological parent status vis-a-vis a child. Fundamental to a finding of the existence of that status is that a parent-child bond has been created. That bond cannot be unilaterally terminated by the legal parent. When there is a conflict over custody and visitation between the legal parent and a psychological parent, the legal paradigm is that of two legal parents and the standard to be applied is the best interests of the child.

Establishing psychological parenthood is not an easy task and the standards we have adopted should be scrupulously applied in order to protect the legal parent-child relationship.

[The concurring opinions of O'HERN, J., and LONG, J., are omitted.]

NOTES AND QUESTIONS

1. *Visitation.* V.C. distinguishes between two entwined concepts, the right to custody and the right to visitation. One Pennsylvania court has referred to a biological parent's unrelated same-sex partner as "certainly fit to exercise partial custody of the child for the purpose of visitation." *T.B. v. L.R.M.*, 874 A.2d 34, 37 (Pa. Super. Ct. 2005). In other words, visitation is a form of temporary custody, although it may be subject to limitations designed to promote consistency where only one parent has decision-making authority.

As you read in Chapter 5 on nonmarital families, after *V.C.* the Supreme Court of California held that where one member of a lesbian couple donated ova to impregnate the other, both are considered mothers and the non-custodial mother is entitled to visitation. *K.M. v. E.G.*, 33 Cal.Rptr.3d 61 (2005).

2. *Other jurisdictions.* A Pennsylvania court observed that "[c]ase law from other jurisdictions demonstrates recognition that nontraditional configurations of the nuclear family have replaced traditional models in recent years, which favors equitable considerations such as the doctrine of *in loco parentis* when deciding third party standing to seek custody/visitation." *T.B. v. L.R.M.*, 753 A.2d 873, 884 n.7 (Pa. Super. Ct. 2000), *aff'd* 786 A.2d 913 (Pa. 2001). On the other hand, some "jurisdictions have denied standing to third parties

seeking custody or visitation based upon a lack of statutory authority to entertain the claim." *Id.* (collecting cases on both points). In Michigan, for example, equitable parenthood doctrines apply only in the context of marriage. *See Van v. Zahorik*, 597 N.W.2d 15 (Mich. 1999).

In 2008 the appellate courts of several states considered equitable parenthood claims, applying distinct analyses that can lead to varying results when third parties seek joint custody or visitation rights in cases with facts similar to those in *V.C.* In *Mason* v. *Dwinnell*, 660 S.E.2d 58 (N.C. Ct. App. 2008), for example, the court applied the best interests of the child standard to award joint legal and physical custody of a child born by artificial insemination to two women who were domestic partners and who had executed a parenting agreement specifying that the woman who was not the biological mother was a "de facto" parent with a psychological tie to the child she was helping to raise. Under these circumstances, the court reasoned, the biological mother's actions were inconsistent with a later assertion of her constitutional right as a parent to exclusive control over her child. The court expressly stated that its decision was not limited to same-sex couples, or to couples prohibited by law from marrying. Without reaching the question of whether North Carolina would recognize parenthood by estoppel, the court held that where the biological parent intentionally created a parent-like relationship between the child and the third party, the third party did not have to be recognized as a legal parent to share custody if such an arrangement was in the child's best interest.

In a second case involving same-sex domestic partners decided the same day, the same court clarified that a North Carolina trial court may consider only the child's best interests in evaluating competing claims of a legal parent and a third party where the parent "acted in a manner inconsistent with his or her constitutionally protected status as a parent" by, for example, demonstrating an intent to create a "permanent parent-like bond" between the third party and the child. *Estroff* v. *Chatterjee*, 660 S.E.2d 73, 75 (N.C. Ct. App. 2008) (finding no such intent).

Applying these rulings, the same court held two months later that "inconsistent acts" need not be bad acts that would disqualify the parent as a custodian, but may refer to the parent's intent with respect to the third party. *Heatzig* v. *MacLean*, 664 S.E.2d 347, 351(N.C. Ct. App. 2008). The court expressly reiterated that North Carolina does not recognize parenthood by estoppel. The sole means of creating "the legal relationship of parent and child" is adoption, the court stated. *Id.* at 353. Is there a practical distinction between the definition of intent in North Carolina and the definition of de facto parenthood set forth in the ALI Principles and the UPA (discussed in notes 3 and 4 below)?

The Court of Appeals of Maryland, the state's highest court, expressly refused to recognize de facto parenthood, and held that a third party's claims to custody or visitation must be decided under the "exceptional circumstances" doctrine discussed in *McDermott* v. *Daugherty* (2005) (p. 669 in Chapter 12). *Janice M.* v. *Margaret K.*, 948 A.2d 73 (Md. 2008). *Janice M.* reversed the decision below and denied visitation to a woman whose partner of 18 years adopted a child they had raised together for five years, from the date of the child's adoption. A Texas intermediate court went further, holding that a domestic partner had no standing to appear in court despite a court order the partners had obtained when the children were infants naming the partners as the children's joint conservators. Reasoning that no controversy existed between the parties at that time, the court concluded that the order was void and unenforceable when the parties split up because the trial court lacked jurisdiction to issue it. *In re Charlena Renee Smith* 262 S.W.3d 463 (Tex. Ct. App. 2008).

3. *Definitions and distinctions among the labels applied to third-party claims of parenthood under the* ALI *Principles.* As *V.C.* makes clear, in jurisdictions that recognize equitable claims to parenthood based on the role a third party has played in the child's life, a biological "stranger" may have standing to claim legal or physical custody as well as visitation rights. Equitable parents may also be obligated to pay child support. *See Chambers v. Chambers,* 2005 WL 645220 (Del. Fam. Ct. 2005) (holding that after a same-sex couple split up, the *de facto* parent is liable for child support).

States vary in the labels they assign to third parties who claim parent-hood, and there are technical distinctions as well. The terms include: (i) "parent by estoppel" or "equitable parent"; and (ii) *de facto* parent. The *V.C.* decision, like many others, uses the terms *"de facto* parent" and "equitable parent" interchangeably, but the ALI distinguishes between them. Section 203 of the Principles defines a *de facto* parent as follows:

(c) A *de facto parent* is an individual other than a legal parent or a parent by estoppel who, for a significant period of time not less than two years,

(i) lived with the child and,

(ii) for reasons primarily other than financial compensation, and with the agreement of a legal parent to form a parent-child relationship, or as a result of a complete failure or inability of any legal parent to perform caretaking functions,

(A) regularly performed a majority of the caretaking functions for the child, or

(B) regularly performed a share of caretaking functions at least as great as that of the parent with whom the child primarily lived.

ALI, Principles § 2.03 (c) (2002).

The Pennsylvania Supreme Court has held that regardless of the nature of the biological parent's relationship with an individual who seeks recognition as a *de facto* parent, a *de facto* parenting relationship is created where "the child has established strong psychological bonds" with a non-biological parent figure who "has lived with the child and provided care, nurture and affection, assuming in the child's eye a stature like that of a parent." *T.B. v. L.R.M.,* 786 A.2d 913, 917 (Pa. 2001). The *de facto* relationship is equivalent to the common law *in loco parentis* doctrine and renders the formalities of legal adoption unnecessary.

Section 2.03 of the ALI Principles defines a parent by estoppel as follows:

(b) A parent by estoppel is an individual who, though not a legal parent,

(i) is obligated to pay child support * * *; or

(ii) lived with the child for at least two years and

    (A) over that period had a reasonable, good faith belief that he was the child's biological father, based on marriage to the mother or on the actions or representations of the mother, and fully accepted parental responsibilities consistent with that belief, and

    (B) if some time thereafter that belief no longer existed, continued to make reasonable, good-faith efforts to accept responsibilities as the child's father; or

(iii) lived with the child since birth, holding out and accepting full and permanent responsibilities as parent, as part of a prior co-parenting agreement with the child's legal parent * * * to raise a child together each with full parental rights and responsibilities, when the court finds that recognition of the individual as a parent is in the child's best interests; or

(iv) lived with the child for at least two years, holding out and accepting full and permanent responsibilities as a parent, pursuant to an agreement with the child's parent * * *, when the court finds that recognition of the individual as a parent is in the child's best interests.

ALI, Principles of the Law of Family Dissolution: Analysis and Recommendations § 2.03(1)(b) (2002). For an argument that the ALI's definition is too narrow and excludes "most nontraditional parents," see Julie Shapiro, *De Facto Parents and the Unfulfilled Promise of the New ALI Principles*, 35 Willamette L. Rev. 769, 770 (1999).

Parent by estoppel cases frequently arise where a married man believes himself to be the biological father of a child in his household, only to discover when the couple breaks up that another man is the biological father. *See, e.g., In re Marriage of Phillips*, 58 P.3d 680 (Kan. 2002) (assigning primary custody to the father, who continued to act as father after genetic testing established that neither of the children he was raising as his own were his biological offspring). In *Soumis v. Soumis*, 553 N.W.2d 619 (Mich. Ct. App. 1996), the court held that the husband stood on equal footing with the mother in his claims for custody and visitation, even where he knew before the child's birth that he might not be the father, he was the only father the child had ever known, the putative biological father was deceased, and the mother had encouraged the parent-child relationship. *Soumis* affirmed the trial court's award of joint custody of the father's non-biological child to the mother and the father by estoppel, and awarded custody of the couple's biological child to the father.

As a matter of public policy, if a married man discovers that he is not the father of a child born during his marriage, is it fair to require him to continue supporting the child? What are the social policy priorities in such a situation?

4. *Uniform Parentage Act.* The Uniform Parentage Act (UPA) recognizes as a parent a person who lives with the child during its first two years of life and openly holds out the child as his or her own. Uniform Parentage Act § 106 cmt.204 (a)(2002), http://www.law.upenn.edu/bll/ulc/upa/final2002.htm. What difference, if any, exists between the ALI approach and the UPA?

5. *Can a neighbor become a psychological parent?* "*V.C.* gave standing, in certain circumstances, to third parties who previously had no right to seek custody or visitation at all, and was not intended to apply only to domestic partners or step-parents." *P.B. v. T.H.*, 851 A.2d 780, 786 (N.J. Super. Ct. App. Div. 2004). *P.B.* involved two children the state had removed from their substance-abusing mother and placed with their aunt, a single mother expecting her second child. When the aunt became overwhelmed, P.B., a neighbor, volunteered to care for the two children, who eventually moved into P.B.'s home. Later, when a custody dispute arose, P.B. claimed that she had been the psychological parent of the younger child, an infant. The trial court held that P.B. was the psychological parent. The appellate court concluded the P.B. had standing to seek custody of the child and remanded the case, indicating that determining who is a psychological parent in third-party custody cases is an issue of law to be decided according to *V.C.*'s four-factor test.

PROBLEM 13–3

You are a state legislator considering what policy your state should adopt with respect to third-party claims to parenthood. What are the competing social policy goals? How should the state balance the goal of encouraging the partners of biological parents to play active roles in the lives of the children in the household with the perceived risk that helping raise a child may impose ongoing responsibilities after the relationship ends?

SECTION 3: MODIFICATION OF CUSTODY OR VISITATION ORDERS

Many of the materials you read earlier in this Chapter concerned modification of custody or visitation orders. This Section focuses on the legal standards that govern modification. First, you will read about the generally applicable grounds for modification. You will then explore one of the most common reasons that a parent petitions for modification–the relocation of the parent who has primary physical custody. As you will see, relocation cases have generated their own subset of legal standards for modification.

A. THE STANDARD

Because of the state's *parens patriae* interest in the welfare of children, courts retain jurisdiction over custody and visitation matters until the child reaches the age of majority. A trial court may modify child custody orders, including consent decrees, but will not do so lightly. To modify a custody arrangement, a trial court in most states must find (i) that circumstances have changed substantially since the original decree was entered; and (ii) that the change in custody will serve the best interests of the child. *See, e.g., Carrasco v. Grubb*, 824 N.E.2d 705, 710 (Ind. Ct. App. 2005). In Oregon, for example, a parent seeking a custody change must show "that (1) after the original judgment or the last order affecting custody, circumstances relevant to the capacity of either the moving party or the legal custodian to take care of the child properly have changed, and (2) considering the asserted changes of circumstance * * *, it would be in the child's best interests to change custody from the legal custodian to the moving party." *In re the Marriage of Boldt*, 176 P.3d 388, 392 (Or. 2008), *cert. denied*, 129 S.Ct. 47 (2008). To avoid re-litigation of issues aired in the initial custody determination, most jurisdictions require that the change of circumstances have occurred after the initial decree, and that it could not have been foreseeable by the parties at the time of the initial decree. A handful of jurisdictions, including Georgia, Kansas and New Hampshire, allow modification based on the child's best interests without any showing of changed circumstances. *E.g.*, Ga. Code Ann. § 19–9–3 (2004); *In re Choy*, 919 A.2d 801 (N. H. 2007) (holding that legislation enacted in 2000 eliminated the changed circumstances requirement for modifying a custody decree). In addition, many state statutes provide that a court may not consider or issue modification orders until a specified period has passed since the initial or prior decree, often two years. *E.g.*, Del. Code Ann. tit. 13, § 729 (1998); *see* ALI Principles, § 2.15 Reporter's Notes to cmt. a (2002).

In most jurisdictions the focus is on the changed circumstances of the custodial parent, not on improvements in the non-custodial parent's circumstances that might have supported that parent's initial custody claim. For example, a non-custodial parent's improved mental health will not ordinarily lead to a change of custody. A material "change of circumstances" often turns out to be a conglomeration of changes, adding up to a different calculation of the child's best interests. ALI Principles, § 2.15 cmt. c.

Some jurisdictions engage in a less stringent inquiry for modifying joint physical custody. *Id.* § 2.15 cmt. a. In considering petitions to modify joint custody decrees, courts may find that the parents' inability to cooperate constitutes a material change of circumstance, or that the children's need for consistency is a changed circumstance when they are old enough to enroll in school.

We do not have exact figures, but anecdotal evidence and court histories suggest that many parents reach informal agreements to modify custody and visitation arrangements as time passes. Because such informal arrangements may later lead to disputes, it is advisable to reduce the new terms to writing, and to have the arrangements approved by the court with jurisdiction over custody matters. *See Hurtt v. Hurtt*, 216 S.W.3d 604 (Ark. Ct. App. 2005). ("The parties cannot modify the divorce decree without permission from the court. Absent a subsequent modification, the language in the divorce decree controls").

PROBLEM 13–4

Martin married Kate in 2000. Three years later she gave birth to a son they named Joey, who was not Martin's biological child. Although Martin was aware that Joey was not his son, he stayed in the marriage and raised the boy with Kate. Three years later, they divorced and received joint legal custody, with primary physical custody going to Kate. After the divorce, Kate became involved with a drug addict and moved in with him. She also began to abuse alcohol and use illegal drugs, and the house fell into chaos. Martin sued for sole legal and physical custody.

Kate's parents intervened in the suit to modify custody, alleging, first, that Martin was not the boy's father, and second that his life as a traveling carnival performer prevented him from providing a suitable home for Joey. Martin responded that he only traveled during the summer months, and that during the rest of the year he parked his mobile home in a trailer community from which he commuted to his performances.

You are the family court judge. Based on what you have learned about child custody in the last chapter and this chapter, what custody order would you issue, and why?

B. RELOCATION

One or both parents commonly relocate after their marriage has ended. Parents frequently move to pursue educational or career opportunities, to establish a home with a new spouse or partner, or to be closer to a support network of family members or friends. Americans in general are increasingly likely to move longer distances, and separated or divorced people are far more likely to move than their married counterparts. Broadcast Release, Tom Edwards, Public Information Office, U.S. Census Bureau, Dep't of Commerce (Sep. 4, 2008) *available at* http://www.census.gov/Press-release/www/releases/archives/mobility_of_the_population/01 2604.html (reporting data from the 2007 Current Population Survey's Annual Social and Economic Supplement); *see also* Leslie Eaton, *Divorced Parents Move, and Custody Gets Trickier*, N.Y. Times, Aug. 8, 2005, at A1. Disputes arising from a custodial parent's proposed relocation frequently lead the other parent to petition for modification of custody on the ground that the proposed move would undermine the petitioner's visitation rights and relationship with the child. The number of relocation cases reaching the courts has risen sharply in recent years.

Most jurisdictions treat relocation cases differently than other petitions for modification of custody or visitation orders. California pioneered the "presumptive right" approach to moves by custodial parents which established a rebuttable presumption that custodial parents have a right to relocate and do not, as a threshold matter, need to convince a court that their reasons for moving are sound. Many other jurisdictions followed suit. In 1996 New York, the state which had been most likely to restrict the custodial parent's freedom to relocate, discarded its requirement that the parent had to establish "exceptional circumstances" for the proposed relocation. Noting that "[l]ike Humpty Dumpty, a family, once broken by divorce, cannot be put back together in precisely the same way," the state's highest court held that "each relocation request must be considered on its own merits * * * with predominant emphasis being placed on what outcome is most likely to serve the best interests of the child." *Tropea v. Tropea*, 642 N.Y.S.2d 575, 580–81 (N.Y. 1996).

Consistent with this trend, the ALI Principles issued in 2002 presume that a parent's relocation does not constitute a substantial change in circumstances permitting modification of custodial arrangements unless the "relocation significantly impairs either parent's ability to exercise responsibilities the parent has been exercising or attempting to exercise under the parenting plan." ALI Principles of the Law of Family Dissolution: Analysis and Recommendations § 2.17(1) (2002). Of course, if one parent moves a long distance, the move may easily "significantly impair" the arrangements of parents with joint physical custody or generous visitation patterns. The ALI Principles expressly provide that the court should allow the parent who exercises "the clear majority of custodial responsibility" to relocate (after giving notice to the other parent) "for a valid purpose, in good faith" to a location that promotes the purpose. *Id*. The ALI lists reasons for moving that should generally be regarded as valid, including the most common purposes generally accepted by courts, such as to be near extended family, to pursue career or educational opportunities, or to join a new spouse or significant other who lives elsewhere. *Id*.

Notwithstanding the ALI recommendations, the pendulum is now moving away from presumptions favoring the custodial parent's freedom to relocate and toward decision-making on a case-by-case basis. Both legislatures and courts have engaged the relocation issue. In its most recent rulings on challenges by noncustodial parents to proposed moves by parents with physical custody, the Supreme Court of California has indicated that a custodial parent's right to relocate with the child is less clear-cut than many believed it to be in that state. In 2003, the California legislature incorporated the court's earlier ruling that a custodial parent who wants to relocate did not need to prove the relocation was "necessary." *In re Marriage of Burgess*, 913 P.2d 473 (Cal. 1996), Cal. Family Code § 7501(b) (West 2004) (expressly affirming *Burgess*). In *LaMusga* v. *LaMusga*, 88 P.3d 81 (Cal. 2004) the court stated that a parent with joint legal custody bears the initial burden to show that a proposed relocation by the parent who has primary physical custody would be to the child's detriment, and that a court could block the relocation or transfer custody where relocation would diminish the child's relationship with the noncustodial parent. In its most recent ruling in a relocation case, the court held that a parent who had neither legal nor physical custody could "seek a change in custody based on the custodial parent's decision to relocate with their child * * *." *In re Marriage of Brown and Yana*, 127 P.3d 28, 35 (Cal. 2006).

Professor Theresa Glennon reviewed all decisions available on Westlaw involving relocation over a five-year period ending June 1, 2006. Her findings confirmed that the reasons for relocating cited by the ALI are reasons given in the bulk of cases, 90% of which involve mothers with custody. This excerpt from her article captures her argument about the uncertainties imposed by the current approach to these cases.

THERESA GLENNON

Still Partners? Examining the Consequences of Post–Dissolution Parenting.
41 Family Law Quarterly 105 (2007).

Parents who divorce or separate are strongly encouraged to co-parent their children. * * *.

The co-parenting approach * * * falls into sharp conflict with the economic clean break model, under which divorced persons and co-habitants who part ways are entirely separate individuals, unencumbered by ongoing legal or financial relationships, free to build new lives and make a fresh start. * * *

* * * Relocation disputes provide a context in which the tension between these two models is most acute.

* * *

Relocation disputes * * * usually develop after dissolution when the parent who has sole custody or is the majority-time residential parent, usually the mother, seeks to move away from the other parent. * * * State approaches to these disputes vary widely, and the outcome of any dispute is far from certain. * * *

* * *

Relocation disputes have spawned their own doctrine. * * * [M}ost states have developed a doctrinal approach that is specific to relocation disputes. Many states now require the parent who seeks to change the child's principal residence to provide notice to the other parent. * * *

* * * [B]road categories fail to capture the diversity of state approaches to relocation. * * *

* * *

* * * Only a small number of states explicitly consider the interests of the parent seeking relocation. * * * Some * * * states take the parent's well-being into account indirectly by finding the child's interest to be interwoven with the interests of the primary custodial parent. In many states, however, the focus is on the best interests of the child, and that focus often centers on the possible disruption a move would cause to the child's relationship with the noncustodial parent.

* * *

Courts granted permission to move in slightly fewer than half—forty-nine percent of the cases [studied] in which a final decision was made. In states with ten or more reported cases in which a decision was made, the percentage of cases in which permission to move was granted varied widely. * * * The percentage of cases in which permission to move was granted is lower if all cases, not just those reaching a final decision, are included. These results mean that for most parents entering litigation, the caselaw in their state is decidedly mixed, and they cannot be confident of the outcome or of receiving a prompt decision.

* * *

To resolve a question of first impression in Florida, an intermediate court summarized several recent decisions from other states that have examined how the law should treat a custodial parent's request to relocate. Consider Professor Glennon's concerns about the needs of the primary custodian as you read the following opinion.

FREDMAN v. FREDMAN

District Court of Appeal of Florida, 2007.
960 So.2d 52.

SILBERMAN, J.

In this postdissolution proceeding, Leslie Ann Fredman * * * (the Mother), appeals a final order denying her supplemental petition and prohibiting her from relocating with the parties' two children to Texas. She contends that section 61.13(2)(d), Florida Statutes (2004), the parental relocation statute,[1] is unconstitutional because it abridges her fundamental rights to privacy and travel and violates her right to equal protection of the law. She also contends that the trial court abused its discretion in denying her request to relocate to Texas. We affirm, holding that the statute is constitutional on its face and that the trial court did not abuse its discretion in denying her request to relocate.

The Mother and David Lynn Fredman (the Father) have two sons, born December 21, 1994, and December 22, 1997. The parties divorced in October of 2002, and the final judgment of dissolution of marriage incorporated the parties' marital settlement agreement (MSA). The parties have shared parental responsibility, with the Mother being the primary residential parent and the Father having liberal visitation, specifically including a minimum of one night per week and every other weekend. * * * At the time the parties entered into the MSA and provided for the specific visitation, the Mother had a relationship with Mike Melton, whom she later married.

The Mother and Mr. Melton met while he was working on a project in Florida for an extended time. Mr. Melton lives in Ponder, Texas, with his son, and he now works in Ponder. The Mother works in Hillsborough County, Florida, and lives with the parties' two sons in a two-bedroom

---

1. The legislature significantly amended the parental relocation statute and moved it to section 61.13001, effective October 1, 2006. * * * The parties did not mention the new statute in their briefs, and the trial court's orders were entered prior to the amendment, pursuant to section 61.13(2)(d). Thus, this opinion does not address section 61.13001 [which in any event would not significantly affect the analysis here].

apartment in Brandon, Florida. On January 23, 2004, the Mother filed a supplemental petition seeking to modify the Father's visitation because she would be marrying Mr. Melton and relocating with the children to Mr. Melton's home in Ponder, Texas. Upon the Father's motion for injunctive relief, the court entered a temporary injunction prohibiting the Mother from moving the children to Texas.

At the final hearing in November 2004, the Mother testified to the benefits of moving the children to the small community of Ponder, Texas, particularly Mr. Melton's new 3000–square-foot home and the amenities at the nearby public school. The Mother testified that she earns $58,000 per year and has the possibility for advancement at her current Florida employment. The Mother testified that she planned to be a stay-at-home mom in Ponder, but if necessary she could find comparable employment there. The only people her children know in Ponder are Mr. Melton and his son. The Mother has no family in Ponder; her family lives in Oklahoma, two and one-half hours away from Ponder.

Mr. Melton testified that he worked in the oil and gas industry * * *, that he earned $70,000 to $90,000 per year, and that he could not find employment in his field of work in Florida.

The Father testified that he works a night shift from 11:00 p.m. to 7:30 a.m., that he exercised visitation with his children on Tuesdays and every other weekend, and that when he did not exercise visitation it was due to his work schedule. Since the Mother filed the supplemental petition, he has increased the overnight visitation because his new wife is home while he is working at night. The Father picks the children up from school on the days he has visitation. He testified that he helps them with their homework and that he enjoys recreational activities with his sons, including bowling and fishing.

The Father has extended family in Hillsborough County, including his mother, grandmother, uncles, aunts, and cousins. The Father testified that the children have seen their grandmother at least once a week throughout their lives. The Father sees his family every weekend, and the children have frequent contact with them, enjoying "boating, fishing, swimming, and just hanging out as a family" at their grandmother's home. The Father's family is also involved in a bowling league in which the children and the Father participate * * * on Tuesday nights. * * * [B]oth the Father and the Mother attend the children's bowling league on Saturdays.

On December 10, 2004, after a final hearing, the trial court rendered an order applying the factors * * * regarding relocation and denying the Mother's request for modification of visitation. On appeal, this court reversed and remanded for the trial court to use the proper legal standard * * * *See Fredman v. Fredman*, 917 So. 2d 1038 (Fla. 2d DCA 2006). On remand, the trial court reconsidered * * * [and] found that the proposed visitation plan was "adequate to foster a continuing, meaningful relationship between the children and the Father" but found, considering all the factors, that the move was not in the children's best interest. Thus, the trial court denied the Mother's * * * request to relocate. The Mother now appeals from the trial court's March 2006 order.

I. CONSTITUTIONALITY OF RELOCATION STATUTE

* * * Mother * * * challenges the facial constitutionality of * * * relocation statute [,] * * * a question of first impression in the State of Florida. * * * [T]his opinion does not address the significantly amended version of the relocation statute in section 61.13001 but applies only to the version of the statute in section 61.13(2)(d).

Section 61.13(2)(d) provides as follows:

No presumption shall arise in favor of or against a request to relocate when a primary residential parent seeks to remove the child and the move will materially affect the current schedule of contact and access with the secondary residential parent. In making a determination as to whether the primary residential parent may relocate with a child, the court must consider the following factors:

1.   Whether the move would be likely to improve the general quality of life for both the residential parent and the child.

2.   The extent to which visitation rights have been allowed and exercised.

3.   Whether the primary residential parent, once out of the jurisdiction, will be likely to comply with any substitute visitation arrangements.

4.   Whether the substitute visitation will be adequate to foster a continuing meaningful relationship between the child and the secondary residential parent.

5.   Whether the cost of transportation is financially affordable by one or both parties.

6.   Whether the move is in the best interests of the child.

The constitutionality of a statute is reviewed de novo; however, a legislative enactment comes to the reviewing court with a presumption of constitutionality, and the reviewing court should, if possible, construe a statute in a manner resulting in a constitutional outcome.

When the legislature enacted section 61.13(2)(d), Florida Statutes, in 1997, it provided, "No presumption shall arise in favor of or against a request to relocate when a primary residential parent seeks to move the child and the move will materially affect the current schedule of contact and access with the secondary residential parent." That provision effectively overruled the Florida Supreme Court's decisions in *Mize v. Mize*, 621 So 2d 417 (Fla. 1993), and *Russenberger v. Russenberger*, 669 So. 2d 1044 (Fla. 1996), which provided that when a primary residential parent is seeking in good faith to relocate, there is a rebuttable presumption in favor of the request to relocate. The Mother contends that this standard was one of constitutional dimension and that by removing the presumption in favor of relocation, the relocation statute "is a clear violation of numerous constitutionally protected rights." Specifically, the Mother raises the right to privacy, the right to travel, and equal protection.

Right to Privacy

The mother contends that the relocation statute violates a primary residential parent's right to privacy because it empowers the State to dictate where the primary residential parent may or may not live. Art. I, § 23, Fla. Const. (providing "the right to be let alone and free from governmental intrusion into the person's private life except as otherwise provided herein"). The argument regarding her fundamental right to privacy seems to be very similar to her argument regarding her fundamental right to travel because the privacy argument is based on her right to choose where she lives. Thus, the discussion on her right to travel will encompass her right to choose where she lives.

To the extent that the mother is arguing that she has a fundamental right as a parent to decide where her children live, she must recognize that the father shares the same fundamental right. * * *

* * * [H]ere, the Mother asserts her right to make childrearing decisions against the Father. The final judgment of dissolution of marriage provides that the parties have shared parental responsibility as to the children and that the Mother is the primary residential parent. As primary residential parent, the Mother does not make all childrearing decisions. Rather, section 61.046(15) defines "shared parental responsibility" as "a court-ordered relationship in which both parents retain full parental rights and responsibilities with respect to their child and in which both parents confer with each other so that major decisions affecting the welfare of the child will be determined jointly." It is obvious that what school a child attends and in what state a child lives are major decisions affecting the child's welfare.

Therefore, when the parties agree to shared parental responsibility in the marital settlement agreement and a court order provides for shared parental responsibility, we conclude that the Mother does not have a reasonable expectation of privacy to decide in what state her children live, with respect to the Father, although she would have a reasonable expectation of privacy as to a third party. Thus, in this particular circumstance, the Mother's right to privacy is not implicated.

Right to Travel

The Mother contends that the relocation statute violates her fundamental right to travel by requiring her to obtain court permission to relocate to another state. The United States Supreme Court has "long 'recognized that the nature of our Federal Union and our constitutional concepts of personal liberty unite to require that all citizens be free to travel throughout the length and breadth of our land uninhibited by statutes, rules, or regulations which unreasonably burden or restrict this movement.' " *Saenz v. Roe*, 526 U.S. 489, 499 (1999) (quoting *Shapiro v. Thompson*, 394 U.S. 618, 629 (1969).

Here, the relocation statute does not prevent the Mother from relocating to another state, but it does restrict her in moving with the parties' children to another state. In *Shapiro*, the Court recognized that "[i]f a law has 'no other purpose * * * than to chill the assertion of constitutional rights by penalizing those who choose to exercise them, then it (is) patently unconstitutional.' " 394 U.S. at 631 (quoting *United States v. Jackson*, 390 U.S. 570, 581 (1968)). In applying this concept to a relocation case, the New Mexico Supreme Court stated that "it makes no difference that the parent who wishes to relocate is not prohibited outright from doing so; a legal rule that operates to chill the exercise of the right, absent a sufficient state interest to do so, is as impermissible as one that bans exercise of the right altogether." *Jaramillo v. Jaramillo*, 823 P.2d 299, 306 (N.M. 1991) (citing *Shapiro*, 394 U.S. at 631). In *In re Marriage of Ciesluk*, 113 P.3d 135, 142 (Colo. 2005), the Colorado Supreme Court, citing *Jaramillo* and *Shapiro*, determined that although the Colorado statute at issue "does not prohibit outright a majority time parent from relocating, it chills the exercise of that parent's right to travel because, in seeking to relocate, that parent risks losing majority parent status with respect to the minor child."

The Colorado Supreme Court in *Ciesluk* discussed the competing interests involved in a relocation by the "majority time parent" and the different approaches courts have taken on the subject. There, an amendment to a Colorado statute replaced a case law "presumption in favor of the majority time parent with a liberal fact-driven analysis." *Id.* at 141. Like the present case, the mother in *Ciesluk* argued that by removing the presumption in favor of relocation, the amended statute "discourages her from relocating, and unconstitutionally infringes upon her right to travel." *Id.* at 142.

Ciesluk recognized, however, that it is not only the relocating parent's fundamental right to travel that is at stake. "In addition, a minority time parent has an equally important constitutional right to the care and control of the child." *Id.* (citing *Troxel v. Granville*, 530 U.S. 57, 65 (2000) (reiterating the fundamental liberty interest that parents have "in the care, custody, and control of their children")). Furthermore, intertwined with the parents' competing rights is the concern for the best interests of the child. *Ciesluk*, 113 P.3d at 142. "Thus, relocation disputes present courts with a unique challenge: to promote the best interest of the child while affording protection equally between a majority time parent's right to travel and a minority time parent's right to parent." *Id.*

The *Ciesluk* court considered and rejected the approach by the Wyoming Supreme Court in *Watt v. Watt*, 971 P.2d 608 (Wyo. 1999), that a custodial parent's right to travel and to relocate the children is not to be denied unless there is a substantial and material change in circumstances and unless detriment to the child can be shown. *Ciesluk*, 113 P.3d at 143.

We agree that this approach fails to take into consideration the other parent's fundamental right to parent, and the Florida relocation statute's fact-driven approach balances all interests, including the best interests of the child.

The *Ciesluk* court also considered and rejected the approach by the Minnesota court in *LaChapelle v. Mitten*, 607 N.W.2d 151 (Minn. Ct. App. 2000), which determined that the deprivation of the right to travel was justified by a compelling state interest: the best interests of the child. *Ciesluk*, 113 P.3d at 144–45. Although this approach has some appeal because the best interests of the child generally is a paramount concern, the Florida Supreme Court has held, albeit in a different context, that the best interests of the child is not a compelling state interest [in the context of a third party visitation dispute]. * * *

* * * Here, the Mother and the Father have competing rights. The Colorado court in *Ciesluk* placed much emphasis on these competing rights, along with the State's concern for the best interests of the child, and chose to adopt the New Mexico Supreme Court's approach in *Jaramillo*. 113 P.3d at 146.

The *Jaramillo* court determined that in a joint custody situation, a parent wishing to relocate should not be burdened by an adverse presumption. 823 P.2d at 305. It also determined that the resisting parent should not be burdened with a presumption in the relocating parent's favor, because the resisting parent has a fundamental liberty interest in parenting. *Id.* at 306. Instead, the court concluded that neither parent will have the burden to show that relocation of the child with the removing parent will be in or contrary to the child's best interests. Each party will have the burden to persuade the court that the new custody arrangement or parenting plan proposed by him or her should be adopted by the court, but that party's failure to carry this burden will only mean that the court remains free to adopt the arrangement or plan that it determines best promotes the child's interests. *Id.* at 309.

The *Ciesluk* court determined that in applying the Colorado statute, a court is not to make a presumption in favor of or against relocation and that neither party has a burden of proof. Rather, " 'both parents share equally the burden of demonstrating how the child's best interest will be served.' " 113 P.3d at 147 (quoting *Jaramillo*, 823 P.2d at 308). The court has the duty to consider and make findings on the twenty-one factors set out in the Colorado statute, with the focus on the child's best interests. *Id.* at 147–48. Therefore, the Colorado court balanced the two competing fundamental rights, along with the child's best interests, and determined that if neither party had a presumption or burden of proof, the rights were appropriately balanced and the child's interests taken into account.

Here, the Florida relocation statute expressly states that there is no presumption in favor of or against relocation. Because the Father's constitutional rights must also be considered, we reject the Mother's argument that the lack of a presumption in favor of the Mother is unconstitutional. Further, section 61.13(2)(d) is silent as to the burden of proof.

When a primary residential parent seeks to relocate a child, section 61.13(2)(d) requires the court to consider all the statutory factors without any presumptions in favor of either party. The factors address, among other things, the relocating parent's quality of life, the other parent's ability to maintain a meaningful relationship with the child, and the child's best interests. Thus, the relocation statute requires the court to consider the competing interests, with an appropriate focus on the parents' rights, along with the best interest of the child. Therefore, the statute does not violate the Mother's right to travel.

Equal Protection

The Mother contends that the relocation statute violates the Equal Protection Clause of the Fourteenth Amendment to the Constitution because it discriminates against primary residential parents. She argues that primary residential parents must obtain permission to relocate, while secondary residential parents need not obtain permission to relocate from the area where their child resides. The Mother cites no equal protection cases in her argument.

An equal protection analysis is appropriate only if similarly situated individuals are treated differently. "Equal protection is not violated merely because some persons are treated differently than other persons. It only requires that persons similarly situated be treated similarly." *Troy v. State*, 948 So. 2d 635, 645 (Fla. 2006) (quoting *Duncan v. Moore*, 754 So. 2d 708, 712 (Fla. 2000)). In a challenge to a Nevada relocation statute on equal protection grounds, the Nevada Supreme Court recognized that custodial and noncustodial parents are not similarly situated. *Reel v. Harrison*, 60 P.3d 480, 483 (Nev. 2002). The court explained that if the noncustodial parent did not consent to the move, the Nevada statute required the custodial parent to obtain court permission to move with the child. The Nevada Supreme Court * * * noted the statute's purpose was " 'to preserve the rights and familial relationship of the noncustodial parent with respect to his or her child.' " *Reel*, 60 P.3d at 483 (footnote omitted).

Here, the Mother, as the primary residential parent, must obtain permission to relocate with the children because relocation would affect the secondary residential parent's fundamental right to parent and would limit the Father's access to the children. However, if the Father chooses to relocate out of state, it does not deny the Mother access to her children. Thus, to the extent that a primary residential parent must seek court permission to relocate, the parties are not similarly situated; thus, the statute does not violate the Equal Protection Clause. Therefore, we conclude that the statute is constitutional on its face.

II. DENIAL OF REQUEST TO RELOCATE

The Mother contends that, in applying section 61.13(2)(d), the trial court abused its discretion in denying her relocation request on remand following the earlier appeal. The standard of review regarding a trial court's order on relocation is abuse of discretion. * * * Here, the record reflects competent, substantial evidence to support the trial court's findings, and we cannot say that the trial court abused its discretion in denying the Mother's request to relocate to Texas.

In this court's prior opinion in *Fredman v. Fredman*, 917 So. 2d 1038, 1041 (Fla. 2d DCA 2006), we reversed and remanded for the trial court to again consider the mother's proposed relocation under section 61.13(2)(d), with directions to use the proper standard as stated in section 61.13(2)(d)(4): "Whether the substitute visitation will be adequate to foster a continuing meaningful relationship between the child and the secondary residential parent."

In its new [March 2006] order, * * * the trial court found that the Mother's proposed substitute visitation schedule "would be adequate to foster a continuing, meaningful relationship between the children and the Father." The trial court adopted the findings in its previous order rendered December 10, 2004 * * *. Although the court found that the substitute visitation would be adequate, the trial court again denied the relocation request. After considering the statutory factors discussed in the 2004 order and the visitation factor that it reconsidered under the proper standard, the court concluded that relocation would not be in the best interest of the children, even though it may be in the best interest of the Former Wife and her new husband. The Court finds that the proposed relocation does not benefit the children inasmuch as there has not been a showing that the proposed relocation would improve the children's school, family or even home life.

In its findings, the court recognized that the family would live in a 3000-square-foot home in Texas and that the Mother currently lives in a two-bedroom apartment in Hillsborough County. On cross-examination, however, the Mother admitted that one could find a house in Hillsborough County, Florida, at a cost comparable to the cost of the home in Ponder. The Father also testified that there were homes available in his community in Brandon at a cost comparable to Mr. Melton's home in Ponder.

With respect to schooling, the court found that although the Mother contended that the children would be in a better school in Texas, the Father testified that comparable public schools are available in Hillsborough and that the children were doing well in their present school. The Mother had testified to all the facilities that the children's small private school in Brandon did not have, but she admitted on cross-examination that good public schools were available in Hillsborough County.

With respect to family life, the court recognized both parents' involvement with the children's sport activities. However, the court emphasized that the Father is actively involved with the children and that he and the children share a "passion for bowling." The court also recognized that the children have frequent contact with the Father's relatives in Hillsborough County, including the Father's mother, grandmother, uncles, aunts, and cousins. The Mother has no family in Texas, and the court noted that Mr. Melton's extended family does not reside in Ponder, Texas. In fact, it appears that the children know no one in Ponder other than their stepfather and stepbrother. This is in stark contrast to the excellent relationship that the children have with the Father's family in Hillsborough County.

The trial court recognized that the move would improve the home life for the Mother and her new husband. * * * However, the Father presented * * * evidence reflecting that the children's best interests would be served by allowing them to remain in Hillsborough County. Based on this record, we cannot say that the trial court abused its discretion in denying the Mother's request to relocate with the children to Texas.

Affirmed.

WHATLEY and KELLY, JJ., Concur.

NOTES AND QUESTIONS

1. *The constitutional right to interstate travel.* In 2008, the Supreme Court of Indiana addressed the constitutional right to interstate travel in the context of relocation cases and, like *Fredman* earlier, endorsed the approach of the Colorado court in *Ciesluk. Baxendale* v. *Raich*, 878 N.E.2d 1252 (Ind. 2008) (surveying opinions of other state supreme courts). The Indiana court stated that while chilling the right to interstate travel "can violate the federal Constitution, * * * other considerations may outweigh an individual's interest in travel. We think it clear that the child's interests are powerful countervailing considerations that cannot be swept aside as irrelevant * * *. In addition, * * * the nonrelocating parent's interest in parenting is itself of constitutional dimension." *Id.* at 1259.

2. *Burdens of proof.* Several jurisdictions employ burden-of-proof rules or rebuttable presumptions highly favorable to a primary residential parent who wishes to relocate. *See, e.g.*, Wis. Stat. Ann. § 767.481(3)(a)(2)(a) (West 2007 & Supp. 2008) (creating a rebuttable presumption that it is in the child's best interests to continue living with the parent with whom the child primarily resides); *Kaiser v. Kaiser*, 23 P.3d 278, 282 (Okla. 2001) ("in the absence of a showing of prejudice to the rights or welfare of a child, a custodial parent has a statutory presumptive right to change their child's residence"). The statute *Fredman* reviewed did not address the burden of proof, but the statute discussed in footnote 1 of the opinion, effective in October 2006, did. The 2006 statute provided that if one parent objects to relocation, the custodial parent who wishes to relocate bears the initial burden "to prove by a preponderance of the evidence that relocation is in the best interest of the child." If that burden is met, "the burden shifts to the nonrelocating parent * * * to show by a preponderance of the evidence that the proposed relocation is not in the best interest of the child." Fla. Stat.§ 61.13001(8) (2006).

3. *What happens to the Fredmans?* Is the mother free to join Mr. Melton in Texas? Under what conditions? Do you think the outcome in this case is

"fair" to the mother? The father? The children? Would any resolution be "fair" to all three? As a public policy matter, how much difference should it make to the outcome of a relocation case whether the parents share joint legal custody? Joint physical custody or serious involvement of the non-custodial parent in the children's lives? How do Professor Glennon's observations, and the concerns about joint custody you were exposed to in Chapter 12 (particularly the excerpts from Professors Singer and Reynolds) affect your understanding of what happened in *Fredman*? What are the strongest counter-arguments to the views of those scholars?

4. *Bad faith.* The ALI and most courts refer to moves undertaken in good faith. If a court suspects that the move is motivated wholly or partly by desire to frustrate the other parents' access to the child, the court will normally refuse to allow the move, either by barring the move, or by modifying custody if the current custodian moves. *See, e.g., In re Marriage of LaMusga,* 88 P.3d 81 (Cal. 2004).

5. *Should the non-custodial parent have unrestricted freedom to relocate?* Limitations on mobility apply only to custodial parents. What argument could be made that it is in the child's best interest for a parent with visitation rights to remain nearby? Would a policy that required parents to remain near each other during a child's minority have an impact on diminution of many relationships between children and non-custodial parents discussed in Chapter 11, child support? Professor Merle H. Weiner argues that proposed relocation by non-custodial parents should be subject to trial court review, as it currently is in only a handful of jurisdictions. Merle H. Weiner, *Inertia and Inequality: Reconceptualizing Disputes Over Parental Relocation,* 40 U.C. Davis L. Rev. 1747 (2007). If either parent relocates far away, who should bear the increased costs of visitation, such as airfare?

6. *Are settlement agreements restricting relocation enforceable?* As part of their 1997 divorce, the parties in *Helton v. Helton,* 2004 WL 63478 (Tenn. Ct. App. Jan. 13, 2004) (unpublished opinion) executed a marital dissolution agreement that contained the wife's promise "not to move the child from Davidson or adjoining counties without husband's written permission." According to the agreement, the wife also acknowledged that "it [was] in the manifest best interest of [the child] that he remain and be raised in Metro–Davidson County or contiguous counties near his father." *Id.* The mother later remarried, and her new husband accepted a job offer in Mississippi. In 2001, the mother informed the father that she intended to relocate to Mississippi with the child to join her husband. Citing the marital dissolution agreement, the father moved to prevent relocation of the child. The court held that the father was not entitled to rely on the marital dissolution agreement:

> A provision in a divorce decree for the care, custody and control of minor children 'shall remain within the control of the court and be subject to such changes or modifications as the exigencies of the case may require.' Tenn. Code Ann. § 36–6–101(a). Our courts have accordingly held that when a marital dissolution agreement with regard to custody is incorporated into a final decree, it is considered to have merged into that decree. Such agreements thereby lose their contractual nature and remain subject to the court's continuing jurisdiction, so that they may be modified as

circumstances change. The parties cannot bargain away the court's continuing jurisdiction over the care of the child and cannot irrevocably agree to the best interests of the child without regard to future developments or changes of circumstances.

Id. at *5.

7. *Court-imposed restrictions on relocation at the time of the initial custody decree.* In *Spahmer v. Gullette*, 113 P.3d 158 (Colo. 2005), the court held that the trial court abused its discretion when it ordered the single mother of an 11–month–old girl, Jordan, to remain in the home state of the child's father as part of the initial allocation of parental rights. *Id.* at 159–60. The parties' relationship lasted 13 months, ending just after Jordan was born. Shortly after their breakup, the father gave the mother permission to spend Christmas with Jordan and the mother's family in Arizona. He subsequently became concerned that the mother was planning to remove Jordan from Colorado permanently, and he filed an action to allocate parental rights and responsibilities. Because the trial court's temporary orders provided that the mother must have the permission of either the father or the court to remove Jordan from Colorado, the mother moved for permission to relocate permanently with Jordan to Arizona. In its subsequent orders allocating parental responsibilities, the trial court ordered the mother to remain in the Denver–Boulder metropolitan area because "Jordan was born here and has spent the entire eleven months of her life to date here. Jordan is to remain a Colorado girl." *Id.* at 160.

Finding on appeal that the trial court had abused its discretion, the state supreme court concluded that "in an initial determination to allocate parental responsibilities, a court has no statutory authority to order a parent to live in a specific location. Rather, the court must accept the location in which each party intends to live, and allocate parental responsibilities accordingly in the best interests of the child." *Id.* at 161.

C. INTERNATIONAL RELOCATION

In *Condon v. Cooper*, 73 Cal.Rptr.2d 33, 46 (Ct. App. 1998), the court upheld the trial court's discretion to permit the mother to relocate with her two sons to Australia, with the father having physical custody of the children in California for 12 weeks each year (corresponding to the Australian school vacation calendar), and in Australia for up to 15 days per month. The court of appeal ordered the trial court to amend its order permitting relocation to include the mother's stipulation to the continuing jurisdiction of California courts and appropriate sanctions to enforce that stipulation.

Condon discussed three problems unique to international relocation cases:

First, the cultural problem. In some cases, to move a child from this country to another is to subject him or her to cultural conditions and practices far different from those experienced by American citizens or to deprive the child of important protections and advantages not available in the other country. To pose an extreme example, who could dispute a proposed relocation of a female child to a country practicing genital mutilation represents a "changed condition" requiring an inquiry whether this move is in the "best interests" of that child? Similarly, how about a move to a country where females were not offered the opportunity for higher education or the freedom to pursue careers? Or a move of any preteen or teenager to a country where the language is one unfamiliar to that child. Or, consider a proposed relocation of any child to a nation governed by a dictator or any nation which denies its citizens the freedoms and rights guaranteed in the United States and other democracies.

Second, the distance problem. Except for Mexico or Canada, foreign relocation cases in this state inevitably involve a move to a different continent—typically 8,000 miles or further and 8 or more time zones away from California. With those great distances come problems of expense, jet lag, and the like. For a person of average income or below, an order relocating his or her child to a faraway foreign country is ordinarily tantamount to an order terminating that parent's custody and visitation rights.

Third, and most difficult, is the jurisdictional problem. California court orders governing child custody lack any enforceability in many foreign jurisdictions and lack guaranteed enforceability even in those which subscribe to the Hague Convention on the Civil Aspects of International Child Abduction. Thus, the California courts cannot guarantee any custody and visitation arrangements they order for the non-moving parent will be honored.

* * *

Id. at 42.

The court proceeded to explain these three problems in practical terms:

[E]xcept for those of considerable means, any relocation to another continent is likely to represent a *de facto* termination of the non-moving parent's rights to visitation and the child's rights to maintain a relationship with that parent. Thus, when a relocation would have this practical effect, before allowing the move-away a trial court should require the moving parent to satisfy the burden of showing the termination of those rights would be in the best interests of the child. If the moving parent cannot satisfy this burden, perhaps he or she could tender an arrangement where the moving parent finances the other parent's visitation or the child spends alternate years in the two countries, or some other plan which accommodates the valuable relationship between the non-moving parent and the child.

Finally, before permitting any relocation which purports to maintain custody and visitation rights in the non-moving parent, the trial court should take steps to insure its orders to that effect will remain enforceable throughout the minority of the affected children. Unless the law of the country where the children are to move guarantees enforceability of custody and visitation orders issued by American courts, and there may be no such country, the court will be required to use its ingenuity to ensure the moving parent adheres to its orders and does not seek to invalidate or modify them in a foreign court.

Id. at 43.

SECTION 4: PARENTS WHO KIDNAP THEIR OWN CHILDREN

When high conflict over custody and visitation persists, some parents take matters into their own hands by absconding with the children.

A. HOW WIDESPREAD A PROBLEM IS KIDNAPPING OF CHILDREN BY THEIR PARENTS?

Precise figures are unavailable because data are not uniformly collected throughout the United States, but emerging data indicate that of the roughly 797,500 children reported missing in 1999, the largest number were runaways; the next largest group were children abducted by parents or relatives, usually in the context of a custody dispute. J. Robert Flores, U.S. Dep't of Justice, Publ'n No. NCJ 196465, National Estimates of Missing Children: An Overview 6 (2002), *available at* http://www. missingkids.com/ en_US/documents/nismart2_overview.pdf. Abduction of children by their parents is illegal in every U.S. jurisdiction, even where statutes are silent about whether kidnapping laws apply to parents. Some authors estimate that as many as one in five parental kidnappings involve crossing an international border, either to return to the parent's native country or to avoid detection. Susan Kreston, *Prosecuting International Parental Kidnapping*, 15 Notre Dame J.L. Ethics & Pub. Pol'y 533, 534 (2001) (citing Rebecca Hegar, *Parental Kidnapping Across International Borders*, 34 Int'l Soc. Work 353 (1991)). You will learn more about federal laws aimed at parental abductions in Chapter 16.

B. CASE NOTE: *STATE OF NEW JERSEY v. FROLAND*

The scheme with which the state charged the defendants in *New Jersey v. Froland*, 874 A.2d 568 (N.J. Super. Ct. App. Div. 2005), *aff'd in part, rev'd in part*, 936 A. 2d 947 (N.J. 2008), was elaborate. John Kindt and his former wife shared legal custody of their two children, ages nine and ten. Pursuant to the parenting agreement, the mother dropped the children off at their father's house on December 27, 2000, with an understanding that he would return the children to her at a doctor's appointment two days later. Due to a snowstorm, they agreed to delay the children's return until noon on the next day, Saturday, December 30. When the mother called the father's home on Friday at about 6 P.M., she discovered that the phone had been disconnected; checking up, she found the house deserted. The mother filed a missing persons report with the police.

When the police searched the father's home they discovered three computers with their hard drives stripped, and express delivery receipts for correspondence with New Jersey and North Carolina boat sales establishments and with an express passport preparation service. Further investigation revealed that during December, the father and stepmother, Stacey Froland Kindt, using an alias, had purchased a boat. The Kindts had also obtained copies of the birth certificates and medical records for three children (the father's two children and the stepmother's 19–year–old nephew who lived with them). They obtained passports for all five stating that they intended to visit New Zealand. The father and stepmother also wrote to their respective parents, explaining that they were taking the children and "intended to flee to a jurisdiction friendly to their position—that Kindt, as the children's father, should have more say in their upbringing." 874 A.2d at 572–73. The stepmother withdrew over $50,000 from a bank account.

On Friday, December 29, Kindt and his wife abandoned the family minivan at Newark airport to throw the police off-track. The family then took an Amtrak train from Newark, New Jersey to North Carolina. Kindt cancelled the boat contract in New Jersey and purchased a 39–foot boat in North Carolina, again using a pseudonym. On January 20, 2001, the group set sail from North Carolina. As luck would have it, the Coast Guard picked them up when their boat became disabled. The police arrested Kindt, Froland–Kindt, and her teenage nephew who had been helping them.

The police search of the boat uncovered a to-do list for the abduction, a global positioning system and charts for North Carolina, Florida and the Bahamas, and several books including "Hide Your Assets and Disappear" and "How to be Invisible." A letter from the stepmother to her mother set up a "safe" messaging system through Yahoo! and explained, "[we] believe very strongly (and the Bible supports us) that the father is the head of the household. He is held personally accountable to God for how his children turn out and is therefore responsible for all instruction, reproof, guidance, and discipline." 874 A.2d at 573–74.

The state charged Kindt, Froland, and Froland's nephew with various counts of kidnapping, interference with custody, and conspiracy and contempt of court. At trial, Kindt argued that he could not be convicted of kidnapping his own children. Following an interlocutory appeal, the jury convicted him of all counts except kidnapping. The court sentenced him to seven years in custody, and confined him to a halfway house pending appeal. Froland, however, was found guilty of first degree kidnapping as well as several other charges. She served sixteen months of a seven-year sentence while her appeal was pending. On appeal she argued that the plain language of the New Jersey statute indicated that a parent cannot be found guilty of kidnapping his own children, and that "she in turn cannot be guilty of kidnapping because she acted with a parent's permission." 936 A.2d at 951. The Supreme Court of New Jersey agreed.

The New Jersey kidnapping statute provides that the removal of a minor without the consent of a parent, or with the use of "force, threat or deception" is unlawful. The state did not present evidence that Kindt and Froland used "force, threat or deception," although it could have, and probably should have, done so. This left the question of parental consent. The court reasoned that if the legislature had intended to limit the term "parent" to parents with sole custody in the context of the kidnapping statute, it could and should have done so expressly. Applying the rule of lenity to the criminal kidnapping statute, the court nonetheless found that Froland was not "immune from punishment" as her "behavior falls squarely within the strictures of the interference with custody statute." *Id.* at 953.

The New Jersey Supreme Court chastised the Appellate Division for treating "kidnapping and interference with custody as overlapping criminal provisions" when "in fact, the statutes were * * * designed to address entirely distinct conduct." *Id.* at 954. The court found that New Jersey intended to follow the approach of the ALI's Model Penal Code, which sought to limit kidnapping charges against parents to situations involving "force, threat or deception." The drafters expressly "posited the irrelevancy of custody arrangements" since the use of force, threat or deception rendered a non-custodial parent vulnerable to kidnapping charges, while enactment of a statute criminalizing interference with custody would cover the remaining ground and protect "the rights of 'the child's other parent.' " *Id.* at 955. Moreover, the court pointed out that the interference with custody statute carries serious penalties, and contemplates imprisonment for a first offense. *Id.*

NOTES AND QUESTIONS

1. *What is the difference between kidnapping and* **civil** *interference with parental custody?* Kidnapping is a criminal offense, prosecuted by the state. As you saw in the discussion of *Froland*, the Model Penal Code endorses criminalizing interference with custody, but it is important to distinguish such criminal statutes from civil actions with the same title. Intentional interference with a custodial relationship was a common law tort, pursued as a civil action to compensate the parent who was wrongfully deprived of his or her custodial relationship with the child. The tort originated in English common law, and the ALI has included the cause of action since the first Restatement of Torts (1938). *See* Restatement (Second) of Torts § 700 (1977). Succinctly stated, the "elements of the cause of action include that the plaintiff had superior custody rights to the child and that the defendant

intentionally interfered with those rights." *Stone v. Wall*, 734 So.2d 1038, 1042 (Fla. 1999). The tort embraces inducements and offers of shelter to adolescents who run away, as well as actions that constitute or resemble kidnapping. The remedy may include reimbursement for the costs of locating and pursuing the child as well as punitive damages.

The clear majority of the courts that have considered the question—courts in at least 16 states and the District of Columbia—have recognized claims for the tort of intentional interference with a custodial relationship. The highest courts of three states, however, have expressly declined to recognize the tort. *Hoblyn v. Johnson*, 55 P.3d 1219, 1225 (Wyo. 2002); *Zaharias v. Gammill*, 844 P.2d 137, 140 (Okla. 1992); *Larson v. Dunn*, 460 N.W.2d 39, 46 (Minn. 1990).

In *Wolf v. Wolf*, 690 N.W.2d 887 (Iowa 2005), the court reaffirmed that the tort remains viable in Iowa. The facts involved what the court termed "a bitter tug of war in Arizona and Iowa courts over the physical custody of Ashley," *id.* at 890, who was 20 years old by the time the Supreme Court of Iowa heard the case. In 1990, Iowa issued the divorce decree, awarding sole legal and primary physical custody to the mother. By 1999, the parents had joint legal custody, and the father had won physical custody in Iowa's intermediate appellate court. By that time, however, the mother had removed Ashley from the jurisdiction. The father obtained a writ of *habeas corpus* in Iowa and went to Arizona to retrieve the child. After Ashley had been at her father's home for a few months, her mother sent her an airline ticket, a credit card and a cell phone. Ashley, then age 15, used these to leave her father and join her mother in Arizona. Mother petitioned for custody in Arizona, but the court ruled that Iowa retained jurisdiction. Ashley and her mother subsequently returned to Iowa to seek modification of custody, but left again during the proceedings in express violation of the court's interim order that they remain in Iowa. The court held that the uncontroverted evidence presented by the father was "substantial and supports the court's finding that [mother] induced Ashley to avoid returning to Iowa." The court expressly rejected the mother's argument that "she was only acting as a good mother by providing Ashley with a protective environment," finding instead that her "affirmative acts * * * demonstrated willful and wanton conduct." *Id* at 892.

Affirmative defenses to the tort have traditionally been available. These include the defendant's reasonable, good faith belief that removing the child was proper, and that the defendant acted to prevent physical harm to the child. *See, e.g., Brown v. Brown*, 800 So.2d 359 (Fla. Dist. Ct. App. 2001) (the defendants, the child's stepmother and aunt, may argue the affirmative defenses where they sheltered a boy who ran away from a residential treatment facility in which his mother had placed him, after the boy told the defendants that the institution drugged him and kept him locked up, and that if forced to return he would run away to live on the streets).

2. *What punishment is appropriate for kidnapping by parents?* Criminal sanctions are generally disfavored in cases involving parental kidnapping. It is widely believed that if authorities find the parent but not the kidnapped child, charging the parent with a crime decreases the likelihood of locating the child. In addition, most criminal penalties are ineffective in compensating the

custodial parent. *See* Richard A. Campbell, *Transition: The Tort of Custodial Interference–Toward a More Complete Remedy to Parental Kidnapping*, 1983 U. Ill. L. Rev. 229, 240 (1983).

Do you think that the New Jersey justice system was correct in sending both Kindt and Froland to jail? Do you agree or disagree with the court's reading of the kidnapping statute as applied to a father and stepmother?

3. *Does it matter how long the child has been with the kidnapper?* Some non-custodial parents may kidnap their children with the hope that after many years, courts would allow them to continue as the custodial parent because the children have been with them for so long. Since preserving continuity in such cases would only encourage child abductions, the social policy of discouraging abductions normally trumps the best-interests emphasis on continuity of care.

A Note on the Hague Convention

The United States ratified the Hague Convention on the Civil Aspects of International Child Abduction and became a signatory state on April 29, 1988; on the same day, Congress enacted the International Child Abduction Remedies Act, 42 U.S.C. §§ 11601–11610 (2002), which implements the Convention in the United States. Sixty-eight of the signatories to the Convention have mutual agreements with the United States as of 2008, but other countries may subscribe to the Convention without an "entry into force" with the U.S. The Hague Convention, as it is known, is intended to discourage international abduction of children age 16 or younger by securing "the prompt return of children wrongfully removed to or retained in any Contracting State." Hague Convention on the Civil Aspects of International Child Abduction art. 1, Oct. 25, 1980, T.I.A.S. No. 11,670, 1343 U.N.T.S. 89.

The State Department administers both "outgoing" and "incoming" cases under the Convention. With respect to the outgoing cases, involving children whose habitual residence is the United States, the State Department helps the custodial parent or guardian to locate the child and to prepare the application for return. The incoming cases involve children wrongfully brought to the United States from a foreign signatory country. As of April 1, 2008, the State Department offers assistance in locating the child and in attempting to secure voluntary return of the child. Efforts to secure return of incoming children were previously delegated to a non-governmental organization, the National Center for Missing and Exploited Children.

Under the Convention, a child is wrongfully removed when removal violates the "custody rights" of another adult under the laws of the country in which the child "habitually resides." Hague Convention, *supra*, at art. IV, V. The Convention expressly prohibits courts hearing petitions for return from examining the underlying merits of the custody case, or from considering the child's best interests, but a court must interpret the meaning of both "habitual residence" and "custody rights." *Id.* at art. XVI; Linda Silberman, *Interpreting the Hague Abduction Convention: In Search of A Global Jurisprudence*, 38 U.C. Davis L. Rev. 1049, 1055–63 (2005). The Convention does not define "habitual residence," which is not necessarily the same as the child's "home state"—a concept used by courts in the United States to determine jurisdiction in various matters related to custody and support (discussed *infra* in Chapter 16).

"Home state" emphasizes the child's physical presence for the six months before removal. Federal appellate decisions are not entirely uniform in their definitions, but the concept of "habitual residence" involves a combination of physical presence and the parents' shared intent as demonstrated by both statements and actions. *See, e.g., Gitter v. Gitter*, 396 F.3d 124, 134 (2d Cir. 2005). Courts also examine whether the child has become acclimated to the new residence. *Id.* at 133. Because of the importance of acclimation, the Convention requires that petitions for return normally be filed within a year of removal. *Id.* at 136. One of the few available defenses to a petition for return is a mature child's consent to removal. Hague Convention, Art. XIII. However, the decision rests in the trial court's discretion, and the child has no right to testify or to have the court credit his or her views. *Kufner* v. *Kufner*, 519 F.3d 33, 40 (1st Cir. 2008). A second defense arises where the petition seeks return of a child to a country that does not observe fundamental freedoms. Silberman, *supra* at 1055.

Denying access to parents who have a right to visitation but no custodial rights is not considered a violation of custodial rights under the Hague Convention. *Croll v. Croll*, 229 F.3d 133, 137–38 (2d Cir. 2000); *In re Vernor*, 94 S.W.3d 201, 208 (Tex. Ct. App. 2002); *Wiggill v. Janicki*, 262 F. Supp.2d 687, 689–90 (S.D. W. Va. 2003). Should it be?

What happens if a parent removes a child from the home state before a custody order has issued? In *Carrascosa* v. *McGuire*, 520 F.3d 249 (3d Cir.), *cert. denied*, 129 S.Ct. 491 (2008) the parents executed an interim parenting agreement while their divorce was pending. The agreement specified that neither parent could remove their daughter, Victoria, from the United States without the other parent's signed consent. In violation of the agreement, the mother took Victoria to Spain and sought and received a divorce there. A federal warrant was issued for the mother's arrest and, when she returned to the U.S. without Victoria, she was jailed for contempt of court. The mother had already remained in jail for two years when the Third Circuit rejected her petition for *habeas corpus*. Victoria had not seen either parent for several years when the matter reached the Court of Appeals. The court concluded that under the law of the child's home state, New Jersey, both parents had equal custody rights until their parental rights were adjudicated in divorce proceedings. The court reasoned that "the Hague Convention is designed to put all participants in a custody dispute back into the positions they would have been in but for one parent's wrongful removal of the child." *Id.* at 260. This requires Victoria's return to New Jersey, whose courts alone can resolve the original custody dispute. Should Victoria be returned to New Jersey, it is likely that the state court will take the mother's initial violation and her continuing contempt of court into consideration when it crafts its custody decree.

CHAPTER 14

PRIVATIZING THE RAMIFICATIONS
OF MARRIAGE AND DIVORCE

■ ■ ■

Previous chapters have shown how the law governs family formation and dissolution. We have considered how law regulates access to dissolution by defining grounds for divorce. And we have seen how law dictates the many consequences that may flow from dissolution, including property distribution, spousal maintenance, child support, custody and visitation. Yet, only a tiny fraction of divorces are actually resolved by courts directly applying these legal rules after litigation.

Ultimately, approximately 90 percent of divorces are uncontested, but many of these begin as contentious proceedings. The outcome of most divorces is controlled directly by some agreement of the parties. The parties may enter into an agreement before the marriage (referred to as a premarital, prenuptial, or antenuptial agreement); after the marriage but before a marital breakdown (known as a postmarital, postnuptial or mid-marriage agreement); or, most frequent, later when the parties are separating or otherwise contemplating divorce (commonly referred to as a separation agreement).

The starting point for deciding financial or other matters in most divorces, then, is not direct judicial application of a statute, but execution of the parties' contract. This circumstance does not mean, of course, that the legal rules applied in court are insignificant: statutes and case law continue to influence private bargains by shaping the parties' expectations of how they might fare if they fail to reach agreement and end up in court. *See* Robert H. Mnookin & Lewis Kornhauser, *Bargaining in the Shadow of the Law: The Case of Divorce*, 88 Yale L.J. 950 (1979), which appears as a main entry in Chapter 15. But "private ordering" is now a central feature of family law practice.

The prominent role of private bargaining in divorce represents a recent and significant development in family law. Historically, as the following section explains, courts categorically refused to enforce agreements that contemplated the possibility of divorce. Courts reasoned that by removing uncertainty about the consequences of divorce, enforcement would violate public policy favoring marriage. Today, the hope of staving off divorce by banning effective planning for its consequences strikes most judges as wrong-headed, and the law in almost all states not only permits but affirmatively *encourages* private settlement in divorce. Indeed, agreed terms concerning alimony or property distribution are now presumptively "binding" on the courts in most jurisdictions; private bargaining over child support, custody and visitation is subject to greater scrutiny.

Notwithstanding broad agreement about the permissibility of divorce-related bargaining, significant controversies remain about the extent to which courts should defer to private agreements. As the succeeding sections show, state laws continue to vary significantly concerning the procedural requirements for negotiating an enforceable agreement, the terms over which parties may bargain, and the extent to which courts will police the agreement's substantive and procedural fairness. Moreover, although law has trended strongly and unmistakably toward permitting greater private ordering in marriage and divorce, scholars and judges recently have voiced reservations about the wisdom of embracing ordinary contract principles in family law. In this sense, debate over public policy limitations on contractual freedom in family formation and dissolution has been redirected, but remains very much alive.

This Chapter considers the movement toward greater contractual freedom in family law by reviewing the courts' treatment of agreements negotiated at different stages of adult relationships: before marriage, during marriage, and at the time of divorce. As you read these materials, consider whether courts should treat these agreements just as any other contract, or whether the parties' intimate relationship creates interpersonal dynamics that justify distinct rules of judicial review and enforcement.

SECTION 1: MARRIAGE—CONTRACT OR STATUS?

A. HISTORICAL PERSPECTIVE

Marriage has always occupied a middle ground between contract and status. Since the 1970s, the conception of marriage has moved unmistakably and dramatically toward contract. "Voluntary changes concerning the marriage have transformed words of intimacy like love, to the language of commerce * * * and self-interest. Spouses became parties, participation became contribution, and divorce became dissolution." Sanford N. Katz, Family Law in America 37 (2003).

Originally, marriage law provided little room for contractual modification by the parties. In 1888, the Supreme Court described marriage as largely a take-it-or-leave-it proposition. In explaining why a divorce granted over a wife's objection did not constitute a governmental impairment of contract in violation of the Contract Clause of the federal Constitution, Justice Stephen J. Field wrote:

> [W]hilst marriage is often termed by text writers and in decisions of courts as a civil contract, generally to indicate that it must be founded

upon the agreement of the parties, and does not require any religious ceremony for its solemnization, it is something more than a mere contract. The consent of the parties is of course essential to its existence, but when the contract to marry is executed by the marriage, a relation between the parties is created which they cannot change. Other contracts may be modified, restricted, or enlarged, or entirely released upon the consent of the parties. Not so with marriage. The relation once formed, the law steps in and holds the parties to various obligations and liabilities.

Maynard v. Hill, 125 U.S. 190, 210–11 (1888). To the Court, the reason for the state's tight control over the essential content of marital status was obvious: Marriage is "an institution, in the maintenance of which in its purity the public is deeply interested, for it is the foundation of the family and of society, without which there would be neither civilization nor progress." *Id.* at 211.

Historically, public control of the marriage relationship played a basic role in establishing bedrock values concerning citizenship and democracy, gender roles, sexual relations, and even racial identity:

> Political and legal authorities endorsed and aimed to perpetuate nationally a *particular* marriage model: lifelong, faithful monogamy, formed by the mutual consent of a man and a woman, bearing the impress of the Christian religion and the English common law in its expectations for the husband to be the family head and economic provider, his wife the dependent partner.

Nancy F. Cott, Public Vows: A History of Marriage and the Nation 3 (2000) (emphasis in original).

Until recent decades, the common law thus tolerated relatively little deviation from the "standard form" marriage. Couples could make enforceable agreements concerning disposition of their property upon the death of either party, but contracts that purported to dictate the parties' rights upon divorce were generally held void *ab initio* as contrary to public policy. *See, e.g., French v. McAnarney*, 195 N.E. 714, 715 (Mass. 1935) (antenuptial agreement waiving alimony upon divorce is absolutely void; "[a] marriage cannot be avoided or the obligations imposed by law as incident to the relation of husband and wife be relaxed by previous agreement between the parties"). Courts saw little danger that waiver of a wife's elective share to her husband's estate would somehow hasten marital dissolution through death; a waiver of alimony, by contrast, might well remove a crucial deterrent to divorce and, in any event, flew in the face of what courts described as the husband's essential and non-negotiable duty to support his wife. *See, e.g., Williams v. Williams*, 243 P. 402 (Ariz. 1926); *French*, 195 N.E. at 715–16.

In the 1960s and 1970s, traditional concerns about "facilitating divorce" began to seem antiquated amid the expansion of the privacy doctrine in marital and family matters (recounted in Chapter 1), the introduction of no-fault divorce, and the growing incidence of divorce generally. As privatization of marriage grew throughout the 1970s and 1980s, state courts moved steadily toward less state regulation of divorce as they began to enforce marital dissolution agreements.

Private ordering is certain to remain a substantial feature of contemporary marriage and divorce, but just how far the law should go in embracing contractual freedom remains a matter of lively debate among judges, legislators and scholars. *See* Howard Fink & June Carbone, *Between Private Ordering and Public Fiat: A New Paradigm for Family Law Decision–Making,* 5 J. L. & Fam. Stud. 1 (2003); Jeffrey Evans Stake *et al., Roundtable: Opportunities for and Limitations of Private Ordering in Family Law,* 73 Ind. L.J. 535 (1998).

B.   THREE FORMS OF AGREEMENTS AFFECTING MARRIAGES

Three basic types of contractual agreements affect marital rights and obligations: premarital agreements executed by prospective spouses; postnuptial agreements by existing spouses who are not currently contemplating divorce; and separation agreements, negotiated in contemplation of agreed-upon marital separation or dissolution, or incident to divorce litigation.

These agreements seek to reduce the chance and cost of potential litigation by defining a couple's property and non-property rights, by clarifying the intended allocation of marital assets, and by planning for property distribution at the death of a spouse or of the marriage. These agreements also often seek to avoid or alter the effect of statutory marital property and spousal support laws. These agreements, however, cannot bind the court on the child-related issues—support, custody and visitation.

Marital agreements are based on contract law, but they do not result from the sort of dispassionate, arms' length bargaining typical of negotiations for commercial and business contracts. As the decisions in the following sections illustrate, most jurisdictions have imposed special duties of disclosure and fair dealing on parties to marriage-related agreements. Most jurisdictions continue to hold that the marital context requires some special limitations on freedom of contract.

A marital separation agreement has two distinct aspects: the first is that the agreement declares the physical separation of the spouses, and the second is that the agreement contains settlement of the rights and obligations arising out of the marriage relationship.

Generally, a contract of physical separation is annulled, voided or rescinded if the parties reconcile and resume marital relations. However, resumption of marital relations does not necessarily rescind a marital settlement agreement about property rights and non-alimony support. These agreements are then reconciliation agreements under which the character of the property changes in consideration for continuation of the marriage.

C. THE LIVING–TOGETHER AGREEMENT

As discussed in Chapter 5, nearly one out of every ten cohabiting couples in the United States consists of unmarried partners. *Marvin v. Marvin*, the landmark California decision discussed in that chapter, and similar decisions in other states have established that unmarried parties may contract with each other to resolve issues relating to property rights, inheritance rights and support. These agreements are generally called living-together, or cohabitation, agreements.

Living-together agreements follow general contract law principles; courts will look closely to ascertain that the agreement has a lawful objective, and that sexual services do not constitute the consideration.

SECTION 2: PREMARITAL AGREEMENTS

Premarital agreements—or antenuptial or prenuptial agreements, as they are also called—once were predominantly for couples in which at least one partner had substantial wealth. These agreements were used most often in second marriages, when an older, wealthy spouse wanted to ensure that assets would pass on to children of a first marriage. *See* Homer H. Clark, Jr., The Law of Domestic Relations in the United States 1 (2d ed. 1987). When married women had fewer protections, wealthy fathers often negotiated prenuptial agreements for their daughters. Today, a far broader range of couples employ premarital agreements. These agreements are now a regular part of family law practice, although most marrying couples do not use them. It is estimated that between five to 10 percent of first marriages and approximately 20 percent of second marriages today involve a prenuptial agreement. *See* Carolyn J. Frantz & Hanoch Dagan, *Properties of Marriage,* 104 Colum. L. Rev. 75, 80 n.12 (2004).

A. MODEL LAWS AND PROPOSED REFORMS

1. THE UNIFORM PREMARITAL AGREEMENT ACT

The widespread acceptance of antenuptial agreements is partly attributable to statutes requiring courts to enforce them. In 1983, the National Conference of Commissioners on Uniform State Laws (NCCUSL) promulgated the Uniform Premarital Agreement Act (UPAA), which facilitates the treatment of premarital agreements as essentially ordinary contracts. To increase the likelihood of enforcement, the UPAA reduces the high burdens of disclosure and conscionability that the common law frequently imposed on premarital agreements. UPAA § 2 cmt., 9C U.L.A. 39, 41 (2001).

The following are two key UPAA provisions directed at both the substance of the agreement and the process by which it is negotiated.

UNIFORM PREMARITAL AGREEMENT ACT

9C U.L.A. 39 (2001).

§ 3. Content.

(a) Parties to a premarital agreement may contract with respect to:

   (1) the rights and obligations of each of the parties in any of the property of either or both of them whenever and wherever acquired or located;

   (2) the right to buy, sell, use, transfer, exchange, abandon, lease, consume, expend, assign, create a security interest in, mortgage, encumber, dispose of, or otherwise manage and control property;

   (3) the disposition of property upon separation, marital dissolution, death, or the occurrence or nonoccurrence of any other event;

   (4) the modification or elimination of spousal support;

   (5) the making of a will, trust, or other arrangement to carry out the provisions of the agreement;

   (6) the ownership rights in and disposition of the death benefit from a life insurance policy;

   (7) the choice of law governing construction of the agreement; and

   (8) any other matter, including their personal rights and obligations, not in violation of public policy or a statute imposing a criminal penalty.

(b) The right of a child to support may not be adversely affected by a premarital agreement.

* * *

§ 6. Enforcement.

(a) A premarital agreement is not enforceable if the party against whom enforcement is sought proves that:

   (1) the party did not execute the agreement voluntarily; or

   (2) the agreement was unconscionable when it was executed and, before execution of the agreement, that party:

      (i) was not provided a fair and reasonable disclosure of the property or financial obligations of the other party;

      (ii) did not voluntarily and expressly waive, in writing, any right to disclosure of the property or financial obligations of the other party beyond the disclosure provided; and

      (iii) did not have, or reasonably could not have had, an adequate knowledge of the property or financial obligations of the other party.

(b) If a provision of a premarital agreement modifies or eliminates spousal support and that modification or elimination causes one party to the agreement to be eligible for support under a program of public assistance at the time of separation or marital dissolution, a court, notwithstanding the terms of the agreement, may require the other party to provide support to the extent reasonably necessary to avoid that eligibility.

(c) An issue of unconscionability of a premarital agreement shall be decided by the court as a matter of law.

* * *

9C U.L.A. 43, 48–49.

Similar to traditional contract law, enforcement under the UPAA requires the parties' voluntary consent to contract. In an effort to enhance the likelihood of enforcement, however, the Act departs from traditional contract law principles by providing for enforcement of an agreement that was unconscionable when executed, provided the affected party received fair and reasonable disclosure, waived disclosure, or reasonably could have had sufficient knowledge of the relevant information. Some commentators have strongly criticized the enforcement provisions of Section 6. Laura W. Morgan, *The Uniform Premarital Agreement Act: What the Law Says, and How Courts are Interpreting It*, 24 Fam. Advoc., Winter 2002, at 13.

The UPAA also requires that the agreement be in writing and executed by both parties, but does not require separate consideration other than the marriage itself. 9C U.L.A. 41. Even in states that have not adopted the UPAA, the Statute of Frauds requires that contracts in contemplation of marriage be evidenced in a writing signed by the party against whom contract enforcement is sought. Why is this requirement a good idea?

Some state statutes go further than the UPAA, requiring that premarital agreements be witnessed, notarized, or formally acknowledged. A New York statute, for instance, requires that any marital contract be "in writing, subscribed by the parties, and acknowledged or proven in the manner required to entitle a deed to be recorded." N.Y. Dom. Rel. L. § 236(B)(3) (McKinney's Supp. 2008). For lack of these formalities, the New York Court of Appeals denied enforcement of a written marital contract that both parties had signed, acknowledged as authentic in open court, and scrupulously observed during their 13–year marriage. *See Matisoff v. Dobi*, 681 N.E.2d 376, 376–78 (N.Y. 1997).

Some states have "softened" this requirement of a writing, however, by applying the rule that partial performance "allows specific enforcement of a contract that lacks the requisite writing." *In re Marriage of Benson*, 116 P.3d 1152, 1159 (Cal. 2005); *see also DewBerry v. George*, 62 P.3d 525 (Wash. Ct. App. 2003).

As of 2008, 26 states and the District of Columbia have adopted some portion of the UPAA. NCCUSL, UPAA Fact Sheet, http://www.nccusl.org/ Update/uniformact_factsheets/uniformacts-fs-upaa.asp.

2. PROPOSAL FOR REFORM: THE ALI PRINCIPLES

AMERICAN LAW INSTITUTE

Principles of the Law of Family Dissolution: Analysis and Recommendations.
2002.

§ 7.04   Procedural Requirements

* * *

(3) A premarital agreement is rebuttably presumed * * * [to satisfy the requirements of informed consent and absence of duress] when the party seeking to enforce the agreement shows that:

    (a) it was executed at least 30 days before the parties' marriage;

    (b) both parties were advised to obtain independent legal counsel, and had reasonable opportunity to do so, before the agreement's execution; and

    (c) in the case of an agreement concluded without the assistance of independent legal counsel for each party, the agreement states, in language easily understandable by an adult of ordinary intelligence with no legal training,

        (i) the nature of any rights or claims otherwise arising at dissolution that are altered by the contract, and the nature of that alteration, and

        (ii) that the interests of the spouses with respect to the agreement may be adverse.

ALI, Principles of the Law of Family Dissolution: Analysis and Recommendations § 7.04(3) (2002).

B. ELEMENTS REQUIRED FOR VALID PREMARITAL AGREEMENTS

Many states have not adopted the UPAA, but have enacted similar laws to recognize and regulate premarital agreements. The UPAA protects only against unconscionability, but other statutes and common law permit closer regulation by requiring that prenuptial agreements be procedurally and substantively fair. To be enforceable in most states, an antenuptial agreement must be (1) voluntary; (2) informed; and (3) tolerably fair so as not to offend public policy. *See, e.g., Friezo v. Friezo*, 914 A.2d 533, 545 (Conn. 2007); *Critchell v. Critchell*, 746 A.2d 282, 287 (D.C. 2000).

The following decision demonstrates how courts determine the enforceability of premarital agreements, where the state legislature has not enacted the UPAA or other standards.

MALLEN v. MALLEN

Supreme Court of Georgia, 2005.
622 S.E.2d 812.

BENHAM, JUSTICE.

At issue in this appeal from a judgment and decree of divorce is the trial court's decision to enforce a prenuptial agreement between the parties. Catherine (Wife) and Peter (Husband) Mallen had lived together unmarried for about four years when Wife got pregnant in 1985. While she was at a clinic to terminate the pregnancy, Husband called to ask her not to have the abortion and to marry him, to both of which requests she agreed. A few days later, nine or ten days before their planned wedding, Husband asked Wife to sign a prenuptial agreement prepared by his attorney. Wife contends Husband told her the agreement was just a formality and he would always take care of her. She took the agreement to an attorney whom she claims Husband paid, who advised her that he did not have time to fully examine it in the days remaining before the wedding. Wife did not consult another attorney or postpone the wedding, but spoke and met with Husband and his counsel about the agreement more than once. She agreed to sign it after a life insurance benefit was increased and the alimony provisions were modified to provide for increases for each year of marriage. The agreement provided that in the event of a divorce, Wife would receive a basic alimony amount to be adjusted for the number of years of marriage, and assets would belong to whomever owned the property originally or received it during the marriage. At the time the agreement was executed, Wife had a high school education and was working as a restaurant hostess, while Husband had a college degree and owned and operated a business. Wife had a net worth of approximately $10,000 and Husband's net worth at the time of the agreement's execution was at least $8,500,000. The record shows that Husband's net worth, as of 2002, appeared to be approximately $22,700,000. After 18 years of marriage and the birth of four children, Husband filed an action for divorce in 2003 and sought to enforce the prenuptial agreement. The trial court held the prenuptial agreement enforceable and incorporated that holding in its final judgment, ruling in accordance with the agreement that Wife was entitled to $2900 per month in alimony for four years and Husband was entitled to all the assets with which he entered the marriage and all assets accumulated during the marriage. This appeal is from that judgment.

Three factors are to be considered in deciding the validity of a prenuptial agreement: "(1) [W]as the agreement obtained through fraud, duress or mistake, or through misrepresentation or nondisclosure of material facts? (2) [I]s the agreement unconscionable? (3) Have the facts and circumstances changed since the agreement was executed, so as to make its enforcement unfair and unreasonable?" *Scherer v. Scherer*, 292 S.E.2d 662, 666 (Ga. 1982). "Whether an agreement is enforceable in light of these criteria is a decision made in the trial court's sound discretion." *Alexander v. Alexander*, 610 S.E.2d 48, 49 (Ga. 2005).

1. With regard to the first factor, Wife claims the agreement is infected with fraud, duress, and nondisclosure of material facts.

A. Fraud. The alleged misrepresentation forming the basis of the fraud claim was a statement Wife avers Husband made to induce her to enter into the agreement, an assertion that the agreement was just a formality and a promise that he would "take care" of her. To avoid the general rule that "in the absence of special circumstances one must exercise ordinary diligence in making an independent verification of contractual terms and representations," Wife asserts that by virtue of their engagement, she and Husband had a confidential relationship which excused her from the duty to verify Husband's statement. While it is true that spouses enjoy a confidential relationship entitling one to repose confidence and trust in the other, Georgia law has not recognized the existence of a confidential relationship between persons who have agreed to marry. A majority of jurisdictions which have addressed the issue have recognized a special relationship between persons engaged to be married that imposes a higher duty with regard to contracts between the parties than exists between other contracting parties. However, we believe Georgia law to be more consistent with the states that have rejected such a protective stance. In deciding that prenuptial agreements should not be considered void as against public policy, this Court in *Scherer v. Scherer*, *supra*, put into place the factors quoted above which are to be considered in judging the validity to such agreements, but did not impose the additional burden of acting in "the utmost good faith," as would be required of persons in confidential relationships. [Ga. Code Ann.] § 23–2–58. Accordingly, we reject Wife's contention that there existed when the agreement was executed a confidential relationship between the parties which would relieve her of responsibility to verify representations regarding the meaning and content of the agreement.

Applying the rule requiring ordinary diligence in making an independent verification of contractual terms and representations, Husband's alleged statement that the agreement was a mere formality cannot serve as a basis for a claim of fraud since Wife could ascertain from the clear terms of the agreement that her rights in the event of divorce would be extremely limited. * * * Husband's alleged promise to take care of Wife is likewise insufficient as a basis for a claim of fraud because it amounts to no more than a promise regarding future action, which is not actionable.

B. Duress. The duress Wife asserts was applied to compel her to execute the agreement was that the marriage would not occur in the absence of the prenuptial agreement and she would be left pregnant and unmarried. * * * [W]e conclude that insistence on a prenuptial agreement as a condition of marriage "does not rise to the level of duress required to void an otherwise valid contract." [*Alexander*, 610 S.E.2d at 50 (Sears, J., concurring)]. *See also Doig v. Doig*, 787 So. 2d 100, 102–103 (Fla. Dist. Ct.

App. 2001) (ultimatum that without the agreement there would be no wedding does not, in itself, constitute duress). Compare *Holler v. Holler*, 612 S.E.2d 469, 475–76 (S.C. Ct. App. 2005) (pregnant, non-English-speaking wife without employment or funds or ability to consult with counsel, and with expiring visa signed agreement written only in English under duress). * * * Nothing in the record of this case suggests that Wife's free will was overcome by the "threat" of not going through with the wedding. In fact, Wife exercised her free will and declined to sign the agreement in the form it was presented to her, acquiescing only when changes were made improving her position in the event of divorce or Husband's death. The fact of Wife's pregnancy does not make Husband's insistence on the agreement rise to the level of duress. She had already demonstrated her willingness to terminate the pregnancy, so she cannot credibly claim the pregnancy put such pressure on her as to overcome her will.

C.   Nondisclosure of material facts. Attached to the prenuptial agreement executed by the parties were financial disclosure forms on which each party set out their assets and liabilities. Neither form listed income. Citing foreign authority based on the existence of a confidential relationship between persons engaged to be married, Wife asserts the absence of Husband's income from the financial statement constituted the nondisclosure of a material fact which would render the agreement unenforceable. In *Posner v. Posner*, 257 So. 2d 530 (Fla. 1972), the Florida Supreme Court held that in light of the confidential relationship of parties to a prenuptial agreement and the inadequate provision for the wife in the agreement under review, the husband's failure to disclose significant sources of income rendered the agreement unenforceable. However, as we held above, parties to prenuptial agreements in Georgia are not by virtue of their planned marriage in a confidential relationship. Wife also cited *DeLorean v. DeLorean*, 511 A.2d 1257 (N.J. Super. Ct. 1986), for the statement in that case that New Jersey law would require a complete written disclosure of all assets and all income. We find that case more persuasive for its holding that under California law, which the agreement specified would be applied and which does not consider persons planning marriage to be in a confidential relationship, a prenuptial agreement is enforceable "[s]o long as the spouse seeking to set aside such an agreement has a general idea of the character and extent of the financial assets and income of the other. . . . Indeed, absent fraud or misrepresentation, there appears to be a duty to make some inquiry to ascertain the full nature and extent of the financial resources of the other." *Id.* [at 1262]. That statement of law is consistent with our holding above that persons planning marriage are not in a confidential relationship that will excuse a party from the duty to "exercise ordinary diligence in making an independent verification of contractual terms and representations[.]" In the present case, although the financial statement did not include income, it did reveal Husband to be a wealthy individual with significant income-producing assets, including an 80% ownership share of a business bearing his name. Wife had lived with Husband for four years and was aware from the standard of living they enjoyed that he received significant income from his business and other sources. Under those circumstances and in light of the authority cited above, Wife cannot be said to have demonstrated that the absence from Husband's financial statement of precise income data constituted the nondisclosure of material facts which would render the prenuptial agreement unenforceable.

2.　Concerning the second inquiry to be made pursuant to *Scherer v. Scherer*, *supra*, Wife asserts that the disparity in financial situation and business experience rendered the prenuptial agreement unconscionable when executed. "An unconscionable contract is one abhorrent to good morals and conscience ... where one of the parties takes a fraudulent advantage of another[,] an agreement that no sane person not acting under a delusion would make and that no honest person would take advantage of." *William J. Cooney, P.C. v. Rowland*, 524 S.E.2d 730, 732 (Ga. Ct. App. 1999). We do not believe the agreement involved here fits that description.

* * * Given our conclusion above that the agreement is not infected with fraud, and given the absence of any suggestion that Wife suffered from any delusion, the disparities between Wife and Husband in financial status and business experience do not demand a conclusion that the agreement was unconscionable.

3.　The remaining factor to be considered is whether circumstances have changed since the execution of the agreement so as to render its enforcement unfair and unreasonable. The changed circumstance which Wife contends in her brief renders enforcement of the agreement unfair and unreasonable is that Husband's net worth increased by 14 million dollars during the marriage.

Since this Court's adoption in *Scherer v. Scherer*, *supra*, of the factors to consider in determining the enforceability of prenuptial agreements, we have not had occasion to address directly the question of what changes in circumstance might render a prenuptial agreement unfair and unreasonable. However, in *Curry v. Curry*, 392 S.E.2d 879, 881 n.2 (Ga. 1990), in considering a trial court's application of those same factors to uphold a reconciliation agreement, this Court found no error in the trial court's holding that there "has been no change in circumstances that [was] not foreseeable at the time that the agreement was entered into...." That element of foreseeability has been recognized by other states as a key element in consideration of changed circumstances. In *Reed v. Reed*, 693 N.W.2d 825, 836 (Mich. Ct. App. 2005), the court held that a significant growth of assets over many years "can hardly be considered an unforeseeable changed circumstance that justifies voiding the ... prenuptial agreement." The Supreme Court of South Carolina, in *Hardee v. Hardee*, 585 S.E.2d 501, 505 (S.C. 2003), agreed with the lower court's holding that the wife's becoming totally disabled was not a change in circumstance that would render the prenuptial agreement unenforceable because "[t]he premarital agreement specifically noted Wife's health problems [and i]t was completely foreseeable to Wife that her health would worsen."

In the present case, Wife was familiar with Husband's financial circumstances from living with him for four years prior to marriage and must have anticipated that his wealth would grow over the ensuing years. Since the continued disparity in their financial situations was plainly foreseeable from the terms of the prenuptial agreement, Wife cannot rely on that as a change in circumstance which renders the agreement unfair.

Because the record in this case supports a finding that none of the factors set forth in *Scherer v. Scherer, supra,* call[s] for a judicial repudiation of the prenuptial agreement signed by the parties, we conclude the trial court did not abuse its discretion in enforcing the agreement.

Judgment affirmed.

SEARS, CHIEF JUSTICE, dissenting.

* * *

In *Scherer v. Scherer*, this Court held that a prenuptial agreement is unenforceable if there was a "nondisclosure of material facts" when the agreement was entered. Thus, under *Scherer*, parties entering a prenuptial agreement have a duty to disclose material facts even absent the presence of a confidential relationship. By necessity, whether a fact is material to a prenuptial agreement will depend on the property and alimony issues that are addressed in the agreement. In the present case, Mr. Mallen's attorney prepared a prenuptial agreement that significantly limited Ms. Mallen's right to alimony. The agreement provides that, in the event of a divorce, Ms. Mallen would be entitled to $1,000 per month in alimony, to be increased $100 a month for each year of the parties' marriage, with Ms. Mallen's right to alimony to terminate four years after the date of the parties' divorce decree. Because a party's income is a critical factor in determining the appropriate amount of alimony, Mr. Mallen's income was material to the prenuptial agreement. In this regard, it is undisputed that, at the time the parties entered the prenuptial agreement, Mr. Mallen did not disclose his income to Ms. Mallen and that his income was approximately $560,000 per year.

Because this material fact was not disclosed to Ms. Mallen, I conclude that the parties' prenuptial agreement is unenforceable. I therefore dissent to the majority opinion. * * *

NOTES AND QUESTIONS

1. *Confidential relationship.* As *Mallen* illustrates, the determination whether parties negotiating a premarital agreement stand in a "confidential relationship" may be relevant to more than one aspect of enforceability. The presence or absence of a confidential relationship may help determine whether the agreement was truly "voluntary," or was instead induced by fraud. It is also often controlling in deciding whether each party's consent is sufficiently

"informed." As *Mallen* indicates, whether the parties stand in a "confidential relationship" affects the scope of their disclosure obligations: the fiduciary duties that spring from a "confidential relationship" ordinarily require much fuller sharing of financial data than is required of other contracting parties.

Deciding when the "confidential relationship" begins is thus a matter of some importance. In Georgia and a handful of other states—including prominently California and New York—the "confidential relationship" commences only upon marriage. *See In re Marriage of Bonds*, 5 P.3d 815 (Cal. 2000); *Eckstein v. Eckstein*, 514 N.Y.S.2d 47 (App. Div. 1987). As *Mallen* concedes, however, the strong majority rule is that an engaged couple negotiating a premarital agreement occupies a confidential relationship. *See, e.g., Bratton v. Bratton*, 136 S.W.3d 595 (Tenn. 2004); *Griffin v. Griffin*, 94 P.3d 96 (Okla. Ct. Civ. App. 2004); *DeMatteo v. DeMatteo*, 762 N.E.2d 797 (Mass. 2002); *In re Marriage of Drag*, 762 N.E.2d 1111 (Ill. App. Ct. 2002). Authorities disagree about whether a confidential relationship exists when parties negotiate an antenuptial agreement before they are actually engaged. *Compare Cannon v. Cannon*, 865 A.2d 563, 573–74 (Md. 2005) (yes), *with Lightman v. Magid*, 394 S.W.2d 151, 156–57 (Tenn. Ct. App. 1965) (no).

2. *Why treat premarital contracts differently from other contracts?* To evaluate whether engaged couples occupy a confidential relationship that imposes special duties of fair dealing, consider the dynamics of bargaining within an intimate relationship. Professor Melvin Eisenberg explains that both economics and morality support excepting confidential relationships from the usual contract rules requiring vigilant self-protection:

> Judge Posner set out an economic justification for that exception in *United States v. Dial*:
>
> > * * * The essence of a fiduciary relationship is that the fiduciary agrees to act as his principal's alter ego rather than to assume the standard arm's length stance of traders in a market. Hence the principal is not armed with the usual wariness that one has in dealing with strangers * * *.
>
> In addition to the economic justification for requiring candor by fiduciaries, there is a moral justification: As a matter of social norms, if A owes B a fiduciary obligation, B will have an expectation of candor by A that is justified by conventional social understandings. The moral norm of relationship-based candor is not limited to fiduciary relationships. Rather, it applies to any ongoing relationship in which as a matter of either the social conventions that apply to the relationship, or the understandings that are implicit in the relationship, one or both parties have a justified expectation that the other will exercise candor in transactions between them.

Melvin A. Eisenberg, *Disclosure in Contract Law*, 91 Cal. L. Rev. 1645, 1682 (2003) (quoting *United States v. Dial,* 757 F.2d 163, 168 (7th Cir. 1985)). Do these rationales support classifying premarital relationships as "confidential"? Is it realistic to expect premarital partners, in the weeks or months before a wedding, to investigate one another's finances and to skeptically challenge assurances about the future? Is such investigation desirable? Would a well-counseled, financially weaker party investigate?

Scholars have identified a number of psychological impediments to effective, clear-eyed bargaining in the context of antenuptial agreements. The crux of the problem is that when couples embark on marriage, they bargain not only in "the shadow of the law," *see* Robert H. Mnookin & Lewis Kornhauser, *Bargaining in the Shadow of the Law: The Case of Divorce*, 88 Yale L.J. 950 (1979), but also in "the shadow of love." Brian Bix, *Bargaining in the Shadow of Love: The Enforcement of Premarital Agreements and How We Think About Marriage*, 40 Wm. & Mary L. Rev. 145 (1998). Professor Eisenberg writes:

> [C]lassical contract law was based on a rational-actor model of psychology, under which actors who make decisions in the face of uncertainty rationally maximize their subjective expected utility, with all future benefits and costs discounted to present value. In particular, the rules of classical contract law were implicitly based on the assumptions that actors are fully knowledgeable, know the law, and act rationally to further their economic self-interest. This model accounts in part for such rules as the duty to read, whose operational significance was that actors were conclusively assumed to have read and understood everything that they signed. It also accounts in part for the rule that bargains would not be reviewed for fairness: if actors always act rationally in their own self-interest, then, in the absence of fraud, duress, or the like, all bargains must be fair.

Melvin A. Eisenberg, *Why There Is No Law of Relational Contracts,* 94 Nw. U. L. Rev. 805, 808 (2000). These assumptions underlying classical contract law may be imperfect even in ordinary commercial settings, but they seem especially inapt in premarital negotiations:

> The limits of cognition have an obvious bearing on the enforceability of prenuptial agreements. To begin with, individuals who plan to marry are often likely to be unduly optimistic about the fate of their marriage. Two people in love are likely to heavily discount the possibility of divorce, because they will overemphasize the concrete evidence of their currently thriving relationship and underemphasize abstract divorce statistics; and because divorce is a risk that, like other risks, people systematically underestimate. As a result, prospective spouses are likely to heavily discount the probability that their prenuptial agreement will come into play.

> Bounded rationality also poses a problem in this context. Because of the exceptionally indefinite nature of marriage, it is almost impossible to predict the impact that a prenuptial agreement will have if it does come into play.

Melvin A. Eisenberg, *The Limits of Cognition and the Limits of Contract*, 47 Stan. L. Rev. 211, 254 (1995).

Empirical studies strongly suggest that people embarking on marriage are likely to grossly underestimate their own risk of divorce. A 1993 survey, for example, showed that most respondents contemplating marriage estimated their chance of divorce as zero, despite knowing that about half of all marriages end in divorce. *See* Lynn A. Baker & Robert E. Emery, *When Every Relationship Is Above Average: Perceptions and Expectations of Divorce at the Time of Marriage*, 17 Law & Hum. Behav. 439, 443 (1993). A similar study 10 years later produced similar results. *See* Heather Mahar, *Why Are There So Few Prenuptial Agreements?,* John M. Olin Center for Law, Economics, and Business Discussion Paper No. 436 (Sept. 2003) (unpublished paper, *available at* http://www.law.harvard.edu/programs/olin_center/papers/436_mahar.php). It may be true that "[p]eople who assume that they will not divorce will not work hard to maintain a fair deal contingent on divorce occurring, just as parties do not bargain hard for reasonable terms on the failure of installment payments, as they do not expect to ever fail in their payments," Bix, *supra*, at 194; but do illusions at marriage provide any reason to deny parties the opportunity to be foolish, or to relieve them of their foolishness?

3. *Overreaching and duress. Mallen* found nothing in the circumstances of the premarital negotiation that impeded the parties' "free will" and rendered the agreement involuntary. Do you agree? *Cf.* Paul Bennett Marrow, *Squeezing Subjectivity from the Doctrine of Unconscionability*, 53 Clev. St. L. Rev. 187, 209 (2005–2006) ("A classic claim is overreaching by a male who demands, as a condition of marriage, a prenuptial agreement from a would-be wife who is already pregnant with his child."). Should the overbearing destruction of "free will" be the measure of "voluntariness" in this context?

In contrast to *Mallen*, the court in the following decision refused to enforce an agreement concluded shortly before a wedding because the circumstances of the negotiation rendered the wife's consent "involuntary." New Hampshire, like Georgia, has not adopted the UPAA.

IN RE ESTATE OF HOLLETT

Supreme Court of New Hampshire, 2003.
834 A.2d 348.

DUGGAN, J.

The petitioner, Erin Hollett, appeals an order by the Merrimack County Probate Court (Patten, J.) declaring the prenuptial agreement made between Erin and the decedent, John Hollett, to be valid. Erin argues that the agreement should be set aside because of duress, undue influence, insufficient financial disclosure, and lack of effective independent counsel. The respondents, Kathryn Hollett, the decedent's first wife, and their five children, argue that the agreement is valid and the probate court's order should be affirmed. We reverse and remand.

The following facts were found by the trial court or are evident from the record. John and Erin married on August 18, 1990. Their courtship had begun in 1984, when John was fifty-two and Erin was twenty-two. John was a successful real estate investor and developer who regularly bought and sold property in New Hampshire and Florida. He had considerable experience with attorneys and accountants because of his business dealings. Erin had dropped out of high school in the eleventh grade, and had no work or business experience aside from several low level jobs. Throughout their relationship and marriage, Erin had almost no involvement in or understanding of John's business.

John had previously been married to Kathryn C. Hollett, with whom he had five children. Under the terms of their divorce, John owed Kathryn a substantial property settlement, and still owed her millions of dollars at the time of his death. Erin was unaware of this property settlement.

In 1988, the same year that John and Erin became engaged, Erin found a newspaper article about prenuptial agreements that John had left on the kitchen counter. When Erin confronted John with the article, he explained that his first wife had given it to him, and stated that he would not get married without a prenuptial agreement. This statement provoked a "heated and unpleasant" discussion during which Erin said she would not sign such an agreement, particularly because John's first wife had insisted upon it. John said nothing to Erin about a prenuptial agreement again until several days before the August 18, 1990 wedding.

In May 1990, apparently in anticipation of the impending marriage, John sent a statement of his net worth to his attorneys in the law firm of McLane, Graf, Raulerson, and Middleton. After meeting with John on July 18, 1990, his lawyers drafted a prenuptial agreement that was sent to him on July 26. Erin testified that she did not learn about the agreement until the evening of August 16, less than forty-eight hours before the wedding. Under the original draft, Erin was to renounce any claim to alimony or a property settlement in the event of a divorce, and would receive only $25,000 and an automobile.

Several days before the wedding, John's lawyers contacted Brian Shaughnessy, a recent law school graduate, and requested that he counsel Erin regarding the prenuptial agreement. The lawyers told Shaughnessy that John would pay his fee. Shaughnessy first called Erin on August 16 to obtain her consent to act as counsel and to set up a meeting at the McLane law firm office the next day. Shaughnessy had never before negotiated a prenuptial agreement, but prior to the meeting he studied the law of prenuptial agreements and reviewed the draft agreement.

Erin, accompanied by her mother, met with Shaughnessy in person for the first and only time at the McLane law firm on August 17, the day before the wedding. At that time, all of the plans and arrangements for the elaborate wedding, at which over 200 guests were expected, had already been made and paid for; Erin's mother and father had already flown in from Thailand. During the meeting and subsequent negotiations with John's attorneys, Shaughnessy noted that Erin was under considerable emotional distress, sobbing throughout the three or four hours he was with her and at times so distressed that he was unable to speak with her. Erin testified that she remembered almost nothing about the conference. Shaughnessy, however, testified that he carefully reviewed John's financial disclosure and draft of the agreement with Erin, explained their legal significance, and asked her what she sought to obtain from the agreement. He testified that he advised her that the settlement offer in the draft was inadequate, and reminded her that the wedding could be put off if necessary.

Shaughnessy also testified that he believed the financial disclosure provided by John, which had not been audited or reviewed by any other party, was inadequate. Shaughnessy, however, had no time to independently verify any of John's finances. In any case, he believed that any failure to disclose was John's problem, as it could lead to the invalidation of the agreement.

At the end of the negotiations, the prenuptial agreement was considerably more favorable to Erin, allowing her to obtain as much as one-sixth of John's estate in the event of a divorce or John's death. John's lawyers prepared a final version of the agreement, which John and Erin signed on the morning of August 18, the day of their wedding.

The parties remained married until John's death on April 30, 2001. John was survived by Erin, his first wife, and his children from his first marriage. Erin subsequently petitioned the probate court to invalidate the prenuptial agreement, while John's first wife and children argued in favor of upholding it. After four days of hearings, the probate court concluded that the prenuptial agreement was valid and enforceable.

On appeal, Erin argues that the prenuptial agreement was invalid for three reasons: (1) the agreement was not voluntary because it was the product of duress and undue influence; (2) John's financial disclosures were inadequate; and (3) she did not have independent counsel. We need only address the issue of duress. * * *

RSA 460:2–a (1997)[1] permits a man and a woman to enter into a written contract "in contemplation of marriage." A prenuptial agreement is presumed valid unless the party seeking the invalidation of the agreement proves that: (1) the agreement was obtained through fraud, duress or mistake, or through misrepresentation or nondisclosure of a material fact; (2) the agreement is unconscionable; or (3) the facts and circumstances have so changed since the agreement was executed as to make the agreement unenforceable. *See In the Matter of Yannalfo and Yannalfo*, 794 A.2d 795, 797 (N.H. 2002).

"As a practical matter, the claim of undue duress is essentially a claim that the agreement was not signed voluntarily." 3 C. Douglas, New Hampshire Practice, Family Law § 1.05, at 12 (2002). To establish duress, a party must ordinarily "show that it involuntarily accepted the other party's terms, that the coercive circumstances were the result of the other party's acts, that the other party exerted pressure wrongfully, and that under the circumstances the party had no alternative but to accept the terms set out by the other party." *Yannalfo*, [794 A.2d at 797]. However, "the State has a special interest in the subject matter" of prenuptial agreements and "courts tend to scrutinize [them] more closely than ordinary commercial contracts." *MacFarlane v. Rich (MacFarlane)*, 567 A.2d 585, 589 (N.H. 1989). Moreover, because such agreements often involve persons in a confidential relationship, "the parties must exercise the highest degree of good faith, candor and sincerity in all matters

---

1. *Ed.'s note*: Section 460:2–a of the New Hampshire Revised States, N.H. Rev. Stat. Ann. § 460:2–a (2007), is the governing statute for antenuptial agreements, which is not based on the UPAA.

bearing on the terms and execution of the proposed agreement, with fairness being the ultimate measure.''

Under the heightened scrutiny afforded to prenuptial agreements, the timing of the agreement is of paramount importance in assessing whether it was voluntary. Fairness demands that the party presented with the agreement have ''an opportunity to seek independent advice and a reasonable time to reflect on the proposed terms.'' * * * Some States, in fact, automatically invalidate any prenuptial agreement signed immediately before a wedding. *See, e.g.*, Minn. Stat. § 519.11 (2002) (agreement ''must be entered into and executed prior to the day of solemnization of marriage'').

In arguing for the validity of the Holletts' agreement, the respondents rely upon *In the Matter of Yannalfo and Yannalfo*, [*supra*]. In that case, the husband and wife, each of whom was employed by the United States Postal Service, signed a prenuptial agreement a ''day or so'' before their wedding. The agreement was limited to a house that the husband and wife had purchased one month before the wedding, for which the husband had contributed $70,000 as a down payment, and the wife had provided $5,000 for closing costs. The agreement stated that the first $70,000 of equity in the house was the property of the husband, and that in the event of a divorce, the house would be sold and $70,000 would be paid to the husband. The agreement did not concern any property other than the $70,000 contribution.

In upholding the agreement in *Yannalfo*, we rejected a *per se* invalidation of agreements signed immediately before the wedding. Instead, we established that each case must be decided upon the totality of its own circumstances. Citing cases from other jurisdictions, however, we suggested that ''additional circumstances coupled with [such] timing'' may compel a finding that a prenuptial agreement was involuntary.

Several important circumstances distinguish the present case from *Yannalfo*. First, the agreement in *Yannalfo* did not involve the entire estates of the parties. Rather, it only concerned money used in a transaction that both parties had participated in one month before the wedding. The agreement in this case, by contrast, involves the post-marriage disbursement of an estate that totaled over six million dollars at the time of the agreement, and the relinquishment of marital rights such as alimony. Such a complicated and important agreement will require more time for negotiation and reflection than the agreement in *Yannalfo*.

Second, unlike the parties in *Yannalfo*, Erin's bargaining position was vastly inferior to that of her husband. John was much older than Erin, and he had already been married. According to their financial disclosures, John had approximately six million dollars in assets, while Erin owned approximately five thousand dollars worth of personal property at the time of the agreement. Erin's work experience during the relationship was limited to stints as a bartender and a grocery store cashier. She had little understanding of and no real involvement in John's business ventures.

According to Erin, in fact, John had encouraged Erin to stop working after they began their relationship. If Erin refused to sign the agreement, she thus not only stood to face the embarrassment of canceling a two hundred guest wedding, but also stood to lose her means of support. Prenuptial agreements that result from such a vast disparity in bargaining power must meet a high standard of procedural fairness.

Finally, John's conduct before the wedding raises serious questions regarding his good faith in dealing with Erin. John had contemplated a prenuptial agreement at least two years before the wedding, as evidenced by his argument with Erin in 1988. Despite Erin's opposition to the idea, however, he did not discuss the agreement with her again. Moreover, although John's lawyers had drafted a prenuptial agreement almost a month before the wedding, John did not obtain counsel for his wife or even inform her of the agreement until several days before the ceremony. * * *

* * *

* * * [In upholding the validity of the prenuptial contract,] the trial court focused upon the assistance Erin received from Brian Shaughnessy before the execution of the agreement. The respondents, in fact, suggest that the presence of counsel should be dispositive of the issue of voluntariness. We note that the trial court itself found that the time constraints limited the quality of Shaughnessy's representation: for example, he was unable to verify the accuracy of John's disclosures. Even assuming, however, that Shaughnessy provided Erin with effective independent counsel, and that the financial representations upon which he relied were accurate, we cannot agree that his counsel by itself was sufficient to validate this agreement.

Independent counsel is useless without the ability and the time to make effective use of such counsel. * * *

In this case, it would be unreasonable to conclude that Erin had "sufficient time" or a "reasonable opportunity" to make use of Brian Shaughnessy's advice. Given the complexity of John's finances and the agreement, and the disparity in the parties' bargaining power, Erin needed more than one day to negotiate and reflect upon his draft proposal. Without such time, we conclude as a matter of law that her signing of the agreement was involuntary under the heightened standard applied to prenuptial agreements.

Reversed and remanded.

Questions

What accounts for the different outcomes in *Mallen* and *Hollett*? Were contrasting facts really determinative—such as the timing of contract negotiations or the different nature of the wedding plans—or are the decisions best understood as driven by differing legal conceptions of voluntariness?

C. SPECIFIC FACTORS IN EVALUATING THE VALIDITY OF PREMARITAL AGREEMENTS

In addition to the general rules governing the enforceability of contracts, antenuptial agreements must satisfy heightened scrutiny. In most jurisdictions, the parties must enter the agreement voluntarily and with full knowledge of the meaning and effect of its terms, the parties must truthfully disclose their assets, and the agreement's terms must be substantively fair and equitable.

1. VOLUNTARINESS OF AN AGREEMENT

Most courts apply heightened scrutiny to determine a premarital agreement's voluntariness, but often differ about how to apply or weight the relevant factors. In addition to individualized circumstances that might be considered coercive, courts often look to the timing of negotiations, the role of counsel, and disparities in the parties' sophistication.

Hollett viewed the timing of contract negotiations as a "paramount" consideration, but declined to adopt a *per se* rule on the issue. Clearly, courts disfavor last-minute prenuptial contract proposals, but many have nevertheless enforced such agreements, depending on other factors. *See, e.g., In re Marriage of Murphy*, 834 N.E.2d 56, 67–68 (Ill. App. Ct. 2005) (enforcing agreement proposed two days before wedding, noting that "[t]he period of time between the execution of the antenuptial agreement and the marriage ceremony is only one factor among many that is considered when determining the validity of the agreement"); *Binek v. Binek*, 673 N.W.2d 594, 598 (N.D. 2004) ("Although it would have been preferable to present the agreement to Ruth Binek more than two days before the wedding, this alone does not render the agreement unenforceable."). Would it be better simply to designate a mandatory timetable, insisting that negotiations commence at least a week—or even a month— before the wedding? A 2001 California law creates a mandatory minimum waiting period by deeming involuntary any prenuptial agreement executed "less than seven calendar days" after it was initially presented. *See* Cal. Fam. Code § 1615(c)(2) (West 2004). As you saw above, the ALI Principles require that a prenuptial agreement be executed at least 30 days before the wedding.

In evaluating timing, many courts consider the nature of the planned wedding ceremony. In Ohio, for instance, "presentation of an agreement a very short time before the wedding ceremony will create a presumption of overreaching or coercion if * * * postponement of the wedding would cause significant hardship, embarrassment or emotional stress." *Fletcher v. Fletcher*, 628 N.E.2d 1343, 1348 (Ohio 1994). Where the planned ceremony is small and informal, courts may be more tolerant of agreements signed on short notice. *See In re Marriage of Bonds*, 5 P.3d 815 (Cal. 2000).

All jurisdictions agree that access to advice of counsel is an important factor in determining the voluntariness of any premarital agreement. Many jurisdictions agree with the view of the California Supreme Court, expressed in a case involving Major League Baseball player Barry Bonds, that "the best assurance of enforceability is independent representation of both parties." *Marriage of Bonds*, 5 P.3d at 833; *accord Binek*, 673 N.W.2d at 598 ("adequate legal representation will often be the best evidence that a spouse signed a premarital agreement knowledgeably and voluntarily"). Nevertheless, *Bonds* and many other decisions have enforced agreements in which one party opted to forgo counsel or met only with an attorney retained by the other spouse. In such cases, courts sometimes emphasize that the unrepresented spouse was advised to seek legal counsel or succeeded in winning concessions even without counsel.

In response to *Bonds*, which held that access to independent counsel was just one factor in assessing the voluntariness of prenuptial agreements, the California legislature amended the state's version of the UPAA in 2001 to require counsel in some instances. The new statute mandates that a premarital agreement will be deemed involuntary unless, among other things, "[t]he party against whom enforcement is sought was represented by independent legal counsel at the time of signing the agreement or, after being advised to seek independent legal counsel, expressly waived, in a separate writing, representation by independent legal counsel." Cal. Fam. Code § 1615(c)(1) (West 2004). Where the issue is waiver of spousal support, the statute strictly requires independent representation for enforceability. *See* Cal. Fam. Code § 1612(c) (West 2004).

In addition to considering the timing of negotiations and each party's access to counsel, courts often consider, as in *Mallen* and *Hollett*, whether one party has significantly more education, experience or business sophistication than the other. Disparity alone does not necessarily establish lack of voluntariness, but may be relevant in evaluating the coercive pressure created by timing or other circumstances.

Most often, courts find lack of voluntariness when some combination of these factors is present. For example, in *In re Marriage of Tamraz*, 2005 WL 1524199 (Cal. Ct. App. June 29, 2005), the court found a lack of voluntary assent where the future husband, an experienced attorney, unexpectedly faxed his fiancée a draft agreement late in the afternoon on the day before the wedding and led her to believe that the agreement's terms were more limited than they actually were.

2.　FINANCIAL DISCLOSURE

As *Mallen* and *Hollett* illustrate, courts widely agree that parties to an antenuptial agreement must fairly disclose to one another material information about their financial status and prospects. Yet jurisdictions often disagree about precisely how much disclosure is required. As *Mallen* notes, part of the disagreement hinges on whether the parties are regarded as occupying a "confidential relationship" which triggers greater disclosure obligations. Even in the majority of jurisdictions that do regard engaged partners as fiduciaries, however, requirements concerning the scope and specificity of disclosure are not uniform. A few jurisdictions insist that each party must provide a detailed listing of assets and income. Most, however, take a more flexible view, requiring only that each spouse have reasonably clear "general knowledge" of the other's financial status. The ALI Principles of the Law of Family Dissolution take this flexible position, considering it sufficient that "the other party knew, at least approximately, the moving party's assets and income, or was provided by the moving party with a written statement containing that information." *Principles*, § 7.04(5). In 2007, the Connecticut Supreme Court agreed with the majority rule that it is enough for parties to provide one another with "a general approximation of their income, assets and liabilities," but added that "a written schedule appended to the agreement itself, although not absolutely necessary, is the most effective method of satisfying the statutory [disclosure] obligation in most circumstances." *Friezo v. Friezo,* 914 A.2d 533, 550 (Conn. 2007).

Aside from differences in the applicable legal standards, it is not always easy to predict whether a court will find disclosure sufficient as a factual matter. In North Dakota, for example—a jurisdiction in which parties to a prenuptial agreement are considered fiduciaries—the state supreme court found adequate disclosure where a wife "testified that before she signed the agreement she knew Theodore Binek owned the Binek coal mine and the equipment thereon, guessed he owned his house, and had been told by her family that he was worth over a million dollars." *Binek,* 673 N.W.2d at 599. Yet, in California—a state in which premarital partners are not considered to occupy a confidential relationship—a court found inadequate disclosure where the parties had been living together for 10 years before the marriage. In *In re Marriage of Tamraz,* 2005 WL 1524199 (Cal. Ct. App. June 29, 2005), the court concluded:

> Although respondent was aware of appellant's interest in the condominium, that he had his own law practice and that he owned three cars, she testified that she did not know anything "about the rest of his financial life." Respondent testified that appellant never disclosed to her all of his assets and debts, that he never shared any information about any investments he had besides the condominium or about the balances in his bank accounts and that he never gave her access to "the books" at his law firm. Appellant admitted that prior to their marriage he never provided respondent with copies of his personal tax returns.

Id. at *6.

What sort of disclosure should be required? Should the test for whether duress invalidates a premarital agreement be stricter than the test for whether duress annuls a marriage, a matter discussed in Chapter 3? Even under the more flexible standard of "general knowledge," do you agree that the disclosure in *Mallen* or *Binek,* adequately enabled a party to make an "informed" decision about whether to waive future claims to maintenance or property?

3. REVIEW FOR "SUBSTANTIVE FAIRNESS" OR "UNCON-SCIONABILITY"

Mallen and *Hollett* both state that courts must undertake some review of the substantive fairness of prenuptial agreements. Jurisdictions differ, however, about the nature and timing of this review. The differences mostly cluster around two issues: first, the *time* at which the agreement's fairness should be measured, and second, how *fairness* should be defined for these purposes.

Ordinary contract law measures unconscionability only at the time of contract formation. Strict UPAA jurisdictions follow this approach with respect to premarital contracts. *See, e.g., Holler v. Holler*, 612 S.E.2d 469 (S.C. Ct. App. 2005); UPAA § 6(a)(2), 9C U.L.A. 49 (2001). Other jurisdictions, as in *Mallen* and *Hollett*, consider also whether circumstances existing at the time of divorce would make enforcement offensive to public policy. This second group includes some states that, in otherwise enacting the UPAA, specifically added language to require an assessment of unconscionability at the time of contract enforcement. *See, e.g., Dornemann v. Dornemann*, 2004 WL 2094746, at *11 (Conn. Super. Ct. Aug. 13, 2004).

The ALI Principles endorse a middle-ground position, which would permit courts to deny enforcement because of changed circumstances during the marriage under only three limited circumstances. Specifically, section 7.05(2) requires court review to ensure that "enforcement would not work a substantial injustice" where:

(a) more than a fixed number of years have passed [the commentary suggests 10 years] * * * ;

(b) a child was born to, or adopted by, the parties, who at the time of execution had no children in common; [or]

(c) there has been a change in circumstances that has a substantial impact on the parties or their children, but when they executed the agreement the parties probably did not anticipate either the change, or its impact.

Principles, § 7.05(2).

The drafters of the ALI Principles conclude that "[p]remarital agreements, with potential long-term application, raise a different kind of fairness concern * * * which is not addressed by the [traditional] unconscionability doctrine":

A premarital agreement that at the time of execution is fair on its face, and is entered into by parties whose consent is truly mutual, may have a very different significance in the parties' lives when enforcement is sought 15 years later, after they have borne and nurtured children. The law's usual assumption that contracting parties are capable judges of their own self-interest is put in doubt when

the judgment is so distant in time and circumstance from its consequences. This capability problem is exacerbated by another uncommon feature of premarital agreements: its principal terms speak
exclusively to a marital dissolution that the parties do not expect to
occur, and so the agreement has no expected application.

Id. at 38. Consider whether the ALI's middle-ground approach is preferable to the approaches taken by the UPAA and jurisdictions that require
enforcement-related review in all cases.

Once a court resolves the timing issue, it must determine the appropriate degree of scrutiny to apply to the prenuptial agreement. Even
ordinary contracts are unenforceable where the terms are "unconscionable," but what should unconscionability mean in the context of prenuptial
agreements? At one end of the spectrum, some jurisdictions stake out an
exceedingly narrow role for judicial review. In *Simeone v. Simeone*, 581
A.2d 162 (Pa. 1990), for example, the court held that courts should
undertake no heightened scrutiny to ensure the "reasonableness" of
prenuptial terms because such efforts would "interfere with the power of
persons contemplating marriage to agree upon, and to act in reliance
upon, what they regard as an acceptable distribution scheme for their
property":

> A court should not ignore the parties' expressed intent by proceeding
> to determine whether a prenuptial agreement was, in the court's
> view, reasonable at the time of its inception or the time of divorce.
> These are exactly the sorts of judicial determinations that such
> agreements are designed to avoid.

Id. at 166; *accord Stoner v. Stoner*, 819 A.2d 529, 532 (Pa. 2003) (affirming
that "prenuptial agreements should be evaluated under the same standards as [a]re other contracts, and * * * that '[a]bsent fraud, misrepresentation, or duress, spouses should be bound by the terms of their
agreements' ").

Most jurisdictions review terms more closely, but still give considerable deference to the agreement as executed. In Massachusetts, for instance, "[a]n agreement, even a one-sided agreement that leaves the
contesting party with 'considerably fewer assets' and imposes a 'far
different lifestyle after divorce' than she had during the marriage, is fair
and reasonable unless 'the contesting party is essentially stripped of
substantially all marital interests.' " *Austin v. Austin*, 839 N.E.2d 837, 841
(Mass. 2005). Some courts play a greater role in ensuring fairness,
especially for waivers of spousal support.

Consider whether it is appropriate to limit the court's evaluation of
fairness only to circumstances that were not reasonably foreseeable by the
parties when they made the agreement. *Cf. Mallen, supra*; *Principles*,
§ 7.05(2)(c). For example, where a wife signed a prenuptial agreement
waiving future support, should a court enforce the agreement if she
becomes "totally disabled" during the marriage so that enforcement
would leave her a public charge? The South Carolina Supreme Court

answered yes, reasoning that the true injustice would be "to permit a party who, fully aware of serious health issues and declining health, knowingly signs a prenuptial agreement against the advice of her attorney, to thereafter recover alimony and/or support." *Hardee v. Hardee*, 585 S.E.2d 501, 505 (S.C. 2003). Would the UPAA permit enforcement of the *Hardee* waiver agreement?

Note that section 6(a) of the UPAA authorizes a court to deny enforcement of an "unconscionable" agreement only where a party has also been denied "fair and reasonable disclosure of the property or financial obligations of the other party." 9C U.L.A. 49. As the reporters of the ALI Principles note, "[t]his remarkable language appears to require enforcement of an unconscionable agreement if it were entered into with the required disclosure." *Principles*, § 7.04, Reporter's Notes to cmt. g. Is such enforcement good policy?

The ALI Principles would permit broader fairness review, at least in cases falling within one of the three categories qualifying for review at enforcement (*see Principles*, § 7.05(2), *supra*). In these cases—including long marriages and marriages in which the couple had children—courts could enforce only contract terms that did not impose a "substantial injustice"; that judgment, in turn, would depend on such factors as "the magnitude of the disparity between the outcome under the agreement and the outcome under otherwise prevailing legal principles," and whether the agreement was intended to make reasonable provision for "children from a prior relationship." *Principles*, § 7.05(3)(a), (c). Applying the ALI Principles, how would you assess the agreements in *Mallen* and *Hollett*?

PROBLEM 14–1

Judy and John Moore were married in June 1987, when Judy was 24 and John was 36. She was a new schoolteacher earning $13,000 annually, and he was a full-time attorney with his own practice and an average annual income of $80,000.

As a condition of the marriage, John asked Judy to sign a premarital agreement drafted by his lawyer. During the course of negotiation, Judy and John disclosed assets of $5,000 and $529,607, respectively. Judy's first lawyer refused to approve of the agreement because he found the terms were one-sided, and he resigned as her counsel because she would not take his advice to reject the terms. Judy retained new counsel who acquiesced to her wish to sign the agreement.

The agreement, which the parties signed six months before the wedding, provided that in the event of divorce: (1) each party would waive any right to alimony beyond that provided under the terms of the agreement, (2) maintenance terms would consist of John's obligation to make a lump-sum payment to Judy of $2,000 for each year of their marriage up to a maximum of $50,000, and (3) each party would retain all separate property owned before the marriage, and each person's earnings from employment during the marriage would remain his or her separate property. The agreement also provided (1) that at execution, Judy would receive $10,000, (2) that John would pay Judy's attorneys' fees to cover the negotiation of the premarital agreement, and (3) that during each year of the marriage, John would contribute $2,000 to an IRA in Judy's name.

Three children were born during the Moores' 21–year marriage. Judy stayed at home to raise the children, and John became the principal shareholder and chief executive officer of his family's successful construction business.

On the parties' cross-petitions for divorce, the court found that the premarital agreement was conscionable and that the parties had entered into it knowingly and with full disclosure. The court enforced the agreement and awarded John $3,551,650 in separate and marital property and Judy $434,454 in property. The court denied separate maintenance for both parties, and ordered John to pay Judy $42,000, or $2,000 for each year of their 21–year marriage.

You are a judge of the state's court of appeals, which has just heard argument on the conscionability of the premarital agreement. If your state has enacted the UPAA, would you find the agreement enforceable? Would your answer be different if your state follows the ALI Principles?

If there were no binding case law or statutes in your state, which standard would you choose to reach the most equitable result?

PROBLEM 14–2

Willie and Maggie married in a relatively informal wedding attended by about 30 family members and friends. The day before the wedding, Willie took Maggie to see a lawyer that he had hired for her. Maggie knew that Willie worked as a delivery truck driver and approximately what he made. The lawyer presented Maggie with a fully drafted antenuptial agreement, explained each of its provisions, and asked her to sign it. Maggie complied. Under the agreement, both parties waived all claims to alimony and property division. In addition, the agreement specifically provided that Willie would retain as his sole and separate property a 19–acre parcel of land in a neighboring county that he had previously purchased "together with any house or structure which may be situated upon said property." There was no house or structure on the property when the parties married, but Willie had hidden away $150,000 in cash that he planned to use to build a home there after the wedding. However, Willie never told Maggie about the $150,000 in cash, and she had no knowledge of the money from any other source.

After eight years of marriage, Willie files for divorce and seeks to enforce the antenuptial agreement. Maggie contends that the agreement is unenforceable and asks the court to divide the couple's marital property. What advice would you give Maggie on her prospects for avoiding enforcement of the agreement in a jurisdiction in which *Mallen* governs?

D. PROVISIONS OF PREMARITAL AGREEMENTS

Parties to a prenuptial agreement may seek to include a variety of terms concerning their respective financial and non-financial obligations. The following material discusses a range of issues that arise in the context of drafting and enforcing prenuptial agreements, including child support, waiver of alimony, and terms governing personal behavior and other non-financial matters.

1. MODIFICATION OF CHILD SUPPORT

All authorities agree that parties may not contractually waive or limit the court's authority to award child support, or to ensure that custody or visitation arrangements remain consistent with the best interests of children. *See, e.g., Principles*, §§ 7.06–7.07; *Werther v. Werther*, 2005 WL 2384722, at *5 (N.Y. Sup. Ct. Sept. 2, 2005) ("In the context of child support, the Court must act as *parens patriae*, and retains jurisdiction to act in the child's best interests. Without question, a provision in an agreement eliminating a party's child support obligation is void as against public policy.").

Section 3(b) of the UPAA prohibits premarital agreements from adversely affecting the right to child support. However, as the next article details, premarital agreements can be powerful tools to set forth a more meaningful understanding of the specific contributions each parent intends to provide their child. If parents elect to bind themselves to more generous support obligations than the law requires, courts will ordinarily hold them to their bargain. *See, e.g., Shortt v. Damron*, 649 S.E.2d 283 (W. Va. 2007) (enforcing terms of separation agreement obligating father to pay children's college expenses). The issues discussed in this article may also arise in negotiations between never married parents, or in negotiations pursuant to divorce.

LINDA J. RAVDIN

Prenups to Protect Children.
24 Fam. Advoc., Winter 2002, at 32, 33–36.

* * *

* * * [P]arties may enter into enforceable premarital agreements that expand the financial rights of children and the financial obligations of one or both parents. Thus, parties may contract to provide material benefits during the marriage, such as private school, summer camp, and other extras. Parents also may contract to pay postmajority periodic support, to pay for college, or to make provisions for a child after a parent's death. To the extent that parties choose to contract beyond the scope of the state-imposed support duty, their obligations will be governed exclusively by the law of contracts.

The law does not preclude parties from being more generous than the law requires, and the courts will generally uphold agreements for the benefit of children that provide a higher level of support or a longer duration than state law requires, or support for a stepchild for whom the obligor would otherwise have no legal obligation. State courts will protect a child from a parental agreement that provides too little support.

* * *

Parties may contract on a variety of material benefits for children that are outside the scope of basic support:

* * *

POSTMAJORITY SUPPORT

* * *

Absent an enforceable contract, courts [in most states] have the authority to require parents to support a child only until that child reaches the age of majority or is otherwise emancipated. * * *

* * *

* * * Once the child reaches the age of majority, the court loses the authority to modify support in either direction. Thus, a change in the payor's ability to pay, for better or for worse, or a change in the child's needs after the child reaches majority, will not provide the basis for a court to increase or decrease the amount.

COLLEGE EXPENSES

A child's undergraduate college education often is the reason parties enter into contractual agreements for postmajority support. Because of high college costs, mistakes resulting from bad substantive terms or poor drafting of college provisions can be quite costly. A court can do little to relieve a party of the consequences of a bad agreement.

A host of issues arise in negotiating and drafting college expense provisions. Insofar as college expense obligations are a matter of contract and not state child support law, the payor has the power to limit the financial obligation. Failure to set limits by contract cannot be unilaterally corrected later.

Defining college expenses. The agreement should define college expenses. That definition may include just the basics, such as tuition, room and board, and books and fees, or may cover additional expenses, such as medical insurance and expenses, the cost of advance placement tests, study abroad, a car, a computer, cable television, the cost of joining a fraternity or sorority, off-campus housing, clothing, laundry, entertainment, a cash allowance, or other incidentals. Failure to define what is included can lead to litigation.

When one party is bound to pay all or most college expenses, the other party has an incentive to define the obligation expansively. It is especially important in these circumstances that the party with no financial obligation not be in a position to incur the expense and bill the obligor later.

* * *

Defining income. If a pre- or post-marital agreement provides for parties to share financial responsibility for college expenses in proportion to their incomes, the agreement should define income and address what is not to be included in *pro rata* shares. Will all income from all sources be included or only salary from primary employment?

* * *

Financial limits. Parties may contract for a limit on their financial obligations. Such a limit will give the parent some control over the choice of school as well as reduce the parent's risk that circumstances, such as a reduction in income or a new family, will adversely affect his or her ability to pay. Such limits can be expressed as a cap tied to a particular school's tuition, such as the local university, a school a parent attended, or some other easily ascertainable benchmark, or the parent's obligation can be expressed in terms of funds available from a specified source, such as a custodial account or other savings. In the absence of contractual limits, a court may infer that the parties intended to obligate themselves for a reasonable amount, but a judge, not the parties, will decide what is reasonable.

School selection. What right will the payor parent have to select or veto the child's choice of school? A parent may contract for the right to participate in the selection or reserve a veto right. In those states, such as Virginia, where a court has no authority to award college expenses, a parent's veto need not be reasonable. Failure to reserve the right to participate in the selection will mean that the party has no such right and may not use the child's school choice to avoid his or her obligation.

When one parent will be solely or primarily responsible for paying college expenses, that parent should reserve the right to approve the school or impose some financial limits on his or her obligation. Failure to contract for any limits means the child may have a blank check.

Time limits. Must education be completed by a certain date? Will the child be required to finish in four years or be given additional time to complete his or her education? As with so many other issues, silence can be costly for the payor. In the absence of any provision, a court may determine a reasonable time limit, not necessarily four years.

The question of time limits relates to other negotiated decisions. It may be reasonable for a party who agrees to pay for four years of college with no financial limits and no financial aid requirements to compel the child to maintain a "C" average and complete school within four years. On the other hand, when the parent's obligation is limited to in-state tuition at a state university, a child may be given a longer period in which to complete his or her education to accommodate a lighter caseload and/or work-study at a more expensive school.

* * *

Savings for future college expenses. Some parties may wish to set aside monies in anticipation of college expenses, such as in a custodial account or in a state tuition contract. When the agreement will include such an obligation, it also should specify whether the parties' obligations are limited to the funds available as a result of their savings.

Child's obligation. Will the child be required to make any financial contribution to his or her own college expenses, such as by working and applying savings to help defray expenses? Will the child be required to apply for financial aid, including loans? An agreement requiring a parent to fully fund a four-year college education with no financial limits would appear not to require the child to be responsible for student loans. Thus, a party must say in the agreement that he or she wants the child to use available financial aid. Similarly, a parent who wants the child to take advantage of other means of reducing costs, such as qualifying for in-state tuition, must say so in the agreement.

Continuation of child support. Will the payor parent continue to make periodic child support payments to the custodial parent in addition to or in lieu of college payments? Where the age of majority is 21 and a court order for child support will not automatically terminate when an 18 year-old goes to college, the agreement should specify whether a child support obligation may be paid in college costs or whether the parent will be required to pay for college and make periodic support payments. An agreement that provides for periodic support and payment of college expenses arguably requires both; yet many obligors may think only one form of payment is required. Ambiguity is likely to hurt the payor.

College expenses after death of obligor. Will the college obligation survive the death of the obligor? In the absence of express provisions in the contract, a college expense obligation will not necessarily survive the death of the obligor. The agreement, therefore, should address this issue. Parties may wish to agree on life insurance or other estate-planning vehicles to meet college obligations. In the absence of such obligations, assume that the college obligation will end with the obligor's death.

* * *

ESTATE PLANNING OBLIGATIONS

Absent a contract, a parent's obligation to support a minor child terminates upon the parent's death. An agreement may provide for life insurance, for creation of trusts, or for testamentary dispositions. Such agreements will be enforced. As with other provisions for children, the drafting of such provisions requires great care and caution.

ENFORCEMENT ISSUES

Unless and until a child support contract is incorporated or otherwise made part of a court order, the obligation is enforceable only as a contract. Thus, the parent receiving payments for the child may obtain a money judgment for breach of contract, specific performance, or other contract remedies. Once a contract is incorporated in a court order, some states will enforce it as a court order for child support, so the obligor may be held in contempt for violating the terms of the contract. Other states will enforce such an obligation only as a contract; contempt will not be a remedy.

* * *

2. WAIVERS OF SPOUSAL SUPPORT

Traditionally, courts were especially hostile to contractual waivers of a future right to alimony. The husband's duty to support his wife—and in its original form, the support duty was indeed gender-specific—was viewed as inherent in marriage and unalterable by any agreement of the parties. Even after the law in all states changed to embrace premarital and marital bargaining about property rights, many jurisdictions continued to treat waivers of spousal support as void, or at least as subject to more searching scrutiny for "fairness." In recent years, many jurisdictions have abandoned the traditional bar against spousal support waivers. *See, e.g., Hardee v. Hardee*, 585 S.E.2d 501, 503–04 (S.C. 2003). 'Forty-one states allow premarital waivers of spousal support, twenty-one by virtue of their legislatures' adoption of all or substantial portions of the UPAA," and another 18 by judicial decision. *Sanford v. Sanford*, 694 N.W.2d 283, 288 n.2 (S.D. 2005).

The trend favoring enforcement of spousal support waivers is so strong that in 2000, the California Supreme Court upheld judicial authority to enforce such waivers even after the state legislature had chosen not to enact the portion of the UPAA authorizing them. *See In re Marriage of Pendleton*, 5 P.3d 839 (Cal. 2000). The legislature later partially acquiesced, but amended the statute to limit enforcement to waivers that are not "unconscionable at the time of enforcement." Cal. Fam. Code § 1612(c) (West 2004). Against this strong current, a handful of jurisdictions still refuse to enforce spousal support waivers. *See, e.g., Sanford*, 694 N.W.2d at 288–89; Iowa Code Ann. § 596.5(2) (West 2001) ("The right of a spouse or child to support shall not be adversely affected by a premarital agreement."). *See also* Susan Wolfson, *Premarital Waiver of Alimony*, 38 Fam. L.Q. 141 (2004). On what rationale might courts consider spousal support rights entirely or partially non-waivable? To help formulate your answer, reconsider the rationales for alimony discussed in Chapter 10.

3. NON–MONETARY CONTRACT TERMS

The UPAA expressly permits parties to negotiate about at least some "personal rights and obligations." UPAA § 3(a)(8), 9C U.L.A. 43. Nevertheless, courts regularly distinguish between monetary and non-monetary terms:

> While property and alimony agreements are enforced, courts are extremely reluctant to enforce provisions dealing with anything else, whether those provisions dictate conduct within the marriage, including the division of labor, cohabitation, or sexual relations; restrict the right to seek a divorce; govern child custody; or specify children's religious training in the event of a divorce.

Katharine B. Silbaugh, *Marriage Contracts and the Family Economy*, 93 Nw. U. L. Rev. 65, 78 (1998). As a result, provisions concerning the non-monetary rights and obligations of the parties occupy, at best, a "legal limbo." Barbara Stark, *Marriage Proposals: From One–Size–Fits–All to Postmodern Marriage Law,* 89 Cal. L. Rev. 1479, 1496–97 (2001).

In *Spires v. Spires*, 743 A.2d 186 (D.C. 1999), a married couple agreed to reconcile after a brief separation and signed a written "marital agreement" including 13 "Articles of Continuance" for their relationship:

> The Articles of Continuance state, among other things, that Mrs. Spires may not withdraw any money from the bank without Mr. Spires' express permission; may not "attempt to influence the status/intensity" of any relationship that Mr. Spires may have "with other individuals outside of the marriage unless the husband verbally requests input from the wife"; may not "dispute" Mr. Spires in public "on any matter"; must "conduct herself in accordance with all scriptures in the Holy Bible applicable to marital relationships germane to wives and in accordance with the husband's specific requests"; must maintain a sexual relationship that "remains spontaneous and solely with the husband"; must "carry out requests of the husband in strict accordance, *i.e.,* timeliness, sequence, scheduling, etc."; and may not receive any loan or gift without first obtaining Mr. Spires' permission. According to the agreement, violation of any of these articles would be considered mental cruelty, abandonment of the marriage, and a request for legal separation and divorce.

Id. at 188 n.2. When the couple later divorced, the trial court refused to enforce the agreement. The court of appeals affirmed, with concurring Judge Frank E. Schwelb condemning the agreement as "deprav[ed]":

> Although, unfortunately, some men abuse, oppress and humiliate their wives, it is surely rare for a husband not only to reduce to writing an instrument requiring total subordination by the wife to the husband's caprice, but also to require his unfortunate spouse to sign it. I find it even more remarkable that a husband who has contrived to secure his wife's formal written assent to the husband's assertion of supremacy would then have the temerity to ask a court to enforce such an oppressive document according to its terms.
>
> In my opinion, a "contract" such as the one between these parties, which formalizes and seeks to legitimize absolute male domi-

nation and female subordination within the marital relationship, is against the public policy of this jurisdiction.

Id. at 192.

What result if the Spires' agreement had not been so one-sided? One Florida couple's prenuptial agreement, for example, set out the personal obligations of both spouses:

> Paragraph 10 reads: "Sally will cook breakfast a minimum of 3 times during the weekdays, and one time per weekend. In return, Renzie will not wake Sally up on her 'off days.'"
>
> Paragraph 11: "Renzie will rub Sally's back/neck 3 times during the weekdays, and one time per weekend for a minimum of 5 minutes, but hopefully more, each time."
>
> Paragraph 17 states that "each time Sally ... regretfully uses the 'F' word, she agrees to do one hour of yardwork within the next 7 days. Likewise, Renzie will put $5 in Sally's cookie jar each time he complains, nags or otherwise makes a fuss about Sally's expenditures...."

Rene Stutzman, *Wife Says Divorce Is News To Her*, Orlando Sentinel, Jan. 3, 2006, at B1.

What about a prenuptial agreement never to have children? According to some lawyers, no-child clauses are becoming more common in family law practice, especially in marriages involving wealthy divorced fathers and younger second wives. *See* Jill Brooke, *A Promise To Love, Honor and Bear No Children*, N.Y. Times, Oct. 13, 2002, at 9–1. If you were a judge, would you enforce a clause imposing a financial penalty in divorce for violating such a pledge? Half a century ago, a New York court held that such an agreement would be void "since it is a matter of public policy that marriage exists primarily for begetting offspring, and the right to normal and proper sex relations is implicit in the marriage contract." *Height v. Height*, 187 N.Y.S.2d 260, 262 (Sup. Ct. 1959). Is that an acceptable rationale for denying enforcement today? *See* Joline F. Sikaitis, Comment, *A New Form of Family Planning?: The Enforceability of No–Child Provisions in Prenuptial Agreements*, 54 Cath. U. L. Rev. 335 (2004) (contending that judicial enforcement would impinge upon fundamental privacy interests in childbearing).

Notwithstanding the particular agreement in *Spires*, Professor Silbaugh contends that the courts' tendency toward "selective enforcement" of premarital contract terms—giving effect only to monetary provisions—generally disadvantages women because they "contribute more nonmonetary wealth [to marriage] than men, and men more money than women, on average." *See* Silbaugh, *supra,* at 99–101. If this observation is accurate, should the law help achieve gender equality by enforcing nonmonetary terms more strongly? Or should the law respond, as Professor Silbaugh suggests, by withdrawing enforcement from monetary terms? Acknowledging "valid reasons for not enforcing nonmonetary agreements, including child welfare concerns," she argues that "treating monetary and nonmonetary components of marriage equally, * * * requires us to deny enforcement of monetary agreements." *Id.* at 123; *see also* Katharine B. Silbaugh, *Gender and Nonfinancial Matters in the ALI Principles of the Law of Family Dissolution*, 8 Duke J. Gender L. & Pol'y 203 (2001).

Courts are regularly called upon to enforce marital agreements concerning religious practice. In some religions, such as Islam and Judaism, written agreements promising payments in the event of divorce can be integral to entry into marriage. *See* Ann Laquer Estin, *Embracing Tradition: Pluralism in American Family Law,* 63 Md. L. Rev. 540, 569–70 (2004); Lindsey E. Blenkhorn, Note, *Islamic Marriage Contracts in American Courts: Interpreting* Mahr *Agreements as Prenuptials and Their Effect on Muslim Women,* 76 S. Cal. L. Rev. 189 (2002). In addition, parties at the time of marriage may agree that dissolution comport with religious law or be referred directly to a religious tribunal.

These faith-based agreements have produced a patchwork of decisions. Courts have enforced agreements requiring payment of money or transfer of property on divorce, provided the promised sum was not so large as to induce the beneficiary to seek divorce. *See, e.g., Odatalla v. Odatalla,* 810 A.2d 93 (N.J. Super. Ct. 2002). Similarly, some courts have honored agreements to refer divorce issues to a religious tribunal. *See, e.g., Avitzur v. Avitzur,* 446 N.E.2d 136 (N.Y. 1983). But disputes over a marital agreement's religious terms can raise sensitive First Amendment questions, particularly where adjudication might require courts to interpret and decide disputed religious doctrine. "Denying enforcement of a marital agreement signed by two individuals in a religious context might infringe their free exercise rights, but interpreting and enforcing such an agreement on the basis of religious law verges dangerously on an establishment of religion." Estin, *supra,* at 542. In interpreting the Establishment Clause, the Supreme Court has sometimes used a test that condemns "excessive entanglement" between courts and religion and is especially wary of resolving disputes over the meaning of religious doctrine. *See, e.g., Sieger v. Sieger,* 2005 WL 2031746, at *51 (N.Y. Sup. Ct. June 29, 2005); Douglas Laycock, *The Supreme Court and Religious Liberty,* 40 Cath. Law. 25 (2000).

NOTES AND QUESTIONS

1. *Who should have a premarital agreement?* Many people may benefit from premarital agreements, especially persons with individual investments and earnings who wish to protect children from prior relationships or other family members. Couples who enter marriage with significant separate assets and who intend to maintain separate finances may benefit from an agreement explicitly stating their intentions. Senior citizens may enjoy similar benefits.

2. *What are the advantages of executing a premarital agreement?* As we have seen, premarital agreements can facilitate private ordering by overriding state laws governing alimony or marital property distribution. Section 3 of the

UPAA, for instance, authorizes parties to a premarital agreement to contract with respect to their rights and obligations "in any property of either or both of them whenever and wherever acquired or located." Moreover, although premarital agreements are often thought of as "a blueprint for divorce," they can also serve "as a plan to preserve a marriage," by clearly defining the spouses' mutual expectations and financial understandings. Fredrica Greene, *Terms of Endearment: Financial Contracts for Couples*, J. Fin. Plan. 78, 78–86 (Mar. 2002).

SECTION 3: POSTNUPTIAL AGREEMENTS

After parties are married, they may enter into contracts governing their respective rights and obligations. Courts commonly enforce separation agreements or reconciliation agreements that married partners negotiate when separation or divorce is imminent. The rules governing these agreements are discussed in the next section.

Far less commonly, spouses negotiate agreements after the wedding but before marital discord has set them on a path to divorce. These contracts, falling in the gap between antenuptial and separation or reconciliation agreements, are sometimes called postnuptial, postmarital or mid-marriage agreements. They remain an infrequent occurrence in most family law practice, but their use is on the rise. Indeed, one commentator predicts that "because of their practical advantages, * * * they will become the dominant form of marital contract" in the years ahead. Sean Hannon Williams, *Postnuptial Agreements*, 2007 Wis. L. Rev. 827, 829.

Lawyers and couples who negotiate postnuptial agreements report that the experience can provide a "midcourse correction" in a marriage. Patricia Wen, *Sealing a Contract After the Marriage*, Boston Globe, Dec. 19, 2005, at A1. The agreements are often used to disentangle the spouses' finances, but may also be used "to codify what is written on the kitchen bulletin board, such as who washes the dishes or who shovels the snow." *Id.* In some cases, couples negotiate agreements to address specific points of conflict that have arisen within a marriage, hammering out their mutual expectations concerning troublesome "behavioral issues—infidelity, gambling, drinking, excess spending, [and] failure to help with the chores or the children." L.A. Johnson, *Another Way to Work it Out: Postnuptial Agreement Can Adjudicate the Disputes Within a Marriage*, Pittsburgh Post–Gazette, Jan. 29, 2006, at F–9. In other cases, the triggering event for negotiations is not discord, but a significant change in one spouse's financial position, such as the receipt of a large inheritance.

In either event, postnuptial agreements seek to clarify the parties' expectations and provide a blueprint for their ongoing marriage. "Therapists who work with couples say the process of drafting postnuptial agreements can help trigger sweeping behavioral changes that might keep couples together." Wen, *supra*, at A1. "Anxiety can suck a tremendous amount of energy out of a relationship because it's rooted in uncertainty," explained one family therapist. "What a post-nup does is eliminate the uncertainty which then reduces the anxiety." *No Pre–Nup? Try a Post–Nuptial*, Amer. Pub. Media, *Marketplace*, June 8, 2006 (quoting Dr. Rob Scuka) (transcript available at http://marketplace.publicradio.org/shows/ 2006/06/08/PM200606085.html).

Anecdotal evidence suggests that for some couples, concluding a postnuptial agreement can be a turning point in a successful marriage. One suburban Boston couple, for example, recounted how their relationship had dissolved into quarreling after 10 years of marriage but rebounded after they sat down at the negotiating table. By specifying their respective financial and family obligations, the agreement reduced tension and the couple recently celebrated their 27th anniversary. *See* Wen, *supra*, at A1.

If a marriage ultimately fails or if the parties breach any term of the postnuptial agreement, most courts enforce these contracts on the same terms as antenuptial agreements. The following two decisions, however, show points of important difference.

1. CONSIDERATION

BRATTON v. BRATTON

Supreme Court of Tennessee, 2004.
136 S.W.3d 595.

WILLIAM M. BARKER, J., delivered the opinion of the court.

We granted permission to appeal in this divorce proceeding to determine whether postnuptial agreements are contrary to public policy and if not, whether the postnuptial agreement entered into by the parties in this case is valid and enforceable. We hold that postnuptial agreements are not contrary to public policy so long as there is consideration for the agreement, it is knowledgeably entered into, and there is no evidence of fraud, coercion or duress. However, the agreement between the parties in this case is invalid because it lacks adequate consideration. * * *

BACKGROUND

The parties, Cynthia Lee Bratton (Ms. Bratton) and Michael Wayne Bratton (Dr. Bratton), were married on June 26, 1982. At the time of the marriage, Dr. Bratton had completed his first year of medical school, and Ms. Bratton was employed as a research technician. Ms. Bratton had a child from a previous marriage. At the time of the trial, the parties had two minor children, ages sixteen and thirteen.

On June 27, 1983, Dr. Bratton handwrote and signed the following letter:

I, Michael W. Bratton, being of sound mind and being married to Cynthia L. Bratton hereby promise never to be the cause of a divorce between us. In the event that I do not fulfill my promise, I will give

Cindy 50% of my present belongings and 50% of my net future earnings.

A more formal "property settlement agreement" was signed by both parties on August 26, 1983. That agreement provided in pertinent part:

WHEREAS, the parties are husband and wife and desire to provide for the future division and distribution of property and support of the Wife in the event of a future divorce; and

WHEREAS, the parties desire that their respective rights and interests in and to all future property to be accumulated be expressly set forth herein and established in accordance with the terms and provisions hereof.

NOW, THEREFORE, IN CONSIDERATION OF THE PREMISES, the mutual benefits accruing to the respective parties and other good and valuable consideration, received or to be received by each of the parties hereto, it is agreed as follows:

1. In the event the Husband is guilty of statutory grounds for divorce under the statutes of the state the parties are domiciled and the Wife institutes divorce proceedings in the state courts of such state, all property jointly owned by the parties, real, personal, or mixed, shall be divided equally between the parties.

2. In the event the Husband is guilty of statutory grounds for divorce under the statutes of the state the parties are domiciled and the Wife institutes divorce proceedings in the state courts of such state, the Husband shall pay to the Wife, one-half (1/2) of all of the Husband's net gross income (after deduction for state and federal income taxes).

The parties' versions as to the events surrounding the execution of the agreement differ substantially. Ms. Bratton testified that prior to their marriage, she and her husband discussed the fact that she would forgo a career as a dentist to stay at home and raise a family if Dr. Bratton would provide one-half of his income to her in the event of a divorce. No written agreement was ever entered into prior to the marriage. One year after the parties married, Ms. Bratton again voiced an interest in dental school to her husband, at which time Dr. Bratton offered to formalize their prior agreement if she would give up the pursuit of a career. * * *

Dr. Bratton testified that there had been no discussion of his wife's interest in dental school prior to their marriage or at any time during the marriage. Instead, he testified that one year into their marriage, Ms. Bratton told him that the doctors with whom she worked warned her that he was likely to leave her once he graduated from medical school and that she needed a legally binding agreement to protect herself from that possibility. After arguing about this with his wife, Dr. Bratton handwrote the letter of July 1983, promising not to leave her and promising that if he did, she would get one-half of his property and future earnings. Dr. Bratton testified that it was Ms. Bratton who contacted an attorney to have the agreement drafted and brought it home for him to sign. At first he refused, but then he relented when she threatened to leave him if he did not sign it. Both parties testified that at the time the agreement was signed, they were not having any marital difficulties.

On March 15, 2000, Ms. Bratton filed for divorce. Dr. Bratton filed a motion for partial summary judgment to have the Property Settlement Agreement declared invalid for lack of consideration. The trial court granted the motion in part. The court found that the agreement was severable and that the portion of the agreement relating to the division of property was valid and enforceable, but that the portion regarding the support was invalid for want of consideration. * * *

The trial court found that in the year 2000, Dr. Bratton, who was an orthopedic surgeon, had a gross annual income of $551,521.00. The court also found that "upon the parties' marriage, Ms. Bratton chose to forgo her career ... in order to support Dr. Bratton's medical career, as well as to serve as homemaker and primary caregiver for the parties' children." While Ms. Bratton is licensed as a real estate broker, the court found that "her business attempts have proved financially unsuccessful."

The trial court granted the divorce to Ms. Bratton based on inappropriate marital conduct on the part of Dr. Bratton in the nature of adultery. Ms. Bratton was designated the primary residential parent of the parties' two minor children. * * * Marital property and marital debt were divided equally between the parties. The court awarded Ms. Bratton alimony in futuro in the amount of $10,500.00 per month until her death or remarriage. Both parties appealed.

The Court of Appeals found that there was consideration for both parts of the postnuptial agreement, but that the whole agreement was in violation of public policy. However, the Court of Appeals affirmed the outcome of the lower court, finding that the evidence did not preponderate against the trial court's division of marital property and marital debt. The court also affirmed the award of alimony *in futuro* to the wife.

Both parties appealed to this Court. * * *

ANALYSIS

Are Postnuptial Agreements Contrary to Public Policy?

The Court of Appeals found that the postnuptial agreement was void as against public policy because it preempted the trial court from equitably assigning marital property and alimony as provided by statute. While this Court has declared valid agreements entered into after marriage if they are incident to a reconciliation, we have not addressed the issue of postnuptial agreements that are entered into before the onset of marital difficulties.

There are several types of agreements entered into by spouses or potential spouses. * * * Courts enforce antenuptial agreements like any other contract provided that they are "entered into freely and knowledgeably, with adequate disclosure, and without undue influence or over-reaching." Likewise, reconciliation agreements have been found to be favored by public policy and are enforceable in a manner similar to antenuptial agreements.

The agreement in the case under submission falls into a third category of agreements—postnuptial agreements. While entered into by spouses after marriage, they differ from reconciliation agreements in that they are entered into before marital problems arise. * * *

Although postnuptial agreements were void and of no effect under the common law, most states to address the issue have now determined such agreements to be valid. These courts have held that generally, spouses may divide their property presently and prospectively by a postnuptial agreement, even without it being incident to a contemplated separation or divorce, provided that the agreement is free from fraud, coercion or undue influence, that the parties acted with full knowledge of the property involved and their rights therein, and that the settlement was fair and equitable.

The rationale behind the decision of the Court of Appeals holding the agreement to be void as against public policy was that the contract * * * preempted the court from equitably assigning marital property or considering the issue of alimony as provided by statute. However, * * * to say that a postnuptial agreement is contrary to public policy due to its invasion into the province of the trial court is inconsistent with the State's acceptance of antenuptial and reconciliation agreements. * * *

Generally, postnuptial agreements will be treated in the same manner as antenuptial and reconciliation agreements. That is to say, they should be interpreted and enforced as any other contract. All contracts must be supported by adequate consideration, and agreements between spouses or potential spouses are no exception. * * * Marriage itself is sufficient consideration for a prenuptial agreement. Similarly, reconciliation in the face of an impending separation or divorce may be adequate consideration. However, with a postnuptial agreement, the marriage itself cannot act as sufficient consideration because past consideration cannot support a current promise. Therefore, there must be consideration flowing to both parties as part of a postnuptial agreement.

* * *

Because of the confidential relationship which exists between husband and wife, postnuptial agreements are likewise subjected to close scrutiny by the courts to ensure that they are fair and equitable. As explained by the court in *Estate of Gab,*

> While it is lawful and not against public policy for husband and wife to enter into such contracts, yet they are not dealing with each other as strangers at arm's length. The relationship of husband and wife is one of special confidence and trust, requiring the utmost good faith and frankness in their dealings with each other.... Transactions of

this character are scrutinized by the courts with great care, to the end that no unjust advantage may be obtained by one over the other by means of any oppression, deception, or fraud. Courts of equity will relieve against any unjust advantage procured by any such means, and less evidence is required in such cases to establish the fraud, oppression, or deception than if the parties had been dealing at arm's length as strangers. . . .

364 N.W.2d [924, 926 (S.D. 1985).]

Is the Agreement Valid and Enforceable?

Having established what is necessary for there to be a valid and enforceable postnuptial agreement, we must determine whether the agreement entered into by the parties in this case meets those requirements. We hold that it does not because it was not supported by adequate consideration.

* * *

It is clear from the agreement that there is consideration flowing from the husband to the wife, as the agreement provides that the wife is to receive one-half of the husband's future income as well as one-half of the jointly owned property. The agreement does not, however, specify what act or forbearance is to be undertaken by the wife as consideration for the contract. * * *

The trial court found that with regard to the property division there was consideration because "a couple'[s] waiver of statutory rights to each other's estate can constitute sufficient consideration." While such a mutual waiver of rights in property may constitute consideration, it does not here. Because the agreement is not severable, we must find consideration for the whole contract. The Court of Appeals found consideration for the whole contract, stating:

> Both parties testified that wife would do something in exchange's [sic] for the husband's promise regarding his future income. The wife testified that she would forego her career to stay home and rear the children. The husband testified that the wife agreed to stay in the marriage in exchange for his signing the Agreement. This could be a benefit flowing to him.

We disagree with the Court of Appeals and hold that, under either fact scenario, there was not adequate consideration flowing from Ms. Bratton to Dr. Bratton. Ms. Bratton's promise not to leave her husband is clearly not consideration for the agreement. Both parties[ ] admitted that they were not having marital difficulties at the time the agreement was signed. Therefore, this was not a reconciliation agreement where separation or divorce was imminent, making the wife's promise to remain in the marriage a meaningful act. According to the husband, the wife's promise was more akin to coercion, in that she threatened to leave him if he did not sign the agreement. Therefore, even if this were to constitute adequate consideration, the agreement would be invalid due to the taint of coercion and duress.[1]

Ms. Bratton's promise to forgo a career as a dentist likewise does not constitute consideration as it is a vague and illusory promise. While the wife testified that she had a desire to become a dentist and had discussed this desire with her husband, she had never enrolled in dental school, had never even taken the dental school admissions tests, nor had she taken any other steps necessary to the pursuit of a career as a dentist. Furthermore, as the trial court noted, Ms. Bratton made the choice to forego a career in order to stay home and support her husband at the time of the marriage, which was prior to any agreement being signed. By basing the agreement on a promise or decision that the wife had already made when entering into the marriage, Ms. Bratton is essentially trying to use past consideration to support a present contract, which this Court has long held to be inadequate consideration. Finally, the benefit received by Dr. Bratton as a result of Ms. Bratton foregoing a career as a dentist was arguably that of having his wife home to look after him, the house, and the children. However, shortly after signing the agreement, Ms. Bratton enrolled in nursing school (although she did not complete more than one semester), and later pursued a career as a real estate agent.

For these reasons, we hold that there was no adequate consideration for the agreement between the parties.[2] Therefore, there is no valid postnuptial agreement.

* * *

CONCLUSION

* * * While the trial court divided the marital property pursuant to the agreement the parties do not contest that division on appeal, and we therefore uphold the trial court's judgment with respect to the property. Because the agreement was not supported by consideration, the trial court properly determined spousal support based upon the statutory guidelines, and we hold that the court's award was not an abuse of discretion. As such, the judgment of the trial court is affirmed.

* * *

---

1. The dissent states that under Dr. Bratton's version of the facts, "the consideration Dr. Bratton bargained for and received was the benefit of domestic tranquility. In addition, Dr. Bratton received Ms. Bratton's promise that she would stay in the marriage." While life may have been "much better" for Dr. Bratton after he signed the agreement, this "domestic tranquility" does not constitute consideration adequate to support the contract. * * * Under the dissent's theory, consideration could be found in many instances which would otherwise amount to or border on coercion. For example, if spouse A wanted to get spouse B to enter into a post-nuptial agreement that was essentially for the sole benefit of A, A could simply create such a hostile environment at home by badgering B until B signed the agreement.

2. While we were unable to find adequate consideration to support the post-nuptial agreement in the case under submission, we can envision many scenarios where there would be adequate consideration. For example, there are many cases upholding post-nuptial agreements in which the parties mutually release claims to each other's property in the event of death. Additionally, there would be adequate consideration where one spouse gives up an existing career to care for the parties' children in exchange for property and support in the event of divorce to protect that spouse from being disadvantaged in re-entering the job market after a potentially long absence.

JANICE M. HOLDER, J., concurring in part and dissenting in part.

I concur in the majority's conclusion that postnuptial agreements are not contrary to public policy. I respectfully dissent, however, from that portion of the majority's opinion concluding that the agreement at issue in the present case was not supported by adequate consideration.

* * *

Under Ms. Bratton's version of the facts, the consideration that flows to Dr. Bratton is Ms. Bratton's promise to forego a career as a dentist. * * *

* * * If Ms. Bratton's promise is illusory because she failed to take steps toward a career that she promised not to pursue, every promise to refrain from activity will suffer from the same infirmity.

* * *

The majority would find adequate consideration when one spouse gives up an existing career to care for the parties' children in exchange for property and support in the event of divorce. I fail to see any meaningful distinction between the facts of this case and those presented in the majority's example. * * *

* * *

Under the[] facts [alleged by Dr. Bratton], the consideration Dr. Bratton bargained for and received was the benefit of domestic tranquility. In addition, Dr. Bratton received Ms. Bratton's promise that she would stay in the marriage.

A majority of this Court, however, disagrees. First, the majority concludes that Ms. Bratton's promise not to leave her husband is not adequate consideration because the parties were not experiencing marital difficulties. While the parties' marital difficulties did not rise to the level of separation, their arguments attest to some amount of tension that was resolved by the execution of the agreement. Moreover, the validity of a postnuptial agreement does not turn on a requirement that parties experience marital difficulties, although this requirement is the hallmark of a reconciliation agreement.

Even assuming the adequacy of consideration, the majority further holds that the agreement, premised on the promise not to leave the marriage, would be invalid as a result of coercion and duress. Yet, promises to stay in or to return to a marriage will not invalidate an agreement to reconcile. Indeed, such promises are considered to be adequate consideration.

By entering into the agreement, Ms. Bratton received one-half of the parties' jointly-owned property and one-half of Dr. Bratton's future earnings. Depending on whose version of the facts is believed, Dr. Bratton received Ms. Bratton's promise to forego her dental career, domestic tranquility, or her promise to stay in the marriage. As such, both parties bargained for and received a benefit by entering into the agreement. Accordingly, I would reverse the Court of Appeals and remand the case for consideration of the issues pretermitted by its holding.

Notes and Questions

1. *Consideration.* Do you agree with the *Bratton* majority that the husband received no legally cognizable consideration for this bargain? The majority acknowledges that courts routinely enforce reconciliation agreements based on the parties' mutual promises to continue the marriage. In 2007, for example, an Illinois appellate court upheld a postnuptial agreement negotiated after the wife discovered that her husband had been having an affair. The court found sufficient consideration for the husband's waiver of property rights in the wife's agreement to remain in the marriage, distinguishing *Bratton* on the ground that the parties negotiated the contract in the midst of genuine "marital difficulties" even though they had not yet separated or filed for divorce. *In re Marriage of Tabassum and Younis,* 881 N.E.2d 396, 407–08 (Ill. Ct. App. 2007). Are the decisions really distinguishable? Why limit legal reliance on promises of marital harmony or forbearance to agreements negotiated when a marriage is already in crisis?

Professor Katharine Silbaugh observes that the "family economy" is "supported by both money and a constant flow of unpaid labor in the form of housekeeping, child, elder and other dependent care, household management, counseling and other emotional support, and entertainment." Katharine B. Silbaugh, *Marriage Contracts and the Family Economy,* 93 Nw. U. L. Rev. 65, 92–93 (1998). *Bratton*'s view of permissible consideration seems to allow spouses to bargain with money but not with promises of non-monetary contributions. To the extent that women continue to make most of the non-monetary contributions in marriage while men contribute most of the money, *see id.* at 99–101, the court's view may disadvantage women. Should gender disparity call for a different view of permissible consideration? If you were an attorney drafting an agreement similar to the one at issue in *Bratton,* how might you revise its terms to ensure that a court would find adequate consideration?

2. *Coercion.* The *Bratton* majority suggests that a threat to divorce if the parties do not conclude a postnuptial agreement is coercive, rendering any resulting agreement unenforceable as involuntary. Courts uniformly hold, however, that threats not to marry without a prenuptial agreement are not coercive. *See, e.g., In re Marriage of Barnes,* 755 N.E.2d 522, 527 (Ill. App. Ct. 2001) ("Both Edward and Sandra could have remained single. Nothing was legally or morally wrong with either of them conditioning marriage upon the execution of a premarital agreement."). Is there a sound reason for distinguishing between the two situations?

If you are inclined to agree with Justice Holder's dissent that Ms. Bratton's "promise to stay in the marriage" furnished sufficient consideration, would you stand by that view on the following facts: Mid-way through a 20–year marriage, the husband, a highly successful entrepreneur with approximately $4.7 million in assets, presented his wife, who had been a 20–year–old immigrant at the time of the marriage, with a non-negotiable demand that she sign an agreement waiving her rights to any property distribution or alimony in the event of divorce. Against the advice of independent counsel, the wife signed the agreement because the husband had threatened to end the marriage if she did not sign and "she wanted to preserve the marriage and did not want her children to grow up in a broken family." *See Pacelli v. Pacelli*, 725 A.2d 56, 58, 62 (N.J. Super. Ct. 1999) (declining to enforce the agreement because its economic provisions were "not fair and just").

3. *Penalties for marital misconduct.* Should a court enforce an agreement imposing a financial penalty for adultery or other misconduct during the marriage? The state supreme court nullified the entire agreement in *Bratton* for want of consideration, but the trial court had enforced the provision specifying a property division based upon the husband's adultery. Similarly, a Wyoming trial court enforced a provision forfeiting a contingent $100,000 payment to the wife based upon her adultery. *See Bradley v. Bradley*, 118 P.3d 984 (Wyo. 2005) (reversing the judgment on other grounds).

The ALI Principles would condition enforceability of misconduct clauses on whether the state permits courts to consider marital fault in dividing property or awarding maintenance. *See* ALI, Principles of the Law of Family Dissolution: Analysis and Recommendations § 7.08(2) (2002) (providing that contract terms "requir[ing] or forbid[ding] a court to evaluate marital conduct in allocating marital property or awarding compensatory payments" are unenforceable "except as the term incorporates principles of state law"). The official commentary notes:

> Modern no-fault divorce laws reflect, among other things, a policy of limiting the role of legal institutions in monitoring and policing the details of intimate relationships, and it would defeat that purpose if parties were permitted, by their own agreement, to require courts to decide if either of them was at fault for their relationship's decline.

Id., cmt. a. The official commentary may be right, but then again an agreement opting out of a state's equitable distribution or support laws may be said similarly to defeat the policy of those laws to promote norms of marital partnership and sharing. *See Developments in the Law—The Law of Marriage and Family: Marriage as a Contract and Marriage as a Partnership: The Future of Antenuptial Agreement Law*, 116 Harv. L. Rev. 2075 (2003). Is there a good reason to consider the latter policy, but not the former, "waivable" by the parties?

2. DEFINING THE SCOPE OF THE UPAA

The Uniform Premarital Agreement Act (UPAA) facially applies only to prenuptial agreements. By court decisions, several states have extended its application to postnuptial agreements. Other states, as in the decision that follows, have held that postnuptial agreements are not subject to statutory standards governing prenuptial agreements. Yet, if postnuptial agreements fall outside the scope of existing statutes, what standards should govern their enforceability? As you read the following decision, consider whether sound policy reasons support distinguishing between the enforcement of prenuptial and postnuptial agreements.

IN RE MARRIAGE OF FRIEDMAN

Court of Appeals of California, 2002.
122 Cal.Rptr.2d 412.

YEGAN, J.

* * *

In this action for marital dissolution, Jill L. Friedman (wife) appeals from an order that a 1991 postnuptial agreement is valid and enforceable. The trial court found that wife voluntarily entered into the agreement and that the agreement was not invalid because of alleged conflict of interest by the attorney who prepared it. We affirm.

FACTS AND PROCEDURAL HISTORY

In December 1990 wife worked as an attorney for a prestigious law firm. She met and fell in love with husband who had just sailed around the world and wanted to start a forensic consulting business. Husband and wife discussed marriage. Wife said that she wanted to keep her law practice as separate property if she married. Husband agreed.

Weeks after meeting wife, husband was diagnosed with leukemia. Lacking insurance for medical treatment, he decided "to go off sailing again and just die." Wife urged husband to undergo a bone marrow transplant and proposed marriage so that he could be placed on her medical insurance. This entreaty saved husband's life. He agreed and the parties married January 27, 1991.

Within days of the marriage, husband called his attorney, S. Timothy Buynak, Jr. Husband wanted to protect wife from creditors if he did not survive the medical treatment, which was a distinct possibility. Husband and wife met Buynak, a partner in the law firm of Hatch and Parent (H & P), on January 31, 1991. Buynak suggested a postnuptial agreement providing that their individual income, business property, and debts would be separate property. Husband's prior marriage ended with a bitter fight over a family business. Buynak explained that he was representing husband and that wife would have to retain separate counsel or represent herself.

* * *

Wife made changes to the postnuptial agreement, which were incorporated into the final draft and signed March 20, 1991. To protect against medical creditors, husband gifted his boat to wife.

Husband underwent a bone marrow transplant and fully recovered. During the marriage, the parties maintained separate bank accounts and separate businesses. Wife started her own law practice but also helped husband in his fledgling business.

Husband's business flourished beyond his and wife's dreams. The limited record on appeal does not disclose the actual value of this asset. It is, however, the source of significant dispute, which gives rise to this interlocutory appeal.

In 1997 or 1998, the parties experienced marital problems. Wife told husband to "get rid" of the postnuptial agreement and that she did not want "that postnuptial agreement hanging over my head anymore." Husband did not agree to do so.

On May 1, 2000, wife filed a petition for marital dissolution. Husband contended that the forensic consulting business was not community property. Wife claimed that the postnuptial agreement was invalid * * *.

* * * The trial court found that Buynak did not represent wife and that she "had ample time (a month) to consult with an attorney, if she chose to do so. Ms. Friedman is a bright woman. She is a trained attorney with three years of experience as a civil litigator at the time this event took place. The courtship, the elopement, the meetings with the attorney, the creation of the postnuptial agreement document, a month to review it—no one held a gun to her head and made her go into the lawyer's office and sign the document on March 20, 1991. She did so freely, voluntarily, intelligently with superior knowledge of the law and the rights that she was relinquishing. . . ."

The trial court stayed the proceedings and certified the matter for interlocutory appeal. * * *

* * *

FAMILY CODE SECTION 1615

In *In re Marriage of Bonds*, 5 P.3d 815 (Cal. 2000), our Supreme Court held that wife's lack of representation was one of several factors to be considered in determining whether a premarital agreement was voluntary under Family Code section 1615. Evidence that the premarital agreement was prepared by husband's attorney and signed by wife without counsel did not automatically void the agreement.

In response to *Bonds*, the Legislature amended Family Code section 1615 to provide that a premarital agreement is not voluntary if a party is not represented by counsel when signing the agreement or the party fails to waive "in a separate writing, representation by independent counsel." * * *

Wife's reliance on Family Code section 1615 is misplaced. This section does not govern postnuptial agreements. Premarital agreements are not interpreted and enforced under the same standards as interspousal agreements. It is well settled that property settlement agreements occupy a favored position in California.

BREACH OF FIDUCIARY DUTY

Wife argues that husband owed a fiduciary duty and that it is presumed that the postnuptial agreement was induced by undue influence. (Fam. Code, § 721, subd. (b)); *In re Marriage of Haines*, [39 Cal. Rptr. 2d

673, 683–84 (Ct. App. 1995)]. That presumption was dispelled by the evidence. The trial court found that as an attorney, wife understood the scope and purpose of the postnuptial agreement. It found that husband "carried the burden of showing that Ms. Friedman was not induced to execute the postnuptial agreement through mistake, undue influence, fraud, misrepresentation, false promise, concealment, nondisclosure or any other breach of the Friedman's confidential relationship. There is no taint." * * *

Substantial evidence supported the trial court's finding[s] * * *. The postnuptial agreement did not favor either party and protected wife's property from husband's creditors. * * *

* * *

FINAL OBSERVATIONS

* * * [W]e review the legality of the 1991 postnuptial agreement at the time it was made. Where, as here, the agreement is lawful, either party may insist upon adhering to its letter. This protects the reasonable expectations of the parties at the time the bargain was struck. Subsequent events, whether unforeseen or fortuitous, and whether they favor one side or the other, should not dictate how we decide the legal issue here presented.

Wife's remaining arguments have been considered and merit no further discussion.

The order declaring the 1991 postnuptial agreement valid is affirmed. Husband is awarded costs on appeal.

NOTES AND QUESTIONS

1. *Procedural safeguards for postnuptial negotiations.* In important respects, California provides fewer procedural safeguards of voluntariness for postnuptial agreements than for antenuptial agreements. This distinction might seem ironic because California is in the minority of jurisdictions that recognize no "confidential relationship" before marriage, but the state follows the universal view that spouses do occupy such a relationship during marriage. *Cf.* Elizabeth Barker Brandt, *The Uniform Premarital Agreements Act and the Reality of Premarital Agreements in Idaho*, 33 Idaho L. Rev. 539, 560–62 (1997) (contrasting the more flexible standards for enforcement of premarital agreements with the "very protective" standards applied to postnuptial and separation agreements).

In antenuptial agreements, California law requires a written waiver of independent counsel for all terms, Cal. Fam. Code § 1615(c) (West 2004); for waivers of spousal support, California law goes further and requires both independent legal representation (non-waivable) and unconscionability review "at the time of enforcement," Cal. Fam. Code § 1612(c) (West 2004). *Friedman* requires none of these safeguards in postnuptial agreements. Even if *Friedman* is correct that California's premarital-agreements statute does not govern postnuptial agreements, is there a sound policy reason for departing from the legislature's assessment of the appropriate protections? Do the cognitive limitations that impede rational bargaining before marriage (for example, the tendencies toward over-optimism and discounting of future benefits) dissipate sufficiently after the wedding to support more deference by courts? *Compare Pacelli v. Pacelli*, 725 A.2d 56, 61–62 (N.J. Super. Ct. 1999) (finding that "the dynamics and pressures involved in a mid-marriage context are qualitatively different" from those involved in premarital bargaining), *with* Rebecca Glass, Comment, *Trading Up: Postnuptial Agreements, Fairness, and a Principled New Suitor for California*, 92 Cal. L. Rev. 215 (2004) (contending that essential similarities in bargaining dynamics support subjecting prenuptial and postnuptial agreements to the same protective standards of enforceability). One commentator has argued that "spousal bargaining dynamics severely limit the extent to which one spouse can take advantage of the other." Sean Hannon Williams contends that, in contrast to premarital partners, spouses have better information about the preferences of their bargaining partners, are less likely to be clouded by excessive optimism about the relationship, and are typically less financially vulnerable to threats by a partner to walk away. Sean Hannon Williams, *Postnuptial Agreements*, 2007 Wis. L. Rev. 827, 830. Do you agree?

Contrary to *Friedman*, some jurisdictions apply the same procedural requirements to determine the voluntariness of prenuptial and postnuptial agreements. *See, e.g., Tibbs v. Anderson*, 580 So.2d 1337, 1339 (Ala. 1991); *Button v. Button*, 388 N.W.2d 546 (Wis. 1986). In at least one sense, California is more protective of postnuptial voluntariness than some other jurisdictions. As *Friedman* acknowledges, California law recognizes a presumption that a waiver of property rights within marriage is the product of undue influence, placing the burden on the spouse who seeks enforcement to prove the bargain's voluntariness. In some other states, the burden of proof on the issue of voluntariness remains with the spouse seeking to avoid enforcement, as in the case of premarital agreements. *See, e.g., Nesmith v. Berger*, 64 S.W.3d 110, 115 (Tex. Ct. App. 2001); *Button*, 388 N.W.2d at 550.

2. *Reconciliation agreements.* As *Bratton* notes, courts have long enforced reconciliation agreements negotiated by married couples following marital strife and separation. These agreements may specify the parties' rights and obligations if the reconciliation fails and the parties divorce. Because of the spouses' confidential relationship, most jurisdictions review reconciliation agreements to ensure that they meet procedural and substantive guarantees of voluntariness, disclosure and fairness:

> Before a reconciliation agreement will be enforced, the court must determine that the promise to resume marital relations was made when the marital rift was substantial. * * * The court must consider whether the circumstances under which the agreement was entered into were fair to the party charged. The terms of the agreement must have been conscionable when the agreement was made. * * * Changed circumstances must not have rendered literal enforcement inequitable.

Pacelli, 725 A.2d at 59–60. Finding basic similarity in the bargaining dynamics producing postnuptial and reconciliation agreements, *Pacelli* held that the same standards should determine the enforceability of postnuptial agreements.

    3. *May courts enforce the terms of a prenuptial or postnuptial agreement while the marriage remains intact?* To the extent that agreements cover the parties' behavior and financial dealings during the marriage, the agreements are treated like any other contract, requiring enforcement through a civil suit. Would you advise a client to file a complaint to enforce the terms of a marital agreement? Why or why not?

    4. *Conditions surrounding negotiation of agreements. Bratton* and *Pacelli* refused to enforce postnuptial agreements because of concerns about the dynamics of the parties' negotiations. Should the context in which the parties negotiated in *Friedman*—amid the specter of the husband's life-threatening illness—have led to a similar result?

SECTION 4: SEPARATION AGREEMENTS

    Because approximately 90 percent of divorces are ultimately uncontested proceedings, the bulk of contemporary family law practice concerns negotiation of marital separation and property settlement agreements. These agreements may set forth the terms of marital dissolution, distribution of real and personal property, support, custody and visitation, and tax consequences. Negotiation is a major component of the next chapter of this casebook.

    Courts once held separation agreements—like antenuptial agreements—to be against public policy for facilitating divorce, but legislatures and courts now strongly favor separation agreements. Negotiated when the marriage is already breaking down or divorce appears inevitable, these agreements are now seen to reduce litigation costs, time and emotional anguish. Also, these agreements may promote the interests of divorcing spouses and their children in ways that court resolution cannot. Many financial and other unique problems arising out of a marital breakup (for instance, who gets the family pet) are beyond the scope of effective judicial resolution. Yet, virtually all matters arising from a marriage relationship can be settled through agreement.

    The following provisions of Section 306 of the Uniform Marriage and Divorce Act reflect the modern consensus.

A. THE UNIFORM MARRIAGE AND DIVORCE ACT

UNIFORM MARRIAGE AND DIVORCE ACT

9A U.L.A. 248–49 (1998).

§ 306. [Separation Agreement].

(a) To promote amicable settlement of disputes between parties to a marriage attendant upon their separation or the dissolution of their marriage, the parties may enter into a written separation agreement containing provisions for disposition of any property owned by either of them, maintenance of either of them, and support, custody, and visitation of their children.

(b) In a proceeding for dissolution of marriage or for legal separation, the terms of the separation agreement, except those providing for the support, custody, and visitation of children, are binding upon the court unless it finds, after considering the economic circumstances of the parties and any other relevant evidence produced by the parties, on their own motion or on request of the court, that the separation agreement is unconscionable.

(c) If the court finds the separation agreement unconscionable, it may request the parties to submit a revised separation agreement or may make orders for the disposition of property, maintenance, and support.

(d) If the court finds that the separation agreement is not unconscionable as to disposition of property or maintenance, and not unsatisfactory as to support:

> (1) unless the separation agreement provides to the contrary, its terms shall be set forth in the decree of dissolution or legal separation and the parties shall be ordered to perform them, or

> (2) if the separation agreement provides that its terms shall not be set forth in the decree, the decree shall identify the separation agreement and state that the court has found the terms not unconscionable.

(e) Terms of the agreement set forth in the decree are enforceable by all remedies available for enforcement of a judgment, including contempt, and are enforceable as contract terms.

(f) Except for terms concerning the support, custody, or visitation of children, the decree may expressly preclude or limit modification of terms set forth in the decree if the separation agreement so provides. Otherwise, terms of a separation agreement set forth in the decree are automatically modified by modification of the decree.

B. THE RELATIONSHIP BETWEEN A SEPARATION AGREEMENT AND THE DIVORCE DECREE

As UMDA section 306(d) suggests, when a court accepts a separation agreement as valid, it will set forth the agreement's terms in some manner in the divorce decree. Depending on the jurisdiction and the procedural rules of the court, separation agreements may be approved, incorporated, or merged into the divorce judgment.

Where the court approves or "ratifies" a separation agreement, the court endorses it as valid under state law and as reasonable; however, the agreement is not part of the judgment and thus is enforceable only under contract principles. "Incorporation" permits the agreement to be part of the judgment, while also remaining contractually binding. "Merger" means that the agreement becomes fully a part of the judgment, and may no longer be enforced as a separate contract. A court may enforce a merged agreement, like other judgments, by contempt of court. *See, e.g., Custis v. Custis*, 2008 WL 2338499 (Va. Ct. App. June 10, 2008).

C. MODIFICATION OF MARITAL SEPARATION AGREEMENTS

Whether the court or parties can modify the terms of a marital separation agreement depends on whether the agreement has been approved, incorporated or merged into a judgment.

Absent a provision barring modification, an incorporated or merged agreement may be modified after entry of the judgment on the same grounds permitted for modification of other court orders. If a separation agreement is not incorporated into the decree, the parties may later modify its terms in accordance with ordinary contract law. *See* Doris Del Tosto Brogan, *Divorce Settlement Agreements: The Problem of Merger or Incorporation and the Status of the Agreement in Relation to the Decree*, 67 Neb. L. Rev. 235 (1988).

Nearly all jurisdictions follow the approach of UMDA section 306(f), which enables parties to bar or limit future modification of contract terms, except terms relating to child custody, visitation, or support. As discussed in the chapters on the child-related issues, terms relating to minor children are always subject to judicial scrutiny and modification. With respect to other terms, if the separation agreement bars subsequent modification, courts honor that directive notwithstanding a later change of circumstances. In one memorable decision, for example, the Missouri Supreme Court held that even an ex-wife's attempt to hire a hit man to murder her ex-husband did not affect his obligation to continue paying her alimony pursuant to a separation agreement that barred future modification. If a separation agreement is found to be conscionable at the time of the divorce decree, the court held, it cannot be reconsidered later on the basis of changed circumstances. The court further rejected the contention that the wife's attempt to kill her ex-husband amounted to a waiver of future support: "Killing Joseph might have resulted in the termination of Ida's ability to collect maintenance," the court reasoned, "but her alleged acts do not establish a clear and unequivocal attempt to relinquish her contractual right to maintenance so long as Joseph is living." *Richardson v. Richardson,* 218 S.W.3d 426, 430 (Mo. 2007). In a small handful of states, however, judicial authority to modify spousal support, like child support, may not be divested by the parties' agreement. *See Toni v. Toni,* 636 N.W.2d 396, 400–401 (N.D. 2001) (collecting decisions).

D. VOIDING A SEPARATION AGREEMENT

Court review of separation agreements is normally minimal. Under the prevailing legal standard, reflected in UMDA section 306(b), the parties' agreement concerning alimony or property rights is presumptively "binding" on the court, absent proof of fraud, duress, or unconscionability. "[A]lthough courts are required in theory to review spousal agreements regarding child support and custody [to ensure their consistency with the best interests of children], courts typically rubber-stamp separation agreements, even in divorces involving children." Jana B. Singer, *The Privatization of Family Law*, 1992 Wis. L. Rev. 1443, 1474–75. Courts have the authority *sua sponte* to probe the parties' economic circumstances to ensure conscionability, but ordinarily rely on the parties' representations. Appellate courts have rejected the suggestion that trial courts have a duty of independent investigation. *See, e.g., Grigsby v. Grigsby*, 2007 WL 1378460 (Ky. Ct. App. May 11, 2007); *Swank v. Swank*, 865 S.W.2d 841, 845 (Mo. Ct. App. 1993). Accordingly, in the great majority of cases, court approval of a separation agreement is "nothing more than a required formality." Eleanor E. Maccoby & Robert H. Mnookin, Dividing the Child: Social and Legal Dilemmas of Custody 40 (1992). Occasionally, however, as in the following decision, a court denies enforcement of a separation agreement.

IN RE MARRIAGE OF THORNHILL

Colorado Court of Appeals.
200 P.3d 1083 (2008).

TERRY, J.

[Antoinette Thornhill executed a separation agreement with her husband, Chuck Thornhill, but later changed her mind and sought to avoid the agreement at the time the trial court granted the divorce. The trial court concluded that the agreement was valid, notwithstanding the wife's change of mind, and divided the couple's property according to its terms. She appealed.] * * *

Wife first argues that the trial court erred in finding the separation agreement conscionable. We agree.

Parties to a marriage, attendant upon their separation or dissolution of the marriage, may enter into a written separation agreement providing for maintenance and the disposition of property. Such provisions are binding on the court unless it finds, after considering the economic circumstances of the parties and any other relevant evidence produced by the parties, that the agreement is unconscionable.

* * *

" '[B]ecause of the fiduciary relationship between husband and wife, separation agreements generally are closely scrutinized by the courts, and such agreements are more readily set aside in equity under circumstances that would be insufficient to nullify an ordinary contract.' " *In re Marriage of Manzo*, 659 P.2d 669, 674 (Colo. 1983).

A court reviewing a separation agreement for conscionability should first review the provisions for fraud, overreaching, concealment of assets, or sharp dealing not consistent with the obligations of marital partners to deal fairly with each other. However, even where the trial court finds no fraud, overreaching, concealment of assets, or sharp dealing, we are still required to review the agreement to determine whether it is "fair, just and reasonable." We do this by looking at the economic circumstances of the parties which result from the agreement.

Here, the parties were married for 27 years before they separated. During most of the marriage, wife cared for the children and held several low-wage jobs while husband worked in the oil business. The family lived for many years in various oil field camps in desolate parts of Wyoming. Although husband earned a sufficient amount to meet his family's needs, his income during most of that time did not approach the substantial sums he began to earn after starting an oil and gas equipment sales and servicing business (the business) in 2001. At the time of the permanent orders hearing, husband's business valuation expert valued his 70.5% ownership share of the business at $1,625,000, after applying a 33% marketability discount. Husband also signed a financial disclosure stating that his total monthly income before expenses was nearly $15,000. Wife's disclosure showed her total monthly income before expenses was less than $5,000.

The parties entered into a separation agreement providing for maintenance to wife and dividing the marital property. However, by the time of the scheduled court hearing to enter a decree based on the agreement, wife realized that at the time she signed the agreement, she had not had a good understanding of the value of the marital assets, and therefore she disavowed the agreement as unfair to her.

Because of wife's disavowal of the agreement, the matter was set for a permanent orders hearing. In its findings after that hearing, the trial court did not find fraud, overreaching, concealment of assets, or sharp dealing. Instead, it found the agreement to be "both enforceable and equitable."

After considering the totality of the circumstances, we conclude the property disposition is not fair, just, or reasonable, and we set it aside and remand for a new permanent orders hearing. The following facts support our conclusion that the agreement is unconscionable:

> ● Importantly, despite the fact that the parties had more than one million dollars in marital assets, wife was not represented by counsel at the time the separation agreement was negotiated and signed. Although in recent years she earned a graduate degree in occupational therapy, the record does not indicate she is sophisticated in legal or financial matters. *See In re Marriage of Seely*, 689 P.2d

1154, 1160 (Colo.App.1984) (court closely scrutinizes separation agreement where one party was not represented by counsel).

• Wife's father, who was chief financial officer of the business, had assisted in negotiating the separation agreement, and in the trial court's ruling following the permanent orders hearing, the court based its determination of conscionability largely on the father's testimony. However, purely by virtue of his role as chief financial officer, the father was required to attempt preservation of the business assets, which necessarily resulted in dual loyalties under the circumstances presented here.

• Wife testified to her lack of mathematical ability, her need to rely on her father to explain financial details of the settlement, her repeated statements that she did not understand the details, and the fact that she was never presented with the promissory note referenced in the agreement concerning payment of husband's obligation to her.

Thus, even accepting the court's implicit finding that there was no fraud, overreaching, concealment of assets, or sharp dealing, we conclude that the agreement is unconscionable. To accomplish the parties' avowed purpose of dividing equally the marital assets that existed at the time of the agreement, it provided that husband would pay wife $752,692, half of what was represented to be the marital assets at the time the agreement was entered into. However, he was not required to pay that sum to wife immediately. Rather, the parties' agreement called for him to pay it in equal monthly installments of $6,272 over ten years, and failed to require him to pay her interest on the total sum or to secure the obligation.

Accordingly, wife lost the ability to obtain the full use and enjoyment, as well as the investment value, of the entire sum, while husband, whose income is substantially greater than wife's, obtained the considerable benefit of retaining the use, enjoyment, and investment value of the unpaid balance. Thus, the present value of the payments to wife was considerably less than $756,692. As wife testified, "[husband] wants me to be [his] bank." Even applying a modest interest rate, the accumulated interest on $752,692 over ten years would be a considerable sum.

We conclude that this combination of factors—wife's lack of understanding of the value of the marital assets; her lack of legal representation and independent financial advice; her father's conflicting roles as her financial advisor and chief financial officer of the business in which husband was majority shareholder; and the failure to provide for interest on such a large obligation over such a lengthy period—results in a property distribution that is not "fair, just and reasonable."

* * *

Because the issues of property, maintenance, and the payment of attorney fees and costs, are inextricably intertwined, we remand to the trial court with directions to vacate the property settlement and to enter new permanent orders. * * *

* * *

NOTES AND QUESTIONS

1. *Unconscionability.* Do you agree with the outcome in *Thornhill*? Courts are usually unwilling to rescue parties from ill-advised bargains. *See* Judith T. Younger, *Across Curricular Boundaries: Searching for a Confluence Between Marital Agreements and Indian Land Transactions*, 26 Law & Inequality 495, 511–12 (2008) (concluding that courts are broadly inclined to enforce even draconian marital agreements, and that recent decisions "display a lamentable disregard for the spouse who, in the interest of the relationship, gives up the production of income to devote herself to the family enterprise"). A New York appellate court captured the prevailing sentiment: "The fact that the defendant was not represented by independent counsel when the stipulation of settlement was executed does not, without more, establish overreaching or require automatic nullification of the agreement. * * * 'An agreement will not be overturned merely because, in retrospect, some of its provisions were improvident or one-sided' or because 'a party had a change of heart.'" *Brennan–Duffy v. Duffy*, 804 N.Y.S.2d 399, 400 (App.Div. 2005).

If the bargain is exceptionally one-sided, however, courts may withhold enforcement. The Kentucky Supreme Court, for example, invalidated as unconscionable a separation agreement in which a divorcing psychiatrist agreed to pay his former wife $5,500 per month in maintenance and $8,000 per month in child support (under a formula by which each figure would be gradually reduced over time), and to cover his children's educational and insurance costs. "Under the agreement, [the wife] was entitled to remain in the marital residence with the children [though she was obligated to pay the $5,200 monthly mortgage payment] and to receive most of the household goods and a vehicle. [The husband] was to receive his medical practice, his retirement account, an automobile, and a $30,000 wine collection." *Shraberg v. Shraberg*, 939 S.W.2d 330, 331 (Ky. 1997). The court emphasized that "the single most important fact is that while [the husband] had a pre-tax income of about $200,000 annually, by the agreement he obligated himself to pay in excess of $160,000 annually for the support of his children and former wife." *Id.* at 333. Two judges dissented, arguing that the case involved nothing more than "the striking of a bad bargain entered into by a highly educated professional spouse, who was unrepresented by counsel." *Id.* at 335 (Stumbo, J., dissenting).

2. *Disclosure obligations.* Like most jurisdictions, Colorado holds that the "confidential relationship" occasioned by marriage continues until the marriage is formally dissolved. Under the majority rule, "[p]arties to a separation agreement stand as fiduciaries to each other, and will be held to the highest standards of good faith and fair dealing in the performance of their contractual obligations." *Krapf v. Krapf*, 786 N.E.2d 318, 323 (Mass. 2003). These standards include an affirmative obligation to disclose all material information relating to one's financial assets and income. Breach of this

duty constitutes fraud, which under ordinary civil procedure rules exposes even a settled judgment accepting a separation agreement to potential reopening when the fraud is discovered. Thus, for example, where a husband negotiated a separation agreement without mentioning to his wife that he had won the lottery four days before filing for divorce, the court reopened the divorce judgment and voided their separation agreement after the ex-husband appeared on television with his girlfriend to claim the prize:

> Petitioner's failure to apprise respondent that he had won $5.38 million in the lottery during their marriage is unequivocally the nondisclosure of a material fact. This fraudulent concealment directly induced respondent into agreeing to a settlement she never would have agreed to had she known the truth. She also would not have agreed to waive maintenance.

In re Marriage of Palacios, 656 N.E.2d 107, 112 (Ill. App. Ct. 1995).

By contrast, some jurisdictions hold that the spouses' confidential relationship may end before divorce, removing any heightened duties of disclosure when a separation agreement is brokered. A North Carolina court explained:

> [W]hile a husband and wife generally share a confidential relationship, this relationship ends when the parties become adversaries. It is well established that when one party to a marriage hires an attorney to begin divorce proceedings, the confidential relationship is usually over, although the mere involvement of an attorney does not automatically end the confidential relationship. Further, when one party moves out of the marital home, this too is evidence that the confidential relationship is over, although it is not controlling.

Lancaster v. Lancaster, 530 S.E.2d 82, 84–85 (N.C. Ct. App. 2000); *cf. Barnes v. Barnes*, 340 S.E.2d 803, 804 (Va. 1986); Amanda K. Esquibel, *Fiduciary Duties: The Legal Effect of the Beneficiary's Retention of Counsel on the Fiduciary Relationship*, 33 Rutgers L.J. 329 (2002). Without a confidential relationship, the divorcing parties are not obligated to volunteer material financial information, but must respond truthfully to specific inquiries. *See Daughtry v. Daughtry*, 497 S.E.2d 105, 107 (N.C. Ct. App. 1998).

Should parties also be required to disclose material non-financial information? In *Barnes*, *supra*, an ex-husband sought to repudiate a separation agreement because his ex-wife had not disclosed that she had twice committed adultery during the marriage. The court rejected the husband's challenge on the ground that, because the spouses negotiated the agreement when they were separated and represented by independent counsel, they were no longer in a confidential relationship. *Barnes*, 340 S.E.2d at 804–05; *accord Winborne v. Winborne*, 255 S.E.2d 640, 643 (N.C. Ct. App. 1979). What result if the parties resided in a jurisdiction that considered spouses to be fiduciaries until entry of the final divorce decree? Does it make sense to apply a stricter fiduciary duty to married persons who are estranged than to engaged persons who are arguably at the height of their commitment to one another?

3. *Terms fixing parental rights and obligations.* Section 306 of the UMDA directs that contract terms relating to spousal property or support are ordinarily binding upon the courts, while terms "providing for the support, custody, and visitation of children" are subject to additional review to ensure

consistency with the interests of affected children. (The ALI Principles adopt a similar position. *See Principles*, § 7.09(5).) As you learned in Chapter 11, when settlement provides for greater child support than the amount required by the child support guidelines, courts generally grant or enforce the greater obligation, unless evidence of involuntariness or manifest unfairness appears. Not surprisingly, courts are unlikely to permit agreed terms that set a child support obligation at an amount lower than prevailing law would otherwise impose. *See Upchurch v. Upchurch*, 624 S.E.2d 643, 647 (S.C. 2006) (holding that "an agreement between the parents may not affect the basic support rights of minor children," and that "[n]otwithstanding any provisions of a separation agreement, the family court retains jurisdiction to do whatever is in the best interest of the children"). Courts often give substantial deference to parental agreements about visitation and child custody, even though courts must similarly ensure their consistency with the child's best interests. *See* Brian Bix, *Domestic Agreements*, 35 Hofstra L. Rev. 1753, 1761 (2007). Is there a compelling reason to be less deferential with respect to child support?

In an influential study excerpted in Chapter 15, Professors Robert Mnookin and Lewis Kornhauser observed that "marital property, alimony, and child-support issues are all basically problems of money, and the distinctions among them become very blurred" in real-world divorce negotiations. Robert H. Mnookin & Lewis Kornhauser, *Bargaining in the Shadow of the Law: The Case of Divorce*, 88 Yale L.J. 950, 959 (1979). What if one party agrees to give the other substantially more marital property in exchange for a lower child support obligation? *See Hammack v. Hammack*, 60 P.3d 663 (Wash. Ct. App. 2003) (holding exchange to be void as against public policy, but acknowledging that parties may characterize a disproportionate award of community property as an "advance payment" of child support if they establish that it is tailored to meet the amount due under prevailing child support guidelines).

4. *Coercion and duress.* Common factors that determine coercion and duress include whether both parties had the assistance of independent counsel, had read and understood the agreement's terms and obligations, and had negotiated changes in the draft agreement. No one factor is determinative. Indeed, agreements have been upheld where each of these factors would tend to suggest coercion or duress. A New York court, for example, enforced a separation agreement against a wife who, without advice of counsel, signed after only a "cursory review" of the document:

> She testified that defendant presented her with the agreement for signing as she was preparing to go out for the night. After she advised him that she did not have time to read the agreement that night, he "ma[d]e a scene" in front of the children, threatening to prevent her from going out unless it was signed. At no time was she fearful or stressed by his behavior. In fact, plaintiff testified that she was determined to go out and had no intentions of changing her plans. * * * While her decision to hastily sign the agreement may have been unwise, her claim of duress is unsupported.

Morand v. Morand, 767 N.Y.S.2d 523, 525 (App. Div. 2003).

5. *Contrast with other marital agreements.* Case law often reflects a greater willingness to enforce separation agreements than antenuptial agree-

ments or postnuptial agreements. The commentary to the ALI Principles suggests that the difference "may * * * reflect the different negotiating context":

> The parties to a premarital agreement are contracting about a speculative contingent future event (dissolution), in a setting dominated by a quite different and immediate event (marriage). By contrast, in an impending family dissolution, the parties are contracting for the event at hand and are better able to anticipate the circumstances within which the agreement will be enforced, and thus to understand the significance of the terms of the agreement. It may also generally be assumed that each party is less naïve about the beneficent intentions of the other party and, given the demise of the relationship, is bargaining at arm's length.

ALI, Principles of the Law of Family Dissolution: Analysis and Recommendations § 7.09 cmt. b (2002). Do these considerations support enforcement of agreements like the one in *Johnson*?

6. *Section 7.09 of the Principles.* Like the UMDA, section 7.09(1) of the ALI Principles generally would make agreed financial terms "binding" on the court if the parties voluntarily entered into a written separation agreement with a "full and fair opportunity to be informed" about each party's financial assets and earning potential. In contrast to the UMDA's open-ended provision against "unconscionable" bargains, section 7.09(2) of the ALI Principles provides:

> Except as provided in the last sentence of this Paragraph, the terms of a separation agreement providing for the disposition of property or for compensatory payments are unenforceable if they substantially limit or augment property rights or compensatory payments otherwise due under law, and enforcement of those terms would substantially impair the economic well-being of a party who has or will have
>
> > (a) primary or dual residential responsibility for a child or
> >
> > (b) substantially fewer economic resources than the other party.

Nevertheless, the court may enforce such terms if it finds, under the particular circumstances of the case, that enforcement of the terms would not work an injustice.

Does section 7.09(2) differ in substance from the understanding of "unconscionability" reflected in the UMDA? If a divorcing spouse enters into an onerous agreement freely and knowingly, what policy rationale supports overriding the parties' free choice? The official commentary to section 7.09(2) states:

> When a residential parent's economic well-being is substantially impaired by contractual relinquishment of legal rights, the interests of a child with whom that parent shares a household are equally impaired. When the economic well-being of a spouse with substantially fewer economic resources than the other spouse is similarly impaired, the public-policy purposes underlying the law of property distribution and compensatory payments [*i.e.,* spousal support] may be completely frustrated.

Are you persuaded?

* * *

How do parties reach the agreements described in this chapter? Negotiation, of course, is central to private ordering. When circumstances ripen into a family law dispute, parties often also participate in mediation or submit the dispute to arbitration. Since the mid–1990s, many couples have turned to "collaborative law" to help determine the resolution of the parties' adversarial relationship. Chapter 15 now takes a closer look at these methods of "alternative dispute resolution," which remain central to family law practice.

CHAPTER 15

ALTERNATIVE DISPUTE RESOLUTION

■ ■ ■

Historically parties seeking divorce or resolution of other family law disputes had few alternatives beyond the courthouse steps. Often the "direct and indirect costs of going to court were staggering, and the emotional scars of a hard-fought court battle made it difficult, if not impossible, for couples to move on with their lives or to cooperatively raise their children." Joan H. McWilliams, *Your ADR Options: Mediation, Arbitration and Collaborative Law*, 24 Fam. Advoc., Spring 2002, at 2, 2.

In contemporary family law, however, litigation is "useful in only a small minority of cases." Mary E. O'Connell & J. Herbie DiFonzo, *The Family Law Education Reform Project Final Report*, 44 Fam. Ct. Rev. 524, 525 (2006). Domestic relations attorneys and divorcing parties typically perceive "settlement as the solution, and the judicial process as the alternative." Marygold S. Melli et al., *The Process of Negotiation: An Exploratory Investigation in the Context of No–Fault Divorce*, 40 Rutgers L. Rev. 1133, 1143 (1988). Court trials have receded to the background as "a blunt, adversarial option of last resort for unresolved issues when, after the exhaustion of all other available remedies, parents remain deadlocked over fundamental issues of values and parental role." Lucy S. McGough, *Protecting Children in Divorce: Lessons From Caroline Norton*, 57 Me. L. Rev. 13, 35 (2005). "Unlike the highly contested divorces reported in the mass media, the average divorcing couple lacks the resources to support—or the property to justify—extended legal combat. Furthermore, even among affluent couples, the long-term interest in family harmony for the sake of children discourages the escalation of combat." Lynn Mather et al., Divorce Lawyers at Work 111 (2001).

The decline of family law litigation has not occurred in a vacuum because "[a]lternative dispute resolution has become a substantial part of the civil justice system" generally. ABA Model Rules of Prof'l Conduct, Model Rule 2.4 cmt.1 (2008). Professor Galanter has assembled abundant data showing that at both the state and federal levels, the percentage of legal disputes resolved by trials is "declining precipitously." Marc Galanter, *A World Without Trials?*, 2006 J. Disput. Resol. 7, 7. The term "the vanishing trial" has entered the legal lexicon. *See, e.g.*, Symposium, *The Vanishing Trial*, 1 J. Empirical Legal Stud. v (2004). Rather than proceed to court, parties to civil disputes today are much more likely to opt for direct give-and-take in negotiation, for enlisting a third party to facilitate the give-and-take in mediation, or for submitting the dispute to a private third-party decisionmaker for binding resolution in arbitration.

This Chapter explores the place of these three traditional alternative dispute resolution (ADR) methods in family law practice, both for married and unmarried parties. The Chapter also introduces a fourth alternative, "collaborative law," which has emerged since the early 1990s as a new ADR method for parties who seek a less adversarial divorce. As you proceed through the Chapter, consider the capacity of each of the four ADR methods to serve (or disserve) interests of spouses, unmarried parents, or unmarried partners and children in proceedings frequently marked by emotion, power imbalance, and the prospect that some rights and obligations will endure past the dissolution or custody decree.

SECTION 1: NEGOTIATION

A. THE NATURE OF DOMESTIC RELATIONS NEGOTIATION

In direct negotiations, disputants meet in an effort to resolve their differences without pursuing a final court decision. Upwards of 90% of filed federal and state civil actions are settled each year, prompting one commentator to assert that negotiation cannot properly be termed "alternative" dispute resolution: "The settlement process is not some marginal, peripheral aspect of disputing in America; it is the central core. * * * Lawyers spend more time on settlement discussions than on research or on trials and appeals." Marc Galanter, *Worlds of Deals: Using Negotiation to Teach About Legal Process*, 34 J. Legal Educ. 268, 269 (1984).

Family law proceedings have featured negotiation for decades, but most prominently since the 1960s. The prevalence of negotiation has doubtless been fueled by clogged court dockets, the uncertainties inherent in judicial application of statutory standards steeped in discretion, and the emotional and financial strains of domestic relations litigation. No-fault divorce has also "effectively changed the core story about divorce from one about guilt and innocence to one that minimized the importance of fault and instead created a complex forward-looking inquiry. This new regime effectively discouraged parties from seeking judicial resolution of their disputes and encouraged them to resolve their disputes through negotiation or mediation." Ray D. Madoff, *Lurking in the Shadow: The Unseen Hand of Doctrine In Dispute Resolution*, 76 S. Cal. L. Rev. 161, 166 (2002).

Mirroring the overwhelming percentage of civil disputants who settle out of court, more than 90% of divorcing spouses and other domestic relations disputants resolve financial and child-related matters alike by negotiation before requesting the court to enter the final decree in accordance with their agreement. Unlike other civil litigants who often consider settlement only after an interlocutory court decision such as denial of summary judgment makes trial imminent, disputing domestic relations parties today typically negotiate with little outside pressure.

Negotiation in family law practice often occurs before suit is filed and routinely continues after filing, during trial, and even while an appeal is pending. Once the parties retain counsel, the lawyers typically participate in the give-and-take. Recognizing that litigation is "expensive and emotionally draining," the American Academy of Matrimonial Lawyers (AAML) says that the "vast majority of cases should be resolved by lawyers negotiating settlements on behalf of their clients." AAML, *Bounds of Advocacy, Goals for Family Lawyers* § 1.5 cmt. (2000), http://www.aaml. org/files/public/Bounds_of_Advocacy.htm. The ABA Section of Family Law urges counsel to "[e]xplore settlement possibilities at the earliest reasonable date." *American Bar Association Section of Family Law Civility Standards*, 40 Fam. L.Q. xv, xvi (Winter 2007).

Substantive law has consumed most of this casebook, but what role remains for that law in the vast bulk of domestic relations cases, which conclude without trial in accordance with the parties' negotiated agreement? Substantive law remains central because the parties know the court will apply these standards if negotiations fail. Negotiation is strongly influenced by the parties' own predictions and expectations about what the court would do in the absence of agreement, and "litigants use courts as bargaining leverage, rather than as decision makers." Eleanor Holmes Norton, *Bargaining and the Ethics of Process*, 64 N.Y.U. L. Rev. 493, 497 (1989).

ROBERT H. MNOOKIN & LEWIS KORNHAUSER

Bargaining in the Shadow of the Law: The Case of Divorce.
88 Yale L.J. 950, 950–51, 959, 968–75 (1979).

* * * We see the primary function of contemporary divorce law not as imposing order from above, but rather as providing a framework within which divorcing couples can themselves determine their postdissolution rights and responsibilities. This process by which parties to a marriage are empowered to create their own legally enforceable commitments is a form of "private ordering."

* * *

* * * "Typically, the parties do not go to court at all, until they have worked matters out and are ready for the rubber stamp." Both in the United States and in England, the overwhelming majority of divorcing couples resolve distributional questions concerning marital property, alimony, child support, and custody without bringing any contested issue to court for adjudication.

* * *

II. The Elements of a Bargaining Model

＊　＊　＊

2. *How Legal Rules Create Bargaining Endowments*

Divorcing parents do not bargain over the division of family wealth and custodial prerogatives in a vacuum; they bargain in the shadow of the law. The legal rules governing alimony, child support, marital property, and custody give each parent certain claims based on what each would get if the case went to trial. In other words, the outcome that the law will impose if no agreement is reached gives each parent certain bargaining chips—an endowment of sorts.

A simplified example may be illustrative. Assume that in disputed custody cases the law flatly provided that all mothers had the right to custody of minor children and that all fathers only had the right to visitation two weeks a month. Absent some contrary agreement acceptable to both parents, a court would order this arrangement. Assume further that the legal rules relating to marital property, alimony, and child support gave the mother some determinate share of the family's economic resources. In negotiations under this regime, neither spouse would ever consent to a division that left him or her worse off than if he or she insisted on going to court. The range of negotiated outcomes would be limited to those that leave both parents as well off as they would be in the absence of a bargain.

If private ordering were allowed, we would not necessarily expect parents to split custody and money the way a judge would if they failed to agree. The father might well negotiate for more child-time and the mother for less. This result might occur either because the father made the mother better off by giving her additional money to compensate her for accepting less child-time, or because the mother found custody burdensome and considered herself better off with less custody. Indeed, she might agree to accept less money, or even to pay the father, if he agreed to relieve her of some child-rearing responsibilities. In all events, because the parents' tastes with regard to the trade-offs between money and child-time may differ, it will often be possible for the parties to negotiate some outcome that makes both better off than they would be if they simply accepted the result a court would impose.

3. *Private Ordering Against a Backdrop of Uncertainty*

Legal rules are generally not as simple or straightforward as is suggested by the last example. Often, the outcome in court is far from certain, with any number of outcomes possible. Indeed, existing legal standards governing custody, alimony, child support, and marital property are all striking for their lack of precision and thus provide a bargaining backdrop clouded by uncertainty. The almost universal judicial standard for resolving custody disputes is the "best interests of the child." Except in situations when one parent poses a substantial threat to the child's well-being, predicting who will get custody under this standard is difficult indeed, especially given the increasing pressure to reject any presumption in favor of maternal custody. Similarly, standards governing alimony and child support are also extraordinarily vague and allow courts broad discretion in disputed cases.

Analyzing the effects of uncertainty on bargaining is an extremely complicated task. It is apparent, however, that the effects in any particular case will depend in part on the attitudes of the two spouses toward risk—what economists call "risk preferences." * * *

Because drawing straws, like flipping a coin, gives each parent a fifty percent chance of receiving full custody, economic theory suggests that for each parent the "expected" outcome is half-custody. We cannot, however, simply assume that each parent will bargain as if receiving half of the child's time were certain. Attitudes toward risk may be defined by asking a parent to compare two alternatives: (1) a certainty of having one-half of the child's time; or (2) a gamble in which the "expected" or average outcome is one-half of the child's time. By definition, a parent who treats these alternatives as equally desirable is risk-neutral. A parent who would accept a certain outcome of less than half-custody in order to avoid the gamble—the chance of losing the coin flip and receiving no custody—is risk-averse. Other parents may be risk preferers: they would rather take the gamble and have a fifty percent chance of winning full custody than accept the certain outcome of split custody.

The reality of custody litigation is more complicated, and the knowledge of the parties much less complete, than in our hypothetical. The parties in the example know the standard for decision and the odds of winning custody in court. But in real situations, the exact odds of various possible outcomes are not known by the parties; often they do not even know what information or criteria the judge will use in deciding.

4. *Transaction Costs*

Costs are involved in resolving the distributional consequences of separation or divorce, and in securing the divorce itself. The transaction costs that the parties must bear may take many forms, some financial and some emotional. The most obvious and tangible involve the expenditure of money. Professional fees—particularly for lawyers—must be paid by one or both parties. In addition, there are filing fees and court costs. More difficult to measure, but also important, are the emotional and psychological costs involved in the dispute-settlement process. Lawsuits generally are emotionally burdensome; the psychological costs imposed by bargaining (and still more by litigation) are particularly acute in divorce.

The magnitude of these transaction costs, both actual and expected, can influence negotiations and the outcome of bargaining. In the dissolution process, one spouse, and that spouse's attorney, can substantially affect the magnitude of the transaction costs that must be borne by the other spouse. As is generally the case, the party better able to bear the transaction costs, whether financial or emotional, will have an advantage in divorce bargaining.

In divorce, transaction costs will generally tend to be (1) higher if there are minor children involved, because of the additional and intensely emotional allocational issues to be determined; (2) an increasing function of the amount of property and income the spouses have, since it is rational to spend more on negotiation when the possible rewards are higher; and (3) higher when there is a broad range of possible outcomes in court.

5. *Strategic Behavior*

The actual bargain that is struck through negotiations—indeed, whether a bargain is struck at all—depends on the negotiation process. During this process, each party transmits information about his or her own preferences to the other. This information may be accurate or intentionally inaccurate; each party may promise, threaten, or bluff. Parties may intentionally exaggerate their chances of winning in court in the hope of persuading the other side to accept less. Or they may threaten to impose substantial transaction costs—economic or psychological—on the other side. In short, there are a variety of ways in which the parties may engage in strategic behavior during the bargaining process.

Opportunities for strategic behavior exist because the parties often will not know with certainty (1) the other side's true preferences with regard to the allocational outcomes; (2) the other spouse's preference or attitudes towards risk; and (3) what the outcome in court will be, or even what the actual odds in court are. Although parents may know a great deal about each other's preferences for money and children, complete knowledge of the other spouse's attitudes is unlikely.

How do parties and their representatives actually behave during the process? Two alternative models are suggested by the literature: (1) a *Strategic Model*, which would characterize the process as "a relatively norm-free process centered on the transmutation of underlying bargaining strength into agreement by the exercise of power, horse-trading, threat, and bluff"; and (2) a *Norm–Centered Model*, which would characterize the process by elements normally associated with adjudication—the parties and their representatives would invoke rules, cite precedents, and engage in reasoned elaboration. Anecdotal observation suggests that each model captures part of the flavor of the process. The parties and their representatives do make appeals to legal and social norms in negotiation, but they frequently threaten and bluff as well.

C. The Task Facing the Spouses and the Process of Negotiation

The task facing divorcing spouses can be summarized, based on the preceding analysis, as one of attempting through bargaining to divide money and child-rearing responsibilities to reflect personal preferences. Even though the interests of the two parents may substantially conflict, opportunities for making both parents better off through a negotiated agreement will exist to the extent that parental preferences differ.

This analysis suggests why most divorcing couples never require adjudication for dispute settlement. The parties gain substantial advantages when they can reach an agreement concerning the distributional consequences of divorce. They can minimize the transaction costs involved in adjudication. They can avoid its risks and uncertainties, and negotiate an agreement that may better reflect their individual preferences.

Furthermore, divorcing spouses usually have no incentive to take cases to court for their precedential value. Unlike insurance companies, public-interest organizations, and other "repeat players," a divorcing spouse will generally have no expectation that an adjudicated case will create precedent, or that any precedent created will be of personal benefit in future litigation.

Given the advantages of negotiated settlements, why do divorcing spouses ever require courtroom adjudication of their disputes? There are a variety of reasons why some divorce cases will be litigated:

1. *Spite.* One or both parties may be motivated in substantial measure by a desire to punish the other spouse, rather than simply to increase their own net worth.

2. *Distaste for Negotiation.* Even though it costs more, one or both parties may prefer the adjudicative process (with third-party decision) to any process that requires a voluntary agreement with the other spouse. Face-to-face contact may be extremely distasteful, and the parties may not be able to negotiate—even with lawyers acting as intermediaries—because of distrust or distaste.

3. *Calling the Bluff—The Breakdown of Negotiations.* If the parties get heavily engaged in strategic behavior and get carried away with making threats, a courtroom battle may result, despite both parties' preference for a settlement. Negotiations may resemble a game of "chicken" in which two teenagers set their cars on a collision course to see who turns first. Some crack-ups may result.

4. *Uncertainty and Risk Preferences.* The exact odds for any given outcome in court are unknown, and it has been suggested that litigants typically overestimate their chances of winning. To the extent that one or both of the parties typically overestimate their chances of winning, more cases will be litigated than in a world in which the outcome is uncertain but the odds are known. * * *

5. *No Middle Ground.* If the object of dispute cannot be divided into small enough increments—whether because of the law, the practical circumstances, or the nature of the subject at issue—there may be no middle ground on which to strike a feasible compromise. Optimal bargaining occurs when, in economic terminology, nothing is indivisible.

* * *

NOTES AND QUESTIONS

1. *The "shadow's" staying power.* The "shadow" cast by statutory standards and other substantive family law may last beyond the court's initial

decree. "Attorneys generally discover that the most obvious measures of achievement in legal practice—winning a case or securing high dollar outcomes—simply do not apply in family law. * * * Divorcing parties, linked together indefinitely through on-going child support, visitation, or alimony payments, have ample opportunity to challenge or undermine one-sided legal outcomes. Winning, especially winning 'big,' may simply mean * * * 'a lifetime annuity for the attorneys as parties continue to battle through post-divorce litigation." Lynn Mather et al., Divorce Lawyers at Work 159 (2001).

2. *The scope of "private ordering."* When parties negotiate the terms of their divorce, they engage in "private ordering," largely substituting their own decisionmaking for that of the court. Is private ordering in divorce actions appropriate? What limits should the law place on the parties' capacity to order their own affairs in the shadow of the law? Consider this article:

ROBERT H. MNOOKIN

Divorce Bargaining: The Limits on Private Ordering.
18 U. Mich. J.L. Reform 1015, 1017–21, 1024–26, 1031–33 (1985).

* * *

I. THE ADVANTAGES OF PRIVATE ORDERING

* * * The core justification [for private ordering] is rooted in notions of human liberty. The liberal ideal that individuals have fundamental rights, and should freely choose to make of their lives what they wish supports private ordering. * * *

Private ordering is also justified on grounds of efficiency. Ordinarily, the parties themselves are in the best position to evaluate the comparative advantages of alternative arrangements. * * * Through negotiations, opportunities exist for making *both* spouses better off than either would be if a court or some third party simply imposed a result. A consensual solution, by definition, more likely conforms with the preferences of each spouse than would a result imposed by a court. Parental preferences often vary with regard to money and child-rearing responsibilities. Through negotiations, a greater likelihood exists that divorcing spouses can divide money and child-rearing responsibilities to reflect their own individual preferences.

Finally, obvious and substantial savings occur when a couple can resolve the distributional consequences of divorce without resort to formal adjudication. The financial cost of litigation, both private and public, lessens. A negotiated settlement allows the parties to avoid the pain of the formal adversarial proceedings and the risks and uncertainties of litigation, which may involve all-or-nothing consequences. Given the substantial delays that often characterize contested judicial proceedings, agreement often saves time and allows each spouse to proceed with his or her life. In short, against a backdrop of fair standards in the shadow of which a couple bargains, divorcing couples should have very broad powers to make their own arrangements. Additionally, significant limitations are inconsistent with the premises of no-fault divorce. The state should encourage parties to settle the distributional consequences of divorce for themselves. The state should also provide an efficient and fair mechanism for enforcing such agreements and for settling disputes when the parties are unable to agree.

II.   JUSTIFICATIONS FOR LIMITATIONS ON PRIVATE ORDERING

A.   *Capacity*

* * * [T]he general defense of private ordering * * * is premised on the notion that divorce bargaining involves rational, self-interested individuals—that the average adult has the intelligence and experience to make a well-informed judgment concerning the desirability of entering into a particular divorce settlement. Given the tasks facing an individual at the time of divorce, and the characteristics of the relationship between divorcing spouses, there are reasons to fear that this may not always be the case.

Informed bargaining requires a divorcing spouse to assess his or her own preferences concerning alternative arrangements. Radical changes in life circumstances complicate such assessments. Within a short period of time, separation and divorce often subject spouses to the stresses of many changes. "[S]pouses need to adjust to new living arrangements, new jobs, new financial burdens, new patterns of parenting, and new conditions of social and sexual life." It may be particularly difficult for a parent to assess custodial alternatives. The past will supply a very incomplete guide to the future. Preferences may stem from past experiences in which child-rearing tasks were performed in an ongoing two-parent family, and dissolution or divorce inevitably alters this division of responsibilities. Childrearing may have new advantages or disadvantages for the parents' own needs. A parent interested in dating may find the child an intrusion in a way that the child never was during marriage. Because children and parents both change, and changes occur unpredictably, projecting parental preferences for custody into the future presents a formidable task. Nevertheless, most parents have some self-awareness, however imperfect, and no third party (such as a judge) is likely to have better information about a parent's tastes, present or future.

Separation often brings in its wake psychological turmoil and substantial emotional distress that can make deliberative and well-informed judgments unlikely. It can arouse "feelings about the (former) spouse, such as love, hate, bitterness, guilt, anger, envy, concern, and attachment; feelings about the marriage, such as regret, disappointment, bitterness, sadness, and failure; and more general feelings such as failure, depression, euphoria, relief, guilt, lowered self-esteem, and lowered self-confidence." * * * "Emotional roller-coasters are common at this stage, causing many people to feel permanent emotional instability." "[T]his is the worst possible time to make any permanent decisions—especially legal ones. * * *"

Such emotional turmoil may prevent for a time any negotiated settlement. Or it may lead to a settlement that a party later regrets.

* * *

B. Unequal Bargaining Power

A second possible justification for imposing limits on private ordering lies in a simple idea. In negotiations between two competent adults, if great disparity in bargaining power exists, some bargains may arise that are unconscionably one-sided. The notion of bargaining power has intuitive appeal, but defies easy definition. Moreover, to speak of "unequal" bargaining power implies that one can know when parties have "equal" bargaining power. * * * [I]t is possible to suggest why one divorcing spouse may be seen as having greater ability to bring about an outcome favorable to himself or herself.

First, bargaining is influenced by the partners' respective legal endowments. The legal rules governing marital property, alimony, child support, and custody give each spouse certain claims based on what each would get if the case goes to trial. * * * These endowments themselves can create unequal bargaining power. * * * To the extent that negotiated settlements simply reflect differences in bargaining power based on the legal rules themselves, no justification arises for a claim of unfairness in an individual case. Instead, the state should consider changing the legal endowments.

Second, bargaining is very much influenced by each party's preferences, i.e., how each party subjectively evaluates alternative outcomes. These preferences are not simply matters of taste. A party's economic resources and life circumstances mold them. The parties' relative bargaining power depends on how each spouse subjectively evaluates the outcome a court would impose. * * *

A third element that affects bargaining concerns uncertainty, and the parties' attitudes towards risk. Often the outcome in court is far from certain, and the parties are negotiating against a backdrop clouded by substantial uncertainty. Because the parties may have different risk preferences, this uncertainty can differentially affect the two spouses. If substantial variance exists among the possible court-imposed outcomes, the relatively more risk-averse party is comparatively disadvantaged.

A fourth element that affects bargaining relates to the differential ability to withstand the transaction costs—both emotional and economic—involved in negotiations. A party who has no immediate need for settlement, enjoys negotiations, and has plenty of resources to pay a lawyer, has an obvious advantage over an impatient opponent who hates negotiations, and cannot afford to wait.

A fifth element concerns the bargaining process itself, and strategic behavior. In divorce bargaining, the spouses may not know each other's true preferences. Negotiations often involve attempts by each side to discern the other side's true preferences, while making credible claims about their own preferences and their intentions if a particular proposal is not accepted. "Bargainers bluff, argue for their positions, attempt to deceive or manipulate each other, and make power plays to gain advantage." Some people are more skilled negotiators than others. They are better at manipulating information and managing impressions. They have a more refined sense of tactical action. These differences can create inequalities in negotiations.

* * *

C. Externalities—Third Party Effects

Third party effects provide the last set of reasons that justify limiting private ordering. A legal system that gives divorcing couples freedom to determine for themselves their postdissolution rights and responsibilities may lead to settlements that reflect the spouses' interests. But negotiated agreements can also have important consequences for third parties, and affect social interests that private negotiations fail to consider adequately.

* * * The most important third party effects concern the children, although externalities can exist with respect to other family members as well. At a conceptual level, one can easily see how a negotiated settlement may reflect parental preferences but not the child's desires or needs. * * * For example, a father may threaten a custody fight over the child, not because he wants custody, but because he wants to push his wife into accepting less support, even though this will have a detrimental effect on the child. A custodial parent, eager to escape an unhappy marriage, may offer to settle for a small amount in order to sever relations soon. A custodial parent may negotiate to eliminate largely the child's contact with the other parent, not because of the child's wants or needs, but because the custodial parent despises his ex-spouse and wants nothing more to do with her.

Concerns about the effects of divorce on children underlie many of the formal limitations on private ordering, e.g., the requirement of court review of private agreements relating to custody and child support; the legal rules prohibiting parents from making nonmodifiable and binding agreements concerning these elements. * * *

* * *

NOTES AND QUESTIONS

1. *Questions about* pro se *divorce litigation.* (a) Because divorcing parties bargain in the shadow of the law, what advice would you give a friend who told you she was considering appearing *pro se* in her upcoming divorce proceeding? To help formulate your advice, what questions would you ask her? (b) If you were a lawyer representing a dissolution client, what would you say to an opponent who was proceeding *pro se*? *See* ABA Model Rule 4.3, discussed in Chapter 2, at page 60.

2. *Negotiation and trial.* What advice would you provide a family law client concerning the relative advantages and disadvantages of negotiating terms with the spouse rather than proceeding to trial? To help formulate your advice, what questions would you ask the client? In what ways is matrimonial negotiation typically different from negotiation in business and commercial cases?

B. THE LAWYER'S ROLE IN DOMESTIC RELATIONS NEGOTIATION

In one recent survey, domestic relations lawyers rated "being a skillful negotiator" as one of their two most important professional skills, a close second only to "being a sensitive listener to the client." Lynn Mather et al., Divorce Lawyers at Work 66–67 (2001). Family law negotiation may take place amid emotional turmoil largely absent in business or commercial litigation, but the family lawyer's obligations to the client remain similar to the obligations that prevail in law practice generally.

ZIEGELHEIM v. APOLLO

Supreme Court of New Jersey, 1992.
607 A.2d 1298.

HANDLER, J.

In this case we must decide what duties an attorney owes a client when negotiating a settlement and whether a client's agreement to a negotiated settlement bars her from recovering from her attorney for the negligent handling of her case.

I

Miriam Ziegelheim, plaintiff, and Irwin Ziegelheim were married on September 11, 1955, and were divorced by a final decree dated August 5, 1983. During the early years of their marriage, Mrs. Ziegelheim was gainfully employed, assisting her husband in his business ventures and working for other employers as well. After the Ziegelheims adopted two infant sons she became a full-time homemaker. The couple separated in August 1979.

In September 1979, Mrs. Ziegelheim retained defendant, attorney Stephen Apollo, to represent her in her anticipated divorce action. * * * According to Mrs. Ziegelheim, she and Apollo met on several occasions to plan various aspects of her case. She told him about all of the marital and separate assets of which she was aware, and they discussed her suspicion that Mr. Ziegelheim was either concealing or dissipating certain other assets as well. In particular, Mrs. Ziegelheim told Apollo that she thought her husband had $500,000 hidden in the form of cash savings and bonds. Accordingly, she asked Apollo to make a thorough inquiry into her husband's assets, including cash, bonds, patents, stocks, pensions, life insurance, profit-sharing plans, and real estate.

When Mrs. Ziegelheim contacted Apollo, she also was aware of a tax deficiency that had been assessed by the Internal Revenue Service against the Ziegelheims on their joint returns. She specifically advised Apollo of her desire that any property settlement agreement absolve her of responsibility for the deficiency. She also insisted that the divorce end with her retention of the marital home, free and clear, with Mr. Ziegelheim assuming the mortgage; that she be awarded $45,630 per year in alimony (with adjustments for inflation); and that Mr. Ziegelheim obtain a life insurance policy in the amount of $500,000 to secure payment of alimony.

In September 1990, Irwin Ziegelheim filed for divorce in the Superior Court, Chancery Division. Through Apollo, Mrs. Ziegelheim filed her answer and a counterclaim. Because both Mr. and Mrs. Ziegelheim sought to terminate their marriage, the only issues to be resolved at the consolidated trial were the payment of alimony, the identification of the marital property, and the equitable distribution of that property.

According to Mrs. Ziegelheim, Apollo failed to discover important information about her husband's assets before entering into settlement negotiations with Mr. Ziegelheim's attorney, Sheldon Liebowitz. Apollo hired an accountant who valued the marital estate at approximately $2,413,000. Mrs. Ziegelheim claims that the accountant substantially underestimated the estate because of several oversights by Apollo, including his failure to locate a bank vault owned by Mr. Ziegelheim; to locate or determine the value of his tax-free municipal bonds; to verify the value of his profit-sharing plan at Pilot Woodworking, a company in which he was the primary shareholder; to search for an estimated $500,000 in savings; to contact the United States Patent Office to verify the existence of certain patents he held; to inquire into a $1,000,000 life insurance policy naming an associate of his as the beneficiary; to verify the value of certain lake-front property; and to verify the value of his stock holdings. She alleges that had Apollo made a proper inquiry, it would have been apparent that the marital estate was worth approximately $2,562,000, or about $149,000 more than the accountant found.

On November 4, 1982, Apollo, Mrs. Ziegelheim, and her accountant commenced settlement discussions with Liebowitz, Mr. Ziegelheim, and Mr. Ziegelheim's accountant. Several proposals and counter-proposals were made over several days, and the discussions culminated on November 8, 1982, when the parties entered into a property settlement agreement governing distribution of the marital estate as well as arrangements for payment of alimony. Later that day, the agreement was orally entered into the record before the judge presiding over the divorce action. Liebowitz recited to the court what he understood to be the terms of the settlement, asking Apollo to interrupt if the recitation contained any errors. Apollo never interrupted to indicate that he thought Liebowitz's representations were inaccurate. Under the agreement, Mrs. Ziegelheim was granted alimony for fifteen years, totalling approximately $330,000 and averaging approximately $22,000 per year. Mrs. Ziegelheim received the marital home and Mr. Ziegelheim received the couple's lake house.

(The parties subsequently disagreed over which of them was to assume the mortgage on the marital home; two transcripts of the hearing differed on the point. The conflict was resolved at a subsequent hearing, in which the court determined that audio recordings of Liebowitz's recitation revealed that Mrs. Ziegelheim was to assume the mortgage.) The Ziegelheims' other personal property also was allocated between them. Mrs. Ziegelheim received shares in Pilot Woodworking, which the company would redeem according to a set schedule, and Mr. Ziegelheim promised to contribute $400 per year toward the purchase of a life term insurance policy. Mr. Ziegelheim also agreed to indemnify Mrs. Ziegelheim for any tax liabilities incurred for the years 1979, 1980, and 1981 "except for liabilities created by Mrs. Ziegelheim." In sum, Mrs. Ziegelheim was to receive approximately $333,000 in alimony, $6,000 in contributions to insurance costs, and $324,000 in property, the last figure representing approximately fourteen percent of the value of the estate (as appraised by Apollo and the accountant). Mr. Ziegelheim was to receive approximately $2,088,000 in property, approximately eighty-six percent of the value of the estate.

When testifying before the court immediately after the settlement was read into the record, both Mrs. Ziegelheim and Mr. Ziegelheim stated that they understood the agreement, that they thought it was fair, and that they entered into it voluntarily. Mrs. Ziegelheim now asserts, however, that she accepted the agreement only after Apollo advised her that wives could expect to receive no more than ten to twenty percent of the marital estate if they went to trial. She claims that Apollo's estimate was unduly pessimistic and did not comport with the advice that a reasonably competent attorney would have given under the circumstances. Had she been advised competently, she says, she would not have accepted the settlement.

The settlement was not finalized until August 2, 1983. According to Mrs. Ziegelheim, the written agreement failed to conform with the oral agreement in that it did not indemnify her for tax deficiencies for which she claims her former husband was wholly responsible. She also claims that the nine-month delay in putting the agreement into final written form was unnecessary, and that it caused her to lose one year's interest on the first $75,000 owed to her pursuant to the stock-redemption clause.

In 1984, Mrs. Ziegelheim filed a malpractice action against Apollo * * *.

Mrs. Ziegelheim filed a five-count complaint against Apollo. Under the first count, she alleged that he was negligent in handling her case because he delayed in securing a final written settlement and thereby caused her to lose interest on the payments due under the settlement; because the written settlement did not contain the tax indemnification clause she wanted; and because the written settlement did not require Mr. Ziegelheim to make as large a contribution to the life insurance costs as she wanted. In the second and third counts she alleged that defendant was negligent in handling her case because he permitted it to settle for less than it should have. In the fourth count she alleged that defendant was negligent in handling her case because he permitted the case to settle under circumstances that ensured an unfair outcome; because he failed to use proper procedures in preparing and negotiating the case; and because he convinced her to accept an agreement that a reasonably prudent attorney would have advised against accepting. In the fifth count she alleged that he was negligent in handling her case because he failed to reduce the complex settlement proposal to writing, compromising her ability to understand its terms and to give informed and reasoned consent to them.

Apollo moved [successfully] for summary judgment. * * *

* * *

II

Like most professionals, lawyers owe a duty to their clients to provide their services with reasonable knowledge, skill, and diligence. We have consistently recited that command in rather broad terms, for lawyers' duties in specific cases vary with the circumstances presented. "What constitutes a reasonable degree of care is not to be considered in a vacuum but with reference to the type of service the attorney undertakes to perform." The lawyer must take "any steps necessary in the proper handling of the case." Those steps will include, among other things, a careful investigation of the facts of the matter, the formulation of a legal strategy, the filing of appropriate papers, and the maintenance of communication with the client.

In accepting a case, the lawyer agrees to pursue the goals of the client to the extent the law permits, even when the lawyer believes that the client's desires are unwise or ill-considered. At the same time, because the client's desires may be influenced in large measure by the advice the lawyer provides, the lawyer is obligated to give the client reasonable advice. As a legal matter progresses and circumstances change, the wishes of the client may change as well. Accordingly, the lawyer is obligated to keep the client informed of the status of the matter for which the lawyer has been retained, and is required to advise the client on the various legal and strategic issues that arise.

In this case, Mrs. Ziegelheim made several claims impugning Apollo's handling of her divorce, and the trial court dismissed all of them on Apollo's motion for summary judgment. As we explain, we believe that the trial court's rulings on several of her claims were erroneous.

* * *

On Mrs. Ziegelheim's claim that Apollo negligently advised her with respect to her chances of winning a greater proportion of the marital estate if she proceeded to trial, we conclude * * * that there was a genuine dispute regarding the appropriate advice that an attorney should give in cases like hers. According to the expert retained by Mrs. Ziegelheim, women in her position—who are in relatively poor health, have little earning capacity, and have been wholly dependent on their husbands—often receive upwards of fifty percent of the marital estate. The expert said that Mrs. Ziegelheim's chances of winning such a large fraction of the estate had she gone to trial would have been especially good because the couple had enjoyed a high standard of living while they were together and because her husband's earning capacity was "tremendous" and would remain so for some time. Her expert's opinion was brought to the trial court's attention, as was the expert report of Mr. Ziegelheim. If plaintiff's expert's opinion were credited, as it should have been for purposes of summary judgment, then Apollo very well could have been found negligent in advising her that she could expect to win only ten to twenty percent of the marital estate.

Apollo urges us to adopt the rule enunciated by the Pennsylvania Supreme Court in *Muhammad v. Strassburger, McKenna, Messer, Shilobod and Gutnick*, 587 A.2d 1346 (Pa. 1991), that a dissatisfied litigant may not recover from his or her attorney for malpractice in negotiating a settlement that the litigant has accepted unless the litigant can prove actual fraud on the part of the attorney. Under that rule, no cause of action can be made based on negligence or contract principles against an attorney for malpractice in negotiating a settlement. The Pennsylvania Supreme Court rationalized its severe rule by explaining that it had a "longstanding public policy which encourages settlements."

New Jersey, too, has a longstanding policy that encourages settlements, but we reject the rule espoused by the Pennsylvania Supreme Court. Although we encourage settlements, we recognize that litigants rely heavily on the professional advice of counsel when they decide whether to accept or reject offers of settlement, and we insist that the lawyers of our state advise clients with respect to settlements with the same skill, knowledge, and diligence with which they pursue all other legal tasks. Attorneys are supposed to know the likelihood of success for the types of cases they handle and they are supposed to know the range of possible awards in those cases.

* * * "One who undertakes to render services in the practice of a profession or trade is required to exercise the skill and knowledge normally possessed by members of that profession in good standing in similar communities." * * * Like most courts, we see no reason to apply a more lenient rule to lawyers who negotiate settlements. After all, the negotiation of settlements is one of the most basic and most frequently undertaken tasks that lawyers perform.

* * *

The fact that a party received a settlement that was "fair and equitable" does not mean necessarily that the party's attorney was competent or that the party would not have received a more favorable settlement had the party's incompetent attorney been competent. * * *

Moreover, another aspect of the alleged professional incompetence that led to the improvident acceptance of the settlement was the attorney's own failure to discover hidden marital assets. When Mrs. Ziegelheim sought to reopen her divorce settlement, the family court denied her motion with the observation that "[a]mple opportunity existed for full discovery," and that "the parties had their own accountants as well as counsel." The court did not determine definitively that Mr. Ziegelheim had hidden no assets, but stated instead that it "suspected that everything to be known was known to the parties." The earlier ruling did not implicate the competence of counsel and, indeed, was premised on the presumptive competence of counsel. Hence, defendant cannot invoke that ruling now to bar a challenge to his competence. Mrs. Ziegelheim should have been allowed to prove that Apollo negligently failed to discover certain assets concealed by her former husband.

The Appellate Division also affirmed the trial court's dismissal of Mrs. Ziegelheim's claims that Apollo negligently delayed in finalizing the settlement and that the written settlement differed from the one recited by Mr. Ziegelheim's lawyer. Again we conclude that she should have been allowed to litigate those claims on the merits. * * *

Mrs. Ziegelheim's final claim is that Apollo was negligent in not writing down the terms of the settlement prior to the hearing in which the settlement was recited and approved by her and Mr. Ziegelheim. She asserts that a competent attorney would have written them down so that she could review them and make an informed and reasoned assessment of their fairness. * * * [O]n this record, her final claim, too, presents genuine issues of material fact and should not have been resolved on summary judgment.

In holding as we do today, we do not open the door to malpractice suits by any and every dissatisfied party to a settlement. Many such claims could be averted if settlements were explained as a matter of record in open court in proceedings reflecting the understanding and assent of the parties. Further, plaintiffs must allege particular facts in support of their claims of attorney incompetence and may not litigate complaints containing mere generalized assertions of malpractice. We are mindful that attorneys cannot be held liable simply because they are not successful in persuading an opposing party to accept certain terms. Similarly, we acknowledge that attorneys who pursue reasonable strategies in handling their cases and who render reasonable advice to their clients cannot be held liable for the failure of their strategies or for any unprofitable outcomes that result because their clients took their advice. The law demands that attorneys handle their cases with knowledge, skill, and diligence, but it does not demand that they be perfect or infallible, and it does not demand that they always secure optimum outcomes for their clients.

* * *

[The dissenting opinion of CLIFFORD, J., is omitted.]

NOTES AND QUESTIONS

1. *A difference of opinion. Ziegelheim* disagreed with the Pennsylvania Supreme Court's *Muhammad* decision, which held that a litigant who accepted a settlement agreement could sue the lawyer who negotiated it only where the lawyer had fraudulently induced the client to accept. *Muhammad* concluded that "[t]he essence of a settlement is contractual in nature. * * * [A]lthough a party to a contract believes he might have made a better deal after he agreed to the original contract, he is nonetheless bound by the terms of that primary agreement." 587 A.2d 1346, 1349 (Pa. 1991).

Muhammad concluded that permitting a divorce client's negligence or breach of contract suit against the lawyer who negotiated the settlement would "create chaos in our civil litigation system" by discouraging settlements and "increasing substantial[ly] the number of legal malpractice cases": "Lawyers would be reluctant to settle a case for fear some enterprising attorney representing a disgruntled client will find a way to sue them for something that 'could have been done, but was not.'" "[S]ettlement of civil litigation," the Pennsylvania Supreme Court concluded, "is critical to the courts' management of caseloads. Without settlement of cases, litigants would have to wait years, if not decades, for their day in court." *Id.* at 1349–51.

Which decision, *Ziegelheim* or *Muhammad*, has the better of the argument? Would your answer to this question depend on whether you are the lawyer or the litigant?

2. What specifically should lawyer Apollo have done differently?

SECTION 2: MEDIATION

A. THE NATURE OF DOMESTIC RELATIONS MEDIATION

Mediation is "facilitated negotiation." In domestic relations mediation, the parties present all or part of their dispute before a third-party neutral, the mediator, who helps the parties "identify the issues, reduce misunderstandings, vent emotions, clarify priorities, find points of agreement, and explore new areas of compromise and possible solutions." Jessica Pearson & Nancy Thoennes, *Mediating and Litigating Custody Disputes: A Longitudinal Evaluation*, 17 Fam. L.Q. 497, 498 (1984). Unlike arbitrators, mediators have no authority to impose a binding decision, or even to require that the parties reach an agreement.

Because decisionmaking authority rests with the parties, mediation is a "consensual" process, rather than an "adjudicative" process like litigation or arbitration. Mediation differs from direct negotiation, which, whether or not conducted by the parties' lawyers, is done face-to-face without facilitation by a third-party neutral. Like other negotiated outcomes, a mediated outcome can reflect the parties' emotional needs and desires, which may not prevail when a court determines a winner and a loser by applying substantive law conferring considerable discretion. Mediating parties "may address any issue they wish, not limited to legal causes of action; they may bring in any information they wish, not limited by rules of evidence and procedure to probative evidence, relevant to legal causes of action and meeting evidentiary requirements for authenticity and accuracy." Jonathan M. Hyman & Lela P. Love, *If Portia Were A Mediator: An Inquiry Into Justice in Mediation*, 9 Clinical L. Rev. 157, 161 (2002).

Parties sometimes settle all issues during family mediation. Where the parties reach no settlement or only a partial settlement, unsettled issues proceed to other forms of dispute resolution, including perhaps trial. At the end of each session that results in tentative points of agreement, the mediator generally drafts a memorandum of understanding identifying these points and sends the memorandum to the parties for their review. At the end of mediation, the mediator sends the parties any completed terms of the agreement. Once the parties execute the agreement, they submit it to the court for entry as a binding order, or for incorporation into the judgment or decree. Joan H. McWilliams, *Your ADR Options: Mediation, Arbitration and Collaborative Law*, 24 Fam. Advoc., Spring 2002, at 2, 2.

Traditionally family mediation, like other mediation, was based on the parties' private agreement to mediate. In 1980, however, California became the first state to mandate mediation in contested child custody disputes in divorce proceedings. Cal. Civ. Code § 4607 (West 1993) (repealed 1994) (current version at Cal. Civ. Code § 3170 (West 2008)). Statutes mandating family law mediation have spread so rapidly that "today a divorce or child custody matter not going to mediation is the exception rather than the rule." Art Hinshaw, *Mediators As Mandatory Reporters of Child Abuse: Preserving Mediation's Core Values*, 34 Fla. St. U. L. Rev. 271, 275 (2007).

The ranks of family mediators today include not only lawyers, but also mental health professionals trained in conflict resolution and such disciplines as child psychology, social work, marriage counseling, education, and family systems. Clergy also sometimes serve as mediators. Because parties often bring both legal issues and emotional needs to the table, mediators may work as a team in "co-mediation." Lawyer-mental health professional teams and male-female teams are available in some communities.

As family mediation has grown more prominent in the past thirty years with the advent of no-fault divorce, researchers have tested the advantages claimed by its proponents and the disadvantages identified by critics. Studies of divorce mediation indicate that parties reach agreement between 50% and 85% of the time, with most studies finding the agreement rate in the mid to upper range. (Prescreening to eliminate some couples for such reasons as a history of domestic violence, high conflict or one party's unwillingness to divorce apparently increases the rate of agreement.)

Studies also indicate (1) that mediation results in more joint legal (but not more joint physical) custody arrangements than adversarial processes; (2) that mediation and litigation yield no difference in child support amounts, though non-custodial parents who mediated agreements have higher rates of compliance with support orders, pay for more "extras" for their children and are more likely to agree to pay college expenses; (3) that mediated property agreements do not differ significantly from agreements reached in negotiation or litigation, but mediation clients view their agreements as fairer; (4) that men and women in mediation reported more satisfaction with their spousal support agreements than did men and women using the adversarial process; (5) that mediated agreements are much more detailed and specific than lawyer-negotiated or litigated agreements; (6) that parties comply with mediated agreements at a higher rate than with agreements reached in the adversarial process; (7) that client satisfaction with the mediation process and mediated outcomes is quite high, in the 60% to 85% range, while 40–60% satisfaction rates with mediation have been reported even among parties unable to reach agreement; (8) that male and female mediation clients emerge more satisfied than comparison groups who pursued traditional adversarial divorce; (9) that participants generally give mediators high marks for their impartiality, sensitivity and skill; (10) that after custody mediation, parties experience small but often short-lived increases in cooperation and improvement in their communications; and (11) that mediation does not affect in a statistically meaningful manner parents' or children's initial psychological adjustment to divorce. Joan B. Kelly, *A Decade of Divorce Mediation Research: Some Questions and Answers*, 34 Fam. & Conciliation Cts. Rev. 373, 375–80 (1996).

Despite the final point in Kelly's summary, one 12–year follow-up study found that "mediation led to several substantial long-term benefits for parents and children, particularly for the relationships between children and nonresidential parents, and between the parents themselves." Robert E. Emery, David Sbarra & Tara Grover, *Divorce Mediation: Research and Reflections*, 43 Fam. Ct. Rev. 22, 23–33 (2005). The study found that "[i]ncreased contact between nonresidential parents (mostly fathers) and children proved to be one notable and very important benefit of mediation. * * * In the mediation group, 54% of nonresidential parents spoke to their children on the telephone once a week or more often in contrast to 13% in the adversary group." *Id.* at 30. Another study found that mandatory child-custody mediation is most likely to produce these positive results in low-conflict cases, that is, cases in which neither party has alleged unfitness or domestic violence. *See* Ralph A. Peeples, Suzanne Reynolds & Catherine T. Harris, *It's the Conflict, Stupid: An Empirical Study of Factors That Inhibit Successful Mediation in High–Conflict Custody Cases*, 43 Wake Forest L. Rev. 505, 528 (2008).

NOTES AND QUESTIONS

1. *The challenges facing family mediators.* Amid the simmering emotions that typically accompany dissolution, family mediators have been likened to "traffic cops" who "direct the flow of dialog to control angry outbursts, interruptions, accusations, and inflammatory remarks." "By enforcing ground rules and bringing structure to the discussions, by paraphrasing contentious remarks, and by permitting one person to speak at a time, the mediator steers parties on a constructive course." Lois Gold, Between Love and Hate: A Guide to Civilized Divorce 247 (1992). Family mediators face a daunting task:

> With regard to the parties, the mediator is expected: to establish and maintain trust and confidence; to demonstrate empathy and understanding for the positions of each side; to be highly expert on substantive and procedural issues, but to use that expertise to guide and counsel, not to impose personal views or take sides. With regard to the process, the mediator is expected to foster a procedure of dispute resolution: in which neither party gets all that it is asking, although neither ends by being humiliated or defeated; that engages all parties in an active process of give and take, albeit one that is sufficiently controlled so that the risks of conflict escalation are kept to a minimum; and that is based on objective and realistic assessment of the forces and interests at play. With regard to the settlement, the mediator is expected to promote agreements that both sides can defend publicly; that each can view as reasonably fair; and that lay the groundwork for improved interaction.

Kenneth Kressel, The Process of Divorce: How Professionals and Couples Negotiate Settlements 203–04 (1985).

2. *Questions about court-annexed mediation.* (a) Should courts have authority to mandate mediation, traditionally a consensual process, as a precondition to judicial resolution? (b) Where a court encourages or recommends mediation, might a party feel pressured into mediating and perhaps settling rather than face the judge after spurning the encouragement or recommendation? (c) In mandatory court-annexed family mediation, what happens if one party appears for the mediation session, sits down at the table, declines to speak and does nothing more?

3. *Mandatory mediation and individual choice.* If family mediation is beneficial for some parties, why should courts need to mandate it? Professor Joshua D. Rosenberg argues that "[t]he unfortunate truth about human behavior * * * is that left to our own devices, we often choose to act in ways that are not profoundly wise." Joshua D. Rosenberg, *In Defense of Mediation*, 33 Ariz. L. Rev. 467, 503–04 (1991). On the other hand, Professor Tina Grillo finds it "indefensible" to require divorcing parties to mediate because "[i]t is presumptuous to assume that the state has a better idea than the parties themselves about whether mediation will work in their particular case." Tina Grillo, *The Mediation Alternative: Process Dangers For Women*, 100 Yale L.J. 1545, 1582–83 (1991). Which argument do you find more persuasive?

4. *Mandatory mediation and access to the courts.* Where mandatory court-annexed family mediation does not resolve the parties' disputes, the parties may proceed to court. Because the judicial process remains available, courts have generally rejected arguments that mediation unconstitutionally denies parties access to the courts or violates due process. *See* Richard C. Reuben, *Public Justice: Toward a State Action Theory of Alternative Dispute Resolution*, 85 Cal. L. Rev. 577, 641 n.42 (1997).

At least where the mediation process is relatively brief, courts reason that mandatory mediation only delays court resolution. *See, e.g., Bauer v. Bauer*, 28 S.W.3d 877, 886–87 (Mo. Ct. App. 2000) (finding no constitutional violation because either spouse could terminate mediation at any time after two hours and proceed to court). Statutes or rules prescribing or anticipating lengthy delays for mandatory family mediation might raise constitutional concerns. Even lengthy delays, however, may survive constitutional scrutiny because litigation also imposes significant delays on litigants. *See* Dwight Golann, *Making Alternative Dispute Resolution Mandatory: The Constitutional Issues*, 68 Or. L. Rev. 487, 548–49 (1989).

5. *Time and cost comparison.* "[A]s litigation becomes extremely expensive, as it is today in major metropolitan areas, middle class divorcing couples may be forced to choose mediation for purely economic considerations and failing that, to represent themselves in court, now seen more and more." Sanford N. Katz, *Family Law at the End of the Twentieth Century: Prologue*, 33 Fam. L.Q. 435, 439 (1995). One study found that "parents settled their disputes in about half the time when assigned to mediation versus adversary settlement." Emery et al., *supra*, at 27. Several studies have reported that private divorce mediation is indeed considerably less expensive than litigation, at least where mediation produces full settlement. *See* Kelly, *supra*, at 376. One study found that parties who successfully mediated their divorce spent only about one-fifth as much on legal fees as parties who followed the traditional court process. Marygold S. Melli et al., *The Process of Negotiation: An Exploratory Investigation in the Context of No–Fault Divorce*, 40 Rutgers L. Rev. 1133, 1142 (1988).

Where mediation is mandatory and court-annexed rather than consensual, further cost-related issues arise. Does mandatory mediation, followed by litigation or other procedure where mediation does not produce final resolution, unfairly increase the costs borne by a divorcing party who might have rejected mediation if left to his or her own devices? Might some spouses, strapped for funds and facing diminished post-divorce lifestyles, be coerced into settling rather than pay counsel fees and other litigation expenses after paying for mandatory mediation? Where a party feels coerced, has mandatory mediation deprived the party of the substantive law's protections?

6. *Mediators' qualifications.* Mediation may be done under the auspices of a private provider or a publicly funded court-annexed program. Minimum qualifications of private mediation providers often depend on standards set by the providers themselves, and some commentators have complained that these standards are not uniformly high. By statute or court rule, several states provide minimum qualifications for mediators in court-annexed programs, which may include a specified number of hours of training.

In 2001, the American Bar Association House of Delegates approved the Model Standards of Practice for Family and Divorce Mediation. *See* Symposium on Standards of Practice, Model Standards of Practice for Family and Divorce Mediation (2001), http://www.abanet.org/family/reports/mediation.pdf. The Model Standards are 13 general principles designed to guide family law mediators. The Model Standards do not have binding regulatory effect, but they may affect the thinking of legislatures, courts and private professional groups. Model Standard II states that: "A family mediator shall be qualified by education and training to undertake the mediation." The Model Standards further indicate that private and court-appointed family mediators should:

1. have knowledge of family law;

2. have knowledge of and training in the impact of family conflict on parents, children and other participants, including knowledge of child development, domestic abuse and child abuse and neglect;

3. have education and training specific to the process of mediation; [and]

4. be able to recognize the impact of culture and diversity.

Id., Overview and Definitions, Standard II, at iii–iv. The Model Standards of Conduct for Mediators, prepared by a joint committee of the American Arbitration Association, the ABA's Section of Dispute Resolution, and the Association of Conflict Resolution, provide similar guidelines, which were revised in 2005. *See* ABA, Am. Arbitration Ass'n, Ass'n for Conflict Resolution, Model Standards of Conduct for Mediators (2005), http://www.abanet.org/dispute/news/ModelStandardsofConductforMediatorsfinal05.pdf.

7. *Some ethical questions for lawyer-mediators.* Lawyer-mediators may be trained in tax law, pension law, bankruptcy law and other specialties central to the divorcing parties' circumstances. When parties seek legal advice from the mediator during the mediation, does the lawyer-mediator run the risk of violating ethical rules concerning dual representation, conflicts of interest, and offering legal advice in the role of a neutral?

The ABA Model Rules of Professional Conduct specify that "a lawyer may serve as a third-party neutral, a nonrepresentational role helping the parties to resolve a dispute or other matter." Model Rules of Prof'l Conduct, Preamble [3]. "Service as a third-party neutral may include service as * * * a mediator." Model Rule 2.4(a). To avoid confusion by lay parties, the lawyer serving as a third-party neutral must "inform unrepresented parties that the lawyer is not representing them. When the lawyer knows or reasonably should know that a party does not understand the lawyer's role in the matter, the lawyer shall explain the difference between the lawyer's role as a third-party neutral and the lawyer's roles as one who represents a client." Model Rule 2.4(b).

Ethics committees nationwide have generally advised lawyer-mediators not to represent a mediating party in the later family law proceeding if the mediation fails to resolve some or all of the issues. The advice amounts to a virtual prohibition. *See, e.g.*, Prof'l Ethics Advisory Comm., Kan. Bar Ass'n, Formal Op. 3 (1983). Later representation would create a conflict of interest because of the mediator's close relationship with both spouses during the mediation process: "If the mediation seems near failure, but one spouse seems impressed by the lawyer's skills, the lawyer may be torn between the duty to impartially explain the law to both spouses and the possibility of bringing in a new client." Prof'l Guidance Comm., Philadelphia Bar Ass'n, Formal Op. 93–24 (1994). The Philadelphia Committee also observed that because the attorney-client privilege would likely not protect discussions between the mediator and the parties during mediation, a lawyer-mediator might be required to testify about admissions made by a spouse during the process if the matter reached trial. The prospect of such testimony would implicate Model Rule 3.7, which provides that "[a] lawyer shall not act as an advocate at a trial in which the lawyer is likely to be a necessary witness unless: (1) the testimony relates to an uncontested issue, * * * or (3) disqualification of the lawyer would work substantial hardship on the client."

The 2008 ABA Model Rules of Professional Conduct may work a change in the virtual prohibition articulated by ethics opinions on the later-representation issue. The Model Rules still provide a mediator rationales for declining later representation, but Model Rule 1.12(a) now permits parties to waive objections to conflicts involving such representation: "[A] lawyer shall not represent anyone in connection with a matter in which the lawyer participated personally and substantially as a * * * mediator or other third-party neutral, unless all parties to the proceeding give informed consent, confirmed in writing."

8. *Unauthorized practice of law.* Professor Jacqueline Nolan–Haley reports that non-lawyer mediators still operate under the "haunting shadows" of threats by the organized bar to suppress competition from non-lawyer mediators by invoking unauthorized-practice-of-law (UPL) regulations, which may lead to criminal or civil sanction. Jacqueline Nolan–Haley, *Lawyers, Non–Lawyers and Mediation: Rethinking the Professional Monopoly From a Problem–Solving Perspective*, 7 Harv. Neg. L. Rev. 235, 235, 239 (2002).

The UPL doctrine restricts the practice of law to persons who hold law licenses and have been admitted to the state bar after examination for education and character. *See* Restatement (Third) of the Law Governing Lawyers §§ 2, 4 (2000). The line of demarcation between the legal and mediation professions remains hazy. The doctrine's application may depend on whether the non-lawyer mediator provides merely "facilitative" mediation, or whether the mediator also provides "evaluative" mediation. The mediator might employ strategies and techniques that facilitate the parties' negotiation, such as helping the parties develop, exchange and evaluate proposals from one another. The mediator might also employ strategies intended to evaluate or direct matters important to the mediation, such as predicting court or other outcomes, and assessing the strengths and weaknesses of the other side's case. *See* Leonard L. Riskin, *Decisionmaking in Mediation: The New Old Grid and the New New Grid System*, 79 Notre Dame L. Rev. 1 (2003). Non-lawyer mediators may find themselves giving legal advice (and thus arguably engaging in UPL) under either model, but the likelihood of giving legal advice increases considerably when the mediator evaluates.

The ABA's Model Standards do not take a position on the appropriateness of facilitative or evaluative mediation, but one veteran mediator observes that "mediators today are much more evaluative than were traditional mediators."

Eric R. Galton, *Mediation With Children: Two Lawyers' Views*, Disp. Resol. Mag., Fall 1996, at 5–6. Other commentators report that at least in court-annexed mediation, parties often select mediators for their ability to evaluate and assess the strengths and weaknesses of the legal case.

9. *Mediation of child custody and visitation issues.* With mediation of custody and visitation disputes now quite common, some commentators have raised warning signals. For one thing, research indicates that joint or shared physical custody arrangements are much more common in mediated cases than in cases resolved by negotiation or litigation, and indeed that some mediators openly state their preferences for such arrangements. *See, e.g.,* Carol Bohmer & Marilyn Ray, *Effects of Different Dispute Resolution Methods on Women and Children After Divorce*, 28 Fam. L. Q. 223, 227, 233–34 (1994). Chapter 12 discusses how joint or shared custody can harm children when the parents are not emotionally equipped for it. Chapter 13 discusses the domestic strife that may result between parties who are more cooperative during and immediately after mediation than afterwards.

Second, bargaining during mediation may lead one spouse to trade financial claims for custody rights. Where the tradeoff leaves the custodial spouse with an inadequate financial arrangement, the children may find themselves in a single-parent household that faces dire financial straits, a predicament sometimes worsened when child support payments from the noncustodial parent are not forthcoming.

In some jurisdictions, the court may (on its own motion or on a party's request) appoint a neutral "parenting coordinator" to assist the parties in resolving ongoing disputes concerning implementation of the parenting plan. Appointments frequently come in high-conflict cases, but no appointment may be made where the court finds that domestic violence occurred during the marriage. *See, e.g.,* Tex. Fam. Code §§ 153.601–.611 (Vernon 2008).

10. *Should family lawyers attend their clients' mediation sessions or advise clients during mediation?* At least in the short run, lawyers' participation in family mediation can dramatically increase the costs incurred by the parties, who must now pay both the mediator and their own counsel. Some commentators argue, however, that overall costs would probably remain unchanged because settlements would come earlier and would more likely be comprehensive, and because discovery costs may be reduced. *See, e.g.,* Craig A. McEwen et al., *Bring in the Lawyers: Challenging the Dominant Approaches in Divorce Mediation*, 79 Minn. L. Rev. 1317, 1394–95 (1995).

One writer takes the position that "ADR will not succeed unless the advocates are engaged and willing to participate on behalf of their clients." Kelly Browe Olson, *The Importance of Using Alternative Dispute Resolution Techniques and Processes in the Ethical and Informed Representation of Children*, 6 Nev. L. Rev. 1333, 1346 (2006). Several commentators urge counsel's full participation because mediation, whether mandatory or consensual, remains an integral part of overall case strategy and development, regardless of whether the sessions produce full, partial or no settlement. Professor Elrod urges participation because "[m]ediation works best when each party is fully advised of his or her legal rights." Linda D. Elrod, Child Custody Practice and Procedure § 1608 (2004). Professor Subrin adds that "having lawyers present at the mediation, and encouraging mediators to explore the law with the litigants, makes it more likely that the vulnerable will gain whatever advantage the law allows." Stephen N. Subrin, *A Traditionalist Looks at Mediation: It's Here to Stay and Much Better Than I Thought*, 3 Nev. L.J. 196, 221 (2002/2003). For example, an unrepresented party may reveal privileged or irrelevant material in mediation, or may agree to something from nervousness, intimidation or fatigue.

Legislatures and courts have adopted rules requiring good faith in court-annexed mediation, but the rules do not define what qualifies as bad faith and often do not provide expressly for sanctions. A few states authorize the court to consider bad faith participation in mediation as a factor in determining child custody or visitation, e.g., Utah Code Ann. § 30–3–38(7) (2008), but these provisions have limited teeth because the dispositive standard remains the best interests of the child. In this posture, sanctions for lawyers' bad faith participation in family mediation are relatively rare. *See* John Lande, *Using Dispute System Design Methods to Promote Good–Faith Participation In Court Connected Mediation Programs*, 50 UCLA L. Rev. 69 (2002).

As a family lawyer, would you recommend to your client that you attend the client's mediation sessions?

11. *Should children participate in their parents' divorce mediation?* Divorce acts typically authorize the court to hear and consider the child's wishes as a persuasive, but not necessarily determinative, factor in fashioning custody and visitation arrangements. Mediators disagree, however, about whether—and if so, how—minor dependent children should participate in their parents' mediation concerning custody and visitation issues.

Two non-lawyer mediators agree that involving children "has a powerful impact on both parents and children." "Children are afforded the opportunity to communicate their concerns and feelings with an understanding person. They tend to leave less anxious and burdened. Many parents become more willing to focus on their children's needs and on their new parental roles rather than on past hurts and disappointments." Robin Drapkin & Florence Bienenfeld, *The Power of Including Children in Custody Mediation, in* Divorce Mediation: Perspectives on the Field 63, 63 (Craig A. Everett ed., 1985).

On the other hand, two psychologists counsel against involving the children in divorce mediation because a child's stated preferences may create a lasting emotional burden and jeopardize future relations with one or both parents. For one thing, "[y]oungsters who state their preferences and see them realized come to believe that they were the determining factor in the decisions made. In drawing such a conclusion, they make themselves vulnerable to guilt because they believe that their statements deprived the parent of something he or she desired (*e.g.*, custody, visitation time)." Guilt can be immediate or long-term: "[W]hen they see their parents cry, complain of loneliness, or experience difficulties of any kind, guilt may lead the youngsters to blame themselves for the unhappiness, misfortune, or conflicts that ensue." Andrew I. Schwebel & Milton Schwebel, *Mediating With Children: Two Psychologists' Views*, Disp. Resol. Mag., Fall 1996, at 3.

A lawyer-mediator concludes that "the dangers of including minors in the mediation process probably * * * outweigh the benefits" because (1) "the modest training requirements for mediators and the lack of standards, regulations and sanctions which apply to mediators clear the way for unskilled and possibly insensitive mediators to inappropriately involve children," (2) "[a]n evaluative and aggressive mediator could present greater risks than benefits to minor participants [who] might feel coerced or betrayed," and (3) "lawyer-mediators, who tend to legalize disputes as much as the lawyers representing the parties do, often pay less attention to the emotional needs and interests of the parties." Galton, *supra*, at 5–7.

In fact, children frequently participate in their parents' family mediation. The child's age may play a critical role in determining whether mediators seek children's input, as it does when a court determines whether to solicit the child's views and how much weight to accord these views. *See* Gary W. Paquin, *The Child's Input in the Mediation Process: Promoting the Best Interests of the Child*, 22 Mediation Q. 69, 74 (Winter 1988).

Children can participate in their parents' family mediation in a variety of ways. The mediator or a mental health professional may ascertain the child's preferences in a private interview and then report to the parents; the child may participate personally in the mediation and state preferences; or the child may state preferences in a videotaped statement. After the parents have reached a settlement, the mediator may explain the arrangements to the child and seek the child's cooperation, though the child might benefit more at that stage from a session with a psychologist or therapist.

As counsel, would you advise your client to permit the children to participate in the mediation? Would you provide the same advice in all cases? What factors might influence your advice in a particular case? What sort of participation would you recommend?

12. *Confidentiality in mediation.* The Uniform Mediation Act (UMA), which was drafted by the National Conference of Commissioners of Uniform State Laws in 2001 and approved by the American Bar Association a year later, takes the position that "frank exchange can be achieved only if the participants know that what is said in the mediation will not be used to their detriment through later court proceedings and other adjudicatory processes." UMA prefatory note 1 (2001), http://www.law.upenn.edu/bll/ulc/mediat/UMA 2001.htm. To encourage states to recognize a uniform testimonial privilege nationally, section 4(a) of the UMA states the general rule that "[a] mediation communication is privileged * * * and is not subject to discovery or admissible in evidence in a proceeding." The Act defines "mediation communication" broadly to include oral, written and nonverbal statements made while convening a mediation, while selecting a mediator or during the mediation itself. *Id.* § 2(a).

Despite the uniform act's initiative, Professor Philip J. Harter reports that "[t]he law governing the confidentiality of mediation is currently a mess":

> Parties regularly expect that what they tell the mediator in confidence will remain just between them, and mediators regularly promise virtually complete confidentiality to the participants. * * * [T]he law governing confidentiality varies by subject matter within a state and by jurisdiction within a substantive area. Moreover, the differences can be quite signifi-

cant. And, the parties to a mediation can never know just where a challenge to confidentiality might be brought or even whether it will be directly related to the subject on the table. As a result, the parties cannot know whether what they think is confidential will be in another jurisdiction when an action might take place or as to parts of a mediation that might fall outside a narrowly drawn statute. Further, mediators often promise more confidentiality than they can actually deliver as a matter of law and since many parties are unrepresented by counsel, they may rely on this assurance to their detriment.

Philip J. Harter, *The Uniform Mediation Act: An Essential Framework For Self–Determination*, 22 N. Ill. U. Rev. 251, 251 (2002).

Offers to compromise or settle a claim, and responses to such offers, are inadmissible in later civil proceedings to prove or disprove the claim. This general inadmissibility rule would cover offers and responses made during mediation. On the other hand, civil discovery rules generally require pretrial disclosure of non-privileged matter relevant to a claim or defense, including arguably inadmissible matter that appears reasonably calculated to lead to discovery of admissible evidence. The rules of evidence then permit introduction of relevant non-privileged evidence at trial. Unless a statute or rule cloaks mediation in confidentiality, parties to family mediation hold no greater privilege than other civil litigants.

A number of states provide for confidentiality of some or all matters arising during the mediation. Some states also recognize a testimonial privilege covering some or all statements made to or by a mediator during mediation. Where mediation does not resolve a dispute, the mediator in these states may not testify (voluntarily or by subpoena of a party or the court) about covered matters discussed in mediation, or about recommendations the mediator made to the parties. *See, e.g.*, Cal. Evid. Code § 1119 (2008); Sarah R. Cole, Nancy A. Rogers & Craig A. McEwen, Mediation—Law, Policy and Practice § 9.12 (2d ed. 1994). Confidentiality may be breached, however, when attendees at the mediation session include the child's court-appointed guardian *ad litem*, who may be bound to report to the court matters within the GAL's knowledge that bear on the best interests of the child. *See* Suzanne J. Schmitz, *Guardians ad Litem Do Not Belong in Family Mediations*, 8 Pepp. Disput. Resol. L.J. 221 (2008).

If you were representing a party in family mediation in a state that has enacted section 4(a) of the UMA, what cautionary advice would the section lead you to provide your client before beginning mediation?

13. *Should mediators be mandatory child abuse and neglect reporters?* Where a parent in mediation alleges or intimates that the other parent has committed acts of physical, sexual or emotional abuse on the children, must the mediator report the suspected acts to law enforcement or child protective authorities? All states have statutes requiring a broad array of enumerated professionals (so-called "mandatory reporters") to report acts of child abuse or neglect that they suspect to have occurred. Persons other than mandatory reporters are "permissive reporters," who may report suspected acts if they wish. Failure to report exposes mandatory reporters to criminal sanction.

Because so much child maltreatment occurs in the home or otherwise outside public view, reporting statutes seek to protect children by alerting authorities. "Some states explicitly identify mediators as mandatory reporters, others implicitly require mediators to report abuse by requiring all persons suspecting abuse to report their suspicions, and others split their mediators into ranks of mandatory reporters and permissive reporters by virtue of their professional training and practice in fields outside of mediation." Art Hinshaw, *Mediators As Mandatory Reporters of Child Abuse: Preserving Mediation's Core Values*, 34 Fla. St. U. L. Rev. 271, 309 (2007).

Professor Hinshaw argues that states should classify all domestic relations mediators as mandatory reporters. He recognizes that mandatory reporting may strain mediation's core values (party self-determination, mediator neutrality, and confidentiality of mediation communications) because "[e]xpectations of mediation confidentiality are dashed, an accused party is likely to believe the mediator is biased, and the parties are at the mercy of what CPS [child protective services] determines should happen next." *Id.* at 297. But he argues that the child protective impulses inherent in family law mediation outweigh these values:

> The primary policy goal in family mediation is to improve outcomes for all parties affected by the mediation, which includes improving outcomes for children. In fact, the importance of mediation outcomes as they affect children manifests in legal and ethical directives requiring mediators to take the best interests of children into account when mediating family disputes. If mediators have reasonable suspicions of child abuse, it is all but impossible to follow those directives without reporting suspected abuse. * * *

Id. at 309. Professor Hinshaw acknowledges that mandatory reporting "may make mediators unwitting conduits for dubious or fraudulent allegations of abuse and could add to the structural problems inherent in the child protection system. Experience from current practice, however, suggests that these potential problems would be minimal." *Id.* at 311.

14. *Conciliation and therapy.* Another ADR device, "conciliation," is sometimes discussed almost as a synonym for mediation. Conciliation, however, is often a less formal process in which the third-party neutral seeks to encourage the parties to negotiate their differences. Matrimonial conciliation programs began as efforts to provide marriage counseling and encourage spouses to reconcile. Today about half the states offer matrimonial conciliation programs, which encourage or require parties to participate in an effort to prepare emotionally for divorce if reconciliation proves impossible.

Mediation also should not be confused with family therapy, which couples may employ if they wish to explore whether and how they may resolve their differences and remain together. A therapist assists the parties' efforts at reconciliation, without facilitating their divorce negotiations. Even if a mediator is a psychotherapist, the mediator's task is to facilitate the couple's divorce negotiations without trying to effect reconciliation.

PROBLEM 15–1

You are an experienced family lawyer and mediator retained by Jack and Judy King to mediate the terms of their divorce. The Kings cannot agree on many things lately, but you would like to encourage them to speak freely and openly about circumstances relating to their property, their future economic prospects, and the needs of their two young children.

(a) If the Kings ask you whether each should retain a lawyer before the first mediation session, what would you say? If they begin mediation without having retained counsel, what advice would you provide as the mediation proceeds and concludes?

(b) If the Kings ask you during the mediation about the relative strengths or weaknesses of one or more of their claims, would you provide that advice?

(c) What would you tell the Kings about whether the statements they make and documents they produce would remain confidential if the mediation does not produce final resolution and they proceed to trial? When would you tell them?

(d) If the Kings ask you whether their children should participate in the mediation, what would you tell them? What questions might you ask?

(e) What would you recommend if the parties cannot agree about whether their children should participate?

PROBLEM 15–2

Bob and Roberta Ricketts are acquaintances of yours from the country club. They visit your law office together one afternoon to say that they wish to dissolve their marriage after 14 years. They would like you to represent them in the divorce proceedings and begin drawing up the papers as soon as possible but, citing ethical concerns, you decline to undertake common representation. If Bob and Roberta agree, may you serve as a mediator seeking to resolve the issues that arise in their dissolution proceeding? If you agree, what ground rules would you set for the mediation?

B.   GENDER AND CULTURE

Proponents praise mediation as a consensual process that reduces the hostility that marks so many family law disputes, and that helps level the playing field for women and children. By enabling parties to fashion their own outcomes, proponents say, mediation offers reorganizing families a measure of self-determination and self-esteem. Proponents also argue that parties are more likely to comply with an arrangement that each helped fashion. In turn, voluntary compliance fosters cooperation and diminishes stress that threatens the children's well-being and the parties' own efforts to proceed with their lives. Family mediation is also seen as an alternative to clogged dockets and the uncertainties and high costs of litigation.

Family mediation's consensual process, lauded as a virtue, has also been condemned as a vice. Critics assert that mediation's relative informality may produce subtle pressures to settle, and thus may deprive the emotionally or financially weaker party and the children of protections afforded by the substantive law. Critics also assert that mediation may perpetuate power imbalances grounded in gender or culture.

1. GENDER

Feminists have been among the most vocal critics of family mediation's essential fairness. For example, Professor Penelope E. Bryan argues that mediation has "insidious" effects for divorcing women:

> * * * [M]ediation exploits wives by denigrating their legal entitlements, stripping them of authority, encouraging unwarranted compromise, isolating them from needed support, and placing them across the table from their more powerful husbands and demanding that they fend for themselves. The process thus perpetuates patriarchy by freeing men to use their power to gain greater control over children, to implant more awareness of male dominance into women's consciousness, and to retain more of the marital financial assets than men would obtain if lawyers negotiated divorce agreements.

Penelope E. Bryan, *Killing Us Softly: Divorce Mediation and the Politics of Power*, 40 Buff. L. Rev. 441, 523 (1992).

Feminists have directed their strongest criticisms at mandatory court-annexed mediation, which they contend holds the greatest potential to deprive vulnerable spouses of the protections the divorce laws seek to provide them and their children:

> Mediation permits persons to speak for themselves and make their own decisions. This self-determination can be empowering. Patterns of domination characteristic of adversary adjudication are challenged in two ways: no outside decisionmaker is present, and the client need not be the passive recipient of a lawyer's advice and decisionmaking. Instead, he can explore alternatives, create options, and make decisions. In private, voluntary mediation, * * * many say that they have chosen mediation so that they, and not a lawyer, will be in charge of their own destinies. In this very immediate way, mediation can challenge the hierarchical, professionalized way that family law is usually practiced.

> This dynamic is fundamentally altered when mediation is imposed rather than sought or offered. When mandatory mediation is part of the court system, the notion that parties are actually making their own decisions is purely illusory. First, the parties have not chosen or timed the process according to their ability to handle it. Second, they are not allowed to decide themselves how much their lawyers should participate, but instead are deprived of whatever protection their lawyers have to offer. Finally, they are not permitted to choose the mediator, and they often cannot leave without endangering their legal position even if they believe the mediator is biased against them.

Tina Grillo, *The Mediation Alternative: Process Dangers For Women*, 100 Yale L.J. 1545, 1581–82 (1991). Can power imbalances be reduced or cured when parties' lawyers participate in their clients' mediation?

MARGARET F. BRINIG
Does Mediation Systematically Disadvantage Women?
2 Wm. & Mary J. Women & L. 1, 4–5, 6, 33–34 (1995).

* * *

Despite their initial objections, attorneys seem to have adjusted to mediation. Interestingly, as the attorneys are disarming, feminists in both the United States and Canada are attacking the process. Feminists have raised a number of objections to the use of mediation instead of the adversarial process. Some writers argue that because women, more than men, seek connection through relationships, women might systematically fare worse. Others argue that women might trade custody for money to avoid litigation because, where custody is concerned, women are more risk averse than their husbands. There is also a more generalized fear that husbands will take advantage of their wives' lack of power within the marital relationship.

* * *

* * * [A] divorce mediator must be conscious of power imbalances brought about by the difference in men's and women's earning power and by physical abuse if present in the relationship. Given this awareness, mediation remains a fair, as well as an inexpensive and time-saving, process for marriage dissolution. There is nothing inherent in being a woman that precludes a successful mediation of marital problems.

* * *

From an empirical standpoint, it is unclear whether gender differences impede women's ability to mediate successfully. Women are apparently not more risk averse. They do not trade money for more custodial time because of risk aversion, but just appear to want to be with their children more than their husbands do. Since mothers get more child support as visitation time with fathers increases, fathers are willing to "pay" for time with their children up to a point.

Feminists who claim that women are more altruistic than men also will have difficulty supporting their conclusions according to the data. Women do not give more in terms of percentages or money than men. Women seem to do more volunteer work and a larger share of housework and child care than their husbands. This difference in utilization of "leisure time," or more accurately, non-labor market activity, may not be due to unselfish and caring behavior. Greater time spent with children may occur because women derive more utility from them than their husbands do, other things being equal. Because of the husbands' greater earning potential, it is more efficient for women, with their lower opportunity costs, to work less or more flexible hours. This accommodates not only child care, with its positive value, but also housework, which most women do not actually enjoy.

The difference in earning power and consequently power within the relationship appears to be the real culprit in this story. Men have an easier exit from marriage because their investments are readily transferable. Therefore they can behave opportunistically during the marriage and can have less to lose during mediation at dissolution. Women's threats are not as credible, so they may have to settle for less. They also have a higher marginal utility of income, since their income on average is lower than their husbands'.

Because mediation is swifter, less expensive, and easier on children, it is a good alternative to litigation in many divorce cases. Many women who have tried mediation liked it. However, congested courts cannot justify mandatory mediation in cases where one spouse holds a monopoly on marital power. No one should order mediation when there has been abuse within the family, substance abuse, or systematic hiding of assets.

NOTES AND QUESTIONS

1. *The research record.* Joan B. Kelly's comprehensive review of divorce mediation research finds "no empirical support for the claims advanced by critics of mediation that mediators force women to give away custody or primary care 'entitlements' or that women are disadvantaged financially by the strategic use of custody conflicts by men." Joan B. Kelly, *A Decade of Divorce Mediation Research: Some Questions and Answers*, 34 Fam. & Conciliation Cts. Rev. 373, 377 (1996). Kelly also reports that "[w]omen were more likely to view mediation as more helpful in empowering them to stand up to their spouses than using attorneys, and they rated themselves as more financially capable and knowledgeable as a result of the mediation process." Kelly found that, "compared to both men and women in the adversarial process, men and women in mediation more often reported that they felt their rights were protected in mediation." *Id.* at 378. Indeed, another study found that 50% to 70% of divorcing parties, men and women alike, found the adversarial process "impersonal, intimidating, and intrusive." U.S. Comm'n on Child and Family Welfare, Parenting Our Children: In the Best Interest of the Nation 39 (1996).

2. *Domestic violence.* Violence occurs in at least a quarter of American households, and, as Chapter 6 reports, approximately 80% of domestic abuse victims are women. Compelling evidence indicates that domestic violence is present in at least half the custody and visitation disputes referred to court-annexed mediation programs. *See* Jessica Pearson, *Mediating When Domestic Violence Is a Factor: Policies and Practices in Court-Based Divorce Mediation Programs*, 14 Mediation Q. 319, 320 (1997).

Commentators disagree about the advisability of mandatory court-annexed mediation where domestic violence is alleged. Many feminists and battered women's advocates argue that courts should never order mediation in the face of domestic violence allegations because "mediation not only fails to protect women from subsequent violence, but also perpetuates their continued victimization." Lisa G. Lerman, *Mediation of Wife Abuse Cases: The Adverse Impact of Informal Dispute Resolution on Women*, 7 Harv. Women's L.J. 57, 61 (1984). These advocates argue that victims should not bear the risk that a mediator or court administrator, through inexperience or sheer human error, will fail to screen out a truly dangerous case. They argue that mediation in effect decriminalizes spousal abuse by providing abusers a conciliatory method of ending the marriage, without further public consequences unless authorities pursue criminal prosecution. A history of domestic violence in a relationship arguably also creates a power imbalance that disables the abused spouse from effectively pursuing her position in mediation.

Mediation, the argument continues, also requires the victim to maintain contact with the abuser in a setting that highlights conflict and disagreement. Mediation lets the abuser learn the battered spouse's whereabouts if she has left the home, lets the abuser know when and where she will appear for mediation, and gives the abuser new cause for anger and physical retribution against her when she openly questions his authority and position in the mediation. Because mediated settlements so often produce joint custody arrangements, mediation may also continue the relationship between victim and abuser while compromising the children's safety.

Other commentators argue, however, that where domestic violence is alleged, the appropriateness of court-annexed mediation should be determined on a case-by-case basis. The answer may depend on what realistic alternatives exist. Judges may not have sufficient training in domestic violence issues, or sufficient sensitivity about the plight of battered women. Adversarial proceedings may worsen family tensions and place the battered woman in greater danger. Enraged partners may ignore restraining orders.

Some observers argue that mediation is not necessarily bad for a battered spouse and may even be good, and that properly trained mediators can be effective in the face of domestic violence allegations. "Victims of domestic violence should have the opportunity to make an informed choice about which divorce process—mediated or adversarial—will best meet the needs of their families. Because families are different and because both adversarial and mediated proceedings vary in quality and accessibility, decisions about what process to use must be made on an individual basis in light of the real, not theoretical, options available to the family." Nancy Ver Steegh, *Yes, No and Maybe: Informed Decision Making About Divorce Mediation in the Presence of Domestic Violence*, 9 Wm. & Mary J. Women & L. 145, 147 (2003). "Women often find mediation to be empowering," and mediation may work for domestic abuse victims if the decision to proceed is made "on a voluntary basis with a highly skilled mediator using a specialized procedure." *Id.* at 183, 204.

To proponents of case-by-case determination, mediation's appropriateness may turn on whether violent incidents have been prevalent or isolated. "[I]f the parties can reach agreement on equal terms and neither party controls the other, family mediation, including matters such as child custody, visitation, and support, may be appropriate even though some abuse has occurred in a relationship." Alison E. Gerencser, *Family Mediation: Screening For Domestic Abuse*, 23 Fla. St. U. L. Rev. 43, 47 (1995). Proponents of case-by-case determination note that litigation, with parties staking out extreme positions to avoid "losing," may also encourage future violence. Several studies indicate high levels of satisfaction with family mediation even where physical and emotional abuse occurred during the marriage or after separation. *See* Kelly, *A Decade of Divorce Mediation Research: Some Questions and Answers, supra,* at 381.

The ABA Model Standards opt for case-by-case determination: "A family mediator shall recognize a family situation involving domestic abuse and take appropriate steps to shape the mediation process accordingly." *Model Standards, supra,* Standard X. Most states that encourage or authorize courts to order divorce mediation provide an exemption where domestic violence is alleged. *E.g.,* 13 Del. Code Ann. tit. 13, § 711A (2008). Some states permit the alleged domestic violence victim to decide whether to attempt mediation and even provide for in-session protection. *See, e.g.,* Haw. Rev. Stat. § 580–41.5 (2008).

2. CULTURE

The ABA Model Standards call on mediators to "be sensitive to the impact of culture * * * on parenting philosophy and other decisions," and to "continuously strive to understand the impact of culture and diversity on the mediator's practice." *Model Standards, supra,* Overview and Definitions, Standards VIII & XIII, at viii, xi.

Professor Cynthia R. Mabry argues that family mediation must "reflect cultural values of people of color and their divergent social and physical environments." Cynthia R. Mabry, *African Americans "Are Not Carbon Copies" of White Americans—The Role of African American Culture in Mediation of Family Disputes,* 13 Ohio St. J. on Disp. Resol. 405, 421 (1998). She argues that after generations of racism, mistrust, biases and stereotypes, whites and African Americans have "different views of the world, different family values, different ways of responding to the dispute resolution process and different ways of rearing children." "[M]ediators should be educated about cultural practices and issues that affect how African American families operate. * * * More specifically, mediators involved in resolution of family disputes should endeavor to understand dissimilarities between African American and white familial experiences." *Id.* at 423, 459. For example, Professor Mabry urges mediators to refrain from calling adult African Americans by their first names without permission. "By referring to older persons by their first names, the mediator innocently may be attempting to be friendly and casual. Without permission to be informal, however, African American participants may be offended, harbor unverbalized anger or view the mediator as disrespectful." *Id.* at 432.

Two commentators observe that in mediation with Hispanic couples, "it may be increasingly important to gather family history, including migration and socioeconomic standing for several generations, so as to full understand the meaning of the presenting problems and the most likely range of outcomes. Unless we have a true understanding of the cultural background and worldview of the participants, we will be ineffective in creating outcomes that are culturally consistent and able to withstand the economic and social pressures that will be placed on them." Alison Taylor & Ernest A. Sanchez, *Out of the White Box: Adapting Mediation to the Needs of Hispanic and Other Minorities Within American Society*, 29 Fam. & Concil. Cts. Rev. 114, 119 (1991).

SECTION 3: ARBITRATION
A. THE NATURE OF DOMESTIC RELATIONS ARBITRATION

In arbitration, parties agree to submit a dispute to a private decision-maker—a single arbitrator or an arbitral panel—who renders a binding decision after hearing each side's witnesses and other evidence. The Federal Arbitration Act (FAA), 9 U.S.C. §§ 1–16 (2003), and its state counterparts mandate enforcement of arbitration agreements reached by the parties either before or after the dispute arises. Some states have enacted legislation specifically authorizing and regulating domestic relations arbitration. *See, e.g.*, N.C. Gen. Stat. §§ 50–41 to–62 (2008). Where a party seeks to sue on a claim covered by the arbitration agreement, the court stays or dismisses judicial proceedings and issues an order compelling arbitration. The arbitral decision is subject to judicial review only where the arbitrator engaged in fraud, corruption or other serious misconduct (or, in some jurisdictions, where the arbitrator "manifestly disregarded" the applicable law).

Only the court may grant a divorce and enter the decree, but parties may agree to arbitrate one or more of the incidents of the divorce, such as topics covered in this casebook in Chapters 9 through 13, that is, property distribution, alimony or the child-related issues of support, custody and visitation. The parties may sign an arbitration agreement before they seek divorce (for example, in a premarital agreement), when they separate, while the divorce action is pending, or even after the court enters the divorce decree. Some parties contemplating divorce turn immediately to arbitration; other parties agree to arbitrate only matters they fail to resolve by negotiation; still others agree to mediation-arbitration ("med/arb"), which has the mediator or another designated person decide—as an arbitrator—any matters not settled in mediation.

Parties may agree to arbitrate under the rules of the American Arbitration Association, or they may agree to tailor these or other rules to suit their circumstances. The parties may select an arbitrator or arbitral panel familiar with family law or the sorts of issues likely to arise before the court enters the decree. The American Academy of Matrimonial Lawyers (AAML) urges that lawyers serving as arbitrators comply with all relevant rules applicable to judges, including the Code of Judicial Conduct. AAML, *Bounds of Advocacy, Goals for Family Lawyers* § 9.2 (2000), http://www.aaml.org/files/public/Bounds_of_Advocacy.htm.

Arbitration frequently provides a speedier resolution than can be had in court. "The parties do not have to wait to be 'reached' on a court calendar, some of which are over two years behind. Not only can the parties virtually choose their date, but they can also get a full-day (or more) without interruptions by other court matters. Because a matter submitted to arbitration usually results in a quick hearing and award, the costs of the decision-making process are greatly reduced. The swiftness of the process may also reduce the time in which children are victims of the stress and tension occasioned by lack of certainty as to the outcome." Joan F. Kessler et al., *Why Arbitrate Family Law Matters?*, 14 J. Am. Acad. Matrimonial Law. 333, 337 (1997).

"Court-annexed" family arbitration, mandated by some statutes and court rules without the parties' agreement, is essentially a nonbinding settlement and conciliation device designed to encourage parties to resolve their differences short of trial based on clearer perceptions of the merits of their relative positions. Binding family arbitration without the parties' agreement to arbitrate would likely violate constitutional rights of access to the courts. *Cf. Nationwide Mut. Fire Ins. Co. v. Pinnacle Medical, Inc.*, 753 So.2d 55, 59 (Fla. 2000) (striking down statute authorizing mandatory commercial arbitration for denying access to the courts).

Whether arbitration is conducted by the parties' agreement or by a court-annexed procedure, lawyers who represent clients in arbitration are governed by ethical canons such as the ABA Model Rules of Professional Conduct. Arbitration practice is likely to be an important skill for domestic relations lawyers in future years because arbitrating parties rarely appear without counsel. A 1997 national survey of domestic relations lawyers reported that arbitration was not yet widely used in matrimonial disputes, but appeared to have been well received where it was available. Arbitration was used most frequently to resolve disputes concerning the economic incidents of divorce, namely property distribution, spousal support and child support. Arbitration was less prevalent in disputes about custody and visitation, evidently because of uncertainty about the enforceability of arbitral awards in such disputes. *See* Mary Kay Kisthardt, *The Use of Mediation and Arbitration for Resolving Family Conflicts: What Lawyers Think About Them*, 14 J. Am. Acad. Matrimonial L. 353, 389–92 (1997). Use of matrimonial arbitration appears to be on the rise, and the American Academy of Matrimonial Lawyers adopted a Model Family Law Arbitration Act in 2005.

Arbitration may also play an important role in resolving post-dissolution disputes between parents prone to continuing bitter conflict about child custody and visitation. The parties' separation agreement may contain an arbitration clause covering future disputes arising under the agreement. The arbitrator may be named by the parties or appointed by the court. In either event, the court holds final statutory authority to determine these child-related matters, so jurisdictions may have arbitrators make a recommendation to the court rather than a final decision. Joan B. Kelly has reported that post-dissolution arbitration dramatically reduces relitigation, and that most parents report satisfaction with their mediator/arbitrator, and decreased conflict with the other parent. *See* Joan B. Kelly, *Psychological and Legal Interventions for Parents and Children in Custody and Access Disputes: Current Research and Practice*, 10 Va. J. Soc. Pol'y & L. 129, 146–47 (2002).

B. DOMESTIC RELATIONS ARBITRATION AND CHILDREN

Family arbitration has had a long history marked by clashes with the state's *parens patriae* authority to protect children. Courts have enforced agreements to arbitrate the financial incidents of divorce, such as property distribution and alimony. But courts have generally not permitted arbitrators—private decisionmakers engaged by the parties—to have the final word on child custody, visitation or support.

Until the late 1970s, courts held that agreements to arbitrate various classes of disputes—including agreements by divorcing parties to arbitrate child-related issues—were unenforceable as contrary to public policy. Courts applying the judicially created "public policy" exception to arbitrability stated various policy grounds for unenforceability. In the domestic relations context, courts reasoned that because children were not parties to their parents' arbitration agreement, the arbitrator's decision should not bind the children on matters vitally affecting their lives. Child protection should remain vested in publicly constituted courts exercising *parens patriae* authority, rather than in essentially unreviewable decisions by privately empowered decisionmakers. Finally, the interests of one or both arbitrating parents might diverge from the best interests of their children; where neither parent would be a fit custodian, for example, a court might award third-party custody but the arbitrator, who serves only by the parents' agreement, might have no authority to do so. *See, e.g.,* Stewart E. Sterk, *Enforceability of Agreements to Arbitrate: An Examination of the Public Policy Defense*, 2 Cardozo L. Rev. 481 (1981).

Beginning in the early 1980s, the Supreme Court rejected the "public policy" doctrine. Today, federal courts must enforce arbitration agreements under the FAA unless an exception to enforcement is found in the FAA itself or in another statute. Federal decisions interpreting the FAA do not necessarily bind state courts in the interpretation of state arbitration acts, but most state court decisions have similarly held that only the legislature may create exceptions to arbitrability.

Abandonment of the public policy doctrine leaves children potentially vulnerable in family arbitration because only a few state arbitration and divorce acts expressly create exceptions to the enforceability of arbitral support, custody or visitation decisions. *See, e.g.,* Mo. Rev. Stat. § 435.405.5 (2008) (where an arbitration award "determines an issue regarding a child of the marriage, such determination shall be subject to de novo judicial review").

Despite the demise of the public policy doctrine generally, some courts still hold that parties may not arbitrate support, custody or visitation at all, even where no statute removes these matters from arbitration. By statute or court decision in other states (such as Missouri, noted above), parties may arbitrate the child-related issues, but only subject to de novo or other close judicial review grounded in *parens patriae. See, e.g., Faherty v. Faherty*, 477 A.2d 1257, 1263 (N.J. 1984) (divorcing parties may arbitrate child support disputes, but courts conduct de novo review "unless it is clear on the face of the award that the award could not adversely affect the substantial best interests of the child"). In any event, courts and not arbitrators have the final word on the child-related issues. The following decision discusses the relationship between arbitration and court review concerning these issues.

HARVEY v. HARVEY

Supreme Court of Michigan, 2004.
680 N.W.2d 835.

PER CURIAM.

In this divorce proceeding, the parties agreed that the friend of the court would determine the custody of their children and that the circuit court could not review the decision.[1] Honoring this, the circuit court entered the friend of the court's recommended order awarding sole custody of the children to defendant and denied plaintiff's motion for a hearing to review the matter.

The Court of Appeals vacated the circuit court's order and remanded the case for a hearing de novo. We affirm that opinion, but write to provide clarification. Regardless of the type of alternative dispute resolution that parties use, the Child Custody Act requires the circuit court to determine independently what custodial placement is in the best interests of the children.[2] * * *

I. BACKGROUND

A. Trial Court Proceedings

Two daughters were born during the parties' marriage, one in 1994 and the other in 1996. In February 2000, plaintiff filed a complaint for divorce with the Family Division of the Oakland Circuit Court. A variety of issues were disputed, including custody of the children.

---

1. Because the "friend of the court" was authorized to hear the parties' evidence and render a binding decision, the friend of the court sat as an arbitrator [eds.]

2. We recognize that parents sometimes reach agreements regarding custody and visitation matters either informally through direct negotiations or through mediation procedures made available by dispute resolution organizations. Our decision does not restrict the ability of parties to address disputes through alternative dispute resolution processes. We hold only that the statutory "best interests" factors control whenever a court enters an order affecting child custody. An initial agreement between the parties cannot relieve the court of its statutory responsibility to ensure that its adjudication of custody disputes is in a child's best interests.

Instead of proceeding directly to trial, the parties opted for a form of alternative dispute resolution. On May 15, 2001, the circuit court entered a consent order, approved by both parties' counsel, for binding arbitration. Its object was to resolve all property matters and provide for an evidentiary hearing and binding decision by the friend of the court referee regarding custody, parenting time, and child support issues. The order stated that the referee's decision could not be reviewed by the circuit court * * *.

Following an evidentiary hearing, the friend of the court submitted findings to the circuit court with a recommended order awarding legal and physical custody of the children solely to defendant. Plaintiff filed timely written objections to the order.

The circuit court entered the recommended order, over plaintiff's objection, changing the existing custodial arrangement. The court denied her motion for an evidentiary hearing de novo and refused to set aside the order when defendant argued that the parties' stipulation restricted its authority to review the order.

B. Appellate Court Proceedings

* * *

In its opinion, the Court of Appeals acknowledged that the Child Custody Act governs all child custody disputes and gives the circuit court continuing jurisdiction over custody proceedings. The Court discussed two statutory schemes that operate concurrently with the Child Custody Act to provide the parties with alternative methods of dispute resolution: the domestic relations arbitration act and the Friend of the Court Act.

The domestic relations arbitration act permits parties to agree to binding arbitration of child custody disputes. It contains numerous protections for them, including mandatory prearbitration disclosures and detailed procedural requirements. The parties can seek circuit court review of the arbitration award. [Mich. Comp. L.] 600.5080 specifically addresses awards concerning child custody:

> (1) Subject to subsection (2), the circuit court shall not vacate or modify an award concerning child support, custody, or parenting time unless the court finds that the award is adverse to the best interests of the child who is the subject of the award or under the provisions of section 5081.

> (2) A review or modification of a child support amount, child custody, or parenting time shall be conducted and is subject to the standards and procedures provided in other statutes, in other applicable law, and by court rule that are applicable to child support amounts, child custody, or parenting time. * * *

Alternatively, parties to a custody dispute can present the issue to a friend of the court referee. If they elect this option, the circuit court may review the referee's recommendation in accordance with MCL 552.507(5) [Friend of the Court Act]. That subsection provides that the circuit court "shall hold a de novo hearing on any matter that has been the subject of a referee hearing" if either party requests such a hearing within twenty-one days after receiving the referee's recommendation.

The Court of Appeals concluded that, under either statute, the parties were entitled to have the circuit court review the custody determination. For this reason, it held, "an agreement for a binding decision in a domestic-relations matter with no right of review in the court, as in this case, is without statutory support under either scheme."

The Court then determined that the parties had not complied with the detailed procedural requirements of the domestic relations arbitration act. As a consequence, it held that the parties' agreement was governed by the Friend of the Court Act. The trial court should have addressed plaintiff's objections by holding a hearing de novo to review whether the custody recommendation was in the best interests of the children. * * * The Court of Appeals summed up as follows:

> In the absence of any review by the trial court, as discussed above, and in the absence of a valid agreement for binding arbitration or an otherwise valid waiver of procedural requirements, plaintiff was improperly denied a hearing regarding her objections to the friend of the court's findings and recommendation.

It vacated the custody order and remanded for a hearing de novo in the circuit court.

* * *

III. ANALYSIS

The Child Custody Act is a comprehensive statutory scheme for resolving custody disputes. With it, the Legislature sought to "promote the best interests and welfare of children." The act applies to all custody disputes and vests the circuit court with continuing jurisdiction.

The act makes clear that the best interests of the child control the resolution of a custody dispute between parents * * *. It places an affirmative obligation on the circuit court to "declare the child's inherent rights and establish the rights and duties as to the child's custody, support, and parenting time in accordance with this act" whenever the court is required to adjudicate an action "involving dispute of a minor child's custody." Taken together, these statutory provisions impose on the trial court the duty to ensure that the resolution of any custody dispute is in the best interests of the child.

Thus, we affirm the Court of Appeals decision to remand this case to the circuit court for a hearing de novo, but not for the reason stated by the Court of Appeals. It is irrelevant that the parties did not have a "valid agreement for binding arbitration or an otherwise valid waiver of procedural requirements. . . ." The Child Custody Act *required* the circuit court to determine the best interests of the children before entering an order resolving the custody dispute.

Our holding should not be interpreted, where the parties have agreed to a custody arrangement, to require the court to conduct a hearing or otherwise engage in intensive fact-finding. Our requirement under such circumstances is that the court satisfy itself concerning the best interests of the children. When the court signs the order, it indicates that it has done so. A judge signs an order only after profound deliberation and in the exercise of the judge's traditional broad discretion.

However, the deference due parties' negotiated agreements does not diminish the court's obligation to examine the best interest factors and make the child's best interests paramount. Nothing in the Child Custody Act gives parents or any other party the power to exclude the legislatively mandated "best interests" factors from the court's deliberations once a custody dispute reaches the court.

Furthermore, neither the Friend of the Court Act nor the domestic relations arbitration act relieves the circuit court of its duty to review a custody arrangement once the issue of a child's custody reaches the bench. The Friend of the Court Act states that the circuit court "shall" hold a hearing de novo to review a friend of the court recommendation if either party objects to that recommendation in writing within twenty-one days.

Likewise, MCL 600.5080 authorizes a circuit court to modify or vacate an arbitration award that is not in the best interests of the child. It requires the circuit court to review the arbitration award in accordance with the requirements of other relevant statutes, including the Child Custody Act. The court retains authority over custody until the child reaches the age of majority.

Thus, even when parties initially elect to submit a custody dispute to an arbitrator or to the friend of the court, they cannot waive the authority that the Child Custody Act confers on the circuit court. As the Court of Appeals has previously explained, parties "cannot by agreement usurp the court's authority to determine suitable provisions for the child's best interests." Permitting the parties, by stipulation, to limit the trial court's authority to review custody determinations would nullify the protections of the Child Custody Act and relieve the circuit court of its statutorily imposed responsibilities.

IV. Conclusion

We agree with the Court of Appeals that parties cannot stipulate to circumvent the authority of the circuit court in determining the custody of children. In making its determination, the court must consider the best interests of the children. Child custody determinations or agreements are not binding until entered by court order.

* * *

NOTES AND QUESTIONS

1. *Questions about* Harvey. (a) Because support, custody and visitation awards are inherently modifiable, should agreements to arbitrate the child-related issues be enforceable like any other arbitration agreement, unenforceable as contrary to public policy, or enforceable subject to de novo judicial review? (b) If the law prohibits parties from arbitrating child-related issues or provides for de novo judicial review of arbitral decisions concerning these issues, does it normally make sense financially or emotionally for parties with minor children to arbitrate property distribution or maintenance? (c) Should the law permit parties to mediate disputes concerning child support, custody or visitation even where agreements to arbitrate these matters would be unenforceable as contrary to public policy? What is the critical distinction between the two ADR processes?

2. *Is child support different?* Some decisions permit arbitration of child support issues (subject to de novo judicial review), but hold agreements to arbitrate custody or visitation unenforceable. *See, e.g., Kelm v. Kelm*, 749 N.E.2d 299 (Ohio 2001). In *Masters v. Masters*, 513 A.2d 104, 113 (Conn. 1986), the court explained that arbitral custody awards "go to the very core of the child's welfare and best interests," but that support awards "generally do not involve 'the delicate balancing of the factors composing the best interests of the child.'" Do you agree that agreements to arbitrate child support implicate different policy considerations than agreements to arbitrate custody or visitation? What would happen if an arbitrator awarded child support in an amount lower than the minimum amount required by the state's child support guidelines?

3. *"Minority culture" arbitration.* Professor E. Gary Spitko urges cultural minorities, such as gay and lesbian co-parents, to use arbitration to avoid the law's "cultural biases." Because arbitration's ground rules depend so heavily on the parties' arbitration agreement, he says, these co-parents might "opt out of substantive law that was developed without regard to their special circumstances and to opt into substantive law custom made for them." For example, Professor Spitko says the co-parents' predispute arbitration agreement might stipulate that if their partnership dissolves, custody or visitation disputes would be resolved by rules favorable to their circumstances as gays or lesbians. The agreement might expand the definition of parenthood to include "anyone who maintains a functional parental relationship with a child when a legally recognized parent created that relationship with the intent that the relationship be parental in nature." Or the agreement might displace the ordinary "best interests of the child" standard in favor of a standard that uses past parental roles to guide the custody and visitation decision. The co-parents could even name a gay or lesbian arbitrator. *See* E. Gary Spitko, *Judge Not: In Defense of Minority–Culture Arbitration*, 77 Wash. U. L.Q. 1065, 1077, 1081–82 (1999).

Professor Ronald J. Krotoszynski, Jr., criticizes the Spitko proposal: "Rather than attempting to flee the court system, cultural minorities should attempt to secure meaningful reforms that lead to a higher degree of confidence in the basic fairness and reliability of these institutions." Ronald J.

Krotoszynski, Jr., *The New Legal Process: Games People Play and the Quest for Legitimate Judicial Decision Making*, 77 Wash. U. L.Q. 993, 1037 (1999).

In the vast majority of states, gay or lesbian co-parents would have no marriage for the court to dissolve. But assume the arbitrator decided support, custody or visitation in a manner inconsistent with general domestic relations law, such as by displacing or modifying the best interests of the child standard, or by opting out of constitutional or statutory rules favoring parental prerogative in custody and visitation matters. Could the court engage in plenary review of the arbitral decision? Should it do so? Would the answer depend on whether the jurisdiction permits courts to overturn decisions by arbitrators who "manifestly disregard the law"?

4. *Arbitration before religious panels.* In *Glauber v. Glauber*, 600 N.Y.S.2d 740 (App. Div. 1993), the court refused to enforce the divorcing parties' agreement that future child custody disputes be decided not by a civil court, but by a specified rabbi. The court held that "an issue found to be appropriate for arbitration may be arbitrated before a religious forum," but that child custody was not arbitrable in New York. To avoid First Amendment restrictions on the authority of civil courts to interpret religious doctrine or practice, *Glauber* stressed that the decision vesting custody decisions solely in the courts was "a neutral one." *Id.* at 743.

PROBLEM 15–3

When Bill and Brenda Brown divorced a few years ago, their marital settlement agreement, which was incorporated into the divorce decree, provided for arbitration in the event that they could not agree about whether their two children should attend private school in a particular year. The arbitration clause stated:

> By April 1 of each year, the parties shall reach agreement as to whether or not private school is necessary for the children for the next school year. If they cannot agree, they will go to arbitration. If the arbitrator finds a need for private school for the children, Husband will pay 60% of the private school tuition and expenses, and Wife shall pay the remaining 40%.

When the parties failed to agree about private school, Bill moved to compel arbitration. Brenda argues that the parties' arbitration clause is unenforceable under state law, which provides that parties may not arbitrate "any dispute involving child custody, visitation or support." Is the dispute between Bill and Brenda arbitrable?

SECTION 4:   COLLABORATIVE FAMILY LAW: THE NEW FRONTIER?

Section 6.603 of the Texas Family Code

COLLABORATIVE LAW.

(a) On a written agreement of the parties and their attorneys, a dissolution of marriage proceeding may be conducted under collaborative law procedures.

(b) Collaborative law is a procedure in which the parties and their counsel agree in writing to use their best efforts and make a good faith attempt to resolve their dissolution of marriage dispute on an agreed basis without resorting to judicial intervention except to have the court approve the settlement agreement, make the legal pronouncements, and sign the orders required by law to effectuate the agreement of the parties as the court determines appropriate. The parties' counsel may not serve as litigation counsel except to ask the court to approve the settlement agreement.

(c) A collaborative law agreement must include provisions for:

(1) full and candid exchange of information between the parties and their attorneys as necessary to make a proper evaluation of the case;

(2) suspending court intervention in the dispute while the parties are using collaborative law procedures;

(3) hiring experts, as jointly agreed, to be used in the procedure;

(4) withdrawal of all counsel involved in the collaborative law procedure if the collaborative law procedure does not result in settlement of the dispute; and

(5) other provisions as agreed to by the parties consistent with a good faith effort to collaboratively settle the matter.

* * *

Tex. Fam. Code § 6.603(a)–(c) (Vernon 2008)

JOHN LANDE & GREGG HERMAN

Fitting the Forum to the Family Fuss: Choosing Mediation, Collaborative
Law, or Cooperative Law for Negotiating Divorce Cases.
42 Fam. Ct. Rev. 280, 280–284 (2004).

Not long ago, divorce lawyers and clients had few alternatives available to negotiate a settlement. Some divorcing parties would negotiate an agreement and complete the legal process of divorce without hiring any professionals. Others would negotiate an agreement themselves, and one of them would hire a lawyer to write the agreement and process the divorce papers in court. These processes often happened when the couple did not have enough resources to afford hiring two lawyers for contested litigation or when the couple preferred to negotiate for themselves. When both spouses hired lawyers, they typically used a process that Marc Galanter called "litigotiation,"[1] * * * the routine process in which lawyers privately expect to settle by using litigation to gain strategic advantage in negotiation. In typical litigotiation, lawyers try to build strong cases for trial and often engage in a ritual charade of being reluctant to negotiate out of fear of losing advantage by appearing weak. Most cases

---

1. *See* Marc Galanter, *Worlds of Deals: Using Negotiation to Teach About Legal Process*, 34 J. Legal Educ. 268, 268 (1984).

eventually do settle, but this process often adds unnecessary costs and harms family members, particularly minor children.

* * *

Starting in the 1990s, family lawyers and other professionals in the United States and Canada developed collaborative law as an alternative to traditional litigotiation and mediation. Collaborative law practitioners seek to provide a civilized process, produce outcomes meeting the needs of both parties, minimize costs, and increase clients' control, privacy, and compliance with agreements. In collaborative law, both parties hire lawyers who focus exclusively on negotiation from the outset of the case. Under a written agreement, the lawyers and parties explicitly commit to avoid litigation by providing that the lawyers are disqualified from representing parties in litigation and must withdraw if either party chooses to litigate or even threatens to litigate. Thus, by using this "disqualification agreement," lawyers and parties reject the litigation-as-usual process of litigotiation. * * *

* * *

COLLABORATIVE LAW

Collaborative law provides each side with a lawyer who can provide legal advice and advocacy that mediators cannot offer. As advocates, collaborative lawyers are not required to be neutral and thus can strongly present clients' interests and positions, compensating for clients' difficulties in doing so. Although the lawyers serve as advocates, the disqualification agreement and collaborative law culture create incentives to satisfy their clients' interests through negotiation. Thus, collaborative law clients may get the "best of both worlds" with strong advocacy and collaborative problem-solving negotiation. Although some believe that zealous advocacy requires lawyers to seek every possible partisan advantage for their clients, lawyers often best serve their clients' interests by negotiating agreements that satisfy important interests of the other parties. This is especially true in divorce cases involving minor children because both parties have strong interests in future cooperation. If either party seeks to maximize its gain at the expense of the other party, such action can stimulate a spiral of retaliatory actions and undermine the potential for cooperation. Thus, collaborative lawyers believe that they can best advance their clients' interest through agreements that satisfy both parties' interests.

Collaborative lawyers and parties negotiate primarily in "four-way" meetings in which all are expected to participate actively. Lawyers are committed to "keep the process honest, respectful, and productive on both sides." The parties are expected to be respectful, provide full disclosure of all relevant information, and address each other's legitimate needs. Under collaborative law theory, parties have "shadow" feelings (such as anger, fear, and grief), which are "expected and accepted, but not permitted to direct the dispute-resolution process." Collaborative law theory provides that each lawyer is responsible for moving parties from artificial bargaining positions to focus on their real needs and interests to seek "win-win" solutions. Some theorists suggest that the collaborative law agreement effectively "amounts to a 'durable power of attorney,' directing the lawyers to take instructions from the client's higher-functioning self, and to politely disregard the instructions that may emerge from time to time during the divorce process when a less high-functioning self takes charge of the client." The collaborative law process may include other professionals such as coaches, who are mental health professionals hired by each client to help identify and change unproductive communication patterns and to educate clients about the divorce process and coparenting. Coaches may help clients distinguish what they believe are their shadow selves and true selves. Collaborative law clients may also hire joint experts such as accountants, appraisers, and child development specialists, who may attend the negotiation meetings if desired.

Virtually all collaborative law leaders and practitioners believe that the disqualification agreement is the "irreducible minimum condition" for calling a practice collaborative law. * * * Under collaborative law theory, the disqualification agreement creates a metaphorical container around the lawyers and clients to help focus on negotiation. Proponents say that lawyers are so used to litigating that at the first sign of disagreement, many lawyers would quickly threaten legal action if not precluded from doing so by an enforceable mechanism like the disqualification agreement. If clients feel angry and want to litigate, the disqualification agreement gives the lawyers an absolute excuse why they cannot do so.

Collaborative law proponents argue that the disqualification agreement is intended to align parties' and lawyers' incentives to promote settlement. The agreement eliminates lawyers' financial incentives to receive increased fees by litigating rather than settling cases early in the process. Thus, the disqualification agreement focuses the lawyers on settling in collaborative law because termination of the process would end their income from the case. The agreement focuses the clients on settling in collaborative law because termination of the process would raise the cost, end the representation by lawyers who they have educated and may trust, and require hiring new lawyers who are likely to be more adversarial. Although collaborative law theory calls for interest-based negotiation, the disqualification agreement increases the incentive to continue negotiations and reach any agreement, not merely agreements satisfying parties' interests.

Many collaborative law clients appreciate feeling protected from adversarial pressures by negotiating in the container created by the disqualification agreement. On the other hand, the disqualification agreement can harm clients if they feel trapped in a collaborative law container. Withdrawal of lawyers can harm clients when they trust their lawyers and/or do not want to invest the time and money required to find, hire, and educate new lawyers about their case. If collaborative law clients want to discontinue with collaborative law but retain their lawyers, the clients must either continue using a collaborative law process that they would prefer to leave or forego continued representation by their lawyers. Thus, parties who have invested a lot of time and money in a collaborative law process may feel stuck there because it is too expensive or damaging to hire new litigation attorneys.

Although parties may feel that the disqualification agreement protects against pressure from the threat of litigation, some may feel heavy pressure to accept agreements that they believe are not in their interests. Some of the pressure may come from their own lawyers because of the lawyers' incentives to press for settlement. Although the collaborative law structure is not inherently inconsistent with lawyers' professional responsibility related to zealous advocacy, some clients may feel dissatisfied with their representation due to the incentives created by the disqualification agreement and the norms of some practitioners to press for settlement.

COOPERATIVE LAW

The cooperative law movement is much smaller than the collaborative law movement, with local groups of practitioners in only a few areas. Cooperative law uses the same principles as collaborative law, except that cooperative law does not involve the disqualification agreement. Thus, cooperative law includes a written agreement to make full, voluntary disclosure of all financial information, avoid formal discovery procedures, utilize joint rather than unilateral appraisals, and use interest-based negotiation.

The choice not to use a disqualification agreement offers advantages and disadvantages. In some cases, parties and lawyers may act reasonably only if they face a credible threat of litigation. Thus, like collaborative law, cooperative law focuses on negotiation, but the lack of a disqualification agreement makes it easier to threaten litigation. Some clients may especially appreciate the security of knowing that they can retain their lawyers if the parties engage in contested litigation. A party who believes that the other party is being unreasonable always retains the power to litigate without having to hire and educate a new lawyer. Cooperative law clients forego the benefits of a disqualification agreement with its strong incentives to settle and avoid litigation. And although parties who use a cooperative law procedure may eventually settle, the implicit or explicit threat of litigation may taint the negotiation by undermining a problem-solving atmosphere.

* * *

NOTES AND QUESTIONS

1. *The growth of collaborative family law.* Proponents claim that collaborative law is "a revolutionary new way to practice family law that is spreading like wildfire across North America." Richard W. Shields et al., Collaborative Law: Another Way to Resolve Family Disputes xiii (2003). Hyperbole aside, in

just a few years collaborative family law has won a place in alternative dispute resolution in the United States, Canada, Australia, and Western Europe. Some lawyers report that their domestic relations practices consist largely or entirely of collaborative law, and some law firms train all their domestic relations lawyers in this new method. Growing numbers of lawyers and law firms list collaborative family law among their specialties. Continuing legal education programs frequently offer instruction about collaborative law. Collaborative practitioners are often organized in local practice groups, which develop standard forms and procedures. Lawyers have formed collaborative law councils and institutes in most states.

In 2001, Texas became the first state to enact legislation recognizing and regulating collaborative law in divorce cases. By prohibiting judges from entering scheduling orders or dismissing divorce cases for as much as two years when parties certify that they are proceeding under a written collaborative agreement, the Texas statute quoted above gives parties and their lawyers an opportunity to make collaboration work without pressure from a judge using a "rocket docket" or similar approach to reduce the court calendar. *See* Tex. Fam. Code § 6.603(e)-(g). A few other states have followed Texas with collaborative law legislation or court rules. *See, e.g.*, N.C. Gen. Stat. §§ 50–70 to–79 (2008); Utah Code Jud. Admin. R. 4–510(1)(D) (2008). Some local jurisdictions have also promulgated court rules authorizing collaborative law and governing its use in divorce cases. The National Conference of Commissioners on Uniform State Laws is drafting a Uniform Collaborative Law Act, which the commissioners hope to complete in 2009.

2. *Collaborative law proponents from the bench and bar*. A Louisiana judge calls collaborative law "divorce with dignity." Kris Axtman, *"Friendly" Divorce Movement Gains Ground*, Christian Sci. Mon., May 21, 2004, at 2. In 2007, New York opened the nation's first Collaborative Family Law Center to "train attorneys, provide space for participants, and connect families with professional services * * *." Chief Judge Judith S. Kaye anticipates that "spouses who choose this approach will find that the financial and emotional cost of divorce is reduced for everyone involved." Judith S. Kaye, N.Y. State Unified Court Sys., The State of the Judiciary 2007, at 11–12.

> After nearly a half century practicing family law, a Texas lawyer agrees:
>
> [A] few family lawyers have prided themselves on being "bombers" able to decimate the other side. I've seen the family fabric—and especially children—irretrievably damaged, court dockets jammed and divorce costs escalate. * * *
>
> As a society, we realize that the process of burying a dead marriage often is unnecessarily painful and scarring to husbands, wives and their children. We know that fighting in divorce court about property, custody and support almost always is emotionally draining, expensive and complicates post-divorce communication. As a helping professional, a lawyer has an obligation to try to minimize the collateral damage that occurs when one or both spouses decides that a marriage no longer works and wants a divorce. * * *

Louise B. Raggio, *Trying to Find a Better Way: Collaborative Law Process Is a Good Thing For Young Lawyers to Know*, Tex. Law., Nov. 3, 2003, at 30. A few years earlier, Ms. Raggio said that she had " 'been dragged, kicking and screaming, into every [divorce] trial because I knew in my heart that litigation would destroy the fabric of the family.' " John McShane & Larry Hance, *Collaborative Family Law On the Rise*, Tex. Law., July 3, 2000, at 29.

3. *Collaborative law critics.* Many lawyers and commentators question the efficacy of collaborative law, including one who maintains that "[a]nything you can do inside the collaborative model you can do outside the collaborative model." David Crary, *Some Couples Find a Less–Contentious Route to Divorce*, Wash. Post, Dec. 23, 2007, at A34. Professor Susan B. Apel argues that the disqualification agreement requires rejection of collaborative law:

> * * * It is not that litigation has to be the favored approach, or that it is the perfect tool in resolving disputes. Even if it has but marginal value in some cases, the good problem-solver should not reject any rational means of achieving an end, particularly at the very beginning of representation. * * * [P]roblem-solving approaches should recognize that until there is ample and demonstrated reason to forego an option, that option should remain open. * * * No responsible lawyer believes that litigation is the only answer. But even without collaborative law, lawyers can and will continue to negotiate and find non-litigation based solutions to client problems. * * *

Susan B. Apel, *Collaborative Law: A Skeptic's View*, Vt. B. J., Spring 2004, at 41, 43. Opponents also often urge that collaborative law violates, or holds the potential to violate, ethical rules, a matter discussed in the Note below.

4. *Is collaborative law different from the traditional settlement process?* Supporters of collaborative law report that most parties settle cases without trial under this new approach. But more than 90% of divorce cases also settle without trial after traditional non-collaborative negotiation. How does collaborative law differ from traditional negotiation?

Pauline H. Tesler says that traditional family law settlements are "fashioned in the shadow of the law, with the litigation matrix shaping the representation from the first attorney-client contact. Often, family law litigators settle these cases virtually, if not literally, on the courthouse steps, after expenditure of enormous emotional and financial resources on *pendente lite* motions and discovery. The settlement may be on the eve of trial, supervised by a settlement conference judge who applies evaluative pressure on parties and counsel in the interests of lightening the court's docket." On the other hand, collaborative lawyers focus on negotiation from the first client interview. "[G]ood collaborative practitioners begin by educating clients about the negotiating process and the divorce recovery process, and eliciting agreements about good faith bargaining and management of conflicts and strong emotions, so that clients are empowered to participate actively and effectively in direct negotiations." Pauline H. Tesler, *Collaborative Family Law*, 4 Pepp. Disp. Resol. L.J. 317, 326–28 (2004).

5. *The needs of family lawyers.* Some lawyers have reportedly embraced collaborative law to help cure their own disillusionment and incipient emotional burnout with traditional domestic relations practice. Many lawyers cringe especially at emotional tugs-of-war that can leave the parties' innocent

children standing helpless on the sidelines. Law school teaches lawyers to "win," but domestic relations cases often leave the field strewn only with "losers." " 'Winning' would be a marriage that worked out; by the time divorcing clients reach us, it is normally too late for that. In the dissolution process, we are often dealing more with 'damage control' than winning." Marjorie Carter, *Mediation is Appropriate Way to Settle Marriage Dissolution*, St. Louis Daily Record/St. Louis Countian, May 1, 2003 (discussing collaborative law).

One practitioner attributes the growth of collaborative law to lawyers who "want their work to be consistent with their personal, real-life values." Jill Schachner Chanen, *Collaborative Counselors*, 92 A.B.A.J. 52 (June 2006). Professor Leonard L. Riskin explains that dissolution clients often have "needs and interests that cannot be addressed through litigation or through an adversarial perspective. All too frequently, however, lawyers fail to learn about or try to satisfy their clients' real needs. Instead, they 'transform' complex, human situations into a dry set of facts that fit into legal rules. When this happens, lawyers may miss opportunities to serve their clients and themselves." Leonard L. Riskin, *The Contemplative Lawyer: On the Potential Contributions of Mindfulness Meditation To Law Students, Lawyers, and Their Clients*, 7 Harv. Negot. L. Rev. 1, 13 (2002).

Professor Barbara Glesner Fines warns, however, that the "burnout factor" means that "some attorneys practice collaborative law for themselves as much as for their clients. While these attorneys may reject traditional representation in family law litigation, they must nonetheless respect the value of these approaches for some clients." Barbara Glesner Fines, *Ethical Issues in Collaborative Lawyering*, 21 J. Am. Acad. Matrim. Lawyers 141, 147 (2008). "If attorneys practicing collaborative law allow their own personal distaste for litigation to cloud their judgment regarding the suitability of collaborative law for their clients," they may vitiate the client's voluntary informed consent by " 'selling' a dispute resolution approach" to the client. *Id.*

6. *Is procedural reform sufficient?* Professor Penelope Eileen Bryan criticizes collaborative law for "retard[ing] meaningful reform * * * by allegedly offering a procedural cure for substantive ills." "Many of the negative consequences of divorce for women and children," she argues, "seem related to poor substantive results rather than to the process used to resolve divorce disputes. * * * [R]eforms like collaborative divorce that focus on emotions and relationship preservation, almost to the exclusion of substantive concerns, and that fail to acknowledge and address many of the problems that cause poor outcomes, are likely to do little to alleviate the postdivorce suffering of women and dependent children." Penelope E. Bryan, *"Collaborative Divorce": Meaningful Reform Or Another Quick Fix?*, 5 Psych., Pub. Pol. & L. 1001, 1001–03 (1999).

PROBLEM 15–4

After seven years of marriage, John and Jane Smith are seeking a divorce. They have two children, ages five and three. The Smiths would like to explore the prospect of mediating or arbitrating incidents of the impending divorce. They are also intrigued by friends' descriptions of collaborative and cooperative divorce law.

As John's lawyer, what advice would you provide concerning the relative advantages and disadvantages of collaborative and cooperative law, and of traditional litigation? What advice would you provide concerning the advantages and disadvantages of these ADR devices, and of negotiation or mediation? Would your advice differ if you were Jane's lawyer? What further information would you seek from your client? What if your client expresses concern whether his or her spouse can be trusted not to hide assets or other information during a collaborative process? Would your advice depend in some measure on the fact that the Smiths have young children? For what sorts of divorcing couples is collaborative law a bad option? For what sorts of divorcing couples is cooperative law (collaborative law, without the disqualification agreement) a better option than collaborative law?

A NOTE ON THE ETHICAL ISSUES RAISED
BY COLLABORATIVE LAW

The ABA Model Rules of Professional Conduct are silent about collaborative law practice. Ethics committees have begun to weigh in, however, and the verdict has generally been guardedly supportive. In 2007, the American Bar Association's Standing Committee on Ethics and Professional Responsibility concluded: "Before representing a client in a collaborative law process, a lawyer must advise the client of the benefits and risks of participation in the process. If the client has given his or her informed consent, the lawyer may represent the client in the collaborative law process. A lawyer who engages in collaborative resolution processes still is bound to the rules of professional conduct, including the duties of competence and diligence." Formal Opinion 07–447 (Aug. 9, 2007). Bar ethics opinions in several states (including Kentucky, New Jersey, North Carolina and Pennsylvania) have likewise concluded that collaborative divorce law processes are not inherently inconsistent with the Model Rules of Professional Conduct; the Colorado Bar Association has reached a contrary conclusion, which the ABA Formal Opinion expressly rejected. *Id.* & n.7.

The ABA Formal Opinion came with a warning. "Most authorities treat collaborative law practice as a species of limited scope representation and discuss the duties of lawyers in those situations, including communication, competence, diligence, and confidentiality. However, even those opinions are guarded, and caution that collaborative practice carries with it a potential for significant ethical difficulties," including ones arising under Model Rules covered in Chapter 2 of this book. *Id.*

1. *Scope of representation.* Pursuant to the collaborative law disqualification agreement, may a lawyer agree to cease representing the client if one party decides to commence litigation? "A lawyer may limit the scope of the representation if the limitation is reasonable and the client gives informed consent." Model Rule 1.2(c). A lawyer must "abide by a client's decisions concerning the objectives of representation and * * * consult with the client as to the means by which they are to be pursued." Model Rule 1.2(a). If the client gives informed consent to collaborative law after full disclosure from

counsel, "[n]othing in [Model Rule 1.2] or its Comment suggest[s] that limiting a representation to a collaborative effort to reach a settlement is per se unreasonable." ABA Formal Opinion 07–447.

If representation terminates, the lawyer must take all reasonable steps to protect the client's interests, including allowing time for employment of other counsel, returning the client's papers and property, and returning any advance payment of fee or expense that has not been earned or incurred. *See* Model Rule 1.16(d) ("Upon termination of representation, a lawyer shall take steps to the extent reasonably practicable to protect a client's interests.")

2. *Diligence.* "A lawyer shall act with reasonable diligence and promptness in representing a client." Model Rule 1.3. The lawyer has an obligation "zealously to protect and pursue a client's legitimate interests, within the bounds of the law * * *." *Id.*, Preamble [9]. "Loyalty and independent judgment are essential elements in the lawyer's relationship to a client." Model Rule 1.7 cmt.1.

Some commentators warn that collaborative law requires lawyers to stray from diligence, loyalty and independence toward neutrality. James Lawrence, for example, argues that collaborative lawyers "straddle the line between advocacy and neutrality," and thus find themselves in a "unique ethical position." "Although the collaborative lawyer is not actually a neutral, his responsibilities shift away from those associated with 'pure' advocacy and toward the creative, flexible representation that characterizes neutrality." James Lawrence, *Collaborative Lawyering: A New Development In Conflict Resolution*, 17 Ohio St. J. on Disp. Resol. 431, 438–39, 442 (2002).

Supporters of collaborative law counter that a diligent lawyer "is not bound * * * to press for every advantage that might be realized for a client." Model Rule 1.3 cmt.1. "Just as lawyers in traditional negotiation may ethically negotiate to accept less than their clients might get in a court judgment, CL lawyers may negotiate under the same understanding of zealous advocacy." John Lande, *Possibilities For Collaborative Law: Ethics and Practice of Disqualification in a New Model of Lawyering*, 64 Ohio St. L.J. 1315, 1335–36 (2003). Supporters also argue that the collaborative lawyer "continues to guard her client's interests above all else. Her commitment is to her client and, by agreement, to the process. Nothing about the collaborative law participation agreement * * * suggests that the collaborative lawyer bears any duty to the interests of the other party. * * * What is missing from the lawyer's role in the collaborative process is the puffing, posturing, and positioning that is confused by many with effective advocacy or zeal." Sandra S. Beckwith & Sherri Goren Slovin, *The Collaborative Lawyer As Advocate: A Response*, 18 Ohio St. J. on Disp. Resol. 497, 498–99 (2003).

3. *Confidentiality.* Model Rule 1.6(a) provides that with narrow exceptions, "[a] lawyer shall not reveal information relating to the representation of a client unless the client gives informed consent." As the Lande and Herman article reproduced above notes, parties to a collaborative law agreement promise each other full disclosure of all relevant information. This promise would include waiver of the attorney-client privilege. If signed following full disclosure, the client's agreement itself would constitute informed consent to disclosure. If the client then objects to disclosure during the proceedings, the

lawyer could seek to withdraw from representation, and might even terminate the collaborative law proceedings under the rules set forth in the agreement. *See* William H. Schwab, *Collaborative Lawyering: A Closer Look at an Emerging Practice*, 4 Pepp. Disp. Resol. L.J. 351 (2004).

4. *Conflicts of interest.* On full disclosure, clients generally may give informed written consent to a conflict of interest. *See* Lande, *Possibilities For Collaborative Law, supra,* at 1340. As quoted above, the ABA Ethics Opinion rejected suggestions that collaborative law practice establishes a non-waivable conflict of interest.

5. *Withdrawal from representation.* The disqualification agreement is the cornerstone of collaborative law. Model Rule 1.16 permits or requires a lawyer to withdraw from representation for a variety of reasons. "When a client has given informed consent to a representation limited to collaborative negotiation toward settlement, the lawyer's agreement to withdraw if the collaboration fails is not an agreement that impairs her ability to represent the client, but rather is consistent with the client's limited goals for the representation." ABA Formal Opinion 07–447.

On withdrawal, the lawyer must "take steps to the extent reasonably practicable to protect a client's interests, such as giving reasonable notice to the client, allowing time for employment of other counsel, [and] surrendering papers and property to which the client is entitled. * * * " Model Rule 1.16(d). Whether the collaborative lawyer withdraws because a party triggers the disqualification clause by requesting litigation, or whether the lawyer withdraws for other reasons, Model Rule 1.16 obligates the lawyer to help the client find new counsel, and to otherwise facilitate the transition.

A CONCLUDING NOTE ABOUT A LAWYER'S ETHICAL DUTY TO INFORM CLIENTS ABOUT ADR

The typical domestic relations client is not a lawyer, has never been a party in a legal proceeding, has never retained a lawyer, and may never before even have walked into a courtroom. Because litigation is "useful in only a small minority of cases" in contemporary family law, should lawyers have an ethical duty to inform their domestic relations clients about ADR alternatives to litigation? Mary E. O'Connell & J. Herbie DiFonzo, *The Family Law Education Reform Project Final Report*, 44 Fam. Ct. Rev. 524, 525 (2006).

The ABA Model Rules of Professional Conduct do not clearly impose this duty to inform the client, in family law cases or otherwise. Model Rule 1.2(a) provides that with limited exceptions, "[a] lawyer shall abide by a client's decisions concerning the objectives of representation and * * * shall consult with the client as to the means by which they are to be pursued." Model Rule 1.4(a)(2) requires the lawyer to "reasonably consult with the client about the means by which the client's objectives are to be accomplished." Model Rule 1.4(b) requires the lawyer to "explain a matter to the extent reasonably necessary to permit the client to make informed decisions regarding the representation." Where litigation is likely, "it may be necessary under Rule 1.4 to inform the client of forms of dispute resolution that might constitute reasonable alternatives to litigation." Model Rule 2.1 cmt.5.

As of 2007, ten states have court rules mandating that lawyers discuss alternatives to litigation with their clients. *See* Andrew Schepard, *Kramer v. Kramer* Revisited: *A Comment on* The Miller Commission Report *and the Obligation of Divorce Lawyers for Parents to Discuss Alternative Dispute Resolution with Their Clients*, 27 Pace L. Rev. 677, 679 n.8 (2007). Minnesota specifies, for example, that "[a]ttorneys shall provide clients with the ADR information." Minn. Gen. Rules of Practice for the District Cts., R. 114.03(b) (2008). The mandatory notice requires the court administrator to provide the attorneys of record and any unrepresented parties with "information about ADR processes available to the county and the availability of a list of neutrals who provide ADR services in that county." R. 114.03(a).

A few other states are inching toward imposing a duty to inform the client about ADR, though the standard is only aspirational in most. *See, e.g.*, Colo. Rules of Prof'l Conduct R. 2.1 (2008) ("[i]n a matter involving or expected to involve litigation, a lawyer should advise the client of alternative forms of dispute resolution that might reasonably be pursued to attempt to resolve the legal dispute or to reach the legal objective sought"). The ABA Section of Family Law urges counsel to "[c]onsider the availability and appropriateness of forms of alternative dispute resolution." *American Bar Association Section of Family Law Civility Standards*, 40 Fam. L.Q. xv, xv (Winter 2007).

Proponents of an ethical duty to inform clients about ADR draw analogies to medical ethics: "We expect a doctor treating a patient for cancer to discuss the benefits and costs of all reasonable treatment options before securing a patient's consent to treatment. The lawyer-client relationship is also based on the client's informed consent to the course of action that the lawyer proposes." Schepard, *supra*, at 689. Professor Frank E.A. Sander, a supporter of a mandatory duty to inform clients about ADR alternatives, says that "[w]e might be surprised by the choices some clients will make when they are candidly told the costs and benefits of pursuing various courses." Frank E.A. Sander, *Should There Be a Duty to Advise of ADR Options? Yes: An Aid to Clients*, A.B.A. J., Nov. 1990, at 50.

Another commentator, however, argues that a mandate to inform clients would be "overkill and unfair micromanagement of the practice of law." "For some clients and some disputes, ADR options may prove more satisfactory. Yet our knowledge of which clients and which disputes are more likely to benefit is woefully inadequate. * * * [T]he time required to properly explain all options in every dispute, would add some cost to each representation, which would be more of a factor in smaller disputes." Michael L. Prigoff, *Should There Be a Duty to Advise of ADR Options? No: An Unreasonable Burden*, A.B.A. J., Nov. 1990, at 51.

PROBLEM 15–5

You are a member of a state bar association task force charged with reviewing the state's rules of professional responsibility. The task force is considering a proposed rule concerning an obligation of lawyers, in representations in which litigation may result, to inform clients about ADR options, including collaborative and cooperative law. The proposed amendment would state that "[a] lawyer has an obligation to recommend alternatives to litigation when an alternative is a reasonable course of action to further the client's interests." *See* Standing Comm. on Prof'l and Judicial Ethics, State Bar of Mich., Informal Op. RI–262 (1996).

As a family law practitioner, you have been asked to present your views on how such an obligation would affect lawyers practicing in your field. Would you vote to adopt the proposed amendment? If not, would you leave as-is the Model Rules quoted in the Concluding Note above, or would you change the proposal? Obligation or not, would you inform your own domestic relations clients of ADR options? In some cases or all?

CHAPTER 16

FAMILY LAW JURISDICTION

■ ■ ■

This Chapter considers a number of complex jurisdictional issues that arise in actions for divorce, property distribution, child support, or child custody. Jurisdictional issues occur throughout family actions, beginning with where a party can make an initial filing, and arising as well in actions seeking to modify an earlier order. The Chapter considers whether actions raising family law claims may be heard in state or federal court, and whether they should be heard by a unified family court that hears all actions relating to a particular family.

Just as in civil litigation generally, domestic relations litigants may proceed only in a court that has personal and subject matter jurisdiction under constitutional prescriptions and applicable statutes and court rules. As you know from Civil Procedure, personal jurisdiction, which limits who may be sued in a particular geographic location, may rest on domicile, consent, physical presence, or another basis. *International Shoe v. Washington*, 326 U.S. 310 (1945), established that personal jurisdiction extends to a state in which the defendant's "minimum contacts" make issuance of a binding judgment fair. For its part, subject matter jurisdiction concerns the court's constitutional and statutory authority to hear and decide the particular claims raised in the case. Because we live in a mobile society and parties frequently move from state to state during separation or after dissolution, jurisdictional issues are pervasive in domestic relations cases. This Chapter first considers whether state or federal courts provide the appropriate forum for most family law cases, and then turns to look at the differing standards for initial and continuing jurisdiction in various types of domestic relations proceedings you learned about in Chapters 8 through 13, namely, divorce, property distribution, alimony, child support, and child custody and visitation. Finally, the Chapter introduces unified family courts, which hear a variety of family law issues in one forum.

The following excerpt introduces some of the complicated jurisdictional issues that can arise in domestic relations cases, including the complexity of having different jurisdictional rules govern each type of claim.

RHONDA WASSERMAN

Parents, Partners, and Personal Jurisdiction.
1995 U. Ill. L. Rev. 813, 813–15.

* * *

The intersection between family law and jurisdiction is messy. If a married couple with children decides to divorce, a court may be asked to resolve at least three different sets of family law issues: whether to grant the divorce itself; how to resolve financial matters (such as alimony, child support and division of marital property); and how to allocate child custody and visitation rights. Although often it would make sense to resolve all of these issues in a single proceeding, each set of issues is governed by a unique set of jurisdictional principles. With respect to the divorce itself, a state has power, consistent with the Due Process Clause, to enter a divorce decree as long as one of the spouses is domiciled there, even if the state lacks *in personam* jurisdiction over the other spouse. But a state cannot resolve the financial matters of alimony or child support without first acquiring *in personam* jurisdiction over the spouse charged with payment. Yet it can adjudicate child custody disputes as long as it is the child's " "home state," " regardless of whether the child or either parent is domiciled there or whether it has *in personam* jurisdiction over the parents.

What explains this smorgasbord of jurisdictional rules governing family matters? Why are alimony, child support, and marital property matters governed by standard jurisdictional rules—*International Shoe's* minimum contacts test—while divorce and child custody issues are not?

It is easy to understand why financial matters—alimony, child support and marital property—are governed by standard jurisdictional rules. After all, the minimum contacts test was devised to assure that defendants were not deprived of *property* without due process of law, and money and marital assets are clearly property. But the Due Process Clause protects against deprivations of liberty as well as property, and the rights to marry and to bear and raise children are constitutionally protected liberty interests. Why then are divorce and child custody suits not governed by the same jurisdictional rules as alimony actions?

* * *

SECTION 1: THE DOMESTIC RELATIONS EXCEPTION TO DIVERSITY JURISDICTION

Congress has conferred federal diversity-of-citizenship jurisdiction in cases or controversies between citizens of different states where the amount in controversy exceeds $75,000. 28 U.S.C. § 1332(a) (2008). Under the court-created "domestic relations exception," however, federal courts will not exercise diversity jurisdiction to grant or deny a divorce, alimony, property distribution or child custody or visitation. *Ankenbrandt v. Richards* discusses the exception's history and present application.

ANKENBRANDT v. RICHARDS

Supreme Court of the United States, 1992.
504 U.S. 689.

JUSTICE WHITE delivered the opinion of the Court.

This case presents the issue whether the federal courts have jurisdiction or should abstain in a case involving alleged torts committed by the former husband of petitioner and his female companion against petitioner's children, when the sole basis for federal jurisdiction is the diversity-of-citizenship provision of 28 U.S.C. § 1332.

I

Petitioner Carol Ankenbrandt, a citizen of Missouri, brought this lawsuit on September 26, 1989, on behalf of her daughters L.R. and S.R. against respondents Jon A. Richards and Debra Kesler, citizens of Louisiana, in the United States District Court for the Eastern District of Louisiana. Alleging federal jurisdiction based on the diversity-of-citizenship provision of § 1332, Ankenbrandt's complaint sought monetary damages for alleged sexual and physical abuse of the children committed by Richards and Kesler. Richards is the divorced father of the children and Kesler his female companion. On December 10, 1990, the District Court granted respondents' motion to dismiss this lawsuit. Citing *In re Burrus*, 136 U.S. 586, 593–594 (1890), for the proposition that "[t]he whole subject of the domestic relations of husband and wife, parent and child, belongs to the laws of the States and not to the laws of the United States," the court concluded that this case fell within what has become known as the "domestic relations" exception to diversity jurisdiction, and that it lacked jurisdiction over the case. * * *

* * *

II

The domestic relations exception upon which the courts below relied to decline jurisdiction has been invoked often by the lower federal courts. The seeming authority for doing so originally stemmed from the announcement in *Barber v. Barber*, 21 How 582 (1859), that the federal courts have no jurisdiction over suits for divorce or the allowance of alimony. * * *

* * *

A

Counsel argued in *Barber* that the Constitution prohibited federal courts from exercising jurisdiction over domestic relations cases. An examination of Article III, *Barber* itself, and our cases since *Barber* makes clear that the Constitution does not exclude domestic relations cases from the jurisdiction otherwise granted by statute to the federal courts.

Article III, Sec. 2, of the Constitution provides in pertinent part:

"Section 2—The judicial Power shall extend to all Cases, in Law and Equity, arising under this Constitution, the Laws of the United States, and Treaties made, * * * to Controversies between two or more States; between a State and Citizens of another State;—between Citizens of different States;—between Citizens of the same State claiming Land under Grants of different States, and between a State, or the Citizens thereof, and foreign States, Citizens or Subjects."

This section delineates the absolute limits on the federal courts' jurisdiction. But in articulating three different terms to define jurisdiction "Cases in Law and Equity," "Cases," and "Controversies"—this provision contains no limitation on subjects of a domestic relations nature. Nor did *Barber* purport to ground the domestic relations exception in these constitutional limits on federal jurisdiction. The Court's discussion of federal judicial power to hear suits of a domestic relations nature contains no mention of the Constitution, and it is logical to presume that the Court based its statement limiting such power on narrower statutory, rather than broader constitutional, grounds.

* * *

B

That Article III, § 2, does not mandate the exclusion of domestic relations cases from federal-court jurisdiction, however, does not mean that such courts necessarily must retain and exercise jurisdiction over such cases. * * *

* * *

The Judiciary Act of 1789 provided that "the circuit courts shall have original cognizance, concurrent with the courts of the several States, of *all suits of a civil nature at common law or in equity, where the matter in dispute exceeds*, exclusive of costs, the sum or value of *five hundred dollars*, and . . . an alien is a party, or the suit is *between a citizen of the State where the suit is brought, and a citizen of another State*." Act of Sept. 24, 1789, § 11, 1 Stat. 78 (emphasis added). The defining phrase, "all suits of a civil nature at common law or in equity," remained a key element of statutory provisions demarcating the terms of diversity jurisdiction until 1948, when Congress amended the diversity jurisdiction provision to eliminate this phrase and replace in its stead the term "all civil actions." 1948 Judicial Code and Judiciary Act, 62 Stat. 930, 28 U.S.C. § 1332.

The *Barber* majority itself did not expressly refer to the diversity statute's use of the limitation on "suits of a civil nature at common law or in equity." The dissenters in *Barber*, however, implicitly made such a reference, for they suggested that the federal courts had no power over certain domestic relations actions because the court of chancery [in

England] lacked authority to issue divorce and alimony decrees. * * * Because the *Barber* Court did not disagree with this reason for accepting the jurisdictional limitation over the issuance of divorce and alimony decrees, it may be inferred fairly that the jurisdictional limitation recognized by the Court rested on this statutory basis and that the disagreement between the Court and the dissenters thus centered only on the extent of the limitation.

We have no occasion here to join the historical debate over whether the English court of chancery had jurisdiction to handle certain domestic relations matters, though we note that commentators have found some support for the *Barber* majority's interpretation. * * * We thus are content to rest our conclusion that a domestic relations exception exists as a matter of statutory construction not on the accuracy of the historical justifications on which it was seemingly based, but rather on Congress' apparent acceptance of this construction of the diversity jurisdiction provisions in the years prior to 1948, when the statute limited jurisdiction to "suits of a civil nature at common law or in equity." * * *

When Congress amended the diversity statute in 1948 to replace the law/equity distinction with the phrase "all civil actions," we presume Congress did so with full cognizance of the Court's nearly century-long interpretation of the prior statutes, which had construed the statutory diversity jurisdiction to contain an exception for certain domestic relations matters. With respect to the 1948 amendment, the Court has previously stated that "no changes of law or policy are to be presumed from changes of language in the revision unless an intent to make such changes is clearly expressed." *Fourco Glass Co. v. Transmirra Products Corp.*, 353 U.S. 222, 227 (1957). With respect to such a longstanding and well-known construction of the diversity statute, and where Congress made substantive changes to the statute in other respects, we presume, absent any indication that Congress intended to alter this exception, that Congress "adopt[ed] that interpretation" when it reenacted the diversity statute. *Lorillard v. Pons*, 434 U.S. 575, 580 (1978).

III

In the more than 100 years since this Court laid the seeds for the development of the domestic relations exception, the lower federal courts have applied it in a variety of circumstances. Many of these applications go well beyond the circumscribed situations posed by *Barber* and its progeny. *Barber* itself disclaimed federal jurisdiction over a narrow range of domestic relations issues involving the granting of a divorce and a decree of alimony * * *.

* * *

The *Barber* Court did thus not intend to strip the federal courts of authority to hear cases arising from the domestic relations of persons unless they seek the granting or modification of a divorce or alimony decree. The holding of the case itself sanctioned the exercise of federal jurisdiction over the enforcement of an alimony decree that had been properly obtained in a state court of competent jurisdiction. Contrary to the *Barber* dissenters' position, the enforcement of such validly obtained orders does not "regulate the domestic relations of society" and produce an "inquisitorial authority" in which federal tribunals "enter the habitations and even into the chambers and nurseries of private families, and inquire into and pronounce upon the morals and habits and affections or antipathies of the members of every household." [*Barber*, 21 How. at 602] (Daniel, J., dissenting). * * *

Subsequently, this Court expanded the domestic relations exception to include decrees in child custody cases. * * *

* * *

* * * We conclude, therefore, that the domestic relations exception, as articulated by this Court since *Barber*, divests the federal courts of power to issue divorce, alimony, and child custody decrees. Given the long passage of time without any expression of congressional dissatisfaction, we have no trouble today reaffirming the validity of the exception as it pertains to divorce and alimony decrees and child custody orders.

Not only is our conclusion rooted in respect for this long-held understanding, it is also supported by sound policy considerations. Issuance of decrees of this type not infrequently involves retention of jurisdiction by the court and deployment of social workers to monitor compliance. As a matter of judicial economy, state courts are more eminently suited to work of this type than are federal courts, which lack the close association with state and local government organizations dedicated to handling issues that arise out of conflicts over divorce, alimony, and child custody decrees. Moreover, as a matter of judicial expertise, it makes far more sense to retain the rule that federal courts lack power to issue these types of decrees because of the special proficiency developed by state tribunals over the past century and a half in handling issues that arise in the granting of such decrees.

By concluding, as we do, that the domestic relations exception encompasses only cases involving the issuance of a divorce, alimony, or child custody decree, we necessarily find that the Court of Appeals erred by affirming the District Court's invocation of this exception. This lawsuit in no way seeks such a decree; rather, it alleges that respondents Richards and Kesler committed torts against L.R. and S.R., Ankenbrandt's children by Richards. Federal subject-matter jurisdiction pursuant to § 1332 thus is proper in this case. * * *

* * *

[The concurring opinions of BLACKMUN, J. and STEVENS, J. are omitted.]

NOTES AND QUESTIONS

1. *Basis for the domestic relations exception.* Commentators have struggled to define a solid basis for the domestic relations exception because, as *Ankenbrandt* acknowledges, nothing in Article III or the diversity statute explicitly creates the exception. Does the Court provide a compelling basis for the exception? What other interests might be at stake? Consider whether contemporary justifications for the exception are the same as the justifications that likely moved the Court in *Barber.* Does the judge-made exception indicate that the federal courts, and Congress by its long silence, consider domestic relations cases not worthy of federal judicial attention? Are ordinary slip-and-fall or mortgage foreclosure cases more deserving of a federal judge's time? Are domestic relations cases inherently matters of state concern? What effects would congressional or judicial repeal of the exemption have on the federal court system or on the state court system?

In light of the domestic relations exception, why did a federal district court and the Supreme Court hear and decide *Zablocki v. Redhail,* which you read as a lead case in Chapter 3? And why did the Supreme Court hear and decide *Orr v. Orr,* a case discussed in Chapter 10, which concerned a specific request for alimony?

2. *Fairness to out-of-state litigants.* The Framers may have included diversity jurisdiction in Article III based on a concern that out-of-state parties would suffer discrimination if they were forced to litigate in state court. Can this concern be dealt with in domestic relations proceedings even if these proceedings are excluded from the federal courts entirely?

SECTION 2: DIVORCE JURISDICTION

Ankenbrandt explains why it is the state courts that hear domestic relations proceedings, including divorce. Before granting a divorce, of course, the state court must have both subject matter and personal jurisdiction.

If both parties are domiciled in the same state, then it seems clear that the state can assert jurisdiction to grant a divorce. But under what circumstances does a court have jurisdiction if only one party is domiciled in the state? This issue became particularly significant during World War II. The 1940s witnessed "a 'divorce boom,' fueled by 'migratory divorce'—divorce granted by one State (typically labeled a 'divorce mill') to a spouse or spouses who had recently moved there from another State (typically one that took a dim and sparing view of divorce)." Parnian Toofanian, *Three's a Crowd?* Sherrer v. Sherrer, 14 J. Contemp. Legal Issues 185, 185–86 (2004). Nevada's requirement of a six-week residency period before a litigant could file for divorce was the shortest in the country, followed by Florida's 90–day residency requirement, which was the second shortest. Some divorcing couples obtained fast divorces in the courts of other countries, including Mexico and the Dominican Republic. Because of the confusion caused by out-of-state divorce decrees, the Supreme Court decided a number of cases involving complex issues of federalism and family law during these years.

A. *EX PARTE* DIVORCE: *WILLIAMS I* AND *WILLIAMS II*

A marriage requires a commitment from two spouses. Must a court have jurisdiction over both parties to grant the divorce? In the following two opinions, the Supreme Court decided the authority of all states to exercise jurisdiction over the "res" (the marital status) of individuals in dissolving marriages by granting divorces on an *ex parte* basis.

In *Williams v. North Carolina*, 317 U.S. 287 (1942) (*Williams I*), the Court considered the validity of a Nevada divorce decree issued to O.B. Williams. Williams married Carrie Wyke in 1916 in North Carolina and lived with her until May 1940, when he went to Las Vegas. Coincidentally, Lillie Shaver Hendrix, who had been married to Thomas Hendrix since 1920, and who also lived in North Carolina, also moved to Las Vegas in May 1940. Both Williams and Hendrix filed for divorce in Nevada in June 1940. Williams was granted a divorce in August, and, on October 4, 1940, the same day that Hendrix was granted her decree, Williams and Hendrix married each other. A North Carolina court subsequently convicted them both of bigamous cohabitation, rejecting their defense based on the Nevada divorce decrees. The Supreme Court held:

> * * * Each state as a sovereign has a rightful and legitimate concern in the marital status of persons domiciled within its borders. The marriage relation creates problems of large social importance. Protection of offspring, property interests, and the enforcement of marital responsibilities are but a few of the commanding problems in the field of domestic relations with which the state must deal. Thus it is plain that each state, by virtue of its command over its domiciliaries and its large interest in the institution of marriage, can alter within its own borders the marriage status of the spouse domiciled there, even though the other spouse is absent. * * *

Id. at 298–99. The Court held that North Carolina was bound to accept the Nevada divorces as lawful, finding: "[I]f decrees of a state altering the marital status of its domiciliaries are not valid throughout the Union even though the requirements of procedural due process are wholly met, a rule would be fostered which could not help but bring 'considerable disaster to innocent persons' " and ' "bastardize children hitherto supposed to be the offspring of lawful marriage.' " *Id.* at 299–301 (quoting *Haddock v. Haddock*, 201 U.S. 562, 628 (1906) (Holmes, J., dissenting)). Relying on the Full Faith and Credit Clause of the U.S. Constitution,[1] *Williams I* held that any state had jurisdiction to grant a divorce to an individual who was

---

1. The Full Faith and Credit Clause provides that "Full Faith and Credit shall be given in each State to the public Acts, Records, and judicial Proceedings of every other State. And the Congress may by general Laws prescribe the Manner in which such Acts, Records and Proceedings shall be proved, and the Effect thereof." U.S. Const. art. IV, § 1.

legally domiciled in that state *and* that all other states must recognize these divorces. Following remand to the North Carolina Supreme Court, the parties were again convicted of bigamy and sentenced to prison terms. Again they appealed.

Williams v. North Carolina, 325 U.S. 226 (1945) (*Williams II*), considered the validity of the spouses' Nevada domicile, an issue that had not been addressed in the previous case:

> What is immediately before us is the judgment of the Supreme Court of North Carolina. We have authority to upset it only if there is want of foundation for the conclusion that that Court reached. The conclusion it reached turns on its finding that the spouses who obtained the Nevada decrees were not domiciled there. The fact that the Nevada court found that they were domiciled there is entitled to respect, and more. The burden of undermining the verity which the Nevada decrees import rests heavily upon the assailant. But simply because the Nevada court found that it had power to award a divorce decree cannot, we have seen, foreclose reexamination by another State. Otherwise, as was pointed out long ago, a court's record would establish its power and the power would be proved by the record. Such circular reasoning would give one State a control over all the other States which the Full Faith and Credit Clause certainly did not confer. If this Court finds that proper weight was accorded to the claims of power by the court of one State in rendering a judgment the validity of which is pleaded in defense in another State, that the burden of overcoming such respect by disproof of the substratum of fact—here domicil—on which such power alone can rest was properly charged against the party challenging the legitimacy of the judgment, that such issue of fact was left for fair determination by appropriate procedure, and that a finding adverse to the necessary foundation for any valid sister-State judgment was amply supported in evidence, we cannot upset the judgment before us. * * *

> When this case was first here, North Carolina did not challenge the finding of the Nevada court that petitioners had acquired domicils in Nevada. * * * Upon retrial, however, the existence of domicil in Nevada became the decisive issue. * * * The burden, it was charged, then devolved upon petitioners "to satisfy the trial jury, not beyond a reasonable doubt nor by the greater weight of the evidence, but simply to satisfy" the jury from all the evidence, that petitioners were domiciled in Nevada at the time they obtained their divorces. The court further charged that "the recitation" of *bona fide* domicil in the Nevada decree was "prima facie evidence" sufficient to warrant a finding of domicil in Nevada but not compelling "such an inference." If the jury found, as they were told, that petitioners had domicils in North Carolina and went to Nevada "simply and solely for the purpose of obtaining" divorces, intending to return to North Carolina on obtaining them, they never lost their North Carolina domicils nor acquired new domicils in Nevada. Domicil, the jury was instructed,

was that place where a person "has voluntarily fixed his abode ... not for a mere special or temporary purpose, but with a present intention of making it his home, either permanently or for an indefinite or unlimited length of time."

* * *

Id. at 233–36. *Williams II* upheld the convictions of Williams and Hendrix for bigamous cohabitation because the left-at-home spouses in North Carolina never participated in the divorce proceedings, and North Carolina was thus not bound by the Nevada decree.

NOTES AND QUESTIONS

1. *Domicile and the validity of the Nevada decree.* Domicile is generally defined as the place where a person resides with the intent to remain indefinitely. Did O.B. Williams and Lillie Shaver Hendrix establish domicile in Nevada? Did the Court hold that the Nevada divorce was entirely invalid?

2. *Remarriage.* If you have an *ex parte* divorce decree from one state, under what circumstances could you remarry?

B. CASE NOTE ON SHAM DOMICILE: *SHERRER v. SHERRER*

Williams concerned the validity of an *ex parte* divorce decree, that is, a decree issued when only one spouse was present. Three years after *Williams II,* the Supreme Court considered a challenge to a decree issued when both spouses were present before the divorce court.

In *Sherrer v. Sherrer,* 334 U.S. 343 (1948), Edward Sherrer alleged that his wife's petition for a Florida divorce was invalid because she had never been domiciled in Florida. After 14 years of marriage, Margaret Sherrer left the couple's Massachusetts home in 1944 for what she claimed was a Florida vacation with the parties' two children. Once in Florida, Margaret informed her husband that she intended to remain there. She found housing there, sent their older daughter to school, worked as a waitress, and filed for divorce 93 days after arriving in Florida, three days beyond the state's 90–day minimum residency requirement for filing divorce actions.

Margaret's complaint alleged that she was domiciled in Florida. Edward retained a Florida attorney and filed a general appearance in the divorce action. He denied the allegations of the complaint, including that Margaret was domiciled in Florida. The Florida court granted the divorce, finding that Margaret was, in fact, a Florida resident and that the court had jurisdiction. Three days later, Margaret married Henry Phelps, who had followed her to Florida from Massachusetts. They lived in Florida for two months before returning together to Massachusetts.

Edward did not appeal the Florida divorce decree. In a later action to clear title to land in Massachusetts, however, he alleged that Margaret had deserted him. The lower courts held that the Florida divorce decree was not entitled to full faith and credit in the Massachusetts courts because Margaret had not validly established domicile in Florida. Margaret appealed to the Supreme Court, which reversed on the ground that the Florida divorce judgment was entitled to full faith and credit.

The Court distinguished *Sherrer* from *Williams I* and *II* because Edward was involved in the divorce proceedings and, consequently, had had the opportunity to challenge domicile at that time. The "obligation of full faith and credit" required that Massachusetts respect the Florida judgment. Margaret's actions might indicate that she never intended to remain in Florida, but Edward could not challenge the domicile issue in a second action.

NOTES AND QUESTIONS

1. *Why a domicile rule?* *Williams I* and *II* were decided during the fault-based era of divorce, when states were concerned that individuals unable to prove fault in a state with strict divorce laws would establish domicile elsewhere to obtain a divorce, and then return to the home state. What purposes, if any, does the domicile rule serve today under a no-fault regime? Consider the views of Professor Rhonda Wasserman:

> The domicile rule (together with the status exception) supposedly assures the parties' convenience by guaranteeing the petitioning spouse an opportunity to sue for divorce in her home state. Without the domicile rule and the status exception, abandoned spouses would have had to travel to the deserting spouses' new home state to obtain jurisdiction over them, at least until the Supreme Court's decision in *International Shoe*. Today, states possess wide latitude to assert *in personam* jurisdiction and many states have enacted special long-arm provisions for matrimonial litigation. Therefore, the status exception and the domicile rule are no longer necessary to ensure that spouses abandoned in a state will have recourse to its divorce courts. Petitioning spouses simply can invoke long-arm jurisdiction over the deserting spouses and sue at home *irrespective* of domicile. Put differently, because the deserting spouse typically will have minimum contacts with the state in which the couple lived together, the abandoned spouse can sue at home, relying upon standard minimum contacts analysis. The assurance of a convenient forum requires neither the status exception nor the domicile rule.

Rhonda Wasserman, *Divorce and Domicile: Time to Sever the Knot*, 39 Wm. & Mary L. Rev. 1, 32–33 (1997). Do you agree with Professor Wasserman that the domicile rule is no longer necessary? Does it matter that many jurisdictions retain both fault and no-fault regimes?

2. *Uniformity among states.* Should states enact a uniform divorce jurisdiction act that would accord full faith and credit to *ex parte* divorce decrees where the petitioner satisfied a brief residency requirement, such as 90 days? Pursuant to the Full Faith and Credit Clause, should Congress enact legislation establishing such a requirement as a federal standard?

3. *The long view.* The divisible divorce cases involve state efforts to control the status of their citizens. Do the Supreme Court's opinions mark a significant change in "state power to set the normative boundaries of family life by extending to individual citizens the ability to choose which jurisdiction would control their marital status"? *See* Ann Laquer Estin, *Family Law Federalism: Divorce and the Constitution*, 16 Wm. & Mary Bill Rts. J. 381, 383 (2007).

C. RESIDENCE REQUIREMENTS

As you learned in Chapter 8, in addition to the domicile requirement, almost all states have enacted statutes requiring residency for a specified period before a court may issue a divorce decree. *See* Charts, 41 Fam. L.Q. 709, 713 (2008) (Chart 4). While the two words may often be used interchangeably in casual communication, the terms have different legal significance. Intent distinguishes residency, which is simply the physical inhabitance of a place, from domicile, which is the place a person considers his or her permanent home.

In the following case, the Supreme Court upheld the constitutionality of state residency requirements for purposes of divorce jurisdiction.

SOSNA v. IOWA

Supreme Court of the United States, 1975.
419 U.S. 393.

MR. JUSTICE REHNQUIST delivered the opinion of the Court.

Appellant Carol Sosna married Michael Sosna on September 5, 1964, in Michigan. They lived together in New York between October 1967 and August 1971, after which date they separated but continued to live in New York. In August 1972, appellant moved to Iowa with her three children, and the following month she petitioned the District Court of Jackson County, Iowa, for a dissolution of her marriage. Michael Sosna, who had been personally served with notice of the action when he came to Iowa to visit his children, made a special appearance to contest the jurisdiction of the Iowa court. The Iowa court dismissed the petition for lack of jurisdiction, finding that Michael Sosna was not a resident of Iowa and appellant had not been a resident of the State of Iowa for one year preceding the filing of her petition. In so doing the Iowa court applied the provisions of Iowa Code § 598.6 (1973) requiring that the petitioner in such an action be "for the last year a resident of the state."

* * *

II

The durational residency requirement under attack in this case is a part of Iowa's comprehensive statutory regulation of domestic relations, an area that has long been regarded as a virtually exclusive province of the States. * * *

The statutory scheme in Iowa, like those in other States, sets forth in considerable detail the grounds upon which a marriage may be dissolved and the circumstances in which a divorce may be obtained. Jurisdiction over a petition for dissolution is established by statute in "the county where either party resides," Iowa Code § 598.2 (1973), and the Iowa courts have construed the term "resident" to have much the same meaning as is ordinarily associated with the concept of domicile. Iowa has recently revised its divorce statutes, incorporating the no-fault concept, but it retained the one-year durational residency requirement.

* * *

Appellant contends that the Iowa requirement of one year's residence is unconstitutional for two separate reasons: *first*, because it establishes two classes of persons and discriminates against those who have recently exercised their right to travel to Iowa, thereby contravening the Court's holdings in [prior cases]; and, *second*, because it denies a litigant the opportunity to make an individualized showing of bona fide residence and therefore denies such residents access to the only method of legally dissolving their marriage.

State statutes imposing durational residency requirements were, of course, invalidated when imposed by States as a qualification for [welfare payments, for voting,] and for medical care. But none of those cases intimated that the States might never impose durational residency requirements, and such a proposition was in fact expressly disclaimed. What those cases had in common was that the durational residency requirements they struck down were justified on the basis of budgetary or recordkeeping considerations which were held insufficient to outweigh the constitutional claims of the individuals. But Iowa's divorce residency requirement is of a different stripe. Appellant was not irretrievably foreclosed from obtaining some part of what she sought[.] * * * She would eventually qualify for the same sort of adjudication which she demanded virtually upon her arrival in the State. Iowa's requirement delayed her access to the courts, but, by fulfilling it, she could ultimately have obtained the same opportunity for adjudication which she asserts ought to have been hers at an earlier point in time.

Iowa's residency requirement may reasonably be justified on grounds other than purely budgetary considerations or administrative convenience. A decree of divorce is not a matter in which the only interested parties are the State as a sort of "grantor," and a divorce petitioner such as appellant in the role of "grantee." Both spouses are obviously interested in the proceedings, since it will affect their marital status and very likely their property rights. Where a married couple has minor children, a decree of divorce would usually include provisions for their custody and support. With consequences of such moment riding on a divorce decree issued by its courts, Iowa may insist that one seeking to initiate such a proceeding have the modicum of attachment to the State required here.

Such a requirement additionally furthers the State's parallel interests both in avoiding officious intermeddling in matters in which another State has a paramount interest, and in minimizing the susceptibility of its own divorce decrees to collateral attack. A State such as Iowa may quite reasonably decide that it does not wish to become a divorce mill for unhappy spouses who have lived there as short a time as appellant had when she commenced her action in the state court after having long resided elsewhere. Until such time as Iowa is convinced that appellant intends to remain in the State, it lacks the "nexus between person and place of such permanence as to control the creation of legal relations and responsibilities of the utmost significance." [*Williams II.*] Perhaps even more important, Iowa's interests extend beyond its borders and include the recognition of its divorce decrees by other States under the Full Faith and Credit Clause of the Constitution, Art. IV, § 1. For that purpose, this Court has often stated that "judicial power to grant a divorce—jurisdiction, strictly speaking—is founded on domicil." [*Williams II*]. Where a divorce decree is entered after a finding of domicile in *ex parte* proceedings, this Court has held that the finding of domicile is not binding upon another State and may be disregarded in the face of "cogent evidence" to the contrary. [*Williams II*]. For that reason, the State asked to enter such a decree is entitled to insist that the putative divorce petitioner satisfy something more than the bare minimum of constitutional requirements before a divorce may be granted. The State's decision to exact a one-year residency requirement as a matter of policy is therefore buttressed by a quite permissible inference that this requirement not only effectuates state substantive policy but likewise provides a greater safeguard against successful collateral attack than would a requirement of bona fide residence alone. * * *

We therefore hold that the state interest in requiring that those who seek a divorce from its courts be genuinely attached to the State, as well as a desire to insulate divorce decrees from the likelihood of collateral attack, requires a different resolution of the constitutional issue presented than [those cases invalidating state statutes imposing durational requirements in the contexts of welfare payments, voting, and medical care].

Nor are we of the view that the failure to provide an individualized determination of residency violates the Due Process Clause of the Fourteenth Amendment. * * *

In *Boddie v. Connecticut*, [401 U.S. 371 (1971)], this Court held that Connecticut might not deny access to divorce courts to those persons who could not afford to pay the required fee. Because of the exclusive role played by the State in the termination of marriages, it was held that indigents could not be denied an opportunity to be heard "absent a countervailing state interest of overriding significance." [*Id.*] at 377. But the gravamen of appellant Sosna's claim is not total deprivation, as in *Boddie*, but only delay. The operation of the filing fee in *Boddie* served to exclude forever a certain segment of the population from obtaining a divorce in the courts of Connecticut. No similar total deprivation is present in appellant's case, and the delay which attends the enforcement of the one-year durational residency requirement is, for the reasons previously stated, consistent with the provisions of the United States Constitution.

Affirmed.

* * *

[The dissenting opinion of WHITE, J., is omitted.]

MR. JUSTICE MARSHALL, with whom MR. JUSTICE BRENNAN joins, dissenting.

* * *

As we have made clear in *Shapiro* [*v. Thompson,* 394 U.S. 618 (1969)], and subsequent cases, any classification that penalizes exercise of the constitutional right to travel is invalid unless it is justified by a compelling governmental interest. * * *

* * *

I

The Court omits altogether what should be the first inquiry: whether the right to obtain a divorce is of sufficient importance that its denial to recent immigrants constitutes a penalty on interstate travel. In my view, it clearly meets that standard. The previous decisions of this Court make it plain that the right of marital association is one of the most basic rights conferred on the individual by the State. The interests associated with marriage and divorce have repeatedly been accorded particular deference, and the right to marry has been termed "one of the vital personal rights essential to the orderly pursuit of happiness by free men." *Loving v. Virginia,* 388 U.S. 1, 12 (1967). * * *

II

Having determined that the interest in obtaining a divorce is of substantial social importance, I would scrutinize Iowa's durational residency requirement to determine whether it constitutes a reasonable means of furthering important interests asserted by the State. * * *

The Court proposes three defenses for the Iowa statute: first, the residency requirement merely delays receipt of the benefit in question—it does not deprive the applicant of the benefit altogether; second, since significant social consequences may follow from the conferral of a divorce, the State may legitimately regulate the divorce process; and third, the State has interests both in protecting itself from use as a "divorce mill" and in protecting its judgments from possible collateral attack in other States. In my view, the first two defenses provide no significant support for the statute in question here. Only the third has any real force.

A

With the first justification, the Court seeks to distinguish [earlier] cases. Yet the distinction the Court draws seems to me specious. Iowa's residency requirement, the Court says, merely forestalls access to the courts; applicants seeking welfare payments, medical aid, and the right to vote, on the other hand, suffer unrecoverable losses throughout the waiting period. This analysis, however, ignores the severity of the deprivation suffered by the divorce petitioner who is forced to wait a year for relief. *See Stanley v. Illinois*, 405 U.S. 645, 647 (1972). The injury accompanying that delay is not directly measurable in money terms like the loss of welfare benefits, but it cannot reasonably be argued that when the year has elapsed, the petitioner is made whole. The year's wait prevents remarriage and locks both partners into what may be an intolerable, destructive relationship. * * *

B

I find the majority's second argument no more persuasive. The Court forgoes reliance on the usual justifications for durational residency requirements—budgetary considerations and administrative convenience. * * * The critical importance of the divorce process, however, weakens the argument for a long residency requirement rather than strengthens it. The impact of the divorce decree only underscores the necessity that the State's regulation be evenhanded.

It is not enough to recite the State's traditionally exclusive responsibility for regulating family law matters; some tangible interference with the State's regulatory scheme must be shown. Yet in this case, I fail to see how any legitimate objective of Iowa's divorce regulations would be frustrated by granting equal access to new state residents. To draw on an analogy, the States have great interests in the local voting process and wide latitude in regulating that process. Yet one regulation that the States may not impose is an unduly long residency requirement. * * *

C

The Court's third justification seems to me the only one that warrants close consideration. Iowa has a legitimate interest in protecting itself against invasion by those seeking quick divorces in a forum with relatively lax divorce laws, and it may have some interest in avoiding collateral attacks on its decree in other States. These interests, however, would adequately be protected by a simple requirement of domicile—physical presence plus intent to remain—which would remove the rigid one-year barrier while permitting the State to restrict the availability of its divorce process to citizens who are genuinely its own.

* * *

For several reasons, the year's waiting period seems to me neither necessary nor much of a cushion. First, the *Williams* opinion was not aimed at States seeking to avoid becoming divorce mills. Quite the opposite, it was rather plainly directed at States that had cultivated a "quickie divorce" reputation by playing fast and loose with findings of domicile. If Iowa wishes to avoid becoming a haven for divorce seekers, it is inconceivable that its good-faith determinations of domicile would not meet the rather lenient full faith and credit standards set out in *Williams*.

A second problem with the majority's argument on this score is that *Williams* applies only to *ex parte* divorces. This Court has held that if both spouses were before the divorcing court, a foreign State cannot recognize a collateral challenge that would not be permissible in the divorcing State. *Sherrer v. Sherrer*, 334 U.S. 343 (1948). Therefore, the Iowa statute sweeps too broadly even as a defense to possible collateral attacks, since it imposes a one-year requirement whenever the respondent does not reside in the State, regardless of whether the proceeding is *ex parte*.

Third, even a one-year period does not provide complete protection against collateral attack. It merely makes it somewhat less likely that a second State will be able to find "cogent evidence" that Iowa's determination of domicile was incorrect. But if the Iowa court has erroneously determined the question of domicile, the year's residence will do nothing to preclude collateral attack under *Williams*.

* * * In sum, concerns about the need for a long residency requirement to defray collateral attacks on state judgments seem more fanciful than real. If, as the majority assumes, Iowa is interested in assuring itself that its divorce petitioners are legitimately Iowa citizens, requiring petitioners to provide convincing evidence of bona fide domicile should be more than adequate to the task.

* * *

NOTES AND QUESTIONS

1. *Reasons for residency requirements.* Residency is only one element of domicile, so satisfying durational residency requirements does not necessarily suffice to establish domiciliary status. Given the full faith and credit requirements of domicile, why do states retain separate residency periods for divorce?

2. *Iowa or Nevada?* Many mid-twentieth century decisions concerning divorce jurisdiction involve a spouse who ran to Nevada for a divorce. Nevada's six-week residency requirement is still viewed as fairly short, but that state is no longer the quickest place for divorce. As of early 2008, Alaska, Massachusetts, South Dakota, and Washington did not impose any minimum period of residency before divorce, Nevada requires only six weeks' residency, and some states only require 60 or 90 days of state residency. *Chart 4: Grounds for Divorce and Residency Requirements*, 41 Fam. L.Q. 709, 713 (2008). Absence of a residency requirement essentially means that a spouse with money can travel to one of these states, instantly declare domicile, file for divorce, and then re-establish domicile in the original state. But while a number of states have eliminated the residency requirement or implemented more lenient requirements, some states continue to impose stringent residen-

cy requirements. For example, in *Barth v. Barth*, 862 N.E.2d 496 (Ohio 2007), the Ohio Supreme Court held that a wife seeking a divorce did not meet the state's six-month residency requirement when she had moved to California for a little over a month to join her husband, and returned to Ohio and then immediately filed for divorce. Do you agree with the *Sosna* majority or the dissent? Should states retain their residency requirements for divorce? Why or why not?

3. *Service of process.* As in all civil litigation, to obtain jurisdiction, the plaintiff must serve the defendant in accordance with the applicable statutory requirements. In most states, service of process may be made on an individual outside the jurisdiction either by personal service or by mailing a copy of the summons and complaint to the individual by registered or certified mail, return receipt requested. At a minimum, due process requires that notice be reasonably calculated, under all the circumstances, to apprise interested parties of the pendency of the action and afford them an opportunity to be heard. Some jurisdictions explicitly allow service by publication in domestic relations cases when the defendant cannot be located. For example, the Washington statute provides:

> When the defendant cannot be found within the state, and upon the filing of an affidavit of the plaintiff * * * stating that he believes that the defendant is not a resident of the state, or cannot be found therein, and that he has deposited a copy of the summons * * * and complaint in the post office, directed to the defendant at his place of residence, unless it is stated in the affidavit that such residence is not known to the affiant * * * the service may be made by publication * * * : * * * When the action is for [divorce] in the cases prescribed by law[.]

Wash. Rev. Code Ann. § 4.28.100 (West 2008). Does this statute adequately protect the interests at stake in divorce?

D. COVENANT MARRIAGE

Under covenant marriage statutes in Louisiana, Arizona and Arkansas, a small number of couples have agreed to a marriage with strong restraints against divorce (discussed *supra*, Chapter 8, at p. 460). The question then arises as to whether one spouse may file for conventional divorce in a state that has not adopted a covenant marriage statute.

While running to another state to obtain divorce seems to resemble a *Williams*-type dilemma, establishing residency and domiciliary status in the second state is not the problem in covenant marriage cases. The problem instead concerns the specific provisions of the covenant marriage itself; for example, in Louisiana, the couples agree that Louisiana law will control their marriage. Many commentators see no reason to give covenant marriage less deference than any other issue requiring application of another state's laws:

> "The right of each state to experiment with rules of its own choice for governing matrimonial and social life" is one of the basic tenets of American federalism. In exercising this right, Louisiana concluded

that the free availability of unilateral no-fault divorce is a serious enough social problem to warrant the use of some new alternatives. * * * [O]ther states may be able to draw valuable conclusions by watching this experiment. For this to be possible, however, the experiment must be allowed to work. The experiment cannot work if it can be defeated by a short trip across the border. In engaging in this experiment, Louisiana does not seek to impose its value judgments on citizens of other states, nor does it deny the right of other states to insist on their value judgments in cases involving their own citizens. The question is simply one of delineating the respective states' spheres of law-making competence. * * *

Katherine Shaw Spaht & Symeon C. Symeonides, *Covenant Marriage and the Law of Conflict of Laws*, 32 Creighton L. Rev. 1085, 1120 (1999) (quoting Williams I). Thus, regardless of the couple's intent to create a covenant marriage with strict requirements for divorce, covenant marriage still may not prevent one spouse from traveling to another state to take advantage of that state's no-fault divorce laws. The second state, because of its connection to the divorce petitioner, appears likely to apply its own laws instead of the covenant marriage laws. *See* Peter Hay, *The American "Covenant Marriage" in the Conflict of Laws*, 64 La. L. Rev. 43, 62 (2003).

QUESTIONS

In applying its divorce laws, should a state be required to respect other states' conceptions of "covenant marriage"? Why or why not? Are the same policy concerns applicable to respect for same-sex marriage? This issue is discussed next.

E. JURISDICTION OVER PROCEEDINGS INVOLVING CIVIL UNIONS OR SAME–SEX MARRIAGES

As you know from Chapter 3, an increasing number of states are according legal status to same-sex unions. As of early 2009, several states permit same-sex couples to marry. California permitted same-sex marriage from June until November 2008, when voters approved a ballot measure to restore the prohibition on same-sex marriage. California and four other states now grant state-level spousal rights to same-sex couples through civil unions or domestic partnerships. In addition, Hawaii, Maine, and Washington offer some state-level spousal rights. Forty-five states have some prohibition against marriage for same-sex couples. Human Rights Campaign, Maps of State Laws and Policies, *available at* www.hrc.org/maps.

Given the variety of state approaches toward same-sex marriages and civil unions, it is unclear what most states will do when they are presented with issues arising from the dissolution of such unions. The following examples from New York illustrates possible approaches.

In *Langan v. St. Vincent's Hosp.*, 765 N.Y.S.2d 411 (Sup.Ct. 2003), a lower court honored John Langan's legal status as Neal Spicehandler's "spouse" after the two were joined in a Vermont civil union. In a wrongful death suit based on Spicehandler's death, the court held that New York must provide Langan with the regular compensation that a spouse would receive under the state's wrongful death statute. New York itself does not permit civil unions or same-sex marriages, but the court held that both full faith and credit and equal protection analysis required the state to recognize Vermont's civil unions and provide the wrongful death recovery. However, on appeal, the decision was reversed, with the appellate court holding that New York was not required to accord the same rights and benefits to a civil union couple as to a married couple. Langan v. St. Vincent's Hosp., 802 N.Y.S.2d 476, 479–80 (App. Div. 2005).

Following *Langan* and a number of other cases involving same-sex marriage, New York Governor David Paterson issued an executive order to the heads of the state's government agencies requiring them to recognize same-sex marriages performed outside the state.

That memo stated, in part:

[A]gencies that do not afford comity or full faith and credit to same-sex marriages that are legally performed in other jurisdictions could be subject to liability. In addition, extension of such recognition is consistent with State policy. In April 2007, the Department of Civil Service extended recognition to same-sex spouses in legal marriages from other jurisdictions for purposes of spousal benefits under the New York Health Insurance Program. * * *

As a result of the above, it is now timely to conduct a review of your agency's policy statements and regulations, and those statutes whose construction is vested in your agency, to ensure that terms such as "spouse," "husband" and "wife" are construed in a manner that encompasses legal same-sex marriages, unless some other provision of law would bar your ability to do so. * * *

In many instances, comity can be extended to legal same-sex marriages through an internal memorandum or policy statement directing staff on the construction of relevant terms in statute or regulation. In other cases, regulatory changes may be necessary.

Currently, same-sex marriages are legal in Canada, South Africa, Spain, Belgium, the Netherlands and Massachusetts. Some decisional law in Massachusetts has called into question whether individuals domiciled in states where same-sex marriage is not legally recognized may marry in Massachusetts. Nonetheless, when a Massachusetts official vested with legal authority, such as a clerk, has recognized such marriage, it should be afforded the same recognition as any other legally performed union.

While New York has decided to recognize same-sex marriages from another jurisdiction, other states have responded in different ways. *Miller–Jenkins v. Miller Jenkins*, a case involving an interstate child custody dispute and the dissolution of a civil union, illustrates another way that states may react when deciding how to recognize the results of same-sex marriages and civil unions. This case is discussed in more detail later in the Chapter.

QUESTIONS

1. *What rights?* Even if a state does not allow its own residents to enter into same-sex marriage or civil unions, why might it accord rights to members of such couples? Why not?

2. *The relevance of the parties' residence.* In deciding whether to recognize a civil union or same-sex marriage, should a state consider the parties' residence at the time of the union? For example, if two residents of a state that does not permit civil unions are lawfully united in another state, should the validity of that union be evaluated differently than if they had both resided in the other state at the time of their union? *See* Linda Silberman, *Current Debates in the Conflict of Laws: Recognition and Enforcement of Same–Sex Marriage: Same–Sex Marriages: Refining the Conflict of Laws Analysis*, 153 U. Pa. L. Rev. 2195 (2005).

F. COMITY

The New York Executive Order emphasizes the possibility of granting "comity" to same-sex marriages from other jurisdictions. As the next decision shows, comity has been an important concept in recognizing decrees from other countries, supplementing the constitutional obligations of granting full faith and credit to another state's orders.

CASON v. CASON

Circuit Court of Virginia.
2001 WL 1830006 (Oct. 16, 2001)[1].

NEY, J.

* * *

Elfenesh Cason married Gerald Cason on August 4, 1964 in Ethiopia. Mr. Cason, a noncommissioned officer in the United States Army, traveled frequently and was often stationed overseas. After his marriage, Elfenesh Cason accompanied him on his various assignments, including tours of duty in Germany and Italy. In 1975, Mr. Cason was stationed at Fort Belvoir in Northern Virginia and he and Elfenesh moved to Fairfax County where they purchased a home * * *.

---

1. Unreported opinion.

On October 25, 1975 the parties separated.

Win–Win Cho testified that she met Gerald Cason in 1975 when he was in Taiwan, Republic of China. She testified that she socialized with him but told him that she would not become involved with a married man. * * *

[Mr. Cason obtained a divorce in the Dominican Republic.]

Mr. Cason returned to Taiwan where, according to Win–Win Cho, he had his Dominican Republic divorce decree literally in hand. She and Mr. Cason were married on July 9, 1976, three days after his return to Taiwan. After the marriage, the parties moved to Tacoma Park, Maryland where they lived with Mr. Cason's sister.

On December 1, 1976, this Court entered an agreed Order for Temporary Support. The order required Gerald Cason to pay to Elfenesh Cason support in the amount of $100 per month and, in addition, to provide all mortgage and other operating costs of the * * * home. He was also to pay for food for Elfenesh Cason. The Order did not state whether the parties were married or not married.

In May of 1989, Gerald Cason drafted a will naming Win–Win Cho (Cason) as his wife, and heir to his property. That same year Win–Win Cho (Cason) became ill and returned to Taiwan to live with her family. She did not resume living with Mr. Cason at any time in the eight years prior to his death.

In 1993, Gerald Cason and Elfenesh Cason obtained a joint loan from the Fairfax County Department of Housing & Community Development for improvements to their residence. In a letter to the Department, Gerald Cason asserted that the couple wanted to add "two one-bedroom in-law apartments" to their home, as "[we] intend to move our Mothers and Fathers in with us." A Deed of Trust securing the loan was executed in the names of "Gerald Cason and Elfenesh Cason, husband and wife" and placed of record. * * *

[At a trial arising out of questions concerning Gerald Cason's estate,] Mr. Al Wood testified that he and Gerald Cason first met during their service in Vietnam and were in contact throughout the years. They acted as employer-employee in a local company after their army service, and they met a few times a year as friends. Mr. Wood testified that during the time that he and Gerald were friends, Gerald never told him that he had obtained a divorce, or that he had left Elfenesh Cason, even though they discussed Elfenesh on occasion. Mr. Wood testified that his wife and Elfenesh Cason were friends and that during the period from 1976 to 1986 Mrs. Wood was in constant contact with Elfenesh Cason. Mrs. Wood never said anything to her husband that might have suggested that she believed that Elfenesh Cason and Gerald Cason were divorced. Mr. Wood testified that he never met Win–Win Cho (Cason).

In 1997, Gerald * * * was killed in an automobile accident in Missouri.

* * *

Elfenesh Cason testified that she had never heard of 'Win–Win Cason' until after Gerald had died.

Elfenesh Cason contends that the divorce obtained in the Dominican Republic is invalid on multiple grounds, that Gerald Cason continued to present himself as her husband up until the time of his death, and that she had no knowledge until after his death that Gerald Cason ever attempted to obtain a divorce from her. Win–Win Cho (Cason) argues that in Virginia there is a rebuttable presumption that a second marriage is valid, and that this Court should recognize as valid the Dominican Republic divorce.

ANALYSIS

Validity of the Dominican Republic Divorce

Win–Win Cho (Cason) relies upon the Dominican divorce decree to invalidate the marriage of Elfenesh and Gerald Cason, thereby validating her own marriage to Gerald Cason. This Court is not required to recognize foreign decrees; however, it may choose to do so under principles of comity.

> "Comity", in the legal sense, is neither a matter of absolute obligation, on the one hand, nor one of mere courtesy and good will, upon the other. But it is the recognition which one nation allows within its territory to the legislative, executive or judicial acts of another * * * having due regard both to international duty and convenience, and to the rights of its own citizens or of other persons who are under the protection of its laws.

Oehl v. Oehl, [272 S.E.2d 441, 443 (Va.] 1980). Courts in Virginia may look behind a foreign decree and make an independent determination as to the sufficiency of the foreign order. Three factors come into play in such an analysis—domicile, notice, and consent.

a. Domicile

Under Virginia law, "each state has exclusive control of the matrimonial status of those domiciled within its borders." [*Howe v. Howe,* 18 S.E. 2d 294, 297 (Va.] 1942). Domicile requirements are jurisdictional in Virginia.

> [Domicile] as used in statutes dealing in divorce, contemplates intention to live in the adopted home permanently or certainly for an indefinite period. *Abiding in one place for a definite time, until the accomplishment of a certain purpose, unaccompanied by any intention to remain permanently or indefinitely, is not sufficient to give a person statutory residence.*

[*Id.*]

* * *

The law of the Dominican Republic explicitly addresses domicile. Under Dominican Republic law, the appropriate court to dissolve a marriage "is that of the domicile of the defendant if a resident of the Republic, otherwise the domicile of the plaintiff. Domicile is considered to be bona fide residence in the Republic."

At no time did Gerald Cason or Elfenesh Cason reside or establish domicile within the Dominican Republic. The divorce decree from the Dominican Republic states "Gerald Cason, of legal age, married, *US Citizen, domiciled and resident in United States* of America…" (Emphasis added.) Domicile was not established by Gerald Cason in the Dominican Republic.

b. Notice

There is no clear evidence before the Court as to whether or not Gerald Cason provided any notice to his wife. At best, the evidence is in conflict. The divorce decree recites that notice was given. Yet, Elfenesh Cason testified that she never received any notice, written or otherwise, pertaining to any divorce. She stated that she never even heard of the Dominican Republic divorce until after Gerald Cason's death.

* * *

* * * Ms. Cason said she had no notice. There was no evidence that she responded to the divorce action. No other evidence of notice was offered beyond the recital in the decree. On balance, the weight of the evidence defeats the notion that notice was given.

c. Consent

In order for a nonresident foreigner to obtain a valid divorce in the Dominican Republic, both parties must consent to the divorce. * * *

For the Dominican Republic court to obtain jurisdiction, the absent defendant

> must execute a power of attorney in the presence of a Notary Public or a Dominican Consul… This power of attorney provides evidence to the Dominican court that the non-appearing spouses accept the jurisdiction of that court.

* * *

Therefore, under the laws of the Dominican Republic, Elfenesh Cason must have consented to the divorce for it to be valid. The evidence is absolutely uncontradicted—both from the Divorce Decree itself and from her testimony—that she did not so consent. Without her doing so, the divorce is invalid under the laws of the Dominican Republic and will not be recognized by this Court.

Finally, the Dominican divorce lacks 'any indicia of reliability'. Gerald Cason was a member of the Army, and later a contractor to the military, and as such, had to travel on a frequent basis. When he left to go overseas, Elfenesh Cason knew only that he was going to work. She had no knowledge of his visit to the Dominican Republic or of his intention to attempt to obtain a divorce there. Under the laws of the Dominican Republic and in conjunction with the public policy of this Commonwealth, she was entitled to notice of the proceedings or had to give her consent to them. Neither notice nor consent occurred.

* * *

CONCLUSION

In summary, the Court finds the Dominican Republic divorce to be a nullity and void. As a result, Gerald Cason could not have lawfully married Win–Win Cho. Additionally, the Court finds that there is sufficient evidence to overcome any presumption that Gerald Cason was married to Win–Win Cho. The Court finds that the evidence is clear that Elfenesh Cason and Gerald Cason were lawfully married at the time of his death.

* * *

NOTES AND QUESTIONS

1. *Strength of comity.* The doctrine of "comity" is based on respect for the sovereignty of other states or countries. Even when the forum state is not required to recognize a judgment issued by a foreign jurisdiction, the forum state may do so pursuant to the principles of comity. As a matter of respect, convenience, and expediency, there is a strong presumption in favor of recognizing foreign judicial decrees. 44B Am. Jur. 2d, Int'l Law § 8 (2008).

2. *Policies of comity.* The comity doctrine seeks to support pre-existing expectations, but how do courts treat foreign degrees that violate U.S. law? Would a U.S. court, for example, grant a divorce to the second wife of a man who has three wives, if bigamous marriages are lawful in the country where the parties married?

3. *Virginia precedents concerning comity.* In an earlier decision, the Virginia Supreme Court had held that comity should be granted to the orders of any "foreign court of competent jurisdiction, entered in accordance with the procedural and substantive law prevailing in its judicatory domain, when that law, in terms of moral standards, societal values, personal rights, and public policy, is reasonably comparable to that of Virginia." *Oehl v. Oehl*, 272 S.E.2d 441, 444 (Va. 1980). Did *Cason* properly apply this holding?

SECTION 3:   JURISDICTION OVER ALIMONY AND PROPERTY DISTRIBUTION

Although a divorce decree can be granted without personal jurisdiction over both parties, issues concerning alimony awards and distribution of property present different jurisdictional issues.

A.   PERSONAL JURISDICTION REQUIREMENT FOR ALIMONY AND PROPERTY DISTRIBUTION

Divorce is available based on one spouse's domicile, regardless of whether a court has personal jurisdiction over both spouses, but a court may award alimony or property distribution only where it has personal jurisdiction over both spouses.

Estin v. Estin, 334 U.S. 541 (1948), was the Supreme Court's first discussion of personal jurisdiction in the alimony-property distribution context. Gertrude and Joseph Estin married and then separated in New York. Gertrude Estin sued her husband in a New York court, and, after Mr. Estin appeared, the court granted the wife a separation decree that included an award of permanent alimony. The husband subsequently moved to Nevada, obtained an absolute divorce—which did not provide for the payment of alimony—and stopped paying alimony. The Supreme Court upheld the validity of the husband's divorce judgment, but found that only a court with personal jurisdiction over the wife could change the New York alimony decree's effect:

> In this case New York evinced a concern with this broken marriage when both parties were domiciled in New York and before Nevada had any concern with it. New York was rightly concerned lest the abandoned spouse be left impoverished and perhaps become a public charge. The problem of her livelihood and support is plainly a matter in which her community had a legitimate interest. The New York court, having jurisdiction over both parties, undertook to protect her by granting her a judgment of permanent alimony. Nevada, however, apparently follows the rule that dissolution of the marriage puts an end to a support order. But the question is whether Nevada could under any circumstances adjudicate rights of respondent under the New York judgment when she was not personally served or did not appear in the proceeding.

* * *

> The New York judgment is a property interest of respondent, created by New York in a proceeding in which both parties were present. It imposed obligations on petitioner and granted rights to respondent. The property interest which it created was an intangible,

jurisdiction over which cannot be exerted through control over a physical thing. Jurisdiction over an intangible can indeed only arise from control or power over the persons whose relationships are the source of the rights and obligations.

Id. at 547–48. *Estin* thus recognized the jurisdictional concept of "divisible divorce," which treats property, support and custodial rights arising from marriage differently than the marital status itself.

In 1957, the Court extended the divisible divorce doctrine to instances in which support rights had not been established by a support order prior to the divorce. In *Vanderbilt v. Vanderbilt*, 354 U.S. 416 (1957), the Court held that a state with the requisite jurisdictional contacts may grant support to an ex-spouse, even after another state had issued a valid divorce decree. During the marriage, the couple had resided in California; the wife moved to New York after the parties separated. Mr. Vanderbilt secured a final divorce in Nevada, without serving process on his wife and without her appearance. Mrs. Vanderbilt then sued in New York for separation and maintenance, sequestering Mr. Vanderbilt's New York property to satisfy personal jurisdiction. The Court rejected the husband's argument that New York had no jurisdiction to order support after dissolution of the spouses' marriage:

> Since the wife was not subject to its jurisdiction, the Nevada divorce court had no power to extinguish any right which she had under the law of New York to financial support from her husband. It has long been the constitutional rule that a court cannot adjudicate a personal claim or obligation unless it has jurisdiction over the person of the defendant. Here, the Nevada divorce court was as powerless to cut off the wife's support right as it would have been to order the husband to pay alimony if the wife had brought the divorce action and he had not been subject to the divorce court's jurisdiction.

Id. at 418–19.

As the following decision shows, state courts continue to use the principles enunciated in *Estin* and *Vanderbilt* to decide cases involving "divisible divorces."

SNIDER v. SNIDER

Supreme Court of Appeals of West Virginia, 2001.
551 S.E.2d 693.

S<small>TARCHER</small>, J<small>USTICE</small>:

* * * [W]e are asked to examine the jurisdiction of a circuit court to award alimony to the appellee and to equitably divide the parties' marital property, when one party to the marriage had previously been granted a divorce decree in a foreign jurisdiction. The appellant, who obtained a divorce in a jurisdiction that could not assert personal jurisdiction over the appellee, contends that the foreign divorce decree voided West Virginia's jurisdiction to adjudicate the parties' property interests. In sum, the appellant argues that the foreign decree extinguished West Virginia's personal jurisdiction over the appellant, and its subject matter jurisdiction over any interests incidental to the parties' marriage.

* * *

The parties to the instant divorce action are the appellant, Mr. Snider, and the plaintiff below and appellee, Rebecca C. Snider. The parties were married on January 20, 1973, in Garrett County, Maryland. * * *

* * * [F]rom 1987 until 1993, Mr. Snider was employed by a glass company in New Jersey.

During the marriage, Ms. Snider was an "at-home mom," raising the children, cooking, and cleaning. Ms. Snider was also charged with arranging for the selling of each house and packing up its contents whenever Mr. Snider took a job in another state.

At some time during 1993, a colleague of Mr. Snider moved to a new job in Elgin, Illinois, and asked Mr. Snider to join him. Mr. Snider apparently agreed to seek a new job with a glass company in Illinois.

Shortly thereafter, in January 1994, the parties traveled to West Virginia to visit with Ms. Snider's family. During the visit, Mr. Snider inspected a townhouse that was being offered for sale in Bridgeport, West Virginia. Mr. Snider informed his wife that he liked the townhouse, and would like to live there when he retired. After several weeks, the parties returned to New Jersey, contacted a realtor, and placed their New Jersey home on the market. The parties also made an offer to purchase the townhouse in West Virginia.

In March 1994, Mr. Snider began working as a consultant, ostensibly under a 6–month contract, for a glass company in Elgin, Illinois. During his time in Illinois, Mr. Snider lived in a motel at company expense. Three months later, the parties were able to complete the purchase of the townhouse in Bridgeport, West Virginia. Mr. Snider arranged the financing for the townhouse, by phone, with a bank in West Virginia.

During the Thanksgiving and Christmas 1994 holidays, the parties spent time in the West Virginia townhouse with other family members. * * *

Ms. Snider contends that, throughout 1995 and 1996, Mr. Snider would routinely stay with her for extended weekends, 3 and 4 days at a time, and for several weeks around holidays, at the townhouse in Bridgeport. * * *

In January and again in April 1997, Mr. Snider visited his wife in Bridgeport, and informed her he was retiring—and returning to West Virginia—in July. Unfortunately, in June 1997, Mr. Snider announced that he wanted a divorce.

Mr. Snider filed for divorce in the Circuit Court of Kane County, Illinois on October 3, 1997, alleging that the parties had been separated on a continuous basis since March 1994. Ms. Snider countered by filing the instant divorce action in the Circuit Court of Harrison County, West Virginia on October 24, 1997.

The Illinois circuit court granted a "judgment dissolving the parties' marriage" on April 1, 1998. However, the Illinois circuit court did not address any other matters, such as the equitable distribution of the parties' marital property or spousal support.

Mr. Snider then moved to dismiss the West Virginia divorce action, contending that because of the Illinois ruling, the West Virginia courts lacked personal jurisdiction over him. On August 8, 1998, the family law master entered an order rejecting Mr. Snider's motion, concluding that the Illinois courts had exercised jurisdiction only over the marriage of the parties. The family law master ruled that West Virginia courts had jurisdiction over the assets of the parties located in West Virginia, and over Mr. Snider personally due to his numerous contacts with the State of West Virginia.

* * * [T]he circuit court adopted the family law master's findings and conclusions, and ordered the equitable distribution of the marital assets of the parties. The circuit court also required Mr. Snider to pay Ms. Snider $2,500.00 per month in spousal support, and to pay her attorney's fees.

* * *

The appellant, Mr. Snider, argues that the circuit court's order is void because the court had neither personal jurisdiction over Mr. Snider, nor subject matter jurisdiction over the equitable distribution of the parties' marital property and any spousal support.

It is a common occurrence for one party to a marriage to seek a divorce in a jurisdiction that is foreign to the other party. This practice, where one spouse obtains a divorce in a foreign jurisdiction without the participation of the other spouse, is known as an "*ex parte* divorce." Courts examining these occurrences have developed the "divisible divorce" doctrine, thereby allowing courts to separate resolution of the *ex parte* divorce from the resolution of the parties' other marital interests—such as child custody and support, spousal support, and the distribution of marital property. * * *

Jurisdiction over an action to dissolve a marriage may be based on the domicil of just one spouse. However, if a court has jurisdiction over only one spouse but not the other, "the 'divisible divorce' concept permits the court to dissolve the marital relationship of the parties ... without addressing the property rights and obligations of the parties." 24 Am. Jur. 2d Divorce and Separation, § 206 (1998). By allowing one state to grant an *ex parte* divorce of the marriage, and another state with jurisdiction over both parties to address the property rights and obligations of the parties, the interests of both states are accommodated, "restricting each

State to the matters of her dominant concern." *Estin v. Estin,* 334 U.S. 541, 549 (1948).

* * *

* * * [W]e are asked to address the validity of a *preceding* divorce decree that has been obtained *ex parte* in a foreign state, and its effect upon the jurisdiction of a West Virginia court seeking to adjudicate the property rights and obligations of the parties to a marriage.

We begin our analysis by noting that West Virginia courts have jurisdiction over domestic relations actions when at least "one of the parties ... at the time the cause of action arose" has been "an actual bona fide resident of this state and has continued so to be for at least one year next preceding the commencement of the action[.]" W.Va. Code, § 48–2–7(b) [1985]. * * *

In the instant case, the record clearly establishes that Ms. Snider was an actual, *bona fide* resident of West Virginia for more than 1 year prior to the date she filed the instant action. Accordingly, the family law master and the circuit court were correct to find jurisdiction could be asserted over Mr. Snider and, more specifically, his marriage to Ms. Snider.

Mr. Snider contends, however, that he has insufficient contacts with the State of West Virginia, such that personal jurisdiction may not fairly and constitutionally be asserted over him. As we stated in * * * *Pries v. Watt*, 410 S.E.2d 285 ([W.Va.] 1991):

* * *

In order to obtain personal jurisdiction over a nonresident defendant, reasonable notice of the suit must be given the defendant. There also must be a sufficient connection or minimum contacts between the defendant and the forum state so that it will be fair and just to require a defense to be mounted in the forum state.

Mr. Snider asserts that he is a "nonresident defendant," and goes on to argue that he has only minimal contacts with the State of West Virginia.

We reject Mr. Snider's position. The family law master plainly concluded, and the circuit court adopted, as a matter of fact, that Mr. Snider maintained a marital relationship with Ms. Snider in West Virginia, repeatedly leading her and others to believe that the marriage was viable, that the parties would reunite upon his retirement from his job in Illinois, and the marriage would continue indefinitely. Mr. Snider purchased marital real estate—the townhouse—in West Virginia, secured a loan for the property through a West Virginia bank, and lived at the townhouse exclusively when he was in West Virginia. * * *

We therefore hold that the family law master and circuit court correctly found contacts sufficient to constitutionally support the personal jurisdiction of a West Virginia court over Mr. Snider.

Mr. Snider also challenges the subject matter jurisdiction of the circuit court over the issues of spousal support and the equitable distribution of the marital property. * * *

* * * *W. Va. Code*, 48–2–15(a) [(1999)] states, in part, that:

Upon ordering a divorce . . . the court may require either party to pay alimony in the form of periodic installments, or a lump sum, or both, for the maintenance of the other party.

Furthermore, *W. Va. Code*, 48–2–15(b) states, in part, that:

Upon ordering . . . a divorce . . . the court may further order all or any part of the following relief: . . .

(7) When the pleadings . . . raise issues concerning the equitable distribution of marital property . . . the court shall order such relief as may be required to effect a just and equitable distribution of the property and to protect the equitable interests of the parties therein;

. . . .

Mr. Snider argues that, under *W. Va. Code*, 48–2–15, West Virginia courts are only empowered to grant relief "upon ordering a divorce"—and conversely, he argues they cannot grant relief when a foreign jurisdiction, which has jurisdiction over the marriage and personal jurisdiction over one party, grants the party an *ex parte* divorce. * * * In essence, Mr. Snider is arguing that, because he filed his action in Illinois first, Ms. Snider is now compelled to travel to the foreign jurisdiction and submit to its laws and authority to obtain any relief. We disagree.

The consequence of accepting Mr. Snider's position would be that our State, where Ms. Snider is domiciled and where the parties ostensibly maintained their marriage, would be forced by a foreign jurisdiction to abdicate its interest in protecting its own residents—married or otherwise. Furthermore, Ms. Snider would be placed in a manifestly unfair predicament:

On the one hand, she may submit to the jurisdiction of a foreign court, where, as an out-of-state defendant, she is under a distinct disadvantage in seeking to recover alimony. On the other hand, she can disregard the foreign action altogether, thereby foregoing all right to alimony payments in the state of her domicile. Putting any spouse to such a choice is palpably unconscionable.

Altman v. Altman, 386 A.2d 766, 772 ([Md.] 1978) (citations omitted).

The seminal case which generally guides our decision is *Vanderbilt v. Vanderbilt*, 354 U.S. 416 (1957). * * *

* * * As in the instant case, the husband appealed, arguing that the Nevada divorce decree had terminated the wife's right to seek any relief under any other state's laws.

* * * Based on *Vanderbilt*, we can discern a general rule that personal rights, which include property and support rights in domestic relations

cases, may not be adjudicated or extinguished by a court lacking personal jurisdiction over a defendant.

It does not appear from the record that the Illinois court could assert personal jurisdiction over Ms. Snider, and Mr. Snider's counsel makes no argument that it could. While we must give full faith and credit to the Illinois decree insofar as it terminates the marriage of the parties, we hold that the Illinois court was without power to adjudicate the issues of spousal support and the equitable distribution of the parties' marital property. The question remains, however, whether our courts, under *W. Va. Code*, 48–2–15, have the authority to adjudicate those issues.

* * *

The position urged by the appellant—that we construe *W. Va. Code*, 48–2–15 in a manner that allows an *ex parte* foreign divorce decree to oust West Virginia courts of authority to address unresolved domestic relations issues arising within its borders—would produce an absurd and unfair predicament for West Virginia domiciliaries. Such a construction would force West Virginia domiciliaries to submit to the personal jurisdiction of a foreign state to resolve their personal and property rights, or forever waive those rights. * * *

* * * We hold, therefore, that under the divisible divorce doctrine, where a foreign jurisdiction does not have personal jurisdiction over both parties to a marriage, the personal and property rights of the parties may be litigated in West Virginia separately from a divorce decree issued in another jurisdiction. Spousal support and marital property rights, available under *W. Va. Code*, 48–2–15, survive such an *ex parte* foreign divorce decree when the foreign court did not have personal jurisdiction over the defendant in the foreign proceeding.

In sum, we conclude that the family law master and the circuit court properly asserted jurisdiction over the parties, and properly asserted jurisdiction over the spousal support for Ms. Snider and the equitable distribution of the parties' marital property.

* * *

NOTES AND QUESTIONS

1. *Divisible divorce: The traditional effect of an* ex parte *divorce on alimony. Snider's* holding—that the court could award alimony to one spouse even after the other spouse obtained an *ex parte* divorce in another jurisdiction—is not necessarily the rule in other states. Many older decisions have held that the right to request maintenance terminates once one party has obtained a valid *ex parte* divorce. In *Starkey v. Starkey*, 209 So.2d 593 (La. Ct. App. 1967), for example, the court held that regardless of where a divorce is obtained, a spouse has no surviving cause of action for alimony once a valid divorce is granted. *Contra* Lewis v. Lewis, 404 So.2d 1230, 1233 (La. 1981) (''When a needy spouse has not been at fault, he or she has a right to alimony

after divorce, *which shall not be denied on the ground that one spouse obtained a valid divorce in a court of another state or country which had no jurisdiction* over the person of the claimant spouse.") (emphasis added). In *Madden v. Madden*, 269 N.E.2d 89, 94 (Mass. 1971), the court held that "[s]eparate support [under state law] is dependent on the existence of the marriage relation, and termination of that relation by a valid divorce decree rendered in another State entitles the husband to a discharge from his liability for payments which had not become due at the time of the divorce."

2. *Contemporary view*. Most decisions denying alimony after an *ex parte* divorce decree were decided more than 30 years ago. These cases have not been overruled, but more recent decisions tend to award alimony even after one spouse obtains a foreign *ex parte* divorce. In *Scharer v. Scharer*, 2001 WL 1203408 (Conn. Super. Ct. Sept. 17, 2001) (unpublished opinion), for example, the court upheld the husband's California *ex parte* divorce decree because he had established domicile there and thus could file for divorce in the state. However, because California lacked personal jurisdiction over the wife, the Connecticut court did not recognize the California court's alimony order, and held that Connecticut courts, which had personal jurisdiction over both spouses, provided the appropriate forum.

What is the justification for awarding alimony or dividing property after a court in another state has validly dissolved the marriage?

3. *Different standards for divorce and property*. Why should a court have jurisdiction to dissolve a marriage *ex parte*, but be required to have personal jurisdiction over both parties before dividing marital assets and debts?

A NOTE ON OBTAINING PERSONAL JURISDICTION THROUGH LONG–ARM STATUTES

State long-arm statutes expand the availability of personal jurisdiction over parties not physically present within the state. Some states have enacted long-arm statutes that apply specifically to domestic relations matters. For example, New York provides for personal jurisdiction over a non-resident defendant in divorce cases:

> [N]otwithstanding the fact that he or she no longer is a resident or domiciliary of this state, * * * provided that this state was the matrimonial domicile of the parties before their separation, or the defendant abandoned the plaintiff in this state, or the claim for support, alimony, maintenance, distributive awards or special relief in matrimonial actions accrued under he laws of this state or under an agreement executed in this state.

N.Y. C.P.L.R. § 302(b) (McKinney 2008). In addition, all states have enacted the Uniform Interstate Family Support Act (UIFSA), discussed in Section 4, which applies to alimony and child support.

QUESTIONS

Should spousal support long-arm statutes be more restrictive than general long-arm statutes? Should the state court be able to assert jurisdiction over a party who is no longer a resident, cannot be found in that state, or does not own property in the state?

B. LIMITS ON OUT-OF-STATE PROPERTY DISTRIBUTION

The Constitution requires states to give full faith and credit to decisions entered in the courts of other states, but this requirement does not extend to judgments over real property located in other states. Because property distribution is central to many domestic relations cases, this jurisdictional restriction is crucial in dissolution proceedings.

The Supreme Court first addressed this property issue in *Fall v. Eastin*, 215 U.S. 1 (1909). After the husband and wife jointly acquired property in Nebraska, they moved to Washington state where they separated a few years later. The Washington court had personal jurisdiction over both parties, but could not convey land that the couple owned in another state.

Later decisions, however, have held that a court may order disposition of real property located outside the state, provided the judgment is directed at the person rather than the property: "courts with personal jurisdiction over a party are understood to have power to make that party do things with respect to out-of-state property." Rochelle Strub, *Marital Property Division in Divorce Proceedings: Full Faith & Credit Clause and Jurisdiction*, 11 J. Contemp. Legal Issues 220, 222 (2000).

In *Breitenstine v. Breitenstine*, 62 P.3d 587 (Wyo. 2003), for example, the court struggled with its limited jurisdiction over property when it sought to divide the marital estate, including real property. The court could not require the husband to transfer his out-of-state property directly to the wife because it did not have jurisdiction over the real property. Instead, the court held that property must be divided "to the extent necessary to satisfy the judgment hereby awarded in favor of the [wife], provide for the alimony payments herein ordered, provide for the child support payments herein ordered, or to comply otherwise with the orders of this Court." *Id.* at 595. Without directly disposing of the out-of-state property, the court nonetheless was able to make a determination affecting it. Similarly, the Washington Supreme Court upheld a lower court's award of title to an apartment and farm located in Poland. It observed that while "a court in one state does not have power directly to affect title to real property located outside the state" based on the principle that "jurisdiction in rem (directly over the thing itself) exists only in the state where the real property is located," a court may nonetheless "indirectly affect title by means of an in personam decree operating on the person over whom it has jurisdiction." In re Marriage of Kowalewski, 182 P.3d 959, 962 (Wash. 2008). You may remember similar contentious issues from Chapter 9 concerning equitable distribution of marital property.

PROBLEM 16–1

Sally and James have been married for 15 years, and are now seeking a divorce. They have lived in Michigan during the entire marriage. Ten years ago, the couple bought a condominium in Florida as an investment, which they have rented out to families visiting the Orlando area. Sally and James have not been to their condo in seven years, and all their rentals take place through an agent. Which state courts can assert jurisdiction to determine ownership issues of the Florida condo?

SECTION 4: CHILD CUSTODY JURISDICTION

Child custody jurisdiction includes a series of issues concerning where a decree can be entered, when other states must respect that decree, which state may modify that decree, and the international impact of these decisions.

A. WHICH STATE HAS JURISDICTION TO ISSUE A CUSTODY ORDER?

1. THE CONSTITUTIONAL CONTEXT FOR JURISDICTION

Like other civil litigants, child custody litigants must ensure that the court hearing their case has personal jurisdiction. All standards governing personal jurisdiction, and all applications of these standards, must satisfy due process. As discussed above, jurisdiction has a variety of bases, including domicile, consent, physical presence, or the requisite "minimum contacts" with the forum state.

The traditional view of custody jurisdiction was that only a court of the state where the child was domiciled could enter a custody decree. *See* Restatement, Conflict of Laws §§ 1, 17 (1934). Because a custody proceeding was viewed as being in rem, jurisdiction followed the child's location. Barbara Ann Atwood, *Child Custody Jurisdiction and Territoriality*, 52 Ohio St. L.J. 369, 377 (1991). This domicile rule was based on the theory that only the child's domiciliary state could issue a binding judgment. In the following case, the Supreme Court considered issues of child custody jurisdiction. As you read the opinions, considers which bases might be appropriate in order for a court to exercise jurisdiction over a child custody dispute.

MAY v. ANDERSON
Supreme Court of the United States, 1953.
345 U.S. 528.

Mr. Justice Burton delivered the opinion of the Court.

The question presented is whether, in a habeas corpus proceeding attacking the right of a mother to retain possession of her minor children, an Ohio court must give full faith and credit to a Wisconsin decree awarding custody of the children to their father when that decree is obtained by the father in an *ex parte* divorce action in a Wisconsin court which had no personal jurisdiction over the mother. For the reasons hereafter stated, our answer is no.

This proceeding began July 5, 1951, when Owen Anderson, here called the appellee, filed a petition for a writ of habeas corpus in the Probate Court of Columbiana County, Ohio. He alleged that his former wife, Leona Anderson May, here called the appellant, was illegally restraining the liberty of their children, Ronald, Sandra and James, aged, respectively, 12, 8 and 5, by refusing to deliver them to him in response to a decree issued by the County Court of Waukesha County, Wisconsin

* * * * * *

* * * [T]he Probate Court decided that it was obliged by the Full Faith and Credit Clause of the Constitution of the United States to accept the Wisconsin decree as binding upon the mother. Accordingly, proceeding to the merits of the case upon the issues presented by the stipulations of counsel, it ordered the children discharged from further restraint by her. That order has been held in abeyance and the children are still with her.

* * *

* * *

The parties were married in Wisconsin and, until 1947, both were domiciled there. After marital troubles developed, they agreed in December, 1946, that appellant should take their children to Lisbon, Columbiana County, Ohio, and there think over her future course. By New Year's Day, she had decided not to return to Wisconsin and, by telephone, she informed her husband of that decision.

Within a few days he filed suit in Wisconsin, seeking both an absolute divorce and custody of the children. The only service of process upon appellant consisted of the delivery to her personally, in Ohio, of a copy of the Wisconsin summons and petition. Such service is authorized by a Wisconsin statute for use in an action for a divorce but that statute makes no mention of its availability in a proceeding for the custody of children. Appellant entered no appearance and took no part in this Wisconsin proceeding which produced not only a decree divorcing the parties from the bonds of matrimony but a decree purporting to award the custody of the children to their father, subject to a right of their mother to visit them at reasonable times. Appellant contests only the validity of the decree as to custody.

Armed with a copy of the decree and accompanied by a local police officer, appellee, in Lisbon, Ohio, demanded and obtained the children from their mother. The record does not disclose what took place between 1947 and 1951, except that the children remained with their father in Wisconsin until July 1, 1951. He then brought them back to Lisbon and permitted them to visit their mother. This time, when he demanded their return, she refused to surrender them.

Relying upon the Wisconsin decree, he promptly filed in the Probate Court of Columbiana County, Ohio, the petition for a writ of habeas corpus now before us. Under Ohio procedure that writ tests only the immediate right to possession of the children. It does not open the door for the modification of any prior award of custody on a showing of changed circumstances. Nor is it available as a procedure for settling the future custody of children in the first instance.

* * *

* * * [W]e have before us the elemental question whether a court of a state, where a mother is neither domiciled, resident nor present, may cut off her immediate right to the care, custody, management and companionship of her minor children without having jurisdiction over her *in personam*. Rights far more precious to appellant than property rights will be cut off if she is to be bound by the Wisconsin award of custody. * * *

In [earlier cases], this Court upheld the validity of a Nevada divorce obtained *ex parte* by a husband, resident in Nevada, insofar as it dissolved the bonds of matrimony. At the same time, we held Nevada powerless to cut off, in that proceeding, a spouse's right to financial support under the prior decree of another state. In the instant case, we recognize that a mother's right to custody of her children is a personal right entitled to at least as much protection as her right to alimony.

In the instant case, the Ohio courts gave weight to appellee's contention that the Wisconsin award of custody binds appellant because, at the time it was issued, her children had a technical domicile in Wisconsin, although they were neither resident nor present there. We find it unnecessary to determine the children's legal domicile because, even if it be with their father, that does not give Wisconsin, certainly as against Ohio, the personal jurisdiction that it must have in order to deprive their mother of her personal right to their immediate possession.[8]

The judgment of the Supreme Court of Ohio, accordingly, is reversed and the cause is remanded to it for further proceedings not inconsistent with this opinion.

Reversed and remanded.

MR. JUSTICE CLARK, not having heard oral argument, took no part in the consideration or decision of this case.

MR. JUSTICE FRANKFURTER, concurring.

The views expressed by my brother JACKSON make it important that I state, in joining the Court's opinion, what I understand the Court to be deciding and what it is not deciding in this case.

What is decided—the only thing the Court decides—is that the Full Faith and Credit Clause does not require Ohio, in disposing of the custody of children in Ohio, to accept, in the circumstances before us, the disposition made by Wisconsin. The Ohio Supreme Court felt itself so bound. This Court does not decide that Ohio would be precluded from recogniz-

---

8. * * *

The instant case does not present the special considerations that arise where a parent, with or without minor children, leaves a jurisdiction for the purpose of escaping process or otherwise evading jurisdiction, and we do not have here the considerations that arise when children are unlawfully or surreptitiously taken by one parent from the other.

ing, as a matter of local law, the disposition made by the Wisconsin court. For Ohio to give respect to the Wisconsin decree would not offend the Due Process Clause. Ohio is no more precluded from doing so than a court of Ontario or Manitoba would be, were the mother to bring the children into one of these provinces.

Property, personal claims, and even the marriage status (*see, e.g., Sherrer v. Sherrer*, 334 U.S. 343 (1948)), generally give rise to interests different from those relevant to the discharge of a State's continuing responsibility to children within her borders. Children have a very special place in life which law should reflect. Legal theories and their phrasing in other cases readily lead to fallacious reasoning if uncritically transferred to determination of a State's duty towards children. There are, of course, adjudications other than those pertaining to children, as for instance decrees of alimony, which may not be definitive even in the decreeing State, let alone binding under the Full Faith and Credit Clause. Interests of a State other than its duty towards children may also prevail over the interest of national unity that underlies the Full Faith and Credit Clause. But the child's welfare in a custody case has such a claim upon the State that its responsibility is obviously not to be foreclosed by a prior adjudication reflecting another State's discharge of its responsibility at another time. Reliance on opinions regarding out-of-State adjudications of property rights, personal claims or the marital status is bound to confuse analysis when a claim to the custody of children before the courts of one State is based on an award previously made by another State. Whatever light may be had from such opinions, they cannot give conclusive answers.

MR. JUSTICE JACKSON, whom MR. JUSTICE REED joins, dissenting.

The Court apparently is holding that the Federal Constitution prohibits Ohio from recognizing the validity of this Wisconsin divorce decree insofar as it settles custody of the couple's children. In the light of settled and unchallenged precedents of this Court, such a decision can only rest upon the proposition that Wisconsin's courts had no jurisdiction to make such a decree binding upon appellant.

* * *

The Court's decision holds that the state in which a child and one parent are domiciled and which is primarily concerned about his welfare cannot constitutionally adjudicate controversies as to his guardianship. The state's power here is defeated by the absence of the other parent for a period of two months. The convenience of a leave-taking parent is placed above the welfare of the child, but neither party is greatly aided in obtaining a decision. The Wisconsin courts cannot bind the mother, and the Ohio courts cannot bind the father. A state of the law such as this, where possession apparently is not merely nine points of the law but all of them and self-help the ultimate authority, has little to commend it in legal logic or as a principle of order in a federal system.

Nor can I agree on principle with the Court's treatment of the question of personal jurisdiction of the wife. I agree with its conclusion and that of the Ohio courts that Wisconsin never obtained jurisdiction of the person of the appellant in this action and therefore the jurisdiction must be rested on domicile of the husband and children. And I have heretofore expressed the view that such personal jurisdiction is necessary in cases where the domicile is obviously a contrived one or the claim of it a sham. But here the Court requires personal service upon a spouse who decamps before the State of good-faith domicile can make provision for custody and support of the children still legally domiciled within it. Wisconsin had a far more real concern with the transactions here litigated than have many of the divorce-mill forums whose judgments we have commanded their sister states to recognize.

In spite of the fact that judges and law writers long have recognized the similarity between the jurisdictional requirements for divorce and for custody, this decision appears to equate the jurisdictional requirements for a custody decree to those for an *in personam* money judgment. One reads the opinion in vain to discover reasons for this choice, unless it is found in the remark that for the wife "rights far more precious than property will be cut off" in the custody proceeding. The force of this cardiac consideration is self-evident, but it seems to me to reflect a misapprehension as to the nature of a custody proceeding or a revision of the views that have heretofore prevailed. * * *

The difference between a proceeding involving the status, custody and support of children and one involving adjudication of property rights is too apparent to require elaboration. In the former, courts are no longer concerned primarily with the proprietary claims of the contestants for the *"res"* before the court, but with the welfare of the *"res"* itself. Custody is viewed not with the idea of adjudicating rights *in* the children, as if they were chattels, but rather with the idea of making the best disposition possible for the welfare of the children. To speak of a court's "cutting off" a mother's right to custody of her children, as if it raised problems similar to those involved in "cutting off" her rights in a plot of ground, is to obliterate these obvious distinctions. Personal jurisdiction of all parties to be affected by a proceeding is highly desirable, to make certain that they have had valid notice and opportunity to be heard. But the assumption that it overrides all other considerations and in its absence a state is constitutionally impotent to resolve questions of custody flies in the face of our own cases. The wife's marital ties may be dissolved without personal jurisdiction over her by a state where the husband has a genuine domicile because the concern of that state with the welfare and marital status of its domiciliary is felt to be sufficiently urgent. Certainly the claim of the domiciled parent to relief for himself from the leave-taking parent does not exhaust the power of the state. The claim of children as well as the home-keeping parent to have their status determined with reasonable certainty, and to be free from an incessant tug of war between squabbling parents, is equally urgent.

* * *

I fear this decision will author new confusions. The interpretative concurrence, if it be a true interpretation, seems to reduce the law of custody to a rule of seize-and-run. I would affirm the decision of the Ohio courts that they should respect the judgment of the Wisconsin court, until it or some other court with equal or better claims to jurisdiction shall modify it.

[The dissenting opinion of MINTON, J., is omitted.]

NOTES AND QUESTIONS

1. *Jurisdictional concerns in practice.* Five justices joined the *May* opinion; one of them, Justice Frankfurter, also wrote a separate concurrence. According to the various opinions, what was the effect of the father's Wisconsin court decree? Based on *May*, when must a second state honor a first state's custody decree? Must a court in the second state have personal jurisdiction over both parents to issue a custody decree that is valid in the issuing state? Must a court have personal jurisdiction over both parties to issue a custody decree that is valid in a second state?

2. *Lingering effects of* May. *May* lead to considerable debate and criticism, just as Justice Jackson predicted. Many critics agreed with him that "[c]ustody is viewed not with the idea of adjudicating rights in the children, as if they were chattels." Moreover, most state decisions appeared to reject *May* where personal jurisdiction could be obtained over one party. Before the promulgation in 1997 of the Uniform Child Custody Jurisdiction and Enforcement Act (UCCJEA) (which is discussed in the next section), these decisions held that the courts of the state having the most significant connections with the child and the child's family had personal jurisdiction over a parent not residing in that state and could issue a custody order. *See, e.g.*, Robert E. Oliphant, *Jurisdiction in Family Law Matters: The Minnesota Perspective*, 30 Wm. Mitchell L. Rev. 557, 573 (2003). However, the UCCJEA, "like the UCCJA and the PKPA [which are explained *infra*] is based on Justice Frankfurter's concurrence in *May v. Anderson.* * * * [J]urisdiction to make a child custody determination is subject matter jurisdiction * * * " UCCJEA § 201, cmt. 2, 9 U.L.A., pt. IA, 649, 673 (1999).

2. STATE COURTS AND JURISDICTION

Following *May v. Anderson*, a parent unhappy with one state's custody decree could move to another state and seek relitigation of the custody decision. The search for a legislative solution to achieve consistency in interstate jurisdictional child custody disputes resulted in promulgation of the Uniform Child Custody Jurisdiction Act (UCCJA) by the National Conference of Commissioners on Uniform State Law (NCCUSL) in 1968. The American Bar Association approved the Act in the same year. UCCJA, 9 U.L.A., pt. IA, 261, 262 (1999). All 50 states, the District of Columbia, and the U.S. Virgin Islands adopted the Act. UCCJEA, prefatory note, 9 U.L.A. 650.

The UCCJA was drafted, in part, because of states' inability to cooperate in interstate custody matters. Under the UCCJA, a state had jurisdiction to determine child custody if: (1) the state was the child's home state or had been the home state within six months prior to the commencement of the proceedings ("home state jurisdiction"); (2) taking jurisdiction was in the best interest of the child and at least one parent had a significant connection to the state ("significant connection jurisdiction"); (3) the child was present in the state and had been abandoned or abused or was in danger ("emergency jurisdiction"); or (4) no other state had jurisdiction. The UCCJA did not otherwise prioritize these four bases of jurisdiction.

Despite widespread state adoption of the UCCJA, differing interpretations of its provisions produced uncertainty regarding enforcement of custody decisions. The Act also had several other problems. First, the UCCJA gave states jurisdiction to resolve custody and visitation disputes if at least one contestant had a significant connection to the state and the state had the best opportunity to hear all the interested parties and to evaluate all the relevant evidence. This grant essentially allowed an adult to create jurisdiction in a new state simply by moving there with the child, as in *May*. A parent's relocation did not cause the former state to lose jurisdiction immediately, but the new state did acquire jurisdiction relatively shortly thereafter, creating periods when concurrent jurisdiction existed. Second, the UCCJA did not provide mechanisms for enforcing child custody determinations, and did not require courts to give full faith and credit to other states' custody decrees. Other uncertainties in the UCCJA included: whether the forum state must have personal jurisdiction over both parents; what constituted adequate notice to the contestants; and what type of "custody" proceedings were subject to the Act. *See, e.g.,* Russell M. Coombs, *Child Custody and Visitation by Non–Parents Under the New Uniform Child Custody Jurisdiction and Enforcement Act: A Rerun of Seize-and-Run,* 16 J. Am. Acad. Matrim. Law. 1 (1999).

In response to the problems that arose when courts did not feel compelled to give full faith and credit to other states' custody decrees under the UCCJA, Congress enacted the Parental Kidnapping Prevention Act (PKPA) in 1980. Pub. L. No. 96–611, 94 Stat. 3568 (1980) (codified at 28 U.S.C. § 1738A (2006)). Despite its name, the Act is not limited to parental kidnapping cases, but applies to all interstate custody disputes. The PKPA mandates that states give full faith and credit to a custody order that substantially complies with the statute's provisions. The PKPA's language establishing the bases for jurisdiction is almost identical to the UCCJA language. Unlike the UCCJA, however, the PKPA clearly gives preference to home state jurisdiction, and allows another state to exercise jurisdiction only where no state qualifies as a home state. The PKPA further authorizes continuing exclusive jurisdiction in the state where the custody order was issued as long as one parent or the child remains there. The PKPA's provisions are still in effect today and are discussed in more detail later in the Chapter.

The PKPA did not settle all interstate jurisdictional problems. To resolve these issues, the NCCUSL promulgated the Uniform Child Custody Jurisdiction and Enforcement Act (UCCJEA) in 1997. NCCUSL, UCCJEA (draft for approval) (1997), http://www.law.upenn.edu/bll/ulc/fnact 99/1990s/uccjea97.htm. As of mid–2008, 46 states, the District of Columbia, and the U.S. Virgin Islands had adopted the UCCJEA, and it had been introduced in three of the remaining states. The UCCJA remains law in states that have not yet adopted the UCCJEA.

The UCCJEA is designed to: (1) prioritize home-state jurisdiction; (2) clarify emergency jurisdictional issues; (3) clarify the meaning of exclusive continuing jurisdiction for the state that entered the child-custody decree; and (4) specify the types of custody proceedings that are subject to the act. UCCJEA, prefatory note, 9 U.L.A. 650. Portions of the UCCJEA are set out below. As the decisions in this Section show, however, even the UCCJEA and the PKPA together have not yet resolved all jurisdictional issues.

UNIFORM CHILD CUSTODY JURISDICTION & ENFORCEMENT ACT

9 U.L.A., pt. IA, 649 (1999).

§ 102.   Definitions.

* * *

(7) "Home State" means the State in which a child lived with a parent or a person acting as a parent for at least six consecutive months immediately before the commencement of a child-custody proceeding. In the case of a child less than six months of age, the term means the State in which the child lived from birth with any of the persons mentioned. A period of temporary absence of any of the mentioned persons is part of the period.

§ 201.   Initial Child–Custody Jurisdiction.

(a) * * * [A] court of this State has jurisdiction to make an initial child-custody determination only if:

>   (1) this State is the home State of the child on the date of the commencement of the proceeding, or was the home State of the child within six months before the commencement of the proceeding and the child is absent from this State but a parent or person acting as a parent continues to live in this State;

>   (2) a court of another State does not have jurisdiction under paragraph (1), or a court of the home State of the child has declined to exercise jurisdiction on the ground that this State is the more appropriate forum under Section 207 or 208, and:

>   >   (A) the child and the child's parents, or the child and at least one parent or a person acting as a parent, have a significant

connection with this State other than mere physical presence; and

    (B) substantial evidence is available in this State concerning the child's care, protection, training, and personal relationships;

(3) all courts having jurisdiction under paragraph (1) or (2) have declined to exercise jurisdiction on the ground that a court of this State is the more appropriate forum to determine the custody of the child under [other provisions of this Act]; or

(4) no court of any other State would have jurisdiction under the criteria specified in paragraph (1), (2), or (3).

(b) Subsection (a) is the exclusive jurisdictional basis for making a child-custody determination by a court of this State.

(c) Physical presence of, or personal jurisdiction over, a party or a child is not necessary or sufficient to make a child-custody determination.

§ 202.   Exclusive, Continuing Jurisdiction.

(a) Except as otherwise provided in Section 204, a court of this State which has made a child-custody determination consistent with Section 201 or 203 has exclusive, continuing jurisdiction over the determination until:

(1) a court of this State determines that neither the child, nor the child and one parent, nor the child and a person acting as a parent have a significant connection with this State and that substantial evidence is no longer available in this State concerning the child's care, protection, training, and personal relationships; or

(2) a court of this State or a court of another State determines that the child, the child's parents, and any person acting as a parent do not presently reside in this State.

(b) A court of this State which has made a child-custody determination and does not have exclusive, continuing jurisdiction under this section may modify that determination only if it has jurisdiction to make an initial determination under Section 201.

§ 204.   Temporary Emergency Jurisdiction.

(a) A court of this State has temporary emergency jurisdiction if the child is present in this State and the child has been abandoned or it is necessary in an emergency to protect the child because the child, or a sibling or parent of the child, is subjected to or threatened with mistreatment or abuse. * * *

§ 206.   Simultaneous Proceedings.

(a) Except as otherwise provided in Section 204, a court of this State may not exercise its jurisdiction under this [article] if, at the time of the commencement of the proceeding, a proceeding concerning the custody of the child has been commenced in a court of another State having jurisdiction substantially in conformity with this [Act], unless the proceeding has been terminated or is stayed by the court of the other State because a court of this State is a more convenient forum [].

* * *

(c) In a proceeding to modify a child-custody determination, a court of this State shall determine whether a proceeding to enforce the determination has been commenced in another State. If a proceeding to enforce a child-custody determination has been commenced in another State, the court may:

(1) stay the proceeding for modification pending the entry of an order of a court of the other State enforcing, staying, denying, or dismissing the proceeding for enforcement;

(2) enjoin the parties from continuing with the proceeding for enforcement; or

(3) proceed with the modification under conditions it considers appropriate.

9 U.L.A. 657–58, 671, 673–74, 676, 680–81.

In the following case, the court had to decide whether the state had subject matter jurisdiction over child custody issues, despite the fact that it was not the child's "home state" under the UCCJEA. Consider the effect of the preceding UCCJEA sections, as adopted into Texas statutory law, on the reasoning of the appellate court.

IN RE BRILLIANT

Court of Appeals of Texas, 2002.
86 S.W.3d 680.

ANN CRAWFORD MCCLURE, JUSTICE.

* * *

FACTUAL SUMMARY

Kaylee Lynn–Marie Brilliant was born in Massachusetts on June 15, 1999. She was conceived when her mother, Kristen Lynn Fox (Kristen), was a seventeen-year-old high school student. Reginald Brilliant (Regi) is Kaylee's father but he and Kristen have never married. Kristen moved in with Regi in March 1999 and they continued living together [in Massachusetts] until April 16, 2000, when Regi moved to Texas. Regi grew up in El Paso and his family continued to live here. The record reveals that the couple had planned to relocate to El Paso and Regi, an employee of Home Depot, requested a job transfer. When the transfer came through, Regi loaded a U–Haul truck with all of his new family's belongings, except for the clothing Kristen needed to finish the last two months of high school. During their brief separation, Kristen lived with her mother and wrote letters in which she told Regi she was anxious "to start my new life down there with you." As planned, Kristen and Kaylee arrived in El Paso on June 12.

On June 15, 2000, Kristen completed and signed a rental application adding her name to the lease on their apartment. She filled out job applications with Blockbuster and Payless Shoe Source, although neither of these is signed nor dated. Kaylee's immunization records were transferred to an El Paso clinic and Regi discovered that the child's shots had not been kept current. While the record does not indicate when the parties applied for a social security card in Kaylee's name, the Social Security Administration mailed Kaylee's card—postmarked April 1, 2000 to Regi's father's home in El Paso.

Kristen soon expressed displeasure with Texas. She wrote Regi a letter on July 10, telling him "that it just wasn't working out, she was leaving, she and the baby were going back to Massachusetts." Regi filed suit on July 19 and on July 21, he obtained a temporary restraining order preventing Kristen from removing Kaylee from El Paso County. Kristen was served with the restraining order on July 22 but she did not move out of the couple's apartment until July 24, when her mother arrived in town. Kristen and Kaylee stayed in the motel with Kristen's mother until July 27, when all three of them left El Paso for Massachusetts in violation of the restraining order. Kristen and Kaylee spent a total of forty-five days in Texas.

Kristen filed a paternity suit in Massachusetts on August 3. She did not file an answer in the Texas suit but instead [contested jurisdiction].
* * *

* * * [The trial court held that it had jurisdiction and] appointed Regi as sole managing conservator of Kaylee, appointed Kristen as possessory conservator and entered a standard possession order.[1] Child support was fixed at $150 per month. From this order, Kristen [appeals, arguing that] * * * Texas lacked subject matter jurisdiction to make an initial child custody determination under the Uniform Child Custody Jurisdiction and Enforcement Act (UCCJEA) * * *.

* * *

UNIFORM CHILD CUSTODY JURISDICTION AND ENFORCEMENT ACT

* * * Kristen contends that the trial court lacked subject matter jurisdiction to make an initial child custody determination. Generally, there are three jurisdictional elements: (1) jurisdiction over the subject matter; (2) jurisdiction over the person or *res*; and (3) power to render the particular relief awarded. Subject matter jurisdiction is essential to the authority of a court to decide a case; it is never presumed and cannot be waived.

Jurisdiction here is predicated upon the UCCJEA which Texas adopted effective September 1, 1999. The Act was designed to address the

---

1. *Ed.'s note*: According to Texas law, a "managing conservator has the right to establish the child's residence and has primary custody of the child. A possessory conservator typically has visitation rights under the terms and conditions set by the court." *In re* V.L.K., 24 S.W.3d 338, 340 n.1 (Tex. 2000); *see, e.g.*, Tex. Fam. Code Ann. §§ 153.132, 153.192 (Vernon 2005).

"inconsistency of interpretation of the [former] UCCJA and the technicalities of applying the PKPA." *McGuire v. McGuire*, 18 S.W.3d 801, 806 (Tex. App. 2000). The clear purpose of the UCCJEA, like that of the former UCCJA, is to discourage and eliminate child snatching, to avoid jurisdictional competition, to avoid continued relitigation of custody decisions, and to promote cooperation between the states to ensure that a custody decision is rendered in the state that can better determine the best interest of the child.

* * *

Framing the Issue

Both parties agree that Texas was not Kaylee's home state as she had not resided here for the requisite six month period. Kristen contends that Massachusetts has home state status because her 45–day residence in Texas was merely a "temporary absence" as that term is used in [the Texas version of Section 102(7) of the UCCJEA, quoted above]. Regi contends that Kristen "moved" from Massachusetts to Texas so that no parent continued to live in Massachusetts; consequently, neither Texas nor Massachusetts has home state jurisdiction and Texas may assert "significant connections" jurisdiction under [the state version of Section 201(a)(2) of the UCCJEA, quoted above]. We must first consider the meaning of "temporary absence."

Temporary Absence

Kristen claims that she is not and never was a resident of the State of Texas, nor was their daughter. She contends that a temporary absence from the home state does not constitute new residency when the stay is less than six months. * * *

* * *

We are faced here with a situation in which Kristen moved from Massachusetts to Texas. Had she returned to Massachusetts before suit was filed, we might be more inclined to find her absence temporary. But at the time suit was filed in Texas, no one lived in Massachusetts—Kristen, Regi, and Kaylee were all living in Texas. Although Kristen and Kaylee returned to Massachusetts, Kristen was restrained from removing the child from El Paso County. She did so anyway. The UCCJEA was designed to prevent the gamesmanship and forum shopping that has occurred here. Kristen chose to relocate to Texas and although, regrettably, she did not wish to remain, she cannot bootstrap her relocation to a "temporary absence" from Massachusetts by skipping town with the child in direct violation of a court order. Consequently, neither Texas nor Massachusetts had home state jurisdiction.

Kristen argues that Massachusetts has already determined it has home state status and has expressed its intent to exercise jurisdiction. By letter dated August 15, 2000, a judge of the Probate and Family Court

Department, Norfolk Division, advised the associate judge below as follows:

> Given the facts set forth in Ms. Fox's Affidavit, which in pertinent part are essentially undisputed, it would appear that Massachusetts and not Texas is the child's home state under the UCCJA. Massachusetts was the child's home state within six months of the date(s) upon which the actions were filed in each court. It would, therefore, appear that the fact that the mother and child resided briefly in Texas (June July 2000) would not confer subject matter jurisdiction in Texas. Moreover, the child was born in Massachusetts, and mother and the child currently reside in, and have significant lifelong connections to, Massachusetts.
>
> After reviewing the enclosed, and your, [sic] file, I respectfully submit that for the reasons set forth above, you decline to take further action and dismiss the action pending before you in order that any question of subject matter jurisdiction can be put to rest.

* * *

We must next consider whether it was appropriate for Texas to exercise jurisdiction on the basis of significant connections. This necessitates a showing by Regi that (1) the child has no home state or the home state has declined to exercise jurisdiction; (2) it is in the best interest of the child because the child and at least one of its parents have a significant connection with Texas beyond mere physical presence; and (3) there is available in Texas substantial evidence concerning the child's present or future care, protection, training, and personal relationships.

Significant Connections

At the hearing, Regi and his father testified concerning Kaylee's connections to Texas. Bruce Brilliant testified that he has lived in El Paso since 1975 and is employed with United States Customs. He has seven other children besides Regi, five of whom still live at home. These four girls and one boy range from two to eleven years of age. The extended family saw Kaylee on a frequent basis and the children would play together. His home featured "a great big play room and there's nothing but toys." Kaylee had a place in their family and "[s]he loved it there." He also explained Regi's and Kristen's plans to raise their family in Texas:

> [T]hey were going to go ahead and go get a house. As a matter of fact, I had the ticket to bring her down here. And after that, she was going to get a job. And my wife even said I'll go over, pick up the baby, take you to work, bring the baby to the house and the baby can play with the kids all day long.
>
> Q: Was that acceptable to Kristen?
>
> A: Yes.

* * *

Regi testified that Kaylee's medical records were transferred to Texas and that the child was behind in her immunizations. He brought her current "except for the TB. She had an appointment for the 14th, but she wasn't here." The Social Security Administration was advised that Kaylee's residence was in Texas.

As we have noted, Kristen did not appear at the hearing so the record contains only the affidavit attached to her plea to the jurisdiction. In it, she claimed that Regi obtained the temporary restraining order by making fraudulent representations to the court. She also alleged that he had made misrepresentations to her concerning "life in his home state of Texas." The affidavit does not specify what those misrepresentations were, nor did Kristen offer evidence to establish any. With regard to significant connections, she made the following statements without elaboration:

I have lived in Quincy, Massachusetts all of my life and was living in Quincy when I met Reginald Brilliant.

. . .

I was 17 years old when I became pregnant and was living at home with my mother in Quincy, Massachusetts.

When I was six months pregnant, Reginald Brilliant and I moved in together.

We lived together at 81 Island Street, Marshfield, Massachusetts for approximately one year and four months.

. . .

I always had reservations about making such a drastic move [to Texas] with my young baby as I had always been extremely close to my mother; and my ties in Massachusetts, where I had lived all of my life, were very strong.

. . .

I intend to stay in the Commonwealth of Massachusetts permanently.

I have been the sole caretaker of my daughter, Kaylee, since her birth.

Kaylee has become extremely attached to my mother, Lynn Fox, with whom we both live.

Kaylee lived with both of her parents from the time of her birth until April 15, 2000 and again from June 12, 2000 until July 24, 2000. She lived with her mother and her maternal grandmother from mid-April until June 12, 2000. Lynn Fox did not testify in person or by affidavit. There was no evidence presented concerning the environment in Massachusetts, other than that Kaylee's medical care had been neglected. Certainly, evidence of Kaylee's connections to Massachusetts could have been presented but Kristen, electing not to appear, offered nothing more than conclusory comments about her attachments to Massachusetts and her mother, and Kaylee's attachment to her grandmother. We are disinclined to accord much weight to attachments Kaylee may have developed in the months following her return to Massachusetts in July 2000 when the move was in complete and utter disregard of a court order. Moreover, jurisdiction is determined based upon the existing circumstances at the time suit is filed in Texas. We thus conclude that it was in Kaylee's best interest for Texas to assume jurisdiction because she and her father had a significant connection to Texas other than mere physical presence, and, based on the record before us, Texas was a repository of substantial evidence concerning her present or future care, training, and personal relationships. Consequently, Texas was authorized to exercise its jurisdiction based on significant connections. * * *

  * * *

NOTES AND QUESTIONS

  1. *Home state preference.* Which court is correct about the existence of a home state? Why?

  2. *Defining a "custody proceeding."* Courts applying the UCCJA were not consistent in specifying the kinds of custody cases to which it applied. The result was a lack of uniformity among the states in determining what types of proceedings were governed by the Act. The UCCJEA remedies this issue with a comprehensive definition of custody proceedings that "includes a proceeding for divorce, separation, neglect, abuse, dependency, guardianship, paternity, termination of parental rights, and protection from domestic violence, in which the issue may appear." UCCJEA § 102(4), 9 U.L.A., pt. IA, 649, 658 (1999). The UCCJEA explicitly excludes juvenile delinquency actions and adoption cases. Juvenile delinquency proceedings are not "custody proceedings" because they do not relate to civil aspects of access to a child, and adoption cases are excluded because adoption is a specialized area covered by the Uniform Adoption Act promulgated in 1994. 9 U.L.A. 11 (1999).

  3. *Notice.* Under Section 205 of the UCCJEA, a child custody determination is enforceable only where notice and opportunity to be heard have been given to any parent whose parental rights have not been terminated, anyone who has physical custody of the child, or anyone else entitled to notice in child-custody proceedings under state law. Section 108(a) of the Act requires that notice to parties outside the state "must be given in a manner reasonably calculated to give actual notice but may be made by publication if other means are not effective." Because the notice provisions also require that respondents be given an opportunity to be heard, *ex parte* orders (including temporary protection orders related to domestic violence) do not satisfy the UCCJEA's notice provision.

  4. *Emergency jurisdiction.* Expansion of emergency jurisdiction was one of the most significant changes in the UCCJEA. Section 204 was drafted to permit states to codify the common trend in UCCJA and PKPA case law to allow emergency jurisdiction where the child is subjected to or threatened with mistreatment or abuse. The section allows a court to take jurisdiction even without either home state or significant connection jurisdiction. This emergency jurisdiction protects victims who flee across state lines and seek legal relief, even where the children have not been abused. However, the UCCJEA limits emergency jurisdiction to temporary orders, which protect the

child until a state with initial and exclusive jurisdiction enters an order. Where there is no existing child custody decree and no custody proceeding has been filed in the home state (or other state with jurisdiction under Sections 201–203), then an emergency custody determination can become final when the issuing state becomes the child's home state and the order so provides. UCCJEA § 204, cmt., 9 U.L.A. 677. In *Button v. Waite*, 208 S.W.3d 366 (Tenn. 2006), the Tennessee Supreme Court held that the trial court erred in exercising temporary emergency jurisdiction where there was no threat of immediate mistreatment or abuse to the child. The alleged danger to the child was terminating the services of the child's therapist and providing an alternate therapist for her. Should this have been an adequate basis for emergency jurisdiction?

5. *Inconvenient forum and declining jurisdiction.* Section 207 of the UCCJEA allows a court in the state with preferred jurisdiction to decline to exercise jurisdiction if it determines, after considering all relevant factors, that it is an inconvenient forum and that another more appropriate forum exists. Which factors would you consider relevant?

6. *Unclean hands and declining jurisdiction.* Section 208 of the UC-CJEA also requires a court to decline to exercise its jurisdiction when a person seeking to invoke jurisdiction has "engaged in unjustifiable conduct." This provision, codifying the equitable "clean hands doctrine," was designed to ensure that parents who kidnap their children do not subsequently benefit from the abduction. The UCCJEA's exclusive, continuing jurisdiction provision ensures that one state will retain jurisdiction, and reduces the likelihood that one parent will take the child to another jurisdiction in an effort to find a more favorable forum. However, the clean hands provision may apply if, for example, one parent abducts a child and establishes a new home state before the entry of a custody decree. In such a situation, the second state must decline to hear the case. The clean hands doctrine does not apply in cases of emergency jurisdiction. Thus, when a parent flees a state based on a threat of abuse to the child and violates an existing custody decree, the refuge state may not decline jurisdiction if the requirements for emergency jurisdiction have been met.

7. *Uniform Child Abduction Prevention Act (UCAPA).* The UCAPA was promulgated in 2006 in order to provide courts with a means to prevent child abduction even before a custody decree is issued. The court may, on its own, direct that certain child abduction prevention measures be taken; one of the parties or a prosecutor may also petition the court for such measures. The court must have jurisdiction pursuant to the UCCJEA (including emergency jurisdiction). Upon a finding that there is a "credible risk" of abduction, section 8 of UCAPA allows courts to order a range of possible abduction prevention measures, including travel or visitation restrictions. http://www. law.upenn.edu/bll/archives/ulc/ucapa/2006_finalact.htm. As of late 2008, UCA-PA had been enacted in seven states and legislation to adopt it was pending in numerous others.

PROBLEM 16–2

Susan and Brad were married in New York and had a daughter, Mary. The two were later divorced by a New York court, which awarded Susan sole physical and legal custody of Mary, and granted Brad reasonable rights of visitation. Susan moved to Wyoming with Mary, while Brad remained in New York. Several years later, a New York trial court modified the original custody order and awarded Brad sole physical and legal custody of Mary, based on the mother's refusal to encourage Mary to visit her father. Susan then sought custody in a Wyoming court, which dismissed the claim for lack of jurisdiction. Susan appealed. Under the UCCJEA, how should the Wyoming appellate court handle the case?

PROBLEM 16–3

Alison feared that her child's father, Daniel, would abuse both her and their daughter. Alison, Daniel and their child all lived in Kentucky, where a court entered a temporary order for protection from abuse and a temporary custody award to Alison. Alison fled to Maine after Daniel threatened to kill her and their child. As soon as she arrived in Maine, Alison filed a complaint for determination of parental rights and child support. In Kentucky, Daniel filed his own motion to establish physical and legal custody. The Maine court issued a temporary custody order to Alison, who later sought a permanent order. Assuming both jurisdictions have adopted the UCCJEA, did Maine have jurisdiction to issue the temporary custody order? Does Maine have jurisdiction to issue a permanent order? If you were Alison's lawyer, what arguments would you make that Maine has jurisdiction? If you were Daniel's lawyer, what arguments would you make that Kentucky retained jurisdiction? What additional information might you want to have?

PROBLEM 16–4

Carol and Juan were married in Arizona. When Carol was 7 months pregnant, she moved to Texas. Within a month of Carol's departure, Juan sued her in Arizona, seeking custody of the child in advance of her birth. The baby, Dana, was subsequently born in Texas, and, when Dana was four months old, Carol filed a custody action in Texas. What arguments might the mother and father each make in the Texas courts? In the Arizona courts?

B. WHEN MUST A STATE GIVE FULL FAITH AND CREDIT TO ANOTHER STATE'S CUSTODY DECREE?

A custody order validly issued in one state should be enforceable in other states. Indeed, enforcement of custody determinations is seemingly required by federal law under the PKPA. Moreover, the UCCJEA also requires that states enforce a custody determination that is consistent with the PKPA. UCCJEA § 303, cmt., 9 U.L.A., pt. IA, 690–91 (1999). The UCCJEA not only establishes when a court has initial jurisdiction, but also when a court must give full faith and credit to proceedings in another state; the PKPA, which is federal law, provides a uniform law concerning full faith and credit, not initial jurisdiction. As mentioned earlier, however, notwithstanding the PKPA and the UCCJEA, jurisdictional conflicts may still occur. Two courts in different states can each assert that they are appropriately exercising jurisdiction, with each asserting that another state must give full faith and credit to the resulting custody decree.

1. THE PARENTAL KIDNAPPING PREVENTION ACT

As discussed above, the Parental Kidnapping Prevention Act (PKPA) requires states to give full faith and credit to other states' child custody determinations. Pub. L. No. 96–611, 94 Stat. 3568 (1980) (codified at 28 U.S.C. § 1738A (2006)). The PKPA establishes a hierarchy of jurisdictional bases; requires states to enforce orders issued by the court in the state with preferred jurisdiction; and prohibits a court from exercising initial jurisdiction when a valid custody proceeding is pending in another state.

PARENTAL KIDNAPPING PREVENTION ACT

28 U.S.C. § 1738A (2006).

§ 1738A. Full faith and credit given to child custody determinations

(a) The appropriate authorities of every state shall enforce according to its terms * * * any custody determination or visitation determination made consistently with the provisions of this section by a court of another State.

* * *

(c) A child custody or visitation determination made by a court of a State is consistent with the provisions of this section only if—

(1) such court has jurisdiction under the law of such State; and

(2) one of the following conditions is met:

(A) such State (i) is the home State of the child on the date of the commencement of the proceeding, or (ii) had been the child's home State within six months before the date of the commencement of the proceeding and the child is absent from such State because of his removal or retention by a contestant or for other reasons, and a contestant continues to live in such State;

(B) (i) it appears that no other State would have jurisdiction under subparagraph (A), and (ii) it is in the best interest of the child that a court of such State assume jurisdiction because (I) the child and his parents, or the child and at least one contestant, have a significant connection with such State other than mere physical presence in such State, and (II) there is available in such State substantial evidence concerning the child's present or future care, protection, training, and personal relationships;

(C) the child is physically present in such State and (i) the child has been abandoned, or (ii) it is necessary in an emergency to protect the child because the child, a sibling, or parent of the child has been subjected to or threatened with mistreatment or abuse;

(D) (i) it appears that no other State would have jurisdiction under subparagraph (A), (B), (C), or (E), or another State has declined to exercise jurisdiction on the ground that the State whose jurisdiction is in issue is the more appropriate forum to determine the custody or visitation of the child, and (ii) it is in the best interest of the child that such court assume jurisdiction; or

(E) the court has continuing jurisdiction pursuant to subsection (d) of this section.

(d) The jurisdiction of a court of a State which has made a child custody or visitation determination consistently with the provisions of this section continues as long as the requirement of subsection (c)(1) of this section continues to be met and such State remains the residence of the child or of any contestant.

* * *

(f) A court of a State may modify a determination of the custody of the same child made by a court of another State, if—

(1) it has jurisdiction to make such a child custody determination; and

(2) the court of the other State no longer has jurisdiction, or it has declined to exercise such jurisdiction to modify such determination.

* * *

2. THE UCCJEA'S ENFORCEMENT PROVISIONS

The provisions of Article 3 of the UCCJEA create a duty to enforce and, unlike the UCCJA, also provide several enforcement remedies for interstate custody determinations.

UNIFORM CHILD CUSTODY JURISDICTION AND ENFORCEMENT ACT

9 U.L.A., pt. IA, 649, 690 (1999).

§ 303. Duty To Enforce.

(a) A court of this State shall recognize and enforce a child-custody determination of a court of another State if the latter court exercised jurisdiction in substantial conformity with this [Act] or the determination was made under factual circumstances meeting the jurisdictional standards of this [Act] and the determination has not been modified in accordance with this [Act].

* * *

Thus, under the UCCJEA, a state is not required to enforce a custody determination of another state where the issuing state exercises custody jurisdiction that does not comport with the UCCJEA. In addition, the

UCCJEA provides five enforcement remedies: (1) a simplified process for registration of custody orders issued by another state; (2) authorization for courts to issue temporary visitation or parenting time orders; (3) authorization for a state to take physical custody of a child in imminent danger of being harmed or removed from the state; (4) a swift enforcement mechanism for violations of custody and visitation provisions, and (5) authorization of public officials to assist in enforcement of child custody determinations.

NOTES AND QUESTIONS

1. *No federal cause of action.* In *Thompson v. Thompson*, 484 U.S. 174 (1988), the Court considered whether the PKPA furnished an implied right of action in federal courts to determine which of two conflicting state custody statutes is valid. In July 1978, Susan Clay (then Thompson) filed a petition in Los Angeles Superior Court for divorce against David Thompson, asking for custody of their son, Matthew. The court initially awarded joint custody to Susan and David, but awarded Susan full custody after she obtained a job in Louisiana. This custody arrangement was supposed to be temporary until an investigator reported back to the court. But after moving to Louisiana, Susan filed a petition there for enforcement of the California custody decree, and for modification of visitation rights; the Louisiana court subsequently awarded Susan sole custody of Matthew in April 1981. In June 1981, the California court, after receiving its investigatory report, awarded sole custody to David. In August 1983, David brought an action in California federal district court seeking a declaration that the Louisiana order was invalid, and enforcement of the new California order. The district court rejected David's claims, and the Ninth Circuit held that the PKPA did not create a private right of action in federal court to determine the validity of competing custody orders. 798 F.2d 1547, 1552–59 (9th Cir. 1986).

The Supreme Court affirmed, stating that the PKPA's context, language, and legislative history did not support a private right of action in federal courts. *Thompson*, 484 U.S. at 187. The Court observed that the problem of jurisdictional deadlocks among states in custody cases, and a national problem of interstate parental abductions at the time of the PKPA's passage, suggested congressional intent only to extend the Full Faith and Credit clause to custody decisions, not to create an entirely new cause of action. The Act's language and legislative history likewise did not support David's claim. In response to the contention that failure to imply a cause of action would diminish the force of the Act, Justice Marshall, writing for the Court, explained:

> * * * [U]ltimate review remains available in this Court for truly intractable jurisdictional deadlocks. * * * [T]he unspoken presumption in petitioner's argument is that the States are either unable or unwilling to enforce the provisions of the Act. * * * State courts faithfully administer the Full Faith and Credit Clause every day; now that Congress has extended full faith and credit requirements to child custody orders, we can think of no reason why the courts' administration of federal law in custody disputes will be any less vigilant. Should state courts prove as

obstinate as petitioner predicts, Congress may choose to revisit the issue. But any more radical approach to the problem will have to await further legislative action * * *.

Id. Should Congress revisit the issue?

2. *Not following the PKPA.* What are the consequences if one court acts contrary to the PKPA by modifying an earlier custody decree from another state?

C. MODIFICATION OF CUSTODY ORDERS

Both the PKPA and Section 203 of the UCCJEA specify the limited circumstances in which one court may modify the custody provisions of another court's decree.

UNIFORM CHILD CUSTODY JURISDICTION AND ENFORCEMENT ACT

9 U.L.A. pt. IA, 649, 676 (1999).

§ 203.   Jurisdiction to Modify Determination.

* * * [A] court of this State may not modify a child-custody determination made by a court of another State unless a court of this State has jurisdiction to make an initial determination under Section 201(a)(1) or (2) and:

(1) the court of the other State determines it no longer has exclusive, continuing jurisdiction under Section 202 or that a court of this State would be a more convenient forum under Section 207; or

(2) a court of this State or a court of the other State determines that the child, the child's parents, and any person acting as a parent do not presently reside in the other State.

* * *

The next decision considers the application of Section 203 of the UCCJEA to a contested custody dispute.

ATCHISON v. ATCHISON

Court of Appeals of Michigan, 2003.
664 N.W.2d 249.

PER CURIAM.

Plaintiff Dennis Atchison appeals as of right from the trial court's order denying his petition for change of custody. We affirm.

The parties were married in June 1985, and resided in Michigan. A daughter was born in 1988, and a son was born in 1992. In 1994, defendant Teresa L. Atchison moved with the two children to Toronto to care for her terminally ill father. After her father's death, defendant and the children continued to live in Ontario, Canada. On January 2, 1998, plaintiff filed a complaint for divorce. Defendant filed an answer to the complaint and her own countercomplaint for divorce. In these pleadings, defendant alleged that proceedings regarding physical custody of the children were pending in an Ontario court. On September 1, 1998, the trial court entered a consent judgment of divorce by withdrawal. The judgment of divorce divided the parties' assets and set forth the payment of child support. * * * [T]he judgment of divorce contained the following provision regarding child custody:

> IT IS FURTHER ORDERED AND ADJUDGED that custody and visitation of the minor children shall be awarded pursuant to the Order of the Ontario Court Provincial Division Case #D84/98–A–A1 entered on February 9, 1998 a copy of which is attached hereto and made a part hereof and marked Exhibit A, and the Ontario Court shall retain jurisdiction with respect to the issue of custody and visitation.

The order of the Ontario Court Provincial Division provided, in relevant part:

> 1. The parties shall have joint custody of the children of the marriage. . . .
>
> 2. The primary residence of the children shall be with the Applicant [defendant], in the Province of Ontario, the Respondent husband [plaintiff] having acknowledged and agreed that the children have habitually resided in the Province of Ontario since April, 1994, and that the children will retain the Province of Ontario as their domicile, and the parties having further agreed that should any issues respecting custody or access arise in future, those issues will be heard and determined by the Ontario Court.

The parties formally modified the child-support payments by court order to account for "temporary" placements of the minor daughter with plaintiff between September 2000 and September 2001. In July 2002, plaintiff petitioned for change of custody with respect to the minor daughter. * * *

Plaintiff alleges that the trial court committed clear legal error by refusing to accept jurisdiction of the custody petition involving the minor daughter in light of her two-year residency in this state. We disagree. Whether a trial court has subject-matter jurisdiction presents a question of law that this Court reviews de novo. This issue also involves interpretation of the Uniform Child Custody Jurisdiction and Enforcement Act, (UCCJEA) * * *. * * *

* * * The UCCJEA became effective in Michigan on April 1, 2002. * * *

A foreign country is treated as a state of the United States when applying the general and jurisdictional provisions of the UCCJEA. Once a court of another state has rendered a child-custody determination, a

Michigan court shall not modify this order, unless certain criteria are established. MCL 722.1203[1] provides:

> * * * [A] court of this state shall not modify a child-custody determination made by a court of another State unless a court of this state has jurisdiction to make an initial determination under section 201(1)(a) or (b) and either of the following applies:
>
> (a) The court of the other state determines it no longer has exclusive, continuing jurisdiction under section 202 or that a court of this state would be a more convenient forum under section 207.
>
> (b) A court of this state or a court of the other state determines that neither the child, nor a parent of the child, nor a person acting as a parent presently reside in the other state.

Thus, to modify a child-custody determination from another state, the Michigan court must have jurisdiction to make the initial child-custody determination, and the other state must determine that it no longer has exclusive, continuing jurisdiction or that a Michigan court would be a more convenient forum. Alternatively, a Michigan court may modify a child-custody determination when it is determined that the child, parent of the child, or person acting as a parent to the child no longer resides in the other state. The satisfaction of this criteria before any modification is mandatory as evidenced by the use of the term "shall."

Review of the record reveals that the criteria for modification of the Canadian child-custody determination was not established. Once an initial child-custody determination occurs, exclusive, continuing jurisdiction generally remains with the decreeing court. A review of the available record indicates that the Ontario court did not determine that it had relinquished its exclusive, continuing jurisdiction or that Michigan was a more convenient forum for the child-custody proceeding. Furthermore, defendant continued to reside in Ontario, Canada, and thus, the Ontario court maintained an interest in retaining its exclusive, continuing jurisdiction. The rules regarding home-state priority and retention of continuing, exclusive jurisdiction for the state that entered the decree are designed to rectify conflicting proceedings and orders in child-custody disputes.

* * *

Affirmed.

NOTE AND QUESTIONS

Other states' judgments. The court treated the Canadian judgment as if it had been issued by another state, and refused to modify it. Did this refusal lead to the appropriate result? Did the court properly apply the UCCJEA's modification provision?

---

1. *Ed.'s note*: Section 722.1203 of the Michigan Compiled Laws, Mich. Comp. Laws Ann. § 722.1203 (West 2005), is the state statute adopting, as modified, Section 203 of the UCCJEA, reproduced above.

PROBLEM 16–5

A California court awarded Jack and Shawna joint legal custody of their son, Michael, and awarded Shawna primary physical custody. Shawna and Michael moved to Norway for two years, so Shawna could pursue an education, while Jack remained in California. At the end of the two-year period, Shawna informed Jack that she wished to remain in Norway permanently with Michael. A year later, when Michael returned to visit his father in California for a visit, Jack filed a motion to modify custody to award him sole custody of Michael. Shawna argued that California, which has enacted the UCCJEA, lacked jurisdiction to consider the motion because California was no longer Michael's home state. How should a California court rule?

PROBLEM 16–6

During their marriage, John and Nancy had two children and lived in Illinois for six years. In 2000, the couple divorced and an Illinois court issued a custody order providing for shared parental rights and responsibilities, with Nancy having primary physical of the children. In 2004, the children moved to Colorado to live with their father, who had moved there and remarried. Nancy claims that this arrangement was temporary, while John claims that the relocation was permanent. The children lived with John until 2006, at which time John moved to modify the Illinois custody judgment in a Colorado court, arguing that Illinois no longer had jurisdiction under the UCCJEA. Nancy later filed a similar modification motion in a court in Illinois, where she continued to reside. John moved to dismiss the Illinois action claiming that Colorado was the proper jurisdiction and that Illinois no longer had continuing, exclusive jurisdiction. If you were the judge in Colorado, how would you handle the situation? If you were the judge in Illinois, how would you rule? According to the UCCJEA, did Illinois retain continuing, exclusive jurisdiction over the children? Would you want any further information before making your decision?

D.   CHILD CUSTODY DISPUTES INVOLVING CIVIL UNIONS OR SAME–SEX MARRIAGES

In issuing a child custody decree, the court must decide between the appropriate parties who are entitled to petition for such a decree. Because many states do not recognize same-sex partnerships lawfully created in other states, the dissolution of these same-sex relationships can result in legal confusion concerning parental status and the jurisdiction of the court. *See Miller–Jenkins v. Miller–Jenkins*, 912 A.2d 951 (Vt. 2006); *Miller–Jenkins v. Miller–Jenkins*, 637 S.E.2d 330 (Va. Ct. App. 2006). In 2000, Lisa Miller–Jenkins and Janet Miller–Jenkins, two Virginia residents, entered into a civil union in Vermont. The two women continued to reside in Virginia. They also had a child in Virginia. Two years later, the couple and child moved to Vermont. In 2003, the couple decided to separate. Lisa filed a petition to dissolve the civil union in Vermont family court and requested that the Court award her parental rights. The Court dissolved the civil union and awarded Lisa temporary custody of the child and gave Janet visitation rights. Shortly after, Lisa filed a petition in a Virginia court, asking the Court to establish the parentage of the child.

A circuit court in Virginia claimed jurisdiction to determine the parentage and parental rights of the child. That court held that Janet's claims to parental status were based on rights under Vermont's civil union laws and were null under the Virginia Marriage Protection Act. The court found that Lisa was the "sole biological and natural parent" of the child and held that Janet had "no claims of parentage or visitation rights over" the child.

Then, the Vermont court issued a ruling refusing to give full faith and credit to the Virginia decision and found that both Janet and Lisa had parental interests in the child.

Both decisions were appealed.

On appeal, the Vermont Supreme Court held that the civil union between Lisa and Janet was valid, even though Lisa and Janet were not residents of Vermont when they entered into the civil union. The Court also addressed the conflict between the Vermont and Virginia courts' child custody decisions and held that the Vermont court had exercised "home state" jurisdiction. While the Vermont proceeding was pending, another court could not exercise jurisdiction over a proceeding to determine custody of or visitation with the child. Therefore, the Virginia court did not have jurisdiction to modify the Vermont order.

The Virginia Court of Appeals reversed the lower court decision finding that Lisa was the "sole parent," holding that Vermont had sole jurisdiction over the custody and visitation determination. The Court of Appeals did not address whether the civil union would have been recognized under Virginia law.

E.   INTERNATIONAL CHILD ABDUCTION

Chapter 13 introduced you to the 1980 Hague Convention on the Civil Aspects of International Child Abduction ("Hague Convention"), which governs all civil cases of international child abduction where the petitioning parent and the child are in different countries, so long as the countries are parties to the Convention and have executed reciprocal agreements. Hague Convention, Oct. 25, 1980, 1343 U.N.T.S. 89 (1983). In 1988, the United States became a signatory state, ratified the Convention, and implemented it through the International Child Abduction Remedies Act (ICARA), 42 U.S.C. §§ 11601–10 (2006). The Convention seeks to "secure the prompt return of children wrongfully removed to or retained in any Contracting State," and to "ensure the rights of custody and of access under the law of one Contracting State are effectively respected in the other Contracting States." Today, the Convention has been enacted in more than 80 countries. *See* Hague Conference on Private International Law, Child Abduction Section, http://hcch.e-vision.nl/index_en.php?act= text.display & tid=21; Merle H. Weiner, *The Potential and Challenges of Transnational Litigation for Feminists Concerned About Domestic Violence Here and Abroad*, 11 Am. U.J. Gender Soc. Pol'y & L. 749, 761–66 (2003).

Generally, a person invoking the Hague Convention seeks the "remedy of return," the return of his or her child to the habitual residence. This remedy applies only in cases of wrongful removal or retention of a child, and requires that the parent seeking return of the child have legal custody. Article 3 of the Convention defines removal as "wrongful" when it occurs "in breach of rights of custody." The "remedy of return" was designed to return the abducted child quickly to his or her habitual residence. The remedy was also designed to discourage abductions and provide for a full hearing in the forum with the most relevant evidence, *i.e.*, the jurisdiction from which the child was originally abducted.

There are several defenses to a "remedy of return" claim. Article 12 permits a court to deny a petition for return of a child if one year has elapsed since the wrongful removal or retention; the child is presumed to be settled in the new environment. Additionally, Article 13(a) permits a court to deny a petition if the person seeking the remedy of return did not have custody rights at the time of removal or retention, or "consented to or subsequently acquiesced in the removal or retention." Article 13(b) provides that a court may deny return if a grave risk exists that return "would expose the child to physical or psychological harm or otherwise place the child in an intolerable situation." Finally, Article 20 allows a court to refuse return if the refusal is required by "the fundamental principles of the requested State relating to the protection of human rights and fundamental freedoms."

ICARA authorizes a party seeking return of a child to file a petition in a court of appropriate jurisdiction where the child is located. ICARA grants state and federal courts concurrent jurisdiction to hear Hague Convention cases.

1. THE HAGUE CONVENTION

CONVENTION ON THE CIVIL ASPECTS OF INTERNATIONAL CHILD ABDUCTION, 1980

T.I.A.S. No. 11,670, 1343 U.N.T.S. 89.

CHAPTER I—SCOPE OF THE CONVENTION

* * *

Article 3

The removal or the retention of a child is to be considered wrongful where:

a) it is in breach of rights of custody attributed to a person, an institution or any other body, either jointly or alone, under the law of the State in which the child was habitually resident immediately before the removal or retention; and

b) at the time of removal or retention those rights were actually exercised, either jointly or alone, or would have been so exercised but for the removal or retention.

The rights of custody mentioned in sub-paragraph *a* above, may arise in particular by operation of law or by reason of a judicial or administrative decision, or by reason of an agreement having legal effect under the law of that State.

Article 4

The Convention shall apply to any child who was habitually resident in a Contracting State immediately before any breach of custody or access rights. The Convention shall cease to apply when the child attains the age of 16 years.

* * *

Article 8

Any person, institution or other body claiming that a child has been removed or retained in breach of custody rights may apply either to the Central Authority of the child's habitual residence or to the Central Authority of any other Contracting State for assistance in securing the return of the child. * * *

* * *

Article 12

Where a child has been wrongfully removed or retained in terms of Article 3 and, at the date of the commencement of the proceedings before the judicial or administrative authority of the Contracting State where the child is, a period of less than one year has elapsed from the date of the wrongful removal or retention, the authority concerned shall order the return of the child forthwith.

The judicial or administrative authority, even where the proceedings have been commenced after the expiration of the period of one year referred to in the preceding paragraph, shall also order the return of the child, unless it is demonstrated that the child is now settled in its new environment.

* * *

Article 13

Notwithstanding the provisions of the preceding Article, the judicial or administrative authority of the requested State is not bound to order the return of the child if the person, institution or other body which opposes its return establishes that:

> *a)* the person, institution or other body having the care of the person of the child was not actually exercising the custody rights at the time of removal or retention, or had consented to or subsequently acquiesced in the removal or retention; or

> *b)* there is a grave risk that his or her return would expose the child to physical or psychological harm or otherwise place the child in an intolerable situation.

The judicial or administrative authority may also refuse to order the return of the child if it finds that the child objects to being returned and has attained an age and degree of maturity at which it is appropriate to take account of its views.

* * *

T.I.A.S. No. 11,670, 4–5, 6–8, 1343 U.N.T.S. 89, 98–99, 100–101.

NOTES AND QUESTIONS

1. *How do courts respond when countries have not signed the Hague Convention?* The Hague Convention has been widely adopted, but it is not in force in many countries where religious courts exercise jurisdiction over child custody matters. One exception is Israel, where religious courts do decide custody issues. Under United States law and the Convention, respect for a foreign court's jurisdiction and custody is not affected by whether the court applies secular or religious law. However, American courts often determine custody based on analysis of the best interests of the child and are wary of foreign custody decrees that appear to be based solely on religious principle. *See* Ann Laquer Estin, *Embracing Tradition: Pluralism in American Family Law*, 63 Md. L. Rev. 540, 593–99 (2004).

2. *Using the Convention.* If you regularly represent parents seeking return of children from another country, would you seek any changes to the Convention?

2. THE INTERNATIONAL PARENTAL KIDNAPPING CRIME ACT (IPKCA)

In 1993, Congress enacted the International Parental Kidnapping Crime Act (IPKCA), 18 U.S.C. § 1204 (2006). Under the IPKCA, it is a crime to "remove" or "retain" a child outside of the United States with the purpose of obstructing another person's lawful exercise of parental rights.

In *United States v. Cummings*, 281 F.3d 1046 (9th Cir. 2002), the defendant argued that the Act was unconstitutional. Defendant Cole Cameron Cummings had three children with his wife, Dana Hopkins. After their divorce, she was granted primary custody of the children. In 1997, Cummings began to suspect that his children were at risk of physical abuse by their new stepfather in their mother's home. During a scheduled visitation, he removed the children to Germany, where his second wife lived and worked. A German court denied Hopkins's petition, made pursuant to the Hague Convention, to return the children. Hopkins filed a civil contempt action against Cummings in Washington state. The U.S. government indicted Cummings under the IPKCA on four counts of kidnapping. As part of a plea agreement, Cummings entered a conditional guilty plea to two of the counts, preserving his right to appeal the district court's denial of his motion to dismiss the indictment.

On appeal, Cummings argued that Congress did not have Commerce Clause authority to criminalize *retention* of an American child in a foreign country. (Cummings did not challenge Congress' authority to criminalize *removal* of a child.) Cummings argued that although the Commerce Clause applied to target conduct directly involved in moving people or things in foreign commerce, the channels of commerce are no longer affected once the movement ceases. The Ninth Circuit Court of Appeals disagreed:

> The cessation of movement does not preclude Congress's reach if the person or goods traveled in the channels of foreign commerce. * * * Likewise, [the IPKCA] reaches conduct once the unlawful foreign transportation has ended. * * * We are satisfied that Congress can act to prohibit the transportation of specified classes of persons in foreign commerce and thus proscribe conduct such as retention of those persons, even though transportation is complete. Not only does [the IPKCA] target activity after the use of channels of foreign commerce is complete, but it also removes an impediment to the use of those channels. If a child is wrongfully retained in a foreign country, he or she cannot freely use the channels of commerce to return. Congress has authority to prevent individuals from impeding commerce, * * * and, as to those who 'retain' children outside the United States, to prevent them from traveling back to this country via the channels of commerce.

Id. at 1050. The court also rejected Cummings' argument that the IPKCA unconstitutionally interfered with a parent's individual rights, which he argued are traditionally left to the states. Acknowledging that family law issues are usually reserved to the states, the court concluded that the IPKCA deals primarily with international kidnapping, which is not an area traditionally reserved to the states. Is the court correct here, or does the IPKCA overextend Congress' Commerce Clause powers? Can you formulate additional arguments that Cummings could have made regarding the IPKCA's unconstitutionality? Subsequent courts have affirmed the *Cummings* holding that the criminalization of the retention of an American child in a foreign country is constitutional. *E.g.*, U.S. v. Fazal Raheman, 355 F.3d 40 (1st Cir. 2004); *U.S. v. Maddox*, 2006 WL 1207964 (D. Or. 2006).

SECTION 5: CHILD SUPPORT JURISDICTION

As with custody decisions, support determinations also must comply with due process, and there are jurisdictional issues relating to the initial order and to suits for modification and enforcement. However, because child support involves financial obligations—that is, who should pay and what amount—the jurisdictional analysis differs from that concerning interstate child custody disputes. The most significant decision concerning due process and personal jurisdiction over modification and enforcement of interstate child support obligations is *Kulko v. Superior Court of California.*

A. WHERE MAY A CHILD SUPPORT ORDER BE ISSUED?

1. CONSTITUTIONAL LIMITS

KULKO v. SUPERIOR COURT

Supreme Court of the United States, 1978.
436 U.S. 84.

MR. JUSTICE MARSHALL delivered the opinion of the Court.

The issue before us is whether, in this action for child support, the California state courts may exercise *in personam* jurisdiction over a nonresident, nondomiciliary parent of minor children domiciled within the State. For reasons set forth below, we hold that the exercise of such jurisdiction would violate the Due Process Clause of the Fourteenth Amendment.

I

Appellant Ezra Kulko married appellee Sharon Kulko Horn in 1959, during appellant's three-day stopover in California en route from a military base in Texas to a tour of duty in Korea. At the time of this marriage, both parties were domiciled in and residents of New York State. Immediately following the marriage, Sharon Kulko returned to New York, as did appellant after his tour of duty. Their first child, Darwin, was born to the Kulkos in New York in 1961, and a year later their second child, Ilsa, was born, also in New York. The Kulkos and their two children resided together as a family in New York City continuously until March 1972, when the Kulkos separated.

Following the separation, Sharon Kulko moved to San Francisco, Cal. A written separation agreement was drawn up in New York; in September 1972, Sharon Kulko flew to New York City in order to sign this agreement. The agreement provided, *inter alia*, that the children would remain with their father during the school year but would spend their Christmas, Easter, and summer vacations with their mother. While Sharon Kulko waived any claim for her own support or maintenance, Ezra Kulko agreed to pay his wife $3,000 per year in child support for the periods when the children were in her care, custody, and control. Immediately after execution of the separation agreement, Sharon Kulko flew to Haiti and procured a divorce there; the divorce decree incorporated the terms of the agreement. She then returned to California, where she remarried and took the name Horn.

The children resided with appellant during the school year and with their mother on vacations, as provided by the separation agreement, until December 1973. At this time, just before Ilsa was to leave New York to spend Christmas vacation with her mother, she told her father that she wanted to remain in California after her vacation. Appellant bought his daughter a one-way plane ticket, and Ilsa left, taking her clothing with her. Ilsa then commenced living in California with her mother during the school year and spending vacations with her father. In January 1976, appellant's other child, Darwin, called his mother from New York and advised her that he wanted to live with her in California. Unbeknownst to appellant, appellee Horn sent a plane ticket to her son, which he used to fly to California where he took up residence with his mother and sister.

Less than one month after Darwin's arrival in California, appellee Horn commenced this action against appellant in the California Superior Court. She sought to establish the Haitian divorce decree as a California judgment; to modify the judgment so as to award her full custody of the children; and to increase appellant's child-support obligations. Appellant appeared specially and moved to quash service of the summons on the ground that he was not a resident of California and lacked sufficient "minimum contacts" with the State under *International Shoe Co. v. Washington*, 326 U.S. 310 (1945), to warrant the State's assertion of personal jurisdiction over him.

[The lower California courts rejected appellant's claims.]

* * *

The California Supreme Court granted appellant's petition for review, and in a 4–2 decision sustained the rulings of the lower state courts. It noted first that the California Code of Civil Procedure demonstrated an intent that the courts of California utilize all bases of *in personam* jurisdiction "not inconsistent with the Constitution." Agreeing with the court below, the Supreme Court stated that, where a nonresident defendant has caused an effect in the State by an act or omission outside the State, personal jurisdiction over the defendant in causes arising from that effect may be exercised whenever "reasonable." It went on to hold that such an exercise was "reasonable" in this case because appellant had "purposely availed himself of the benefits and protections of the laws of California" by sending Ilsa to live with her mother in California. While noting that appellant had not, "with respect to his other child, Darwin, caused an effect in [California]"—since it was appellee Horn who had arranged for Darwin to fly to California in January 1976—the court concluded that it was "fair and reasonable for defendant to be subject to personal jurisdiction for the support of both children, where he has committed acts with respect to one child which confers [*sic*] personal jurisdiction and has consented to the permanent residence of the other child in California."

* * *

* * * [W]e hereby grant the petition and reverse the judgment below.

II

* * *

Like any standard that requires a determination of "reasonableness," the "minimum contacts" test of *International Shoe* is not susceptible of mechanical application; rather, the facts of each case must be weighed to determine whether the requisite "affiliating circumstances" are present. *Hanson v. Denckla*, 357 U.S. 235, 246 (1958). * * *

A

In reaching its result, the California Supreme Court did not rely on appellant's glancing presence in the State some 13 years before the events that led to this controversy, nor could it have. Appellant has been in California on only two occasions, once in 1959 for a three-day military stopover on his way to Korea, and again in 1960 for a 24–hour stopover on his return from Korean service. To hold such temporary visits to a State a basis for the assertion of *in personam* jurisdiction over unrelated actions arising in the future would make a mockery of the limitations on state jurisdiction imposed by the Fourteenth Amendment. Nor did the California court rely on the fact that appellant was actually married in California on one of his two brief visits. We agree that where two New York domiciliaries, for reasons of convenience, marry in the State of California and thereafter spend their entire married life in New York, the fact of their California marriage by itself cannot support a California court's exercise of jurisdiction over a spouse who remains a New York resident in an action relating to child support.

Finally, in holding that personal jurisdiction existed, the court below carefully disclaimed reliance on the fact that appellant had agreed at the time of separation to allow his children to live with their mother three months a year and that he had sent them to California each year pursuant to this agreement. As was noted below, to find personal jurisdiction in a State on this basis, merely because the mother was residing there, would discourage parents from entering into reasonable visitation agreements. Moreover, it could arbitrarily subject one parent to suit in any State of the Union where the other parent chose to spend time while having custody of their offspring pursuant to a separation agreement. * * *

The "purposeful act" that the California Supreme Court believed did warrant the exercise of personal jurisdiction over appellant in California was his "actively and fully consent[ing] to Ilsa living in California for the school year ... and ... sen[ding] her to California for that purpose." We cannot accept the proposition that appellant's acquiescence in Ilsa's desire to live with her mother conferred jurisdiction over appellant in the California courts in this action. A father who agrees, in the interests of family harmony and his children's preferences, to allow them to spend more time in California than was required under a separation agreement can hardly be said to have "purposefully availed himself" of the "benefits and protections" of California's laws.[7]

Nor can we agree with the assertion of the court below that the exercise of *in personam* jurisdiction here was warranted by the financial benefit appellant derived from his daughter's presence in California for nine months of the year. This argument rests on the premise that, while appellant's liability for support payments remained unchanged, his yearly expenses for supporting the child in New York decreased. But this circumstance, even if true, does not support California's assertion of jurisdiction here. Any diminution in appellant's household costs resulted, not from the child's presence in California, but rather from her absence from appellant's home. Moreover, an action by appellee Horn to increase support payments could now be brought, and could have been brought when Ilsa first moved to California, in the State of New York; a New York court would clearly have personal jurisdiction over appellant and, if a judgment were entered by a New York court increasing appellant's child-support obligations, it could properly be enforced against him in both New York and California. Any ultimate financial advantage to appellant thus results not from the child's presence in California, but from appellee's failure earlier to seek an increase in payments under the separation agreement. The argument below to the contrary, in our view, confuses the question of appellant's liability with that of the proper forum in which to determine that liability.

B

* * *

The circumstances in this case clearly render "unreasonable" California's assertion of personal jurisdiction. There is no claim that appellant has visited physical injury on either property or persons within the State of California. The cause of action herein asserted arises, not from the defendant's commercial transactions in interstate commerce, but rather from his personal, domestic relations. It thus cannot be said that appellant has sought a commercial benefit from solicitation of business from a resident of California that could reasonably render him liable to suit in state court; appellant's activities cannot fairly be analogized to an insurer's sending an insurance contract and premium notices into the State to an insured resident of the State. *Cf. McGee v. International Life Insurance Co.,* 355 U.S. 220 (1957). Furthermore, the controversy between the

---

7. The court below stated that the presence in California of appellant's daughter gave appellant the benefit of California's "police and fire protection, its school system, its hospital services, its recreational facilities, its libraries and museums...." But, in the circumstances presented here, these services provided by the State were essentially benefits to the child, not the father, and in any event were not benefits that appellant purposefully sought for himself.

parties arises from a separation that occurred in the State of New York; appellee Horn seeks modification of a contract that was negotiated in New York and that she flew to New York to sign. As in *Hanson v. Denckla*, 357 U.S. at 252, the instant action involves an agreement that was entered into with virtually no connection with the forum State.

Finally, basic considerations of fairness point decisively in favor of appellant's State of domicile as the proper forum for adjudication of this case, whatever the merits of appellee's underlying claim. It is appellant who has remained in the State of the marital domicile, whereas it is appellee who has moved across the continent. *Cf. May v. Anderson*, 345 U.S. 528, 534–35, n.8 (1953). Appellant has at all times resided in New York State, and, until the separation and appellee's move to California, his entire family resided there as well. As noted above, appellant did no more than acquiesce in the stated preference of one of his children to live with her mother in California. This single act is surely not one that a reasonable parent would expect to result in the substantial financial burden and personal strain of litigating a child-support suit in a forum 3,000 miles away, and we therefore see no basis on which it can be said that appellant could reasonably have anticipated being "haled before a [California] court," *Shaffer v. Heitner*, 433 U.S. [186, 216 (1977)]. To make jurisdiction in a case such as this turn on whether appellant bought his daughter her ticket or instead unsuccessfully sought to prevent her departure would impose an unreasonable burden on family relations, and one wholly unjustified by the "quality and nature" of appellant's activities in or relating to the State of California. *International Shoe Co. v. Washington*, 326 U.S. at 319.

III

In seeking to justify the burden that would be imposed on appellant were the exercise of *in personam* jurisdiction in California sustained, appellee argues that California has substantial interests in protecting the welfare of its minor residents and in promoting to the fullest extent possible a healthy and supportive family environment in which the children of the State are to be raised. These interests are unquestionably important. But while the presence of the children and one parent in California arguably might favor application of California law in a lawsuit in New York, the fact that California may be the "center of gravity" for choice-of-law purposes does not mean that California has personal jurisdiction over the defendant. * * *

California's legitimate interest in ensuring the support of children resident in California without unduly disrupting the children's lives, moreover, is already being served by the State's participation in the Revised Uniform Reciprocal Enforcement of Support Act of 1968. This statute provides a mechanism for communication between court systems in different States, in order to facilitate the procurement and enforcement of child-support decrees where the dependent children reside in a State that cannot obtain personal jurisdiction over the defendant. California's version of the Act essentially permits a California resident claiming support from a nonresident to file a petition in California and have its merits adjudicated in the State of the alleged obligor's residence, without either party's having to leave his or her own State. Cal. Civ. Proc. Code Ann. § 1650 *et seq.* (West 1972 and Supp. 1978).[13] * * *

It cannot be disputed that California has substantial interests in protecting resident children and in facilitating child-support actions on behalf of those children. But these interests simply do not make California a "fair forum," *Shaffer v. Heitner, supra,* at 215, in which to require appellant, who derives no personal or commercial benefit from his child's presence in California and who lacks any other relevant contact with the State, either to defend a child-support suit or to suffer liability by default.

* * *

Reversed.

MR. JUSTICE BRENNAN, with whom MR. JUSTICE WHITE and MR. JUSTICE POWELL join, dissenting.

* * * I cannot say that the Court's determination against state-court *in personam* jurisdiction is implausible, but, though the issue is close, my independent weighing of the facts leads me to conclude, in agreement with the analysis and determination of the California Supreme Court, that appellant's connection with the State of California was not too attenuated, under the standards of reasonableness and fairness implicit in the Due Process Clause, to require him to conduct his defense in the California courts. I therefore dissent.

NOTES AND QUESTIONS

1. *Physical presence.* Given the location of the children and relevant evidence in California, why didn't the Supreme Court hold that the California courts had ruled correctly?

2. *Purposeful act.* How does sending a child to live in another state differ from sending an insurance contract to another state?

2. STATE LAWS

There have been repeated efforts to develop uniform state laws on child support jurisdiction. In 1950, the National Conference of Commissioners on Uniform State Laws (NCCUSL) drafted the Uniform Reciprocal Enforcement of Support Act (URESA). URESA was amended in 1968, and retitled the Revised Uniform Reciprocal Enforcement of Support Act

---

13. * * * Under the Act, an "obligee" may file a petition in a court of his or her State (the "initiating court") to obtain support. 9 U.L.A. §§ 11, 14 (1973). If the court "finds that the [petition] sets forth facts from which it may be determined that the obligor owes a duty of support and that a court of the responding state may obtain jurisdiction of the obligor or his property," it may send a copy of the petition to the "responding state." § 14. This has the effect of requesting the responding State "to obtain jurisdiction over the obligor." § 18 (b). If jurisdiction is obtained, then a hearing is set in a court in the responding State at which the obligor may, if he chooses, contest the claim. * * *

(RURESA). As you noticed in *Kulko*, the Court relied on RURESA to reach its decision. By 1957, some version of URESA was in effect in every state and provided a method for interstate enforcement of support orders without commencing a new legal proceeding. URESA allowed a party to file a complaint in his or her jurisdiction, and have the complaint forwarded to the obligor's jurisdiction. A court in the obligor's jurisdiction tried the case, and then rendered and enforced a judgment. This system created many problems. For example, URESA allowed the original order to remain in effect even after that order was registered in another state, and had been modified by the second state. Consequently, two or more valid court orders from different states could require different support obligations for the same obligor and child. Unif. Interstate Family Support Act, prefatory note, 9 U.L.A., pt. IB, 159, 161–63 (2005).

The Uniform Interstate Family Support Act (UIFSA), first promulgated in 1992 and ratified by the American Bar Association in 1993, has completely replaced URESA. UIFSA provides uniform rules for enforcement and modification of family support orders by setting jurisdictional standards for state courts, determining the basis for a state to exercise exclusive jurisdiction over a child support proceeding, and creating rules for determining which state issues a controlling order if proceedings are initiated in multiple jurisdictions. In 1996, Congress mandated that states enact some parts of UIFSA as a condition of remaining eligible for federal funding of child support enforcement. By 1998, all U.S. jurisdictions had complied. UIFSA, prefatory note, 9 U.L.A., 162; *see* UIFSA Home Page, http://www.uifsa.com/.

NCCUSL amended UIFSA in 1996. In 2001, the NCCUSL drafted further amendments to UIFSA that, among other things, limited the ability of parties to seek modification orders in states other than the issuing state, and clarified the appropriate procedures in the event of multiple court orders. Most states have not yet adopted the 2001 version.

UIFSA provides procedural and jurisdictional rules for proceedings to establish, enforce, and modify a child support order. Only one state has continuing jurisdiction to modify a child support order. Unlike the UC-CJEA, which addressed only subject matter jurisdiction, UIFSA addresses both personal and subject matter jurisdiction. For example, Section 202 of the 2001 model act, reproduced below, provides that personal jurisdiction continues as long as a tribunal has continuing, exclusive jurisdiction to modify or enforce an order.

UNIFORM INTERSTATE FAMILY SUPPORT ACT[1]

9 U.L.A., pt. IB, 159, 175, 185, 189, 192–93 (2005).

§ 102. Definitions.

* * *

---

1. *Ed.'s note*: Brackets are reproduced as they appear in the original material.

(4) "Home State" means the State in which a child lived with a parent or a person acting as parent for at least six consecutive months immediately preceding the time of filing of a [petition] or comparable pleading for support and, if a child is less than six months old, the State in which the child lived from birth with any of them. A period of temporary absence of any of them is counted as part of the six-month or other period.

* * *

§ 201.   Bases For Jurisdiction Over Nonresident.

(a) In a proceeding to establish or enforce a support order or to determine parentage, a tribunal of this State may exercise personal jurisdiction over a nonresident individual [or the individual's guardian or conservator] if:

(1) the individual is personally served with [citation, summons, notice] within this State;

(2) the individual submits to the jurisdiction of this State by consent in a record, by entering a general appearance, or by filing a responsive document having the effect of waiving any contest to personal jurisdiction;

(3) the individual resided with the child in this State;

(4) the individual resided in this State and provided prenatal expenses or support for the child;

(5) the child resides in this State as a result of the acts or directives of the individual;

(6) the individual engaged in sexual intercourse in this State and the child may have been conceived by that act of intercourse;

(7) the individual asserted parentage in the [putative father registry] maintained in this State by the [appropriate agency]; or

(8) there is any other basis consistent with the constitutions of this State and the United States for the exercise of personal jurisdiction.

§ 202.   Duration Of Personal Jurisdiction.

Personal jurisdiction acquired by a tribunal of this State in a proceeding under this [Act] or other law of this State relating to a support order continues as long as a tribunal of this State has continuing, exclusive jurisdiction to modify its order or continuing jurisdiction to enforce its order as provided by Sections 205, 206, and 211.

* * *

§ 205.   Continuing, Exclusive Jurisdiction To Modify Child–Support Order.

(a) A tribunal of this State that has issued a support order consistent with the law of this State has and shall exercise continuing, exclusive jurisdiction to modify its child-support order if the order is the controlling order and:

　(1) at the time of the filing of a request for modification this State is the residence of the obligor, the individual obligee, or the child for whose benefit the support order is issued; or

　(2) even if this State is not the residence of the obligor, the individual obligee, or the child for whose benefit the support order is issued, the parties consent in a record or in open court that the tribunal of this State may continue to exercise jurisdiction to modify this order.

(b) A tribunal of this State that has issued a child-support order consistent with the law of this State may not exercise its continuing jurisdiction to modify the order if :

　(1) all the parties who are individuals file consent in a record with the tribunal of this State that a tribunal of another State that has jurisdiction over at least one of the parties who is an individual or that is located in the State of residence of the child may modify the order and assume continuing, exclusive jurisdiction; or

　(2) its order is not the controlling order.

(c) If a tribunal of another State has issued a child-support order pursuant to [UIFSA] or a law substantially similar to [that Act] which modifies a child-support order of this State, tribunals of this State shall recognize the continuing, exclusive jurisdiction of the tribunal of the other State.

(d) A tribunal of this State that lacks continuing, exclusive jurisdiction to modify a child-support order may serve as an initiating tribunal to request a tribunal of another State to modify a support order issued in that State.

(e) A temporary support order issued *ex parte* or pending resolution of a jurisdictional conflict does not create continuing, exclusive jurisdiction in the issuing tribunal.

* * *

　The following decision demonstrates a state court's struggle with interstate support issues.

CASE v. CASE

Court of Appeals of Utah, 2004.
103 P.3d 171.

Greenwood, Judge:

* * *

Background

　Father and Mother were married in California, in 1992. During their marriage, two children were born. In March 2002, the parties obtained a Judgment of Dissolution (Divorce Judgment) in the Superior Court of Stanislaus County, California. At the time of the divorce, and as reflected in the Divorce Judgment, Mother and the two children had moved to Utah, and Father had moved to Maryland. Under the Divorce Judgment, [child support was reserved until further order of the court]. * * *

* * *

In March 2003, Mother filed a * * * [petition asking a Utah court to issue a child support order. A Utah trial court found in her favor.] Father filed a timely appeal. * * *

* * *

ANALYSIS

I. Trial Court's Subject Matter Jurisdiction Under UIFSA

Father argues that the Utah trial court lacked subject matter jurisdiction to modify the Divorce Judgment and order him to pay child support. * * *

* * *

UIFSA regulates the establishment, enforcement, or modification of support orders across state lines. The primary purpose of UIFSA is to provide uniform child support enforcement laws between the states. * * *

Utah's UIFSA confers subject matter jurisdiction upon Utah courts to modify child support orders issued by another state as long as certain conditions are met. *See* Utah Code Ann. § 78–45f–611 (2002). Section 78–45F–611[1] provides:

> (1) After a child support order issued in another state has been registered in this state, the responding tribunal of this state may modify that order only if * * * after notice and hearing it finds that:
>
> * * *
>
> (i) the child, the individual obligee, and the obligor do not reside in the issuing state;
>
> (ii) *a petitioner who is a nonresident of this state seeks modification*; and
>
> (iii) the respondent is subject to the personal jurisdiction of the tribunal of this state.

Id. § 78–45f–611(1)(a)(i)–(iii) (emphasis added).

Although Mother stated in her petition that she sought modification of the California child support order, the State, in its amicus memorandum, contends that Mother more appropriately seeks an initial order of support because the California court did not do so, but rather reserved the issue of child support. [Section 401 of] UIFSA similarly grants jurisdiction to Utah courts to establish a support order where an order otherwise entitled to recognition under UIFSA has not been issued if:

> (a) *the individual seeking the order resides in another state*; or
>
> (b) the support enforcement agency seeking the order is located in another state.

. . . . .

---

1. *Ed.'s note*: This statute reflects the model wording of Section 611 of UIFSA (1996).

(3) Upon finding, after notice and opportunity to be heard, that an obligor owes a duty of support, the tribunal shall issue a support order directed to the obligor * * *.

Id. § 78–45f–401 (emphasis added). Both sections 78–45f–611 and 78–45f–401 clearly and unequivocally require that a petitioner be a nonresident of Utah in order to seek an initial order or a modification of child support under UIFSA in the State of Utah.

In this case, Mother and Father were divorced in California, and a California court issued the Divorce Judgment. The parties agreed at that time to reserve the issue of child support. After Father moved to Maryland and Mother moved to Utah, Mother sought a modification of the California order in a Utah court. Because she sought to modify the Divorce Judgment in Utah, the requirements of UIFSA were triggered. Whether the trial court was asked to modify the Divorce Judgment, or establish a new child support order, it lacked jurisdiction over the matter because Mother, as a resident of Utah, fails to meet the necessary requirements to establish a new support order or modify an existing order from another state.

Mother does not dispute that she does not meet the[se] requirements. Rather, she argues that those sections are inapplicable because under 78–45f–202 [the state's Section 202 of UIFSA], the trial court obtained subject matter jurisdiction over the case by virtue of its personal jurisdiction over Father. * * *

Mother argues that under 78–45f–202, parts 3, 4, 5, 6, and 7 of UIFSA do not apply to this case because the trial court obtained personal jurisdiction over Father. * * * [Parts 4 and 6 require] the petitioner to be a nonresident. Accordingly, it is necessary to determine if 78–45f–202 trumps the subject matter jurisdiction requirements found in sections 78–45f–401 and 78–45f–611. We conclude that the statutory language is ambiguous. Without any Utah case law on the subject, in order to determine the meaning of 78–45f0202, we first turn to the official comments by the drafters of UIFSA. * * *

The official comments to UIFSA sections 201 and 202 do not mention subject matter jurisdiction. Rather, they appear to assume that the forum state's court already has subject matter jurisdiction over the case. Instead, the comment to section 201 states that the purpose of sections 201 and 202 is to address long-arm jurisdiction over a nonresident respondent. *See* UIFSA, U.L.A., 18, (1996) (comment § 201). The drafters' intent was to "insure that every enacting State has a long-arm statute as broad as constitutionally permitted." *Id.* Thus, when a state has subject matter jurisdiction over a case, and the respondent lives in another state, sections 201 and 202 provide the basis for asserting the forum state's long-arm jurisdiction over the respondent.

* * * Accordingly, section 202 only applies to proceedings to establish, enforce, or modify support orders of the forum state against an out-of-

state respondent. It is not applicable when the support order was rendered by a state other than the forum state.

This analysis of the UIFSA drafters' intent is consistent with *LeTellier v. LeTellier*, 40 S.W.3d 490 (Tenn. 2001), where the Tennessee Supreme Court faced a similar factual scenario and the same statutory interpretation question as is presented in this case. In *LeTellier*, a District of Columbia court had entered an order adjudging paternity and ordering the father to pay child support. The mother later moved to Tennessee, and the father moved to Virginia. Some years later, the mother filed a petition in Tennessee seeking to modify the child support award. The trial court granted the father's motion to dismiss for lack of subject matter jurisdiction. The Tennessee Court of Appeals reversed on the basis that UIFSA was preempted by federal law on the question of jurisdiction. On appeal to the Tennessee Supreme Court, the mother argued that under section 202 of UIFSA, when a Tennessee court has personal jurisdiction over a nonresident, the other jurisdictional provisions of UIFSA are not applicable. The Tennessee Supreme Court rejected this argument, holding that section 202 applied only to "proceedings to establish, enforce, or modify Tennessee support decrees against an out-of-state resident." *Id.* at 494. The mother in *LeTellier* argued that because personal jurisdiction was obtained, she should be able to obtain a modification in Tennessee. The supreme court stated:

> [T]he order [the mother] sought to modify was issued by a state other than Tennessee. Tennessee courts lack subject matter jurisdiction to modify out-of-state orders when the provisions of UIFSA are not satisfied. Because this case still retains its interstate character, [section 202] has no application to this case. The remaining provisions of UIFSA, including the subject matter jurisdiction provisions of [section 611], still apply.

Id. [at 495] (footnote omitted).

The Tennessee court also observed that the comments to section 201 and 202 "make no reference to subject matter jurisdiction and appear to presume that subject matter jurisdiction exists." *Id.* at 494. The court further observed that UIFSA "attempts to achieve a rough justice between the parties * * *by preventing a litigant from choosing to seek modification in a local tribunal to the marked disadvantage of the other party." *Id.* at 495. We agree with the analysis of the Tennessee Supreme Court and find it to be consistent with the UIFSA drafters' intent.

A petitioner under UIFSA must first establish subject matter jurisdiction under section 401 or 611. Without such compliance, the petition must be dismissed. Personal jurisdiction achieved under sections 201 and 202 does not confer the prerequisite subject matter jurisdiction. In the case before us, Mother asked a Utah court to modify a California support decree and order Father, a Maryland resident, to pay child support. Because this case does not involve a Utah support order, it still retains its interstate character, and Mother must satisfy the jurisdiction requirements of UIFSA for modifying an out-of-state support decree. Mother's residency in Utah precludes a Utah court from establishing or modifying child support pursuant to the parties' California Divorce Decree. Mother's remedies are to initiate proceedings in a Maryland court, which would have both personal jurisdiction over Father and subject matter jurisdiction over the case pursuant to UIFSA, or in California where the court would have continuing jurisdiction.

CONCLUSION

The trial court lacked subject matter jurisdiction over this case because under UIFSA, a Utah court cannot establish, modify, or enforce a foreign support order unless the petitioner is a nonresident of Utah. Accordingly, we reverse the trial court's grant of summary judgment and its order requiring Father to pay child support and remand with instructions to dismiss Mother's petition.

NOTES AND QUESTIONS

1. *Long-arm jurisdiction.* UIFSA contains a broad provision for asserting long-arm jurisdiction over an absent respondent in the state of residence of the other parent, the child's custodian or the child entitled to support. Sections 201 and 202 of UIFSA (reproduced above) allow an issuing state to assert long-arm jurisdiction over a nonresident respondent to establish a support order or to determine parentage. UIFSA § 201, cmt., 9 U.L.A., pt. IB, 159, 185 (2005). Such jurisdiction ensures that child support can be established through a one-state proceeding. Where the long-arm statute can be satisfied, the petitioner (either the obligor or obligee) can: (1) use the long-arm statute to obtain personal jurisdiction over the respondent; or (2) initiate a two-state proceeding seeking to establish a support order in the respondent's state of residence. *Id.*

2. Kulko *and UIFSA.* Are all of the provisions in Section 201 of UIFSA concerning personal jurisdiction constitutional under *Kulko*?

3. *Enforcing a support order.* A keystone of UIFSA is that power to enforce the issuing state's order is not "exclusive" to that state. Instead, if requested, one or more states may also enforce the order. UIFSA provides two direct enforcement procedures that do not require court assistance. First, section 501 permits a notice to be sent directly to the obligor's employer in another state, triggering income withholding by the employer, without a hearing unless the employee objects. Second, Section 507 also provides for direct administrative enforcement by the support enforcement agency in the obligor's state.

When enforcement of a support order in another state requires court involvement, the obligee must first register the existing support order in the responding state. The responding state must enforce the order except in a few limited circumstances in which modification is permitted.

4. *Modification jurisdiction.* Why are the requirements for initial jurisdiction and modification jurisdiction different?

B. WHEN MUST A STATE GIVE A CHILD SUPPORT ORDER FULL FAITH AND CREDIT?

Congress enacted the Full Faith and Credit for Child Support Orders Act (FFCCSOA) in 1994. 28 U.S.C. § 1738B (2006). The legislation, which is similar to the PKPA, is designed: (1) to facilitate enforcement of child support orders among the states; (2) to discourage continuing interstate controversies over child support in the interest of greater financial stability and secure family relationships for the child; and (3) to avoid jurisdictional competition and conflict among the state courts in establishing child support orders.

The FFCCSOA generally requires state courts to enforce the terms of a child support order issued by courts in a different state. "Child support order" is defined as "a judgment, decree or order of a court requiring the payment of child support in periodic amounts or in a lump sum." The Act broadly defines support as "a payment of money, continuing support, or arrearages or the provision of a benefit (including payment of health insurance, child care, and educational expenses) for the support of a child."

The FFCCSOA requires a state to give full faith and credit to any valid child support order. A support order is valid where: (1) it was issued by a court pursuant to the laws of the state in which the court was located; (2) the court had subject matter jurisdiction to hear and resolve the matter; and (3) the court had personal jurisdiction over the contestants, provided that the contestants had reasonable notice and an opportunity to be heard.

FULL FAITH AND CREDIT FOR CHILD SUPPORT ORDERS ACT

28 U.S.C. § 1738B (2006).

* * *

(c) Requirements of child support orders.—A child support order made by a court of a State is made consistently with this section if—

    (1) a court that makes the order, pursuant to the laws of the State in which the court is located and subsections (e), (f), and (g)—

        (A) has subject matter jurisdiction to hear the matter and enter such an order; and

        (B) has personal jurisdiction over the contestants; and

    (2) reasonable notice and opportunity to be heard is given to the contestants.

(d) Continuing jurisdiction.—A court of a State that has made a child support order consistently with this section has continuing, exclusive jurisdiction over the order if the State is the child's State [of residence] or the residence of any individual contestant unless the court of another State, acting in accordance with subsections (e) and (f), has made a modification of the order.

* * *

(f) Recognition of child support orders.—If 1 or more child support orders have been issued with regard to an obligor and a child, a court shall apply the following rules in determining which order to recognize for purposes of continuing, exclusive jurisdiction and enforcement:

(1) If only 1 court has issued a child support order, the order of that court must be recognized.

(2) If 2 or more courts have issued child support orders for the same obligor and child, and only 1 of the courts would have continuing, exclusive jurisdiction under this section, the order of that court must be recognized.

(3) If 2 or more courts have issued child support orders for the same obligor and child, and more than 1 of the courts would have continuing, exclusive jurisdiction under this section, an order issued by a court in the current home State of the child must be recognized, but if an order has not been issued in the current home State of the child, the order most recently issued must be recognized.

(4) If 2 or more courts have issued child support orders for the same obligor and child, and none of the courts would have continuing, exclusive jurisdiction under this section, a court having jurisdiction over the parties shall issue a child support order, which must be recognized.

(5) The court that has issued an order recognized under this subsection is the court having continuing, exclusive jurisdiction under subsection (d).

(g) Enforcement of modified orders.—A court of a State that no longer has continuing, exclusive jurisdiction of a child support order may enforce the order with respect to nonmodifiable obligations and unsatisfied obligations that accrued before the date on which a modification of the order is made under subsections (e) and (f).

(h) Choice of law.—

(1) In general.—In a proceeding to establish, modify, or enforce a child support order, the forum State's law shall apply except as provided in paragraphs (2) and (3).

(2) Law of state of issuance of order.—In interpreting a child support order including the duration of current payments and other obligations of support, a court shall apply the law of the State of the court that issued the order.

* * *

Note and Questions

The FFCCSOA contains several choice of law provisions that courts must apply. First, the Act states that the forum state's law applies in proceedings to establish, modify or enforce a child support order unless otherwise provided. 28 U.S.C. § 1738B(h)(1). Second, the law of the issuing court's state applies in interpreting a child support order, such as determining the duration of current payments and other obligations. 28 U.S.C. § 1738B(h)(2). However, the court must apply the statute of limitations that provides the longer period of limitation of either the forum state or the issuing state. 28 U.S.C. § 1738B(h)(3). What policies support these choice of law provisions?

PROBLEM 16–7

Susan and Michael were married and had three children, ages 25, 21, and 19. The couple, who lived in New York throughout their marriage, recently divorced, and a New York court issued a child support order. Under New York law, a child is eligible for child support until she reaches the age of 21 and therefore the youngest child was eligible for support. Susan and the youngest child moved to Virginia, where the law mandates child support only until the age of 18. Does the Virginia court have jurisdiction to enforce the New York support order? Is the youngest child entitled to child support in Virginia?

C. WHERE MAY A CHILD SUPPORT ORDER BE MODIFIED?

1. UIFSA

Under UIFSA, a party who requests a tribunal in another state to modify an existing child support order must register the original order in the other state. Because UIFSA provides continuing, exclusive jurisdiction in the court exercising original jurisdiction, generally only that court may modify the support order. However, if modification jurisdiction is no longer appropriate in the issuing court, a second tribunal may become vested with the continuing, exclusive jurisdiction necessary to modify the order. This vesting can occur when neither the individual parties nor the child reside in the issuing state, or when the parties agree that another tribunal may assume modification jurisdiction. The 2001 amendment to Section 205 allows parties to agree that the issuing tribunal will continue to exercise its continuing, exclusive jurisdiction even if the parties and child have moved from that state. Can you think of any reason why the parties might request this option? Why would the UIFSA drafters have added this to the original Act?

2. FFCCSOA

The FFCCSOA also limits one state's authority to modify a support order issued by another state. A court has modification jurisdiction only where: (1) that court would now have initial jurisdiction to issue a child support order if this were a new case; and (2) the other state's court can no longer exercise continuing and exclusive jurisdiction over the order. A state loses continuing, exclusive jurisdiction if it is no longer the residence state of the child or any contestant, or if all contestants have filed written consents to modification by another state. *See* 28 U.S.C. § 1738B(a)(2)(2006); 28 U.S.C. § 1738B(e)(2006); Margaret Campbell Haynes, *Federal Full Faith and Credit for Child Support Orders Act*, 14 SPG–Del. Law. 26 (1996).

FULL FAITH & CREDIT FOR CHILD SUPPORT ORDERS ACT

28 U.S.C. § 1738B (2006).

* * *

(e) Authority to modify orders. A court of a State may modify a child support order issued by a court of another State if—

(1) the court has jurisdiction to make such a child support order pursuant to subsection (i); and

(2) (A) the court of the other State no longer has continuing, exclusive jurisdiction of the child support order because that State no longer is the child's State or the residence of any individual contestant; or

(B) each individual contestant has filed written consent with the State of continuing, exclusive jurisdiction for a court of another State to modify the order and assume continuing, exclusive jurisdiction over the order.

* * *

AUCLAIR v. BOLDERSON

Supreme Court of New York, Appellate Division, 2004.
775 N.Y.S.2d 121.

MERCURE, J.

* * *

Petitioner and respondent were divorced in 1987. Pursuant to a judgment entered in Florida, the Circuit Court of Okaloosa County granted petitioner physical custody of the parties' two children and ordered that respondent pay child support of $200 per month per child until the children reached 18 years of age. During the divorce proceedings, petitioner and the children moved to New York. Respondent moved to Missouri after the divorce.

In 1994, respondent, by order to show cause, sought to hold petitioner in contempt of court for violating a 1993 order of protection issued by [New York] Supreme Court. Upon petitioner's cross motion to modify child support, Supreme Court * * * issued a temporary order increasing respondent's support obligation (hereinafter the 1994 order). In 1995, Supreme Court * * * issued a final order (hereinafter the 1995 order) following the terms of the 1994 order. Respondent appeals from the 1995 order, which was not entered until 2001.

In 1998, petitioner sought to modify the Florida judgment to extend the duration of support until the parties' children reached 21 years of age. A Support Magistrate dismissed the petition for modification on the ground that the duration of support is governed by the law of Florida, as the state issuing the divorce judgment.

In 2002, petitioner filed two petitions seeking enforcement of the 1995 order and an upward modification of child support. Petitioner also commenced a separate proceeding seeking a new order of support for the parties' daughter Rebecca. Petitioner argued that the Florida judgment and 1995 order expired when Rebecca reached her 18th birthday and, thus, the new support proceeding was not governed by the terms of that judgment. Respondent challenged the petitions, arguing that New York did not have personal jurisdiction over him or subject matter jurisdiction to modify the Florida judgment. A Support Magistrate rejected respondent's arguments, granted the petitions seeking enforcement and modification, and dismissed the separate petition for an order of support for Rebecca as moot. Family Court subsequently dismissed respondent's objections regarding jurisdiction. Respondent also appeals from that order.

Respondent argues that this state's courts lack subject matter jurisdiction to modify the Florida judgment by operation of two statutes—the Federal Full Faith and Credit for Child Support Orders Act (hereinafter FFCCSOA) and the Uniform Interstate Family Support Act (hereinafter UIFSA). FFCCSOA "follow[s] the contours of UIFSA" (*LeTellier v. LeTellier*, 40 S.W.3d 490, 498 [Tenn. 2001]), which is in effect in all 50 states. The two statutes have complementary goals. UIFSA is intended "to eliminate the problems arising from multiple support orders from various States by providing for one tribunal to have continuing and exclusive jurisdiction to establish or modify a child support order" (*Matter of Reis v. Zimmer*, 700 N.Y.S.2d 609 [1999]). FFCCSOA requires that states give full faith and credit to out-of-state child support orders and restrains states from modifying those out-of-state orders except in limited circumstances. The two statutes are to be read together, and their "parallel jurisdictional provisions * * * provide a virtually iron-clad structure for" enforcing or modifying an out-of-state child support order (Sobie Practice Commentaries, Introductory Commentary, McKinney's Cons Laws of N.Y., Book 29A, Family Ct. Act art. 5–B, at 204–205).

Initially, both FFCCSOA and UIFSA grant "continuing, exclusive jurisdiction over" a child support order to the state that issued the order (28 U.S.C. § 1738B [d]). The issuing state loses such jurisdiction where, as here, none of the parties or children continues to reside in that state. The issuing state will also be deprived of continuing, exclusive jurisdiction when all parties file written consents that allow another state to assume continuing, exclusive jurisdiction over the order.

The absence of such continuing, exclusive jurisdiction, however, while an essential prerequisite, does not, by itself, confer upon another state the power to modify the child support order. If no written consent to the change in jurisdiction has been filed, FFCCSOA requires that the modifying state have personal jurisdiction over the nonmoving party. Additionally, "the party or support enforcement agency seeking to modify, or to modify and enforce [the initial order must] register that order" with the modifying state (28 U.S.C. § 1738B [i]).

UIFSA also requires that the initial child support order be registered in the modifying state. UIFSA then confers subject matter jurisdiction upon the modifying state if the issuing state was deprived of continuing, exclusive jurisdiction by virtue of the written consent of the parties. If no such consent exists, however, UIFSA requires that: (1) none of the parties or children continues to reside in the issuing state; (2) the party seeking modification is not a resident of the modifying state; and (3) the nonmoving party is subject to personal jurisdiction in the modifying state.

With this framework in mind, we find that New York courts lack subject matter jurisdiction to either modify the Florida judgment or to subsequently enforce that modification. Pursuant to UIFSA and FFCCSOA, Florida lost "continuing, exclusive jurisdiction" over its judgment by virtue of the fact that neither the parties nor the children continued to reside there. As such, the courts of a nonissuing state may modify the judgment if it has been registered in that state and certain other criteria have been met. Here, petitioner failed to demonstrate that the Florida judgment was registered in New York. In itself, this failure to prove registration prevents New York courts from obtaining subject matter jurisdiction under both UIFSA and FFCCSOA.

* * *

Additionally, because petitioner and the children are residents of New York, "all of the parties [must] have filed written consents [in the Florida court to allow New York courts] to modify the support order and assume continuing, exclusive jurisdiction over the order" under UIFSA (Unif. Interstate Family Support Act [1996] § 611, official comment, 9 [part 1] ULA 348, 430–431 [Supp. 1999]).[2] There is no indication in the record, however, that the parties have filed any documents in the Florida Circuit Court consenting to New York's jurisdiction. Thus, under UIFSA and FFCCSOA, both Supreme Court and Family Court lacked subject matter jurisdiction to modify the Florida judgment. Accordingly, the courts erred in failing to dismiss the petitions seeking modification of the Florida judgment and enforcement of the modifications.

---

2. It should be noted that if both parties resided in New York, there would be jurisdiction to enforce and to modify an order issued in another state.

With respect to the separate 2002 petition seeking a new support order for Rebecca, we agree with respondent that Family Court lacked personal jurisdiction over him. While respondent, through his appearance, consented to personal jurisdiction in the proceedings that led to the 1994 and 1995 orders modifying the Florida judgment he disputed Family Court's exercise of personal jurisdiction over him in the separate 2002 proceeding seeking a new order of support for Rebecca. Given that he did not appear other than to dispute Family Court's exercise of personal jurisdiction over him, respondent did not consent to personal jurisdiction with regard to petitioner's commencement of a new proceeding for a support order. Therefore, the petition seeking a new support order for Rebecca was properly dismissed.

Respondent's remaining arguments are either academic or meritless.

* * *

QUESTIONS

Modification jurisdiction. Under what circumstances may a court in one state modify a child support decree issued by a court in another state? Do you think that *Auclair* was correctly decided? What policy considerations influence your assessment?

PROBLEM 16–8

New Mexico issued a support order requiring John Vincent to pay $2000 monthly to his ex-wife to support their child. John has resided in California for three years since the issuance of this order because he was assigned to active duty there in the Air Force. If John filed his income tax returns in New Mexico and intended to return to New Mexico after he retired from the military, does that state retain continuing, exclusive jurisdiction over child support? Does California have jurisdiction to modify New Mexico's order? Under what circumstances would California have jurisdiction? What further information would you need to make your decision? Does California have jurisdiction to enforce the order? What information would you need to make that determination?

PROBLEM 16–9

In 1994, Mark and Tammy were divorced in Colorado, where a court issued a child support order for their two children. The Colorado court later modified this order three times. In 2006, Tammy and her children moved to Washington state, where she filed a petition seeking to modify the child support order. Mark moved to dismiss for lack of subject matter jurisdiction under UIFSA. If you were Mark's lawyer, what arguments would you make that Washington does not have jurisdiction? If you were the judge, what further information would you need to make your decision?

SECTION 6: UNIFIED FAMILY COURTS

Domestic relations cases are the largest and fastest growing segment of state court caseloads. Approximately 30% of the civil cases in state courts involve family problems, a percentage exceeded only by that for traffic offenses. Courts that hear family matters, however, are often overburdened and inefficient. The late nineteenth century innovation of juvenile courts, which were designed to provide a supportive atmosphere for adjudicating cases involving delinquency, abuse and neglect, status offenses and (in most states) adoption, ironically turned out to be one source of inefficiency. Legal scholars have long observed that a court that treats a range of family problems "as a series of single separate controversies may often not do justice to the whole or the several separate parts." Roscoe Pound, *The Place of the Family Court in the Judicial System*, 5 Nat'l Probation & Parole Ass'n J. 161, 164 (1959).

In an effort to avoid the delays, duplication and unnecessary expense that frequently arise when troubled families must proceed in both juvenile court and general jurisdiction court, several jurisdictions have implemented unified family courts. Unified family courts have existed since the early twentieth century, but gained prominence in a few states, such as Rhode Island and Hawaii, starting in the 1960s. In 1991, the National Council of Juvenile and Family Court Judges recommended a model family court. Three years later, the American Bar Association adopted a policy endorsing unified family courts. In addition to the children's cases traditionally heard in juvenile court, the family court's subject matter jurisdiction typically includes divorce proceedings, paternity suits, emancipation proceedings, proceedings for protective orders under child abuse and adult abuse statutes, and, in some jurisdictions, criminal prosecutions charging abuse or neglect or domestic violence.

Proponents also assert that unified family courts can produce consistency and efficiency that serve the best interests of children, families and courts. Families and the judicial system save time, effort and resources when one decisionmaker remains familiar with the family's circumstances and resolves all family-related matters. Family members are spared the ordeal of appearing in multiple courts that determine frequently interrelated factual and legal issues. Children are spared the discomfort of testifying in multiple proceedings. Consider, for example, the plight of a young child allegedly molested by her father. In a jurisdiction without a unified family court, the child may be forced to testify about the same or similar events in multiple proceedings if the mother files for divorce after learning of the sexual assault, if child protective authorities file a civil abuse proceeding to remove the child from the home, and if the prosecutor files criminal charges.

Proponents argue that the one-judge-one-family approach enables family courts to treat family distress efficiently while minimizing the risk of inconsistent judgments or of multiple initiatives that each overlook a basic need. On the other hand, family court critics are particularly skeptical of removing the criminal court's jurisdiction over domestic violence. They fear that removal diminishes the impact of sanction because unified family courts are primarily civil courts.

The philosophy and structure of the unified family court are discussed in the following excerpt.

CATHERINE J. ROSS

Unified Family Courts: Good Sense, Good Justice.
Trial, Jan. 1999, at 30, 30–31.

* * * Unfortunately, all is not well in the traditional family courts found in most jurisdictions.

* * *

In most jurisdictions today, a child's family may appear in front of 6, 8 or even 14 different judges, special masters, and hearing officers on issues including divorce, child custody and visitation, child and spousal support, paternity, adoption, domestic violence, child abuse and neglect, juvenile delinquency and termination of parental rights.

In this chaos, no one gets a complete picture of the child and family. Decision makers may not know about parallel hearings and certainly do not have information that would enable them to understand how the matters relate to each other. The parties must miss work repeatedly to attend separate hearings that should have been consolidated. Attorneys fees mount.

* * *

What is a unified family court? There is no one definition. These courts take many forms, each reflecting the judicial and political culture of its jurisdiction. * * *

Successful unified family courts have four elements in common: (1) comprehensive jurisdiction; (2) efficient, modern administration designed to support the concept of "one family, one team"; (3) multidisciplinary training for all court personnel, from intake staff to judges; and (4) ability to ensure that family members receive the services they need.

* * *

* * * Sophisticated intake and case-management teams determine in large part a court's success. Each member of the team–whether intake worker, case manager, social worker, court clerk or judge–needs preliminary and ongoing training in nonlegal fields such as child development, psychology, and medicine that regularly come up in family legal matters. * * *

* * *

Unified family courts must preserve the civil and procedural rights of the parties who appear before them, even as they encourage alternative forms of dispute resolution, education for divorcing parents, and access to needed services. A holistic vision of justice for families ultimately rests on the rule of law, a system in which both lawyers and judges will continue to play a critical role.

* * *

NOTES AND QUESTIONS

1. *The current status of unified family courts.* As of 2006, thirteen states had no unified family courts, nor plans to create them. Thirty-seven states and the District of Columbia had one of the following: a statewide family court system, family courts in some parts of the state, family court pilot programs, or plans to establish a family court system. Within those states that have unified family courts, these courts vary in their definition and structure. In assigning cases, many of these states follow one of three models—a traditional calendar assignment system, a one judge/one family system, or a one judge/one case system. Other states use a variety of these assignment methods. *See* Barbara Babb, *Unified Family Court: Reevaluating Where We Stand: A Comprehensive Survey of America's Family Justice System*, 46 Fam. Ct. Rev. 230 (2008). Can you think of any reasons why other states might be reluctant to initiate reform?

2. *Criminal matters.* Although most unified family courts have jurisdiction over juvenile delinquency cases, only about half have jurisdiction over criminal matters involving adults. *See* James W. Bozzomo & Gregory Scolieri, *A Survey of Unified Family Courts: An Assessment of Different Jurisdictional Models*, 42 Fam. Ct. Rev. 12, 15 (2004). What reasons support including adult family criminal matters in unified family courts? Why might states have chosen not to include these matters?

CHAPTER 17

ADOPTION AND ASSISTED REPRODUCTIVE TECHNOLOGY

■ ■ ■

Domestic relations law concerns the rights and obligations of persons as they create, maintain and dissolve their households. Whether created by marriage or a nonmarital relationship, "households" typically include children. This final Chapter concerns adoption and assisted reproductive technology, methods that bring children into the family without the sexual intimacy between spouses or nonmarital partners that normally attends household creation.

Adoption opens the Chapter. All states have comprehensive acts providing for adoption of children. In most states, the juvenile or family court holds exclusive original jurisdiction to decide adoption petitions, though some states vest adoption jurisdiction in the probate or surrogate's court. A child may not be adopted unless a court enters an order decreeing that the adoption complies with the act and is in the best interests of the child.

Adoption is "the legal equivalent of biological parenthood." *Smith v. OFFER*, 431 U.S. 816, 844 n.51 (1977). Except in a stepparent adoption, or in an adoption by a parent's nonmarital partner in states that permit such adoptions, a valid adoption permanently extinguishes the parent-child relationship between the child and both biological parents and creates in its place a new legal relationship between the child and the adoptive parents. In a stepparent or partner adoption, the parent-child relationship continues with the custodial biological parent, and the adoption permanently displaces only the biological parent whose rights have been terminated.

Adoptive parents acquire the constitutional rights of parenthood and family autonomy discussed elsewhere in this book, including the Fourteenth Amendment substantive due process right to direct the child's upbringing free from unreasonable state interference. *See, e.g., In re Adoption of C.A.*, 137 P.3d 318, 326 (Colo. 2006). By creating a new parent-child relationship, the adoptive parents and the adoptee also secure new rights and obligations under a variety of federal and state laws, including tax laws, workers' compensation laws, Social Security and other entitlement laws, public assistance laws, inheritance laws, and family leave laws.

This Chapter closes with an examination of assisted reproductive technology (ART), which "started out as an effort to help married couples fulfill their dreams of having genetically related children [but] has, within just a few short years, triggered a revolution about how we think about parentage, marriage, and even gender identification." Bruce Lord Wilder, *Current Status of Assisted Reproductive Technology 2005: An Overview and Glance at the Future*, 39 Fam. L.Q. 573, 573 (2005). In stark contrast to adoption, family creation through ART requires no court supervision or decree. Indeed, ART is a multibillion dollar business, with comparatively little federal or state regulation. The National Organ Transplant Act of 1984, as amended, 42 U.S.C. § 274e (2003 & Supp. 2008), prohibits purchase and sale of human organs in interstate commerce, but has not been applied to gametes.

The U.S. Centers for Disease Control and Prevention (CDC) defines ART to include "all fertility treatments in which both eggs and sperm are handled" to establish a pregnancy without sexual intercourse. CDC, 2005 Assisted Reproductive Technology Success Rates 3 (2007). ART thus sometimes involves "collaborative reproduction," the participation of third parties in achieving parenthood. These third parties may include donors who provide eggs, sperm, or embryos, as well as fertility clinics, sperm banks, egg recruiters, or other actors.

Married and unmarried couples, and single women and men, may now turn to assisted reproductive technology, not necessarily because they are infertile, but because they are gay or lesbian, because they fear the risks or inconvenience of gestation and childbirth, because they have postponed childbirth, or because they fear transmitting a genetic disease or defect to their offspring. Adoption may have proved unavailing, or the intended parents may wish a child who can continue the bloodline of least one of the parents.

NOTES

1. *A national adoption profile.* Adopted children represent about 2.5% of children living with a parent-householder in the United States, and U.S. courts grant more than a million adoption petitions each decade. For example, courts approved 151,332 adoptions of children (130,269 domestic adoptions and 21,063 international adoptions) in 2002, the latest year for which figures are available. *See* National Council For Adoption, Adoption Factbook IV, at 5 (Lee A. Allen & Virginia C. Ravenal eds., 2007), http://www.adoptioncouncil. org/documents/AdoptionFactbookIV.pdf ("Adoption Factbook").

2. *A national ART profile.* ART has proliferated in the United States since the first American ART infant was born in 1981. The CDC estimates that slightly more than 1% of U.S. infants born in 2005 were born following ART cycles. The agency further reports that between 1996 and 2005, "[t]he number of ART cycles performed in the United States has more than doubled,

from 64,681 cycles in 1996 to 134,260 in 2005." CDC, 2005 Assisted Reproductive Technology Success Rates, *supra*, at 13, 61. (Because ART consists of several steps for two weeks or so, an ART procedure is typically considered a "cycle" of treatment, rather than one procedure at a single point in time.) "The number of [ART] live-birth deliveries in 2005 (38,910) was more than two and a half times higher than in 1996 (14,507)." *Id.* at 61.

SECTION 1:   ADOPTION

A.   CONTEMPORARY ATTITUDES AND HISTORICAL BACKGROUND

Americans today generally think positively of adoption of children. Results of the comprehensive *National Adoption Attitudes Survey* found (1) that 63% of Americans hold "very favorable" opinions about adoption, (2) that 39% of Americans have "very seriously," or "somewhat seriously," considered adopting a child, and (3) that 57% of Americans believe that adoptive parents receive the same satisfaction from raising adoptive children as biological children. *See National Adoption Attitudes Survey* 1–3 (2002).

Formal adoption did not exist at common law, which had no procedure for severing a child's legal relationship with biological parents and replacing it by a legal relationship with other parents. Children might be transferred informally from one household to another, sometimes by apprenticeship or guardianship to a family that agreed to provide care and education, perhaps in return for needed labor. Children sometimes assumed the new family's surname, but before enactment of adoption statutes in the second half of the nineteenth century, informal transfer did not sever existing legal parent-child relationships and create new ones.

JAMIL S. ZAINALDIN

The Emergence of a Modern American Family Law: Child
Custody, Adoption, and the Courts, 1796–1851.
73 Nw. U. L. Rev. 1038, 1042–45 (1979).

* * * [U]nlike most historical phenomena, the first instance of departure from the traditional model of adoption can be isolated by location, day, and year. On April 2, 1847, the Massachusetts House of Representatives ordered that the Committee on the Judiciary consider "the expediency of providing by law for the adoption of children." On May 13, 1851, the Committee reported to the House "A Bill for the Adoption of Children." There seems to have been little or no opposition. Eleven days later the Massachusetts legislature passed the first general "Act to Provide for the Adoption of Children" in America.

The Massachusetts adoption statute of 1851 was the first *modern* adoption law in history. It is notable for two reasons. First, it contradicted the most fundamental principles of English domestic relations law, and overruled centuries of English precedent and legislation which prohibited the absolute, permanent, and voluntary transfer of parental power to third persons. Second, the traditional status of adoption allocated benefits between the giver and taker, while the Massachusetts statute distinguished the adoptee as the prime beneficiary. The heart of the adoption transaction became the judicially monitored transfer of rights with due regard for the *welfare of the child* and the *parental qualifications* of the adopters.

Within the next twenty-five years, more than a score of states would enact some form of adoption law, and in most cases the Massachusetts statute served as a model. Strangely, it would seem, the passage of the first Massachusetts act attracted little public attention. Little or no debate over the issue occurred in the legislature, apparently no social reform movements advocated passage of the law, and, when the law did appear, few newspapers bothered to take note of the event. And for several years after the passage of the statute, few adopters took advantage of the law. There is, then, no clear explanation for why the legislature passed the law when it did. Nor at first glance would there seem to be any explanation for the casual reception accorded such an apparently radical statute.

The new law may have been part of the larger legislative trend of substituting private enactments with general statutes. Private laws granting divorce, legitimacy, incorporation, and change of name were becoming particularly cumbersome in the 1840s. And there is ample evidence that children throughout the United States were being "adopted" through private acts, especially those concerning change of name. A contemporary of the nineteenth century—and an advocate of statutory adoption— thought that the law would secure important rights to the adopters. A modern commentator, however, suggests that the first general adoption statute may have evolved out of a desire to protect the perceived right of inheritance of nonlegally adopted children.

Just why the Massachusetts legislature moved in 1851 may never be known. Perhaps all of these reasons prompted the lawmakers to action. At once they endeavored to protect the child and to endow his standing in the family with status, while conferring upon adopters the rights and duties of parents. The discretionary proceeding in the probate court was perceived as the soundest, most efficient method for effecting adoption.

B. WHEN MAY A CHILD BE ADOPTED?

A child is adopted only when the court enters a final decree approving the adoption in the best interests of the child. The court may grant an adoption petition only where, under the adoption act, the child is available for adoption and the would-be adoptive parent has standing because he or she is within the class of persons eligible to adopt. *Adoption of M.A.* concerned standing—the would-be adoptive parents' right to petition the court—because the two children were available for adoption once the court entered an order terminating the parental rights of their biological parents.

ADOPTION OF M.A.

Supreme Judicial Court of Maine, 2007.
930 A.2d 1088.

LEVY, J.

A.C. and M.K. appeal from the judgment of the Cumberland County Probate Court dismissing their joint petitions for adoption and name change as to their foster children, M.A. and R.A. * * * [W]e vacate court's judgment and remand for further proceedings.

I. BACKGROUND

* * * In early 2001, A.C. and M.K., an unmarried, same-sex couple, became foster parents to the minor children and biological siblings, M.A. and R.A. At the time, M.A. was one week shy of her fourth birthday and R.A. was four months old. The Department of Health and Human Services received the custody of the children as a result of a jeopardy order entered in a child protection proceeding in the District Court. The parental rights of the children's birth parents were subsequently terminated by the court with their consent. Both children have been diagnosed with post-traumatic stress disorder, reactive attachment disorder, and attention deficit and hyperactivity disorder.

Nearly two years after the children came into the Department's custody, A.C. and M.K. applied to the Department to adopt the children. An independent home study * * * report recommended that A.C. and M.K. be approved to jointly adopt the children, concluding that:

> [A.C. and M.K.] are able to parent children with moderate to severe special needs that include attachment disorders, mental illness, ADHD/ADD, learning disabilities and delays. They are able to parent children who require a wide range of services and may not live independently as ... adult[s].

The children's court-appointed guardian ad litem recommended in favor of the adoption, concluding that "[h]aving two legal parents forever will clearly be in the children's best interests." The Department's adoption worker and adoption supervisor responsible for the children also issued reports strongly supporting the adoptions, recommending that the adoptions "be legalized as soon as possible to provide [each child] with the security that only permanence can provide." In April 2006, the Department, acting through its Commissioner, consented to the joint adoption of both children by A.C. and M.K.

A.C. and M.K. filed two petitions for adoption in the Cumberland County Probate Court in May 2006: one to jointly adopt M.A., and the other to jointly adopt R.A. * * * The following month, the court denied the petitions in a written order that simply stated that each was "denied for lack of jurisdiction pursuant to 18–A M.R.S.A. [§] 9–301,'' without addressing the merits of the petitions. Section 9–301 provides: "A husband and wife jointly or an unmarried person, resident or nonresident of the State, may petition the Probate Court to adopt a person, regardless of age, and to change that person's name.'' * * *

II. DISCUSSION

* * *

Because the Probate Court has personal jurisdiction over the parties and the children, and subject-matter jurisdiction to act on petitions for adoption, the Probate Court erred in dismissing the petitions for lack of jurisdiction. However, to the extent the Probate Court inferred that a joint petition by unmarried persons is prohibited by section 9–301, we must still determine whether a joint petition for adoption filed by two unmarried persons is procedurally barred because the statute addresses joint petitions only in connection with a husband and wife, but not in connection with two unmarried persons.

A.   The Plain Meaning of Section 9–301

* * *

The petitioners and the Attorney General both assert that section 9–301 is clear and unambiguous. They observe that the statute does not expressly prohibit two unmarried persons from jointly petitioning to adopt a child. The petitioners urge us to treat the statute's language permitting a petition to adopt by a "husband and wife jointly" as functioning solely as a restriction on petitions brought by married persons. They note that other jurisdictions have construed similar statutes on this basis and have recognized that the purpose of requiring a married person to join his or her spouse to an adoption petition is "specific to the marital relationship and its attendant legal obligations.''

In support of their view that the statute is unambiguous, the petitioners also cite the statutory rule of construction, stated in 1 M.R.S. § 71(9) (2006), that "[w]ords of the singular number may include the plural; and words of the plural number may include the singular." If applied to section 9–301, the statute's reference to petitions by "an unmarried person" includes the plural "unmarried persons." We perceive two problems, however, with resting a reading of section 9–301 squarely on the rule of construction stated in section 71(9).

First, * * * [a] reasonable argument can be made, counter to that advanced by the petitioners, that because section 9–301 mentions joint petitions only in connection with married persons, the plain meaning of the statute is that joint petitions are permitted to be filed only by married persons. In addition, even if the rule is determined to be applicable, it cannot be applied to produce a result that is contrary to the adoption statute's purpose or design. Accordingly, contrary to the petitioner's contention, the application of the rule of construction in section 71(9) does not end our inquiry in this case.

Second, construing the phrase "unmarried person" to include the plural "unmarried persons" would not only permit a joint petition by two unmarried persons, but would also arguably permit an indefinite number of persons to join in a single adoption petition. *See In re K.M.*, 653 N.E.2d [888,] 894 [(Ill. App. Ct. 1995)] (citing lower court's concern in this regard). *But see Adoption of Tammy*, 619 N.E.2d [315,] 318–19 [(Mass. 1993)] (relying on the rule of statutory construction that words of the singular include the plural in concluding that two unmarried persons may file a joint adoption petition). In the unique context of a child adoption statute, a strict application of section 71(9) could lead to a construction of section 9–301 that would produce illogical results.

Although we are not persuaded that the construction of section 9–301 should rest on section 71(9), we are equally unpersuaded that the plain language of section 9–301 is reasonably susceptible to only one construction. The statute is silent as to whether an unmarried person may or may not be a party to a joint petition. As a general principle of statutory construction, if a statute does not contain "a limiting adverb such as 'solely,' we refuse to imply such a restriction." One cannot conclude that the statute prohibits two unmarried persons from proceeding by way of a joint petition without reaching beyond the actual language of the statute so as to interpret it to state: "[a] husband and wife jointly or an unmarried person, resident or nonresident of the State, [individually, but not jointly,] may petition the Probate Court to adopt a person."

A plain reading of the statute is not only saddled by the need to engage in an inference that introduces the restriction "individually, but not jointly," into the text, but also leads to possibly absurd or illogical results. The adoption statute expressly permits unmarried persons to adopt children and does not expressly prohibit a child from being adopted by two unmarried persons. Therefore, unless one reads section 9–301 as also implicitly establishing a bar that prohibits more than one unmarried person from adopting a particular child, A.C. and M.K. could achieve a joint adoption of the children by filing separate individual petitions for adoption, and then moving to consolidate the petitions into a single adoption proceeding * * *. In addition, A.C. and M.K. could also proceed by having one file an individual petition to adopt the children and, if successful, that person consenting to a second adoption petition filed by the other, resulting in the adoption of the children by both. In short, if we infer that section 9–301 prohibits joint petitions by unmarried persons, but does not prohibit joint adoption by two unmarried persons, unmarried persons can still accomplish a joint adoption through successive or consolidated individual petitions. With this in mind, construing section 9–301 as prohibiting a joint petition by unmarried persons elevates form over substance to an illogical degree.

Accordingly, we do not accept the petitioners' contention that the plain language of section 9–301 is free from ambiguity and requires no further inquiry beyond the application of the rule of construction stated in 1 M.R.S. § 71(9). Because the statute is reasonably susceptible of different constructions, it is ambiguous, and we turn to consider its history and purpose for further guidance.

B.   Legislative History and Purpose

     1.   History

* * *

The legislative history establishes that the provision regarding joint petitions by husbands and wives began with the 1855 Act and was intended to restrict petitions brought by married persons. There is nothing in the legislative history * * * to suggest that the statute, in its current form, should impose a restriction on petitions by unmarried persons.

* * *

C.   Purpose of Adoption Law

When we find a statute ambiguous, we may also look to the statute's underlying purpose to ascertain legislative intent. * * *

Although statutes adopted in derogation of the common law are to be strictly construed, we have previously recognized that "[w]e construe our adoption statutes to protect the rights and privileges of the child being adopted."[13] This is consistent with the central role the best interests of the children play in the statutory factors the court is required to consider in evaluating an adoption petition. Accordingly, it is established in our jurisprudence that:

> Adoption statutes, as well as matters of procedure leading up to adoption, should be liberally construed to carry out the beneficent purposes of the adoption institution and to protect the adopted child in the rights and privileges coming to it as a result of the adoption.

* * *

The construction of section 9–301 that will most promote the rights and privileges of children such as M.A., R.A., and other similarly situated children, and will simplify and clarify the law of adoption, is one that does not infer a procedural bar that would disqualify the joint petitions filed by A.C. and M.K. In contrast to a narrow reading of section 9–301 that infers a restriction not expressed in the statute, a broader construction is more in keeping with the statute's overriding objective of protecting the welfare of children. A joint adoption assures that in the event of either adoptive parent's death, the children's continued relationship with the surviving

---

13. Many other courts have likewise rejected the application of strict construction to adoption statutes, favoring instead a broader construction that promotes the best interests of the child.

adoptive parent is fixed and certain. A joint adoption also enables the children to be eligible for a variety of public and private benefits, including Social Security, worker's compensation, and intestate succession, as well as employment benefits such as health insurance and family leave, on account of not one, but two legally recognized parents. Most importantly, a joint adoption affords the adopted children the love, nurturing, and support of not one, but two parents.

* * *

There is also a broader, systemic reason for opting in favor of a construction of section 9–301 that permits the joint petitions filed in this case. The Probate Code requires the court to evaluate the best interest factors in order "to give the adoptee a *permanent home* at the earliest possible date." 18–A M.R.S. § 9–308(b) (emphasis added). * * * "[P]ermanency planning was embraced by Congress in the Adoption and Safe Families Act of 1997 (ASFA) in direct response to the documented inability of state child welfare systems to bring about stable and final outcomes for children within a timeframe reasonably designed to meet their needs." * * * [B]ecause of "the strong public policy favoring permanency for children [that] must inform the trial court's exercise of judicial discretion associated with determining a child's best interest," a disposition that will result in a child remaining in long-term foster care can only be sustained if there is a compelling reason for it.

* * *

Viewing the petitions and the supporting reports and documents in the light most favorable to the petitioners, it is clear that a construction of section 9–301 that imposes a procedural bar that would further complicate and delay, or even prohibit, the court from considering a joint adoption petition is inimical to the children's interests and bears no connection to the child welfare goals of our adoption and child protection statutes. When faced with competing constructions of a statute, we choose the construction "that avoids a result adverse to the public interest." We conclude that section 9–301 does not prohibit a joint adoption petition by two unmarried persons.

* * *

NOTES AND QUESTIONS

1. *The "best interests of the child."* Once the child is available for adoption and the prospective adoptive parents' standing is established, attention turns to whether granting the adoption petition would be in the best interests of the child. As Chapter 12 explained, the "best interests" standard triggers a fact-specific inquiry that vests considerable discretion in the court.

"[C]ourts have not demanded perfection in adoptive parents." *George L v. Commissioner*, 599 N.Y.S.2d 319, 320 (App. Div. 1993). Adoption may be in the child's best interests, for example, even where the prospective adoptive parents have relatively modest means. Adoption seeks "to provide the *best* home that is available. By that is not meant the wealthiest home, but the home which * * * the court deems will best promote the welfare of the particular child." *State ex rel. St. Louis Children's Aid Soc'y v. Hughes*, 177 S.W.2d 474, 477 (Mo. 1944) (emphasis in original).

Even a prospective adoptive parent's criminal record does not necessarily defeat the adoption petition. *See, e.g., In re Alison VV*, 621 N.Y.S.2d 739, 739–40 (App. Div. 1995) (holding that the 34–year–old prospective adoptive parent's convictions for disorderly conduct and hindering prosecution when she was seventeen did not preclude adoption because she had engaged in no further criminal activity, had been steadily employed by the same employer for twelve years, had been certified as a foster parent and had had foster children placed in her home).

What general factors should the court examine in determining whether a proposed adoption would be in the best interests of the child? If you were the probate judge on remand in *Adoption of M.A.*, would you have granted the adoption petitions in the best interests of the two children? How should the court respond if the prospective adoptive parents testify that they need to adopt the child for their own emotional well-being or to help shore up their shaky marriage?

Does the law on the books always reflect the law in practice? As you proceed through this Chapter, consider Professor Jana B. Singer's observation that recent years have seen "a change in the perceived purpose of American adoption law, from promoting the welfare of children in need of parents * * * to fulfilling the needs and desires of couples who want children." Jana B. Singer, *The Privatization of Family Law*, 1992 Wis. L. Rev. 1443, 1478.

2. *Determining standing and the best interests of the child.* The following examples illustrate some judicial decisions and policy directives affecting standing to adopt and the best interests of the child:

a. *Gays and lesbians.* As in *Adoption of M.A.*, gays or lesbians may wish to adopt children of persons other than their partners. One member of a gay or lesbian partnership may also file a "second parent" or "co-parent" petition seeking to adopt the other's child, who may have been born or adopted before the partnership began. The number of gays and lesbians who adopt is unknown because many applicants may hide their sexual orientation for fear that agencies and courts would hold it against them. *See, e.g.,* Patricia J. Falk, *Second–Parent Adoption*, 48 Cleve. St. L. Rev. 93 (2000).

Standing to adopt in "second parent" or "co-parent" cases turns on interpretation of the state's adoption act. Results in the courts have been mixed. *Adoption of M.A.* is typical of decisions that have granted standing; decisions denying standing include *In re Angel Lace M.*, 516 N.W.2d 678 (Wis. 1994). *See also* Richard F. Storrow, *Rescuing Children From the Marriage Movement: The Case Against Marital Status Discrimination in Adoption and Assisted Reproduction,* 39 U.C. Davis L. Rev. 305, 339 (2006), which reported that twenty-six states recognize second-parent adoption. Once the court enters an adoption decree, the second parent or co-parent assumes the rights and obligations of parenthood, including the obligation to support the child.

A same-sex partnership is not necessarily a homosexual partnership, but two states expressly bar homosexuals from adopting children. *See* Fla. Stat. § 63.042(3) (2008); Miss. Code Ann. § 93–17–3(5) (2008). Utah and Arkansas also prohibit adoption of a child by a gay or lesbian couple because both states permit adoption only by persons legally married to each other, or by single persons not living in a cohabitation relationship outside marriage. *See* Utah Code Ann. § 78–30–1(3) (2008); http://www.arelections.org/index.php?ac:show:contest_statewide=1 & elecid=181 & contestid=5 (Ark. statewide ballot initiative, 2008). In *Lofton v. Secretary of the Dep't of Children and Family Services*, 358 F.3d 804 (11th Cir. 2004), the court rejected due process and equal protection challenges to Florida's prohibition.

In other states, the best-interests-of-the-child standard determines adoption petitions filed by gays or lesbians with standing to adopt. A 2003 study found that 60% of public and private adoption agencies now accept applications from gays and lesbians, that some adoption agencies actively reach out to gays and lesbians, and that about 40% of adoption agencies have placed children with gay or lesbian parents. The study concluded that the numbers were probably higher because most agencies do not keep specific statistics on their clients' sexual orientation. *See* Evan B. Donaldson Adoption Inst., *Expanding Resources for Children* 11 (2006) ("Expanding Resources").

The 2000 Census found that more than 594,000 households are headed by same-sex partners, and that more than 400,000 children under 18 (whether adopted or not) live in these households. *See* U.S. Census Bureau, *Married–Couple and Unmarried–Partner Households: 2000*, at 1 (2003); U.S. Census Bureau, *Characteristics of Children Under 18 Years By Age, Race, and Hispanic or Latino Origin, for the United States: 2000* (PHC–T–30) (2004). The numbers are likely low estimates because they do not include, for example, households whose adult partners did not state their relationship or households headed by a single parent who is gay or lesbian. "Using the most conservative definition, it can be safely concluded that at minimum 1 million American children under the age of 18 have at least one gay or lesbian parent." *See* Expanding Resources, *supra*, at 11.

The number of studies on gay and lesbian parenting is comparatively limited, but "social science research concludes that children reared by gay and lesbian parents fare comparably to those of children raised by heterosexuals on a range of measures of social and psychological adjustment. * * * [V]irtually every valid study reaches the same conclusion: The children of gays and lesbians adjust positively and their families function well. The limited research on gay/lesbian adoption points in the same direction." *Id. See, e.g.*, Michael S. Wald, *Same–Sex Couple Marriage: A Family Policy Perspective*, 9 Va. J. Soc. Pol. & L., 291, 319–29 (2001); Charlotte J. Patterson, *Adoption of Minor Children by Lesbian and Gay Adults: A Social Science Perspective*, 2 Duke J. Gender L. & Pol'y 191 (1995). *But see* Lynn D. Wardle, *Considering the Impacts on Children and Society of "Lesbigay" Parenting*, 23 Quinnipiac L. Rev. 541 (2004) (suggesting that social science studies have ignored significant potential effects of gay childrearing on children, including increased development of homosexual orientation in children, emotional and cognitive disadvantages caused by the absence of opposite-sex parents, and economic security).

The American Academy of Pediatrics supports legislation permitting gays and lesbians to adopt their partners' children because these children "deserve the security of 2 legally recognized parents." The AAP concludes that adoption would provide these children not only the "psychological and legal security that comes from having 2 willing, capable, and loving parents," but also access to health insurance benefits from both parents, Social Security survivor benefits if either parent dies, and a continuing legal relationship with (and a right to continuing support from) both parents if the parents separate. *See* American Academy of Pediatrics, *Coparent or Second–Parent Adoption by Same–Sex Parents*, 109 Pediatrics 339 (2002). The AAP position is consistent with research findings that "have attributed the advantage in adoptive families partly to the added measure of legal security and social legitimacy associated with entry into formal legal parenthood"; where the law denies children adoptive status and thus consigns them to an informal relationship, "[t]he perceived insecurity of their status, at least when compared to the privileged status of adoption, sometimes results in a holding back of emotional investment in the relationship in order to protect against the trauma of potential family disruption." David D. Meyer, *A Privacy Right to Public Recognition of Family Relationships? The Cases of Marriage and Adoption*, 51 Vill. L. Rev. 891, 911 (2006).

b. *Single persons.* As Maine's statute at issue in *Adoption of M.A.* demonstrated, most states permit a single person to petition to adopt a child who is available for adoption but require married couples to petition jointly unless the petitioner is the child's stepparent. In some states, two unmarried adults may be unable to petition jointly to adopt a child even if neither adult is a biological parent of the child. *See, e.g., In re Jason C.*, 533 A.2d 32 (N.H. 1987) (opinion by Souter, J.).

Adoption by single persons can be in the best interests of some children who would otherwise be consigned to prolonged institutional or foster care: "[S]ingle adoptive parents are * * * most likely to adopt older children than infants, and * * * tend[ ] to adopt 'special needs' children who [are] older, minority, and/or handicapped." W. Bradford Wilcox & Robin Fretwell Wilson, *Bringing Up Baby: Adoption, Marriage, and the Best Interests of the Child*, 14 Wm. & Mary Bill of Rts. J. 883, 884 n.4 (2006), quoting *Adoption Statistics: Single Parents*, http://statistics.adoption.com/information/adoption-statistics-single-parents.html.

c. *Foster parents.* A substantial number of adoptions each year are by the child's foster parents. Until relatively recently, public and private child placement agencies often required prospective foster parents to agree in writing not to seek to adopt foster children placed in their homes. The purpose was to discourage development of emotional bonds between foster parent and child while the agency sought to reunify the child with the biological family or to find a permanent adoptive placement. In the past generation, courts have refused to enforce no-adoption agreements where adoption by the foster parents was in the best interests of the child. *See, e.g., Knight v. Deavers*, 531 S.W.2d 252 (Ark. 1976); *C.S. v. S.H.*, 671 So.2d 260 (Fla. Dist. Ct. App. 1996). Does *Adoption of M.A.* suggest any reasons why such agreements might be contrary to the best interests of the child?

Some state adoption acts now even grant a preference to foster parents who have cared for the child for a specified period, though the court retains ultimate authority to grant or deny the adoption petition in the best interests of the child. *See, e.g.*, N.Y. Social Servs. Law § 383(3) (McKinney 2003 & Supp. 2008) (preference for foster parents who have cared for the child continuously for one year or more). Courts may grant the foster parents' adoption petition even where a competing petitioner is the child's blood relative. *See, e.g. In re Adoption of CF*, 120 P.3d 992 (Wyo. 2005) (over objection of the biological mother whose parental rights had been terminated, court granted the foster parents' adoption petition and denied the paternal grandfather's petition for custody or visitation; adoption by the foster parents was in the boy's best interests because he had been placed with them when he was less than two years old, had lived with them for about two and one-half years, had developed a strong bond with them, and had made vast improvements in his numerous physical and emotional problems).

Adoption restrictions on foster parents have not disappeared. Tennessee's Department of Children's Services, for example, requires prospective foster parents to sign an agreement that "we will not attempt to adopt, file a petition to adopt, or take any steps whatsoever to adopt this child, unless, after consultation with the Department staff, the decision is made that adoption is in the child's best interests." Only after the child has been in the foster home for at least a year do foster parents enjoy a preference to adopt. *See In re Adoption of A.K.S.R.*, 71 S.W.3d 715, 718 (Tenn. Ct. App. 2001). Who should make the best-interests determination when foster parents seek to adopt, the agency or the court?

d. *Grandparents and other "kin."* Grandparents or other relatives sometimes seek to adopt a child whose biological parents have died, have had their parental rights terminated, or have become unable to care for the child because of mental disability, substance abuse or other cause. Courts show a marked inclination to honor the wishes of biological parents to place a child with fit relatives, but the best interests of the child remain determinative and relatives hold no substantive due process right to adopt. *See, e.g., In re Adoption of T.J.D.*, 186 S.W.3d 488 (Mo. Ct. App. 2006) (granting the foster parents' petition, and denying the grandfather's petition, to adopt four children; the grandfather lacked sufficient parenting skills to raise the children and intended to permit contact with the biological parents who had drug problems, while the foster parents loved the children and had provided them with a stable home in which they were thriving).

Some decisions create a preference or rebuttable presumption in favor of relatives who wish to adopt a child. *See, e.g., In re Welfare of D.L.*, 486 N.W.2d 375, 379 (Minn. 1992). In most states, however, the relative holds a preference or presumption only where a statute or rule grants one. *See, e.g., Clark County District Atty. v. Eighth Judicial Dist. Ct.*, 167 P.3d 922 (Nev. 2007). The preference or presumption created by statute or rule usually depends on the duration of the relative's relationship with the child. *See, e.g.*, Fla. Stat. § 63.0425 (2005 & Supp. 2008) (where child placed for adoption has lived with grandparent for at least six months, grandparent has priority to adopt the grandchild unless the deceased parent has indicated a different preference by will or unless the stepparent wishes to adopt).

e. *Stepparents*. Stepparents cannot adopt their stepchildren until the court terminates the parental rights of the noncustodial biological parent by consent or in a contested proceeding. Most stepparent adoptions involve stepfathers adopting their wives' children born in or out of wedlock. An uncontested stepparent adoption generally gives the law's imprimatur to a family structure already in existence.

The best-interests-of-the-child standard determines the outcome where the biological custodial parent dies, the other fit biological parent has no parental rights or consents to termination, and the surviving stepparent wishes to adopt the child. If no competing petition is filed, the court is likely to approve the adoption unless the stepparent appears unfit. If a close relative also petitions to adopt the child, the stepparent may lose because he (like the close relative) is a legal stranger to the child. The stepparent's position would appear most tenuous where the adoption act grants the relative a preference. On the other hand, the stepparent's position would appear stronger if the child has resided with him for a significant period and if uprooting would likely cause the child psychological harm.

f. *The petitioners' age*. In most states, a person must be eighteen or older to adopt a child, unless he or she is the child's stepparent or is married to an adult petitioner. *See, e.g.*, Md. Code Ann., Fam. Law § 5–331 (2006 & Supp. 2008). A few states establish a higher minimum age or set other requirements. *See, e.g.*, Ga. Code Ann. § 19–8–3 (2008) (requiring that the petitioner be "at least 25 years of age or * * * married and living with his spouse," and "at least ten years older than the child"). In states with no minimum age, courts determine on a case-by-case basis whether adoption by a minor would be in the best interests of the child.

Older persons frequently petition to adopt children. Courts determine these petitions in accordance with the best-interests standard because adoption statutes do not establish a maximum permissible age for adoptive parents. *See, e.g.*, *In re A.C.G.*, 894 A.2d 436 (D.C. 2006) (approving adoption by sexually abused 10–year–old child's 78–year–old great aunt, who had made financial arrangements for the child and arranged for two family members well known to the child, aged 67 and 41, to care for her if the aunt died or became disabled; the court found that removing the child from the aunt's care would likely have had a severe impact on child's emotional development because the aunt had cared for her since she was two months old). Where the petitioners are the child's grandparents or other relatives, the factors discussed in note 2.d above may affect the outcome.

g. *Disabled petitioners*. Several states have enacted adoption statutes prohibiting discrimination based on physical disability. *See, e.g.*, Wis. Stat. Ann. § 48.82(5) (2008) ("Although otherwise qualified, no person shall be denied the [right to adopt a child] because the person is deaf, blind or has other physical handicaps.").

3. *Incest*. Incest prohibitions are a major exception to the principle that a valid adoption extinguishes the child's legal relationship with the biological parents and creates a new legal relationship with the adoptive parents. Proof that one of the parties had been validly adopted is not necessarily a defense under incest statutes prohibiting marriage or sexual relations between parent

and child, brothers and sisters, and other close relatives of the whole or half blood. In *State v. Sharon H.*, 429 A.2d 1321 (Del. Super. Ct. 1981), for example, a half-sister and half-brother (born of the same mother but of different fathers) married. The sister had been adopted by a non-family-member when she was ten days old. *Sharon H.* rejected the couple's defense that the adoption rendered the otherwise incestuous marriage lawful.

4. *Adoption of siblings.* Must siblings be adopted into the same home, or may the court separate siblings by approving adoptions into different homes? Neither the U.S. Supreme Court nor any state supreme court has articulated a constitutional right of "sibling association," that is, a child's right not to be separated from siblings in adoption. In a handful of states, statutes require courts to consider sibling bonds when determining placement, or to make "reasonable efforts" to place siblings together. *See, e.g.*, 10 Okl. St. Ann. § 7202 (2008). But no state statute prohibits separate adoptions of siblings or even creates a rebuttable presumption against separation. As in custody decisions, "a sibling relationship is but one factor, albeit an important one, that a judge should consider" in determining the best interests of the child. *Adoption of Hugo*, 700 N.E.2d 516, 524 (Mass. 1998).

Courts prefer to keep siblings together in adoption. *See, e.g., In re Shanee Carol B.*, 550 S.E.2d 636, 642–43 (W. Va. 2001). The principle also applies to half-siblings. *See, e.g., Crouse v. Crouse*, 552 N.W.2d 413, 418 (S.D. 1996). Courts nonetheless separate roughly 35,000 children from their brothers and sisters in foster and adoptive homes each year. *See* William Wesley Patton, *The Status of Siblings' Rights: A View Into the New Millennium*, 51 DePaul L. Rev. 1, 1–2 (2001). Courts and agencies are sometimes torn between the desire to keep siblings together and the difficulty of finding adoptive parents willing and able to adopt siblings as a group. The court may subordinate the children's long-term interest in sibling association to their short-term interest in permanency. Should courts strive to keep siblings together in adoption whenever possible? Why?

A few states expressly grant separated siblings standing to petition for visitation with one another. *See* Ellen Marrus, *"Where Have You Been, Fran?" The Right of Siblings To Seek Court Access To Override Parental Denial of Visitation*, 66 Tenn. L. Rev. 977, 1013 (1999). Post-adoption visitation orders grounded in the best interests of the child but opposed by the adoptive parents face careful constitutional scrutiny after *Troxel v. Granville*, 530 U.S. 57 (2000), the third-party visitation decision presented in Chapter 13.

PROBLEM 17–1

Section 1–102 of the Uniform Adoption Act creates broad standing to adopt: "Subject to this [Act], any individual may adopt or be adopted by another individual for the purpose of creating the relationship of parent and child between them." If a prospective adoptive parent is married, his or her spouse must join the petition. UAA § 3–301(b).

Under Section 1–102, "[n]o one is categorically excluded * * * from being considered as a prospective adoptee or as a prospective adoptive parent." The drafters are explicit that "[m]arital status, like other general characteristics such as race, ethnicity, religion, or age, does not preclude an individual from adopting." *Id.* § 1–102 cmt. Parties with standing may adopt only where the Act's many requirements are satisfied. For example, a child would become available for adoption only where the biological parents consent to a direct adoptive placement, relinquish their parental rights to an agency, or have their parental rights terminated by a court. The court may approve the adoption only if it finds that the prospective adoptive parents are fit to adopt and that the adoption would be in the best interests of the child.

If you were a state legislator, would you vote to enact Section 1–102 of the UAA in your state?

A NOTE ABOUT "EQUITABLE ADOPTION"

Suppose an adult intends to adopt a child but fails to complete the adoption process and secure an adoption decree. The child continues to live in the adult's household, and the adult raises and educates the child and holds him out as a member of the family. If the adult dies intestate, may the child inherit?

More than half the states recognize equitable adoption, sometimes also called adoption by estoppel, virtual adoption or de facto adoption. The equitable adoption doctrine enables courts to enforce agreements to adopt where the adult failed to complete the adoption process through negligence or by design. The agreement may be with the child, the child's biological parents, or someone *in loco parentis*.

Most claimants invoking the equitable adoption doctrine have sought to share in the intestate adult's estate. Courts have also applied the doctrine in suits to recover damages for the adult's wrongful death, to recover support from the adult, to establish adoptive status under inheritance tax laws, or to recover life insurance, workers' compensation or other death benefits following the adult's death. The adult might also seek to invoke the doctrine, for example, in suits seeking workers' compensation benefits for the child's death, inheritance from the child, or damages for the child's wrongful death. Should courts be more willing to invoke the doctrine in a suit by the putative adoptee than in a suit by the putative adoptor?

Equitable adoption does not confer adoptive status but, in accordance with the maxim that equity regards as done that which ought to be done, confers the benefit the claimant seeks. Most decisions recognizing equitable adoption require proof of (1) the adult's express or implied agreement to adopt the child, (2) the child's reliance on the agreement, (3) performance by the child's biological parents in relinquishing custody, (4) performance by the child in living in the adults' home and acting as their child, and (5) partial performance by the adults in taking the child into their home and treating the child as their own. *See, e.g., Lankford v. Wright*, 489 S.E.2d 604, 605, 606–07 (N.C. 1997). Rather than rely on contract law, some decisions base equitable adoption on "inherent justice" because "the child 'should have been' adopted and would have been but for the [adult's] 'inadvertence or fault.'" *Estate of Ford*, 82 P.3d 747, 752, 753 n.4 (Cal. 2004).

Some states refuse to recognize the equitable adoption doctrine on the ground that establishing the parameters of adoption law is for the legislature and not the courts. *See, e.g., Sowers v. Tsamolias*, 929 P.2d 188, 193 (Kan. Ct. App. 1996). In jurisdictions that do recognize the doctrine, the judicial embrace has been lukewarm. Most recognizing jurisdictions require that the claimant prove the agreement to adopt by a heightened standard of proof, such as clear and convincing evidence. *See, e.g., Reutter ex rel. Reutter v. Barnhart*, 372 F.3d 946, 951–52 (8th Cir. 2004). Claimants "rarely" establish the requisite agreement. *J.N.H. v. N.T.H. II*, 705 So.2d 448, 452 (Ala. Ct. Civ. App. 1997). What explains the lukewarm judicial embrace?

C. THE ADOPTION PROCESS

1. AGENCY ADOPTIONS AND PRIVATE PLACEMENTS

The biological and adoptive parents may arrange an adoption by working through an adoption agency, or they may contact each other privately. The next article explains arrangements that lead to adoption.

JANA B. SINGER

The Privatization of Family Law.
1992 Wis. L. Rev. 1443, 1444, 1478–86.

* * *

1. AGENCY-FACILITATED ADOPTION

American law recognizes two methods of placing children for adoption with non-relatives: agency placement and independent or private placement, sometimes referred to as "gray market" adoption. In an agency adoption, the biological parents generally relinquish their parental rights to a public or private adoption agency, after they have been counseled about their options for raising the child. The agency is then responsible for placing the child with adoptive parents. Traditionally, in agency adoptions, the birth parents played little or no role in selecting adoptive parents and had no contact with the adoptive parents once they had been selected by the agency. This is changing, however, largely in response to competition from private placement adoption. Thus, many adoption agencies now permit birth parents to play a more active role in selecting an adoptive family. State laws relaxing the confidentiality of adoption records have also facilitated contact between the biological and the adoptive parents in agency adoptions.

Adoption agencies are also generally responsible for investigating the fitness of prospective adoptive parents. Traditionally, many adoption agencies restricted eligibility for adoption based on factors such as age, marital status, race, religion, financial stability and emotional health. These restrictions disqualified many prospective parents from participating in agency adoptions and discouraged others from even applying to agencies.

Once an agency approves prospective parents for adoption, those parents are typically placed on a waiting list until a suitable child becomes available for adoption. The waiting period for a healthy infant today can be as long as four to six years. When a possible child becomes available, the agency often performs additional studies on the biological parents and adoptive parents in an effort to ensure the success of the adoption. Agencies also provide for the care of the child should problems arise in the adoption process, and may perform follow-up studies after placing the child in the adoptive home, to ensure that the child and family are adjusting well.

Adoption agencies are heavily regulated by the state. In all states, such agencies must be licensed and, in most, they must operate as nonprofit entities. Some adoption agencies are dedicated exclusively to the provision of adoption services; others are part of multi-service agencies or government entities. * * *

2. INDEPENDENT OR PRIVATE–PLACEMENT ADOPTION

Independent or private-placement adoptions occur without the assistance of a licensed adoption agency. Instead, birth mothers and prospective adoptive parents deal directly with each other or, more commonly, through an intermediary such as a physician or a lawyer.[172] Often, potential adoptive parents seek out pregnant women who are considering adoption by placing advertisements in newspapers or magazines. These advertisements typically promise a loving and financially secure home for the baby, along with payment of the pregnant woman's medical and legal expenses. Some lawyers specializing in private adoptions engage in similar advertising directed at expectant mothers. Couples seeking to adopt privately are also counseled to send their resumes to obstetricians and to post their resumes in public places, particularly on college campuses.

Over the past ten years, there has been a marked increase in private-placement adoptions, particularly for healthy white infants. A recent treatise on adoption asserts that today "[t]he overwhelming majority of healthy infants are adopted through private placements." Other commentators report that, in California and other states that allow private adoption, up to eighty percent of all newborn adoptions are handled privately. * * *

Private-placement adoption differs from illegal baby-selling primarily in that payments to the birth mother are limited to her pregnancy-related expenses, and payments to the intermediary (if any) are restricted to the provision of professional services. The line between such permissible and

---

172. Some states explicitly permit third party intermediaries to assist a birth parent in locating prospective adopters and in arranging for the actual physical transfer of the child. These states supposedly hold intermediaries to strict accounting requirements for their fees and expenses. Other states permit private placements by parents, but prohibit unlicensed intermediaries, including lawyers, from engaging in "child-placement" activities. Even in these states, however, it is considered appropriate for lawyers representing prospective adoptive parents to advise them on how to locate a child, and for lawyers representing birth parents to advise them on how to evaluate prospective adopters.

impermissible payments, however, is often difficult to draw. State laws differ substantially on what qualifies as a compensable pregnancy-related expense on the part of the birth mother. Similarly, the distinction between legitimate professional services and illegal "child placement activities" on the part of an adoption intermediary is neither clear nor uniform across the country.

* * *

NOTES AND QUESTIONS

1. *An adoption profile.* In 2002, 56.5% of domestic adoptions of children by non-relatives were processed by public agencies, 22.4% were processed by private agencies, and 21.1% were processed by private individuals. *See* Adoption Factbook, *supra*, at 6. The increasing volume of private-placement adoptions is fueled by the contemporary shortage of white adoptable children without special needs, which has produced intense competition for these children among potential adoptive parents. The shortage stems from several factors. Abortion and birth control are more widely available to unmarried women than in the past; the stigma of single parenting and out-of-wedlock births has markedly diminished in the past generation or so; and 98% of unmarried women who deliver babies now choose to parent them. *Id.* at 11.

2. *Agency regulations.* In the past, many adoption agencies have excluded prospective adoptive parents based on such factors as age, marital status, religion, financial stability and emotional health. Today officially sanctioned discrimination is becoming the rare exception in American life, but discrimination in adoptive placement persists because it frequently results from exercise of agency discretion rather than from express rules and regulations. Where discrimination is charged, courts appear reluctant to second guess the agency determination, which is normally granted deference because of the agency's expertise. In light of society's general commitment to end officially sanctioned discrimination, what state interests support continued discriminatory treatment of prospective adoptive parents who are otherwise fit parents for a child available for adoption?

3. *Adoption fees.* "Earlier in the century it was considered inappropriate to charge couples seeking to adopt lest the arrangement appear too commercial; charitable donations were routinely sought and accepted. Since the 1950s fees have been charged to defray the administrative costs incurred by agencies: the costs for counseling biological parents and adoptive parents, for providing temporary care for the child, for handling termination of parental rights actions and for supervising placements after they are made." Joan Heifetz Hollinger, *Introduction to Adoption Law and Practice* § 1.05[3][a], *in* 1 Adoption Law and Practice (Joan Heifetz Hollinger ed., 1996 & Supp. 2007). Today the cost of a public agency adoption may range from zero to $2500; the cost of a domestic private agency adoption ranges from $4,000 to more than $30,000; the cost of a domestic independent adoption ranges from $8,000 to more than $30,000, and perhaps as much as $50,000. *See* Elizabeth J. Samuels, *Time to Decide? The Laws Governing Mothers' Consents to the Adoption of Their Newborn Infants*, 72 Tenn. L. Rev. 509, 522 (2005). Some

observers believe that in independent adoptions, "under the table" payments may boost the amount.

4. *Federal and state adoption subsidies.* In 2002, about 60% of unrelated domestic adoptions were of special-needs children. *See* Adoption Factbook, *supra*, at 8. The definition of "special needs" differs from state to state, but all states' definitions include older children; children of racial or ethnic minority groups; children with siblings who should be placed together if possible; and children with behavioral, developmental, mental health or medical challenges dating from birth, or from prolonged physical or emotional abuse inflicted by their biological or foster parents.

Child psychologists recognize that children freed for adoption thrive best in permanent adoptive homes rather than in prolonged foster or institutional care, but adoption agencies frequently experience considerable difficulty placing special-needs children. In 2003, an estimated 119,000 children were awaiting adoption from the child welfare system but only about 20,000 were in pre-adoptive homes. The waiting children were disproportionately minorities and older children who had been in substitute care for most of their lives. *See* U.S. Children's Bureau, *The AFCARS Report* (2005).

Special-needs children may require expensive professional care and treatment beyond the means of many prospective adoptive parents. In an effort to facilitate adoption of special-needs children needing permanency, federal and state laws provide financial assistance for parents willing to shoulder the responsibility. Some states grant tax credits to adults who adopt children. The state initiatives generally cover medical, maintenance and special services costs. Eligibility for state assistance generally depends on the adoptive parents' financial circumstances and the child's special needs.

5. *The Internet.* The Internet continues to revolutionize many aspects of the adoption process. Official federal and state websites provide photographs and profiles of children awaiting adoption; one such site is http://www.Adopt USKids.org, maintained by the U.S. Children's Bureau, which is part of the U.S. Department of Health and Human Services. Various private websites also offer advice, education and assistance for biological parents and prospective adoptive parents.

As in other fields, reliance on private Internet websites for information comes with both advantages and potential risks: "On the one hand, there is unrestricted access to information, along with convenience and privacy. On the other hand, there is the possibility of misinterpretation, inaccurate information, and deceit. The lack of adoption expertise can lead to serious misunderstandings. The failure to take into account the reputation of information sources, including Web sites themselves—and their owners and authors—raises the likelihood of reliance on incorrect information. Similarly, not 'knowing' your sources increases susceptibility to fraud and other misrepresentation." Nathan Gwilliam, *The Pros and Cons of the Internet's Impacts on Adoption Practice*, in Adoption Factbook, *supra*, at 425.

6. *Investigations or home studies.* In agency adoptions and private placements alike, adoption acts require at least one investigation or home study. In some states, courts may waive this requirement for good cause.

Many states do not impose the requirement where the prospective adoptive parent is the child's stepparent or other close relative.

The investigation or home study enables the court to determine whether the parents would be suitable for the child, helps the parents probe their capacity to be adoptive parents and the strength of their desire to adopt, and helps reveal factors about the parents or the child that might affect the adoption. The investigation or home study may also protect the child from a placement that is risky because of the parents' circumstances, such as a history of abuse or neglect or the parents' likely inability to cope with the child's special needs.

In agency adoptions, the agency must make an investigation or home study before placing the child with the prospective adoptive parents, with the child sometimes placed in temporary foster care in the interim. The agency must follow up with a further inspection shortly after placement. In private placements, however, no investigation or home study normally takes place until after the parent or intermediary has made the placement, and sometimes not until long afterwards. Concern about lax regulation of private placements has led some states to require that at least where the prospective adoptive parent is not the child's stepparent or other relative, a notice to adopt must be filed and an investigation or home study must be conducted before transfer of the child. Transfer may not be made until the parents are certified as qualified. *See, e.g.,* N.Y. Dom. Rel. L. §§ 115, 115–c, 115–d (McKinney 2003 & Supp. 2008). These requirements recognize that because of the child's need for continuity, a meaningful post-transfer study may not be possible.

Except in stepparent adoptions and other unusual circumstances, the adoption does not become final until the child has been in the adoptive parents' custody for a probationary period which, depending on the state, may range from three months to a year. The court signs the final adoption order if circumstances warrant after a final home investigation. Should states require home investigations and probationary periods in stepparent adoptions?

A NOTE ON THE INTERSTATE COMPACT ON THE PLACEMENT OF CHILDREN

In light of the sometimes significant differences among state adoption laws, parties seeking advantages from comparatively favorable provisions may move a child from one state to another. Forum shopping remains an option because only a few states have enacted the Uniform Adoption Act of 1994 (UAA), 9 U.L.A. 11 (1994 & Supp. 2006).

In 2002, about 14,000 children entered or exited states for adoption, implicating the Interstate Compact on the Placement of Children (ICPC), which all states have enacted since it was first proposed in 1960. *See* Adoption Factbook, *supra,* at 8–9. The Compact seeks to protect children transported between states for foster care or adoption, and to maximize their opportunity for a suitable placement. Most decisions hold that the Compact applies to both private and agency adoptions. *See, e.g., In re Baby Girl ___,* 850 S.W.2d 64, 68 n.6 (Mo. 1993) (citing decisions).

The Compact prohibits individuals and entities, except specified close relatives of the child, from bringing or sending a child into another state for foster or adoptive placement unless the sender complies with its terms and the receiving state's child placement laws. Before placing a child, senders must notify the receiving state's compact administrator, who must investigate and, if satisfied, notify the sending state that the proposed placement does not appear contrary to the child's interests. The child may not be sent or brought into the receiving state until notification is given. The sending agency retains jurisdiction over the child in matters relating to custody, supervision, care and disposition until the child is adopted, reaches majority, becomes self-supporting or is discharged with the receiving state's concurrence. The sending agency also continues to have financial responsibility for support and maintenance of the child during the period of the placement.

The Compact provides two penalties for sending or bringing a child across state lines in violation of its provisions. Violations are punishable under the child placement laws of either state, and may be grounds for suspending or revoking a license to place or care for children. ICPC Art. IV. The Compact does not specify whether violation may also be a ground for dismissing the adoption petition, and only a few decisions have entered dismissal orders. Should violation result in dismissal?

Where an attorney representing a party to the adoption overlooks or violates the Compact, the attorney may face professional discipline, sanctions under the civil procedure code's bad-faith pleading rule, or reduction of fees otherwise awardable. Counsel's noncompliance may be unintentional because "[m]any persons, including attorneys, who are inexperienced in interstate adoptions are simply unaware of the existence of the ICPC and its provisions." Bernadette W. Hartfield, *The Role of the Interstate Compact on the Placement of Children in Interstate Adoption*, 68 Neb. L. Rev. 292, 303 (1989).

2. BABY SELLING

All states have enacted statutes prohibiting baby selling and baby brokering. The statutes can operate against lawyers, who may act as intermediaries in private-placement adoptions by bringing together biological mothers (often unmarried teenagers) and prospective adoptive parents. The policy is that adoption should not be a commercial transaction for profit, but some observers believe that these statutes are frequently ineffective in preventing "under the table" payments by would-be adoptive parents desperate for healthy adoptable babies. As you read *State v. Brown*, consider why baby selling prosecutions are few and far between, and why sanctions imposed on biological and adoptive parents are quite rare and usually quite minor.

STATE v. BROWN
Supreme Court of Kansas, 2001.
35 P.3d 910.

McFARLAND, C.J.:

* * *

Defendant operated an escort service named "Blaze" out of her home in Wichita. Upon hearing that a former employee, Samantha Pruitt, had given birth to a child in Oklahoma and was considering putting the child up for adoption, defendant told her to wait. Defendant then went to Oklahoma and brought the mother and child to her home.

Defendant made arrangements for another employee (Teresa Lawrence) and Tina Black to acquire the child from Pruitt in exchange for a new car, $800, and a cell phone. Defendant was to receive half of the cash as compensation for her part in putting the deal together. The transfer of the child took place, but none of the agreed-upon compensation was paid or delivered. Pruitt became dissatisfied with the delay and complained to a friend who happened to be the girlfriend of a police officer.

Ultimately, Pruitt and the police officer reported the incident. In cooperation with the Wichita Police Department, Pruitt made a monitored telephone call to the defendant, wherein the following was said:

"Pruitt: So uh . . . what happened to the money that I was supposed to get and the car and cell phone. What did they . . . .

"Brown: Hey, you can get all that when you get the fucking uh . . . uh . . . birth certificate.

"Pruitt: . . . did they just . . . but what about you . . . your half of the money, did they give it all to you?

"Brown: Not yet they haven't. They're waiting for the birth certificate. I get to wait just like you get to wait.

"Pruitt: Yeah.

"Brown: You know, you produce what you're suppose and everything will go cool. All you have to go over you fucking . . . boyfriend's house and get it out of the garage . . . he has to wait 21 days . . . that's bullshit."

The conversation then disintegrated into name calling.

It was further stipulated: "None of the money was intended for any bill or expense incidental to birth or adoption proceedings." Ultimately, the child was found and taken into protective custody.

* * *

THE STATUTE

K.S.A. 59–2121 provides:

"(a) Except as otherwise authorized by law, no person shall request, receive, give or offer to give any consideration in connection with an adoption, or a placement for adoption, other than:

> (1) Reasonable fees for legal and other professional services rendered in connection with the placement or adoption not to exceed customary fees for similar services by professionals of equivalent experience and reputation where the services are

performed, except that fees for legal and other professional services as provided in this section performed outside the state shall not exceed customary fees for similar services when performed in the state of Kansas;

(2) reasonable fees in the state of Kansas of a licensed child-placing agency;

(3) actual and necessary expenses, based on expenses in the state of Kansas, incident to placement or to the adoption proceeding;

(4) actual medical expenses of the mother attributable to pregnancy and birth;

(5) actual medical expenses of the child; and

(6) reasonable living expenses of the mother which are incurred during or as a result of the pregnancy.

"(b) In an action for adoption, a detailed accounting of all consideration given, or to be given, and all disbursements made, or to be made, in connection with the adoption and the placements for adoption shall accompany the petition for adoption. Upon review of the accounting, the court shall disapprove any such consideration which the court determines to be unreasonable or in violation of this section and, to the extent necessary to comply with the provisions of this section, shall order reimbursement of any consideration already given in violation of this section.

"(c) Knowingly and intentionally receiving or accepting clearly excessive fees or expenses in violation of subsection (a) shall be a severity level 9, nonperson felony. Knowingly failing to list all consideration or disbursements as required by subsection (b) shall be a class B nonperson misdemeanor."

* * *

Discussion
* * *

It is clear that the legislature intended to discourage "the marketing of children by limiting the profitability of such activity" and to provide penalties for fees which are "of questionable legitimacy."

* * *

* * * Professor Linda Elrod and Judge James Buchele offer this insight into independent adoptions and the "baby broker":

"The extent of regulation of independent adoptions varies in those other states which allow them. A few states have no legislative restrictions. Some will not process an adoption if the child is found through an 'intermediary' or 'baby broker' not licensed as an adoption agency. Some limit the amount of money that can be obtained by those involved in placing a child for adoption. Other states, in addition to limiting fees, require extensive background investigations of all adoptive parents. All states find that selling a human being, especially a child, violates public policy. Additionally, engaging in adoptions for profit fails to take into consideration the best interests standard that applies in placing children generally. The highest bidder rather than the 'best home' gets the child."

* * *

Defendant draws our attention to the fact that in K.S.A. 59–2121(a) the prohibited conduct is that "no person shall request, receive, give or offer to give any consideration in connection with an adoption," followed by six exceptions thereto. However, subsection (c) speaks only of "[k]nowingly and intentionally receiving or accepting clearly excessive fees." Thus, she argues, the legislature has only criminalized the prohibited conduct of receiving or accepting such fees. From there she contends that as she did not actually receive or accept the agreed upon fee, she did not violate K.S.A. 59–2121(c). Defendant treats "accepting" and "receiving" as being synonymous. We disagree. "Receive" is listed in subsection (a), but "accept" is not. One must conclude that the legislature intended to criminalize more than "receiving" excessive fees by adding "accepting." Otherwise "accepting" would be a redundant term pulled from the air rather than subsection (a).

* * *

* * * [T]he purpose of K.S.A. 59–2121 is to discourage the marketing of children by limiting the profitability of such activity. The welfare of children lies at the heart of the legislation. The fact that defendant had not yet received the money she bargained for in brokering the child when law enforcement officials stepped in does not change the nature of the transaction. The child had changed hands pursuant to the deal defendant brokered. Defendant sold Pruitt's child * * *.

* * *

We conclude such conduct constituted "[k]nowingly and intentionally receiving or accepting clearly excessive fees or expenses in violation of subsection (a)," as set forth in K.S.A. 59–2121(c).

The judgment [of conviction] is affirmed.

* * *

NOTES AND QUESTIONS

1. *Discipline of lawyer intermediaries.* Lawyers and other intermediaries must heed the baby-selling statutes, which (like the Kansas statute quoted in *Brown*) permit payment of "reasonable" legal fees. In *In re Thacker*, 881 S.W.2d 307 (Tex. 1994), the court upheld disbarment of a lawyer convicted of purchasing five children from the same mother, including a set of unborn

twins. Lawyer Thacker, the sole proprietor of a state-licensed adoption agency, found biological mothers who wanted to relinquish their children for adoption and matched the children with adoptive parents. For her services, adoptive parents paid her an $11,000 fee for a placement, or $2,500 for a "hard-to-place" child. The biological mother would relinquish her parental rights in favor of the lawyer, who would then go to court with the adoptive parents and finalize the adoption.

In the case that led to Thacker's conviction, the biological mother was a prostitute and drug user who gave birth to her first child when she was fifteen and who commonly lived on the streets. The court of appeals found that the lawyer paid her about $12,000 for the five children. The court held that violation of the baby-selling statute constitutes a crime involving moral turpitude, a predicate for disbarment. *See Thacker v. State*, 889 S.W.2d 380, 384–85 (Tex. Ct. App. 1994), *denying writ of habeas corpus*, 999 S.W.2d 56 (Tex. Ct. App. 1999).

Unlike private agency intermediaries, lawyers need no license or certification specifically authorizing participation in adoptive placements. Adoption lawyers are licensed by the state to practice their profession, however, and remain subject to the ethical rules governing lawyers generally, and to discipline for professional misconduct. Should states require a special license for lawyers and other intermediaries who facilitate private placements?

2. *Questions about baby selling.* Does Samantha Pruitt, the biological mother in *Brown*, strike you as the sort of person who would be a good parent to her baby? If not, would everyone have been better off if the state had encouraged her to consent to the child's adoption by a devoted couple willing to pay her for the child? Do you agree with one judge who called baby selling a victimless crime: "Even if baby selling does exist, what's so horrible about that? If the child is going to a home with good parents who can give it all the love and security it will ever need, why should we care if the parents paid $50,000 for the privilege? The child is happy, the parents are happy, so what is the harm?" *Newborn Fever: Flocking to An Adoption Mecca*, Time, Mar. 12, 1984, at 31.

Judge Richard A. Posner argues that a regulated free market in adoptable infants would serve the best interests of the children involved. *See* Richard A. Posner & Elizabeth Landes, *The Economics of the Baby Shortage*, 7 J. Legal Stud. 323 (1978). Judge Posner finds that the existing adoption system countenances baby selling, marked by "a high black-market price conjoined with an artificially low price for babies obtained from adoption agencies and through lawful independent adoptions." Richard A. Posner, *The Regulation of the Market in Adoptions*, 67 B.U. L. Rev. 59, 65 (1987). He argues that a regulated market, with adoptions effective only on ultimate court approval, would be an antidote to the "the painful spectacle of mass abortion and illegitimacy in a society in which, to a significant extent, children are not available for adoption by persons unwilling to violate the law." *Id*. at 71.

If the thought of buying and selling babies offends sensibilities, does the law indeed permit money to count for too much under the present adoption system? Consider these thoughts:

ELIZABETH BARTHOLET

Family Bonds: Adoption, Infertility, and the New World of Child Production.
73–74 (1999).

The parental screening system applies only to those who do not possess the money to buy their way around it. Prospective adopters with money can escape all but minimal screening. They can also exercise extensive choice among the children available for adoption, and it is they who are most likely to end up adopting the healthy infants who are most in demand. The more money prospective adopters have, the greater their ability to shop around and escape the strictures of the system.

Without money, you are limited to the public adoption agency system, which deals primarily with the children in foster care and applies the classic screening and matching criteria. With money, you can venture into the private adoption agency world, where a great variety of screening systems are used and a much larger proportion of healthy infants and young children are available. Some private agencies screen and match according to the classic home study criteria, but others are much more sympathetic to nontraditional parents. Still others are willing to place children with virtually all adoptive applicants who satisfy minimal criteria. Prospective adopters can shop among the private agencies and select the one most sympathetic to their personal profile and most likely to provide the kind of child they are looking for. Fees vary significantly, with the agencies that are most open to nontraditional parents tending to charge higher fees.

Money also gives access to the world of independent adoption, which accounts for roughly one third of all nonrelative adoption in this country. Here home studies are not required at all. Some intermediaries and some birth parents apply their own screening criteria, and nontraditional parents have a harder time adopting than young married couples do. But many of those who place children in the independent process do little or no screening, and those who are more selective have a wide variety of views on what qualities they are looking for. A great many parents who surrender infants at birth are attracted to independent adoption, so prospective adopters with enough money to explore the possibilities are able both to avoid classic screening and to find their way to a healthy newborn. The state subjects these parents to only the most minimal scrutiny in the court process that formalizes the adoption. Even when a postplacement home study is required, its purpose is to determine whether the adopter satisfies minimum fitness criteria, not to decide whether he or she ranks high enough to be assigned a particular child, as is the case in the agency process.

Independent adoptions are allowed in all but a handful of states. Even those states that outlaw them as a formal matter and require home studies prior to adoptive placement permit a form of adoption that enables those with money to bypass key aspects of the screening system. In what are known as identified adoptions, prospective adopters are allowed to find their own child as long as they satisfactorily complete a home study before taking the child home. Since they can generally exercise some choice as to who will do the study, and since they will not be compared with other potential adopters, they must satisfy only minimal standards for parental fitness.

Judged in terms of the very values it purports to serve, the screening system fails. Together with the rule against baby-buying, parental screening is supposed to ensure that children are assigned not to the highest bidder but to those deemed most fit to parent. The fact that money enables those deemed least fit to buy their way to the children who are most in demand makes a farce of the entire system.

* * *

PROBLEM 17–2

Your state is one of the handful that does not permit private placement adoptions to adoptive parents unrelated to the child. You chair the state bar association's family law committee. A leading newspaper's editorial page editor has asked you to write an op-ed article that fairly summarizes the arguments for and against private placement adoptions to non-relatives, with your conclusions about whether the legislature should enact legislation permitting such adoptions, subject of course to the court's ultimate authority to approve or reject particular adoptions. What will you say?

D. THE CONSENT REQUIREMENT

1. REQUIREMENT OF INFORMED AND VOLUNTARY CONSENT

The general rule is that on a petition by persons with standing to adopt, the court may not proceed unless consents to adoption have been secured from all persons with a right to give or withhold consent. The required consents do not complete the adoption, but merely enable the court to order the adoption in the best interests of the child if it concludes all other requirements have been satisfied.

Knowing and voluntary consent (or, as some statutes call it, "release," "relinquishment" or "surrender") generally must be secured from both biological parents. Most states specify that consent to adoption may not be executed until the child is born. *See, e.g.,* Ariz. Rev. Stat. § 8–107(B) (2008) ("A consent given before seventy-two hours after the birth of the child is invalid."). In some states, this specification applies only to the biological mother; the biological father may consent before or after the child's birth. *See, e.g.,* 23 Pa. Cons. Stat. § 2711(c) (2008). Why would states distinguish between mothers and fathers in this respect?

A parent may execute a specific consent (authorizing adoption only by particular persons named in the consent), or a general consent (authorizing adoption by persons chosen by the agency, an authorized intermediary, or the court). To preserve confidentiality, general consents are normally used in adoptions in which a child placement agency is the intermediary.

Consent is not required from a biological parent who has died, who a court determines is incompetent, whose parental rights have been terminated by consent or court order, or who has abandoned or neglected the child for a specified period. If the biological parent is incompetent, the court may appoint a guardian of the child's person, with authority to consider whether to consent in the parent's stead. In some states, the court in the adoption proceeding itself may determine whether to terminate parental rights. Other states require that where contested or consensual termination is a predicate for adoption, the termination proceeding must take place before the adoption proceeding.

The right of unwed fathers to withhold consent to an adoption can present particularly thorny questions. The biological mother has traditionally held the right to veto an adoption by withholding consent, unless consent was excused by operation of law. The right applied regardless of whether the mother was married to the father at conception and birth. Before *Stanley v. Illinois*, 405 U.S. 645 (1972), however, unwed fathers held no right to notice of the child's impending adoption and no right to veto the adoption under the federal Constitution or the constitutions or statutes of most states. By conferring due process and equal protection rights on the unwed father with respect to the child, *Stanley* and its progeny raise the specter that the father whose rights have not been terminated (including a father who cannot be located now) may appear sometime in the future and contest the adoption. The *Stanley* line of decisions is discussed in Chapters 5 and 12.

Because valid consent to adoption may terminate the parent-child relationship, statutes prescribe formalities designed to emphasize to the biological parent the gravity of consent. In almost all states, consent must be in writing. The adoption act may specify that the consent be signed before a judge, notary or other designated officer. A particular number of witnesses may be required. *See, e.g.*, Mass. Gen. Laws ch. 210 § 2 (2008) ("two competent witnesses, one of whom shall be selected by" the consenter). The consent may have to be under oath. *See, e.g.*, 750 Ill. Comp. Stat. 50/11 (2008). Where failure to comply with one or more of these formalities leaves the validity of the consent open to question, failure may invalidate the adoption itself. *Compare In re Adoption of Infant Child Baxter*, 799 N.E.2d 1057, 1058 (Ind. 2003) (where biological parents' written consents to adoption of their newborn were not properly notarized, the consents' validity may be satisfied by evidence that the signatures are authentic and genuine and manifest present intention to give up the child for adoption), *with Bridges v. Bush*, 220 S.W.3d 259, 261–62 (Ark. Ct. App. 2005) (because the notary was not present when the biological parents signed the consent and relinquishment forms, a fraud was practiced on the trial court and the adoption would be set aside because the biological mother testified that she did not know what she was signing). Why might a court strain to approve the adoption despite technical failure to comply with consent formalities?

In most states, consent to the adoption must also be secured from the child over a specified age. *See, e.g.*, Cal. Fam. Code § 8602 (West 2008) (twelve). Some statutes authorize the court to dispense with the child's consent for good cause. *See, e.g.*, Idaho Code Ann. § 16–1504(1) (2008) ("Consent to adoption is required from: (a) The adoptee, if he is more than twelve (12) years of age, unless he does not have the mental capacity to consent."). Why should consent of older adoptees be a condition of adoption? Should the court have authority to dispense with this consent in appropriate cases? Should the court consider the wishes of a child below the age of consent?

Where a child has been committed to the custody of a public or private child placement agency, the agency's consent may also be a factor. In a few states, agency refusal to consent operates as a veto, divesting the court of authority to grant the adoption. Many states make the agency's consent a prerequisite to adoption, but authorize judicial scrutiny by providing that the agency may not unreasonably withhold consent. *See, e.g.*, Minn. Stat. § 259.24(1)(e), (7) (2008). Under the familiar judicial approach to review of administrative decisionmaking, the court will likely accord deference to the agency because of its expertise. Even where the consent statute seemingly makes agency consent mandatory without condition, many decisions hold that the agency's refusal to consent is nonetheless persuasive only. The court holds authority to grant the adoption if it finds that the agency's refusal to consent is contrary to the best interests of the child. *See, e.g.*, *In re M.L.M.*, 926 P.2d 694, 697 (Mont. 1996).

2. THE NOTICE REQUIREMENT

The right to give or withhold consent to the adoption must be distinguished from the right to notice of the adoption proceeding. A person with the right to consent, such as a parent, may veto the adoption by withholding consent. The court may not enter the adoption decree until knowing and voluntary consent has been secured from all persons or agencies holding the right.

Notice of the adoption proceeding must be provided to persons whose consent to the adoption is required. The adoption act, however, may also require notice to other persons, who may have the right to address the court concerning the best interests of the child, but who do not hold the right to veto the adoption. To expedite the adoption process, some states provide that notice of the adoption proceeding need not be given to a person who has executed a valid consent to adoption. Do these provisions excusing notice make good sense? Most states permit minor biological parents to execute valid out-of-court consents without the advice of their parents or guardians, other family members or counsel. To help reduce the adoption's vulnerability to later collateral attack, however, counsel for the adoptive parents may wish the minor to acknowledge her desires in open court.

3. REVOKING CONSENT

In many states, the biological parents' consent to adoption may be revoked within the first few days after execution, or within the first few hours or days after the child's birth. The court may then have authority to determine whether to permit revocation in the best interests of the child. *See, e.g., In re Baby Girl P.*, 188 S.W.3d 6 (Mo. Ct. App. 2006) (denying mother's motion to withdraw her consent to newborn's adoption). Professor Elizabeth J. Samuels concludes that the brief "windows" (considerably shorter than the approximate six-week windows afforded by most European nations) stem from policy decisions to "value an increase in infant adoptions over the goal of encouraging careful deliberation" by the biological parent, usually the mother. Elizabeth J. Samuels, *Time to Decide? The Laws Governing Mothers' Consents to the Adoption of Their Newborn Infants*, 72 Tenn. L. Rev. 509, 511–12, 513 (2005). Whose interests are at stake when the state establishes the length of the "window" within which a biological parent may revoke consent to an adoption? Do the brief windows established in many states satisfactorily accommodate these interests?

E. OPEN ADOPTION

In an "open adoption," the child has continuing post-decree contact with the biological parents or other relatives. The continuing contact may include visitation, correspondence, telephone calls or other relations. Informal adoption, frequently with arrangements for openness, was the norm for the first several decades after Massachusetts enacted the first modern adoption act in 1851. Only in the early years of the twentieth century did states begin to mandate sealing of adoption records to insure confidentiality and complete severance of the legal and social relationship between adoptees and their biological parents.

In recent years, the shortage of readily adoptable children has helped encourage open adoptions based on agreements between biological parents and adoptive parents. The shortage has provided leverage to biological mothers who seek a future right of contact with the child before consenting to a private-placement adoption. Most adoption agencies also now accommodate birth mothers who seek open arrangements and might opt for private adoption in the absence of such accommodation. *See* Evan B. Donaldson Adoption Inst., Safeguarding the Rights and Well–Being of Birthparents in the Adoption Process 2 (2006). Because the *Stanley v. Illinois* line of decisions, discussed in Chapter 5, gives many unwed fathers a constitutional right to withhold consent to adoption, unwed fathers concerned about adoption arrangements may also have a voice.

The growth of privately arranged open adoptions has also resulted from the changing demographics of adoption. In recent years, smaller percentages of adoptions have involved newborns and greater percentages have involved children over the age of two, including considerably older children and other children with special needs. More and more children have been adopted by their stepparents, relatives and foster parents. The result is that in a growing number of adoptions, the biological parents, adoptees and adoptive parents know one another's identities and whereabouts before the petition is filed. The child may have had a relationship with his or her parents and other relatives that cannot be undone by a stroke of the judge's pen.

Where practical necessity or private arrangement does not produce openness, however, confidentiality and complete severance of prior legal relationships may still mark adoption. The next decision, which concerned an eight-year-old child, determines whether the court may order an open adoption in the absence of an agreement between the biological and adoptive parents, and perhaps over the adoptive parents' objection.

ADOPTION OF VITO

Supreme Judicial Court of Massachusetts, 2000.
728 N.E.2d 292.

MARSHALL, C.J.

* * *

* * * [W]e hold that a judge may order limited postadoption contact, including visitation, between a child and a biological parent where such contact is currently in the best interests of the child. The judge has the authority to ensure that such contact in the best interests of the child is maintained during an appropriate transitional period.

Judicial exercise of equitable power to require postadoption contact is not warranted in this case, however, because there is little or no evidence of a significant, existing bond between Vito and his biological mother, and no other compelling reason for concluding that postadoption contact is currently in his best interests. Vito has formed strong, nurturing bonds with his preadoptive family; and the record supports little more than speculation that postadoption contact will be important for his adjustment years later, in adolescence. * * *

I

* * * In 1990 Vito's biological mother began using crack cocaine, which she continued to do until 1995, with occasional periods of nonuse. Prior to May, 1991, when a judge in the Boston Juvenile Court awarded temporary custody of her three oldest children to the [Department of Social Services], she had been trading food stamps and using public welfare benefits to purchase crack cocaine. Her children were often left at home alone. When Vito tested positive for cocaine at birth, an abuse and neglect report concerning him was filed two days after his birth, alleging his positive cocaine screen and his mother's failure to obtain prenatal care. The report was substantiated. In February, 1992, the existing care and protection petition for Vito's three older siblings was amended to include Vito, and he was placed in the temporary custody of the department.

* * *

From the time of his removal from his mother's care in January, 1992, while in the hospital, until January, 1995, his biological mother visited Vito only once. During that ninety-minute visit, Vito responded minimally to his biological mother, withdrew from her and attached himself to his foster mother. At the end of that visit, the mother agreed to visit Vito again at the end of the month, on his first birthday, but although the foster mother and Vito arrived for the birthday visit, the mother failed to attend; she did not telephone to cancel the visit. Following the failed January, 1993, birthday visit, the biological mother made no request for a visit with her son for the remainder of 1993. During 1994 there were no visits with Vito, and little contact between the biological mother and the department; she told the department she had relocated to Florida.

In 1995, while back in Massachusetts in prison on shoplifting charges, Vito's mother signed a department service plan, entered a drug rehabilitation program and began visits with Vito and his siblings. Vito's mother was released from prison in October, 1995. The judge found that the mother's visits with Vito have been generally consistent since March, 1995, and that she has attended monthly supervised visits since her release. The judge found that Vito and his biological mother have "no emotional sharing" between them and remain dissociated, despite pleasant play and conversation. The judge found that Vito did not show any genuine interest in his biological siblings and did not appear to have formed any emotional attachment to his biological mother; he did not appear to be excited to see her and separated from her with no difficulties or emotional overtones. * * *

In contrast, the judge found that Vito is "fully integrated into his foster family both emotionally and ethnically." The judge found that it was "important" to Vito to belong to his foster family "because that was the only family he had known," and that "[t]he foster parents are invested in adopting [Vito]; they perceive him as their own son." She found that Vito "has a significant attachment to his foster family," and that separating Vito from his foster family could result in a range of negative responses, from severe depression to less severe trauma.

The judge concluded that, by clear and convincing evidence, Vito's mother is currently unfit to parent him. * * *

The judge further determined that "racial issues *may* at sometime in the future" become a problem for Vito (emphasis added). She found that Vito's relationship with his biological mother is "crucial" for his "racial and cultural development and adjustment," that his best interests will be served by continued "significant" contact with her after any adoption, and that under the department's adoption plan Vito would have limited or no connection to his African–American family or culture. She found that the department's plan is not in Vito's "best interest so long as it does not provide for significant ongoing contact with [his][m]other and [biological] siblings."

II

A

* * *

* * * [There exists] centuries-old equitable authority of courts to act in the best interests of children, even absent express or inferable statutory directives, when those children are properly under the courts' jurisdiction, as they plainly are here. * * * [There are also] years of precedent involving a long line of cases basing the authority of judges to order postadoption and other visitation on the Probate Court's equitable authority.

* * * [R]ecent legislative amendments * * * [do not] amount to a legislative repudiation of the view that postadoption contact may be judicially ordered.[17] * * *

* * *

A judge's equitable power to order postadoption contact, however, is not without limit. This equitable authority does not derive from the statutory adoption scheme, but it must necessarily be attentive to the policy directives inherent in that scheme, as well as to constitutional limitations on intrusions on the prerogatives of the adoptive family. The adoption statute contemplates, for example, that after an adoption decree, 'all rights, duties and other legal consequences of the natural relation of child and parent ... shall, except as regards marriage, incest or cohabitation, terminate between the child so adopted and his natural parents." This provision strongly suggests that in ordinary circumstances adoption is meant to sever most enforceable obligations involving the biological parent with the child. This statutory language is not a bar to judicial orders for postadoption contact, however, because an order for postadoption contact is grounded in the over-all best interests of the child, based on emotional bonding and other circumstances of the actual personal relationship of the child and the biological parent, not in the rights of the biological parent nor the legal consequences of their natural relation.

---

17. * * * In 1999, the Legislature amended provisions * * * to allow biological parents and adoptive parents to enter into an agreement for postadoption contact. The amendment provides that "such agreement may be approved by the court issuing the termination [of parental rights] decree * * * ; provided, however, that an agreement * * * shall be finally approved by the court issuing the adoption decree." Conditions for court approval of such an agreement include that it has been knowingly and voluntarily entered by all parties. * * * [I]n enforcing that agreement a court may later limit, restrict, condition, or decrease contact between the biological parents and the child, but may not increase that contact.

Constitutional considerations also guide the exercise of this equitable power. Adoptive parents have the same legal rights toward their children that biological parents do. Parental rights to raise one's children are essential, basic rights that are constitutionally protected.[22] *See, e.g., Wisconsin v. Yoder*, 406 U.S. 205 (1972); *Stanley v. Illinois*, 405 U.S. 645 (1972); *Meyer v. Nebraska*, 262 U.S. 390 (1923). "It is cardinal with us that the custody, care and nurture of the child reside first in the parents," and in most circumstances we "have respected the private realm of family life which the state cannot enter." *Prince v. Massachusetts*, 321 U.S. 158, 166 (1944). State intrusion in the rearing of children by their parents may be justified only in limited circumstances.

At a pragmatic level, unnecessary involvement of the courts in long-term, wide-ranging monitoring and enforcement of the numerous postadoption contact arrangements could result from too ready an application of the court's equitable power to issue contact orders. * * * [C]ourts are not often the best place to monitor children's changing needs, particularly the needs of young children. What may be in Vito's best interest at the age of five says little about his best interests at age ten or fifteen.

We also recognize the concern raised by the department and the amici that untrammeled equitable power used to impose postadoption contact might reduce the number of prospective parents willing to adopt. Any practice that potentially reduces the pool of prospective adoptive parents raises grave concerns. * * *

Where, as here, the child has formed strong, nurturing bonds with his preadoptive family, and there is little or no evidence of a significant, existing bond with the biological parent, judicial exercise of equitable power to require postadoption contact would usually be unwarranted. On the other hand, a judicial order for postadoption contact may be warranted where the evidence readily points to significant, existing bonds between the child and a biological parent, such that a court order abruptly disrupting that relationship would run counter to the child's best interests. Cases warranting a postadoption contact order are more likely to occur where no preadoptive family has yet been identified, and where a principal, if not the only, parent-child relationship in the child's life remains with the biological parent. A necessary condition is a finding, supported by the evidence, that continued contact is currently in the best interests of the child.[25] Because an order of postadoption contact affects the rights of the adoptive parents to raise their children, the order should

---

22. In some circumstances, of course, these rights are balanced with the rights and needs of the child.

25. We focus here on an order requiring postadoption contact between a child and his biological parents. Similar limitations apply to postadoption contact between a child and his biological siblings. * * * While contact with siblings and contact with biological parents may pose different challenges in the adoptive setting, and may be governed by different statutory considerations, in terms of intrusion on the prerogatives of the adoptive family, judicial requirement of contact with biological siblings might not differ significantly from a requirement for contact with parents.

be carefully and narrowly crafted to address the circumstances giving rise to the best interests of the child.

In such cases, the judge has the equitable authority to ensure that contact in the best interests of the child is maintained during an appropriate transitional period posttermination, or even postadoption. The purpose of such contact is not to strengthen the bonds between the child and his biological mother or father, but to assist the child as he negotiates, often at a very young age, the tortuous path from one family to another. Each day judges must grapple with the consequences of significant relationships that develop between young children and the adults in whose care or custody they are placed. It is for that reason that our jurisprudence has always made the interest of the child paramount.

Transitional provision for posttermination or postadoption contact in the best interests of the child, however, is a far different thing from judicial meddling in the child's and adoptive family's life, based not on evidence of the emotional ties and current dynamics between the child and the biological parent, but on speculation concerning some hypothetical dynamic between parent and child several years hence, later in adolescence, for example. * * * That is a matter that is properly left to the wise guidance of Vito's new family.

* * *

COWIN, J. (concurring, with whom LYNCH, J., joins).

* * *

In 1999, the Legislature added new provisions to the adoption statutes. * * * By enacting these amendments, the Legislature recognized that adoptive and biological parents may make agreements for postadoption contact. * * * The judge must approve the agreement as long as it is in the best interests of the child, is fair and reasonable, and has been entered into knowingly and voluntarily by the parties. A judge may order specific enforcement of the agreement; however, during an enforcement proceeding the judge may only limit, restrict, condition, or decrease contact with the biological parents, but may not increase the amount of contact or place new obligations on the adoptive parents. The Legislature instructed that these new sections should not be interpreted to "abrogate the right of an adoptive parent to make decisions on behalf of his child."
* * *

These amendments have a specific scope. Their purpose is to permit agreements between biological and adoptive parents that provide for postadoptive contact. The judge's power is limited to approving the agreement and reducing or conditioning the contact between the child and the biological parents. The judge is not empowered to expand the agreement. It is incongruous to believe that the Legislature would expressly deprive the court of the right to expand postadoption visitation when an agreement exists, but yet, in the absence of an agreement, grant the court broad power to order visitation.

* * *

NOTES AND QUESTIONS

1. *Questions about this decision. Adoption of Vito* was decided less than three weeks before the Supreme Court decided *Troxel v. Granville*, which appears as a lead decision in Chapter 13. Courts have not yet had occasion to apply *Troxel* to requests for post-adoption visitation with biological parents. (a) Does *Troxel* permit courts, over the adoptive parents' objections, to order post-adoption visitation? (b) If post-adoption visitation orders remain constitutional after *Troxel*, what showing must be made to secure the order?

2. *Statutory authorization.* About twenty states expressly authorize courts to order visitation between the child and specified persons—usually the biological parents, grandparents, siblings or other close relatives—when visitation would be in the best interests of the child. *See* Annette R. Appell, *The Endurance of Biological Connection: Heteronormativity, Same–Sex Parenting and the Lessons of Adoption*, 22 BYU J. Pub. L. 289, 305 n. 106 (2008). Some states expressly preclude visitation orders following adoption. *See, e.g.*, Tenn. Code Ann. § 36–1–121(f) (2008).

Where the adoption act is silent about post-adoption visitation, decisions have disagreed about whether courts may exercise inherent authority to order visitation with siblings, biological parents, or other third parties. Some decisions have authorized courts to enter more than the transitional visitation orders authorized in *Adoption of Vito*, at least in some circumstances. In *In re S.A.H.*, 537 N.W.2d 1, 7 (S.D. 1995), for example, the court held that visitation may be ordered with persons who previously acted in a custodial or parental role for the child when three factors indicate, by clear and convincing evidence, that such an arrangement would be in the best interests of the child: (1) the child's psychological need to know his or her ancestral, ethnic and cultural background, (2) the effect of open adoption on the child's integration with the adoptive family, and (3) the effect open adoption will have on the pool of prospective adoptive parents. Decisions such as *In re Adoption of C.H.*, 554 N.W.2d 737 (Minn. 1996), however, preclude courts from exercising equitable authority to enter post-adoption visitation orders on the ground that the adoption act terminates all legal rights and obligations between the adoptee and persons other than the adoptive parents.

Aside from the constitutional questions raised by *Troxel*, court-mandated openness stirs policy disagreements. Why might openness in appropriate cases serve the best interests of the child? What interests might be served by precluding courts, as a matter of law, from ordering openness?

3. *"Contact" agreements. Adoption of Vito* discusses a 1999 Massachusetts statute, which is typical of state laws that authorize specific enforcement of "contact" agreements that the court finds are in the best interests of the child. States without such statutes disagree about specific enforcement. In *Groves v. Clark*, 920 P.2d 981, 985 (Mont. 1996), for example, the court held

that a written visitation agreement between the biological mother and the adoptive parents would be specifically enforced where the agreement was in the best interests of the child. On the other hand, *Birth Mother v. Adoptive Parents*, 59 P.3d 1233 (Nev. 2002), refused to enforce an agreement purporting to give the biological parent post-adoption visitation rights because the adoption decree granted no such rights; a biological parent had no rights to the child except rights recited in the decree.

Should courts grant specific performance of agreements providing for post-adoption visitation between the biological parent and the child? Would *Troxel v. Granville* pose a barrier to specific performance in some or all cases?

F. CULTURAL AND RELIGIOUS IDENTITY

1. TRANSRACIAL ADOPTION

The term "transracial adoption" (TRA) literally describes any adoption in which the adoptive parents and child are of different races, including adoptions in which the child is white. As a practical matter, however, nearly all transracial adoptions in the United States involve white parents and black or biracial children. It is estimated that domestic transracial adoptions amount to less than one percent of completed adoptions. *See* Cynthia G. Hawkins–Leon and Carla Bradley, *Race and Transracial Adoption: The Answer is Neither Simply Black or White Nor Right or Wrong,* 51 Cath. U.L. Rev. 1227, 1264 n.257 (2002). According to the 2000 Census, about 17% of adoptive families in the U.S. are multiracial and about 271,000 children under eighteen have been adopted transracially. *See* U.S. Census Bureau, *Facts For Features: National Adoption Month* (2004); U.S. Census Bureau, Statistical Abstract of the United States 2006, at 54 tbl. 61.

The Howard M. Metzenbaum Multiethnic Placement Act of 1994 (MEPA), Pub. L. No. 103–382, 553(a)(1), 108 Stat. 3518, 4056 (amended 1996), was a federal funding statute that sought to encourage transracial adoption by ending the practice of matching adoptive parents with children of the same race in foster care and adoptive placement. MEPA prohibited states and private agencies from delaying or denying an adoptive placement "solely on the basis of race."

Experience quickly demonstrated that the word "solely" actually encouraged race-matching by permitting agencies and courts to consider the potential adoptive family's financial status and other cultural, ethnic and social factors. Congress amended MEPA in the Small Business Job Protection Act of 1996, Pub. L. No. 104–188, 110 Stat. 1755. As amended, MEPA prohibits private and public child placement agencies from denying any person the opportunity to become an adoptive or foster parent, or from delaying or denying the placement of a child for adoption or into foster care, "on the basis of the race, color, or national origin of the adoptive or foster parent, or the child." 42 U.S.C. § 1996b(1) (2003). The amended Act applies to any agency that receives federal funds, and makes violations actionable under Title VI of the Civil Rights Act of 1964. *Id.* § 1996b(2).

MEPA has not muted the national debate about transracial adoption. *See, e.g.,* Symposium, *Black Children and Their Families in the 21st Century: Surviving the American Nightmare or Living the American Dream?*, 26 B.C. Third World L.J. (2006). Professor Ruth–Arlene W. Howe, for example, argues that "[b]y according no legitimacy to the group interests of African–Americans and focusing just on the individual rights of African–American children, [TRA proponents] assure a supply of children to meet the market demands of white adults seeking to parent whatever children they select. These actions rob African–Americans of the privilege and responsibility of caring for their own children. No group can be assured continued existence and vitality if it does not bear and rear its own children." Ruth–Arlene W. Howe, *Transracial Adoption (TRA): Old Prejudices and Discrimination Float Under a New Halo*, 6 B.U. Pub. Int. L.J. 409, 417 (1997).

Professors Cynthia Hawkins–Leon and Carla Bradley contend that "although most White adoptive families provide loving homes for their African–American children, only a few of these families are able to effectively educate and prepare their African–American children for the realities of racism in this country." Hawkins–Leon & Bradley, *supra,* 51 Cath. U.L. Rev. at 1274.

On the other hand, Professor Randall Kennedy calls race-matching "a destructive practice in *all* its various guises, from moderate to extreme. It ought to be replaced by a system under which children in need of homes may be assigned to the care of foster or adoptive parents as quickly as reasonably possible, *regardless* of perceived racial differences. Such a policy would greatly benefit vulnerable children. It would also benefit American race relations." Professor Kennedy favors a system under which "race would not be allowed to play any part in the selection of adoptive families, unless there was some compelling justification substantiated by specific evidence directly relevant to the case at hand." Randall Kennedy, Interracial Intimacies: Sex, Marriage, Identity, and Adoption 402, 416 (2003).

In 2008, the Evan B. Donaldson Adoption Institute concluded that by mandating "an unyielding color-blindness," MEPA runs counter to sound adoption practice and the best interests of children. *See* Evan B. Donaldson Adoption Inst., Finding Families for African American Children: The Role of Race & Law in Adoption From Foster Care 7 (2008). The comprehensive Donaldson report criticized MEPA for inhibiting agencies from assessing a family's readiness and capacity to help a transracially adopted child cope with being "different," develop a positive racial/ethnic identity, and face discrimination. *Id.* at 6–7.

The Donaldson Institute argued that TRA law and practice must be grounded in "acknowledgement of race-related realities—not 'color blindness.' " *Id.* at 8. The Institute recommended that Congress reinstate the original MEPA standard that race may be one factor, but not the sole factor, considered in determining whether to approve a transracial adoption. *Id.*

Notes and Questions

1. *A bit of history.* The first recorded adoption in the United States of a black child by white parents took place in 1948. *See* Joyce A. Ladner, Mixed Families: Adopting Across Racial Boundaries 59 (1977). In 1972, the National Association of Black Social Workers condemned transracial adoption as "cultural genocide":

> * * * Black children should be placed only with Black families whether in foster care or for adoption. Black children belong, physically, psychologically and culturally in Black families in order that they receive the total sense of themselves and develop a sound projection of their future. Human beings are products of their environment and develop their sense of values, attitudes and self concept within their family structures. Black children in white homes are cut off from the healthy development of themselves as Black people.

> Our position is based on:

> 1. the necessity of self-determination from birth to death, of all Black people.

> 2. the need of our young ones to begin at birth to identify with all Black people in a Black community.

> 3. the philosophy that we need our own to build a strong nation.

> The socialization process for every child begins at birth. Included in the socialization process is the child's cultural heritage which is an important segment of the total process. This must begin at the earliest moment; otherwise our children will not have the background and knowledge which is necessary to survive in a racist society. This is impossible if the child is placed with white parents in a white environment.

Nat'l Ass'n of Black Soc. Workers, *Position Paper* (Apr. 1972), *in* Rita James Simon & Howard Altstein, Transracial Adoption 50–52 (1977). The ensuing nationwide decline in the number of transracial adoptive placements is generally attributed to this position paper, which led some states to enact legislation granting preferences to prospective adoptive parents who were of the same race as the child, and reportedly deterred some public and private adoption agencies from advancing transracial placements. Professor Howe also attributes the decline to reduced federal subsidies to social services agencies. Howe, *supra*, at 465.

2. Palmore. In *Palmore v. Sidoti*, 466 U.S. 429 (1984), discussed in Chapter 12, the white divorced mother lost custody of her young daughter after she married a black man. On the motion to modify the order granting custody to the mother, the trial court found neither biological parent unfit but placed the child with the biological father because "it is inevitable that [she] will, if allowed to remain in her present situation and attains school age and

thus more vulnerable to peer pressures, suffer from the social stigmatization that is sure to come." *Id.* at 431 (quoting the trial court).

Palmore held that the decision modifying custody violated equal protection. "It would ignore reality to suggest that racial and ethnic prejudices do not exist or that all manifestations of those prejudices have been eliminated," Chief Justice Burger wrote for the unanimous Court. "The Constitution cannot control such prejudices but neither can it tolerate them. Private biases may be outside the reach of the law, but the law cannot, directly or indirectly, give them effect." *Id.* at 433.

The Supreme Court has never considered whether *Palmore* prohibits judicial enforcement of race-matching in adoption cases, which raise child placement issues at least as profound as those raised in custody disputes between biological parents. Professor David D. Meyer concludes that "[s]trict scrutiny would not permit routine reliance on race as a factor in placement decisions, but leaves room for reliance where considerations of race are demonstrably necessary to achieving substantial gains in the welfare of an affected child":

> The available social science does not suggest that children are commonly harmed by transracial placements; indeed, in certain respects they appear to enjoy distinct benefits. Yet, studies also suggest that the readiness of transracial adoptive parents to anticipate and address issues relating to race is an important factor in ensuring that success. At a minimum, then, some specialized inquiry into the preparedness of transracial adoptive parents seems justifiable. Beyond that, considerations of race in child placement must depend upon empirical proof that, for a particular child, the benefits of preferring a same-race placement would be sufficiently significant to justify the social costs of race-conscious decisionmaking. While the available evidence suggests this will not be often, it remains incomplete and recognizes-as should the Constitution-that the circumstances and needs of some individual children are exceptional.

David D. Meyer, Palmore *Comes of Age: The Place of Race In the Placement of Children*, 18 U. Fla. J. L. & Pub. Pol'y 183, 206–07 (2007). Under what circumstances, if any, should race be a permissible consideration in adoption? Should the child's age matter?

3. *Native American adoption.* Congress' rejection of race-matching in child placement and adoption in MEPA stands in contrast to the lawmakers' recognition of tribal identity in the Indian Child Welfare Act of 1978 (ICWA), Pub. L. No. 95–608, 92 Stat. 3069 (codified as amended at 25 U.S.C. §§ 1901–1963 (2003)). MEPA expressly exempts the ICWA from its provisions.

The ICWA provides that "[i]n any adoptive placement of an Indian child under State law, a preference shall be given, in the absence of good cause to the contrary, to a placement with (1) a member of the child's extended family; (2) other members of the Indian child's tribe; or (3) other Indian families." *Id.* § 1915(b). By thus expressly recognizing children as tribal resources, the ICWA seeks to protect the best interests of Indian children, and to promote the security, survival and stability of Indian families and tribes. *Id.* §§ 1901(1),(3); 1902. Professor Barbara Atwood reports that the ICWA has produced "greater respect for tribal authority over the placement of Indian children and an expansion of tribal family preservation programs," while decreasing the rate at which Indian children are removed from their homes and the rate of placement with non-Indian caregivers. Barbara Atwood, *The Voice of the Indian Child: Strengthening the Indian Child Welfare Act Through Children's Participation*, 50 Ariz. L. Rev. 127, 128 (2008).

4. *Religion.* By statute in some states and case law in others, courts are mandated or authorized to consider the religion of the prospective adoptive parent and of the child (or the child's biological parents) in determining whether to approve the adoption. Religious matching raises two fundamental questions:

a. *Religious differences.* The first question is whether the court may deny an adoption on the ground that the adoptive parent and the child (or the child's biological parents) are of different religions. Courts generally hold that where the statute requires religious matching when "feasible" or "practicable" without creating an inflexible rule requiring matching, religion may be considered in determining the best interests of the child. *See, e.g., Petition of Gally,* 107 N.E.2d 21, 25 (Mass. 1952). Where the child is too young to express a religious preference, courts consider the biological parents' religious preferences for the child, but such preferences too are not determinative. *See, e.g., Cooper v. Hinrichs,* 140 N.E.2d 293, 297 (Ill. 1957). Religious differences are less significant where the biological parents consent to adoption by a petitioner of a different faith. *See, e.g., Adoption of Anonymous,* 261 N.Y.S.2d 439 (Fam. Ct. 1965).

Should the child's age affect the weight the court gives to the adoptive parents' different religion? Consider, for example, a twelve-year-old who has practiced a religion for as long as the child can remember and wishes to continue practicing. On the other hand, why should the court consider religion at all in determining whether to grant adoption of a newborn or infant by an otherwise qualified petitioner? Do you agree with the court in *Petitions of Goldman,* 121 N.E.2d 843, 846 (Mass. 1954): "[A] child too young to understand any religion, even imperfectly, nevertheless may have a religion. * * * [T]he statute was intended to apply to such children, and * * * the words 'religious faith * * * of the child' mean the religious faith of the parents, or in case of 'dispute' the faith of the mother"?

Should the feasibility or practicability of religious-matching depend on the availability of adoptive parents who share the faith of the child or the biological parents? If a special-needs child is difficult to place because of a physical or mental disability, religious matching may not be "practicable" if no such adoptive parents appear. *See, e.g., Frantum v. Dep't of Public Welfare,* 133 A.2d 408 (Md. 1957) (denying adoption by Lutheran petitioners of physically disabled infant whose biological mother wished him to be raised as a Catholic; denial was without prejudice to renewal of petition if the infant was not adopted by others in six months); *Petition of Gally,* 107 N.E.2d at 24 (holding that religious matching was not practicable where it was unlikely that the physically disabled two-year-old would be adopted by anyone other than the petitioners). On the other hand, where prospective adoptive parents of the same religion as the child or biological parents are available, religious differences may be a factor in determining the best interests of the child. *See, e.g., Petitions of Goldman*, 121 N.E.2d at 844–45.

b.   *Belief in a Supreme Being*. The second fundamental religious-matching question is whether a court may deny an adoption because a prospective adoptive parent does not believe in a Supreme Being. Some decisions consider a parent's non-belief in God as indicating inability or unwillingness to direct the child's religious and moral upbringing. However, *In re Adoption of E*, 279 A.2d 785 (N.J. 1971), is typical of decisions holding that without other facts, a court may not find failure to believe in God controlling. The court concluded that "[s]incere belief in and adherence to the tenets of a religion may be indicative of moral fitness to adopt in a particular case," but that morality does not lie "in the exclusive province of one or of all religions or of religiosity in general." *Id.* at 792–93.

Religious-matching statutes invite challenges that they violate the First Amendment by establishing a religion or by prohibiting the free exercise of religion. Where religious matching is merely one factor but not dispositive, courts reject these challenges on the ground that the statute seeks only to determine the best interests of the child. *See, e.g., Dickens v. Ernesto*, 281 N.E.2d 153 (N.Y. 1972). Some courts have held, however, that the First Amendment is violated when courts invoke religious matching as the sole ground for denying an adoption. *See, e.g., Adoption of E*, 279 A.2d at 793–96; *Orzechowski v. Perales*, 582 N.Y.S.2d 341, 347–48 (Fam. Ct. 1992).

G.   INTERNATIONAL ADOPTION

The post-World War II years saw growing numbers of Americans adopt children from other nations. Largely unknown in the United States before the war, international adoption began in earnest with returning soldiers and with media accounts of desperate European and Asian refugee children during and immediately after the conflict. The Korean and Vietnam wars increased Americans' interest, but soon international adoption was no longer a product solely of war.

Today the United States is the greatest "receiver" of children adopted across national borders. The increase in international adoptions by Americans appears to result, at least partly, from the shortage of readily adoptable children in the United States and, according to some observers, from the growth of open adoption that permits biological mothers to maintain contact with their adopted children born in the United States. Professor Solangel Maldonado contends that racial preferences—specifically, an aversion by whites to adopting African–American children—drives some of the demand. Solangel Maldonado, *Discouraging Racial Preferences in Adoptions,* 39 U.C. Davis L. Rev. 1415, 1467–68 (2006).

The growth of international adoption has generated spirited worldwide debate. Many child advocates argue that international adoption offers a future to abandoned, homeless and sometimes starving children in many corners of the world while also serving the needs of loving parents in the United States who face a shortage of adoptable American children without special needs. "Untold millions of children in foreign countries live in desperate need for a nurturing home. Their only real-world alternative to adoption is life or death on the streets or in orphanages." Elizabeth Bartholet, *Beyond Biology: The Politics of Adoption & Reproduction*, 2 Duke J. Gender L. & Pol'y 5, 11 (1995). Professor Bartholet recognizes that "[i]nternational adoption is not a panacea":

> It will never be more than a very partial solution for the problems of the homeless children of the world. There are millions on millions of those children. The best solution in any event would be to solve the problems of social and economic injustice that prevent so many birth parents from being able to raise their children themselves. But given the realities of today's world, and the existence of so many children who will not be raised by their birth parents, international adoption does provide a very good solution for virtually all of those homeless children lucky enough to get placed.

Elizabeth Bartholet, *International Adoption: Thoughts On the Human Rights Issues*, 13 Buff. Hum. Rts. L. Rev. 151, 158 (2007).

Critics have charged, however, that international adoption has fueled child trafficking and "often results in the transfer of children from the least advantaged women to the most advantaged," while "do[ing] nothing to alleviate the conditions in the societies or communities from which the children come and thus do[ing] nothing to change the conditions that place some women in the position of being unable to care for their children themselves." Twila L. Perry, *Transracial and International Adoption: Mothers, Hierarchy, Race, and Feminist Legal Theory*, 10 Yale J.L. & Feminism 101, 102 (1998). *See generally* David M. Smolin, *The Two Faces of Intercountry Adoption: The Significance of the Indian Adoption Scandals*, 35 Seton Hall L. Rev. 403 (2005).

International adoptions today account for nearly 15% of United States adoptions annually. The numbers have increased rapidly since 1990, when the State Department issued only 7,093 immigrant visas to orphans coming to the United States; in 2008, the Department issued more than 17,000 immigrant visas to orphans. From 2004 to 2007, China was the greatest source of intercountry adoptions, though Guatemala was the greatest source in 2008. *See* U.S. Dep't of State, *Total Adoptions to the United States* (2008), http://travel.state.gov/family/adoption/stats/stats_451.html.

For each of the past four years for which statistics are available, however, the number of U.S. visas issued for international adoptees has declined, and the decline is projected to continue. *See, e.g., Cuts In Foreign Adoptions Causing Anxiety In USA*, USA Today, Aug. 12, 2008, at 1. For one thing, some traditional "sending" nations have restricted or terminated adoptions by foreigners amid reports that children were being kidnapped from their biological mothers, even on public streets, because the children were worth thousands of dollars in the international adoption market. Professor D. Marianne Brower Blair finds international adoption marked by a recent "migration of entrepreneurs into a field once dominated by humanitarian and philanthropic organizations." D. Marianne Brower Blair, *Safeguarding the Interests of Children in Intercountry Adoption: Assessing the Gatekeepers*, 34 Cap. U. L. Rev. 349, 402 (2005). "[L]ack of regulation and oversight, particularly in the countries of origin, coupled with the potential for financial gain, has spurred the growth of an industry around adoption, where profit, rather than the best interests of children, takes centre stage. Abuses include the sale and abduction of children, coercion of parents, and bribery." *See UNICEF's Position on Inter–Country Adoption*, http://www.unicef.org/media/media_41918.html.

The recent declines in international adoptions is also partially attributable to close United States application of the Hague Convention on Protection of Children and Co-operation in Respect of Intercountry Adoption, which the nation formally ratified in 2007. On the one hand, the Convention recognizes adoption as a positive alternative for children unable to remain with their biological families but unlikely to be adopted in their own nations; on the other, the Convention seeks to stem trafficking in children by establishing minimal international adoption standards and procedures to safeguard the interests of children, biological parents and adoptive parents.

Even before U.S. ratification of the Convention, the federal Intercountry Adoption Act of 2000, Pub. L. No. 106–279, 114 Stat. 825 (codified in scattered sections of 42 U.S.C.), enabled the nation to participate in the Convention and secured its benefits for U.S. adoptive parents and adoptees in international adoptions. The State Department has promulgated implementing regulations requiring, among other things, that prospective adoptive parents receive pre-adoption training and counseling concerning the child's cultural, racial, religious, ethnic and linguistic background. U.S. Dep't of State, Final Rules, 22 C.F.R. Pts. 96–98, 71 Fed. Reg. 8161–64 (2006). The Child Citizenship Act of 2000, Pub. L. No. 106–395, 114 Stat. 1631, confers United States citizenship automatically on thousands of foreign-born children who do not acquire citizenship at birth, including certain children adopted by American citizens.

H. POST–ADOPTION DISPUTES

Uncontested adoptions are a refreshing aspect of juvenile and family court dockets, which are otherwise laden with abuse, neglect and delinquency cases and hotly contested divorces. "Unlike other cases where all too often we see people at their worst and the conflicts presented seem irreconcilable and the solutions we have to offer are less than satisfactory," judges in adoption cases "see people at their best, and the only complications are those in tying up the legal loose ends to ensure that the adoptive child will have the blessing of a safe home and loving family." Stephen N. Limbaugh, Jr., *State of the Judiciary Address*, 58 J. Mo. Bar 14, 17 (2002).

Adoption is a particularly enduring method of family creation because "the rate of failed adoptions is quite small compared to the rate of failed marriages." Barbara Bennett Woodhouse, *Waiting For Loving: The Child's Fundamental Right to Adoption*, 34 Cap. U. L. Rev. 297, 319 (2005). An adoption may fail, however, when the child manifests severe physical or emotional problems previously unknown to the adoptive parents. Adoption law faces its greatest challenge when a party sues to annul an adoption or to recover damages for negligence or fraudulent misrepresentation by an adoption agency or other intermediary.

Adoption codes normally establish a short period within which finalized adoptions may be challenged. *See, e.g.,* Md. Ann. Code, Fam. Law § 5–353 (2008) (one year). The period is not tolled during the child's minority because tolling would defeat the purpose of the short period, which is to produce finality and thus to protect children from the psychological trauma occasioned by disrupted lives. *See, e.g., Wimber v. Timpe*, 818 P.2d 954, 957 (Or. Ct. App. 1991).

Limitations statutes, however, frequently reach only challenges for procedural irregularities or defects in the adoption proceeding itself. A few states also expressly create a limitations period for fraud challenges. *See, e.g.,* Colo. Rev. Stat. § 19–5–214(1) (2008). Other states have enacted broad statutes of limitations that reach all challenges. *See, e.g.,* 10 Okla. Stat. § 58 (2008).

Where the adoption code's statute of limitations reaches only procedural irregularities or defects, courts usually permit challenges for fraud or other substantive irregularity under the state's civil procedure statute or rules relating to vacatur of final judgments generally. *See, e.g., Green v. Sollenberger*, 656 A.2d 773 (Md. 1995). Under general limitations doctrines, the limitations period for a fraud claim may be tolled until the allegedly defrauded party discovered or should reasonably have discovered the fraud. *See, e.g., McAdams v. McAdams*, 109 S.W.3d 649, 651–53 (Ark. 2003).

Burr v. Board of County Commissioners, 491 N.E.2d 1101 (Ohio 1986), was the first decision to impose civil liability on an adoption intermediary for nondisclosure of information about the adopted child's physical or mental condition. A number of jurisdictions have now permitted recovery for fraud or negligence, or both. Courts generally avoid the term "wrongful adoption" because application of settled negligence and fraud doctrines makes creation of a new tort unnecessary. The measure of compensatory damages sought is normally the extraordinary costs of raising the child in light of the fraudulently or negligently concealed physical or mental condition.

Lawsuits will likely continue because today's adoption dockets include greater numbers of emotionally and physically disabled foster children and of international adoptees. Complete information about foster children is sometimes unavailable because of poor recordkeeping, rapid turnover of social welfare agency personnel, and frequent movement of the child from home to home. Private adoption agencies frequently do not receive full information from foster care authorities. International adoptees may have been anonymously abandoned by their parents or may have come from poorly administered orphanages that did not maintain adequate medical histories. *See* D. Marianne Brower Blair, *Getting the Whole Truth and Nothing But the Truth: The Limits of Liability For Wrongful Adoption*, 67 Notre Dame L. Rev. 851, 868 (1992); Juju Chang et al., *From Russia With Love—Dealing With Difficult Adoptions*, http://abcnews.go.com/2020/story?id=6322100 & page=1 (Nov. 28, 2008).

Adoptive parents may seek to annul the adoption rather than merely recover damages. Annulment makes the adoption a nullity from the outset, and thus frees the adoptive parents from the rights and obligations that adoption creates; a damage action, on the other hand, leaves the adoptive family intact but awards compensatory or punitive damages, or both, for the defendant's fraud or negligence. Suits to annul adoptions tend to arise in three situations. An adopting stepparent may seek annulment when he or she later divorces the biological parent; the adoptive parents may find the child ungovernable and beyond their control; or the child may manifest undisclosed severe emotional or physical disabilities unknown to the parents when they adopted.

Except where the adoptive parents appear defrauded or where other extreme circumstances appear, courts normally deny annulment as contrary to the best interests of the child. An annulment order is particularly unlikely where the child has been in the adoptive home for a substantial period, or where the child's likely alternative is a return to state custody. "[P]ublic policy disfavors a revocation of an adoption because an adoption is intended to bring a parent and child together in a permanent relationship, to bring stability to the child's life, and to allow laws of intestate succession to apply with certainty to adopted children." *In re Adoption of T.B.*, 622 N.E.2d 921, 924 (Ind. 1993). Because "the law abhors the idea of being able to 'send the child back,'" *id.*, a number of decisions grant annulment only on a strong showing of fraud proved by clear and convincing evidence. *See, e.g., In re Lisa Diane G.*, 537 A.2d 131, 132–33 (R.I. 1988).

I.   ADOPTEES' RIGHTS TO "LEARN THEIR ROOTS"

"Closed adoption"—the practice of sealing of adoption records to insure confidentiality and complete severance of the legal and social relationship between adoptees and their biological parents—is "a relatively recent phenomenon":

> * * * The first "modern" adoption statutes were enacted around the middle part of the nineteenth century. * * * These statutes were not * * * concerned with secrecy or confidentiality. Adoption evolved over the next century, becoming more bureaucratic and professionalized. * * * The purpose of these early [20th century] confidentiality restrictions was *not* to prevent those involved in the adoption from

having access to information, but to keep the public from viewing these files to determine whether a child was born outside of marriage.

* * *

Similarly, during the 1930s and 1940s, when states began issuing new birth certificates to adopted children, the states' goals were to improve the collection of children's vital statistics and reduce the stigma of illegitimacy, not to prevent adopted children from gaining access to their original birth certificates. * * *

A number of social and professional pressures fueled the shift from confidentiality to secrecy during the post-World War II era. Adoption agencies used the promise of secrecy as a way to distinguish themselves from less respectable adoption sources. Social workers argued that secrecy would help insure the integrity of the adoptive family by preventing disgruntled biological parents from later attempting to reclaim their children. In addition, social workers believed that the secrecy of records would help biological mothers "recover" from their "indiscretion" and continue with their lives as though they had never had a child.

The changing demographic composition of birth parents also contributed to the rise of secrecy. Prior to World War II, a majority of the birth mothers who surrendered children for adoption were either married or divorced, and often relinquished children only after struggling to support them financially. In the postwar era, birth mothers were younger and predominantly single; the vast majority of their children were born outside of marriage and were relinquished within days of their birth. These changing demographics were accompanied by a shift in attitudes toward unwed mothers. Before World War II, out-of-wedlock pregnancy was often explained as the product of inherent and immutable biological and moral deficiencies. Children born under such circumstances were biologically suspect and women who gave birth outside of marriage were permanently marked as outcast mothers. In the post-World War II era, this biological explanation was replaced with a psychological paradigm that asserted that illegitimacy reflected an emotional rather than a biological disorder, and that such a "maladjusted" female could be "rehabilitated" and reintegrated into society. Key to this rehabilitation was the immediate relinquishment of the child and the permanent severing of ties between the biological mother and the adoptive family. * * *

Secrecy was thus seen as critical to the successful rehabilitation of unwed (white) mothers and to their reentry into the marriage market, as well as to the child's successful integration into her adoptive family. Secrecy also served the interests of childless couples, who sought adoption in unprecedented numbers during an era of celebratory pronatalism, which viewed parenthood as a patriotic necessity and a prerequisite to marital success. Adoption protected these couples from the shame of infertility and created families for them that were seemingly indistinguishable from their biological counterparts. By the mid–1960s, these factors had combined to transmute traditional confidentiality requirements into a regime of sealed records and secrecy which prevented all members of the adoption triad from accessing information about the connection between adopted children and their biological families.

Naomi Cahn & Jana Singer, *Adoption, Identity, and the Constitution: The Case For Opening Closed Records*, 2 U. Pa. J. Const. L. 150, 154–56 (1999).

Confidentiality legislation today is grounded in the policy determination that closed records serve the interests of all parties to the adoption. The biological parents can put the past behind them, secure from embarrassment, and sometimes shame, arising from the adoption itself and perhaps the circumstances of the pregnancy and birth. The adoptive parents can raise the child as their own, free from outside interference and fear that the biological parent might try to "reclaim" the child. The adoptee avoids any shame from out-of-wedlock birth and can develop a relationship with the adoptive parents. By serving these interests of the members of the adoption triangle, confidentiality is also said to serve a state interest in encouraging persons to participate in the adoption process. *See* Elizabeth J. Samuels, *The Idea of Adoption: An Inquiry into the History of Adult Adoptee Access to Birth Records*, 53 Rutgers L. Rev. 367 (2001).

When the court decrees an adoption, the child is issued a new birth certificate naming the adoptive parents as the only parents and the child assumes their surname. The original birth certificate and all other court records are permanently sealed and may be released only on court order for good cause (or in some states, on consent of the adoptive parents, the biological parents, and the adoptee). In the absence of the severe necessity that establishes good cause, the biological parents may not learn the identity or whereabouts of the child or adoptive parents, and the adoptive parents and the child may not learn the identities or whereabouts of the biological parents. An adoptee inquisitive about his or her heritage may learn only what the adoptive parents reveal, and they may not know very much themselves.

The good-cause requirement permits disclosure of identifying information (that is, information which includes the birth parents' name, birth date, place of birth and last known address) only where the adoptee shows an urgent need for medical, genetic or other reasons. Even without such a showing, most states mandate or allow disclosure to adoptive families of an adopted child's health and genetic information, which can be critical in an age of rapid advances in medicine and genetic counseling. Some states also grant adoptees, when they reach majority, the right to nonidentifying information concerning their biological parents (that is, information about the parents' physical description, age at the time of adoption, race, nationality, religious background, and talents and hobbies, without revealing the parents' identities).

A vast array of statutes and rules may help assure confidentiality. Adoption proceedings are not open to the public. Adoption records are exempt from state freedom of information acts or open records laws. The adoption agency, the attorneys and other participants face criminal or contempt sanction for making unauthorized disclosure. *See, e.g.*, Or. Rev. Stat. § 109.440 (2008).

Confidentiality statutes lose their force when the court orders an open adoption, or specifically enforces a private agreement for such an arrangement. As a practical matter, confidentiality may also be impossible where the birth mother insists on maintaining contact with the child as a condition of her consent, where the adoption is otherwise concluded informally before the parties seek the decree, or where the child has had a pre-adoption relationship with the biological parents or other relatives.

In the absence of privately negotiated, practical or court-mandated openness, confidentiality statutes impede or thwart the efforts of many adoptees to locate their birth parents. The adoption act's mandate that the child assume a new identity and a new life, however, cannot extinguish the desire of many adoptees for disclosure. Recent years have witnessed the growth of advocacy and support groups to assist adoptees' efforts to locate their birth families, to lobby for legislation easing confidentiality standards, and to challenge the constitutionality of sealed-records statutes.

Federal and state courts have rebuffed a variety of challenges to the constitutionality of statutes that mandate confidentiality of adoption records in the absence of good cause for disclosure. Courts find a rational basis for upholding the birth parents' interest in privacy, the adoptive parents' interest in finality, and the state's interest in fostering adoption. *See, e.g.*, *Alma Society, Inc. v. Mellon*, 601 F.2d 1225 (2d Cir. 1979); *In re Adoption of S.J.D.*, 641 N.W.2d 794 (Iowa 2002).

Practical impossibility is sometimes the greatest barrier to an adoptee's search for his or her roots. Poor recordkeeping at some adoption agencies may make any sustained search fruitless, particularly after the passage of decades. Children adopted from orphanages overseas, sometimes after surreptitious abandonment by their biological parents, may have been subject to no recordkeeping in their native lands; an abandoned child might not even have a birth certificate or other proof of exact date of birth.

NOTES AND QUESTIONS

1. *Questions about sealed records.* (a) Are the interests of the biological parents, adoptive parents and the state sufficiently strong to thwart an adoptee's request for disclosure of identifying information? (b) Given the recent growth in open adoptions, do confidentiality statutes continue to serve

worthwhile purposes when adoptees seek disclosure of their sealed adoption records after they reach adulthood? (c) Given the contemporary shortage of healthy adoptable children and the long waiting lists of desirous adoptive parents, does the state still have a strong interest in sealing records to protect the sensibilities of prospective adoptive parents and thereby encourage adoption? (d) Does the state deny adoptees personal autonomy when it creates an adoption process by operation of law and denies them information concerning their heritage for the rest of their lives? Or does the state do enough when it assures release of non-identifying information needed for medical or other such purposes? (e) Would state-mandated openness lead some biological mothers to choose abortion rather than adoption?

2. *Psychological need.* In *Matter of Linda F.M. v. Department of Health*, 418 N.E.2d 1302, 1304 (N.Y. 1981), the adoptee unsuccessfully sought release of her forty-year-old adoption records. She alleged that her inability to discover her natural parents' identity had caused psychological problems because "I feel cut off from the rest of humanity. * * * I want to know who I am. The only person in the world who looks like me is my son. I have no ancestry. Nothing." *Linda F.M.* acknowledged that "desire to learn about one's ancestry should not be belittled," but held that "mere desire to learn the identity of one's natural parents cannot alone constitute good cause, or the requirement * * * would become a nullity." The court did state that "concrete psychological problems, if found by the court to be specifically connected to the lack of knowledge about ancestry, might constitute good cause." *Id.*

3. *Medical necessity.* In *Golan v. Louise Wise Services*, 507 N.E.2d 275 (N.Y. 1987), the 54–year–old movant had been adopted when he was less than fifteen months old. Suffering from a heart condition that produced a heart attack before the trial court heard the disclosure motion, he and his attending physicians asserted that genetic information would assist treatment and help enable the physicians to evaluate the severity of his condition. The movant asserted that without this information, the Federal Aviation Administration would not certify him to continue his career as a commercial pilot because the risk posed by his condition was unknown. Both of Golan's adoptive parents were deceased, and his biological mother and father would have been 75 and 80 years old respectively if they were still alive.

The adoption agency supplied movant Golan with all medical and historical information it possessed concerning his biological parents, except his biological father's name and hometown and the name of the college the biological father allegedly attended. (Golan already knew his birth mother's name.) The court denied the disclosure motion because "[a] rule which automatically gave full disclosure to any adopted person confronted with a medical problem with some genetic implications would swallow New York's strong policy against disclosure as soon as adopted people reached middle age." *Id.* at 279.

4. *Registry statutes.* Many states have enacted registry statutes, which provide for release of identifying information where the birth parents, the adoptive parents and the adoptee all register their desire for release. Passive

registry statutes allow parties to register their desires, and active registry statutes authorize state authorities to seek out parties' desires when one party expresses a desire for disclosure. *See, e.g.*, Colo. Rev. Stat. § 25–2–113.5 (2008) (passive); Or. Rev. Stat. § 109.503 (2008) (active). In states without registry statutes, the parties' unanimous consent to disclosure may still be insufficient to establish "good cause" and overcome the state's interest in secrecy. *See, e.g.*, *In re Estate of McQuesten*, 578 A.2d 335, 339 (N.H. 1990).

5. *Disclosure legislation.* A handful of states grant adoptees an absolute right to their original birth certificates when they reach adulthood, *e.g.*, Alaska Stat. § 18.50.500 (2006), or to the court records of their adoption proceeding, e.g., 9 S.D. Cod. L. § 25–6–15 (2006). In *Doe v. Sundquist*, 2 S.W.3d 919 (Tenn. 1999), the court upheld the constitutionality of legislation that allowed disclosure of sealed adoption records to adoptees twenty-one or older. The court held that the legislation did not impair the vested rights of birth parents who had surrendered children under the prior law, or violate the rights to familial and procreational privacy and to nondisclosure of personal information.

If you were a member of the Tennessee legislature when it considered the legislation at issue, how would you have voted? What objections to openness might be raised now by birth parents or adoptive parents who were promised confidentiality in adoptions finalized years ago? Why might birth parents or adoptive parents now welcome openness?

SECTION 2:   ASSISTED REPRODUCTIVE TECHNOLOGY

A.   OVERVIEW

This Section surveys assisted reproductive technology (ART) and discusses the promises and challenges that its growth poses for families and family law practitioners. As you proceed through the Section, notice the strains that rapid technological change places on traditional sources of common law and statutory enactment. As you consider whether Congress or state legislatures should regulate ART, weigh the vexing legal and ethical questions that ART poses for lawmakers seeking to balance the rights and obligations of the adults, with the best interests of the children and potential children. Consider also whether the constitutional rights of persons aspiring to become parents limit government authority to regulate ART. *See* Linda J. Lacey, *The Law of Artificial Insemination and Surrogate Parenthood in Oklahoma: Roadblocks to the Right to Procreate*, 22 Tulsa L.J. 281 (1987); Radhika Rao, *Reconceiving Privacy: Relationships and Reproductive Technology*, 45 UCLA L. Rev. 1077 (1998); John A. Robertson, *Embryo Culture and the "Culture of Life": Constitutional Issues in the Embryonic Stem Cell Debate*, 2000 U. Chi. Legal F. 1.

The following article provides an overview of some ART methods.

MARSHA GARRISON

Law Making For Baby Making: An Interpretive Approach
to the Determination of Legal Parentage.
113 Harv. L. Rev. 835, 845–52 (2000).

I.   THE REVOLUTION IN REPRODUCTION * * *

A.   Artificial Insemination

Artificial insemination (AI) is the oldest and most popular means of technological conception. An estimated 20,000 to 30,000 children are born in the United States each year following AI with sperm provided by donors (AID), and tens of thousands more following AI with sperm donated by husbands (AIH). AI first came into widespread use during the 1950s. Until the 1980s, it was almost invariably sought by married couples, either to enhance the probability of conception by bypassing the cervical barrier (AIH) or to "remedy" the husband's infertility (AID).

Although AIH and AID both offer an infertile couple increased odds of conceiving a child, they produce different results and different legal issues. The husband and wife who conceive using AIH are both genetic parents of the child, and thus, under traditional family law principles, they are also his legal parents. With AID, however, only the wife is genetically related to the child. Thus, under prevailing law at the time AID came into widespread use, her husband's parental status was unclear.

During the 1970s, the states began to enact legislation that clarified the AID child's legal parentage. The 1973 Uniform Parentage Act (UPA), for example, provided that "[i]f, under the supervision of a licensed physician and with the consent of her husband, a wife is inseminated artificially with semen donated by a man not her husband, the husband is treated in law as if he were the natural father of a child thereby conceived." As of 1998, fifteen states had adopted the UPA or a virtually identical standard, and fifteen others had enacted similar statutes that varied by eliminating the licensed physician requirement.

Although the AID statutes resolved the status issue that courts initially confronted, they failed to resolve a host of other legal questions that might arise from the use of AID—and which increasingly do. The status issues posed by AID today reflect a shift in its usage. Advances in the treatment of male infertility have markedly reduced the number of married couples who seek AID, while a remarkable change in parenting norms has greatly expanded the number of would-be parents who seek AID for reasons unrelated to infertility: many of these new AID applicants are single women who wish to achieve pregnancy but have no male partner; others are parties to a surrogate parenting agreement; and an occasional applicant wishes to become pregnant using sperm from a deceased partner. Many of these new users continue to employ sperm banks and physician assistance in order to ensure donor screening and anonymity, but others rely on known donors and perform AID at home without physician involvement.

The larger legal context has also shifted. As AID developed during the 1950s and 60s, its practitioners followed the model pioneered by adoption agencies. In both contexts, the goal was to provide would-be parents with the closest possible substitute for their own biological child; secrecy, participant anonymity, and physical-trait "matching" were employed to achieve these ends. But while AID practitioners still follow the old model, adoption practice has turned away from it. The federal government has severely restricted racial matching in adoption, and disclosure increasingly replaces secrecy; agencies and experts now counsel openness about the adopted child's origins, and adoption statutes have accordingly moved toward open records and even "open adoption," in which the biological parent retains some form of contact with the child after her adoptive placement.

The legal status of unmarried biological fathers has shifted even more dramatically. Although both AID users and adoptive parents could afford to ignore biological fathers during the 1950s and 60s—in most states unmarried fathers had no legal rights whatsoever—the Supreme Court has since held that an unmarried father who has "grasp[ed] th[e] opportunity [to develop a relationship with his child] and accept[ed] some measure of responsibility for the child's future" is entitled to constitutional protection. A number of state courts have accordingly voided adoptions when the unmarried father had no notice of the proceeding and promptly came forward to obtain custody. Courts have also permitted challenges to the marital presumption of legitimacy, and even sperm donors who have asserted claims to visitation or custody have sometimes been recognized as legal parents.

Current AID statutes were not drafted with an eye to either the new users or the new legal context in which AID occurs. Most do not address the paternity of an AID child born to an unmarried woman. Nor do current statutes typically provide guidance either on the AI donor's rights to a relationship with his biological child or the child's rights to information about her origins. In sum, current law on artificial insemination provides an extremely limited response to an isolated legal issue; it fails to assimilate AID into the broader set of legal principles governing parental rights and relationships.

B. *In Vitro Fertilization*

While AI avoids sex, in vitro fertilization (IVF) moves the entire process of conception outside the body. In IVF, ovarian stimulation is followed by the collection of eggs ready for fertilization. The process of fertilization takes place in vitro in a laboratory; some or all of the resulting preembryos are then implanted into the uterus or fallopian tubes. The first IVF birth occurred in 1978 in Great Britain. Since then, tens of thousands of children conceived through IVF have been born in the United States alone.

Like AI, IVF was originally employed by married couples with infertility problems; thus the first IVF baby, Louise Brown, was conceived using

Mrs. Brown's ova in combination with her husband's sperm. But as with AI, the uses of IVF have expanded. Because IVF takes the process of conception outside the body, it permits the use of donated eggs (the analog to AID); this practice has expanded dramatically because IVF success rates for older women substantially increase when the eggs of younger women are employed. IVF also permits the use of another woman to gestate the fetus; although less common than IVF with donated ova, this practice, too, has increased. The net result is a confusing array of "parents"; for example, would-be parents *A* and *B* might obtain sperm from Man *C* and eggs from Woman *D*, then have a doctor implant the resulting preembryos in Woman *E* to be carried to term. And, as with AI, today's IVF users are not necessarily married couples with fertility problems. *A* and *B* might be a gay couple, or *A* and *B* might be simply *A*, a single man or woman.

The parenting possibilities created by IVF present a host of legal issues. One set of questions relates to the legal parentage of children born through IVF. While arguably more complex, these questions are similar to those raised by AID. But IVF also poses altogether new legal problems relating to the status of preembryos created in vitro. Were these preembryos within her body, the pregnant woman could choose to abort them or carry them to term. When they are outside the womb, the woman's rights are less clear.

Courts have begun to address the legal issues raised by IVF, but legislatures have thus far been almost entirely inactive. The Tennessee Supreme Court has ruled that preembryos created through IVF and frozen for future use are neither persons nor property; when a married couple that had donated genetic material for the creation of such preembryos later divorced, the court held that, based on the facts and lack of an agreement regarding disposition of the preembryos, the spouse who wished to destroy the preembryos was entitled to do so over the objection of the other spouse.[63] The California Supreme Court has held that a baby born using IVF and a gestational surrogate was the legal child of the genetic parents,[64] and a lower court in New York has ruled that a woman who bore a child through IVF using donated ova was the child's legal mother. * * *

C.   Pregnancy for Another: The Various Forms of Surrogacy

Surrogacy—bearing a child for someone else—stands in contrast to AI and IVF in that it requires no technology at all. The Biblical Sarah, Rachel, and Leah all made use of surrogates—their handmaids—in order to produce children for their husbands; conception was achieved sexually rather than technologically. Modern surrogacy, however, invariably involves conception through AI. In the case of gestational surrogacy, in

---

63. *See* Davis v. Davis, 842 S.W.2d 588, 597, 604 (Tenn. 1992); *cf.* Kass v. Kass, 696 N.E.2d 174, 182 (N.Y. 1998) (upholding a preembryo disposition contract and noting the importance of effecting the parties' intentions). * * *

64. *See* Johnson v. Calvert, 851 P.2d 776, 778 (Cal. 1993).

which the woman who gives birth is not genetically related to the child she bears, IVF is employed as well.

Modern surrogacy also differs from that of Biblical times in its reliance on contract. Biblical surrogacy involved an informal understanding between the infertile woman, her husband, and her handmaid, but surrogacy today is almost invariably conducted on the basis of a formal, written document specifying rights and obligations. Surrogacy today is also commercial: contracts almost always require payments both to the woman who will bear the child and to a service that has brokered the arrangement.

Commercial, contract surrogacy emerged in the United States in the late 1970s. Although its use has spread, the number of surrogate births remains small in comparison to those obtained through AI and IVF alone; in 1993 the Center for Surrogate Parenting estimated that 4000 surrogate births had occurred in the United States.

Public attention became focused on surrogacy as a result of the widely-publicized case of *In re Baby M*, involving the legality of an agreement by a "surrogate" mother to relinquish the child she had conceived through AI to the sperm donor and his wife in return for $10,000. Perhaps because of the media attention, state legislatures reacted to surrogacy with greater speed than they have reacted to AI and IVF. By 1987, at least seventy-two bills pertaining to surrogacy had been introduced in Congress, state legislatures and the District of Columbia; today, nearly half of the states have statutes regulating surrogacy. Almost all of these statutes declare commercial surrogacy contracts void and unenforceable. Some additionally criminalize participation in and/or brokering of a surrogacy agreement. A few explicitly permit noncommercial surrogacy. And three states (New Hampshire, Nevada, and Virginia) permit some forms of commercial surrogacy, although all allow the birth mother to rescind the surrogacy contract within a specified time period.

Most surrogacy laws assume that the "surrogate" birth mother is genetically related to the child; they thus fail to address the increasingly common phenomenon of gestational surrogacy. With gestational surrogacy, it is possible for a child to have three "mothers"—one who is genetically related to the child, one who gave birth to the child, and one who planned the pregnancy and intended the child to be hers. It is also possible for a child to have three "fathers"—one related to the child genetically, one married to the woman who gave birth to it, and one who planned the pregnancy and intended it to be his. Current law, even in states with statutes governing surrogacy, typically fails to offer clear (or even murky) answers as to the rights and obligations of these various parties.

* * *

NOTES AND QUESTIONS

1. *Types of ART.* Professor Garrison identified artificial insemination, IVF, and surrogacy; in addition, ART may involve donor eggs and donor embryos.

2. *Infertility rates.* Assisted reproductive technology is fueled in part by significant rates of adult infertility, a condition that most experts define as being unable to get pregnant after at least one year of trying. Indeed, fertility has been called "one of the fastest growing areas of medicine." Jennifer L. Rosato, *The Children of ART (Assisted Reproductive Technology): Should the Law Protect Them From Harm?*, 2004 Utah L. Rev. 57, 58.

The U.S. Centers for Disease Control and Prevention reports that of the approximately 62 million American women of reproductive age in 2002, about 1.2 million (2%) had an infertility-related medical appointment in the prior year and an additional 10% had received infertility services at some time in their lives. Seven percent of married couples with the woman of reproductive age (2.1 million couples) reported that they had not used contraception for twelve months, but that the woman had not become pregnant. *See* CDC, 2005 Assisted Reproductive Technology Success Rates 3 (2007). The rate of female infertility in the United States is projected to continue increasing until at least 2025. *See* Ellen Hardy & Maria Yolanda Makuch, *Gender, Infertility & ART*, in World Health Organization, Current Practices and Controversies in Assisted Reproduction (Effy Vayena et al. eds., WHO 2002).

Infertility is often seen primarily as a woman's condition, but infertility due to the woman (a "female factor," such as tubal or ovulatory dysfunction) occurs in only about one-third of infertility cases. In another third of cases, infertility is due to the man (a "male factor," such as abnormal sperm or low sperm count). In the remaining infertility cases, the cause is a mixture of male and female factors or unknown factors. *See* CDC, 2005 Assisted Reproductive Technology Success Rates, *supra*, at 31; U.S. Dep't of Health & Hum. Servs., *Infertility* 1, www.womenshealth.gov.

3. *Deferred parenthood.* ART has also assumed greater importance as more and more women in recent years have postponed having children until their 30s and 40s. About 20% of women in the United States now have their first child after age 35, and about one-third of couples have fertility problems when the woman is over 35. *See* U.S. Dep't of Health & Hum. Servs., *Infertility, supra,* at 1. In 2005, the average age of women using ART services was 36." CDC, 2005 Assisted Reproductive Technology Success Rates, *supra*, at 15.

4. *Potential dangers.* "Rates of ART-associated birth defects are 1.4–to 2–fold higher than the overall rate of 3% to 4% of births in general." Nancy S. Green, *Risks of Birth Defects and Other Adverse Outcomes Associated With Assisted Reproductive Technology*, 114 Pediatrics 256 (2004). Much of increased risk is directly attributable to the significantly higher rates of multiple-infant births from ART cycles, which stem from the common medical practices of increasing the likelihood of conception by using stimulation hormones or transferring multiple pre-embryos. In 2005, nearly one-third of

live ART births were multiple-infant births (30% twins and about 2% triplets or more). These numbers contrast sharply with a multiple-infant birth rate of slightly more than 3% in the general U.S. population. *See* CDC, 2005 Assisted Reproductive Technology Success Rates, *supra*, at 22.

The CDC reports that "[m]ultiple-infant births are associated with greater problems for both mothers and infants, including higher rates of caesarian section, prematurity, low birth weight, and infant disability or death." *Id.*

5. *Sparse legal regulation.* Despite the substantial health risks to children of ART, "reproduction proceeds virtually unregulated" by federal or state law, and remains "bound only by the ethics of the fertility specialist and the financial and emotional limits of the infertile couple." Jennifer L. Rosato, *The Children of ART (Assisted Reproductive Technology): Should the Law Protect Them From Harm?*, 2004 Utah L. Rev. 57, 62. Professor Storrow reports that some private fertility clinics do little or nothing to screen applicants, though some clinics do apply "gatekeeper mechanisms" grounded in parental fitness and the best interests of the child. "On average, clinics turn away four percent of applicants each year. Three percent are turned away due to medical concerns that run the gamut from the near futility of treatment to the high risk of transmitting serious genetically based disorders to offspring. One percent are refused treatment due to psychosocial concerns." Richard F. Storrow, *The Bioethics of Prospective Parenthood: In Pursuit of the Proper Standard For Gatekeeping in Infertility Clinics*, 28 Cardozo L. Rev. 2283, 2286 (2007).

Federal law regulates ART in the Fertility Clinic Success Rate and Certification Act of 1992, Pub. L. No. 102–493, 106 Stat. 3146 (codified as amended at 42 U.S.C. 263a–1 to 7 (2003)); without establishing standards of practice, the Act requires fertility clinics to provide information about their success rates, which the U.S. Centers for Disease Control and Prevention publishes annually. Federal law also requires that donor gametes undergo tests for some diseases, such as HIV. Only a few states have ART statutes, which usually regulate only particular aspects of ART such as in vitro fertilization and surrogacy. In February 2008, the American Bar Association House of Delegates approved the Model Act Governing Assisted Reproductive Technology, which a committee of the ABA's Section of Family Law had drafted over several years, http://www.abanet.org/family/committees/artmodelact.pdf.

Professor Rosato urges more comprehensive public regulation to help protect the children of ART. "Many healthy children have been born to loving families using [ART] methods. However, these important decisions must be made more responsibly than in the past to ensure the safety and well-being of future children. Focused state regulation and federal oversight of developing technologies are central to remedying the problems created by the lack of regulation over the last twenty-five years." Rosato, *supra*, at 62. The prospects for enactment of comprehensive federal or state ART legislation in the foreseeable future, however, appear dim because the core issues underlying ART are "politically controversial and often mixed with religious, moral, medical, political, social, and legal disagreement." Charles P. Kindregan, Jr. &

Maureen McBrien, Assisted Reproductive Technology: A Lawyer's Guide to Emerging Law and Science 25 (2006).

PROBLEM 17–3

In 2007, the Victorian Law Reform Commission issued a report with recommendations for amending existing ART legislation in Australia. *See* Victorian Law Revision Comm'n, Assisted Reproductive Technology & Adoption: Final Report, www.lawreform.vic.gov.au. The Commission recommended, among other things, amendments that:

1) would prohibit ART treatment unless a woman is "in the circumstances in which she finds herself, unlikely to become pregnant other than by a treatment procedure";

2) would presume that people who have been convicted for sexual and serious violent offences, or who have had child protection orders entered against them, may not have access to ART treatment; and

3) would permit physicians or civil authorities who believe that a child born as a result of ART would be at risk of abuse or neglect to petition a clinical ethics committee, which would have authority to decide whether to prohibit ART treatment.

Could Congress or a state legislature constitutionally enact these restrictions under United States law?

B. DONOR GAMETES

In each of the various ART methods discussed in Professor Garrison's article, the genetic material may belong to the intended parents, or it may have been "donated" by another person. This latter form of reproduction is often called "collaborative" or "third-party" reproduction, because it typically involves people who are not seeking parenthood, but who donate gametes (sperm or eggs) or embryos, or assist in gestating an embryo.

Gamete or embryo donation and gestation assistance raise troublesome legal issues that lawmakers have frequently been loathe to confront. "In vitro fertilization is highly commercialized, and there appears to be no serious interest in regulating the sale of sperm, eggs, or even embryos. Donors of sperm receive relatively low compensation, but donors of eggs possessing highly desirable characteristics of beauty, intelligence, race or even religion are sometimes well compensated. While the word 'donors' is commonly used to describe gamete donors, in truth, the gametes are usually being sold based on market demand rather than being donated in an altruistic sense." Kindregan & McBrien, *supra*, at 79. Commercial sperm banks have proliferated, and "[b]uying sperm over the Internet * * * is not much different from buying shoes." Jennifer Egan, *Wanted: A Few Good Sperm*, N.Y. Times Mag., Mar. 19, 2006, at 46.

1. LEGAL RIGHTS OF DONORS, RECIPIENTS AND OFFSPRING

Anonymity. In a state without ART legislation, donors' parental rights and obligations depend on the wishes and circumstances of the parties, and of any private clinic that provides genetic material. A donor may be a "known donor," such as a friend or acquaintance of the recipient, or an "anonymous donor" whose identity the clinic protects. Known donors may be entitled to claim full parental rights, regardless of the terms of their agreement with the recipient.

Clinics have traditionally assumed that anonymity is best for everyone concerned, and have resisted entreaties to disclose donors' identities. Children's desire to "learn their roots," however, may be as strong after an ART birth as after an adoption. Many children conceived by ART wish to learn their heritage, including any medical history that might enable them to live productive lives.

Recipients of genetic material may also want their children to know the provider's identity. Either initially or after the passage of time, many donors wish to have knowledge of, or even to establish a relationship with, their offspring. Some sperm banks offer donors who provided sperm anonymously the option of allowing their identity to be revealed to their offspring after the offspring reach the age of majority. "Identity-release donors" (or "open donors") are gamete donors who state their willingness at the outset to be contacted by any offspring after the offspring turn eighteen.

Where a child is conceived through egg or sperm donation, should the law guarantee the child the right to learn the donor's identity? Or should the law mandate anonymity, just as the law has closed and sealed adoption records for much of the past century? Should the law permit egg or sperm donors, like biological parents in open adoptions, the option to remain in contact with the child they help conceive? In a regime generally governed by anonymity, should the law nonetheless permit the child or parent access to the anonymous donor's identity where the child needs medical information about the donor, for example because the child manifests a disease or defect that might be within the donor's genetic history?

Parentage. Traditionally, genetics has been the cornerstone of parentage. Where a husband and wife use their own sperm and eggs to conceive a child carried by the wife, of course, the wife is the child's mother by gestation and genetics, and the husband is the father by genetics and presumption. As *Michael H.* taught in Chapter 5, however, where a woman delivers a child with the sperm of a man other than her husband, she is the mother and her husband, if any, is the presumed father.

In collaborative reproduction, biological connections are even more complicated and less dispositive in determining parentage. A sperm donor may assert his biological paternity, or the husband may seek to rebut the marital presumption of his paternity by proving through genetic testing that he is not the genetic father. By the same token, where the child is born from an egg of a woman other than the mother, the egg donor might claim maternity or the wife could theoretically try to deny maternity for lack of a genetic relationship. *See* Uniform Parentage Act, art. 7, prefatory cmt. (2000, as amended 2002). ART even separates genetics from gestation.

Is a sperm or egg donor a parent of the child, entitled to the rights and obligations of parenthood (including the support obligation)? Or should the donor be assured protection from such rights and responsibilities? In addition to the "intended parent" or "intended parents," might the child have a second "father" or second "mother" (the sperm donor or egg donor respectively)? The Uniform Parentage Act, as amended in 2002, seeks to produce a measure of clarity. Consider these questions in light of the materials below—Delaware's enactment of the UPA provisions relating to sperm or egg donation, and a recent state supreme court decision in Pennsylvania, which has not enacted the UPA provisions.

Delaware Parentage Act

* * *

§ 8–102. Definitions.

In this chapter:

* * *

(4) "Assisted reproduction" means a method of causing pregnancy other than sexual intercourse. The term includes:

(i) Intrauterine insemination;

(ii) Donation of eggs;

(iii) Donation of embryos; [and]

(iv) In-vitro fertilization and transfer of embryos * * *

* * *

(8) "Donor" means an individual who produces eggs or sperm used for assisted reproduction, whether or not for consideration. The term does not include:

(i) A husband who provides sperm, or a wife who provides eggs, to be used for assisted reproduction by the wife;

(ii) A woman who gives birth to a child by means of assisted reproduction, or

(iii) A parent under subchapter VII of this chapter [relating to "child of assisted reproduction"].

§ 8–702. Parental status of donor.

A donor is not a parent of a child conceived by means of assisted reproduction.

§ 8–703. Paternity of a child of assisted reproduction.

A man who provides sperm for, or consents to, assisted reproduction by a woman as provided in § 8–704 of this title with intent to be the parent of her child, is a parent of the resulting child.

§ 8–704. Consent to assisted reproduction.

(a) Consent by a woman and a man who intends to be a parent of a child born to the woman by assisted reproduction must be in a record signed by the woman and the man. This requirement does not apply to a donor.

(b) Failure to sign a consent required by subsection (a) of this section, before or after birth of the child, does not preclude a finding of paternity if the woman and man, during the first 2 years of the child's life, resided together in the same household with the child and openly held out the child as their own.

§ 8–705. Limitation on husband's dispute of paternity.

(a) Except as otherwise provided in subsection (b) of this section, the husband of a wife who gives birth to a child by means of assisted reproduction may not challenge his paternity of the child unless:

(1) Within 2 years after learning of the birth of the child he commences a proceeding to adjudicate his paternity; and

(2) The court finds that he did not consent to the assisted reproduction, before or after birth of the child.

(b) A proceeding to adjudicate paternity may be maintained at any time if the court determines that:

(1) The husband did not provide sperm for, or before or after the birth of the child consent to assisted reproduction by his wife;

(2) The husband and the mother of the child have not cohabited since the probable time of assisted reproduction; and

(3) The husband never openly held out the child as his own.

(c) The limitation provided in this section applies to a marriage declared invalid after assisted reproduction.

§ 8–706. Effect of dissolution of marriage or withdrawal of consent.

(a) If a marriage is dissolved before placement of eggs, sperm or embryos, the former spouse is not a parent of the resulting child unless the former spouse consented in a record that if assisted reproduction were to occur after a divorce, the former spouse would be a parent of the child.

(b) The consent of a woman or a man to assisted reproduction may be withdrawn by that individual in a record at any time before placement of eggs, sperm or embryos. An individual who withdraws consent under this section is not a parent of the resulting child.

§ 8–707. Parental status of deceased individual.

If an individual who consented in a record to be a parent by assisted reproduction dies before placement of eggs, sperm, or embryos, the deceased individual is not a parent of the resulting child unless the deceased individual consented in a record that if assisted reproduction were to occur after death, the deceased individual would be a parent of the child.

* * *

Del. Code Ann. tit. 13, §§ 8–102, 8–702 to–707 (2005).

Note and Questions

Questions about the UPA. (a) Should sperm donation present an exception to the black-letter law (presented in Chapter 11) that a biological parent is liable for child support? (b) If the man "donates" sperm by having sexual intercourse with a woman, does the UPA apply? If not, what law determines the man's rights and obligations with respect to the child conceived by sexual intercourse? (c) Does the UPA distinguish between sperm donors who are known to the donee and anonymous sperm donors? Should it? (d) If the man and woman agree that the sperm donor shall be the father of any child born from the donation, is the agreement enforceable under the UPA? (e) The common law presumes that where a child born to a married woman, her husband is the father. If a woman is inseminated with a donor's sperm without her husband's knowledge, is the husband the "father" of the child and thus liable for child support? (f) What rights does the UPA grant the child who is born by assisted reproduction? Does the UPA adequately protect these children? (g) The law imposed a child support obligation on 13–year–old Shane Seyer (Chapter 11, page 589 above) who, as a matter of law, was incapable of consenting to the sexual assault that led to his child's conception and birth; why should the law not impose the support obligation on competent adults who knowingly and voluntarily donate their sperm?

FERGUSON v. McKIERNAN
Supreme Court of Pennsylvania, 2007.
940 A.2d 1236.

Justice Baer.

We are called upon to determine whether a sperm donor involved in a private sperm donation—*i.e.*, one that occurs outside the context of an institutional sperm bank—effected through clinical rather than sexual means may be held liable for child support, notwithstanding the formation of an agreement between the donor and the donee that she will not hold the donor responsible for supporting the child that results from the arrangement. The lower courts effectively determined that such an agreement, even where bindingly formed, was unenforceable as a matter of law. Faced with this question of first impression in an area of law with profound importance for hundreds, perhaps thousands of Pennsylvania families, we * * * reverse.

Former paramours Joel McKiernan (Sperm Donor) and Ivonne Ferguson (Mother) agreed that Sperm Donor would furnish his sperm in an arrangement that, by design, would feature all the hallmarks of an anonymous sperm donation: it would be carried out in a clinical setting; Sperm Donor's role in the conception would remain confidential; and neither would Sperm Donor seek visitation nor would Mother demand from him any support, financial or otherwise. At no time prior to conception, during Mother's pregnancy, or after the birth of the resultant twins did either party behave inconsistently with this agreement, until approximately five years after the twins' birth, when Mother filed a motion seeking child support from Sperm Donor. The trial court, recognizing the terms of the agreement outlined above and expressing dismay at what it found to be Mother's dishonest behavior, nevertheless found that the best interests of the twins rendered the agreement unenforceable as contrary to public policy. * * *

* * * Sperm Donor met Mother in May 1991, when he began his employment with Pennsylvania Blue Shield, where Mother also worked. At that time, Mother was married to and living with Paul Ferguson (Husband), although whether their sexual relations continued at that point is subject to dispute. Mother was raising two children she had conceived with Husband, while he provided little if any emotional or financial support.

Later that year, Sperm Donor's and Mother's friendly relations turned intimate, and in or around November 1991 their relationship took on a sexual aspect. Mother assured Sperm Donor that she was using birth control, and the couple did not use condoms. Although Mother variously indicated to Sperm Donor that she was taking birth control pills or using injectable or implanted birth control, in fact she had undergone tubal ligation surgery in or around 1982, following the birth of her second child by Husband.

* * *

* * * In September 1993, after learning that her tubal ligation was irreversible, Mother approached physician William Dodson at Hershey Medical Center, to discuss alternative methods of conception, specifically in vitro fertilization (IVF) using donor sperm followed by implantation of the fertilized eggs. Mother did not inform Sperm Donor of either consultation, and continued to mislead him by referring to one or more alternative methods of contraception she claimed to be using or considering using.

Toward the end of 1993, the parties' relationship had changed in character from an intimate sexual relationship to a friendship without the sexual component. At about that time, late in 1993, Mother broached the topic of bearing Sperm Donor's child. Even though Mother biologically was incapable of conceiving via intercourse due to her irreversible tubal ligation, and notwithstanding that the parties were no longer in a sexual relationship, she inexplicably suggested first that they conceive sexually. Sperm Donor, evidently unaware that the point was moot, refused. He made clear that he did not envision marrying Mother, and thus did not wish to bear a child with her.

Revising her approach, Mother then suggested that Sperm Donor furnish her with his sperm for purposes of IVF. Initially, Sperm Donor expressed his reluctance to do so. He relented, however, once Mother convinced him that she would release him from any of the financial burdens associated with conventional paternity; that she was up to the task of raising an additional child in a single-parent household and had the financial wherewithal to do so; and that, were he not to furnish his own sperm, she would seek the sperm of an anonymous donor instead.[4]

* * *

On February 14, 1994, Sperm Donor traveled to Hershey Medical Center to provide a sperm sample.[6] This sample was used, in turn, to fertilize Mother's eggs, which then were implanted. The procedure succeeded, enabling Mother to become pregnant. Sperm Donor in no way subsidized the IVF procedure.

* * *

* * * Even during the birth on August 25, 1994, * * * Sperm Donor maintained his anonymity regarding his biological role in the pregnancy, an effort Mother affirmatively supported when she named Husband as the father on the twins' birth certificates, and reinforced by the fact that Sperm Donor neither was asked, nor offered, to contribute to the costs associated with Mother's delivery of the twins.

Regarding Sperm Donor's and Mother's post-partum interactions, the trial court found that,

> [a]fter the twins were born, [Sperm Donor] saw [Mother] and the boys on a few occasions in the hospital. Approximately two years after the births, [Sperm Donor] spent an afternoon with [Mother] and the twins while visiting his parents in Harrisburg. [Sperm Donor] never provided the children with financial support or gifts, nor did he assume any parental identity. [Sperm Donor] had no further contact with either [Mother] or the children until May 1999 when [Mother] randomly obtained [Sperm Donor's] phone number and subsequently filed for child support.

* * *

Based on this recitation of facts, the trial court found that the parties had formed a binding oral agreement prior to the twins' conception * * *

* * *

The court nevertheless found the agreement unenforceable [because] "a parent cannot bind a child or bargain away that child's right to support" * * *. Relying on the support guidelines, * * *, the court im-

---

4. In testimony uncontradicted by Mother, Sperm Donor stated that Mother preferred him to an anonymous sperm donor because "[s]he knew my background. She just knew my makeup, and just said that she preferred to have that anonymous donor known to her."

6. Coincidentally, the paperwork for Mother's divorce from Husband was filed the same day.

posed on Sperm Donor an ongoing support obligation of $1384 per month effective retroactively to January 1, 2001, with a corresponding arrear of $66,033.66 due immediately upon issuance of the order.

A panel of the Superior Court affirmed the trial court's ruling in a unanimous opinion that echoed the trial court's ruling. * * *

* * * We must determine whether a would-be mother and a willing sperm donor can enter into an enforceable agreement under which the donor provides sperm in a clinical setting for IVF and relinquishes his right to visitation with the resultant child(ren) in return for the mother's agreement not to seek child support from the donor. * * *

* * *

* * * The inescapable reality is that all manner of arrangements involving the donation of sperm or eggs abound in contemporary society, many of them couched in contracts or agreements of varying degrees of formality. An increasing number of would-be mothers who find themselves either unable or unwilling to conceive and raise children in the context of marriage are turning to donor arrangements to enable them to enjoy the privilege of raising a child or children, a development neither our citizens nor their General Assembly have chosen to proscribe despite its growing pervasiveness.

Of direct relevance to the instant case, women, single and otherwise, increasingly turn to anonymous sperm donors to enable them to conceive either in vitro or through artificial insemination. In these arrangements, the anonymous donor and the donee respectively enter into separate contracts with a sperm bank prior to conception and implantation of an embryo or embryos. The contract releases the mother from any obligation to afford the sperm donor a father's access to the child for visitation or custody while releasing the donor from any obligation to support the child.

Thus, two potential cases at the extremes of an increasingly complicated continuum present themselves: dissolution of a relationship (or a mere sexual encounter) that produces a child via intercourse, which requires both parents to provide support; and an anonymous sperm donation, absent sex, resulting in the birth of a child. These opposed extremes produce two distinct views that we believe to be self-evident. In the case of traditional sexual reproduction, there simply is no question that the parties to any resultant conception and birth may not contract between themselves to deny the child the support he or she requires. In the institutional sperm donation case, however, there appears to be a growing consensus that clinical, institutional sperm donation neither imposes obligations nor confers privileges upon the sperm donor. Between these poles lies a spectrum of arrangements that exhibit characteristics of each extreme to varying degrees-informal agreements between friends to conceive a child via sexual intercourse; non-clinical non-sexual insemination; and so on.

Although locating future cases on this spectrum may call upon courts to draw very fine lines, courts are no strangers to such tasks, and the instant case, which we must resolve, is not nearly so difficult. The facts of this case, as found by the trial court and supported by the record, reveal the parties' mutual intention to preserve all of the trappings of a conventional sperm donation, including formation of a binding agreement. Indeed, the parties could have done little more than they did to imbue the transaction with the hallmarks of institutional, non-sexual conception by sperm donation and IVF. They negotiated an agreement outside the context of a romantic relationship; they agreed to terms; they sought clinical assistance to effectuate IVF and implantation of the consequent embryos, taking sexual intercourse out of the equation; they attempted to hide Sperm Donor's paternity from medical personnel, friends, and family; and for approximately five years following the birth of the twins both parties behaved in every regard consistently with the intentions they expressed at the outset of their arrangement, Sperm Donor not seeking to serve as a father to the twins, and Mother not demanding his support, financial or otherwise. * * *

Assuming that we do not wish to disturb the lives of the many extant parties to anonymous, institutional sperm donation, we can only rule in Mother's favor if we are able to draw a legally sustainable distinction between the negotiated, clinical arrangement that closely mimics the trappings of anonymous sperm donation that the trial court found to have existed in this case and institutional sperm donation, itself. Where such a distinction hinges on something as trivial as the parties' success in preserving the anonymity they took substantial steps to ensure, however, we can discern no principled basis for such a distinction.

Moreover, even if, arguendo, such a distinction were tenable, it would mean that a woman who wishes to have a baby but is unable to conceive through intercourse could not seek sperm from a man she knows and admires, while assuring him that he will never be subject to a support order and being herself assured that he will never be able to seek custody of the child. Accordingly, to protect herself and the sperm donor, that would-be mother would have no choice but to resort to anonymous donation or abandon her desire to be a biological mother, notwithstanding her considered personal preference to conceive using the sperm of someone familiar, whose background, traits, and medical history are not shrouded in mystery. To much the same end, where a would-be donor cannot trust that he is safe from a future support action, he will be considerably less likely to provide his sperm to a friend or acquaintance who asks, significantly limiting a would-be mother's reproductive prerogatives. There is simply no basis in law or policy to impose such an unpleasant choice, and to do so would be to legislate in precisely the way Mother notes this Court has no business doing.

Moreover, we cannot agree with the lower courts that the agreement here at issue is contrary to the sort of manifest, widespread public policy that generally animates the courts' determination that a contract is unenforceable. The absence of a legislative mandate coupled to the constantly evolving science of reproductive technology and the other considerations highlighted above illustrate the very opposite of unanimity with regard to the legal relationships arising from sperm donation, whether anonymous or otherwise. This undermines any suggestion that the agreement at issue violates a "dominant public policy" or "obvious ethical or moral standards," sufficient to warrant the invalidation of an otherwise binding agreement.

This Court takes very seriously the best interests of the children of this Commonwealth, and we recognize that to rule in favor of Sperm Donor in this case denies a source of support to two children who did not ask to be born into this situation. Absent the parties' agreement, however, the twins would not have been born at all, or would have been born to a different and anonymous sperm donor, who neither party disputes would be safe from a support order. Further, we cannot simply disregard the plight of Sperm Donor's marital child, who also did not ask to be born into this situation, but whose interests would suffer under the trial court's order.

* * *

Former JUSTICES NIGRO and NEWMAN did not participate in the decision of this case.

CHIEF JUSTICE CAPPY and JUSTICE CASTILLE join the opinion.

[DISSENTING OPINION by JUSTICE SAYLOR is omitted].

JUSTICE EAKIN, dissenting.

I respectfully dissent from the majority's conclusion appellee can bargain away her children's right to support from their father merely because he fathered the children through a clinical sperm donation. The majority concludes this is possible because the parties intended "to preserve all of the trappings of a conventional sperm donation * * * [and] negotiated an agreement outside the context of a romantic relationship * * *." To this, I say, "So what?" The only difference between this case and any other is the means by which these two parents conceived the twin boys who now look for support. Referring to Joel McKiernan as "Sperm Donor" does not change his status—he is their father.

It is those children whose rights we address, not the rights of the parents. Do these children, unlike any other, lack the fundamental ability to look to both parents for support? If the answer is no, and the law changes as my colleagues hold, it must be for a reason of monumental significance. Is the means by which these parents contracted to accomplish conception enough to overcome that right? I think not.

* * *

Speculating about an anonymous donor's reluctance is irrelevant—there is no anonymity here and never has been. There was no effort at all to insulate the identity of the father—he was a named party to the contract! This is not a case of a sperm clinic where donors have their identity concealed. The only difference between this case and any other conception is the intervention of hardware between one identifiable would-be parent and the other.

* * *

Indeed, it is not our place to legislate, yet the refusal to recognize a traditional and just right to support because of "evolving" notions (which are not directly applicable to the facts) is surely legislation from the Court. To deny these children their right to support from their father changes long-standing law—if the legislature wishes to disenfranchise children whose conception utilizes clinical procedures, it may pass such a law, but we should not. The legislature can best undertake consideration of all the policy and personal ramifications of "evolving" notions and "alternative reproductive technologies in contemporary American society."

While conception is accomplished in ways our forbearers could never have imagined, and will in the future be accomplished in ways we cannot now imagine, that simply is not the issue with a private contract between these identifiable parents. We do not have anonymity—we have a private contract between parents who utilized a clinical setting to accomplish those private aims, the creation of a child. The issue is not anyone's ability or future reluctance to utilize anonymous sperm banks-the issue is the right of these two boys to support, and whether there are compelling reasons to remove that right from them. The children point and say, "That is our father. He should support us." What are we to reply? "No! He made a contract to conceive you through a clinic, so your father need not support you." I find this unreasonable at best.

This private contract involves traditional support principles not abrogated by the means chosen by the parents to inseminate the mother, and I would apply the well-settled precedent that the best interest of the children controls. A parent cannot bargain away the children's right to support. These children have a right to support from both parents, including the man who is not an anonymous sperm donor, but their father.

* * *

NOTE AND QUESTIONS

Questions about Ferguson. (a) How would *Ferguson* have come out if Pennsylvania, like Delaware, had enacted the UPA provisions relating to gamete donation? (b) Should the law distinguish private sperm donations from donations made to a sperm bank? (c) Now that Joel McKiernan is not the twins' father in the eyes of the law, who is? (d) If the state supreme court had held the agreement unenforceable and affirmed the order imposing child support, what other rights and obligations concerning the twins would McKiernan have held? (e) Do you agree with McKiernan's argument, seeking to avoid a child support obligation, that "the Commonwealth should not concern itself with the question of anonymity if the parties to the agreement themselves are not concerned" (f) Do you agree with the *Ferguson* majority's argument that, but for the law's willingness to release donors from the child support obligation, many children conceived through sperm donation would not be born at all? (g) If Ivonne Ferguson dies of a terminal disease two years after the *Ferguson* decision, what will happen to the twins? (h) Who—courts or the legislature—should determine whether a sperm donor incurs a child support obligation?

2.   LEGAL DISPUTES ABOUT OWNERSHIP

Eggs or sperm, or embryos resulting from them, may be cryopreserved (frozen and stored) for future use. A person may turn to cryopreservation, for example, where the person faces cancer treatment that might damage reproductive organs, faces military service in a war zone, receives diagnosis of a terminal illness, experiences difficulties conceiving naturally, or fears approaching an age when prospects of successful conception would diminish. Cryopreserved embryos may be used in successive cycles, increasing the likelihood of child birth if implantation in a particular cycle proves unsuccessful.

An estimated 400,000 embryos have been cryopreserved in the United States, and the numbers grow each year. Frozen embryos were used in about 15% of all ART cycles performed in 2005. CDC, 2005 Assisted Reproductive Technology Success Rates, *supra*, at 54 (2007). At the same time, sharp legal and ethical disputes have arisen about whether the embryos are persons entitled to legal rights, or whether they are the property of the parties who created them but may later disagree about their use or disposal. Who is entitled to a voice in determining the embryos' use or disposal if one or both parties die, the parties divorce, or the parties later disagree about use or disposal? Whose interests are at stake when a court must resolve the disagreement? In a state without legislation on the subject, the next decision grapples with these questions and demonstrates the disagreements that characterize the few decisions on point. These issues revisit the controversies you saw in Chapter 10 over distribution of marital "property."

IN RE MARRIAGE OF WITTEN

Supreme Court of Iowa, 2003.
672 N.W.2d 768.

Ternus, Justice.

The primary issue raised on appeal of the district court's decree in this dissolution action is whether the court properly determined the rights of Arthur (known as Trip) and Tamera Witten with respect to the parties' frozen human embryos stored at a medical facility. While we agree with Tamera that the informed consent signed by the parties at the request of the medical facility does not control the current dispute between the donors over the use or disposition of the embryos, we reject Tamera's request that she be allowed to use the embryos over Trip's objection. Therefore, we affirm the trial court's order that neither party may use or dispose of the embryos without the consent of the other party.

* * *

I. BACKGROUND FACTS AND PROCEEDINGS.

The appellee, Arthur (Trip) Witten, and the appellant, Tamera Witten, had been married for approximately seven and one-half years when Trip sought to have their marriage dissolved in April 2002. One of the contested issues at trial was control of the parties' frozen embryos. During the parties' marriage they had tried to become parents through the process of *in vitro* fertilization. Because Tamera was unable to conceive children naturally, they had eggs taken from Tamera artificially fertilized with Trip's sperm. Tamera then underwent several unsuccessful embryo transfers in an attempt to become pregnant. At the time of trial seventeen fertilized eggs remained in storage at the University of Nebraska Medical Center (UNMC).

Prior to commencing the process for *in vitro* fertilization, the parties signed informed consent documents prepared by the medical center. These documents included an "Embryo Storage Agreement," which was signed by Tamera and Trip as well as by a representative of UNMC. It provided in part:

> *Release of Embryos.* The Client Depositors [Trip and Tamera] understand and agree that containers of embryos stored pursuant to this agreement will be used for transfer, release or disposition only with the signed approval of both Client Depositors. UNMC will release the containers of embryos only to a licensed physician recipient of written authorization of the Client Depositors.

The agreement * * * provided for termination of UNMC's responsibility to store the embryos upon several contingencies: (1) the client depositors' written authorization to release the embryos or to destroy them; (2) the death of the client depositors; (3) the failure of the client depositors to pay the annual storage fee; or (4) the expiration of ten years from the date of the agreement.

At trial, Tamera asked that she be awarded "custody" of the embryos. She wanted to have the embryos implanted in her or a surrogate mother in an effort to bear a genetically linked child. She testified that upon a successful pregnancy she would afford Trip the opportunity to exercise parental rights or to have his rights terminated. She adamantly opposed any destruction of the embryos, and was also unwilling to donate the eggs to another couple.

Trip testified at the trial that while he did not want the embryos destroyed, he did not want Tamera to use them. He would not oppose donating the embryos for use by another couple. Trip asked the court to enter a permanent injunction prohibiting either party from transferring, releasing, or utilizing the embryos without the written consent of both parties.

* * *

III. *DISPOSITION OF EMBRYOS.*

A. *Scope of storage agreement.* We first consider Tamera's contention that the storage agreement does not address the situation at hand. As noted earlier, the agreement had a specific provision governing control of the embryos if one or both parties died, but did not explicitly deal with the possibility of divorce. Nonetheless, we think the present predicament falls within the general provision governing "release of embryos," in which the parties agreed that the embryos would not be transferred, released, or discarded without "the signed approval" of both Tamera and Trip. This provision is certainly broad enough to encompass the decision-making protocol when the parties are unmarried as well as when they are married.

The only question, then, is whether such agreements are enforceable when one of the parties later changes his or her mind with respect to the proper disposition of the embryos. In reviewing the scarce case law from other jurisdictions on this point, we have found differing views of how the parties' rights should be determined. There is, however, abundant literature that has scrutinized the approaches taken to date. * * * From these various sources, we have identified three primary approaches to resolving disputes over the disposition of frozen embryos, which we have identified as (1) the contractual approach, (2) the contemporaneous mutual consent model, and (3) the balancing test.

Tamera's argument that her right to bear children should override the parties' prior agreement as well as Trip's current opposition to her use of the embryos resembles the balancing test. As for Tamera's alternative argument, we have found no authority supporting a "best interests" analysis in determining the disposition of frozen embryos. * * *

B. *"Best interests" test.* Iowa Code section 598.41 sets forth various standards governing a court's determination of the custody of the parties' children in a dissolution case, including the requirement that any custody award reflect "the best interest of the child." Tamera contends the embryos are children and their best interest demands placement with her. Trip argues the frozen embryos are not children and should not be considered as such for purposes of applying chapter 598 in dissolution actions.

* * *

Our first step is to consider the legislature's definition of "child" as that term is used in chapter 598. The term "minor child" is defined in section 598.1(6) as "any *person* under legal age." Iowa Code §§ 598.1(6) (emphasis added). Whether frozen embryos fall within this definition is an issue of first impression for this court.

* * *

* * * [W]e conclude the principles contained in section 598.41 do not govern the dispute before us. First, we note the purposes of the "best interest" standard set forth in that statute are to "assure the child the opportunity for the maximum continuing physical and emotional contact with both parents" and to "encourage parents to share the rights and responsibilities of raising the child." The principles developed under this statute are simply not suited to the resolution of disputes over the control of frozen embryos. Such disputes do not involve maximizing physical and emotional contact between both parents and the child; they involve the more fundamental decision of whether the parties will be parents at all. Moreover, it would be premature to consider which parent can most effectively raise the child when the "child" is still frozen in a storage facility.

The principles of section 598.41 do not fit because what is really at issue here is not the custody of children as that concept is generally viewed and analyzed in dissolution cases. Rather, the issue here is who will have decision-making authority with respect to the fertilized eggs. Thus, the factors that are relevant in determining the custody of children in dissolution cases are simply not useful in determining how decisions will be made with respect to the disposition and use of a divorced couple's fertilized eggs. For these reasons, we conclude the legislature did not intend to include fertilized eggs or frozen embryos within the scope of section 598.41.

C. *Enforcement of storage agreement.* We now consider the appropriateness of the trial court's decision to allow Tamera and Trip's agreement with the medical center to control the current dispute between them. As we noted above, there are three methods of analysis that have been suggested to resolve disputes over frozen embryos. We will discuss them separately.

1. *Contractual approach.* The currently prevailing view—expressed in three states—is that contracts entered into at the time of *in vitro* fertilization are enforceable so long as they do not violate public policy. The New York Court of Appeals expressed the following rationale for this contractual approach:

> [It is] particularly important that courts seek to honor the parties' expressions of choice, made before disputes erupt, with the parties' over-all direction always uppermost in the analysis. Knowing that advance agreements will be enforced underscores the seriousness and integrity of the consent process. Advance agreements as to disposition would have little purpose if they were enforceable only in the event the parties continued to agree. To the extent possible, it should be the progenitors—not the State and not the courts—who by their prior directive make this deeply personal life choice.

Kass [*v. Kass*, 696 N.E.2d 174, 180 (N.Y. 1998)].

This approach has been criticized, however, because it "insufficiently protects the individual and societal interests at stake":

First, decisions about the disposition of frozen embryos implicate rights central to individual identity. On matters of such fundamental personal importance, individuals are entitled to make decisions consistent with their contemporaneous wishes, values, and beliefs. Second, requiring couples to make binding decisions about the future use of their frozen embryos ignores the difficulty of predicting one's future response to life-altering events such as parenthood. Third, conditioning the provision of infertility treatment on the execution of binding disposition agreements is coercive and calls into question the authenticity of the couple's original choice. Finally, treating couples' decisions about the future use of their frozen embryos as binding contracts undermines important values about families, reproduction, and the strength of genetic ties.

[Carl H. Coleman, *Procreative Liberty and Contemporaneous Choice: An Inalienable Rights Approach to Frozen Embryo Disputes*, 84 Minn. L. Rev. 55, 88–89 (1999).] * * * In response to such concerns, one commentator has suggested an alternative model requiring contemporaneous mutual consent. We now examine that approach.

2. *Contemporaneous mutual consent.* * * * Proponents of the mutual-consent approach suggest that, with respect to "decisions about intensely emotional matters, where people act more on the basis of feeling and instinct than rational deliberation," it may "be impossible to make a knowing and intelligent decision to relinquish a right in advance of the time the right is to be exercised." One's erroneous prediction of how she or he will feel about the matter at some point in the future can have grave repercussions. * * * To accommodate these concerns, advocates of the mutual-consent model propose "no embryo should be used by either partner, donated to another patient, used in research, or destroyed without the [contemporaneous] mutual consent of the couple that created the embryo." Under this alternate framework,

> advance instructions would not be treated as binding contracts. If either partner has a change of mind about disposition decisions made in advance, that person's current objection would take precedence over the prior consent. If one of the partners rescinds an advance disposition decision and the other does not, the mutual consent principle would not be satisfied and the previously agreed-upon disposition decision could not be carried out.

> . . . . .

> When the couple is unable to agree to any disposition decision, the most appropriate solution is to keep the embryos where they are—in frozen storage. Unlike the other possible disposition decisions—use by one partner, donation to another patient, donation to research, or destruction—keeping the embryos frozen is not final and irrevocable. By preserving the status quo, it makes it possible for the partners to reach an agreement at a later time.

[Coleman, 84 Minn. L. Rev.] at 110–12; *see also id.* at 89 (suggesting "the embryo would remain in frozen storage until the parties reach a new agreement, the embryo is no longer viable, or storage facilities are no longer available"). Although this model precludes one party's use of the embryos to have children over the objection of the other party, the outcome under the contractual approach and the balancing test would generally be the same. *See A.Z. v. B.Z.*, 725 N.E.2d 1051, 1057–58 (Mass. 2000) ("As a matter of public policy, . . . forced procreation is not an area amenable to judicial enforcement."); *Davis* [*v. Davis*, 842 S.W.2d 588, 604 (Tenn. 1992)] ("Ordinarily, the party wishing to avoid procreation should prevail.").

3. *Balancing test.* The New Jersey Supreme Court appears to have adopted an analysis regarding the disposition of frozen human embryos that incorporates the idea of contemporaneous decision-making, but not that of mutual consent. In *J.B.* [*v. M.B.*, 783 A.2d 707 (N.J. 2001)], the New Jersey court * * * stated:

> We believe that the better rule, and the one we adopt, is to enforce agreements entered into at the time in vitro fertilization is begun, *subject to the right of either party to change his or her mind about disposition up to the point of use or destruction of any stored preembryos.*

Id. at 719 (emphasis added). The court based its decision on "[t]he public policy concerns that underlie limitations on contracts involving family relationships." *Id.*

The New Jersey court did not, however, adopt the requirement for mutual consent as a prerequisite for any use or disposition of the preembryos. Rather, that court stated that "if there is a disagreement between the parties as to disposition . . ., the interests of both parties must be evaluated" by the court. This balancing test was also the default analysis employed by the Tennessee Supreme Court in *Davis* where the parties had not executed a written agreement.

The obvious problem with the balancing test model is its internal inconsistency. Public policy concerns similar to those that prompt courts to refrain from enforcement of contracts addressing reproductive choice demand even more strongly that we not substitute the courts as decision makers in this highly emotional and personal area. Nonetheless, that is exactly what happens under the decisional framework based on the balancing test because the court must weigh the relative interests of the parties in deciding the disposition of embryos when the parties cannot agree.

D. *Discussion.* With these alternative approaches in mind, we turn to the present case. Trip asks that the contractual provision requiring mutual consent be enforced; Tamera claims this agreement is against the public policy of Iowa because it allows Trip to back out of his prior agreement to become a parent. We first consider whether there is any merit to Tamera's public policy argument. * * *

* * *

Tamera contends the contract at issue here violates public policy because it allows a person who has agreed to participate in an in vitro fertilization program to later change his mind about becoming a parent. While there is some question whether Trip's participation constitutes an implied agreement to become a father, we accept Tamera's assertion for purposes of the present discussion and proceed to consider whether there is any public policy against an agreement allowing a donor to abandon *in vitro* fertilization attempts when viable embryos remain. Tamera cites to no Iowa statute or prior case that articulates such a policy in the factual context we face here. While Iowa statutes clearly impose responsibilities on parents for the support and safekeeping of their children, such statutes, as we have already discussed in connection with chapter 598, do not contemplate the complex issues surrounding the disposition and use of frozen human embryos. The public policy evidenced by our law relates to the State's concern for the physical, emotional, and psychological well being of children who have been born, not fertilized eggs that have not even resulted in a pregnancy.

Nor can we say that the "morals of the times" are such that a party participating in an in vitro fertilization process has the duty to use or facilitate the use of each fertilized egg for purposes of pregnancy. To the contrary, courts that have considered one party's desire to use frozen embryos over the objection of the other progenitor have held that the objecting party's fundamental right not to procreate outweighs the other party's procreative rights, even in the face of a prior agreement allowing one party to use the embryos upon the parties' divorce. Thus, we find no public policy that requires the use of the frozen embryos over one party's objection.

That brings us to the more complex issue: are prior agreements regarding the future disposition of embryos enforceable when one of the donors is no longer comfortable with his or her prior decision? We first note our agreement with other courts considering such matters that the partners who created the embryos have the primary, and equal, decision-making authority with respect to the use or disposition of their embryos. We think, however, that it would be against the public policy of this state to enforce a prior agreement between the parties in this highly personal area of reproductive choice when one of the parties has changed his or her mind concerning the disposition or use of the embryos.

Our statutes and case law evidence an understanding that decisions involving marital and family relationships are emotional and subject to change. For example, Iowa law imposes a seventy-two hour waiting period after the birth of a child before the biological parents can release parental rights. In addition, although this court has not abolished claims for breach of promise to marry, only recovery of monetary damages is permitted; the court will not force a party to actually consummate the marriage. It has also long been recognized in this state that agreements for the purpose of bringing about a dissolution of marriage are contrary to public policy and therefore void.

This court has also expressed a general reluctance to become involved in intimate questions inherent in personal relationships. * * * Certainly reproductive decisions are likewise not proper matters of judicial inquiry and enforcement.

We have considered and rejected the arguments of some commentators that embryo disposition agreements are analogous to antenuptial agreements and divorce stipulations, which courts generally enforce. Whether embryos are viewed as having life or simply as having the potential for life, this characteristic or potential renders embryos fundamentally distinct from the chattels, real estate, and money that are the subjects of antenuptial agreements. Divorce stipulations are also distinguishable. While such agreements may address custody issues, they are contemporaneous with the implementation of the stipulation, an attribute noticeably lacking in disposition agreements.

In addition to decisional and statutory authority supporting a public policy against judicial enforcement of personal decisions concerning marriage, family, and reproduction, our statutes also anticipate the effect of a couple's dissolution on their prior decisions. For example, Iowa Code section 633.271 provides that if a testator is divorced after making a will, "all provisions in the will in favor of the testator's spouse" are automatically revoked. Similarly, Iowa Code section 633.3107 revokes all provisions in a revocable trust in favor of the settlor's spouse upon divorce or dissolution of the marriage. Similar considerations make enforcement of contracts between partners involving such personal decisions as the use and disposition of their combined genetic material equally problematic. As noted by one commentator, embryos are originally created as "a mutual undertaking by [a] couple to have children together." Coleman, 84 Minn. L.Rev. at 83. Agreements made in that context are not always consistent with the parties' wishes once the mutual undertaking has ended.

We think judicial decisions and statutes in Iowa reflect respect for the right of individuals to make family and reproductive decisions based on their current views and values. They also reveal awareness that such decisions are highly emotional in nature and subject to a later change of heart. For this reason, we think judicial enforcement of an agreement *between a couple* regarding their future family and reproductive choices would be against the public policy of this state.

* * *

In view of these competing needs, we reject the contractual approach and hold that agreements entered into at the time *in vitro* fertilization is commenced are enforceable and binding on the parties, "subject to the right of either party to change his or her mind about disposition up to the point of use or destruction of any stored embryo." *J.B.*, 783 A.2d at 719. This decisional model encourages prior agreements that can guide the actions of all parties, unless a later objection to any dispositional provision is asserted. It also recognizes that, *absent a change of heart by one of the partners,* an agreement governing disposition of embryos does not violate public policy. Only when one person makes known the agreement no longer reflects his or her current values or wishes is public policy implicated. Upon this occurrence, allowing either party to withdraw his or her agreement to a disposition that person no longer accepts acknowledges the public policy concerns inherent in enforcing prior decisions of a fundamentally personal nature. In fairness to the medical facility that is a party to the agreement, however, any change of intention must be communicated in writing to all parties in order to reopen the disposition issues covered by the agreement.

That brings us, then, to the dilemma presented when one or both partners change their minds and the parties cannot reach a mutual decision on disposition. We have already explained the grave public policy concerns we have with the balancing test, which simply substitutes the court as decision maker. A better principle to apply, we think, is the requirement of contemporaneous mutual consent. Under that model, no transfer, release, disposition, or use of the embryos can occur without the signed authorization of both donors. If a stalemate results, the status quo would be maintained. The practical effect will be that the embryos are stored indefinitely unless both parties can agree to destroy the fertilized eggs. Thus, any expense associated with maintaining the status quo should logically be borne by the person opposing destruction.

Turning to the present case, we find a situation in which one party no longer concurs in the parties' prior agreement with respect to the disposition of their frozen embryos, but the parties have been unable to reach a new agreement that is mutually satisfactory. Based on this fact, under the principles we have set forth today, we hold there can be no use or disposition of the Wittens' embryos unless Trip and Tamera reach an agreement. Until then, the party or parties who oppose destruction shall be responsible for any storage fees. Therefore, we affirm the trial court's ruling enjoining both parties from transferring, releasing, or utilizing the embryos without the other's written consent.

* * *

NOTES AND QUESTIONS

1. *Questions about cryopreservation.* (a) Where parties disagree about the use or disposition of frozen embryos created with their genetic material, whose rights should prevail: the rights of the party who opposes destruction of potential offspring, or the rights of the party who opposes unwanted parenthood controlled by the other party's decisionmaking? (b) Does the state have an interest in the outcome of such disagreements? (c) Should the court

appoint a guardian *ad litem* to protect the best interests of the embryo? (d) Where the parties whose genetic material created the embryo wish to dispose of the embryo, should the law free the embryo for adoption by others?

2. *Posthumous children, probate, and trust administration.* Cryopreservation permits birth of a child through ART months or years after the death of one or both biological parents whose genetic material produced the embryo. Sperm may even be harvested from a deceased man's cadaver and cryopreserved for future use. Where a "posthumous child" is born from cryopreserved genetic material implanted after the death of one or both genetic parents, mutual rights and obligations may outlive death.

Wills. A testator may leave a will providing for "my children," "my grandchildren," or "my issue," or some similar designation. Unless the testator specifies how posthumous children born through ART should be treated, the probate court seeks to determine the testator's intent.

Intestacy. State intestacy laws typically provide for "afterborn children." In Arkansas, for example, "[p]osthumous descendants of the intestate conceived before or after his or her death but born thereafter shall inherit in the same manner as if born in the lifetime of the intestate." Ark. Code Ann. 28–9–210(a) (2008). The dispositive question is when "conception" occurs, which the laws typically do not define.

At the least, state legislatures intended these provisions to operate when the father dies during pregnancy or the mother dies in childbirth. Only a handful of states have enacted some version of § 707 of the Uniform Parentage Act (2000), which (as amended in 2002) provides this definition of the inheritance rights of posthumously conceived children: "If a spouse dies before placement of eggs, sperm, or embryos, the deceased spouse is not a parent of the resulting child unless the deceased spouse consented in a record that if assisted reproduction were to occur after death, the deceased spouse would be a parent of the child." With the term "spouse," section 707 reaches only married biological parents. A few states have enacted the term "individual" instead, thus extending the reach to unmarried biological parents. *See, e.g.*, Del. Code § 8–707 (2008).

In *Finley v. Astrue*, 372 Ark. 103 (2008), the married couple cryopreserved ten embryos using the wife's eggs and the husband's sperm. Less than a year after he died intestate, she thawed two of the embryos and had them implanted in her uterus, resulting in a single pregnancy. She filed a federal lawsuit alleging that the Social Security Administration wrongfully denied her claims for spousal or children's survivor benefits, which under federal law depend on whether the child could inherit from the deceased parent under the state intestacy law.

Answering a question certified by the federal district court, the state supreme court rejected the wife's claim that under the state intestacy statute, her child was "conceived" when the husband's sperm fertilized her egg during his lifetime. The court declined to define the term "conception" because it concluded that the legislature did not intend that the statute, enacted in 1969 before the advent of ART, reach in vitro fertilization. Defining the term "would implicate many public policy concerns, including, but certainly not limited to, the finality of estates. * * * The determination of public policy lies almost exclusively with the legislature." *Id.*

Trusts. A posthumous ART child's rights under a trust agreement depend on the grantor's intent. *See, e.g., In re Martin B.*, 841 N.Y.S.2d 207 (Surr. Ct. 2007) (held that the terms "issue" and "descendants" in seven trust agreements included children born from in vitro fertilization with cryopreserved semen of the grantor's son, who had died of Hodgkin's Lymphoma a few years before the children's birth).

What advice would you give a client who has cryopreserved genetic material and may (or may not) wish to provide for a child conceived from it after the client's death?

3. *The "intended parenthood" doctrine. Witten* decided the frozen embryos' future after the parties had signed a storage agreement requiring mutual approval for use, and before either divorcing party had used any embryo to conceive a child. Assume that Iowa had previously enacted section 706 of the Uniform Parentage Act, which provides that:

(a) If a marriage is dissolved before placement of eggs, sperm, or embryos, the former spouse is not a parent of the resulting child unless the former spouse consented in a record that if assisted reproduction were to occur after a divorce, the former spouse would be a parent of the child.

(b) The consent of a woman or a man to assisted reproduction may be withdrawn by that individual in a record at any time before placement of eggs, sperm, or embryos. An individual who withdraws consent under this section is not a parent of the resulting child.

How would *Witten* have come out under section 706? On the facts presented, would each ex-spouse be a "parent" of the child, with all the rights and obligations that attend parenthood? Does the section sufficiently protect the interests of the child born from the cryopreserved embryo?

PROBLEM 17–4

Richard and Jean Griffin seek to divorce after eight years of marriage. Shortly after their son was born six years ago, Jean had a hysterectomy that left her unable to produce eggs or give birth naturally to a child. A few months later, Richard and Jean decided to have another child through *in vitro* fertilization. At the nearby Center For Surrogate Parenting, four preembryos were created with Richard's sperm and eggs received from an egg donor. Two of the embryos were implanted in a surrogate mother, producing a daughter. The two remaining preembryos were frozen and stored at the center.

Richard and Jean signed an agreement with the egg donor and the donor's husband. The agreement contained the following provision: "All eggs produced by the Egg Donor shall be deemed the property of the Intended Parents [Richard and Jean] and as such, the Intended Parents shall have the sole right to determine the disposition of the Egg(s). In no event may the Intended Parents allow any other party the use of the eggs without the Egg Donor's express written permission." The agreement defines Richard as the Intended Father and Jean as the Intended Mother.

Richard and Jean also signed an agreement with the Center For Surrogate Parenting, which provided in part, "If the Intended Parents are unable to reach a mutual decision concerning disposition of their preembryos, they must petition a court of competent jurisdiction to determine the appropriate disposition." The agreement with the Center further directed that remaining embryos be "thawed out but not allowed to undergo further development," and be disposed of when the embryos have been maintained in cryopreservation for five years, unless the Center agreed at the couple's request to extend cryopreservation for an additional period.

In the divorce proceedings, Richard expressed his wish that the two frozen embryos be donated to research or to others undergoing IVF. Jean expressed her wish that the embryos be implanted in a surrogate mother and brought to term. You are the trial court judge. How would you decide the case?

C. SURROGACY

In the typical surrogate birth, the child is carried to term in the womb of a woman who agrees to bear the child for another couple. The woman is a "genetic surrogate" when she contributes her egg to conception. The woman is a "gestational surrogate" when she carries the embryo created from the egg of another woman, who may be the intended mother. A genetic surrogate thus has both a genetic and gestational connection to the embryo she is carrying, but the gestational surrogate has no genetic connection.

Surrogacy has been assailed as "reproductive prostitution," John Lawrence Hill, *Exploitation*, 79 Cornell L. Rev. 631, 638 n.32 (1994) (discussing commentators), but the process has also resulted in the births of healthy children who would not otherwise have been born because one or both of the intended parents were infertile or gay, the intended mother was unable to carry a child to term, or the intended parents were fearful of gestation or of transmitting genetic disease or defect through natural conception and child birth. Controversy aside, "a greater acceptance of the practice, and advances in science, find more women than ever before having babies for those who cannot," including "military wives who have taken on surrogacy to supplement the family income, some while their husbands are serving overseas." Lorraine Ali & Raina Kelley, *The Curious Lives of Surrogates*, Newsweek, Apr. 7, 2008, at 44.

1. GENETIC SURROGACY

The Baby M saga, described in the decision below, dominated the headlines for months as it worked its way through the New Jersey court system in the late 1980s. The New Jersey Supreme Court's unanimous opinion, delivered when the child was nearly two years old, demonstrates the profound human emotions that may attend surrogate motherhood, and also the strains that surrogacy imposes on legal doctrines developed based on traditional assumptions about conception and birth.

Because no state had surrogacy legislation at the time, *Baby M's* bases for decision were traditional law and policies regulating contracts, adoption, custody, visitation and termination of parental rights. In this "genetic surrogacy" case, consider whether the *Baby M* court reached a suitable resolution from these sources. Consider too whether the actual "surrogate" mother was Mary Beth Whitehead (who provided the egg and carried the child in her uterus) or Mrs. Stern (the sperm provider's wife, who contributed no genetic material herself and did not otherwise participate in the pregnancy).

IN RE BABY M

Supreme Court of New Jersey, 1988.
537 A.2d 1227.

WILENTZ, C.J.

In this matter the Court is asked to determine the validity of a contract that purports to provide a new way of bringing children into a family. For a fee of $10,000, a woman agrees to be artificially inseminated with the semen of another woman's husband; she is to conceive a child, carry it to term, and after its birth surrender it to the natural father and his wife. The intent of the contract is that the child's natural mother will thereafter be forever separated from her child. The wife is to adopt the child, and she and the natural father are to be regarded as its parents for all purposes. The contract providing for this is called a "surrogacy contract," the natural mother inappropriately called the "surrogate mother."

We invalidate the surrogacy contract because it conflicts with the law and public policy of this State. While we recognize the depth of the yearning of infertile couples to have their own children, we find the payment of money to a "surrogate" mother illegal, perhaps criminal, and potentially degrading to women. Although in this case we grant custody to the natural father, the evidence having clearly proved such custody to be in the best interests of the infant, we void both the termination of the surrogate mother's parental rights and the adoption of the child by the wife/stepparent. We thus restore the "surrogate" as the mother of the child. We remand the issue of the natural mother's visitation rights to the trial court, since that issue was not reached below and the record before us is not sufficient to permit us to decide it *de novo*.

We find no offense to our present laws where a woman voluntarily and without payment agrees to act as a "surrogate" mother, provided that she is not subject to a binding agreement to surrender her child. Moreover, our holding today does not preclude the Legislature from altering the current statutory scheme, within constitutional limits, so as to permit surrogacy contracts. Under current law, however, the surrogacy agreement before us is illegal and invalid.

I.

FACTS

In February 1985, William Stern and Mary Beth Whitehead entered into a surrogacy contract. It recited that Stern's wife, Elizabeth, was infertile, that they wanted a child, and that Mrs. Whitehead was willing to provide that child as the mother with Mr. Stern as the father.

The contract provided that through artificial insemination using Mr. Stern's sperm, Mrs. Whitehead would become pregnant, carry the child to term, bear it, deliver it to the Sterns, and thereafter do whatever was necessary to terminate her maternal rights so that Mrs. Stern could thereafter adopt the child. Mrs. Whitehead's husband, Richard, was also a party to the contract; Mrs. Stern was not. Mr. Whitehead promised to do all acts necessary to rebut the presumption of paternity under the Parentage Act. Although Mrs. Stern was not a party to the surrogacy agreement, the contract gave her sole custody of the child in the event of Mr. Stern's death. Mrs. Stern's status as a nonparty to the surrogate parenting agreement presumably was to avoid the application of the baby-selling statute to this arrangement.

Mr. Stern, on his part, agreed to attempt the artificial insemination and to pay Mrs. Whitehead $10,000 after the child's birth, on its delivery to him. In a separate contract, Mr. Stern agreed to pay $7,500 to the Infertility Center of New York ("ICNY"). The Center's advertising campaigns solicit surrogate mothers and encourage infertile couples to consider surrogacy. ICNY arranged for the surrogacy contract by bringing the parties together, explaining the process to them, furnishing the contractual form, and providing legal counsel.

The history of the parties' involvement in this arrangement suggests their good faith. William and Elizabeth Stern were married in July 1974, having met at the University of Michigan, where both were Ph.D. candidates. Due to financial considerations and Mrs. Stern's pursuit of a medical degree and residency, they decided to defer starting a family until 1981. Before then, however, Mrs. Stern learned that she might have multiple sclerosis and that the disease in some cases renders pregnancy a serious health risk. Her anxiety appears to have exceeded the actual risk, which current medical authorities assess as minimal. Nonetheless that anxiety was evidently quite real, Mrs. Stern fearing that pregnancy might precipitate blindness, paraplegia, or other forms of debilitation. Based on the perceived risk, the Sterns decided to forego having their own children. The decision had special significance for Mr. Stern. Most of his family had been destroyed in the Holocaust. As the family's only survivor, he very much wanted to continue his bloodline.

Initially the Sterns considered adoption, but were discouraged by the substantial delay apparently involved and by the potential problem they saw arising from their age and their differing religious backgrounds. They were most eager for some other means to start a family.

The paths of Mrs. Whitehead and the Sterns to surrogacy were similar. Both responded to advertising by ICNY. * * *

Both parties, undoubtedly because of their own self-interest, were less sensitive to the implications of the transaction than they might otherwise have been. Mrs. Whitehead, for instance, appears not to have been concerned about whether the Sterns would make good parents for her child; the Sterns, on their part, while conscious of the obvious possibility that surrendering the child might cause grief to Mrs. Whitehead, overcame their qualms because of their desire for a child. At any rate, both the Sterns and Mrs. Whitehead were committed to the arrangement; both thought it right and constructive.

* * * On February 6, 1985, Mr. Stern and Mr. and Mrs. Whitehead executed the surrogate parenting agreement. After several artificial inseminations over a period of months, Mrs. Whitehead became pregnant. The pregnancy was uneventful and on March 27, 1986, Baby M was born.

* * * Her birth certificate indicated her name to be Sara Elizabeth Whitehead and her father to be Richard Whitehead. * * *

Mrs. Whitehead realized, almost from the moment of birth, that she could not part with this child. She had felt a bond with it even during pregnancy. * * * She talked about how the baby looked like her other daughter, and made it clear that she was experiencing great difficulty with the decision.

Nonetheless, Mrs. Whitehead was, for the moment, true to her word. Despite powerful inclinations to the contrary, she turned her child over to the Sterns on March 30 at the Whiteheads' home.

The Sterns were thrilled with their new child. They had planned extensively for its arrival, far beyond the practical furnishing of a room for her. It was a time of joyful celebration—not just for them but for their friends as well. The Sterns looked forward to raising their daughter, whom they named Melissa. * * *

* * *

The depth of Mrs. Whitehead's despair surprised and frightened the Sterns. She told them that she could not live without her baby, that she must have her, even if only for one week, that thereafter she would surrender her child. The Sterns, concerned that Mrs. Whitehead might indeed commit suicide, not wanting under any circumstances to risk that, and in any event believing that Mrs. Whitehead would keep her word, turned the child over to her. * * *

The struggle over Baby M began when it became apparent that Mrs. Whitehead could not return the child to Mr. Stern. Due to Mrs. Whitehead's refusal to relinquish the baby, Mr. Stern filed a complaint seeking enforcement of the surrogacy contract. * * *

Eventually the Sterns discovered where the Whiteheads were staying, commenced supplementary proceedings in Florida, and obtained an order requiring the Whiteheads to turn over the child. Police in Florida enforced the order, forcibly removing the child from her grandparents' home. She was soon thereafter brought to New Jersey and turned over to the Sterns. The prior order of the court, issued *ex parte*, awarding custody of the child to the Sterns *pendente lite*, was reaffirmed by the trial court after consideration of the certified representations of the parties (both represented by counsel) concerning the unusual sequence of events that had unfolded. Pending final judgment, Mrs. Whitehead was awarded limited visitation with Baby M.

* * *

II.

INVALIDITY AND UNENFORCEABILITY OF SURROGACY CONTRACT

* * *

A. Conflict with Statutory Provisions

The surrogacy contract conflicts with: (1) laws prohibiting the use of money in connection with adoptions; (2) laws requiring proof of parental unfitness or abandonment before termination of parental rights is ordered or an adoption is granted; and (3) laws that make surrender of custody and consent to adoption revocable in private placement adoptions.

(1) Our law prohibits paying or accepting money in connection with any placement of a child for adoption. Violation is a high misdemeanor. Excepted are fees of an approved agency (which must be a non-profit entity) and certain expenses in connection with childbirth.

Considerable care was taken in this case to structure the surrogacy arrangement so as not to violate this prohibition. * * * Nevertheless, it seems clear that the money was paid and accepted in connection with an adoption.

* * *

* * * The evils inherent in baby-bartering are loathsome for a myriad of reasons. The child is sold without regard for whether the purchasers will be suitable parents. The natural mother does not receive the benefit of counseling and guidance to assist her in making a decision that may affect her for a lifetime. In fact, the monetary incentive to sell her child may, depending on her financial circumstances, make her decision less voluntary. Furthermore, the adoptive parents may not be fully informed of the natural parents' medical history.

* * *

(2) The termination of Mrs. Whitehead's parental rights, called for by the surrogacy contract and actually ordered by the court fails to comply with the stringent requirements of New Jersey law. * * *

* * *

In order to terminate parental rights under the private placement adoption statute, there must be a finding of "intentional abandonment or a very substantial neglect of parental duties without a reasonable expectation of a reversal of that conduct in the future." * * *

* * *

In this case a termination of parental rights was obtained not by proving the statutory prerequisites but by claiming the benefit of contractual provisions. * * *

Since the termination was invalid, it follows, as noted above, that adoption of Melissa by Mrs. Stern could not properly be granted.

(3) The provision in the surrogacy contract stating that Mary Beth Whitehead agrees to "surrender custody ... and terminate all parental rights" contains no clause giving her a right to rescind. It is intended to be an irrevocable consent to surrender the child for adoption—in other words, an irrevocable commitment by Mrs. Whitehead to turn Baby M over to the Sterns and thereafter to allow termination of her parental rights. * * *

* * *

The provision in the surrogacy contract whereby the mother irrevocably agrees to surrender custody of her child and to terminate her parental rights conflicts with the settled interpretation of New Jersey statutory law. * * *

B. Public Policy Considerations

* * * The contract's basic premise, that the natural parents can decide in advance of birth which one is to have custody of the child, bears no relationship to the settled law that the child's best interests shall determine custody. * * *

The surrogacy contract guarantees permanent separation of the child from one of its natural parents. Our policy, however, has long been that to the extent possible, children should remain with and be brought up by both of their natural parents. * * * This is not simply some theoretical ideal that in practice has no meaning. The impact of failure to follow that policy is nowhere better shown than in the results of this surrogacy contract. A child, instead of starting off its life with as much peace and security as possible, finds itself immediately in a tug-of-war between contending mother and father.

The surrogacy contract violates the policy of this State that the rights of natural parents are equal concerning their child, the father's right no greater than the mother's. * * * The whole purpose and effect of the surrogacy contract was to give the father the exclusive right to the child by destroying the rights of the mother.

The policies expressed in our comprehensive laws governing consent to the surrender of a child stand in stark contrast to the surrogacy contract and what it implies. Here there is no counseling, independent or otherwise, of the natural mother, no evaluation, no warning.

* * *

Although the interest of the natural father and adoptive mother is certainly the predominant interest, realistically the *only* interest served, even they are left with less than what public policy requires. They know little about the natural mother, her genetic makeup, and her psychological and medical history. Moreover, not even a superficial attempt is made to determine their awareness of their responsibilities as parents.

Worst of all, however, is the contract's total disregard of the best interests of the child. There is not the slightest suggestion that any inquiry will be made at any time to determine the fitness of the Sterns as custodial parents, of Mrs. Stern as an adoptive parent, their superiority to Mrs. Whitehead, or the effect on the child of not living with her natural mother.

This is the sale of a child, or, at the very least, the sale of a mother's right to her child, the only mitigating factor being that one of the purchasers is the father. Almost every evil that prompted the prohibition on the payment of money in connection with adoptions exists here.

* * *

Intimated, but disputed, is the assertion that surrogacy will be used for the benefit of the rich at the expense of the poor. In response it is noted that the Sterns are not rich and the Whiteheads not poor. Nevertheless, it is clear to us that it is unlikely that surrogate mothers will be as proportionately numerous among those women in the top twenty percent income bracket as among those in the bottom twenty percent. Put differently, we doubt that infertile couples in the low-income bracket will find upper income surrogates.

In any event, even in this case one should not pretend that disparate wealth does not play a part simply because the contrast is not the dramatic "rich versus poor." At the time of trial, the Whiteheads' net assets were probably negative * * *. The Sterns are both professionals, she a medical doctor, he a biochemist. Their combined income when both were working was about $89,500 a year and their assets sufficient to pay for the surrogacy contract arrangements.

* * *

The long-term effects of surrogacy contracts are not known, but feared—the impact on the child who learns her life was bought, that she is the offspring of someone who gave birth to her only to obtain money; the impact on the natural mother as the full weight of her isolation is felt along with the full reality of the sale of her body and her child; the impact on the natural father and adoptive mother once they realize the conse-quences of their conduct. * * *

The surrogacy contract is based on principles that are directly contrary to the objectives of our laws. * * *

Beyond that is the potential degradation of some women that may result from this arrangement. In many cases, of course, surrogacy may bring satisfaction, not only to the infertile couple, but to the surrogate mother herself. The fact, however, that many women may not perceive surrogacy negatively but rather see it as an opportunity does not diminish its potential for devastation to other women.

* * *

IV.

CONSTITUTIONAL ISSUES

Both parties argue that the Constitutions—state and federal—mandate approval of their basic claims. * * * The right asserted by the Sterns is the right of procreation; that asserted by Mary Beth Whitehead is the right to the companionship of her child. * * *

* * *

* * * The right to procreate very simply is the right to have natural children, whether through sexual intercourse or artificial insemination. It is no more than that. Mr. Stern has not been deprived of that right. Through artificial insemination of Mrs. Whitehead, Baby M is his child. The custody, care, companionship, and nurturing that follow birth are not parts of the right to procreation; they are rights that may also be constitutionally protected, but that involve many considerations other than the right of procreation. To assert that Mr. Stern's right of procreation gives him the right to the custody of Baby M would be to assert that Mrs. Whitehead's right of procreation does not give her the right to the custody of Baby M; it would be to assert that the constitutional right of procreation includes within it a constitutionally protected contractual right to destroy someone else's right of procreation.

* * *

Mr. Stern also contends that he has been denied equal protection of the laws by the State's statute granting full parental rights to a husband in relation to the child produced, with his consent, by the union of his wife with a sperm donor. The claim really is that of Mrs. Stern. It is that she is in precisely the same position as the husband in the statute: she is presumably infertile, as is the husband in the statute; her spouse by agreement with a third party procreates with the understanding that the child will be the couple's child. The alleged unequal protection is that the understanding is honored in the statute when the husband is the infertile party, but no similar understanding is honored when it is the wife who is infertile.

It is quite obvious that the situations are not parallel. A sperm donor simply cannot be equated with a surrogate mother. The State has more than a sufficient basis to distinguish the two situations—even if the only difference is between the time it takes to provide sperm for artificial insemination and the time invested in a nine-month pregnancy—so as to justify automatically divesting the sperm donor of his parental rights without automatically divesting a surrogate mother. Some basis for an equal protection argument might exist if Mary Beth Whitehead had contributed her egg to be implanted, fertilized or otherwise, in Mrs. Stern, resulting in the latter's pregnancy. That is not the case here, however.

Mrs. Whitehead, on the other hand, * * * claims the right to the companionship of her child. This is a fundamental interest, constitutionally protected. * * * By virtue of our decision Mrs. Whitehead's constitutional complaint * * * is moot. * * *

* * *

V.

Custody

* * *

* * * Our reading of the record persuades us that the trial court's decision awarding custody to the Sterns (technically to Mr. Stern) should be affirmed * * *.

* * *

* * * Mrs. Whitehead was * * * guilty of a breach of contract, and indeed, she did break a very important promise, but we think it is expecting something well beyond normal human capabilities to suggest that this mother should have parted with her newly born infant without a struggle. Other than survival, what stronger force is there? We do not know of, and cannot conceive of, any other case where a perfectly fit mother was expected to surrender her newly born infant, perhaps forever, and was then told she was a bad mother because she did not. We know of no authority suggesting that the moral quality of her act in those circumstances should be judged by referring to a contract made before she became pregnant. We do not countenance, and would never countenance, violating a court order as Mrs. Whitehead did, even a court order that is wrong; but her resistance to an order that she surrender her infant, possibly forever, merits a measure of understanding. We do not find it so clear that her efforts to keep her infant, when measured against the Sterns' efforts to take her away, make one, rather than the other, the wrongdoer. * * *

* * *

VI.

Visitation

* * *

* * * Mrs. Whitehead spent the first four months of this child's life as her mother and has regularly visited the child since then. Second, she is

not only the natural mother, but also the legal mother, and is not to be penalized one iota because of the surrogacy contract. Mrs. Whitehead, as the mother (indeed, as a mother who nurtured her child for its first four months—unquestionably a relevant consideration), is entitled to have her own interest in visitation considered. * * *

* * *

We have decided that Mrs. Whitehead is entitled to visitation at some point, and that question is not open to the trial court on this remand. The trial court will determine what kind of visitation shall be granted to her, with or without conditions, and when and under what circumstances it should commence. * * *

* * *

CONCLUSION

* * *

If the Legislature decides to address surrogacy, consideration of this case will highlight many of its potential harms. We do not underestimate the difficulties of legislating on this subject. In addition to the inevitable confrontation with the ethical and moral issues involved, there is the question of the wisdom and effectiveness of regulating a matter so private, yet of such public interest. Legislative consideration of surrogacy may also provide the opportunity to begin to focus on the overall implications of the new reproductive biotechnology—*in vitro* fertilization, preservation of sperm and eggs, embryo implantation and the like. The problem is how to enjoy the benefits of the technology—especially for infertile couples— while minimizing the risk of abuse. The problem can be addressed only when society decides what its values and objectives are in this troubling, yet promising, area.

* * *

NOTES AND QUESTIONS

1. *Aftermath.* On remand, the trial court found that Melissa's best interests would be served by unsupervised, uninterrupted, liberal visitation with her genetic mother, Mary Beth Whitehead. *See In re Baby M*, 542 A.2d 52, 53 (N.J. Super. Ct. 1988). The parties agreed not to appeal the decision.

After Mary Beth and Richard Whitehead were divorced in 1987, she married New York accountant Dean Gould, with whom she had two more children. She wrote a book about her experiences, appeared on television talk shows, became the subject of full-length magazine stories and made-for-television movies, and became an outspoken critic of surrogacy. By the time Melissa Stern turned 13 in 1999, she was reportedly calling Mary Beth "mom," William Stern "dad," Elizabeth Stern "Betsy," and Dean Gould,

"Dean." *See* Cori Anne Natoli, *"Baby M," Focus Of Custody Fight Turns 13*, Asbury Park (N.J.) Press, Mar. 28 1999, at 1A. In 2008, Melissa was a college senior majoring in religion. *See* Susannah Cahalan, *Tug O' Love: Baby M All Grown Up*, N.Y. Post, Apr. 13, 2008, at 9.

2. *The scorecard in the states.* In the wake of *Baby M*, a number of states have enacted surrogacy legislation. Other states, however, continue to avoid such legislation because of the ethical, religious and moral questions that would arise during debate. "Absent adequate regulation, many participants in surrogacy agreements find themselves in the Wild West of family law." Theresa Glennon, *Surrogacy Agreements: Inaction Causes Harm*, Nat'l L.J., July 24, 2006, at 31.

Among the states with legislation, no one approach has achieved unanimity. Some states deny enforcement of surrogacy agreements in all circumstances. *See, e.g.*, Ariz. Rev. Stat. Ann. § 25–218(A) (2005). Other states deny enforcement only where the surrogate is compensated. *See, e.g.*, Ky. Rev. Stat. Ann. § 199.590(4) (2005). Some states have exempted surrogacy agreements from baby-selling statutes. *See, e.g.*, Ala. Code § 26–10A–34 (2005). A few states have expressly made unpaid surrogacy agreements lawful. *See, e.g.*, Fla. Stat. § 742.15 (2005). A few states permit surrogacy only where the intended mother is infertile. *See id.* § 742.15(2)(a). New Hampshire and Virginia restrict who may act as a surrogate and require advance judicial approval of the agreement. *See* N.H. Rev. Stat. Ann. §§ 168–B:16(I)(b), 168–B:17 (2005); Va. Code Ann. §§ 20–159(B), 20–160(B)(6) (2005). Arkansas presumes that a child born to a surrogate mother is the child of the intended parents and not the surrogate. *See* Ark. Code Ann. § 9–10–201(b)–(c) (2005). Most states with surrogacy legislation "permit only married couples to hire surrogates," thus excluding gay and lesbian individuals and couples. Richard F. Storrow, *Rescuing Children From the Marriage Movement: The Case Against Marital Status Discrimination in Adoption and Assisted Reproduction*, 39 U.C. Davis L. Rev. 305, 314 (2006). For a survey of state surrogacy laws, see Am. Surrogacy Center, Inc., *Individual State Laws Governing Surrogacy*, http://www.surrogacy.com/legals/states.html.

The National Conference of Commissioners on Uniform State Laws (NCCUSL) has also found consensus on surrogacy laws elusive. NCCUSL has advanced the Uniform Parentage Act (2000), which (1) permits written "gestational agreements," including ones providing for payment of consideration (§ 801), (2) provides for judicial validation of the agreement where the court finds the consideration reasonable and where, unless waived by the court, a home study of the intended parents establishes that they "meet the standards of suitability applicable to adoptive parents" (§§ 802–03), and (3) provides for a court order confirming the validated agreement when the child is born (§ 807). The Commissioners and the ABA representatives could not agree on further details, including whether surrogacy should be limited to married couples, as the Commissioners had initially proposed. *See* 9B U.L.A. 297 (2001 & Supp. 2005).

PROBLEM 17–5

Sam Richards has filed for divorce from his wife Sue after sixteen years of marriage. They have one child, a 14–year–old daughter Cindy who was conceived by artificial insemination between Sam and a surrogate mother, who provided her egg. The surrogate turned over the child to Sam and Sue shortly after birth, and Sam and Sue have raised the girl as their own. The parental rights of the surrogate mother, and of her husband, have been terminated. Sue has never filed to adopt Cindy.

A state statute provides: "In any dispute about the custody of a minor child involving a parent and a nonparent, there shall be a presumption that it is the child's best interests to be in the custody of the parent, which presumption may be rebutted by showing that it would be detrimental to the child to permit the parent to have custody."

May the court grant Sue custody of the child? To secure custody or visitation, what showing would Sue have to make?

2. GESTATIONAL SURROGACY

Gestational surrogacy, where the surrogate carries a fetus conceived with another woman's egg, has become a more popular reproductive option than genetic surrogacy. Indeed "surrogacy agreements now almost always stipulate that the woman who carries the baby cannot also donate the egg." Lorraine Ali & Raina Kelley, *The Curious Lives of Surrogates*, Newsweek, Apr. 7, 2008, at 44.

Legal uncertainties remain concerning the enforceability of genetic surrogacy agreements when the biologically-related woman resists relinquishing the child; the growth of in vitro fertilization makes gestational surrogacy safer and more likely to succeed, based on agreements that courts are more likely to enforce in the absence of such biological relationship. In 2005, gestational surrogates were used in 1% of ART cycles using fresh non-donor embryos. *See* CDC, 2005 Assisted Reproductive Technology Success Rates 52 (2007).

The following gestational surrogacy decision demonstrates that years after *Baby M*, surrogacy and collaborative reproduction still strain the capacity of contract law and other traditional sources of law to determine the parentage of children conceived by these ART methods. As you read this decision in light of *Baby M* and other ART materials in this Chapter, consider the need for maternity and surrogacy legislation.

J.F. v. D.B.

Superior Court of Pennsylvania, 2006.
897 A.2d 1261.

Opinion by MCCAFFERY, J.:

Appellant, J.F. ("Father"), asks us to determine whether the trial court erred in holding that D.B. ("gestational carrier") has standing to seek custody of the triplet boys she carried and delivered, after having taken them from the hospital against Father's wishes when they were eight days old. In a companion case, an action initiated by gestational carrier, Father appeals from the trial court's order terminating the parental rights of J.R. ("egg donor"). * * * [W]e decline to comment on the validity of surrogacy contracts, either specifically in this case or generally in this Commonwealth. That task is for the legislature. Our holding today is limited to our conclusion that gestational carrier lacked standing to seek custody or challenge Father's custody of the triplets. As a result, gestational carrier also lacked standing to seek termination of egg donor's parental rights. Accordingly, we vacate the order of the trial court and remand the matter with directions.

FACTS AND PROCEDURAL HISTORY

The unique facts and procedural history underlying these appeals are as follows. Father is a math professor and department chair at Cleveland State University in Cleveland, Ohio. He lives with E.D., who was a practicing dentist and is now retired. Father and E.D., who live together in a home they built in Ohio, are in a long-term relationship and they want to have children. E.D. is a widow, with two grown children: a daughter, who is married with four children, and a son. Father has no children. After enduring infertility treatments and learning that E.D. was incapable of conceiving any more children, the couple considered other options. Although willing, E.D.'s daughter was incapable of serving as a surrogate for the couple.

Father and E.D. eventually contacted Surrogate Mothers, Inc. ("SMI"), a private surrogacy agency in Indiana. The couple entered into an agreement with SMI listing Father as "Biological Father or Adoptive Father", E.D. as "Biological Mother, Adoptive Mother, or Partner", and the couple as "Client". * * *

SMI matched the couple with gestational carrier, a married resident of Pennsylvania with three children of her own, and egg donor, a single woman residing in Texas. E.D. met gestational carrier in April 2002. In August 2002, Father, egg donor, gestational carrier and her husband executed a surrogacy contract ("the Contract" or "the Surrogacy Contract") * * *. By virtue of the Contract Father agreed, *inter alia,* to pay gestational carrier the sum of $15,000.00 for a single birth, $20,000.00 for multiple births, plus medical expenses, travel expenses, and life insurance for the duration of the pregnancy. Gestational carrier agreed, *inter alia,* that she would not attempt to form a parent-child relationship with any child or children she might bear; [and] that she would voluntarily relinquish any parental rights to any such child or children * * *. In the event that custody was somehow awarded to either gestational carrier or egg donor, each agreed to indemnify Father for any and all monies paid for child support, and reimburse him for any and all monies paid to either one pursuant to the Surrogacy Contract. Father agreed to assume legal responsibility for any child or children of his, born pursuant to the Contract, and the Contract also provided that any such child or children should be placed in the sole custody of E.D. if Father were to die before the birth of the child or children. * * *

Pursuant to the Surrogacy Contract, the parties underwent extensive medical and psychological testing. Finally, in April 2003, three of egg donor's eggs, fertilized *in vitro* with Father's sperm, were implanted in gestational carrier. Father and E.D., the intended parents, were present for this procedure as well as four weeks later for the sonogram confirming that gestational carrier was carrying triplets. Intended parents also attended gestational carrier's first few doctor's appointments in Erie, Pennsylvania, but were later told by gestational carrier not to come to any more appointments. Thereafter, E.D. called to check on gestational carrier and the triplets she was carrying, apparently more often than gestational carrier liked. She asked E.D. not to call so often, and E.D. complied, as she had complied with the request to stop going to the doctor's appointments. When it became necessary for gestational carrier to go on bed rest on her doctor's advice, she requested additional money for that period of time. Even though they were not required to do so by the contract, intended parents sent gestational carrier an additional $1,000 for each of the four months she was on bed rest.

As the triplets grew, the doctor became concerned that gestational carrier would go into labor prematurely. Gestational carrier scheduled a caesarean delivery ("C-section") at Hamot Medical Center ("Hamot" or "the hospital") in Erie, Pennsylvania, for November 19, 2003, approximately thirty-five (35) weeks into the pregnancy. Although E.D. expressed her desire to be in the delivery room for the birth, gestational carrier wanted her husband there instead, and so gestational carrier did not tell intended parents about the scheduled C-section. Gestational carrier knew the triplets' gender, but intended parents chose to wait to find out until the birth.

On the morning of November 19th, gestational carrier called SMI to inform the agency that she would be undergoing a C-section later that day. SMI called intended parents and informed them of this fact. The triplets were, indeed, born on that date, but their early delivery caused minor medical problems that warranted their placement in Hamot's neonatal intensive care unit ("NICU"). Intended parents, who had only learned about the birth on that same day, drove from Ohio to Erie that evening to visit the babies.

* * * [SMI informed the hospital] that a court order naming Father and E.D. as the parents would be forthcoming; however, Hamot did not receive such order. As a result, the hospital insisted that intended parents have permission from gestational carrier to see the triplets in the NICU, which gestational carrier gave. In addition, gestational carrier signed a form satisfactory to Hamot that allowed Hamot to discharge the triplets to Father. On the night of the triplets' birth, intended parents were able to hold only one son, as the other two were on oxygen.

Over the next few days, while the children were being monitored and cared for by Hamot doctors and nurses in the NICU, intended parents purchased a mini-van, car seats, toys, and clothing, all for the care and benefit of the triplets. E.D. made repeated telephone calls to their insurance company to secure medical insurance for the infants and arrange for apnea monitors, which the babies required before they could be discharged from the hospital. E.D. spoke with gestational carrier on November 20th and the 21st.[7] E.D. also telephoned Hamot at least once a day, often more frequently, to speak with the babies' doctors, NICU nurses, and social services personnel. Hamot discharged gestational carrier on Saturday, November 22nd, and she went home. Prior to and at that time, gestational carrier claimed to have had no intention of taking the triplets home with her. She also knew that E.D. was planning to adopt them.

* * *

[A few days later, the gestation carrier arranged] to take the triplets home with her. Gestational carrier expressed her concern about what was going to happen to the children if they were discharged to people who had not visited them frequently in the NICU. Gestational carrier also stated that she believed Father and E.D. were "not fit to be parents." At that time, gestational carrier revoked her consent for intended parents to visit the children. She also arranged to nest with the triplets that night, along with her husband, so that they could take the babies home when they were discharged.

Although gestational carrier notified * * * SMI of her decision to take the triplets home, she did not contact intended parents, who were expecting to arrive at Hamot that evening for nesting and training. Anticipating a confrontation, Hamot staff contacted security to alert them to intended parents' impending arrival. Unaware of these events, intended parents arrived at Hamot late on Tuesday afternoon ready for training and nesting. They were met by Hamot security at the NICU nurses' station. At the direction of Huckno, Hamot staff told intended parents that the triplets had been discharged to gestational carrier, and they should seek legal advice. E.D. insisted on speaking with Huckno, who verified that the triplets had been discharged to gestational carrier with his consent. In fact, the triplets had not been discharged and gestational carrier was present at the hospital at this time, preparing for her own nesting and training with the babies that evening. Even though Hamot staff had represented to intended parents that the triplets had been discharged to gestational carrier, the triplets remained at Hamot for an additional two days, until Thursday, November 27th. On that day, gestational carrier took the babies from Hamot to her home in Corry, Pennsylvania.

After being informed of the purported "discharge" of the babies, the bewildered intended parents returned to Ohio and promptly began calling

---

7. During these calls, gestational carrier purportedly expressed concern that the couple was not coming to the hospital frequently to visit the triplets. E.D. explained that her daughter was away for the week and E.D.'s four young grandchildren were staying with them, and it was difficult to travel from their home to Erie to visit the triplets in the NICU with four young children. Because gestational carrier had unilaterally scheduled the C-section for November 19th and had deliberately chosen not to inform intended parents, E.D. did not have any opportunity to make other plans for the care of her grandchildren.

gestational carrier. Each time, they left messages asking for an explanation of gestational carrier's actions. Gestational carrier did not return any of the calls.

* * *

The trial court held hearings on the issue of standing * * *. [T]he court, *sua sponte*, voided the surrogacy contract as against public policy for, among other things, failure to specifically name a "legal mother", "particularly if something were to happen to [intended parents], or if they were to decide not to take custody of the children." The court summarily eliminated both E.D. and egg donor as possible legal mothers, without sending either woman notice of her right to be heard or to intervene. The court further found gestational carrier was the "legal mother" of the triplets. Finally, the court concluded that gestational carrier "would most likely still have third[-]party standing *in loco parentis*" to seek custody, even if she were not the "legal mother" of the children.

The court then entered its order finding that gestational carrier had standing to pursue custody and child support based both on her court-conferred status as "legal mother" and her *in loco parentis* status. * * *

* * *

* * * [T]he court issued an order * * * awarding primary physical custody to gestational carrier * * * [and] also granted Father partial custody/visitation, and ordered that legal custody be shared between Father and gestational carrier. In addition, the court entered a stipulated order for child support. * * * [Later,] the court entered an order * * * terminating egg donor's parental rights. * * *

* * *

* * * Because we find that gestational carrier has no standing to pursue custody of the children on either an *in loco parentis* basis or as the children's "legal mother", we do not reach the issue of whether the evidence presented at the custody hearings was sufficient to support the court's award of primary physical custody to gestational carrier.

STANDING BASED ON IN LOCO PARENTIS STATUS
* * *

Well-settled Pennsylvania law provides that persons other than a child's biological or natural parents are "third parties" for purposes of custody disputes. In addition, natural parents have a *prima facie* right to custody. * * * Even when standing to seek custody is conferred upon a third party, the natural parent has a "*prima facie* right to custody," which will be forfeited only if clear and "convincing reasons appear that the child's best interest will be served by an award to the third party. Thus, even before the proceedings start, the evidentiary scale is tipped, and tipped hard to the [biological] parents' side." *Jones v. Jones*, 884 A.2d 915, 917 (Pa. Super. [Ct.] 2005).

[T]here is a stringent test for standing in third-party suits for . . . custody due to the respect for the traditionally strong right of parents to raise their children as they see fit. The courts generally find standing in third-party visitation and custody cases only where the legislature specifically authorizes the cause of action. A third party has been permitted to maintain an action for custody, however, where that party stands *in loco parentis* to the child.

* * *

The phrase *"in loco parentis"* refers to a person who puts oneself in the situation of a lawful parent by assuming the obligations incident to the parental relationship without going through the formality of a legal adoption. . . . The third party in this type of relationship, however, cannot place himself *in loco parentis* in defiance of the parents' wishes and the parent/child relationship.

Liebner [*v. Simcox*, 834 A.2d 606, 609 (Pa. Super. Ct. 2003)].

* * *

* * * There was no acquiescence or participation by Father in gestational carrier's unilateral decision to take custody of the triplets. The requirement of a natural parent's participation and acquiescence is critical to the determination of whether to accord a third party *in loco parentis* status. The law simply cannot permit a third party to act contrary to the natural parent's wishes in obtaining custody and then benefit from that defiant conduct in a subsequent custody action. * * *

* * *

* * * Accordingly, gestational carrier's standing to pursue custody of the babies cannot be sustained on the basis of *in loco parentis* status and the trial court erred in ruling otherwise.

STANDING BASED ON "LEGAL MOTHER" STATUS

* * *

* * * Father challenges the trial court's authority to void the Surrogacy Contract *sua sponte* * * *

* * * [C]ourts may not rule on matters not before them:

Due process requires that the litigants receive notice of the issues before the court and an opportunity to present their case in relation to those issues. * * *

Fallaro v. Yeager, 528 A.2d 222, 224 (Pa. Super. [Ct.] 1987).

* * *

* * * [T]he trial court herein proceeded to declare the Contract void despite the absence of some of the parties to the Contract. The court compounded its error by naming gestational carrier the "legal mother" without even *notifying* egg donor, the person all parties concede is the biological mother of the babies. Plainly, egg donor was an indispensable party in this action. Thus, not only was it necessary to notify egg donor because she was a party to the Contract, it was also imperative that she have notice because she is the biological mother of the triplets. In light of these facts, the court lacked jurisdiction to rule on the issue of who was the "legal mother."

Even if we were to ignore the fact that the court *sua sponte* addressed the validity of the Contract without a request from the parties and without all indispensable parties present, we would conclude that the court's analysis of the issue was seriously flawed. * * *

* * * Only in the clearest of cases may a court declare a contract void as against public policy.

The trial court herein struck down the Contract primarily because the parties failed to name a legal mother. However, the designation of who is a "legal mother" is one ultimately determined by statute and/or judicial ruling. Had the parties named a legal mother in the Contract, that designation surely would not have been binding on the court. We find the trial court's basis for invalidating the Contract unsupportable.[24]

* * *

In summary, we hold that, with regard to the custody matter, Father was entitled to obtain custody of his biological children from the third party gestational carrier who has no biological connection to the children and who took custody of the children in flagrant defiance of Father's wishes. The trial court erred in finding that gestational carrier had *in loco parentis* status to challenge Father's right to custody. Gestational carrier's defiant conduct precluded such a finding. Moreover, the trial court erred in *sua sponte* voiding the Surrogacy Contract as contrary to public policy and in naming gestational carrier as the "legal mother". None of the bases upon which the trial court relied for standing can be sustained.

* * *

* * * We have vacated the trial court's finding that gestational carrier is the legal mother here. We have also vacated the court's finding that gestational carrier had *in loco parentis* status. As a result, there is no need to assess the merits of the trial court's termination decision, as the matter itself should not have proceeded to a hearing due to gestational carrier's lack of standing to bring the action.

* * *

---

24. Because of the resolution of standing, we decline to address the merits of any other issue in the trial court opinion. We are aware that the trial court voided the Surrogacy Contract on another ground, to wit, because it found that the terms of the contract allowed the parties to "bargain away" the children's rights in violation of long-standing public policy in this Commonwealth. We do not review this ruling by the trial court because we believe review is unnecessary. * * *

NOTES AND QUESTIONS

1. *Intent-based parentage.* The *J.F.* surrogacy contract recited the gestational carrier's apparent intent not to form a parental bond with any child born, yet the carrier's feelings changed after she gave birth. Do you believe that intent-based parentage is possible in collaborative reproduction? How is such parentage different from intent-based parentage in adoptions?

In denying the gestational surrogate standing to seek custody because she does not stand *in loco parentis* to the triplets, how does the court credit the gestational surrogate's physical and emotional stake in the triplets' gestation and births?

2. *The children's interests.* Notice that as *J.F.* decides the standing of adults, the court nowhere weighs the triplets' interests in the determination of their parentage. Footnote 24 closes the courthouse door on the children.

What interests do children conceived by ART have in the determination of their parentage? Are these interests distinguishable from the interests of children who are the subjects of custody litigation in divorce proceedings (discussed in Chapter 12), and, if so, how? With gestational surrogacy, genetic surrogacy, and gamete donations happening across the country, is *J.F.* accurate that this case is marked by "unique facts and procedural history"?

If *J.F.* had proceeded beyond standing, perhaps the court's only realistic alternatives would have been to hold the underlying contract unenforceable (as *Baby M* did), or to determine parentage by applying traditional principles of law. In the end, *J.F.*'s most perspicacious conclusion may be its recognition that maternity and surrogacy legislation is a "task * * * for the legislature." Statutory resolution, however, is also no easy task in light of the ethical, religious and moral questions that have dominated debate in states that have considered such legislation.

PROBLEM 17–6

You are a state senator in a state that is considering surrogacy legislation for the first time. You sit on the Families and Children Committee, which has just concluded hearings on this bill:

BILL

1. Surrogate parenting contracts are hereby declared contrary to the public policy of this state, and are void and unenforceable.

2. "Surrogate parenting contract" shall mean any agreement, oral or written, in which:

(a) a woman agrees either to be inseminated with the sperm of a man who is not her husband or to be impregnated with an embryo that is the product of an ovum fertilized with the sperm of a man who is not her husband; and

(b) the woman agrees to, or intends to, surrender or consent to the adoption of the child born as a result of such insemination or impregnation.

3. No person or other entity shall knowingly request, accept, receive, pay or give any fee, compensation or other remuneration, directly

or indirectly, in connection with any surrogate parenting contract, or induce, arrange or otherwise assist in arranging a surrogate parenting contract for a fee, compensation or other remuneration, except for:

(a) payments in connection with the adoption of a child permitted by law and disclosed pursuant to law; or

(b) payments for reasonable and actual medical fees and hospital expenses for artificial insemination or *in vitro* fertilization services incurred by the mother in connection with the birth of the child.

4. (a) A birth mother or her husband, a genetic father and his wife, and, if the genetic mother is not the birth mother, the genetic mother and her husband who violate this section shall be subject to a civil penalty not to exceed five hundred dollars.

(b) Any other person or entity who or which induces, arranges or otherwise assists in the formation of a surrogate parenting contract for a fee, compensation or other remuneration or otherwise violates this section shall be subject to a civil penalty not to exceed ten thousand dollars and forfeiture to the state of any such fee, compensation or remuneration for the first such offense. Any person or entity who or which induces, arranges or otherwise assists in the formation of a surrogate parenting contract for a fee, compensation or other remuneration or otherwise violates this section, after having been once subject to a civil penalty for violating this section, shall be guilty of a felony.

Would you vote to send this bill to the floor as currently drafted? If not, how would you amend the bill in committee?

Assume that after hearings on the bill, a majority of the Families and Children Committee rejects the bill's total prohibition on compensated surrogacy. A majority of the committee wants a bill that regulates, without totally prohibiting, such surrogacy. You have been assigned to help draft regulatory legislation. How would you respond to the following questions concerning regulation, which arose during hearings on the initial bill?:

1. *Questions about limiting the potential class of intended parents.* (a) Should the state permit surrogacy only where the intended parents are infertile? Where pregnancy might endanger the intended mother's health? Where the intended parents are a married couple? Where one intended parent is genetically related to the child? (b) Should the state permit a surrogacy contract by an 80–year–old seeking heirs? By fertile 25–year–olds who themselves could conceive children in long-term relationships, but who may not want the inconvenience, perhaps because it might burden their career plans?

2. *Questions about judicial oversight.* Should the state permit surrogacy agreements only where a court, after a hearing, gives prior approval to the agreement? If the answer is yes, (a) who should be required to join in the petition to the court? (b) what factors should the court consider in determining whether to grant approval? (c) should the court appoint a guardian *ad litem* for the anticipated child? (d) should the court order an inspection and evaluation of the intended parents' household, similar to the procedures that precede court approval of an adoption?

3. *What if the baby is born with a serious birth defect and the intended parents no longer want her?* If the intended parents change their minds before or upon birth, what happens to the child being carried by the surrogate? Should the answer depend on the terms of the surrogacy agreement, or should legislation provide the answer?

PROBLEM 17–7

Two longtime friends, John and Judy Jones, stop by your law office seeking your advice. They have been married for seven years, and both are in their late twenties. They are childless, and they have been trying unsuccessfully to conceive a child for the past two years. They are thinking about whether to adopt a child or to attempt some form of surrogacy arrangement. What would you advise concerning the relative merits of each avenue to parenthood?

D. CLONING: THE "BRAVE NEW WORLD"?

"Great potential for causing harm exists in assisted reproduction. In a sense, the biological revolution brought about by assisted reproductive technology holds the potential of affecting the evolution of human life itself. * * * [R]eproductive science is already being employed to attempt to customize children to be more intelligent or more beautiful than is likely by natural reproduction. Certainly the technology is already being used to produce children of a preferred gender." Charles P. Kindregan, Jr. & Maureen McBrien, Assisted Reproductive Technology: A Lawyer's Guide to Emerging Law and Science 25 (2006).

Initiatives such as these smack of eugenics, a matter of concern to students of history. At the forefront of public debate today is the prospect of human cloning, which was largely the preserve of science fiction aficionados when Aldous Huxley anticipated it in his 1932 novel, *Brave New World*, sixty-four years before scientists cloned the first mammal, the sheep Dolly. Dolly's birth led the *New York Times* to describe cloning as "the one bit of genetic engineering that has been anticipated and dreaded more than any other." Gina Kolata, *Scientist Reports First Cloning Ever of Adult Mammal*, N.Y. Times, Feb. 23, 1997, at 11.

The term "cloning" encompasses two distinct activities—reproductive cloning and therapeutic cloning:

> They begin the same way. Nuclear material is taken from a woman's egg while nuclear material from a donor's somatic cells is introduced in its place. The egg then begins to develop just as a traditional fertilized ovum does. In reproductive cloning (which may or may not be possible with humans), however, this developing embryo is implanted in a uterus and brought to term. If a baby is born it would have essentially the same genetic make-up as the donor. Reproductive cloning is intensely controversial and has very few supporters.

In therapeutic cloning, however, no one plans to bring the embryo to term. After a few weeks, the stem cells are removed and used for research. This technique, while controversial, has many supporters, as does stem cell research generally. It may have the advantage over ordinary stem cell research in that an individual suffering from a disease could be the donor, resulting in stem cells that might be particularly useful for studying or treating his ailment because they would match his genetic code.

Proponents of therapeutic cloning would very much like to separate it from reproductive cloning in the public mind, since the latter conjures up images of hundreds of genetically identical people created for some nefarious purpose. * * *

Steven Goldberg, *MRIs and the Perception of Risk*, 33 Am. J. L. & Med. 229, 233–34 (2007).

About a dozen states have enacted cloning legislation. Most of these states prohibit reproductive cloning but permit therapeutic cloning. *See* Kindregan, Jr. & McBrien, *supra*, at 249. In 2004, the ABA House of Delegates adopted a resolution that "supports law and public policy, both national and international, that oppose or prohibit reproductive cloning." Recognizing that reproductive cloning has been attempted and might prove successful "in the near future" despite legislative prohibition, the resolution also supported national law and policy that "establish a presumption that a live birth resulting from such attempts is a human being; [g]uarantee that any such human being is a person, legally separate and distinct from its biological progenitor, with all rights accorded to any other live born human being under existing law; and [e]stablish[] legal parentage, including the legal rights and obligations that flow therefrom, of such person." ABA, Human Cloning Resolution (Aug. 9–10, 2004).

POSTSCRIPT: YOUR FUTURE IN FAMILY LAW

This casebook's Preface advised that "[t]his is an exciting time to * * * practice family law." Chapter 2 describes family law practice, and Chapter 15 treats the realities of alternative dispute resolution in that practice. Most of the rest of the book treats substantive family law doctrine and policy. Now that you have nearly completed the course, use this final Problem to ponder whether practicing family law would enable you to find professional fulfillment.

PROBLEM

You teach family law at State University School of Law, and you make yourself readily available to students who wish to discuss their future career plans. A student stops by your office to make an appointment to talk with you about whether to accept an offer to become an associate in a leading local firm that practices family law exclusively. The student is not certain about whether to make a commitment to a long-term career practicing family law. What advice will you provide?

*

INDEX

References are to Pages

References are to Pages

†